The Nasdaq Stock Market℠
Nasdaq-100®
ADRs
Foreign Securities
1997 Edition

S0-AIW-353

Moody's Investors Service
Financial Information Services

NASDAQ®

Contents

NOTE: All company business and financial data was provided by Moody's Investors Service. For information about Nasdaq companies not included in this book, visit Nasdaq's web site at www.nasdaq.com or refer to Moody's Handbook of Nasdaq Stocks.

Introduction

The Nasdaq Stock Market Nasdaq-100, ADRs and Foreign Securities
is a comprehensive resource of investing information about companies
listed on The Nasdaq Stock Market℠ (Nasdaq). Three types of Nasdaq®
companies are profiled: those in the Nasdaq-100 Index® those that list
their shares on Nasdaq in the form of American Depositary Receipts
(ADRs), and foreign securities listed on the Nasdaq National Market®
In total, 415 leading-edge companies were chosen for this book based
on three important investment considerations: size, growth and
international diversity.

In the beginning of the Nasdaq-100 section, the companies are ranked
by market value. The sections on ADRs and Foreign Securities begin
with a list of companies arranged alphabetically, followed by a list of
companies grouped by country. In all sections, the lists are followed
by company profiles in alphabetical order. Each profile includes a
description of the company's business, a list of corporate officers, current
and historical earnings and dividends information, annual financial
data, a trading volume chart, and other pertinent financial and contact
information. All the data has been compiled as a guide to investors
who are either acting on investment advice or making independent
investment decisions about any of the companies profiled in this book.

The Nasdaq Stock Market

By combining advanced computer and telecommunications technology
with a system of competing market makers, Nasdaq has created a
uniquely effective equities trading environment – one that provides
listed companies with high visibility and that fosters growth. As a
result of Nasdaq's exacting listing requirements, company reviews
and sophisticated system of market surveillance, investors can have
confidence in the integrity of the market.

Companies listed on Nasdaq are separated into two tiers – the Nasdaq
National Market for larger companies with higher capitalization, and the
Nasdaq SmallCap Market℠ for small- to medium-sized companies. The
Nasdaq Stock Market is operated by The Nasdaq Stock Market, Inc., and
is regulated by NASD Regulation, Inc. (NASDR℠). Both Nasdaq and
NASDR are wholly-owned subsidiaries of the National Association of
Securities Dealers, Inc. (NASD®).

How To Use This Book

The presentation of background information plus current and historical data provides the answers to three basic questions for each company:

1. What does the company do?
   (See G.)

2. How has the company done in the past?
   (See B, D, E, I, J.)

3. How is the company doing now?
   (See D, E, F, H.)

The following information is highlighted:

A. CAPSULE STOCK INFORMATION –
This section shows the stock symbol, plus the approximate yield afforded by the indicated dividend based on a recent price, and the price/earnings ratio. The recent price is expressed in U.S. dollars for all companies. Also included for U.S. companies is an indication whether the company's stock can be purchased on margin. Price/earnings ratios for ADRs have been adjusted to reflect the underlying multiple shares, where applicable.

B. LONG-TERM PRICE CHART – This chart illustrates the pattern of monthly stock price movements, fully adjusted for stock dividends and splits. For non-U.S. companies issuing ADRs, the chart shows monthly price movements for their Nasdaq-listed ADRs. The chart points out the degree of volatility in the price movement of the company's stock and reveals its long-term trend. It indicates areas of price support and resistance, plus other technical points to be considered by the investor. The bars at the base of the long-term price chart indicate the monthly trading volume. Monthly trading volume can provide an indication of the periods when stock accumulation occurs, and what percent of a company's outstanding shares are traded.

C. PRICE SCORES – Below each U.S. company's price/volume chart are **Moody's Price Scores.** These are two basic measures of the stock's performance. Each stock is measured against the New York Stock Exchange Composite Index. A score of 100 indicates that the stock did as well as the New York Stock Exchange Composite Index during the time period. A score of less than 100 means that the stock did not do as well; a score of more than 100 means that the stock outperformed the NYSE Composite Index.

Thus, **Moody's Price Scores** allow the user to make easy, across-the-board comparisons of various stocks' historical performances. Because each stock is measured against the New York Stock Exchange Index, its score may be compared with that of any other stock.

The **7-YEAR PRICE SCORE** mirrors the common stock's price growth over the previous 7 years. The higher the price score, the better the relative performance. The score is based on the ratio of the latest 12-month average price to the current 7-year average. This ratio is then indexed against the same ratio for the New York Stock Exchange Index, which is expressed as 100.

12-MONTH PRICE SCORE is a similar measurement but for a shorter period of time. It indicates the recent vigor or sluggishness of a stock's price movement. It is based on the ratio of the latest 2-month average price to the current 12-month average. As was done for the 7-Year Price Score, this ratio is also indexed to the same ratio for the New York Stock Exchange. In both cases, all prices are adjusted for all stock dividends and splits.

D. EARNINGS PER SHARE – These figures are as reported by the company. For U.S. companies, figures are shown before the effect of extraordinary items, discontinued operations and cumulative effects of accounting changes (unless otherwise noted). All figures are adjusted for all stock dividends and splits. For U.S. companies, interim quarterly earnings are shown. For non-U.S. companies, if no earnings per share have been reported, figures are calculated by dividing net income by average or year-end shares outstanding.

E. INTERIM DIVIDENDS PER SHARE –
The cash dividends shown, all expressed in U.S. dollars unless noted, are the amounts

ILLUSTRATIVE INC.

YIELD 2.2%
P/E RATIO 12.5

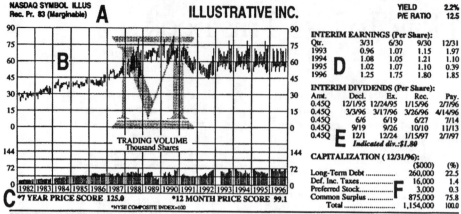

B

TRADING VOLUME
Thousand Shares

C
| 1982 | 1983 | 1984 | 1985 | 1986 | 1987 | 1988 | 1989 | 1990 | 1991 | 1992 | 1993 | 1994 | 1995 | 1996 |

*7 YEAR PRICE SCORE 125.0   *12 MONTH PRICE SCORE 99.1
*NYSE COMPOSITE INDEX=100

INTERIM EARNINGS (Per Share):

Qtr.	3/31	6/30	9/30	12/31
1993	0.96	1.07	1.15	1.97
1994	1.08	1.05	1.21	1.10
1995	1.02	1.07	1.10	0.39
1996	1.25	1.75	1.80	1.85

D

INTERIM DIVIDENDS (Per Share):

Amt.	Decl.	Ex.	Rec.	Pay.
0.45Q	12/1/95	12/24/95	1/15/96	2/7/96
0.45Q	3/3/96	3/17/96	3/26/96	4/14/96
0.45Q	6/6	6/19	6/27	7/14
0.45Q	9/19	9/26	10/10	11/13
0.45Q	12/1	12/24	1/15/97	2/7/97

Indicated div.:$1.80

E

CAPITALIZATION (12/31/96):

	($000)	(%)
Long-Term Debt	260,000	22.5
Def. Inc. Taxes	16,000	1.4
Preferred Stock	3,000	0.3
Common Surplus	875,000	75.8
Total	1,154,000	100.0

F

RECENT DEVELOPMENTS: For the year ended 12/31/96 net income was $185.4 million or $5.15 per share versus $178.0 million or $4.63 per share a year ago. Net sales totaled $3.68 billion, compared with $3.40 billion in the previous year. Increased sales were due in part to widespread acceptance of the Company's new products. The start-up costs of these new products limited net income growth. Sales and earnings in foreign markets advanced 17% and 20%, respectively, over the year-earlier results.

H

G   BUSINESS

ILLUSTRATIVE INC. is engaged in the research, manufacture and marketing of ethical pharmaceuticals, proprietary drugs and other products used in human and animal health care. It also provides medical services and manufactures medical instruments. Products are distributed in the U.S. and most free-world countries. Major products include tranquilizers, amphetamines, specialty antibiotics and vaccines; animals health products include vaccines and feed additives; medical services include a full range of pathology services. Sales (operating income) in 1996 were as follows: pharmaceutical products, 55% (48%); medical services and instruments 20% (18%); industrial products, 7% (8%); and others, 18% (26%).

ANNUAL EARNINGS AND DIVIDENDS PER SHARE

	1996	1995	1994	1993	1992	1991
Earnings Per Share	5.15	4.63	5.10	4.80	4.16	4.10
Dividends Per Share	1.80	1.36	1.32	1.23	1.16	1.06
Dividend Payout %	35.0	29.4	25.9	30.7	27.9	25.6

I

ANNUAL FINANCIAL DATA

RECORD OF EARNINGS (IN MILLIONS):

	1996	1995	1994	1993	1992	1991
Net Sales	3,675.0	3,400.0	3,214.2	2,526.3	2,500.6	2,234.8
Costs and Expenses	3,200.2	3,100.0	2,900.1	2,399.1	2,210.4	2,074.3
Depreciation	20.0	18.0	19.0	17.4	15.3	16.4
Operating Profit	455.0	282.0	295.1	109.4	274.9	144.1
Income Before Taxes	242.4	230.0	220.1	123.6	251.3	133.6
Income Taxes	57.0	52.0	75.1	70.2	84.0	41.1
Net Income	185.4	178.0	145.5	53.3	167.3	92.5
Aver. Com. Shs. (000)	36,000	17,500	17,000	15,250	15,200	14,530

J

BALANCE SHEET (IN MILLIONS):

	1996	1995	1994	1993	1992	1991
Cash, Securities, Etc.	380.0	350.0	310.6	270.3	290.4	282.0
Receivables	140.0	120.0	125.0	120.9	130.3	126.3
Inventories	250.0	230.0	220.2	206.5	200.6	202.4
Gross Property	1,600.0	1,500.9	1,000.7	1,100.0	1,004.5	980.6
Depreciation Reserve	513.1	510.1	500.1	510.1	475.0	450.3
Long-Term Debt	260.0	249.0	229.4	300.5	296.1	301.6
Net Stockholders' Equity	875.0	540.0	530.1	523.7	518.2	504.6
Total Assets	2,800.0	2,700.0	2,432.0	2,031.6	1,963.4	1,825.4
Total Current Assets	1,960.0	1,400.0	1,021.4	926.2	700.1	626.3
Total Current Liabs.	973.0	470.0	426.5	400.1	296.4	251.4
Net Working Capital	987.0	930.0	594.9	526.1	403.7	374.9
Yr.-End Com. Shs. (000)	35,000	16,500	16,000	15,063	15,047	14,490

STATISTICAL RECORD:

	1996	1995	1994	1993	1992	1991
Operating Profit Margin %	12.4	8.3	9.2	4.3	11.0	6.4
Book Value Per Share	25.00	32.73	33.13	34.53	34.31	34.80
Return on Equity %	21.2	33.0	27.4	10.2	32.3	18.3
Return on Assets %	6.6	6.6	5.9	2.6	8.5	5.1
Average Yield %	2.3	2.3	2.1	1.7	1.7	2.1
P/E Ratio	16.5-9.5	15.6-9.5	15.2-9.4	21.1-14.9	18.0-14.4	19.8-9.3
Price Range	85-49	72-44	77½-48	84½-59½	75-59¾	81-38

Statistics are as originally reported.

OFFICERS:
S. Polland, Chmn.
B. Armbruster, Vice Chmn.
M. Golden, Pres. & C.E.O.
S. Munn, V.P.-Fin
G. Cox, Secretary

INCORPORATED: DE, June, 1929

PRINCIPAL OFFICE: 99 Church St., New York, NY 10007

TELEPHONE NUMBER: (212) 885-2160

NO. OF EMPLOYEES: 24,000 (approx.)

ANNUAL MEETING: In July

SHAREHOLDERS: 15,500

INSTITUTIONAL HOLDINGS:
No. of Institutions: 15
Shares Held: 5,700,675

K

REGISTRAR(S): First National Bank of N.Y.

TRANSFER AGENT(S): First National Bank of N.Y.

How To Use This Book (Continued)

declared by the companies. No adjustments have been made for stock dividends or splits. For non-U.S.companies, the amount shown is net of a 15% tax to U.S. residents, to indicate the actual amount received by U.S. investors. For companies issuing ADRs, the dividend shown is per ADR. **Ex-Dividend Date:** a stockholder must purchase the stock prior to this date in order to be entitled to the dividend. The **Record Date** indicates the date on which the shareholder had to have been a holder of record in order to have qualified for the dividend. The **Payable Date** indicates the date the company paid or intends to pay the dividend. For U.S. companies, the cash amount shown in the first column is followed by a letter (example: "Q" for quarterly) to indicate the frequency of the dividend. The **Indicated Dividend** is the annualized rate, fully adjusted, of the latest regular cash dividend.

F. CAPITALIZATION – These are certain items in the company's capital account. Both the U.S. dollar amounts and their respective percentages are given.
Long-Term Debt is the total amount of debt owed by the company due beyond one year.
Capital Lease Obligations is shown as a separate caption when indicated on the balance sheet as such.
Deferred Income Taxes represent the company's tax liability arising from accelerated depreciation and investment tax credit.
Preferred Stock and/or Preference Stock is the sum of equity issues, exclusive of common stock, the holders of which have a prior claim ahead of common shareholders, to the income of the company while it continues to operate and to the assets in the event of dissolution.
Minority Interest is a capital item that reflects the share of ownership by an outside party in a consolidated subsidiary of the company.
Common and Surplus is the sum of the stated or par value of the common stock, plus additional paid-in capital and retained earnings less the dollar amount of treasury shares. For non-U.S. companies, Preferred Stock and Common and Surplus are generally combined under **Stockholders' Equity.**

G. COMPANY BUSINESS – This section is a summary of the company's operations:

the products or services it sells, its markets and production facilities.

H. RECENT DEVELOPMENTS – This section discusses the latest information on the company. In addition to analysis of recently released sales and earnings figures, items covered may include, where applicable and available, new product introductions, capital expenditures, expanded operations, acquisitions, labor developments, equity and debt financing, the rate of incoming orders and the level of backlog.

I. ANNUAL EARNINGS AND DIVIDENDS PER SHARE – These figures are adjusted for all stock dividends and splits. **Earnings Per Share** are as reported by the company, except for adjustments for certain items where footnoted. If no earnings per share have been reported, the figures are calculated by dividing net income by average or year-end shares outstanding.
Dividends Per Share, shown for U.S. companies, represent the sum of all cash payments on a calendar year basis. Any fiscal year ending prior to June 30, for example, is shown with dividends paid in the prior calendar year.
Dividend Payout %, shown for U.S. companies, is the percentage of cash paid out of earnings per share.

J. ANNUAL FINANCIAL DATA – Here is pertinent earnings and balance sheet information essential to analyzing a corporation's performance. The figures are shown as reported by the company in its annual report, and the year-to-year comparisons provide the necessary historical perspective to intelligently review the various operating and financial trends. Some items have been combined in an effort to simplify and standardize accounts. For non-U.S. companies, figures appear in both U.S. dollars and native currency. Generic definitions follow:

RECORD OF EARNINGS:

For U.S. companies, **Net Sales** indicate total income from operations, excluding all non-operating revenues. **Revenues** indicate the total income from operations, including

9

How To Use This Book (Continued)

all non-operating revenues. For non-U.S. companies, **Total Revenues** indicate total income from operations, exclusive of all non-operating revenues.

Costs and Expenses is the total of all costs related to the operation of the business, including cost of sales, and selling, general and administrative expenses. Excluded items are depreciation, interest and other financial costs (except for financial institutions), and other non-operating expenses.

Depreciation & Amortization includes all non-cash charges such as depletion as well as depreciation and amortization.

Operating Profit and **Operating Income** are the profit remaining after deducting depreciation as well as all operating costs and expenses from the company's revenues and net sales. This figure is before interest expenses, extraordinary gains and charges, and income and expense items of a non-operating nature.

Income Before Taxes is the remaining income after deducting all costs, expenses, property charges, interests, etc., but before deducting income taxes.

Income Taxes are shown as reported by the company and include both the amount of current taxes actually paid out and the amount deferred to future years.

Minority Interest in the income statement is that portion of profits of a consolidated subsidiary that is allocated to a minority owner of that subsidiary.

Net Income for U.S. companies is as reported by the corporation, before extraordinary gains and losses, discontinued operations and accounting changes, which are appropriately footnoted. For non-U.S. companies, figures may include extraordinary gains and losses according to accounting practices in the specific countries.

Average Common Shares is the weighted average number of shares, including common equivalent shares outstanding during the year, as reported by the corporation and fully adjusted for all stock dividends and splits. The use of average shares minimizes the distortion in earnings per share that could result from issuance of a large amount of stock or the company's purchase of a large amount of its own stock during the year.

BALANCE SHEET:

Cash, Cash Equivalents and Securities include unrestricted cash and temporary investments in marketable securities, such as government securities, certificates of deposit and short-term investments.

Receivables and Net Receivables are all accounts due from customers, etc., that the company shows as current assets.

Inventories indicate the sum of the raw materials, work in progress and finished goods as valued by the company.

Gross Property is the total fixed assets, including all property, land, plants, buildings, equipment, fixtures, etc.

Depreciation and Accumulated Depreciation are the accumulation of annual charges to income representing a computed decline in the value of an asset due to wear and tear or obsolescence.

Long-Term Debt is the total long-term debt (due beyond one year) reported by the company, including bonds, capital lease obligations, notes, mortgages, debentures, etc.

Stockholders' Equity is the sum of all capital stock accounts – stated values of preferred and common stock, paid in capital, earned surplus (retained earnings), etc., net of all treasury stock.

Total Assets represent the sum of all tangible and intangible assets as reported by the company.

Total Current Assets are all of the company's short-term assets such as cash, marketable securities, inventories, etc., as reported by the company.

Total Current Liabilities are all of the obligations of the company due within one year, as reported.

Net Working Capital is derived by subtracting Current Liabilities from Current Assets.

Year-End Shares Outstanding represent the number of shares outstanding as of the date of the company's annual report, exclusive of treasury stock. For U.S. companies these figures are adjusted for subsequent stock dividends and splits.

How To Use This Book (Continued)

STATISTICAL RECORD:

Operating Profit Margin indicates operating profit as a percentage of net sales or revenues. **Book Value Per Share** is calculated for U.S. companies by taking the aggregate dollar value of tangible assets as carried on the corporation's books and dividing it by the outstanding shares of common stock at year end. This figure is fully adjusted for all stock dividends and splits. For non-U.S. companies, book value is calculated by dividing stockholders' equity by year-end share outstanding. Book value for banks and public utilities is as reported by the companies. Book value is expressed in U.S. dollars for all companies.

Return on Equity is one of several measures of profitability. It is the ratio of net income to net stockholders' equity, expressed as a percentage. This ratio illustrates how effectively the investment of the stockholders is being utilized to earn a profit. In pertaining to banks it is a measure of annualized return on each $100 of average stockholder equity.

Return on Assets is another means of measuring profitability. It is the ratio of net income to total assets, expressed as a percentage. This indicates how effectively the corporate assets are being used to generate profits.

Net Profit Margin, shown for non-U.S. companies, is the ratio of net income to total revenues, expressed as a percentage. This ratio measures management's overall efficiency, not only in managing operations but in terms of borrowing money at favorable rates, investing idle cash to produce extra income, and taking advantage of tax benefits.

Average Yield, shown for U.S. companies, is the ratio (expressed as a percentage) of the annual dividend to the mean price of the common stock (average of the high and low for the year). Both prices and dividends are for calendar years.

Price/Earnings Ratio, shown for U.S. companies, is given as a range. The figures are calculated by dividing the stock's highest price for the calendar year and its lowest price by the year's earnings per share. Earnings used in the calculation for a particular calendar year

are for the fiscal year in which the majority of the company's business took place. As a rule, for companies whose fiscal years end before June 30, the ratio is calculated by using the price range of the prior calendar year. For those with fiscal years ending on June 30 or later, the current year's price range is used. *Editor's note: For U.S. companies, statistics are as originally reported. For non-U.S. companies, financial information may be restated to reflect subsequent events.*

K. ADDITIONAL INFORMATION –

For each stock, listings are provided for the company's officers, date of incorporation, its address, telephone number, annual meeting date, the number of employees, the number of stockholders, and institutional holdings. For U.S. companies, the registrar and transfer agent are given; for non-U.S. companies, the registrar or depositary bank is given. **Institutional Holdings** indicate the number of investment companies, insurance companies, bank trust and college endowment funds holding the stock and the total number of shares held as last reported.

American Depositary Receipts – For the relevant non-U.S. companies, this section describes how many shares, and what kind of shares, their **American Depositary Receipts** (ADRs) represent. It also shows whether their ADRs are sponsored or unsponsored.

ABBREVIATIONS AND SYMBOLS

cr	Credit
d	Deficit
dr	Debit
E	Extra
M	Monthly
N/A	Not Available
N.M.	Not Meaningful
p	Preliminary
P.F.	Pro Forma
Q	Quarterly
r	Revised
S	Semi-Annual
Sp	Special Dividend

Percentage of Total U.S. Share Volume

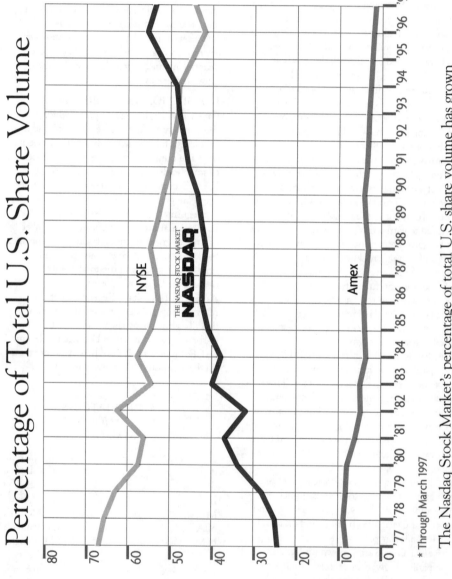

* Through March 1997

The Nasdaq Stock Market's percentage of total U.S. share volume has grown substantially since its inception, more than doubling over the last 20 years.

Percentage of Total U.S. Dollar Volume

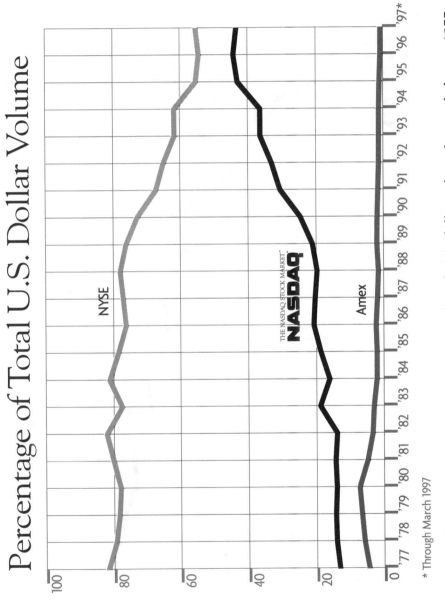

NYSE

THE NASDAQ STOCK MARKET
NASDAQ

Amex

'77 '78 '79 '80 '81 '82 '83 '84 '85 '86 '87 '88 '89 '90 '91 '92 '93 '94 '95 '96 '97*

100 80 60 40 20 0

* Through March 1997

The Nasdaq Stock Market's percentage of total U.S. dollar volume has tripled since 1977.

Comparative Index Performance

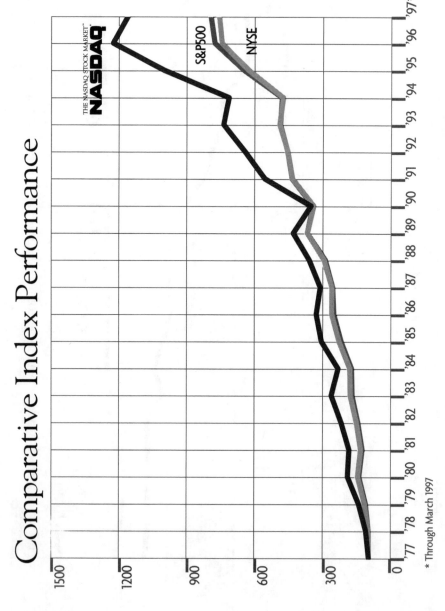

* Through March 1997

Over the last 20 years, The Nasdaq Stock Market composite index has outperformed the market composite indices of both the S&P 500 and the New York Stock Exchange.

14

Nasdaq-100

Rank	Symbol	Company Name	
			$114,44...
			109,583,800,0
			...88,...40,0
			...5,37...
1	INTC	Intel Corporation	
2	MSFT	Microsoft Corporation	
3	CSCO	Cisco Systems, Inc.	
4	ORCL	Oracle Corporation	
5	MCIC	MCI Communications Corporation	19,776,720,0
6	WCOM	WorldCom, Inc.	19,283,572,0
7	AMGN	Amgen Inc.	14,776,367,0
8	DELL	Dell Computer Corporation	11,891,315,0
9	SUNW	Sun Microsystems, Inc.	10,605,730,0
10	AMAT	Applied Materials, Inc.	8,358,398,0
11	TCOMA	Tele-Communications, Inc.	7,013,412,0
12	TLAB	Tellabs, Inc.	6,822,206,0
13	COMS	3Com Corporation	5,762,756,0
14	PMTC	Parametric Technology Corporation	5,752,941,0
15	COST	Costco Companies Inc.	5,426,545,0
16	ASND	Ascend Communications, Inc.	4,775,330,0
17	BMCS	BMC Software, Inc.	4,631,504,0
18	OXHP	Oxford Health Plans, Inc.	4,461,011,0
19	HBOC	HBO & Company	4,311,433,0
20	PSFT	PeopleSoft, Inc.	4,038,000,0
21	ADPT	Adaptec, Inc.	3,972,647,0
22	QCOM	QUALCOMM Incorporated	3,788,682,0
23	ALTR	Altera Corporation	3,758,028,0
24	XLNX	Xilinx, Inc.	3,560,846,0
25	NWAC	Northwest Airlines Corporation	3,516,809,0
26	ADCT	ADC Telecommunications, Inc.	3,496,115,0
27	LLTC	Linear Technology Corporation	3,312,732,0
28	ANDW	Andrew Corporation	3,284,088,0
29	NOVL	Novell, Inc.	3,266,290,0
30	SPLS	Staples, Inc.	3,238,958,0
31	CMCSK	Comcast Corporation	3,215,109,
32	CHIR	Chiron Corporation	3,175,82...
33	SIAL	Sigma-Aldrich Corporation	
34	MXIM	Maxim Integrated Products, Inc.	
35	NOBE	Nordstrom, Inc.	
36	PAYX	P...	

The Nasdaq-100

The Nasdaq-100 Index includes 100 of the largest non-financial domestic companies listed on the Nasdaq National Market tier of The Nasdaq Stock Market. Each security in the Index is proportionately represented by its market capitalization in relation to the total market value of the Index.

Launched in January 1985, the Index reflects Nasdaq's largest growth companies across a variety of major industry groups, including airlines, biotechnology, computer and software manufacturing, office products, semiconductors and steel. All Index components have a minimum market capitalization of $500 million and an average daily trading volume of at least 100,000 shares.

The number of securities in the Nasdaq-100 Index makes it an effective vehicle for arbitrageurs and securities traders. In October 1993, the Nasdaq-100 Index began trading on the Chicago Board Options Exchange. On April 10, 1996, the Chicago Mercantile Exchange began trading futures and futures options on the Nasdaq-100 Index.

As of the end of 1996, the Nasdaq-100 Index had outperformed other major indices. The Nasdaq-100 Index was up 43%, while the Dow Jones Index rose 26%, and the Standard and Poor's 500 Index climbed 20%. Individual stocks within the Nasdaq-100 Index varied, with 69 stocks finishing the year with higher prices. Dell Computer was the best performing stock in the Index, increasing 206.9% – from $17.31 per share to $53.12 per share.

For quick reference, the companies listed in this section are ranked by market capitalization and then profiled in alphabetical order.

Nasdaq-100 Companies

(as of March 31, 1997)

RANK	SYMBOL	COMPANY NAME	MARKET VALUE
1	INTC	Intel Corporation	$114,448,955,000
2	MSFT	Microsoft Corporation	109,583,800,000
3	CSCO	Cisco Systems, Inc.	31,638,145,000
4	ORCL	Oracle Corporation	25,370,732,000
5	MCIC	MCI Communications Corporation	19,776,720,000
6	WCOM	WorldCom, Inc.	19,283,572,000
7	AMGN	Amgen Inc.	14,776,367,000
8	DELL	Dell Computer Corporation	11,891,315,000
9	SUNW	Sun Microsystems, Inc.	10,605,730,000
10	AMAT	Applied Materials, Inc.	8,358,398,000
11	TCOMA	Tele-Communications, Inc.	7,013,412,000
12	TLAB	Tellabs, Inc.	6,822,206,000
13	COMS	3Com Corporation	5,762,756,000
14	PMTC	Parametric Technology Corporation	5,752,941,000
15	COST	Costco Companies Inc.	5,426,545,000
16	ASND	Ascend Communications, Inc.	4,775,330,000
17	BMCS	BMC Software, Inc.	4,631,504,000
18	OXHP	Oxford Health Plans, Inc.	4,461,011,000
19	HBOC	HBO & Company	4,311,433,000
20	PSFT	PeopleSoft, Inc.	4,038,000,000
21	ADPT	Adaptec, Inc.	3,972,647,000
22	QCOM	QUALCOMM Incorporated	3,788,682,000
23	ALTR	Altera Corporation	3,758,028,000
24	XLNX	Xilinx, Inc.	3,560,846,000
25	NWAC	Northwest Airlines Corporation	3,516,809,000
26	ADCT	ADC Telecommunications, Inc.	3,496,115,000
27	LLTC	Linear Technology Corporation	3,312,732,000
28	ANDW	Andrew Corporation	3,284,088,000
29	NOVL	Novell, Inc.	3,266,290,000
30	SPLS	Staples, Inc.	3,238,958,000
31	CMCSK	Comcast Corporation	3,215,109,000
32	CHIR	Chiron Corporation	3,175,823,000
33	SIAL	Sigma-Aldrich Corporation	3,087,500,000
34	MXIM	Maxim Integrated Products, Inc.	3,084,245,000
35	NOBE	Nordstrom, Inc.	3,005,798,000
36	PAYX	Paychex, Inc.	2,967,087,000
37	ADBE	Adobe Systems Incorporated	2,873,231,000
38	NXTL	Nextel Communications, Inc.	2,804,470,000
39	CPWR	Compuware Corporation	2,691,097,000
40	BGEN	Biogen, Inc.	2,688,085,000
41	PCAR	PACCAR Inc.	2,594,573,000
42	QNTM	Quantum Corporation	2,509,853,000
43	NSCP	Netscape Communications Corporation	2,540,101,000
44	CTAS	Cintas Corporation	2,504,623,000
45	DIGI	DSC Communications Corporation	2,454,482,000
46	STRY	Stryker Corporation	2,407,427,000
47	CSCC	Cascade Communications Corp.	2,369,978,000
48	ATML	Atmel Corporation	2,353,272,000
49	SBUX	Starbucks Corporation	2,310,276,000
50	FORT	Fort Howard Corporation	2,302,783,000

Nasdaq-100 Companies (Continued)

RANK	SYMBOL	COMPANY NAME	MARKET VALUE
51	IFMX	Informix Corporation	2,269,673,000
52	PHSYB	PacifiCare Health Systems, Inc.	2,266,305,000
53	AAPL	Apple Computer, Inc.	2,259,076,000
54	AGREA	American Greetings Corporation	2,250,508,000
55	TYSNA	Tyson Foods, Inc.	2,224,037,000
56	PETM	PETsMART, Inc.	2,130,219,000
57	MCAF	McAfee Associates, Inc.	2,128,248,000
58	CNTO	Centocor, Inc.	2,108,160,000
59	EFII	Electronics for Imaging, Inc.	2,053,722,000
60	APCC	American Power Conversion Corporation	2,036,340,000
61	BOST	Boston Chicken, Inc.	1,949,042,000
62	GART	Gartner Group, Inc.	1,938,919,000
63	BMET	Biomet, Inc.	1,930,804,000
64	PAIR	PairGain Technologies, Inc.	1,891,675,000
65	FDLNB	Food Lion, Inc.	1,870,506,000
66	KLAC	KLA-Tencor Corp.	1,863,763,000
67	WCLX	Wisconsin Central Transportation Corporation	1,788,550,000
68	MUEI	Micron Electronics, Inc.	1,768,584,000
69	MOLX	Molex Incorporated	1,763,960,000
70	QTRN	Quintiles Transnational Corp.	1,761,874,000
71	WTHG	Worthington Industries, Inc.	1,738,424,000
72	FISV	Fiserv, Inc.	1,684,929,000
73	GNCI	General Nutrition Companies, Inc.	1,681,803,000
74	MCCRK	McCormick & Company, Incorporated	1,661,198,000
75	BBBY	Bed Bath & Beyond Inc.	1,656,989,000
76	VKNG	Viking Office Products, Inc.	1,623,489,000
77	GENZ	Genzyme Corporation	1,616,738,000
78	MLHR	Herman Miller, Inc.	1,607,424,000
79	CBRL	Cracker Barrel Old Country Store, Inc.	1,590,307,000
80	KMAG	Komag, Incorporated	1,561,397,000
81	MCHP	Microchip Technology Inc.	1,539,510,000
82	PHYC	PhyCor, Inc.	1,484,771,000
83	ERTS	Electronic Arts Inc.	1,433,623,000
84	ADSK	Autodesk, Inc.	1,389,513,000
85	HCCC	HealthCare COMPARE Corp.	1,367,153,000
86	FORE	FORE Systems, Inc.	1,358,820,000
87	FAST	Fastenal Company	1,327,865,000
88	RPOW	RPM, Inc.	1,289,053,000
89	ROST	Ross Stores, Inc.	1,249,161,000
90	CEXP	Corporate Express, Inc.	1,201,925,000
91	SYBS	Sybase, Inc.	1,095,892,000
92	INTU	Intuit Inc.	1,075,638,000
93	CEFT	Concord EFS, Inc.	1,060,144,000
94	SNPS	Synopsys, Inc.	1,006,850,000
95	ADTN	ADTRAN, Inc.	967,925,000
96	OSSI	Outback Steakhouse, Inc.	959,000,000
97	PAGE	Paging Network, Inc.	833,251,000
98	CRUS	Cirrus Logic, Inc.	787,604,000
99	GEMS	Glenayre Technologies, Inc.	591,147,000
100	IDXX	IDEXX Laboratories, Inc.	526,554,000

ADAPTEC INC.

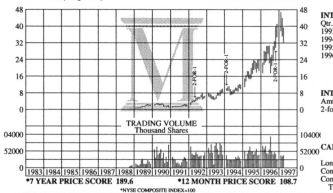

INTERIM EARNINGS (Per Share):

Qtr.	June	Sept.	Dec.	Mar.
1993-94	0.13	0.12	0.15	0.20
1994-95	0.16	0.18	0.26	0.28
1995-96	0.29	0.01	0.28	0.37
1996-97	0.16	0.01	0.36	0.40

INTERIM DIVIDENDS (Per Share):

Amt.	Decl.	Ex.	Rec.	Pay.
2-for-1	10/17/96	11/18/96	11/1/96	11/15/96

CAPITALIZATION (3/31/97):

	($000)	(%)
Long-Term Debt	850	0.1
Conv. Sub. Notes	230,000	25.0
Common & Surplus	688,325	74.9
Total	919,175	100.0

RECENT DEVELOPMENTS: For the fiscal year ended 3/31/97, net income increased 4.0% to $107.6 million. This compares with $103.4 million a year earlier. Net revenues were up 41.6% to $933.9 million from $659.3 million the previous year. The year-end results included write-offs of acquired in-process technology totaling $92.2 million versus $52.3 million the year before. For the fourth quarter ended 3/31/97, net income rose 14.0% to $46.8 million from $41.1 million in the corresponding prior-year quarter.

Net revenues increased 35.2% to $265.1 million compared with $196.0 million a year earlier. The current quarter's results included an $11.5 million write-off for acquired in-process technology. On 3/27/97, the Company agreed to purchase privately-held Skipstone Inc., a supplier of software, engineering services and developer toolkits associated with FireWire connectivity technology, in a $7.5 million cash transaction.

BUSINESS

ADAPTEC, INC. is a supplier of high-performance intelligent subsystems and associated software and VLSI circuits used to control the flow of data between a microcomputer's central processing unit (CPU) and its peripherals, such as optical and tape storage devices, and network-file servers. The Company's product families include host-adapters using extensive proprietary software, proprietary VLSI circuits and software-based development systems. The host-adapter products are based on the Small Computer Systems Interface (SCSI) standard, which interfaces with all standard microcomputer architectures. The single-chip disk controller products interface with both SCSI and AT, Industry Standard Architecture, disk drives. The Company's products include intelligent subsytems and associated software, proprietary VLSI circuits, and a family of SCSI test and development systems. Through Cognet Data Technologies, Inc. ADPT provides high-performance Fast Ethernet products for the networking market. ADPT supports all major IBM-compatible microcomputer architectures and intends to support new major architectures as they emerge.

ANNUAL EARNINGS AND DIVIDENDS PER SHARE

	3/31/97	3/31/96	3/31/95	3/31/94	3/31/93	3/31/92	3/31/91
Earnings Per Share	0.93	0.95	0.88	0.55	0.48	0.17	0.15
Dividends Per Share	①...	Nil	Nil	②...	③...	Nil	Nil

① 2-for-1 stk. split, 11/15/96 ② 2-for-1 stk. split, 1/28/94 ③ 2-for-1 stk. split, 4/6/92

ANNUAL FINANCIAL DATA

RECORD OF EARNINGS (IN THOUSANDS):

	3/31/97	3/31/96	3/31/95	3/31/94	3/31/93	3/31/92	3/31/91
Total Revenues	933,868	659,347	466,194	372,245	311,339	150,315	128,865
Costs and Expenses	⑤772,640	515,619	332,748	283,621	241,626	129,175	111,696
Depreciation & Amort	...	17,593	15,662	11,489	6,970	4,743	3,781
Operating Income	161,228	126,135	117,784	77,135	62,743	16,397	13,388
Income Bef Income Taxes	171,781	137,989	124,537	78,603	65,854	19,486	17,135
Income Taxes	64,220	34,614	31,135	19,653	16,464	4,872	4,931
Net Income	107,561	103,375	93,402	58,950	49,390	14,614	12,204
Aver. Shs. Outstg.	115,062	109,138	106,714	107,204	103,304	83,328	82,296

⑤ Incl. Depr. & Amort.

BALANCE SHEET (IN THOUSANDS):

Cash and Cash Equivalents	548,441	295,494	246,746	183,007	146,715	66,824	59,803
Receivables, Net	132,571	89,487	56,495	55,334	44,383	26,773	16,754
Inventories	53,184	55,028	31,712	38,940	33,377	20,964	13,585
Gross Property	⑤141,599	132,961	95,111	72,114	59,449	24,311	19,642
Accumulated Depreciation	...	40,183	27,248	20,592	14,849	10,856	8,352
Long-Term Debt	850	4,250	7,650	11,050	14,450	423	996
Net Stockholders' Equity	688,325	511,945	371,644	297,616	225,155	116,486	94,558
Total Assets	1,043,494	646,486	435,708	358,475	282,896	138,615	109,142
Total Current Assets	817,948	465,280	350,472	293,260	234,984	122,822	96,264
Total Current Liabilities	124,319	130,291	56,414	38,489	35,693	17,151	10,190
Net Working Capital	693,629	334,989	294,058	254,771	199,291	105,671	86,074
Year End Shares Outstg	...	106,040	103,354	104,582	101,428	82,672	78,208

① Net.

STATISTICAL RECORD:

Operating Profit Margin %	17.3	19.1	25.3	20.7	20.2	10.9	10.4
Book Value Per Share	...	4.83	3.60	2.84	2.22	1.41	1.21
Return on Equity %	15.6	20.2	25.1	19.8	21.9	12.5	12.9
Return on Assets %	10.3	16.0	21.4	16.4	17.5	10.5	11.2
P/E Ratio	44.2-18.8	25.6-11.5	13.9-8.0	18.2-8.4	16.2-4.5	13.9-6.1	20.3-7.6
Price Range	41⅛-17½	24⅛-10⅞	12⅛-7	10-4⅝	7¾-2⅛	2½-1⅛	3-1⅛

Statistics are as originally reported.
Figures for 3/31/97 are preliminary.

OFFICERS:
J.G. Adler, Chmn.
F.G. Saviers, Pres. & C.E.O.
P.G. Hansen, V.P.-Fin., C.F.O. & Asst. Sec.
C.G. O'Meara, V.P. & Treas.

INCORPORATED: CA, May, 1981

PRINCIPAL OFFICE: 691 S. Milpitas Blvd., Milpitas, CA 95035

TELEPHONE NUMBER: (408) 945-8600
FAX: (408) 945-9095
NO. OF EMPLOYEES: 2,211
ANNUAL MEETING: In August
SHAREHOLDERS: 724
INSTITUTIONAL HOLDINGS:
No. of Institutions: 183
Shares Held: 95,279,964

REGISTRAR(S):

TRANSFER AGENT(S): Chemical Trust Co. of California, San Francisco, CA

ADC TELECOMMUNICATIONS INC.

YIELD ...%
P/E RATIO 39.8

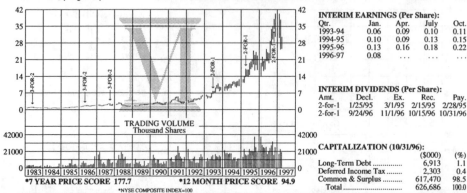

TRADING VOLUME
Thousand Shares

| 1983 | 1984 | 1985 | 1986 | 1987 | 1988 | 1989 | 1990 | 1991 | 1992 | 1993 | 1994 | 1995 | 1996 | 1997 |

*7 YEAR PRICE SCORE 177.7   *12 MONTH PRICE SCORE 94.9

*NYSE COMPOSITE INDEX=100

INTERIM EARNINGS (Per Share):

Qtr.	Jan.	Apr.	July	Oct.
1993-94	0.06	0.09	0.10	0.11
1994-95	0.10	0.09	0.13	0.15
1995-96	0.13	0.16	0.18	0.22
1996-97	0.08	...	...	...

INTERIM DIVIDENDS (Per Share):

Amt.	Decl.	Ex.	Rec.	Pay.
2-for-1	1/25/95	3/1/95	2/15/95	2/28/95
2-for-1	9/24/96	11/1/96	10/15/96	10/31/96

CAPITALIZATION (10/31/96):

	($000)	(%)
Long-Term Debt	6,913	1.1
Deferred Income Tax	2,303	0.4
Common & Surplus	617,470	98.5
Total	626,686	100.0

RECENT DEVELOPMENTS: On 3/31/97, the Company announced the completion of its acquisition of The Apex Group, Inc., a software development and information management company based in Columbia, Maryland. The stock-for-stock purchase was valued at approximately $26.0 million and accounted for as a pooling of interests. On 2/3/97, ADCT announced intentions to develop, with CAI Wireless Systems Inc. (CAI) a fixed two-way broadband wireless test system for the transmission of video,

voice and data using the ADCT's Homework™ platform and CAI's Multichannel Multipoint Distribution Services spectrum. For the first quarter ended 1/31/97, net income declined 36.3% to $10.4 million. This compares with $16.3 million in the corresponding prior-year quarter. Net sales grew 57.9% to $256.8 million from $162.6 million in the comparable quarter the year before. The operating results included non-recurring charges of $22.7 million.

BUSINESS

ADC TELECOMMUNICATIONS INC. designs, manufactures and markets products that serve a broad range of transmission, networking and cable management functions in telecommunications networks utilizing copper and fiber optic transmission media. The Company markets its products worldwide through its own direct sales force, as well as through distributors, dealer organizations and original equipment manufacturers. The Company's products are designed primarily for use in the public telecommunications networks maintained by telephone operating companies, other telecommunications common carriers and broadcast networks, and for use in private telecommunications networks maintained by large businesses, government agencies, and educational and other non-profit institutions.

ANNUAL EARNINGS AND DIVIDENDS PER SHARE

	10/31/96	10/31/95	10/31/94	10/31/93	10/31/92	10/31/91	10/31/90
Earnings Per Share	0.68	0.47	③0.37	0.29	0.19	0.20	0.22
Dividends Per Share	①...	②...	Nil	④...	Nil	Nil	Nil

① 2-for-1 stk. split, 10/31/96 ② 2-for-1 stk. split, 2/28/95 ③ Before extra. item ④ 2-for-1 stk. split, 6/29/93

ANNUAL FINANCIAL DATA

RECORD OF EARNINGS (IN THOUSANDS):

Total Revenues	828,009	586,222	448,735	366,118	316,496	293,839	259,802
Costs and Expenses	689,590	502,765	381,221	312,871	277,903	237,344	207,751
Depreciation & Amort	33,794	26,341	23,366	20,587	19,878	17,954	14,306
Operating Income	133,184	80,324	64,379	50,449	35,873	38,541	37,745
Income Bef Income Taxes	136,663	86,229	64,321	49,737	34,726	36,405	38,172
Income Taxes	49,200	31,043	23,800	18,101	13,700	14,380	15,269
Net Income	87,463	55,186	①40,521	31,636	21,026	22,025	22,903
Aver. Shs. Outstg.	128,314	117,094	111,220	109,996	108,352	106,952	106,120

① Before extra. item dr$1,450,000.

BALANCE SHEET (IN THOUSANDS):

Cash and Cash Equivalents	183,221	238,491	49,512	16,324	20,484	30,109	25,978
Receivables, Net	163,219	107,255	75,348	66,830	47,414	41,373	37,338
Inventories	130,582	86,559	64,203	48,278	39,063	40,427	33,845
Gross Property	275,631	191,537	162,189	146,528	127,441	116,779	94,965
Accumulated Depreciation	144,551	112,851	96,057	83,652	69,496	58,971	49,581
Long-Term Debt	6,913	...	410	810	14,110	43,634	4,841
Net Stockholders' Equity	617,470	510,866	264,758	220,394	182,188	158,374	134,013
Total Assets	768,765	601,083	334,684	280,054	240,762	247,169	181,665
Total Current Assets	499,501	447,747	199,368	142,531	115,355	119,530	102,525
Total Current Liabilities	142,079	88,961	67,353	54,901	40,071	40,525	37,335
Net Working Capital	357,422	358,786	132,015	87,630	75,284	79,005	65,190
Year End Shares Outstg	130,354	125,474	111,552	110,788	108,880	107,432	106,312

STATISTICAL RECORD:

Operating Profit Margin %	16.1	13.7	14.3	13.8	11.3	13.1	14.5
Book Value Per Share	3.68	3.48	1.75	1.32	1.05	0.82	0.94
Return on Equity %	14.2	10.8	15.3	14.4	11.5	13.9	17.1
Return on Assets %	11.4	9.2	12.1	11.3	8.7	8.9	12.6
P/E Ratio	59.2-21.0	52.7-24.2	34.5-21.6	37.9-15.9	30.6-14.4	25.6-12.5	14.8-8.5
Price Range	40¼-14¼	24¾-11⅜	12¾-8	11-4⅝	6⅛-2⅞	5⅜-2⅝	3¼-1⅞

Statistics are as originally reported.

OFFICERS:
W.J. Cadogan, Chmn., Pres., C.E.O. & C.O.O.
R.E. Switz, V.P. & C.F.O.

INCORPORATED: MN, 1953

PRINCIPAL OFFICE: 12501 Whitewater Dr., Minnetonka, MN 55343

TELEPHONE NUMBER: (612) 938-8080
FAX: (612) 946-3292
NO. OF EMPLOYEES: 4,620
ANNUAL MEETING: In February
SHAREHOLDERS: 3,232 (approx.)
INSTITUTIONAL HOLDINGS:
No. of Institutions: 188
Shares Held: 98,085,416

REGISTRAR(S): Norwest Bank Minnesota, N.A., South St. Paul, MN

TRANSFER AGENT(S): Norwest Bank Minnesota, N.A., South St. Paul, MN

ADOBE SYSTEMS INC.

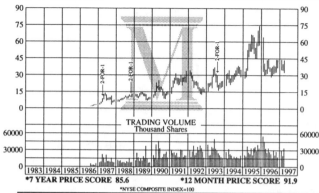

TRADING VOLUME
Thousand Shares

1983 1984 1985 1986 1987 1988 1989 1990 1991 1992 1993 1994 1995 1996 1997

*7 YEAR PRICE SCORE 85.6   *12 MONTH PRICE SCORE 91.9
*NYSE COMPOSITE INDEX=100

INTERIM EARNINGS (Per Share):

Qtr.	Feb.	May	Aug.	Nov.
1993-94	0.30	0.27	0.29	d0.65
1994-95	0.50	0.47	0.44	d0.16
1995-96	0.44	0.29	0.40	0.92
1996-97	0.63	. . .	. . .	. . .

INTERIM DIVIDENDS (Per Share):

Amt.	Decl.	Ex.	Rec.	Pay.
0.05Q	3/21/96	4/2/96	4/4/96	4/18/96
0.05Q	6/25	7/3	7/8	7/22
0.05Q	9/25	9/30	10/2	10/16
0.05Q	12/18	1/14/97	1/16/97	1/30/97
0.05Q	3/18/97	3/27	4/1	4/15

Indicated div.: $0.20

CAPITALIZATION (11/29/96):

	($000)	(%)
Deferred Income Tax	3,809	0.5
Common & Surplus	706,514	99.5
Total	710,323	100.0

RECENT DEVELOPMENTS: For the first quarter ended 2/28/97, net income grew 38.1% to $46.5 million from $33.7 million in the comparable quarter the year before. Total revenues were up 16.9% to $226.5 million compared with $193.6 million in the corresponding year-earlier period. Application products revenue increased 19.3% to $175.0 million, with 50% of retail products revenue coming from the sale of products for Windows platforms and 50% coming from those for Macintosh platforms. Licensing revenues for the quarter totaled $51.5 million, up 9.7% over the prior year. Operating expenses in the current quarter included $2.4 million for non-recurring items. The prior-year results included sales, marketing and customer support expenses of $62.6 million and amortization of software development costs of $626,000 that were not reported in the current year.

BUSINESS

ADOBE SYSTEMS INCORPORATED develops and supports computer software products and technologies that enable users to create, display, print and communicate all forms of electronic documents. The Company's principal products are: (1) Photoshop digital editing software for photographs to be used in print and electronic documents and web sites; and (2) PostScript, which displays, interprets and implements page layouts with multiple and mixed type fonts, graphics, illustrations and diagrams.

QUARTERLY DATA

(11/29/96)($000)	Rev	Inc
1st Quarter	193,642	33,663
2nd Quarter	204,337	22,009
3rd Quarter	180,909	29,847
4th Quarter	207,675	67,758

ANNUAL EARNINGS AND DIVIDENDS PER SHARE

	11/29/96	12/1/95	11/25/94	11/26/93	11/27/92	11/29/91	11/30/90
Earnings Per Share	2.04	1.26	0.22	1.22	0.94	1.13	0.91
Dividends Per Share	0.20	0.20	0.20	0.19	0.16	0.15	0.115
Dividend Payout %	9.8	15.9	90.9	15.6	17.1	13.3	12.6

ANNUAL FINANCIAL DATA

RECORD OF EARNINGS (IN MILLIONS):

	11/29/96	12/1/95	11/25/94	11/26/93	11/27/92	11/29/91	11/30/90
Total Revenues	786.6	762.3	675.6	313.5	265.9	229.7	168.7
Costs and Expenses	584.2	567.3	575.3	206.5	178.5	136.5	95.4
Depreciation & Amort	55.6	60.4	57.8	26.0	19.0	15.2	11.1
Operating Income	146.8	134.6	42.5	81.0	68.4	77.9	62.2
Income Bef Income Taxes	244.8	163.9	52.9	91.1	69.5	83.6	66.3
Income Taxes	91.5	70.4	37.6	34.0	25.9	32.0	26.2
Net Income	153.3	93.5	15.3	57.0	43.6	51.6	40.1
Aver. Shs. Outstg. (000)	75,064	74,253	70,169	46,627	46,650	45,882	43,846

BALANCE SHEET (IN MILLIONS):

	11/29/96	12/1/95	11/25/94	11/26/93	11/27/92	11/29/91	11/30/90
Cash and Cash Equivalents	564.1	516.0	444.8	236.3	159.8	116.3	69.7
Receivables, Net	126.7	133.2	111.3	49.8	48.9	37.9	31.3
Inventories	. . .	. . .	10.1	4.1	4.8	3.9	4.0
Gross Property	157.6	155.9	136.7	62.5	48.9	32.0	24.8
Accumulated Depreciation	77.4	104.2	90.1	39.2	28.1	19.3	12.7
Net Stockholders' Equity	706.5	698.4	514.3	272.3	224.6	182.8	107.8
Total Assets	1,012.3	884.7	710.0	352.9	281.3	221.2	145.7
Total Current Assets	736.7	692.8	598.5	304.3	224.4	161.6	109.1
Total Current Liabilities	230.6	186.3	195.7	73.7	56.8	36.9	37.0
Net Working Capital	506.1	506.5	402.8	230.6	167.6	124.7	72.1
Year End Shs Outstg (000)	71,476	72,834	61,150	45,167	44,449	44,266	41,913

STATISTICAL RECORD:

	11/29/96	12/1/95	11/25/94	11/26/93	11/27/92	11/29/91	11/30/90
Operating Profit Margin %	18.7	17.7	6.3	25.8	25.7	33.9	36.8
Book Value Per Share	9.88	9.59	8.41	6.03	5.05	4.13	2.57
Return on Equity %	21.7	13.4	3.0	20.9	19.4	28.2	37.2
Return on Assets %	15.1	10.6	2.2	16.2	15.5	23.3	27.5
Average Yield %	0.4	0.4	0.7	0.7	0.7	0.6	0.7
P/E Ratio	31.5-14.0	58.9-21.6	N.M.	30.3-12.8	36.4-13.4	30.0-11.8	27.9-9.3
Price Range	64¼-28½	74¼-27¼	38½-20½	37-15⅝	34¼-12⅝	33⅞-13⅜	25⅜-8½

Statistics are as originally reported.

OFFICERS:
J.E. Warnock, Chmn. & C.E.O.
C.M. Geschke, Pres.
P.J. Bell, Exec. V.P., C.F.O. & C.A.O.
C.M. Pouliot, V.P., Gen. Couns. & Sec.

INCORPORATED: CA, Oct., 1983

PRINCIPAL OFFICE: 345 Park Ave., San Jose, CA 95110-2704

TELEPHONE NUMBER: (408) 536-6000

FAX: (408) 537-4032

NO. OF EMPLOYEES: 2,266

ANNUAL MEETING: In April

SHAREHOLDERS: 2,238

INSTITUTIONAL HOLDINGS:
No. of Institutions: 173
Shares Held: 50,044,380

REGISTRAR(S): Harris Trust Co. of California, Chicago, IL

TRANSFER AGENT(S): Harris Trust Co. of California, Chicago, IL

ADTRAN, INC.

YIELD ...%
P/E RATIO 29.6

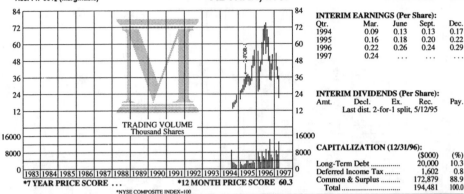

*7 YEAR PRICE SCORE ... *12 MONTH PRICE SCORE 60.3

*NYSE COMPOSITE INDEX=100

TRADING VOLUME
Thousand Shares

INTERIM EARNINGS (Per Share):

Qtr.	Mar.	June	Sept.	Dec.
1994	0.09	0.13	0.13	0.17
1995	0.16	0.18	0.20	0.22
1996	0.22	0.26	0.24	0.29
1997	0.24	...	...	...

INTERIM DIVIDENDS (Per Share):

Amt.	Decl.	Ex.	Rec.	Pay.
Last dist. 2-for-1 split, 5/12/95				

CAPITALIZATION (12/31/96):

	($000)	(%)
Long-Term Debt	20,000	10.3
Deferred Income Tax	1,602	0.8
Common & Surplus	172,879	88.9
Total	194,481	100.0

RECENT DEVELOPMENTS: For the quarter ended 3/31/97, net income rose 10.4% to $9.5 million. This compares with $8.6 million in the corresponding quarter the year before. Sales increased 12.3% to $61.2 million from $54.5 million in the comparable year-earlier period. Contributing to the improved results were a 14.9% increase in Integrated Services Digital Network (ISDN) revenues and a 39.3% increase in High bit-rate Digital Subscriber Line/T1 shipments. These improvements were partially offset by a 15.2% decline in DDS/Frame Relay revenues. The Company's Total Reach product has been made available in commercial quantities, with ADTN receiving one significant order. On 4/3/97, the Company announced a distribution partnership with Tech Data Corp., a distributor of personal computer products. Tech Data will distribute ADTN's full-line of ISDN, T1 and DDS network access products to its resellers and retail dealers throughout the United States.

BUSINESS

ADTRAN, INC. designs, develops, manufactures, markets and services a broad range of high-speed digital transmission products utilized by telephone companies and corporate end-users to implement advanced digital data services over existing telephone networks. The Company also customizes many of its products for private label distribution and for original equipment manufacturers to incorporate into their own products. ADTN's product lines are comprised of more than 200 product lines and are built around a core technology development by the Company to address the Local Loop and Central Office digital communications marketplace.

ANNUAL EARNINGS AND DIVIDENDS PER SHARE

	1996	1995	1994	1993	1992	1991
Earnings Per Share	1.01	0.75	0.52	0.25	0.26	...
Dividends Per Share	Nil	①...	Nil	Nil	Nil	...

① 2-for-1 stk. split, 5/12/95

ANNUAL FINANCIAL DATA

RECORD OF EARNINGS (IN THOUSANDS):

	1996	1995	1994	1993	1992	1991
Total Revenues	250,121	181,478	123,440	72,411	57,042	42,621
Costs and Expenses	184,019	136,345	92,056	56,973	42,036	31,079
Depreciation & Amort	4,890	3,053	2,253	1,727	1,319	1,193
Operating Income	61,212	42,080	29,132	13,710	13,687	10,349
Income Bef Income Taxes	63,502	44,291	29,099	13,281	13,733	...
Income Taxes	23,682	14,834	6,289	...	...	...
Net Income	39,820	29,458	22,811	13,281	13,733	10,376
Aver. Shs. Outstg.	39,566	39,290	36,132	34,061	34,125	33,900

BALANCE SHEET (IN THOUSANDS):

	1996	1995	1994	1993	1992	1991
Cash and Cash Equivalents	77,395	59,680	27,265	162	90	...
Receivables, Net	35,787	31,161	18,791	12,470	7,635	...
Inventories	40,793	44,997	27,524	15,598	9,848	...
Gross Property	67,608	38,123	25,594	21,871	16,574	...
Accumulated Depreciation	13,637	8,878	6,063	3,987	2,349	...
Long-Term Debt	20,000	20,000	...	...	...	...
Capital Lease Obligations	...	...	...	7,922	5,567	...
Net Stockholders' Equity	172,879	130,743	85,233	29,757	21,974	...
Total Assets	210,207	165,767	94,347	46,304	31,947	...
Total Current Assets	156,236	136,522	74,817	28,420	17,722	...
Total Current Liabilities	15,726	14,056	8,449	8,624	4,407	...
Net Working Capital	140,510	122,466	66,368	19,795	13,315	...
Year End Shares Outstg	38,770	37,462	36,147	31,204	31,203	...

STATISTICAL RECORD:

	1996	1995	1994	1993	1992	1991
Operating Profit Margin %	24.5	23.2	23.6	18.9	24.0	24.3
Book Value Per Share	4.46	3.49	2.36	0.95	0.70	...
Return on Equity %	23.0	22.5	26.8	44.6	62.5	...
Return on Assets %	18.9	17.8	24.2	28.7	43.0	...
P/E Ratio	74.5-25.5	74.0-26.7	45.0-25.5	...	...	...
Price Range	75¼-25¾	55½-20	23⅜-13¼	...	...	...

Statistics are as originally reported.

OFFICERS:
M.C. Smith, Chmn. & C.E.O.
H.A. Thrailkill, Pres. & C.O.O.
J.R. Cooper, V.P.-Fin. & C.F.O.
L.S. McMillian, Sr. V.P. & Sec.

INCORPORATED: DE, Nov., 1985

PRINCIPAL OFFICE: 901 Explorer Boulevard, Huntsville, AL 35807

TELEPHONE NUMBER: (205) 971-8000
FAX: (205) 971-8699
NO. OF EMPLOYEES: 894
ANNUAL MEETING: In April
SHAREHOLDERS: 561
INSTITUTIONAL HOLDINGS:
No. of Institutions: 57
Shares Held: 4,690,402

REGISTRAR(S): First Union National Bank of N.C., Charlotte, NC

TRANSFER AGENT(S): First Union National Bank of N.C., Charlotte, NC

NASDAQ SYMBOL ALTR
Rec. Pr. $46\frac{5}{8}$ (Marginable)

ALTERA CORP.

YIELD ...%
P/E RATIO 37.9

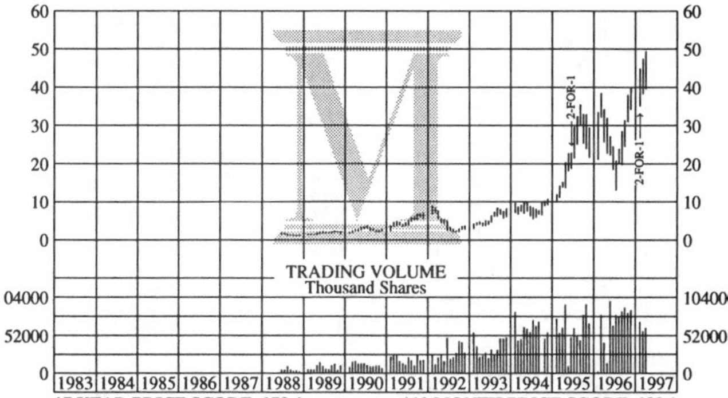

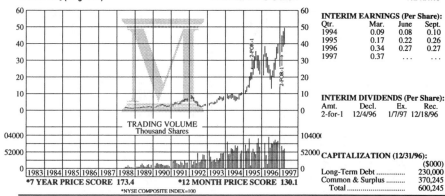

*7 YEAR PRICE SCORE 173.4 *12 MONTH PRICE SCORE 130.1

*NYSE COMPOSITE INDEX=100

INTERIM EARNINGS (Per Share):

Qtr.	Mar.	June	Sept.	Dec.
1994	0.09	0.08	0.10	d0.11
1995	0.17	0.22	0.26	0.31
1996	0.34	0.27	0.27	0.32
1997	0.37	...	...	...

INTERIM DIVIDENDS (Per Share):

Amt.	Decl.	Ex.	Rec.	Pay.
2-for-1	12/4/96	1/7/97	12/18/96	1/6/97

CAPITALIZATION (12/31/96):

	($000)	(%)
Long-Term Debt	230,000	38.3
Common & Surplus	370,245	61.7
Total	600,245	100.0

RECENT DEVELOPMENTS: For the three months ended 3/31/97, net income increased 8.3% to $34.1 million compared with $31.4 million in the corresponding period the year before. Sales were up 3.9% to $142.4 million from $137.1 million the previous year. The strongest sales increase was reported in the Company's domestic business, while international operations also posted sales growth. Sales in the computer segment paced overall sales growth, and sales to the communications marketplace continued to be strong. Gross margin as a percentage of sales rose to 62.0% from 61.3% a year earlier due to improved yields and wafer price reductions. During the quarter, ALTR added $81.9 million of cash to its balance sheet, after expenditures of $18.7 million toward the construction of the Company's new San Jose headquarters facility, and $4.6 million for routine capital expenditures.

BUSINESS

ALTERA CORPORATION designs, develops, and markets CMOS (complementary-metal-oxide-semiconductor) programmable logic integrated circuits and associated computer-aided engineering development software and hardware. The Company's semiconductor products, which are generally known as EPLD's (Erasable Programmable Logic Devices) and FLEX (Flexible Logic Element matriX) devices, are standard logic chips that customers configure for specific end-use applications using the Company's proprietary software.

ANNUAL EARNINGS AND DIVIDENDS PER SHARE

	1996	1995	1994	1993	1992	1991	1990
Earnings Per Share	**1.18**	**0.96**	**0.17**	**0.25**	**0.14**	**0.22**	**0.17**
Dividends Per Share	**Nil**	**[1]...**	**Nil**	**Nil**	**Nil**	**Nil**	**Nil**

Note: 2-for-1 stk. split, 1/6/97. [1] 2-for-1 stk. split, 5/31/95

ANNUAL FINANCIAL DATA

	1996	1995	1994	1993	1992	1991	1990
RECORD OF EARNINGS (IN THOUSANDS):							
Total Revenues	497,306	401,598	198,796	140,279	101,470	106,862	78,304
Costs and Expenses	308,329	255,149	159,909	102,705	77,616	74,843	54,947
Depreciation & Amort	20,884	12,166	9,528	7,814	7,351	5,807	4,621
Operating Income	168,093	134,283	29,359	29,760	16,503	26,212	18,736
Income Bef Income Taxes	169,137	137,891	31,496	31,392	18,024	27,845	20,717
Income Taxes	60,002	51,020	16,888	10,197	6,485	10,038	7,332
Net Income	109,135	86,871	14,608	21,195	11,539	17,807	13,385
Aver. Shs. Outstg.	96,631	91,154	86,492	83,984	82,572	82,268	79,968
BALANCE SHEET (IN THOUSANDS):							
Cash and Cash Equivalents	280,850	365,219	92,594	81,637	50,578	40,149	23,285
Receivables, Net	113,888	91,857	44,027	29,656	18,499	20,241	15,489
Inventories	75,798	55,421	38,477	16,242	15,031	10,896	12,122
Gross Property	141,334	94,653	50,260	41,235	37,221	32,001	26,136
Accumulated Depreciation	51,530	39,807	32,048	27,542	22,315	16,533	12,955
Long-Term Debt	230,000	288,600	...	...	...	...	...
Net Stockholders' Equity	370,245	255,189	158,019	121,699	95,606	81,450	61,010
Total Assets	778,212	715,554	213,882	155,757	114,693	102,206	74,947
Total Current Assets	472,987	518,007	177,342	128,953	85,595	72,170	51,908
Total Current Liabilities	177,967	171,765	55,863	34,058	19,087	20,756	13,937
Net Working Capital	295,020	346,242	121,479	94,895	66,508	51,414	37,971
Year End Shares Outstg	87,604	87,116	85,952	81,632	80,304	79,176	77,656
STATISTICAL RECORD:							
Operating Profit Margin %	33.8	33.4	14.8	21.2	16.3	24.5	23.9
Book Value Per Share	2.12	2.93	1.84	1.49	1.19	1.03	0.79
Return on Equity %	29.5	34.0	9.2	17.4	12.1	21.9	21.9
Return on Assets %	14.0	12.1	6.8	13.6	10.1	17.4	17.9
P/E Ratio	33.6-11.0	37.4-10.4	31.6-15.8	16.4-5.9	32.1-7.1	16.2-5.1	11.0-5.1
Price Range	40-$13\frac{1}{8}$	$35\frac{1}{2}$-$9\frac{7}{8}$	$10\frac{3}{4}$-$5\frac{3}{8}$	$8\frac{3}{8}$-3	9-2	$7\frac{1}{8}$-$2\frac{1}{4}$	$3\frac{3}{4}$-$1\frac{3}{4}$

Statistics are as originally reported.

OFFICERS:
R. Smith, Chmn., Pres. & C.E.O.
D. Berlan, Exec. V.P. & C.O.O.
C.W. Bergere, V.P., Couns. & Sec.
N. Sarkisian, V.P.-Fin. & C.F.O.

INCORPORATED: CA, Jan., 1984

PRINCIPAL OFFICE: 2610 Orchard Parkway, San Jose, CA 95134-2020

TELEPHONE NUMBER: (408) 894-7000

FAX: (408) 428-0463

NO. OF EMPLOYEES: 918

ANNUAL MEETING: In April

SHAREHOLDERS: 20,000 (approx.)

INSTITUTIONAL HOLDINGS:
No. of Institutions: 158
Shares Held: 71,384,850 (adj.)

REGISTRAR(S): Bank of Boston, Boston, MA

TRANSFER AGENT(S): Bank of Boston, Boston, MA

AMERICAN GREETINGS CORP.

YIELD 2.3%
P/E RATIO 13.5

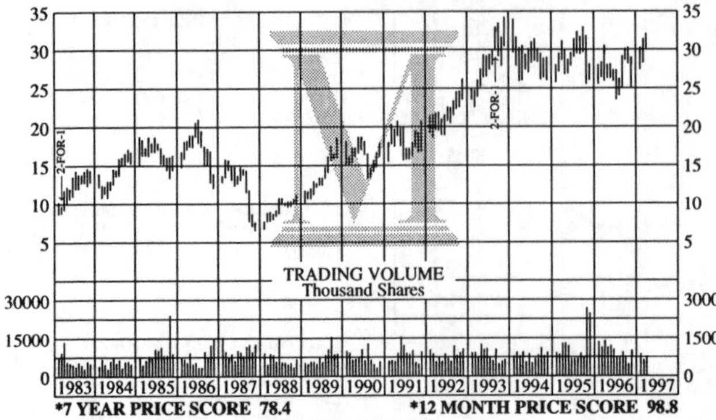

TRADING VOLUME
Thousand Shares

| 1983 | 1984 | 1985 | 1986 | 1987 | 1988 | 1989 | 1990 | 1991 | 1992 | 1993 | 1994 | 1995 | 1996 | 1997 |

*7 YEAR PRICE SCORE 78.4   *12 MONTH PRICE SCORE 98.8

*NYSE COMPOSITE INDEX=100

INTERIM EARNINGS (Per Share):

Qtr.	May	Aug.	Nov.	Feb.
1993-94	0.40	0.16	0.70	0.53
1994-95	0.45	0.18	0.79	0.58
1995-96	0.50	0.20	0.24	0.60
1996-97	0.37	0.15	1.00	0.71

INTERIM DIVIDENDS (Per Share):

Amt.	Decl.	Ex.	Rec.	Pay.
0.16Q	4/22/96	5/22/96	5/27/96	6/10/96
0.17Q	6/28	8/23	8/27	9/10
0.17Q	10/28	11/22	11/26	12/10
0.17Q	1/27/97	2/20/97	2/24/97	3/10/97
0.17Q	4/7	5/22	5/27	6/10

Indicated div.: $0.68

CAPITALIZATION (2/29/96):

	($000)	(%)
Long-Term Debt	231,073	15.3
Deferred Income Tax	45,084	3.0
Common & Surplus	1,235,022	81.7
Total	1,511,179	100.0

RECENT DEVELOPMENTS: For the fiscal year ended 2/28/97, net income rose 45.1% to $167.1 million from $115.1 million the year before. Net sales were up 7.9% to $2.16 billion compared with $2.00 billion a year earlier. The increase in sales was attributed to growth in the Company's core everyday and seasonal greeting card business. AGRE's greeting card operations reported increases in sales and operating income that were near double-digit levels. Results from the Consumer Products Group, particu-larly Magnivision and AG Industries, were below the Company's expectations. For the fourth quarter ended 2/28/97, net income grew 17.6% to $53.3 million from $45.3 million in the corresponding prior-year quarter. Net sales were up 11.5% to $608.6 million compared with $545.8 million the previous year. The Company has absorbed costs associated with testing its Learning Horizons educational products and is completing the re-engineering of its Danville, Kentucky distribution center.

BUSINESS

AMERICAN GREETINGS CORPO-RATION is engaged in the design, manufacture and sale of everyday and seasonal greeting cards and other social expression products. The Company has operations, subsidiaries and licensees in more than 75 countries, and prints its products in 23 languages.

ANNUAL EARNINGS AND DIVIDENDS PER SHARE

	2/29/96	2/28/95	2/28/94	2/28/93	2/29/92	2/28/91	2/28/90
Earnings Per Share	1.54	2.00	① 1.77	1.55	1.40	1.32	1.14
Dividends Per Share	0.60	0.53	② 0.465	0.42	0.38	0.345	0.34
Dividend Payout %	39.0	26.5	26.3	26.5	26.4	26.4	29.4

① Before acctg. change ② 2-for-1 stk. split, 9/13/93

ANNUAL FINANCIAL DATA

RECORD OF EARNINGS (IN MILLIONS):

	2/29/96	2/28/95	2/28/94	2/28/93	2/29/92	2/28/91	2/28/90
Total Revenues	2,012.0	1,878.4	1,780.8	1,688.2	1,573.1	1,431.8	1,309.0
Costs and Expenses	1,737.3	1,566.0	1,494.9	1,431.7	1,344.1	1,227.7	1,124.6
Depreciation & Amort	75.3	68.4	59.6	48.5	45.5	42.2	40.3
Operating Income	199.3	244.0	226.3	208.0	183.4	161.9	144.1
Income Bef Income Taxes	175.0	227.2	209.4	181.1	153.0	130.5	116.4
Income Taxes	59.9	78.4	78.5	68.8	55.5	48.0	44.2
Net Income	115.1	148.8	① 130.9	112.3	97.5	82.5	72.2
Aver. Shs. Outstg. (000)	74,529	74,305	73,809	72,440	69,514	63,291	64,059

① Before acctg. change dr$17,182,000.

BALANCE SHEET (IN MILLIONS):

	2/29/96	2/28/95	2/28/94	2/28/93	2/29/92	2/28/91	2/28/90
Cash and Cash Equivalents	30.1	87.2	101.0	235.2	177.4	80.5	122.7
Receivables, Net	456.6	390.7	384.8	343.3	323.3	348.0	305.6
Inventories	335.1	279.3	243.4	228.1	276.0	277.6	242.3
Gross Property	851.1	862.0	794.0	708.2	658.9	612.6	576.7
Accumulated Depreciation	410.9	413.2	365.0	320.7	288.4	255.5	224.4
Long-Term Debt	231.1	74.5	54.2	169.4	255.7	246.2	235.5
Net Stockholders' Equity	1,235.0	1,159.5	1,053.4	952.5	865.0	656.6	604.6
Total Assets	2,005.8	1,761.8	1,565.2	1,548.4	1,437.8	1,255.7	1,141.0
Total Current Assets	970.2	893.4	850.2	911.9	847.5	738.4	680.9
Total Current Liabilities	453.8	362.3	375.9	330.2	218.5	254.2	200.8
Net Working Capital	516.3	531.2	474.3	581.7	629.0	484.2	480.2
Year End Shs Outstg (000)	74,708	74,302	74,119	72,902	71,768	63,219	64,018

STATISTICAL RECORD:

	2/29/96	2/28/95	2/28/94	2/28/93	2/29/92	2/28/91	2/28/90
Operating Profit Margin %	9.9	13.0	12.7	12.3	11.7	11.3	11.0
Book Value Per Share	16.53	15.61	14.21	13.07	12.05	10.39	9.44
Return on Equity %	9.3	12.8	12.4	11.8	11.3	12.6	11.9
Return on Assets %	5.7	8.4	8.4	7.3	6.8	6.6	6.3
Average Yield %	2.1	1.8	1.6	1.9	2.1	2.1	2.4
P/E Ratio	21.4-16.6	17.0-12.9	19.4-12.7	16.9-12.0	14.8-11.1	14.3-10.2	16.6-9.1
Price Range	33-25½	34-25⅞	34¼-22½	26¼-18⅝	20¾-15½	18¾-13⅜	18⅝-10¼

Statistics are as originally reported.

OFFICERS:
I.I. Stone, Founder-Chmn.
M. Weiss, Chmn. & C.E.O.
E. Fruchtenbaum, Pres. & C.O.O.
W.S. Meyer, Sr. V.P. & C.F.O.

INCORPORATED: OH, Jan., 1944

PRINCIPAL OFFICE: One American Road, Cleveland, OH 44144-2398

TELEPHONE NUMBER: (216) 252-7300
FAX: (216) 252-6777
NO. OF EMPLOYEES: 16,300 full-time; 20,500 part-time
ANNUAL MEETING: In June
SHAREHOLDERS: 21,010 (approx.)
INSTITUTIONAL HOLDINGS:
No. of Institutions: 220
Shares Held: 60,036,709

REGISTRAR(S): National City Bank, Corporate Trust Administration, Cleveland, OH

TRANSFER AGENT(S): National City Bank, Corporate Trust Administration, Cleveland, OH

NASDAQ SYMBOL APCC
Rec. Pr. 21⅞ (Marginable)

AMERICAN POWER CONVERSION CORP.

YIELD ...%
P/E RATIO 21.0

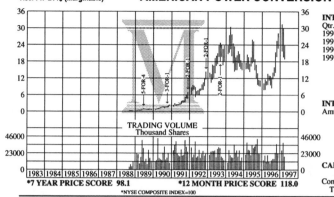

*7 YEAR PRICE SCORE 98.1 *12 MONTH PRICE SCORE 118.0
*NYSE COMPOSITE INDEX=100

TRADING VOLUME Thousand Shares

INTERIM EARNINGS (Per Share):

Qtr.	Mar.	June	Sept.	Dec.
1994	0.15	0.17	0.21	0.25
1995	0.20	0.19	0.18	0.18
1996	0.16	0.20	0.30	0.32
1997	0.22	...	...	...

INTERIM DIVIDENDS (Per Share):

Amt.	Decl.	Ex.	Rec.	Pay.
Last dist. 2-for-1 split, 9/24/93				

CAPITALIZATION (12/31/96):

	($000)	(%)
Common & Surplus	391,898	100.0
Total	391,898	100.0

RECENT DEVELOPMENTS: For the first quarter ended 3/30/97, net earnings increased 38.2% to $21.0 million. This compares with $15.2 million in the corresponding quarter the previous year. Sales for the quarter were up 21.5% to $172.0 million from $141.6 million in the comparable year-earlier quarter. Domestic sales rose 29.0% for the quarter, while international sales grew 10.0%. During the quarter, APCC made its first entry into the above 5 kVA power protection market with the introduction of the

Symmetra Power Array, which combines high-availability power protection with remote manageability, predictive failure and proactive alerts for data centers. Also during the quarter, the Company announced the acquisition of Systems Enhancement Corporation, which develops and markets power management software solutions to the uninterruptible power supply market. Systems Enhancement was purchased for approximately $12.6 million in APCC stock.

BUSINESS

AMERICAN POWER CONVERSION CORP. designs, manufactures and markets Uninterruptible Power Supplies (UPS), power protection equipment, including surge protectors, power conditioning equipment and related software for computer and computer-related equipment. A UPS provides surge suppression, line filtering and instantaneous battery backup power in the event of a complete power loss. By keeping the power supplied to the computer within safe limits, a UPS prevents hardware damage and keeps vital data intact.

ANNUAL EARNINGS AND DIVIDENDS PER SHARE

	1996	1995	1994	1993	1992	1991	1990
Earnings Per Share	0.98	0.74	0.77	0.53	0.31	0.18	0.11
Dividends Per Share	Nil	Nil	Nil	⑪...	⑫...	⑬...	⑭...

⑪ 2-for-1 stk. split, 9/27/93 ⑫ 2-for-1 stk. split, 12/18/92 ⑬ 2-for-1 stk. split, 12/9/91 ⑭ 3-for-1 stk. split, 9/28/90

ANNUAL FINANCIAL DATA

RECORD OF EARNINGS (IN THOUSANDS):

	1996	1995	1994	1993	1992	1991	1990
Total Revenues	706,877	515,262	378,295	250,298	157,462	93,624	59,247
Costs and Expenses	559,576	401,455	266,541	172,413	112,809	68,570	43,799
Depreciation & Amort	13,511	10,102	6,105	2,988	1,823	897	759
Operating Income	133,790	103,705	105,649	74,898	42,830	24,156	14,689
Income Bef Income Taxes	138,979	104,565	109,350	75,875	43,073	24,186	14,741
Income Taxes	46,558	35,029	38,075	27,316	15,291	8,619	5,395
Net Income	92,421	69,536	71,275	48,559	27,782	15,567	9,346
Aver. Shs. Outstg.	94,347	93,867	92,913	91,588	91,004	90,869	87,193

BALANCE SHEET (IN THOUSANDS):

Cash and Cash Equivalents	153,234	39,040	41,480	47,752	20,984	12,169	3,007
Receivables, Net	128,828	82,522	68,050	37,645	23,222	13,785	9,559
Inventories	130,443	147,541	92,416	49,072	38,166	20,661	16,674
Gross Property	114,353	89,348	66,563	30,659	19,718	13,288	7,792
Accumulated Depreciation	35,655	22,144	13,109	7,004	4,016	2,193	1,595
Net Stockholders' Equity	391,898	289,766	211,928	131,904	75,959	43,652	25,552
Total Assets	504,002	346,588	265,163	158,971	98,454	58,173	35,850
Total Current Assets	424,115	278,381	210,866	135,267	82,733	46,909	29,453
Total Current Liabilities	106,324	51,923	50,254	25,397	21,457	14,007	7,138
Net Working Capital	317,791	226,458	160,612	109,870	61,276	32,902	22,315
Year End Shares Outstg	94,292	93,271	92,452	90,869	87,850	86,086	84,750

STATISTICAL RECORD:

Operating Profit Margin %	18.9	20.1	27.9	29.9	27.2	25.8	24.8
Book Value Per Share	4.16	3.11	2.29	1.45	0.86	0.51	0.30
Return on Equity %	23.6	24.0	33.6	36.8	36.6	35.7	36.6
Return on Assets %	18.3	20.1	26.9	30.5	28.2	26.8	26.1
P/E Ratio	28.7-8.0	35.0-12.3	39.6-18.8	46.7-19.8	46.4-16.9	41.9-10.3	21.6-5.7
Price Range	28⅛-7⅞	25⅞-9⅛	30½-14½	24¾-10½	14⅜-5¼	7⅛-1¾	2⅜-⅝

Statistics are as originally reported.

OFFICERS:
R.B. Dowdell, Jr., Chmn., Pres. & C.E.O.
E.W. Machala, V.P.-Oper. & Treas.
D.M. Muir, C.F.O.
E.E. Landsman, V.P. & Clerk

INCORPORATED: MA, Mar., 1981

PRINCIPAL OFFICE: 132 Fairgrounds Road, West Kingston, RI 02892

TELEPHONE NUMBER: (401) 789-5735

FAX: (401) 789-3710

NO. OF EMPLOYEES: 2,650 (approx.)

ANNUAL MEETING: In June

SHAREHOLDERS: 2,823 (approx.)

INSTITUTIONAL HOLDINGS:
No. of Institutions: 158
Shares Held: 48,100,512

REGISTRAR(S):

TRANSFER AGENT(S): Bank of Boston, Boston, MA

25

NASDAQ SYMBOL AMGN
Rec. Pr. 56 (Marginable)

AMGEN, INC.

YIELD ...%
P/E RATIO 21.8

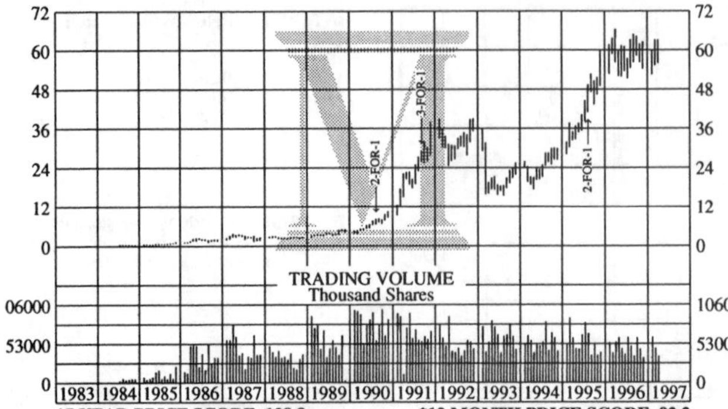

72
60
48
36
24
12
0
2-FOR-1
3-FOR-1
2-FOR-1
TRADING VOLUME
Thousand Shares
106000
53000
0
1983 1984 1985 1986 1987 1988 1989 1990 1991 1992 1993 1994 1995 1996 1997

***7 YEAR PRICE SCORE 128.8** ***12 MONTH PRICE SCORE 92.2**

*NYSE COMPOSITE INDEX=100

INTERIM EARNINGS (Per Share):

Qtr.	Mar.	June	Sept.	Dec.
1994	0.33	0.39	0.41	0.02
1995	0.39	0.49	0.52	0.52
1996	0.51	0.64	0.64	0.64
1997	0.65	...	...	...

INTERIM DIVIDENDS (Per Share):

Amt.	Decl.	Ex.	Rec.	Pay.
0.0008rts	2/19/97	3/24/97	3/21/97	3/21/97

CAPITALIZATION (12/31/96):

	($000)	(%)
Long-Term Debt	59,000	3.0
Common & Surplus	1,906,300	97.0
Total	1,965,300	100.0

RECENT DEVELOPMENTS: For the three months ended 3/31/97, net income grew 25.6% to $180.3 million from $143.6 million in the corresponding period the year before. Total revenues were up 13.3% to $575.5 million compared with $507.9 million the previous year. Product sales increased 12.4% for the quarter as sales of EPOGEN® rose 19.7% to $292.0 million and sales of NEUPOGEN® advanced 4.7% to $244.0 million. Sales of EPOGEN and NEUPOGEN were strengthened by recently-issued patents as well as a new strategic agreement. The Company's investment in research and development rose 13.1% to $147.7 million, representing 27.6% of product sales, from $130.6 million in the comparable prior-year quarter. AMGN has filed a License Application with the Food and Drug Administration for STEMGEN®, an early-acting blood cell growth factor. The Company is also performing clinical studies of INFERGEN®, which treats Hepatitis C patients.

BUSINESS

AMGEN, INC. is a global biotechnology company that develops, manufactures, and markets human therapeutics based on advanced cellular and molecular biology. The Company manufactures and markets NEUPOGEN®, a product that selectively stimulates the production of neutrophils, a type of white blood cell. Another product AMGN manufactures is EPOGEN®, a product that stimulates red blood cell production. EPO® is marketed in the U.S. and the People's Republic of China to dialysis patients in treatment for anemia disorders.

ANNUAL EARNINGS AND DIVIDENDS PER SHARE

	12/31/96	12/31/95	12/31/94	12/31/93	12/31/92	12/31/91	3/31/91
Earnings Per Share	**2.42**	**1.67**	**1.15**	**[2] 1.31**	**1.22**	**0.34**	**0.13**
Dividends Per Share	**Nil**	**[1]...**	**Nil**	**Nil**	**Nil**	**[3]...**	**[4]...**

[1] 2-for-1 stk. split, 8/15/95 [2] Before acctg. change [3] 3-for-1 stk. split, 9/11/91 [4] 2-for-1 stk. split, 8/13/90

ANNUAL FINANCIAL DATA

	12/31/96	12/31/95	12/31/94	12/31/93	12/31/92	12/31/91	3/31/91
RECORD OF EARNINGS (IN MILLIONS):							
Total Revenues	2,239.8	1,939.9	1,647.9	1,373.8	1,093.0	682.0	381.2
Costs and Expenses	d100.3	d84.2	d74.5	d50.7	d33.6	d21.5	d17.7
Depreciation & Amort	100.3	84.2	74.5	50.7	33.6	21.5	17.7
Operating Profit	904.9	743.6	578.8	1,373.8	1,093.0	682.0	381.2
Income Bef Income Taxes	962.3	794.4	588.3	592.4	563.1	157.9	72.4
Provision for Inc Taxes	282.5	256.7	268.6	217.8	205.5	60.1	38.1
Net Income	679.8	537.7	319.7	[1] 374.6	357.6	97.9	34.3
Aver. Shs. Outstg. (000)	280,700	280,700	279,580	287,222	294,594	292,094	265,314
[1] Before acctg. change cr$8,738,000.							
BALANCE SHEET (IN MILLIONS):							
Inventories	97.4	88.8	98.0	74.7	56.8	40.2	35.9
Gross Property	1,301.2	1,033.4	873.4	730.7	522.2	309.8	218.1
Accumulated Depreciation	390.7	289.6	208.1	143.7	96.2	64.1	52.4
Long-Term Debt	59.0	177.2	183.4	181.2	129.9	39.7	12.8
Net Stockholders' Equity	1,906.3	1,671.8	1,274.3	1,172.0	933.7	531.1	398.0
Total Assets	2,765.6	2,432.8	1,994.1	1,765.5	1,374.3	865.5	514.0
Total Current Assets	1,502.6	1,454.1	1,115.6	1,054.5	873.1	589.6	326.9
Total Current Liabilities	642.9	583.8	536.4	412.3	310.7	294.7	103.2
Net Working Capital	859.7	870.3	579.2	642.2	562.4	294.9	223.7
Year End Shs Outstg (000)	246,700	265,700	264,656	268,428	272,642	263,728	253,322
STATISTICAL RECORD:							
Operating Profit Margin %	40.4	38.3	35.1	100.0	100.0	100.0	100.0
Book Value Per Share	7.73	6.29	4.81	4.37	3.42	2.01	1.57
Return on Equity %	35.7	32.2	25.1	32.0	38.3	18.4	8.6
Return on Assets %	24.6	22.1	16.0	21.2	26.0	11.3	6.7
P/E Ratio	27.5-21.2	31.1-14.6	26.2-15.1	27.4-11.8	32.1-20.2	N.M.	81.7-27.9
Price Range	66½-51⅜	59¾-28⅛	30⅛-17⅜	35⅞-15½	39⅛-24⅝	38-9⅜	10⅝-3⅝

Statistics are as originally reported.

OFFICERS:
G.M. Binder, Chmn. & C.E.O.
K.W. Sharer, Pres. & C.O.O.

INCORPORATED: DE, Apr., 1980

PRINCIPAL OFFICE: 1840 DeHavilland Dr., Thousand Oaks, CA 91320-1789

TELEPHONE NUMBER: (805) 447-1000
FAX: (805) 447-1010
NO. OF EMPLOYEES: 4,646
ANNUAL MEETING: In May
SHAREHOLDERS: 14,000 (approx.)
INSTITUTIONAL HOLDINGS:
No. of Institutions: 480
Shares Held: 154,349,662

REGISTRAR(S): American Stock Transfer & Trust Co., New York, NY

TRANSFER AGENT(S): American Stock Transfer & Trust Co., New York, NY

ANDREW CORP.

YIELD ...%
P/E RATIO 31.0

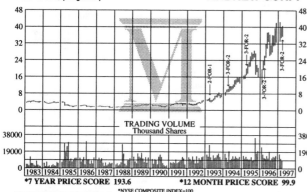

INTERIM EARNINGS (Per Share):

Qtr.	Dec.	Mar.	June	Sept.
1993-94	0.07	0.10	0.13	0.20
1994-95	0.13	0.15	0.21	0.27
1995-96	0.18	0.20	0.26	0.34
1996-97	0.27	0.28	...	...

INTERIM DIVIDENDS (Per Share):

Amt.	Decl.	Ex.	Rec.	Pay.
3-for-2	2/8/95	3/9/95	2/22/95	3/8/95
3-for-2	2/7/96	3/7/96	2/21/96	3/6/96
3-for-2	2/11/97	3/12/97	2/25/97	3/11/97

CAPITALIZATION (9/30/96):

	($000)	(%)
Long-Term Debt	40,423	8.0
Minority Interest	9,291	1.8
Common & Surplus	456,214	90.2
Total	505,928	100.0

RECENT DEVELOPMENTS: For the second quarter ended 3/31/97, net income was up 39.5% to $25.5 million compared with $18.3 million in the corresponding quarter the previous year. Sales for the period rose 13.7% to $208.2 million from $183.2 million in the comparable year-earlier period. Orders increased 17.8% to $222.3 million from $188.8 million the year before. The growth in second-quarter sales and orders was driven by worldwide wireless infrastructure markets. U.S. sales growth was paced by personal communications infrastructure construction. International sales were also strong, most notably in Asia and Europe. The higher amount of orders was attributed in part to a number of significant longer-term contracts scheduled for shipment over the next four quarters. These contracts were for coaxial cable, antennas, broadcast systems, towers and services principally in South America and Asia.

BUSINESS

ANDREW CORP. is a global supplier of communications systems equipment and services. The Company serves the wireless communications market, which includes cellular personal communications systems, and the land mobile radio market, which includes broadcast and common carriers.

BUSINESS LINE ANALYSIS

(9/30/96)($000)	Rev	Inc
Commercial	731,347	170,401
Government	34,063	1,154
Network	27,568	(3,143)
Corporate and Other	597	(22,427)
Total	793,575	145,985

ANNUAL EARNINGS AND DIVIDENDS PER SHARE

	9/30/96	9/30/95	9/30/94	9/30/93	9/30/92	9/30/91	9/30/90
Earnings Per Share	0.99	0.77	0.50	0.33	0.26	0.23	0.18
Dividends Per Share	①...	②...	③...	④...	Nil	Nil	Nil

Note: 3-for-2 stk. split, 3/11/97. ① 3-for-2 stk. split, 3/6/96 ② 3-for-2 stk. split, 3/8/95 ③ 3-for-2 stk. split, 3/2/94 ④ 2-for-1 stk. split, 3/4/93

ANNUAL FINANCIAL DATA

RECORD OF EARNINGS (IN THOUSANDS):

Total Revenues	793,575	626,463	558,457	430,820	442,008	416,229	365,990
Costs and Expenses	613,256	491,408	459,552	362,958	377,305	355,491	313,640
Depreciation & Amort	34,334	24,960	22,387	21,186	20,863	20,256	17,421
Operating Income	145,985	110,095	76,518	46,676	43,840	40,482	34,929
Income Bef Income Taxes	141,245	105,952	69,366	43,591	39,979	35,876	29,611
Income Taxes	50,848	38,143	24,971	15,729	14,992	13,698	11,450
Net Income	90,397	67,809	44,395	27,862	24,987	22,178	18,161
Aver. Shs. Outstg.	91,782	88,415	88,149	86,475	97,079	98,549	102,051

BALANCE SHEET (IN THOUSANDS):

Cash and Cash Equivalents	31,295	45,085	40,267	21,729	7,433	17,081	13,823
Receivables, Net	197,589	141,732	126,821	107,276	111,125	109,056	102,013
Inventories	166,609	119,434	87,587	70,306	68,675	64,670	70,333
Gross Property	334,088	273,510	230,634	207,511	199,063	187,688	165,595
Accumulated Depreciation	201,388	172,970	155,668	139,398	128,234	115,252	100,957
Long-Term Debt	40,423	44,710	45,455	50,000	52,556	52,556	63,447
Net Stockholders' Equity	456,214	351,378	272,854	219,570	192,224	217,471	198,524
Total Assets	631,229	491,029	415,163	337,103	313,932	343,018	319,542
Total Current Assets	401,984	310,681	260,649	202,620	190,308	209,855	189,258
Total Current Liabilities	117,382	87,854	91,628	63,931	65,444	59,525	53,190
Net Working Capital	284,602	222,827	169,021	138,689	124,864	150,330	136,068
Year End Shares Outstg	90,648	87,762	86,216	85,028	82,652	96,755	97,455

STATISTICAL RECORD:

Operating Profit Margin %	18.4	17.6	13.7	10.8	9.9	9.7	9.5
Book Value Per Share	4.56	5.39	4.08	3.15	2.70	2.66	2.34
Return on Equity %	19.8	19.3	16.3	12.7	13.0	10.2	9.1
Return on Assets %	14.3	13.8	10.7	8.3	8.0	6.5	5.7
P/E Ratio	42.7-12.8	24.9-13.1	21.1-9.4	17.9-8.0	12.5-5.6	10.8-5.9	9.7-5.6
Price Range	42½-12⅝	28⅝-15⅛	15⅞-7⅛	8⅝-3¾	4¾-2⅛	3⅝-2	2½-1½

Statistics are as originally reported.

OFFICERS:
F.L. English, Chmn., Pres. & C.E.O.
C.R. Nicholas, Exec. V.P.-Fin. & Admin. & C.F.O.
J.F. Petelle, Sec.

INCORPORATED: IL, Aug., 1947; reincorp., DE, Nov., 1986

PRINCIPAL OFFICE: 10500 W. 153rd St., Orland Park, IL 60462

TELEPHONE NUMBER: (708) 349-3300

FAX: (708) 349-5943

NO. OF EMPLOYEES: 4,622

ANNUAL MEETING: In February

SHAREHOLDERS: 3,242

INSTITUTIONAL HOLDINGS:
No. of Institutions: 204
Shares Held: 52,217,678 (adj.)

REGISTRAR(S): Harris Trust & Savings Bank, Chicago, IL

TRANSFER AGENT(S): Harris Trust & Savings Bank, Chicago, IL

NASDAQ SYMBOL AAPL
Rec. Pr. 18⅝ (Marginable)

APPLE COMPUTER, INC.

YIELD ...%
P/E RATIO ...

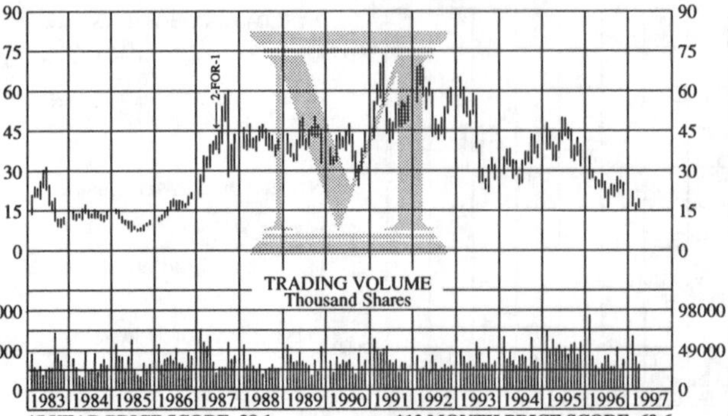

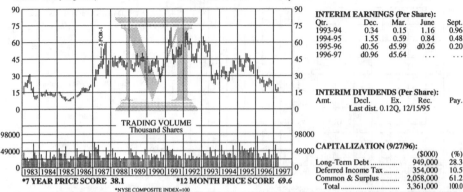

***7 YEAR PRICE SCORE 38.1** ***12 MONTH PRICE SCORE 69.6**

*NYSE COMPOSITE INDEX=100

INTERIM EARNINGS (Per Share):

Qtr.	Dec.	Mar.	June	Sept.
1993-94	0.34	0.15	1.16	0.96
1994-95	1.55	0.59	0.84	0.48
1995-96	d0.56	d5.99	d0.26	0.20
1996-97	d0.96	d5.64	...	...

INTERIM DIVIDENDS (Per Share):

Amt. Decl. Ex. Rec. Pay.

Last dist. 0.12Q, 12/15/95

CAPITALIZATION (9/27/96):

	($000)	(%)
Long-Term Debt	949,000	28.3
Deferred Income Tax	354,000	10.5
Common & Surplus	2,058,000	61.2
Total	3,361,000	100.0

RECENT DEVELOPMENTS: For the quarter ended 3/28/97, AAPL incurred a net loss of $708.0 million. This compares with a net loss of $740.0 million in the corresponding quarter the year before. Net sales dropped 26.7% to $1.60 billion from $2.19 billion the previous year. The Company recorded a charge of $375.0 million in the current quarter for the write-off of in-process research and development related to its 4/4/97 acquisition of NeXT Software, Inc. AAPL also recorded a charge of $155.0 million to increase reserves to cover the costs of restructuring activities. This compares with a restructuring charge of $207.0 million in the prior year. The Company is divesting its non-core assets and is executing a plan that is expected to reduce annual operating expenses by $500.0 million. Several new products have recently been introduced, including the Power Macintosh 6500 series of computers for home and small business customers, the PowerBook 3400 for mobile professionals, and the eMate 300 for students.

BUSINESS

APPLE COMPUTER, INC. develops, manufactures, licenses and markets products, technologies, services and solutions based on personal computers, servers, peripherals, software, Internet content and personal digital assistants. The Company serves business, education, consumer, entertainment, scientific and engineering and government customers in more than 140 countries.

QUARTERLY DATA

(9/27/96)($000)	Rev	Inc
1st Quarter	3,148,000	(69,000)
2nd Quarter	2,185,000	(740,000)
3rd Quarter	2,179,000	(32,000)
4th Quarter	2,321,000	25,000

ANNUAL EARNINGS AND DIVIDENDS PER SHARE

	9/27/96	9/29/95	9/30/94	9/24/93	9/25/92	9/27/91	9/28/90
Earnings Per Share	**d6.59**	**3.45**	**2.61**	**0.73**	**4.33**	**2.58**	**3.77**
Dividends Per Share	**Nil**	**0.48**	**0.48**	**0.48**	**0.48**	**0.48**	**0.45**
Dividend Payout %	**...**	**13.9**	**18.5**	**65.8**	**11.1**	**18.6**	**14.3**

ANNUAL FINANCIAL DATA

RECORD OF EARNINGS (IN MILLIONS):							
Total Revenues	9,833.0	11,062.0	9,188.7	7,977.0	7,086.5	6,308.8	5,558.4
Costs and Expenses	11,060.0	10,251.0	8,498.5	7,700.5	6,063.6	5,657.1	4,643.7
Depreciation & Amort	156.0	127.0	168.0	166.1	217.2	204.4	202.7
Operating Income	d1,383.0	684.0	522.3	110.3	805.8	447.3	712.0
Income Bef Income Taxes	d1,295.0	674.0	500.3	139.7	855.4	499.7	778.5
Income Taxes	cr479.0	250.0	190.1	53.1	325.1	189.9	303.6
Net Income	d816.0	424.0	310.2	86.6	530.4	309.8	474.9
Aver. Shs. Outstg. (000)	123,734	123,047	118,735	119,125	122,490	120,283	125,813
BALANCE SHEET (IN MILLIONS):							
Cash and Cash Equivalents	1,745.0	952.0	1,257.9	892.3	1,435.5	892.7	997.1
Receivables, Net	1,496.0	1,931.0	1,581.3	1,381.9	1,087.2	907.2	761.9
Inventories	662.0	1,775.0	1,088.4	1,506.6	580.1	671.7	355.5
Gross Property	1,348.0	1,492.0	1,452.2	1,412.7	1,135.6	1,036.0	844.9
Accumulated Depreciation	750.0	781.0	785.1	753.1	673.4	588.0	446.7
Long-Term Debt	949.0	303.0	304.5	...	...	...	...
Net Stockholders' Equity	2,058.0	2,901.0	2,383.3	2,026.4	2,187.4	1,766.7	1,446.8
Total Assets	5,364.0	6,231.0	5,302.7	5,171.4	4,223.7	3,493.6	2,975.7
Total Current Assets	4,515.0	5,224.0	4,476.5	4,338.4	3,558.4	2,863.6	2,403.3
Total Current Liabilities	2,003.0	2,325.0	1,944.3	2,515.2	1,425.5	1,217.1	1,027.1
Net Working Capital	2,512.0	2,899.0	2,532.1	1,823.2	2,132.9	1,646.6	1,376.3
Year End Shs Outstg (000)	124,497	122,922	119,543	116,147	118,479	118,386	115,359
STATISTICAL RECORD:							
Operating Profit Margin %	...	6.2	5.7	1.4	11.4	7.1	12.8
Book Value Per Share	16.53	23.60	19.94	17.45	18.46	14.92	12.54
Return on Equity %	...	14.6	13.0	4.3	24.2	17.5	32.8
Return on Assets %	...	6.8	5.8	1.7	12.6	8.9	16.0
Average Yield %	...	1.2	1.4	1.1	0.9	0.8	1.3
P/E Ratio	...	14.5-9.2	16.8-9.4	89.4-30.1	16.2-9.6	28.4-15.6	12.7-6.4
Price Range	35½-16	50⅛-31⅝	43¾-24⅝	65¼-22	70-41½	73¼-40¼	47¾-24¼

Statistics are as originally reported.

OFFICERS:
Dr. G.F. Amelio, C.E.O. & Chmn.
F.D. Anderson, Exec. V.P. & C.F.O.
G. DeLuca, Exec. V.P.-Mktg.
D. Manovich, Exec. V.P.-Sales
E. Hancock, Exec. V.P.-Adv. Tech.

INCORPORATED: CA, Jan., 1977

PRINCIPAL OFFICE: 1 Infinite Loop, Cupertino, CA 95014

TELEPHONE NUMBER: (408) 996-1010

NO. OF EMPLOYEES: 10,896 (perm.); 2,502 (temp.)

ANNUAL MEETING: In February

SHAREHOLDERS: 30,008

INSTITUTIONAL HOLDINGS:
No. of Institutions: 204
Shares Held: 55,378,888

REGISTRAR(S): First National Bank of Boston, Shareholder Services Division, Boston, MA

TRANSFER AGENT(S): First National Bank of Boston, Shareholder Services Division, Boston, MA

NASDAQ SYMBOL AMAT
Rec. Pr. 50¼ (Marginable)

APPLIED MATERIALS, INC.

YIELD ...%
P/E RATIO 24.9

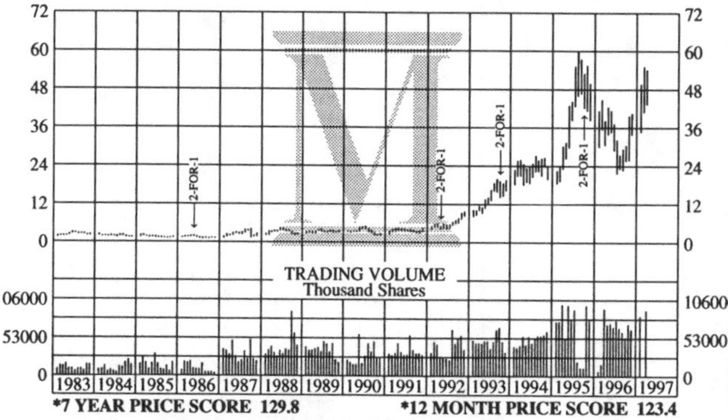

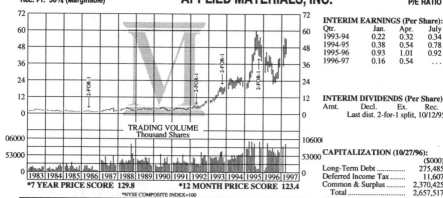

***7 YEAR PRICE SCORE 129.8** ***12 MONTH PRICE SCORE 123.4**

*NYSE COMPOSITE INDEX=100

INTERIM EARNINGS (Per Share):

Qtr.	Jan.	Apr.	July	Oct.
1993-94	0.22	0.32	0.34	0.37
1994-95	0.38	0.54	0.78	0.84
1995-96	0.93	1.01	0.92	0.40
1996-97	0.16	0.54	...	...

INTERIM DIVIDENDS (Per Share):

Amt.	Decl.	Ex.	Rec.	Pay.

Last dist. 2-for-1 split, 10/12/95

CAPITALIZATION (10/27/96):

	($000)	(%)
Long-Term Debt	275,485	10.4
Deferred Income Tax	11,607	0.4
Common & Surplus	2,370,425	89.2
Total	2,657,517	100.0

RECENT DEVELOPMENTS: For the second quarter ended 4/27/97, net income declined 45.0% to $102.1 million from $185.8 million in the comparable prior-year quarter. Net sales were down 20.1% to $900.9 million compared with $1.13 billion the previous year. The decrease in operating results was primarily attributed to reduced business volume and increased investment in product development for AMAT's 300mm wafer processing system. New orders of $1.00 billion were booked during the quarter, down from $1.30 billion a year earlier. On 3/24/97, the Company announced the formation of its new Process Diagnostics and Control (PDC) Business Group, which is comprised of AMAT's recently-acquired Israeli companies, Opal, Inc. and Orbot Instruments, Ltd. The PDC Group will develop, manufacture, market and service critical dimension-scanning electron microscope and automated wafer and reticle inspection systems for use in the production of semiconductor devices.

BUSINESS

APPLIED MATERIALS INC. is the leading independent producer of wafer fabrication systems for the worldwide semiconductor industry. The Company manufactures systems for chemical vapor deposition, plasma etching, epitaxial deposition, ion implantation and physical vapor deposition, and is developing thin film transistor fabrication systems for flat panel displays. In addition to corporate facilities in Santa Clara, California, the Company maintains research, development and manufacturing centers in the United States, Europe, Japan, and Israel. To support a growing worldwide customer base, sales and service offices are located in the U.S., Japan, Europe, South Korea, Taiwan, Singapore, and the People's Republic of China.

ANNUAL EARNINGS AND DIVIDENDS PER SHARE

	10/27/96	10/29/95	10/30/94	10/31/93	10/25/92	10/27/91	10/28/90
Earnings Per Share	**3.27**	**2.56**	**[2] 1.26**	**0.61**	**0.27**	**0.19**	**0.25**
Dividends Per Share	**Nil**	**[1]...**	**Nil**	**[3]...**	**[4]...**	**Nil**	**Nil**

[1] 2-for-1 stk. split, 10/12/95 [2] Before acctg. change [3] 2-for-1 stk. split, 10/6/93 [4] 2-for-1 stk. split, 4/7/92

ANNUAL FINANCIAL DATA

RECORD OF EARNINGS (IN MILLIONS):							
Total Revenues	4,144.8	3,061.9	1,659.8	1,080.0	751.4	638.6	567.1
Costs and Expenses	3,092.4	2,284.7	1,261.5	880.2	654.1	561.4	492.2
Depreciation & Amort	148.9	83.2	59.1	38.9	28.9	24.5	16.0
Operating Income	903.6	693.9	339.2	161.0	68.4	52.7	59.0
Income Bef Income Taxes	922.4	698.5	334.5	153.6	58.9	40.4	54.1
Income Taxes	322.9	244.5	117.1	50.7	19.4	14.1	20.0
Net Income	599.6	454.1	[1] 213.7	99.7	39.5	26.2	34.1
Aver. Shs. Outstg. (000)	183,607	177,348	170,042	164,588	145,360	137,800	136,288
[1] Before acctg. change cr$7,000,000.							
BALANCE SHEET (IN MILLIONS):							
Cash and Cash Equivalents	1,037.6	769.3	422.3	266.2	222.7	140.1	72.0
Receivables, Net	822.4	817.7	405.8	256.0	191.5	152.8	147.3
Inventories	478.6	427.4	245.7	154.6	110.7	101.5	102.3
Gross Property	1,265.6	859.7	622.6	449.6	344.1	285.8	236.8
Accumulated Depreciation	346.6	228.9	170.1	121.9	85.6	72.6	55.3
Long-Term Debt	275.5	279.8	209.1	121.1	118.4	124.0	53.6
Net Stockholders' Equity	2,370.4	1,783.5	966.3	598.8	474.1	325.5	300.3
Total Assets	3,638.0	2,965.4	1,702.7	1,120.2	853.8	660.8	558.0
Total Current Assets	2,693.1	2,311.6	1,230.5	775.9	581.8	434.2	366.9
Total Current Liabilities	935.2	861.7	496.4	380.5	248.2	200.0	195.2
Net Working Capital	1,757.8	1,449.9	734.1	395.4	333.6	234.2	171.7
Year End Shs Outstg (000)	180,235	179,278	168,208	160,750	156,392	134,968	133,080
STATISTICAL RECORD:							
Operating Profit Margin %	21.8	22.7	20.4	14.9	9.1	8.3	10.4
Book Value Per Share	13.15	9.95	5.74	3.73	3.03	2.41	2.26
Return on Equity %	25.3	25.5	22.1	16.7	8.3	8.1	11.3
Return on Assets %	16.5	15.3	12.6	8.9	4.6	4.0	6.1
P/E Ratio	13.7-6.7	23.4-7.2	21.6-14.4	32.8-13.3	18.1-7.4	12.5-6.6	10.3-4.3
Price Range	44¾-21¾	59⅞-18½	27¼-18⅛	20-8⅛	9¾-4	4¾-2½	5⅛-2⅛

Statistics are as originally reported.

OFFICERS:
J.C. Morgan, Chmn. & C.E.O.
J.W. Bagley, Vice-Chmn.
D. Mayden, Pres.
G.F. Taylor, Sr. V.P. & C.F.O.

INCORPORATED: CA, Nov., 1967; reincorp., DE, 1987

PRINCIPAL OFFICE: 3050 Bowers Avenue, Santa Clara, CA 95054

TELEPHONE NUMBER: (408) 727-5555

FAX: (408) 986-7825

NO. OF EMPLOYEES: 11,403 (approx.)

ANNUAL MEETING: In March

SHAREHOLDERS: 3,832 (approx.)

INSTITUTIONAL HOLDINGS:
No. of Institutions: 336
Shares Held: 106,973,468

REGISTRAR(S): Harris Trust Co. of California, Los Angeles, CA

TRANSFER AGENT(S): Harris Trust Co. of California, Los Angeles, CA

ASCEND COMMUNICATIONS, INC.

YIELD ...%
P/E RATIO 42.5

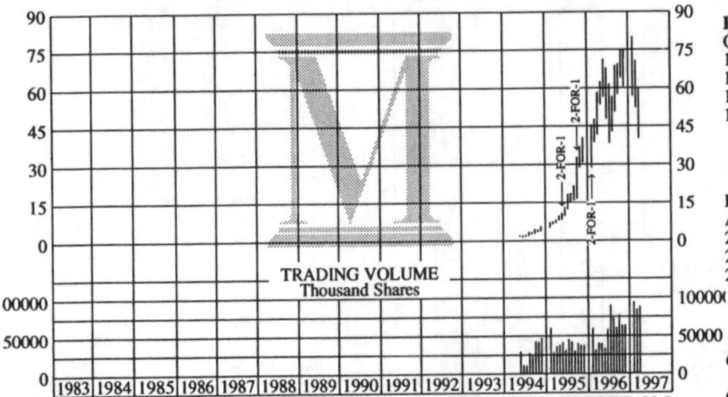

90 75 60 45 30 15 0

TRADING VOLUME
Thousand Shares

00000
50000
0

1983|1984|1985|1986|1987|1988|1989|1990|1991|1992|1993|1994|1995|1996|1997

*7 YEAR PRICE SCORE ... *12 MONTH PRICE SCORE 83.8

*NYSE COMPOSITE INDEX=100

INTERIM EARNINGS (Per Share):

Qtr.	Mar.	June	Sept.	Dec.
1994	----	0.09	----	----
1995	0.04	0.05	0.07	0.12
1996	0.15	0.24	0.20	0.32
1997	0.27	...	...	...

INTERIM DIVIDENDS (Per Share):

Amt.	Decl.	Ex.	Rec.	Pay.
2-for-1	4/20/95	5/12/95	5/1/95	5/11/95
2-for-1	9/25	10/6	9/25	10/5
2-for-1	12/15	1/8/96	12/15	1/5/96

CAPITALIZATION (12/31/96):

	($000)	(%)
Common & Surplus	547,450	100.0
Total	547,450	100.0

RECENT DEVELOPMENTS: For the quarter ended 3/31/97, net income soared 81.0% to $35.1 million compared with $19.4 million in the corresponding prior-year quarter. Net sales were $202.4 million. This compares with $92.0 million in the comparable quarter the year before. The results included an $18.0 million charge for purchased research and development related to the acquisition of InterCon Systems Corp. The stronger operating results were attributed to customer acceptance and demand for the Company's MAX TNT product, which contributed to revenues for the first time during the quarter, as well as first-time revenue contributions from the GRF 400 product. On 3/30/97, ASND announced that it will acquire Cascade Communications Corp. in a stock exchange valued at approximately $3.70 billion. The acquisition is expected to close in the third quarter of 1997.

BUSINESS

ASCEND COMMUNICATIONS, INC. develops, manufactures, sells and supports a broad range of high-speed digital wide-area network access products. The Company's products use bandwidth on demand to enhance and extend existing corporate networks for applications such as videoconferencing remote access, Internet access, bulk file transfer, imaging and integrated voice, video and data access. The Company's products also use bandwidth on demand to provide automatic emergency backup and bandwidth capacity for peak-period overflow to complement private leased line, frame relay and ATM networks.

ANNUAL EARNINGS AND DIVIDENDS PER SHARE

	1996	1995	1994	1993	1992	1991
Earnings Per Share	0.89	0.28	0.09	0.02	d0.33	d0.21
Dividends Per Share	①...	②...	Nil	Nil	Nil	Nil

① 2-for-1 stk. split, 1/5/96 ② 2-for-1 stk. splits, 5/11/95 & 10/5/95

ANNUAL FINANCIAL DATA

RECORD OF EARNINGS (IN THOUSANDS):

	1996	1995	1994	1993	1992	1991
Total Revenues	549,297	149,590	39,343	16,215	7,236	3,156
Costs and Expenses	365,960	103,651	29,709	14,520	10,754	5,523
Depreciation & Amort	8,801	2,114	621	398	373	205
Operating Income	174,536	43,825	9,013	1,297	d3,891	d2,572
Income Bef Income Taxes	186,415	49,318	9,905	1,349	d3,766	...
Income Taxes	73,304	18,745	1,206	...	...	...
Net Income	113,111	30,573	8,699	1,349	d3,766	d2,393
Aver. Shs. Outstg.	127,809	108,976	92,800	82,152	11,488	11,472

BALANCE SHEET (IN THOUSANDS):

Cash and Cash Equivalents	373,151	211,080	35,548	6,261	6,595	...
Receivables, Net	136,634	36,427	9,131	3,636	1,664	...
Inventories	49,241	24,855	5,256	1,211	710	...
Gross Property	53,600	12,583	3,708	1,845	1,401	...
Accumulated Depreciation	13,566	3,652	1,568	947	569	...
Capital Lease Obligations	...	...	108	316	389	...
Net Stockholders' Equity	547,450	296,130	43,655	9,560	8,140	...
Total Assets	651,866	335,450	53,272	12,392	10,032	...
Total Current Assets	572,299	274,541	50,866	11,318	9,084	...
Total Current Liabilities	104,416	39,320	9,509	2,516	1,503	...
Net Working Capital	467,883	235,221	41,357	8,802	7,581	...
Year End Shares Outstg	119,417	110,086	95,720	10,416	8,376	...

STATISTICAL RECORD:

Operating Profit Margin %	31.8	29.3	22.9	8.0	...	...
Book Value Per Share	4.58	2.69	0.46	...	...	...
Return on Equity %	20.7	10.3	19.9	14.1	...	...
Return on Assets %	17.4	9.1	16.3	10.9	...	...
P/E Ratio	84.6-32.3	N.M.-17.9	62.5-15.3	...	...	...
Price Range	75¼-28¾	40⅝-5	5⅝-1⅜	...	...	...

Statistics are as originally reported.

OFFICERS:
M. Ejabat, C.E.O. & Pres.
R.K. Dahl, V.P.-Fin., C.F.O. & Sec.

INCORPORATED: CA, Feb., 1989; reincorp., DE, May, 1994

PRINCIPAL OFFICE: 1701 Harbor Bay Parkway, Alameda, CA 94502

TELEPHONE NUMBER: (510) 769-6001

FAX: (510) 814-2300

NO. OF EMPLOYEES: 721

ANNUAL MEETING: In May

SHAREHOLDERS: 1,144

INSTITUTIONAL HOLDINGS:
No. of Institutions: 209
Shares Held: 103,621,225

REGISTRAR(S): First Interstate Bank, San Francisco, CA

TRANSFER AGENT(S): First Interstate Bank, San Francisco, CA

ATMEL CORP.

YIELD ...%
P/E RATIO 12.6

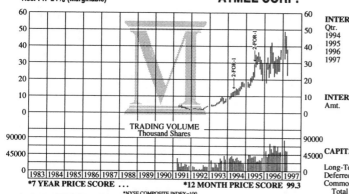

INTERIM EARNINGS (Per Share):

Qtr.	Mar.	June	Sept.	Dec.
1994	0.14	0.16	0.18	0.19
1995	0.21	0.26	0.31	0.38
1996	0.45	0.50	0.53	0.53
1997	0.38	...	...	...

INTERIM DIVIDENDS (Per Share):

Amt.	Decl.	Ex.	Rec.	Pay.
Last dist. 2-for-1 split, 8/8/95				

TRADING VOLUME
Thousand Shares

1983 1984 1985 1986 1987 1988 1989 1990 1991 1992 1993 1994 1995 1996 1997

*7 YEAR PRICE SCORE ...   *12 MONTH PRICE SCORE 99.3
*NYSE COMPOSITE INDEX=100

CAPITALIZATION (12/31/96):

	($000)	(%)
Long-Term Debt	278,576	25.5
Deferred Income Tax	22,935	2.1
Common & Surplus	789,751	72.4
Total	1,091,262	100.0

RECENT DEVELOPMENTS: For the first quarter ended 3/31/97, net income declined 13.7% to $38.7 million. This compares with $44.9 million in the corresponding quarter the previous year. Net revenues for the period were up 5.4% to $252.9 million from $240.1 million in the comparable year-earlier period. While revenues increased for the quarter, a stronger dollar, pricing pressure in the Company's non-volatile business and delays in the qualification of ATML's new Flash products hindered revenue growth.

Many of the Company's new 49 series Flash and Data Flash and the AVR Flash Microcontroller products are being sampled by customers in computer peripheral, wireless phone, answering machine and consumer product applications. Operating income for the quarter totaled $61.5 million, or 24.3% of revenues, down from $68.0 million, or 28.3% of revenues, the year before, reflecting higher cost of sales and research and development expenses.

BUSINESS

ATMEL CORP. designs, develops, manufactures and markets a broad range of high performance non-volatile memory and logic integrated circuits using its proprietary CMOS (complementary metal-oxide semiconductor) technologies. The Company's products are used in a range of applications in the computing, telecommunications, datacommunications, industrial/instrumentation, consumer electronics, automotive and military/avionics markets. ATML designs, develops, manufactures and markets on a worldwide basis a broad line of complex integrated circuits. The Company manufactures EEP-ROMS (Both parallel-interface and serial interface), EPROMs, and Flash, as well as programmable logic, microcontrollers, and application-specific devices.

ANNUAL EARNINGS AND DIVIDENDS PER SHARE

	1996	1995	1994	1993	1992	1991	1990
Earnings Per Share	2.01	1.16	0.66	0.37	0.20	0.16	0.09
Dividends Per Share	Nil	①...	②...	Nil	Nil	Nil	Nil

① 2-for-1 stk. split, 8/8/95 ② 2-for-1 stk. split, 4/11/94

ANNUAL FINANCIAL DATA

RECORD OF EARNINGS (IN MILLIONS):

	1996	1995	1994	1993	1992	1991	1990
Total Revenues	1,070.3	634.2	375.1	221.7	139.8	120.4	76.9
Costs and Expenses	653.8	407.9	253.2	162.3	111.3	96.8	61.2
Depreciation & Amort	111.0	58.9	34.1	15.3	9.5	8.2	6.1
Operating Income	305.5	167.4	87.8	44.1	19.0	15.4	9.5
Income Bef Income Taxes	309.2	172.3	90.1	44.8	19.9	14.9	7.1
Income Taxes	107.4	58.6	30.6	14.8	6.0	4.5	2.8
Net Income	201.7	113.7	59.5	30.0	13.9	10.3	4.2
Aver. Shs. Outstg. (000)	100,584	95,214	89,566	81,404	73,060	68,200	48,328

BALANCE SHEET (IN MILLIONS):

Cash and Cash Equivalents	157.3	180.0	79.3	67.6	24.9	45.3	21.7
Receivables, Net	174.5	101.6	51.6	34.0	30.4	21.5	20.3
Inventories	70.3	48.5	35.0	33.5	41.4	38.3	28.3
Gross Property	1,081.0	590.4	326.5	125.5	52.4	38.6	31.3
Accumulated Depreciation	213.6	118.1	61.7	35.3	23.6	16.0	7.8
Long-Term Debt	278.6	88.5	46.5	24.0	23.0	21.2	34.4
Net Stockholders' Equity	789.8	588.8	358.1	218.2	132.0	114.8	36.7
Total Assets	1,455.9	919.6	540.9	300.9	183.5	159.5	101.4
Total Current Assets	460.0	366.1	188.4	143.7	99.6	109.9	76.6
Total Current Liabilities	336.4	233.5	123.8	54.8	27.9	23.6	29.6
Net Working Capital	123.6	132.6	64.6	88.9	71.7	86.4	47.0
Year End Shs Outstg (000)	98,752	97,207	90,762	82,988	70,312	67,132	28,648

STATISTICAL RECORD:

Operating Profit Margin %	28.5	26.4	23.4	19.9	13.6	12.8	12.4
Book Value Per Share	8.00	6.06	3.95	2.63	1.88	1.71	1.28
Return on Equity %	25.5	19.3	16.6	13.8	10.6	9.0	11.5
Return on Assets %	13.9	12.4	11.0	10.0	7.6	6.5	4.2
P/E Ratio	21.1-9.0	30.7-12.9	28.0-12.3	26.0-10.5	22.4-9.9	31.7-10.8	...
Price Range	42⅜-18⅛	36½-15⅜	18¾-8¼	9⅝-3⅞	4¼-1⅞	4¾-1⅝	...

Statistics are as originally reported.

OFFICERS:
G. Perlegos, Chmn., Pres. & C.E.O.
K. Chellam, V.P.-Fin. & Admin. & C.F.O.
M. Bertelsen, Sec.

INCORPORATED: CA, Dec., 1984

PRINCIPAL OFFICE: 2325 Orchard Parkway,
San Jose, CA 95131

TELEPHONE NUMBER: (408) 441-0311
FAX: (408) 436-4200
NO. OF EMPLOYEES: 3,914
ANNUAL MEETING: In April
SHAREHOLDERS: 1,848 (approx.)
INSTITUTIONAL HOLDINGS:
No. of Institutions: 183
Shares Held: 56,728,119

REGISTRAR(S): Chemical Trust Co. of
America, San Francisco, CA

TRANSFER AGENT(S): Chemical Trust Co.
of America, San Francisco, CA

NASDAQ SYMBOL ADSK
Rec. Pr. 31⅛ (Marginable)

AUTODESK, INC.

YIELD 0.8%
P/E RATIO 35.8

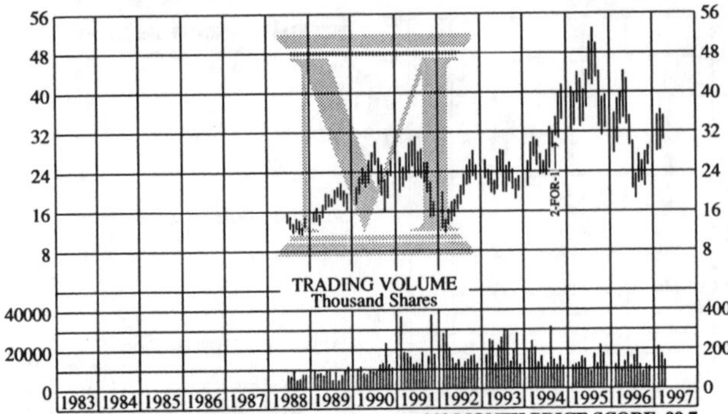

*7 YEAR PRICE SCORE 74.9 *12 MONTH PRICE SCORE 99.7

*NYSE COMPOSITE INDEX=100

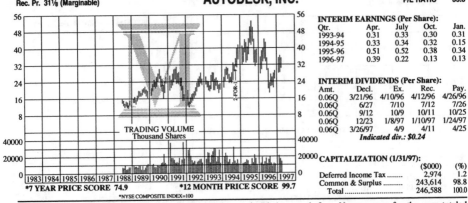

INTERIM EARNINGS (Per Share):

Qtr.	Apr.	July	Oct.	Jan.
1993-94	0.31	0.33	0.30	0.31
1994-95	0.33	0.34	0.32	0.15
1995-96	0.51	0.52	0.38	0.34
1996-97	0.39	0.22	0.13	0.13

INTERIM DIVIDENDS (Per Share):

Amt.	Decl.	Ex.	Rec.	Pay.
0.06Q	3/21/96	4/10/96	4/12/96	4/26/96
0.06Q	6/27	7/10	7/12	7/26
0.06Q	9/12	10/9	10/11	10/25
0.06Q	12/23	1/8/97	1/10/97	1/24/97
0.06Q	3/26/97	4/9	4/11	4/25

Indicated div.: $0.24

CAPITALIZATION (1/31/97):

	($000)	(%)
Deferred Income Tax	2,974	1.2
Common & Surplus	243,614	98.8
Total	246,588	100.0

RECENT DEVELOPMENTS: On 3/31/97, the Company's acquisition of Softdesk Inc. closed with ADSK issuing 0.477327 shares of stock for each outstanding share of Softdesk stock. The acquisition of Softdesk, a leading supplier of architecture, engineering and construction application software, was accounted for using the purchase method. For the fiscal year ended 1/31/97, net income dropped to $41.6 million. This compares with $87.8 million the previous year. Net income per share was $0.88 versus $1.76 the year before. Net revenues for the year totaled $496.7 million, down 7.0% compared with $534.2 million a year earlier. For the fourth quarter ended 1/31/97, net income fell to $6.0 million from $16.3 million in the corresponding prior-year quarter. Net income per share was $0.13 versus $0.34 the previous year. Fourth-quarter net revenues declined 8.9% to $115.0 million from $126.3 million in the comparable year-earlier quarter.

BUSINESS

AUTODESK INC. develops, markets and supports a family of design automation and multimedia software products for use on personal computers. The Company's 2D and 3D products, geographic information systems and data management tools are used in many industries for mapping, architectural design, mechanical design, film and video production, video/game development and Web content development. ADSK's Kinetix™ division develops PC-based 3D modeling and animation software, providing a full range of products for digital media and design professionals. The Company's principal software products are: AutoCAD, AutoCAD LT, 3D Studio Max and Mechanical Desktop. ADSK's products are used by more than three million customers in more than 140 countries and are sold through Autodesk Systems Centers, Dealers and Distributors.

ANNUAL EARNINGS AND DIVIDENDS PER SHARE

	1/31/97	1/31/96	1/31/95	1/31/94	1/31/93	1/31/92	1/31/91
Earnings Per Share	**0.88**	**1.76**	**1.14**	**1.25**	**0.88**	**1.16**	**1.15**
Dividends Per Share	**0.24**	**0.24**	**[1] 0.24**	**0.24**	**0.24**	**0.22**	**0.20**
Dividend Payout %	**27.3**	**13.6**	**21.1**	**19.2**	**27.3**	**19.0**	**17.4**

[1] 2-for-1 stk. split, 10/94

ANNUAL FINANCIAL DATA

RECORD OF EARNINGS (IN THOUSANDS):							
Total Revenues	496,693	534,167	454,612	405,596	353,154	273,974	237,850
Costs and Expenses	402,043	379,893	322,212	295,325	278,571	178,960	143,363
Depreciation & Amort	34,833	25,247	24,989	20,568	16,386	14,783	13,533
Operating Income	59,817	129,027	107,411	89,703	58,197	80,231	80,954
Income Bef Income Taxes	66,512	138,280	89,144	96,758	69,763	92,294	91,977
Income Taxes	24,941	50,492	32,538	34,592	25,890	34,500	35,222
Net Income	41,571	87,788	56,606	62,166	43,873	57,794	56,755
Aver. Shs. Outstg.	47,190	49,800	49,840	49,740	49,800	49,980	49,368
BALANCE SHEET (IN THOUSANDS):							
Cash and Cash Equivalents	182,785	193,306	240,354	177,608	153,339	170,752	124,466
Receivables, Net	68,577	93,919	86,340	71,245	62,685	50,526	40,354
Inventories	7,340	9,685	5,769	8,803	16,844	11,200	10,588
Gross Property	121,721	127,743	111,605	92,952	71,241	63,428	55,588
Accumulated Depreciation	77,671	78,778	65,090	51,003	39,168	31,247	22,428
Net Stockholders' Equity	243,614	342,328	323,484	296,879	267,833	267,305	218,285
Total Assets	492,233	517,929	482,076	404,874	358,283	328,026	265,234
Total Current Assets	310,528	347,834	373,085	279,557	249,341	247,538	187,631
Total Current Liabilities	150,171	144,295	154,990	102,316	84,080	56,984	43,773
Net Working Capital	160,357	203,539	218,095	177,241	165,261	190,554	143,858
Year End Shares Outstg	45,108	46,351	47,241	47,480	48,022	49,176	48,824
STATISTICAL RECORD:							
Operating Profit Margin %	12.0	24.2	23.6	22.1	16.5	29.3	34.0
Book Value Per Share	5.05	6.91	6.29	5.66	5.09	5.12	4.35
Return on Equity %	17.1	25.6	17.5	20.9	16.4	21.6	26.0
Return on Assets %	8.4	16.9	11.7	15.4	12.2	17.6	21.4
Average Yield %	0.8	0.6	0.8	1.0	1.2	1.0	0.9
P/E Ratio	50.3-21.0	30.1-17.8	36.4-18.5	22.7-14.8	32.1-13.2	26.9-12.8	26.2-13.9
Price Range	44¼-18½	53-31¼	41½-21⅛	28⅜-18½	28¼-11⅝	31⅛-14¾	30⅛-16

Statistics are as originally reported.

OFFICERS:
C.A. Bartz, Chmn., Pres. & C.E.O.
E.B. Herr, Pres. & C.O.O.
C. Tsingos, V.P. & Treas.

INCORPORATED: CA, Apr., 1982; reincorp., DE, Aug., 1994

PRINCIPAL OFFICE: 111 McInnis Parkway, San Rafael, CA 94903

TELEPHONE NUMBER: (415) 507-5000

NO. OF EMPLOYEES: 2,044

ANNUAL MEETING: In June

SHAREHOLDERS: 1,430 (approx.)

INSTITUTIONAL HOLDINGS:
No. of Institutions: 163
Shares Held: 32,166,181

REGISTRAR(S): Harris Trust & Savings Bank, Chicago, IL

TRANSFER AGENT(S): Harris Trust & Savings Bank, Chicago, IL

BED BATH & BEYOND INC.

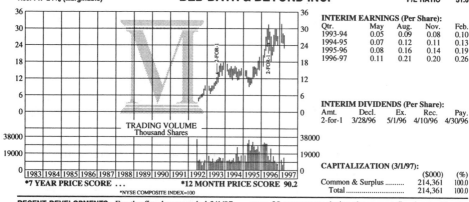

*7 YEAR PRICE SCORE ... *12 MONTH PRICE SCORE 90.2
*NYSE COMPOSITE INDEX=100

INTERIM EARNINGS (Per Share):

Qtr.	May	Aug.	Nov.	Feb.
1993-94	0.05	0.09	0.08	0.10
1994-95	0.07	0.12	0.11	0.13
1995-96	0.08	0.16	0.14	0.19
1996-97	0.11	0.21	0.20	0.26

INTERIM DIVIDENDS (Per Share):

Amt.	Decl.	Ex.	Rec.	Pay.
2-for-1	3/28/96	5/1/96	4/10/96	4/30/96

CAPITALIZATION (3/1/97):

	($000)	(%)
Common & Surplus	214,361	100.0
Total	214,361	100.0

RECENT DEVELOPMENTS: For the fiscal year ended 3/1/97, net earnings increased 39.4% to $55.0 million. This compares with $39.5 million a year earlier. Net sales were up 36.9% to $823.2 million from $601.3 million the previous year. During the year, BBBY opened 28 new superstores and expanded two stores, operating a total of 108 stores at year's end. Since the end of the fiscal year, the Company has opened seven new superstores as part of its plan to open 30 new stores during the current fiscal year. For the fourth quarter ended 3/1/97, net earnings grew 42.9% to $18.3 million from $12.8 million in the comparable quarter the year before. Net sales rose 39.4% to $245.2 million from $175.9 million the previous year. The fiscal year and fourth quarter ended 3/1/97 included an extra six days of reporting not included in the prior-year results.

BUSINESS

BED BATH & BEYOND INC. is a nationwide operator of "superstores" selling domestics merchandise and home furnishings typically. The domestics merchandise line includes bed-linens and related items (sheets, comforters, comforter covers, bedspreads, draperies, decorative pillows, blankets, bed pillows and mattress pads), bath accessories (towels, shower curtains, waste-baskets, hampers, bathroom rugs and wall hardware), and kitchen textiles (tablecloths, placemats, cloth napkins, dish towels and chair pads). Home furnishings include kitchen and tabletop items (cookware, cutlery, kitchen gadgets, small electric appliances, dinnerware, flatware and glassware), basic housewares (storage items, closet-related items, general housewares, and lifestyle accessories), and miscellaneous gifts, picture frames, juvenile items and seasonal merchandise. The Company offers leading brand name merchandise including Wamsutta, Martex, Fieldcrest, Mikasa, Krups, Henckels and Black & Decker. As of May 1997, Bed Bath & Beyond operated 115 stores in 26 states.

ANNUAL EARNINGS AND DIVIDENDS PER SHARE

	3/1/97	2/25/96	2/26/95	2/27/94	2/28/93	3/1/92	3/3/91
Earnings Per Share	0.78	0.57	0.43	0.32	0.24	0.19	...
Dividends Per Share	①...	Nil	Nil	②...	Nil	Nil	...

① 2-for-1 stk. split, 4/30/96. ② 2-for-1 stk. split, 7/93

ANNUAL FINANCIAL DATA

RECORD OF EARNINGS (IN THOUSANDS):

	3/1/97	2/25/96	2/26/95	2/27/94	2/28/93	3/1/92	3/3/91
Total Revenues	823,178	601,252	440,261	305,767	216,712	167,595	134,219
Costs and Expenses	719,132	523,765	381,383	265,002	187,749	146,143	116,007
Depreciation & Amort	13,439	9,902	7,193	4,200	2,630	1,804	1,427
Operating Income	90,607	67,585	51,685	36,565	26,333	19,648	16,785
Income Bef Income Taxes	91,311	66,880	50,869	36,940	26,600	19,920	17,269
Income Taxes	36,296	27,421	20,856	15,053	10,640	7,968	6,908
Net Income	55,015	39,459	30,013	21,887	15,960	11,952	10,361
Aver. Shs. Outstg.	70,555	69,412	69,138	68,820	67,304	65,508	...

BALANCE SHEET (IN THOUSANDS):

Cash and Cash Equivalents	38,765	10,267	6,463	2,672	10,095	551	144
Inventories	187,185	148,383	108,388	74,982	43,089	40,609	25,226
Gross Property	130,469	95,333	71,415	46,975	28,099	17,717	11,837
Accumulated Depreciation	42,137	28,698	19,214	12,075	8,454	5,824	4,020
Long-Term Debt	...	5,000	16,800	13,300	...	11,780	...
Net Stockholders' Equity	214,361	151,446	108,939	77,305	54,643	30,853	23,655
Total Assets	329,925	235,810	176,678	121,468	76,654	55,477	36,231
Total Current Assets	227,555	160,280	118,011	81,977	53,856	42,627	26,703
Total Current Liabilities	105,876	72,553	46,109	27,545	19,355	10,672	11,110
Net Working Capital	121,679	87,727	71,902	54,432	34,501	31,955	15,593
Year End Shares Outstg	68,603	68,068	67,768	67,592	67,500	58,250	58,250

STATISTICAL RECORD:

Operating Profit Margin %	11.0	11.2	11.7	12.0	12.2	11.7	12.5
Book Value Per Share	3.12	2.22	1.61	1.14	0.81	0.53	0.41
Return on Equity %	25.7	26.1	27.6	28.3	29.2	38.7	43.8
Return on Assets %	16.7	16.7	17.0	18.0	20.8	21.5	28.6
P/E Ratio	40.4-23.0	34.9-15.8	40.1-26.5	55.5-20.3	40.4-16.0	...	...
Price Range	31½-16⅜	19⅞-9	17¼-11⅜	17¾-6½	9½-3¾	...	...

Statistics are as originally reported.

OFFICERS:
W. Eisenberg, Chmn. & Co-C.E.O.
L. Feinstein, Pres. & Co-C.E.O.
R. Curwin, C.F.O. & Treas.
S.H. Temares, Exec. V.P.-C.O.O.

INCORPORATED: NY, 1971

PRINCIPAL OFFICE: 650 Liberty Avenue, Union, NJ 07083

TELEPHONE NUMBER: (908) 688-0888

NO. OF EMPLOYEES: 4,500 (full-time); 2,500 (part-time)

ANNUAL MEETING: In June

SHAREHOLDERS: 500 (approx.)

INSTITUTIONAL HOLDINGS:
No. of Institutions: 124
Shares Held: 65,903,707

REGISTRAR(S):

TRANSFER AGENT(S): American Stock Transfer & Trust Co., New York, NY

BIOGEN, INC.

YIELD ...%
P/E RATIO 40.6

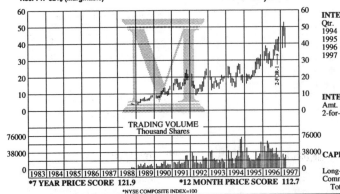

*7 YEAR PRICE SCORE 121.9   *12 MONTH PRICE SCORE 112.7

*NYSE COMPOSITE INDEX=100

INTERIM EARNINGS (Per Share):

Qtr.	Mar.	June	Sept.	Dec.
1994	0.15	0.01	d0.40	0.15
1995	0.04	0.01	0.02	0.02
1996	d0.05	d0.13	0.61	0.11
1997	0.22	...	...	...

INTERIM DIVIDENDS (Per Share):

Amt.	Decl.	Ex.	Rec.	Pay.
2-for-1	10/22/96	11/18/96	11/4/96	11/15/96

CAPITALIZATION (12/31/96):

	($000)	(%)
Long-Term Debt	62,254	11.4
Common & Surplus	484,370	88.6
Total	546,624	100.0

RECENT DEVELOPMENTS: For the three months ended 3/31/97, net income totaled $17.0 million compared with a net loss of $3.7 million in the corresponding period a year earlier. Total revenues jumped to $99.7 million from $38.8 million the previous year. Revenues for the 1997 quarter included $52.6 million from sales of AVONEX®, the Company's treatment for relapsing forms of multiple sclerosis. No product revenues were reported in the prior-year period. AVONEX® is currently available by prescription in the United Kingdom, Germany, Sweden and Finland, and is also on the market in Israel and Cyprus. In March 1997, BGEN signed an agreement with CV Therapeutics for the development of CVT-124, a treatment for congestive heart failure, in which BGEN will hold exclusive marketing rights. As of April 1997, CVT-124 was in a multi-center phase II clinical trial. Clinical trials have also begun for CD40, treating lupus and other autoimmune diseases, and LFA3TIP, treating psoriasis.

BUSINESS

BIOGEN, INC. is a biopharmaceutical company principally engaged in developing and manufacturing drugs for human health care through genetic engineering. Biogen derives revenues from five products sold by licensees around the world. These products include alpha interferon and hepatitis B vaccines and diagnostic products. Biogen's research is focused on biological systems and processes in which its scientific expertise in molecular biology, cell biology, immunology and protein chemistry can lead to a greater understanding of disease processes and, as a result, to the creation of new pharmaceuticals. The Company is primarily concerned with developing and testing products for the treatment of cardiovascular disease, inflammatory diseases, AIDS, and certain cancers and viruses. Presently in clinical trials is BGEN's Recombinant Beta Interferon, an antiviral and anticancer agent. The Company also has several major research programs in progress.

ANNUAL EARNINGS AND DIVIDENDS PER SHARE

	1996	1995	1994	1993	1992	1991	1990
Earnings Per Share	0.55	0.08	d0.07	0.47	0.56	0.08	0.04
Dividends Per Share	①...	Nil	Nil	Nil	Nil	Nil	Nil

① 2-for-1 stk. split, 11/15/96

ANNUAL FINANCIAL DATA

RECORD OF EARNINGS (IN THOUSANDS):

	1996	1995	1994	1993	1992	1991	1990
Total Revenues	277,090	151,691	156,344	149,287	135,114	69,577	59,415
Costs and Expenses	220,997	133,330	150,195	108,013	88,042	57,067	47,619
Depreciation & Amort	15,264	10,916	8,056	6,657	7,141	5,064	3,786
Operating Profit	174,933	100,894	121,710	119,912	108,745	51,216	46,286
Income Bef Income Taxes	40,829	7,445	d1,907	34,617	39,931	7,446	8,010
Income Taxes	299	1,785	2,990	2,200	1,620	260	290
Net Income	40,530	5,660	d4,897	32,417	38,311	7,186	7,720
Aver. Shs. Outstg.	73,221	72,890	65,548	69,440	68,396	59,928	50,860

BALANCE SHEET (IN THOUSANDS):

	1996	1995	1994	1993	1992	1991	1990
Cash and Cash Equivalents	321,381	307,948	267,802	270,351	227,888	185,990	104,146
Receivables, Net	90,840	19,612	18,502	31,695	33,415	40,918	27,877
Gross Property	217,926	155,014	104,651	64,111	53,341	47,261	38,837
Accumulated Depreciation	52,603	39,966	31,489	25,611	21,035	18,575	15,201
Long-Term Debt	62,254	32,826	...	...	...	...	...
Net Stockholders' Equity	484,370	382,980	329,934	325,174	284,953	238,989	145,742
Total Assets	634,572	469,201	377,862	356,950	311,192	253,067	158,485
Total Current Assets	435,754	340,309	294,784	309,424	268,447	209,164	120,774
Total Current Liabilities	87,948	53,395	47,928	31,776	26,239	14,078	12,743
Net Working Capital	347,806	286,914	246,856	277,648	242,208	195,086	108,031
Year End Shares Outstg	72,526	71,012	66,258	64,600	63,468	61,558	45,864

STATISTICAL RECORD:

	1996	1995	1994	1993	1992	1991	1990
Operating Profit Margin %	14.7	4.9	...	23.2	29.6	10.7	13.5
Book Value Per Share	6.53	5.28	4.86	4.92	4.39	3.76	3.04
Return on Equity %	8.4	1.5	...	10.0	13.4	3.0	5.3
Return on Assets %	6.4	1.2	...	9.1	12.3	2.8	4.9
P/E Ratio	79.5-46.4	N.M.	...	50.8-25.8	44.4-16.3	N.M.	N.M.
Price Range	43¾-25½	33¼-16	27⅞-13⅝	23⅞-12⅛	24⅞-9⅛	24½-12⅛	14¾-7¼

Statistics are as originally reported.

OFFICERS:
J.L. Vincent, Chmn.
J.R. Tobin, Pres. & C.E.O.
T.M. Kish, V.P.-Fin., C.F.O. & Treas.
M.J. Astrue, V.P., Gen. Couns. & Sec.

INCORPORATED: MA, 1978

PRINCIPAL OFFICE: 14 Cambridge Center, Cambridge, MA 02142

TELEPHONE NUMBER: (617) 679-2000
FAX: (617) 252-9617
NO. OF EMPLOYEES: 675
ANNUAL MEETING: In June
SHAREHOLDERS: 2,759 (approx.)
INSTITUTIONAL HOLDINGS:
No. of Institutions: 185
Shares Held: 50,069,930

REGISTRAR(S):

TRANSFER AGENT(S): State Street Bank & Trust Co., Boston, MA

34

BIOMET INC.

YIELD ...%
P/E RATIO 17.3

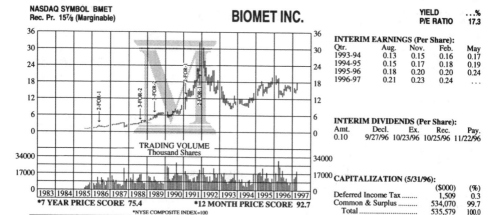

INTERIM EARNINGS (Per Share):

Qtr.	Aug.	Nov.	Feb.	May
1993-94	0.13	0.15	0.16	0.17
1994-95	0.15	0.17	0.18	0.19
1995-96	0.18	0.20	0.20	0.24
1996-97	0.21	0.23	0.24	...

INTERIM DIVIDENDS (Per Share):

Amt.	Decl.	Ex.	Rec.	Pay.
0.10	9/27/96	10/23/96	10/25/96	11/22/96

CAPITALIZATION (5/31/96):

	($000)	(%)
Deferred Income Tax	1,509	0.3
Common & Surplus	534,070	99.7
Total	535,579	100.0

RECENT DEVELOPMENTS: For the third quarter ended 2/28/97, net income increased 16.1% to $27.3 million. This compares with $23.5 million in the corresponding quarter the year before. Net sales were up 9.5% to $146.2 million from $133.5 million in the prior year. Reconstructive sales totaled $87.2 million, or 59.7% of total sales, compared with $81.0 million a year earlier, an increase of 7.7%. Electro-Biology, Inc. (EBI) sales grew 5.4% to $29.0 million from $27.5 million the previous year. Sales of other products rose 20.0% to $29.9 million compared with $25.0 million in the corresponding year-earlier quarter. Pacing the sales and net income increases for the quarter were continued market penetration of the Company's primary and revision reconstructive devices in both international and domestic markets. Reconstructive sales were led by BMET's Maxim Total Knee and Alliance Hip Systems. EBI's sales were driven by increased sales of bone healing products.

BUSINESS

BIOMET INC. and its subsidiaries design, develop, manufacture, and market products used primarily by orthopedic medical specialists in both surgical and nonsurgical therapy, including reconstructive and trauma devices, electrical bone growth stimulators, orthopedic support devices, operating room supplies, powered surgical instruments, general surgical instruments, arthroscopy products, and oral-maxillofacial products and instruments. Headquartered in Warsaw, Indiana, the Company and its subsidiaries currently distribute products in approximately 100 countries.

ANNUAL EARNINGS AND DIVIDENDS PER SHARE

	5/31/96	5/31/95	5/31/94	5/31/93	5/31/92	5/31/91	5/31/90
Earnings Per Share	0.82	0.69	0.61	0.56	0.46	0.36	0.27
Dividends Per Share	Nil	Nil	Nil	Nil	① ...	② ...	Nil

① 2-for-1 stk. split, 12/17/91 ② 2-for-1 stk. split, 1/15/91

ANNUAL FINANCIAL DATA

RECORD OF EARNINGS (IN THOUSANDS):

	5/31/96	5/31/95	5/31/94	5/31/93	5/31/92	5/31/91	5/31/90
Total Revenues	535,159	452,272	373,295	335,373	274,795	209,690	162,379
Costs and Expenses	377,067	318,875	259,495	233,219	196,813	150,240	116,609
Depreciation & Amort	20,812	14,370	12,046	11,687	8,159	6,496	5,654
Operating Income	137,280	119,027	101,754	90,467	69,823	52,954	40,116
Income Bef Income Taxes	149,669	124,942	107,032	94,272	76,511	58,600	43,828
Income Taxes	55,563	45,742	37,214	30,311	24,702	19,126	13,895
Net Income	94,106	79,200	69,818	63,961	51,809	39,474	29,933
Aver. Shs. Outstg.	115,461	115,459	115,215	114,934	113,009	111,892	111,136

BALANCE SHEET (IN THOUSANDS):

Cash and Cash Equivalents	136,902	90,445	140,842	93,623	74,585	50,679	42,875
Receivables, Net	154,055	140,283	96,800	84,708	69,448	54,960	39,934
Inventories	151,465	140,885	92,263	83,003	56,933	41,171	28,122
Gross Property	132,697	121,018	83,460	77,678	60,528	46,688	34,167
Accumulated Depreciation	52,533	40,710	32,336	24,609	17,167	12,320	8,405
Net Stockholders' Equity	534,070	444,617	357,283	301,319	232,467	172,928	129,374
Total Assets	598,469	539,084	418,077	354,409	279,234	210,660	155,348
Total Current Assets	462,916	391,902	342,227	271,039	209,727	152,082	115,204
Total Current Liabilities	62,099	89,150	53,819	46,652	42,020	33,570	22,631
Net Working Capital	400,817	302,752	288,408	224,387	167,707	118,512	92,573
Year End Shares Outstg	146,322	115,188	114,424	115,288	113,462	112,378	111,446

STATISTICAL RECORD:

Operating Profit Margin %	25.7	26.3	27.3	27.0	25.4	25.3	24.7
Book Value Per Share	3.50	3.59	2.94	2.43	1.89	1.38	1.04
Return on Equity %	17.6	17.8	19.5	21.2	22.3	22.8	23.1
Return on Assets %	15.7	14.7	16.7	18.0	18.6	18.7	19.3
P/E Ratio	24.2-16.0	20.7-13.0	27.0-13.7	54.5-24.6	70.4-17.7	27.9-14.3	25.9-14.8
Price Range	19⅞-13⅛	14¼-9	16½-8⅜	30½-13¾	32⅜-8⅛	9¾-5	7-4

Statistics are as originally reported.

OFFICERS:
N.L. Noblitt, Chmn.
D.A. Miller, Ph.D, Pres. & C.E.O.
G.D. Hartman, V.P.-Fin. & Treas.

INCORPORATED: IN, Nov., 1977

PRINCIPAL OFFICE: Airport Industrial Park, P.O. Box 587, Warsaw, IN 46581-0587

TELEPHONE NUMBER: (219) 267-6639
FAX: (219) 267-8137
NO. OF EMPLOYEES: 2,280 (approx.)
ANNUAL MEETING: In September
SHAREHOLDERS: 11,500 (approx.)
INSTITUTIONAL HOLDINGS:
No. of Institutions: 176
Shares Held: 60,374,805

REGISTRAR(S):

TRANSFER AGENT(S): Lake City Bank, Warsaw, IN

NASDAQ SYMBOL BMCS
Rec. Pr. 44⅛ (Marginable)

BMC SOFTWARE, INC.

YIELD	...%
P/E RATIO	28.7

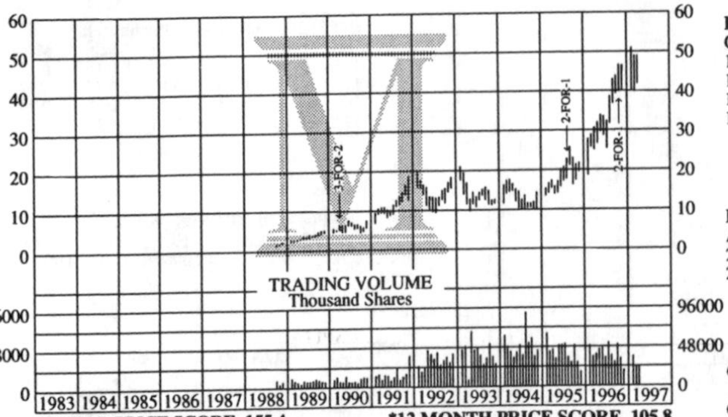

60
50
40
30
20
10
0
3-FOR-2
2-FOR-1
2-FOR-1
TRADING VOLUME
Thousand Shares
96000
48000
0
1983 1984 1985 1986 1987 1988 1989 1990 1991 1992 1993 1994 1995 1996 1997

*7 YEAR PRICE SCORE 155.4 *12 MONTH PRICE SCORE 105.8

*NYSE COMPOSITE INDEX=100

INTERIM EARNINGS (Per Share):

Qtr.	June	Sept.	Dec.	Mar.
1993-94	0.17	0.19	0.22	d0.05
1994-95	0.21	0.24	0.28	0.03
1995-96	0.27	0.25	0.13	0.37
1996-97	0.26	0.33	0.45	0.50

INTERIM DIVIDENDS (Per Share):

Amt.	Decl.	Ex.	Rec.	Pay.
2-for-1	7/19/95	8/15/95	8/4/95	8/14/95
2-for-1	10/23/96	11/19/96	11/4/96	11/18/96

CAPITALIZATION (3/31/97):

	($000)	(%)
Common & Surplus	546,212	100.0
Total	546,212	100.0

RECENT DEVELOPMENTS: For the fiscal year ended 3/31/97, net earnings were up 55.2% to $163.9 million compared with $105.6 million a year earlier. Total revenues grew 31.3% to $563.2 million from $428.9 million the previous year. The operating results included acquired research and development costs of $11.3 million compared with $23.6 million the year before. Revenues for the year were fueled by a 37.0% increase in North American revenues and a 23.0% rise in international revenues. License revenues accounted for 67.6% of total revenues. For the fourth quarter ended 3/31/97, net earnings rose 37.8% to $53.4 million from $38.8 million in the comparable prior-year quarter. Total revenues for the quarter increased 25.2% to $160.6 million compared with $128.3 million in the corresponding quarter the previous year. License revenues accounted for 69.9% of fourth-quarter revenues.

BUSINESS

BMC SOFTWARE, INC. is a worldwide developer and vendor of more than 100 software solutions for automating application and data management across host-based and open systems environments. The Company's products are primarily designed to facilitate database and network management, maintenance and recovery and to increase the speed and efficiency of data-communications. The products aim to allow customers to achieve performance benefits and cost savings by operating data-processing centers and data-communications networks more efficiently.

ANNUAL EARNINGS AND DIVIDENDS PER SHARE

	3/31/97	3/31/96	3/31/95	3/31/94	3/31/93	3/31/92	3/31/91
Earnings Per Share	**1.53**	**1.01**	**0.76**	**0.54**	**0.63**	**0.47**	**0.32**
Dividends Per Share	[1]...	[2]...	**Nil**	**Nil**	**Nil**	**Nil**	**Nil**

[1] 2-for-1 stk. split, 11/18/96 [2] 2-for-1 stk. split, 8/14/95 [2] 3-for-2 stk. split, 3/7/90

ANNUAL FINANCIAL DATA

	3/31/97	3/31/96	3/31/95	3/31/94	3/31/93	3/31/92	3/31/91
RECORD OF EARNINGS (IN THOUSANDS):							
Total Revenues	563,210	428,850	345,000	288,500	238,500	188,696	139,531
Costs and Expenses	[1] 346,186	266,857	217,581	194,195	141,544	114,045	90,325
Depreciation & Amort	...	14,404	18,791	14,401	10,871	8,579	6,231
Operating Income	217,024	147,589	108,628	79,904	86,085	66,072	42,975
Income Bef Income Taxes	237,074	163,035	120,332	90,612	93,408	70,451	47,008
Income Taxes	73,202	57,464	42,815	34,123	28,022	21,840	15,625
Net Income	163,872	105,571	77,517	56,489	65,386	48,611	31,383
Aver. Shs. Outstg.	107,155	104,572	101,952	104,608	104,708	103,372	100,424
[1] Incl. Depr. & Amort.							
BALANCE SHEET (IN THOUSANDS):							
Cash and Cash Equivalents	138,953	130,158	93,824	80,269	130,630	137,912	91,575
Receivables, Net	98,823	87,022	70,382	65,330	55,986	42,090	12,873
Gross Property	[1] 116,296	144,730	127,848	113,265	80,676	41,120	22,127
Accumulated Depreciation	...	36,818	26,560	20,110	18,842	14,558	9,858
Net Stockholders' Equity	546,212	383,708	306,154	250,400	223,386	149,531	100,583
Total Assets	844,159	608,218	502,649	417,527	378,652	241,554	141,147
Total Current Assets	248,382	227,972	182,900	160,699	197,813	191,209	112,948
Total Current Liabilities	204,663	184,197	147,734	127,130	123,364	74,531	29,542
Net Working Capital	43,719	43,775	35,166	33,569	74,449	116,678	83,406
Year End Shares Outstg	...	105,010	101,000	102,976	104,928	102,580	97,520
[1] Net.							
STATISTICAL RECORD:							
Operating Profit Margin %	38.5	34.4	31.5	27.7	36.1	35.0	30.8
Book Value Per Share	...	3.40	2.87	2.29	1.99	1.33	0.92
Return on Equity %	30.0	27.5	25.3	22.6	29.3	32.5	31.2
Return on Assets %	19.4	17.4	15.4	13.5	17.3	20.1	22.2
P/E Ratio	30.6-12.2	25.5-13.4	23.4-13.3	38.9-18.1	31.3-14.9	39.9-14.4	23.8-14.1
Price Range	46¾-18⅝	25¾-13½	17¾-10⅛	21-9¾	19¾-9⅜	18¾-6¾	7⅝-4½

Statistics are as originally reported.
Figures for 3/31/97 are preliminary.

OFFICERS:
M.P. Watson, Jr., Chmn., Pres. & C.E.O.
W. Austin, Sr. V.P. & C.F.O.
M.B. Morse, V.P., Gen. Couns. & Sec.
S.B. Solcher, Treas.

INCORPORATED: TX, 1980; reincorp., DE, Jul., 1988

PRINCIPAL OFFICE: 2101 CityWest Boulevard, Houston, TX 77042-2827

TELEPHONE NUMBER: (713) 918-8800

FAX: (713) 242-9312

NO. OF EMPLOYEES: 1,185

ANNUAL MEETING: In August

SHAREHOLDERS: 271 (approx.)

INSTITUTIONAL HOLDINGS:
No. of Institutions: 212
Shares Held: 97,453,802

REGISTRAR(S): First National Bank of Boston, Shareholder Services Division, Boston, MA

TRANSFER AGENT(S): First National Bank of Boston, Shareholder Services Division, Boston, MA

BOSTON CHICKEN, INC.

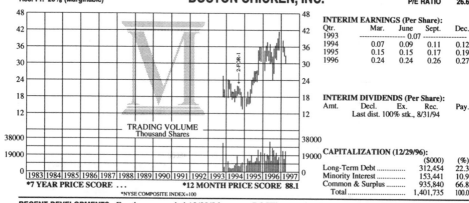

INTERIM EARNINGS (Per Share):

Qtr.	Mar.	June	Sept.	Dec.
1993	------- 0.07 -------			
1994	0.07	0.09	0.11	0.12
1995	0.15	0.15	0.17	0.19
1996	0.24	0.24	0.26	0.27

INTERIM DIVIDENDS (Per Share):

Amt.	Decl.	Ex.	Rec.	Pay.
	Last dist. 100% stk., 8/31/94			

CAPITALIZATION (12/29/96):

	($000)	(%)
Long-Term Debt	312,454	22.3
Minority Interest	153,441	10.9
Common & Surplus	935,840	66.8
Total	1,401,735	100.0

TRADING VOLUME Thousand Shares

*7 YEAR PRICE SCORE ...   *12 MONTH PRICE SCORE 88.1

*NYSE COMPOSITE INDEX=100

RECENT DEVELOPMENTS: For the year ended 12/29/96, net income advanced 99.5% to $67.0 million from $33.6 million in 1995. Earnings for 1996 included a gain of $38.2 million related to the sale of a subsidiary's stock. Total revenue was up 65.9% to $264.5 million from $159.5 million a year earlier. For the quarter ended 12/29/96, net income climbed 77.2% to $18.1 million from $10.2 million in the same prior-year period. Total revenue grew 70.6% to $78.3 million from $45.9 million in 1995. During 1996,

BOST's area developers tripled their development commitments, with plans to open approximately 3,600 Boston Markets in the U.S. in the next five to seven years. In addition, Boston Market International, a new venture formed to license the Boston Market brand outside the U.S., signed a letter of intent with an international financed area developer. Under this agreement, 600 stores will be built in Taiwan and the People's Republic of China over the next ten years.

BUSINESS

BOSTON CHICKEN, INC., based in Golden, CO, operates and franchises Boston Market restaurants that specialize in home-style meals featuring rotisserie-roasted Boston Chicken and turkey breast, Hearth Honey hams, double-sauced meat loaf, hand-carved Boston Carver sandwiches and fresh vegetables, salads and other side dishes, including mashed potatoes made from scratch. As of 1/28/97 there were 1,087 Boston Market stores in operation in 38 states and the District of Columbia. The Company also owns approximately 60% of Einstein/Noah Bagel Corp., which operates and franchises 315 retail bagel stores in 27 states primarily under the Einstein Bros.™ Bagels and Noah's New York Bagels® brands.

ANNUAL EARNINGS AND DIVIDENDS PER SHARE

	12/29/96	12/31/95	12/25/94	12/26/93	12/27/92	12/29/91	12/30/90
Earnings Per Share	1.01	0.66	0.38	0.07	d0.21	...	...
Dividends Per Share	Nil	Nil	①...	Nil	Nil	...	...

① 2-for-1 stk. split, 8/31/94.

ANNUAL FINANCIAL DATA

RECORD OF EARNINGS (IN MILLIONS):

	12/29/96	12/31/95	12/25/94	12/26/93	12/27/92	12/29/91	12/30/90
Total Revenues	264.5	159.5	96.2	42.5	8.3	5.2	3.4
Costs and Expenses	150.3	80.8	65.5	38.6	14.3	7.6	4.7
Depreciation & Amort	22.9	11.4	6.1	2.0	0.3	0.2	0.1
Operating Income	91.3	67.2	24.6	1.9	d6.3	d2.6	d1.4
Inc Fr Cont Opers Bef Income Taxes	115.2	54.4	20.5	1.6	d5.9	...	...
Income Taxes	43.0	20.8	4.3	...	...	...	...
Net Income	67.0	33.6	16.2	1.6	d5.9	d2.6	d1.3
Aver. Shs. Outstg. (000)	66,501	50,972	42,861	32,667	28,495	18,775	16,859

BALANCE SHEET (IN MILLIONS):

Cash and Cash Equivalents	100.8	310.4	25.3	4.5	9.7	2.9	...
Receivables, Net	41.6	31.8	31.7	6.7	0.9	0.2	...
Inventories				0.6	0.2	①0.0	...
Gross Property	357.8	268.9	167.7	53.6	10.5	2.4	...
Accumulated Depreciation	23.1	10.3	4.4	2.2	0.5	0.3	...
Long-Term Debt	312.5	307.2	130.0	...	...	...	...
Net Stockholders' Equity	935.8	716.8	259.8	94.9	17.0	3.0	...
Total Assets	1,543.6	1,073.9	427.0	110.1	22.7	5.6	...
Total Current Assets	146.5	343.8	59.3	13.1	11.0	3.2	...
Total Current Liabilities	87.6	30.3	27.3	10.3	3.2	2.1	...
Net Working Capital	58.8	313.5	32.0	2.8	7.8	1.1	...
Year End Shs Outstg (000)	64,246	59,129	44,700	34,705	22,305	13,476	...
① Equal to $44,000.							

STATISTICAL RECORD:

Operating Profit Margin %	34.5	42.2	25.6	4.5	...	...	...
Book Value Per Share	11.60	12.12	5.81	2.73	0.76	0.22	...
Return on Equity %	7.2	4.7	6.2	1.7	...	...	...
Return on Assets %	4.3	3.1	3.8	1.5	...	...	...
P/E Ratio	41.1-23.9	54.4-22.0	63.8-35.5	N.M.	...	...	...
Price Range	41½-24⅛	35⅞-14½	24¼-13½	25½-17¾	...	...	...

Statistics are as originally reported.

OFFICERS:
S.A. Beck, Co-Chmn., C.E.O. & Pres.
M.W. Stephens, Vice-Chmn. & C.F.O.

INCORPORATED: MA, Mar., 1988; reincorp., DE, Sep., 1993

PRINCIPAL OFFICE: P.O. Box 4086, Golden, CO 80401-4086

TELEPHONE NUMBER: (303) 278-9500

NO. OF EMPLOYEES: 975 (approx.)

ANNUAL MEETING: In May

SHAREHOLDERS: 2,900 (approx.)

INSTITUTIONAL HOLDINGS:
No. of Institutions: 132
Shares Held: 48,108,008

REGISTRAR(S): Harris Trust & Savings Bank, Chicago, IL

TRANSFER AGENT(S): Harris Trust & Savings Bank, Chicago, IL

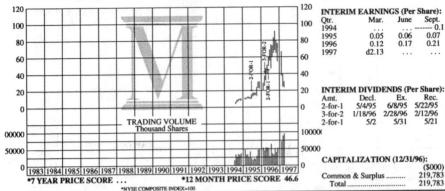

NASDAQ SYMBOL CSCC
Rec. Pr. 31⅜ (Marginable)

CASCADE COMMUNICATIONS CORP.

YIELD ...%
P/E RATIO ...

TRADING VOLUME
Thousand Shares

| 1983 | 1984 | 1985 | 1986 | 1987 | 1988 | 1989 | 1990 | 1991 | 1992 | 1993 | 1994 | 1995 | 1996 | 1997 |

*7 YEAR PRICE SCORE ...   *12 MONTH PRICE SCORE 46.6
*NYSE COMPOSITE INDEX=100

INTERIM EARNINGS (Per Share):

Qtr.	Mar.	June	Sept.	Dec.
1994	...	...	------ 0.11 ------	
1995	0.05	0.06	0.07	0.10
1996	0.12	0.17	0.21	0.24
1997	d2.13	...	...	...

INTERIM DIVIDENDS (Per Share):

Amt.	Decl.	Ex.	Rec.	Pay.
2-for-1	5/4/95	6/8/95	5/22/95	6/6/95
3-for-2	1/18/96	2/28/96	2/12/96	2/27/96
2-for-1	5/2	5/31	5/21	5/30

CAPITALIZATION (12/31/96):

	($000)	(%)
Common & Surplus	219,783	100.0
Total	219,783	100.0

RECENT DEVELOPMENTS: On 3/30/97, CSCC announced that it will be acquired by Ascend Communications, Inc. in a stock-for-stock exchange valued at approximately $3.70 billion. This acquisition is expected to be completed in the third quarter of 1997. For the quarter ended 3/29/97, the Company reported a net loss of $198.3 million compared with net income of $10.4 million in the corresponding period of the previous year. Earnings for 1997 included a one-time charge of $213.1 million related to the purchase of in-process technology. Revenue advanced 61.2% to $90.3 million from $56.0 million the year before. Gross profit as a percentage of revenue fell to 63.5% from 64.7% a year earlier. Research and development expenses climbed 96.9% to $17.7 million from $9.0 million the previous year. Sales and marketing expenses increased 58.5% to $13.8 million from $8.7 million the year before. CSCC incurred a loss from operations of $190.8 million versus income of $16.4 million in 1996.

BUSINESS

CASCADE COMMUNICATIONS CORP. is a global provider of wide area networking ("WAN") products for the public carrier, Internet Service Provider and enterprise markets. The Company delivers multi-service WAN switches and network management solutions that enable customers to seamlessly integrate existing technologies with Asynchronous Transfer Mode for cost-effective network expansion and investment protection. On 1/29/97, the Company acquired Sahara Networks, Inc. in a stock transaction valued at approximately $216.5 million. On 3/30/97, the Company announced that it will be acquired by Ascend Communications, Inc. in a stock-for-stock exchange valued at approximately $3.70 billion.

ANNUAL EARNINGS AND DIVIDENDS PER SHARE

	1996	1995	1994	1993	1992	1991
Earnings Per Share	0.72	0.28	0.11	...	...	...
Dividends Per Share	①...	②...	Nil	...	...	...

① 3-for-2 stk. split, 2/27/96 & 2-for-1 stk. split, 5/30/96. ② 2-for-1 stk. split, 6/6/95.

ANNUAL FINANCIAL DATA

RECORD OF EARNINGS (IN THOUSANDS):

	1996	1995	1994	1993	1992	1991
Total Revenues	340,976	134,834	50,060	6,960	816	...
Costs and Expenses	217,032	91,253	38,093	9,311	3,855	1,086
Depreciation & Amort	13,662	5,503	1,651	369	185	47
Operating Income	110,282	38,078	10,317	d2,720	d3,224	d1,133
Inc Fr Cont Opers Bef Income Taxes	115,589	41,316	11,098	d2,613	d3,145	d1,055
Income Taxes	44,810	15,906	1,832	...	...	...
Net Income	70,779	25,410	9,266	d2,613	d3,145	d1,055
Aver. Shs. Outstg.	97,767	91,220	81,072	...	...	...

BALANCE SHEET (IN THOUSANDS):

Cash and Cash Equivalents	112,319	60,594	41,580	7,616	5,332	...
Receivables, Net	91,999	25,720	9,736	2,201	193	...
Inventories	19,303	7,645	7,937	4,761	582	...
Gross Property	52,209	21,204	8,179	1,924	784	...
Accumulated Depreciation	19,197	7,224	2,225	601	232	...
Long-Term Debt	...	...	...	256	113	...
Net Stockholders' Equity	219,783	86,306	52,480	11,428	6,173	...
Total Assets	270,261	111,859	65,764	16,070	6,709	...
Total Current Assets	235,042	94,740	59,592	14,652	6,126	...
Total Current Liabilities	50,478	25,553	13,284	4,386	423	...
Net Working Capital	184,564	69,187	46,308	10,266	5,703	...
Year End Shares Outstg	90,155	91,220	81,072	...	...	...

STATISTICAL RECORD:

Operating Profit Margin %	32.3	28.2	20.6	...	...	...
Book Value Per Share	2.44	2.06	1.29	...	...	...
Return on Equity %	32.2	29.4	17.7	38.2	74.2	...
Return on Assets %	26.2	22.7	14.1	...	...	...
P/E Ratio	N.M.	N.M.	98.9-35.2	...	...	...
Price Range	91¼-20⅜	30⅞-9½	10⅞-3⅞	...	...	...

Statistics are as originally reported.

OFFICERS:
G. Deshpande, Chmn.
D.E. Smith, Pres. & C.E.O.
P.E. Blondin, V.P.-Fin., C.F.O., Treas. & Sec.

INCORPORATED: DE, Oct., 1994

PRINCIPAL OFFICE: 5 Carlisle Road, Westford, MA 01886

TELEPHONE NUMBER: (508) 692-2600

NO. OF EMPLOYEES: 833

ANNUAL MEETING: In May

SHAREHOLDERS: 625

INSTITUTIONAL HOLDINGS:
No. of Institutions: 176
Shares Held: 73,764,540

REGISTRAR(S): Boston Equiserv, Boston, MA

TRANSFER AGENT(S): Boston Equiserv, Boston, MA

38

CENTOCOR, INC.

NASDAQ SYMBOL CNTO
Rec. Pr. 32½ (Marginable)

YIELD ...%
P/E RATIO ...

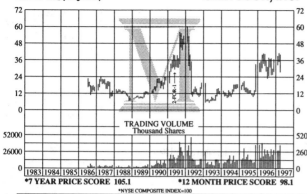

*7 YEAR PRICE SCORE 105.1   *12 MONTH PRICE SCORE 98.1
*NYSE COMPOSITE INDEX=100

INTERIM EARNINGS (Per Share):

Qtr.	Mar.	June	Sept.	Dec.
1994	d1.13	d0.30	d0.34	d0.83
1995	d0.14	d0.30	d0.21	d0.32
1996	d0.16	d0.07	d0.02	0.04
1997	0.05	...	...	...

INTERIM DIVIDENDS (Per Share):

Amt.	Decl.	Ex.	Rec.	Pay.
Last dist. 2-for-1 stk. split, 5/24/91.				

CAPITALIZATION (12/31/96):

	($000)	(%)
Long-Term Debt	54,765	18.6
Minority Interest	3,839	1.3
Common & Surplus	235,910	80.1
Total	294,514	100.0

RECENT DEVELOPMENTS: For the quarter ended 3/31/97, the Company reported net income of $3.3 million compared with a net loss of $9.7 million in the corresponding period of the previous year. Total revenues advanced to $45.0 million from $21.9 million the year before. Product sales climbed to $44.9 million from $21.7 million a year earlier. Costs and expenses totaled $41.9 million versus $30.5 million the prior year. Other income amounted to $244,000 compared with other expense of $1.1 million the previous year. Income taxes were $70,000 versus none for 1995. On 3/3/97, the Company entered into a research and commercialization agreement with GenPharm International, Inc. This agreement is based on GenPharm's HuMAb-Mouse™ strain, which contains functional human antibody genes that wil be generated against antigens, including human antigens. CNTO will develop completely human antibodies to several unnamed antigens, and will have worldwide marketing and manufacturing rights to any of the antibodies that enter the clinic.

BUSINESS

CENTOCOR, INC. is a biotechnology company that develops therapeutic and diagnostic human health care products for cardiovascular, autoimmune and infectious diseases, and cancer. The Company concentrates on research and development, manufacturing and market development, with a primary technological focus on monoclonal antibodies, with additional programs in genetic vaccines and peptides.

ANNUAL EARNINGS AND DIVIDENDS PER SHARE

	1996	1995	1994	1993	1992	1991	1990
Earnings Per Share	d0.20	d0.98	d2.55	d1.79	d4.90	d5.72	d5.10
Dividends Per Share	Nil	Nil	Nil	Nil	Nil	☐...	Nil

☐ 2-for-1 stk. split, 5/28/91.

ANNUAL FINANCIAL DATA

RECORD OF EARNINGS (IN THOUSANDS):

	1996	1995	1994	1993	1992	1991	1990
Total Revenues	135,485	78,916	67,226	75,930	126,232	53,197	64,634
Costs and Expenses	136,894	111,441	118,160	104,879	271,761	158,828	86,172
Depreciation & Amort	13,921	14,778	18,164	25,804	24,217	18,176	16,319
Operating Profit	41,457	18,932	905	11,360	17,030	d52,106	15,097
Inc Fr Cont Opers Bef Income Taxes	d13,468	d57,132	d126,658	d74,379	...	...	d134,380
Income Taxes	...	...	...	...	...	...	cr2,200
Net Income	d12,763	d57,132	d126,658	d74,379	d194,146	d195,555	d132,180
Aver. Shs. Outstg.	66,475	58,207	49,597	41,482	39,623	34,172	25,930

BALANCE SHEET (IN THOUSANDS):

Cash and Cash Equivalents	176,315	131,437	181,588	122,872	150,159	180,905	95,719
Receivables, Net	29,587	13,137	12,924	12,549	14,445	18,089	18,743
Inventories	23,815	20,783	16,682	13,874	16,858	76,188	33,771
Gross Property	141,491	142,864	131,808	143,216	170,030	154,021	123,259
Accumulated Depreciation	79,954	74,727	61,768	58,533	51,840	36,722	24,290
Long-Term Debt	54,765	231,640	231,640	238,100	238,166	259,368	42,083
Net Stockholders' Equity	235,910	d29,396	5,278	d19,194	30,721	144,027	168,664
Total Assets	341,121	260,284	305,915	281,039	349,268	472,929	273,080
Total Current Assets	234,748	168,969	214,957	152,711	187,164	284,260	157,673
Total Current Liabilities	45,480	56,137	67,247	59,604	77,106	63,618	43,632
Net Working Capital	189,268	112,832	147,710	93,107	110,058	220,642	114,041
Year End Shares Outstg	69,177	58,538	57,081	43,672	41,192	37,681	27,998

STATISTICAL RECORD:

Operating Profit Margin %	30.6	24.0	1.3	15.0	13.5	...	23.4
Book Value Per Share	3.41	...	0.09	...	0.75	3.82	6.02
Price Range	40⅞-23	33⅛-9⅝	18¾-8⅞	19½-5¼	60¼-9½	56¼-19⅜	24⅛-11⅞

Statistics are as originally reported.

OFFICERS:
H.J. Schoemaker, Chmn.
D.P. Holveck, Pres. & C.E.O.
D.J. Caruso, V.P.-Fin. & C.F.O.

INCORPORATED: PA, May, 1979

PRINCIPAL OFFICE: 200 Great Valley Parkway, Malvern, PA 19355

TELEPHONE NUMBER: (610) 651-6000
FAX: (610) 651-6100
NO. OF EMPLOYEES: 545 (approx.)
ANNUAL MEETING: In June
SHAREHOLDERS: 3,534 (approx.)
INSTITUTIONAL HOLDINGS:
No. of Institutions: 138
Shares Held: 49,340,510

REGISTRAR(S): Boston Equiserv, Boston, MA

TRANSFER AGENT(S): Boston Equiserv, Boston, MA

CHIRON CORP.

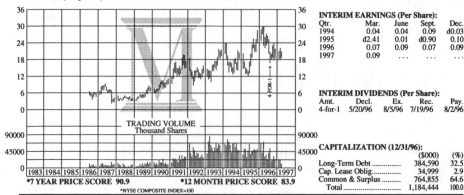

INTERIM EARNINGS (Per Share):

Qtr.	Mar.	June	Sept.	Dec.
1994	0.04	0.04	0.09	d0.03
1995	d2.41	0.01	d0.90	0.10
1996	0.07	0.09	0.07	0.09
1997	0.09	...	...	...

INTERIM DIVIDENDS (Per Share):

Amt.	Decl.	Ex.	Rec.	Pay.
4-for-1	5/20/96	8/5/96	7/19/96	8/2/96

*7 YEAR PRICE SCORE 90.9   *12 MONTH PRICE SCORE 83.9
*NYSE COMPOSITE INDEX=100

CAPITALIZATION (12/31/96):

	($000)	(%)
Long-Term Debt	384,590	32.5
Cap. Lease Oblig.	34,999	2.9
Common & Surplus	764,855	64.6
Total	1,184,444	100.0

RECENT DEVELOPMENTS: For the quarter ended 3/31/97, net income advanced 20.3% to $15.3 million from $12.7 million in the same prior-year period. Total revenues improved 8.0% to $330.3 million from $305.8 million in 1995. Net product sales grew 4.7% to $251.1 million from $239.8 million the prior year, despite unfavorable currency exchange rates. Without the impact of foreign currency, product sales growth would have been 9%. Income from operations climbed 25.0% to $30.4 million from $24.3 mil-

lion a year earlier. This improvement was primarily due to a significant increase in the Company's sales fee income from sales of Aredia® (pamidronate disodium), increased performance from CHIR's joint blood screening business, and higher royalties. During the quarter, CHIR and Ortho Diagnostic Systems, Inc. announced that their joint business was awarded a contract to provide 100% of the reagents, systems and support required by the American Red Cross for viral disease blood screening.

BUSINESS

CHIRON CORPORATION applies biotechnology and other techniques of modern biology to develop products that diagnose, prevent and treat human disease. The Company is building a healthcare business to address needs in four markets: diagnostics, including immunodiagnostics and new quantitative tests based on nucleic-acid probe-technology; vaccines, emphasizing adult and pediatric infectious diseases; therapeutics, with an emphasis on oncology and serious infectious diseases; and ophthalmic surgical products for a number of uses in eye-care, including the correction of vision. CHIR focuses its research in two areas: understanding of the human immune system related to infectious disease and cancer; and pharmaceuticals. The Company is researching additional therapeutic products, including a new generation of chemical therapeutics developed through advanced techniques of drug discovery and design.

ANNUAL EARNINGS AND DIVIDENDS PER SHARE

	1996	1995	1994	1993	1992	1991	1990
Earnings Per Share	0.31	d3.16	0.13	0.14	② d0.80	② d5.55	② 0.06
Dividends Per Share	①...	Nil	Nil	Nil	Nil	Nil	Nil

① 4-for-1 stk. split, 8/2/96. ② Before extraord. item.

ANNUAL FINANCIAL DATA

RECORD OF EARNINGS (IN MILLIONS):

	1996	1995	1994	1993	1992	1991	1990
Total Revenues	1,312.8	1,100.6	454.0	317.5	248.1	118.5	78.5
Costs and Expenses	1,110.1	1,483.9	362.2	277.4	323.3	548.7	73.0
Depreciation & Amort	112.3	99.1	49.4	25.0	24.7	8.3	5.1
Operating Income	90.4	d482.4	42.4	15.1	d99.8	d438.6	0.4
Inc Fr Cont Opers Bef Income Taxes	80.0	d490.8	32.0	23.1	d92.4	d424.4	7.1
Income Taxes	24.8	21.7	13.7	4.7	3.6	0.8	3.0
Net Income	55.1	d512.5	18.3	18.4	① d96.0	② d425.2	③ 4.0
Aver. Shs. Outstg. (000)	177,052	162,440	137,172	134,724	120,800	76,904	68,708

① Before extra. item dr$6,657,000. ② Before extra. item cr$100,000. ③ Before extra. item cr$2,805,000.

BALANCE SHEET (IN MILLIONS):

	1996	1995	1994	1993	1992	1991	1990
Cash and Cash Equivalents	106.8	135.4	222.5	238.1	256.8	558.3	154.2
Receivables, Net	352.0	285.8	140.5	76.4	62.7	35.4	14.6
Inventories	180.5	165.9	47.6	35.5	21.7	...	...
Gross Property	796.8	658.6	362.5	259.1	129.6	100.9	44.2
Accumulated Depreciation	213.2	140.8	76.3	55.1	40.0	22.9	19.8
Long-Term Debt	384.6	374.3	308.3	333.0	107.2	238.6	121.5
Capital Lease Obligations	35.0	38.9	29.7	...	...	...	...
Net Stockholders' Equity	764.9	672.4	572.6	522.3	492.9	524.4	120.3
Total Assets	1,688.7	1,490.2	1,049.7	968.6	712.4	895.3	265.4
Total Current Assets	696.8	637.0	433.8	362.0	349.1	617.0	174.1
Total Current Liabilities	473.2	368.6	119.6	105.6	105.4	124.6	21.0
Net Working Capital	223.6	268.4	314.2	256.4	243.7	492.4	153.1
Year End Shs Outstg (000)	170,675	166,952	133,516	130,708	127,132	117,364	65,128

STATISTICAL RECORD:

	1996	1995	1994	1993	1992	1991	1990
Operating Profit Margin %	6.9	...	9.3	4.8	...	...	0.5
Book Value Per Share	3.65	3.12	3.65	3.69	3.50	4.05	1.81
Return on Equity %	7.2	...	3.2	3.5	...	...	3.3
Return on Assets %	3.3	...	1.7	1.9	...	...	1.5
P/E Ratio	96.4-54.0	...	N.M.	N.M.	...	...	N.M.
Price Range	29⅞-16¾	28½-12	24-12¾	21¾-10	18⅝-8¾	19¾-9⅜	11¼-5⅞

Statistics are as originally reported.

OFFICERS:
W.J. Rutter, Ph.D., Chmn.
E.E. Penhoet, Ph.D., Pres. & C.E.O.
D.L. Winger, Sr. V.P.-Fin. & Admin. & C.F.O.

INCORPORATED: CA, May, 1981; reincorp., DE, Feb., 1987

PRINCIPAL OFFICE: 4560 Horton Street, Emeryville, CA 94608-2916

TELEPHONE NUMBER: (510) 655-8730
FAX: (510) 655-9910
NO. OF EMPLOYEES: 7,434
ANNUAL MEETING: In May
SHAREHOLDERS: 8,139 (approx.)
INSTITUTIONAL HOLDINGS:
No. of Institutions: 140
Shares Held: 30,780,959

REGISTRAR(S): Continental Stock Transfer & Trust Co., New York, NY

TRANSFER AGENT(S): Continental Stock Transfer & Trust Co., New York, NY

NASDAQ SYMBOL CTAS
Rec. Pr. 55½ (Marginable)

CINTAS CORP.

YIELD 0.5%
P/E RATIO 30.3

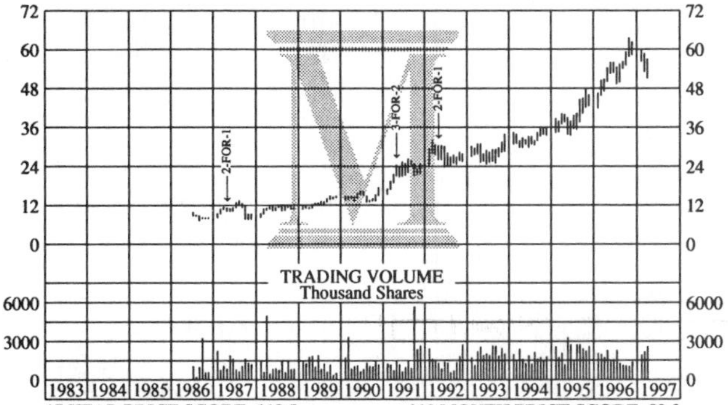

***7 YEAR PRICE SCORE 118.5** ***12 MONTH PRICE SCORE 89.3**

*NYSE COMPOSITE INDEX=100

INTERIM EARNINGS (Per Share):

Qtr.	Aug.	Nov.	Feb.	May
1993-94	0.23	0.29	0.28	0.32
1994-95	0.29	0.34	0.33	0.38
1995-96	0.35	0.40	0.39	0.46
1996-97	0.42	0.48	0.47	...

INTERIM DIVIDENDS (Per Share):

Amt.	Decl.	Ex.	Rec.	Pay.
0.20A	2/15/95	3/6/95	3/10/95	4/3/95
0.25A	2/14/96	3/6/96	3/8/96	4/2/96
0.30A	2/18/97	3/5/97	3/7/97	4/4/97

Indicated div.: $0.30

CAPITALIZATION (5/31/96):

	($000)	(%)
Long-Term Debt	117,924	20.8
Deferred Income Tax	18,747	3.3
Common & Surplus	429,497	75.9
Total	566,168	100.0

RECENT DEVELOPMENTS: For the quarter ended 2/28/97, net income advanced 21.2% to $22.5 million versus $18.5 million in the same prior-year period. Revenues climbed 14.7% to $210.0 million from $183.0 million in 1996. Income before income taxes rose 19.8% to $36.3 million from $30.3 million the prior year. For the nine months ended 2/28/97, net income grew 20.9% to $64.8 million from $53.7 million the year before. Revenue rose 14.1% to $611.3 million compared with $535.7 million a year earlier. Income before income taxes advanced 19.4% to $104.6 million versus $87.6 million in 1996. During its third quarter, CTAS opened a new operation in Salt Lake City, Utah. On 3/6/97, the Company announced that it acquired Micron-Clean Uniform Service, Inc. in Newburgh, New York. Micron provides uniforms to the growing technology, biotechnology, pharmaceutical, electronics, and food-processing industries.

BUSINESS

CINTAS CORPORATION designs, manufactures and implements corporate identity uniform programs, which it rents or sells to customers throughout the United States and Canada. Currently, the Company occupies 132 uniform rental locations in the United States and the provinces of Ontario and British Columbia, Canada. The Company operates processing plants that house administrative, sales and service personnel and the necessary equipment involved in the cleaning of uniforms and bulk items. Branch operations provide administrative, sales and service functions. The Company operates three distribution facilities and has four manufacturing plants, two of which produce trousers and two producing uniform shirts. The Company owns or leases approximately 2,765 vehicles.

ANNUAL EARNINGS AND DIVIDENDS PER SHARE

	5/31/96	5/31/95	5/31/94	5/31/93	5/31/92	5/31/91	5/31/90
Earnings Per Share	**1.60**	**1.34**	**1.12**	**0.97**	**[1] 0.79**	**0.74**	**0.63**
Dividends Per Share	**0.25**	**0.20**	**0.17**	**0.14**	**0.11**	**[2] 0.095**	**[3] 0.075**
Dividend Payout %	**15.6**	**14.9**	**15.2**	**14.4**	**13.9**	**12.8**	**11.9**

[1] Before acctg. chg. [2] 2-for-1 stk. split, 4/3/92. [3] 3-for-2 stk. split, 4/3/91.

ANNUAL FINANCIAL DATA

	5/31/96	5/31/95	5/31/94	5/31/93	5/31/92	5/31/91	5/31/90
RECORD OF EARNINGS (IN THOUSANDS):							
Total Revenues	730,130	615,098	523,216	452,722	401,563	322,479	284,536
Costs and Expenses	570,695	482,761	408,520	352,648	319,006	255,953	229,251
Depreciation	30,586	26,179	24,271	23,149	19,359	16,402	12,258
Operating Profit	293,320	243,833	209,871	183,068	158,268	129,016	112,815
Inc Fr Cont Opers Bef Income Taxes	122,230	100,961	85,451	71,303	58,206	48,777	41,626
Income Taxes	47,047	38,218	33,281	26,430	21,716	17,345	15,020
Net Income	75,183	62,743	52,170	44,873	[1] 36,490	31,432	26,606
Aver. Shs. Outstg.	47,099	46,891	46,706	46,411	46,145	42,876	42,476
[1] Before acctg. change cr$2,705,000.							
BALANCE SHEET (IN THOUSANDS):							
Cash and Cash Equivalents	82,543	45,482	60,782	54,969	22,912	18,439	30,374
Receivables, Net	78,244	69,032	56,347	48,075	40,721	35,261	31,841
Inventories	34,678	36,883	29,059	21,452	25,165	23,209	19,847
Gross Property	366,478	333,390	288,402	263,053	240,462	197,255	144,984
Accumulated Depreciation	113,881	105,393	95,899	82,206	67,507	44,689	33,668
Long-Term Debt	117,924	120,275	84,184	103,611	67,790	58,919	43,568
Net Stockholders' Equity	429,497	364,344	309,652	264,914	225,864	185,632	157,441
Total Assets	668,762	596,181	501,632	454,165	361,261	305,822	254,162
Total Current Assets	297,502	241,422	221,453	187,133	138,729	117,524	115,385
Total Current Liabilities	102,594	95,012	91,484	65,176	51,910	53,368	46,797
Net Working Capital	194,908	146,410	129,969	121,957	86,819	64,156	68,588
Year End Shares Outstg	47,199	47,005	46,801	46,579	46,190	43,421	42,518
STATISTICAL RECORD:							
Operating Profit Margin %	17.6	17.3	17.3	17.0	15.7	15.5	15.1
Book Value Per Share	9.10	7.75	6.62	5.69	4.89	4.28	3.70
Return on Equity %	17.5	17.2	16.8	16.9	16.2	16.9	16.9
Return on Assets %	11.2	10.5	10.4	9.9	10.1	10.3	10.5
Average Yield %	0.5	0.5	0.5	0.4	0.5	0.5	0.4
P/E Ratio	35.0-20.9	30.0-22.2	30.4-22.1	33.1-24.5	33.4-19.5	23.8-17.4	23.8-16.9
Price Range	56-33½	40¼-29¾	34-24¾	32⅛-23¾	26⅜-15⅜	17⅝-12⅞	15-10⅝

Statistics are as originally reported.

OFFICERS:
R.T. Farmer, Chmn.
R.J. Kohlhepp, C.E.O.
S.D. Farmer, Pres. & C.O.O.

INCORPORATED: OH, 1968; reincorp., WA, Dec., 1987

PRINCIPAL OFFICE: 6800 Cintas Boulevard P.O. Box 625737, Cincinnati, OH 45262-5737

TELEPHONE NUMBER: (513) 459-1200

FAX: (513) 573-4130

NO. OF EMPLOYEES: 10,803

ANNUAL MEETING: In October

SHAREHOLDERS: 1,700 (approx.)

INSTITUTIONAL HOLDINGS:
No. of Institutions: 190
Shares Held: 18,304,210

REGISTRAR(S): Fifth Third Bank, Cincinnati, OH 45263

TRANSFER AGENT(S): Fifth Third Bank, Cincinnati, OH 45263

CIRRUS LOGIC, INC.

YIELD ...%
P/E RATIO ...

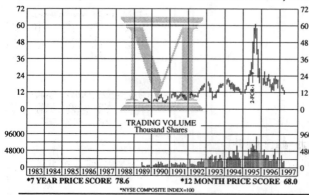

INTERIM EARNINGS (Per Share):

Qtr.	June	Sept.	Dec.	Mar.
1993-94	----------	---------- 0.70	----------	
1994-95	----------	---------- 0.96	----------	
1995-96	0.34	0.47	d0.06	d1.38
1996-97	d0.12	0.05	0.16	d0.79

INTERIM DIVIDENDS (Per Share):

Amt.   Decl.   Ex.   Rec.   Pay.
Last dist. 2-for-1 split, 7/17/95.

CAPITALIZATION (3/30/96):

	($000)	(%)
Long-Term Debt	65,571	13.1
Cap. Lease Oblig.	6,258	1.3
Common & Surplus	428,666	85.6
Total	500,495	100.0

TRADING VOLUME
Thousand Shares

*7 YEAR PRICE SCORE 78.6   *12 MONTH PRICE SCORE 68.0
*NYSE COMPOSITE INDEX=100

RECENT DEVELOPMENTS: For the year ended 3/29/97, CRUS reported a net loss of $46.2 million compared with a net loss of $36.2 million the previous year. The net loss in fiscal 1997 included fourth quarter restructuring charges of $21.0 million and $14.5 million of other charges to cost of sales. The loss for fiscal 1996 included restructuring costs of $21.0 million and a gain on sale of assets of $16.6 million. Earnings for fiscal 1995 included restructuring costs of $11.6 million and non-recurring costs of $1.2 mil-

lion. Net sales fell 20.0% to $917.2 million from $1.15 billion in 1995. Net interest and other expense totaled $8.1 million versus income of $2.5 million the year before. For the quarter ended 3/29/97, CRUS incurred a net loss of $51.9 million compared with a net loss of $88.4 million in the corresponding period of the prior year. Net sales dropped 8.6% to $212.9 million from $233.1 million a year earlier. Net interest and other expense amounted to $2.7 million versus an expense of $493,000 in 1995.

BUSINESS

CIRRUS LOGIC, INC. is a major manufacturer of advanced integrated circuits for the personal computer, consumer and industrial markets. The Company's software-rich "Systems in Silicon" are designed to add high value to major brands worldwide in applications that span multimedia (graphics, video, audio), communications (enterprise networking and remote data access) and mass storage (magnetic and optional moving media). On 10/2/96, the Company and Lucent Technologies entered into a joint venture named Cirent Semiconductor, which manufactures advanced computer chips in Orlando, Florida.

ANNUAL EARNINGS AND DIVIDENDS PER SHARE

	3/30/96	4/1/95	4/2/94	3/31/93	3/31/92	3/31/91	3/31/90
Earnings Per Share	d0.58	0.96	0.70	0.41	0.41	0.59	0.52
Dividends Per Share	Nil	①...	Nil	Nil	Nil	Nil	Nil

2-for-1 stk. split, 7/17/95.

ANNUAL FINANCIAL DATA

RECORD OF EARNINGS (IN MILLIONS):

Total Revenues	1,146.9	889.0	544.1	354.8	171.6	141.8	85.0
Costs and Expenses	1,126.9	776.7	478.1	308.3	142.0	110.2	65.1
Depreciation & Amort	64.3	34.3	26.9	15.2	8.4	5.1	3.8
Operating Income	d44.2	78.0	39.2	31.3	21.2	26.6	16.1
Inc Fr Cont Opers Bef Income Taxes	d41.7	89.6	54.8	32.9	23.0	29.1	18.0
Income Taxes	cr5.5	28.2	17.8	12.3	7.4	10.3	2.6
Net Income	d36.2	61.4	①37.1	20.6	15.6	18.8	15.4
Aver. Shs. Outstg. (000)	62,761	63,680	26,728	25,447	38,214	31,736	29,952

① Before acctg. change cr$7,550,000.

BALANCE SHEET (IN MILLIONS):

Cash and Cash Equivalents	175.3	187.0	237.0	72.7	48.3	54.9	40.8
Receivables, Net	186.4	182.1	81.8	64.2	29.4	20.8	14.0
Inventories	134.5	103.6	73.1	48.5	15.8	10.0	11.2
Gross Property	283.7	173.3	118.3	78.4	39.5	25.6	14.7
Accumulated Depreciation	113.5	73.1	48.6	31.5	17.8	9.8	5.6
Long-Term Debt	65.6	16.6	11.4	12.8	7.3	9.1	2.5
Capital Lease Obligations	6.3	9.6	7.8	5.3	4.9	0.5	1.1
Net Stockholders' Equity	428.7	419.0	337.6	142.6	95.5	73.5	52.3
Total Assets	917.6	673.5	502.2	256.4	140.5	109.0	77.6
Total Current Assets	594.8	479.9	413.0	193.5	98.5	90.5	67.0
Total Current Liabilities	412.2	228.3	145.4	95.8	32.9	25.9	21.7
Net Working Capital	182.6	251.6	267.6	97.8	65.6	64.6	45.3
Year End Shs Outstg (000)	63,951	60,594	28,313	23,963	36,420	30,346	29,774

STATISTICAL RECORD:

Operating Profit Margin %	...	8.8	7.2	8.8	12.3	18.8	19.0
Book Value Per Share	6.70	6.92	11.93	5.95	2.62	2.42	1.76
Return on Equity %	...	14.7	11.0	14.4	16.4	25.6	29.4
Return on Assets %	...	9.1	7.4	8.0	11.1	17.2	19.9
P/E Ratio	...	23.3-10.9	11.9-4.0	22.8-9.9	29.9-14.9	18.2-6.8	15.3-8.7
Price Range	61⅛-11⅛	22⅜-10½	19⅞-6⅝	18½-8	12¼-6⅛	10¾-4	7⅞-4½

Statistics are as originally reported.

OFFICERS:
S.S. Patil, Chairman
M.L. Hackworth, Pres. & C.E.O.
R.K. Shelton, V.P.-Fin. & Admin., C.F.O. & Treas.

INCORPORATED: CA, Feb., 1984

PRINCIPAL OFFICE: 3100 West Warren Avenue, Fremont, CA 94538

TELEPHONE NUMBER: (510) 623-8300

FAX: (510) 226-2180

NO. OF EMPLOYEES: 2,654

ANNUAL MEETING: July 31, 1997

SHAREHOLDERS: 2,146 (approx.)

INSTITUTIONAL HOLDINGS:
No. of Institutions: 96
Shares Held: 21,137,705

REGISTRAR(S): First National Bank of Boston, Shareholder Services Division, Boston, MA

TRANSFER AGENT(S): First National Bank of Boston, Shareholder Services Division, Boston, MA

NASDAQ SYMBOL CSCO
Rec. Pr. 48⅜ (Marginable)

CISCO SYSTEMS, INC.

YIELD ...%
P/E RATIO 28.3

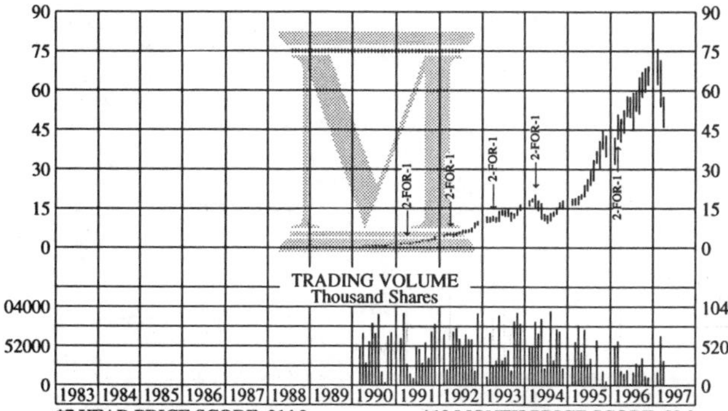

*7 YEAR PRICE SCORE 214.2 *12 MONTH PRICE SCORE 89.0

*NYSE COMPOSITE INDEX=100

INTERIM EARNINGS (Per Share):

Qtr.	Oct.	Jan.	Apr.	July
1993-94	0.12	0.15	0.16	0.17
1994-95	0.17	0.10	0.21	0.24
1995-96	0.28	0.31	0.37	0.41
1996-97	0.26	0.49	0.55	...

INTERIM DIVIDENDS (Per Share):

Amt.	Decl.	Ex.	Rec.	Pay.
2-for-1	2/9/94	3/21/94	3/4/94	3/15/94
2-for-1	1/23/96	2/20/96	2/2/96	2/16/96

CAPITALIZATION (7/28/96):

	($000)	(%)
Common & Surplus	2,819,622	100.0
Total	2,819,622	100.0

RECENT DEVELOPMENTS: For the quarter ended 4/26/97, net income advanced 54.0% to $378.3 million from $245.6 million in the same prior-year period. Earnings for 1997 included a realized gain of $32.3 million related to the sale of an investment. Net sales climbed 51.6% to $1.65 billion from $1.09 billion in 1996. During its second and third quarters, CSCO participated in various alliances with Hewlett-Packard Company, Intel Corporation, Microsoft Corporation, and GTE for the development of advanced network and Internet business solutions. On 3/3/97, CSCO acquired a minority equity interest in Software.com. In addition, the Company acquired Telesend in a stock-for-stock exchange. On 5/21/97, CSCO purchased a minority equity stake in TIBCO Software, Inc. On 6/9/97, Cisco signed a definitive agreement to acquire Skystone Systems Corporation for 1.0 million shares of Cisco common stock, worth approximately $66.5 million, and $22.6 million in cash.

BUSINESS

CISCO SYSTEMS, INC. develops, manufactures, markets, and supports high-performance multiprotocol internetworking systems that enable its customers to build large-scale integrated networks. The Company's products connect and manage communications among local and wide area networks that employ a variety of network protocols, media interfaces, network topologies and cabling systems. Cisco's principal products, a family of multiprotocol routers that support a wide variety of network protocols and media, simultaneously offer routing and bridging functions at rapid speeds, and offer a high level of network intelligence through Cisco's Internetwork Operating System (IOS) software. On 9/19/96, Cisco and Macmillan Publishing USA formed Cisco Press, a joint publishing agreement.

ANNUAL EARNINGS AND DIVIDENDS PER SHARE

	7/28/96	7/30/95	7/31/94	7/25/93	7/26/92	7/28/91	7/29/90
Earnings Per Share	**1.37**	**0.76**	**0.60**	**0.33**	**0.17**	**0.09**	**0.03**
Dividends Per Share	①...	Nil	②...	③...	④...	⑤...	Nil

① 2-for-1 stk. split, 2/16/96. ② 2-for-1 stk. split, 3/15/94. ③ 2-for-1 stk. split, 3/19/93. ④ 2-for-1 stk. split, 3/20/92. ⑤ 2-for-1 stk. split, 3/15/91.

ANNUAL FINANCIAL DATA

	7/28/96	7/30/95	7/31/94	7/25/93	7/26/92	7/28/91	7/29/90
RECORD OF EARNINGS (IN MILLIONS):							
Total Revenues	4,096.0	1,978.9	1,243.0	649.0	339.6	183.2	69.8
Costs and Expenses	2,695.2	1,534.7	754.9	385.4	210.2	117.0	48.4
Depreciation & Amort	132.6	58.5	30.8	13.6	6.7	3.0	1.0
Operating Income	1,400.8	642.9	488.1	263.6	129.4	66.2	21.4
Inc Fr Cont Opers Bef Income Taxes	1,464.8	679.0	509.5	275.1	136.1	70.8	23.5
Income Taxes	551.5	258.0	194.6	103.2	51.7	27.6	9.6
Net Income	913.3	421.0	314.9	172.0	84.4	43.2	13.9
Aver. Shs. Outstg. (000)	666,586	554,596	530,102	516,268	508,144	500,640	444,064
BALANCE SHEET (IN MILLIONS):							
Cash and Cash Equivalents	1,038.2	439.5	182.8	89.0	156.4	91.4	56.9
Receivables, Net	622.9	421.7	237.6	129.1	61.3	34.7	15.9
Inventories	301.2	71.2	27.9	23.5	9.1	6.1	3.7
Gross Property	575.5	242.9	131.8	72.2	38.3	16.5	5.2
Accumulated Depreciation	244.2	106.2	54.4	23.5	10.3	3.8	1.1
Net Stockholders' Equity	2,819.6	1,378.7	848.2	475.2	245.6	127.5	69.2
Total Assets	3,630.2	1,757.3	1,053.7	595.2	323.9	154.1	82.7
Total Current Assets	2,159.6	996.0	507.7	268.3	247.1	141.0	78.2
Total Current Liabilities	769.4	337.8	205.5	120.0	78.3	26.3	13.2
Net Working Capital	1,390.3	658.2	302.2	148.3	168.8	114.7	65.0
Year End Shs Outstg (000)	849,284	544,492	515,394	494,832	480,888	456,304	428,352
STATISTICAL RECORD:							
Operating Profit Margin %	34.2	32.5	39.3	40.6	38.1	36.1	30.7
Book Value Per Share	3.32	2.53	1.65	0.96	0.51	0.28	0.16
Return on Equity %	32.4	30.5	37.1	36.2	34.4	33.9	20.1
Return on Assets %	25.2	24.0	29.9	28.9	26.1	28.0	16.8
P/E Ratio	48.9-23.4	58.9-21.4	34.2-15.8	49.3-28.4	61.4-24.2	50.0-14.7	45.8-20.8
Price Range	67-32	44¾-16¼	20⅜-9⅜	16½-9½	10⅛-4	4¼-1¼	1⅜-⅝

Statistics are as originally reported.

OFFICERS:
J.P. Morgridge, Chmn.
D.T. Valentine, Vice-Chmn.
J.T. Chambers, Pres. & C.E.O.

INCORPORATED: CA, Dec., 1984

PRINCIPAL OFFICE: 170 West Tasman Drive, San Jose, CA 95134

TELEPHONE NUMBER: (408) 526-4000

FAX: (408) 526-4100

NO. OF EMPLOYEES: 10,400

ANNUAL MEETING: In November

SHAREHOLDERS: 8,300 (approx.)

INSTITUTIONAL HOLDINGS:
No. of Institutions: 644
Shares Held: 479,077,016

REGISTRAR(S): First National Bank of Boston, Boston, MA

TRANSFER AGENT(S): First National Bank of Boston, Boston, MA

COMCAST CORP.

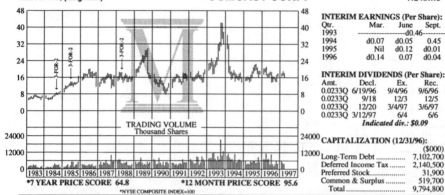

7 YEAR PRICE SCORE 64.8 *NASDAQ SYMBOL INDEX=100* **12 MONTH PRICE SCORE 95.6** *NYSE COMPOSITE INDEX=100*

INTERIM EARNINGS (Per Share):

Qtr.	Mar.	June	Sept.	Dec.
1993	----	----d0.46----		
1994	d0.07	d0.05	0.45	d0.65
1995	Nil	d0.12	d0.01	d0.03
1996	d0.14	0.07	d0.04	d0.10

INTERIM DIVIDENDS (Per Share):

Amt.	Decl.	Ex.	Rec.	Pay.
0.0233Q	6/19/96	9/4/96	9/6/96	9/27/96
0.0233Q	9/18	12/3	12/5	12/26
0.0233Q	12/20	3/4/97	3/6/97	3/27/97
0.0233Q	3/12/97	6/4	6/6	6/27

Indicated div.: $0.09

CAPITALIZATION (12/31/96):

	($000)	(%)
Long-Term Debt	7,102,700	72.5
Deferred Income Tax	2,140,500	21.9
Preferred Stock	31,900	0.3
Common & Surplus	519,700	5.3
Total	9,794,800	100.0

RECENT DEVELOPMENTS: For the year ended 12/31/96, CMCS incurred a net loss of $52.5 million compared with a net loss of $37.8 million in 1995. The increase in net loss resulted principally from financing costs and non-cash charges, which included depreciation and amortization, primarily from acquisitions. Earnings for 1996 and 1995 included equity in net losses of affiliates of $144.8 million and $86.6 million, respectively, and extraordinary losses of $1.0 million and $6.1 million, respectively. Earnings for 1996 included a gain of $40.6 million from an equity offer-

ing of an affiliate. Revenues advanced 20.1% to $4.04 billion from $3.36 billion in 1995. For the quarter ended 12/31/96, CMCS reported a net loss of $25.7 million versus a net loss of $5.9 million in the same prior-year period. Revenues climbed 16.1% to $1.17 million from $1.01 billion in 1995. On 4/1/97, Comcast announced that its joint venture with The Walt Disney Co., Comcast Entertainment LLC, acquired a majority interest in E! Entertainment Television from Time Warner.

BUSINESS

COMCAST CORPORATION is primarily engaged in the development, operation and management of cable and cellular communications systems. Cable communication systems generally offer subscribers the signals of all national television networks; local and distant independent, specialty and educational television stations; satellite-delivered non-broadcast channels; locally originated programs; educational programs; home shopping; and public service announcements and continuous time, news and weather services. In addition, each of the Company's systems offer, for an extra monthly charge, one or more special services such as Home Box Office, Cinemax, Showtime, The Movie Channel, and the Disney Channel. Comcast also constructs, develops, manages and operates cellular telephone systems pursuant to licenses granted by the FCC for markets in Pennsylvania, New Jersey, Delaware and Illinois. The Company provides cellular telephone services to markets that serve a population in excess of 7.5 million. In February 1995, Comcast acquired a majority stake (57.4%) in QVC, Inc., an electronic retailer of consumer products.

ANNUAL EARNINGS AND DIVIDENDS PER SHARE

	1996	1995	1994	1993	1992	1991	1990
Earnings Per Share	d0.21	d0.16	d0.32	d0.46	☐ d1.08	d0.87	d1.05
Dividends Per Share	0.093	0.093	0.093	0.14	0.14	0.135	0.12

☐ Before extraord. item.

ANNUAL FINANCIAL DATA

RECORD OF EARNINGS (IN MILLIONS):

	1996	1995	1994	1993	1992	1991	1990
Total Revenues	4,038.4	3,362.9	1,375.3	1,338.2	900.3	721.0	657.0
Costs and Expenses	2,831.2	2,344.1	799.0	731.8	503.2	411.8	385.9
Depreciation & Amort	698.3	689.1	336.5	341.5	232.0	164.3	161.2
Operating Income	508.9	329.8	239.8	264.9	165.1	145.0	109.9
Inc Fr Cont Opers Bef Income Taxes	d16.1	d45.4	d84.6	d83.6	d203.9	d142.8	d183.1
Income Taxes	84.4	42.2	cr9.2	15.2	14.0	12.8	cr4.7
Net Income	☐ d52.5	☐ d37.8	☐ d75.3	☐ d98.9	☐ d217.9	d155.6	d178.4
Aver. Shs. Outstg. (000)	247,600	239,679	236,262	213,939	201,815	178,715	169,365

☐ Before extra. item dr$1,000,000. ☐ Before extra. item dr$6,084,000. ☐ Before extra. item dr$11,703,000. ☐ Before extra. item dr$17,620,000. ☐ Before extra. item dr$52,297,000.

BALANCE SHEET (IN MILLIONS):

	1996	1995	1994	1993	1992	1991	1990
Cash and Cash Equivalents	539.6	910.0	465.5	679.8	347.9	595.7	206.2
Receivables, Net	439.3	450.5	108.2	72.2	57.8	30.1	27.5
Inventories	258.4	243.4	18.6	...	...	...	...
Gross Property	3,600.1	2,575.6	2,081.3	1,722.6	1,522.5	845.5	790.4
Accumulated Depreciation	1,061.3	932.0	823.6	701.6	565.4	340.6	271.3
Long-Term Debt	7,102.7	6,943.8	4,810.5	4,162.9	3,973.5	2,452.9	2,248.2
Net Stockholders' Equity	551.6	d827.7	d726.8	d870.5	d181.6	19.5	d21.7
Total Assets	12,088.6	9,580.3	6,763.0	4,948.3	4,271.9	2,793.6	2,456.6
Total Current Assets	1,405.8	1,653.7	608.5	776.6	428.6	645.5	251.5
Total Current Liabilities	1,364.9	1,122.1	660.6	594.6	391.7	264.3	187.0
Net Working Capital	40.9	531.6	d52.1	182.0	36.9	381.2	64.5
Year End Shs Outstg (000)	326,027	239,338	239,037	221,686	135,606	193,163	169,886

STATISTICAL RECORD:

	1996	1995	1994	1993	1992	1991	1990
Operating Profit Margin %	12.6	9.8	17.4	19.8	18.3	20.1	16.7
Book Value Per Share	...	...	...	...	...	0.10	...
Average Yield %	0.5	0.5	0.4	0.5	0.8	0.9	1.0
Price Range	21⅛-13¾	22½-13¾	36⅜-13¾	42¼-17½	19¾-13½	18¼-10⅞	17⅝-7⅝

Statistics are as originally reported.

OFFICERS:
R.J. Roberts, Chairman
J.A. Brodsky, Vice-Chairman
B.L. Roberts, President

INCORPORATED: PA, Mar., 1969

PRINCIPAL OFFICE: 1500 Market Street, Philadelphia, PA 19102-2148

TELEPHONE NUMBER: (215) 665-1700
NO. OF EMPLOYEES: 16,400
ANNUAL MEETING: In June
SHAREHOLDERS: 1,973 cl. A com., 2,672 special cl. A com., 1 cl. B. com.
INSTITUTIONAL HOLDINGS:
No. of Institutions: 98
Shares Held: 19,727,905

REGISTRAR(S): Pittsburgh National Bank, Pittsburgh, PA 15230

TRANSFER AGENT(S): Pittsburgh National Bank, Pittsburgh, PA 15265

COMPUWARE CORP.

YIELD ...%
P/E RATIO 19.4

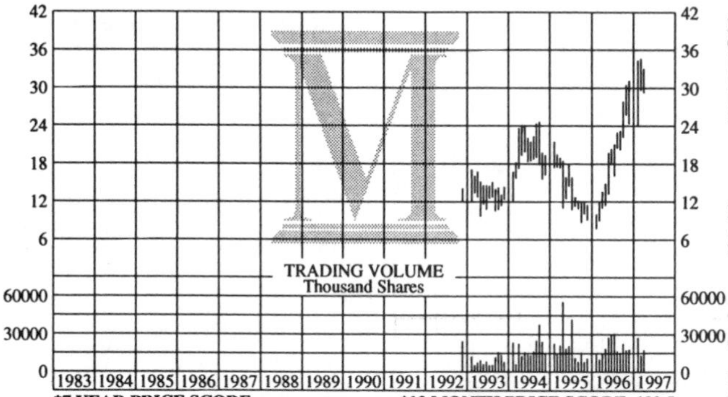

TRADING VOLUME
Thousand Shares

| | 1983 | 1984 | 1985 | 1986 | 1987 | 1988 | 1989 | 1990 | 1991 | 1992 | 1993 | 1994 | 1995 | 1996 | 1997 |

*7 YEAR PRICE SCORE ...   *12 MONTH PRICE SCORE 120.5
*NYSE COMPOSITE INDEX=100

INTERIM EARNINGS (Per Share):

Qtr.	June	Sept.	Dec.	Mar.
1993-94	0.09	0.17	0.21	0.21
1994-95	d0.06	0.19	0.29	0.23
1995-96	0.09	0.16	d0.03	0.29
1996-97	0.04	0.18	0.36	...

INTERIM DIVIDENDS (Per Share):

Amt.	Decl.	Ex.	Rec.	Pay.
2-for-1	1/22/97	4/15/97	4/4/97	4/14/97

CAPITALIZATION (3/31/96):

	($000)	(%)
Deferred Income Tax	991	0.3
Common & Surplus	318,985	99.7
Total	319,976	100.0

RECENT DEVELOPMENTS: For the year ended 3/31/97, net income soared to $97.4 million from $44.2 million the previous year. Earnings for 1997 amd 1996 included purchased research and development charges of $21.8 million and $24.9 million, respectively. Earnings for 1996 included restructuring costs of $10.7 million. Total revenues rose 32.3% to $812.9 million from $614.4 million a year earlier. Software license revenues advanced 40.7% to $318.9 million from $226.7 million the prior year. Professional ser-vices revenue grew 39.7% to $284.5 million from $203.6 million in 1996. Income from operations climbed to $143.7 million from $71.8 million the previous year. For the quarter ended 3/31/97, net income advanced to $45.9 million from $25.0 million in the same prior-year period. Total revenues grew 35.1% to $252.6 million from $186.9 million in 1996. On 4/15/97, CPWR acquired Vine Systems, a privately held consulting firm located in London, England.

BUSINESS

COMPUWARE CORP. develops, markets and supports an integrated line of systems software products, which improves programmer productivity in testing, debugging and maintaining application software. In addition, the Company develops, markets and supports products to manage database applications, computers and networks in client/server computing environments. The Company also provides professional services to plan, develop, implement and maintain computer systems for large corporate and public sector clients.

ANNUAL EARNINGS AND DIVIDENDS PER SHARE

	3/31/96	3/31/95	3/31/94	3/31/93	3/31/92	3/31/91	3/31/90
Earnings Per Share	0.50	0.65	0.67	0.45	d0.79	...	...
Dividends Per Share	Nil	Nil	Nil	Nil	...	...	...

Note: 2-for-1stk. split, 4/14/97.

ANNUAL FINANCIAL DATA

RECORD OF EARNINGS (IN THOUSANDS):

Total Revenues	614,359	533,877	330,338	234,940	175,025	141,772	127,993
Costs and Expenses	534,024	427,112	239,110	175,438	193,171	129,003	115,647
Depreciation & Amort	8,567	8,858	6,759	9,405	10,743	2,430	1,174
Income From Operations	71,768	97,907	84,469	50,097	d28,889	10,339	11,172
Income Bef Income Taxes	78,783	95,181	87,701	50,764	d28,850	13,098	12,315
Income Taxes	34,541	33,084	28,595	15,567	cr5,026	3,588	2,810
Net Income	44,242	62,097	59,106	35,197	d23,824	9,510	9,505
Aver. Shs. Outstg.	89,738	95,370	77,706	67,864	61,630	...	...

BALANCE SHEET (IN THOUSANDS):

Cash and Cash Equivalents	107,922	165,116	122,032	113,243	5,068	43,857	...
Receivables, Net	245,449	191,593	136,485	96,279	79,139	55,937	...
Gross Property	88,583	72,468	29,629	19,506	14,515	10,006	...
Accumulated Depreciation	31,980	25,352	13,004	8,609	6,280	3,683	...
Long-Term Debt	...	...	...	...	2,349	847	...
Net Stockholders' Equity	318,985	336,201	240,313	168,284	29,104	56,090	...
Total Assets	555,726	524,095	365,752	266,110	135,490	117,911	...
Total Current Assets	361,767	370,224	263,055	211,597	85,184	100,883	...
Total Current Liabilities	219,925	179,614	119,897	89,262	100,623	58,524	...
Net Working Capital	141,842	190,610	143,158	122,335	d15,439	42,359	...
Year End Shares Outstg	84,596	91,014	74,762	70,126	47,390	47,594	53,894

STATISTICAL RECORD:

Operating Profit Margin %	11.7	18.3	25.6	21.3	...	7.3	8.7
Book Value Per Share	3.01	3.11	2.42	...	...	...	...
Return on Equity %	13.9	18.5	24.6	20.9	...	20.9	...
Return on Assets %	8.0	11.8	16.2	13.2	...	8.1	...
P/E Ratio	43.0-17.5	37.9-18.8	22.5-12.7	27.4-23.3	...	...	...
Price Range	21½-8¾	24⅝-12¼	17⅛-9⅝	14⅛-12	...	...	...

Statistics are as originally reported.

OFFICERS:
P. Karmanos, Jr., Chmn. & C.E.O.
J.A. Nathan, Pres. & C.O.O.
R. Caponigro, Sr. V.P., C.F.O. & Treas.

INCORPORATED: MI, 1973

PRINCIPAL OFFICE: 31440 Northwestern Highway, Farmington Hills, MI 48334-2564

TELEPHONE NUMBER: (810) 737-7300

NO. OF EMPLOYEES: 4,105

ANNUAL MEETING: In August

SHAREHOLDERS: 401 approx.

INSTITUTIONAL HOLDINGS:
No. of Institutions: 124
Shares Held: 65,046,190 (adj.)

REGISTRAR(S):

TRANSFER AGENT(S): National Bank of Detroit, Detroit, MI

45

CONCORD EFS, INC.

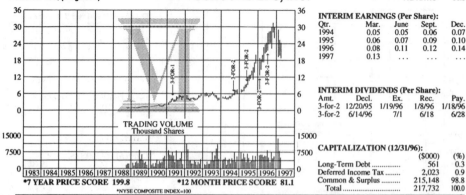

INTERIM EARNINGS (Per Share):

Qtr.	Mar.	June	Sept.	Dec.
1994	0.05	0.05	0.06	0.07
1995	0.06	0.07	0.09	0.10
1996	0.08	0.11	0.12	0.14
1997	0.13	...	...	...

INTERIM DIVIDENDS (Per Share):

Amt.	Decl.	Ex.	Rec.	Pay.
3-for-2	12/20/95	1/19/96	1/8/96	1/18/96
3-for-2	6/14/96	7/1	6/18	6/28

TRADING VOLUME
Thousand Shares

1983 1984 1985 1986 1987 1988 1989 1990 1991 1992 1993 1994 1995 1996 1997

*7 YEAR PRICE SCORE 199.8   *12 MONTH PRICE SCORE 81.1

*NYSE COMPOSITE INDEX=100

CAPITALIZATION (12/31/96):

	($000)	(%)
Long-Term Debt	561	0.3
Deferred Income Tax	2,023	0.9
Common & Surplus	215,148	98.8
Total	217,732	100.0

RECENT DEVELOPMENTS: For the first quarter ended 3/31/97, net income advanced 70.2% to $7.9 million, or $0.13 per share. This compared with $4.7 million, or $0.08 per share, in the corresponding period of the previous year. Revenues increased 38.8% to $47.0 million from $33.9 million the year before. Operating income climbed 52.0% to $10.1 million from $6.6 million a year earlier. On 2/12/97, CEFT announced that it entered into an agreement in principle with Comdata Corporation to provide cash advance transactions at Concord's ATM network at truckstops across the United States. Under this agreement, approximately 500,000 drivers at Concord ATMs will be provided automated cash advances. Drivers will no longer have to spend time on the phone registering their Comcheck cards nor spend additional time waiting in line at the fuel desk to receive their cash.

BUSINESS

CONCORD EFS, INC. and its subsidiaries provide transaction processing services and P.O.S. equipment to retailers, financial institutions and trucking companies. The Company's subsidiaries include Concord Computing Corporation, EFS National Bank, and Concord Equipment Sales.

ANNUAL EARNINGS AND DIVIDENDS PER SHARE

	12/31/96	12/31/95	12/31/94	12/31/93	12/31/92	12/31/91	9/30/91
Earnings Per Share	0.45	0.31	0.23	0.18	0.17	⑤0.04	0.13
Dividends Per Share	①...	②...	③...	Nil	Nil	...	④...

① 3-for-2 stk. split, 6/28/96 & 1/18/96. ② 3-for-2 stk. split, 5/22/95. ③ 3-for-3 stk. split, 9/16/94. ④ 3-for-1 stk. split, 4/9/91. ⑤ For three months due to fiscal year-end change.

ANNUAL FINANCIAL DATA

RECORD OF EARNINGS (IN THOUSANDS):

Total Revenues	166,700	127,762	96,213	75,444	65,562	14,291	48,145
Costs and Expenses	129,399	101,493	78,152	61,050	51,993	11,115	36,710
Operating Income	37,301	26,270	18,061	14,394	13,569	3,175	11,435
Inc Fr Cont Opers Bef Income Taxes	41,315	28,386	19,650	15,219	14,072	3,325	12,096
Income Taxes	14,526	10,146	6,979	5,357	5,011	1,267	4,718
Net Income	26,789	18,315	12,713	9,863	8,974	2,039	7,273
Aver. Shs. Outstg.	59,935	57,858	55,898	55,676	55,167	55,244	54,770

BALANCE SHEET (IN THOUSANDS):

Cash and Cash Equivalents	159,509	60,012	35,144	28,894	24,005	...	20,772
Receivables, Net	38,894	64,425	34,666	18,859	15,234	...	11,542
Inventories	4,353	4,765	2,908	3,350	540	...	413
Gross Property	73,819	57,750	49,790	40,339	32,364	...	23,285
Accumulated Depreciation	46,782	37,831	30,151	22,727	17,068	...	11,863
Long-Term Debt	561	978	1,371	...	...	...	55
Net Stockholders' Equity	215,148	89,545	61,935	50,251	39,573	...	26,289
Total Assets	292,813	156,887	99,462	71,033	56,316	...	44,562
Total Current Assets	205,687	132,102	75,626	53,421	41,019	...	33,140
Total Current Liabilities	75,081	63,889	34,106	18,766	14,780	...	16,822
Net Working Capital	130,606	68,213	41,520	34,655	26,240	...	16,318
Year End Shares Outstg	60,817	37,412	54,356	54,099	...	52,896	

STATISTICAL RECORD:

Operating Profit Margin %	22.4	20.6	18.8	19.1	20.7	22.2	23.8
Book Value Per Share	3.54	3.59	1.14	0.93	0.74	...	0.50
Return on Equity %	12.5	20.5	20.5	19.6	22.7	...	27.7
Return on Assets %	9.1	11.7	12.8	13.9	15.9	...	16.3
P/E Ratio	70.0-27.8	64.5-21.0	32.6-16.8	36.8-19.4	37.5-21.9	N.M	42.3-15.4
Price Range	31½-12½	20-6½	7½-3⅞	6⅝-3½	6-3½	5½-2	5½-2

Statistics are as originally reported.

OFFICERS:
D.M. Palmer, Chmn. & C.E.O.
E.A. Labry, III, Pres. & Chief Mktg. Off.
W.E. Lucado, Sr. V.P., Investment & Compliance Off.
T.J. Dowling, V.P. & Contr.

INCORPORATED: MA, Jan., 1970; reincorp., DE, 1990

PRINCIPAL OFFICE: 2525 Horizon Lake Dr. Suite 120, Memphis, TN 38133

TELEPHONE NUMBER: (901) 371-8000

FAX: (901) 371-8050

NO. OF EMPLOYEES: 447

ANNUAL MEETING: In May

SHAREHOLDERS: 11,500

INSTITUTIONAL HOLDINGS:
No. of Institutions: 111
Shares Held: 45,476,310

REGISTRAR(S): State Street Bank & Trust Co., Boston, MA 02266

TRANSFER AGENT(S): State Street Bank & Trust Co., Boston, MA 02266

CORPORATE EXPRESS, INC.

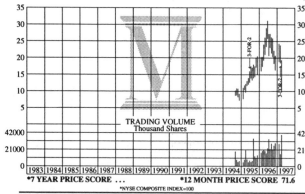

7 YEAR PRICE SCORE ... **12 MONTH PRICE SCORE 71.6**

NYSE COMPOSITE INDEX=100

TRADING VOLUME
Thousand Shares

INTERIM EARNINGS (Per Share):

Qtr.	May	Aug.	Nov.	Feb.
1994-95	----	0.11	----	
1995-96	0.07	0.06	0.09	d0.19
1996-97	0.09	0.10	0.06	0.05

INTERIM DIVIDENDS (Per Share):

Amt.	Decl.	Ex.	Rec.	Pay.
3-for-2	6/15/95	6/22/95	6/16/95	6/21/95
3-for-2	1/22/97	2/3/97	1/24/97	1/31/97

CAPITALIZATION (3/2/96):

	($000)	(%)
Long-Term Debt	118,332	18.2
Cap. Lease Oblig.	9,568	1.5
Minority Interest	24,843	3.8
Common & Surplus	496,514	76.5
Total	649,257	100.0

RECENT DEVELOPMENTS: For the year ended 3/1/97, the Company reported net income of $42.0 million compared with income from continuing operations of $6.8 million the previous year. Earnings for 1997 and 1996 included merger and other non-recurring charges of $19.8 million and $36.8 million, respectively. Net sales advanced 69.0% to $3.20 billion from $1.89 billion the year before. Gross profit as a percentage of net sales fell slightly to 24.4% from 24.7% a year earlier. Operating profit soared to $100.5 million from $38.2 million the prior year. For the quarter ended 3/1/97, the Company produced net income of $7.2 million versus a loss from continuing operations of $19.9 million in the corresponding period of the previous year. Net sales grew 63.7% to $900.6 million from $550.3 million the year before. Results for both the year and quarter ended 3/1/97 increased due to acquisitions and internal growth. In February 1997, CEXP entered the Italian market.

BUSINESS

CORPORATE EXPRESS, INC. distributes office products to large corporations. The Company operates in over 750 locations, including 100 distribution centers, utilizing a fleet of approximately 10,000 delivery vehicles throughout the United States, Canada, the United Kingdom, New Zealand, Australia, France, Germany, and Italy.

ANNUAL EARNINGS AND DIVIDENDS PER SHARE

	3/2/96	2/25/95	2/28/94	2/28/93	2/29/92
Earnings Per Share	0.03	0.11	0.06	...	...
Dividends Per Share	Nil	①...	...	...	...

Note: 3-for-2 stk. split, 1/31/97. ① 3-for-2 stk. split, 6/21/95.

ANNUAL FINANCIAL DATA

RECORD OF EARNINGS (IN MILLIONS):

	3/2/96	2/25/95	2/28/94	2/28/93	2/29/92
Total Revenues	1,590.1	621.5	164.8	103.1	77.7
Costs and Expenses	1,533.5	593.7	166.0	100.9	72.9
Depreciation & Amort	26.8	10.4	2.9	2.9	1.7
Operating Income	29.8	17.4	d4.0	d0.8	3.1
Inc Fr Cont Opers Bef Income Taxes	15.1	5.6	d7.9	d5.1	d0.4
Income Taxes	11.0	0.9	...	cr0.2	⑤0.1
Net Income	2.7	①4.7	②d7.9	③d5.0	④d0.4
Aver. Shs. Outstg. (000)	102,086	73,793	48,398	...	...

① Before extra. item cr$586,000. ② Before disc. op. cr$138,000; and extra. item dr$1,169,000. ③ Before disc. op. dr$4,571,000. ④ Before disc. op. dr$435,000. ⑤ Equal to $53,000.

BALANCE SHEET (IN MILLIONS):

	3/2/96	2/25/95	2/28/94	2/28/93	2/29/92
Cash and Cash Equivalents	28.7	11.5	11.4	5.0	...
Receivables, Net	311.6	137.9	91.8	20.3	...
Inventories	102.0	54.6	34.0	6.5	...
Gross Property	159.0	46.6	27.8	13.3	...
Accumulated Depreciation	49.5	9.3	4.7	3.4	...
Long-Term Debt	118.3	114.5	137.2	23.5	...
Capital Lease Obligations	9.6	6.4	3.4	1.3	...
Net Stockholders' Equity	496.5	196.8	76.5	2.1	...
Total Assets	910.5	445.7	320.5	51.1	...
Total Current Assets	459.5	217.2	140.3	32.5	...
Total Current Liabilities	242.2	117.1	94.1	21.8	...
Net Working Capital	217.2	100.2	46.2	10.7	...
Year End Shs Outstg (000)	103,632	84,695	31,178	19,728	...

STATISTICAL RECORD:

	3/2/96	2/25/95	2/28/94	2/28/93	2/29/92
Operating Profit Margin %	1.9	2.8	...	...	3.9
Book Value Per Share	2.49	1.66	0.30	...	...
Return on Equity %	0.6	2.4	...	...	...
Return on Assets %	0.3	1.0	...	...	...
Price Range	30¾-11½	20½-7⅝	10⅞-7¼	...	...

Statistics are as originally reported.

OFFICERS:
J. Rysavy, Chmn. & C.E.O.
R.L. King, Pres. & C.O.O.
S.R. Leno, Exec. V.P. & C.F.O.

INCORPORATED: CO, 1985

PRINCIPAL OFFICE: 325 Interlocken Parkway, Broomfield, CO 80021

TELEPHONE NUMBER: (303) 373-2800

NO. OF EMPLOYEES: 25,000 (approx.)

ANNUAL MEETING: In July

SHAREHOLDERS: 140

INSTITUTIONAL HOLDINGS:
No. of Institutions: 128
Shares Held: 63,754,353

REGISTRAR(S): Chemical Trust Co. of California

TRANSFER AGENT(S): Chemical Trust Co. of California

COSTCO COS., INC.

*7 YEAR PRICE SCORE 52.1   *12 MONTH PRICE SCORE 109.3

*NYSE COMPOSITE INDEX=100

INTERIM EARNINGS (Per Share):

Qtr.	Nov.	Feb.	May	Aug.
1993-94	d0.17	0.27	0.14	0.27
1994-95	0.22	0.31	0.17	0.35
1995-96	0.25	0.35	0.21	0.42
1996-97	0.16	0.46	...	...

INTERIM DIVIDENDS (Per Share):

Amt.	Decl.	Ex.	Rec.	Pay.
	No dividends paid.			

CAPITALIZATION (9/1/96):

	($000)	(%)
Long-Term Debt	1,229,221	39.2
Deferred Income Tax	56,734	1.8
Minority Interest	72,346	2.3
Common & Surplus	1,777,798	56.7
Total	3,136,099	100.0

RECENT DEVELOPMENTS: For the 12 weeks ended 2/16/97, net income advanced 36.4% to $97.4 million versus $71.4 million in the same prior-year period. Earnings for 1996 and 1995 included pre-opening costs of $6.1 million and $6.0 million, respectively. Total revenue for the period was $5.24 billion, up 11.7% from $4.69 billion in 1995. Net sales, representing 98.3% of total revenues, were up 11.8% to $5.15 billion from $4.61 billion a year earlier. On a comparable warehouse basis, that is warehouses open for at least one year, sales increased 9%. For the 24 weeks ended 2/16/97, net income grew 6.8% to $129.3 million from $121.0 million the prior year. Earnings for 1996 reflected a $65.0 million provision for impaired assets, resulting from the adoption of an accounting standard, and warehouse closing costs of $5.0 million. Also, earnings for 1996 and 1995 included pre-opening costs of $16.3 million and $15.4 million, respectively. Total revenues rose 11.6% to $10.12 billion from $9.07 billion in 1995.

BUSINESS

COSTCO COMPANIES, INC. (formerly Price/Costco, Inc.) was formed on 10/21/93 as a result of a merger of the Price Company and Costco Wholesale Corporation. PCCW operates a chain of cash and carry membership warehouses that sell nationally-branded and selected private-label merchandise at low prices to businesses purchasing for commercial use, personal use, or resale, and also to individuals who are members of selected employee groups. PCCW's business is based upon achieving high sales volumes and rapid inventory turnover by offering a limited assortment of merchandise in a wide variety of product categories at very competitive prices. As of 3/13/97, PCCW operated a chain of 258 warehouses in the United States, Canada, the United Kingdom, and Taiwan as well as 13 warehouses in Mexico through a 50%-owned joint venture.

ANNUAL EARNINGS AND DIVIDENDS PER SHARE

	9/1/96	9/3/95	8/28/94	8/29/93	8/31/92	8/31/91	8/31/90
Earnings Per Share	1.22	① 1.05	① 0.51	0.92	2.61	2.68	2.47
Dividends Per Share	Nil	Nil	Nil	Nil	Nil	Nil	Nil

① Before disc. oper.

ANNUAL FINANCIAL DATA

RECORD OF EARNINGS (IN MILLIONS):

Total Revenues	19,566.5	18,247.3	16,480.6	15,497.7	7,511.8	6,756.0	5,412.3
Costs and Expenses	18,914.1	17,671.9	15,984.2	14,986.9	7,234.5	6,501.6	5,185.5
Depreciation & Amort	161.6	142.0	136.3	112.1	54.0	40.6	27.4
Operating Income	490.7	433.3	360.1	398.7	223.4	213.8	199.4
Inc Fr Cont Opers Bef Income Taxes	423.5	368.2	203.6	370.3	215.2	219.8	205.5
Income Taxes	174.7	151.0	92.7	147.1	86.1	85.7	80.2
Net Income	248.8	① 217.2	② 110.9	223.2	129.1	134.1	125.4
Aver. Shs. Outstg. (000)	205,242	210,962	219,332	227,331	51,691	52,197	53,485

① Before disc. op. dr$83,363,000. ② Before disc. op. dr$223,266,000.

BALANCE SHEET (IN MILLIONS):

Cash and Cash Equivalents	102.0	45.7	62.9	210.3	99.3	305.4	51.3
Receivables, Net	137.5	146.7	130.3	149.7	61.4	63.5	41.0
Inventories	1,500.8	1,422.3	1,260.5	993.7	381.5	338.0	262.2
Gross Property	3,543.5	3,062.0	2,571.5	2,361.8	1,070.0	758.6	550.6
Accumulated Depreciation	655.2	526.4	425.1	330.2	144.0	113.8	75.6
Long-Term Debt	1,229.2	1,094.6	795.5	812.6	509.0	496.5	193.5
Net Stockholders' Equity	1,777.8	1,530.7	1,685.0	1,796.7	802.0	763.0	616.3
Total Assets	4,911.9	4,437.4	4,235.7	3,940.1	1,923.7	1,845.5	1,210.1
Total Current Assets	1,828.3	1,702.3	1,534.3	1,389.0	557.0	738.3	379.3
Total Current Liabilities	1,771.6	1,692.9	1,647.3	1,258.3	587.4	568.4	392.3
Net Working Capital	56.7	9.4	d113.0	130.7	d30.4	169.8	d13.0
Year End Shs Outstg (000)	196,436	195,164	217,795	217,074	46,208	48,736	48,591

STATISTICAL RECORD:

Operating Profit Margin %	2.5	2.4	2.2	2.6	3.0	3.2	3.7
Book Value Per Share	9.05	7.58	7.56	8.28	16.29	14.58	12.49
Return on Equity %	14.0	14.2	6.6	12.4	16.1	17.6	20.3
Return on Assets %	5.1	4.9	2.6	5.7	6.7	7.3	10.4
P/E Ratio	21.0-11.8	17.7-11.3	42.4-24.5	41.8-17.0	21.1-11.3	24.3-14.1	19.5-10.7
Price Range	26-14⅝	18¾-12	21⅝-12½	42¼-17⅛	55-29½	65¼-37¾	48¼-26½

Statistics are as originally reported.

OFFICERS:
J.H. Brotman, Chmn.
J.D. Sinegal, Pres. & C.E.O.
R.A. Galanti, Exec. V.P. & C.F.O.

INCORPORATED: CA, Feb., 1976; reincorp., DE, Oct., 1993

PRINCIPAL OFFICE: 999 Lake Drive, Issaquah, WA 98027

TELEPHONE NUMBER: (206) 313-8100

NO. OF EMPLOYEES: 53,000

ANNUAL MEETING: In February

SHAREHOLDERS: 8,324

INSTITUTIONAL HOLDINGS:
No. of Institutions: 246
Shares Held: 149,239,837

REGISTRAR(S):

TRANSFER AGENT(S): First Interstate Bank of Wash., N.A., Seattle, WA 98111

CRACKER BARREL OLD COUNTRY STORE, INC.

YIELD 0.1%
P/E RATIO 22.1

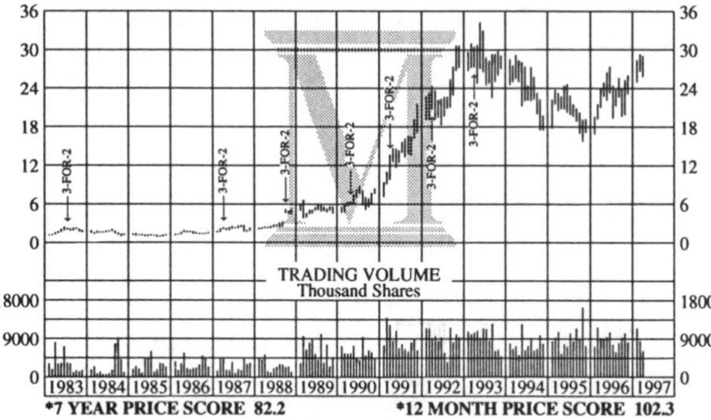

7 YEAR PRICE SCORE 82.2 **12 MONTH PRICE SCORE 102.3**

*NYSE COMPOSITE INDEX=100

INTERIM EARNINGS (Per Share):

Qtr.	Oct.	Jan.	Apr.	July
1993-94	------------------ 0.94 ------------------			
1994-95	0.26	0.20	0.25	0.38
1995-96	0.28	0.21	0.27	0.29
1996-97	0.31	0.26	...	...

INTERIM DIVIDENDS (Per Share):

Amt.	Decl.	Ex.	Rec.	Pay.
0.005Q	5/29/96	6/12/96	6/14/96	6/28/96
0.005Q	8/30	9/11	9/13	9/27
0.005Q	11/26	12/11	12/13	1/2/97
0.005Q	2/28/97	3/12/97	3/14/97	3/28

Indicated div.: $0.02

CAPITALIZATION (8/2/96):

	($000)	(%)
Long-Term Debt	15,500	2.6
Cap. Lease Oblig.	1,468	0.3
Deferred Income Tax	10,043	1.7
Common & Surplus	566,221	95.4
Total	593,232	100.0

RECENT DEVELOPMENTS: For the quarter ended 1/31/97, net income climbed 27.5% to $16.0 million from $12.5 million in the corresponding period of the previous year. Total sales advanced 22.0% to $267.9 million compared with $219.5 million the year before. Same-store restaurant sales increased 5.0%, and same-store retail sales grew 13.2%. Same-store sales improved due to the more normal weather conditions versus the extreme winter weather conditions the prior year. Gross profit as a percentage of total sales rose to 63.6% from 63.3% in 1996. Operating income totaled $25.3 million, up 28.2% from $19.7 million a year earlier. During the quarter, the Company opened sixteen new stores. CBRL plans to open a total of fifteen stores in the third quarter and nine in the fourth quarter. For the six months ended 1/31/97, net income climbed 18.8% to $34.8 million from $29.3 million the previous year. Total sales advanced 19.6% to $526.8 million from $440.5 million the year before.

BUSINESS

CRACKER BARREL OLD COUNTRY STORE, INC. owns and operates 287 full service "country store" restaurants located in the southeast, midwest, mid-Atlantic and southwest United States along interstate highways. These family restaurants serve breakfast, lunch and dinner between the hours of 6:00 a.m. and 10:00 p.m. and feature home-style country cooking prepared on the premises from CBRL's own recipes. Menu items are moderately priced. The restaurants do not serve alcoholic beverages. The stores are constructed in a rustic, country store design and feature a separate gift shop area offering a wide variety of items specializing in hand-blown glassware, cast-iron cookware, toys and wood crafts as well as various old-fashioned candies, jellies and other foods.

ANNUAL EARNINGS AND DIVIDENDS PER SHARE

	8/2/96	7/28/95	7/29/94	7/30/93	7/31/92	8/2/91	8/3/90
Earnings Per Share	1.04	1.09	0.94	0.78	0.60	0.45	0.31
Dividends Per Share	0.02	0.02	0.02	①0.019	②0.016	③0.015	④0.014
Dividend Payout %	1.9	1.8	2.1	2.4	2.6	3.3	4.5

① 3-for-2 stk. split, 3/93. ② 3-for-2 stk. split, 3/23/92. ③ 3-for-2 stk. split, 3/25/91. ④ 3-for-2 stk. split, 4/2/90.

ANNUAL FINANCIAL DATA

RECORD OF EARNINGS (IN THOUSANDS):

Total Revenues	943,287	783,093	640,899	517,616	400,577	300,209	225,518
Costs and Expenses	811,156	653,885	531,397	428,584	332,849	253,179	194,381
Depreciation & Amort	31,433	26,488	20,401	15,802	12,497	9,339	6,658
Operating Income	100,698	102,720	89,100	73,229	55,231	37,691	24,479
Inc Fr Cont Opers Bef Income Taxes	102,380	105,333	90,568	72,944	54,222	36,551	24,063
Income Taxes	38,865	39,289	33,609	27,292	20,279	13,679	8,796
Net Income	63,515	66,043	①56,959	45,652	33,943	22,872	15,267
Aver. Shs. Outstg.	60,813	60,557	60,607	58,789	56,204	51,497	48,360

① Before acctg. change cr$988,262.

BALANCE SHEET (IN THOUSANDS):

Cash and Cash Equivalents	33,706	59,228	78,581	103,647	50,530	67,376	5,397
Receivables, Net	9,775	8,712	6,214	2,437	1,708	1,774	540
Inventories	61,470	51,515	41,990	28,426	23,192	15,746	12,628
Gross Property	692,243	576,854	460,134	362,588	280,927	213,743	153,150
Accumulated Depreciation	123,670	97,336	74,175	56,992	44,233	35,074	27,665
Long-Term Debt	15,500	19,500	23,500	36,576	41,449	42,516	13,762
Capital Lease Obligations	1,468	1,598	1,709	1,802	1,876	2,032	2,188
Net Stockholders' Equity	566,221	496,083	429,846	366,785	222,110	180,443	99,941
Total Assets	676,379	604,515	530,064	469,073	313,460	264,666	145,156
Total Current Assets	106,436	120,366	127,880	135,342	76,065	85,304	18,916
Total Current Liabilities	83,147	76,766	67,158	59,227	43,531	35,024	24,724
Net Working Capital	23,289	43,600	60,721	76,115	32,533	50,280	d5,808
Year End Shares Outstg	60,594	59,992	59,901	59,570	54,778	53,915	47,535

STATISTICAL RECORD:

Operating Profit Margin %	10.7	13.1	13.9	14.1	13.8	12.6	10.9
Book Value Per Share	9.34	8.27	7.18	6.16	4.05	3.35	2.10
Return on Equity %	11.2	13.3	13.3	12.4	15.3	12.7	15.3
Return on Assets %	9.4	10.9	10.7	9.7	10.8	8.6	10.5
Average Yield %	0.1	0.1	0.1	0.1	0.1	0.1	0.2
P/E Ratio	26.3-16.2	22.6-14.4	31.0-18.6	43.9-28.6	51.0-30.6	47.8-15.8	28.6-15.3
Price Range	27⅜-16⅞	24⅝-15¾	29⅛-17½	34¼-22½	30⅝-18⅜	21½-7⅛	8⅞-4¾

Statistics are as originally reported.

OFFICERS:
D. Evins, Chmn. & C.E.O.
R.N. Magruder, Pres. & C.O.O.
M.A. Woodhouse, Sr. V.P.-Fin. & C.F.O.

INCORPORATED: TN, Oct., 1969

PRINCIPAL OFFICE: P.O. Box 787 Hartmann Drive, Lebanon, TN 37087-0787

TELEPHONE NUMBER: (615) 444-5533

NO. OF EMPLOYEES: 31,683

ANNUAL MEETING: In November

SHAREHOLDERS: 19,011

INSTITUTIONAL HOLDINGS:
No. of Institutions: 130
Shares Held: 26,044,337

REGISTRAR(S):

TRANSFER AGENT(S): Trust Company Bank, Atlanta, GA

DELL COMPUTER CORP.

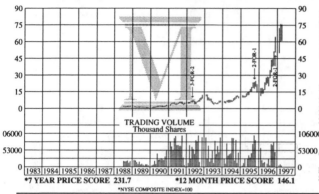

TRADING VOLUME
Thousand Shares

*7 YEAR PRICE SCORE 231.7   *12 MONTH PRICE SCORE 146.1
*NYSE COMPOSITE INDEX=100

INTERIM EARNINGS (Per Share):

Qtr.	Apr.	July	Oct.	Jan.
1994-95	0.10	0.16	0.23	0.34
1995-96	0.28	0.33	0.38	0.35
1996-97	0.42	⑤0.58	⑤0.78	1.01
1997-98	1.08	...	...	...

INTERIM DIVIDENDS (Per Share):

Amt.	Decl.	Ex.	Rec.	Pay.
3-for-2	3/6/92	4/10/92	3/23/92	4/9/92
2-for-1	10/9/95	10/30/95	10/20/95	10/27/95
2-for-1	11/12/96	12/9/96	11/25/96	12/6/96

CAPITALIZATION (2/2/97):

	($000)	(%)
Long-Term Debt	18,104	2.2
Stockholders' Equity	805,907	97.8
Total	824,011	100.0

RECENT DEVELOPMENTS: For the quarter ended 5/4/97, net income advanced to $198 million from $82 million in the same prior-year period. Net sales climbed 58.0% to $2.59 billion from $1.64 billion a year earlier. Sales in Europe rose 38% to $644 million compared with the year before. Sales in the Americas grew 64% to over $1.7 billion due to continued success with major corporate customers in the U.S., while sales in the Asia-Pacific region, including Japan, increased 90% to $199 million versus 1996. Gross margin grew 74.9% to $558 million, or 21.6% of net sales, from $319 million, or 19.5% of net sales, in 1996. Operating income increased to $277 million from $112 million a year earlier. For the fiscal year 1997 ended 2/2/97, net income advanced 95.2% to $531 million from $272 million in fiscal 1996. Earnings for fiscal 1997 excluded an extraordinary loss of $13 million. Net sales climbed 46.5% to $7.76 billion compared with $5.30 billion the year before.

BUSINESS

DELL COMPUTER CORPORATION, together with its subsidiaries, designs, develops, manufactures, markets, services and supports a wide range of computer systems, including desktops, notebooks and network servers, and also markets software, peripherals and service and support programs. With revenue of approximately $7.8 billion for fiscal 1997 (which ended on 2/2/97), the Company is a major direct marketer of computer systems and a computer vendor. DELL designs and customizes products and services to end-user requirements, and offers an extensive selection of peripherals and software. DELL's complete range of computer systems include Dell Dimension® and OptiPlex® desktop computers, Latitude® notebook computers, and PowerEdge® network servers. The Company's products and services are sold in more than 140 countries and territories to customers extending from major corporations, government agencies, and medical and education institutions to small businesses and individuals.

ANNUAL EARNINGS AND DIVIDENDS PER SHARE

	2/2/97	1/28/96	1/29/95	1/30/94	1/31/93	2/2/92	2/3/91
Earnings Per Share	①2.77	1.34	0.85	d0.27	0.65	0.35	0.23
Dividends Per Share	②...	Nil	③...	Nil	Nil	④...	Nil

① Before extraord. charge. ② 2-for-1 stk. split, 12/6/96. ③ 2-for-1 stk. split, 10/27/95. ④ 3-for-2 stk. split, 4/9/92

ANNUAL FINANCIAL DATA

RECORD OF EARNINGS (IN MILLIONS):

Total Revenues	7,759	5,296	3,475	2,873	2,014	890	546
Costs and Expenses	6,998	4,881	3,193	2,882	1,855	809	493
Depreciation & Amort	47	38	33	31	20	14	9
Operating Income	714	377	249	d39	139	67	45
Inc Fr Cont Opers Bef Income Taxes	747	383	213	d39	143	73	44
Income Taxes	216	111	64	cr3	42	23	16
Net Income	①531	272	149	d36	102	51	27
Aver. Shs. Outstg. (000)	191,799	194,170	166,168	149,332	156,940	145,096	120,256

① Before extraord. item of approx. dr$13 million.

BALANCE SHEET (IN MILLIONS):

Cash and Cash Equivalents	1,352	646	527	337	95	155	37
Receivables, Net	903	726	538	411	374	165	90
Inventories	251	429	293	220	303	127	89
Gross Property	374	292	208	152	114	72	43
Accumulated Depreciation	139	113	91	65	44	28	17
Long-Term Debt	18	113	113	100	48	42	...
Net Stockholders' Equity	806	973	652	471	369	274	112
Total Assets	2,993	2,148	1,594	1,141	927	560	264
Total Current Assets	2,747	1,957	1,470	1,048	853	512	236
Total Current Liabilities	1,658	939	751	538	494	230	141
Net Working Capital	1,089	1,018	719	510	359	283	95
Year End Shs Outstg (000)	173,047	186,893	158,719	151,716	147,432	143,206	116,072

STATISTICAL RECORD:

Operating Profit Margin %	9.2	7.1	7.2	...	6.9	7.5	8.2
Book Value Per Share	4.66	5.21	4.11	3.10	2.50	1.91	0.96
Return on Equity %	65.9	28.0	22.9	...	27.6	18.6	24.1
Return on Assets %	17.7	12.7	9.3	...	11.0	9.1	10.2
P/E Ratio	23.2-4.2	18.5-7.4	14.1-5.7	...	18.7-5.8	17.3-7.5	13.7-3.3
Price Range	64⅜-11½	24¾-9⅞	11⅞-4¾	12½-3⅛	12⅛-3¾	6⅛-2	3⅛-¾

Statistics are as originally reported.

OFFICERS:
M.S. Dell, Chmn. & C.E.O.
M.L. Topfer, Vice-Chmn.
T.J. Meredith, Sr. V.P. & C.F.O.

INCORPORATED: TX, May, 1984; reincorp., DE, Oct., 1987

PRINCIPAL OFFICE: One Dell Way, Round Rock, TX 78682

TELEPHONE NUMBER: (512) 338-4400
FAX: (512) 728-3653
NO. OF EMPLOYEES: 11,000 (approx.)
ANNUAL MEETING: In July
SHAREHOLDERS: 3,680 (approx.)
INSTITUTIONAL HOLDINGS:
No. of Institutions: 285
Shares Held: 101,578,904

REGISTRAR(S): American Stock Transfer & Trust Co., 40 Wall Street, New York, NY 10005

TRANSFER AGENT(S): American Stock Transfer & Trust Co., 40 Wall Street, New York, NY 10005

NASDAQ SYMBOL DIGI
Rec. Pr. 21¾ (Marginable)

DSC COMMUNICATIONS CORP.

YIELD ...%
P/E RATIO ...

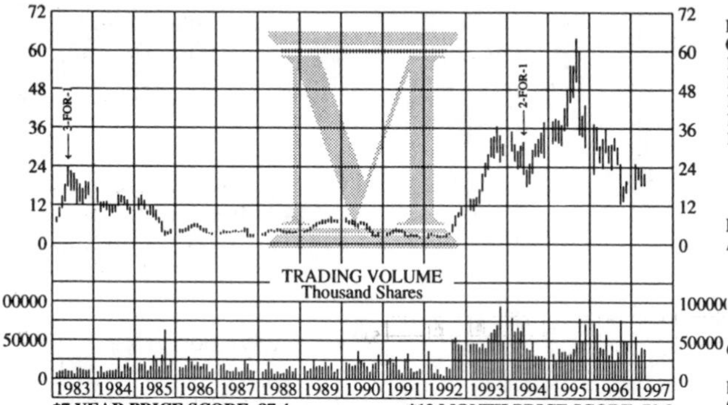

*7 YEAR PRICE SCORE 87.4 *12 MONTH PRICE SCORE 79.8

*NYSE COMPOSITE INDEX=100

INTERIM EARNINGS (Per Share):

Qtr.	Mar.	June	Sept.	Dec.
1993	0.12	0.17	0.22	0.26
1994	0.25	0.31	0.37	0.46
1995	0.36	0.44	0.42	0.42
1996	0.10	0.18	d0.49	0.15
1997	0.14	...	...	...

INTERIM DIVIDENDS (Per Share):

Amt.	Decl.	Ex.	Rec.	Pay.

Last dist. 100% stk., 5/25/94

CAPITALIZATION (12/31/96):

	($000)	(%)
Long-Term Debt	274,602	19.3
Common & Surplus	1,147,636	80.7
Total	1,422,238	100.0

RECENT DEVELOPMENTS: For the quarter ended 3/31/97, net income advanced 42.0% to $16.4 million from $11.5 million in the same prior-year period. Revenue climbed 8.5% to $334.2 million from $307.9 million the year before. This improvement resulted from a higher volume of access product deliveries and increased sales of the Company's transmission products. Gross profit as a percentage of revenue fell to 41.7% from 42.0% a year earlier. This decrease reflected a higher content of lower-margin access and international transmission product revenues. Operating income increased 33.5% to $24.0 million compared with $18.0 million the prior year. Net other income totaled $3.2 million versus $689,000 the previous year. Income before income taxes improved 41.9% to $26.4 million from $18.6 million the year before. On 3/13/97, DIGI announced the signing of a multi-year agreement with Bell Atlantic for the purchase of telecommunications equipment. This agreement extends from 1998 to 2001.

BUSINESS

DSC COMMUNICATIONS CORP. designs, manufactures, markets and services telecommunications systems and products for domestic and international long-distance carriers, local exchange carriers, and private network customers. The Company's principal products are large, complex microprocessor-controlled systems, which incorporate sophisticated hardware and software technology. The Company develops such systems to meet United States and international telecommunications standards, and the specific requirements of the Bell Operating Companies, independent telephone companies, long-distance carriers, private networks, and companies operating public and private communication networks in other countries. The switching and intelligent network products include the MegaHub product line, the DSC DEX 200, DSC DEX 400 and the BASIS service platform. Other products include radio systems, network management systems, eco cancelers, and transcoders.

ANNUAL EARNINGS AND DIVIDENDS PER SHARE

	1996	1995	1994	1993	1992	1991	1990
Earnings Per Share	**[1] d0.06**	**1.63**	**1.39**	**0.77**	**0.13**	**d1.31**	**[3] 0.24**
Dividends Per Share	**Nil**	**Nil**	**[2] ...**	**Nil**	**Nil**	**Nil**	**Nil**

[1] Incl. special charges [2] 100% stk. div., 5/25/94 [3] Bef. extraord. item

ANNUAL FINANCIAL DATA

	1996	1995	1994	1993	1992	1991	1990
RECORD OF EARNINGS (IN MILLIONS):							
Total Revenues	1,380.9	1,422.0	1,003.1	730.8	536.3	461.5	519.3
Operating Expenses	1,299.0	1,039.8	716.0	576.3	450.3	449.6	437.8
Depreciation	94.0	102.8	73.2	44.3	43.6	45.6	37.9
Operating Income	d12.2	279.4	214.0	110.2	42.4	d81.9	43.6
Inc Fr Cont Opers Bef Income Taxes	d12.2	290.0	223.2	109.5	16.9	d106.8	27.2
Income Taxes	...	97.3	60.6	27.8	5.3	1.5	6.9
Net Income	d7.6	192.7	162.6	81.7	11.6	d108.3	[1] 20.3
Aver. Shs. Outstg. (000)	116,514	118,126	116,889	106,650	93,198	82,678	84,638
[1] Before extra. item dr$209,000.							
BALANCE SHEET (IN MILLIONS):							
Cash and Cash Equivalents	334.0	569.3	271.3	313.8	69.8	26.4	35.0
Receivables, Net	411.9	277.0	239.7	140.0	90.4	116.8	164.5
Gross Property	764.7	675.7	526.2	380.5	324.0	306.2	305.5
Accumulated Depreciation	361.1	305.2	243.3	200.7	174.8	143.7	118.0
Long-Term Debt	274.6	210.4	25.3	56.7	128.6	109.0	209.0
Prop, Plant & Equip, Net	403.6	370.5	283.0	179.8	149.2	162.5	187.5
Net Stockholders' Equity	1,147.6	1,124.1	851.1	617.8	202.6	174.7	279.2
Total Assets	1,925.7	1,865.3	1,268.5	900.4	547.7	599.9	759.4
Total Current Assets	1,202.9	1,220.5	738.5	602.0	274.8	306.9	405.3
Total Current Liabilities	432.9	481.6	345.4	195.3	195.8	301.9	252.0
Net Working Capital	770.0	739.0	393.0	406.8	79.0	5.0	153.3
Year End Shs Outstg (000)	117,252	110,613	108,536	110,036	88,230	83,350	81,390
STATISTICAL RECORD:							
Operating Profit Margin %	...	19.6	21.3	15.1	7.9	...	8.4
Book Value Per Share	8.54	8.36	6.08	9.71	2.52	1.90	4.18
Return on Equity %	...	17.1	19.1	13.2	5.7	...	7.3
Return on Assets %	...	10.3	12.8	9.1	2.1	...	2.7
P/E Ratio	...	39.3-18.5	27.2-12.9	23.9-6.9	46.0-7.5	...	17.6-4.8
Price Range	37⅜-12⅝	64-30⅛	37⅞-17⅞	36⅝-10½	11½-1⅞	4⅞-1⅞	8¼-2¼

Statistics are as originally reported.

OFFICERS:
J.L. Donald, Chmn., Pres. & C.E.O.
G.F. Montry, Sr. V.P. & C.F.O.
C.J. Ornes, V.P. & Treas.

INCORPORATED: DE, Sep., 1976

PRINCIPAL OFFICE: 1000 Coit Road, Plano, TX 75075-5813

TELEPHONE NUMBER: (972) 519-3000

NO. OF EMPLOYEES: 6,367

ANNUAL MEETING: In April

SHAREHOLDERS: 5,242

INSTITUTIONAL HOLDINGS:
No. of Institutions: 209
Shares Held: 56,762,450

REGISTRAR(S): Society National Bank, Dallas, TX

TRANSFER AGENT(S): Society National Bank, Dallas, TX

ELECTRONIC ARTS, INC.

YIELD ...%
P/E RATIO 23.2

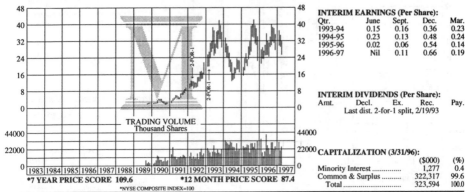

INTERIM EARNINGS (Per Share):

Qtr.	June	Sept.	Dec.	Mar.
1993-94	0.15	0.16	0.36	0.23
1994-95	0.23	0.13	0.48	0.24
1995-96	0.02	0.06	0.54	0.14
1996-97	Nil	0.11	0.66	0.19

INTERIM DIVIDENDS (Per Share):

Amt.	Decl.	Ex.	Rec.	Pay.
Last dist. 2-for-1 split, 2/19/93				

CAPITALIZATION (3/31/96):

	($000)	(%)
Minority Interest	1,277	0.4
Common & Surplus	322,317	99.6
Total	323,594	100.0

RECENT DEVELOPMENTS: For the fiscal year ended 3/31/97, net income rose 30.9% to $53.0 million. This compares with $40.5 million a year earlier. Net revenues for the year totaled $624.8 million, up 17.5% from $531.9 million the previous year. The Company's worldwide CD business for personal computers grew 27.0% during the year to more than $175.0 million. During the year, ERTS shipped 26 products for the newer 32-bit game systems. For the fourth quarter ended 3/31/97, net income increased 40.0% to $10.4 million compared with $7.4 million in the corresponding prior-year quarter. Net revenues were up 22.6% to $143.8 million from $117.3 million in the comparable period the year before. Fourth-quarter revenues grew 35.0% in Europe and 21.0% in North America, reflecting strong growth in the PlayStation market as well as the launch of the Nintendo 64 machine. During the fourth quarter, the Company introduced 11 new products on four different platforms.

BUSINESS

ELECTRONIC ARTS, INC. develops, publishes and distributes interactive entertainment software worldwide for personal computers and advanced entertainment systems such as the Sony PlayStation™ and Sega Saturn™. ERTS markets its products under five brand names: EA Sports, Electronic Arts Studio, Orgin Systems Inc., Bullfrog Productions Ltd. and Jane's® Combat Simulations.

ANNUAL EARNINGS AND DIVIDENDS PER SHARE

	3/31/96	3/31/95	3/31/94	3/31/93	3/31/92	3/31/91	3/31/90
Earnings Per Share	0.75	1.07	0.90	0.65	0.37	0.23	③0.17
Dividends Per Share	Nil	Nil	Nil	①...	②...	Nil	Nil

① 2-for-1 stk. split, 2/22/93   ② 2-for-1 stk. split, 3/27/92   ③ Before extraord. item

ANNUAL FINANCIAL DATA

RECORD OF EARNINGS (IN THOUSANDS):

Total Revenues	531,887	493,346	418,289	298,386	162,129	101,753	72,445
Costs and Expenses	462,497	417,755	349,925	253,213	137,527	87,614	62,241
Depreciation & Amort	15,859	10,763	7,865	3,994	1,743	1,507	1,187
Operating Income	53,531	64,828	60,499	41,179	22,859	12,632	9,017
Inc Fr Cont Opers Bef Income Taxes	59,552	78,078	64,281	43,716	24,269	13,837	9,631
Income Taxes	18,759	24,980	19,450	13,421	8,615	4,701	3,591
Net Income	40,489	55,718	44,737	30,858	15,654	9,136	①6,040
Aver. Shs. Outstg.	54,163	52,230	52,219	49,925	44,859	40,218	36,326

① Before extra. item cr$485,000.

BALANCE SHEET (IN THOUSANDS):

Cash and Cash Equivalents	185,852	184,846	142,249	98,029	56,890	27,632	22,023
Receivables, Net	73,075	59,531	70,399	33,240	22,226	18,171	10,920
Inventories	14,704	12,358	9,691	12,578	8,547	5,545	5,344
Gross Property	108,812	54,662	40,663	27,930	10,658	7,328	5,840
Accumulated Depreciation	38,750	24,134	15,516	9,031	6,143	4,792	3,632
Net Stockholders' Equity	322,317	237,073	172,178	110,571	65,213	43,809	32,584
Total Assets	424,219	341,239	273,651	181,257	101,101	63,050	46,811
Total Current Assets	300,338	272,160	233,729	152,781	91,179	53,663	39,793
Total Current Liabilities	100,625	103,018	97,988	67,687	35,888	19,126	14,021
Net Working Capital	199,713	169,142	135,741	85,094	55,291	34,537	25,772
Year End Shares Outstg	52,742	50,863	47,669	46,197	43,965	38,231	37,391

STATISTICAL RECORD:

Operating Profit Margin %	10.1	13.1	14.5	13.8	14.1	12.4	12.4
Book Value Per Share	6.11	4.66	3.61	2.39	1.48	1.15	0.87
Return on Equity %	12.6	23.5	26.0	27.9	24.0	20.9	18.5
Return on Assets %	9.5	16.3	16.3	17.0	15.5	14.5	12.9
P/E Ratio	56.3-20.5	31.3-11.9	48.8-23.0	35.1-14.9	26.0-6.1	18.5-6.5	14.0-10.3
Price Range	42¼-15⅜	33½-12¾	42-19¾	21¾-9¼	9⅝-2¼	4¼-1½	2⅜-1¾

Statistics are as originally reported.

OFFICERS:
L.F. Probst, III, Chmn., Pres. & C.E.O.
E.S. McKee, Jr., Sr. V.P., C.F.O. & Chief Admin. Off.
R.A. Kennedy, V.P., Gen. Couns. & Sec.
INCORPORATED: CA, May, 1982; reincorp., DE, Sept., 1991
PRINCIPAL OFFICE: 1450 Fashion Island Blvd., San Mateo, CA 94404

TELEPHONE NUMBER: (415) 571-7171
NO. OF EMPLOYEES: 1,500 (approx.)
ANNUAL MEETING: In July
SHAREHOLDERS: 2,085 (approx.)
INSTITUTIONAL HOLDINGS:
No. of Institutions: 133
Shares Held: 43,771,154

REGISTRAR(S):

TRANSFER AGENT(S): First Interstate Bank, Ltd., San Francisco, CA

ELECTRONICS FOR IMAGING, INC.

YIELD ...%
P/E RATIO 32.6

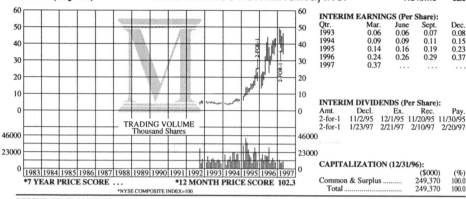

TRADING VOLUME
Thousand Shares

*7 YEAR PRICE SCORE ...   *12 MONTH PRICE SCORE 102.3
*NYSE COMPOSITE INDEX=100

INTERIM EARNINGS (Per Share):

Qtr.	Mar.	June	Sept.	Dec.
1993	0.06	0.06	0.07	0.08
1994	0.09	0.09	0.11	0.15
1995	0.14	0.16	0.19	0.23
1996	0.24	0.26	0.29	0.37
1997	0.37	...	...	...

INTERIM DIVIDENDS (Per Share):

Amt.	Decl.	Ex.	Rec.	Pay.
2-for-1	11/2/95	12/1/95	11/20/95	11/30/95
2-for-1	1/23/97	2/21/97	2/10/97	2/20/97

CAPITALIZATION (12/31/96):

	($000)	(%)
Common & Surplus	249,370	100.0
Total	249,370	100.0

RECENT DEVELOPMENTS: For the three months ended 3/31/97, net income surged 62.2% to $20.4 million, or $0.37 per share, from $12.6 million, or $0.23 per share, in the corresponding quarter of the previous year. Revenue totaled $91.0 million, up 43.0% from $63.6 million the prior year. Higher revenue and earnings were driven by continued strong demand for all of the Company's Fiery™ products coupled with rapid market acceptance of the low-cost Fiery™ controllers that were introduced in late 1996. Research and development expenses jumped 95.6% to $8.1 million, while sales and marketing expenses were up 63.1% to $9.6 million. Income from operations soared 62.9% to $29.4 million from $18.0 million the year before.

BUSINESS

ELECTRONICS FOR IMAGING, INC. develops products and technologies that enable high-quality digital color printing over computer networks. The Company's Fiery™ Color Servers incorporate hardware and software technologies that transform digital color copiers from the leading copier manufacturers into fast, high-quality color printers. EFII now has sales offices in France, Germany, Holland, Italy, Spain, Tokyo and the United Kingdom. EFII has developed strong sales, technical and distribution relationships with major color copier vendors including Canon, Kodak, Minolta, Xerox and Ricoh. EFII began introducing its new Fiery XJ family of products in early 1995.

ANNUAL EARNINGS AND DIVIDENDS PER SHARE

	1996	1995	1994	1993	1992	1991	1990
Earnings Per Share	1.13	0.71	0.43	0.26	0.19	0.03	d0.21
Dividends Per Share	Nil	①...	Nil	Nil	Nil	Nil	Nil

Note: 2-for-1 stk. split, 2/20/97. ① 2-for-1 stk. split, 11/30/95

ANNUAL FINANCIAL DATA

RECORD OF EARNINGS (IN THOUSANDS):

	1996	1995	1994	1993	1992	1991	1990
Total Revenues	298,013	190,451	130,381	89,526	53,690	16,426	2,000
Costs and Expenses	202,683	133,920	96,871	68,963	43,596	15,090	5,471
Depreciation & Amort	5,484	3,414	3,140	1,846	1,532	548	324
Operating Income	89,846	53,117	30,370	18,717	8,562	788	d3,795
Inc Fr Cont Opers Bef Income Taxes	97,164	58,593	33,301	20,551	8,763	766	d4,121
Income Taxes	34,980	21,093	11,995	7,800	2,175	148	...
Net Income	62,184	37,500	21,306	12,751	6,588	618	d4,121
Aver. Shs. Outstg.	54,828	53,100	49,836	49,156	35,788	29,072	20,004

BALANCE SHEET (IN THOUSANDS):

	1996	1995	1994	1993	1992	1991	1990
Cash and Cash Equivalents	212,100	144,018	106,974	79,491	45,193	3,048	65
Receivables, Net	40,875	27,588	8,739	11,050	5,263	666	...
Inventories	11,004	7,809	8,423	4,388	2,618	642	...
Gross Property	25,808	15,153	11,336	8,492	5,265	2,611	1,034
Accumulated Depreciation	15,168	9,684	6,981	3,841	1,995	923	375
Long-Term Debt	...	...	...	...	...	1,579	1,236
Net Stockholders' Equity	249,370	163,940	113,529	88,342	47,411	d1,662	d3,323
Total Assets	298,953	194,469	135,461	104,044	58,533	6,519	1,126
Total Current Assets	286,949	187,588	130,003	98,482	54,784	4,565	429
Total Current Liabilities	49,583	30,529	21,932	15,702	11,122	6,602	3,213
Net Working Capital	237,366	157,059	108,071	82,780	43,662	d2,037	d2,784
Year End Shares Outstg	51,503	49,942	47,956	46,388	38,348	13,416	12,520

STATISTICAL RECORD:

	1996	1995	1994	1993	1992	1991	1990
Operating Profit Margin %	30.1	27.9	23.3	20.9	15.9	4.8	...
Book Value Per Share	4.84	3.29	2.37	1.91	1.24	...	...
Return on Equity %	24.9	22.9	18.8	14.4	13.9	...	...
Return on Assets %	20.8	19.3	15.7	12.3	11.3	9.5	...
P/E Ratio	39.0-11.8	35.4-8.5	17.2-7.6	21.6-13.5	31.6-17.8	...	...
Price Range	44⅛-13⅜	25⅛-6	7⅜-3⅜	5⅝-3½	6-3½	...	...

Statistics are as originally reported.

OFFICERS:
D. Avida, Pres. & C.E.O.
J. Lenches, Exec. V.P.
F. Rosenzweig, V.P.-Mfg.
E. Saltzman, V.P.-Strategic Rel.

INCORPORATED: DE, Nov., 1988

PRINCIPAL OFFICE: 2855 Campus Drive, San Mateo, CA 94403

TELEPHONE NUMBER: (415) 286-8600

FAX: (415) 286-8686

NO. OF EMPLOYEES: 370

ANNUAL MEETING: In May

SHAREHOLDERS: 252 (approx.)

INSTITUTIONAL HOLDINGS:
No. of Institutions: 134
Shares Held: 46,097,034

REGISTRAR(S): Boston EquiServe, Shareholder Services Division, Boston, MA

TRANSFER AGENT(S): Boston EquiServe, Shareholder Services Division, Boston, MA

FASTENAL CO.

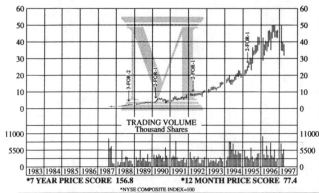

*7 YEAR PRICE SCORE 156.8 *12 MONTH PRICE SCORE 77.4
*NYSE COMPOSITE INDEX=100

INTERIM EARNINGS (Per Share):

Qtr.	Mar.	June	Sept.	Dec.
1993	0.06	0.08	0.09	0.09
1994	0.09	0.12	0.13	0.15
1995	0.16	0.18	0.19	0.19
1996	0.20	0.22	0.23	0.21
1997	0.23	...	...	...

INTERIM DIVIDENDS (Per Share):

Amt.	Decl.	Ex.	Rec.	Pay.
0.02A	1/26/96	2/28/96	3/1/96	3/15/96
0.02A	2/4/97	2/26/97	2/28/97	3/14/97

Indicated div.: $0.02

CAPITALIZATION (12/31/96):

	($000)	(%)
Common & Surplus	125,967	100.0
Total	125,967	100.0

RECENT DEVELOPMENTS: For the three months ended 3/31/97, net earnings increased 17.9% to $8.8 million, or $0.23 per share, from $7.4 million, or $0.20 per share, the previous year. Net sales climbed 38.1% to $87.1 million compared with $63.1 million in the corresponding quarter a year earlier. Gross profit advanced 37.1% to $45.8 million, or 52.6% of net sales, from $33.4 million, or 53.0% of net sales, the year before. Operating income rose 23.3% to $14.7 million from $11.9 million the prior year. Earnings before income taxes totaled $14.7 million, up 17.7% versus $12.5 million a year ago. During the first quarter, FAST opened 44 new stores. Of the 44 stores added, 30 were Fastenal® stores and 14 were satellite stores.

BUSINESS

FASTENAL COMPANY sells thousands of different types of threaded fasteners and other industrial and construction supplies through 528 Company-operated Fastenal stores located in the U.S. and in Canada. Threaded fasteners include products such as nuts, bolts, screws, studs, and related washers. The Company also operates FastTool stores that sell hand, power, and specialty tools, and also safety supplies. FastTool has its own marketing personnel and repair facilities, and are located adjacent to existing Company stores.

ANNUAL EARNINGS AND DIVIDENDS PER SHARE

	1996	1995	1994	1993	1992	1991	1990
Earnings Per Share	0.86	0.72	0.49	0.31	0.23	0.18	0.17
Dividends Per Share	0.02	①0.02	0.02	0.015	②0.015	0.013	③...
Dividend Payout %	2.3	2.8	4.1	4.7	6.3	7.2	...

① 100% stk. div., 3/29/95 ② 2-for-1 stk. split, 3/31/92 ③ 2-for-1 stk. split, 2/90.

ANNUAL FINANCIAL DATA

RECORD OF EARNINGS (IN THOUSANDS):

	1996	1995	1994	1993	1992	1991	1990
Total Revenues	287,691	222,555	161,886	110,307	81,263	62,305	52,290
Costs and Expenses	226,935	171,655	127,303	87,847	64,950	50,772	41,657
Depreciation & Amort	7,349	5,404	3,619	2,603	1,890	1,285	788
Operating Income	53,407	45,496	30,964	19,857	14,423	10,248	9,845
Inc Fr Cont Opers Bef Income Taxes	54,432	46,206	31,391	20,075	14,735	10,748	10,312
Income Taxes	21,893	18,795	12,725	8,165	5,902	4,142	3,992
Net Income	32,539	27,411	18,666	11,910	8,833	6,606	6,320
Aver. Shs. Outstg.	37,939	37,939	37,939	37,939	37,939	37,939	37,939

BALANCE SHEET (IN THOUSANDS):

Cash and Cash Equivalents	426	6,583	3,133	1,976	1,316	3,407	4,572
Receivables, Net	42,772	32,813	24,335	16,154	11,035	8,378	6,770
Inventories	56,526	40,178	30,911	22,234	15,220	11,231	8,409
Gross Property	64,611	42,381	28,086	20,577	15,119	9,871	5,897
Accumulated Depreciation	20,681	15,291	11,098	7,838	5,307	3,527	2,242
Net Stockholders' Equity	125,967	94,323	67,649	49,809	38,468	30,204	23,854
Total Assets	151,545	109,320	81,795	57,463	43,937	34,103	27,959
Total Current Assets	103,455	81,097	59,487	40,973	28,038	23,453	19,970
Total Current Liabilities	25,038	14,997	14,146	7,654	5,469	3,899	3,362
Net Working Capital	78,417	66,100	45,341	33,319	22,569	19,554	16,608
Year End Shares Outstg	37,939	37,939	37,939	37,939	37,939	37,939	37,939

STATISTICAL RECORD:

Operating Profit Margin %	18.6	20.4	19.1	18.0	17.7	16.4	18.8
Book Value Per Share	3.32	2.49	1.78	1.31	1.01	0.80	0.63
Return on Equity %	25.8	29.1	27.6	23.9	23.0	21.9	26.5
Return on Assets %	21.5	25.1	22.8	20.7	20.1	19.4	22.6
Average Yield %	0.1	0.1	0.2	0.2	0.3	0.4	...
P/E Ratio	58.1-33.4	59.7-27.6	46.9-29.6	51.2-30.6	47.8-30.4	45.8-22.2	37.5-18.4
Price Range	50-28¾	43-19⅞	23-14½	15⅞-9½	11-7	8¼-4	6⅜-3⅛

Statistics are as originally reported.

OFFICERS:
R.A. Kierlin, Chmn., Pres. & C.E.O.
D.L. Florness, Treas., C.F.O. & C.A.O.
W.D. Oberton, V.P. & C.O.O.
S.M. Slaggie, Sec.

INCORPORATED: MN, 1968

PRINCIPAL OFFICE: 2001 Theurer Blvd., Winona, MN 55987

TELEPHONE NUMBER: (507) 454-5374

FAX: (507) 454-6542

NO. OF EMPLOYEES: 3,073

ANNUAL MEETING: In April

SHAREHOLDERS: 2,200 (approx.)

INSTITUTIONAL HOLDINGS:
No. of Institutions: 108
Shares Held: 17,904,919

REGISTRAR(S): Norwest Bank Minnesota, N.A., St. Paul, MN

TRANSFER AGENT(S): Norwest Bank Minnesota, N.A., St. Paul, MN

FISERV, INC.

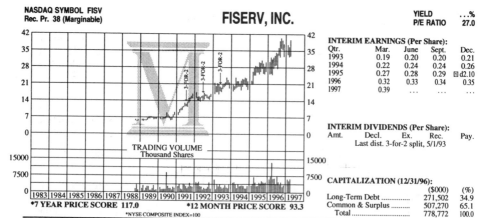

INTERIM EARNINGS (Per Share):

Qtr.	Mar.	June	Sept.	Dec.
1993	0.19	0.20	0.20	0.21
1994	0.22	0.24	0.24	0.26
1995	0.27	0.28	0.29	⑤d2.10
1996	0.32	0.33	0.34	0.35
1997	0.39	...	...	...

INTERIM DIVIDENDS (Per Share):

Amt.   Decl.   Ex.   Rec.   Pay.
Last dist. 3-for-2 split, 5/1/93

CAPITALIZATION (12/31/96):

	($000)	(%)
Long-Term Debt	271,502	34.9
Common & Surplus	507,270	65.1
Total	778,772	100.0

*7 YEAR PRICE SCORE 117.0   *12 MONTH PRICE SCORE 93.3
*NYSE COMPOSITE INDEX=100

RECENT DEVELOPMENTS: For the three months ended 3/31/97, net income totaled $18.1 million, or $0.39 per share, up 23.7% compared with $14.7 million, or $0.32 per share, the previous year. Revenues increased 6.0% to $206.5 million from $194.7 million the year before. Higher revenues were primarily attributed to the addition of new clients and cross-sales of multiple products and services. Income before income taxes climbed 23.7% to $30.7 mil-

lion from $24.9 million in the corresponding prior-year quarter. In March 1997, the Company announced an agreement to acquire BHC Financial, Inc., a provider of securities processing and support services to banks, insurance companies, brokerage firms, money managers and mutual fund companies. On 4/1/97, FISV acquired AdminaStar Communications, a commercial provider of laser printing and mailing services.

BUSINESS

FISERV, INC. is a full-service provider of data processing, software system development, item processing and check imaging, multiple technology support and related information management services and products to banks, credit unions, savings institutions and other financial intermediaries worldwide.

ANNUAL EARNINGS AND DIVIDENDS PER SHARE

	1996	1995	1994	1993	1992	1991	1990
Earnings Per Share	1.34	①d1.36	0.95	0.80	0.67	0.56	0.47
Dividends Per Share	Nil	Nil	Nil	②...	③...	④...	Nil

① Incl. one-time charges of $109.6 million, or $2.49 per share, related to the acquisition of Information Technology, Inc. ② 3-for-2 stk. split, 5/3/93 ③ 3-for-2 stk. split, 6/1/92 ④ 3-for-2 stk. split, 7/2/91

ANNUAL FINANCIAL DATA

RECORD OF EARNINGS (IN MILLIONS):

	1996	1995	1994	1993	1992	1991	1990
Total Revenues	798.3	703.4	579.8	467.9	332.1	281.3	183.2
Costs and Expenses	611.4	718.7	463.3	378.8	270.2	229.2	145.2
Depreciation & Amort	42.2	38.5	31.4	21.5	16.1	14.9	10.4
Operating Income	123.6	d79.7	74.3	57.5	39.2	31.7	23.4
Inc Fr Cont Opers Bef Income Taxes	104.5	d98.5	67.3	53.2	37.1	28.7	21.5
Income Taxes	42.9	cr38.7	26.9	20.5	14.1	10.3	7.7
Net Income	61.7	d59.9	40.4	32.7	23.0	18.3	13.8
Aver. Shs. Outstg. (000)	46,198	44,008	40,735	39,455	34,539	32,580	29,090

BALANCE SHEET (IN MILLIONS):

	1996	1995	1994	1993	1992	1991	1990
Cash and Cash Equivalents	80.8	59.7	29.7	35.9	57.6	24.4	21.6
Receivables, Net	192.8	291.6	123.0	104.7	54.9	48.2	29.4
Gross Property	304.8	279.1	220.2	168.8	106.4	90.3	64.5
Accumulated Depreciation	161.2	130.7	105.2	72.1	53.5	43.8	34.1
Long-Term Debt	271.5	381.4	143.9	111.1	52.6	51.6	33.6
Net Stockholders' Equity	507.3	434.3	358.7	307.7	192.5	166.9	99.7
Total Assets	1,908.5	1,885.3	1,661.3	1,182.4	898.2	740.1	565.2
Total Current Assets	328.0	415.2	187.4	170.5	130.8	88.9	61.6
Total Current Liabilities	1,128.4	1,067.6	1,129.8	745.9	635.5	508.5	418.3
Net Working Capital	d800.4	d652.4	d942.4	d575.4	d504.8	d419.6	d356.7
Year End Shs Outstg (000)	45,348	44,887	39,157	38,780	33,933	33,523	28,868

STATISTICAL RECORD:

	1996	1995	1994	1993	1992	1991	1990
Operating Profit Margin %	15.5	...	12.8	12.3	11.8	11.3	12.8
Book Value Per Share	2.08	0.06	2.71	2.28	2.51	1.89	1.10
Return on Equity %	12.2	...	11.3	10.6	11.9	11.0	13.8
Return on Assets %	3.2	...	2.4	2.8	2.6	2.5	2.4
P/E Ratio	30.1-18.7	...	25.0-18.9	29.7-20.9	26.1-20.3	30.1-14.3	19.7-12.2
Price Range	40⅜-25	31-21	23¾-18	23¾-16¾	17½-13⅝	16⅞-8	9¼-5¾

Statistics are as originally reported.

OFFICERS:
G.D. Dalton, Chmn. & C.E.O.
L.M. Muma, Pres. & C.O.O.
C.W. Sprague, Exec. V.P., Gen. Counsel & Sec.
K.R. Jensen, Sr. Exec. V.P., C.F.O. & Treas.
E.P. Alberts, Sr. V.P.-Fin. & Contr.

INCORPORATED: DE, 1984

PRINCIPAL OFFICE: 255 Fiserv Drive, P.O. Box 979, Brookfield, WI 53045

TELEPHONE NUMBER: (414) 879-5000

NO. OF EMPLOYEES: 8,590

ANNUAL MEETING: In March

SHAREHOLDERS: 30,000 (approx.)

INSTITUTIONAL HOLDINGS:
No. of Institutions: 155
Shares Held: 31,460,702

REGISTRAR(S): Firstar Trust Company, Milwaukee, WI

TRANSFER AGENT(S): Firstar Trust Company, Milwaukee, WI

FOOD LION, INC.

YIELD 2.0%
P/E RATIO 14.7

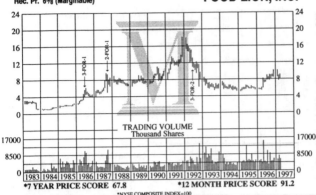

INTERIM EARNINGS (Per Share):

Qtr.	Mar.	June	Sept.	Dec.
1993	0.05	0.06	0.05	d0.15
1994	0.06	0.07	0.08	0.11
1995	0.08	0.08	0.09	0.12
1996	0.09	0.10	0.11	0.14
1997	0.10	...	...	...

INTERIM DIVIDENDS (Per Share):

Amt.	Decl.	Ex.	Rec.	Pay.
0.0276Q	7/1/96	7/11/96	7/15/96	7/29/96
0.0276Q	9/23	10/3	10/7	10/21
0.0332Q	2/6/97	2/20/97	2/24/97	3/10/97
0.0332Q	4/7	4/17	4/21	5/5

Indicated div.: $0.13

CAPITALIZATION (12/28/96):

	($000)	(%)
Long-Term Debt	495,111	22.7
Cap. Lease Oblig.	469,035	21.5
Common & Surplus	1,215,938	55.8
Total	2,180,084	100.0

RECENT DEVELOPMENTS: For the 12 weeks ended 3/22/97, net income advanced 11.4% to $45.5 million, or $0.10 per share, from $40.9 million, or $0.09 per share, the previous year. Net sales climbed 12.5% to $2.28 billion from $2.02 billion the year before. Same-store sales were essentially flat compared with the corresponding prior-year period. Sales were negatively affected by competitive pressures and mild winter weather in the southeast. Sales should benefit from increased levels of advertising and targeted marketing programs in the second quarter. Gross profit improved 20.7% to $496.9 million, or 21.8% of net sales, from $411.6 million, or 20.3% of net sales, the prior year. Operating income totaled $101.3 million, up 17.9% versus $86.0 million a year earlier. During the first quarter, FDLN opened nine new stores and closed 15 underperforming stores and one Kash n' Karry store.

BUSINESS

FOOD LION, INC. operates 1,202 retail food supermarkets in the Southeastern U.S. The stores are located in North Carolina, South Carolina, Virginia, Tennessee, Georgia, Florida, Louisiana, Maryland, Texas, Delaware, Kentucky, West Virginia, Pennsylvania and Oklahoma. The Company sells in its stores a wide variety of groceries, produce, meats, dairy products, seafood, frozen food, delibakery and non-food items such as tobacco, health and beauty aids and other household and personal products. Through its supermarkets, the Company offers nationally and regionally advertised brand name merchandise as well as products manufactured and packaged for the Company under the private label of "Food Lion."

ANNUAL EARNINGS AND DIVIDENDS PER SHARE

	12/28/96	12/30/95	12/31/94	1/1/94	1/2/93	12/28/91	12/29/90
Earnings Per Share	0.44	0.36	0.32	0.01	0.37	0.42	0.36
Dividends Per Share	0.11	0.095	0.09	0.09	① 0.088	0.099	0.088
Dividend Payout %	25.0	26.4	29.0	N.M.	29.7	23.1	24.4

① 3-for-2 stk. split, 6/8/92

ANNUAL FINANCIAL DATA

RECORD OF EARNINGS (IN MILLIONS):

Total Revenues	9,005.9	8,210.9	7,932.6	7,609.8	7,195.9	6,438.5	5,584.4
Costs and Expenses	8,422.4	7,708.2	7,453.5	7,388.1	6,734.6	5,958.8	5,185.9
Depreciation & Amort	165.3	146.2	139.8	143.0	121.6	104.6	81.4
Operating Profit	418.3	356.5	339.3	249.2	339.7	375.1	317.1
Inc Fr Cont Opers Bef Income Taxes	337.8	283.1	252.7	6.4	290.6	340.7	284.5
Income Taxes	131.7	110.7	99.8	2.5	112.6	135.5	111.9
Net Income	206.1	172.4	152.9	3.9	178.0	205.2	172.6
Aver. Shs. Outstg. (000)	470,216	481,154	483,708	483,701	483,663	483,516	483,210

BALANCE SHEET (IN MILLIONS):

Cash and Cash Equivalents	102.4	70.0	66.9	46.1	105.1	4.3	10.4
Receivables, Net	227.0	128.0	140.6	110.0	96.0	97.1	77.0
Inventories	1,065.7	881.0	855.7	929.1	896.4	844.5	673.6
Gross Property	2,689.6	2,333.7	2,101.5	1,993.3	1,873.6	1,426.3	1,094.8
Accumulated Depreciation	917.1	840.9	744.8	621.9	499.9	389.5	303.0
Long-Term Debt	469.0	372.6	305.0	301.5	245.7	195.2	153.8
Capital Lease Obligations	495.1	355.3	355.3	569.4	248.1	247.2	97.9
Net Stockholders' Equity	1,215.9	1,102.5	1,027.4	917.6	955.7	826.6	668.6
Total Assets	3,488.6	2,645.3	2,487.8	2,503.7	2,521.5	1,992.2	1,559.5
Total Current Assets	1,428.1	1,152.4	1,131.1	1,139.5	1,147.8	955.4	767.7
Total Current Liabilities	1,154.2	698.7	697.2	619.3	986.3	688.1	602.8
Net Working Capital	274.5	453.7	433.9	520.2	161.6	267.3	164.8
Year End Shs Outstg (000)	469,068	475,134	483,713	483,703	483,693	483,609	483,351

STATISTICAL RECORD:

Operating Profit Margin %	4.6	4.3	4.3	1.0	4.7	5.8	5.7
Book Value Per Share	2.00	2.32	2.12	1.90	1.98	1.71	1.38
Return on Equity %	16.9	15.6	14.9	0.4	18.6	24.8	25.8
Return on Assets %	5.9	6.5	6.1	0.2	7.1	10.3	11.1
Average Yield %	1.4	1.6	1.4	1.3	0.9	0.8	1.0
P/E Ratio	23.0-12.2	18.4-13.9	23.4-16.0	N.M	48.6-16.9	43.2-19.3	30.9-19.1
Price Range	10⅛-5⅜	6⅝-5	7½-5⅛	8½-5⅜	18-6¼	18⅛-8⅛	11⅛-6⅞

Statistics are as originally reported.

OFFICERS:
T.E. Smith, Chmn., Pres. & C.E.O.
J.C. Hall, Jr., Sr. V.P.-Oper. & C.O.O.
R.W. McCanless, Sr. V.P., Chief Admin.
Off. & Sec.
M.J. Price, Treas.

INCORPORATED: NC, Aug., 1957

PRINCIPAL OFFICE: 2110 Executive Drive
P.O. Box 1330, Salisbury, NC 28145-1330

TELEPHONE NUMBER: (704) 633-8250
FAX: (704) 636-5024
NO. OF EMPLOYEES: 27,924 (full-time);
45,246 (part-time).
ANNUAL MEETING: In May
SHAREHOLDERS: 30,753 (Cl. A); 20,945
(Cl. B.)
INSTITUTIONAL HOLDINGS:
No. of Institutions: 63
Shares Held: 22,483,389

REGISTRAR(S): First Chicago Trust
Company of New York, Jersey City, NJ
07303-2500

TRANSFER AGENT(S): First Chicago Trust
Company of New York, Jersey City, NJ
07303-2500

FORE SYSTEMS, INC.

YIELD ...%
P/E RATIO 31.4

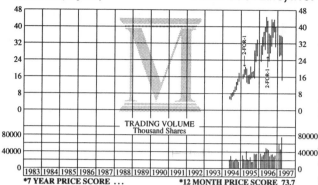

*7 YEAR PRICE SCORE ...   *12 MONTH PRICE SCORE 73.7
*NYSE COMPOSITE INDEX=100

INTERIM EARNINGS (Per Share):

Qtr.	June	Sept.	Dec.	Mar.
1994-95	0.02	0.04	0.05	0.06
1995-96	0.05	0.08	0.09	d0.11
1996-97	0.12	0.14	0.13	0.04

INTERIM DIVIDENDS (Per Share):

Amt.	Decl.	Ex.	Rec.	Pay.
2-for-1	5/6/96	6/4/96	5/20/96	6/3/96

CAPITALIZATION (3/31/97):

	($000)	(%)
Common & Surplus	454,179	100.0
Total	454,179	100.0

RECENT DEVELOPMENTS: For the fiscal year ended 3/31/97, net income totaled $41.5 million, or $0.41 per share, compared with $9.7 million, or $0.11 per share, in the corresponding prior-year period. Revenue surged 68.1% to $395.3 million from $235.2 million the previous year. Results for fiscal 1997 included a one-time charge of $8.3 million related to a litigation settlement by FORE's ALANTEC subsidiary. Earnings were also negatively affected by merger-related expenses of $1.7 million and $29.4 million in fiscal 1997 and fiscal 1996, respectively. Gross profit was $226.2 million, or 57.2% of revenue, compared with $136.5 million, or 58.0% of revenue, the prior year. For the three months ended 3/31/97, net income totaled $3.9 million versus a net loss of $9.6 million a year earlier. The 1997 results included the aforementioned litigation charge, while 1996 results included $27.1 million of merger-related expenses. Revenue climbed 34.6% to $101.3 million from $75.3 million a year ago.

BUSINESS

FORE SYSTEMS, INC. designs, develops, manufactures and sells high-performance networking products based on asynchronous transfer mode (ATM) technology. These products include ForeRunner® ATM switches and adapter cards, PowerHub® LAN switches, CellPath™ WAN multiplexers for ATM connectivity, ForeThought™ Internetworking Software and ForeView® Network Management Software. FORE has delivered ATM and LAN switching solutions to over 4,000 customers, including Fortune 500 companies, telecommunications service providers, government agencies, research institutions and universities.

ANNUAL EARNINGS AND DIVIDENDS PER SHARE

	3/31/97	3/31/96	3/31/95	3/31/94	3/31/93	3/31/92
Earnings Per Share	0.41	0.11	0.18	③ 0.06	...	...
Dividends Per Share	①...	Nil	②...	Nil	...	...

① 2-for-1 stk. split, 6/3/96.   ② 2-for-1 stk. split, 2/15/95   ③ Pro forma

ANNUAL FINANCIAL DATA

RECORD OF EARNINGS (IN THOUSANDS):

	3/31/97	3/31/96	3/31/95	3/31/94	3/31/93	3/31/92
Total Revenues	395,347	235,189	75,611	23,506	5,482	1,043
Costs and Expenses	① 334,025	216,051	62,019	19,809	4,912	883
Depreciation & Amort	...	8,490	2,831	489	88	29
Income From Operations	61,322	10,648	10,761	3,208	482	131
Income Bef Income Taxes	65,492	20,554	11,908	3,280	520	134
Income Taxes	24,022	10,817	4,548	1,202	222	41
Net Income	41,470	9,737	7,360	2,078	298	93
Aver. Shs. Outstg.	99,949	86,432	55,314	45,660	...	...

BALANCE SHEET (IN THOUSANDS):

Cash and Cash Equivalents	299,682	296,155	33,741	3,089	4,556	59
Receivables, Net	84,997	69,564	21,657	8,068	1,555	178
Inventories	50,769	27,495	14,511	4,423	1,094	134
Gross Property	② 47,906	36,131	8,894	2,158	347	124
Accumulated Depreciation	...	11,365	2,779	549	119	31
Long-Term Debt	...	...	...	289	...	...
Net Stockholders' Equity	454,179	335,990	54,614	2,060	369	111
Total Assets	538,577	424,362	78,774	18,416	7,435	468
Total Current Assets	490,651	399,596	72,659	16,541	7,205	373
Total Current Liabilities	84,398	88,372	24,160	10,538	1,966	357
Net Working Capital	406,273	311,224	48,499	6,003	5,239	16
Year End Shares Outstg	97,552	86,432	51,902	24,316	24,032	24,000

① Incl. depr.   ② Net

STATISTICAL RECORD:

Operating Profit Margin %	15.5	4.5	14.2	13.6	8.8	12.6
Book Value Per Share	4.66	3.89	1.05	0.07	0.02	...
Return on Equity %	9.1	2.9	13.5	N.M.	80.8	83.8
Return on Assets %	7.7	2.3	9.3	11.3	4.0	19.9
Price Range	44¾-23⅜	33⅞-12¾	17⅞-5	...	...	...

Statistics are as originally reported.

OFFICERS:
E.C. Cooper, Chmn. & C.E.O.
O. Menzilcioglu, Pres.
T.J. Gill, C.O.O. & C.F.O.
M.I. Green, V.P.-Worldwide Sales

INCORPORATED: PA, Apr., 1990; reincorp., DE, Nov., 1992

PRINCIPAL OFFICE: 1000 FORE Drive, Warrendale, PA 15086-7502

TELEPHONE NUMBER: (412) 742-4444
FAX: (412) 742-7704
NO. OF EMPLOYEES: 1,361
ANNUAL MEETING: In July
SHAREHOLDERS: 1,481
INSTITUTIONAL HOLDINGS:
No. of Institutions: 193
Shares Held: 60,671,669

REGISTRAR(S): Chase Mellon Shareholder Services, Pittsburgh, PA

TRANSFER AGENT(S): Chase Mellon Shareholder Services, Pittsburgh, PA

FORT HOWARD CORP.

YIELD ...%
P/E RATIO 12.5

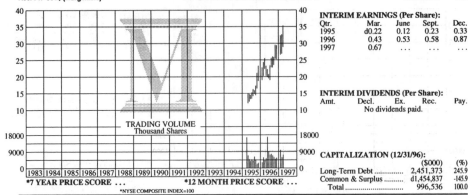

*NYSE COMPOSITE INDEX=100

INTERIM EARNINGS (Per Share):

Qtr.	Mar.	June	Sept.	Dec.
1995	d0.22	0.12	0.23	0.33
1996	0.43	0.53	0.58	0.87
1997	0.67	...	...	...

INTERIM DIVIDENDS (Per Share):

Amt.	Decl.	Ex.	Rec.	Pay.
No dividends paid.				

CAPITALIZATION (12/31/96):

	($000)	(%)
Long-Term Debt	2,451,373	245.9
Common & Surplus	d1,454,837	-145.9
Total	996,536	100.0

*7 YEAR PRICE SCORE ... *12 MONTH PRICE SCORE ...

RECENT DEVELOPMENTS: On 5/5/97, the Company announced it had signed a definitive agreement to be acquired by James River Corp. for the formation of new company named Fort James Corporation. FORT shareholders will recieve 1.375 shares of Fort James common stock for every share of FORT held. For the three months ended 3/31/97, income before an extraordinary charge totaled $49.7 million, up 84.7% compared with net income of $26.9 million the prior year. Net sales advanced 3.9% to $400.8 million from $385.7 million a year earlier. Domestic tissue sales grew 3.7% compared with the first quarter of 1996. Sales of converted products climbed 8.6% from the year before, partially offset by lower selling prices stemming from industry-wide price decreases occurring in mid-1996. Gross income advanced 16.5% to $171.7 million, or 42.8% of net sales, from $147.4 million, or 38.2% of net sales, a year earlier. Operating income increased 21.0% to $138.2 million from $114.2 million in 1996, reflecting higher sales volume and lower wastepaper costs in domestic and international operations.

BUSINESS

FORT HOWARD CORPORATION manufactures and markets consumer tissue products in the United States and the United Kingdom. FORT's products include Mardi Gras® printed napkins and paper towels; So-Dri® paper towels; Soft 'N Gentle® and Green Forest® bath and facial tissues. The Company also markets products under the Preference® Ultra, Preference®, and Envision® brands.

ANNUAL EARNINGS AND DIVIDENDS PER SHARE

	1996	1995	1994	1993	1992
Earnings Per Share	① 2.44	① 0.57	...	...	...
Dividends Per Share	Nil	Nil	...	...	...

① Before extraord. item

ANNUAL FINANCIAL DATA

RECORD OF EARNINGS (IN MILLIONS):

	1996	1995	1994	1993	1992
Total Revenues	1,580.8	1,620.9	1,274.4	1,187.4	1,151.4
Costs and Expenses	984.8	1,161.9	881.9	2,861.4	824.0
Depreciation & Amort	101.6	98.9	95.7	130.7	138.0
Operating Income	476.4	360.1	276.8	d1,716.6	270.7
Inc Fr Cont Opers Bef Income Taxes	214.5	51.9	d61.0	d2,056.4	d69.8
Income Taxes	43.8	18.4	cr18.9	cr16.3	cr0.4
Net Income	① 170.7	② 33.5	③ d42.1	④ d2,040.1	⑤ d69.4
Aver. Shs. Outstg. (000)	70,088	58,228	38,103	38,107	...

① Before extra. item dr$8,136,000. ② Before extra. item dr$18,748,000. ③ Before extra. item dr$28,170,000. ④ Before extra. item dr$11,964,000. ⑤ Before extra. item dr$10,587,000.

BALANCE SHEET (IN MILLIONS):

	1996	1995	1994	1993	1992
Cash and Cash Equivalents	0.8	0.9	0.4	0.2	...
Receivables, Net	133.3	127.4	148.4	129.3	...
Inventories	151.2	163.1	130.8	118.3	...
Gross Property	2,057.4	1,971.6	1,932.7	1,845.1	...
Accumulated Depreciation	809.7	706.4	611.8	516.9	...
Long-Term Debt	2,451.4	2,903.3	3,189.6	3,109.8	...
Net Stockholders' Equity	d1,454.8	d1,838.4	d2,148.4	d2,080.9	...
Total Assets	1,615.4	1,652.4	1,680.9	1,649.8	...
Total Current Assets	285.3	291.4	279.6	247.8	...
Total Current Liabilities	321.7	326.2	377.1	339.5	...
Net Working Capital	d36.4	d34.7	d97.5	d91.7	...
Year End Shs Outstg (000)	74,381	63,371	...	...	...

STATISTICAL RECORD:

	1996	1995	1994	1993	1992
Operating Profit Margin %	30.1	22.2	21.7	...	23.5
Return on Assets %	10.6	2.0	...	...	...
P/E Ratio	12.1-7.8	40.8-21.1	...	...	...
Price Range	29½-19	23¼-12	...	...	...

Statistics are as originally reported.

OFFICERS:
M.T. Riordan, Chmn., Pres. & C.E.O.
K.J. Hempel, Vice-Chmn. & C.F.O.
J.W. Nellen, II, V.P. & Sec.

INCORPORATED: DE, 1967

PRINCIPAL OFFICE: 1919 South Broadway, Green Bay, WI 54304

TELEPHONE NUMBER: (414) 435-8821
FAX: (414) 435-3703
NO. OF EMPLOYEES: 7,000 (approx.)
ANNUAL MEETING: In May
SHAREHOLDERS: 935 (approx.)
INSTITUTIONAL HOLDINGS:
No. of Institutions: 110
Shares Held: 63,272,343

REGISTRAR(S): ChaseMellon Shareholder Services, L.L.C., New York, NY

TRANSFER AGENT(S): ChaseMellon Shareholder Services, L.L.C., New York, NY

GARTNER GROUP, INC.

YIELD ...%
P/E RATIO 83.1

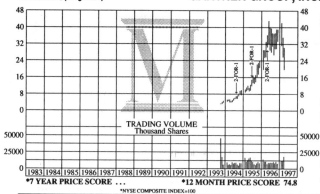

INTERIM EARNINGS (Per Share):				
Qtr.	Dec.	Mar.	June	Sept.
1993-94	------------------ 0.17 ------------------			
1994-95	0.08	0.08	0.08	0.03
1995-96	0.12	0.12	0.13	d0.19
1996-97	0.19	0.18	...	...

INTERIM DIVIDENDS (Per Share):				
Amt.	Decl.	Ex.	Rec.	Pay.
2-for-1	1/25/96	4/1/96	3/16/96	3/29/96

CAPITALIZATION (9/30/96):	($000)	(%)
Common & Surplus	150,235	100.0
Total	150,235	100.0

*7 YEAR PRICE SCORE ...   *12 MONTH PRICE SCORE 74.8
*NYSE COMPOSITE INDEX=100

RECENT DEVELOPMENTS: For the three months ended 3/31/97, net income jumped 55.4% to $18.2 million from $11.7 million the previous year. Total revenues climbed 31.1% to $119.1 million from $90.8 million in the corresponding year-earlier quarter. Revenues from research, advisory and benchmarking services totaled $96.0 million, up 28.1% compared with $75.0 million the year before. Other revenues grew 45.8% to $23.1 million from $15.8 million the prior year, reflecting strong gains from the

Company's technology-based training business. Operating income was $29.6 million compared with $19.7 million in 1996, representing an increase of 50.2%. For the six months ended 3/31/97, net income surged 60.5% to $37.2 million from $23.2 million a year ago. Total revenues rose 30.5% to $244.5 million from $187.3 million the previous year. The 1996 results included a non-recurring charge taken in the first quarter of $1.7 million related to the acquisition of Dataquest.

BUSINESS

GARTNER GROUP, INC. is an independent provider of research and analysis on the computer hardware, software, communications and related information technology ("IT") industries. GART's core business is researching and analyzing significant IT industry trends and developments, packaging such analysis into annually renewable subscription-based products and distributing such products through print and electronic media. GART's business is also comprised of the following entities: Dataquest, a provider of IT market research and consulting; Real Decisions, a provider of benchmarking, continuous improvement and best practices services; and Gartner Group Learning, a developer and publisher of education training products and services for computer desktop and technical applications professionals. Cognizant Corp. owned approximately 51% of GART's common stock.

ANNUAL EARNINGS AND DIVIDENDS PER SHARE

	9/30/96	9/30/95	9/30/94	9/30/93	9/30/92	9/30/91
Earnings Per Share	0.17	0.27	0.17	④ 0.09	d0.08	...
Dividends Per Share	①...	②...	③...	Nil	Nil	...

① 2-for-1 stk. split, 3/29/96 ② 2-for-1 stk. split, 6/28/95 ③ 2-for-1 stk. split, 8/26/94 ④ Before extraord. item

ANNUAL FINANCIAL DATA

RECORD OF EARNINGS (IN THOUSANDS):

Total Revenues	394,672	229,152	169,002	122,544	100,353	84,422
Costs and Expenses	332,353	177,829	134,329	101,572	87,849	78,697
Depreciation & Amort	12,879	8,087	7,265	6,368	10,455	9,421
Operating Income	49,440	43,236	27,357	14,604	2,049	d3,696
Inc Fr Cont Opers Bef Income Taxes	53,130	45,605	27,355	12,178	d3,476	d8,924
Income Taxes	36,692	20,066	12,380	5,412	1,075	714
Net Income	16,438	25,539	14,975	① 6,766	d4,551	d9,638
Aver. Shs. Outstg.	98,612	91,762	92,008	72,000	55,592	56,584

① Before extra. item dr$765,000.

BALANCE SHEET (IN THOUSANDS):

Cash and Cash Equivalents	126,809	91,096	50,654	6,385	12,277	...
Receivables, Net	143,762	99,176	92,964	57,238	36,874	...
Gross Property	68,937	41,234	23,725	19,239	16,210	...
Accumulated Depreciation	36,119	21,414	14,145	10,402	7,014	...
Long-Term Debt	...	...	6,419	4,952	32,556	...
Capital Lease Obligations	...	...	...	...	233	...
Net Stockholders' Equity	150,235	85,499	49,028	12,869	d13,729	...
Total Assets	444,108	300,598	232,557	133,685	109,489	...
Total Current Assets	310,150	217,802	164,509	76,610	57,680	...
Total Current Liabilities	291,408	211,799	171,333	113,291	90,429	...
Net Working Capital	18,742	6,003	d6,824	d36,681	d32,749	...
Year End Shares Outstg	92,927	85,552	83,336	...	...	...

STATISTICAL RECORD:

Operating Profit Margin %	12.5	18.9	16.2	11.9	2.0	...
Book Value Per Share	0.61	0.32	...	...	...	...
Return on Equity %	10.9	29.9	30.5	52.6	33.1	...
Return on Assets %	3.7	8.5	6.4	5.1	...	...
P/E Ratio	N.M.	89.4-32.9	58.1-23.5	51.4-34.7	...	...
Price Range	43⅛-19¾	24⅛-8⅞	9⅞-4	4⅝-3⅛	...	...

Statistics are as originally reported.

OFFICERS:
M.A. Fernandez, Chmn., Pres. & C.E.O.
W.T. Clifford, Exec. V.P. & C.O.O.
E.F. Carter, Exec. V.P. & Chief Mktg. Off.
J.F. Halligan, Exec. V.P., C.F.O., Treas. & Sec.

INCORPORATED: DE, 1990

PRINCIPAL OFFICE: P.O. Box 10212 56 Top Gallant Road, Stamford, CT 06904-2212

TELEPHONE NUMBER: (203) 964-0096
FAX: (203) 316-1100
NO. OF EMPLOYEES: 2,129
ANNUAL MEETING: Jan. 22, 1998
SHAREHOLDERS: 271 (approx.) Class A; 1 Class B
INSTITUTIONAL HOLDINGS:
No. of Institutions: 110
Shares Held: 39,084,618

REGISTRAR(S):

TRANSFER AGENT(S): Boston EquiServe, Boston, MA

GENERAL NUTRITION COS., INC.

YIELD ...%
P/E RATIO N.M.

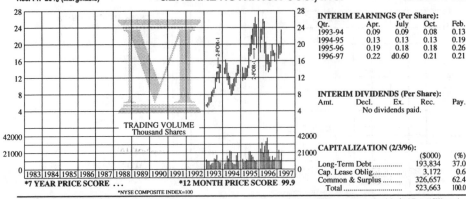

*7 YEAR PRICE SCORE ...   *12 MONTH PRICE SCORE 99.9

*NYSE COMPOSITE INDEX=100

TRADING VOLUME
Thousand Shares

INTERIM EARNINGS (Per Share):

Qtr.	Apr.	July	Oct.	Feb.
1993-94	0.09	0.09	0.08	0.13
1994-95	0.13	0.13	0.13	0.19
1995-96	0.19	0.18	0.18	0.26
1996-97	0.22	d0.60	0.21	0.21

INTERIM DIVIDENDS (Per Share):

Amt.	Decl.	Ex.	Rec.	Pay.
		No dividends paid.		

CAPITALIZATION (2/3/96):

	($000)	(%)
Long-Term Debt	193,834	37.0
Cap. Lease Oblig...............	3,172	0.6
Common & Surplus	326,657	62.4
Total	523,663	100.0

RECENT DEVELOPMENTS: For the fifty-two weeks ended 2/1/97, the Company reported net earnings of $3.9 million compared with $69.1 million a year earlier. Net revenue totaled $990.8 million, up 17.1% from $846.0 million in the same period the year before. The fiscal 1996 results included one-time charges of $92.1 million related primarily to the discontinuance of the Nature's Food Centre concept and the fitness and apparel lines. Operating earn-ings were $60.3 million compared with $137.1 million the previous year. For the 16 weeks ended 2/1/97, net earnings slipped 22.8% to $17.8 million from $23.0 million the prior year. Net revenue climbed 18.9% to $316.3 million from $266.0 million a year earlier. Same-store sales rose 2.4% versus the fourth quarter the year before, due to improve-ments in the Company's core supplement business.

BUSINESS

GENERAL NUTRITION COMPA-NIES, INC. is a nationwide specialty retailer of vitamin, mineral and sports nutrition supplements, and is also a provider of personal care, and other health-related products. As of 5/13/97, the Company operated 3,121 com-pany and franchised General Nutrition Center stores. The stores are located primarily in regional shopping malls in all 50 states, Puerto Rico and 17 foreign countries. The Company's marketing emphasis is on its high-margin, value-added vitamin, mineral and sports nutrition supplements sold under the Company's proprietary GNC®, Pro Performance®, Chal-lenge™, Preventive Nutrition™, Herbal Plus™ and Vita Worth™ brands and other nationally recog-nized third-party brand names.

ANNUAL EARNINGS AND DIVIDENDS PER SHARE

	2/3/96	2/4/95	2/5/94	2/6/93	2/1/92	2/2/91
Earnings Per Share	0.81	②0.57	②0.39	②d0.01	④d0.38	④d1.02
Dividends Per Share	①...	Nil	③...	Nil	Nil	Nil

① 2-for-1 stk. split, 10/17/95   ② Before extraord. item   ③ 2-for-1 stk. split, 10/5/93   ④ Before disc. oper. & extraord. item

ANNUAL FINANCIAL DATA

RECORD OF EARNINGS (IN THOUSANDS):

Total Revenues	845,952	672,945	546,253	453,527	393,568	346,818
Costs and Expenses	700,317	567,241	463,719	402,667	353,519	317,376
Depreciation & Amort	32,196	24,850	20,171	19,795	18,488	18,583
Operating Income	137,116	95,750	75,766	43,392	33,265	23,079
Inc Fr Cont Opers Bef Income Taxes	117,040	78,081	52,439	10,355	d2,505	d19,799
Income Taxes	47,894	32,337	22,851	5,595	4,212	cr4,137
Net Income	69,146	①45,744	②29,588	③4,760	④d6,717	⑤d15,662
Aver. Shs. Outstg.	90,257	79,774	77,132	49,288	48,228	26,104

① Before extra. item dr$8,550,000. ② Before extra. item dr$6,119,000. ③ Before extra. item dr$2,576,000. ④ Before disc. op. cr$170,536,000; and extra. item cr$182,000. ⑤ Before disc. op. dr$142,448,000; and extra. item cr$6,375,000.

BALANCE SHEET (IN THOUSANDS):

Cash and Cash Equivalents	961	1,095	1,144	48,325	4,015	...
Receivables, Net	47,939	43,227	5,719	...	260	...
Inventories	147,723	140,960	94,917	69,493	58,995	...
Gross Property	206,724	160,545	113,434	90,854	76,360	...
Accumulated Depreciation	60,755	47,325	39,384	30,695	23,241	...
Long-Term Debt	193,834	293,178	211,437	267,328	288,542	...
Capital Lease Obligations	3,172	5,301	...	...	...	...
Net Stockholders' Equity	326,657	202,837	160,231	79,333	41,533	...
Total Assets	683,812	626,571	466,726	465,669	398,351	...
Total Current Assets	210,322	197,486	135,246	139,051	80,638	...
Total Current Liabilities	157,641	123,212	92,735	119,008	68,276	...
Net Working Capital	52,681	74,274	42,511	20,043	12,362	...
Year End Shares Outstg	87,744	79,084	75,836	68,770	48,232	48,144

STATISTICAL RECORD:

Operating Profit Margin %	16.2	14.5	13.9	9.6	8.5	6.7
Return on Equity %	21.2	22.6	18.5	6.0	...	...
Return on Assets %	10.1	7.3	6.3	1.0	...	...
P/E Ratio	32.7-13.9	28.5-13.6	39.1-12.5	...	...	...
Price Range	26½-11¼	16¼-7¾	15¼-4⅞	...	...	...

Statistics are as originally reported.

OFFICERS:
J.D. Horn, Chmn.
W.E. Watts, Pres. & C.E.O.
E.J. Kozlowski, Exec. V.P. & C.F.O.
J.M. Sander, V.P.-Law, Chief Legal Off. & Sec.

INCORPORATED: DE, Jun., 1989

PRINCIPAL OFFICE: 300 6th Ave., Pittsburgh, PA 15222

TELEPHONE NUMBER: (412) 288-4600

NO. OF EMPLOYEES: 9,610 (approx.)

ANNUAL MEETING: In June

SHAREHOLDERS: 312 (approx.)

INSTITUTIONAL HOLDINGS:
No. of Institutions: 133
Shares Held: 68,089,724

REGISTRAR(S): Fleet National Bank, Providence, RI

TRANSFER AGENT(S): Fleet National Bank, Providence, RI

GENZYME CORP.

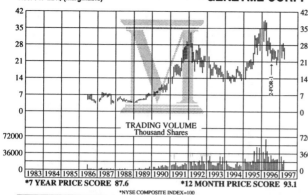

*7 YEAR PRICE SCORE 87.6   *12 MONTH PRICE SCORE 93.1
*NYSE COMPOSITE INDEX=100

TRADING VOLUME
Thousand Shares

INTERIM EARNINGS (Per Share):

Qtr.	Mar.	June	Sept.	Dec.
1993	0.21	0.22	0.26	d0.87
1994	0.19	0.19	0.19	0.05
1995	0.22	0.23	0.27	0.04
1996	0.27	0.28	d0.09	0.91
1997	0.27	...	...	...

INTERIM DIVIDENDS (Per Share):

Amt.	Decl.	Ex.	Rec.	Pay.
2-for-1	6/7/96	7/26/96	7/11/96	7/25/96

CAPITALIZATION (12/31/96):

	($000)	(%)
Long-Term Debt	241,359	21.1
Cap. Lease Oblig.	639	0.1
Common & Surplus	902,309	78.8
Total	1,144,307	100.0

RECENT DEVELOPMENTS: For the three months ended 3/31/97, net income advanced 11.6% to $21.2 million, or $0.27 per share, from $19.0 million, or $0.27 per share, a year earlier. Total revenues climbed 29.4% to $144.6 million from $111.8 million the year before. The increase in revenues was partially attributed to the addition of sales from Deknatel Snowden Pencer Inc. (DSP), which was acquired in July 1996. Sales of the Company's Ceredase® and Cerezyme® enzymes, that are used in the treatment of Gaucher disease, jumped 30% to a record $76.4 million versus the first quarter in 1996. Revenue from research and development contracts dropped 72.1% to $1.7 million from $6.1 million, stemming from the cessation of funding from Neozyme II Corp. Gross profit rose 35.7% to $87.1 million from $64.2 million the previous year. Operating income totaled $27.4 million, up 21.3% compared with $22.6 million the prior year.

BUSINESS

GENZYME CORPORATION is a diversified, integrated human health care products company operating in five major business areas. The Company's business activities in the areas of therapeutics, diagnostic services, diagnostic products, and pharmaceuticals are organized as the Genzyme General Division. The Company's activities to develop, manufacture and market products for the treatment and prevention of serious tissue damage are conducted through the Genzyme Tissue Repair Division. On 12/16/94, the Company redesignated its common stock into two classes, General Division common stock (GENZ) and Tissue Repair Division common stock (GENZL).

ANNUAL EARNINGS AND DIVIDENDS PER SHARE

	1996	1995	1994	1993	1992	1991	1990
Earnings Per Share ☐	d0.45	0.73	0.61	d0.13	③ d0.69	③ 0.25	d0.85
Dividends Per Share	②...	Nil	Nil	Nil	Nil	Nil	Nil

☐ All earnings per share figures are for the General Division. ② 2-for-1 stk. split, 7/25/96
③ Before extraord. item

ANNUAL FINANCIAL DATA

RECORD OF EARNINGS (IN MILLIONS):

	1996	1995	1994	1993	1992	1991	1990
Total Revenues	518.8	383.8	311.1	270.4	219.1	121.7	54.8
Costs and Expenses	555.0	320.7	258.7	285.0	236.1	96.6	75.5
Depreciation & Amort	30.2	22.6	18.2	16.8	11.0	6.8	5.0
Operating Profit	d75.3	35.8	34.1	d31.5	d28.1	45.5	13.7
Inc Fr Cont Opers Bef Income Taxes	d69.6	43.3	30.8	d12.6	d11.5	22.9	d27.2
Income Taxes	3.2	21.6	14.5	cr6.5	18.8	11.7	...
Net Income	d72.8	21.7	16.3	d6.1	☐ d30.3	② 11.2	d27.2
Aver. Shs. Outstg. (000)	80,814	69,844	59,494	58,990	44,740	45,176	31,888

☐ Before extra. item cr$471,000. ② Before extra. item cr$8,387,000.

BALANCE SHEET (IN MILLIONS):

	1996	1995	1994	1993	1992	1991	1990
Cash and Cash Equivalents	149.7	256.7	76.6	57.5	116.4	107.2	42.9
Receivables, Net	134.3	96.7	82.2	67.1	58.3	31.8	11.3
Inventories	125.3	53.0	36.8	23.2	20.3	16.3	13.0
Gross Property	482.7	393.9	343.6	230.9	112.5	48.5	40.6
Accumulated Depreciation	88.8	64.5	46.8	34.7	24.6	16.4	11.2
Long-Term Debt	241.4	124.3	126.4	144.7	104.9	100.0	0.3
Capital Lease Obligations	0.6	0.1	0.3	...	0.5	1.0	1.7
Net Stockholders' Equity	902.3	705.2	419.0	334.1	322.6	259.9	96.2
Total Assets	1,270.5	905.2	658.4	542.1	480.7	390.5	118.1
Total Current Assets	509.6	418.9	206.7	156.4	202.9	159.0	68.9
Total Current Liabilities	114.0	66.5	102.9	56.8	36.6	23.3	10.4
Net Working Capital	395.6	352.4	103.9	99.6	166.3	135.7	58.5
Year End Shs Outstg (000)	88,593	74,432	70,242	48,484	47,560	41,420	32,290

STATISTICAL RECORD:

	1996	1995	1994	1993	1992	1991	1990
Operating Profit Margin %	...	9.3	11.0	...	...	15.0	...
Book Value Per Share	7.39	9.07	5.55	6.28	5.77	5.95	2.81
Return on Equity %	...	3.1	3.9	...	...	4.3	...
Return on Assets %	...	2.4	2.5	...	...	2.9	...
P/E Ratio	...						
Price Range	38½-19¾	35-13⅝	19⅛-12	23⅛-12⅝	33¼-16¼	29⅜-11¾	14⅜-6¼

Statistics are as originally reported.

OFFICERS:
H.A. Termeer, Chmn., Pres. & C.E.O.
D.J. McLachlan, Exec. V.P.-Fin. & C.F.O.

INCORPORATED: DE, Jun., 1981; reincorp., MA, Nov., 1991

PRINCIPAL OFFICE: One Kendall Square, Cambridge, MA 02139-1562

TELEPHONE NUMBER: (617) 252-7500
FAX: (617) 252-7600
NO. OF EMPLOYEES: 3,516
ANNUAL MEETING: In May
SHAREHOLDERS: 2,908 General Division; 3,665 Tissue Repair Division
INSTITUTIONAL HOLDINGS:
No. of Institutions: 178
Shares Held: 45,235,614

REGISTRAR(S): American Stock Transfer & Trust Co., 40 Wall Street, New York, NY 10005

TRANSFER AGENT(S): American Stock Transfer & Trust Co., 40 Wall Street, New York, NY 10005

GLENAYRE TECHNOLOGIES, INC.

YIELD ...%
P/E RATIO 10.2

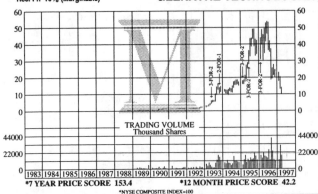

TRADING VOLUME
Thousand Shares

*7 YEAR PRICE SCORE 153.4   *12 MONTH PRICE SCORE 42.2

*NYSE COMPOSITE INDEX=100

INTERIM EARNINGS (Per Share):

Qtr.	Mar.	June	Sept.	Dec.
1993	0.11	0.13	0.15	0.08
1994	0.13	0.13	0.14	0.16
1995	0.23	0.29	0.33	0.37
1996	0.27	0.36	0.22	0.27
1997	0.22	...	...	...

INTERIM DIVIDENDS (Per Share):

Amt.	Decl.	Ex.	Rec.	Pay.

Last dist. 3-for-2 split, 12/29/95

CAPITALIZATION (12/31/96):

	($000)	(%)
Common & Surplus	455,861	100.0
Total	455,861	100.0

RECENT DEVELOPMENTS: For the three months ended 3/31/97, net income was $13.4 million, down 21.3% compared with $17.1 million the year before. Net sales climbed 18.3% to $105.8 million from $89.4 million a year earlier. Sales from the Company's Wireless Messaging group rose 3.7% to $83.5 million from $80.5 million the previous year. Sales from the Integrated Network group totaled $13.5 million, up sharply versus $3.8 million a year ago, while Wire-less Interconnect sales jumped 71.8% to $8.8 million from $5.1 million in 1996. Income from operations slipped 16.1% to $18.6 million from $22.1 million the prior year. Financial performance was hampered by lower margins stemming from a greater mix of international turn-key projects, a higher effective tax rate, and increased costs for research and development, selling, depreciation and amortization.

BUSINESS

GLENAYRE TECHNOLOGIES INC. is a worldwide supplier of telecommunications equipment and related software used in the wireless personal communications service markets. The Company designs, manufactures, markets and services switches, transmitters, controls and software used in personal communications systems, including wireless messaging, voice processing, mobile data systems and point-to-point wireless interconnection products.

ANNUAL EARNINGS AND DIVIDENDS PER SHARE

	1996	1995	1994	1993	1992	1991	1990
Earnings Per Share	1.11	1.22	②0.56	③0.48	③0.03	②0.03	③d0.03
Dividends Per Share	Nil	①...	Nil	④...	Nil	Nil	⑤...

① 50% stk. div., 1/5/95; 3-for-2 stk. split, 6/19/95 & 12/29/95 ② Before disc. oper. ③ Before disc. oper. & extraord. item ④ 3-for-2 stk. split, 5/14/93 & 2-for-1 stk. split, 11/29/93 ⑤ 1-for-200 reverse stk. split & 100-for-1 stk. split, 6/6/90

ANNUAL FINANCIAL DATA

RECORD OF EARNINGS (IN THOUSANDS):

Total Revenues	390,246	321,404	172,107	136,139	15,586	72,316	19,146
Costs and Expenses	289,879	219,320	129,978	104,042	14,635	67,942	15,579
Depreciation & Amort	13,482	8,571	5,884	5,059	725	1,228	507
Operating Income	86,885	93,513	36,245	27,038	226	1,605	d1,007
Inc Fr Cont Opers Bef Income Taxes	96,651	101,745	40,295	24,161	960	1,597	d505
Income Taxes	26,207	25,297	7,200	461	95	263	cr233
Net Income	70,444	76,448	①33,095	②23,700	③865	④523	⑤d967
Aver. Shs. Outstg.	60,597	62,479	58,703	49,401	37,511	36,786	37,853

① Before disc. op. cr$388,000. ② Before disc. op. cr$100,000; and extra. item dr$1,695,000. ③ Before disc. op. dr$7,990,000. ④ Before disc. op. dr$19,000. ⑤ Before disc. op. dr$3,000; and extra. item cr$1,064,000.

BALANCE SHEET (IN THOUSANDS):

Cash and Cash Equivalents	131,801	114,654	91,505	66,099	5,681	47,564	44,007
Receivables, Net	149,378	104,793	49,041	30,833	28,293	11,456	5,043
Inventories	50,460	50,045	24,261	19,053	19,667	...	...
Gross Property	100,917	58,726	23,595	15,715	29,440	①7,753	①7,325
Accumulated Depreciation	20,416	10,806	5,888	3,167	10,364	...	...
Long-Term Debt	...	...	...	2,007	60,671	1,751	7,005
Net Stockholders' Equity	455,861	390,694	245,435	198,708	64,022	59,964	59,328
Total Assets	521,210	447,580	284,961	228,244	174,964	80,650	81,531
Total Current Assets	339,596	276,681	170,333	120,762	57,041	59,020	49,050
Total Current Liabilities	60,565	53,194	35,124	27,264	40,537	12,755	9,828
Net Working Capital	279,031	223,487	135,209	93,498	16,504	46,265	39,222
Year End Shares Outstg	59,868	60,045	55,992	53,792	42,222	36,728	36,728

① Net

STATISTICAL RECORD:

Operating Profit Margin %	22.3	29.1	21.1	19.9	1.5	2.2	...
Book Value Per Share	6.33	5.17	3.29	2.50	1.52	1.63	1.62
Return on Equity %	15.5	19.6	13.5	11.9	1.4	0.9	...
Return on Assets %	13.5	17.1	11.6	10.4	0.5	0.6	...
P/E Ratio	48.4-16.8	40.3-13.1	33.5-17.2	34.1-4.4	N.M.	N.M.	...
Price Range	53¾-18⅝	49⅛-16	18¾-9⅝	16⅜-2⅛	2½-1⅛	1½-1⅛	1⅜-⅜

Statistics are as originally reported.

OFFICERS:
R.D. Ardizzone, Chmn.
G.B. Smith, Pres. & C.E.O.
S. Ciepcielinski, Exec. V.P.-Fin. & Admin., C.F.O. & Treas.

INCORPORATED: DE, Sep., 1987

PRINCIPAL OFFICE: 5935 Carnegie Boulevard, Charlotte, NC 28209

TELEPHONE NUMBER: (704) 553-0038

NO. OF EMPLOYEES: 2,150

ANNUAL MEETING: In May

SHAREHOLDERS: 1,800 (approx.)

INSTITUTIONAL HOLDINGS:
No. of Institutions: 108
Shares Held: 40,717,517

REGISTRAR(S): American Stock Transfer & Trust Co., New York, NY

TRANSFER AGENT(S): American Stock Transfer & Trust Co., New York, NY

HBO & CO.

YIELD 0.1%
P/E RATIO 58.2

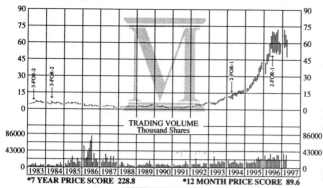

INTERIM EARNINGS (Per Share):

Qtr.	Mar.	June	Sept.	Dec.
1994	0.09	0.10	0.12	0.13
1995	0.15	d0.97	0.11	0.39
1996	0.24	0.27	0.14	0.13
1997	0.38	...	...	...

INTERIM DIVIDENDS (Per Share):

Amt.	Decl.	Ex.	Rec.	Pay.
100%	5/14/96	6/11/96	5/27/96	6/10/96
0.02Q	5/14	6/26	6/28	7/19
0.02Q	8/13	9/26	9/30	10/22
0.02Q	11/12	12/27	12/31	1/20/97
0.02Q	2/11/97	3/26/97	3/31/97	4/22

Indicated div.: $0.08

CAPITALIZATION (12/31/96):

	($000)	(%)
Long-Term Debt	192	0.0
Common & Surplus	525,343	100.0
Total	525,535	100.0

RECENT DEVELOPMENTS: On 6/13/97, the Company completed the acquisition of Amisys Managed Care Systems, Inc., a provider of managed care software for the commercial HMO market. On 6/26/97, HBOC acquired Enterprise Systems, Inc., a developer of material and resource management software for the healthcare market. For the three months ended 3/31/97, net income advanced 63.4% to $35.7 million from $21.9 million the previous year. Total revenue climbed 27.5% to $219.9 million from $172.5 million a year earlier. Software revenue surged 54.5% to $67.9 million, hardware revenue rose 28.6% to $30.4 million, and services revenue grew 15.9% to $121.6 million from the year before. Operating income soared 65.1% to $57.8 million from $35.0 million the prior year. Results benefited from a shift by healthcare organizations to a single vendor solution for information management solutions.

BUSINESS

HBO & COMPANY is a healthcare information service company that provides a variety of computer-based information systems and services to hospitals, multi-hospital groups and hospital affiliates. The Company designs, sells and services information systems and software packages for a variety of applications within healthcare organizations and also sells, installs and services Local Area Networks (LANs), Metropolitan Area Networks (MANs) and Wide Area Network (WANs). In addition, the Company provides information system (IS) management services under contract management agreements whereby it staffs, manages and operates healthcare IS facilities.

ANNUAL EARNINGS AND DIVIDENDS PER SHARE

	1996	1995	1994	1993	1992	1991	1990
Earnings Per Share	0.79	d0.34	0.43	0.30	0.22	③ d0.06	0.13
Dividends Per Share	① 0.08	0.08	② 0.079	0.075	0.075	0.075	0.075
Dividend Payout %	10.1	...	18.4	25.0	34.1	...	57.7

① 100% stk. div., 6/10/96 ② 2-for-1 stk. split, 3/28/94 ③ Before disc. oper.

ANNUAL FINANCIAL DATA

RECORD OF EARNINGS (IN THOUSANDS):

Total Revenues	796,578	495,595	327,201	237,129	202,221	170,725	201,490
Costs and Expenses	629,149	506,101	261,685	196,676	173,543	164,052	174,065
Depreciation & Amort	49,179	30,253	17,496	9,261	8,297	9,763	15,053
Operating Income	118,250	d40,759	48,020	31,192	20,381	d3,090	12,372
Inc Fr Cont Opers Bef Income Taxes	122,352	d42,058	46,989	30,533	19,875	d4,325	10,666
Income Taxes	48,398	cr16,823	18,830	12,186	6,758	cr1,470	3,526
Net Income	① 73,954	① d25,235	28,159	18,347	13,117	③ d2,855	① 7,140
Aver. Shs. Outstg.	93,055	75,644	65,946	61,956	61,012	55,328	57,480

① Incl. non-recurring merger-related charges of: 1996, $61,414,000 ($0.40 per sh.); 1995, $136,481,000 ($1.77 per sh.); 1991, $10,883,000 ($0.13 per sh.); 1990, 731,000 ($0.03 per sh.). ② Before disc. op. dr$544,000.

BALANCE SHEET (IN THOUSANDS):

Cash and Cash Equivalents	183,613	65,263	5,825	23,158	7,569	2,711	2,323
Receivables, Net	316,371	174,004	106,590	45,430	56,759	58,320	61,310
Inventories	6,993	6,757	1,280	1,335	2,648	6,719	3,878
Gross Property	153,663	104,872	87,764	73,785	75,799	79,904	102,721
Accumulated Depreciation	104,244	71,263	61,166	55,348	60,917	62,785	69,685
Long-Term Debt	192	582	...	...	...	20,010	37,457
Net Stockholders' Equity	525,343	318,730	91,475	50,023	40,791	22,600	26,703
Total Assets	848,947	535,134	233,877	119,084	102,800	103,201	132,979
Total Current Assets	519,763	252,370	122,663	73,227	69,243	70,719	70,174
Total Current Liabilities	316,358	205,120	131,382	59,586	54,617	53,214	50,992
Net Working Capital	203,405	47,250	d8,719	13,641	14,626	17,505	19,182
Year End Shares Outstg	90,601	80,238	63,546	59,048	60,228	56,444	54,604

STATISTICAL RECORD:

Operating Profit Margin %	14.8	...	14.7	13.2	10.1	...	6.1
Book Value Per Share	3.19	1.68	0.53	0.85	0.68	0.40	0.49
Return on Equity %	14.1	...	30.8	36.7	32.2	...	26.7
Return on Assets %	8.7	...	12.0	15.4	12.8	...	5.8
Average Yield %	0.2	0.3	0.6	1.0	1.7	3.6	3.2
P/E Ratio	91.8-41.5	...	42.7-21.8	38.8-14.2	29.5-10.8	...	28.8-7.7
Price Range	72½-32¾	43¼-16½	18⅜-9⅜	11⅝-4¼	6½-2⅜	3-1¼	3¾-1

Statistics are not restated for acquisitions.

OFFICERS:
H.T. Green, Jr., Chmn.
C.W. McCall, Pres. & C.E.O.
J.P. Gilbertson, Exec. V.P.-Fin., C.F.O., Treas. & Sec.

INCORPORATED: DE, Nov., 1974

PRINCIPAL OFFICE: 301 Perimeter Center North, Atlanta, GA 30346

TELEPHONE NUMBER: (770) 393-6000

FAX: (770) 393-6092

NO. OF EMPLOYEES: 4,404

ANNUAL MEETING: In May

SHAREHOLDERS: 2,528

INSTITUTIONAL HOLDINGS:
No. of Institutions: 214
Shares Held: 79,428,130

REGISTRAR(S): SunTrust Bank, Atlanta, GA

TRANSFER AGENT(S): SunTrust Bank, Atlanta, GA

NASDAQ SYMBOL HCCC
Rec. Pr. 44 (Marginable)

HEALTHCARE COMPARE CORP.

YIELD ...%
P/E RATIO 19.0

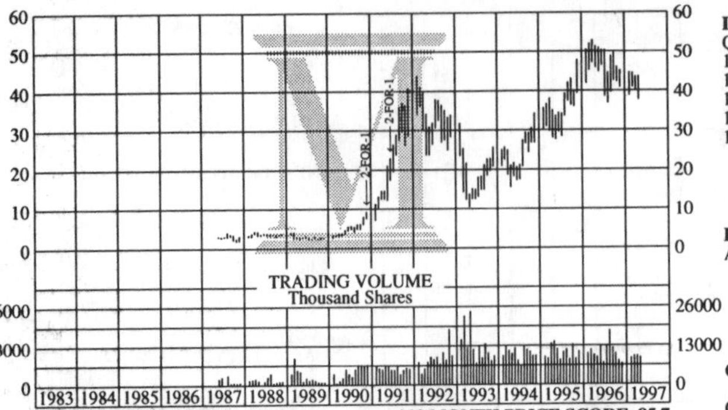

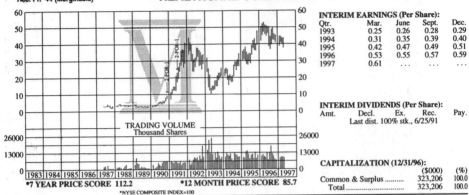

*7 YEAR PRICE SCORE 112.2 *12 MONTH PRICE SCORE 85.7

*NYSE COMPOSITE INDEX=100

INTERIM EARNINGS (Per Share):

Qtr.	Mar.	June	Sept.	Dec.
1993	0.25	0.26	0.28	0.29
1994	0.31	0.35	0.39	0.40
1995	0.42	0.47	0.49	0.51
1996	0.53	0.55	0.57	0.59
1997	0.61	...	...	...

INTERIM DIVIDENDS (Per Share):

Amt.	Decl.	Ex.	Rec.	Pay.

Last dist. 100% stk., 6/25/91

CAPITALIZATION (12/31/96):

	($000)	(%)
Common & Surplus	323,206	100.0
Total	323,206	100.0

RECENT DEVELOPMENTS: For the three months ended 3/31/97, net income climbed 9.9% to $20.8 million from $19.0 million a year earlier. Earnings per share were $0.61 compared with $0.53 in the first quarter in 1996. Revenues advanced 8.2% to $64.9 million from $60.0 million the previous year. PPO services revenue rose 10.4% to $50.9 million from $46.1 million the prior year, while fee schedule services remained essentially flat at $6.3 million versus a year ago. Revenues from utilization management services slid 12.7% to $4.8 million from $5.5 million in 1996. Revenues from net premiums more than doubled to $2.9 million from $1.4 million a year earlier. However, the Company received no revenue from government contract services during the quarter compared with $770,000 the previous year. Income before income taxes totaled $33.8 million, up 9.9% from $30.8 million the prior year.

BUSINESS

HEALTHCARE COMPARE CORP. provides full-service medical cost management services to corporate employers, government employee groups, unions, third party administrators, group health and workers' compensation insurance carriers. HCCC provides utilization management (COMPARE Medical Review Programs), computer assisted bill review and pricing services (OUCH Systems) and enters into fixed-price contracts with medical providers in the form of preferred provider networks (The AFFORDABLE Medical Networks) for the exclusive use of clients.

ANNUAL EARNINGS AND DIVIDENDS PER SHARE

	1996	1995	1994	1993	1992	1991	1990
Earnings Per Share	**2.24**	**1.89**	**1.45**	**1.08**	**0.51**	**0.50**	**0.23**
Dividends Per Share	**Nil**	**Nil**	**Nil**	**Nil**	**Nil**	**[1]...**	**[2]...**

[1] 2-for-1 stk. split, 6/26/91 [2] 2-for-1 stk. split, 12/18/90

ANNUAL FINANCIAL DATA

	1996	1995	1994	1993	1992	1991	1990
RECORD OF EARNINGS (IN THOUSANDS):							
Total Revenues	247,804	214,338	186,606	157,650	133,501	70,910	42,238
Costs and Expenses	120,656	100,686	95,575	90,398	96,967	49,677	33,660
Depreciation & Amort	14,092	12,049	11,001	7,994	6,609	3,414	2,666
Operating Profit	114,814	103,110	80,030	59,258	45,925	17,819	5,912
Inc Fr Cont Opers Bef Income Taxes	128,395	111,094	85,023	63,409	32,343	20,292	8,234
Income Taxes	49,400	44,557	34,354	24,938	14,227	7,535	2,720
Net Income	78,995	66,537	50,669	38,471	18,116	12,757	5,514
Aver. Shs. Outstg.	35,244	35,123	35,002	35,480	35,386	25,357	23,946
BALANCE SHEET (IN THOUSANDS):							
Cash and Cash Equivalents	152,262	145,233	66,455	50,585	73,109	25,882	34,782
Receivables, Net	24,515	22,255	24,386	22,625	25,639	13,076	6,357
Gross Property	95,128	79,886	73,411	74,323	63,600	38,756	16,199
Accumulated Depreciation	48,472	36,472	28,111	26,431	18,622	10,111	6,706
Net Stockholders' Equity	323,206	280,270	199,557	170,776	130,305	61,422	43,112
Total Assets	353,338	297,194	215,009	187,491	146,093	69,346	52,128
Total Current Assets	188,471	173,922	93,794	75,846	100,069	40,001	41,565
Total Current Liabilities	28,135	16,798	15,350	16,678	15,630	7,758	7,387
Net Working Capital	160,336	157,124	78,444	59,168	84,439	32,243	34,178
Year End Shares Outstg	33,697	34,635	35,942	35,033	34,959	23,789	23,156
STATISTICAL RECORD:							
Operating Profit Margin %	46.3	48.1	42.9	37.6	22.4	25.1	14.0
Book Value Per Share	9.59	8.09	5.55	4.87	3.73	2.58	1.86
Return on Equity %	24.4	23.7	25.4	22.5	13.9	20.8	12.8
Return on Assets %	22.4	22.4	23.6	20.5	12.4	18.4	10.6
P/E Ratio	23.7-16.4	25.3-14.6	23.7-10.7	29.5-9.7	86.3-46.6	81.5-14.3	40.8-11.4
Price Range	53-36¾	47⅞-27⅝	34⅜-15½	31⅞-10½	44-23¾	40¾-7⅛	9⅜-2⅝

Statistics are as originally reported.

OFFICERS:
T.J. Pritzker, Chmn.
J.C. Smith, Pres. & C.E.O.
J.E. Whitters, V.P.-Fin. & C.F.O.
S.T. Smith, Esq., Gen. Coun.

INCORPORATED: DE, 1982

PRINCIPAL OFFICE: 3200 Highland Ave., Downers Grove, IL 60515-1223

TELEPHONE NUMBER: (630) 241-7900

NO. OF EMPLOYEES: 1,500 (approx.)

ANNUAL MEETING: In May

SHAREHOLDERS: 1,117

INSTITUTIONAL HOLDINGS:
No. of Institutions: 138
Shares Held: 22,999,285

REGISTRAR(S): LaSalle National Bank, Chicago, IL

TRANSFER AGENT(S): LaSalle National Bank, Chicago, IL

NASDAQ SYMBOL IDXX
Rec. Pr. $12\frac{1}{4}$ (Marginable)

IDEXX LABORATORIES, INC.

YIELD ...%
P/E RATIO 14.8

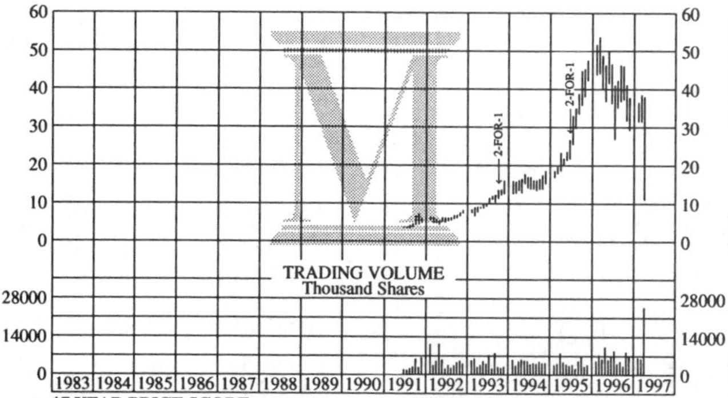

*7 YEAR PRICE SCORE ... *12 MONTH PRICE SCORE 72.0

*NYSE COMPOSITE INDEX=100

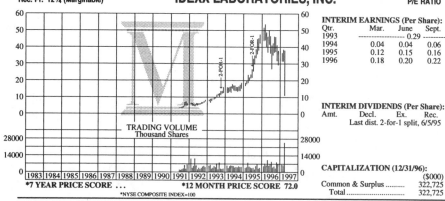

INTERIM EARNINGS (Per Share):

Qtr.	Mar.	June	Sept.	Dec.
1993	----------	0.29	----------	
1994	0.04	0.04	0.06	0.27
1995	0.12	0.15	0.16	0.18
1996	0.18	0.20	0.22	0.23

INTERIM DIVIDENDS (Per Share):

Amt.	Decl.	Ex.	Rec.	Pay.

Last dist. 2-for-1 split, 6/5/95

CAPITALIZATION (12/31/96):

	($000)	(%)
Common & Surplus	322,725	100.0
Total	322,725	100.0

RECENT DEVELOPMENTS: On 2/14/97, IDXX announced that it had entered into an agreement to acquire Advanced Veterinary Systems, a supplier of veterinary practice management computer systems. For the twelve months ended 12/31/96, net income jumped 51.9% to $32.6 million from $21.5 million in the corresponding period the previous year. Revenue totaled $267.7 million, up 41.9% compared with $188.6 million a year earlier. Higher revenues were attributed to increased sales of veterinary clinical chemistry consumables, veterinary laboratory services stemming from acquisitions of veterinary reference laboratories, canine test products, and a quantitative thyroid instrument introduced in the first quarter of 1996. Income from operations surged 42.5% to $47.0 million from $33.0 million the prior year. For the three months ended 12/31/96, net income advanced 29.6% to $9.2 million from $7.1 million in the same quarter the previous year. Revenue was $74.6 million, up 37.6% versus $54.2 million a year earlier.

BUSINESS

IDEXX LABORATORIES, INC. produces diagnostic tests for diseases in animal food (salmonella and Johne's disease), pets (feline leukemia), and other agricultural and environmental contaminants (E. coli and aflatoxin). The Company's products use biotech processes such as DNA testing and immunoassay testing. IDXX, which sells more than 400 products to customers in more than 50 countries, also owns AMIS International, a supplier of testing services to Japanese veterinarians.

ANNUAL EARNINGS AND DIVIDENDS PER SHARE

	1996	1995	1994	1993	1992	1991	1990
Earnings Per Share	**0.83**	**0.61**	**0.40**	**0.29**	**0.18**	**0.16**	**d0.30**
Dividends Per Share	**Nil**	**1 ...**	**Nil**	**2 ...**	**Nil**	**Nil**	**Nil**

1 2-for-1 stk. split, 6/5/95 2 2-for-1 stk. split, 10/9/93

ANNUAL FINANCIAL DATA

	1996	1995	1994	1993	1992	1991	1990
RECORD OF EARNINGS (IN THOUSANDS):							
Total Revenues	267,677	188,602	126,363	93,062	57,653	30,454	24,510
Costs and Expenses	210,296	149,892	99,140	75,364	51,699	26,822	28,384
Depreciation & Amort	10,390	5,742	4,518	3,783	896	1,025	896
Operating Income	46,991	32,968	22,705	13,915	5,058	2,606	d4,770
Inc Fr Cont Opers Bef Income Taxes	55,323	37,036	22,834	15,042	6,100	3,452	d4,077
Income Taxes	22,682	15,542	9,498	5,388	1,177	300	...
Net Income	32,640	21,494	13,336	9,654	4,923	3,152	d4,077
Aver. Shs. Outstg.	39,519	35,362	33,525	33,118	27,906	20,108	13,879
BALANCE SHEET (IN THOUSANDS):							
Cash and Cash Equivalents	173,637	183,662	50,413	39,400	31,182	14,770	7,860
Receivables, Net	66,633	47,321	25,754	21,389	11,907	5,102	4,375
Inventories	48,402	28,192	20,789	14,619	12,794	5,125	3,441
Gross Property	59,257	40,339	24,480	20,038	17,534	14,851	5,678
Accumulated Depreciation	22,863	14,844	11,082	8,085	5,835	3,877	3,453
Net Stockholders' Equity	322,725	279,125	99,786	83,631	70,372	31,466	14,188
Total Assets	373,852	312,540	121,741	97,967	79,745	38,089	18,744
Total Current Assets	301,717	261,980	98,531	76,818	57,422	26,395	16,084
Total Current Liabilities	51,127	33,415	21,955	14,336	9,367	6,613	4,548
Net Working Capital	250,590	228,565	76,575	62,483	48,055	19,783	11,536
Year End Shares Outstg	37,774	36,549	31,543	31,102	27,640	20,452	635
STATISTICAL RECORD:							
Operating Profit Margin %	17.6	17.5	18.0	15.0	8.8	8.6	...
Book Value Per Share	8.54	7.64	3.16	2.40	2.17	1.51	...
Return on Equity %	10.1	7.7	13.4	11.5	7.0	10.0	...
Return on Assets %	8.7	6.9	11.0	9.9	6.2	8.3	...
P/E Ratio	64.8-32.4	77.9-27.7	46.6-31.6	55.2-22.8	45.8-25.0	45.3-21.1	...
Price Range	$53\frac{3}{4}$-$26\frac{7}{8}$	$47\frac{1}{2}$-$16\frac{7}{8}$	$18\frac{5}{8}$-$12\frac{5}{8}$	16-$6\frac{5}{8}$	$8\frac{1}{4}$-$4\frac{1}{2}$	$7\frac{1}{4}$-$3\frac{3}{8}$	...

Statistics are as originally reported.

OFFICERS:
D.E. Shaw, Chmn. & C.E.O.
E.F. Workman, Jr. Ph.D, Pres. & C.O.O.
R.K. Carlton, Sr. V.P.-Fin. & Admin. & C.F.O.
M. Raines, V.P.-Fin. & Treas.

INCORPORATED: DE, 1983

PRINCIPAL OFFICE: One Idexx Drive, Westbrook, ME 04092

TELEPHONE NUMBER: (207) 856-0300

FAX: (207) 856-0346

NO. OF EMPLOYEES: 1,515

ANNUAL MEETING: In May

SHAREHOLDERS: 1,333

INSTITUTIONAL HOLDINGS:
No. of Institutions: 120
Shares Held: 32,012,183

REGISTRAR(S): Bank of Boston, Boston, MA

TRANSFER AGENT(S): Bank of Boston, Boston, MA

NASDAQ SYMBOL IFMX
Rec. Pr. 7⅞ (Marginable)

INFORMIX CORP.

YIELD ...%
P/E RATIO ...

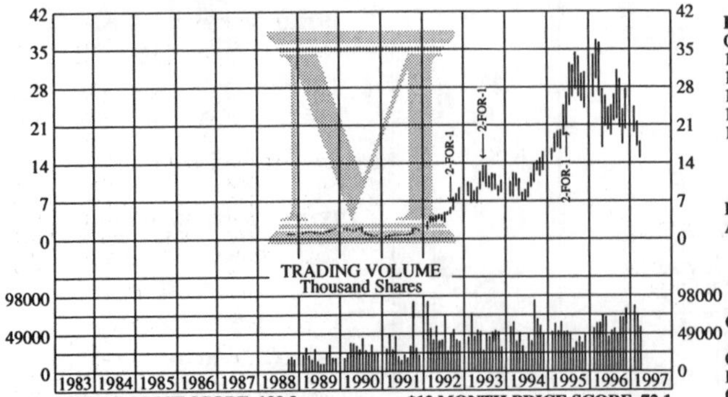

42
35
28
21
14
7
0
2-FOR-1
2-FOR-1
2-FOR-1
TRADING VOLUME
Thousand Shares
98000
49000
0
1983 1984 1985 1986 1987 1988 1989 1990 1991 1992 1993 1994 1995 1996 1997

*7 YEAR PRICE SCORE 133.3 *12 MONTH PRICE SCORE 72.1

*NYSE COMPOSITE INDEX=100

INTERIM EARNINGS (Per Share):

Qtr.	Mar.	June	Sept.	Dec.
1993	0.09	0.09	0.11	0.13
1994	0.10	0.10	0.12	0.18
1995	0.14	0.16	0.18	0.28
1996	0.10	0.14	0.17	0.22
1997	d0.93	...	...	...

INTERIM DIVIDENDS (Per Share):

Amt.	Decl.	Ex.	Rec.	Pay.

Last dist. 2-for-1 split, 6/23/95

CAPITALIZATION (12/31/96):

	($000)	(%)
Cap. Lease Oblig.	1,462	0.2
Deferred Income Tax	31,203	5.2
Common & Surplus	570,714	94.6
Total	603,379	100.0

RECENT DEVELOPMENTS: For the quarter ended 3/30/97, the Company reported a loss of $140.1 million, or $0.93 per share, compared with net income of $15.9 million, or $0.10 per share, the previous year. Net revenues fell 34.5% to $133.7 million from $204.0 million a year earlier. Results for 1997 included a one-time charges of $30.5 million related to the write-off of goodwill and other long-term assets and $7.0 million from the acquisition of Centerview Software. Results for 1996 included nonrecurring merger expenses of $5.9 million. Revenues from licenses dropped 52.6% to $71.7 million from $151.2 million the year before, while revenues from services totaled $62.0 million, up 17.3% versus $52.8 million the prior year. The Company attributed the lower revenues to weakness in all geographic regions, especially in Europe, coupled with the failure to close several large transactions before the end of the quarter. Operating loss was $164.4 million compared with operating income of $23.3 million a year ago.

BUSINESS

INFORMIX CORP. develops and markets high performance relational database management and office automation software. The Advanced Products Division's popular relational database management system (RDBMS) and fourth-generation language (4GL) application development products are available for the UNIX, DOS, OS/2, VMS, and MVS operating systems. The Workstation Products Division develops and markets high performance office productivity software. Products include the SmartWare system which combines word processing, database management, spreadsheet, business graphics, and communications modules for DOS, UNIX, and XENIX operating environments, and Wings, a recently introduced graphic spreadsheet for Apple Macintosh computers.

ANNUAL EARNINGS AND DIVIDENDS PER SHARE

	1996	1995	1994	1993	1992	1991	1990
Earnings Per Share	0.63	0.76	0.49	0.42	0.38	[4] 0.11	[5] d0.23
Dividends Per Share	Nil	[1]...	Nil	[2]...	[3]...	Nil	Nil

[1] 2-for-1 stk. split, 6/23/95 [2] 2-for-1 stk. split, 6/14/93 [3] 2-for-1 stk. split, 9/16/92 [4] Before extraord. item [5] Before acctg. chg.

ANNUAL FINANCIAL DATA

	1996	1995	1994	1993	1992	1991	1990
RECORD OF EARNINGS (IN THOUSANDS):							
Total Revenues	939,311	708,985	468,697	352,915	283,594	179,811	146,107
Costs and Expenses	754,760	520,701	349,930	256,112	196,019	146,509	153,640
Depreciation & Amort	47,207	29,031	16,206	11,414	15,593	16,499	12,809
Operating Income	137,344	159,253	102,561	85,389	71,982	16,803	d20,342
Inc Fr Cont Opers Bef Income Taxes	148,209	166,140	103,430	87,679	61,712	13,859	d22,663
Income Taxes	50,391	60,807	37,234	31,564	13,930	1,670	460
Net Income	97,818	105,333	66,196	56,115	47,782	[1] 12,189	d46,410
Aver. Shs. Outstg.	155,573	138,896	134,610	135,202	127,324	114,696	101,696
[1] Before extra. item cr$421,000.							
BALANCE SHEET (IN THOUSANDS):							
Cash and Cash Equivalents	261,020	252,164	191,526	143,527	119,454	41,854	20,509
Receivables, Net	267,425	194,424	141,526	114,889	67,745	47,267	39,861
Inventories	...	...	...	...	2,682	3,637	4,746
Gross Property	293,318	147,163	96,309	72,378	55,641	46,864	42,067
Accumulated Depreciation	106,591	69,935	52,188	39,597	33,843	25,059	16,593
Long-Term Debt	...	...	...	...	...	22,575	23,750
Capital Lease Obligations	1,462	770	343	451	1,252	2,808	6,312
Net Stockholders' Equity	570,714	423,055	275,644	207,405	132,652	54,179	38,071
Total Assets	903,842	674,416	444,410	326,633	231,459	132,924	109,534
Total Current Assets	557,924	471,898	348,016	269,417	195,696	96,563	69,307
Total Current Liabilities	299,566	225,560	153,552	113,404	97,010	53,362	41,401
Net Working Capital	258,358	246,338	194,464	156,013	98,686	43,201	27,906
Year End Shares Outstg	150,782	135,329	130,948	129,472	125,670	112,332	107,568
STATISTICAL RECORD:							
Operating Profit Margin %	14.6	22.5	21.9	24.2	25.4	9.3	...
Book Value Per Share	3.42	2.85	1.92	1.47	0.95	0.36	0.23
Return on Equity %	17.1	24.9	24.0	27.1	36.0	22.5	...
Return on Assets %	10.8	15.6	14.9	17.2	20.6	9.2	...
P/E Ratio	58.3-26.8	45.2-19.2	32.9-14.5	32.4-16.1	25.0-4.3	18.2-3.4	...
Price Range	36¾-16⅞	34⅜-14⅝	16⅛-7⅛	13⅝-6¾	9½-1⅝	2-⅜	2¼-½

Statistics are as originally reported.

OFFICERS:
P.E. White, Chmn., Pres. & C.E.O.
D.H. Stanley, V.P., Gen. Counsel & Sec.
M.R. Brauns, V.P. & Treas.

INCORPORATED: CA, 1980; reincorp., DE, Aug., 1986

PRINCIPAL OFFICE: 4100 Bohannon Dr., Menlo Park, CA 94025

TELEPHONE NUMBER: (415) 926-6300

NO. OF EMPLOYEES: 4,491

ANNUAL MEETING: In May

SHAREHOLDERS: 3,400 (approx.)

INSTITUTIONAL HOLDINGS:
No. of Institutions: 221
Shares Held: 89,508,753

REGISTRAR(S): First National Bank of Boston, Shareholder Services Division, Boston, MA

TRANSFER AGENT(S): First National Bank of Boston, Shareholder Services Division, Boston, MA

INTEL CORP.

YIELD 0.1%
P/E RATIO 19.7

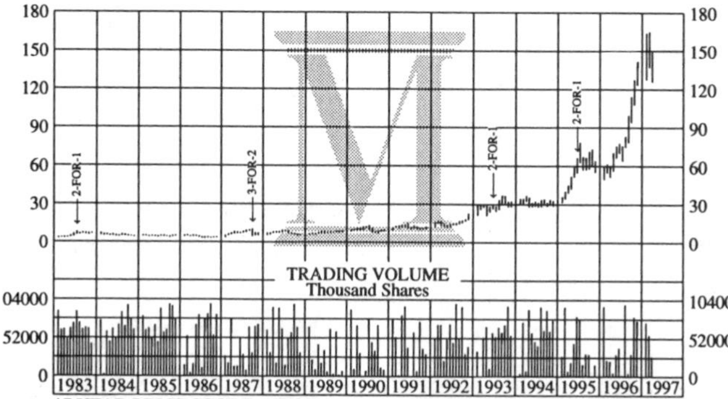

*7 YEAR PRICE SCORE 187.8   *12 MONTH PRICE SCORE 126.7
*NYSE COMPOSITE INDEX=100

TRADING VOLUME
Thousand Shares

INTERIM EARNINGS (Per Share):

Qtr.	Mar.	June	Sept.	Dec.
1993	0.31	0.33	0.34	0.34
1994	0.35	0.37	0.38	0.22
1995	0.51	0.50	0.53	0.49
1996	0.51	0.59	0.74	1.07
1997	1.10	...	...	...

INTERIM DIVIDENDS (Per Share):

Amt.	Decl.	Ex.	Rec.	Pay.
0.05Q	5/22/96	7/30/96	8/1/96	9/1/96
0.05Q	9/19	10/30	11/1	12/1
0.05Q	11/13	1/29/97	2/1/97	3/1/97
0.05Q	3/26/97	4/29	5/1	6/1
2-for-1	3/26	...	6/10	7/13

Indicated div.: $0.10

CAPITALIZATION (12/28/96):

	($000)	(%)
Long-Term Debt	728,000	3.9
Deferred Income Tax	997,000	5.4
Common & Surplus	16,872,000	90.7
Total	18,597,000	100.0

RECENT DEVELOPMENTS: For the three months ended 3/29/97, net income more than doubled to $1.98 billion from $894.0 million the previous year. Net revenues totaled $6.45 billion, up 38.3% from $4.64 billion a year earlier. Sales to the Americas slid to 40% of total revenues from 42% the prior year. Meanwhile, sales to the Asia-Pacific region jumped to 20% of total revenues from 14% a year ago. Higher revenues were driven by strong demand for

INTC's recently-introduced Pentium® processor with MMX™ media enhancement technology and the Pentium® Pro processor. As a percentage of net revenue, gross margin improved to 64% compared with 48% in the corresponding quarter the year before due to a more favorable product mix. Operating income was $2.87 billion, up sharply versus $1.31 billion in 1996. In May 1997, the Company plans to introduce the Pentium II processor.

BUSINESS

INTEL CORP. and its subsidiaries are engaged primarily in the business of designing, developing, manufacturing and marketing microcomputer components and related products at various levels of integration. Such components consist of silicon-based semiconductors etched with complex patterns of transistors. Each one of these integrated circuits can perform the functions of thousands—even millions—of individual transistors, diodes, capacitors and resistors. INTC's major products include: microprocessors, including the Pentium®, and related board-level products, chipsets, embedded processors and microcontrollers, flash memory chips, network and communications products and conferencing products.

ANNUAL EARNINGS AND DIVIDENDS PER SHARE

	12/28/96	12/30/95	12/31/94	12/25/93	12/26/92	12/28/91	12/29/90
Earnings Per Share	2.91	2.02	1.31	1.30	0.62	0.49	0.40
Dividends Per Share	0.09	①0.07	0.057	②0.05	0.013	Nil	Nil
Dividend Payout %	3.1	3.5	4.4	3.8	2.1	...	...

Note: 2-for-1 stk. split, 7/13/97 ① 2-for-1 stk. split, 6/16/95 ② 2-for-1 stk. split, 6/6/93

ANNUAL FINANCIAL DATA

RECORD OF EARNINGS (IN MILLIONS):

Total Revenues	20,847.0	16,202.0	11,521.0	8,782.0	5,844.0	4,779.0	3,921.0
Costs and Expenses	11,406.0	9,579.0	7,106.0	4,673.0	3,836.0	3,281.0	2,771.0
Depreciation & Amort	1,888.0	1,371.0	1,028.0	717.0	518.0	418.0	292.0
Operating Income	7,553.0	5,252.0	3,387.0	3,392.0	1,490.0	1,080.0	858.0
Inc Fr Cont Opers Bef Income Taxes	7,934.0	5,638.0	3,603.0	3,530.0	1,569.0	1,195.0	986.0
Income Taxes	2,777.0	2,072.0	1,315.0	1,235.0	502.0	376.0	336.0
Net Income	5,157.0	3,566.0	2,288.0	2,295.0	1,067.0	819.0	650.0
Aver. Shs. Outstg. (000)	1,776,000	1,768,000	1,748,000	1,764,000	1,716,000	1,672,000	1,624,000

BALANCE SHEET (IN MILLIONS):

Cash and Cash Equivalents	7,907.0	2,458.0	2,410.0	3,136.0	2,835.0	2,277.0	1,785.0
Receivables, Net	4,293.0	3,524.0	2,530.0	1,758.0	1,069.0	698.0	710.0
Inventories	1,293.0	2,004.0	1,169.0	838.0	535.0	422.0	415.0
Gross Property	14,262.0	11,792.0	8,516.0	6,313.0	4,648.0	3,644.0	2,814.0
Accumulated Depreciation	5,775.0	4,321.0	3,149.0	2,317.0	1,832.0	1,481.0	1,156.0
Long-Term Debt	728.0	400.0	392.0	426.0	249.0	363.0	345.0
Net Stockholders' Equity	16,872.0	12,140.0	9,267.0	7,500.0	5,445.0	4,418.0	3,592.0
Total Assets	23,735.0	17,504.0	13,816.0	11,344.0	8,089.0	6,292.0	5,376.0
Total Current Assets	13,684.0	8,097.0	6,167.0	5,802.0	4,691.0	3,604.0	3,119.0
Total Current Liabilities	4,863.0	3,619.0	3,024.0	2,433.0	1,842.0	1,228.0	1,314.0
Net Working Capital	8,821.0	4,478.0	3,143.0	3,369.0	2,849.0	2,376.0	1,805.0
Year End Shs Outstg (000)	1,642,000	1,642,000	1,654,000	1,672,000	1,676,000	1,632,000	1,596,000

STATISTICAL RECORD:

Operating Profit Margin %	36.2	32.4	29.4	38.6	25.5	22.6	21.9
Book Value Per Share	10.28	7.40	5.61	4.49	3.25	2.71	2.25
Return on Equity %	30.6	29.4	24.7	30.6	19.6	18.5	18.1
Return on Assets %	21.7	20.4	16.6	20.2	13.2	13.0	12.1
Average Yield %	0.2	0.3	0.4	0.3	0.2	...	...
P/E Ratio	24.3-8.5	19.4-7.8	14.0-10.7	14.3-8.2	18.5-9.3	15.3-9.7	16.3-8.8
Price Range	70¾-24⅞	39¼-15¾	18⅜-14	18⅝-10⅝	11½-5¾	7½-4¾	6½-3½

Statistics are as originally reported.

OFFICERS:
G.E. Moore, Chmn.
A.S. Grove, Pres. & C.E.O.
C.R. Barrett, Exec. V.P. & C.O.O.
A.D. Bryant, V.P. & C.F.O.

INCORPORATED: CA, Jul., 1968; reincorp., DE, May, 1989

PRINCIPAL OFFICE: 2200 Mission College Blvd. P.O. Box 58119, Santa Clara, CA 95052-8119

TELEPHONE NUMBER: (408) 765-8080

FAX: (408) 765-1402

NO. OF EMPLOYEES: 48,500 (approx.)

ANNUAL MEETING: In April

SHAREHOLDERS: 124,000 (approx.)

INSTITUTIONAL HOLDINGS:
No. of Institutions: 902
Shares Held: 963,104,460 (Adj.)

REGISTRAR(S): Harris Trust & Savings Bank, Chicago, IL

TRANSFER AGENT(S): Harris Trust & Savings Bank, Chicago, IL

INTUIT

YIELD ...%
P/E RATIO ...

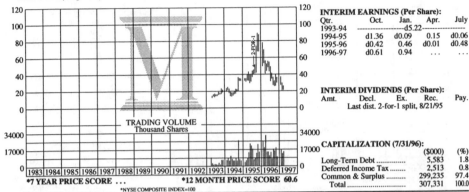

INTERIM EARNINGS (Per Share):

Qtr.	Oct.	Jan.	Apr.	July
1993-94	--------------d5.22--------------			
1994-95	d1.36	d0.09	0.15	d0.06
1995-96	d0.42	0.46	d0.01	d0.48
1996-97	d0.61	0.94	...	...

INTERIM DIVIDENDS (Per Share):

Amt.	Decl.	Ex.	Rec.	Pay.
Last dist. 2-for-1 split, 8/21/95				

TRADING VOLUME
Thousand Shares

*7 YEAR PRICE SCORE ...   *12 MONTH PRICE SCORE 60.6
*NYSE COMPOSITE INDEX=100

CAPITALIZATION (7/31/96):

	($000)	(%)
Long-Term Debt	5,583	1.8
Deferred Income Tax	2,513	0.8
Common & Surplus	299,235	97.4
Total	307,331	100.0

RECENT DEVELOPMENTS: On 3/31/97, the Company announced that its Japanese subsidiary, Intuit KK, had completed the acquisition of Japan-based Nihon Micom KK for $39.0 million. Nihon Micom, which develops and markets small business accounting software in Japan, will be merged into Intuit KK in early May, 1997. For the three months ended 1/31/96, the Company reported income from continuing operations of $44.7 million compared with income from continuing operations of $24.1 million the previous year. These results included acquisition-related charges, net of taxes, of $7.6 million and $16.8 million for the respective 1996 and 1995 periods. Net revenue totaled $266.0 million, up 21.5% versus $219.0 million a year earlier. Revenues were fueled by strong growth in the Business Products segment, boosted by the December launch of QuickBooks 5.0 and QuickBooks Pro 5.0. On 1/27/97, the Company sold Intuit Services Corp. to CheckFree Corp. for 12.6 million shares of CheckFree common stock.

BUSINESS

INTUIT INC. develops, markets and supports software products that enable households and small businesses to automate commonly performed financial tasks. The Company's products are designed to help users to organize, understand and manage their finances through the preparation of financial data for analysis and planning. Intuit's first product, Quicken®, simplifies data entry by using an easily recognizable on-screen image of a checkbook and automates transactions such as printing checks, calculating account balances, creating budgets, reconciling bank statements and preparing reports and graphs. Its second major product, QuickBooks®, is tailored to small business users unfamiliar with complex double-entry accounting methods. It has a design based on user-friendly on-screen invoices and forms rather than debit-and-credit entry. Its third major product, Turbo Tax® and MacInTax® are personal tax programs. Intuit's products are sold through retail software outlets, computer superstores, general mass merchandisers and also via direct sales to end users.

ANNUAL EARNINGS AND DIVIDENDS PER SHARE

	7/31/96	7/31/95	7/31/94	9/30/93	9/30/92	9/30/91	9/30/90
Earnings Per Share	① d0.46	d1.11	③ d5.22	0.37	0.25	0.21	0.18
Dividends Per Share	② ...	Nil	Nil	Nil	Nil	Nil	Nil

① Before disc. oper. ② 2-for-1 stk. split, 8/21/95 ③ For 10 months due to fiscal year-end change.

ANNUAL FINANCIAL DATA

RECORD OF EARNINGS (IN THOUSANDS):

Total Revenues	538,608	395,729	194,126	121,372	83,793	44,539	33,059
Costs and Expenses	504,592	421,782	351,206	104,561	74,166	37,046	26,805
Depreciation & Amort	23,853	64,011	42,884	3,580	1,773	1,112	758
Operating Income	d5,776	d66,228	d177,058	13,231	7,854	6,381	5,496
Income Bef Income Taxes	1,870	d21,122	d174,561	13,755	8,142	6,651	5,621
Income Taxes	16,225	24,241	1,752	5,344	2,866	2,353	2,062
Net Income	① d14,355	d45,363	d176,313	8,411	5,276	4,298	3,559
Aver. Shs. Outstg.	45,149	40,762	33,804	22,700	21,016	20,570	20,036

① Before disc. op. dr$6,344,000.

BALANCE SHEET (IN THOUSANDS):

Cash and Cash Equivalents	198,018	191,375	83,886	39,540	9,030	7,181	...
Receivables, Net	68,678	57,866	26,779	32,246	10,274	7,022	...
Inventories	4,448	6,040	2,320	2,936	2,580	668	...
Gross Property	145,695	76,209	36,739	12,892	8,802	5,455	...
Accumulated Depreciation	50,084	27,360	12,543	5,470	3,209	1,755	...
Long-Term Debt	5,583	4,426	...	...	162	266	...
Capital Lease Obligations	...	...	...	...	162	266	...
Net Stockholders' Equity	299,235	281,186	185,823	49,244	17,345	11,940	...
Total Assets	418,020	384,202	244,582	83,281	29,634	19,100	...
Total Current Assets	280,413	259,381	119,942	75,511	22,516	15,110	...
Total Current Liabilities	110,689	98,083	50,816	34,037	12,127	6,894	...
Net Working Capital	169,724	161,298	69,126	41,474	10,389	8,216	...
Year End Shares Outstg	45,807	43,867	38,472	22,410	12,928	12,818	20,036

STATISTICAL RECORD:

Operating Profit Margin %	...	...	...	10.9	9.4	14.3	16.6
Book Value Per Share	5.84	4.71	2.26	2.20	0.32	...	...
Return on Equity %	...	...	...	17.1	30.4	36.0	...
Return on Assets %	...	...	...	10.1	17.8	22.5	...
P/E Ratio	...	...	...	62.8-32.4	...	...	...
Price Range	78-25⅞	89¼-29¾	36⅝-13½	23¼-12	...	...	...

Statistics are as originally reported.

OFFICERS:
S.D. Cook, Chmn.
W.V. Campbell, Pres. & C.E.O.
J.J. Heeger, Sr. V.P. & C.F.O.
C.L. Valentine, Sec. & Gen. Couns.
INCORPORATED: CA, Mar., 1983; reincorp., DE, Mar., 1993
PRINCIPAL OFFICE: 2535 Garcia Avenue, Mountain View, CA 94043

TELEPHONE NUMBER: (415) 944-6000
NO. OF EMPLOYEES: 3,474
ANNUAL MEETING: In June
SHAREHOLDERS: 1,000 (approx.)
INSTITUTIONAL HOLDINGS:
No. of Institutions: 101
Shares Held: 25,712,730

REGISTRAR(S): American Stock Transfer & Trust Co., New York, NY

TRANSFER AGENT(S): American Stock Transfer & Trust Co., New York, NY

KLA-TENCOR CORPORATION

YIELD ...%
P/E RATIO 20.8

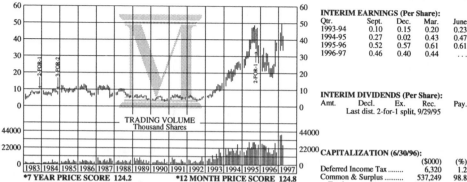

TRADING VOLUME
Thousand Shares

INTERIM EARNINGS (Per Share):

Qtr.	Sept.	Dec.	Mar.	June
1993-94	0.10	0.15	0.20	0.23
1994-95	0.27	0.02	0.43	0.47
1995-96	0.52	0.57	0.61	0.61
1996-97	0.46	0.40	0.44	...

INTERIM DIVIDENDS (Per Share):

Amt.	Decl.	Ex.	Rec.	Pay.
	Last dist. 2-for-1 split, 9/29/95			

CAPITALIZATION (6/30/96):

	($000)	(%)
Deferred Income Tax	6,320	1.2
Common & Surplus	537,249	98.8
Total	543,569	100.0

RECENT DEVELOPMENTS: For the third quarter ended 3/31/97, net income decreased 25.5% to $23.7 million. This compares with $31.8 million in the corresponding prior-year quarter. Net sales dropped 15.9% to $157.8 million from $187.5 million in the comparable quarter a year earlier. New orders for the period were up, continuing to recover from first-quarter lows, led by improvements in the wafer inspection and metrology areas. Orders in the U.S. were much stronger, while orders from Japan were about the same and orders in Eurpoe and Asia-Pacific were lower. The Company's merger with Tencor Instruments closed on 4/30/97, creating a combined company providing comprehensive measurement and analysis systems for yield management available to the semiconductor industry. The transaction was accounted for as a pooling-of-interests under a one-for-one stock exchange, with the new entity being named KLA-Tencor Corporation.

BUSINESS

KLA-TENCOR CORPORATION was formed through the 4/30/97 merger of KLA Instruments Corp. and Tencor Instruments. The Company designs, manufactures, markets and services yield-management and process-monitoring systems for the semiconductor industry for wafer, reticle, and metrology inspection equipment. KLAC's systems are used to analyze product and process quality at critical steps in the manufacture of integrated circuits, providing feedback so that fabrication problems can be identified, addressed and contained.

ANNUAL EARNINGS AND DIVIDENDS PER SHARE

	6/30/96	6/30/95	6/30/94	6/30/93	6/30/92	6/30/91	6/30/90
Earnings Per Share	1.20	1.20	0.69	0.18	②d0.45	②0.07	0.26
Dividends Per Share	①...	Nil	Nil	Nil	Nil	Nil	Nil

① 2-for-1 stk. split, 9/29/95 ② Before disc. oper.

ANNUAL FINANCIAL DATA

RECORD OF EARNINGS (IN THOUSANDS):

Total Revenues	694,867	442,416	243,737	167,236	155,963	148,432	167,916
Costs and Expenses	501,096	349,723	192,921	146,100	158,816	134,364	146,233
Depreciation & Amort	16,267	10,642	10,734	9,646	10,732	9,088	8,705
Operating Income	177,504	82,051	40,082	11,490	d13,585	4,980	12,978
Income Bef Income Taxes	188,894	88,814	40,251	9,281	d16,292	3,499	14,000
Income Taxes	68,010	30,196	10,063	2,320	318	1,084	4,620
Net Income	120,884	58,618	30,188	6,961	①d16,610	②2,415	9,380
Aver. Shs. Outstg.	52,329	48,870	44,088	39,414	36,902	37,104	36,076

① Before disc. op. cr$2,800,000. ② Before disc. op. dr$13,000,000.

BALANCE SHEET (IN THOUSANDS):

Cash and Cash Equivalents	123,683	118,740	139,126	52,362	23,711	31,254	42,099
Receivables, Net	230,716	147,429	81,721	51,994	56,747	54,418	52,056
Inventories	132,377	79,759	53,265	42,489	48,575	47,942	44,611
Gross Property	120,773	88,643	74,151	72,589	76,016	72,921	48,337
Accumulated Depreciation	48,948	39,639	37,002	33,205	31,217	24,793	24,002
Long-Term Debt	...	...	20,000	20,000	24,000	24,000	...
Net Stockholders' Equity	537,249	403,969	227,382	114,050	103,032	113,161	122,136
Total Assets	712,772	546,296	321,570	199,089	188,457	198,023	179,276
Total Current Assets	493,559	360,877	278,455	151,569	134,734	140,731	144,849
Total Current Liabilities	169,203	132,851	65,582	57,958	50,773	49,615	45,698
Net Working Capital	324,356	228,026	212,873	93,611	83,961	91,116	99,151
Year End Shares Outstg	51,030	50,160	45,728	39,006	37,392	36,486	35,974

STATISTICAL RECORD:

Operating Profit Margin %	25.5	18.5	16.4	6.9	...	3.4	7.7
Book Value Per Share	10.53	8.05	4.97	2.92	2.76	3.10	3.40
Return on Equity %	22.5	14.5	13.3	6.1	...	2.1	7.7
Return on Assets %	17.0	10.7	9.4	3.5	...	1.2	5.2
P/E Ratio	15.3-7.6	40.6-19.4	39.4-17.9	80.7-29.3	...	N.M.	24.0-11.1
Price Range	35¼-17½	48¾-23¼	27-12¼	14⅛-5⅛	6⅞-3	7¼-4	6¼-2⅞

Statistics are as originally reported. Figures for 6/30/96 and before are for KLA Instruments Corp.

OFFICERS:
K. Levy, Chmn. & C.E.O.
K.L. Schroeder, Pres. & C.O.O.
R.J. Boehlke, V.P.-Fin. & Admin., & C.F.O.
C. Stoddart, Treas.

INCORPORATED: DE, Jul., 1975

PRINCIPAL OFFICE: 160 Rio Robles, P.O. Box 49055, San Jose, CA 95134

TELEPHONE NUMBER: (408) 468-4200

NO. OF EMPLOYEES: 2,500 (approx.)

ANNUAL MEETING: In November

SHAREHOLDERS: 1,167 (approx.)

INSTITUTIONAL HOLDINGS:
No. of Institutions: 126
Shares Held: 37,512,589

REGISTRAR(S): First National Bank of Boston, Shareholder Services Division, Boston, MA

TRANSFER AGENT(S): First National Bank of Boston, Shareholder Services Division, Boston, MA

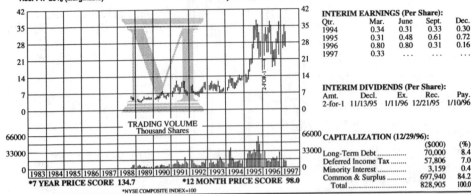

NASDAQ SYMBOL KMAG
Rec. Pr. 28⅛ (Marginable)

KOMAG, INCORPORATED

YIELD ...%
P/E RATIO 17.6

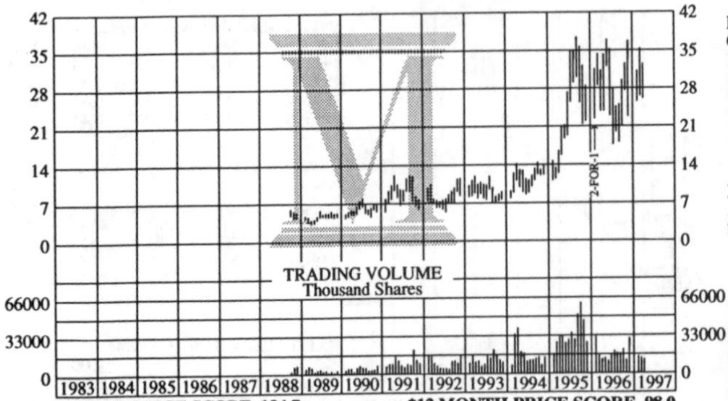

*7 YEAR PRICE SCORE 134.7 *12 MONTH PRICE SCORE 98.0

*NYSE COMPOSITE INDEX=100

INTERIM EARNINGS (Per Share):

Qtr.	Mar.	June	Sept.	Dec.
1994	0.34	0.31	0.33	0.30
1995	0.31	0.48	0.61	0.72
1996	0.80	0.80	0.31	0.16
1997	0.33	...	...	...

INTERIM DIVIDENDS (Per Share):

Amt.	Decl.	Ex.	Rec.	Pay.
2-for-1	11/13/95	1/11/96	12/21/95	1/10/96

CAPITALIZATION (12/29/96):

	($000)	(%)
Long-Term Debt	70,000	8.4
Deferred Income Tax	57,806	7.0
Minority Interest	3,159	0.4
Common & Surplus	697,940	84.2
Total	828,905	100.0

RECENT DEVELOPMENTS: For the three months ended 3/30/97, net income totaled $17.8 million. This compares with $42.5 million in the corresponding prior-year period. First-quarter net sales were up 9.4% to $167.2 million from $152.8 million the previous year. The lower net income reflects a sharp decline in gross profit as a percentage of net sales, which fell to 23.5% from 42.2% in 1996. Lower manufacturing yields on new products and reduced equipment utilization rates contributed to the lower gross profit percentage. In January 1997, the Company commenced operations at its second Penang, Malaysia plant with the first production line from that facility. In addition, KMAG's new San Jose, California plant began production in the latter part of the fourth quarter of 1996. The output from these new facilities, combined with added volume from yield improvements, led to a 16.0% increase in unit production for the quarter compared with the fourth quarter of 1996.

BUSINESS

KOMAG, INCORPORATED designs and manufactures thin-film disks, the primary storage medium used to store digital data in computer disk drives. The Company's products are used in disk arrays, network file servers, high-end personal computers and engineering workstations. Komag has facilities in the United States, Japan, Malaysia and Thailand.

QUARTERLY DATA

(12/29/96)($000)	Rev	Inc
1st Quarter	152,839	42,504
2nd Quarter	152,208	42,560
3rd Quarter	131,533	16,498
4th Quarter	141,211	8,412

ANNUAL EARNINGS AND DIVIDENDS PER SHARE

	12/29/96	12/31/95	1/1/95	1/2/94	1/3/93	12/29/91	12/31/90
Earnings Per Share	**2.07**	**2.14**	**1.27**	**d0.23**	**0.40**	**0.38**	**[1] 0.44**
Dividends Per Share	**Nil**	**Nil**	**Nil**	**Nil**	**Nil**	**Nil**	**Nil**

[1] Before extra. item

ANNUAL FINANCIAL DATA

	12/29/96	12/31/95	1/1/95	1/2/94	1/3/93	12/29/91	12/31/90
RECORD OF EARNINGS (IN THOUSANDS):							
Total Revenues	577,791	512,248	392,391	385,375	326,801	279,194	149,884
Costs and Expenses	378,370	317,681	267,855	341,673	270,938	221,975	112,784
Depreciation & Amort	86,928	65,483	47,591	49,025	36,431	29,744	18,414
Operating Income	112,493	129,084	76,945	d5,323	19,432	27,475	18,686
Income Bef Income Taxes	121,148	135,219	77,366	d7,313	22,638	28,607	18,149
Income Taxes	20,595	33,809	23,210	26,425	18,375	14,293	6,741
Net Income	109,974	106,815	58,522	d9,901	16,893	15,359	[1] 13,376
Aver. Shs. Outstg.	53,132	49,905	45,994	42,744	42,824	40,926	30,430
[1] Before extra. item cr$371,000.							
BALANCE SHEET (IN THOUSANDS):							
Cash and Cash Equivalents	93,241	213,678	93,948	91,559	89,343	91,014	45,187
Receivables, Net	64,125	66,694	44,778	43,007	35,357	30,823	24,035
Inventories	61,960	29,021	24,101	31,082	20,197	21,991	9,552
Gross Property	933,059	543,842	382,652	375,883	292,688	188,098	121,828
Accumulated Depreciation	289,353	214,668	153,769	188,616	100,637	67,194	43,623
Long-Term Debt	70,000	...	16,250	29,482	24,821	11,881	19,656
Capital Lease Obligations	...	...	...	...	2,792	4,635	240
Net Stockholders' Equity	697,940	574,564	331,215	255,331	248,738	202,077	115,126
Total Assets	938,357	686,315	424,095	382,297	355,849	276,979	163,103
Total Current Assets	251,097	323,158	171,507	178,273	153,430	149,460	82,025
Total Current Liabilities	108,955	70,940	53,277	85,883	55,536	51,652	23,950
Net Working Capital	142,142	252,218	118,230	92,390	97,894	97,808	58,075
Year End Shares Outstg	51,696	50,714	45,803	43,532	42,162	40,996	29,324
STATISTICAL RECORD:							
Operating Profit Margin %	19.5	25.2	19.6	...	5.9	9.8	12.5
Book Value Per Share	13.50	11.33	7.23	5.87	5.90	4.93	3.93
Return on Equity %	15.8	18.6	17.7	...	6.8	7.6	11.6
Return on Assets %	11.7	15.6	13.8	...	4.7	5.5	8.2
P/E Ratio	17.9-8.5	17.5-5.2	11.4-6.2	...	29.1-13.4	32.2-14.1	18.5-9.7
Price Range	37-17⅝	37½-11⅛	14½-7⅞	12-6⅞	11⅝-5⅜	12¼-5⅜	8⅛-4¼

Statistics are as originally reported.

OFFICERS:
T. Chen, Chmn.
S.C. Johnson, Pres. & C.E.O.
W.L. Potts, Jr., Sr. V.P., C.F.O. & Sec.

INCORPORATED: CA, Jun., 1983; reincorp., DE, Jan., 1987

PRINCIPAL OFFICE: 1704 Automation Parkway, San Jose, CA 95131

TELEPHONE NUMBER: (408) 576-2000

NO. OF EMPLOYEES: 4,800

ANNUAL MEETING: In May

SHAREHOLDERS: 483 (approx.)

INSTITUTIONAL HOLDINGS:
No. of Institutions: 100
Shares Held: 35,915,537

REGISTRAR(S): Chase Mellon Shareholder Services

TRANSFER AGENT(S): Chase Mellon Shareholder Services

LINEAR TECHNOLOGY CORP.

YIELD 0.4%
P/E RATIO 30.1

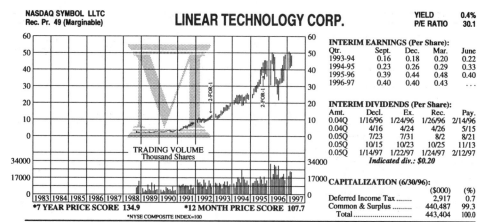

TRADING VOLUME
Thousand Shares

*7 YEAR PRICE SCORE 134.9   *12 MONTH PRICE SCORE 107.7
*NYSE COMPOSITE INDEX=100

INTERIM EARNINGS (Per Share):

Qtr.	Sept.	Dec.	Mar.	June
1993-94	0.16	0.18	0.20	0.22
1994-95	0.23	0.26	0.29	0.33
1995-96	0.39	0.44	0.48	0.40
1996-97	0.40	0.40	0.43	...

INTERIM DIVIDENDS (Per Share):

Amt.	Decl.	Ex.	Rec.	Pay.
0.04Q	1/16/96	1/24/96	1/26/96	2/14/96
0.04Q	4/16	4/24	4/26	5/15
0.05Q	7/23	7/31	8/2	8/21
0.05Q	10/15	10/23	10/25	11/13
0.05Q	1/14/97	1/22/97	1/24/97	2/12/97

Indicated div.: $0.20

CAPITALIZATION (6/30/96):

	($000)	(%)
Deferred Income Tax	2,917	0.7
Common & Surplus	440,487	99.3
Total	443,404	100.0

RECENT DEVELOPMENTS: For the third quarter ended 3/30/97, net income decreased 10.0% to $34.0 million compared with $37.8 million in the corresponding prior-year quarter. Net sales fell 9.2% to $95.0 million from $104.7 million the year before. Compared with second-quarter results, net income rose 7.0% and net sales were up 5.0%. This sequential growth reflects increasing customer demand throughout the quarter and stronger results across all of the Company's major end application markets, partic-ularly communications. LLTC has commenced production operations at its new Camas, Washington wafer fabrication facility. In addition, the Company will be ramping up fabrication operations in Miltipas, California, assembly operations in Penang and test operations in Singapore. For the nine months ended 3/30/97, net income was down 5.5% to $97.0 million from $102.6 million in the comparable period a year earlier. Net sales dropped 4.4% to $275.2 million from $287.7 million the previous year.

BUSINESS

LINEAR TECHNOLOGY CORP. is a manufacturer of high-performance linear integrated circuits. The Company's products include operational, instrumentation and audio amplifiers; voltage regulators, power management devices, references, comparators and convertors; switched-capacitor filters; communications interface circuits; one-chip data acquisition subsystems; pulse-width modulators and sample-and-hold devices. Applications for LLTC's products include telecommunications, notebook and desktop computers, video/multimedia, computer peripherals, cellular telephones, industrial automotive and process controls, network and factory automation products and satellites.

ANNUAL EARNINGS AND DIVIDENDS PER SHARE

	6/30/96	7/2/95	7/3/94	6/27/93	6/28/92	6/30/91	7/1/90
Earnings Per Share	1.71	1.11	0.75	0.49	0.35	0.24	0.17
Dividends Per Share	☐ 0.18	0.15	0.125	☑ 0.105	0.025	Nil	Nil
Dividend Payout %	10.5	13.5	16.7	21.4	7.1	...	...

☐ 2-for-1 stk. split, 9/1/95   ☑ 2-for-1 stk. split, 11/25/92

ANNUAL FINANCIAL DATA

RECORD OF EARNINGS (IN THOUSANDS):

Total Revenues	377,771	265,023	200,538	150,867	119,440	94,152	75,620
Costs and Expenses	176,754	136,498	112,303	92,316	79,303	67,255	56,431
Depreciation & Amort	10,263	8,563	6,339	5,806	4,542	3,838	3,999
Operating Income	190,754	119,962	81,896	52,745	35,595	23,059	15,190
Income Bef Income Taxes	203,902	128,450	86,495	55,715	38,488	26,222	17,492
Income Taxes	69,938	43,754	29,668	19,280	13,471	9,283	6,191
Net Income	133,964	84,696	56,827	36,435	25,017	16,939	11,301
Aver. Shs. Outstg.	77,888	76,328	75,352	73,814	72,432	70,416	67,448

BALANCE SHEET (IN THOUSANDS):

Cash and Cash Equivalents	322,472	250,222	176,801	127,878	95,278	69,225	53,438
Receivables, Net	48,395	29,770	26,517	20,006	19,719	14,094	14,619
Inventories	12,930	9,719	10,016	8,376	7,921	7,543	5,882
Gross Property	164,805	94,490	74,014	57,970	50,454	40,613	32,464
Accumulated Depreciation	53,883	43,688	36,741	30,601	24,903	20,361	16,534
Long-Term Debt	...	...	...	259	1,726	6,439	8,170
Net Stockholders' Equity	440,487	308,530	223,475	162,515	123,531	89,682	68,769
Total Assets	529,802	367,553	268,399	196,492	159,799	120,742	96,354
Total Current Assets	418,880	316,751	231,126	169,123	134,248	100,490	80,424
Total Current Liabilities	86,398	55,828	42,921	32,372	33,514	23,718	18,600
Net Working Capital	332,482	260,923	188,205	136,751	100,734	76,772	61,824
Year End Shares Outstg	74,662	73,586	72,616	71,348	70,022	67,394	65,660

STATISTICAL RECORD:

Operating Profit Margin %	50.5	45.3	40.8	35.0	29.8	24.5	20.1
Book Value Per Share	5.90	4.19	3.08	2.28	1.76	1.33	1.05
Return on Equity %	30.4	27.5	25.4	22.4	20.3	18.9	16.4
Return on Assets %	25.3	23.0	21.2	18.5	15.7	14.0	11.7
Average Yield %	0.5	0.4	0.6	0.7	0.2	...	...
P/E Ratio	29.2-12.6	41.1-20.7	34.3-24.3	40.3-21.2	37.0-22.8	34.4-13.0	21.3-12.5
Price Range	50¼-21¾	45⅝-23	25¾-18¼	19¾-10⅜	12¾-7⅞	8¼-3¹⁄₈	3⅝-2⅛

Statistics are as originally reported.

OFFICERS:
R.H. Swanson, Jr., Pres. & C.E.O.
P. Coghlan, V.P.-Fin. & C.F.O.
A.F. Schneiderman, Sec.

INCORPORATED: CA, Sept., 1981

PRINCIPAL OFFICE: 1630 McCarthy Blvd.,
Milpitas, CA 95035-7417

TELEPHONE NUMBER: (408) 432-1900

NO. OF EMPLOYEES: 1,638

ANNUAL MEETING: In October

SHAREHOLDERS: 789 (approx.)

INSTITUTIONAL HOLDINGS:
No. of Institutions: 210
Shares Held: 62,002,184

REGISTRAR(S): First National Bank of
Boston, Boston, MA

TRANSFER AGENT(S): First National Bank
of Boston, Boston, MA

MAXIM INTEGRATED PRODUCTS, INC.

YIELD ...%
P/E RATIO 25.4

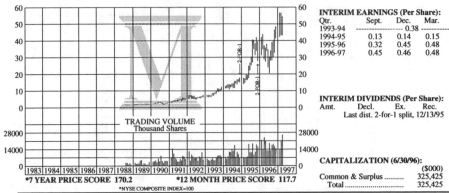

INTERIM EARNINGS (Per Share):

Qtr.	Sept.	Dec.	Mar.	June
1993-94	------------	0.38	------------	
1994-95	0.13	0.14	0.15	0.17
1995-96	0.32	0.45	0.48	0.49
1996-97	0.45	0.46	0.48	...

INTERIM DIVIDENDS (Per Share):

Amt.	Decl.	Ex.	Rec.	Pay.
Last dist. 2-for-1 split, 12/13/95				

CAPITALIZATION (6/30/96):

	($000)	(%)
Common & Surplus	325,425	100.0
Total	325,425	100.0

RECENT DEVELOPMENTS: For the third quarter ended 3/31/97, net income increased 3.6% to $35.4 million compared with $34.2 million in the corresponding quarter the year before. Net revenues rose 1.8% to $111.0 million from $109.0 million the previous year. Gross margin and operating income as percentages of sales fell 1.3% and 1.1%, respectively, as cost of goods sold outpaced revenue growth and research and development expenses rose 16.5%. During the quarter, backlog shippable within twelve months grew to $124.0 million. This compares with $103.0 million at the beginning of the quarter. Of the $124.0 million backlog, 76.0% was for orders with requested delivery in the fourth quarter of the Company's present fiscal year. Net bookings for the third quarter were up 30.0% when compared with those in the second fiscal quarter, reflecting growth across all geographic regions and business units. MXIM completed construction of a 140,000 square-foot facility in the Philippines during the third quarter.

BUSINESS

MAXIM INTEGRATED PRODUCTS, INC. designs, develops, manufactures and markets a broad range of linear and mixed-signal integrated circuits, commonly referred to as analog circuits. The Company also provides a range of high-frequency design processes and capabilities that can be used in custom design.

GEOGRAPHIC DATA

(6/30/96)	Rev(%)
United States	42.1
Europe	28.5
Pacific Rim...............	26.0
Other........................	3.4
Total	100.0

ANNUAL EARNINGS AND DIVIDENDS PER SHARE

	6/30/96	6/30/95	6/30/94	6/30/93	6/30/92	6/30/91	6/30/90
Earnings Per Share	1.74	0.59	0.38	0.29	0.24	0.19	0.15
Dividends Per Share	①...	Nil	Nil	Nil	Nil	Nil	Nil

① 2-for-1 stk. split, 12/13/95

ANNUAL FINANCIAL DATA

RECORD OF EARNINGS (IN THOUSANDS):

Total Revenues	421,626	250,820	153,932	110,184	86,954	73,806	55,960
Costs and Expenses	222,837	181,969	112,409	80,126	60,539	51,957	40,714
Depreciation & Amort	12,899	11,617	5,949	4,610	5,949	5,864	4,554
Operating Income	185,890	57,234	35,574	25,448	20,466	15,985	10,692
Income Bef Income Taxes	190,457	59,855	37,628	26,588	21,036	15,597	10,173
Income Taxes	67,112	20,949	13,546	9,306	7,363	5,459	2,570
Net Income	123,345	38,906	24,082	17,282	13,673	10,138	7,603
Aver. Shs. Outstg.	70,927	66,502	63,628	60,050	58,160	54,540	52,120

BALANCE SHEET (IN THOUSANDS):

Cash and Cash Equivalents	129,253	92,295	48,430	49,079	33,686	14,875	4,935
Receivables, Net	80,664	27,714	17,950	19,177	14,599	10,967	9,971
Inventories	30,471	19,105	18,330	15,485	15,169	14,643	12,652
Gross Property	197,425	131,709	97,353	50,355	43,321	40,008	38,656
Accumulated Depreciation	50,357	43,784	19,657	15,898	14,305	12,229	10,405
Capital Lease Obligations	...	...	40	174	683	2,745	4,921
Net Stockholders' Equity	325,425	178,710	130,192	97,336	72,277	51,234	37,716
Total Assets	417,794	256,133	178,523	126,902	95,546	71,840	60,681
Total Current Assets	264,551	161,822	99,480	91,257	67,898	42,144	29,190
Total Current Liabilities	88,369	65,844	43,435	27,210	20,218	15,881	17,120
Net Working Capital	176,182	95,978	56,045	64,047	47,680	26,263	12,070
Year End Shares Outstg	61,446	58,873	57,346	55,676	53,284	50,456	47,964

STATISTICAL RECORD:

Operating Profit Margin %	44.1	22.8	23.1	23.1	23.5	21.7	19.1
Book Value Per Share	5.30	3.04	2.27	1.75	1.36	1.00	0.77
Return on Equity %	37.9	21.8	18.5	17.8	18.9	19.8	20.2
Return on Assets %	29.5	15.2	13.5	13.6	14.3	14.1	12.5
P/E Ratio	27.7-11.9	71.0-23.9	47.0-28.6	42.2-21.1	31.3-20.3	30.9-14.5	11.6-6.5
Price Range	48¼-20⅝	41⅞-14⅛	17⅞-10⅞	12¼-6⅛	7½-4⅞	5⅞-2¾	3⅜-1⅞

Statistics are as originally reported.

OFFICERS:
J.F. Gifford, Chmn., Pres. & C.E.O.
M.J. Byrd, V.P. & C.F.O.

INCORPORATED: CA, Apr., 1983; reincorp. Aug., DE,, 1987

PRINCIPAL OFFICE: 120 San Gabriel Drive, Sunnyvale, CA 94086

TELEPHONE NUMBER: (408) 737-7600

NO. OF EMPLOYEES: 1,987

ANNUAL MEETING: In November

SHAREHOLDERS: 1,362 (approx.)

INSTITUTIONAL HOLDINGS:
No. of Institutions: 127
Shares Held: 54,762,006

REGISTRAR(S): Boston Equiserve, Boston, MA

TRANSFER AGENT(S): Boston Equiserve, Boston, MA

MCAFEE ASSOCIATES, INC.

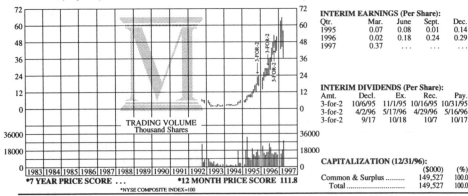

INTERIM EARNINGS (Per Share):

Qtr.	Mar.	June	Sept.	Dec.
1995	0.07	0.08	0.01	0.14
1996	0.02	0.18	0.24	0.29
1997	0.37	...	...	...

INTERIM DIVIDENDS (Per Share):

Amt.	Decl.	Ex.	Rec.	Pay.
3-for-2	10/6/95	11/1/95	10/16/95	10/31/95
3-for-2	4/2/96	5/17/96	4/29/96	5/16/96
3-for-2	9/17	10/18	10/7	10/17

TRADING VOLUME
Thousand Shares

*7 YEAR PRICE SCORE ...   *12 MONTH PRICE SCORE 111.8

*NYSE COMPOSITE INDEX=100

CAPITALIZATION (12/31/96):

	($000)	(%)
Common & Surplus	149,527	100.0
Total	149,527	100.0

RECENT DEVELOPMENTS: For the three months ended 3/31/97, net income soared to $19.7 million. This compares with $1.1 million in the corresponding period the year before. The prior-year net income reflects acquisition and related costs of $8.3 million. Net revenue for the period more than doubled to $73.4 million from $33.8 million a year earlier. During the quarter, MCAF introduced VirusScan 3.0, the latest version of its desktop anti-virus software. The Company also introduced GroupScan 3.0 and GroupShield 3.0, stand-alone anti-virus solutions for the Lotus

Notes and Domino web server. The Company extended its global presence during the quarter by adding research sites in Amsterdam, Tokyo and Santa Clara, CA that provide customers with 24-hour virus response. Also during the quarter, MCAF acquired Jade KK, an anti-virus software vendor in Japan. In March 1997, the Company entered the diagnostic software utility market with the introduction of PC Medic 97, which addresses common Windows 95 problems.

BUSINESS

MCAFEE ASSOCIATES, INC., founded in 1989, is a worldwide vendor of network security and management solutions for enterprise-enabled client/server PC networks and stand-alone PCs. The Company offers integrated security suites consisting of anti-virus, encryption and firewall products. Coupled with network management suites comprised of help desk with metering, distribution, inventory and desktop management tools, the Company serves the emerging NT-centric networking market.

ANNUAL EARNINGS AND DIVIDENDS PER SHARE

	1996	1995	1994	1993	1992	1991	1990
Earnings Per Share	0.73	0.30	0.04	0.20	③ 0.38	...	...
Dividends Per Share	①...	②...	Nil	Nil	Nil	...	...

① 3-for-2 stk. splits, 10/17/96 & 5/16/96 ② 3-for-2 stk. split, 10/31/95 ③ Pro forma

ANNUAL FINANCIAL DATA

RECORD OF EARNINGS (IN THOUSANDS):

	1996	1995	1994	1993	1992	1991	1990
Total Revenues	181,126	90,065	32,900	17,911	13,683	6,915	1,594
Costs and Expenses	110,688	64,451	30,018	6,197	3,168	1,647	568
Depreciation & Amort	3,169	1,356	1,198	165	61	17	3
Operating Income	67,269	24,258	1,684	11,549	10,454	5,251	1,023
Income Bef Income Taxes	70,730	25,971	2,315	12,194	6,080	4,314	1,023
Income Taxes	31,713	11,055	928	4,890	cr5,012	...	...
Net Income	39,011	14,916	1,387	7,304	11,092	4,314	1,023
Aver. Shs. Outstg.	53,207	49,365	37,156	35,946	33,286	32,490	32,490
BALANCE SHEET (IN THOUSANDS):							
Cash and Cash Equivalents	126,731	55,357	26,545	27,695	18,935	2,297	574
Receivables, Net	30,251	25,891	16,201	9,254	2,701	1,331	978
Gross Property	14,061	6,818	1,870	777	305	89	34
Accumulated Depreciation	6,575	3,419	669	228	81	20	3
Long-Term Debt	...	...	...	...	...	10,000	...
Net Stockholders' Equity	149,527	63,542	23,015	18,363	10,333	d17,740	d3,718
Total Assets	194,485	104,020	56,398	39,074	28,512	3,777	1,586
Total Current Assets	163,948	90,685	45,178	37,258	26,594	3,639	1,553
Total Current Liabilities	41,295	35,853	24,720	15,696	14,072	8,734	3,424
Net Working Capital	122,653	54,832	20,458	21,562	12,522	d5,095	d1,871
Year End Shares Outstg	48,662	46,130	35,028	33,600	33,196	...	...
STATISTICAL RECORD:							
Operating Profit Margin %	37.1	26.9	5.1	64.5	76.4	75.9	64.2
Book Value Per Share	3.05	1.31	0.57	0.55	0.31	...	...
Return on Equity %	26.1	23.5	6.0	39.8	N.M.	...	...
Return on Assets %	20.1	14.3	2.5	18.7	38.9	N.M.	64.5
P/E Ratio	72.4-19.0	78.3-14.6	N.M.	30.0-6.9	18.1-8.9	...	...
Price Range	52⅞-13⅞	23½-4⅜		6-2	6-1⅜	6⅞-3⅞	...	...

Statistics are as originally reported.

QUARTERLY DATA

(12/31/96)($000)	Rev	Inc
1st Quarter	33,845	1,083
2nd Quarter	40,767	9,400
3rd Quarter	47,290	12,898
4th Quarter	59,224	15,636

OFFICERS:
W.L. Larson, Chmn., Pres. & C.E.O.
P.K. Goyal, V.P.-Admin., C.F.O., Treas. & Sec.

INCORPORATED: DE, Aug., 1992

PRINCIPAL OFFICE: 2805 Bowers Ave., Santa Clara, CA 95051-0963

TELEPHONE NUMBER: (408) 988-3832
FAX: (408) 970-9727
NO. OF EMPLOYEES: 481
ANNUAL MEETING: In June
SHAREHOLDERS: 250
INSTITUTIONAL HOLDINGS:
No. of Institutions: 148
Shares Held: 46,112,963

REGISTRAR(S): First National Bank of Boston, c/o Boston EquiServe, Boston, MA

TRANSFER AGENT(S): First National Bank of Boston, c/o Boston EquiServe, Boston, MA

NASDAQ SYMBOL MCCR K
Rec. Pr. 24 (Marginable)

MCCORMICK & CO., INC.

YIELD 2.5%
P/E RATIO 36.4

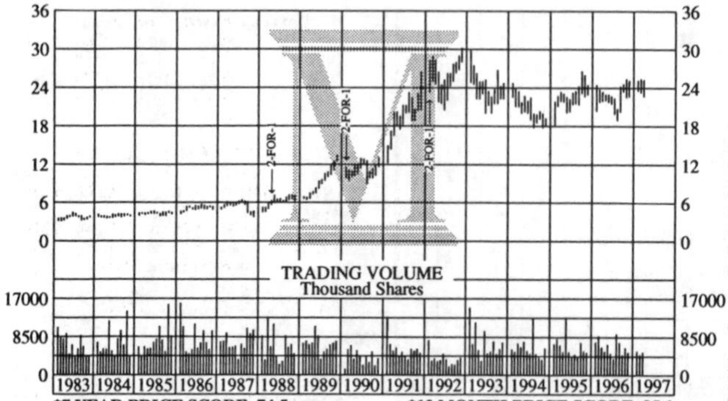

36
30
24
18
12
6
0
2-FOR-1
2-FOR-1
2-FOR-1
TRADING VOLUME
Thousand Shares
17000
8500
0
1983 1984 1985 1986 1987 1988 1989 1990 1991 1992 1993 1994 1995 1996 1997

*7 YEAR PRICE SCORE 74.5 *12 MONTH PRICE SCORE 95.1

*NYSE COMPOSITE INDEX=100

INTERIM EARNINGS (Per Share):

Qtr.	Feb.	May	Aug.	Nov.
1993-94	0.23	0.24	0.33	d0.03
1994-95	0.24	0.20	0.25	0.47
1995-96	0.12	0.14	d0.26	0.58
1996-97	0.20	...	...	...

INTERIM DIVIDENDS (Per Share):

Amt.	Decl.	Ex.	Rec.	Pay.
0.14Q	3/20/96	3/28/96	4/1/96	4/10/96
0.14Q	6/18	6/26	6/28	7/10
0.14Q	9/16	9/26	9/30	10/10
0.15Q	12/16	12/27	12/31	1/20/97
0.15Q	3/19/97	3/26/97	3/31/97	4/10

Indicated div.: $0.60

CAPITALIZATION (11/30/96):

	($000)	(%)
Long-Term Debt	291,194	39.0
Deferred Income Tax	4,937	0.7
Common & Surplus	450,043	60.3
Total	746,174	100.0

RECENT DEVELOPMENTS: For the first quarter ended 2/28/97, net income was up 55.1% to $15.2 million. This compares with income of $9.8 million, before a $462,000 loss from discontinued operations, in the corresponding quarter the year before. Net sales for the quarter grew 2.9% to $407.4 million from $395.8 million the previous year. Sales for the Company's U.S. retail business were negatively affected by price increases. The balance of MCCR's businesses, however, showed strong growth for the quarter. During the quarter, the Company signed an agreement to sell Giza National Dehydration Co. of Cairo, Egypt to Kato Investment Co., also of Cairo. MCCR has also sold a unit of its Packaging Group, Minipack Systems Ltd. of Southampton, England, to a management buyout group with equity financing from the venture capital group 3i. The Company's Canadian subsidiary has acquired several product lines from Reckitt & Colman Canada, Inc. to be marketed using the FRENCH'S brand name.

BUSINESS

McCORMICK & COMPANY, INCORPORATED is a diversified specialty food company and a worldwide leader in the marketing, manufacturing and distribution of seasoning, flavoring and food products to the food industry—retail outlets, food service and food processors. A packaging group markets and manufactures plastic bottles and tubs for food, personal care, and other industries. McCormick's products are processed at 52 facilities throughout the world and are sold in 84 countries. The Company operates five divisions. Consumer Products consist of spices, extracts, flavorings and seasonings. The Industrial Products segment manufactures and sells food ingredients and custom food flavoring systems to major food manufacturers. Food Service supplies spices, condiments, seasonings and related flavor systems to the foodservice market. International offers a variety of products to the consumer, industrial and foodservice markets. Packaging markets and manufactures plastic bottles and tubes.

ANNUAL EARNINGS AND DIVIDENDS PER SHARE

	11/30/96	11/30/95	11/30/94	11/30/93	11/30/92	11/30/91	11/30/90
Earnings Per Share	**[1] 0.54**	**1.20**	**0.75**	**[2] 1.22**	**1.16**	**0.98**	**0.83**
Dividends Per Share	**0.56**	**0.52**	**0.48**	**0.44**	**[3] 0.38**	**0.28**	**[4] 0.23**
Dividend Payout %	**N.M.**	**43.3**	**64.0**	**36.1**	**32.8**	**28.6**	**27.7**

[1] Before disc. oper. & extra. item [2] Before acctg. change [3] 2-for-1 stk. split, 1/21/92 [4] 2-for-1 stk. split, 1/19/90

ANNUAL FINANCIAL DATA

RECORD OF EARNINGS (IN MILLIONS):							
Total Revenues	1,732.5	1,858.7	1,694.8	1,556.6	1,471.4	1,427.9	1,323.0
Costs and Expenses	1,575.4	1,590.0	1,504.0	1,325.6	1,260.3	1,241.8	1,159.3
Depreciation & Amort	63.8	63.7	62.5	50.5	43.8	40.5	36.6
Operating Income	93.3	205.0	128.2	180.5	167.2	145.6	127.1
Income Bef Income Taxes	61.7	149.2	87.0	149.9	138.3	114.9	104.3
Income Taxes	23.9	53.7	33.8	60.5	53.0	42.8	38.6
Net Income	[1] 43.5	97.5	61.2	[2] 99.7	95.2	80.9	69.4
Aver. Shs. Outstg. (000)	80,641	81,181	81,240	80,799	80,116	82,396	80,856

[1] Before disc. op. cr$6,249,000; and extra. item dr$7,806,000. [2] Before acctg. change dr$26,626,000.

BALANCE SHEET (IN MILLIONS):							
Cash and Cash Equivalents	22.4	12.5	15.6	12.8	1.8	6.0	5.3
Receivables, Net	251.3	257.9	252.3	188.1	164.4	149.7	144.3
Inventories	245.1	383.2	374.5	321.3	282.2	268.6	238.8
Gross Property	693.8	897.4	837.1	754.8	670.0	605.3	556.4
Accumulated Depreciation	293.4	372.6	332.5	289.2	251.5	226.8	202.4
Long-Term Debt	291.2	349.1	374.3	346.4	201.1	207.6	211.5
Net Stockholders' Equity	450.0	519.3	490.0	466.8	437.9	389.2	364.4
Total Assets	1,326.6	1,614.3	1,568.7	1,313.2	1,130.9	1,032.0	946.9
Total Current Assets	534.4	670.7	657.7	540.2	468.1	445.2	408.9
Total Current Liabilities	499.3	646.9	600.8	392.9	419.6	360.2	305.9
Net Working Capital	35.1	23.9	56.8	147.3	48.5	85.0	103.0
Year End Shs Outstg (000)	78,205	81,218	81,206	80,999	80,308	79,682	79,866

STATISTICAL RECORD:							
Operating Profit Margin %	5.4	11.0	7.6	11.6	11.4	10.2	9.6
Book Value Per Share	3.64	4.17	3.62	4.15	4.36	4.00	3.61
Return on Equity %	9.7	18.8	12.5	21.4	21.7	20.8	19.0
Return on Assets %	3.3	6.0	3.9	7.6	8.4	7.8	7.3
Average Yield %	2.5	2.3	2.3	1.8	1.5	1.4	2.1
P/E Ratio	47.0-35.0	24.9-16.9	33.0-23.7	24.4-16.4	26.1-17.7	27.0-12.5	15.8-10.8
Price Range	25⅜-18⅞	26⅝-18⅛	24¾-17¾	29¾-20	30¼-20½	26½-12¼	13⅛-9

Statistics are as originally reported.

OFFICERS:
C.P. McCormick, Jr., Chmn.
R.J. Lawless, Pres. & C.E.O.
R.G. Davey, Exec. V.P. & C.F.O.
R.W. Single, Sr., V.P. & Sec.

INCORPORATED: MD, Nov., 1915

PRINCIPAL OFFICE: 18 Loveton Circle, Sparks, MD 21152-6000

TELEPHONE NUMBER: (410) 771-7301
FAX: (410) 771-7462
NO. OF EMPLOYEES: 7,300 (approx.)
ANNUAL MEETING: In March
SHAREHOLDERS: 2,900 (vot. com.); 9,900 (non-vot. com.)
INSTITUTIONAL HOLDINGS:
No. of Institutions: 147
Shares Held: 41,847,193

REGISTRAR(S): At Company's Office

TRANSFER AGENT(S): At Company's Office

NASDAQ SYMBOL MCIC
Rec. Pr. 39 (Marginable)

MCI COMMUNICATIONS CORP.

YIELD 0.1%
P/E RATIO 22.5

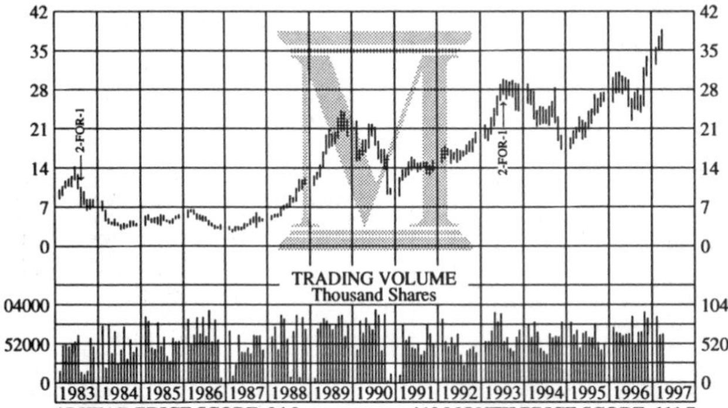

*7 YEAR PRICE SCORE 94.9 *12 MONTH PRICE SCORE 111.7
*NYSE COMPOSITE INDEX=100

INTERIM EARNINGS (Per Share):

Qtr.	Mar.	June	Sept.	Dec.
1994	0.36	0.37	0.38	0.22
1995	0.36	0.38	d0.35	0.41
1996	0.42	0.43	0.44	0.44
1997	0.42	...	...	...

INTERIM DIVIDENDS (Per Share):

Amt.	Decl.	Ex.	Rec.	Pay.
0.025S	5/10/95	5/26/95	6/2/95	6/23/95
0.025S	11/1	11/15	11/17	12/8
0.025S	4/3/96	5/29/96	5/31/96	6/21/96
0.025S	11/1	11/20	11/22	12/13

Indicated div.: $0.05

CAPITALIZATION (12/31/96):

	($000)	(%)
Long-Term Debt	4,294,000	26.5
Cap. Lease Oblig.	504,000	3.1
Redeemable Pfd Stock	750,000	4.6
Common & Surplus	10,661,000	65.8
Total	16,209,000	100.0

RECENT DEVELOPMENTS: The Company's merger with British Telecommunications, plc (BT) was approved by MCIC's shareholders on 4/2/97. The combined entity will be named Concert plc and will operate under the BT and MCI brand names in the United Kingdom and the United States, respectively. Concert's ordinary shares will trade on the London Stock Exchange, and it will list American Depositary Shares on the New York Stock Exchange. The merger is expected to be completed in Fall 1997. For the first quarter ended 3/31/97, net income remained flat at $295.0 million compared with the corresponding prior-year quarter. Revenue for the quarter was up 8.7% to $4.88 billion from $4.49 billion in the comparable period the year before. The increase in revenues was led by double-digit growth in the Company's Business Markets, driven by especially strong growth in value-added services such as data, Internet, conferencing and pre-paid calling cards.

BUSINESS

MCI COMMUNICATIONS CORPORATION, primarily through its subsidiaries, is a carrier of domestic long-distance telecommunications services, including dial 1 access and dial access long-distance telephone service; voice and data services over software-defined virtual private networks; private line and switched access services; toll free or 800 services; and 900 services. The Company also provides domestic record communications service and electronic messaging service. Domestic services are marketed through MCI's Multinational Account unit and its Communications Services unit. MCI also provides international long-distance telephone service, international record communications service, international data service and international electronic messaging service. International services are marketed through MCI International, Inc. The Company also markets its services, domestically and internationally, through arrangements with third parties. The Company's services are provided to nearly 21 million customers.

ANNUAL EARNINGS AND DIVIDENDS PER SHARE

	1996	1995	1994	1993	1992	1991	1990
Earnings Per Share	**1.73**	**0.80**	**1.32**	**[1] 1.12**	**1.11**	**1.00**	**0.53**
Dividends Per Share	**0.05**	**0.05**	**0.05**	**[2] 0.05**	**0.05**	**0.05**	**0.05**
Dividend Payout %	**2.9**	**6.3**	**3.8**	**4.5**	**4.5**	**5.0**	**9.4**

[1] Before extra. item [2] 2-for-1 stk. split, 7/12/93

ANNUAL FINANCIAL DATA

	1996	1995	1994	1993	1992	1991	1990
RECORD OF EARNINGS (IN MILLIONS):							
Total Revenues	18,494.0	15,265.0	13,338.0	11,921.0	10,562.0	8,433.0	7,680.0
Costs and Expenses	14,517.0	12,839.0	10,706.0	9,683.0	8,478.0	6,566.0	6,317.0
Depreciation & Amort	1,722.0	1,367.0	1,230.0	1,019.0	955.0	776.0	743.0
Operating Income	2,313.0	1,118.0	1,456.0	1,268.0	1,211.0	1,091.0	620.0
Income Bef Income Taxes	1,990.0	897.0	1,280.0	1,045.0	963.0	848.0	440.0
Income Taxes	753.0	349.0	485.0	418.0	354.0	297.0	141.0
Net Income	1,202.0	548.0	795.0	[1] 627.0	609.0	551.0	299.0
Aver. Shs. Outstg. (000)	695,000	687,000	604,000	562,000	532,000	520,000	510,000
[1] Before extra. item dr$45,000,000.							
BALANCE SHEET (IN MILLIONS):							
Cash and Cash Equivalents	348.0	844.0	2,268.0	165.0	232.0	41.0	231.0
Receivables, Net	4,047.0	3,402.0	2,491.0	2,366.0	1,764.0	1,587.0	1,447.0
Gross Property	18,709.0	15,547.0	13,408.0	11,618.0	10,316.0	9,684.0	8,708.0
Accumulated Depreciation	6,535.0	5,238.0	4,349.0	4,297.0	4,151.0	3,987.0	3,675.0
Long-Term Debt	4,294.0	2,855.0	2,401.0	2,366.0	3,432.0	3,104.0	3,147.0
Capital Lease Obligations	504.0	589.0	596.0	...	...	...	...
Net Stockholders' Equity	11,411.0	9,602.0	9,004.0	4,713.0	3,150.0	2,959.0	2,340.0
Total Assets	22,978.0	19,301.0	16,366.0	11,276.0	9,678.0	8,834.0	8,249.0
Total Current Assets	4,716.0	4,505.0	4,888.0	2,601.0	2,181.0	1,758.0	1,811.0
Total Current Liabilities	5,046.0	4,870.0	3,137.0	3,201.0	2,464.0	2,300.0	2,422.0
Net Working Capital	d330.0	d365.0	1,751.0	d600.0	d283.0	d542.0	d611.0
Year End Shs Outstg (000)	685,000	686,000	680,000	541,000	526,000	518,000	508,000
STATISTICAL RECORD:							
Book Value Per Share	12.03	10.38	11.62	6.69	3.88	3.51	2.36
Return on Equity %	11.3	5.7	8.8	13.3	19.3	18.6	12.8
Average Yield %	0.2	0.2	0.2	0.2	0.3	0.4	0.3
P/E Ratio	19.6-12.9	34.4-21.7	22.0-13.1	26.7-16.9	18.5-13.3	16.0-9.0	42.5-17.5
Price Range	33⅞-22⅜	27½-17⅜	29-17¼	29⅞-18⅞	20½-14¾	16-9	22½-9¼

Statistics are as originally reported.

OFFICERS:
B.C. Roberts, Jr., Chmn.
G.H. Taylor, C.E.O.
T.F. Price, Pres. & C.O.O.
D.L. Maine, Exec. V.P. & C.F.O.

INCORPORATED: DE, Aug., 1968

PRINCIPAL OFFICE: 1801 Pennsylvania Ave., N.W., Washington, DC 20006

TELEPHONE NUMBER: (202) 872-1600
FAX: (202) 887-2967
NO. OF EMPLOYEES: 55,000 (approx.)
ANNUAL MEETING: In April
SHAREHOLDERS: 48,015
INSTITUTIONAL HOLDINGS:
No. of Institutions: 417
Shares Held: 373,048,135

REGISTRAR(S): Mellon Securities Trust Co., New York, NY

TRANSFER AGENT(S): Mellon Securities Trust Company, New York, NY

NASDAQ SYMBOL MCHP
Rec. Pr. 35½ (Marginable)

MICROCHIP TECHNOLOGY, INC.

YIELD ...%
P/E RATIO 37.8

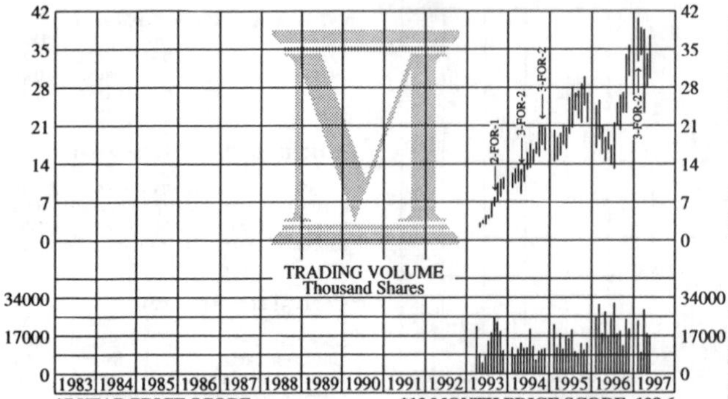

42
35
28
21
14
7
0
2-FOR-1
3-FOR-2
3-FOR-2
3-FOR-2
TRADING VOLUME
Thousand Shares
34000
17000
0
1983 1984 1985 1986 1987 1988 1989 1990 1991 1992 1993 1994 1995 1996 1997

*7 YEAR PRICE SCORE ... *12 MONTH PRICE SCORE 108.6

*NYSE COMPOSITE INDEX=100

INTERIM EARNINGS (Per Share):

Qtr.	June	Sept.	Dec.	Mar.
1993-94	0.06	0.08	0.12	0.15
1994-95	0.15	0.17	0.18	0.20
1995-96	0.21	0.23	0.11	0.25
1996-97	0.12	0.25	0.27	0.30

INTERIM DIVIDENDS (Per Share):

Amt.	Decl.	Ex.	Rec.	Pay.
3-for-2	12/9/96	1/7/97	12/20/96	1/6/97

CAPITALIZATION (3/31/97):

	($000)	(%)
Long-Term Debt	3,616	1.1
Cap. Lease Oblig.	2,383	0.7
Deferred Income Tax	6,169	1.9
Common & Surplus	316,584	96.3
Total	328,752	100.0

RECENT DEVELOPMENTS: For the fiscal year ended 3/31/97, net income totaled $51.1 million, up 16.9% compared with $43.8 million a year earlier. Net sales for the year rose 16.9% to $334.3 million from $285.9 million the year before. The current-year's results included a write-off of purchased in-process technology of $1.6 million, compared with a write-off of $11.4 million in the prior year, and restructuring costs of $6.0 million. For the fourth quarter ended 3/31/97, net income grew 20.7% to $16.6 million from $13.7 million in the comparable quarter the previous year. Net sales were up 29.8% to $93.5 million compared with $72.1 million in the corresponding year-earlier quarter. The fourth-quarter results were paced by strong microcontroller development system shipments, a high level of new customer design win activity, and a stream of new product introductions.

BUSINESS

MICROCHIP TECHNOLOGY, INC. develops, manufactures and markets field programmable microcontrollers and related specialty memory products for high-volume embedded control applications. Field programmable microcontrollers are standard products that can be configured by customers using the Company's proprietary development systems to provide integrated solutions for application-specific control requirements. MCHP supplies its products for the consumer, automotive, office automation, communications and industrial markets.

ANNUAL EARNINGS AND DIVIDENDS PER SHARE

	3/31/97	3/31/96	3/31/95	3/31/94	3/31/93	3/31/92	3/31/91
Earnings Per Share	**0.94**	**0.80**	**0.70**	**0.41**	**0.13**	**0.01**	...
Dividends Per Share	1 ...	Nil	Nil	2 ...	3 ...	Nil	...

1 3-for-2 stk. split, 1/6/97. 2 3-for-2 stk. split, 4/5/94 & 11/8/94 3 2-for-1 stk. split, 9/14/93

ANNUAL FINANCIAL DATA

	3/31/97	3/31/96	3/31/95	3/31/94	3/31/93	3/31/92	3/31/91
RECORD OF EARNINGS (IN THOUSANDS):							
Total Revenues	334,252	285,888	207,961	138,742	88,652	73,058	73,515
Costs and Expenses	223,042	195,601	158,830	116,174	84,722	73,204	76,950
Depreciation & Amort	40,153	29,975	17,196	9,310	4,749	3,649	1,633
Operating Income	71,057	60,312	49,201	24,204	5,566	1,490	d1,800
Income Bef Income Taxes	69,493	59,934	49,128	24,133	4,555	535	d2,049
Income Taxes	18,361	16,182	12,829	4,974	337	175	145
Net Income	51,132	43,752	36,299	19,159	4,218	360	d2,194
Aver. Shs. Outstg.	54,683	54,533	51,640	46,155	33,420	30,767	1,404
BALANCE SHEET (IN THOUSANDS):							
Cash and Cash Equivalents	42,999	31,059	46,194	42,618	24,835	4,463	7,219
Receivables, Net	61,102	47,208	37,868	26,416	14,554	12,840	9,650
Inventories	56,813	56,127	40,201	24,730	19,239	21,293	18,959
Gross Property	333,525	259,426	148,011	73,539	27,374	23,732	15,076
Accumulated Depreciation	99,467	62,043	36,498	19,302	10,210	5,472	1,838
Long-Term Debt	3,616	27,086	6,233	5,368	1,743	2,008	1,431
Capital Lease Obligations	2,383	6,164	9,107	9,056	2,006	3,755	2,087
Net Stockholders' Equity	316,584	219,632	161,825	87,864	43,834	18,030	13,396
Total Assets	428,092	358,187	249,480	151,425	76,919	57,879	50,102
Total Current Assets	189,536	156,431	137,582	97,012	59,175	39,157	36,564
Total Current Liabilities	98,360	100,576	66,275	43,428	26,730	29,054	25,849
Net Working Capital	91,176	55,855	71,307	53,584	32,445	10,103	10,715
Year End Shares Outstg	53,196	51,580	49,955	46,236	41,810	1,188	338
STATISTICAL RECORD:							
Operating Profit Margin %	21.3	21.1	23.7	17.4	6.3	2.0	...
Book Value Per Share	5.95	4.26	3.24	1.90	1.05	15.13	39.57
Return on Equity %	16.2	19.9	22.4	21.8	9.6	2.0	...
Return on Assets %	11.9	12.2	14.5	12.7	5.5	0.6	...
P/E Ratio	38.0-14.0	37.5-18.1	30.1-12.3	28.0-5.6	...	...	...
Price Range	35¾-13⅛	30-14½	21⅛-8⅝	11⅝-2⅜	...	...	...

Statistics are as originally reported.

OFFICERS:
S. Sanghi, Chmn., Pres. & C.E.O.
C.P. Chapman, V.P., C.F.O. & Sec.

INCORPORATED: DE, Feb., 1989

PRINCIPAL OFFICE: 2355 West Chandler Boulevard, Chandler, AZ 85224-6199

TELEPHONE NUMBER: (602) 786-7200

NO. OF EMPLOYEES: 1,900

ANNUAL MEETING: In July

SHAREHOLDERS: 570 (approx.)

INSTITUTIONAL HOLDINGS:
No. of Institutions: 235
Shares Held: 44,872,526

REGISTRAR(S): Harris Trust & Savings Bank, Chicago, IL

TRANSFER AGENT(S): Harris Trust & Savings Bank, Chicago, IL

MICRON ELECTRONICS INC.

YIELD ...%
P/E RATIO 22.6

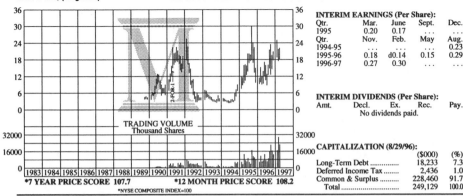

*7 YEAR PRICE SCORE 107.7   *12 MONTH PRICE SCORE 108.2

*NYSE COMPOSITE INDEX=100

INTERIM EARNINGS (Per Share):

Qtr.	Mar.	June	Sept.	Dec.
1995	0.20	0.17	...	...
Qtr.	Nov.	Feb.	May	Aug.
1994-95	...	...	...	0.23
1995-96	0.18	d0.14	0.15	0.29
1996-97	0.27	0.30	...	...

INTERIM DIVIDENDS (Per Share):

Amt.	Decl.	Ex.	Rec.	Pay.
No dividends paid.				

CAPITALIZATION (8/29/96):

	($000)	(%)
Long-Term Debt	18,233	7.3
Deferred Income Tax	2,436	1.0
Common & Surplus	228,460	91.7
Total	249,129	100.0

RECENT DEVELOPMENTS: For the second quarter ended 2/27/97, net income was $27.8 million. This compares with a net loss of $12.6 million in the corresponding quarter the year before. The prior-year loss reflects a restructuring charge of $29.5 million. Net sales for the quarter were up 11.8% to $510.3 million from $456.6 million in the comparable period a year earlier. Sales of PC systems grew 18.4% to $409.6 million from $298.2 million the previous year primarily as a result of increased name recognition and market acceptance as well as continued acceptance of the direct sales channel. Contract manufacturing revenues were approximately 38.0% higher in the quarter due to growth in business from the Company's five largest contract manufacturing customers. Sales of reduced specification memory products were also up for the quarter, benefiting from an increase in average selling prices and a slight increase in megabits shipped.

BUSINESS

MICRON ELECTRONICS, INC. is a provider of PC systems in the United States through direct sales. The Company's PC operations develop, manufacture, market and support a range of memory-intensive, high-performance desktop and notebook PC systems and networks under the Micron brand name. In addition to its PC operations, MUEI has contract manufacturing and component recovery operations. The Company's wholly-owned subsidiary, Micron Custom Manufacturing Services, Inc., is a contract manufacturer specializing in the assembly of custom complex printed circuit boards, memory modules and system level products. The Company's component recovery operation, SpecTek, recovers, assembles, tests, grades and markets nonstandard random access memory components not meeting full industry standard specifications.

ANNUAL EARNINGS AND DIVIDENDS PER SHARE

	8/29/96	8/31/95	12/31/94	1/1/94	12/31/92	12/31/91	12/31/90
Earnings Per Share	0.04	0.74	d0.74	d1.39	d3.28	1.33	0.70
Dividends Per Share	Nil	Nil	Nil	Nil	Nil	①...	Nil

① 2-for-1 stk. split, 4/23/91

ANNUAL FINANCIAL DATA

RECORD OF EARNINGS (IN MILLIONS):

Total Revenues	1,764.9	1,000.0	266.3	216.2	206.1	230.9	127.1
Costs and Expenses	1,667.2	880.3	271.3	226.6	234.9	214.0	119.5
Depreciation & Amort	22.2	13.2	1.8	2.0	5.5	1.0	0.4
Operating Income	76.0	106.5	d6.8	d12.4	d34.3	15.9	7.2
Income Bef Income Taxes	79.6	108.5	d6.3	d12.1	d33.8	16.2	6.6
Income Taxes	35.1	43.4	...	...	cr5.6	6.0	2.4
Net Income	44.6	65.1	d6.3	d12.1	d28.2	10.3	4.2
Aver. Shs. Outstg. (000)	92,495	87,422	8,729	8,680	8,585	7,756	5,990

BALANCE SHEET (IN MILLIONS):

Cash and Cash Equivalents	115.8	69.4	25.3	9.2	10.7	24.7	0.5
Receivables, Net	211.6	144.8	24.0	11.0	20.6	17.5	7.0
Inventories	69.9	92.7	24.6	28.5	30.7	51.2	21.2
Gross Property	175.1	95.4	10.3	9.5	11.7	5.1	2.4
Accumulated Depreciation	45.9	37.1	8.1	6.5	7.0	1.5	0.5
Long-Term Debt	18.2	5.8	...	...	...	...	3.4
Net Stockholders' Equity	228.5	173.7	23.5	24.8	36.7	64.4	8.2
Total Assets	529.9	382.7	77.6	53.6	68.6	100.1	32.6
Total Current Assets	399.1	308.8	74.9	50.1	63.3	95.6	30.1
Total Current Liabilities	277.4	202.3	54.1	28.7	31.7	35.5	20.9
Net Working Capital	121.8	106.5	20.8	21.4	31.7	60.1	9.2
Year End Shs Outstg (000)	92,473	91,431	8,804	8,705	8,651	8,513	4,930

STATISTICAL RECORD:

Operating Profit Margin %	4.3	10.6	...	...	...	6.9	5.7
Book Value Per Share	2.47	1.76	2.13	2.85	4.24	7.57	1.66
Return on Equity %	19.5	37.5	...	...	...	16.0	51.4
Return on Assets %	8.4	17.0	...	...	...	10.3	12.9
P/E Ratio	49.0-18.2	40.4-10.1	...	...	...	16.9-5.2	18.4-5.2
Price Range	23½-8¾	29⅞-7½	9-2⅜	7-2½	25½-2¾	22½-6⅞	12⅞-3⅝

Statistics are as originally reported.

OFFICERS:
J.M. Daltoso, Chmn., Pres. & C.E.O.
T. E. Oaas, V.P.-Fin. & C.F.O.
G.A. Haneke, V.P. & Chief Info. Off.

INCORPORATED: MN, May, 1981

PRINCIPAL OFFICE: 900 East Karcher Road, Nampa, ID 83687

TELEPHONE NUMBER: (208) 893-3434

NO. OF EMPLOYEES: 3,000 (approx.)

ANNUAL MEETING: In May

SHAREHOLDERS: 2,228 (approx.)

INSTITUTIONAL HOLDINGS:
No. of Institutions: 47
Shares Held: 5,714,141

REGISTRAR(S):

TRANSFER AGENT(S): Norwest Bank Minnesota, N.A., South St. Paul, MN

NASDAQ SYMBOL MSFT
Rec. Pr. 98¼ (Marginable)

MICROSOFT CORP.

YIELD ...%
P/E RATIO 43.3

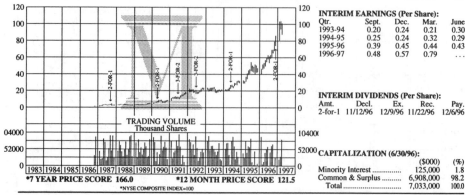

INTERIM EARNINGS (Per Share):

Qtr.	Sept.	Dec.	Mar.	June
1993-94	0.20	0.24	0.21	0.30
1994-95	0.25	0.24	0.32	0.29
1995-96	0.39	0.45	0.44	0.43
1996-97	0.48	0.57	0.79	...

INTERIM DIVIDENDS (Per Share):

Amt.	Decl.	Ex.	Rec.	Pay.
2-for-1	11/12/96	12/9/96	11/22/96	12/6/96

TRADING VOLUME
Thousand Shares

*7 YEAR PRICE SCORE 166.0   *12 MONTH PRICE SCORE 121.5
*NYSE COMPOSITE INDEX=100

CAPITALIZATION (6/30/96):

	($000)	(%)
Minority Interest	125,000	1.8
Common & Surplus	6,908,000	98.2
Total	7,033,000	100.0

RECENT DEVELOPMENTS: For the third quarter ended 3/31/97, net income soared 85.4% to $1.04 billion. This compares with $562.0 million in the corresponding quarter a year earlier. Net revenues for the quarter were up 45.5% to $3.21 billion from $2.21 billion in the comparable prior-year quarter. The improved operating results were mainly attributed to the success of Microsoft® Office 97, which was introduced in January 1997. The Company sold approximately eight million licenses of Office 97 applica-

tions during the quarter, selling at three times the rate of any previous version of this productivity suite. In March 1997, MSFT and Intel introduced the Network PC Reference Platform, an effort to reduce the cost of managing a distributed PC environment while delivering business flexibility, performance range, and network and application compatibility. The Company continues to make significant investments in Internet integration.

BUSINESS

MICROSOFT CORPORATION is engaged in the development, manufacture, marketing, licensing and support of a wide range of software products, including operating systems for personal computers, office machines and personal information devices; applications programs; and languages; as well as personal computer books, hardware, and multimedia products. MSFT's primary operating systems for PCs are: the Microsoft MS-DOS® operating system, the Microsoft Windows™ and Windows™ 95 operating systems, and Microsoft Windows™ for Workgroups. Software titles include Microsoft Word, a word processing application; Microsoft Excel, MSFT's spreadsheet application; Microsoft PowerPoint®, a graphics presentation program; and Microsoft Money, a financial organization program. The Company markets its products to end users, organizations and original equipment manufacturers.

ANNUAL EARNINGS AND DIVIDENDS PER SHARE

	6/30/96	6/30/95	6/30/94	6/30/93	6/30/92	6/30/91	6/30/90
Earnings Per Share	1.72	1.16	0.94	0.79	0.60	0.42	0.26
Dividends Per Share	Nil	Nil	①...	Nil	②...	③...	④...

Note: 2-for-1 stk. split, 12/6/96. ① 2-for-1 stk. split, 5/94 ② 3-for-2 stk. split, 6/15/92 ③ 3-for-2 stk. split, 6/27/91 ④ 100% stk. div., 4/13/90

ANNUAL FINANCIAL DATA

RECORD OF EARNINGS (IN MILLIONS):

Total Revenues	8,671.0	5,937.0	4,649.0	3,753.0	2,758.7	1,843.4	1,183.4
Costs and Expenses	5,113.0	3,630.0	2,686.0	2,276.0	1,650.4	1,117.8	743.9
Depreciation & Amort	480.0	269.0	237.0	151.0	112.3	75.8	46.3
Operating Income	3,078.0	2,038.0	1,726.0	1,326.0	996.0	649.8	393.2
Income Bef Income Taxes	3,379.0	2,167.0	1,722.0	1,401.0	1,041.3	670.6	410.6
Income Taxes	1,184.0	714.0	576.0	448.0	333.2	207.9	131.4
Net Income	2,195.0	1,453.0	1,146.0	953.0	708.1	462.7	279.2
Aver. Shs. Outstg.	1,280.0	1,254.0	1,220.0	1,212.0	1,176.9	1,126.0	1,074.7

BALANCE SHEET (IN MILLIONS):

Cash and Cash Equivalents	6,940.0	4,750.0	3,614.0	2,290.0	1,344.9	686.3	449.2
Receivables, Net	639.0	581.0	475.0	338.0	270.2	243.3	181.0
Inventories	...	...	102.0	127.0	85.9	47.1	55.6
Gross Property	2,346.0	1,907.0	1,445.0	1,181.0	977.2	648.6	399.4
Accumulated Depreciation	1,020.0	715.0	515.0	314.0	210.6	118.5	73.9
Net Stockholders' Equity	6,908.0	5,333.0	4,450.0	3,242.0	2,193.0	1,350.8	918.6
Total Assets	10,093.0	7,210.0	5,363.0	3,805.0	2,639.9	1,644.2	1,105.3
Total Current Assets	7,839.0	5,620.0	4,312.0	2,850.0	1,769.7	1,028.5	719.9
Total Current Liabilities	2,425.0	1,347.0	913.0	563.0	446.9	293.4	186.8
Net Working Capital	5,414.0	4,273.0	3,399.0	2,287.0	1,322.8	735.2	533.1
Year End Shs Outstg	1,194.0	1,176.0	1,162.0	1,128.0	1,088.6	1,045.4	1,023.3

STATISTICAL RECORD:

Operating Profit Margin %	35.5	34.3	37.1	35.3	36.1	35.3	33.2
Book Value Per Share	5.79	4.54	3.83	2.88	2.02	1.29	0.90
Return on Equity %	31.8	27.2	25.8	29.4	32.3	34.3	30.4
Return on Assets %	21.7	20.2	21.4	25.0	26.8	28.1	25.3
P/E Ratio	42.6-23.3	47.1-25.1	34.6-20.7	31.1-22.4	39.4-27.3	45.6-19.8	34.6-18.0
Price Range	73⅛-40	54⅝-29⅛	32⅝-19½	24½-17⅝	23¾-16½	18⅝-8⅛	9-4⅝

Statistics are as originally reported.

OFFICERS:
William H. Gates, Chmn. & C.E.O.
M.W. Brown, V.P.-Fin. & C.F.O.
G. Maffei, Treas.

INCORPORATED: WA, Jun., 1981

PRINCIPAL OFFICE: One Microsoft Way, Redmond, WA 98052-6399

TELEPHONE NUMBER: (206) 882-8080

NO. OF EMPLOYEES: 17,801

ANNUAL MEETING: In October

SHAREHOLDERS: 35,643

INSTITUTIONAL HOLDINGS:
No. of Institutions: 742
Shares Held: 411,812,462

REGISTRAR(S): First Interstate Bank of California, Ltd., Calabasas, CA

TRANSFER AGENT(S): First Interstate Bank of California, Ltd., Calabasas, CA

NASDAQ SYMBOL MLHR
Rec. Pr. 40 (Marginable)

MILLER (HERMAN) INC.

YIELD	0.7%
P/E RATIO	30.5

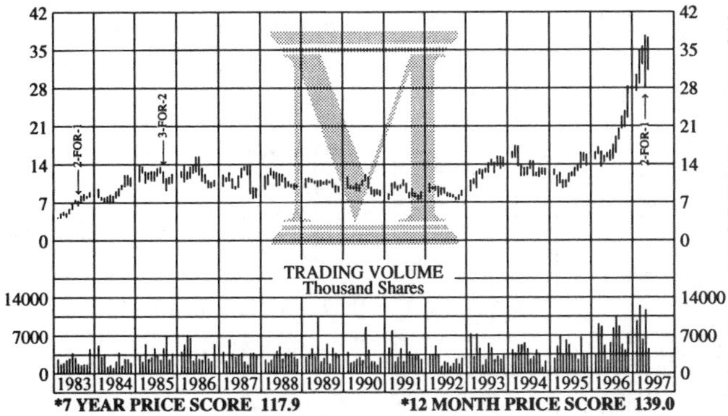

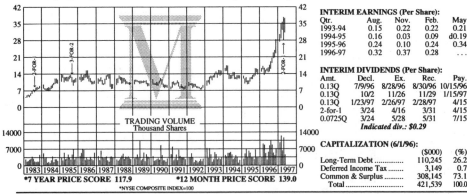

*7 YEAR PRICE SCORE 117.9 *12 MONTH PRICE SCORE 139.0

*NYSE COMPOSITE INDEX=100

INTERIM EARNINGS (Per Share):

Qtr.	Aug.	Nov.	Feb.	May
1993-94	0.15	0.22	0.22	0.21
1994-95	0.16	0.03	0.09	d0.19
1995-96	0.24	0.10	0.24	0.34
1996-97	0.32	0.37	0.28	...

INTERIM DIVIDENDS (Per Share):

Amt.	Decl.	Ex.	Rec.	Pay.
0.13Q	7/9/96	8/28/96	8/30/96	10/15/96
0.13Q	10/2	11/26	11/29	1/15/97
0.13Q	1/23/97	2/26/97	2/28/97	4/15
2-for-1	3/24	4/16	3/31	4/15
0.0725Q	3/24	5/28	5/31	7/15

Indicated div.: $0.29

CAPITALIZATION (6/1/96):

	($000)	(%)
Long-Term Debt	110,245	26.2
Deferred Income Tax	3,149	0.7
Common & Surplus	308,145	73.1
Total	421,539	100.0

RECENT DEVELOPMENTS: For the third quarter ended 3/1/97, net income increased 13.7% to $13.5 million compared with $11.9 million in the corresponding quarter the year before. Net sales advanced 16.7% to $365.1 million from $312.9 million a year earlier. Net sales of international operations and exports from the U.S. rose 7.0% to $175.3 million compared with $163.9 million the previous year. The current quarter's operating results included a pre-tax charge of $13.7 million for the restructuring of the Company's German operations. The restructuring efforts in Germany included the discontinuation of manufacturing operations, with a small team remaining to serve MLHR's existing client base in Germany, Eastern Europe and the Netherlands. New orders for the third quarter increased 30.1% to $358.6 million. The backlog of unfilled orders at the end of the quarter totaled $200.2 million.

BUSINESS

HERMAN MILLER, INC. is engaged primarily in the design, manufacture and sale of furniture systems, products and related services principally for offices, and to a lesser extent, for health care facilities and other uses. Through research and design, the Company strives to develop innovative solutions to operational problems in the office, institution, health care, materials handling and other environments in which its products and systems are used.

ANNUAL EARNINGS AND DIVIDENDS PER SHARE

	6/1/96	6/3/95	5/28/94	5/29/93	5/30/92	6/1/91	6/2/90
Earnings Per Share	**0.92**	**0.09**	**0.80**	**0.44**	**[1] d0.07**	**0.28**	**0.91**
Dividends Per Share	**0.26**	**0.26**	**0.26**	**0.26**	**0.26**	**0.26**	**0.26**
Dividend Payout %	**28.4**	**N.M.**	**32.5**	**59.1**	**N.M.**	**94.5**	**28.6**

Note: 2-for-1 stk. split, 4/15/97. [1] Before extra. item & acctg. change

ANNUAL FINANCIAL DATA

	6/1/96	6/3/95	5/28/94	5/29/93	5/30/92	6/1/91	6/2/90
RECORD OF EARNINGS (IN MILLIONS):							
Total Revenues	1,283.9	1,083.1	953.2	855.7	804.7	878.7	865.0
Costs and Expenses	1,164.0	1,034.3	858.2	780.3	772.2	806.8	754.3
Depreciation & Amort	45.0	39.7	33.2	31.6	30.5	32.8	28.0
Operating Income	74.9	9.1	61.8	43.8	2.0	39.2	82.7
Income Bef Income Taxes	70.1	4.0	63.5	42.4	d1.0	33.2	75.0
Income Taxes	24.2	cr0.3	23.1	20.3	2.5	19.1	28.4
Net Income	45.9	4.3	40.4	22.1	[1] d3.5	14.1	46.6
Aver. Shs. Outstg. (000)	50,258	49,584	50,510	49,986	50,326	51,370	51,286
[1] Before extra. item dr$2,681,000; and acctg. chg dr$7,976,000.							
BALANCE SHEET (IN MILLIONS):							
Cash and Cash Equivalents	57.1	16.5	22.7	16.5	16.9	15.4	11.8
Receivables, Net	170.1	165.1	121.6	111.2	109.8	122.3	134.1
Inventories	65.7	71.1	59.8	56.0	59.9	69.4	83.5
Gross Property	536.1	513.5	454.9	431.4	411.7	389.6	367.4
Accumulated Depreciation	267.3	243.3	215.9	203.0	191.4	170.8	147.8
Long-Term Debt	110.2	60.1	20.6	21.1	29.4	54.7	89.0
Net Stockholders' Equity	308.1	286.9	296.3	283.9	280.1	314.8	314.3
Total Assets	694.9	659.0	533.7	484.3	471.3	492.9	534.0
Total Current Assets	334.9	297.1	228.7	207.6	205.3	221.6	243.1
Total Current Liabilities	219.0	257.5	177.7	144.9	138.8	107.6	116.1
Net Working Capital	115.9	39.6	50.9	62.7	66.5	114.0	127.0
Year End Shs Outstg (000)	49,672	49,672	49,180	50,008	50,296	51,062	51,228
STATISTICAL RECORD:							
Operating Profit Margin %	5.8	0.8	6.5	5.1	0.2	4.5	9.6
Book Value Per Share	6.21	5.78	6.03	5.68	5.57	6.17	5.91
Return on Equity %	14.9	1.5	13.6	7.8	...	4.5	14.8
Return on Assets %	6.6	0.7	7.6	4.6	...	2.9	8.7
Average Yield %	2.0	1.8	2.1	2.9	2.8	2.6	2.5
P/E Ratio	17.7-10.5	N.M.	19.4-11.3	24.0-16.8	...	44.3-29.8	12.7-9.8
Price Range	16⅛-9⅝	17½-11⅝	15½-9	10⅝-7⅜	11¼-7½	12⅛-8⅛	11⅝-8⅞

Statistics are as originally reported.

OFFICERS:
D.L. Nelson, Chmn.
M.A. Volkema, Pres. & C.E.O.
B.C. Walker, V.P.-Fin.
J.E. Christenson, V.P., Gen. Couns. & Sec.

INCORPORATED: MI, 1905

PRINCIPAL OFFICE: 855 East Main Ave., P.O. Box 302, Zeeland, MI 49464-0302

TELEPHONE NUMBER: (616) 654-3000

NO. OF EMPLOYEES: 6,964 (full-time); 491 (part-time)

ANNUAL MEETING: In October

SHAREHOLDERS: 14,000 (approx.)

INSTITUTIONAL HOLDINGS:
No. of Institutions: 225
Shares Held: 30,675,306 (adj.)

REGISTRAR(S): First Chicago Trust Co. of New York, Jersey City, NJ

TRANSFER AGENT(S): First Chicago Trust Co. of New York, Jersey City, NJ

MOLEX, INC.

	YIELD	0.2%
	P/E RATIO	23.0

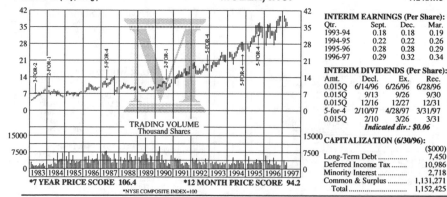

INTERIM EARNINGS (Per Share):

Qtr.	Sept.	Dec.	Mar.	June
1993-94	0.18	0.18	0.19	0.23
1994-95	0.22	0.22	0.26	0.30
1995-96	0.28	0.28	0.29	0.31
1996-97	0.29	0.32	0.34	...

INTERIM DIVIDENDS (Per Share):

Amt.	Decl.	Ex.	Rec.	Pay.
0.015Q	6/14/96	6/26/96	6/28/96	7/25/96
0.015Q	9/13	9/26	9/30	10/25
0.015Q	12/16	12/27	12/31	1/27/97
5-for-4	2/10/97	4/28/97	3/31/97	4/25
0.015Q	2/10	3/26	3/31	4/25

Indicated div.: $0.06

CAPITALIZATION (6/30/96):

	($000)	(%)
Long-Term Debt	7,450	0.6
Deferred Income Tax	10,986	1.0
Minority Interest	2,718	0.2
Common & Surplus	1,131,271	98.2
Total	1,152,425	100.0

TRADING VOLUME
Thousand Shares

1983 1984 1985 1986 1987 1988 1989 1990 1991 1992 1993 1994 1995 1996 1997

*7 YEAR PRICE SCORE 106.4   ***12 MONTH PRICE SCORE 94.2**

*NYSE COMPOSITE INDEX=100

RECENT DEVELOPMENTS: For the third quarter ended 3/31/97, net income was up 19.6% to $43.2 million. This compares with $36.1 million in the corresponding quarter the year before. Net revenue rose 11.5% to $387.1 million from $347.1 million in the comparable prior-year period. The net return on sales for the quarter was 11.2%, boosted by the Company's operations in the Far East North, the Far East South and the Americas regions as well as improve-

ment in Europe. Currency translation decreased revenues and net income by $19.5 million and $2.0 million, respectively. The reduction in net income due to currency translation was largely offset by lower cost of sales and by transaction gains that resulted from the lower value of the Japanese yen. The Company's order backlog at the end of the quarter totaled $246.8 million, up 9.0% compared with $226.4 million a year earlier.

BUSINESS

MOLEX INCORPORATED is engaged in the manufacture and sale of electrical components. The Company designs, manufactures, and distributes electrical and electronic devices such as terminals, connectors, planer cables, cable assemblies, interconnection systems, fiber optic interconnection systems, backplanes and mechanical and electronic switches. Crimping machines and terminal inserting equipment are offered on a lease or purchase basis to the Company's customers for the purpose of applying the Company's components to the customers' products.

ANNUAL EARNINGS AND DIVIDENDS PER SHARE

	6/30/96	6/30/95	6/30/94	6/30/93	6/30/92	6/30/91	6/30/90
Earnings Per Share	1.16	0.99	0.77	③ 0.61	0.55	0.53	0.51
Dividends Per Share	① 0.048	② 0.031	0.017	④ 0.012	0.006	⑤ 0.006	0.005
Dividend Payout %	4.1	3.1	2.2	2.0	1.2	1.2	0.9

Note: 5-for-4 stk. split, 4/25/97. ① 25% stk. div., 9/15/95 ② 25% stk. div., 11/94 ③ Before acctg. change ④ 5-for-4 stk. split, 12/1/92 ⑤ 2-for-1 stk. split, 7/25/90

ANNUAL FINANCIAL DATA

RECORD OF EARNINGS (IN MILLIONS):

Total Revenues	1,382.7	1,197.7	964.1	859.3	776.2	708.0	594.4
Costs and Expenses	1,046.5	885.7	717.9	650.2	596.4	536.9	435.3
Depreciation & Amort	119.9	104.9	88.8	76.2	67.6	58.7	54.4
Operating Income	216.3	207.2	157.4	132.9	112.2	112.4	104.6
Income Bef Income Taxes	229.0	214.5	159.5	133.5	117.4	117.9	110.0
Income Taxes	83.3	90.3	63.2	58.4	49.8	53.4	47.5
Net Income	145.6	124.0	94.9	① 74.7	67.5	64.6	62.1
Aver. Shs. Outstg. (000)	125,931	125,019	123,720	123,049	122,366	121,695	122,119

① Before acctg. change dr$3,605,000.

BALANCE SHEET (IN MILLIONS):

Cash and Cash Equivalents	282.7	313.1	228.9	186.1	157.2	149.6	143.7
Receivables, Net	296.6	302.7	240.3	205.5	182.2	157.8	136.6
Inventories	147.6	150.8	113.3	104.5	93.7	83.6	71.8
Gross Property	1,292.9	1,266.3	1,000.4	854.2	758.7	601.5	483.5
Accumulated Depreciation	679.8	699.0	559.4	468.3	396.0	320.8	254.5
Long-Term Debt	7.5	8.1	7.4	7.5	7.9	9.1	8.0
Net Stockholders' Equity	1,131.3	1,107.3	881.6	751.7	660.4	550.7	481.3
Total Assets	1,461.0	1,441.0	1,138.5	961.8	849.7	709.7	606.9
Total Current Assets	734.6	773.0	586.6	500.2	436.5	395.3	355.1
Total Current Liabilities	275.2	278.0	205.4	180.5	168.2	143.8	110.0
Net Working Capital	459.4	495.0	381.2	319.7	268.3	251.5	245.2
Year End Shs Outstg (000)	126,020	126,173	124,216	123,358	122,786	122,073	121,731

STATISTICAL RECORD:

Operating Profit Margin %	15.6	17.3	16.3	15.5	14.5	15.9	17.6
Book Value Per Share	8.98	8.78	7.10	6.10	5.38	4.51	3.95
Return on Equity %	12.9	11.2	10.8	9.9	10.2	11.7	12.9
Return on Assets %	10.0	8.6	8.3	7.8	7.9	9.1	10.2
Average Yield %	0.2	0.1	0.1	0.1	0.1	0.1	0.1
P/E Ratio	26.6-18.8	29.8-20.0	29.9-20.2	32.2-21.7	29.3-21.9	27.8-16.9	20.7-13.4
Price Range	30¾-21¾	29⅝-19¾	23-15½	19⅝-13¼	16¼-12⅛	14¾-9	10½-6¾

Statistics are as originally reported.

OFFICERS:
F.A. Krehbiel, Chmn. & C.E.O.
J.H. Krehbiel, Jr., Pres. & C.O.O.
R.B. Mahoney, V.P., C.F.O. & Treas.
L.A. Hecht, Sec. & Gen. Coun.

INCORPORATED: IL, 1957; reincorp., DE, Sep., 1972

PRINCIPAL OFFICE: 2222 Wellington Court, Lisle, IL 60532

TELEPHONE NUMBER: (630) 969-4550

FAX: (630) 969-1352

NO. OF EMPLOYEES: 10,100

ANNUAL MEETING: In October

SHAREHOLDERS: 6,159 com.; 4,565 Cl. A com.

INSTITUTIONAL HOLDINGS:
No. of Institutions: 170
Shares Held: 25,261,253 (adj.)

REGISTRAR(S):

TRANSFER AGENT(S): Harris Trust & Savings Bank of Chicago, Chicago, IL

NETSCAPE COMMUNICATIONS CORP.

YIELD ...%
P/E RATIO N.M.

105 90 75 60 45 30 15

72000 36000 0

*7 YEAR PRICE SCORE ...   *12 MONTH PRICE SCORE 57.3

TRADING VOLUME
Thousand Shares

1983 1984 1985 1986 1987 1988 1989 1990 1991 1992 1993 1994 1995 1996 1997

*NYSE COMPOSITE INDEX=100

INTERIM EARNINGS (Per Share):

Qtr.	Mar.	June	Sept.	Dec.
1995	d0.06	d0.04	0.01	0.03
1996	0.04	0.01	0.09	0.10
1997	0.09	...	...	...

INTERIM DIVIDENDS (Per Share):

Amt.	Decl.	Ex.	Rec.	Pay.
2-for-1	11/15/95	2/7/96	1/23/96	2/6/96

CAPITALIZATION (12/31/96):

	($000)	(%)
Long-Term Debt	484	0.1
Common & Surplus	390,650	99.9
Total	391,134	100.0

RECENT DEVELOPMENTS: For the three months ended 3/31/97, net income totaled $7.9 million, or $0.09 per share, compared with $3.6 million, or $0.04 per share, in the corresponding prior-year quarter. Total revenues more than doubled to $120.2 million from $56.1 million the previous year. Product revenues jumped 83.0% to $89.8 million from $49.1 million a year earlier. Service revenues were $30.5 million, up significantly versus $7.1 million in the first quarter in 1996. Results benefited from strong growth in the Company's server business, primarily in the email and groupware areas. NSCP is planning to release Netscape Communicator™ and SuiteSpot™ 3.0 in the second quarter of 1997. Gross profit totaled $104.4 million, or 86.8% of total revenues, compared with $47.6 million, or 84.9% of total revenues, the year before. Operating income was $11.7 million versus $2.5 million a year ago.

BUSINESS

NETSCAPE COMMUNICATIONS CORP. is a provider of application software that supports information exchange and commercial transactions over the Internet. The Company developed Netscape Navigator™, a popular tool for accessing the World Wide Web and also produces Netsite Commerce Server, a secure method of paying for Internet purchases. The Company also offers a full line of clients, servers, development tools and commercial applications to create a complete platform for next-generation, live on-line applications.

ANNUAL EARNINGS AND DIVIDENDS PER SHARE

	1996	1995	1994
Earnings Per Share	0.24	d0.05	...
Dividends Per Share	[1] ...	Nil	...

[1] 2-for-1 stk. split, 2/6/96.

ANNUAL FINANCIAL DATA

RECORD OF EARNINGS (IN THOUSANDS):

Total Revenues	346,195	80,656	696
Costs and Expenses	298,354	82,800	[1] 9,221
Depreciation & Amort	18,776	3,203	...
Operating Income	22,715	d7,380	d8,525
Income Bef Income Taxes	29,453	d2,943	...
Income Taxes	8,545	498	...
Net Income	20,908	d3,441	d8,470
Aver. Shs. Outstg.	87,861	73,784	64,513

[1] Incl. Dep.

BALANCE SHEET (IN THOUSANDS):

Cash and Cash Equivalents	200,564	148,505	3,244
Receivables, Net	110,627	28,467	702
Gross Property	105,899	23,423	2,663
Accumulated Depreciation	19,332	2,827	216
Long-Term Debt	484	1,198	725
Net Stockholders' Equity	390,650	173,350	1,084
Total Assets	537,450	227,748	7,159
Total Current Assets	348,430	182,491	4,012
Total Current Liabilities	146,316	53,200	5,350
Net Working Capital	202,114	129,291	d1,338
Year End Shares Outstg	87,941	81,063	9,022

STATISTICAL RECORD:

Operating Profit Margin %	6.6	...	...
Book Value Per Share	4.44	2.14	0.12
Return on Equity %	5.4	...	...
Return on Assets %	3.9	...	...
P/E Ratio	N.M.	...	...
Price Range	86-34½	87-23	...

Statistics are as originally reported.

OFFICERS:
J.H. Clark, Chmn.
J.L. Barksdale, Pres. & C.E.O.
P.L. Currie, Sr. V.P. & C.F.O.
R.R. Katz, Sr. V.P., Gen. Couns. & Sec.

INCORPORATED: DE, Apr., 1994

PRINCIPAL OFFICE: 501 East Middlefield Road, Mountain View, CA 94043

TELEPHONE NUMBER: (415) 254-1900

NO. OF EMPLOYEES: 1,811 (approx.)

ANNUAL MEETING: In June

SHAREHOLDERS: 2,468

INSTITUTIONAL HOLDINGS:
No. of Institutions: 224
Shares Held: 22,039,574

REGISTRAR(S):

TRANSFER AGENT(S): The First National Bank of Boston, Palo Alto, CA

NASDAQ SYMBOL NXTL
Rec. Pr. 14⅜ (Marginable)

NEXTEL COMMUNICATIONS, INC.

YIELD ...%
P/E RATIO ...

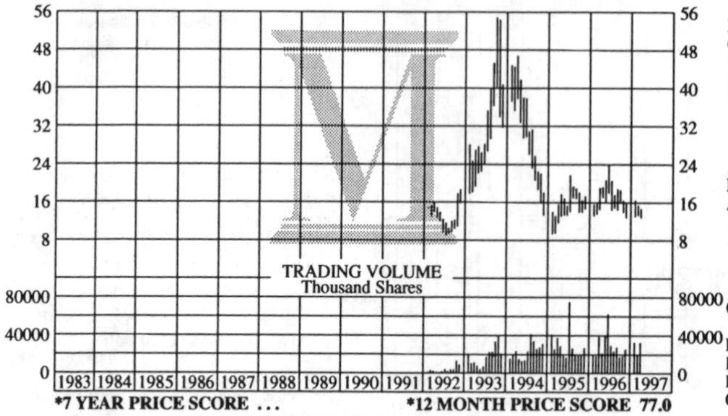

56
48
40
32
24
16
8
TRADING VOLUME
Thousand Shares
80000
40000
0
1983 1984 1985 1986 1987 1988 1989 1990 1991 1992 1993 1994 1995 1996 1997

*7 YEAR PRICE SCORE ... *12 MONTH PRICE SCORE 77.0

*NYSE COMPOSITE INDEX=100

INTERIM EARNINGS (Per Share):

Qtr.	Mar.	June	Sept.	Dec.
1995	d0.50	d0.53	d0.61	d0.62
1996	d0.56	d0.28	d0.66	d0.70
1997	d0.93	...	...	...

INTERIM DIVIDENDS (Per Share):

Amt. Decl. Ex. Rec. Pay.

No dividends paid.

CAPITALIZATION (12/31/96):

	($000)	(%)
Long-Term Debt	2,783,041	45.7
Deferred Income Tax	505,516	8.3
Preferred Stock	300,000	4.9
Common & Surplus	2,508,138	41.1
Total	6,096,695	100.0

RECENT DEVELOPMENTS: For the three months ended 3/31/97, NXTL incurred a net loss of $220.9 million. This compares with a net loss of $118.7 million in the corresponding period the year before. Revenues for the period were up 62.0% to $110.7 million from $68.3 million in the prior year. Radio service revenue, which reflects airtime usage and monthly fees, rose 78.5% to $103.7 million as the Company added approximately 122,600 digital mobile units in service during the quarter. In addition, the monthly average revenue per digital unit increased to $59 from $37 a year earlier. During the quarter, NXTL launched its National Network guaranteed all-digital coverage in the U.S with an aggressive national advertising campaign. The National Network is attributed to the large gain in the number of digital subscribers. The larger net loss for the quarter reflects significant increases in selling, general and administrative and depreciation and amortization expenses, as well as a 44.5% lower tax benefit.

BUSINESS

NEXTEL COMMUNICATIONS, INC. provides wireless communications services such as mobile phones, paging, private networks (dispatch), and data to businesses, professionals, and consumers in large metropolitan areas in the United States. The Company is primarily engaged in the acquisition and operation of specialized mobile radio systems, as well as sales and servicing of two-way radio equipment. As of 3/31/97, the Company had a subscriber base of 422,900 digital communications customers and a total number of analog units in service of approximately 715,000.

ANNUAL EARNINGS AND DIVIDENDS PER SHARE

	12/31/96	12/31/95	12/31/94	3/31/94	3/31/93	3/31/92	3/31/91
Earnings Per Share	**d2.50**	**d2.31**	**d1.25**	**d0.73**	**d0.16**	[1] **d0.58**	[1] **d0.30**
Dividends Per Share	**Nil**	**Nil**	**Nil**	**Nil**	**Nil**	**Nil**	**Nil**

[1] Before extra. item

ANNUAL FINANCIAL DATA

	12/31/96	12/31/95	12/31/94	3/31/94	3/31/93	3/31/92	3/31/91
RECORD OF EARNINGS (IN MILLIONS):							
Total Revenues	332.9	225.2	83.7	67.9	53.0	52.5	53.9
Costs and Expenses	578.0	415.9	145.3	69.8	40.0	34.7	34.6
Depreciation & Amort	400.8	236.2	94.1	58.4	[3] 0.0	25.7	24.5
Operating Income	d645.9	d426.9	d155.8	d60.2	d12.9	d7.8	d5.2
Income Bef Income Taxes	d863.2	d531.8	d197.2	d78.3	d10.6	d18.9	d15.4
Income Taxes	cr307.2	cr200.6	cr71.3	cr21.4	cr1.0	cr3.3	cr8.5
Net Income	d556.0	d331.2	d125.8	d56.9	d9.6	[1] d15.7	[2] d7.0
Aver. Shs. Outstg. (000)	222,779	143,283	100,639	78,439	58,736	26,925	23,154

[1] Before extra. item dr$12,765,000. [2] Before extra. item dr$747,000. [3] Equal to $26,000.

	12/31/96	12/31/95	12/31/94	3/31/94	3/31/93	3/31/92	3/31/91
BALANCE SHEET (IN MILLIONS):							
Cash and Cash Equivalents	144.7	409.3	474.0	909.6	31.9	13.4	0.5
Receivables, Net	90.4	41.5	15.4	6.8	5.3	4.5	6.5
Inventories	45.2	21.2	11.7	3.1	1.9	1.8	2.4
Gross Property	2,118.5	1,331.5	807.7	374.5	134.1	37.4	29.5
Accumulated Depreciation	314.8	139.3	49.8	23.8	13.2	9.5	5.8
Long-Term Debt	2,783.0	1,653.4	1,163.2	1,080.7	55.0	1.0	106.1
Net Stockholders' Equity	2,808.1	2,945.1	1,268.6	846.3	255.2	191.1	54.6
Total Assets	6,472.4	5,547.3	2,889.1	2,197.3	333.6	210.8	212.0
Total Current Assets	309.1	504.7	504.2	922.0	39.9	20.2	10.1
Total Current Liabilities	375.7	365.0	216.7	103.2	23.3	17.5	18.2
Net Working Capital	d66.6	139.7	287.5	818.8	16.6	2.7	d8.0
Year End Shs Outstg (000)	227,583	193,579	105,596	87,779	63,173	55,337	21,217
STATISTICAL RECORD:							
Book Value Per Share	12.34	15.21	12.01	3.99	1.75	0.55	...
Price Range	24-12¾	21¾-9⅜	46¾-13¼	54⅞-17⅞	18¾-9	...	...

Statistics are as originally reported.

OFFICERS:
D.F. Akerson, Chmn.
M.E. O'Brien, Vice-Chmn.
B.D. McAuley, Vice-Chmn.
T.M. Donahue, Pres.
S.M. Shindler, Sr. V.P. & C.F.O.

INCORPORATED: DE, Apr., 1987

PRINCIPAL OFFICE: 1505 Farm Credit Dr., McLean, VA 22102

TELEPHONE NUMBER: (703) 394-3000

NO. OF EMPLOYEES: 3,500

ANNUAL MEETING: In September

SHAREHOLDERS: 2,006 (Cl. A); 1 (Cl. B)

INSTITUTIONAL HOLDINGS:
No. of Institutions: 134
Shares Held: 72,601,540

REGISTRAR(S): First Chicago Trust Co. of New York

TRANSFER AGENT(S): First Chicago Trust Co. of New York

NASDAQ SYMBOL NOBE
Rec. Pr. 37⅛ (Marginable)

NORDSTROM, INC.

YIELD 1.3%
P/E RATIO 20.2

30000
15000
0

| 1983 | 1984 | 1985 | 1986 | 1987 | 1988 | 1989 | 1990 | 1991 | 1992 | 1993 | 1994 | 1995 | 1996 | 1997 |

*7 YEAR PRICE SCORE 77.3   ***12 MONTH PRICE SCORE 80.8**

*NYSE COMPOSITE INDEX=100

TRADING VOLUME
Thousand Shares

INTERIM EARNINGS (Per Share):

Qtr.	Apr.	July	Oct.	Jan.
1993-94	0.14	0.52	0.31	0.74
1994-95	0.39	0.77	0.46	0.85
1995-96	0.34	0.65	0.36	0.67
1996-97	0.34	0.55	0.42	0.53

INTERIM DIVIDENDS (Per Share):

Amt.	Decl.	Ex.	Rec.	Pay.
0.125Q	5/21/96	5/29/96	5/31/96	6/14/96
0.125Q	8/20	8/28	8/30	9/16
0.125Q	11/19	11/26	11/29	12/16
0.125Q	2/18/97	2/26/97	2/28/97	3/14/97

Indicated div.: $0.50

CAPITALIZATION (1/31/97):

	($000)	(%)
Long-Term Debt	329,330	18.3
Common & Surplus	1,473,192	81.7
Total	1,802,522	100.0

RECENT DEVELOPMENTS: For the year ended 1/31/97, net earnings fell 10.7% to $147.5 million from $165.1 million in 1996. This decrease reflected higher merchandise markdowns from the reorganization of women's apparel and higher write-offs on NOBE's credit card balances. Net sales grew 8.3% to $4.45 billion from $4.11 billion the year before, led by a 7.0% increase from new stores. The Company opened new full-line stores during 1996 in King of Prussia, Pennsylvania; Dallas, Texas; Troy, Michigan; and

Denver, Colorado. For the quarter ended 1/31/97, net earnings dropped 20.9% to $42.8 million compared with $54.1 million in the corresponding prior-year period. This decrease resulted from lower sales volume in comparable stores, higher inventories than planned, higher markdowns and an increase in inventory shrinkage. Net sales advanced 6.4% to $1.32 billion from $1.24 billion the previous year due to strong sales from four new stores opened during 1996.

BUSINESS

NORDSTROM, INC. operates a total of 83 stores, including large specialty stores in Washington, Oregon, California, Utah, Colorado, Alaska, Texas, Virginia, New York, New Jersey, Pennsylvania, Michigan, Illinois, Indiana, Maryland and Minnesota, selling a wide selection of apparel, shoes and accessories for women, men and children. The Company also operates clearance stores under the name "Nordstrom Rack," which serve as outlets for clearance merchandise from the Company's large specialty stores. The Racks also purchase merchandise directly from manufacturers. The Racks are located in Washington, Oregon, California, Utah, Illinois, Pennsylvania, Virginia and Maryland. The Company also operates a men's specialty store in New York and leased shoe departments in 12 department stores in Hawaii and Guam.

ANNUAL EARNINGS AND DIVIDENDS PER SHARE

	1/31/97	1/31/96	1/31/95	1/31/94	1/31/93	1/31/92	1/31/91
Earnings Per Share	1.82	2.02	2.47	1.71	1.67	1.66	1.42
Dividends Per Share	0.50	0.50	0.385	0.34	0.32	0.31	0.30
Dividend Payout %	27.5	24.8	15.6	19.9	19.2	18.7	21.1

ANNUAL FINANCIAL DATA

RECORD OF EARNINGS (IN MILLIONS):

	1/31/97	1/31/96	1/31/95	1/31/94	1/31/93	1/31/92	1/31/91
Total Revenues	4,453.1	4,113.5	3,894.5	3,589.9	3,422.0	3,179.8	2,893.9
Costs and Expenses	4,143.5	3,792.7	3,512.1	3,306.4	3,138.4	2,904.9	2,662.4
Depreciation & Amort	156.1	134.3	110.8	103.5	102.8	96.0	85.6
Operating Income	153.4	186.5	271.6	180.1	180.8	178.9	145.9
Income Bef Income Taxes	243.5	272.3	335.6	230.9	222.1	217.2	178.3
Income Taxes	96.0	107.2	132.6	90.5	85.5	81.4	62.5
Net Income	147.5	165.1	203.0	140.4	136.6	135.8	115.8
Aver. Shs. Outstg. (000)	80,849	81,920	82,144	82,003	81,893	81,780	81,675

BALANCE SHEET (IN MILLIONS):

	1/31/97	1/31/96	1/31/95	1/31/94	1/31/93	1/31/92	1/31/91
Cash and Cash Equivalents	28.3	24.5	32.5	91.2	29.1	14.7	24.7
Receivables, Net	714.6	893.9	675.9	586.4	603.2	608.2	575.5
Inventories	719.9	626.3	627.9	585.6	536.7	506.6	448.3
Gross Property	2,096.9	1,942.1	1,730.9	1,499.6	1,385.1	1,327.2	1,184.9
Accumulated Depreciation	944.5	838.8	746.7	654.0	560.9	470.8	378.7
Long-Term Debt	329.3	365.7	297.9	336.4	440.6	502.2	457.7
Net Stockholders' Equity	1,473.2	1,423.0	1,343.8	1,166.5	1,052.0	939.2	826.4
Total Assets	2,702.5	2,732.6	2,396.8	2,177.5	2,053.2	2,041.9	1,902.6
Total Current Assets	1,532.4	1,612.8	1,397.7	1,314.9	1,219.8	1,177.6	1,090.4
Total Current Liabilities	787.4	832.3	690.5	627.5	511.2	553.9	551.8
Net Working Capital	745.0	780.5	707.3	687.4	708.6	623.7	538.5
Year End Shs Outstg (000)	79,635	81,113	82,244	82,059	81,975	81,844	81,738

STATISTICAL RECORD:

	1/31/97	1/31/96	1/31/95	1/31/94	1/31/93	1/31/92	1/31/91
Operating Profit Margin %	3.4	4.5	7.0	5.0	5.3	5.6	5.0
Book Value Per Share	18.50	17.54	16.34	14.22	12.83	11.48	10.11
Return on Equity %	10.0	11.6	15.1	12.0	13.0	14.5	14.0
Return on Assets %	5.5	6.0	8.5	6.4	6.7	6.7	6.1
Average Yield %	1.1	1.2	1.2	1.1	1.0	0.8	1.1
P/E Ratio	29.4-18.8	22.4-17.3	20.1-12.6	25.4-14.8	25.6-15.3	31.9-13.3	27.6-12.1
Price Range	53½-34¼	45¼-35	49¾-31	43½-25¼	42¾-25½	53-22	39¼-17¼

Statistics are as originally reported.

OFFICERS:
J.J. Whitacre, Chmn.
B.W. Nordstrom; E.B. Nordstrom; J.D. Nordstrom; J.A. Nordstrom; P.E. Nordstrom; W.E. Nordstrom, Co.-Pres.

INCORPORATED: WA, 1946

PRINCIPAL OFFICE: 1501 Fifth Avenue, Seattle, WA 98101

TELEPHONE NUMBER: (206) 628-2111

FAX: (206) 628-1707

NO. OF EMPLOYEES: 39,600 (approx.)

ANNUAL MEETING: In May

SHAREHOLDERS: 74,000 (approx.)

INSTITUTIONAL HOLDINGS:
No. of Institutions: 208
Shares Held: 39,474,391

REGISTRAR(S): Chase Mellon Shareholder Services, New York, NY

TRANSFER AGENT(S): Chase Mellon Shareholder Services, New York, NY

NORTHWEST AIRLINES CORP.

YIELD ...%
P/E RATIO 7.8

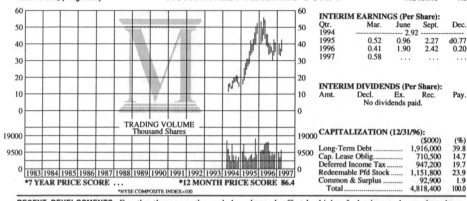

INTERIM EARNINGS (Per Share):

Qtr.	Mar.	June	Sept.	Dec.
1994	-----------	2.92	-----------	
1995	0.52	0.96	2.27	d0.77
1996	0.41	1.90	2.42	0.20
1997	0.58	...	...	...

INTERIM DIVIDENDS (Per Share):

Amt.	Decl.	Ex.	Rec.	Pay.
		No dividends paid.		

CAPITALIZATION (12/31/96):

	($000)	(%)
Long-Term Debt	1,916,000	39.8
Cap. Lease Oblig.	710,500	14.7
Deferred Income Tax	947,200	19.7
Redeemable Pfd Stock	1,151,800	23.9
Common & Surplus	92,900	1.9
Total	4,818,400	100.0

RECENT DEVELOPMENTS: For the three months ended 3/31/97, net income increased 21.0% to $64.6 million. This compares with $53.4 million in the corresponding period the year before. Total revenues were up 4.9% to $2.38 billion from $2.26 billion in the comparable prior-year period. The higher net income reflects, among other things, a 16.5% decline in interest expense as well as an 85.5% higher foreign currency gain at $12.8 million. The 1997 operating results were characterized by strong domestic demand, offset by higher fuel prices and a weakened yen. During the quarter, NWAC carried nearly 12.7 million passengers. This compares with 12.0 million passengers a year earlier. Passenger revenues totaled $2.04 billion, or 85.9% of total revenues, up 5.4% compared with $1.94 billion the previous year. On 4/1/97, the Company acquired Express Airlines I, Inc. of Atlanta, which operates as Northwest Airlink in the Minneapolis/St. Paul and Memphis markets.

BUSINESS

NORTHWEST AIRLINES CORP. is a holding company whose principal operating indirect subsidiary is Northwest Airlines, Inc. The Company operates from four primary hubs at Minneapolis/St. Paul, Detroit, Memphis, and Tokyo and Osaka. The Company, together with major airline alliances and Northwest Airlink partners, serves more than 390 cities in 80 countries on six continents. The airline has more destinations in Asia than any other U.S. airline, including the most non-stop flights between the U.S. and Japan. With KLM Royal Dutch Airlines, the Company serves more than 80 cities in Europe, Africa and the Middle East from 11 U.S. gateways through a European hub in Amsterdam. With Alaska Airlines and its Airlink partners, the Company serves more than 240 U.S. cities.

ANNUAL EARNINGS AND DIVIDENDS PER SHARE

	1996	1995	1994	1993	1992	1991
Earnings Per Share	4.93	① 3.02	2.92	d2.82	② 16.11	d5.97
Dividends Per Share	Nil	Nil	Nil	Nil	Nil	Nil

① Before extra. item ② Before acctg. change

ANNUAL FINANCIAL DATA

RECORD OF EARNINGS (IN MILLIONS):

Total Revenues	9,880.5	9,084.9	9,142.9	8,648.9	8,127.6	7,682.9
Operating Expenses	8,449.0	7,824.6	7,955.1	7,959.2	8,103.4	7,420.4
Depreciation	377.7	358.1	357.4	417.3	400.4	372.4
Operating Income	1,053.8	902.2	830.4	272.4	d376.2	d109.9
Income Bef Income Taxes	872.4	550.6	498.3	d123.2	d1,482.1	d488.0
Income Taxes	336.3	204.0	202.8	cr7.9	cr511.4	cr167.8
Net Income	536.1	① 342.1	295.5	d115.3	② d970.7	d320.2
Aver. Shs. Outstg. (000)	101,090	94,300	80,890	65,450	64,950	64,950

① Before extra. item cr$49,900,000. ② Before acctg. change dr$108,800,000.

BALANCE SHEET (IN MILLIONS):

Cash and Cash Equivalents	812.5	1,111.6	1,069.9	192.3	275.1	...
Receivables, Net	751.6	783.1	728.4	801.7	830.4	...
Gross Property	7,135.6	6,479.0	6,101.8	5,971.9	5,588.5	...
Accumulated Depreciation	1,923.6	1,689.5	1,449.6	1,276.4	974.6	...
Long-Term Debt	1,916.0	2,137.4	3,679.3	4,193.0	4,155.8	...
Prop, Plant & Equip, Net	5,212.0	4,789.5	4,652.2	4,695.5	4,613.9	...
Net Stockholders' Equity	1,244.7	745.1	d575.7	d1,280.6	d1,166.4	...
Total Assets	8,511.7	8,412.3	8,070.1	7,571.3	7,545.4	...
Total Current Assets	2,089.9	2,338.2	2,185.2	1,544.7	1,517.6	...
Total Current Liabilities	2,883.2	2,840.6	2,546.7	2,323.6	2,253.0	...
Net Working Capital	d793.3	d502.4	d361.5	d778.9	d735.4	...
Year End Shs Outstg (000)	97,600	91,350	84,330	58,010	52,700	...

STATISTICAL RECORD:

Operating Profit Margin %	10.7	9.9	9.1	3.1	...	...
Return on Equity %	43.1	45.9	...	...	...	...
Return on Assets %	6.3	3.8	3.7	...	...	...
P/E Ratio	11.3-6.1	17.4-5.3	7.3-3.9	...	...	...
Price Range	55⅞-30⅛	52½-15⅞	21⅜-11½	...	...	...

Statistics are as originally reported.

OFFICERS:
G.L. Wilson, Chairman
J.H. Dasburg, Pres. & C.E.O.
J.A. Lawrence, Exec. V.P. & C.F.O.

INCORPORATED: DE, Feb., 1989

PRINCIPAL OFFICE: 2700 Lone Oak Pkwy, Eagan, MN 55121

TELEPHONE NUMBER: (612) 726-2111

NO. OF EMPLOYEES: 47,500 (approx.)

ANNUAL MEETING: In April

SHAREHOLDERS: 458

INSTITUTIONAL HOLDINGS:
No. of Institutions: 67
Shares Held: 39,024,086

REGISTRAR(S): Norwest Bank Minnesota, N.A., St. Paul, MN

TRANSFER AGENT(S): Norwest Bank Minnesota, N.A., St. Paul, MN

NOVELL, INC.

YIELD ...%
P/E RATIO 27.9

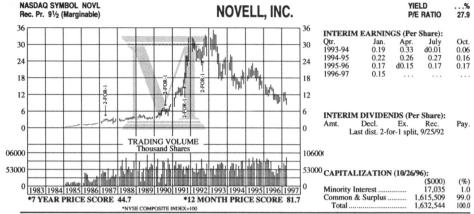

INTERIM EARNINGS (Per Share):

Qtr.	Jan.	Apr.	July	Oct.
1993-94	0.19	0.33	d0.01	0.06
1994-95	0.22	0.26	0.27	0.16
1995-96	0.17	d0.15	0.17	0.17
1996-97	0.15	...	...	...

INTERIM DIVIDENDS (Per Share):

Amt.	Decl.	Ex.	Rec.	Pay.
Last dist. 2-for-1 split, 9/25/92				

TRADING VOLUME
Thousand Shares

*7 YEAR PRICE SCORE 44.7   ***12 MONTH PRICE SCORE 81.7**
*NYSE COMPOSITE INDEX=100

CAPITALIZATION (10/26/96):

	($000)	(%)
Minority Interest	17,035	1.0
Common & Surplus	1,615,509	99.0
Total	1,632,544	100.0

RECENT DEVELOPMENTS: For the quarter ended 1/31/97, net income dropped 20.1% to $50.8 million from $63.6 million in the same prior-year period. Earnings for 1996 included a restructuring charge of $18.4 million. Net sales declined 14.4% to $374.8 million from $437.9 million the year before. The Company's core business, network server operating systems, increased 10.0% to $251.0 million versus 1996. Within this segment, IntranetWare directory-enabled server products for intranets and the Internet rose 41.0% to $185.0 million. During the quarter, NOVL shipped more than 250,000 network server operating systems despite market weakness in Europe and Japan. Gross profit fell 12.6% to $298.9 million from $341.9 million a year earlier; however, gross profit as a percentage of net sales improved to 79.7% versus 78.1% the previous year. Income from operations fell 25.8% to $61.5 million from $82.8 million the year before.

BUSINESS

NOVELL, INC. is a provider of network software designed to enable the connected enterprise, and bring structure to the Internet to make it a business tool. The Company's software provides the infrastructure to manage and maintain distributed information resources on business intranets and the Internet. NOVL helps customers extend LANs and WANs into intranets and extranets that combine the Company's network software with Internet technologies based on open, industry standards. NOVL is also advancing a new "client/server" computing model, in which the network is the primary information asset in business and users gain access to the entire resources of the Internet. The Company's networking services include Novell Directory Services, a universal directory service for organizing accessing, authenticating and managing network information and resources; Novell GroupWise groupware; and ManageWise management products.

ANNUAL EARNINGS AND DIVIDENDS PER SHARE

	10/26/96	10/28/95	10/29/94	10/30/93	10/31/92	10/26/91	10/27/90
Earnings Per Share	0.35	0.90	0.56	d0.11	0.81	0.55	0.34
Dividends Per Share	Nil	Nil	Nil	Nil	①...	②...	③...

① 2-for-1 stk. split, 9/28/92 ② 2-for-1 stk. split, 9/3/91 ③ 2-for-1 stk. split, 8/90

ANNUAL FINANCIAL DATA

RECORD OF EARNINGS (IN MILLIONS):

	10/26/96	10/28/95	10/29/94	10/30/93	10/31/92	10/26/91	10/27/90
Total Revenues	1,374.9	2,041.2	1,998.1	1,122.9	1,512.5	640.1	497.5
Costs and Expenses	1,161.1	1,494.9	1,641.8	1,006.9	543.4	389.6	342.4
Depreciation & Amort	104.8	94.2	86.4	41.7	33.1	24.3	20.9
Operating Income	108.9	452.1	269.9	74.2	356.9	226.1	134.2
Income Bef Income Taxes	180.0	508.7	297.4	104.0	377.3	248.1	145.1
Income Taxes	54.0	170.4	90.7	139.2	128.3	85.6	50.8
Net Income	126.0	338.3	206.7	d35.2	249.0	162.5	94.3
Aver. Shs. Outstg. (000)	357,919	374,584	368,332	314,409	308,104	295,968	276,468

BALANCE SHEET (IN MILLIONS):

Cash and Cash Equivalents	1,024.8	1,321.2	861.8	664.1	545.3	346.8	254.8
Receivables, Net	490.2	530.4	489.8	331.7	290.4	185.3	123.9
Inventories	16.8	23.0	32.2	...	15.5	11.8	12.1
Gross Property	723.1	683.5	701.5	375.3	293.3	211.7	125.6
Accumulated Depreciation	328.4	293.1	306.8	158.5	111.5	69.8	46.3
Long-Term Debt	...	...	...	...	0.5	1.2	2.4
Net Stockholders' Equity	1,615.5	1,938.3	1,487.0	996.5	937.8	598.6	398.3
Total Assets	2,049.5	2,416.8	1,963.5	1,343.9	1,096.7	726.3	494.4
Total Current Assets	1,590.8	1,925.2	1,453.1	1,052.2	866.0	553.1	402.1
Total Current Liabilities	364.8	460.9	462.7	230.4	149.4	118.2	93.8
Net Working Capital	1,226.0	1,464.2	990.4	821.8	716.6	434.9	308.3
Year End Shs Outstg (000)	346,059	371,567	364,535	308,051	300,635	287,973	281,645

STATISTICAL RECORD:

Operating Profit Margin %	7.9	22.1	13.5	6.6	23.6	35.3	27.0
Book Value Per Share	4.67	5.22	4.08	3.23	3.12	2.08	1.41
Return on Equity %	7.8	17.5	13.9	...	26.6	27.1	23.7
Return on Assets %	6.1	14.0	10.5	...	22.7	22.4	19.1
P/E Ratio	44.6-25.0	25.8-15.3	46.9-24.6	...	41.4-27.8	58.9-13.9	25.0-10.3
Price Range	15⅝-8¾	23¼-13¾	26¼-13¾	35¼-17	33½-22½	32⅜-7⅝	8½-3½

Statistics are as originally reported.

OFFICERS:
E. Schmidt, Chmn. & C.E.O.
J.A. Marengi, Pres.
J.R. Tolonen, Exec. V.P. & C.F.O.
D.R. Bradford, Sr. V.P., Sec. & Gen. Couns.

INCORPORATED: DE, Jan., 1983

PRINCIPAL OFFICE: 122 East 1700 South, Provo, UT 84606

TELEPHONE NUMBER: (801) 861-7000

NO. OF EMPLOYEES: 5,818

ANNUAL MEETING: In May

SHAREHOLDERS: 12,631

INSTITUTIONAL HOLDINGS:
No. of Institutions: 222
Shares Held: 123,911,830

REGISTRAR(S): Mellon Bank N.A., Pittsburgh, PA

TRANSFER AGENT(S): Mellon Bank N.A., Pittsburgh, PA

NASDAQ SYMBOL ORCL
Rec. Pr. 37⅜ (Marginable)

ORACLE CORP.

YIELD	...%
P/E RATIO	34.7

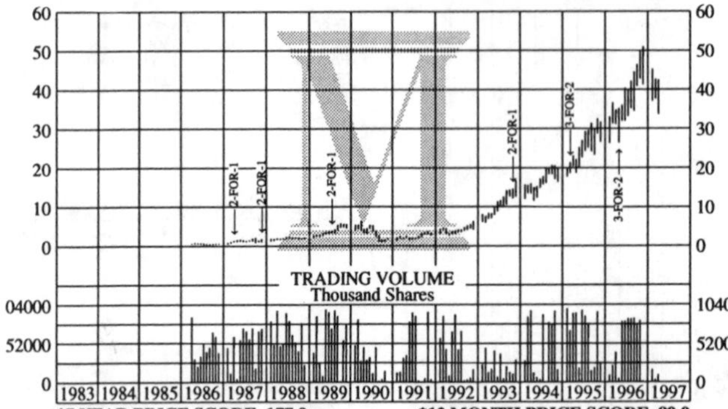

*7 YEAR PRICE SCORE 177.9 *12 MONTH PRICE SCORE 89.9

*NYSE COMPOSITE INDEX=100

INTERIM EARNINGS (Per Share):

Qtr.	Aug.	Nov.	Feb.	May
1993-94	0.06	0.09	0.11	0.17
1994-95	0.09	0.14	0.16	0.27
1995-96	0.08	0.20	0.22	0.40
1996-97	0.17	0.27	0.25	...

INTERIM DIVIDENDS (Per Share):

Amt.	Decl.	Ex.	Rec.	Pay.
3-for-2	1/24/95	2/23/95	2/6/95	2/22/95
3-for-2	3/14/96	4/17/96	4/2/96	4/16/96

CAPITALIZATION (5/31/96):

	($000)	(%)
Long-Term Debt	897	0.0
Deferred Income Tax	9,207	0.5
Common & Surplus	1,870,449	99.5
Total	1,880,553	100.0

RECENT DEVELOPMENTS: For the quarter ended 2/28/97, net income advanced 15.7% to $169.3 million from $146.3 million in the same prior-year period. Earnings for 1996 included special charges of $36.8 million for in-process research and development costs related to the acquisitions of Datalogix and the on-line analytical processing business of Information Resources, Inc. in January 1997 and July 1995, respectively. Total revenues climbed 34.5% to $1.37 billion from $1.02 billion the year before. This increase reflected strong growth in all of the Company's major geographic regions. Operating income grew 18.3% to $260.1 million from $219.9 million a year earlier. Income before taxes rose 19.3% to $264.5 million from $221.7 million in 1995. For the nine months ended 2/28/97, net income rose 37.0% to $461.5 million from $337.0 million the prior year. Total revenues improved 35.4% to $3.74 billion from $2.76 billion the previous year.

BUSINESS

ORACLE CORPORATION designs, develops, markets, and supports computer software products with a wide variety of uses, including database management and network products, applications development productivity tools and end-user applications. The Company's principal product, the ORACLE® Universal Server® is a SQL-based, relational database management system that runs on a broad range of computers, from mainframes to network computers. The Company offers its products, along with related consulting, education and support services, in more than 140 countries around the world.

ANNUAL EARNINGS AND DIVIDENDS PER SHARE

	5/31/96	5/31/95	5/31/94	5/31/93	5/31/92	5/31/91	5/31/90
Earnings Per Share	**0.90**	**0.66**	**0.43**	**③ 0.21**	**0.10**	**d0.02**	**0.19**
Dividends Per Share	**①...**	**②...**	**Nil**	**③...**	**Nil**	**Nil**	**Nil**

① 3-for-2 stk. split, 4/16/96. ② 3-for-2 stk. split, 2/22/95. ③ 2-for-1 stk. split, 11/9/93.

ANNUAL FINANCIAL DATA

RECORD OF EARNINGS (IN MILLIONS):							
Total Revenues	4,223.3	2,966.9	2,001.1	1,502.8	1,178.5	1,027.9	970.8
Costs and Expenses	3,098.9	2,169.4	1,476.6	1,206.6	999.1	939.3	737.0
Depreciation & Amort	219.5	147.8	104.6	79.2	65.8	70.7	44.1
Operating Income	904.9	649.7	420.0	217.0	113.7	17.9	189.8
Inc Fr Cont Opers Bef Income Taxes	919.5	659.0	423.5	218.0	96.1	d13.2	172.7
Income Taxes	316.2	217.5	139.7	76.3	34.6	cr0.8	55.3
Net Income	603.3	441.5	283.7	① 141.7	61.5	d12.4	117.4
Aver. Shs. Outstg. (000)	670,658	665,399	665,402	659,142	642,461	600,305	615,717
① Before acctg. change dr$43,470,000.							
BALANCE SHEET (IN MILLIONS):							
Cash and Cash Equivalents	840.9	585.8	464.8	357.8	176.5	101.5	49.8
Receivables, Net	1,204.0	846.3	515.7	405.6	401.0	423.6	497.0
Gross Property	1,128.6	858.4	614.0	390.5	370.2	305.9	238.6
Accumulated Depreciation	442.8	323.4	235.5	201.3	163.2	111.7	66.6
Long-Term Debt	0.9	81.7	82.8	86.4	95.9	18.0	89.1
Net Stockholders' Equity	1,870.4	1,211.4	740.6	528.0	435.0	344.7	387.6
Total Assets	3,357.2	2,424.5	1,595.0	1,184.0	955.6	857.6	787.2
Total Current Assets	2,284.5	1,617.2	1,075.6	842.3	640.7	586.2	569.3
Total Current Liabilities	1,455.0	1,055.1	682.1	551.3	406.0	479.4	283.6
Net Working Capital	829.5	562.0	393.5	291.0	234.7	106.8	285.7
Year End Shs Outstg (000)	655,826	650,036	644,313	640,026	629,535	613,337	590,121
STATISTICAL RECORD:							
Operating Profit Margin %	21.4	21.9	21.0	14.4	9.6	1.7	19.5
Book Value Per Share	2.70	1.71	0.99	0.67	0.54	0.46	0.60
Return on Equity %	32.3	36.4	38.3	26.8	14.1	...	30.3
Return on Assets %	18.0	18.2	17.8	12.0	6.4	...	14.9
P/E Ratio	27.1-15.0	31.3-17.6	39.0-13.7	30.4-12.5	37.5-12.5	...	30.3-11.2
Price Range	24⅜-13½	20⅝-11⅝	16¾-5⅞	6⅜-2⅝	3¾-1¼	6¼-1⅛	5¾-2⅛

Statistics are as originally reported.

OFFICERS:
L.J. Ellison, Chmn. & C.E.O.
R.J. Lane, Pres. & C.O.O.
J.O. Henley, Exec. V.P. & C.F.O.
R. Shaw, Exec. V.P.—Worldwide Svces.
D. Roux, Exec. V.P.—Corp. Dev.

INCORPORATED: DE, Mar., 1987

PRINCIPAL OFFICE: 500 Oracle Parkway, Redwood City, CA 94065

TELEPHONE NUMBER: (415) 506-7000

FAX: (415) 506-7200

NO. OF EMPLOYEES: 28,844

ANNUAL MEETING: In October

SHAREHOLDERS: 5,461 (approx.)

INSTITUTIONAL HOLDINGS:
No. of Institutions: 477
Shares Held: 337,254,558

REGISTRAR(S): Harris Trust & Savings Bank, Chicago, IL

TRANSFER AGENT(S): Bank of Boston, Boston, MA

NASDAQ SYMBOL OSSI
Rec. Pr. 18¼ (Marginable)

OUTBACK STEAKHOUSE, INC.

YIELD	...%
P/E RATIO	12.4

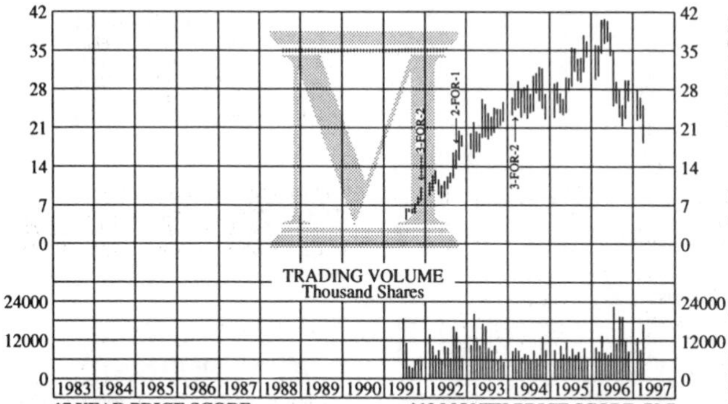

*7 YEAR PRICE SCORE ... *12 MONTH PRICE SCORE 72.7

*NYSE COMPOSITE INDEX=100

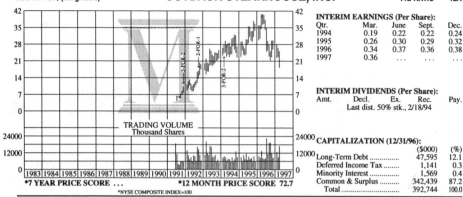

INTERIM EARNINGS (Per Share):

Qtr.	Mar.	June	Sept.	Dec.
1994	0.19	0.22	0.22	0.24
1995	0.26	0.30	0.29	0.32
1996	0.34	0.37	0.36	0.38
1997	0.36	...	...	...

INTERIM DIVIDENDS (Per Share):

Amt.	Decl.	Ex.	Rec.	Pay.
		Last dist. 50% stk., 2/18/94		

CAPITALIZATION (12/31/96):

	($000)	(%)
Long-Term Debt	47,595	12.1
Deferred Income Tax	1,141	0.3
Minority Interest	1,569	0.4
Common & Surplus	342,439	87.2
Total	392,744	100.0

RECENT DEVELOPMENTS: For the quarter ended 3/31/97, net income rose 2.0% to \$17.2 million compared with \$16.9 million in the corresponding period of the previous year. Total revenues advanced 25.4% to \$271.0 million from \$216.1 million a year earlier. Sales for 1997 increased, particularly in the markets where the Company started television advertising. Sales from Company-owned restaurants improved 25.2% to \$269.0 million from \$215.0 million the year before. Sales from franchised and joint venture restaurants rose 41.2% to \$48.0 million from \$34.0 million the prior year. Labor and other related expenses grew 31.8% to \$64.3 million from \$48.8 million the year before. This increase reflected continued back-of-the-house wage rate inflation and higher labor cost at the Company's Carrabba's Italian Grill units. Income from operations climbed 2.1% to \$32.4 million from \$31.7 million the prior year. Income before income taxes rose to \$27.1 million from \$26.5 million the previous year.

BUSINESS

OUTBACK STEAKHOUSE, INC. operates 391 full-service restaurants under the name Outback Steakhouse, 58 of which are franchised. The restaurants serve dinner only and feature a limited menu of high-quality, uniquely seasoned steaks, prime rib, chops, ribs, chicken, fish and pasta. The restaurants also offer specialty appetizers, including the signature Bloomin' Onion, desserts and full liquor service. The Company opened its first Outback Steakhouse in Tampa, Florida in 1988. Since then, the Company has expanded into major metropolitan markets in 39 states. The average sales volume for an Outback Steakhouse is just under \$3.2 million per year. The Company plans to open 70-75 Outback Steakhouses in 1997. The Company is also developing Carrabba's Italian Grills. Carrabba's is a casual restaurant offering freshly prepared, highly flavorful food, with large portions at moderate prices. There are 57 Carrabba's in operation in 11 states averaging annual sales of \$2.1 million. The Company plans to open 20-25 Carrabba's restaurants in 1997.

ANNUAL EARNINGS AND DIVIDENDS PER SHARE

	1996	1995	1994	1993	1992	1991	1990
Earnings Per Share	**1.45**	**1.15**	**0.87**	**0.57**	**0.34**	**0.19**	**0.45**
Dividends Per Share	**Nil**	**1 ...**	**Nil**	**2 ...**	**3 ...**	**Nil**	**Nil**

1 3-for-2 stk. split, 2/18/94. 2 2-for-1 stk. split, 10/15/92. 3 3-for-2 stk. split, 12/17/91.

ANNUAL FINANCIAL DATA

	1996	1995	1994	1993	1992	1991	1990
RECORD OF EARNINGS (IN THOUSANDS):							
Total Revenues	937,400	663,969	451,916	271,164	123,984	55,219	22,713
Costs and Expenses	770,853	541,290	365,978	219,563	102,242	45,444	18,372
Depreciation & Amort	35,528	24,016	15,125	8,863	3,636	2,080	702
Operating Income	130,917	99,105	72,082	43,071	20,961	9,088	4,081
Inc Fr Cont Opers Bef Income Taxes	111,896	83,875	60,894	37,624	19,303	8,427	3,110
Income Taxes	40,283	29,167	21,602	14,297	6,802	2,638	1,175
Net Income	71,613	54,708	39,292	23,327	12,501	5,789	1,935
Aver. Shs. Outstg.	49,289	46,529	43,997	41,207	37,039	31,374	4,282
BALANCE SHEET (IN THOUSANDS):							
Cash and Cash Equivalents	15,661	24,404	23,587	29,434	57,902	16,233	2,583
Inventories	16,637	5,859	4,539	3,325	1,648	904	249
Gross Property	461,003	300,403	183,210	98,141	37,658	13,474	4,906
Accumulated Depreciation	63,244	36,489	20,887	10,239	3,636	1,512	506
Long-Term Debt	47,595	29,006	12,310	664	...	747	754
Net Stockholders' Equity	342,439	255,130	172,300	122,010	92,605	26,648	5,649
Total Assets	469,843	343,757	228,531	141,155	108,561	34,715	10,157
Total Current Assets	41,108	46,430	39,502	36,904	61,490	17,771	3,042
Total Current Liabilities	74,099	55,989	41,098	17,202	13,730	6,328	2,239
Net Working Capital	d32,991	d9,559	d1,596	19,702	47,760	11,443	803
Year End Shares Outstg	48,009	45,164	42,931	39,849	37,712	32,856	698
STATISTICAL RECORD:							
Operating Profit Margin %	14.0	14.9	16.0	15.9	16.9	16.5	18.0
Book Value Per Share	7.13	5.65	4.01	3.06	2.40	0.78	3.69
Return on Equity %	20.9	21.4	22.8	19.1	13.5	21.7	61.4
Return on Assets %	15.2	15.9	17.2	16.5	11.5	16.7	19.1
P/E Ratio	28.1-14.7	32.9-19.9	36.0-25.4	45.8-27.2	60.3-24.6	53.9-23.0	...
Price Range	40¾-21⅜	37⅞-22⅞	32-22⅝	26⅛-15½	20½-8⅜	10¼-4⅜	...

Statistics are as originally reported.

OFFICERS:
C.T. Sullivan, Chmn. & C.E.O.
R.D. Basham, Pres. & C.O.O.
R.S. Merritt, Sr. V.P., C.F.O. & Treas.
J.J. Kadow, V.P., Couns. & Sec.

INCORPORATED: FL, Oct., 1987; reincorp., DE, Apr., 1991

PRINCIPAL OFFICE: 550 North Reo St. Suite 200, Tampa, FL 33609

TELEPHONE NUMBER: (813) 282-1225

FAX: (813) 282-1209

NO. OF EMPLOYEES: 23,000 (approx.)

ANNUAL MEETING: In April

SHAREHOLDERS: 2,742 (approx.)

INSTITUTIONAL HOLDINGS:
No. of Institutions: 121
Shares Held: 23,497,144

REGISTRAR(S): Bank of New York, New York, NY

TRANSFER AGENT(S): Bank of New York, New York, NY

OXFORD HEALTH PLANS, INC.

YIELD ...%
P/E RATIO 47.2

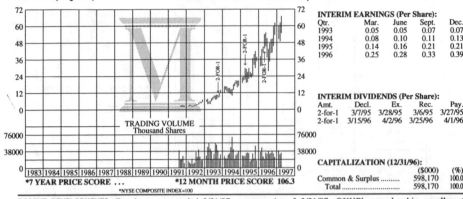

INTERIM EARNINGS (Per Share):

Qtr.	Mar.	June	Sept.	Dec.
1993	0.05	0.05	0.07	0.07
1994	0.08	0.10	0.11	0.13
1995	0.14	0.16	0.21	0.21
1996	0.25	0.28	0.33	0.39

INTERIM DIVIDENDS (Per Share):

Amt.	Decl.	Ex.	Rec.	Pay.
2-for-1	3/7/95	3/28/95	3/6/95	3/27/95
2-for-1	3/15/96	4/2/96	3/25/96	4/1/96

TRADING VOLUME
Thousand Shares

CAPITALIZATION (12/31/96):

	($000)	(%)
Common & Surplus	598,170	100.0
Total	598,170	100.0

*7 YEAR PRICE SCORE ...   *12 MONTH PRICE SCORE 106.3
*NYSE COMPOSITE INDEX=100

RECENT DEVELOPMENTS: For the quarter ended 3/31/97, net earnings advanced 85.7% to $34.4 million from $18.5 million in the same prior-year period. Earnings for 1997 and 1996 included equity in net losses of affiliate of $900,000 and $1.1 million, respectively. Total revenues climbed 50.0% to $987.3 million from $658.1 million in 1996. Premiums earned improved 50.0% to $970.1 million, while net third-party administration revenues fell 3.3% from $3.1 million from the previous year. Operating earnings grew 80.3% to $59.8 million from $33.2 million the prior year. As of 3/31/97, OXHP's membership enrollment increased approximately 45% to 1.7 million versus 1996. OXHP's medical-loss ratio (health care expenses as a percentage of premium revenues) grew to 80.2% from 79.9% a year earlier. This increase reflected higher pharmacy costs and increased hospital reimbursement costs in New York due to the enactment of the Health Care Reform Act of 1996. On 4/8/97, OXHP agreed to acquire a minority interest in Compass PPA, Inc., the parent company of a commercial health plan in Chicago, Illinois.

BUSINESS

OXFORD HEALTH PLANS, INC. is a managed-care company that provides health-benefit plans in New York, New Jersey, Connecticut and Pennsylvania. The Company's product lines include traditional health maintenance organizations, point-of-service plans, third-party administration of employer-funded benefit plans, Medicare and Medicaid plans, and dental plans. OXHP markets its plans through a direct sales force as well as independent insurance agents and brokers.

ANNUAL EARNINGS AND DIVIDENDS PER SHARE

	1996	1995	1994	1993	1992	1991	1990
Earnings Per Share	1.24	0.71	0.41	0.23	4 0.13	5 0.08	...
Dividends Per Share	1 ...	2 ...	Nil	3 ...	Nil	Nil	...

1 2-for-1 stk. split, 4/1/96. 2 2-for-1 stk. split, 3/27/95. 3 2-for-1 stk. split, 10/27/93. 4 Before acctg. chg. 5 Before extraord. item.

ANNUAL FINANCIAL DATA

RECORD OF EARNINGS (IN MILLIONS):

	1996	1995	1994	1993	1992	1991	1990
Total Revenues	3,075.0	1,765.4	720.7	311.8	155.7	94.9	61.4
Costs and Expenses	2,855.7	1,647.3	662.2	282.9	140.7	87.9	58.9
Depreciation & Amort	42.9	23.0	7.1	2.9	1.3	0.8	0.5
Operating Profit	176.5	95.1	51.5	26.0	13.7	6.2	1.9
Inc Fr Cont Opers Bef Income Taxes	172.0	91.5	49.5	26.1	13.8	6.2	1.9
Income Taxes	72.4	39.1	21.6	11.2	5.8	2.7	1.0
Net Income	99.6	52.4	27.9	14.9	1 8.0	2 3.6	3 0.9
Aver. Shs. Outstg. (000)	80,019	73,454	68,284	65,544	61,008	45,784	30,496

1 Before extra. item cr$3,300,000. 2 Before extra. item cr$1,149,000. 3 Before extra. item cr$625,000.

BALANCE SHEET (IN MILLIONS):

	1996	1995	1994	1993	1992	1991	1990
Cash and Cash Equivalents	839.5	368.6	191.1	109.8	73.5	46.1	15.0
Receivables, Net	355.2	120.0	62.7	24.0	16.4	7.1	9.2
Gross Property	174.7	127.5	45.1	14.5	6.5	4.1	3.3
Accumulated Depreciation	69.7	30.1	10.3	3.4	2.9	2.0	1.2
Net Stockholders' Equity	598.2	220.0	127.1	91.0	66.2	43.0	5.9
Total Assets	1,346.7	608.8	314.8	165.6	106.1	66.4	27.1
Total Current Assets	1,200.5	492.2	255.2	134.5	90.4	53.4	24.4
Total Current Liabilities	748.6	388.7	187.7	74.6	39.7	22.7	20.2
Net Working Capital	452.0	103.4	67.5	59.9	50.8	30.7	4.2
Year End Shs Outstg (000)	77,376	68,781	63,692	62,352	60,348	54,728	60,124

STATISTICAL RECORD:

	1996	1995	1994	1993	1992	1991	1990
Operating Profit Margin %	5.7	5.4	7.1	8.3	8.8	6.5	3.1
Book Value Per Share	7.73	3.20	2.00	1.46	1.10	0.79	...
Return on Equity %	16.7	23.8	22.0	16.4	12.1	8.3	16.1
Return on Assets %	7.4	8.6	8.9	9.0	7.5	5.4	3.5
P/E Ratio	50.2-22.4	59.0-27.1	50.9-24.1	60.9-16.8	54.8-16.3	39.1-25.0	...
Price Range	62¼-27¾	41⅞-19¼	20⅞-9⅞	14-3⅞	7⅛-2⅛	3⅛-2	...

Statistics are as originally reported.

OFFICERS:
S.F. Wiggins, Chmn. & C.E.O.
W. M. Sullivan, Pres. & C.O.O.
A.B. Cassidy, C.F.O.

INCORPORATED: DE, Sep., 1984

PRINCIPAL OFFICE: 800 Connecticut Avenue, Norwalk, CT 06854

TELEPHONE NUMBER: (203) 852-1442

NO. OF EMPLOYEES: 5,000 (approx.)

ANNUAL MEETING: In August

SHAREHOLDERS: 571

INSTITUTIONAL HOLDINGS:
No. of Institutions: 173
Shares Held: 70,028,251

REGISTRAR(S): Fleet National Bank, Providence, RI

TRANSFER AGENT(S): Fleet National Bank, Providence, RI

PACCAR INC

YIELD 1.3%
P/E RATIO 14.4

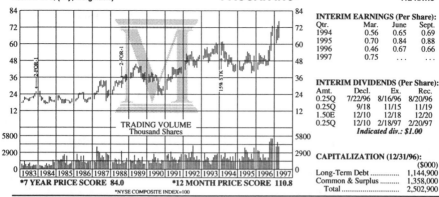

INTERIM EARNINGS (Per Share):

Qtr.	Mar.	June	Sept.	Dec.
1994	0.56	0.65	0.69	0.74
1995	0.70	0.84	0.88	0.84
1996	0.46	0.67	0.66	0.81
1997	0.75	...	...	...

INTERIM DIVIDENDS (Per Share):

Amt.	Decl.	Ex.	Rec.	Pay.
0.25Q	7/22/96	8/16/96	8/20/96	9/5/96
0.25Q	9/18	11/15	11/19	12/5
1.50E	12/10	12/18	12/20	1/6/97
0.25Q	12/10	2/18/97	2/20/97	3/5

Indicated div.: $1.00

TRADING VOLUME
Thousand Shares

*7 YEAR PRICE SCORE 84.0 *12 MONTH PRICE SCORE 110.8
*NYSE COMPOSITE INDEX=100

CAPITALIZATION (12/31/96):

	($000)	(%)
Long-Term Debt	1,144,900	45.7
Common & Surplus	1,358,000	54.3
Total	2,502,900	100.0

RECENT DEVELOPMENTS: For the quarter ended 3/31/97, net income advanced 62.2% to $57.9 million from $35.7 million in the corresponding period of the previous year. Earnings for 1996 included net costs of $11.0 million for the closure of the Company's Canadian truck plant. Manufacturing and parts net sales climbed 40.4% to $1.44 billion from $1.03 billion the year before. Financial services revenues were up 1.8% to $68.1 million from $66.9 million the prior year. Income from manufacturing and parts grew 92.9% to $62.9 million from $32.6 million a year earlier. Net other income totaled $3.6 million compared with $300,000 in 1995. Income before income taxes rose 59.0% to $88.7 million from $55.8 million the previous year. Results for 1997 increased primarily due to the inclusion of DAF Trucks N.V., acquired on 11/15/96, as well as the improvement of the heavy-duty truck market, particularly in North America.

BUSINESS

PACCAR INC designs, manufactures and markets commercial and industrial equipment. The Company has three principal industry segments: (1) manufacture of heavy-duty trucks and related parts; (2) automotive parts sales and related services; and (3) finance and leasing services provided to customers and dealers. Manufactured products also include industrial winches and oilfield extraction pumps. The Company competes in the truck parts aftermarket primarily through its dealer network. PACCAR sells general automotive parts and accessories through Company operated stores. The Company's finance and leasing activities are principally related to Company products and allied equipment. The Company manufactures trucks marketed under the Peterbilt, Kenworth, DAF and Foden nameplates in the class 8 diesel category, as well as smaller categories.

ANNUAL EARNINGS AND DIVIDENDS PER SHARE

	1996	1995	1994	1993	1992	1991	1990
Earnings Per Share	2.59	3.25	2.63	1.83	0.84	① 0.51	0.80
Dividends Per Share	2.00	2.00	② 0.94	0.57	0.479	0.44	1.09
Dividend Payout %	77.4	46.2	33.1	30.9	57.0	85.5	N.M.

Note: 2-for-1 stk. split, 5/21/97. ① Before acctg. chg. ② 15% stk. div., 2/94.

ANNUAL FINANCIAL DATA

RECORD OF EARNINGS (IN MILLIONS):

	1996	1995	1994	1993	1992	1991	1990
Total Revenues	4,599.7	4,848.2	4,499.2	3,553.1	2,756.0	2,374.5	2,791.4
Costs and Expenses	4,226.4	4,401.7	4,116.8	3,284.5	2,620.1	2,269.0	2,645.4
Depreciation & Amort	81.1	73.5	63.2	56.7	47.2	49.2	51.8
Operating Profit	292.2	373.0	319.2	211.9	88.7	56.3	101.8
Inc Fr Cont Opers Bef Income Taxes	312.9	399.6	320.1	219.8	91.6	48.3	94.2
Income Taxes	111.9	146.8	115.6	77.6	26.4	8.6	30.5
Net Income	201.0	252.8	204.5	142.2	65.2	① 39.7	63.7
Aver. Shs. Outstg. (000)	77,800	77,800	77,800	77,800	77,800	77,740	77,774	79,846

① Before acctg. change cr$15,427,000.

BALANCE SHEET (IN MILLIONS):

	1996	1995	1994	1993	1992	1991	1990
Cash and Cash Equivalents	527.8	621.3	553.0	458.9	464.7	496.3	477.8
Receivables, Net	560.5	227.7	232.9	2,207.4	1,789.5	1,737.8	1,904.7
Inventories	406.5	239.5	274.5	193.7	151.0	151.2	191.6
Gross Property	1,261.0	792.3	716.7	669.1	605.0	559.0	534.8
Accumulated Depreciation	528.4	370.0	346.8	324.7	299.8	286.9	261.5
Long-Term Debt	1,144.9	1,160.3	1,008.3	720.8	498.6	501.2	655.2
Capital Lease Obligations	...	...	2.7	...	...	...	...
Net Stockholders' Equity	1,358.0	1,251.2	1,174.5	1,107.5	1,038.4	1,032.3	1,019.2
Total Assets	5,298.8	4,390.5	3,928.2	3,291.2	2,809.3	2,737.6	2,906.2
Total Current Assets	1,568.1	1,148.6	1,125.5	2,917.0	2,476.4	2,459.8	2,645.5
Total Current Liabilities	2,418.6	1,710.3	1,480.6	1,253.2	1,109.0	1,032.8	1,038.7
Net Working Capital	d850.5	d561.7	d355.1	1,663.8	1,367.4	1,426.9	1,606.8
Year End Shs Outstg (000)	77,800	77,724	77,718	77,714	77,800	77,790	77,756

STATISTICAL RECORD:

	1996	1995	1994	1993	1992	1991	1990
Operating Profit Margin %	6.4	7.7	7.1	6.0	3.2	2.4	3.4
Book Value Per Share	16.10	15.11	14.25	13.35	13.27	13.11	
Return on Equity %	14.8	20.2	17.4	12.8	6.3	3.8	6.2
Return on Assets %	3.8	5.8	5.2	4.3	2.3	1.5	2.2
Average Yield %	7.0	6.4	3.4	1.8	1.7	2.1	6.0
P/E Ratio	14.1-8.1	8.4-6.0	11.7-7.6	16.7-12.7	32.6-24.7	42.9-26.7	25.0-14.6
Price Range	36⅝-20⅞	27⅜-19⅝	30⅞-20	30⅝-23¼	27⅜-20¾	21⅞-13⅝	19⅞-11⅝

Statistics are as originally reported.

OFFICERS:
M.C. Pigott, Chmn. & C.E.O.
M.A. Tembreull, Vice-Chmn.
D.J. Hovind, Pres.

INCORPORATED: WA, 1924; reincorp., DE, Nov., 1971

PRINCIPAL OFFICE: PACCAR Building 777 106th Avenue N.E., Bellevue, WA 98004

TELEPHONE NUMBER: (206) 455-7400

FAX: (206) 453-5959

NO. OF EMPLOYEES: 17,000 (approx.)

ANNUAL MEETING: In April

SHAREHOLDERS: 3,099

INSTITUTIONAL HOLDINGS:
No. of Institutions: 155
Shares Held: 32,174,476 (adj.)

REGISTRAR(S): First Chicago Trust Co. of New York, Jersey City, NJ

TRANSFER AGENT(S): First Chicago Trust Co. of New York, Jersey City, NJ

PACIFICARE HEALTH SYSTEMS, INC.

YIELD ...%
P/E RATIO 32.1

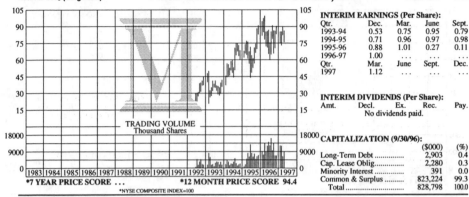

*7 YEAR PRICE SCORE ...   *12 MONTH PRICE SCORE 94.4
*NYSE COMPOSITE INDEX=100

INTERIM EARNINGS (Per Share):

Qtr.	Dec.	Mar.	June	Sept.
1993-94	0.53	0.75	0.95	0.79
1994-95	0.71	0.96	0.97	0.98
1995-96	0.88	1.01	0.27	0.11
1996-97	1.00	...	...	...
Qtr.	Mar.	June	Sept.	Dec.
1997	1.12	...	...	...

INTERIM DIVIDENDS (Per Share):

Amt.	Decl.	Ex.	Rec.	Pay.
		No dividends paid.		

CAPITALIZATION (9/30/96):

	($000)	(%)
Long-Term Debt	2,903	0.4
Cap. Lease Oblig.	2,280	0.3
Minority Interest	391	0.0
Common & Surplus	823,224	99.3
Total	828,798	100.0

RECENT DEVELOPMENTS: For the quarter ended 3/31/97, net income climbed 36.5% to $43.5 million from $31.9 million in the same prior-year period. Total operating revenue advanced 59.3% to $1.84 billion from $1.16 billion the year before. Government premiums grew 58.5% to $1.07 billion, while commercial premiums rose 61.8% to $756.9 million the prior year. Operating income increased 69.5% to $71.1 million from $42.0 million the previous year. Interest expense amounted to $9.7 million versus $829,000

the year before. Income before income taxes climbed 48.2% to $79.1 million from $53.3 million a year earlier. Results for 1997 included the acquisition of FHP International on 2/14/97. As of 3/31/97, total membership increased 102% to over 3.9 million, while commercial enrollment and Medicare membership grew 112% and 92%, respectively, versus the prior year. On 6/20/97, PHSY signed a non-binding letter of intent to sell its FHP of Illinois health plan operations to Principal Health Care, Inc.

BUSINESS

PACIFICARE HEALTH SYSTEMS, INC. is a managed care organization. The Company's primary operations include managed-care products for employer groups and Medicare beneficiaries in 13 states and Guam, serving over 4.0 million members. Other specialty managed care operations include Medicare risk management services, pharmacy benefit management, military health care management, coordination of managed-care products for multi-region employers, health and life insurance, behavioral health, worker's compensation, dental and vision services and health promotion.

ANNUAL EARNINGS AND DIVIDENDS PER SHARE

	9/30/96	9/30/95	9/30/94	9/30/93	9/30/92	9/30/91	9/30/90
Earnings Per Share	2.27	3.62	① 3.02	2.25	1.78	1.10	0.74
Dividends Per Share	Nil	Nil	Nil	Nil	②...	Nil	Nil

① Before acctg. change ② 2-for-1 stk split, 6/11/92

ANNUAL FINANCIAL DATA

RECORD OF EARNINGS (IN MILLIONS):

Total Revenues	4,637.3	3,731.0	2,893.3	2,221.1	1,686.3	1,242.4	975.8
Costs and Expenses	4,549.5	3,575.6	2,768.9	2,130.3	1,623.5	1,206.0	957.2
Depreciation & Amort	22.9	21.4	17.9	11.9	8.4	6.3	3.9
Operating Income	78.6	148.2	120.9	87.2	60.5	30.1	14.7
Inc Fr Cont Opers Bef Income Taxes	122.8	182.1	145.5	108.3	74.9	44.5	29.4
Income Taxes	50.8	74.0	60.9	45.6	31.3	18.8	11.8
Net Income	72.0	108.1	① 84.6	62.7	43.6	25.7	17.6
Aver. Shs. Outstg. (000)	31,671	29,864	28,004	27,847	24,509	23,346	23,770

① Before acctg. change cr$5,658,000.

BALANCE SHEET (IN MILLIONS):

Cash and Cash Equivalents	700.1	811.5	710.6	437.2	272.1	205.8	160.4
Receivables, Net	225.8	140.6	102.4	67.0	53.9	33.5	34.6
Gross Property	186.1	172.4	149.5	114.3	89.3	72.8	26.9
Accumulated Depreciation	92.3	73.1	52.5	35.2	25.1	14.8	9.4
Long-Term Debt	2.9	6.3	91.4	21.8	18.5	2.3	0.3
Capital Lease Obligations	2.3	5.7	9.7	...	...	...	...
Net Stockholders' Equity	823.2	732.0	413.4	319.3	198.9	99.7	74.6
Total Assets	1,299.5	1,385.4	1,105.5	693.6	498.1	322.3	231.6
Total Current Assets	934.2	961.6	821.9	514.9	329.5	241.2	198.6
Total Current Liabilities	470.7	641.0	590.6	352.1	279.9	219.4	155.5
Net Working Capital	463.5	320.6	231.2	162.8	49.6	21.8	43.1
Year End Shs Outstg (000)	31,292	30,882	27,528	27,256	25,617	22,770	22,762

STATISTICAL RECORD:

Operating Profit Margin %	1.7	4.0	4.2	3.9	3.6	2.4	1.5
Book Value Per Share	18.99	14.13	8.95	8.79	4.52	4.00	2.94
Return on Equity %	8.7	14.8	20.5	19.6	21.9	25.8	23.7
Return on Assets %	5.5	7.8	7.7	9.0	8.8	8.0	7.6
P/E Ratio	43.8-26.3	25.1-12.2	24.8-12.3	22.2-9.1	25.3-12.6	...	...
Price Range	99½-59¾	91-44	75-37¼	50-20½	45-22½	...	...

Statistics are as originally reported.

OFFICERS:
T. Hartshorn, Chmn.
A.R. Hoops, Pres. & C.E.O.
W.B. Lowell, Exec. V.P., Chief Admin. Off. & C.F.O.

INCORPORATED: DE, Feb., 1985; reincorp., CA, Nov., 1983

PRINCIPAL OFFICE: 5995 Plaza Drive, Cypress, CA 90630-5028

TELEPHONE NUMBER: (714) 229-2636

NO. OF EMPLOYEES: 10,000 full and part-time

ANNUAL MEETING: In June

SHAREHOLDERS: 222 class A; 196 class B

INSTITUTIONAL HOLDINGS:
No. of Institutions: 141
Shares Held: 22,053,375

REGISTRAR(S): Chase Mellon Shareholder Services, Los Angeles, CA

TRANSFER AGENT(S): Chase Mellon Shareholder Services, Los Angeles, CA

PAGING NETWORK, INC.

YIELD ...%
P/E RATIO ...

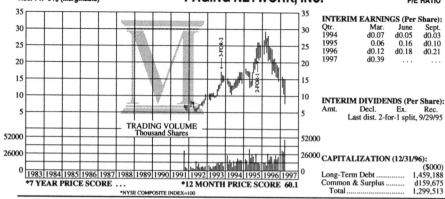

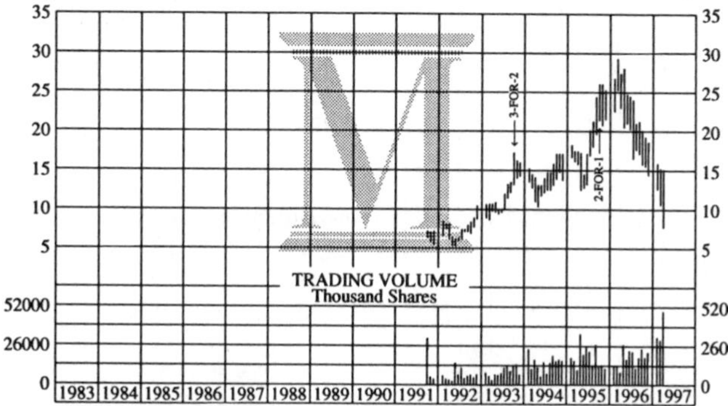
35
30
25
20
15
10
5
3-FOR-2
2-FOR-1
TRADING VOLUME
Thousand Shares
52000
26000
0
1983 1984 1985 1986 1987 1988 1989 1990 1991 1992 1993 1994 1995 1996 1997

*7 YEAR PRICE SCORE ... *12 MONTH PRICE SCORE 60.1
*NYSE COMPOSITE INDEX=100

INTERIM EARNINGS (Per Share):

Qtr.	Mar.	June	Sept.	Dec.
1994	d0.07	d0.05	d0.03	d0.02
1995	0.06	0.16	d0.10	d0.11
1996	d0.12	d0.18	d0.21	d0.28
1997	d0.39	...	...	...

INTERIM DIVIDENDS (Per Share):

Amt.	Decl.	Ex.	Rec.	Pay.

Last dist. 2-for-1 split, 9/29/95

CAPITALIZATION (12/31/96):

	($000)	(%)
Long-Term Debt	1,459,188	112.2
Common & Surplus	d159,675	-12.2
Total	1,299,513	100.0

RECENT DEVELOPMENTS: For the quarter ended 3/31/97, PAGE incurred a net loss of $39.9 million versus a net loss of $12.1 million in the same prior-year period. Earnings for 1997 and 1996 included equity in loss of an unconsolidated subsidiary of $292,000 and $115,000, respectively. Total revenues climbed 20.9% to $225.2 million from $186.4 million the prior year. Net revenues (total revenues less cost of products sold) were $193.9 million, up 18.9% from $163.0 million in 1996. Interest expense grew 26.3% to $37.6 million from $29.7 million, while interest income dropped to $745,000 from $2.0 million a year earlier. Results for 1997 included PAGE's VoiceNow service, which commenced February 1997, as well as PAGE's international operations, which commenced service in April 1996. On 4/17/97, PAGE and Motorola, Inc. entered into an agreement, whereby PAGE will place $170.0 million of purchase orders to manufacture one-way, two-way and voice paging infrastructure through 1999. This pact is an expansion of PAGE's existing commitment to buy Motorola equipment.

BUSINESS

PAGING NETWORK, INC., through 95 sales and service offices, provides paging and messaging services to 9.5 million subscribers across the United States. The Company also services the District of Columbia, Toronto, Montreal, Vancouver, and Brazil. The Company actively markets its paging services throughout the United States and its paging transmission capability covers approximately 90% of the United States population. The Company offers its subscribers a wide variety of paging services. The Company also offers news and stock updates, voice mail, fax forwarding and wireless data transmission to palmtop computers.

ANNUAL EARNINGS AND DIVIDENDS PER SHARE

	1996	1995	1994	1993	1992	1991	1990
Earnings Per Share	**d0.80**	**d0.43**	**d0.18**	**d0.20**	**3 d0.07**	**d0.11**	**d0.01**
Dividends Per Share	**Nil**	**1 ...**	**Nil**	**2 ...**	**Nil**	**Nil**	**Nil**

1 2-for-1 stk. split, 9/29/95. 2 3-for-2 stk. split, 10/18/93. 3 Before extraord. item.

ANNUAL FINANCIAL DATA

	1996	1995	1994	1993	1992	1991	1990
RECORD OF EARNINGS (IN MILLIONS):							
Total Revenues	822.5	646.0	489.7	373.9	257.8	166.4	117.8
Costs and Expenses	565.7	444.9	349.6	273.7	182.2	109.1	78.5
Depreciation & Amort	213.4	149.0	107.4	87.4	58.7	41.2	31.8
Operating Income	43.4	52.1	32.7	12.8	16.9	16.1	7.4
Net Income	d81.8	d44.2	d18.0	d20.0	1 d6.8	d9.3	d0.8
Aver. Shs. Outstg. (000)	102,500	101,900	101,200	101,000	101,100	101,100	80,004
1 Before extra. item dr$14,884,000.							
BALANCE SHEET (IN MILLIONS):							
Cash and Cash Equivalents	3.8	198.2	2.5	2.5	1.3	1.9	1.8
Receivables, Net	60.1	41.3	22.4	13.8	16.3	5.2	7.4
Inventories	57.7	14.1	9.9	7.4	8.3	...	...
Gross Property	1,171.1	841.0	583.6	432.9	326.5	227.6	178.7
Accumulated Depreciation	330.1	225.4	161.7	119.3	75.4	65.0	47.6
Long-Term Debt	1,459.2	1,150.0	504.0	342.5	267.0	146.0	234.5
Net Stockholders' Equity	d159.7	d80.8	d39.9	d23.4	d4.8	16.6	d89.9
Total Assets	1,462.1	1,228.3	706.0	371.6	304.7	190.6	162.6
Total Current Assets	130.4	259.1	39.4	29.0	29.8	9.9	11.8
Total Current Liabilities	162.6	159.1	241.9	52.4	42.6	28.0	18.1
Net Working Capital	d32.2	100.0	d202.5	d23.4	d12.7	d18.1	d6.2
Year End Shs Outstg (000)	102,621	102,246	102,246	101,086	100,562	100,458	79,420
STATISTICAL RECORD:							
Operating Profit Margin %	5.3	8.1	6.7	3.4	6.5	9.7	6.3
Return on Equity %	51.2	54.7	45.0	85.6	N.M.	...	0.9
Price Range	29¼-14⅜	26-12½	17⅛-10⅜	17¼-8⅝	10½-5¼	7⅛-5⅜	...

Statistics are as originally reported.

OFFICERS:
G.M. Perrin, Chmn.
G.W. Marschel, Pres. & C.E.O.
K.W. Sanders, Sr. V.P.-Fin., C.F.O., Treas. & Asst. Sec.

INCORPORATED: DE, Sep., 1981

PRINCIPAL OFFICE: 4965 Preston Park Blvd. Suite 600, Plano, TX 75093

TELEPHONE NUMBER: (214) 985-4100

NO. OF EMPLOYEES: 5,728

ANNUAL MEETING: In May

SHAREHOLDERS: 411 (approx.)

INSTITUTIONAL HOLDINGS:
No. of Institutions: 124
Shares Held: 82,500,621

REGISTRAR(S):

TRANSFER AGENT(S): First National Bank of Boston, Shareholder Services Division, Boston, MA

NASDAQ SYMBOL PAIR
Rec. Pr. 24⅞ (Marginable)

PAIRGAIN TECHNOLOGIES, INC.

YIELD ...%
P/E RATIO 42.9

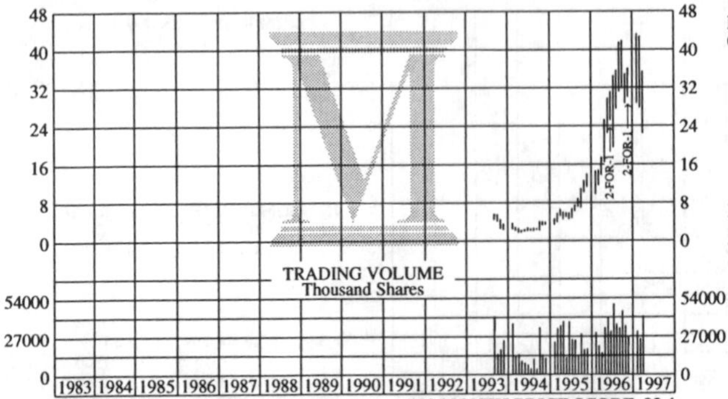

*7 YEAR PRICE SCORE ... *12 MONTH PRICE SCORE 93.4

*NYSE COMPOSITE INDEX=100

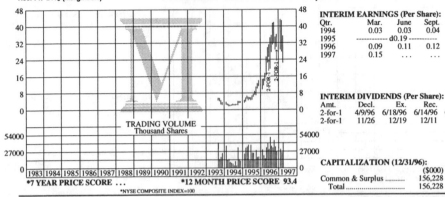

INTERIM EARNINGS (Per Share):

Qtr.	Mar.	June	Sept.	Dec.
1994	0.03	0.03	0.04	0.04
1995	------------ d0.19 ------------			0.21
1996	0.09	0.11	0.12	0.19
1997	0.15	...	...	...

INTERIM DIVIDENDS (Per Share):

Amt.	Decl.	Ex.	Rec.	Pay.
2-for-1	4/9/96	6/18/96	6/14/96	6/17/96
2-for-1	11/26	12/19	12/11	12/18

CAPITALIZATION (12/31/96):

	($000)	(%)
Common & Surplus	156,228	100.0
Total	156,228	100.0

RECENT DEVELOPMENTS: For the quarter ended 3/31/97, net income advanced 82.8% to $11.4 million from $6.2 million in the corresponding period of the previous year. Earnings for 1997 included merger expenses of $2.6 million. Revenues soared 74.6% to $70.7 million from $40.5 million the year before. Gross profit as a percentage of revenues rose to 49.4% from 47.0% in 1996. Research and development expenses increased 68.8% to $6.2 million from $3.6 million a year earlier. Selling and marketing expenses grew 28.9% to $4.8 million from $3.7 million. General and administrative expenses rose 4.2% to $2.4 million from $2.3 million the year before. Operating income more than doubled to $18.9 million from $9.3 million the prior year. Net interest and other income totaled $1.2 million compared with $765,000 in 1996. Income before income taxes climbed to $20.2 million from $10.1 million the previous year.

BUSINESS

PAIRGAIN TECHNOLOGIES, INC. delivers high speed, fiber quality digital transmissions over copper wire. This linkage allows public and private telecommunication service providers to seemlessly connect their fiber optic networks to end users. The Company markets its HiGain and Campus systems under CopperOptics, which indicates their ability to deliver fiber optic quality over the "last mile" in telephone networks. On 2/27/97, the Company acquired AVIDIA Systems for 2.37 million shares of common stock. AVIDIA is a Connecticut-based developer of low cost, Asynchronous Transfer Mode ("ATM") Digital Subscriber Line Access Multiplexers.

ANNUAL EARNINGS AND DIVIDENDS PER SHARE

	1996	1995	1994	1993	1992	1991	1990
Earnings Per Share	0.51	0.02	0.14	0.15	d0.05	d0.12	...
Dividends Per Share	[1]...	Nil	Nil	Nil	Nil	...	...

[1] 2-for-1 stk. split, 6/17/96 & 12/18/96.

ANNUAL FINANCIAL DATA

	1996	1995	1994	1993	1992	1991	1990
RECORD OF EARNINGS (IN THOUSANDS):							
Total Revenues	205,409	107,224	59,518	36,307	9,502	2,361	1,246
Costs and Expenses	147,484	79,644	47,279	27,031	11,248	5,626	3,164
Depreciation & Amort	4,683	4,048	1,726	662	254	128	44
Operating Income	53,242	23,532	10,513	8,614	d2,000	d3,393	d1,962
Inc Fr Cont Opers Bef Income Taxes	59,419	10,238	13,180	8,519	d2,085	d3,418	d1,987
Income Taxes	22,816	9,182	4,613	907	...	...	...
Net Income	36,603	1,056	8,567	7,612	d2,085	d3,418	d1,987
Aver. Shs. Outstg.	72,058	67,280	61,612	49,940	38,084	30,136	21,792
BALANCE SHEET (IN THOUSANDS):							
Cash and Cash Equivalents	112,619	55,725	53,276	49,920	3,302	367	...
Receivables, Net	34,947	16,397	12,301	5,450	1,681	632	...
Inventories	26,010	22,522	16,474	10,499	3,570	1,002	...
Gross Property	18,408	10,883	5,201	3,179	1,540	746	...
Accumulated Depreciation	8,113	4,481	1,770	914	427	196	...
Long-Term Debt	...	...	...	...	2,573	...	...
Capital Lease Obligations	...	...	...	...	104	...	...
Net Stockholders' Equity	156,228	93,931	74,846	65,236	d9,859	d8,068	...
Total Assets	193,016	105,326	86,625	68,203	9,693	2,587	...
Total Current Assets	176,343	96,161	83,147	65,908	8,555	2,019	...
Total Current Liabilities	36,788	11,395	11,779	2,967	3,337	1,050	...
Net Working Capital	139,555	84,766	71,368	62,941	5,218	969	...
Year End Shares Outstg	64,043	60,708	50,836	49,352	2,120	1,732	...
STATISTICAL RECORD:							
Operating Profit Margin %	25.9	21.9	17.7	23.7	...	...	...
Book Value Per Share	2.44	1.55	1.47	1.32	...	...	...
Return on Equity %	23.4	1.1	11.4	11.7	...	...	...
Return on Assets %	19.0	1.0	9.9	11.2	...	...	...
P/E Ratio	82.1-19.1	N.M.	29.5-12.5	37.5-15.8	...	...	...
Price Range	41⅞-9¾	14-3⅜	4⅛-1¾	5⅝-2⅜	...	...	...

Statistics are as originally reported.

OFFICERS:
C.S. Strauch, Chmn. & C.E.O.
H.S. Flagg, Pres.
C.W. McBrayer, V.P.-Fin., Admin. & C.F.O.

INCORPORATED: CA, Feb, 1988; reincorp., DE, 1993

PRINCIPAL OFFICE: 14402 Franklin Avenue, Tustin, CA 92780

TELEPHONE NUMBER: (714) 832-9922

NO. OF EMPLOYEES: 486

ANNUAL MEETING: In June

SHAREHOLDERS: 233

INSTITUTIONAL HOLDINGS:
No. of Institutions: 116
Shares Held: 51,761,771

REGISTRAR(S): U.S. Stock Transfer Corp., Glendale, CA

TRANSFER AGENT(S): U.S. Stock Transfer Corp., Glendale, CA

PARAMETRIC TECHNOLOGY CORP.

YIELD ...%
P/E RATIO 33.3

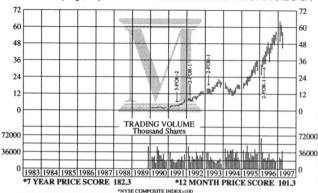

INTERIM EARNINGS (Per Share):

Qtr.	Dec.	Mar.	June	Sept.
1993-94	0.13	0.14	0.15	0.16
1994-95	0.17	0.18	0.11	0.10
1995-96	0.25	0.28	0.31	0.20
1996-97	0.37	0.39	...	...

INTERIM DIVIDENDS (Per Share):

Amt.	Decl.	Ex.	Rec.	Pay.
2-for-1	2/8/96	3/1/96	2/22/96	2/29/96

TRADING VOLUME
Thousand Shares

*7 YEAR PRICE SCORE 182.3   *12 MONTH PRICE SCORE 101.3
*NYSE COMPOSITE INDEX=100

CAPITALIZATION (9/30/96):

	($000)	(%)
Common & Surplus	512,432	100.0
Total	512,432	100.0

RECENT DEVELOPMENTS: For the quarter ended 3/29/97, net income climbed 44.0% to $53.1 million from $36.8 million in the same prior-year period. Total revenue advanced 40.9% to $198.0 million from $140.5 million in 1996. Strong sales in North America more than offset weaker-than-expected sales from international operations, particularly Japan, due to the strong dollar. License revenue was $147.1 million, or 74.3% of total revenue, compared with $103.4 million, or 73.6% of total revenue, a year earlier. Service revenue was $51.0 million, or 25.7% of total revenue, versus $37.1 million, or 26.4% of total revenue, in 1996. Sales and marketing expenses grew 37.2% to $77.3 million from $56.3 million the previous year. Operating income rose 43.7% to $79.2 million from $55.1 million the year before. On 3/18/97, PMTC received a $2.7 million follow-on order for software and services from Case Corporation of Racine, Wisconsin. On 3/26/97, PMTC received a $1.0 million order for software and services from Vickers Shipbuilding & Engineering Ltd. of the United Kingdom.

BUSINESS

PARAMETRIC TECHNOLOGY CORP. develops, markets and supports a family of fully-integrated software products that automate the mechanical design-through-manufacturing process. The Company's Pro/ENGINEER product family is based on a software architecture that integrates the different stages of mechanical design automation and allows changes made in one stage of the design process to be automatically reflected in all other phases of this process. Pro/ENGINEER's use of a single, unified data structure improves interaction among engineers by allowing all members of the product development team to work on the design simultaneously. Products and their manufacturing processes are developed concurrently.

ANNUAL EARNINGS AND DIVIDENDS PER SHARE

	9/30/96	9/30/95	9/30/94	9/30/93	9/30/92	9/30/91	9/30/90
Earnings Per Share	1.04	0.60	0.57	0.38	0.19	0.10	0.06
Dividends Per Share	①...	Nil	Nil	②...	③...	④...	Nil

① 2-for-1 stk. split, 2/26/93. ② 2-for-1 stk. split, 2/26/93. ③ 3-for-2 stk. split, 6/28/91.

ANNUAL FINANCIAL DATA

RECORD OF EARNINGS (IN THOUSANDS):

Total Revenues	600,122	394,310	244,256	163,088	86,739	44,715	25,475
Costs and Expenses	378,666	266,213	136,865	93,603	53,939	29,281	17,259
Depreciation & Amort	16,800	9,466	5,216	3,302	1,833	1,042	747
Operating Income	204,656	118,631	102,175	66,183	30,967	14,392	7,469
Inc Fr Cont Opers Bef Income Taxes	216,157	127,660	106,893	68,470	33,222	15,886	8,570
Income Taxes	78,247	50,298	39,978	25,537	12,155	5,555	2,957
Net Income	137,910	77,362	66,915	42,933	21,067	10,331	5,613
Aver. Shs. Outstg.	133,211	129,046	117,128	114,864	111,996	108,504	103,644

BALANCE SHEET (IN THOUSANDS):

Cash and Cash Equivalents	434,216	308,248	207,469	122,778	73,493	34,472	24,571
Receivables, Net	117,273	80,405	57,554	38,898	22,981	12,292	8,140
Gross Property	66,856	37,888	21,931	12,553	5,526	3,040	2,319
Accumulated Depreciation	30,339	18,077	9,109	4,521	2,125	1,967	1,375
Capital Lease Obligations	...	...	...	...	...	13	219
Net Stockholders' Equity	512,432	370,929	242,079	146,798	78,673	41,990	28,817
Total Assets	659,217	453,727	286,990	176,684	107,165	50,901	34,674
Total Current Assets	562,050	399,732	270,956	165,230	99,217	48,674	33,098
Total Current Liabilities	145,992	82,030	44,273	28,901	26,969	7,700	4,525
Net Working Capital	416,058	317,702	226,683	136,329	72,248	40,974	28,573
Year End Shares Outstg	127,429	125,130	113,834	109,204	104,290	98,974	96,046

STATISTICAL RECORD:

Operating Profit Margin %	34.1	30.1	41.8	40.6	35.7	32.2	29.3
Book Value Per Share	4.02	2.96	2.12	1.34	0.75	0.42	0.30
Return on Equity %	26.9	20.9	27.6	29.2	26.8	24.6	19.5
Return on Assets %	20.9	17.1	23.3	24.3	19.7	20.3	16.2
P/E Ratio	54.6-24.9	60.4-26.7	35.3-18.9	58.9-29.6	74.3-33.6	76.3-18.8	43.8-20.8
Price Range	56¾-25⅞	36¼-16	20⅛-10¾	22⅜-11¼	14⅛-6⅜	7⅝-1⅞	2⅝-1¼

Statistics are as originally reported.

OFFICERS:
S.C. Walske, Chmn. & C.E.O.
C.R. Harrison, Pres. & C.O.O.
E.J. Gillis, Exec V.P.—Fin., C.F.O. & Treas.
INCORPORATED: MA, May, 1985
PRINCIPAL OFFICE: 128 Technology Drive, Waltham, MA 02154

TELEPHONE NUMBER: (617) 398-5000
FAX: (617) 398-6000
NO. OF EMPLOYEES: 2,774
ANNUAL MEETING: In February
SHAREHOLDERS: 2,619
INSTITUTIONAL HOLDINGS:
No. of Institutions: 246
Shares Held: 112,119,931

REGISTRAR(S): American Stock Transfer & Trust Co., 40 Wall Street, New York, NY 10005

TRANSFER AGENT(S): American Stock Transfer & Trust Co., 40 Wall Street, New York, NY 10005

PAYCHEX, INC.

YIELD	0.8%
P/E RATIO	46.0

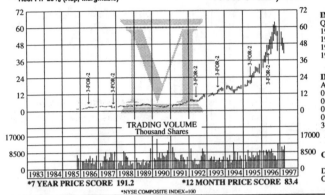

TRADING VOLUME
Thousand Shares

*7 YEAR PRICE SCORE 191.2   *12 MONTH PRICE SCORE 83.4
*NYSE COMPOSITE INDEX=100

INTERIM EARNINGS (Per Share):

Qtr.	Aug.	Nov.	Feb.	May
1993-94	0.07	0.07	0.06	0.07
1994-95	0.09	0.09	0.10	0.10
1995-96	0.12	0.13	0.13	0.14
1996-97	0.16	0.17	0.18	...

INTERIM DIVIDENDS (Per Share):

Amt.	Decl.	Ex.	Rec.	Pay.
0.06Q	7/12/96	7/30/96	8/1/96	8/22/96
0.09Q	10/3	10/24	10/28	11/25
0.09Q	1/9/97	1/28/97	1/30/97	2/20/97
0.09Q	4/10	4/29	5/1	5/22
3-for-2	4/10	5/30	5/8	5/29

Indicated div.: $0.24

CAPITALIZATION (5/31/96):

	($000)	(%)
Deferred Income Tax	416	0.2
Common & Surplus	190,810	99.8
Total	191,226	100.0

RECENT DEVELOPMENTS: For the quarter ended 2/28/97, net income advanced 39.9% to $19.3 million from $13.8 million in the same prior-year period. Total revenue climbed 27.4% to $195.6 million from $153.5 million in 1995. Payroll revenue grew 21.3% to $97.9 million from $80.7 million the prior year. Professional Employer Organization/Human Resources Services ("PEO/HRS") revenues rose 34.2% to $97.6 million from $72.8 million a year earlier. Operating income improved 46.3% to $25.0 million from $17.1 million in 1995. Results for 1996 reflected strong growth in PAYX's payroll client base and an increase in clients using PAYX's Taxpay®, Direct Deposit product and Check Signing option. Comparisons were made with restated 1995 results to reflect the merger between PAYX and National Business Solutions, Inc., as well as the formation of the PEO/HRS business segment during the third quarter of fiscal 1997. On 3/10/97, PAYX introduced Paychex Business Solutions, a PEO, to Southern California.

BUSINESS

PAYCHEX, INC. is primarily engaged in providing computerized payroll accounting services to 256,000 small to medium-sized businesses nationwide. The Company prepares and furnishes paychecks, earnings statements and internal accounting records such as journals, summaries and earnings histories. Paychex prepares for its clients all required monthly, quarterly and annual payroll tax returns for federal, state and local governments. The TAXPAY® service is utilized by approximately 66% of its clients nationwide. This service provides automatic payment of payroll taxes and filing of quarterly and annual returns. The market for the Company's services has evolved primarily as a result of employers being required by law to act as the "tax collectors" for various taxing authorities. This makes employers responsible for complying with a variety of complex, changing regulations and for withholding from the employee's pay and remitting to the taxing authorities all payroll taxes collected.

ANNUAL EARNINGS AND DIVIDENDS PER SHARE

	5/31/96	5/31/95	5/31/94	5/31/93	5/31/92	5/31/91	5/31/90
Earnings Per Share	0.51	0.38	0.28	0.24	0.14	0.10	0.09
Dividends Per Share	① 0.12	② 0.08	0.08	③ 0.05	④ 0.03	0.02	0.02
Dividend Payout %	23.5	21.1	28.6	25.0	21.4	20.0	22.2

Note: 3-for-2 stk. split, 5/29/97. ① 3-for-2 stk. split, 5/23/96. ② 3-for-2 stk. split, 5/25/95. ③ 3-for-2 stk. split, 8/26/93. ④ 3-for-2 stk. split, 5/20/92.

ANNUAL FINANCIAL DATA

RECORD OF EARNINGS (IN THOUSANDS):

Total Revenues	325,285	267,176	224,052	190,032	161,272	137,081	120,200
Costs and Expenses	243,846	205,125	176,064	152,668	132,631	115,384	100,743
Depreciation & Amort	13,940	11,040	11,205	10,707	9,824	8,414	7,330
Operating Income	67,499	51,011	36,783	26,657	18,728	13,283	12,127
Inc Fr Cont Opers Bef Income Taxes	72,687	54,373	38,986	28,027	19,547	14,048	13,208
Income Taxes	20,354	15,333	10,916	8,072	5,845	4,425	4,642
Net Income	52,333	39,040	28,070	19,955	13,702	9,623	8,566
Aver. Shs. Outstg.	102,528	101,083	100,777	100,339	99,629	99,144	99,017

BALANCE SHEET (IN THOUSANDS):

Cash and Cash Equivalents	117,244	83,695	55,596	38,115	20,025	11,037	15,785
Receivables, Net	46,331	38,781	29,114	23,498	20,454	15,644	14,239
Gross Property	110,118	88,726	92,988	88,702	81,955	69,708	53,882
Accumulated Depreciation	60,120	45,019	50,572	46,586	38,080	29,670	23,747
Long-Term Debt	...	523	728	1,237	1,634	2,024	1,653
Net Stockholders' Equity	190,810	139,932	108,508	85,189	67,405	54,491	47,160
Total Assets	220,208	168,437	129,789	106,920	86,242	70,413	62,109
Total Current Assets	165,292	124,219	87,001	64,225	41,621	29,702	31,423
Total Current Liabilities	28,134	26,661	18,970	17,836	13,737	10,481	10,166
Net Working Capital	137,158	97,558	68,031	46,389	27,884	19,221	21,257
Year End Shares Outstg	103,047	101,322	100,938	100,587	100,067	99,206	99,090

STATISTICAL RECORD:

Book Value Per Share	1.85	1.38	1.07	0.85	0.67	0.55	0.47
Return on Equity %	27.4	27.9	25.9	23.4	20.3	17.7	18.2
Return on Assets %	23.8	23.2	21.6	18.7	15.9	13.7	13.8
Average Yield %	0.7	0.8	0.9	0.8	1.0	0.6	1.1
P/E Ratio	43.2-22.2	31.3-21.8	40.1-23.9	39.8-21.4	32.9-13.8	27.2-16.2	41.7-26.2
Price Range	22⅛-11⅜	12⅛-8⅜	11⅛-6⅝	7⅞-4¼	4⅝-1⅞	2⅝-1⅝	3⅝-2¼

Statistics are as originally reported.

OFFICERS:
B.T. Golisano, Chmn., Pres. & C.E.O.
J.M. Morphy, C.F.O. & Sec.

INCORPORATED: DE, Jun., 1979

PRINCIPAL OFFICE: 911 Panorama Trail South, Rochester, NY 14625-0397

TELEPHONE NUMBER: (716) 385-6666
NO. OF EMPLOYEES: 4,097 (approx.)full-time; 231(approx.)part-time
ANNUAL MEETING: In October
SHAREHOLDERS: 5,740
INSTITUTIONAL HOLDINGS:
No. of Institutions: 200
Shares Held: 59,657,318 (adj.)

REGISTRAR(S): American Stock Transfer & Trust Co., 40 Wall Street, New York, NY 10005

TRANSFER AGENT(S): American Stock Transfer & Trust Co., 40 Wall Street, New York, NY 10005

PEOPLESOFT, INC.

YIELD   ...%
P/E RATIO   N.M.

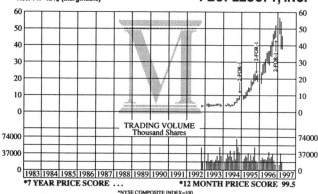

*7 YEAR PRICE SCORE ... *12 MONTH PRICE SCORE 99.5
*NYSE COMPOSITE INDEX=100

INTERIM EARNINGS (Per Share):

Qtr.	Mar.	June	Sept.	Dec.
1994	0.03	0.03	0.04	0.05
1995	0.05	0.06	0.07	0.10
1996	0.09	0.11	0.13	0.01
1997	0.14	...	...	...

INTERIM DIVIDENDS (Per Share):

Amt.	Decl.	Ex.	Rec.	Pay.
2-for-1	10/23/96	12/2/96	11/15/96	11/29/96

CAPITALIZATION (12/31/96):

	($000)	(%)
Common & Surplus	253,248	100.0
Total	253,248	100.0

RECENT DEVELOPMENTS: For the quarter ended 3/31/97, net income advanced 88.6% to $17.8 million from $9.5 million in the corresponding period of the previous year. Total revenues soared 86.7% to $153.7 million from $82.3 million the year before. Revenues from license fees jumped 91.4% to $83.4 million from $43.6 million in 1995. Revenues from services climbed 81.5% to $70.2 million from $38.7 million a year earlier. Revenues from international operations increased 85.9% to $26.4 million, or 17.2% of total revenues, from $14.2 million, or 17.3% of total revenues, the prior year. Total costs and expenses grew 85.6% to $126.5 million from $68.1 million the previous year. Operating income rose 92.2% to $27.2 million from $14.2 million the year before. Income before income taxes improved 85.5% to $29.2 million from $15.8 million in 1995. Results for 1996 were restated to included the acquisition of Red Pepper Software.

BUSINESS

PEOPLESOFT, INC. designs, develops, markets and supports a suite of Enterprise Resource Optimization application software products for large- and medium-sized organizations. PeopleSoft HRMS, PeopleSoft Financials, PeopleSoft Distribution, PeopleSoft Manufacturing and PeopleSoft Student Administration Systems are portable, scalable and integrated families of client/server applications, which incorporate such features as automated workflow, a distributed processing architecture with java- or windows-based clients, a choice of RDEMS platforms, a graphical navigator, development tools, and integrated data management, reporting and analysis capabilities. The Company offers industry-specific software and support solutions through nine business units, individually focused on one of the following markets: discrete manufacturing, retail, healthcare, public sector, federal government, higher education, infrastructure, financial services and industry services. The Company licenses and supports its products through direct offices in over 15 countries across North America, Latin America, Europe, the Far East, and Australia.

ANNUAL EARNINGS AND DIVIDENDS PER SHARE

	1996	1995	1994	1993	1992	1991	1990
Earnings Per Share	0.30	0.27	0.14	0.08	0.06	0.03	0.01
Dividends Per Share	①...	②...	③...	Nil	Nil	...	...

① 2-for-1 stk. split, 11/29/96. ② 2-for-1 stk. split, 11/29/95. ③ 2-for-1 stk. split, 12/9/94.

ANNUAL FINANCIAL DATA

RECORD OF EARNINGS (IN THOUSANDS):

	1996	1995	1994	1993	1992	1991	1990
Total Revenues	450,052	227,568	112,895	58,191	31,565	17,137	6,108
Costs and Expenses	367,537	171,401	83,902	43,130	22,363	13,592	5,363
Depreciation & Amort	26,691	11,282	7,298	2,552	1,075	479	193
Operating Income	55,824	44,885	21,695	12,509	8,127	3,066	552
Inc Fr Cont Opers Bef Income Taxes	61,712	48,929	23,853	13,678	8,082	3,051	431
Income Taxes	25,851	19,570	9,308	5,265	3,240	1,148	11
Net Income	35,861	29,359	14,545	8,413	4,842	1,903	420
Aver. Shs. Outstg.	120,032	109,596	103,852	101,608	72,096	62,60	49,352

BALANCE SHEET (IN THOUSANDS):

	1996	1995	1994	1993	1992	1991	1990
Cash and Cash Equivalents	197,013	125,739	87,953	56,740	42,142	2,086	433
Receivables, Net	191,922	111,943	58,235	39,606	17,691	10,994	2,492
Gross Property	140,279	81,383	28,221	10,048	4,244	2,186	1,038
Accumulated Depreciation	43,581	18,164	8,604	3,348	1,499	682	280
Long-Term Debt	...	1,305	891	989	933	1,397	1,037
Net Stockholders' Equity	253,248	156,701	93,349	72,084	47,676	6,616	d336
Total Assets	540,080	314,151	172,271	108,461	64,313	16,194	3,871
Total Current Assets	396,638	243,590	149,221	97,269	60,253	14,189	2,925
Total Current Liabilities	286,832	156,145	78,031	35,388	15,704	8,181	3,170
Net Working Capital	109,806	87,445	71,190	61,881	44,549	6,008	d245
Year End Shares Outstg	107,639	98,642	95,820	92,944	82,864	54,560	47,408

STATISTICAL RECORD:

	1996	1995	1994	1993	1992	1991	1990
Operating Profit Margin %	12.4	19.7	19.2	21.5	25.7	17.9	9.0
Book Value Per Share	2.25	1.51	0.94	0.75	0.56	0.02	...
Return on Equity %	14.2	18.7	15.6	11.7	10.2	N.M.	...
Return on Assets %	6.6	9.3	8.4	7.8	7.5	11.8	10.8
P/E Ratio	N.M.	87.0-27.8	70.5-23.2	56.9-33.3	66.7-47.9	...	...
Price Range	52¼-17⅛	23½-7½	9⅞-3¼	5⅛-3	4-2⅞	...	...

Statistics are as originally reported.

OFFICERS:
D.A. Duffield, Chmn., Pres. & C.E.O.
R.E. Codd, Sr. V.P.-Fin. & Admin., C.F.O. & Sec.

INCORPORATED: DE, Aug., 1987

PRINCIPAL OFFICE: 4440 Rosewood Drive, Pleasanton, CA 94588

TELEPHONE NUMBER: (510) 225-3000

NO. OF EMPLOYEES: 3,000 (approx.)

ANNUAL MEETING: In May

SHAREHOLDERS: 1,337 (approx.)

INSTITUTIONAL HOLDINGS:
No. of Institutions: 144
Shares Held: 69,478,508

REGISTRAR(S): Bank of Boston, Boston, MA 02102

TRANSFER AGENT(S): Bank of Boston, Boston, MA 02102

PETSMART, INC.

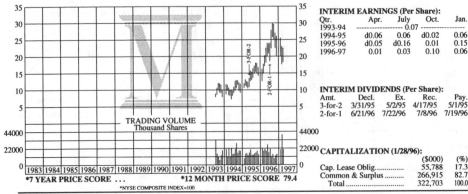

*7 YEAR PRICE SCORE ...   *12 MONTH PRICE SCORE 79.4
*NYSE COMPOSITE INDEX=100

TRADING VOLUME
Thousand Shares

INTERIM EARNINGS (Per Share):

Qtr.	Apr.	July	Oct.	Jan.
1993-94		0.07		
1994-95	d0.06	0.06	d0.02	0.06
1995-96	d0.05	d0.16	0.01	0.15
1996-97	0.01	0.03	0.10	0.06

INTERIM DIVIDENDS (Per Share):

Amt.	Decl.	Ex.	Rec.	Pay.
3-for-2	3/31/95	5/2/95	4/17/95	5/1/95
2-for-1	6/21/96	7/22/96	7/8/96	7/19/96

CAPITALIZATION (1/28/96):

	($000)	(%)
Cap. Lease Oblig.	55,788	17.3
Common & Surplus	266,915	82.7
Total	322,703	100.0

RECENT DEVELOPMENTS: For the 53 weeks ended 2/2/97, PETM reported net income of $20.6 million versus a net loss of $5.4 million for the previous 52-week period. Earnings for 1996 and 1995 included merger and non-recurring charges of $40.7 million and $47.1 million, respectively, and store pre-opening expenses of $10.9 million and $5.4 million, respectively. Net sales grew 28.5% to $1.50 billion from $1.17 billion a year earlier. Income before income taxes totaled $34.3 million versus a loss of $14.9 million.

For the 14 weeks ended 2/2/97, net income dropped 47.4% to $7.6 million from $14.4 million for the same 13-week period the prior year. Earnings for the current year included merger and restructuring charges of $20.4 million. Earnings for 1996 and 1995 included store pre-opening expenses of $3.1 million and $1.6 million, respectively. Net sales advanced 38.1% to $457.4 million from $331.1 million the year before. Comparisons were made with restated 1995 results. During the quarter, PETM opened 17 stores.

BUSINESS

PETSMART, INC. is the nation's leading operator of superstores specializing in pet food, pet supplies and pet services. As of 2/2/97, the Company operated 341 superstores in North America and 56 superstores in the United Kingdom. The average PETsMART superstore is 25,000 square feet. The superstores stock more than 12,000 items and offer the most complete assortment of products and services available for household pets. PETsMART also guarantees its customers the lowest price on each of the products it sells. PETM carries an extensive selection of pet foods and treats, including labels such as Science Diet, Iams, Ralston Purina and Alpo. Pet supplies include collars, leashes, health aids, shampoos, medications, toys, animal carriers, dog houses, cat furniture and equestrian supplies. PETM also sells fresh water tropical fish and domestically bred birds. During 1995, the Company acquired Sporting Dog Specialties, Petstuff, Inc. and The Pet Food Giant, Inc.

ANNUAL EARNINGS AND DIVIDENDS PER SHARE

	1/30/97	1/28/96	1/29/95	1/30/94	1/31/93	2/2/92	2/3/91
Earnings Per Share	0.17	d0.04	0.05	③0.07	④0.05	④d0.15	d0.17
Dividends Per Share	①...	Nil	②...	Nil	Nil	Nil	Nil

① 2-for-1 stk. split, 7/19/96. ② 3-for-2 stk. split, 5/1/95. ③ Before acctg. change. ④ Before extraord. credit.

ANNUAL FINANCIAL DATA

RECORD OF EARNINGS (IN MILLIONS):

Total Revenues	1,501.0	1,030.7	601.0	330.8	187.9	106.6	58.2
Costs and Expenses	...	1,014.9	577.0	313.3	178.0	103.4	58.3
Depreciation & Amort	...	21.8	15.8	8.6	4.9	2.5	1.0
Operating Income	42.6	d6.0	8.3	8.8	5.0	0.7	d1.1
Inc Fr Cont Opers Bef Income Taxes	34.3	d11.7	4.8	7.2	3.9	0.7	d0.5
Income Taxes	13.7	cr8.9	0.8	2.6	1.5	0.3	...
Net Income	20.6	d2.8	4.1	①4.6	②2.4	③0.4	d0.5
Aver. Shs. Outstg. (000)	118,226	108,387	89,710	70,680	58,006	11,934	11,886

① Before acctg. change cr$233,000. ② Before extra. item cr$1,419,000. ③ Before extra. item cr$299,000.

BALANCE SHEET (IN MILLIONS):

Cash and Cash Equivalents	39.9	74.2	76.1	117.9	18.3	18.6	...
Receivables, Net	...	31.0	18.1	10.0	4.8	2.2	...
Inventories	...	190.6	116.0	64.8	38.7	21.2	...
Gross Property	...	214.0	155.4	91.5	51.1	22.7	...
Accumulated Depreciation	...	53.5	29.9	15.5	7.5	3.8	...
Capital Lease Obligations	...	55.8	61.4	36.9	21.3	7.4	...
Net Stockholders' Equity	361.0	266.9	202.6	192.1	60.1	38.6	...
Total Assets	689.8	510.3	358.2	292.6	115.0	64.4	...
Total Current Assets	409.3	305.9	216.0	196.0	63.3	42.5	...
Total Current Liabilities	251.1	176.2	85.8	58.5	30.9	17.0	...
Net Working Capital	158.2	129.8	130.3	137.5	32.4	25.5	...
Year End Shs Outstg (000)	...	101,704	86,640	78,810	7,116	7,004	...

STATISTICAL RECORD:

Operating Profit Margin %	2.8	...	1.4	2.7	2.7	0.6	...
Book Value Per Share	...	2.63	2.34	2.44	3.51	0.80	...
Return on Equity %	5.7	...	2.0	2.4	9.6	6.4	...
Return on Assets %	3.0	...	1.1	1.6	2.1	0.6	...
Price Range	29⅞-12⅜	18⅛-10⅜	12⅞-7⅛	12-7⅞	...	...	...

Statistics are as originally reported.
Figures for 1/30/97 are preliminary.

OFFICERS:
S.J. Parker, Chmn.
M.S. Hansen, Pres. & C.E.O.
S. Schnabel, Sr. V.P. & C.F.O.

INCORPORATED: DE, Aug., 1986

PRINCIPAL OFFICE: 10000 N. 31st Ave., Suite C-100, Phoenix, AZ 85051

TELEPHONE NUMBER: (602) 944-7070

NO. OF EMPLOYEES: 11,000

ANNUAL MEETING: In June

SHAREHOLDERS: 2,810

INSTITUTIONAL HOLDINGS:
No. of Institutions: 145
Shares Held: 75,182,402

REGISTRAR(S): Norwest Bank Minnesota, N.A., South St. Paul, MN

TRANSFER AGENT(S): Norwest Bank Minnesota, N.A., South St. Paul, MN

PHYCOR INC.

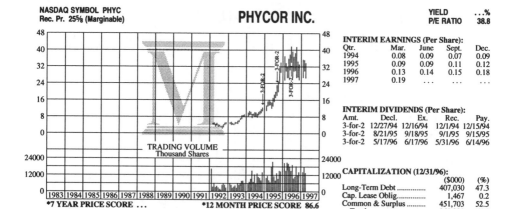

*7 YEAR PRICE SCORE ...   *12 MONTH PRICE SCORE 86.6

*NYSE COMPOSITE INDEX=100

INTERIM EARNINGS (Per Share):

Qtr.	Mar.	June	Sept.	Dec.
1994	0.08	0.09	0.07	0.09
1995	0.09	0.09	0.11	0.12
1996	0.13	0.14	0.15	0.18
1997	0.19	...	...	...

INTERIM DIVIDENDS (Per Share):

Amt.	Decl.	Ex.	Rec.	Pay.
3-for-2	12/27/94	12/16/94	12/1/94	12/15/94
3-for-2	8/21/95	9/18/95	9/1/95	9/15/95
3-for-2	5/17/96	6/17/96	5/31/96	6/14/96

CAPITALIZATION (12/31/96):

	($000)	(%)
Long-Term Debt	407,030	47.3
Cap. Lease Oblig.	1,467	0.2
Common & Surplus	451,703	52.5
Total	860,200	100.0

RECENT DEVELOPMENTS: For the quarter ended 3/31/97, net earnings grew 60.0% to $12.3 million from $7.7 million in the corresponding period of the previous year. Net revenues advanced 54.2% to $250.7 million from $162.5 million the year before. On a base representing 31 clinics and 13 IPA markets, same-market revenue rose 13.2% for the quarter. Operating expenses grew 53.7% to $230.6 million from $150.0 million a year earlier. Earnings before taxes increased 60.0% to $20.0 million compared with $12.5

million the prior year. During the quarter, the Company entered into a definitive agreement with Florida Independent Physician Association ("FIPA") and Mariner Health Group, Inc. Under this agreement, PHYC will assume management responsibilities for FIPA with Florida Physician Services, the IPA management company associated with FIPA. FIPA is a statewide network of regionally based, physician-directed IPAs covering the state of Florida.

BUSINESS

PHYCOR, INC. operates multi-specialty medical clinics by acquiring certain assets of established multi-specialty clinics, such as equipment and accounts receivable, and by operating each clinic under a long-term service agreement with an affiliated multi-specialty physician group that practices exclusively through the clinic. Upon the acquisition of a clinic's operating assets, PhyCor simultaneously enters into a long-term service agreement with the acquired company. PhyCor, under the terms of the service agreement, provides the physician group with the equipment and facilities used in their medical practice, manages clinic operations, employs most of the clinic's non-physician personnel, and receives a service fee. A multi-specialty clinic provides a broad range of medical services through an organized physician group practice representing various medical specialties, ranging from general medicine to highly focused sub-specialties. As of 5/7/97, the Company operates 48 clinics with approximately 3,280 physicians in 28 states and manages independent practice associations with more than 15,800 physicians in 23 markets.

ANNUAL EARNINGS AND DIVIDENDS PER SHARE

	1996	1995	1994	1993	1992	1991	1990
Earnings Per Share	0.60	0.41	0.32	0.27	d0.57	②0.05	②0.01
Dividends Per Share	①...	③...	④...	Nil	Nil	⑤...	Nil

① 3-for-2 stk. split, 6/14/96. ② Before extraord. item. ③ 3-for-2 stk. split, 9/15/95. ④ 3-for-2 stk. split, 2/15/94. ⑤ 1-for-2 rev. stk. split, 11/11/91.

ANNUAL FINANCIAL DATA

RECORD OF EARNINGS (IN MILLIONS):

	1996	1995	1994	1993	1992	1991	1990
Total Revenues	766.3	441.6	242.5	167.4	135.9	90.1	63.9
Costs and Expenses	644.4	374.0	211.1	147.2	139.0	81.0	59.0
Depreciation & Amort	40.2	21.4	12.2	8.4	6.4	4.2	2.7
Operating Profit	81.7	46.1	19.1	11.8	9.1	4.8	2.2
Inc Fr Cont Opers Bef Income Taxes	59.2	35.8	16.5	8.2	d13.3	1.3	0.2
Income Taxes	22.8	13.9	4.8	1.1	0.4	0.6	0.1
Net Income	36.4	21.9	11.7	7.1	d13.7	①0.8	②0.1
Aver. Shs. Outstg. (000)	61,096	53,510	36,329	25,871	23,943	14,237	13,238

① Before extra. item cr$297,000. ② Before extra. item cr$33,000.

BALANCE SHEET (IN MILLIONS):

Cash and Cash Equivalents	30.5	18.8	6.5	3.2	9.2	2.6	3.6
Receivables, Net	295.4	167.0	118.2	61.6	53.1	32.5	26.7
Inventories	15.2	8.9	5.8	4.0	3.4	2.2	1.9
Gross Property	216.3	143.2	79.0	39.4	39.3	28.2	22.1
Accumulated Depreciation	56.0	34.4	20.2	12.7	9.0	5.0	2.3
Long-Term Debt	407.0	125.3	83.6	61.2	13.2	9.5	7.2
Capital Lease Obligations	1.5	1.6	1.3	3.1	3.6	1.3	1.6
Net Stockholders' Equity	451.7	388.8	184.1	70.0	53.9	25.5	24.4
Total Assets	1,118.6	643.6	351.4	171.2	141.4	92.5	78.8
Total Current Assets	383.4	217.5	144.9	77.5	69.4	39.6	33.5
Total Current Liabilities	170.5	106.1	64.3	30.5	33.5	17.7	15.5
Net Working Capital	212.9	111.4	80.5	46.9	35.9	21.8	18.0
Year End Shs Outstg (000)	54,831	53,399	37,899	24,197	22,040	4,365	4,365

STATISTICAL RECORD:

Operating Profit Margin %	10.7	10.4	7.9	7.1	...	5.4	3.5
Book Value Per Share	...	1.49	1.23	0.26	0.61	...	...
Return on Equity %	8.1	5.6	6.3	10.2	...	3.0	0.2
Return on Assets %	3.3	3.4	3.3	4.2	...	0.8	0.1
P/E Ratio	69.6-42.5	82.9-26.5	39.1-23.4	33.8-14.8	...	...	...
Price Range	41¾-25½	34-10⅞	12½-7½	9⅛-4	5¼-2¼	...	...

Statistics are as originally reported.

OFFICERS:
J.C. Hutts, Chmn., Pres. & C.E.O.
T.S. Dent, Exec. V.P.-Corp. Services & Sec.
D.W. Reeves, Exec. V.P.-Devel.
R.D. Wright, Exec. V.P.-Opers.
J.K. Crawford, V.P., Treas. & C.F.O.

INCORPORATED: TN, Jan., 1988

PRINCIPAL OFFICE: 30 Burton Hills Blvd.
Suite 400, Nashville, TN 37215

TELEPHONE NUMBER: (615) 665-9066

NO. OF EMPLOYEES: 15,000 (approx.)

ANNUAL MEETING: In May

SHAREHOLDERS: 2,300 (approx.)

INSTITUTIONAL HOLDINGS:
No. of Institutions: 133
Shares Held: 47,351,255

REGISTRAR(S):

TRANSFER AGENT(S): First Union National
Bank of N.C., Charlotte, NC

QUALCOMM, INC.

YIELD ...%
P/E RATIO 86.5

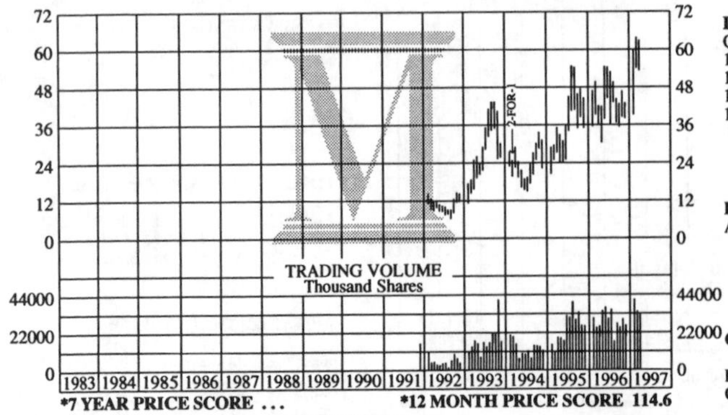

TRADING VOLUME
Thousand Shares

| | 1983 | 1984 | 1985 | 1986 | 1987 | 1988 | 1989 | 1990 | 1991 | 1992 | 1993 | 1994 | 1995 | 1996 | 1997 |

*7 YEAR PRICE SCORE ...   *12 MONTH PRICE SCORE 114.6
*NYSE COMPOSITE INDEX=100

INTERIM EARNINGS (Per Share):

Qtr.	Dec.	Mar.	June	Sept.
1993-94	0.09	0.10	0.12	d0.03
1994-95	0.11	0.11	0.13	0.17
1995-96	0.15	0.02	0.02	0.11
1996-97	0.13	0.23	...	...

INTERIM DIVIDENDS (Per Share):

Amt.	Decl.	Ex.	Rec.	Pay.
Last dist. 2-for-1 split, 2/23/94.				

CAPITALIZATION (9/29/96):

	($000)	(%)
Long-Term Debt	14,458	1.7
Common & Surplus	844,913	98.3
Total	859,371	100.0

RECENT DEVELOPMENTS: For the quarter ended 3/30/97, net income advanced to $16.7 million from $1.5 million in the same prior-year period. Total revenues soared to $586.0 million from $149.0 million the year before. Communications systems revenues jumped to $508.0 million from $104.0 million, reflecting the rapid growth in sales of CDMA phones and ASIC products. Contract services revenue climbed 75.0% to $49.0 million from $28.0 million primarily due to ramp-up of the Globalstar development contract. For the six months ended 3/30/97, net income increased to $25.9 million from $11.6 million a year earlier. Total revenues jumped to $975.0 million from $296.0 million the prior year. On 4/22/97, the Company announced that it acquired a 49% equity stake in Corporacion Nacional de Radiodeterminacion, a Mexican corporation that has been the exclusive operator and distributor of QCOM's OmniTRACS® two-way mobile satellite communications and tracking system in Mexico since 1992.

BUSINESS

QUALCOMM INC. is a provider of digital wireless communications products, technologies and services. QCOM designs, develops, markets and manufactures wireless communications, infrastructure and subscriber equipment and Application Specific Integrated Circuits ("ASICs") based on its Code Division Multiple Access ("CDMA") technology. QCOM manufactures, distributes and operates satellite-based, two-way mobile communications and tracking systems (OmniTRACS) that provide data, position reporting and other services for transportation companies and other mobile and fixed-site customers. QCOM also provides contract development services, including the design and development of subscriber and ground communications equipment for the Globalstar L.P. satellite-based communications system.

ANNUAL EARNINGS AND DIVIDENDS PER SHARE

	9/29/96	9/30/95	9/30/94	9/30/93	9/27/92	9/29/91	9/28/90
Earnings Per Share	0.30	0.53	0.25	0.25	d0.11	d0.27	d0.58
Dividends Per Share	Nil	Nil	①...	Nil	Nil	Nil	...

① 2-for-1 stk. split, 2/23/94.

ANNUAL FINANCIAL DATA

RECORD OF EARNINGS (IN MILLIONS):

	9/29/96	9/30/95	9/30/94	9/30/93	9/27/92	9/29/91	9/28/90
Total Revenues	813.9	386.6	271.6	168.7	107.5	90.3	46.5
Costs and Expenses	764.5	335.1	242.9	146.8	102.3	91.0	56.8
Depreciation & Amort	56.8	30.9	18.8	10.0	7.2	5.8	5.6
Operating Income	d7.4	20.6	10.0	11.9	d2.0	d6.5	d15.8
Inc Fr Cont Opers Bef Income Taxes	26.6	39.9	17.3	13.1	d2.3	d8.3	d17.1
Income Taxes	5.6	9.7	2.1	1.0	0.6	0.1	...
Net Income	21.0	30.2	15.2	12.1	d4.1	d8.4	d17.1
Aver. Shs. Outstg. (000)	70,214	57,420	53,514	48,046	39,058	31,344	29,532

BALANCE SHEET (IN MILLIONS):

	9/29/96	9/30/95	9/30/94	9/30/93	9/27/92	9/29/91	9/28/90
Cash and Cash Equivalents	346.3	567.0	137.5	192.1	54.4	0.1	3.8
Receivables, Net	217.4	82.7	62.9	34.1	24.7	16.8	9.9
Inventories	171.5	44.0	15.6	14.1	6.5	5.9	5.4
Gross Property	470.0	251.9	155.3	89.2	41.3	31.7	20.6
Accumulated Depreciation	117.3	66.4	41.6	26.9	21.0	15.0	9.8
Long-Term Debt	14.5	36.1	26.6	29.0	6.5	9.4	4.1
Capital Lease Obligations	...	...	...	...	2.9	4.2	3.3
Net Stockholders' Equity	844.9	799.6	262.2	236.7	68.8	2.6	9.1
Total Assets	1,185.3	940.7	357.9	306.6	108.3	41.6	32.5
Total Current Assets	751.2	704.6	220.6	241.5	86.7	23.4	19.5
Total Current Liabilities	326.0	105.0	69.2	40.9	30.1	25.5	15.9
Net Working Capital	425.2	599.6	151.4	200.7	56.6	d2.1	3.6
Year End Shs Outstg (000)	66,535	58,194	51,486	50,268	41,772	21,154	19,956

STATISTICAL RECORD:

	9/29/96	9/30/95	9/30/94	9/30/93	9/27/92	9/29/91	9/28/90
Operating Profit Margin %	...	5.3	3.7	7.1	...	...	...
Book Value Per Share	12.70	13.74	5.09	4.71	1.65	0.12	0.46
Return on Equity %	2.5	3.8	5.8	5.1	...	...	...
Return on Assets %	1.8	3.2	4.2	3.9	...	...	...
Price Range	54½-30⅜	54¾-20½	33¾-15	43⅜-11¼	14⅝-6¼	...	...

Statistics are as originally reported.

OFFICERS:
I.M. Jacobs, Chairman & C.E.O.
A.J. Viterbi, Vice-Chmn.
H.P. White, Pres.
R. Sulpizio, Exec. V.P. & C.O.O.
INCORPORATED: CA, Sep., 1981; reincorp., DE, Sep., 1991
PRINCIPAL OFFICE: 6455 Lusk Blvd., San Diego, CA 92121-2779

TELEPHONE NUMBER: (619) 587-1121
NO. OF EMPLOYEES: 8,000
ANNUAL MEETING: In February
SHAREHOLDERS: 2,500
INSTITUTIONAL HOLDINGS:
No. of Institutions: 211
Shares Held: 29,377,067

REGISTRAR(S): Harris Trust & Savings, Chicago, IL

TRANSFER AGENT(S): Harris Trust & Savings, Chicago, IL

QUANTUM CORP.

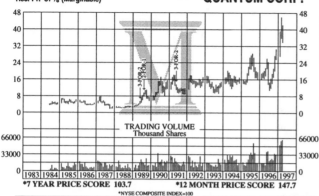

*7 YEAR PRICE SCORE 103.7 *12 MONTH PRICE SCORE 147.7
*NYSE COMPOSITE INDEX=100

INTERIM EARNINGS (Per Share):

Qtr.	June	Sept.	Dec.	Mar.
1993-94	------------------ 0.06 ------------------			
1994-95	1.24	1.03	d1.06	0.48
1995-96	0.25 ------ 0.29 ------			d2.28
1996-97	0.07	0.08	0.85	1.28

INTERIM DIVIDENDS (Per Share):

Amt.   Decl.   Ex.   Rec.   Pay.
Last dist. 3-for-2 split, 4/30/91

CAPITALIZATION (3/31/96):

	($000)	(%)
Long-Term Debt	598,158	52.3
Common & Surplus	544,823	47.7
Total	1,142,981	100.0

RECENT DEVELOPMENTS: For the year ended 3/31/97, QNTM reported net income of $148.5 million versus a net loss of $90.5 million in 1995. Sales climbed 20.3% to $5.32 billion from $4.42 billion the prior year. QNTM's DLT™ tape and related sales soared approximately 117% to $728.0 million versus 1995. Also, QNTM shipped 6.1 million desktop drives due to the strength of Quantum's Fireball TM and Bigfoot product lines. Gross profit as a percentage of sales grew to 14.5% from 12.3% a year earlier. General and administrative expenses dropped 68.5% to $86.5 million. Net interest and other expense advanced 46.1% to $40.8 million. Income before income taxes amounted to $200.7 million versus a loss of $141.3 million. For the quarter ended 3/31/97, QNTM produced net income of $87.7 million compared with a net loss of $122.9 million in the same prior-year period. Sales advanced 26.9% to $1.56 billion from $1.23 billion in 1995. On 5/1/97, Quantum and Matsushita-Kotobuki Electronics, Ltd. signed a definitive agreement to form a joint venture company to design, develop, and manufacture recording heads.

BUSINESS

QUANTUM CORPORATION is a leader in designing, manufacturing and marketing advanced small-form-factor hard disk drives based on Winchester technology, for a broad range of computer systems, including desktop workstations, personal computers and advanced notebook computers. The Company also designs and markets storage enhancement products that upgrade the capacity of existing desktop personal computer systems. The Company markets its products to major OEMS (original equipment manufacturers) through a broad range of distributors, dealers and retail outlets worldwide.

ANNUAL EARNINGS AND DIVIDENDS PER SHARE

	3/31/96	3/31/95	3/31/94	3/31/93	3/31/92	3/31/91	3/31/90
Earnings Per Share	d1.74	1.72	0.06	2.05	1.05	1.69	1.14
Dividends Per Share	Nil	Nil	Nil	Nil	①...	Nil	②...

① 3-for-2 stk. split, 5/1/91. ② 3-for-2 stk. split, 4/89 & 2-for-1 stk. split, 8/89.

ANNUAL FINANCIAL DATA

RECORD OF EARNINGS (IN MILLIONS):

	3/31/96	3/31/95	3/31/94	3/31/93	3/31/92	3/31/91	3/31/90
Total Revenues	4,422.7	3,368.0	2,131.1	1,697.2	1,127.7	877.7	446.3
Costs and Expenses	4,439.0	3,153.6	2,091.4	1,521.4	1,024.4	756.3	374.0
Depreciation & Amort	97.1	53.3	29.3	26.9	28.1	13.2	5.3
Operating Income	d113.4	161.1	10.3	148.9	75.3	108.3	67.0
Inc Fr Cont Opers Bef Income Taxes	d141.3	145.3	3.7	146.6	74.4	116.0	72.1
Income Taxes	cr50.9	63.7	1.0	52.8	27.5	42.1	24.9
Net Income	d90.5	81.6	2.7	93.8	46.8	73.9	47.2
Aver. Shs. Outstg. (000)	51,841	47,319	44,967	45,728	44,672	43,614	41,391

BALANCE SHEET (IN MILLIONS):

Cash and Cash Equivalents	164.8	187.8	330.0	289.0	145.0	114.7	79.3
Receivables, Net	820.7	541.9	357.2	304.5	194.4	161.7	70.0
Inventories	459.5	324.7	194.1	223.2	87.4	101.7	24.1
Gross Property	525.4	399.9	158.7	132.1	107.0	81.5	36.9
Accumulated Depreciation	161.3	119.8	72.8	57.4	41.1	25.4	13.7
Long-Term Debt	598.2	327.5	212.5	212.5	...	...	...
Net Stockholders' Equity	544.8	509.5	411.3	398.2	308.4	238.3	153.6
Total Assets	1,975.4	1,481.0	997.4	926.6	546.8	489.4	243.2
Total Current Assets	1,526.5	1,089.9	895.7	829.7	452.9	396.3	185.4
Total Current Liabilities	821.1	644.0	373.7	315.9	236.1	247.7	83.2
Net Working Capital	705.4	445.9	522.0	513.8	216.8	148.6	102.2
Year End Shs Outstg (000)	54,196	44,164	44,604	43,322	42,893	39,147	37,131

STATISTICAL RECORD:

Operating Profit Margin %	...	4.8	0.5	8.8	6.7	12.3	15.0
Book Value Per Share	8.83	9.37	9.22	9.19	7.19	6.09	3.90
Return on Equity %	...	16.0	0.7	23.6	15.2	31.0	30.7
Return on Assets %	...	5.5	0.3	10.1	8.6	15.1	19.4
P/E Ratio	...	11.8-6.8	N.M.	8.8-5.4	17.3-8.5	10.1-3.5	9.6-2.5
Price Range	28½-13¾	20¼-11⅝	17¾-9⅜	18-11⅛	18⅛-8⅞	17⅛-5⅞	11-2⅞

Statistics are as originally reported.

OFFICERS:
S.M. Berkley, Chmn.
M.A. Brown, Pres. & C.E.O.
R.L. Clemmer, Exec. V.P.-Fin. & C.F.O.
INCORPORATED: CA, Feb., 1980; reincorp., DE, Apr., 1987
PRINCIPAL OFFICE: 500 McCarthy Blvd., Milpitas, CA 95035

TELEPHONE NUMBER: (408) 894-4000
FAX: (408) 894-3223
NO. OF EMPLOYEES: 7,036
ANNUAL MEETING: In July
SHAREHOLDERS: 2,445
INSTITUTIONAL HOLDINGS:
No. of Institutions: 184
Shares Held: 45,344,414

REGISTRAR(S): Harris Trust Co. of California, Chicago, IL 60690

TRANSFER AGENT(S): Harris Trust Co. of California, Chicago, IL 60690

QUINTILES TRANSNATIONAL, CORP.

YIELD ...%
P/E RATIO N.M.

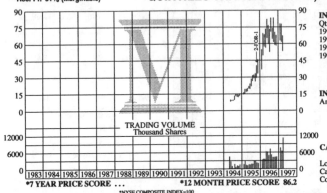

INTERIM EARNINGS (Per Share):

Qtr.	Mar.	June	Sept.	Dec.
1994	0.09	0.09	0.10	0.11
1995	0.11	0.13	0.15	0.16
1996	0.19	0.22	0.24	d0.45
1997	0.30	...	...	...

INTERIM DIVIDENDS (Per Share):

Amt.	Decl.	Ex.	Rec.	Pay.
Last dist. 2-for-1 split, 11/27/95				

CAPITALIZATION (12/31/96):

	($000)	(%)
Long-Term Debt	163,285	52.2
Cap. Lease Oblig.	5,407	1.7
Common & Surplus	144,348	46.1
Total	313,040	100.0

TRADING VOLUME
Thousand Shares

1983 1984 1985 1986 1987 1988 1989 1990 1991 1992 1993 1994 1995 1996 1997

*7 YEAR PRICE SCORE ...   *12 MONTH PRICE SCORE 86.2

*NYSE COMPOSITE INDEX=100

RECENT DEVELOPMENTS: For the quarter ended 3/31/97, net income advanced to $10.4 million from $4.4 million in the corresponding period of the previous year. Earnings for 1996 included restructuring costs of $13.1 million, special pension costs of $2.3 million, and $17.1 million in non-recurring transaction costs. Net revenue was $170.0 million, up 53.7% from $110.6 million a year earlier. Direct costs grew 52.3% to $86.6 million, while general and administrative expense rose 59.4% to $58.4 million versus 1995. Comparisons were made with restated 1996 results to include the acquisitions of BRI International, Inc. and Innovex Ltd. Income from operations increased to $17.1 million compared with $7.0 million the year before. Income before income taxes climbed to $16.4 million versus $7.3 million the prior year. The improved results for 1997 reflected the Company's recent acquisitions, as well as its expansion into Hong Kong.

BUSINESS

QUINTILES TRANSNATIONAL CORP. is a major provider of full-service contract research, sales and marketing services to the worldwide pharmaceutical, biotechnology and medical device industries, and provides healthcare policy consulting and health information management services to the healthcare industry. QTRN has 63 operating units in 22 countries. On April 20, 1994, the Company's stock commenced trading. On 11/22/96, the Company acquired BRI International, Inc., an international contract research organization. On 11/29/96, the Company acquired Innovex Limited, a worldwide contract pharmaceutical organization.

ANNUAL EARNINGS AND DIVIDENDS PER SHARE

	1996	1995	1994	1993	1992	1991
Earnings Per Share	0.13	0.56	0.39	0.29	0.23	...
Dividends Per Share	Nil	①...	Nil	Nil	Nil	...

① 2-for-1 stk. split, 11/27/95.

ANNUAL FINANCIAL DATA

RECORD OF EARNINGS (IN THOUSANDS):

	1996	1995	1994	1993	1992	1991
Total Revenues	537,608	156,437	90,067	61,704	44,296	29,515
Costs and Expenses	①475,610	133,529	76,030	52,225	37,271	24,528
Depreciation & Amort	24,780	7,514	4,538	3,469	2,261	1,883
Operating Income	37,218	15,394	9,499	6,010	4,764	3,104
Inc Fr Cont Opers Bef Income Taxes	②17,125	17,162	10,178	5,822	4,272	2,394
Income Taxes	11,914	5,903	3,506	1,980	1,622	949
Net Income	5,211	11,259	6,672	3,842	2,650	1,445
Aver. Shs. Outstg.	34,050	20,028	17,557	13,535	11,622	10,404

① Incl. $13,100,000 and $2,300,000 in non-recurring restructuring and special pension costs. ② Incl. $17,100,000 in non-recurring transactions relating to the BRI and Innovex acquisitions.

BALANCE SHEET (IN THOUSANDS):

	1996	1995	1994	1993	1992	1991
Cash and Cash Equivalents	99,655	69,146	39,353	9,184	1,911	...
Receivables, Net	178,579	57,165	36,052	29,130	19,248	...
Gross Property	178,466	74,381	36,312	26,285	20,529	...
Accumulated Depreciation	54,286	17,523	12,478	8,974	6,036	...
Long-Term Debt	163,285	19,947	902	3,908	4,954	...
Capital Lease Obligations	5,407	...	...	...	...	...
Net Stockholders' Equity	144,348	158,539	78,846	35,120	19,659	...
Total Assets	518,050	221,290	110,631	66,815	46,496	...
Total Current Assets	290,890	131,481	78,332	40,815	23,003	...
Total Current Liabilities	194,882	37,235	27,371	24,369	18,630	...
Net Working Capital	96,008	94,246	50,961	16,446	4,373	...
Year End Shares Outstg	33,150	21,387	6,253	14,448	12,926	...

STATISTICAL RECORD:

	1996	1995	1994	1993	1992	1991
Operating Profit Margin %	6.9	9.8	10.5	9.7	10.8	10.5
Book Value Per Share	4.35	5.97	11.53	1.97	0.98	...
Return on Equity %	3.6	7.1	8.5	10.9	13.5	...
Return on Assets %	1.0	5.1	6.0	5.8	5.7	...
P/E Ratio	N.M.	82.1-25.9	40.5-21.4	...	...	...
Price Range	83¼-37	46-14½	15⅜-8⅛	...	...	...

Statistics are as originally reported.

OFFICERS:
D.B. Gillings, Chmn. & C.E.O.
S.J. Costa, Pres. & C.O.O.
R.R. Selisker, C.F.O., V.P.-Fin. & Treas.

INCORPORATED: NC, 1982

PRINCIPAL OFFICE: 4709 Creekstone Drive Riverbirch Building Suite 300, Morrisville, NC 27560

TELEPHONE NUMBER: (919) 941-2000
FAX: (919) 941-9113
NO. OF EMPLOYEES: 8,000 (approx.)
ANNUAL MEETING: In April
SHAREHOLDERS: 8,950
INSTITUTIONAL HOLDINGS:
No. of Institutions: 91
Shares Held: 13,305,569

REGISTRAR(S): First Union National Bank of N.C., Charlotte, NC

TRANSFER AGENT(S): First Union National Bank of N.C., Charlotte, NC

ROSS STORES, INC.

YIELD   0.5%
P/E RATIO 18.4

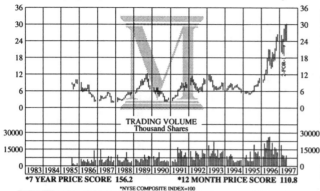

7 YEAR PRICE SCORE 156.2   **12 MONTH PRICE SCORE 110.8**
*NYSE COMPOSITE INDEX=100

TRADING VOLUME
Thousand Shares

INTERIM EARNINGS (Per Share):

Qtr.	Apr.	July	Oct.	Jan.
1994-95	0.09	0.18	0.23	0.26
1995-96	0.08	0.21	0.16	0.43
1996-97	0.27	0.36	0.32	0.63
1997-98	0.47	...	...	...

INTERIM DIVIDENDS (Per Share):

Amt.	Decl.	Ex.	Rec.	Pay.
0.07Q	11/27/96	12/4/96	12/6/96	1/6/97
2-for-1	1/30/97	3/6/97	2/11/97	3/5
0.045Q	2/6	3/6	3/10	4/7
0.045Q	5/22	6/11	6/13	7/7

Indicated div.: $0.18

CAPITALIZATION (2/3/96):

	($000)	(%)
Long-Term Debt	9,806	3.3
Common & Surplus	291,516	96.7
Total	301,322	100.0

RECENT DEVELOPMENTS: For the quarter ended 5/3/97, net earnings advanced 70.4% to $23.8 million compared with $13.9 million for the corresponding period of the previous year. Sales rose 19.4% to $442.8 million from $370.9 million the year before. Comparable-store sales climbed 11% on a day-for-day basis versus the prior year. Interest income amounted to $200,000 compared with an expense of $184,000 in 1996. Earnings before income taxes increased 70.5% to $39.6 million from $23.2 million a year earlier. The results for the quarter ended 5/3/97 reflected a steady growth throughout most of the Company's geographic markets and merchandise categories. In addition, ROST maintained strict control on expenses and inventories. Comparable in-store inventories increased slightly. Total consolidated inventories rose 23% due to a larger number of stores in operation and a higher level of seasonal packaway merchandise.

BUSINESS

ROSS STORES, INC. operates a chain of off-price retail stores offering first quality, in-season, branded apparel, shoes, cosmetics and apparel-related accessories for its target customers, value-conscious men and women between the ages of 25 and 54 and their families. As of 5/3/97, the Company had 315 stores in operation.

ANNUAL EARNINGS AND DIVIDENDS PER SHARE

	2/1/97	2/3/96	1/28/95	1/29/94	1/30/93	2/1/92	2/2/91
Earnings Per Share	0.79	0.88	0.75	0.57	0.66	0.57	0.72
Dividends Per Share	① 0.14	0.12	0.10	Nil	Nil	Nil	Nil
Dividend Payout %	8.9	13.6	13.3	...	...	...	...

① 2-for-1 stk. split, 3/5/97.

ANNUAL FINANCIAL DATA

RECORD OF EARNINGS (IN MILLIONS):

	2/1/97	2/3/96	1/28/95	1/29/94	1/30/93	2/1/92	2/2/91
Total Revenues	1,689.8	1,426.4	1,262.5	1,122.0	1,043.3	926.7	798.9
Costs and Expenses	1,526.6	1,324.5	1,184.0	1,050.3	964.8	859.9	753.6
Depreciation & Amort	28.8	27.0	24.0	20.5	18.7	15.9	13.1
Operating Profit	134.5	74.9	54.5	51.2	59.8	50.8	32.2
Inc Fr Cont Opers Bef Income Taxes	134.8	72.1	61.4	48.9	56.7	45.4	25.2
Income Taxes	53.9	28.8	24.5	19.5	22.7	17.7	8.6
Net Income	80.9	43.3	36.8	29.3	34.0	27.7	16.6
Aver. Shs. Outstg. (000)	51,311	49,504	49,414	51,430	51,366	49,098	46,440

BALANCE SHEET (IN MILLIONS):

Cash and Cash Equivalents	44.8	23.4	23.6	32.3	40.5	16.4	5.3
Receivables, Net	7.8	9.9	5.4	4.0	5.8	4.1	5.9
Inventories	373.7	296.0	275.2	228.9	221.0	185.0	157.9
Gross Property	348.7	321.6	293.3	243.3	208.6	190.8	165.8
Accumulated Depreciation	156.1	140.2	122.0	99.2	80.5	63.9	50.8
Long-Term Debt	...	9.8	46.1	33.3	33.5	40.7	57.6
Net Stockholders' Equity	328.8	291.5	254.6	228.2	209.6	162.6	123.1
Total Assets	659.5	541.2	506.2	437.4	419.9	357.7	309.5
Total Current Assets	439.6	342.8	316.3	280.5	277.7	216.4	179.4
Total Current Liabilities	304.8	221.2	184.5	155.4	156.7	138.9	112.4
Net Working Capital	134.8	121.6	131.8	125.0	121.0	77.4	67.0
Year End Shs Outstg (000)	49,332	49,202	48,866	49,390	50,922	48,982	46,198

STATISTICAL RECORD:

Operating Profit Margin %	8.0	5.2	4.3	4.6	5.7	5.5	4.0
Book Value Per Share	6.67	5.93	5.21	4.62	4.00	3.18	2.50
Return on Equity %	24.6	14.8	14.5	12.8	16.2	17.0	13.5
Return on Assets %	12.3	8.0	7.3	6.7	8.1	7.7	5.4
P/E Ratio	33.5-11.6	12.3-5.4	11.9-7.2	21.1-11.1	17.4-8.2	16.3-4.3	20.3-6.1
Price Range	26½-9⅛	10¾-4¾	8⅞-5⅜	12-6¼	11½-5⅜	9¼-2⅜	7⅜-2⅛

Statistics are as originally reported.

RPM, INC.

YIELD 3.1%
P/E RATIO 17.4

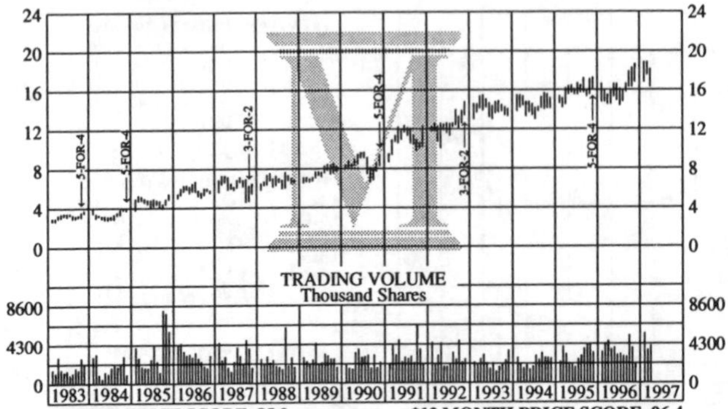

TRADING VOLUME
Thousand Shares

*7 YEAR PRICE SCORE 85.0   *12 MONTH PRICE SCORE 96.4
*NYSE COMPOSITE INDEX=100

INTERIM EARNINGS (Per Share):

Qtr.	Aug.	Nov.	Feb.	May
1993-94	0.21	0.20	0.10	0.24
1994-95	0.26	0.21	0.10	0.28
1995-96	0.27	0.22	0.11	0.32
1996-97	0.31	0.24	0.10	...

INTERIM DIVIDENDS (Per Share):

Amt.	Decl.	Ex.	Rec.	Pay.
0.12Q	7/8/96	7/17/96	7/19/96	7/31/96
0.13Q	10/18	10/24	10/28	10/31
0.13Q	1/10/97	1/15/97	1/20/97	1/31/97
0.13Q	4/7	4/16	4/18	4/30

Indicated div: $0.52

CAPITALIZATION (5/31/96):

	($000)	(%)
Long-Term Debt	447,654	47.0
Deferred Income Tax	57,810	6.1
Common & Surplus	445,833	46.9
Total	951,297	100.0

RECENT DEVELOPMENTS: For the quarter ended 2/28/97, net income fell 6.7% to $7.5 million from $8.0 million in the corresponding period of the previous year. This decrease was due to the results of the operations of Tremco, Inc., acquired on 2/1/97, combined with a slow seasonal period. Net sales advanced 16.5% to $297.2 million compared with $255.2 million a year earlier. All of the Company's operating units, excluding Tremco, Inc., performed at record levels, particularly the industrial lines. In addition, RPOW's internal growth increased from 1995, and accounted for nearly half of the total sales growth. Gross profit as a percentage of sales increased to 42.3% from 41.1% the year before. Income before income taxes dropped 6.1% to $13.1 million from $13.9 million the prior year. For the nine months ended 2/28/97, net income advanced 12.9% to $50.0 million from $44.3 million the previous year. Net sales grew 15.0% to $942.5 million from $819.5 million a year earlier.

BUSINESS

RPM, INC. is a widely-diversified manufacturer of protective coatings, marketing products to approximately 130 countries and operating manufacturing facilities in 59 locations in the United States, Belgium, Canada, China, South Africa, and the Netherlands. The Company participates in two broad market categories worldwide: industrial and consumer. Brand names include RUST-OLEUM®, CARBOLINE®, BONDO®, ZINSSER®, and DAY-GLO®. Approximately 60% of the Company's sales are derived from the industrial market sectors, with the remainder in consumer products. The vast majority of RPM's specialty coatings, both consumer and industrial, protect existing goods or structures and are generally not affected by cyclical movements in the economy.

ANNUAL EARNINGS AND DIVIDENDS PER SHARE

	5/31/96	5/31/95	5/31/94	5/31/93	5/31/92	5/31/91	5/31/90
Earnings Per Share	0.90	0.85	0.74	0.66	0.59	0.55	0.52
Dividends Per Share	0.456	① 0.424	0.392	0.338	② 0.298	0.271	③ 0.246
Dividend Payout %	50.7	49.9	53.0	51.2	50.5	49.3	47.3

① 25% stk. div.,12/8/95.   ② 3-for-2 stk. split, 12/7/92.   ③ 5-for-4 stk. split, 12/7/90.

ANNUAL FINANCIAL DATA

RECORD OF EARNINGS (IN MILLIONS):

	5/31/96	5/31/95	5/31/94	5/31/93	5/31/92	5/31/91	5/31/90
Total Revenues	1,136.4	1,017.0	815.6	625.7	552.1	500.3	444.8
Costs and Expenses	948.1	849.7	688.2	546.1	460.9	427.4	378.2
Depreciation & Amort	42.6	36.9	25.9	① 0.0	19.4	14.4	12.2
Operating Profit	145.7	130.3	101.5	79.5	71.7	58.4	54.4
Inc Fr Cont Opers Bef Income Taxes	119.9	106.9	88.1	66.1	57.3	51.7	45.0
Income Taxes	51.0	45.8	35.5	26.7	22.8	19.8	17.2
Net Income	68.9	61.1	52.6	39.4	34.5	31.8	27.7
Aver. Shs. Outstg. (000)	76,548	71,554	70,896	59,486	58,890	58,176	52,995
① Equal to $21,000.							

BALANCE SHEET (IN MILLIONS):

Cash and Cash Equivalents	34.3	28.0	25.4	24.8	27.3	18.6	2.5
Receivables, Net	231.6	207.5	162.3	127.2	116.5	93.8	90.8
Inventories	178.9	169.2	130.5	115.5	110.9	85.7	87.4
Gross Property	399.6	360.7	263.2	221.7	202.1	134.6	129.7
Accumulated Depreciation	174.9	156.7	112.2	87.4	75.8	52.1	48.2
Long-Term Debt	447.7	406.4	233.0	220.9	238.9	114.5	145.2
Net Stockholders' Equity	445.8	347.6	314.5	239.1	221.8	206.3	161.0
Total Assets	1,155.1	959.1	660.8	584.6	558.9	401.2	375.3
Total Current Assets	465.1	421.3	334.5	280.7	263.0	205.4	185.6
Total Current Liabilities	189.4	151.1	104.0	117.9	90.1	75.7	63.2
Net Working Capital	275.7	270.2	230.5	162.7	173.0	129.7	122.4
Year End Shs Outstg (000)	77,449	71,196	70,939	59,153	58,971	58,265	52,900

STATISTICAL RECORD:

Operating Profit Margin %	12.8	12.8	12.4	12.7	13.0	11.7	12.2
Book Value Per Share	0.23	0.15	2.50	1.70	1.35	1.95	1.13
Return on Equity %	15.5	17.6	16.7	16.5	15.5	15.4	17.2
Return on Assets %	6.0	6.4	8.0	6.7	6.2	7.9	7.4
Average Yield %	2.9	2.9	2.8	2.7	3.2	3.7	3.6
P/E Ratio	19.2-15.8	18.3-15.2	20.8-17.5	22.3-15.2	21.2-14.9	17.6-12.0	16.3-12.7
Price Range	17¼-14¼	15¾-13	15½-13	14¾-10⅛	12⅜-8⅝	9¾-6⅝	8½-6½

Statistics are as originally reported.

OFFICERS:
T.C. Sullivan, Chmn. & C.E.O.
J.A. Karman, Pres. & C.O.O.
F.C. Sullivan, Exec. V.P. & C.F.O.
P.A. Granzier, V.P., Sec. & Gen. Couns.

INCORPORATED: OH, May, 1947

PRINCIPAL OFFICE: 2628 Pearl Road, P.O. Box 777, Medina, OH 44258

TELEPHONE NUMBER: (330) 273-5090
FAX: (330) 225-8743
NO. OF EMPLOYEES: 6,500 (approx.)
ANNUAL MEETING: Oct. 17, 1997
SHAREHOLDERS: 75,000 (approx.)
INSTITUTIONAL HOLDINGS:
No. of Institutions: 160
Shares Held: 28,944,322

REGISTRAR(S): Harris Trust and Savings Bank, Chicago, IL

TRANSFER AGENT(S): Harris Trust and Savings Bank, Chicago, IL

SIGMA-ALDRICH CORP.

YIELD 0.9%
P/E RATIO 18.6

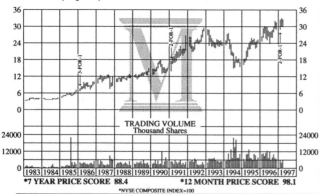

*7 YEAR PRICE SCORE 88.4   *12 MONTH PRICE SCORE 98.1
*NYSE COMPOSITE INDEX=100

INTERIM EARNINGS (Per Share):

Qtr.	Mar.	June	Sept.	Dec.
1994	0.30	0.27	0.27	0.26
1995	0.33	0.34	0.33	0.32
1996	0.37	0.37	0.37	0.37
1997	0.41	...	...	...

INTERIM DIVIDENDS (Per Share):

Amt.	Decl.	Ex.	Rec.	Pay.
0.11Q	5/7/96	5/30/96	6/3/96	6/17/96
0.11Q	8/13	8/28	8/30	9/13
2-for-1	11/12	1/3/97	12/16	1/2/97
0.0625Q	11/12	12/12/96	12/16	1/2
0.0625Q	2/18/97	2/27/97	3/3/97	3/17

Indicated div.: $0.25

CAPITALIZATION (12/31/96):

	($000)	(%)
Long-Term Debt	...	3,787	0.4
Common & Surplus	942,274	99.6
Total	946,061	100.0

RECENT DEVELOPMENTS: For the first quarter ended 3/31/97, net income rose 12.6% to $41.4 million. This compares with $36.7 million in the corresponding period the year before. Revenues climbed 6.3% to $279.1 milion versus $262.4 million a year earlier. On 4/24/97, the Company announced that it will open new plants later in 1997 in the United States and the United Kingdom in order to expand its chemical businesses. In the United States, new facilities and equipment will be built to support the growing demand for the Company's metal products. For the quarter ended 12/31/96, net income advanced 15.2% to $37.2 million from $32.3 million in the corresponding period of the previous year. Net sales grew 10.7% to $257.5 million from $232.6 million in 1995. Sales results were boosted by strong demand for the Company's electrical, mechanical and telecommunication support products and enclosures.

BUSINESS

SIGMA-ALDRICH CORP. is in two lines of business. The Company develops, manufactures and distributes approximately 80,000 biochemicals, organic and inorganic chemicals, diagnostic reagents and related products. These are used primarily in research and development, in the diagnosis of disease, and as specialty chemicals for manufacturing purposes. B-Line Systems, Inc., a subsidiary, manufactures and sells metal components for strut, cable tray, pipe support and telecommunications systems. These components are used in routing electrical and mechanical services in industrial installations and supporting telecommunications applications.

ANNUAL EARNINGS AND DIVIDENDS PER SHARE

	1996	1995	1994	1993	1992	1991	1990
Earnings Per Share	1.48	1.32	1.11	① 1.08	0.96	0.80	0.72
Dividends Per Share	0.283	0.18	0.165	0.145	0.125	② 0.11	0.10
Dividend Payout %	19.1	13.6	14.9	13.5	13.0	13.8	13.9

Note: 2-for-1 stk. split, 1/2/97. ① Before acctg. change. ② 2-for-1 stk. split, 1/3/91.

ANNUAL FINANCIAL DATA

RECORD OF EARNINGS (IN MILLIONS):

	1996	1995	1994	1993	1992	1991	1990
Total Revenues	1,034.6	959.8	851.2	739.4	654.4	589.4	529.1
Costs and Expenses	759.7	714.8	644.2	541.3	478.2	438.7	394.7
Depreciation & Amort	45.2	40.9	36.7	32.5	28.9	26.8	24.4
Operating Profit	229.7	204.2	170.3	165.6	147.3	123.9	110.0
Inc Fr Cont Opers Bef Income Taxes	229.7	204.2	170.3	165.6	147.3	123.9	110.0
Income Taxes	81.8	72.5	60.0	58.5	51.9	44.1	38.8
Net Income	147.9	131.7	110.3	① 107.2	95.5	79.8	71.2
Aver. Shs. Outstg. (000)	99,930	99,714	99,714	99,658	99,604	99,540	99,432	99,236

① Before acctg. change dr$10,806,000.

BALANCE SHEET (IN MILLIONS):

	1996	1995	1994	1993	1992	1991	1990
Cash and Cash Equivalents	103.7	84.0	9.7	10.3	44.9	28.1	6.6
Receivables, Net	165.5	144.7	134.9	113.4	91.9	83.7	79.4
Inventories	362.8	346.4	330.3	305.5	260.1	261.7	233.0
Gross Property	659.4	572.6	506.7	425.5	329.4	311.6	290.7
Accumulated Depreciation	280.3	244.6	204.0	168.2	141.1	119.9	98.4
Long-Term Debt	3.8	13.8	14.5	17.3	18.7	69.3	70.8
Net Stockholders' Equity	942.3	824.7	699.5	591.1	511.8	441.0	368.5
Total Assets	1,100.0	985.2	852.0	753.4	615.8	596.5	546.2
Total Current Assets	666.6	610.0	502.3	450.8	415.8	391.0	340.6
Total Current Liabilities	110.3	108.0	105.0	111.4	66.2	70.9	92.9
Net Working Capital	556.3	502.0	397.3	339.5	349.6	320.1	247.7
Year End Shs Outstg (000)	100,100	99,754	99,664	99,610	99,552	99,492	99,316

STATISTICAL RECORD:

	1996	1995	1994	1993	1992	1991	1990
Operating Profit Margin %	22.2	21.3	20.0	22.4	22.5	21.0	20.8
Book Value Per Share	9.41	8.27	7.02	5.93	5.14	4.43	3.71
Return on Equity %	15.7	16.0	15.8	18.1	18.7	18.1	19.3
Return on Assets %	13.4	13.4	13.0	14.2	15.5	13.4	13.0
Average Yield %	1.0	0.9	0.8	0.6	0.5	0.5	0.7
P/E Ratio	21.7-16.0	20.9-12.3	24.9-13.5	26.9-20.6	30.9-21.7	33.4-17.3	25.0-17.4
Price Range	32⅛-23¾	25⅞-16¼	27⅝-15	29-22¼	29⅝-20⅞	26¾-13⅞	18-12½

Statistics are as originally reported.

OFFICERS:
C.T. Cori, Chmn. & C.E.O.
D.R. Harvey, Pres. & C.O.O.
P.A. Gleich, V.P. & C.F.O.
T.M. Tallarico, V.P. & Sec.
K.A. Richter, Treas.

INCORPORATED: DE, Jul., 1975
PRINCIPAL OFFICE: 3050 Spruce St., St. Louis, MO 63103

TELEPHONE NUMBER: (314) 771-5765

NO. OF EMPLOYEES: 5,984

ANNUAL MEETING: In May

SHAREHOLDERS: 2,086

INSTITUTIONAL HOLDINGS:
No. of Institutions: 299
Shares Held: 64,409,586 (adj.)

REGISTRAR(S): Harris Trust, Chicago, IL 60690

TRANSFER AGENT(S): Harris Trust, Chicago, IL 60690

STAPLES, INC.

YIELD ...%
P/E RATIO 30.9

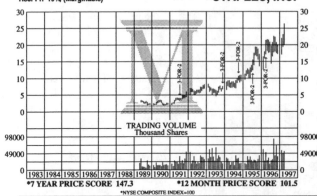

TRADING VOLUME
Thousand Shares

*7 YEAR PRICE SCORE 147.3   *12 MONTH PRICE SCORE 101.5
*NYSE COMPOSITE INDEX=100

INTERIM EARNINGS (Per Share):

Qtr.	Apr.	July	Oct.	Jan.
1993-94	0.02	d0.03	0.11	0.11
1994-95	0.02	0.02	0.08	0.14
1995-96	0.05	0.06	0.13	0.21
1996-97	0.08	0.09	0.19	0.28

INTERIM DIVIDENDS (Per Share):

Amt.	Decl.	Ex.	Rec.	Pay.
3-for-2	3/5/96	3/26/96	3/15/96	3/25/96

CAPITALIZATION (2/1/97):

	($000)	(%)
Long-Term Debt	404,449	34.1
Cap. Lease Oblig..............	19,062	1.6
Common & Surplus	761,686	64.3
Total	1,185,197	100.0

RECENT DEVELOPMENTS: On 6/30/97, a federal judge blocked the Company's proposed acquisition of Office Depot, Inc. contending the combination would be anticompetitive and bring higher prices to consumers. For the 52 weeks ended 2/1/97, net income surged 44.4% to $106.4 million from $73.7 million in the corresponding 53-week period a year earlier. Sales climbed 29.3% to $3.97 billion from $3.07 billion the year before. Comparable-store sales rose 14% from the equivalent prior-year period. Gross profit as a percentage of sales grew to 23.8% from 22.9% the previous year. During fiscal 1996, SPLS opened a record 115 stores and remodeled 78 stores to Staples' new format. For the 13 weeks ended 2/1/97, net income rose 34.5% to $46.9 million from $34.9 million in the same 14-week period the year before. Sales were up 19.3% to $1.16 billion from $975.5 million a year earlier.

BUSINESS

STAPLES, INC. operates high-volume office superstores that provide small and medium-sized businesses with brand name office products, supplies and accessories at discount prices. As of 3/4/97, the Company operated 574 superstores that stocked more than 5,000 brand name office products, including office supplies, business machines, office furniture, computers and related products, janitorial supplies and other products. Staples' stores offer their customers access to approximately 17,000 additional products through a special order department, which allows the Company to broaden its product offering without additional working capital investment.

ANNUAL EARNINGS AND DIVIDENDS PER SHARE

	2/1/97	2/3/96	1/28/95	1/29/94
Earnings Per Share	0.64	0.45	0.26	0.21
Dividends Per Share	①...	②...	③...	④...

① 3-for-2 stk. split, 3/25/96. ② 3-for-2 stk. split, 7/24/95. ③ 3-for-2 stk. split, 10/29/94. ④ 50% stk. div., 12/14/93.

ANNUAL FINANCIAL DATA

RECORD OF EARNINGS (IN MILLIONS):

Total Revenues	3,967.7	3,068.1	2,000.1	1,308.6
Costs and Expenses	3,761.4	2,918.3	1,917.7	1,247.8
Depreciation & Amort	55.9	43.6	28.7	22.6
Operating Income	204.0	147.8	81.7	37.7
Inc Fr Cont Opers Bef Income Taxes	173.0	119.8	63.9	32.4
Income Taxes	66.6	46.1	24.0	12.9
Net Income	106.4	73.7	39.9	19.5
Aver. Shs. Outstg. (000)	166,625	162,078	140,261	134,297

BALANCE SHEET (IN MILLIONS):

Cash and Cash Equivalents	106.1	110.8	71.0	110.5
Receivables, Net	167.1	122.5	75.9	51.6
Inventories	813.7	644.5	463.5	239.8
Gross Property	613.9	413.0	292.9	189.9
Accumulated Depreciation	171.0	120.5	80.3	52.6
Long-Term Debt	404.4	342.9	247.2	144.2
Capital Lease Obligations	19.1	26.9	26.0	...
Net Stockholders' Equity	761.7	611.4	385.0	287.2
Total Assets	1,787.8	1,402.8	1,008.5	650.8
Total Current Assets	1,151.3	925.9	639.7	433.7
Total Current Liabilities	602.6	421.5	350.3	219.4
Net Working Capital	548.8	504.3	289.4	214.3
Year End Shs Outstg (000)	162,238	158,329	141,323	133,178

STATISTICAL RECORD:

Operating Profit Margin %	5.1	4.8	4.1	2.9
Book Value Per Share	4.19	3.35	2.23	2.16
Return on Equity %	14.0	12.1	10.4	6.8
Return on Assets %	6.0	5.3	4.0	3.0
P/E Ratio	35.4-19.7	42.1-20.7	38.6-22.8	56.1-31.5
Price Range	22⅝-12³⁷/₆₄	19⅜-9½	11-6½	8¼-4⅝

Statistics are as originally reported.

OFFICERS:
T.G. Stemberg, Chmn. & C.E.O.
M. Hanaka, Pres. & C.O.O.
J.J. Mahoney, Exec. V.P. & C.F.O.

INCORPORATED: DE, Nov., 1985

PRINCIPAL OFFICE: One Research Drive, Westborough, MA 01581

TELEPHONE NUMBER: (508) 370-8500

FAX: (508) 370-8955

NO. OF EMPLOYEES: 12,473 (full-time); 12,521 (part-time).

ANNUAL MEETING: In June

SHAREHOLDERS: 9,134

INSTITUTIONAL HOLDINGS:
No. of Institutions: 248
Shares Held: 150,749,748

REGISTRAR(S): The First National Bank of Boston, Boston, MA

TRANSFER AGENT(S): The First National Bank of Boston, Boston, MA

NASDAQ SYMBOL SBUX
Rec. Pr. 27¼ (Marginable)

STARBUCKS CORP.

YIELD ...%
P/E RATIO 47.0

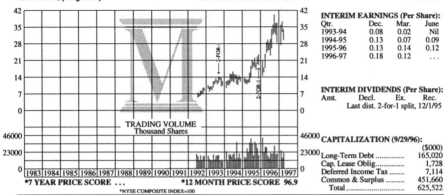

42 ... 42
35 ... 35
28 ... 28
21 ... 21
14 ... 14
7 ... 7
0 ... 0

TRADING VOLUME
Thousand Shares

46000 ... 46000
23000 ... 23000
0 ... 0

|1983|1984|1985|1986|1987|1988|1989|1990|1991|1992|1993|1994|1995|1996|1997|

*7 YEAR PRICE SCORE ...   ***12 MONTH PRICE SCORE 96.9**

*NYSE COMPOSITE INDEX=100

INTERIM EARNINGS (Per Share):

Qtr.	Dec.	Mar.	June	Sept.
1993-94	0.08	0.02	Nil	0.07
1994-95	0.13	0.07	0.09	0.07
1995-96	0.13	0.14	0.12	0.16
1996-97	0.18	0.12	...	...

INTERIM DIVIDENDS (Per Share):

Amt.	Decl.	Ex.	Rec.	Pay.
Last dist. 2-for-1 split, 12/1/95				

CAPITALIZATION (9/29/96):

	($000)	(%)
Long-Term Debt	165,020	26.4
Cap. Lease Oblig.	1,728	0.3
Deferred Income Tax	7,114	1.1
Common & Surplus	451,660	72.2
Total	625,522	100.0

RECENT DEVELOPMENTS: For the three months ended 3/30/97, net earnings slipped 7.2% to $9.6 million from $10.4 million the previous year. Net revenues climbed 39.9% to $214.9 million from $153.6 million the year before. Earnings in the second quarter of 1996 benefited from a pretax gain of $9.2 million stemming from the sale of the Company's investment in Noah's New York Bagels, Inc. Retail sales jumped 40% over the prior-year period to $185.1 million. Specialty sales surged 41% to $25.5 million from a year earlier, while direct response sales were up 33% to $4.4 million compared with a year ago. Comparable-store sales increased 5% versus the same quarter in 1996. Operating income was $14.0 million, up 85.2% from $7.6 million the previous year. For the six months ended 3/30/97, net earnings totaled $24.0 million versus earnings, including the aforementioned one-time gain, of $20.0 million, an increase of 20.4%. Net revenues grew 40.5% to $454.1 million from $323.1 million the year before.

BUSINESS

STARBUCKS CORPORATION is a major retailer and roaster of specialty coffee in North America. As of 5/25/97, SBUX operated 1,237 primarily company-owned retail locations in North America and the Pacific Rim. In addition, the Company has a specialty sales group and a national direct-response business.

ANNUAL EARNINGS AND DIVIDENDS PER SHARE

	9/29/96	10/1/95	10/2/94	10/3/93	9/27/92	9/29/91	9/30/90
Earnings Per Share	0.55	0.37	0.17	0.14	0.09	③0.06	...
Dividends Per Share	①...	Nil	Nil	②...	Nil	Nil	...

① 2-for-1 stk. split, 12/1/95 ② 2-for-1 stk. split, 9/29/93 ③ Pro forma

ANNUAL FINANCIAL DATA

RECORD OF EARNINGS (IN THOUSANDS):

	9/29/96	10/1/95	10/2/94	10/3/93	9/27/92	9/29/91	9/30/90
Total Revenues	696,481	465,213	284,923	163,477	93,078	57,650	35,392
Costs and Expenses	603,538	402,611	249,090	144,328	83,063	52,204	33,074
Depreciation & Amort	35,950	22,486	12,535	6,174	3,644	2,537	1,512
Operating Income	56,993	40,116	23,298	12,975	6,371	2,909	806
Inc Fr Cont Opers Bef Income Taxes	68,501	43,143	17,754	13,919	6,580	2,886	812
Income Taxes	26,373	17,041	7,548	5,416	2,476	477	...
Net Income	42,128	26,102	10,206	8,503	4,104	2,409	812
Aver. Shs. Outstg.	76,964	71,909	59,758	58,056	49,752	40,624	...

BALANCE SHEET (IN THOUSANDS):

	9/29/96	10/1/95	10/2/94	10/3/93	9/27/92	9/29/91	9/30/90
Cash and Cash Equivalents	229,436	62,451	15,921	34,496	37,740	1,120	4,421
Receivables, Net	17,621	10,157	5,394	2,862	1,571	853	529
Inventories	83,370	123,657	56,064	24,247	11,720	8,120	3,282
Gross Property	457,480	296,943	170,759	81,560	42,966	28,182	17,758
Accumulated Depreciation	88,003	52,215	30,005	15,807	9,398	5,844	3,136
Long-Term Debt	165,020	80,398	80,500	80,500	...	7,450	3,900
Capital Lease Obligations	1,728	1,013	...	...	...	...	...
Net Stockholders' Equity	451,660	312,231	109,898	88,073	75,288	7,304	6,258
Total Assets	726,613	468,178	231,421	192,971	87,866	37,810	27,879
Total Current Assets	339,541	205,655	84,580	66,231	53,169	11,437	8,849
Total Current Liabilities	101,091	71,046	40,418	24,398	12,578	8,211	4,379
Net Working Capital	238,450	134,609	44,162	41,833	40,591	3,226	4,470
Year End Shares Outstg	77,584	70,957	57,936	54,670	52,401	16,814	16,458

STATISTICAL RECORD:

	9/29/96	10/1/95	10/2/94	10/3/93	9/27/92	9/29/91	9/30/90
Operating Profit Margin %	8.2	8.6	8.2	7.9	6.8	5.0	2.3
Book Value Per Share	5.82	4.40	1.90	1.61	1.44	0.43	0.38
Return on Equity %	9.3	8.4	9.3	9.7	5.5	33.0	13.0
Return on Assets %	5.8	5.6	4.4	4.4	4.7	6.4	2.9
P/E Ratio	73.2-26.4	63.5-30.1	95.6-55.9	N.M.	N.M.	...	...
Price Range	40¼-14½	23½-11⅛	16¼-9½	14⅛-8	9½-5½	...	...

Statistics are as originally reported.

OFFICERS:
H. Schultz, Chmn. & C.E.O.
O.C. Smith, Pres. & C.O.O.
M. Casey, Sr. V.P. & C.F.O.

INCORPORATED: WA, Nov., 1985

PRINCIPAL OFFICE: 2401 Utah Avenue South, Seattle, WA 98134

TELEPHONE NUMBER: (206) 447-1575
FAX: (206) 682-7570
NO. OF EMPLOYEES: 16,600
ANNUAL MEETING: In March
SHAREHOLDERS: 6,710 (approx.)
INSTITUTIONAL HOLDINGS:
No. of Institutions: 142
Shares Held: 47,657,850

REGISTRAR(S): ChaseMellon Shareholder Services, Seattle, WA 98101

TRANSFER AGENT(S): ChaseMellon Shareholder Services, Seattle, WA 98101

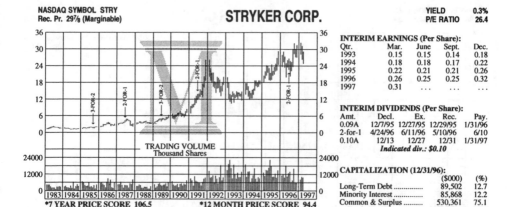

STRYKER CORP.

	YIELD	0.3%
	P/E RATIO	26.4

INTEREST EARNINGS (Per Share):

Qtr.	Mar.	June	Sept.	Dec.
1993	0.15	0.15	0.14	0.18
1994	0.18	0.18	0.17	0.22
1995	0.22	0.21	0.21	0.26
1996	0.26	0.25	0.25	0.32
1997	0.31	...	...	...

INTERIM DIVIDENDS (Per Share):

Amt.	Decl.	Ex.	Rec.	Pay.
0.09A	12/7/95	12/27/95	12/29/95	1/31/96
2-for-1	4/24/96	6/11/96	5/10/96	6/10
0.10A	12/13	12/27	12/31	1/31/97

Indicated div.: $0.10

CAPITALIZATION (12/31/96):

	($000)	(%)
Long-Term Debt	89,502	12.7
Minority Interest	85,868	12.2
Common & Surplus	530,361	75.1
Total	705,731	100.0

TRADING VOLUME
Thousand Shares

*7 YEAR PRICE SCORE 106.5   *12 MONTH PRICE SCORE 94.4

*NYSE COMPOSITE INDEX=100

RECENT DEVELOPMENTS: For the three months ended 3/31/97, net earnings advanced 20.0% to $30.0 million from $25.0 million in the corresponding prior-year quarter. Net sales totaled $239.5 million, up 10.1% versus $217.6 million the previous year. Domestic sales grew 11.9% to $149.6 million from $133.7 million the year before, reflecting strong shipments of orthopaedic implants, powered surgical instruments and endoscopic equipment combined with increased revenue from physical therapy services. International sales rose 7.2% to $89.9 million from $83.9 million in 1996, stemming from strong shipments of surgical products partially offset by an unfavorable currency exchange rate. Gross profit was up 10.6% to $141.9 million, or 59.2% of net sales, from $128.3 million, or 58.9% of net sales, a year earlier. Operating income increased 10.7% to $44.1 million from $39.9 million the prior year.

BUSINESS

STRYKER CORPORATION and its subsidiaries develop, manufacture and market specialty surgical and medical products, including endoscopic systems, orthopedic implants, powered surgical instruments and patient handling equipment, which are sold to hospitals and physicians worldwide. In addition, the Company provides physical therapy services through stand-alone clinics throughout the U.S. The Company through its acquisition of Dimso SA, and its subsidiaries in France and Spain, designs and manufactures the Diapason and Stryker 2S Spinal Implant systems in addition to other orthopedic products. In August 1994, STRY acquired a 51% stake in Matsumoto Medical Instruments, Inc., the Company's Japanese distributor.

ANNUAL EARNINGS AND DIVIDENDS PER SHARE

	1996	1995	1994	1993	1992	1991	1990
Earnings Per Share	1.08	0.90	0.75	0.62	0.50	0.35	③ 0.25
Dividends Per Share	① 0.045	0.04	0.035	0.03	0.025	② ...	Nil
Dividend Payout %	4.2	4.4	4.7	4.8	5.0	...	...

① 2-for-1 stk. split, 6/10/96 ② 2-for-1 stk. split, 6/14/91 ③ Before extraord. item

ANNUAL FINANCIAL DATA

RECORD OF EARNINGS (IN THOUSANDS):

Total Revenues	910,060	871,952	681,920	557,335	477,054	364,825	280,634
Costs and Expenses	756,553	685,987	540,500	449,210	391,971	301,473	237,820
Depreciation & Amort	...	28,654	20,944	16,183	11,382	11,796	7,109
Operating Income	153,507	157,311	120,476	91,942	73,701	51,556	35,705
Inc Fr Cont Opers Bef Income Taxes	160,446	163,093	127,575	96,065	76,940	53,345	38,100
Income Taxes	61,650	66,900	50,770	35,860	29,240	20,270	14,475
Net Income	104,640	87,010	72,400	60,205	47,700	33,075	① 23,625
Aver. Shs. Outstg.	96,838	96,936	96,734	96,712	95,432	95,052	94,792

① Before extra. item cr$9,910,000.

BALANCE SHEET (IN THOUSANDS):

Cash and Cash Equivalents	367,573	264,648	202,045	152,637	91,752	80,029	54,052
Receivables, Net	166,052	163,593	154,590	87,896	76,899	53,268	50,723
Inventories	127,387	133,619	115,757	76,582	79,391	78,194	60,133
Gross Property	290,185	285,501	271,268	125,341	107,537	73,740	59,559
Accumulated Depreciation	117,882	102,909	90,549	57,634	47,888	37,684	30,859
Long-Term Debt	89,502	96,967	95,276	31,282	1,433	1,400	1,900
Net Stockholders' Equity	530,361	454,279	358,266	288,434	232,261	179,875	147,875
Total Assets	993,506	854,891	767,971	454,204	340,272	270,316	209,521
Total Current Assets	753,537	623,253	540,529	343,851	269,605	228,678	175,634
Total Current Liabilities	251,741	174,438	179,211	129,886	101,408	88,382	57,757
Net Working Capital	501,796	448,815	361,318	213,965	168,197	140,296	117,877
Year End Shares Outstg	96,787	97,108	96,738	96,790	96,606	95,194	94,928

STATISTICAL RECORD:

Operating Profit Margin %	16.9	18.0	17.7	16.5	15.4	14.1	12.7
Book Value Per Share	5.01	4.49	3.52	2.90	2.31	1.85	1.51
Return on Equity %	19.7	19.2	20.2	20.9	20.5	18.4	16.0
Return on Assets %	10.5	10.2	9.4	13.3	14.0	12.2	11.3
Average Yield %	0.2	0.2	0.2	0.2	0.1	...	...
P/E Ratio	29.7-18.4	32.5-20.1	25.0-15.8	32.1-16.9	52.3-26.3	74.6-19.6	34.0-19.5
Price Range	32⅛-19⅞	29¼-18⅛	18¾-11⅞	19⅞-10½	26⅛-13⅛	26⅛-6⅞	8½-4⅞

Statistics are as originally reported.

OFFICERS:
J.W. Brown, Chmn., Pres. & C.E.O.
D.J. Simpson, V.P., C.F.O. & Sec.
C.F. Homrich, Treas.
C.E. Hall, Esq., Gen. Counsel
J.R. Winter, Controller

INCORPORATED: MI, Feb., 1946

PRINCIPAL OFFICE: 2725 Fairfield Rd., Kalamazoo, MI 49002

TELEPHONE NUMBER: (616) 385-2600

NO. OF EMPLOYEES: 5,274

ANNUAL MEETING: In April

SHAREHOLDERS: 3,306

INSTITUTIONAL HOLDINGS:
No. of Institutions: 188
Shares Held: 41,124,808

REGISTRAR(S): First National Bank of Chicago, Chicago, IL 60670

TRANSFER AGENT(S): First National Bank of Chicago, Chicago, IL 60670

SUN MICROSYSTEMS, INC.

YIELD ...%
P/E RATIO 17.7

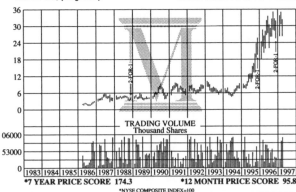

INTERIM EARNINGS (Per Share):

Qtr.	Sept.	Dec.	Mar.	June
1993-94	0.04	0.12	0.15	0.10
1994-95	0.10	0.21	0.27	0.32
1995-96	0.21	0.32	0.37	0.31
1996-97	0.31	0.46	0.58	...

INTERIM DIVIDENDS (Per Share):

Amt.	Decl.	Ex.	Rec.	Pay.
2-for-1	8/8/96	12/11/96	11/18/96	12/10/96

TRADING VOLUME
Thousand Shares

*7 YEAR PRICE SCORE 174.3   ***12 MONTH PRICE SCORE 95.8**
*NYSE COMPOSITE INDEX=100

CAPITALIZATION (6/30/96):

	($000)	(%)
Long-Term Debt	40,000	1.7
Common & Surplus	2,251,486	98.3
Total	2,291,486	100.0

RECENT DEVELOPMENTS: For the three months ended 3/30/97, net income climbed 56.0% to $223.5 million from $143.3 million in the corresponding quarter the previous year. Net revenues increased 14.9% to $2.11 billion from $1.84 billion a year earlier. The 1997 results included a $62.2 million gain from the sale of an equity investment and a non-recurring charge of $22.9 million from purchased in-process technology related to the acquisition of LongView Technologies, LLC. Operating income totaled $257.0 million, up 27.4% compared with $201.8 million a year ago. Results benefited from the introduction of new desktop systems, servers, storage and software products, partially offset by sluggish economic conditions in Japan. For the nine months ended 3/30/97, net income jumped 48.4% to $525.2 million from $354.1 million the year before. Net revenues totaled $6.06 billion, up 19.3% versus $5.08 billion in the same prior-year period.

BUSINESS

SUN MICROSYSTEMS, INC. is one of the world's leading suppliers of client-server computing solutions, which feature networked workstations and servers that store, process, and distribute information. SUNW's product design philosophy is based on the use of industry-standard technologies such as the UNIX® operating system, NFS® file system, OpenWindows™ environment, and SPARC® microprocessor. SUNW has integrated these technologies in an open systems architecture and established a high-performance distributed computing environment. SUNW's systems currently are used in both commercial and technical applications, including financial services, telecommunications, electronic publishing, software engineering, computer-aided design, scientific research, and medical electronics.

ANNUAL EARNINGS AND DIVIDENDS PER SHARE

	6/30/96	6/30/95	6/30/94	6/30/93	6/30/92	6/30/91	6/30/90
Earnings Per Share	1.21	0.90	0.51	0.37	0.43	0.47	0.61
Dividends Per Share	Nil	①...	Nil	Nil	Nil	Nil	Nil

· Note: 2-for-1 stk. split, 12/10/96.   ① 2-for-1 stk. split, 12/11/95.

ANNUAL FINANCIAL DATA

RECORD OF EARNINGS (IN MILLIONS):

Total Revenues	7,094.8	5,901.9	4,689.9	4,308.6	3,588.9	3,221.3	2,466.2
Costs and Expenses	6,077.8	5,160.9	4,164.4	3,835.8	3,112.4	2,705.2	2,104.8
Depreciation & Amort	284.1	240.6	248.2	232.4	215.5	221.2	184.1
Operating Income	675.0	500.4	277.3	240.4	261.1	294.9	177.3
Inc Fr Cont Opers Bef Income Taxes	708.9	523.3	283.4	223.9	254.9	284.0	154.4
Income Taxes	232.5	167.5	87.6	67.2	81.6	93.7	43.2
Net Income	476.4	355.8	195.8	156.7	173.3	190.3	111.2
Aver. Shs. Outstg. (000)	393,380	393,700	387,056	420,500	406,560	412,268	377,476

BALANCE SHEET (IN MILLIONS):

Cash and Cash Equivalents	989.6	1,228.0	882.8	1,138.7	1,220.1	834.3	393.6
Receivables, Net	1,384.2	1,214.6	956.5	749.0	614.3	514.5	523.3
Inventories	460.9	319.7	294.9	256.3	179.7	223.9	204.8
Gross Property	1,282.4	1,045.9	877.3	775.0	788.5	701.3	603.7
Accumulated Depreciation	748.5	616.9	517.0	426.7	428.1	350.1	253.9
Long-Term Debt	40.0	78.1	116.2	177.8	347.6	401.2	358.9
Net Stockholders' Equity	2,251.5	2,122.6	1,628.3	1,642.8	1,485.1	1,212.6	926.8
Total Assets	3,800.9	3,544.6	2,898.0	2,767.6	2,671.6	2,326.3	1,778.6
Total Current Assets	3,033.7	2,934.4	2,305.1	2,272.3	2,148.4	1,801.0	1,297.4
Total Current Liabilities	1,489.3	1,330.8	1,147.8	947.0	838.9	712.6	492.9
Net Working Capital	1,544.5	1,603.6	1,157.3	1,325.3	1,309.5	1,088.4	804.5
Year End Shs Outstg (000)	371,964	394,056	375,404	408,448	400,008	385,440	370,452

STATISTICAL RECORD:

Operating Profit Margin %	9.5	8.5	5.9	5.6	7.3	9.2	7.2
Book Value Per Share	6.06	5.39	4.34	4.02	3.72	3.15	2.50
Return on Equity %	21.2	16.8	12.0	9.5	11.7	15.7	12.0
Return on Assets %	12.5	10.0	6.8	5.7	6.5	8.2	6.3
P/E Ratio	29.0-14.9	28.5-8.3	18.7-9.0	27.5-14.3	21.2-13.2	20.9-11.2	30.8-12.4
Price Range	35⅛-18	25¾-7½	9½-4½	10¼-5¼	9⅛-5⅝	9¾-5⅛	9⅜-3¾

Statistics are as originally reported.

OFFICERS:
S.G. McNealy, Chmn., Pres. & C.E.O.
M.E. Lehman, V.P. & C.F.O.
M.H. Morris, V.P., Gen. Couns. & Sec.

INCORPORATED: CA, Feb., 1982; reincorp., DE, Jul., 1987

PRINCIPAL OFFICE: 2550 Garcia Avenue, Mountain View, CA 94043

TELEPHONE NUMBER: (415) 960-1300
FAX: (415) 969-9131
NO. OF EMPLOYEES: 17,400 (approx.)
ANNUAL MEETING: In November
SHAREHOLDERS: 5,900 (approx.)
INSTITUTIONAL HOLDINGS:
No. of Institutions: 404
Shares Held: 204,157,307

REGISTRAR(S): Bank of Boston, Boston, MA 02102

TRANSFER AGENT(S): Bank of Boston, Boston, MA 02102

SYBASE, INC.

YIELD ...%
P/E RATIO ...

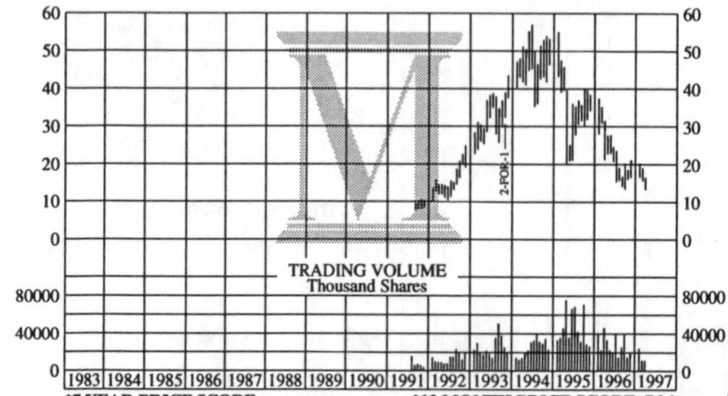

*7 YEAR PRICE SCORE ...   *12 MONTH PRICE SCORE 76.1
*NYSE COMPOSITE INDEX=100

TRADING VOLUME
Thousand Shares

INTERIM EARNINGS (Per Share):

Qtr.	Mar.	June	Sept.	Dec.
1993	0.13	0.18	0.21	0.34
1994	0.22	0.29	0.36	0.52
1995	d0.25	d0.13	0.02	0.08
1996	d0.09	d0.33	d0.69	0.07
1997	0.05	...	...	...

INTERIM DIVIDENDS (Per Share):

Amt.	Decl.	Ex.	Rec.	Pay.
Last dist. 100% stk., 11/19/93				

CAPITALIZATION (12/31/96):

	($000)	(%)
Long-Term Debt	2,871	0.7
Common & Surplus	396,808	99.3
Total	399,679	100.0

RECENT DEVELOPMENTS: For the quarter ended 3/31/97, net income totaled $3.5 million, or $0.05 per share, compared with a loss of $6.9 million, or $0.09 per share, the previous year. Total revenues fell slightly to $241.9 million from $243.7 million the year before. Revenue for services advanced 11.5% to $106.7 million from $95.7 million the prior year, while license fees slipped 8.6% to $135.2 million from $147.9 million a year ago. Operating income was $4.7 million compared with a loss of $11.7 million a year earlier. Income before income taxes totaled $5.7 million versus a loss of $9.2 million in the first quarter of 1996. In April 1997, the Company introduced ImpactNow™, which provides a platform that customers can use to design, develop and deploy Internet and other thin client applications.

BUSINESS

SYBASE, INCORPORATED develops, markets and supports a full line of relational database management software products and services for on-line applications in networked computing environments. The Company offers a broad range of relational database management system (RDBMS) servers, application development tools and connectivity software and complements this product portfolio by providing comprehensive consulting and integration services required to support enterprise-wide on-line applications. Sybase offers three major product families based upon its advanced client/server architecture: the SYBASE SQL Server family, SYBASE SQL Life-cycle tools and SYBASE connectivity interfaces and gateways. The Company markets its products and services worldwide through a direct sales force, distributors, value-added remarketers, systems integrators and original equipment manufacturers.

ANNUAL EARNINGS AND DIVIDENDS PER SHARE

	1996	1995	1994	1993	1992	1991	1990
Earnings Per Share	d1.05	d0.27	1.38	0.86	0.48	②0.19	d0.20
Dividends Per Share	Nil	Nil	Nil	①...	Nil	Nil	Nil

① 100% stk. div., 11/22/93 ② Before extraord. item

ANNUAL FINANCIAL DATA

RECORD OF EARNINGS (IN MILLIONS):

	1996	1995	1994	1993	1992	1991	1990
Total Revenues	1,011.5	956.6	693.8	426.7	264.6	159.4	103.1
Costs and Expenses	987.9	904.8	537.8	332.8	210.2	135.0	100.9
Depreciation & Amort	97.8	75.2	39.6	24.4	16.8	11.6	7.6
Operating Income	d74.2	d23.3	116.4	69.5	37.6	12.8	d5.5
Inc Fr Cont Opers Bef Income Taxes	d66.7	d14.7	121.3	71.2	39.5	12.5	d5.8
Income Taxes	12.3	4.8	46.1	27.1	15.8	5.5	0.2
Net Income	d79.0	d19.5	75.2	44.1	23.7	①7.0	d6.0
Aver. Shs. Outstg. (000)	75,160	71,292	54,422	51,432	49,211	36,974	30,556
① Before extra. item cr$2,172,000.							

BALANCE SHEET (IN MILLIONS):

Cash and Cash Equivalents	174.5	223.7	197.1	138.1	75.0	59.3	12.9
Receivables, Net	253.2	218.9	175.1	112.4	88.6	53.2	36.6
Gross Property	404.9	335.2	186.1	100.6	56.9	33.7	24.8
Accumulated Depreciation	213.5	140.2	75.2	44.8	27.6	16.6	8.4
Long-Term Debt	2.9	5.5	5.4	4.8	6.2	...	...
Net Stockholders' Equity	396.8	439.6	337.2	190.6	118.3	80.0	32.1
Total Assets	751.9	766.3	575.6	332.5	209.6	145.1	78.2
Total Current Assets	445.3	461.5	384.0	257.3	167.1	116.0	50.7
Total Current Liabilities	352.2	321.2	232.4	136.0	83.1	55.1	36.7
Net Working Capital	93.1	140.3	151.6	121.3	83.9	60.9	13.9
Year End Shs Outstg (000)	76,609	72,646	51,647	47,780	44,929	37,468	29,738

STATISTICAL RECORD:

Operating Profit Margin %	...	...	16.8	16.3	14.2	8.0	...
Book Value Per Share	4.25	4.95	6.30	3.82	2.48	1.85	0.77
Return on Equity %	...	...	22.3	23.2	20.0	8.7	...
Return on Assets %	...	...	13.1	13.3	11.3	4.8	...
P/E Ratio	...	...	41.3-25.5	50.6-26.5	51.8-21.4	55.9-40.1	...
Price Range	...	37⅜-13½	55-19⅞	57-35¼	43½-22¾	24⅞-10¼	10⅝-7⅝	...

Statistics are as originally reported.

OFFICERS:
M.B. Hoffman, Chmn.
M.E. Kertzman, Pres & C.E.O.
J. Acosta, Sr. V.P. & C.F.O.
M.L. Gaynor, V.P., Gen. Counsel & Sec.

INCORPORATED: CA, Nov., 1984; reincorp., DE, Jul., 1991

PRINCIPAL OFFICE: 6475 Christie Ave., Emeryville, CA 94608

TELEPHONE NUMBER: (510) 922-3500

FAX: (510) 658-9441

NO. OF EMPLOYEES: 5,484

ANNUAL MEETING: In May

SHAREHOLDERS: 2,257

INSTITUTIONAL HOLDINGS:
No. of Institutions: 86
Shares Held: 43,038,748

REGISTRAR(S): Boston Equiserve LP, Boston, MA

TRANSFER AGENT(S): Boston Equiserve LP, Boston, MA

SYNOPSYS, INC.

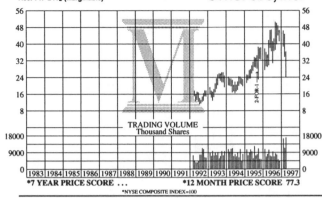

TRADING VOLUME
Thousand Shares

| | 1983 | 1984 | 1985 | 1986 | 1987 | 1988 | 1989 | 1990 | 1991 | 1992 | 1993 | 1994 | 1995 | 1996 | 1997 |

*7 YEAR PRICE SCORE ...   *12 MONTH PRICE SCORE 77.3

*NYSE COMPOSITE INDEX=100

INTERIM EARNINGS (Per Share):

Qtr.	Dec.	Mar.	June	Sept.
1993-94	----------	0.42	----------	
1994-95	0.20	0.21	0.09	0.25
1995-96	0.28	d0.36	0.30	0.32
1996-97	0.38	0.19	...	...

INTERIM DIVIDENDS (Per Share):

Amt.	Decl.	Ex.	Rec.	Pay.
Last dist. 2-for-1 split, 9/8/95				

CAPITALIZATION (9/30/96):

	($000)	(%)
Long-Term Debt	15,970	6.4
Common & Surplus	232,747	93.6
Total	248,717	100.0

RECENT DEVELOPMENTS: For the three months ended 3/31/97, net income totaled $10.4 million compared with a net loss of $12.1 million the previous year. Total revenue climbed 30.0% to $124.2 million from $95.5 million a year earlier. The 1997 results included a charge of $11.4 million related to the acquisition of EPIC Design Technology, Inc. on 2/28/97. The 1996 earnings were negatively affected by a charge of $39.7 million stemming from the acquisition of certain IBM technology. Product revenue rose 21.4% to $79.5 million, while service revenue surged 48.9% to $44.7 million. Gross margin advanced 27.9% to $109.5 million, or 88.2% of total revenue, from $85.6 million, or 89.6% of total revenue, the year before. For the six months ended 3/31/97, net income was $29.5 million, up sharply from $1.5 million the prior year. Total revenue increased 31.0% to $240.9 million from $184.0 million the previous year.

BUSINESS

SYNOPSYS, INC. develops, markets, and supports high-level design automation (HLDA) products for designers of integrated circuits (ICs) and electrical systems. SNPS offers a range of design tools and verification systems that let designers develop, simulate the behavior of, and test the performance of ICs. The Company also provides software that offers libraries of design code to significantly reduce design time. SNPS also provides training, support and consulting services for its customers.

ANNUAL EARNINGS AND DIVIDENDS PER SHARE

	9/30/96	9/30/95	9/30/94	9/30/93	9/30/92	9/30/91	9/30/90
Earnings Per Share	0.57	0.75	0.42	0.42	0.24	0.14	②0.18
Dividends Per Share	Nil	①...	Nil	Nil	Nil	Nil	Nil

① 2-for-1 stk. split, 9/8/95   ② Before extraord. item

ANNUAL FINANCIAL DATA

RECORD OF EARNINGS (IN THOUSANDS):

Total Revenues	353,500	265,500	196,000	108,000	63,000	40,500	22,068
Costs and Expenses	305,879	207,152	160,766	80,255	47,319	31,704	15,758
Depreciation & Amort	18,721	15,548	12,134	7,745	5,181	3,668	1,165
Operating Income	28,900	42,800	23,100	20,000	10,500	5,128	5,145
Inc Fr Cont Opers Bef Income Taxes	35,850	47,708	25,049	20,855	11,167	5,500	5,484
Income Taxes	12,150	17,408	9,299	7,670	4,035	1,980	1,836
Net Income	23,700	30,300	15,750	13,185	7,132	3,520	①3,648
Aver. Shs. Outstg.	41,553	40,416	37,678	31,584	29,412	25,964	23,134

① Before extra. item cr$377,000.

BALANCE SHEET (IN THOUSANDS):

Cash and Cash Equivalents	236,567	209,984	139,099	83,751	42,674	12,169	11,236
Receivables, Net	61,085	42,863	33,928	15,305	18,869	8,742	5,742
Gross Property	92,495	59,493	43,373	23,843	16,407	10,760	5,454
Accumulated Depreciation	40,958	30,773	24,033	10,893	7,589	3,823	1,597
Long-Term Debt	15,970	...	...	...	...	...	...
Capital Lease Obligations	...	...	...	598	2,139	1,433	
Net Stockholders' Equity	232,747	182,302	121,129	82,199	58,142	20,863	11,860
Total Assets	408,967	297,571	208,462	121,795	81,648	35,397	22,019
Total Current Assets	317,627	262,528	180,093	100,888	63,453	22,192	17,656
Total Current Liabilities	160,250	115,269	87,333	39,596	22,908	12,395	8,726
Net Working Capital	157,377	147,259	92,760	61,292	40,545	9,797	8,930
Year End Shares Outstg	40,435	38,971	35,726	29,032	27,098	8,474	7,600

STATISTICAL RECORD:

Operating Profit Margin %	8.2	16.1	11.8	18.5	16.7	12.7	23.3
Book Value Per Share	5.73	4.65	3.32	2.69	1.91	1.82	1.54
Return on Equity %	10.2	16.6	13.0	16.0	12.3	16.9	30.8
Return on Assets %	5.8	10.2	7.6	10.8	8.7	9.9	16.6
P/E Ratio	88.6-48.2	51.3-28.5	58.0-39.3	62.8-30.7	74.0-46.4	...	...
Price Range	50½-27½	38½-21⅜	24⅜-16½	26⅜-12⅞	17¾-11⅛	...	...

Statistics are as originally reported.

OFFICERS:
H.C. Jones, Jr., Chmn.
A.J. de Geus, Pres. & C.E.O.
A.B. Seawell, Sr. V.P., Fin. & Oper., C.F.O.

INCORPORATED: NC, Dec., 1986; reincorp., DE, Aug., 1987

PRINCIPAL OFFICE: 700 East Middlefield Rd., Mountain View, CA 94043-4033

TELEPHONE NUMBER: (415) 962-5000

FAX: (415) 965-8637

NO. OF EMPLOYEES: 1,716

ANNUAL MEETING: In February

SHAREHOLDERS: 277 (approx.)

INSTITUTIONAL HOLDINGS:
No. of Institutions: 104
Shares Held: 37,746,368

REGISTRAR(S): Boston EquiServe, Canton, MA

TRANSFER AGENT(S): Boston EquiServe, Canton, MA

TELE-COMMUNICATIONS, INC.

YIELD ...%
P/E RATIO ...

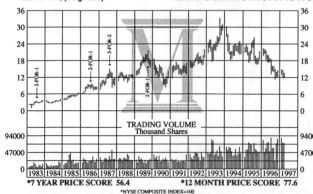

7 YEAR PRICE SCORE 56.4 **12 MONTH PRICE SCORE 77.6**

*NYSE COMPOSITE INDEX=100

TRADING VOLUME
Thousand Shares

INTERIM EARNINGS (Per Share):

Qtr.	Mar.	June	Sept.	Dec.
1993	0.11	0.07	d0.13	d0.08
1994	0.07	0.01	Nil	0.01
1995	d0.08	d0.16	0.12	d0.01
1996	d0.22	d0.29	d0.24	d0.46

INTERIM DIVIDENDS (Per Share):

Amt.	Decl.	Ex.	Rec.	Pay.
stock	10/30/96	12/5/96	11/12/96	12/4/96

CAPITALIZATION (12/31/96):

	($000)	(%)
Long-Term Debt	14,926,000	52.7
Deferred Income Tax	6,012,000	21.2
Minority Interest	1,493,000	5.3
Redeemable Pfd Stock	1,658,000	5.8
Common & Surplus	4,253,000	15.0
Total	28,342,000	100.0

RECENT DEVELOPMENTS: On 3/12/97, TCOM shareholders voted to create two new series of Telephony Group target common stock. For the year ended 12/31/96, the Company reported net earnings of $278.0 million compared with a net loss of $171.0 million in the corresponding 1995 period. Total revenues climbed 23.3% to $8.02 billion from $6.51 billion the previous year. Revenue from communications and programming services was $7.04 billion compared with $5.59 billion the year before, an increase of 26.0%. Net sales from electronic retailing services advanced 7.0% to $984.0 million from $920.0 million in the prior-year period. Operating income rose 16.6% to $632.0 million from $542.0 million a year earlier. For the three months ended 12/31/96, net earnings totaled $724.0 million versus a net loss of $64.0 million in the same quarter in 1995. Total revenues grew 19.8% to $2.16 billion from $1.80 billion the previous year.

BUSINESS

TELE-COMMUNICATIONS, INC., through its subsidiaries, is engaged in the operation of CATV and microwave communications systems. Western Tele-Communications, Inc. provides common carrier communications services by means of terrestrial microwave video relay systems. The transportable earth station provides mobile services by utilizing its capabilities of transmitting and receiving television programs via a communications satellite. Community Tele-Communications, Inc. distributes television signals and special information programs to subscribers within a particular community by means of a coaxial cable network. Pay TV provides, for an extra charge, additional programs, such as recently released movies, special entertainment or selected sporting events to subscribers on a designated channel. In August 1994, the Company merged with Liberty Media Corp. In December 1996, the Company spun-off TCI Satellite Entertainment to holders of TCOMA and TCOMB common stock.

ANNUAL EARNINGS AND DIVIDENDS PER SHARE

	1996	1995	1994	1993	1992	1991	1990
Earnings Per Share	d1.22	d0.11	0.09	d0.02	① d0.08	d0.28	d0.81
Dividends Per Share	Nil	Nil	Nil	Nil	Nil	Nil	Nil

① Before disc. oper.

ANNUAL FINANCIAL DATA

RECORD OF EARNINGS (IN MILLIONS):

	1996	1995	1994	1993	1992	1991	1990
Total Revenues	8,022.0	6,851.0	4,936.0	4,153.0	3,574.0	3,827.0	3,625.0
Costs and Expenses	5,774.0	4,937.0	3,130.0	2,326.0	1,947.0	2,311.0	2,290.0
Depreciation & Amort	1,616.0	1,372.0	1,018.0	911.0	0.7	712.0	681.0
Operating Income	632.0	542.0	788.0	916.0	956.0	804.0	654.0
Inc Fr Cont Opers Bef Income Taxes	540.0	d291.0	171.0	161.0	131.0	d34.0	d264.0
Income Taxes	262.0	cr120.0	116.0	168.0	150.0	68.0	23.0
Net Income	278.0	d171.0	55.0	d7.0	① d19.0	d102.0	d287.0
Aver. Shs. Outstg. (000)	914,000	820,500	540,800	433,000	424,100	359,900	354,860

① Before disc. op. dr$15,000,000.

BALANCE SHEET (IN MILLIONS):

Cash and Cash Equivalents	394.0	118.0	74.0	1.0	34.0	35.0	31.0
Receivables, Net	448.0	407.0	301.0	232.0	203.0	249.0	278.0
Inventories	136.0	226.0	121.0	...	...	...	...
Gross Property	11,696.0	10,679.0	8,942.0	7,520.0	6,591.0	6,249.0	5,979.0
Accumulated Depreciation	4,168.0	3,653.0	3,066.0	2,585.0	2,207.0	1,806.0	1,453.0
Long-Term Debt	14,926.0	13,211.0	11,162.0	9,900.0	10,285.0	9,910.0	9,487.0
Net Stockholders' Equity	5,911.0	5,028.0	2,971.0	2,130.0	1,596.0	1,554.0	622.0
Total Assets	30,244.0	25,130.0	19,528.0	16,520.0	13,164.0	13,010.0	12,310.0
Total Current Assets	1,108.0	863.0	496.0	233.0	237.0	319.0	367.0
Total Current Liabilities	1,649.0	1,515.0	1,193.0	781.0	655.0	618.0	627.0
Net Working Capital	d541.0	d652.0	d697.0	d548.0	d418.0	d299.0	d260.0
Year End Shs Outstg (000)	913,000	820,470	576,060	529,100	430,100	418,580	357,950

STATISTICAL RECORD:

Operating Profit Margin %	7.9	7.9	16.0	22.1	26.7	21.0	18.0
Book Value Per Share	6.47	6.13	5.16	4.03	3.71	3.71	1.74
Return on Equity %	6.5	...	1.9	...	...	...	...
Return on Assets %	0.9	...	0.3	...	...	...	...
Price Range	22⅜-11⅜	26¼-16⅝	30¼-18¼	33¼-17½	22-15⅜	17½-11⅝	18½-8⅜

Statistics are as originally reported.

OFFICERS:
J.C. Malone, Chmn. & C.E.O.
L.J. Hindery, Jr., Pres. & C.O.O.
S.M. Brett, Exec. V.P., Gen. Couns. & Sec.

INCORPORATED: DE, Aug., 1968

PRINCIPAL OFFICE: Terrace Tower II 5619 DTC Parkway, Englewood, CO 80111-3000

TELEPHONE NUMBER: (303) 267-5500

NO. OF EMPLOYEES: 35,000 (approx.)

ANNUAL MEETING: In August

SHAREHOLDERS: 8,437 (A TCI); 587 (B TCI); 7,807 (A Lib.); 570 (B Lib.).

INSTITUTIONAL HOLDINGS:
No. of Institutions: 301
Shares Held: 405,657,741

REGISTRAR(S): The Bank of New York, New York, NY
First Security Bank of Utah, N.A., Salt Lake City, UT 84125

TRANSFER AGENT(S): The Bank of New York, New York, NY
First Security Bank of Utah, N.A., Salt Lake City, UT 84125

TELLABS, INC.

YIELD ...%
P/E RATIO 50.9

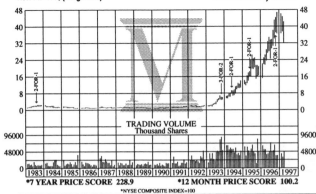

1983 1984 1985 1986 1987 1988 1989 1990 1991 1992 1993 1994 1995 1996 1997
*7 YEAR PRICE SCORE 228.9   *12 MONTH PRICE SCORE 100.2
*NYSE COMPOSITE INDEX=100

INTERIM EARNINGS (Per Share):

Qtr.	Mar.	June	Sept.	Dec.
1993	0.03	0.03	0.04	0.08
1994	0.06	0.09	0.10	0.14
1995	0.13	0.15	0.15	0.21
1996	0.17	d0.10	0.25	0.32
1997	0.34	...	...	...

INTERIM DIVIDENDS (Per Share):

Amt.	Decl.	Ex.	Rec.	Pay.
2-for-1	10/24/96	11/18/96	10/31/96	11/15/96

CAPITALIZATION (12/27/96):

	($000)	(%)
Long-Term Debt	2,850	0.5
Deferred Income Tax	7,109	1.2
Common & Surplus	591,276	98.3
Total	601,235	100.0

RECENT DEVELOPMENTS: For the three months ended 3/28/97, net profit more than doubled to $63.1 million, or $0.34 per share, from $31.1 million, or $0.17 per share, in the first quarter a year earlier. Sales jumped 43.5% to $247.1 million from $172.3 million in the previous year. The 1997 results were positively affected by a pretax gain of $20.8 million related to the sale of stock held as an investment. Sales of the Company's TITAN® 5500 digital cross-connect systems were up approximately 61%, while MartisDXX™ system sales soared approximately 65% compared with the year before. Sales of echo cancellers grew 33% versus the prior-year period. Gross profit surged 55.2% to $151.7 million, or 61.4% of sales, from $97.8 million, or 56.8% of sales, in 1996. Operating profit totaled $71.4 million, up 70.2% compared with $41.9 million a year earlier.

BUSINESS

TELLABS, INC. and its subsidiaries design, assemble, market and service a diverse line of electronic communications equipment used in public and private communications networks worldwide. Products include voice and data communications and networking equipment. TLAB's customers include telephone companies, other common carriers, government agencies and business end-users. TLAB operates in two principal geographic areas: North America and Europe. TLAB's main facility is in Lisle, Illinois, a surburb of Chicago, and houses the corporate offices, which are augmented by major facilities in Bolingbrook, Illinois; Round Rock, Texas; Shannon, Ireland; and Helsinki, Finland.

ANNUAL EARNINGS AND DIVIDENDS PER SHARE

	12/27/96	12/29/95	12/30/94	12/31/93	1/1/93	12/27/91	12/28/90
Earnings Per Share	0.64	0.63	0.39	④ 0.18	0.10	0.04	0.05
Dividends Per Share	①...	②...	③...	⑤...	Nil	Nil	Nil

① 2-for-1 stk. split, 11/15/96 ② 2-for-1 stk. split, 5/19/95 ③ 100% stk. div., 5/20/94 ④ Before acctg. chg. ⑤ 3-for-2 stk. split, 11/19/93

ANNUAL FINANCIAL DATA

RECORD OF EARNINGS (IN THOUSANDS):

	12/27/96	12/29/95	12/30/94	12/31/93	1/1/93	12/27/91	12/28/90
Total Revenues	868,975	635,229	494,153	320,463	258,560	212,751	211,046
Costs and Expenses	696,349	476,008	392,082	287,732	242,461	207,365	202,852
Depreciation & Amort	32,648	23,682	19,502	14,511	11,370	9,856	8,563
Operating Income	168,943	156,653	99,682	32,046	16,099	4,537	8,194
Inc Fr Cont Opers Bef Income Taxes	175,282	162,825	97,824	35,801	19,152	7,025	10,731
Income Taxes	57,317	47,219	25,435	5,334	2,298	394	2,629
Net Income	117,965	115,606	72,389	①30,467	16,854	6,631	8,102
Aver. Shs. Outstg.	184,674	183,420	181,328	176,942	176,936	159,720	151,716

① Before acctg. change cr$1,500,000.

BALANCE SHEET (IN THOUSANDS):

	12/27/96	12/29/95	12/30/94	12/31/93	1/1/93	12/27/91	12/28/90
Cash and Cash Equivalents	226,867	162,236	74,669	45,571	49,351	44,253	38,468
Receivables, Net	167,928	127,565	84,397	74,473	53,440	46,035	37,351
Inventories	78,519	67,715	51,881	49,881	36,212	32,067	30,693
Gross Property	267,014	201,441	166,931	144,206	107,832	90,245	86,329
Accumulated Depreciation	104,254	84,419	69,300	59,326	51,173	43,417	36,227
Long-Term Debt	2,850	2,850	2,850	2,850	3,765	3,992	4,184
Net Stockholders' Equity	591,276	433,233	292,790	207,006	167,144	145,043	130,411
Total Assets	743,823	552,051	390,067	328,766	210,748	185,964	171,538
Total Current Assets	475,464	366,370	220,556	176,400	144,413	127,613	110,755
Total Current Liabilities	131,624	98,564	82,239	112,115	35,476	30,860	32,499
Net Working Capital	343,840	267,806	138,317	64,285	108,937	96,753	78,256
Year End Shares Outstg	179,653	177,597	174,577	171,932	166,065	160,955	153,607

STATISTICAL RECORD:

	12/27/96	12/29/95	12/30/94	12/31/93	1/1/93	12/27/91	12/28/90
Operating Profit Margin %	19.4	24.7	20.2	10.0	6.2	2.1	3.9
Book Value Per Share	2.93	2.19	1.43	0.81	1.01	0.90	0.85
Return on Equity %	20.0	26.7	24.7	14.7	10.1	4.6	6.2
Return on Assets %	15.9	20.9	18.6	9.3	8.0	3.6	4.7
P/E Ratio	73.0-23.8	41.9-18.7	35.9-14.1	37.5-9.0	22.5-13.8	46.9-25.0	25.0-15.0
Price Range	46¾-15¼	26⅜-11¾	14-5½	6¾-1⅝	2¼-1⅜	1⅞-1	1¼-¾

Statistics are as originally reported.

OFFICERS:
M.J. Birck, Pres. & C.E.O.
P.A. Guglielmi, Exec. V.P.-Fin., C.F.O. & Treas.
C.C. Gavin, Sec.

INCORPORATED: IL, 1975; reincorp., DE

PRINCIPAL OFFICE: 4951 Indiana Avenue, Lisle, IL 60532-1698

TELEPHONE NUMBER: (630) 378-8800

NO. OF EMPLOYEES: 3,418

ANNUAL MEETING: In April

SHAREHOLDERS: 3,035 (approx.)

INSTITUTIONAL HOLDINGS:
No. of Institutions: 263
Shares Held: 123,248,352

REGISTRAR(S):

TRANSFER AGENT(S): Harris Trust & Savings Bank, Chicago, IL

3COM CORP.

INTERIM EARNINGS (Per Share):

Qtr.	Aug.	Nov.	Feb.	May
1993-94	0.20	0.16	d0.82	0.34
1994-95	0.21	0.02	0.31	0.32
1995-96	0.38	0.09	0.42	0.17
1996-97	0.52	0.57	0.47	...

INTERIM DIVIDENDS (Per Share):

Amt.	Decl.	Ex.	Rec.	Pay.
Last dist. 2-for-1 split, 8/25/95				

TRADING VOLUME
Thousand Shares

1983 1984 1985 1986 1987 1988 1989 1990 1991 1992 1993 1994 1995 1996 1997

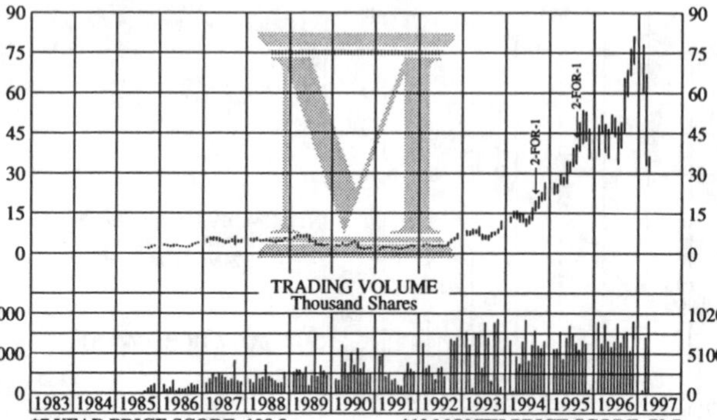

*7 YEAR PRICE SCORE 198.8   ***12 MONTH PRICE SCORE 70.7**

*NYSE COMPOSITE INDEX=100

CAPITALIZATION (5/31/96):

	($000)	(%)
Long-Term Debt	110,000	9.9
Deferred Income Tax	16,299	1.5
Common & Surplus	978,805	88.6
Total	1,105,104	100.0

RECENT DEVELOPMENTS: On 2/26/97, the Company announced that it had entered into a definitive agreement to acquire U.S. Robotics Corp. in a pooling-of-interests transaction. Under the terms of the agreement, each share of U.S. Robotic's stock will be exchanged for 1.75 shares of COMS stock. For the three months ended 2/28/97, net income rose 17.5% to $87.6 million from $74.6 million in the corresponding quarter a year earlier. Sales climbed 29.8% to $786.8 million from $606.0 million the previous year. Sales of systems products, which include switches, hubs, internetworking and remote access products, totaled $432.6 million, up 24% versus the year before. Sales of network adaptors grew 39% to $346.3 million from the same prior-year quarter. Gross margin advanced 33.4% to $428.5 million, or 54.5% of sales, from $321.2 million, or 53.0% of sales, a year earlier. Operating income was $129.4 million, up 14.5% compared with $113.0 million the previous year.

BUSINESS

3COM CORPORATION is a computer networking company, providing multi-vendor connectivity and information sharing for workgroups, departments and corporate environments. The Company designs, manufactures, markets and supports a wide range of networked client-server systems based on industry standards and an open systems architecture. 3Com's computer networking systems consist of products in three broad product categories: client-server systems, which include network operating software, dedicated workgroup servers and network workstations; internetwork or bridges and network control servers; and transmission products, which include network adapters, multi-media transmission systems and transceivers. COMS acquired Synernetics, Inc. and Centrum Communication, Inc. in the fiscal year ending 5/31/94 and Chipcom Corp. in 10/95.

ANNUAL EARNINGS AND DIVIDENDS PER SHARE

	5/31/96	5/31/95	5/31/94	5/31/93	5/31/92	5/31/91	5/31/90
Earnings Per Share	1.01	0.87	d0.23	0.30	0.08	d0.49	0.35
Dividends Per Share	①...	②...	Nil	Nil	Nil	Nil	Nil

① 2-for-1 stk. split, 8/25/95 ② 2-for-1 stk. split, 8/31/94

ANNUAL FINANCIAL DATA

RECORD OF EARNINGS (IN MILLIONS):

Total Revenues	2,327.1	1,295.3	827.0	617.2	408.4	398.6	419.1
Costs and Expenses	1,934.5	1,053.1	793.4	531.1	381.4	422.4	362.3
Depreciation & Amort	91.0	46.7	30.6	25.1	21.6	22.7	22.5
Operating Income	301.7	195.5	2.9	60.9	5.5	d46.5	34.3
Inc Fr Cont Opers Bef Income Taxes	308.5	198.4	19.5	60.2	5.2	d44.6	32.8
Income Taxes	130.6	72.7	48.2	21.7	2.6	cr17.0	12.3
Net Income	177.9	125.7	d28.7	38.6	4.2	d27.7	20.5
Aver. Shs. Outstg. (000)	176,517	145,618	125,240	126,496	112,752	113,364	116,268

BALANCE SHEET (IN MILLIONS):

Cash and Cash Equivalents	499.3	323.5	129.7	117.2	78.7	97.5	86.7
Receivables, Net	438.4	241.0	149.9	103.3	81.9	77.1	87.4
Inventories	241.0	122.1	71.4	68.1	52.3	32.4	45.8
Gross Property	471.0	232.7	161.6	126.3	119.7	98.1	91.7
Accumulated Depreciation	224.3	124.5	94.6	71.1	66.4	47.8	43.3
Long-Term Debt	110.0	110.0	...	...	...	...	...
Net Stockholders' Equity	978.8	464.9	280.8	258.3	199.0	190.3	232.3
Total Assets	1,525.1	839.7	444.3	367.6	293.9	270.8	294.3
Total Current Assets	1,239.7	707.6	361.1	304.4	228.6	218.2	229.5
Total Current Liabilities	414.5	263.7	162.5	108.2	87.1	71.4	59.0
Net Working Capital	825.2	443.9	198.5	196.2	141.5	146.8	170.5
Year End Shs Outstg (000)	168,800	138,462	130,104	123,400	110,392	108,784	116,424

STATISTICAL RECORD:

Operating Profit Margin %	13.0	15.1	0.4	9.9	1.3	...	8.2
Book Value Per Share	5.80	3.36	2.16	2.09	1.80	1.75	2.00
Return on Equity %	18.2	27.0	...	14.9	2.1	...	8.8
Return on Assets %	11.7	15.0	...	10.5	1.4	...	7.0
P/E Ratio	53.1-22.0	30.8-11.7	...	24.6-7.8	82.2-36.2	...	40.7-14.0
Price Range	53⅜-22¼	26⅝-10⅛	12⅛-4⅞	7½-2⅜	3⅛-1⅜	4¾-1⅜	7¼-2½

Statistics are as originally reported.

OFFICERS:
E.A. Benhamou, Chmn., Pres. & C.E.O.
C.B. Paisley, V.P.-Fin. & C.F.O.

INCORPORATED: CA, Jun., 1979

PRINCIPAL OFFICE: 5400 Bayfront Plaza,
Santa Clara, CA 95052-8145

TELEPHONE NUMBER: (408) 764-5000
FAX: (408) 764-5001
NO. OF EMPLOYEES: 5,190
ANNUAL MEETING: In September
SHAREHOLDERS: 2,997 (approx.)
INSTITUTIONAL HOLDINGS:
No. of Institutions: 339
Shares Held: 142,996,214

REGISTRAR(S):

TRANSFER AGENT(S): First National Bank
of Boston, Shareholder Services Division,
Boston, MA

TYSON FOODS, INC.

YIELD 0.5%
P/E RATIO 35.5

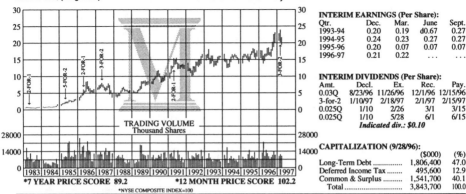

*7 YEAR PRICE SCORE 89.2   *12 MONTH PRICE SCORE 102.2

*NYSE COMPOSITE INDEX=100

TRADING VOLUME
Thousand Shares

INTERIM EARNINGS (Per Share):

Qtr.	Dec.	Mar.	June	Sept.
1993-94	0.20	0.19	d0.67	0.27
1994-95	0.24	0.23	0.27	0.27
1995-96	0.20	0.07	0.07	0.07
1996-97	0.21	0.22	...	...

INTERIM DIVIDENDS (Per Share):

Amt.	Decl.	Ex.	Rec.	Pay.
0.03Q	8/23/96	11/26/96	12/1/96	12/15/96
3-for-2	1/10/97	2/18/97	2/1/97	2/15/97
0.025Q	1/10	2/26	3/1	3/15
0.025Q	1/10	5/28	6/1	6/15

Indicated div.: $0.10

CAPITALIZATION (9/28/96):

	($000)	(%)
Long-Term Debt	1,806,400	47.0
Deferred Income Tax	495,600	12.9
Common & Surplus	1,541,700	40.1
Total	3,843,700	100.0

RECENT DEVELOPMENTS: For the three months ended 3/29/97, net income totaled $48.2 million compared with $14.4 million the previous year. Sales fell slightly to $1.57 billion from $1.59 billion a year ago. Sales for the second quarter of fiscal 1997 did not include revenues from beef and pork due to the sale of certain assets in the first quarter. In addition, results were hampered by sluggish international sales and continued high grain prices. Gross profit advanced 14.3% to $262.2 million from $229.3 million the year before, and improved as a percentage of sales to 16.7% versus 14.4% the prior year. Operating income jumped 89.9% to $104.8 million from $55.2 million the previous year. For the six months ended 3/29/97, net income climbed 60.8% to $92.8 million from $57.7 million a year earlier. Sales were down 1.0% to $3.10 billion versus $3.13 billion the previous year.

BUSINESS

TYSON FOODS, INC. and its various subsidiaries produce, market and distribute a variety of food products consisting of value-enhanced poultry; fresh and frozen poultry; value-enhanced seafood products; fresh and frozen seafood products; flour and corn tortillas, chips and other Mexican food products. Additionally, TYSNA has live swine, animal feed and pet food operations. TYSNA's integrated operations consist of breeding and rearing chickens and hogs, harvesting seafood, as well as the processing, further processing and marketing of these food products. TYSNA's products are marketed and sold to national and regional grocery chains, regional grocery wholesalers, clubs or warehouse stores, military commissaries, industrial food processing companies, national and regional chain restaurants or their distributors, international export companies and distributors who service restaurants, foodservice operations such as plant and school cafeterias, convenience stores, hospitals and other vendors.

ANNUAL EARNINGS AND DIVIDENDS PER SHARE

	9/28/96	9/30/95	10/1/94	10/2/93	10/3/92	9/28/91	9/29/90
Earnings Per Share	0.40	1.01	d0.01	0.81	0.77	0.70	0.60
Dividends Per Share	0.08	0.06	0.053	0.027	0.027	① 0.023	0.013
Dividend Payout %	20.0	5.9	...	3.3	3.5	3.3	2.2

Note: 3-for-2 stk. split, 2/15/97. ① 2-for-1 stk. split, 4/16/91.

ANNUAL FINANCIAL DATA

RECORD OF EARNINGS (IN MILLIONS):

Total Revenues	6,453.8	5,511.2	5,110.3	4,707.4	4,168.8	3,922.1	3,825.3
Costs and Expenses	6,156.6	5,013.6	4,885.4	4,301.1	3,807.6	3,559.6	3,479.4
Depreciation & Amort	239.3	204.9	188.3	176.6	148.9	135.8	123.4
Operating Income	269.6	471.7	195.2	375.5	331.7	333.2	326.7
Inc Fr Cont Opers Bef Income Taxes	132.6	343.6	118.6	309.6	261.0	242.5	200.1
Income Taxes	49.0	131.0	120.7	129.3	100.5	97.0	80.1
Net Income	86.9	219.2	d2.1	180.3	160.5	145.5	120.0
Aver. Shs. Outstg. (000)	218,100	217,650	221,700	222,512	207,593	207,056	199,296

BALANCE SHEET (IN MILLIONS):

Cash and Cash Equivalents	36.6	33.1	27.0	21.5	27.1	25.5	16.9
Receivables, Net	547.1	494.7	444.2	104.8	122.0	96.7	90.8
Inventories	1,027.4	949.4	754.2	675.2	525.1	535.7	472.3
Gross Property	2,978.1	3,046.6	2,509.8	2,186.1	1,758.5	1,677.0	1,498.3
Accumulated Depreciation	1,108.9	1,033.1	899.8	750.8	616.3	515.0	427.2
Long-Term Debt	1,806.4	1,620.5	1,381.5	920.5	726.5	845.9	950.4
Net Stockholders' Equity	1,541.7	1,467.7	1,289.4	1,360.7	980.2	822.5	663.0
Total Assets	4,544.1	4,444.3	3,668.0	3,253.5	2,617.7	2,645.8	2,501.1
Total Current Assets	1,810.3	1,519.8	1,261.3	811.8	679.9	662.0	585.9
Total Current Liabilities	685.8	865.8	539.8	526.7	465.8	550.1	483.2
Net Working Capital	1,124.5	654.0	721.5	285.1	214.1	111.9	102.7
Year End Shs Outstg (000)	217,500	217,200	217,950	220,901	206,246	206,070	204,921

STATISTICAL RECORD:

Operating Profit Margin %	4.2	8.6	3.8	8.0	8.0	8.5	8.5
Book Value Per Share	3.73	3.04	2.51	1.97	1.15	0.29	...
Return on Equity %	5.6	14.9	...	13.3	16.4	17.7	18.1
Return on Assets %	1.9	4.9	...	5.5	6.1	5.5	4.8
Average Yield %	0.4	0.4	0.4	0.2	0.2	0.2	0.1
P/E Ratio	57.8-34.7	18.2-13.7	...	22.4-15.9	21.6-13.1	22.1-13.4	19.6-12.7
Price Range	23⅛-13⅞	18⅝-13⅞	16⅝-12½	18⅛-12⅞	16⅝-10⅛	15½-9⅜	11¾-7⅝

Statistics are as originally reported.

OFFICERS:
L.E. Tollett, Chmn. & C.E.O.
D Tyson, Sr. Chmn.
D.E. Wray, Pres. & C.O.O.
W. Britt, Exec. V.P. & C.F.O.

INCORPORATED: AR, Oct., 1947; reincorp., DE, Feb., 1986

PRINCIPAL OFFICE: 2210 W. Oaklawn Dr., Springdale, AR 72764

TELEPHONE NUMBER: (501) 290-4000
FAX: (501) 290-4061
NO. OF EMPLOYEES: 58,300 (approx.)
ANNUAL MEETING: In January
SHAREHOLDERS: 39,000 Cl. A; 22 Cl. B (approx.)
INSTITUTIONAL HOLDINGS:
No. of Institutions: 130 (approx.)
Shares Held: 56.5 million (approx.)

REGISTRAR(S):

TRANSFER AGENT(S): First Chicago Trust Co. of New York, Jersey City, NJ

VIKING OFFICE PRODUCTS, INC.

YIELD ...%
P/E RATIO 17.6

INTERIM EARNINGS (Per Share):

Qtr.	Sept.	Dec.	Mar.	June
1993-94	0.08	0.08	0.13	0.10
1994-95	0.12	0.11	0.17	0.14
1995-96	0.15	0.15	0.21	0.19
1996-97	0.19	0.19	0.24	...

INTERIM DIVIDENDS (Per Share):

Amt.	Decl.	Ex.	Rec.	Pay.
2-for-1	4/11/96	5/16/96	5/1/96	5/15/96

TRADING VOLUME
Thousand Shares

7 YEAR PRICE SCORE 164.7   **12 MONTH PRICE SCORE 78.1**
*NYSE COMPOSITE INDEX=100

CAPITALIZATION (6/28/96):

	($000)	(%)
Deferred Income Tax	2,532	0.9
Common & Surplus	275,029	99.1
Total	277,561	100.0

RECENT DEVELOPMENTS: For the three months ended 3/31/97, net income climbed 14.3% to $20.7 million from $18.1 million in the corresponding quarter in 1996. Revenues were up 15.1% to $353.1 million from $306.8 million a year earlier. European revenues rose 19% to $207.5 million, while revenues from the Company's Australian division advanced 11% to $15.9 million. European results were hampered by fewer billing days, sluggish growth in France and the U.K., an unfavorable foreign currency exchange rate, and lower paper pricing. U.S. revenues grew 10% to $129.7 million compared with the third quarter in 1996. U.S. revenue growth was negatively affected by one less billing day and lower selling prices of paper products. Gross profit was $121.2 million, or 34.3% of revenues, up 15.9% versus $104.5 million, or 34.1% of revenues, the previous year. For the nine months ended 3/31/97, net income rose 21.0% to $53.6 million from $44.3 million the prior year. Revenues totaled $960.1 million, up 22.0% versus $787.3 million the year before.

BUSINESS

VIKING OFFICE PRODUCTS, INC. markets office related products to small and medium-sized businesses employing fewer than 100 employees. Incorporated in 1960, VKNG has grown nationally through mergers and has become an international distributor of office products with subsidiaries located in Great Britain, France, the Netherlands, Austria, Belgium, Ireland and Australia. The Company's international expansion began in 1990, adding distribution channels in Australia in 1993, cross-border sales in Belgium in May 1994, and Germany in November 1995. Catalog sales and direct mail marketing tailored to meet specific professional needs are developed using VKNG's extensive database. Personalized messaging of catalog mailers is integral to VKNG's micro-marketing practices. Via direct mail, VKNG is able to reach targeted businesses and provide services unavailable from superstores or warehouses.

ANNUAL EARNINGS AND DIVIDENDS PER SHARE

	6/28/96	6/30/95	6/24/94	6/25/93	6/26/92	6/28/91	6/29/90
Earnings Per Share	0.70	0.54	0.38	0.21	0.17	0.12	[4] 0.12
Dividends Per Share	[1] ...	Nil	[2] ...	Nil	[3] ...	Nil	Nil

[1] 2-for-1 stk. split, 5/15/96 [2] 2-for-1 stk. split, 6/14/94 [3] 2-for-1 stk. split, 2/14/92 [4] Before extraord. item

ANNUAL FINANCIAL DATA

RECORD OF EARNINGS (IN MILLIONS):

Total Revenues	1,055.8	811.9	565.1	449.7	320.1	226.3	157.9
Costs and Expenses	960.2	739.3	512.3	416.7	296.0	209.7	141.7
Depreciation & Amort	13.7	8.1	5.0	3.7	3.2	2.6	2.3
Operating Income	81.9	64.5	47.7	29.4	20.9	14.0	13.9
Inc Fr Cont Opers Bef Income Taxes	89.6	72.3	52.1	32.1	22.4	13.5	10.7
Income Taxes	29.2	26.2	20.3	15.0	9.6	5.7	4.6
Net Income	60.5	46.1	31.8	17.2	12.8	7.8	[5] 6.1
Aver. Shs. Outstg. (000)	86,560	85,100	83,700	81,152	76,028	69,468	53,416

[5] Before extra. item dr$941,000.

BALANCE SHEET (IN MILLIONS):

Cash and Cash Equivalents	44.8	47.5	48.5	30.9	12.5	0.8	1.0
Receivables, Net	121.1	96.0	65.1	49.7	37.2	23.9	13.8
Inventories	81.8	64.7	45.3	31.2	32.3	22.1	16.6
Gross Property	123.2	65.9	33.4	18.2	17.7	12.3	8.9
Accumulated Depreciation	28.0	16.8	10.2	7.4	5.9	3.9	2.3
Long-Term Debt	...	...	...	...	...	13.0	13.0
Net Stockholders' Equity	275.0	208.5	150.2	112.7	95.1	55.0	47.9
Total Assets	399.6	308.3	227.2	165.3	135.7	95.9	77.9
Total Current Assets	268.8	227.0	171.9	120.1	88.6	51.6	35.3
Total Current Liabilities	122.1	99.4	76.7	51.4	39.1	26.1	15.1
Net Working Capital	146.8	127.6	95.2	68.7	49.5	25.5	20.2
Year End Shs Outstg (000)	82,964	81,582	80,424	78,152	77,496	66,328	66,328

STATISTICAL RECORD:

Operating Profit Margin %	7.8	7.9	8.4	6.5	6.5	6.2	8.8
Book Value Per Share	2.97	2.19	1.49	1.02	0.79	0.30	0.18
Return on Equity %	22.0	22.1	21.2	15.2	13.5	14.1	12.7
Return on Assets %	15.1	15.0	14.0	10.4	9.5	8.1	7.8
P/E Ratio	48.6-29.8	45.1-23.1	42.8-27.6	58.9-25.6	42.6-22.1	38.7-10.0	16.3-9.8
Price Range	34-20⅞	24⅜-12½	16¼-10½	12⅜-5⅜	7¼-3¾	4⅜-1⅛	1⅞-1⅛

Statistics are as originally reported.

OFFICERS:
I. Helford, Chmn. & C.E.O.
M.B. Nelson, Pres. & C.O.O.
F.R. Jarc, Exec. V.P. & C.F.O.

INCORPORATED: CA, 1960

PRINCIPAL OFFICE: 879 W. 190th St., P.O. Box 61144, Los Angeles, CA 90061

TELEPHONE NUMBER: (310) 225-4500
FAX: (310) 225-4422
NO. OF EMPLOYEES: 3,340
ANNUAL MEETING: In November
SHAREHOLDERS: 1,077 (approx.)
INSTITUTIONAL HOLDINGS:
No. of Institutions: 160
Shares Held: 63,618,784

REGISTRAR(S): American Stock Transfer & Trust Co., 40 Wall Street, New York, NY 10005

TRANSFER AGENT(S): American Stock Transfer & Trust Co., 40 Wall Street, New York, NY 10005

WISCONSIN CENTRAL TRANSPORTATION CORP.

YIELD ...%
P/E RATIO 29.7

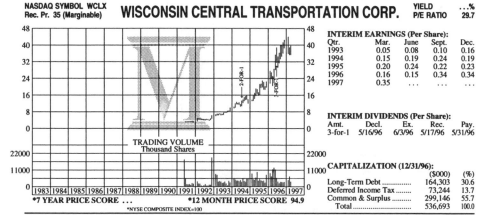

INTERIM EARNINGS (Per Share):

Qtr.	Mar.	June	Sept.	Dec.
1993	0.05	0.08	0.10	0.16
1994	0.15	0.19	0.24	0.19
1995	0.20	0.24	0.22	0.23
1996	0.16	0.15	0.34	0.34
1997	0.35	...	...	...

INTERIM DIVIDENDS (Per Share):

Amt.	Decl.	Ex.	Rec.	Pay.
3-for-1	5/16/96	6/3/96	5/17/96	5/31/96

TRADING VOLUME
Thousand Shares

1983 1984 1985 1986 1987 1988 1989 1990 1991 1992 1993 1994 1995 1996 1997

*7 YEAR PRICE SCORE ...   *12 MONTH PRICE SCORE 94.9

*NYSE COMPOSITE INDEX=100

CAPITALIZATION (12/31/96):

	($000)	(%)
Long-Term Debt	164,303	30.6
Deferred Income Tax	73,244	13.7
Common & Surplus	299,146	55.7
Total	536,693	100.0

RECENT DEVELOPMENTS: For the three months ended 3/31/97, net income more than doubled to $17.6 million, or $0.35 per share, compared with $8.1 million, or $0.16 per share, the previous year. Operating revenues climbed 22.8% to $80.3 million from $65.4 million a year earlier. Earnings for 1996 were negatively affected by a pretax charge of $2.5 million related to the 3/4/96 derailment in Weyauwega, WI. Volume was up 19.8% to a record of more than 137,500 carloads versus the first quarter in 1996 reflecting higher volumes in woodpulp, clay products, sand, stone and minerals, steel and intermodal shipments. Shipments of metallic ore were up 34.0% from the prior year, primarily due to the 1/27/97 acquisition of the Duck Creek North lines from Union Pacific Railroad Company. Income from operations totaled $15.1 million, up sharply compared with $4.8 million the year before.

BUSINESS

WISCONSIN CENTRAL TRANSPORTATION CORP. is a holding company that operates over 3,000 route miles of railway through the following wholly-owned subsidiaries: Wisconsin Central Ltd.; WCL Railcars, Inc.; Fox Valley & Western Ltd.; Wisconsin Central International, Inc.; Sault Ste. Marie Bridge Co.; WC Canada Holdings, Inc. and Algoma Central Railway Inc. Through its subsidiaries, the Company provides railroad services to the state of Wisconsin, the upper peninsula of Michigan, northeastern Illinois, eastern Minnesota and Ontario, Canada. In addition, the Company holds a 23% equity interest in Tranz Rail Holding Limited, which operates 2,400 route miles of railway nationwide in New Zealand and also holds a 34% equity interest in English Welsh & Scottish Railway Holdings Limited, which operates most of the freight railroad services in Great Britian.

ANNUAL EARNINGS AND DIVIDENDS PER SHARE

	1996	1995	1994	1993	1992	1991	1990
Earnings Per Share	[1] 0.99	[1] 0.89	[1] 0.77	[1] 0.38	0.28	[1] 0.26	0.32
Dividends Per Share	[2]...	Nil	[3]...	Nil	Nil	Nil	Nil

[1] Before extraord. item [2] 3-for-1 stk. split, 5/31/96 [3] 2-for-1 stk. split, 7/5/94

ANNUAL FINANCIAL DATA

RECORD OF EARNINGS (IN THOUSANDS):

	1996	1995	1994	1993	1992	1991	1990
Total Revenues	262,160	263,427	211,139	151,691	124,364	113,657	113,289
Costs and Expenses	212,797	188,138	146,008	109,187	90,390	83,705	81,881
Depreciation & Amort	13,591	11,830	10,506	7,656	7,618	7,524	7,711
Operating Income	35,772	63,459	54,625	34,848	26,356	22,428	23,697
Inc Fr Cont Opers Bef Income Taxes	28,735	56,147	47,772	29,290	17,836	14,086	11,697
Income Taxes	11,378	22,170	19,068	11,944	6,955	5,494	...
Net Income	[1] 50,034	[2] 44,632	[3] 38,282	[4] 18,836	10,881	[5] 8,592	7,546
Aver. Shs. Outstg.	50,647	50,241	49,788	49,572	38,904	32,616	24,000

[1] Before extra. item dr$1,602,000. [2] Before extra. item dr$2,123,000. [3] Before extra. item dr$1,587,000. [4] Before extra. item dr$1,398,000. [5] Before extra. item dr$341,000.

BALANCE SHEET (IN THOUSANDS):

	1996	1995	1994	1993	1992	1991	1990
Cash and Cash Equivalents	5,637	1,472	5,247	4,677	37,979	2,582	15,601
Receivables, Net	85,822	66,283	37,338	33,358	23,480	22,783	27,052
Inventories	17,530	17,245	15,738	12,846	9,055	8,442	7,747
Gross Property	528,784	462,669	379,105	345,210	225,935	206,389	176,453
Accumulated Depreciation	63,791	51,174	40,251	31,010	23,544	18,674	15,579
Long-Term Debt	164,303	123,721	102,500	134,155	81,428	96,001	119,008
Net Stockholders' Equity	299,146	237,695	190,478	149,674	133,685	73,619	29,143
Total Assets	691,275	540,732	433,613	389,182	280,822	227,874	219,579
Total Current Assets	111,630	86,148	59,602	52,875	71,668	34,980	51,465
Total Current Liabilities	139,603	102,450	80,789	63,114	39,948	40,152	55,940
Net Working Capital	d27,973	d16,302	d21,187	d10,239	31,720	d5,172	d4,475
Year End Shares Outstg	50,779	50,460	49,941	49,662	49,470	38,490	24,000

STATISTICAL RECORD:

	1996	1995	1994	1993	1992	1991	1990
Operating Profit Margin %	13.6	24.1	25.9	23.0	21.2	19.7	20.9
Book Value Per Share	5.89	4.68	3.78	2.92	2.57	1.78	0.91
Return on Equity %	16.7	18.8	20.1	12.6	8.1	11.7	25.9
Return on Assets %	7.2	8.3	8.8	4.8	3.9	3.8	3.4
P/E Ratio	42.9-20.7	25.7-14.7	20.9-12.5	26.3-15.8	22.3-12.1	13.9-11.1	...
Price Range	41½-20½	22⅞-13⅛	16⅛-9⅝		10-6	6¼-3⅜	3⅝-2⅞

Statistics are as originally reported.

OFFICERS:
E.A. Burkhardt, Chmn., Pres. & C.E.O.
T.F. Power, Jr., Exec. V.P. & C.F.O.
J.R. McCarren, Exec. V.P. & C.O.O.
M.J. Mickey, Treas.

INCORPORATED: DE

PRINCIPAL OFFICE: One O'Hara Center, 6250 North River Rd., Suite 9000, Rosemont, IL 60018

TELEPHONE NUMBER: (847) 318-4600

NO. OF EMPLOYEES: 2,047

ANNUAL MEETING: In May

SHAREHOLDERS: 1,450

INSTITUTIONAL HOLDINGS:
No. of Institutions: 109
Shares Held: 39,320,409

REGISTRAR(S): First National Bank of Boston, Boston, MA

TRANSFER AGENT(S): First National Bank of Boston, Boston, MA

NASDAQ SYMBOL WCOM
Rec. Pr. 22¼ (Marginable)

WORLDCOM, INC.

YIELD . . .%
P/E RATIO . . .

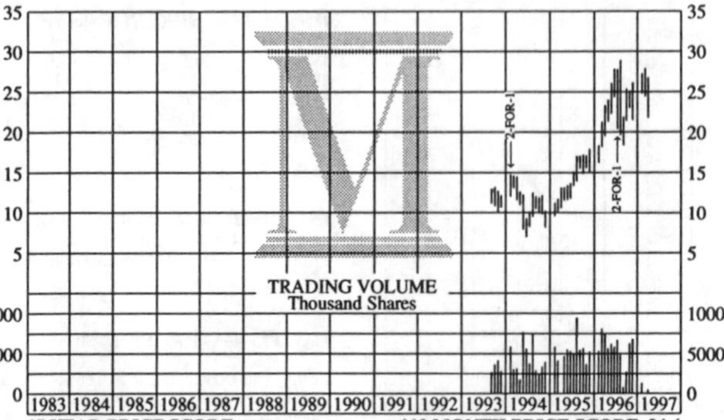

35
30
25
20
15
10
5
2-FOR-1
2-FOR-1
TRADING VOLUME
Thousand Shares
100000
50000
0
1983 1984 1985 1986 1987 1988 1989 1990 1991 1992 1993 1994 1995 1996 1997

***7 YEAR PRICE SCORE . . .** ***12 MONTH PRICE SCORE 94.4**

*NYSE COMPOSITE INDEX=100

INTERIM EARNINGS (Per Share):

Qtr.	Mar.	June	Sept.	Dec.
1993		0.43		
1994	0.10	0.04	d0.38	d0.25
1995	0.14	0.16	0.15	0.20
1996	0.22	d0.62	0.27	d5.22
1997	0.05	. . .	. . .	. . .

INTERIM DIVIDENDS (Per Share):

Amt.	Decl.	Ex.	Rec.	Pay.
2-for-1	5/23/96	7/5/96	6/6/96	7/3/96
rights	. . .	. . .	9/6	. . .

CAPITALIZATION (12/31/96):

	($000)	(%)
Long-Term Debt	4,803,581	27.0
Preferred Stock	128	0.0
Common & Surplus	12,959,848	73.0
Total	17,763,557	100.0

RECENT DEVELOPMENTS: For the three months ended 3/31/97, net income declined 42.5% to $49.7 million, or $0.05 per share, from $86.3 million, or $0.22 per share the previous year. Earnings for 1997 were negatively affected by increased amortization of goodwill of $84.0 million related to the 12/31/96 acquisition of MFS Communications Company, Inc. Revenues jumped 62.2% to $1.68 billion from $1.03 billion a year earlier. Higher revenues were attributed to the acquisition of MFS coupled with strong internal growth across all communications services. Long distance traffic surged 51.8% to 8.52 billion minutes from 5.61 billion minutes the prior year. Operating income totaled $170.5 million, down 12.3% versus $195.9 million the year before.

BUSINESS

WORLDCOM, INC. (formerly LDDS Metromedia Communications, Inc.) is the fourth largest long distance company in the United States. The Company offers domestic and international voice, data and video products and services to business customers, other carriers and the residential market. The Company operates a nationwide digital fiber optic network and has worldwide network capacity. On 10/5/95, the Company completed the acquisition of Williams Telecommunications Group, Inc. for approximately $2.50 billion. The Company merged with IDB Communications Group, Inc. on 12/30/94. On 12/31/96, WCOM acquired MFS Communications Company, Inc.

ANNUAL EARNINGS AND DIVIDENDS PER SHARE

	1996	1995	1994	1993	1992	1991	1990
Earnings Per Share	**[1] d5.50**	**0.65**	**d0.48**	**0.43**	**[1] d0.02**	**0.22**	**0.14**
Dividends Per Share	**[2] . . .**	**Nil**	**Nil**	**[3] . . .**	**[4] . . .**	**[5] . . .**	**[6] . . .**

[1] Before extraord. item [2] 2-for-1 stk. split, 7/3/96 [3] 2-for-1 stk. split, 1/7/94 [4] 3-for-2 stk. split, 1/15/93 [5] 3-for-2 stk. split, 6/26/91 [6] 3-for-2 stk. split, 7/17/90

ANNUAL FINANCIAL DATA

	1996	1995	1994	1993	1992	1991	1990
RECORD OF EARNINGS (IN MILLIONS):							
Total Revenues	4,485.1	3,639.9	2,220.8	1,144.7	800.8	263.4	154.4
Costs and Expenses	6,025.9	2,652.6	1,987.2	866.6	715.8	205.2	118.3
Depreciation & Amort	303.3	311.3	163.8	79.9	53.9	15.4	9.4
Operating Income	d1,844.1	676.0	69.7	198.2	31.1	42.8	26.7
Inc Fr Cont Opers Bef Income Taxes	d2,059.4	438.8	d48.3	175.5	8.2	31.1	17.6
Income Taxes	129.5	171.1	73.8	71.3	8.4	13.4	7.8
Net Income	[1] d2,188.9	267.7	d122.2	104.2	[2] d0.2	17.7	9.8
Aver. Shs. Outstg. (000)	397,890	386,898	315,610	186,944	194,836	83,642	74,374
[1] Before extra. item dr$24,434,000. [2] Before extra. item dr$5,800,000.							
BALANCE SHEET (IN MILLIONS):							
Cash and Cash Equivalents	995.2	41.7	20.3	6.2	4.1	4.1	1.1
Receivables, Net	1,012.5	563.2	532.9	277.6	160.0	50.5	20.9
Gross Property	4,282.6	2,056.4	944.3	525.8	357.1	74.1	41.6
Accumulated Depreciation	385.5	487.1	317.6	181.5	143.9	17.7	9.4
Long-Term Debt	4,803.6	2,278.4	788.0	526.0	333.7	150.5	93.9
Net Stockholders' Equity	12,960.0	2,187.3	1,827.2	1,621.7	343.0	100.1	39.4
Total Assets	19,862.0	6,634.6	3,430.2	2,514.5	869.6	337.3	168.5
Total Current Assets	2,296.1	654.8	589.4	322.0	178.2	56.0	22.6
Total Current Liabilities	1,910.0	1,978.8	710.7	309.0	164.1	72.0	28.4
Net Working Capital	386.1	d1,324.0	d121.2	13.0	14.1	d16.1	d5.8
Year End Shs Outstg (000)	885,080	386,486	319,286	238,510	199,040	85,362	70,726
STATISTICAL RECORD:							
Operating Profit Margin %	. . .	18.6	3.1	17.3	3.9	16.2	17.3
Return on Equity %	. . .	12.2	. . .	6.4	. . .	17.7	24.8
Return on Assets %	. . .	4.0	. . .	4.1	. . .	5.3	5.8
P/E Ratio	. . .	27.7-14.8	. . .	30.8-23.5	. . .	. . .	. . .
Price Range	28⅞-16¼	18-9⅝	14¾-7	13¼-10⅛	. . .	. . .	. . .

Statistics are as originally reported.

OFFICERS:
J.Q. Crowe, Chmn.
J.W. Sidgmore, Vice-Chmn. & C.O.O.
B.J. Ebbers, Pres. & C.E.O.
S.D. Sullivan, C.F.O. & Sec.

INCORPORATED: DE, 1972

PRINCIPAL OFFICE: 515 East Amite Street, Jackson, MS 39201-2702

TELEPHONE NUMBER: (601) 360-8600

NO. OF EMPLOYEES: 13,000 (approx.)

ANNUAL MEETING: In May

SHAREHOLDERS: 8,754

INSTITUTIONAL HOLDINGS:
No. of Institutions: 323
Shares Held: 249,646,019

REGISTRAR(S): First Union National Bank of N.C., Charlotte, NC

TRANSFER AGENT(S): First Union National Bank of N.C., Charlotte, NC

WORTHINGTON INDUSTRIES, INC.

YIELD 2.6%
P/E RATIO 19.8

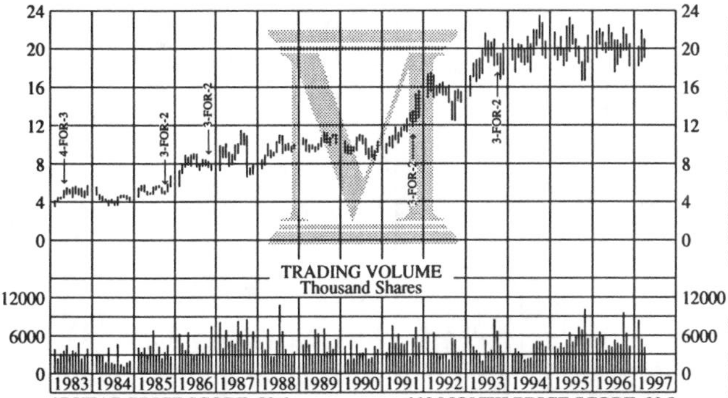

INTERIM EARNINGS (Per Share):

Qtr.	Aug.	Nov.	Feb.	May
1993-94	0.18	0.18	0.22	0.29
1994-95	0.28	0.31	0.32	0.38
1995-96	0.24	0.29	0.23	0.25
1996-97	0.22	0.23	0.23	...

INTERIM DIVIDENDS (Per Share):

Amt.	Decl.	Ex.	Rec.	Pay.
0.12Q	5/16/96	5/30/96	6/3/96	6/21/96
0.12Q	8/16	8/29	9/3	9/27
0.12Q	11/15	12/3	12/5	12/30
0.12Q	2/17/97	2/27/97	3/3/97	3/27/97

Indicated div.: $0.48

TRADING VOLUME
Thousand Shares

1983 | 1984 | 1985 | 1986 | 1987 | 1988 | 1989 | 1990 | 1991 | 1992 | 1993 | 1994 | 1995 | 1996 | 1997

7 YEAR PRICE SCORE 82.6   **12 MONTH PRICE SCORE 90.8**

NYSE COMPOSITE INDEX=100

CAPITALIZATION (5/31/96):

	($000)	(%)
Long-Term Debt	298,742	28.4
Deferred Income Tax	112,662	10.7
Common & Surplus	639,540	60.9
Total	1,050,944	100.0

RECENT DEVELOPMENTS: On 4/16/97, the Company announced the start-up of its 400,000 ton hot dipped galvanizing line in Delta, Ohio. In February, WTHG acquired Gerstenslager Co., an automotive body panel maker, for $113.0 million of WTHG common stock. For the three months ended 2/28/97, net earnings fell slightly to $21.8 million from $22.2 million in the corresponding quarter a year earlier. Net sales climbed 25.9% to $486.6 million from $386.5 million the previous year. Earnings were negatively affected by weak results from WTHG's metal framing business and the Malvern steel facility, partially offset by improved results from the Company's steel processing, automotive body panel, cylinders, plastics and joint venture businesses. For the nine months ended 2/28/97, net earnings rose 7.9% to $66.4 million from $61.6 million the year before. Net sales totaled $1.38 billion, up 24.1% compared with $1.11 billion the prior year.

BUSINESS

WORTHINGTON INDUSTRIES, INC., is a manufacturer of metal and plastic products. The Company is comprised of three segments: (1) Processed Steel Products processes flat-rolled steel coils to customer specifications, and also manufactures low pressure cylinders and suspended ceiling systems; (2) Custom Products makes injection molded plastic parts and precision metal components; and (3) Cast Products produces and machines a wide variety of rail car and industrial steel castings as well as undercarriages for mass transit cars. The Company operates 64 manufacturing facilities in 22 states and seven countries.

ANNUAL EARNINGS AND DIVIDENDS PER SHARE

	5/31/96	5/31/95	5/31/94	5/31/93	5/31/92	5/31/91	5/31/90
Earnings Per Share	1.01	1.29	0.94	0.74	0.63	0.50	③ 0.61
Dividends Per Share	0.43	0.39	① 0.34	0.32	② 0.275	0.258	0.218
Dividend Payout %	42.6	30.2	36.2	43.2	43.7	51.6	35.7

① 3-for-2 stk. split, 10/25/93 ② 3-for-2 stk. split, 10/28/91 ③ Before disc. oper.

ANNUAL FINANCIAL DATA

RECORD OF EARNINGS (IN MILLIONS):

Total Revenues	1,477.8	1,483.6	1,285.1	1,115.7	974.2	874.9	915.9
Costs and Expenses	1,312.5	1,295.6	1,133.3	977.9	856.1	776.3	803.3
Depreciation & Amort	39.2	34.1	32.4	29.2	26.9	23.8	20.8
Operating Profit	126.1	153.8	119.4	177.3	153.6	132.3	147.0
Inc Fr Cont Opers Bef Income Taxes	147.8	186.7	135.6	105.1	87.2	70.0	87.6
Income Taxes	56.5	70.0	50.8	38.9	31.6	25.4	32.4
Net Income	91.3	116.7	84.9	66.2	55.5	44.6	① 55.2
Aver. Shs. Outstg. (000)	90,812	90,730	90,378	89,699	88,989	88,877	90,101

① Before disc. oper dr$2,022,000.

BALANCE SHEET (IN MILLIONS):

Cash and Cash Equivalents	19.0	2.0	13.3	17.6	6.0	9.0	50.0
Receivables, Net	225.0	216.4	189.7	168.9	150.2	126.1	129.3
Inventories	208.0	200.9	184.9	159.5	138.2	124.7	120.3
Gross Property	793.3	589.3	531.5	488.9	464.9	425.3	365.7
Accumulated Depreciation	280.9	254.4	224.0	195.5	171.4	150.0	130.0
Long-Term Debt	298.7	53.5	54.1	55.6	57.3	59.0	42.5
Net Stockholders' Equity	639.5	590.3	503.9	433.1	388.7	355.0	344.4
Total Assets	1,220.1	917.0	798.6	686.1	622.4	563.8	560.6
Total Current Assets	476.0	451.9	413.1	364.0	311.2	275.7	312.9
Total Current Liabilities	151.3	179.2	180.5	147.0	130.9	107.4	133.3
Net Working Capital	324.8	272.7	232.6	217.1	180.4	168.3	179.7
Year End Shs Outstg (000)	90,830	90,840	90,561	90,113	89,308	88,702	88,702

STATISTICAL RECORD:

Operating Profit Margin %	8.5	10.4	9.3	9.7	9.4	8.5	10.0
Book Value Per Share	6.32	6.50	5.56	4.81	4.35	4.00	3.88
Return on Equity %	14.3	19.8	16.8	15.3	14.3	12.6	16.0
Return on Assets %	7.5	12.7	10.6	9.6	8.9	7.9	9.8
Average Yield %	2.2	1.9	1.9	2.6	2.2	2.7	2.1
P/E Ratio	23.0-16.5	18.2-13.6	23.0-16.0	23.8-16.7	24.9-14.4	22.0-16.8	18.6-14.9
Price Range	23¼-16⅝	23½-17½	21⅝-15	17⅝-12⅜	15⅝-9	11-8⅜	11⅜-9⅛

Statistics are as originally reported.

OFFICERS:
J.P. McConnell, Chmn. & C.E.O.
D.H. Malenick, Pres. & C.O.O.
D.G. Barger, Jr., V.P. & C.F.O.

INCORPORATED: OH, Jun., 1955; reincorp., DE, Dec., 1986

PRINCIPAL OFFICE: 1205 Dearborn Dr., Columbus, OH 43085

TELEPHONE NUMBER: (614) 438-3210

NO. OF EMPLOYEES: 12,000 (approx.)

ANNUAL MEETING: In September

SHAREHOLDERS: 10,563

INSTITUTIONAL HOLDINGS:
No. of Institutions: 162
Shares Held: 46,328,899

REGISTRAR(S): First National Bank of Boston, Shareholder Services Division, Boston, MA

TRANSFER AGENT(S): First National Bank of Boston, Shareholder Services Division, Boston, MA

XILINX, INC.

YIELD ...%
P/E RATIO 35.7

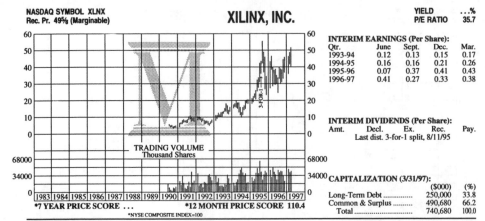

INTERIM EARNINGS (Per Share):

Qtr.	June	Sept.	Dec.	Mar.
1993-94	0.12	0.13	0.15	0.17
1994-95	0.16	0.16	0.21	0.26
1995-96	0.07	0.37	0.41	0.43
1996-97	0.41	0.27	0.33	0.38

INTERIM DIVIDENDS (Per Share):

Amt.	Decl.	Ex.	Rec.	Pay.
Last dist. 3-for-1 split, 8/11/95				

TRADING VOLUME
Thousand Shares

*7 YEAR PRICE SCORE ...   *12 MONTH PRICE SCORE 110.4
*NYSE COMPOSITE INDEX=100

CAPITALIZATION (3/31/97):

	($000)	(%)
Long-Term Debt	250,000	33.8
Common & Surplus	490,680	66.2
Total	740,680	100.0

RECENT DEVELOPMENTS: For the fiscal year ended 3/29/97, net income rose 8.8% to $110.4 million, or $1.39 per share, from $101.5 million, or $1.28 per share, in the corresponding period the previous year. Revenues inched up 1.3% to $568.1 million from $560.8 million a year earlier. The fiscal 1997 results include a charge of $5.0 million related to the write-off of the Company's XC8100 product line. Earnings in fiscal 1996 were hampered by a $19.4 million non-recurring charge for the write-off of in-process technology related to the purchase of NeoCAD, Inc. Operating income slid 4.0% to $159.1 million from $165.8 million the year before. For the quarter ended 3/29/97, net income fell 10.2% to $30.4 million from $33.9 million the prior year. Revenues totaled $151.8 million, up 1.4% versus $149.7 million in the fourth quarter a year ago.

BUSINESS

XILINX, INC. designs, develops and markets complementary metal-oxide-silicon programmable logic devices and related system software. XLNX's programmable logic product lines include field programmable gate arrays (FPGAs) and complex programmable logic devices. These components are standard integrated circuits programmed by manufacturers in the computer, peripherals, telecommunications, networking, industrial control, consumer, instrumentation, and high-reliability/military markets to perform desired logic operations.

ANNUAL EARNINGS AND DIVIDENDS PER SHARE

	3/31/97	3/31/96	3/31/95	3/31/94	3/31/93	3/31/92	3/31/91
Earnings Per Share	1.39	1.28	0.80	0.57	0.38	0.30	0.23
Dividends Per Share	Nil	⑪...	Nil	Nil	Nil	Nil	Nil

⑪ 3-for-1 stk. split, 8/11/95

ANNUAL FINANCIAL DATA

RECORD OF EARNINGS (IN THOUSANDS):

Total Revenues	568,143	560,802	355,130	256,448	177,998	135,827	97,638
Costs and Expenses	⑪ 409,082	372,582	250,841	180,469	127,793	100,132	71,873
Depreciation & Amort	...	22,464	12,241	10,811	8,619	5,558	3,142
Operating Income	159,061	165,756	92,048	65,168	41,586	30,137	22,623
Inc Fr Cont Opers Bef Inc Tax	165,758	170,902	94,845	67,436	43,610	33,758	25,723
Income Taxes	55,382	69,448	35,567	26,157	16,379	12,493	9,791
Net Income	110,376	101,454	59,278	41,279	27,231	21,265	15,932
Aver. Shs. Outstg.	79,675	78,955	74,109	72,237	70,848	71,868	68,652

⑪ Incl. Dep.

BALANCE SHEET (IN THOUSANDS):

Cash and Cash Equivalents	425,847	377,961	122,884	115,645	84,785	81,336	71,762
Receivables, Net	72,248	79,528	43,901	35,942	27,129	21,073	12,839
Inventories	62,367	39,238	25,586	26,597	13,061	9,666	8,952
Gross Property	⑪ 86,580	128,283	70,576	45,105	36,927	27,608	16,837
Accumulated Depreciation	...	45,645	31,336	21,299	16,415	10,776	6,229
Long-Term Debt	250,000	250,000	867	2,195	3,911	4,959	3,813
Net Stockholders' Equity	490,680	368,244	243,971	172,878	123,299	108,662	83,273
Total Assets	847,693	720,880	320,940	226,156	162,899	146,589	111,643
Total Current Assets	601,555	538,706	256,166	194,186	136,789	121,382	99,522
Total Current Liabilities	97,253	102,636	76,102	51,083	35,689	32,968	24,557
Net Working Capital	504,302	436,070	180,064	143,103	101,100	88,414	74,965
Year End Shares Outstg	...	71,933	70,227	68,628	67,242	67,242	67,926

⑪ Net

STATISTICAL RECORD:

Operating Profit Margin %	28.0	29.6	25.9	25.4	23.4	22.2	23.2
Book Value Per Share	...	5.12	3.47	2.52	1.83	1.62	1.23
Return on Equity %	22.5	27.6	24.3	23.9	22.1	19.6	19.1
Return on Assets %	13.0	14.1	18.5	18.3	16.7	14.5	14.3
P/E Ratio	33.5-17.6	43.4-14.2	25.8-12.0	31.8-13.8	27.1-12.7	36.6-13.9	24.1-13.4
Price Range	46½-24½	55½-18⅛	20⅝-9⅝	18⅛-7⅞	10⅜-4⅞	10⅞-4⅛	5⅝-3⅛

Statistics are as originally reported.

OFFICERS:
W.P. Roelantz, C.E.O.
G.M. Steel, V.P.-Fin. & C.F.O.
R.C. Hinckley, V.P.-Strategic Plan. & Sec.

INCORPORATED: CA, Feb., 1984; reincorp., DE, Apr., 1990

PRINCIPAL OFFICE: 2100 Logic Drive, San Jose, CA 95124-3400

TELEPHONE NUMBER: (408) 879-6911

NO. OF EMPLOYEES: 1,201

ANNUAL MEETING: In August

SHAREHOLDERS: 671 (approx.)

INSTITUTIONAL HOLDINGS:
No. of Institutions: 205
Shares Held: 53,980,701

REGISTRAR(S): Boston EquiServe

TRANSFER AGENT(S): Boston EquiServe

ADRs

Company Name	
ABB AB	Sweden
A B Electrolux	Sweden
AB SKF	Sweden
Adecco S A	Switzerland
Akzo Nobel N.V.	Netherlands
Amcor Limited	Australia
Anangel-American Shipholdings Limited	Greece
Anglo American Corporation of South Africa	South Africa
Anglo American Gold Investment Company	South Africa
Atlas Pacific Limited	Australia
Banca Quadrum S.A.	Mexico
Banco de Galicia y Buenos Aires S.A.	Argentina
Biacore International AB	Sweden
Blyvooruitzicht Gold Mining Co	South Africa
Boral Limited	Australia
British Biotech plc	United Kingdom
BT Shipping Limited	United Kingdom
Buffelsfontein Gold Mines, Ltd	South Africa
Burmah Castrol PLC	United Kingdom
Business Objects S.A.	France
Canon Inc.	Japan
Cantab Pharmaceuticals plc	United Kingdom
Carlton Communications Plc	United Kingdom
CBT Group, Plc	Ireland
Central Pacific Minerals N.L.	Australia
Coflexip	France
COLT Telecom Group plc	United Kingdom
Compania Cervecerias Unidas S.A.	Chile
Concordia Paper Holdings, Ltd.	Hong Kong
Cortecs International Limited	Australia
CRH, public limited company	Ireland
CSK Corporation	
Dai'ei, Inc.	
Danka Business Systems	
Dassault S	

ADRs

Nasdaq is a leading financial market for the trading of ADRs in the United States. One hundred thirty-four companies, from 27 countries,[1] list their ADRs on Nasdaq. Among Nasdaq's ADRs are some of the best-known companies in the world, including Japan's Fuji Photo, Nissan and Toyota; France's Moet Hennessy Louis Vuitton; Akzo of the Netherlands; Reuters and Orange plc of the United Kingdom; and Sweden's Volvo, Electrolux and Ericsson Telephone.

What is an ADR?

An American Depositary Receipt (ADR) is a receipt or certificate issued by a U.S. bank that represents title to a specified number of non-U.S. shares of a foreign corporation deposited in a custodian bank in the country of domicile. Since an ADR is evidence of ownership of the underlying shares, it may be freely traded in the U.S. without delivery of the actual non-U.S. shares that it represents.

ADRs began trading in the late 1920s as a means for American investors to invest in foreign securities and to assist non-U.S. companies trying to gain access to U.S. capital markets.

There are two types of ADRs: sponsored and unsponsored. A sponsored ADR is set up when a company decides to promote its ADRs in the U.S. A single depositary bank is chosen, and future ADRs are issued through this bank. The bank typically assumes responsibility for dividend distribution, information dissemination and program administration – with costs borne by the issuer.

An unsponsored ADR program is generally initiated by one or more U.S. brokers because of significant American investor interest in the shares of a non-U.S. corporation. U.S. depositary banks issue the ADRs and receive their compensation from certificate issuance and cancellation fees, which they deduct from dividend payments prior to distribution to ADR holders. In an unsponsored situation, more than one depositary bank may be involved.

The key advantage of an ADR program is that U.S. investors can trade ADRs in the U.S. without the expense and difficulty of having to transfer the underlying shares from the bank in the corporation's country of domicile. Other advantages include: readily available price information; familiarity with the certificate, which conforms to U.S. standards; lower transaction costs; timely dividend distribution in U.S. dollars; and the U.S. system of three-day settlement.

[1] As of December 31, 1996.

ADRs by Company

(as of December 31, 1996)

COMPANY NAME	COUNTRY	SYMBOL
ABB AB	Sweden	ABBBY
A B Electrolux	Sweden	ELUXY
AB SKF	Sweden	SKFRY
Adecco S A	Switzerland	ADECY
Akzo Nobel N.V.	Netherlands	AKZOY
Amcor Limited	Australia	AMCRY
Anangel-American Shipholdings Limited	Greece	ASIPY
Anglo American Corporation of South Africa	South Africa	ANGLY
Anglo American Gold Investment Company	South Africa	AAGIY
Atlas Pacific Limited	Australia	APCFY
Banca Quadrum S.A.	Mexico	QDRMY
Banco de Galicia y Buenos Aires S.A.	Argentina	BGALY
Biacore International AB	Sweden	BCORY
Blyvooruitzicht Gold Mining Co.	South Africa	BLYDY
Boral Limited	Australia	BORAY
British Biotech plc	United Kingdom	BBIOY
BT Shipping Limited	United Kingdom	BTBTY
Buffelsfontein Gold Mines, Ltd.	South Africa	BLGMY
Burmah Castrol PLC	United Kingdom	BURMY
Business Objects S.A.	France	BOBJY
Canon Inc.	Japan	CANNY
Cantab Pharmaceuticals plc	United Kingdom	CNTBY
Carlton Communications Plc	United Kingdom	CCTVY
CBT Group, Plc	Ireland	CBTSY
Central Pacific Minerals N.L.	Australia	CPMNY
Coflexip	France	CXIPY
COLT Telecom Group plc	United Kingdom	COLTY
Compania Cervecerias Unidas S.A.	Chile	CCUUY
Concordia Paper Holdings, Ltd.	Hong Kong	CPLNY
Cortecs International Limited	Australia	DLVRY
CRH, public limited company	Ireland	CRHCY
CSK Corporation	Japan	CSKKY
Dai'ei, Inc.	Japan	DAIEY
Danka Business Systems PLC	United Kingdom	DANKY
Dassault Systemes, S.A.	France	DASTY
De Beers Consolidated Mines	South Africa	DBRSY
Digitale Telekabel AG	Germany	DTAGY
Dr. Solomon's Group, plc	United Kingdom	SOLLY
Driefontein Consolidated, Ltd.	South Africa	DRFNY
Durban Roodepoort Deep, Ltd.	South Africa	DROOY
ECsoft Group plc	United Kingdom	ECSGY
Eidos plc	United Kingdom	EIDSY
Ericsson (LM) Telephone Company	Sweden	ERICY
Ethical Holdings plc	United Kingdom	ETHCY
Flamel Technologies S.A.	France	FLMLY
Free State Consolidated Gold Mining Company	South Africa	FSCNY
Fuji Photo Film Co., Ltd.	Japan	FUJIY
Futuremedia Public Limited Company	United Kingdom	FMDAY
General Cable, PLC	United Kingdom	GCABY
Genset	France	GENXY

ADRs by Company (Continued)

COMPANY NAME	COUNTRY	SYMBOL
Getty Communications, plc	United Kingdom	GETTY
Gold Fields of South Africa Limited	South Africa	GLDFY
Great Central Mines N.L.	Australia	GTCMY
Great Wall Electronic International Limited	United Kingdom	GWALY
Harmony Gold Mining Co., Ltd.	South Africa	HGMCY
Hibernia Foods Public Limited Company	Ireland	HIBNY
Highveld Steel and Vanadium Corporation Limited	South Africa	HSVLY
Insignia Solutions, plc	United Kingdom	INSGY
Instrumentarium Corporation	Finland	INMRY
Instrumentation Laboratory SpA	Italy	ILABY
Israel Land Development Company Limited	Israel	ILDCY
Ito-Yokado Co., Ltd.	Japan	IYCOY
Japan Air Lines Company, Ltd.	Japan	JAPNY
Kirin Brewery Company, Limited	Japan	KNBWY
Kloof Gold Mining Co., Ltd.	South Africa	KLOFY
Learmonth & Burchett Management Systems, Inc.	United Kingdom	LBMSY
Lihir Gold, Limited	New Guinea	LIHRY
London & Overseas Freighters Limited	Bermuda	LOFSY
London International Group plc	United Kingdom	LONDY
London Pacific Group, Limited	United Kingdom	LPGLY
LVMH Moet Hennessy Louis Vuitton	France	LVMHY
Macronix International Co. Ltd.	Taiwan	MXICY
M.A.I.D., plc	United Kingdom	MAIDY
Makita Corp.	Japan	MKTAY
Matav-Cable Systems Media Ltd.	Israel	MATVY
Memtec Limited	Australia	MMTCY
Micro Focus Group PLC	United Kingdom	MIFGY
Mid-States PLC	United Kingdom	MSADY
Minorco	Luxembourg	MNRCY
Mitsui & Company, Ltd.	Japan	MITSY
Multicanal Participacoes, S.A.	Brazil	MPARY
NEC Corporation	Japan	NIPNY
Nera AS	Norway	NERAY
NICE-Systems Limited	Israel	NICEY
Nissan Motor Co., Ltd.	Japan	NSANY
Nord Pacific Limited	Bermuda	NORPY
NYNEX CableComms Group, Plc	United Kingdom	NYNCY
Oce N.V.	Netherlands	OCENY
OLS Asia Holdings, Limited	Hong Kong	OLSAY
Orange, plc	United Kingdom	ORNGY
OzEmail, Limited	Australia	OZEMY
Pacific Dunlop Limited	Australia	PDLPY
Pelsart Resources N.L.	Australia	PELRY
Petsec Energy ltd.	Australia	PSALY
Planning Sciences Intl. plc	United Kingdom	PLNSY
Professional Staff, plc	United Kingdom	PSTFY
P.T. Pasifik Satelit Nusantara	Indonesia	PSNRY
Rank Group Plc. (The)	United Kingdom	RANKY
Reuters Holdings PLC	United Kingdom	RTRSY
Rexam, Plc	United Kingdom	REXMY

COMPANY NAME	COUNTRY	SYMBOL
SAES Getters S.p.A.	Italy	SAESY
Santos, Ltd.	Australia	STOSY
Sanyo Electric Co., Ltd.	Japan	SANYY
Sasol Ltd.	South Africa	SASOY
Saville Systems, plc	Ireland	SAVLY
Sawako Corporation	Japan	SWKOY
Select Appointments Public Limited Company	United Kingdom	SELAY
SELECT Software Tools Limited	United Kingdom	SLCTY
Senetek PLC	United Kingdom	SNTKY
Signet Group plc	United Kingdom	SIGGY
Smallworldwide plc	United Kingdom	SWLDY
Southern Pacific Petroleum N.L.	Australia	SPPTY
St. Helena Gold Mines Limited	South Africa	SGOLY
Stolt-Nielsen S.A.	Luxembourg	STLBY
Swedish Match, AB	Sweden	SWMAY
Telefonos de Mexico, S.A. de C.V	Mexico	TFONY
Telewest Communications plc	United Kingdom	TWSTY
Teva Pharmaceutical Industries Limited	Israel	TEVIY
Thorn plc	United Kingdom	THRNY
Tokio Marine & Fire Insurance Company, Limited	Japan	TKIOY
Toyota Motor Corporation	Japan	TOYOY
Trans-Global Resources N.L.	Australia	TGBRY
Transcom International, Limited	Australia	TRIXY
Tranz Rail Holdings, Limited	New Zealand	TNZRY
Trinity Biotech PLC	Ireland	TRIBY
United News & Media, p.l.c.	United Kingdom	UNEWY
Vaal Reefs Exploration and Mining Company Limited	South Africa	VAALY
Volvo (A B)	Sweden	VOLVY
Wacoal Corp.	Japan	WACLY
Waterford Wedgwood PLC	Ireland	WATFZ
Western Deep Levels Ltd.	South Africa	WDEPY
WPP Group plc	United Kingdom	WPPGY
Xeikon, N.V.	Belgium	XEIKY
Xenova Group plc	United Kingdom	XNVAY

ADRs by Country

(as of December 31, 1996)

COUNTRY	COMPANY NAME	SYMBOL
Argentina	Banco de Galicia y Buenos Aires S.A.	BGALY
Australia	Amcor Limited	AMCRY
Australia	Atlas Pacific Limited	APCFY
Australia	Boral Limited	BORAY
Australia	Central Pacific Minerals N.L.	CPMNY
Australia	Cortecs International Limited	DLVRY
Australia	Great Central Mines N.L.	GTCMY
Australia	Memtec Limited	MMTCY
Australia	OzEmail, Limited	OZEMY
Australia	Pacific Dunlop Limited	PDLPY
Australia	Pelsart Resources N.L.	PELRY
Australia	Petsec Energy ltd.	PSALY
Australia	Santos, Ltd.	STOSY
Australia	Southern Pacific Petroleum N.L	SPPTY
Australia	Trans-Global Resources N.L.	TGBRY
Australia	Transcom International, Limited	TRIXY
Belgium	Xeikon, N.V.	XEIKY
Bermuda	London & Overseas Freighters Limited	LOFSY
Bermuda	Nord Pacific Limited	NORPY
Brazil	Multicanal Participacoes, S.A.	MPARY
Chile	Compania Cervecerias Unidas S.A.	CCUUY
Finland	Instrumentarium Corporation	INMRY
France	Business Objects S.A.	BOBJY
France	Coflexip	CXIPY
France	Dassault Systemes, S.A.	DASTY
France	Flamel Technologies S.A.	FLMLY
France	Genset	GENXY
France	LVMH Moet Hennessy Louis Vuitton	LVMHY
Germany	Digitale Telekabel AG	DTAGY
Greece	Anangel-American Shipholdings Limited	ASIPY
Hong Kong	Concordia Paper Holdings, Ltd.	CPLNY
Hong Kong	OLS Asia Holdings, Limited	OLSAY
Indonesia	P.T. Pasifik Satelit Nusantara	PSNRY
Ireland	CBT Group, Plc	CBTSY
Ireland	CRH, public limited company	CRHCY
Ireland	Hibernia Foods Public Limited Company	HIBNY
Ireland	Saville Systems, plc	SAVLY
Ireland	Trinity Biotech PLC	TRIBY
Ireland	Waterford Wedgwood PLC	WATFZ
Israel	Israel Land Development Company Limited	ILDCY
Israel	Matav-Cable Systems Media Ltd.	MATVY
Israel	NICE-Systems Limited	NICEY
Israel	Teva Pharmaceutical Industries Limited	TEVIY
Italy	Instrumentation Laboratory SpA	ILABY
Italy	SAES Getters S.p.A.	SAESY
Japan	Canon Inc.	CANNY
Japan	CSK Corporation	CSKKY
Japan	Dai'ei, Inc.	DAIEY
Japan	Fuji Photo Film Co., Ltd.	FUJIY
Japan	Ito-Yokado Co., Ltd.	IYCOY

COUNTRY	COMPANY NAME	SYMBOL
Japan	Japan Air Lines Company, Ltd.	JAPNY
Japan	Kirin Brewery Company, Limited	KNBWY
Japan	Makita Corp.	MKTAY
Japan	Mitsui & Company, Ltd.	MITSY
Japan	NEC Corporation	NIPNY
Japan	Nissan Motor Co., Ltd.	NSANY
Japan	Sanyo Electric Co., Ltd.	SANYY
Japan	Sawako Corporation	SWKOY
Japan	Tokio Marine & Fire Insurance Company, Limited	TKIOY
Japan	Toyota Motor Corporation	TOYOY
Japan	Wacoal Corp.	WACLY
Luxembourg	Minorco	MNRCY
Luxembourg	Stolt-Nielsen S.A.	STLBY
Mexico	Banca Quadrum S.A.	QDRMY
Mexico	Telefonos de Mexico, S.A. de C.V.	TFONY
Netherlands	Akzo Nobel N.V.	AKZOY
Netherlands	Oce N.V.	OCENY
New Guinea	Lihir Gold, Limited	LIHRY
New Zealand	Tranz Rail Holdings, Limited	TNZRY
Norway	Nera AS	NERAY
South Africa	Anglo American Corporation of South Africa	ANGLY
South Africa	Anglo American Gold Investment Company	AAGIY
South Africa	Blyvooruitzicht Gold Mining Co	BLYDY
South Africa	Buffelsfontein Gold Mines, Ltd	BLGMY
South Africa	De Beers Consolidated Mines	DBRSY
South Africa	Driefontein Consolidated, Ltd.	DRFNY
South Africa	Durban Roodepoort Deep, Ltd.	DROOY
South Africa	Free State Consolidated Gold Mining Company	FSCNY
South Africa	Gold Fields of South Africa Limited	GLDFY
South Africa	Harmony Gold Mining Co., Ltd.	HGMCY
South Africa	Highveld Steel and Vanadium Corporation Limited	HSVLY
South Africa	Kloof Gold Mining Co., Ltd.	KLOFY
South Africa	Sasol Ltd.	SASOY
South Africa	St. Helena Gold Mines Limited	SGOLY
South Africa	Vaal Reefs Exploration and Mining Company Limited	VAALY
South Africa	Western Deep Levels Ltd.	WDEPY
Sweden	ABB AB	ABBBY
Sweden	A B Electrolux	ELUXY
Sweden	AB SKF	SKFRY
Sweden	Biacore International AB	BCORY
Sweden	Ericsson (LM) Telephone Company	ERICY
Sweden	Swedish Match, AB	SWMAY
Sweden	Volvo (A B)	VOLVY
Switzerland	Adecco S A	ADECY
Taiwan	Macronix International Co. Ltd	MXICY
United Kingdom	British Biotech plc	BBIOY
United Kingdom	BT Shipping Limited	BTBTY
United Kingdom	Burmah Castrol PLC	BURMY
United Kingdom	Cantab Pharmaceuticals plc	CNTBY
United Kingdom	Carlton Communications Plc	CCTVY

ADRs by Country (Continued)

COUNTRY	COMPANY NAME	SYMBOL
United Kingdom	COLT Telecom Group plc	COLTY
United Kingdom	Danka Business Systems PLC	DANKY
United Kingdom	Dr. Solomon's Group, plc	SOLLY
United Kingdom	ECsoft Group plc	ECSGY
United Kingdom	Eidos plc	EIDSY
United Kingdom	Ethical Holdings plc	ETHCY
United Kingdom	Futuremedia Public Limited Company	FMDAY
United Kingdom	General Cable, PLC	GCABY
United Kingdom	Getty Communications, plc	GETTY
United Kingdom	Great Wall Electronic International Limited	GWALY
United Kingdom	Insignia Solutions, plc	INSGY
United Kingdom	Learmonth & Burchett Management Systems, Inc.	LBMSY
United Kingdom	London International Group plc	LONDY
United Kingdom	London Pacific Group, Limited	LPGLY
United Kingdom	M.A.I.D., plc	MAIDY
United Kingdom	Micro Focus Group PLC	MIFGY
United Kingdom	Mid-States PLC	MSADY
United Kingdom	NYNEX CableComms Group, Plc	NYNCY
United Kingdom	Orange, plc	ORNGY
United Kingdom	Planning Sciences Intl. plc	PLNSY
United Kingdom	Professional Staff, plc	PSTFY
United Kingdom	Rank Group Plc. (The)	RANKY
United Kingdom	Reuters Holdings PLC	RTRSY
United Kingdom	Rexam, Plc	REXMY
United Kingdom	Select Appointments Public Limited Company	SELAY
United Kingdom	SELECT Software Tools Limited	SLCTY
United Kingdom	Senetek PLC	SNTKY
United Kingdom	Signet Group plc	SIGGY
United Kingdom	Smallworldwide plc	SWLDY
United Kingdom	Telewest Communications plc	TWSTY
United Kingdom	Thorn plc	THRNY
United Kingdom	United News & Media, p.l.c.	UNEWY
United Kingdom	WPP Group plc	WPPGY
United Kingdom	Xenova Group plc	XNVAY

ABB AB

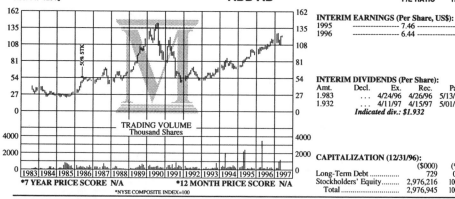

INTERIM EARNINGS (Per Share, US$):

1995	------------------ 7.46 ------------------
1996	------------------ 6.44 ------------------

INTERIM DIVIDENDS (Per Share):

Amt.	Decl.	Ex.	Rec.	Pay.
1.983	...	4/24/96	4/26/96	5/13/96
1.932	...	4/11/97	4/15/97	5/01/97

Indicated div.: $1.932

CAPITALIZATION (12/31/96):

	($000)	(%)
Long-Term Debt	729	0.0
Stockholders' Equity........	2,976,216	100.0
Total	2,976,945	100.0

RECENT DEVELOPMENTS: For the year ended 12/31/96, net income dropped 11.5% to SEK4.1 million from SEK4.7 million in 1995. The Company's share in ABB Group earnings before taxes and after minority interests fell 8.6% to SEK6.7 million from SEK7.3 million the year before. ABB Group is a 50%-owned subsidiary of ABBBY. On 4/15/97, ABB Inc., a subsidiary of ABBBY, was awarded a contract valued at approximately US$16.0 million for the tenth cracking heater project at DuPont Packaging and Industrial Polymers' Orange, Texas facility. On 5/5/97, ABB Inc. and PacifiCorp formed a joint venture named EnergyPact, LLC. EnergyPact will help investor- and publicly-owned utilities and energy companies increase their competitiveness in a deregulated electric industry. On 5/8/97, ABB Lummus Global, a subsidiary of ABBBY, was awarded a turnkey contract valued at approximately US$10.0 million from DSM NV to implement an ethylene furnace project at the DSM Hydrocarbons NAK-III facility in The Netherlands.

BUSINESS

ABB AB, through its 50%-owned company, ABB Asea Brown Boveri Ltd. is engaged in seven business segments, comprised of 37 business areas and 1,000 companies. ABB Asea Brown Boveri Ltd. is the holding company of Asea Brown Boveri Group. The business activities include the production and distribution of nuclear and hydroelectric power, as well as the manufacture and sale of transportation equipment, environmental controls, marine and offshore installations, power generation systems, power transmission networks, low-voltage apparatus, process automation systems, rail transportation systems, semiconductors, tunneling machinery, retarder brakes used in railroad yards, welding and thermal cutting equipment; as well as household appliances. The Company is also engaged in finance and investment activities, including the provision of financial services.

ANNUAL EARNINGS

	12/31/96	12/31/95	12/31/96	12/31/95
	US $		SEK	
Earnings Per Share	6.44	7.46	44.20	49.90

ANNUAL FINANCIAL DATA

RECORD OF EARNINGS (IN THOUSANDS):

Total Revenues	970,007	1,088,465	6,653,000	7,280,700
Costs & Expenses	2,624	3,080	18,000	20,600
Operating Income	967,383	1,085,385	6,635,000	7,260,100
Income Bef Income Tax	971,174	1,089,586	6,661,000	7,288,200
Income Tax	366,979	389,597	2,517,000	2,606,000
Net Income	604,195	699,989	4,144,000	4,682,200

BALANCE SHEET (IN THOUSANDS):

Receivables, Net	437	613	3,000	4,100
Long-Term Debt	729	1,047	5,000	7,000
Stockholders' Equity	2,976,215	2,639,452	20,413,000	17,655,200
Total Assets	2,977,673	2,647,854	20,423,000	17,711,400
Total Current Assets	26,098	32,741	179,000	219,000
Total Current Liabilities	729	1,136	5,000	7,600
Net Working Capital	25,369	31,604	174,000	211,400
Year End Shs Outstg	93,791	93,791	93,791	93,791

STATISTICAL RECORD:

Return on Equity %	20.30	26.52
Return on Assets %	20.29	26.44
Operating Profit Margin %	99.73	99.72
Net Profit Margin %	62.29	64.31
Book Value Per Share	31.73	28.14

Converted at 1996, US$0.1458= 1 Swedish Krona; 1995, US$0.1495= 1 Swedish Krona

OFFICERS:
B. Svedberg, Chmn.
C. Dahlback, Pres.

INCORPORATED: Sweden, 1883

PRINCIPAL OFFICE: P.O. Box 7373, S-10391 Stockholm Sweden

TELEPHONE NUMBER: 46-8-613 65 60

NO. OF EMPLOYEES: N.A.

ANNUAL MEETING: In Apr.

SHAREHOLDERS: 74,737

INSTITUTIONAL HOLDINGS:
No. of Institutions: 50
Shares Held: 3,869,238

AMERICAN DEPOSITARY RECEIPTS:
(Sponsored) Each American Depositary Receipt represents one series B share of par SEK50.

DEPOSITARY BANK(S): Citibank N.A., (212) 657-7800

A B ELECTROLUX

YIELD 2.4%
P/E RATIO 15.7

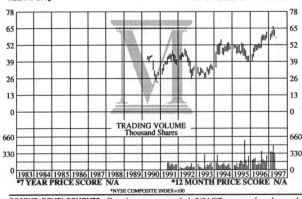

INTERIM EARNINGS (Per Share, US$):

Qtr.	Mar.	June	Sept.	Dec.
1996		3.68		

INTERIM DIVIDENDS (Per Share):

Amt.	Decl.	Ex.	Rec.	Pay.
1.57	...	5/08/96	5/10/96	6/05/96
1.376	...	5/01/97	5/05/97	5/29/97
5.005	...	5/16/97	5/20/97	...

Indicated div.: $1.376

TRADING VOLUME
Thousand Shares

1983 1984 1985 1986 1987 1988 1989 1990 1991 1992 1993 1994 1995 1996 1997
*7 YEAR PRICE SCORE N/A   *12 MONTH PRICE SCORE N/A
*NYSE COMPOSITE INDEX=100

CAPITALIZATION (12/31/96):

	($000)	(%)
Long-Term Debt	2,420,000	42.5
Stockholders' Equity	3,270,003	57.5
Total	5,690,003	100.0

RECENT DEVELOPMENTS: For the quarter ended 3/31/97, net income declined 17.1% to SEK416.0 million compared with SEK502.0 million in the same period of 1996. Sales were SEK28.72 billion, up 4.1% from SEK27.58 billion a year earlier. Operating income slid 3.5% to SEK1.12 billion versus SEK1.16 billion in 1996. Income after financial items slipped 13.8% to SEK777.0 million compared with SEK901.0 million the year before. Income before taxes was SEK694.0 million, down 12.9% from SEK797.0 million in 1996. The decline in earnings was primarily attributable to weaker demand in Europe in most product areas. Although income for Outdoor Products business area improved, results were hampered by a marked decline in demand for Commercial Appliances. The Company attained higher income for white goods on the basis of strong performance improvement in North America and continued good performance in Brazil. In geographical areas, operating income was favorable in North and South America, but declined in Europe and Asia. Asia was negatively affected by the costs of establishing new operations.

BUSINESS

A B ELECTROLUX is the parent company of a group engaged in the manufacture and sale of household appliances, floor-care products and commercial metals. The Household Appliances product business area is engaged in the production and sale of floor-care products, absorption refrigerators, room air-conditioners, sewing machines, as well as kitchen and bathroom cabinets. The Outdoor Product business area is engaged in the production and sale of garden equipment. The Commercial Appliances business area is engaged in the production and sale of food-service equipment for restaurants and institutions; equipment for apartment-house laundry rooms and commercial laundries; vacuum cleaners, as well as wet/dry cleaners for commercial use. The Industrial Products business area is engaged in the development, research, production, sale and distribution of primary aluminum, semi-manufactured aluminum, copper, brass, stainless steel and plastic components. The Company's products are sold under some of the following brand names: Electrolux, Zanussi, AEG, Husqvarna, Elektro Helios, Rex, Tricity-Bendix, Juno, Corbero, Frigidaire, White-Westinghouse, Tappan, Kelvinator, Gibson, Eureka, and Tornado.

ANNUAL EARNINGS

	12/31/96	12/31/95	12/31/96	12/31/95
	---US $---		---SEK---	
Earnings Per Share	3.68	5.61	25.26	37.52

ANNUAL FINANCIAL DATA

RECORD OF EARNINGS (IN MILLIONS):

	12/31/96	12/31/95	12/31/96	12/31/95
Total Revenues	16,038	17,312	110,000	115,800
Costs & Expenses	14,742	15,859	101,114	106,082
Depreciation & Amort	647	659	4,438	4,407
Operating Income	649	794	4,448	5,311
Income Bef Income Tax	474	600	3,250	4,016
Income Tax	172	179	1,182	1,199
Net Income	270	411	1,850	2,748

BALANCE SHEET (IN MILLIONS):

Cash & Cash Equivalents	1,970	2,130	13,510	14,249
Receivables, Net	3,421	3,330	23,462	22,276
Inventories	2,527	2,745	17,334	18,359
Gross Property	8,512	7,812	58,383	52,257
Accumulated Depreciation	4,477	4,032	30,707	26,967
Long-Term Debt	2,420	1,749	16,597	11,696
Stockholders' Equity	3,270	3,185	22,428	21,304
Total Assets	12,477	12,432	85,578	83,156
Total Current Assets	8,257	8,465	56,632	56,620
Total Current Liabilities	5,151	5,301	35,326	35,458
Net Working Capital	3,106	3,164	21,306	21,162
Year End Shs Outstg (000)	73,234	73,234	73,234	73,234

STATISTICAL RECORD:

Return on Equity %	8.26	12.90		
Return on Assets %	N.M.	N.M.		
Operating Profit Margin %	4.05	4.59		
Net Profit Margin %	1.68	2.37		
Book Value Per Share	44.65	43.49		

Converted at 1996, US$0.1458= 1 Swedish Krona; 1995, US$0.1495= 1 Swedish Krona

---

OFFICERS:
M. Treschow, Pres. & C.E.O.
L. Ribohn, Sr. Exec. V.P.
H. G. Backman, Exec. V.P.
M. Palm, Exec. V.P.

INCORPORATED: Sweden, 1919

PRINCIPAL OFFICE: Lilla Essingen, S-105 45, Stockholm Sweden

TELEPHONE NUMBER: 46 8 738 6000

NO. OF EMPLOYEES: 112,140

ANNUAL MEETING: In Apr.

SHAREHOLDERS: 48,300

INSTITUTIONAL HOLDINGS:
No. of Institutions: 26
Shares Held: 971,587

AMERICAN DEPOSITARY RECEIPTS:
(Sponsored) Each American Depositary Receipt represents one series B share of par SEK50.

DEPOSITARY BANK(S): J.P. Morgan, (212) 648-3206

AB SKF

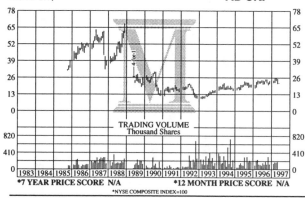

*7 YEAR PRICE SCORE N/A   *12 MONTH PRICE SCORE N/A
*NYSE COMPOSITE INDEX=100

TRADING VOLUME
Thousand Shares

INTERIM EARNINGS (Per Share, US$):

Qtr.	Mar.	June	Sept.	Dec.
1995	------------------	2.72	------------------	
1996	------------------	2.18	------------------	

INTERIM DIVIDENDS (Per Share):

Amt.	Decl.	Ex.	Rec.	Pay.
0.654	...	4/26/96	4/30/96	5/17/96
0.57	...	4/17/97	4/21/97	5/06/97

CAPITALIZATION (12/31/96):

	($000)	(%)
Minority Interests	41,990	1.7
Long-Term Debt	706,547	29.5
Stockholders' Equity	1,648,998	68.8
Total	2,397,535	100.0

RECENT DEVELOPMENTS: For the year ended 12/31/96, net income decreased 17.8% to SEK1.69 billion. This compares with SEK2.06 billion a year earlier. Net sales declined 8.5% to SEK33.59 billion from SEK36.70 billion the year before. The drop in sales was largely attributed to changes in currency exchange rates, which had an adverse effect on sales of approximately SEK2.70 billion. Lower volumes and structural changes also contributed to the sales decline. The decline in sales was offset by a 2.5% increase attributed to price and mix effects, which reflect volume shifts among various customer segments with different price levels. Contributing positively to the year-end operating results was a SEK378.0 million gain related to the sale of a Japanese subsidiary, which mainly contained the property where the Company's Tokyo office is located.

BUSINESS

AB SKF is a manufacturer of rolling bearings, seals and special steels. The Company has 54 rolling-bearing production facilities in 20 countries. Bearings is the Company's largest product area, accounting for 87% of 1996 sales. The Seals division has operating facilities in Italy, Germany and Chicago, Illinois, which operate a combined 11 plants in the U.S. and Europe. In addition, the Seals division has three joint-venture companies in Japan, China and Mexico. The Company's special steel company, Ovako Steel, sells slightly more than half of its production to the Company's bearing manufacturing plants. The balance is sold to manufacturers primarily within Western Europe's machinery and automotive sectors.

ANNUAL EARNINGS

	12/31/96	12/31/95	12/31/96	12/31/95
	-------------US $-------------		------------SEK------------	
Earnings Per Share	2.18	2.72	14.97	18.21

ANNUAL FINANCIAL DATA

RECORD OF EARNINGS (IN MILLIONS):				
Total Revenues	4,951	5,502	33,957	36,806
Costs & Expenses	4,329	4,701	29,691	31,446
Depreciation & Amort	203	203	1,392	1,360
Operating Income	419	598	2,874	4,000
Income Bef Income Tax	352	507	2,412	3,389
Income Tax	102	194	701	1,301
Minority Interests	3	4	19	30
Net Income	247	308	1,692	2,058
BALANCE SHEET (IN MILLIONS):				
Cash & Cash Equivalents	305	433	2,091	2,897
Receivables, Net	953	985	6,534	6,587
Inventories	1,382	1,341	9,476	8,972
Gross Property	4,010	3,862	27,505	25,834
Accumulated Depreciation	2,178	2,175	14,940	14,548
Long-Term Debt	707	685	4,846	4,584
Stockholders' Equity	1,649	1,513	11,310	10,122
Total Assets	4,926	4,933	33,784	32,995
Total Current Assets	2,758	2,862	18,919	19,145
Total Current Liabilities	1,305	1,372	8,950	9,174
Net Working Capital	1,453	1,491	9,969	9,971
Year End Shs Outstg (000)	113,000	113,000	113,000	113,000
STATISTICAL RECORD:				
Return on Equity %	14.96	20.33		
Return on Assets %	5.01	6.24		
Operating Profit Margin %	8.46	10.87		
Net Profit Margin %	4.98	5.59		
Book Value Per Share	14.59	13.39		

Converted at 1996, US$0.1458= 1 Swedish Kronor; 1995, US$0.1495= 1 Swedish Kronor

OFFICERS:
A. Scharp, Chmn.
P. Augustsson, Pres. & C.E.O.
T. Bertilsson, Fin.
K. Thoren, Bus. Dev.

INCORPORATED: N/A

PRINCIPAL OFFICE: SE-415 50 Gothenburg
Sweden

TELEPHONE NUMBER: +46-31-337 10 00

NO. OF EMPLOYEES: 43,123

ANNUAL MEETING: In Apr.

SHAREHOLDERS: 35,472

INSTITUTIONAL HOLDINGS:
No. of Institutions: 16
Shares Held: 1,487,720

AMERICAN DEPOSITARY RECEIPTS: (Sponsored) Each American Depositary Receipt represents one unrestricted ordinary B share of par SEK12.50.

DEPOSITARY BANK(S): Citibank N.A., (212) 657-7800

ADECCO S A

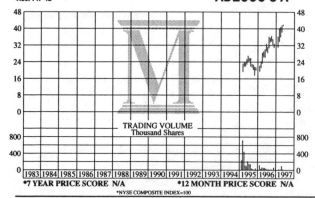

INTERIM EARNINGS (Per Share, US$):

1996 ---------------- d0.87 ----------------

INTERIM DIVIDENDS (Per Share):

Amt.	Decl.	Ex.	Rec.	Pay.
	No dividends paid.			

CAPITALIZATION (12/31/96):

	($000)	(%)
Long-Term Debt	94,490	5.0
Stockholders' Equity........	1,781,365	95.0
Total	1,875,855	100.0

RECENT DEVELOPMENTS: For the year ended 12/31/96, the Company reported a net loss from continuing operations of SFr15.08 million versus income from continuing operations of SFr115.6 million in 1995. Net service revenues advanced to SFr6.39 billion from FFr4.16 billion a year earlier. Results in 1996 included amortization of goodwill of SFr191.8 million (versus SFr2.8 million in 1995) and restructuring costs of SFr21.3 million. In August 1996, Adia and Ecco SA consummated the merger contemplated by the exchange offer agreement dated 5/8/96. Upon consummation of the merger, all of the outstanding shares of the common stock of Ecco were exchanged for 1.028 shares of Adia's common stock, or were purchased at a price of FFr1,720 per share. Pursuant to the exchange offer agreement the cash alternative was limited to 10% of the outstanding Ecco shares, excluding the shares held by Ecco's main shareholder. In connection with the merger, Adia changed its name from Adia SA to Adecco SA.

BUSINESS

ADECCO SA is an international personnel service corporation, providing business solutions for companies at the local, regional, and global levels. The Company was formed in September, 1996 by the merger of Adia SA of Switzerland, and the French company, Ecco SA. Swiss-based Adecco now has over 2,500 office in 40 countries worldwide, and employs approximately 1,500,000 temporary associates each year. The Company offers specialized services under separate brand names to better serve clients, to recruit professional personnel within each category, and to maximize market penetration. Specialty brands include "Accountants on Call," which specializes in temporary and full-time placement of clerical accounting assistants; "Lee Hecht Harrison," an outplacement and career management firm; and "Ajilon," which offers consultants in systems planning, enterprise and process modeling, testing and installation, operations configuration support, software and system maintenance for numerous industries.

ANNUAL EARNINGS

	12/31/96	12/31/95	12/31/96	12/31/95
	US$		SFr	
Earnings Per Share [1]	d0.87	10.00	d1.17	11.54
[1] From cont. opers.				

ANNUAL FINANCIAL DATA

RECORD OF EARNINGS (IN THOUSANDS):

	12/31/96	12/31/95	12/31/96	12/31/95
Total Revenues	4,735,980	3,606,738	6,386,165	4,160,501
Costs & Expenses	4,550,623	3,437,633	6,136,223	3,965,432
Depreciation & Amort.	142,254	2,405	191,820	2,774
Operating Income	43,103	166,701	58,122	192,295
Income Bef Income Tax	82,799	183,766	111,649	211,981
Income Tax	85,734	67,875	115,607	78,296
Minority Interests	8,251	15,652	11,126	18,055
Income from Continuing Opers	d11,186	100,240	d15,084	115,630
Net Income from Discontinued Opers	2,949	12,131	3,977	13,993
Net Income	8,237	112,370	d11,107	129,623
Average Shares Outstg	12,861	10,020	12,861	10,020

BALANCE SHEET (IN THOUSANDS):

Cash & Cash Equivalents	476,669	552,809	642,757	637,685
Receivables, Net	1,163,972	787,286	1,569,541	908,162
Gross Property	293,435	107,655	395,678	124,184
Accumulated Depreciation	170,768	65,018	230,270	75,001
Long-Term Debt	94,490	65,454	127,414	75,504
Stockholders' Equity	1,781,365	599,129	2,402,056	691,117
Total Assets	3,617,249	1,638,458	4,877,628	1,890,020
Total Current Assets	1,802,592	1,391,800	2,430,680	1,605,491
Total Current Liabilities	1,586,071	826,734	2,138,715	953,667
Net Working Capital	216,521	565,066	291,965	651,824
Year End Shs Outstg	16,518	10,020	16,518	10,020

STATISTICAL RECORD:

Return on Equity %	...	16.73		
Return on Assets %	...	6.12		
Operating Profit Margin %	0.91	4.62		
Net Profit Margin %	...	2.78		
Book Value Per Share	107.84	59.79		

Converted at 1996, US$0.7416= 1 Swiss franc; 1995, US$0.8669= 1 Swiss franc

OFFICERS:
P. Foriel-Destezet, Co-Chmn.
K. J. Jacobs, Co-Chmn.
P. Beauviala, Vice-Chmn.
J. P. Bowmer, C.E.O.

INCORPORATED: N/A

PRINCIPAL OFFICE: Rue de Langallerie 11, Case Postale 2 1000 Lausanne 4 Switzerland

TELEPHONE NUMBER: 41-21-321-66-66

NO. OF EMPLOYEES: 10,000 (permanent)

ANNUAL MEETING: N/A

SHAREHOLDERS: N/A

INSTITUTIONAL HOLDINGS:
No. of Institutions: 7
Shares Held: 465,582

AMERICAN DEPOSITARY RECEIPTS: (Sponsored) Eight American Depositary Receipt represents one common share of par SFr10.

DEPOSITARY BANK(S): J.P. Morgan, (212)648-3206

AKZO NOBEL N.V.

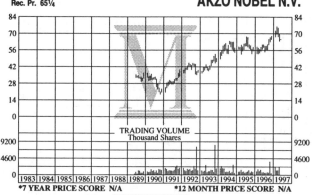

INTERIM EARNINGS (Per Share, US$):

Qtr.	Mar.	June	Sept.	Dec.
1994		9.55		
1995		11.50		
1996		9.61		

INTERIM DIVIDENDS (Per Share):

Amt.	Decl.	Ex.	Rec.	Pay.
1.351	...	4/23/96	4/25/96	5/20/96
0.439	...	11/7	11/12	12/3
1.56	...	4/24/97	4/28/97	5/19/97

Indicated div.: $3.12

TRADING VOLUME
Thousand Shares

*7 YEAR PRICE SCORE N/A   *12 MONTH PRICE SCORE N/A

*NYSE COMPOSITE INDEX=100

CAPITALIZATION (12/31/96):

	($000)	(%)
Minority Interests	d123,308	-2.4
Long-Term Debt	1,112,879	22.3
Stockholders' Equity	3,990,924	80.1
Total	4,980,495	100.0

RECENT DEVELOPMENTS: For the year ended 12/31/96, net income was NLG1.32 billion compared with income before extraordinary items of NLG1.31 billion a year earlier. Net sales rose 4.4% to NLG22.44 billion from NLG21.49 billion the previous year. The sales increase was largely due to a 3.0% positive currency translation effect. Sales volumes were 1.0% higher, while average selling prices were virtually unchanged from 1995. Sales from the Pharma Group were up 4.7% to NLG3.95 billion compared

with NLG3.77 billion last year. Pharma operating income grew as lower results of oral contraceptives were more than offset by higher contributions from other areas. Coatings Group sales of NLG7.44 billion were 8.7% higher than the previous year's sales of NLG6.84 billion, primarily reflecting positive translation and merger effects. Sales of Chemicals grew 4.8% to NLG7.70 billion, fueled by a 2.0% increase in volumes and the currency translation effects of 4.0%.

BUSINESS

AKZO NOBEL N.V. is a holding company. The Company's operations are carried out in business units clustered in four groups on the basis of affinity between activities: Pharma, Coatings, Chemicals and Fibers. The Pharma business has a broad range of products, including oral contraceptives, fertility drugs, antidepressants, muscle relaxants, diagnostic test systems, nonprescription drugs and veterinary products. Regarding the Coatings business, the Company is a producer of paints, finishes and resins for industrial applications, professional uses and the do-it-yourself sector. The Company also supplies to the adhesives, impregnated paper, ink, toner and associated products, and polymer markets. In the Chemicals business, the Company is a producer of specialty, functional and bulk chemicals. Chemicals business products include catalysts and additives for the manufacturing of polymers and elastomers; catalysts for the oil refining, sufactant and intermediates; bleaching chemicals; salt; chlorine; and alkali products. The Company supplies fibers for industrial and textile uses, membranes, nonwovens and other industrial products.

ANNUAL EARNINGS

	12/31/96	12/31/95	12/31/96	12/31/95
	----US $----		----Guilders----	
Earnings Per Share	9.61	11.50	18.54	18.49

ANNUAL FINANCIAL DATA

RECORD OF EARNINGS (IN MILLIONS):

Total Revenues	11,265	13,363	22,438	21,488
Costs & Expenses	10,572	12,136	20,407	19,515
Operating Income	1,052	1,227	2,031	1,973
Income Bef Income Tax	916	1,065	1,768	1,713
Income Tax	263	308	507	495
Eq. Earnings in Affils.	47	85	91	137
Minority Interests	18	27	34	43
Net Income	683	816	1,318	1,312
Net Extraordinary Items	...	1	...	2
BALANCE SHEET (IN MILLIONS):				
Cash & Cash Equivalents	462	435	891	699
Receivables, Net	2,262	2,613	4,366	4,202
Inventories	2,009	2,259	3,878	3,632
Gross Property	10,614	11,582	20,486	18,624
Accumulated Depreciation	5,699	6,309	11,000	10,145
Long-Term Debt	1,113	1,690	2,148	2,718
Stockholders' Equity	3,991	4,108	7,703	6,605
Total Assets	10,573	11,557	20,407	18,583
Total Current Assets	4,733	5,307	9,135	8,533
Total Current Liabilities	3,516	3,532	6,787	5,680
Net Working Capital	1,216	1,775	2,348	2,853
Year End Shs Outstg (000)	71,165	71,080	71,165	71,080
STATISTICAL RECORD:				
Return on Equity %	17.11	19.86		
Return on Assets %	6.46	7.06		
Operating Profit Margin %	9.05	9.18		
Net Profit Margin %	5.88	6.11		
Book Value Per Share	56.08	57.79		

Converted at 1996, US$0.5181= 1 Netherlands guilder; 1995, US$0.6219= 1 Netherlands guilder

OFFICERS:
C. J. van Lede, Chmn.
A. G. Vermeeren, Deputy Chmn.
B. C. Beusmans, Sec.

INCORPORATED: May, 1911

PRINCIPAL OFFICE: Velperweg 76, NL 6824 BM Arnhem Netherlands

TELEPHONE NUMBER: +31 26 366 4433

NO. OF EMPLOYEES: 70,700

ANNUAL MEETING: In Apr.

SHAREHOLDERS: N/A

INSTITUTIONAL HOLDINGS:
No. of Institutions: 60
Shares Held: 4,867,771

AMERICAN DEPOSITARY RECEIPTS: (Sponsored) Each American Depositary Receipt represents one-half of a common share of par NLG 20. ADRs split 2-for-1 in Feb. 1989.

DEPOSITARY BANK(S): J.P. Morgan, (212) 648-3206

AMCOR LTD.

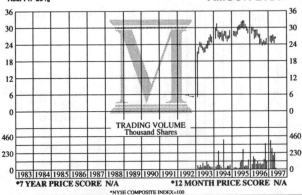

*7 YEAR PRICE SCORE N/A   *12 MONTH PRICE SCORE N/A
*NYSE COMPOSITE INDEX=100

TRADING VOLUME
Thousand Shares

INTERIM EARNINGS (Per Share, US$):

Qtr.	Sept.	Dec.	Mar.	June
1995-96		------------ 0.46 ------------		
1996-97	------ 0.22 ------		...	...

INTERIM DIVIDENDS (Per Share):

Amt.	Decl.	Ex.	Rec.	Pay.
0.601	...	9/25/95	9/27/95	10/27/95
0.565	...	3/27/96	3/27/96	4/26/96
0.631	...	9/23	9/25	10/25
0.529	...	3/21/97	3/25/97	4/25/97

Indicated Div.:$1.06

CAPITALIZATION (6/30/96):

	($000)	(%)
Minority Interests	28,193	0.7
Long-Term Debt	1,076,749	27.1
Stockholders' Equity	2,658,443	66.8
Deferred Income Tax	214,358	5.4
Total	3,977,743	100.0

RECENT DEVELOPMENTS: For the six months ended 12/31/96, income was $140.6 million before an extraordinary charge compared with net income of $213.5 million for the same period in 1995. Net sales were $3.16 billion, down 2.3% from $3.23 billion in the corresponding 1995 period. Operating profit was $202.6 million compared with $306.9 million in the 1995 period, a decrease of 34.0%. Results were negatively affected by strong competitive pressure on prices and margins in the Australian and New Zealand packaging businesses. In addition, international paper prices remained low compared with the very high levels of the previous year and several businesses continued to incur losses.

BUSINESS

AMCOR LTD. and its subsidiaries are engaged in packaging, forest products, tissue and personal care products and international trading. Through the Containers Packaging division, the Company is engaged in the production of aluminum, steel and aerosol cans. Through the Amcor Fibre Packaging division, the Company sellls corrugated packaging for fresh and processed food, beverages, household products and a range of industrial uses. Through the Amcor Paper Group division, the Company is engaged in the production of container materials for fibre boxes and paper sacks; plasterboard liners for the building industry and cartonboards for packaging food and household products.

ANNUAL EARNINGS

	6/30/96	6/30/95	6/30/96	6/30/95
	------------US $------------		------------A$------------	
Earnings Per Share	0.46	0.48	0.58	0.67

ANNUAL FINANCIAL DATA

RECORD OF EARNINGS (IN THOUSANDS):

	6/30/96	6/30/95	6/30/96	6/30/95
Total Revenues	5,353,425	4,758,042	6,798,000	6,704,300
Income Bef Income Tax	392,805	407,155	498,800	573,700
Income Tax	125,843	146,766	159,800	206,800
Minority Interests	158	5,110	200	7,200
Net Income	280,350	285,725	356,000	402,600
Average Shares Outstg	618,700	601,200	618,700	601,200

BALANCE SHEET (IN THOUSANDS):

Cash & Cash Equivalents	98,595	67,989	125,200	95,800
Receivables, Net	876,724	848,943	1,113,300	1,196,200
Inventories	724,500	842,201	920,000	1,186,700
Gross Property	4,239,664	3,591,224	5,383,700	5,060,200
Accumulated Depreciation	1,449,079	1,225,084	1,840,100	1,726,200
Long-Term Debt	1,076,749	1,072,995	1,367,300	1,511,900
Stockholders' Equity	2,658,443	2,430,510	3,375,800	3,424,700
Total Assets	5,485,568	5,014,172	6,965,800	7,065,200
Total Current Assets	1,699,819	1,759,133	2,158,500	2,478,700
Total Current Liabilities	1,485,540	1,293,925	1,886,400	1,823,200
Net Working Capital	214,279	465,208	272,100	655,500
Year End Shs Outstg	632,291	613,317	632,291	613,317

STATISTICAL RECORD:

Return on Equity %	10.55	11.76		
Return on Assets %	5.11	5.69		
Operating Profit Margin %	7.33	8.55		
Net Profit Margin %	5.23	6.00		
Book Value Per Share	4.20	3.96		

Converted at 1996, US$0.7875= 1 Australian $; 1995, US$0.7097= 1 Australian $

OFFICERS:
S. D. M. Wallis, Chairman
D. B. Macfarlane, Managing Director
D. E. Meiklejohn, Exec. Dir., Fin. & Admin.
B. D. S. Canning, Gen. Mgr. Commercial

INCORPORATED: Nov., 1926

PRINCIPAL OFFICE: Southgate Tower-East, 40 City Road, South Melbourne Victoria Australia 3205

TELEPHONE NUMBER: 03-9694-9000

NO. OF EMPLOYEES: 25,300

ANNUAL MEETING: In Oct.

SHAREHOLDERS: 120,600

INSTITUTIONAL HOLDINGS:
No. of Institutions: 6
Shares Held: 1,140,085

AMERICAN DEPOSITARY RECEIPTS: (Sponsored) Each American Depositary Receipt represents four ordinary shares of par A$1.00.

DEPOSITARY BANK(S): J.P. Morgan, (212) 648-3206

ANANGEL-AMERICAN SHIPHOLDINGS LTD.

TRADING VOLUME
Thousand Shares

*7 YEAR PRICE SCORE N/A   *12 MONTH PRICE SCORE N/A
*NYSE COMPOSITE INDEX=100

INTERIM EARNINGS (Per Share, US$):

Qtr.	Sept.	Dec.	Mar.	June
1994-95	------------------	0.86	------------------	
1995-96	------------------	1.39	------------------	
1996-97	0.11	0.08	...	...

INTERIM DIVIDENDS (Per Share):

Amt.	Decl.	Ex.	Rec.	Pay.
0.50	...	9/1/95	9/6/95	10/16/95
0.50	...	3/13/96	3/15/96	4/10/96
0.25	...	6/19	6/21	7/10
0.25	...	8/30	9/4	10/4

Indicated div.: $0.50

CAPITALIZATION (6/30/96):

	($000)	(%)
Long-Term Debt	186,132	45.5
Stockholders' Equity	223,041	54.5
Total	409,173	100.0

RECENT DEVELOPMENTS: For the second quarter ended 12/31/96, net income was US$1.3 million. This compares with US$5.9 million in the corresponding quarter a year earlier. Revenue from voyages totaled US$18.8 million, down 28.9% from US$26.4 million in the comparable prior-year period. Operating profit for the period was US$2.8 million, or 14.8% of revenue, compared with US$7.9 million, or 29.9% of revenue, the year before. The second-quarter results reflect the deterioration in dry cargo freight rates from September 1995 through October 1996, which contributed to the decline in operating profit margin. For the six months ended 12/31/96, net income was US$3.0 million compared with US$10.5 million in the corresponding year-earlier period. Revenue from voyages decreased 22.7% to US$39.5 million from US$51.1 million in the comparable period the year before.

BUSINESS

ANANGEL-AMERICAN SHIPHOLDINGS LTD. is a holding company. Through its subsidiaries, the Company acquires and operates oceangoing ships that principally transport dry bulk commodities on a worldwide basis. The Company's fleet consists of multi-purpose, handy-size and cape-size vessels, as well as product tankers.

ANNUAL EARNINGS

	6/30/96	6/30/95	6/30/96	6/30/95
	-----------US $-----------		-----------Cayman $-----------	
Earnings Per Share	1.39	0.86	1.15	0.71

ANNUAL FINANCIAL DATA

RECORD OF EARNINGS (IN THOUSANDS):

Total Revenues	100,114	85,646	82,917	70,934
Costs & Expenses	51,251	45,838	42,447	37,964
Depreciation & Amort	22,400	20,481	18,552	16,963
Operating Income	26,463	18,492	21,917	15,316
Net Income	21,024	12,866	17,413	10,656
Average Shares Outstg	15,983	15,983	15,983	15,983

BALANCE SHEET (IN THOUSANDS):

Cash & Cash Equivalents	72,319	22,612	59,896	18,728
Receivables, Net	2,127	2,820	1,762	2,336
Inventories	999	989	827	819
Gross Property	481,525	486,768	398,811	403,154
Accumulated Depreciation	99,093	94,736	82,071	78,463
Long-Term Debt	186,132	158,234	154,159	131,054
Stockholders' Equity	223,041	217,999	184,728	180,552
Total Assets	460,500	419,310	381,398	347,283
Total Current Assets	78,068	27,278	64,658	22,592
Total Current Liabilities	40,658	28,214	33,674	23,368
Net Working Capital	37,410	d936	30,984	d775
Year End Shs Outstg	15,983	15,983	15,983	15,983

STATISTICAL RECORD:

Return on Equity %	9.95	6.32
Return on Assets %	4.82	3.28
Operating Profit Margin %	26.43	21.59
Net Profit Margin %	21.00	15.02
Book Value Per Share	13.95	13.64

Converted at 1996, US$1.2074= 1 Caymanian $; 1995, US$1.2074= 1 Caymanian $

OFFICERS:
J. A. Angelicoussis, Chmn.
C. F. Kanellakis, Pres.
M. C. Costeletos, V.P.
K. H. Sparkes, Sec.

INCORPORATED: Apr., 1987

PRINCIPAL OFFICE: The Huntlaw Building, P.O. Box 1350, Grand Cayman Cayman Islands

TELEPHONE NUMBER: 301-422 4501

NO. OF EMPLOYEES: N/A

ANNUAL MEETING: In Oct.

SHAREHOLDERS: N/A

INSTITUTIONAL HOLDINGS:
No. of Institutions: 15
Shares Held: 2,331,784

AMERICAN DEPOSITARY RECEIPTS: (Sponsored) Each American Depositary Receipt represents one ordinary share of US$1.

DEPOSITARY BANK(S): The Bank of New York, (212) 250-8500

ANGLO AMERICAN CORP. OF SOUTH AFRICA LTD.

*7 YEAR PRICE SCORE N/A   *12 MONTH PRICE SCORE N/A
*NYSE COMPOSITE INDEX=100

INTERIM EARNINGS (Per Share, US$):
1995-96 ------------------ 4.73 ------------------

INTERIM DIVIDENDS (Per Share):

Amt.	Decl.	Ex.	Rec.	Pay.
0.806	...	6/13/95	6/15/95	8/07/95
0.337	...	12/13	12/15	1/30/96
0.964	...	6/19/96	6/21/96	8/12
0.321	...	12/11	12/13	1/28/97

Indicated div.: 0.642

CAPITALIZATION (3/31/96):

	($000)	(%)
Stockholders' Equity	7,185,325	97.5
Deferred Income Tax	186,139	2.5
Total	7,371,464	100.0

RECENT DEVELOPMENTS: For the year ended 3/31/96, net income increased 30.5% to R4,397 million compared with R3,369 million in 1995. The Company noted that associates' contribution to net income of R6,084 million, representing 78% of net income before taxation, was 39% higher than the prior year largely as a result of much improved operating results from diamonds, industrial interests and international mining finance. Minorco, De Beers/Centenary, Anglo American Industrial Corporation and Mondi all contributed significantly to the improvement. Income from interests in financial services, particularly Southern Life, First National Bank and SA Eagle, was higher. Platinum income was lower, while base metals producers Palobora and Samancor provided significantly higher income. Income from gold and uranium holdings was substantially reduced from the prior year, reflecting the productivity and cost pressures of this sector.

BUSINESS

ANGLO AMERICAN CORPORATION OF SOUTH AFRICA LTD. is a mining finance house. Through its subsidiaries and associated companies, the Company is involved in mining, financial, industrial and commercial enterprises worldwide, but principally in southern Africa. It provides administrative and technical services, and financial support to many of these companies and has investments over a wide range of associated and non-administered companies. The Company has extensive interests in precious metal mining and coal, uranium, diamond, base metal, platinum and other minerals mining and prospecting. The Company is also engaged in steel and heavy engineering, paper, pulp and packaging, timber, chemicals, electronics, motor manufacturing, food, financial services and property.

ANNUAL EARNINGS

	3/31/96	3/31/95	3/31/96	3/31/95
	-------------US $-------------		-------------Rand-------------	
Earnings Per Share	4.73	4.02	18.83	14.45

ANNUAL FINANCIAL DATA

RECORD OF EARNINGS (IN THOUSANDS):

	3/31/96	3/31/95	3/31/96	3/31/95
Total Revenues	① 1,995,533	1,645,378	7,944,000	5,908,000
Costs & Expenses	45,467	42,332	181,000	152,000
Income Bef Income Tax	1,950,066	1,603,046	7,763,000	5,756,000
Income Tax	406,442	305,236	1,618,000	1,096,000
Minority Interests	439,098	359,544	1,748,000	1,291,000
Net Income	1,104,526	938,267	4,397,000	3,369,000

① Includes sale of US real estate, US$1,200,000.

BALANCE SHEET (IN THOUSANDS):

Cash & Cash Equivalents	1,065,590	901,783	4,242,000	3,238,000
Receivables, Net	359,467	373,190	1,431,000	1,340,000
Inventories	93,949	97,754	374,000	351,000
Gross Property	① 1,306,491	1,497,495	5,201,000	5,377,000
Accumulated Depreciation	311,739	343,391	1,241,000	1,233,000
Stockholders' Equity	7,185,325	6,965,285	28,604,000	25,010,000
Total Assets	8,790,995	8,606,764	34,996,000	30,904,000
Total Current Assets	1,519,006	1,372,727	6,047,000	4,929,000
Year End Shs Outstg ②	233,637	233,554	233,637	233,554

① Includes sale of US real estate, US$1,200,000. ② Adjusted for stock split, 2/4/95.

STATISTICAL RECORD:

Return on Equity %	15.4	13.5
Return on Assets %	12.6	10.9
Operating Profit Margin %	. . .	. . .
Net Profit Margin %	55.4	57.0
Book Value Per Share	30.75	29.82

Converted at 1996, US$0.2512= 1 South African Rand; 1995, US$0.2785= 1 South African Rand

OFFICERS:
J. O. Thompson, Chmn.
N. F. Oppenheimer, Deputy Chmn.
W. G. Boustred, Deputy Chmn.
E. P. Gush, Deputy Chmn.

INCORPORATED: South Africa, Sep. 25, 1917

PRINCIPAL OFFICE: 44 Main Street Johannesburg South Africa 2001

TELEPHONE NUMBER: (011) 638-9111
NO. OF EMPLOYEES: N/A
ANNUAL MEETING: In Aug.
SHAREHOLDERS: 15,916
INSTITUTIONAL HOLDINGS:
No. of Institutions: 29
Shares Held: 993,504
AMERICAN DEPOSITARY RECEIPTS: (Unsponsored) Each American Depositary Receipt represents one ordinary share of par R0.10.

DEPOSITARY BANK(S): The Bank of New York, (212) 815-2175; Bankers Trust Co., (212) 250-8500; Citibank N.A., (212) 657-7800

ANGLO AMERICAN GOLD INVESTMENT CO. LTD.

YIELD 4.6
P/E RATIO 13.8

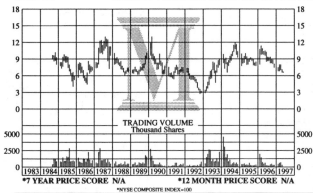

INTERIM EARNINGS (Per Share, US$):

	June	Sept.	Dec.	Mar.
1994-95			6.32	
1995-96			4.91	

INTERIM DIVIDENDS (Per Share):

Amt.	Decl.	Ex.	Rec.	Pay.
0.13	...	5/26/95	6/02/95	7/24/95
0.164	...	11/08/95	11/10/95	1/03/96
0.093	...	5/29/96	5/31/96	7/22/96
0.146	...	10/30/96	11/01/96	12/23/96
0.156	...	4/30/97	5/02/97	6/23/97

Indicated Div.: $0.31

TRADING VOLUME
Thousand Shares

1983 1984 1985 1986 1987 1988 1989 1990 1991 1992 1993 1994 1995 1996 1997

*7 YEAR PRICE SCORE N/A   ***12 MONTH PRICE SCORE N/A**

*NYSE COMPOSITE INDEX=100

CAPITALIZATION (3/31/96):

	($000)	(%)
Stockholders' Equity	383,331	100.0
Total	383,331	100.0

RECENT DEVELOPMENTS: For the year ended 3/31/96, net income declined 13.9% to R472.0 million compared with R548.0 million in the same period of 1995. Total revenue slipped 11.7% to R529.0 from R599.0 million in the prior year. Investment income decreased 24.0% to R263.0 from R346.0 million the year before. Interest earned jumped 17.4% to R54.0 million from R46.0 million a year earlier.

Surplus on the realization on investments inched up 2.4% to R212.0 million versus R207.0 million in 1995. The cost of prospecting during the year was R26.0 million in both 1996 and 1995. Increased expenditure outside South Africa was offset by a decline in expenditure in South Africa. Results, should be favorably affected by strong demand for gold jewelry in the United States.

BUSINESS

ANGLO AMERICAN GOLD INVESTMENT CO. LTD. is an investment holding company, which through its subsidiaries, has interests in gold and gold/uranium mines and prospecting programs, as well as the ownership of mineral rights.

ANNUAL EARNINGS

	3/31/96	3/31/95	3/31/96	3/31/95
	-----US $-----		-----Rand-----	
Earnings Per Share	4.91	6.32	19.55	22.69

ANNUAL FINANCIAL DATA

RECORD OF EARNINGS (IN THOUSANDS):

Total Revenues	132,885	166,822	529,000	599,000
Costs & Expenses	10,299	11,140	41,000	40,000
Operating Income	122,586	155,682	488,000	559,000
Income Bef Income Tax	122,586	155,682	488,000	559,000
Income Tax	4,019	3,064	16,000	11,000
Net Income	118,566	152,618	472,000	548,000

BALANCE SHEET (IN THOUSANDS):

Cash & Cash Equivalents	5,526	5,013	22,000	18,000
Receivables, Net	754	557	3,000	2,000
Stockholders' Equity	383,331	367,063	1,526,000	1,318,000
Total Assets	422,518	414,687	1,682,000	1,489,000
Total Current Assets	70,587	130,617	281,000	469,000
Total Current Liabilities	39,187	47,624	156,000	171,000
Net Working Capital	31,400	82,993	125,000	298,000
Year End Shs Outstg	24,147	26,147	24,147	26,147

STATISTICAL RECORD:

Return on Equity %	30.93	41.58
Return on Assets %	28.06	36.80
Operating Profit Margin %	92.25	93.32
Net Profit Margin %	89.22	91.49
Book Value Per Share	15.87	15.20

Converted at 1996, US$0.2512= 1 South African Rand; 1995, US$0.2785= 1 South African Rand

OFFICERS:
N. F. Oppenheimer, Chmn.

INCORPORATED: Jan., 1937

PRINCIPAL OFFICE: 44 Main Street, Johannesburg, 2001 South Africa

TELEPHONE NUMBER: 011-638-9111

NO. OF EMPLOYEES: N/A

ANNUAL MEETING: In Jun.

SHAREHOLDERS: 3,085

INSTITUTIONAL HOLDINGS:
No. of Institutions: 19
Shares Held: 555,142

AMERICAN DEPOSITARY RECEIPTS: (Unsponsored) Ten American Depositary Receipts represent one ordinary share of par R1.

DEPOSITARY BANK(S): The Bank of New York, (212) 815-2175; Bankers Trust Co., (212) 250-8500; Citibank, (212) 657-7800; DST Systems Inc.

ATLAS PACIFIC LIMITED

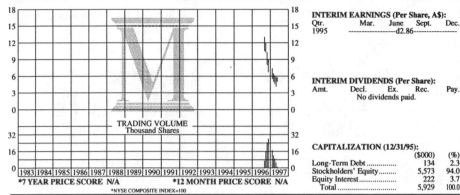

*7 YEAR PRICE SCORE N/A   *12 MONTH PRICE SCORE N/A
*NYSE COMPOSITE INDEX=100

INTERIM EARNINGS (Per Share, A$):

Qtr.	Mar.	June	Sept.	Dec.
1995		d2.86		

INTERIM DIVIDENDS (Per Share):

Amt.	Decl.	Ex.	Rec.	Pay.
	No dividends paid.			

CAPITALIZATION (12/31/95):

	($000)	(%)
Long-Term Debt	134	2.3
Stockholders' Equity........	5,573	94.0
Equity Interest..................	222	3.7
Total	5,929	100.0

RECENT DEVELOPMENTS: For the year ended 12/31/95, the Company incurred a net loss of A$768,000 compared with net income of A$459,000 a year earlier. Revenues were A$681,000 down 42.3% from A$1.2 million in the prior year. The decrease in revenue was due to a reduction in the sale of investment securities during 1995. Contributions to revenue during 1995 were: mineral exploration, 2.0%; share trading, 88.0%; and other, 11.0% of total revenues, respectively in 1995. The Company incurred expenses totaling A$0.7 million related to corporate consulting and public relations services.

BUSINESS

ATLAS PACIFIC LIMITED is engaged in pearl farming. In 1993, the Company invested in the Kupang pearling project located in Indonesia. The Kupang Project operates an oyster hatchery for the purpose of cultivating South Sea pearls. Prior to 1993, the Company prospected for gold and other precious and semi-precious minerals in Australia and New Zealand. The Company has disposed of all of its mining interest except its 75.0% interest in the Forrest Belle/Boudie Rat tenement located in the Eastern Goldfields area of Western Australia. The Company is currently attempting to sell its interest in this tenement. The Company owns a 100.0% interest in both Sharcon Pty. Ltd. and Tansim Pty. Ltd. as well as a 75.0% interest in P.T. Cendana Indopearls, who owns and operates the Kupang project.

ANNUAL EARNINGS

	12/31/95	12/31/94	12/31/95	12/31/94
	US $		A$	
Earnings Per Share	d2.12	1.64	d2.86	2.12

ANNUAL FINANCIAL DATA

RECORD OF EARNINGS (IN THOUSANDS):

Total Revenues	504	915	681	1,180
Income Bef Income Tax	d568	356	d768	459
Net Income	d568	356	d768	459
Average Shares Outstg(000)	26,841	21,676	26,841	21,676

BALANCE SHEET (IN THOUSANDS):

Cash & Cash Equivalents	797	1,503	1,072	1,938
Receivables, Net	428	1	575	1
Gross Property	1,325	615	1,782	793
Accumulated Depreciation	239	73	321	94
Long-Term Debt	134	...	181	...
Stockholders' Equity	5,791	4,701	7,789	6,061
Total Assets	6,013	4,729	8,087	6,098
Total Current Assets	1,225	1,505	1,648	1,940
Total Current Liabilities	87	28	118	37
Net Working Capital	1,138	1,476	1,530	1,903
Year End Shs Outstg(000)	31,283	24,992	31,283	24,992

STATISTICAL RECORD:

Return on Equity %	...	7.6		
Return on Assets %	...	7.5		
Operating Profit Margin %	...	7.5		
Net Profit Margin %	...	38.9		
Book Value Per Share	0.2	0.2		

Converted at 1995, US$0.7435= 1 Australian $; 1994, US$0.7756= 1 Australian $

OFFICERS:
A. A. Trevisan, Chmn.
L. F. Petersen, C.E.O.
T. P. Purchas, Project Manager
B. P. Panos, Sec.

INCORPORATED: Feb., 1987

PRINCIPAL OFFICE: Level 4, South Shore Centre, 83 South Perth Esplanade, South Perth Australia

TELEPHONE NUMBER: N/A

NO. OF EMPLOYEES: 204

ANNUAL MEETING: N/A

SHAREHOLDERS: N/A

INSTITUTIONAL HOLDINGS:
No. of Institutions: 2
Shares Held: 2,026

AMERICAN DEPOSITARY RECEIPTS: Each American Depositary Receipt represents 20 ordinary shares of par A$0.20.

DEPOSITARY BANK(S): The Bank of New York, (212) 815-2175

NASDAQ SYMBOL QDRMY
Rec. Pr. 3⅜

BANCA QUADRUM S.A.

YIELD ...
P/E RATIO N.M.

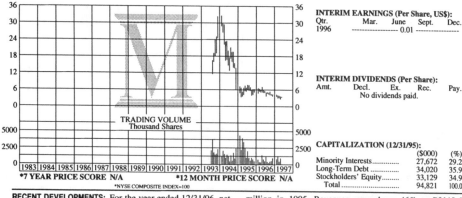

*7 YEAR PRICE SCORE N/A   ***12 MONTH PRICE SCORE N/A**
*NYSE COMPOSITE INDEX=100

INTERIM EARNINGS (Per Share, US$):

Qtr.	Mar.	June	Sept.	Dec.
1996	------------------ 0.01 ------------------			

INTERIM DIVIDENDS (Per Share):

Amt.	Decl.	Ex.	Rec.	Pay.
	No dividends paid.			

CAPITALIZATION (12/31/95):

	($000)	(%)
Minority Interests..............	27,672	29.2
Long-Term Debt	34,020	35.9
Stockholders' Equity........	33,129	34.9
Total	94,821	100.0

RECENT DEVELOPMENTS: For the year ended 12/31/96, net income slipped to P$347,000 compared with P$1.4 million in the corresponding period a year earlier. Revenues were P$550.0 million versus P$627.3 million in 1995. Earnings were pressured by the cost of carrying repossessed property, past due loans and other non-revenue generating assets at market interest rates. For the fourth quarter ended 12/31/96, net income was P$63,000 versus a loss of P$9.1 million in 1995. Revenues were down 46% to P$119.6 million versus P$175.2 million a year earlier. Gross non-performing assets expressed as a percentage of the portfolio declined during the quarter from 16.2% to 14.8%, and the net non-performing asset ratio decreased from 10.5% to 9.6%. Loans past due by more than 60 days declined from 15.6% to 14.1%.

BUSINESS

BANCA QUADRUM S.A. is engaged in the provision of multiple banking services, asset-based financing and credit-related services for small, medium-sized and large companies. Services and products provided include secured and unsecured financing, purchase of accounts receivable, short-term promissory notes, bills of exchange and import-export services. Through its subsidiaries, the Company provides asset-based financing and credit-related services to both industrial companies and individuals, to finance the purchase of transportation equipment, including automobiles, buses and trucks; industrial machinery; office equipment, including furniture and computer equipment; and industrial and commercial real estate, including plants, offices and buildings.

ANNUAL EARNINGS

	12/31/95	12/31/94	12/31/95	12/31/94
	------------US $------------		------------Pesos------------	
Earnings Per Share	d0.07	0.02	d0.52	0.10

ANNUAL FINANCIAL DATA

RECORD OF EARNINGS (IN THOUSANDS):

	12/31/95	12/31/94	12/31/95	12/31/94
Total Revenues	82,764	46,116	636,647	227,847
Costs & Expenses	73,397	36,557	564,590	180,616
Depreciation & Amort	10,285	4,587	79,115	22,661
Operating Income	d918	4,973	d7,058	24,570
Income Bef Income Tax	d1,011	4,973	d7,779	24,570
Income Tax	165	1,083	1,270	5,352
Eq. Earnings in Affils.	. . .	d3,137	. . .	d15,501
Minority Interests	550	253	4,232	1,249
Net Income	d1,727	500	d13,281	2,468

BALANCE SHEET (IN THOUSANDS):

Cash & Cash Equivalents	35,735	16,686	274,884	82,439
Receivables, Net	184,625	184,861	1,420,193	913,345
Gross Property	8,363	8,675	64,328	42,863
Accumulated Depreciation	1,791	1,338	13,774	6,613
Long-Term Debt	34,020	57,253	261,692	282,873
Stockholders' Equity	33,129	45,613	254,839	225,359
Total Assets	263,604	244,820	2,027,725	1,209,584
Total Current Assets	220,360	201,547	1,695,077	995,784
Total Current Liabilities	194,579	140,854	1,496,764	695,918
Net Working Capital	25,781	60,693	198,313	299,866
Year End Shs Outstg	25,537	25,537	25,537	25,537

STATISTICAL RECORD:

Return on Equity %	. . .	1.10		
Return on Assets %	. . .	0.20		
Operating Profit Margin %	. . .	10.78		
Net Profit Margin %	. . .	1.08		
Book Value Per Share	9.98	8.82		

Converted at 1995, US$0.1300= 1 Mexican Peso; 1994, US$0.2024= 1 Mexican Peso

OFFICERS:
M. J. Delmont Macphaee
L. A. Cantu Gottwald, Sec.
L. F. Ahumada Russek
J. R. Bellot Castro

INCORPORATED: Mar., 1993

PRINCIPAL OFFICE: Anillo Periferico Sur 4249 Fracc. Jardines en la Montana, Mexico

TELEPHONE NUMBER: 5-723-9000; 596-9388

NO. OF EMPLOYEES: N/A

ANNUAL MEETING: In Apr.

SHAREHOLDERS: N/A

INSTITUTIONAL HOLDINGS:
No. of Institutions: 7
Shares Held: 551,950

AMERICAN DEPOSITARY RECEIPTS: (Sponsored) Each American Depositary Share represents one Unit, each consisting of one Series C share and one Series L share.

DEPOSITARY BANK(S): The Bank of New York, (212) 815-2175

137

BANCO DE GALICIA Y BUENOS AIRES

YIELD ...
P/E RATIO 4.5

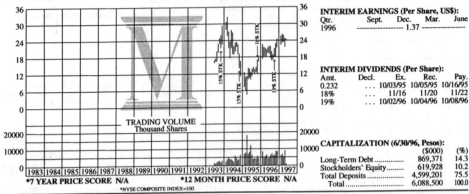

INTERIM EARNINGS (Per Share, US$):

Qtr.	Sept.	Dec.	Mar.	June
1996	----------------	1.37	----------------	

INTERIM DIVIDENDS (Per Share):

Amt.	Decl.	Ex.	Rec.	Pay.
0.232	...	10/03/95	10/05/95	10/16/95
18%	...	11/16	11/20	11/22
19%	...	10/02/96	10/04/96	10/08/96

CAPITALIZATION (6/30/96, Pesos):

	($000)	(%)
Long-Term Debt	869,371	14.3
Stockholders' Equity.........	619,928	10.2
Total Deposits	4,599,201	75.5
Total	6,088,500	100.0

RECENT DEVELOPMENTS: For the third quarter ended 3/31/97, net income was Ps. 28.0 million, 26.7% higher than the Ps. 22.1 million of the corresponding period of fiscal 1995. The improvement in earnings was primarily attributed to higher net financial income and lower income tax, partially compensated by higher administrative expenses and provision for loan losses. The increase in net financial income was the result of an increase of approximately 35% in interest-earning assets, partially offset by a reduction of the financial margin. During the quarter, and following the authorizations granted by the central Bank of Argentina and the Bank of England, a representative office was opened in the City of London.

BUSINESS

BANCO DE GALICIA Y BUENOS AIRES is engaged in commercial and investment banking activities. Services provided include deposits, checking and savings accounts, automatic teller machines (ATMs), debit cards, telephone operation services, electronic banking, letters of credit, credit cards, mortgage financing, foreign currency transactions, investment advisory services, commercial and personal loans, car loans, electronic collections, pension fund management, custody of securities, and travelers' checks. The Company also provides insurance coverage for its customers.

ANNUAL EARNINGS

	6/30/96	6/30/95	6/30/96	6/30/95
	---------------US $-------------		-----------Pesos-----------	
Earnings Per Share	0.30	0.25	0.30	0.25

ANNUAL FINANCIAL DATA

RECORD OF EARNINGS (IN MILLIONS):

Total Revenues	968	841	967	841
Costs & Expenses	856	750	855	750
Income Bef Income Tax	112	90	112	90
Income Tax	35	26	35	26
Net Income	77	64	77	64
Average Shares Outstg (000)	255,765	255,765	255,765	255,765

BALANCE SHEET (IN MILLIONS):

Cash & Cash Equivalents	972	640	971	640
Loan & Other Receivables	6,461	4,627	6,453	4,626
Gross Property	169	166	169	166
Deposits & Other Liabilities	7,120	4,998	7,111	4,997
Stockholders' Equity	620	554	619	554
Total Assets	7,780	5,553	7,771	5,551
Year End Shs Outstg (000)	255,765	255,765	255,765	255,765

STATISTICAL RECORD:

Return on Equity %	12.42	11.55		
Return on Assets %	N.M.	N.M.		
Book Value Per Share	2.42	2.16		

Converted at 1996, US$1.0012= 1 Argentine peso; 1995, US$1.0003= 1 Argentine peso

OFFICERS:
E. J. Escasany, C. E. O.
D. A. Llambias, Sr. Exec. V.P.
E. E. Arrobas, Sr. Exec. V.P.
L. A. Diaz, Chief Planning Off. & Contr.

INCORPORATED: Argentina, Nov. 1905

PRINCIPAL OFFICE: Tte. Gral. Juan D. Peron 407 Buenos Aires Argentina

TELEPHONE NUMBER: (54) 1 329 6000

NO. OF EMPLOYEES: 5,101

ANNUAL MEETING: In Sep.

SHAREHOLDERS: 5,000

INSTITUTIONAL HOLDINGS:
No. of Institutions: 47
Shares Held: 90,575,449

AMERICAN DEPOSITARY RECEIPTS: (Sponsored) Each American Depositary Receipt represents four Class B ordinary shares.

DEPOSITARY BANK(S): The Bank of New York, (212) 815-2175

BIACORE INTERNATIONAL AB

YIELD ...
P/E RATIO 23.77

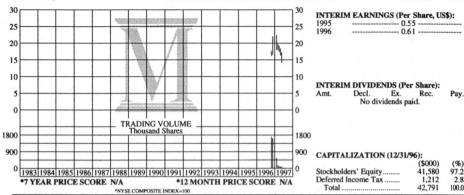

INTERIM EARNINGS (Per Share, US$):
1995 ----------------- 0.55 -----------------
1996 ----------------- 0.61 -----------------

INTERIM DIVIDENDS (Per Share):

Amt.	Decl.	Ex.	Rec.	Pay.
		No dividends paid.		

CAPITALIZATION (12/31/96):

	($000)	(%)
Stockholders' Equity........	41,580	97.2
Deferred Income Tax	1,212	2.8
Total	42,791	100.0

RECENT DEVELOPMENTS: For the year ended 12/31/96, net income was SEK40.7 compared with SEK36.1 million in the corresponding period a year earlier. Net sales were SEK260.4 million, up 25% versus SEK209.0 million in 1995. In North and South America sales rose 62%. Sales in the Asia-Pacific region were favorable, but rose only 9% following very strong sales in the final quarter of 1995 that were largely attributable to a supplementary budget for universities and colleges in Japan during their budget year. In Europe sales advanced 13%. The strengthening of the Swedish krona had an adverse impact on sales and income growth, due to the Company's invoicing being principally in foreign currency, while most costs are incurred in Sweden.

BUSINESS

BIACORE INTERNATIONAL AB and its subsidiaries develop, manufacture and market advanced scientific instruments that employ affinity-based biosensor technology to analyze biomolecular interactions for a wide range of life science applications. BCORY pioneered the development of this technology, which is used for determining the function concentration of biomolecules (substances related to biological processes). The Company's integrated detection systems are designed to measure the rates at which biomolecules associate and dissociate, to determine the presence and concentration of a biomolecule in a given sample, to measure the strength of the interactions between molecules and to localize the binding sites in the interaction.

ANNUAL EARNINGS

	12/31/96	12/31/95	12/31/96	12/31/95
	----------US $----------		----------SEK----------	
Earnings Per Share	0.61	0.55	4.17	3.70

ANNUAL FINANCIAL DATA

RECORD OF EARNINGS (IN THOUSANDS):

Total Revenues	38,102	31,590	261,329	211,303
Costs & Expenses	27,603	21,580	189,320	144,351
Depreciation & Amort	1,060	1,138	7,273	7,613
Operating Income	9,439	8,871	64,736	59,339
Income Bef Income Tax	9,095	7,803	62,380	52,197
Income Tax	3,168	2,413	21,725	16,141
Net Income	5,927	5,390	40,655	36,056

BALANCE SHEET (IN THOUSANDS):

Cash & Cash Equivalents	35,092	1,208	240,683	8,083
Receivables, Net	14,294	12,749	98,039	85,276
Inventories	1,555	1,572	10,663	10,512
Gross Property	17,296	21,376	118,627	142,985
Accumulated Depreciation	6,751	10,440	46,305	69,830
Long-Term Debt	...	6,746	...	45,127
Stockholders' Equity	41,580	7,389	285,183	49,423
Total Assets	61,524	26,465	421,972	177,026
Total Current Assets	50,940	15,529	349,385	103,871
Total Current Liabilities	16,696	9,851	114,515	65,891
Net Working Capital	34,244	5,678	234,870	37,980
Year End Shs Outstg	9,750	9,750	9,750	9,750

STATISTICAL RECORD:

Return on Equity %	14.26	72.95		
Return on Assets %	9.63	20.37		
Operating Profit Margin %	24.77	28.08		
Net Profit Margin %	15.56	17.06		
Book Value Per Share	4.26	0.76		

Converted at 1996, US$0.1458= 1 Swedish Krona; 1995, US$0.1495= 1 Swedish Krona

OFFICERS:
L. Andren, Pres. & C.E.O.
L. Forslund, C.F.O. & Exec. V.P.
C. Ekstrom, Human Resource Mgr.
J. Fineman, Head of Research & Prod.

INCORPORATED: Oct. 1996

PRINCIPAL OFFICE: Rapsgatan 7, S-754 50 Uppsala Sweden

TELEPHONE NUMBER: (011)-46-1867-5700

NO. OF EMPLOYEES: 141

ANNUAL MEETING: N/A

SHAREHOLDERS: 3,572

INSTITUTIONAL HOLDINGS:
No. of Institutions: 15
Shares Held: 964,500

AMERICAN DEPOSITARY RECEIPTS: Each American Depositary Share represents one ordinary share of par value SEK10.

DEPOSITARY BANK(S): J.P. Morgan, (212) 648-3206

BLYVOORUITZICHT GOLD MINING CO. LTD.

YIELD ...
P/E RATIO ...

*7 YEAR PRICE SCORE N/A   *12 MONTH PRICE SCORE N/A

*NYSE COMPOSITE INDEX=100

INTERIM EARNINGS (Per Share, US$):

Qtr.	Sept.	Dec.	Mar.	June
1994-95		d0.27		
1995-96		d0.06		

INTERIM DIVIDENDS (Per Share):

Amt.	Decl.	Ex.	Rec.	Pay.
	No dividends paid.			

CAPITALIZATION (6/30/96):

	($000)	(%)
Stockholders' Equity	51,905	100.0
Total	51,905	100.0

RECENT DEVELOPMENTS: For the fiscal year ended 6/30/96, the Company reported a net loss of R11.5 million (US$2.6 million). This compares with a net loss of R23.8 million (US$6.6 million) a year earlier. Total revenues grew 56.7% to R312.5 million (US$72.2 million) from R199.4 million (US$54.8 million) the year before. The Company's average gold sales price during the year was R46,954 per kilogram (US$378 per ounce) compared with R43,867 per kilogram (US$382 per ounce) the previous year. The Company's Doornfontein mine produced 7.7% more ounces of gold than the prior year, reflecting an increase in tonnage at the expense of grades. The ounces of gold produced from surface operations, however, declined by 8.2% due primarily to a reduction of the recovery grade from tailings material. A larger decline in ounces of gold produced, 30.8%, was reported at the Company's Blyvooruitzicht mine, which was the result of a restructuring of that mine.

BUSINESS

BLYVOORUITZICHT GOLD MIN-ING CO. LTD is engaged in the operations of gold mining on the West Wits Line and has a common boundary with Doornfontein. Silver is recovered as a by-product.

ANNUAL EARNINGS

	6/30/96	6/30/95	6/30/96	6/30/95
	US $		Rand	
Earnings Per Share	d0.06	d0.27	d0.25	d0.99

ANNUAL FINANCIAL DATA

RECORD OF EARNINGS (IN THOUSANDS):

	6/30/96	6/30/95	6/30/96	6/30/95
Total Revenues	72,179	54,827	312,463	199,372
Costs & Expenses	64,955	55,577	281,189	202,098
Depreciation & Amort	2,973	3,017	12,868	10,970
Operating Income	4,251	d3,767	18,406	d13,696
Income Bef Income Tax	d2,903	d10,358	d12,569	d37,667
Income Tax	cr258	cr3,803	cr1,115	cr13,829
Net Income	d2,646	d6,555	d11,454	d23,838
Average Shares Outstg	45,650	24,000	45,650	24,000

BALANCE SHEET (IN THOUSANDS):

Cash & Cash Equivalents	16,384	3,333	70,925	12,120
Receivables, Net	1,848	1,015	8,002	3,691
Inventories	7,928	8,776	34,319	31,913
Gross Property	201,411	95,597	871,911	347,625
Accumulated Depreciation	150,498	61,829	651,505	224,833
Stockholders' Equity	51,905	26,223	224,697	95,355
Total Assets	81,342	48,908	352,131	177,848
Total Current Assets	26,160	13,124	113,246	47,724
Total Current Liabilities	15,933	11,816	68,975	42,969
Net Working Capital	10,227	1,308	44,271	4,755
Year End Shs Outstg	50,602	24,000	50,602	24,000

STATISTICAL RECORD:

Return on Equity %	...	...		
Return on Assets %	...	...		
Operating Profit Margin %	5.90	...		
Net Profit Margin %	...	...		
Book Value Per Share	1.03	1.09		

Converted at 1996, US$0.2310= 1 South African Rand; 1995, US$0.2750= 1 South African Rand

OFFICERS:
R.A.R. Kebble, Chairman
R.J. Drummond, General Mgr.
M.B. Cripps, Financial Dir.

INCORPORATED: June, 1937

PRINCIPAL OFFICE: Randgold House, 5 Press Avenue, Selby Johannesburg South Africa 2025

TELEPHONE NUMBER: (011) 837-0706

NO. OF EMPLOYEES: 4,877

ANNUAL MEETING: In Nov.

SHAREHOLDERS: 7,733 (ADRs)

INSTITUTIONAL HOLDINGS:
No. of Institutions: 11
Shares Held: 704,798

AMERICAN DEPOSITARY RECEIPTS: (Sponsored) Each American Depositary Receipt represents three ordinary shares of par R0.25.

DEPOSITARY BANK(S): Bank of New York, (212) 815-2175

BORAL LIMITED

YIELD 3.8%
P/E RATIO 20.0

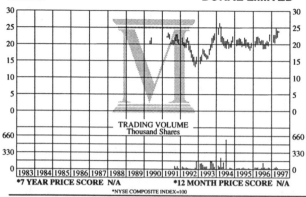

TRADING VOLUME
Thousand Shares

1983|1984|1985|1986|1987|1988|1989|1990|1991|1992|1993|1994|1995|1996|1997
*7 YEAR PRICE SCORE N/A   ***12 MONTH PRICE SCORE N/A**
*NYSE COMPOSITE INDEX=100

INTERIM EARNINGS (Per Share, US$):

Qtr.	Sept.	Dec.	Mar.	June
1995-96	------------------ 0.15 -----------------			

INTERIM DIVIDENDS (Per Share):

Amt.	Decl.	Ex.	Rec.	Pay.
0.628	...	10/05/95	10/10/95	11/10/95
0.662	...	4/19/96	4/23/96	5/24/96
0.465	...	10/08	10/10	11/12
0.457	...	4/04/97	4/08/97	5/12/97

Indicated div.: $0.91

CAPITALIZATION (6/30/96):

	($000)	(%)
Long-Term Debt	1,083,547	32.1
Stockholders' Equity	2,288,900	67.9
Total	3,372,447	100.0

RECENT DEVELOPMENTS: For the half year ended 12/31/96, profit after tax and minority interests but before abnormal declined 20.0% to A$96.0 million compared with A$120.0 million in the prior-year period of 1995. Earnings before interest and tax were A$221.0 million, down 9.8% from A$245.0 million in the corresponding 1995 period. The Company had an abnormal net loss of A$2.7 million result-ing from the sale of the German roof tiles business com-pared with a gain of A$49.5 million in the previous corre-sponding period of 1995 from the sale of the elevators business. The decline in results was primarily attributable to the decline in housing activity, which has squeezed mar-gins even further than previously.

BUSINESS

BORAL LIMITED and its subsidiar-ies are engaged in producing the fol-lowing: Building products: bricks, roof tiles, timber, plasterboard, win-dows, masonry and woodchips; Con-struction materials: quarries, concrete, cememnt, transport, asphalt, con-tracting, recycling, flyash, scaffolding and concrete placing; Energy: LPG and natural gas, LPG shipping, oil and gas exploration and production. Ser-vices and engineering: elevators, engi-neering, tyres, materials handling, formwork and dimension stone. The Company has operations in North America, Europe and Asia as well as Australia.

ANNUAL EARNINGS

	6/30/96	6/30/95	6/30/96	6/30/95
	--------------US $--------------		--------------A$--------------	
Earnings Per Share	0.15	0.19	0.19	0.27

ANNUAL FINANCIAL DATA

RECORD OF EARNINGS (IN MILLIONS):

Total Revenues	3,938	3,581	5,001	5,045
Costs & Expenses	3,621	3,186	4,598	4,489
Operating Income	317	394	403	556
Income Bef Income Tax	209	315	266	443
Income Tax	41	102	53	144
Minority Interests	6	4	7	6
Net Income	162	209	206	294
Average Shares Outstg (000)	875,336	779,612	1,111,538	1,098,509

BALANCE SHEET (IN MILLIONS):

Cash & Cash Equivalents	79	41	100	58
Receivables, Net	624	519	792	731
Inventories	485	443	616	624
Gross Property	3,958	3,548	5,027	4,999
Accumulated Depreciation	1,197	1,028	1,521	1,449
Long-Term Debt	1,084	899	1,376	1,266
Stockholders' Equity	2,289	2,042	2,907	2,877
Total Assets	4,771	4,243	6,059	5,979
Total Current Assets	1,228	1,038	1,559	1,463
Total Current Liabilities	1,034	979	1,313	1,380
Net Working Capital	193	59	245	83
Year End Shs Outstg (000)	1,128,175	1,100,804	1,128,175	1,100,804

STATISTICAL RECORD:

Return on Equity %	7.1.2			
Return on Assets %	3.4	4.9		
Operating Profit Margin %	8.1	11.0		
Net Profit Margin %	4.1	5.8		
Book Value Per Share	2.03	1.86		

Converted at 1996, US$0.7875= 1 Australian$; 1995, US$0.7097= 1 Australian$

OFFICERS:
P. J. W. Cottrell, Chairman
A. R. Berg, Managing Director

INCORPORATED: Australia, 1946

PRINCIPAL OFFICE: Level 39, AMP Centre, 50 Bridge Street, Sydney, 2000 Australia

TELEPHONE NUMBER: (02) 9220 6300

NO. OF EMPLOYEES: 21,735

ANNUAL MEETING: In Nov.

SHAREHOLDERS: N/A

INSTITUTIONAL HOLDINGS:
No. of Institutions: 5
Shares Held: 403,963

AMERICAN DEPOSITARY RECEIPTS: Each American Depositary Receipt represents eight ordinary shares of par A$0.50.

DEPOSITARY BANK(S): The Bank of New York, (212-815-2729)

NASDAQ SYMBOL BBIOY
Rec. Pr. 39⅛

BRITISH BIOTECH PLC

YIELD 1.5
P/E RATIO 4.7

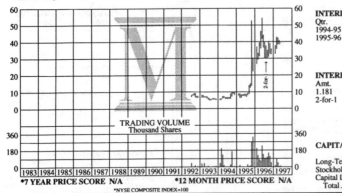

TRADING VOLUME Thousand Shares

1983 1984 1985 1986 1987 1988 1989 1990 1991 1992 1993 1994 1995 1996 1997
*7 YEAR PRICE SCORE N/A   *12 MONTH PRICE SCORE N/A
*NYSE COMPOSITE INDEX=100

INTERIM EARNINGS (Per Share, US$):

Qtr.	July	Oct.	Jan.	Apr.
1994-95		0.85		
1995-96		0.84		

INTERIM DIVIDENDS (Per Share):

Amt.	Decl.	Ex.	Rec.	Pay.
1.181	...	7/08/96	7/10/96	7/24/96
2-for-1	...	8/05/96	7/26/96	8/02/96

Indicated div.: $0.59

CAPITALIZATION (4/30/96):

	($000)	(%)
Long-Term Debt	4,899	3.8
Stockholders' Equity	125,485	96.1
Capital Lease Oblgs.	210	0.2
Total	130,594	100.0

RECENT DEVELOPMENTS: For the year ended 4/30/96, the Company reported a net loss of £25.2 million compared with a net loss of £26.3 million the previous year. Turnover on continuing operations more than doubled to £8.5 million from £3.2 million the year before. Total expenditure climbed 11.3% to £35.9 million from £32.2 million a year earlier. This increase was primarily due to higher expenses related to clinical trials for the development of new products. Research and development income advanced to £8.5 million from £3.2 million the prior year. This growth resulted from the collaborative agreement with Glaxo Wellcome to develop BB-2983 for the treatment of arthritis. Other income was received during the current year under the EUREKA grant from the United Kingdom government, as well as under a research agreement from Techne Inc. Operating loss totaled £27.4 million versus a loss of £29.1 million the previous year.

BUSINESS

BRITISH BIOTECH PLC is engaged in pharmaceutical research and product development, conducted both on its own behalf and in connection with various collaborative research and development agreements with other companies. The Company is currently pursuing research and development in four medical areas: (i) inflammation and inflammatory diseases such as asthma and arthritis; (ii) cancer, particularly tumor invasion and spread; (iii) vascular diseases such as thrombosis and myocardial infarction; and (iv) immunotherapy of cancer and viral disease, particularly AIDS.

ANNUAL EARNINGS

	4/30/96	4/30/95	4/30/96	4/30/95
	------US $------		------£------	
Earnings Per Share	d0.76	d0.89	d0.50	d0.55

ANNUAL FINANCIAL DATA

RECORD OF EARNINGS (IN THOUSANDS):

Total Revenues	12,795	5,144	8,462	3,191
Costs & Expenses	54,252	51,976	35,881	32,243
Operating Income	d41,458	d46,832	d27,419	d29,052
Income Bef Income Tax	d38,013	d42,446	d25,141	d26,331
Income Tax	56	11	37	7
Net Income	d38,069	d42,457	d25,178	d26,338
Average Shares Outstg	50,883	48,075	50,883	48,075

BALANCE SHEET (IN THOUSANDS):

Cash & Cash Equivalents	105,982	67,731	70,094	42,017
Receivables, Net	4,028	5,658	2,664	3,510
Inventories	151	116	100	72
Gross Property	50,269	50,833	33,247	31,534
Accumulated Depreciation	17,876	13,546	11,823	8,403
Long-Term Debt	5,109	6,008	3,379	3,727
Stockholders' Equity	125,485	95,248	82,993	59,087
Total Assets	142,554	110,793	94,282	68,730
Total Current Assets	110,161	73,506	72,858	45,599
Total Current Liabilities	11,960	9,537	7,910	5,916
Net Working Capital	98,201	63,969	64,948	39,683
Year End Shs Outstg	57,956	48,352	57,956	48,352

STATISTICAL RECORD:

Book Value Per Share	2.17	1.97		

Converted at 1996, US$1.5120= 1 British pound; 1995, US$1.6120= 1 British pound.

OFFICERS:
J. M. Raisman, Chmn.
K. G. McCullagh, C.E.O.
J. J. Noble, Fin. Dir.
P. J. Lewis, Res. & Dev. Dir.

INCORPORATED: United Kingdom, 1986

PRINCIPAL OFFICE: Watlington Road, Oxford OX4 5LY United Kingdom

TELEPHONE NUMBER: 01865-748747
FAX: 01865-781047
NO. OF EMPLOYEES: 335
ANNUAL MEETING: In Sep.
SHAREHOLDERS: 4,175
INSTITUTIONAL HOLDINGS:
No. of Institutions: 11
Shares Held: 2,530,710

AMERICAN DEPOSITARY
RECEIPTS: (Sponsored) Each American Depositary Receipt represents ten ordinary shares or par £0.05 each.

DEPOSITARY BANK(S): The Bank of New York, (212) 815-2175

142

NASDAQ SYMBOL BTBTY
Rec. Pr. 3⅞

BT SHIPPING LIMITED

YIELD ...
P/E RATIO ...

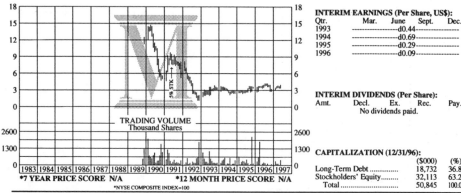

*7 YEAR PRICE SCORE N/A *12 MONTH PRICE SCORE N/A

*NYSE COMPOSITE INDEX=100

TRADING VOLUME
Thousand Shares

INTERIM EARNINGS (Per Share, US$):

Qtr.	Mar.	June	Sept.	Dec.
1993		d0.44		
1994		d0.69		
1995		d0.29		
1996		d0.09		

INTERIM DIVIDENDS (Per Share):

Amt.	Decl.	Ex.	Rec.	Pay.
	No dividends paid.			

CAPITALIZATION (12/31/96):

	($000)	(%)
Long-Term Debt	18,732	36.8
Stockholders' Equity	32,113	63.2
Total	50,845	100.0

RECENT DEVELOPMENTS: For the year ended 12/31/96, the Company reported a net loss of $779,000 compared with a net loss of $2.3 million the year before. Revenue from voyages declined 8.0% to $29.3 million from $31.8 million a year earlier. Voyage expenses were $6.2 million versus $10.2 million the previous year, resulting in a 6.8% increase in net operating revenue to $23.1 million from $21.6 million the year before. Ship operating expenses were $14.0 million compared with $13.4 million a year earlier. Operating profit soared to $1.1 million from $82,000 the previous year. The Company reported a net loss before taxes of $739,000 compared with a net loss of $2.3 million in the prior-year period.

BUSINESS

BT SHIPPING LIMITED owns and operates, through its subsidiaries, a fleet of six product tankers that are specifically designed to carry refined oil products, including fuel oil, diesel oil, gas oil, kerosene, gasoline, jet fuel and napthas. The Company operates the vessels on the spot voyage market or on short time charters (three months or less), unless opportunities arise to time charter one or more vessels at acceptable rates.

ANNUAL EARNINGS

	12/31/96	12/31/95	12/31/94	12/31/93	12/31/92	12/31/91
			US $			
Earnings Per Share	d0.09	d0.29	d0.69	d0.44	d4.52	0.62

ANNUAL FINANCIAL DATA

RECORD OF EARNINGS (IN THOUSANDS):

	12/31/96	12/31/95	12/31/94	12/31/93	12/31/92	12/31/91
Total Revenues	23,072	21,608	22,476	23,283	17,026	31,535
Costs & Expenses	15,872	15,413	15,870	17,364	16,509	14,498
Depreciation & Amort	6,113	6,113	6,558	6,777	8,116	8,066
Operating Income	1,087	82	48	d858	d7,599	8,971
Income Bef Income Tax	d739	d2,310	d2,555	d3,377	d10,584	4,206
Income Tax	40	36	33	38	30	28
Eq. Earnings in Affils.	146	24	...	...	...	...
Net Income	d779	d2,346	d2,588	d3,415	d10,614	4,178
Net Extraordinary Items	...	...	3,111	...	20,000	...
Average Shares Outstg	8,217	8,217	8,217	7,774	7,198	6,789

BALANCE SHEET (IN THOUSANDS):

Cash & Cash Equivalents	6,587	3,166	8,381	10,916	5,606	18,318
Receivables, Net	2,383	2,517	2,310	1,273	1,102	1,648
Inventories	1,731	1,150	1,216	1,558	1,277	1,449
Gross Property	113,601	113,601	113,601	130,800	130,800	130,800
Accumulated Depreciation	62,146	56,033	49,920	51,478	44,701	16,585
Long-Term Debt	18,732	22,304	27,516	39,634	48,592	52,720
Stockholders' Equity	32,113	32,899	35,245	40,936	41,378	72,068
Total Assets	64,651	67,538	79,093	97,678	100,537	140,673
Total Current Assets	12,666	9,644	15,332	18,142	14,193	26,047
Total Current Liabilities	13,806	12,335	16,332	17,108	10,567	15,885
Net Working Capital	d1,140	d2,691	d1,000	1,034	3,626	10,162
Year End Shs Outstg	8,217	8,217	8,217	8,217	6,573	6,573

STATISTICAL RECORD:

Return on Equity %	...	...	...	...	...	5.8
Return on Assets %	...	...	...	...	...	3.0
Operating Profit Margin %	4.7	0.4	0.2	...	...	28.4
Net Profit Margin %	...	...	...	...	...	12.8
Book Value Per Share	3.91	4.00	4.29	4.98	6.30	10.96

OFFICERS:
S. E. N. Pollock, Chmn., Pres. & Dir.
A. Jones, V.P. & C.F.O.
J. P. Gray, V.P. & Dir.

INCORPORATED: Bermuda, April, 1989

PRINCIPAL OFFICE: Cedar House 41 Cedar Ave. Hamilton Bermuda HM 09

TELEPHONE NUMBER: (441) 295-2244

NO. OF EMPLOYEES: 164

ANNUAL MEETING: In July

SHAREHOLDERS: N/A

INSTITUTIONAL HOLDINGS:
No. of Institutions: 5
Shares Held: 1,511,452

AMERICAN DEPOSITARY RECEIPTS: (Sponsored) Each American Depositary Receipt represents one ordinary share of par US$1.00.

DEPOSITARY BANK(S): The Bank of New York, (212) 815-2175

143

BUFFELSFONTEIN GOLD MINES LIMITED

YIELD ...
P/E RATIO ...

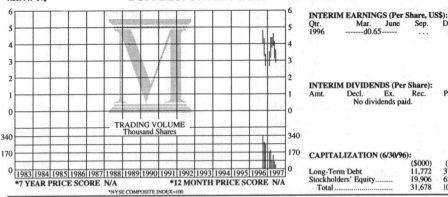

INTERIM EARNINGS (Per Share, US$):

Qtr.	Mar.	June	Sep.	Dec.
1996	-------d0.65------		...	...

INTERIM DIVIDENDS (Per Share):

Amt.	Decl.	Ex.	Rec.	Pay.
	No dividends paid.			

TRADING VOLUME
Thousand Shares

*7 YEAR PRICE SCORE N/A   *12 MONTH PRICE SCORE N/A

*NYSE COMPOSITE INDEX=100

CAPITALIZATION (6/30/96):

	($000)	(%)
Long-Term Debt	11,772	37.2
Stockholders' Equity	19,906	62.8
Total	31,678	100.0

RECENT DEVELOPMENTS: For the six months ended 6/30/96, net loss was $7.2 million. This compares with a loss of $570,000 for the six months ended 12/31/95. Revenues were $50.8 million, down 9.9% from $55.9 million in the equivalent period six months earlier. Product sales were down 9.3% to $48.9 million, while interest and dividends rose 35.1% to $873,000. Costs and expenses were down 2.8% to $61.9 million from $63.7 million. The decline in revenues and earnings resulted from a major restructuring undertaken in January 1996. The restructuring resulted in the close or sale of certain mining operations and a reduction in the Company's workforce.

BUSINESS

BUFFELSFONTEIN GOLD MINES LIMITED (formerly a division of Buffelsfontein Gold Mining Company Limited) is engaged in gold mining from underground reserves, the treatment of surface reserves and related activities, including extraction, processing and smelting. The Company's mine operations are located in the Klerksdorp area, North West Province, approximately 100 miles southwest of Johannesburg. The Company has extensive underground workings and mines the Vaal Reef. The Company's main activity is deep-levle mining. In addition, the Company has surface mining operations that consist of the milling of low grade surface dumps. The metallurgical plant on site has a capacity of 2.9 million tons per annum.

ANNUAL EARNINGS

	6/30/96 [1] --US $--	6/30/96 --Rand--
Earnings Per Share	d0.61	d2.66

ANNUAL FINANCIAL DATA

RECORD OF EARNINGS (IN THOUSANDS):

Total Revenues	47,805	206,948
Income Bef Income Tax	d10,409	d45,061
Income Tax	cr3,653	cr15,812
Net Income	d6,757	d29,249

[1] Results are for the six months ended 6/30/96.

BALANCE SHEET (IN THOUSANDS):

Cash & Cash Equivalents	13,983	60,533
Receivables, Net	3,817	16,523
Inventories	6,395	27,682
Gross Property	136,112	589,229
Long-Term Debt	11,772	50,960
Stockholders' Equity	19,906	86,172
Total Assets	55,377	239,728
Total Current Assets	27,359	118,437
Total Current Liabilities	23,700	102,596
Net Working Capital	3,659	15,841
Year End Shs Outstg	11,117	11,117

STATISTICAL RECORD:

Return on Equity %	...	
Return on Assets %	...	
Operating Profit Margin %	...	
Net Profit Margin %	...	
Book Value Per Share	1.79	

Converted at 1996, US$0.2310= 1 South African Rand.

OFFICERS:
R. A. R. Kebble, Chairman
J. Botha, General Manager
J. Schoonhoven, Fin. Dir.

INCORPORATED: Republic of South Africa, Sept. 20, 1995.

PRINCIPAL OFFICE: Randgold House, 5 Press Avenue, Selby, Johannesburg, South Africa, 2025

TELEPHONE NUMBER: (011) 837-0706

NO. OF EMPLOYEES: 2,500

ANNUAL MEETING: N/A

SHAREHOLDERS: N/A

INSTITUTIONAL HOLDINGS:
No. of Institutions: N/A
Shares Held: N/A

AMERICAN DEPOSITARY RECEIPTS: (Sponsored) Each American Depositary Receipt represents one ordinary share of R0.01.

DEPOSITARY BANK(S): The Bank of New York, (212) 815-2175

NASDAQ SYMBOL BURMY
Rec. Pr. 33⅜

BURMAH CASTROL PLC

YIELD 2.6%
P/E RATIO 13.4

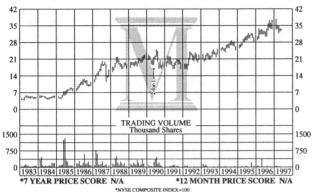

*7 YEAR PRICE SCORE N/A   *12 MONTH PRICE SCORE N/A

*NYSE COMPOSITE INDEX=100

INTERIM EARNINGS (Per Share, US $):

Qtr.	Mar.	June	Sept.	Dec.
1995	------------------	1.04	------------------	
1996	------------------	1.25	------------------	

INTERIM DIVIDENDS (Per Share):

Amt.	Decl.	Ex.	Rec.	Pay.
0.806	...	4/15/96	4/17/96	7/22/96
0.429	...	10/10	10/15	1/21/97

Indicated div.: $0.86

CAPITALIZATION (12/31/96):

	($000)	(%)
Stockholders' Equity........	1,435,411	96.6
Deferred Income Tax	18,131	1.2
Preferred Stock.................	32,196	2.2
Total	1,485,738	100.0

RECENT DEVELOPMENTS: For the year ended 12/31/96, net earnings from continuing operations were £155.1 million compared with £135.0 million the year before. Results for the recent period included a net gain of £11.0 million related to the disposal of the group's fuels retailing businesses in Turkey, Chile and Sweden and the group's plans to dispose of a number of businesses in the construction

chemicals division. Turnover from continuing operations, net of duties, rose 3.8% to £3.05 billion from £2.93 billion a year earlier. Turnover results for the current and prior-year periods exlude £12.7 million and £114.1 million, respectively, from discontinued operations. Operating profit from continuing operations increased 3.6% to £280.6 million from £270.9 million the previous year.

BUSINESS

BURMAH CASTROL PLC is an international manufacturer and marketer of specialized lubricants and chemicals. The Company has two principal business groups: lubricants, which is centered on the Castrol brand of automotive, industrial and marine products; and chemicals, which markets high performance, specialty products to a wide range of industries under internationally recognized brand names. The Company also operates petrol service stations in a number of countries and is joint operator of the world's largest liquefied natural gas transportation project.

ANNUAL EARNINGS

	12/31/96	12/31/95	12/31/96	12/31/95
	-------------US $------------		-------------British £-----------	
Earnings Per Share	1.25	1.04	0.74	0.67

ANNUAL FINANCIAL DATA

RECORD OF EARNINGS (IN MILLIONS):

Total Revenues	5,184	4,734	3,060	3,049
Costs & Expenses	4,730	4,327	2,791	2,786
Operating Income	455	407	268	262
Income Bef Income Tax	462	393	272	253
Income Tax	165	152	98	98
Minority Interests	33	31	20	20
Net Income	263	210	155	135
Average Shares Outstg (000)	207,700	200,400	207,700	200,400

BALANCE SHEET (IN MILLIONS):

Cash & Cash Equivalents	697	525	411	338
Receivables, Net	1,084	1,026	640	661
Inventories	489	509	289	328
Gross Property	1,754	1,670	1,035	1,075
Accumulated Depreciation	715	699	422	450
Stockholders' Equity	1,435	1,225	847	789
Total Assets	3,819	3,574	2,254	2,301
Total Current Assets	2,271	2,060	1,340	1,327
Total Current Liabilities	1,551	1,368	915	881
Net Working Capital	720	692	425	446
Year End Shs Outstg (000)	211,500	201,700	211,500	201,700

STATISTICAL RECORD:

Return on Equity %	18.3	17.1		
Return on Assets %	6.9	5.9		
Operating Profit Margin %	8.8	8.6		
Net Profit Margin %	5.1	4.4		
Book Value Per Share	6.78	6.07		

Converted at 1996, US$1.6945= 1 British pound; 1995, US$1.5530= 1 British pound

OFFICERS:
L. Urquhart, Non-Executive Chmn.
J. Fry, C.E.O.
B. Hardy, Fin. Dir.

INCORPORATED: 1886

PRINCIPAL OFFICE: Burmah Castrol House Pipers Way Swindon United Kingdom SN3 1RE

TELEPHONE NUMBER: (01793) 511 521

NO. OF EMPLOYEES: 21,180

ANNUAL MEETING: In May

SHAREHOLDERS: 52,934

INSTITUTIONAL HOLDINGS:
No. of Institutions: 6
Shares Held: 262,787

AMERICAN DEPOSITARY RECEIPTS: (Sponsored) Each American Depository Receipt represents 2 ordinary shares of par £1. American Depositary Receipts underwent a 1-for-4 reverse split on Nov. 17, 1987 and a 2-for-1 split on May 25, 1990.

DEPOSITARY BANK(S): J.P. Morgan, (212) 648-3206

BUSINESS OBJECTS S.A.

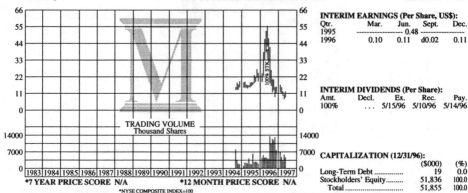

*7 YEAR PRICE SCORE N/A   *12 MONTH PRICE SCORE N/A

*NYSE COMPOSITE INDEX=100

INTERIM EARNINGS (Per Share, US$):

Qtr.	Mar.	Jun.	Sept.	Dec.
1995	---------------- 0.48 ----------------			
1996	0.10	0.11	d0.02	0.11

INTERIM DIVIDENDS (Per Share):

Amt.	Decl.	Ex.	Rec.	Pay.
100%	...	5/15/96	5/10/96	5/14/96

CAPITALIZATION (12/31/96):

	($000)	(%)
Long-Term Debt	19	0.0
Stockholders' Equity.........	51,836	100.0
Total	51,855	100.0

RECENT DEVELOPMENTS: For the year ended 12/31/96, net income was $5.1 million compared with $8.0 million the year before. Total revenues advanced 40.5% to $85.1 million from $60.6 million a year earlier. License fees revenuesincreased 32.1% to $64.5 million, while services revenues soared 74.9% to $20.7 million. As a percentage of total revenues, gross profit margin was 88.2% versus 89.9% the previous year. Income from operations declined 29.6% to $7.0 million. For the quarter ended12/31/96, net income was $1.8 million compared with $3.3 million the year before. Total revenues increased 30.7% to $25.8 million from $19.8 million a year earlier.

BUSINESS

BUSINESS OBJECTS S.A. is engaged in the development, marketing, and support of enterprise-wide decision support software tools for the client/server market. The Company's products are designed to allownon-technical end-users to perform queries by using 'objects' as representations of data as well as to prepare reports and graphs and to conduct multi-dimensional analysis. The Company's products are available for Microsoft Windows, Apple Macintosh and Unix Motif andcharacter workstations, with access to most large relational databases such as Oracle, Sybase, Informix, and IBM DB2. The Company's software is designed for medium to large business organizations andgovernmental institutions.

ANNUAL EARNINGS

	12/31/96	12/31/95	12/31/96	12/31/95
	----------US $----------		----------FFr----------	
Earnings Per Share	0.31	0.48	0.84	1.23

ANNUAL FINANCIAL DATA

RECORD OF EARNINGS (IN THOUSANDS):

	12/31/96	12/31/95	12/31/96	12/31/95
Total Revenues	85,137	60,606	446,445	297,234
Costs & Expenses	78,089	50,594	409,486	248,131
Operating Income	7,048	10,012	36,959	49,103
Income Bef Income Tax	8,897	12,011	46,654	58,906
Income Tax	3,737	3,963	19,596	19,436
Net Income	5,160	8,048	27,058	39,470

BALANCE SHEET (IN THOUSANDS):

Cash & Cash Equivalents	42,171	46,702	221,138	229,044
Receivables, Net	24,176	17,174	126,775	84,228
Inventories	510	260	2,674	1,275
Gross Property	10,101	3,961	52,968	19,426
Long-Term Debt	19	121	100	593
Stockholders' Equity	51,836	46,461	271,820	227,862
Total Assets	80,770	71,013	423,545	348,274
Total Current Assets	70,057	66,669	367,368	326,969
Total Current Liabilities	28,915	24,431	151,626	119,819
Net Working Capital	41,142	42,238	215,742	207,151
Year End Shs Outstg	16,385	16,083	16,385	16,083

STATISTICAL RECORD:

Return on Equity %	9.95	17.32
Return on Assets %	6.39	11.33
Operating Profit Margin %	8.28	16.52
Net Profit Margin %	6.06	13.28
Book Value Per Share	1.56	1.42

Converted at 1996, US$0.1907 = 1 French franc; 1995, US$0.2039 = 1 French franc

OFFICERS:
B. Liautaud, Chmn., Pres. & C.E.O.
R. P. Verheecke, C.F.O. & Sr. Group V.P.
A. Dayon, Group V.P.
D. Kellogg, Group V.P.

INCORPORATED: France, Aug., 1990

PRINCIPAL OFFICE: 1 square Chaptal 92300 Levallois-Perret France

TELEPHONE NUMBER: (33-1) 41 25 21 21

NO. OF EMPLOYEES: 552

ANNUAL MEETING: In June

SHAREHOLDERS: 85

INSTITUTIONAL HOLDINGS:
No. of Institutions: 41
Shares Held: 7,544,327

AMERICAN DEPOSITARY RECEIPTS: (Sponsored) Each American Depositary Share represents one ordinary share of par FFr1.

DEPOSITARY BANK(S): The Bank of New York, (212) 815-2175

CANON INC.

YIELD 0.5%
P/E RATIO 27.3

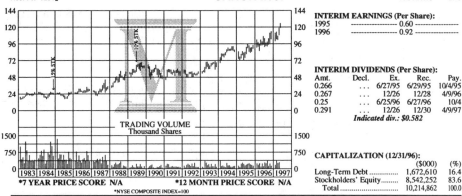

*7 YEAR PRICE SCORE N/A   *12 MONTH PRICE SCORE N/A

*NYSE COMPOSITE INDEX=100

INTERIM EARNINGS (Per Share):

1995	0.60
1996	0.92

INTERIM DIVIDENDS (Per Share):

Amt.	Decl.	Ex.	Rec.	Pay.
0.266	...	6/27/95	6/29/95	10/4/95
0.267	...	12/26	12/28	4/9/96
0.25	...	6/25/96	6/27/96	10/4
0.291	...	12/26	12/30	4/9/97

Indicated div.: $0.582

CAPITALIZATION (12/31/96):

	($000)	(%)
Long-Term Debt	1,672,610	16.4
Stockholders' Equity	8,542,252	83.6
Total	10,214,862	100.0

RECENT DEVELOPMENTS: For the year ended 12/31/96, net income jumped 71.1% to Y94,177 million ($811.9 million) from Y55,036 million the previous year. Net sales totaled Y2,558,227 million ($22.05 billion), up 18.1% versus Y2,165,626 million a year earlier. Results benefited from strong sales growth of computer peripherals, steppers, computers, facsimiles, and still cameras combined with a favorable exchange rate compared with the U.S. dollar.

Sales in the Americas region climbed 20.3% in 1996, while sales advanced 15.5% in both Japan and Europe compared with the prior year. Gross profit was up 23.2% to Y1,092,790 million ($9.42 billion) from Y887,271 million the year before. As a percentage of net sales, gross profit improved to 42.7% versus 41.0% a year earlier. Operating profit surged 43.7% to Y221,036 million ($1.91 billion) from Y153,838 million the previous year.

BUSINESS

CANON INC. is a manufacturer of copying machines and computer peripherals, mainly laser beam and bubble jet printers. The Company's products also include business systems such as faxes, computers, electronic typewriters, micrographs, Japanese-language word processors and calculators. The Company's camera business consists mainly of 35mm cameras and 8mm video camcorders. Optical related products include steppers and aligners used in semiconductor chip production, broadcasting lenses and medical equipment. Revenues in 1996 were derived as follows: computer peripherals, 34.3%; copying machines, 32.0%; business systems, 17.2%; cameras, 8.4%; and optical and other products, 8.1%.

ANNUAL EARNINGS

	12/31/96	12/31/95	12/31/96	12/31/95
	--------------US $--------------		--------------Yen--------------	
Earnings Per Share	0.92	0.60	106.32	62.13

ANNUAL FINANCIAL DATA

RECORD OF EARNINGS (IN MILLIONS):

	12/31/96	12/31/95	12/31/96	12/31/95
Total Revenues	22,257	21,007	2,558,227	2,165,626
Costs & Expenses	20,334	19,514	2,337,191	2,011,788
Operating Income	1,923	1,492	221,036	153,838
Income Bef Income Tax	1,728	1,206	198,669	124,290
Income Tax	702	569	80,636	58,670
Minority Interests	69	34	7,952	3,528
Net Income	819	534	94,177	55,036
Average Shares Outstg (000)	885,763	885,779	885,763	885,779

BALANCE SHEET (IN MILLIONS):

Cash & Cash Equivalents	5,762	6,235	662,272	642,832
Receivables, Net	2,755	2,825	316,638	291,213
Inventories	4,566	4,910	524,832	506,157
Gross Property	11,707	11,935	1,345,579	1,230,364
Accumulated Depreciation	6,259	6,415	719,452	661,297
Long-Term Debt	1,673	2,891	192,254	298,055
Stockholders' Equity	8,542	8,242	981,868	849,674
Total Assets	22,779	23,874	2,618,298	2,461,225
Total Current Assets	15,195	16,180	1,746,544	1,668,076
Total Current Liabilities	10,386	10,705	1,193,836	1,103,571
Net Working Capital	4,809	5,476	552,708	564,505
Year End Shs Outstg (000)	853,614	836,243	853,614	836,243

STATISTICAL RECORD:

Return on Equity %	9.59	6.48
Return on Assets %	3.60	2.24
Operating Profit Margin %	8.64	7.10
Net Profit Margin %	3.68	2.54
Book Value Per Share	10.01	9.86

Converted at 1996, US$0.0087= 1 Japanese Yen; 1995, US$0.0097= 1 Japanese Yen

OFFICERS:
R. Kaku, Chmn.
F. Mitarai, Pres.

INCORPORATED: Aug., 1937

PRINCIPAL OFFICE: 30-2, Shimomaruko 3-chome, Ohta-ku, Tokyo 146 Japan

TELEPHONE NUMBER: 81-3-3758-2111

NO. OF EMPLOYEES: 75,628

ANNUAL MEETING: In March

SHAREHOLDERS: N/A

INSTITUTIONAL HOLDINGS:
No. of Institutions: 43
Shares Held: 1,767,483

AMERICAN DEPOSITARY RECEIPTS: (Sponsored) Each American Depositary Receipt (new) represents five common shares of par Y50.

DEPOSITARY BANK(S): J.P. Morgan, (212) 648-3206

CANTAB PHARMACEUTICALS PLC

YIELD ...
P/E RATIO ...

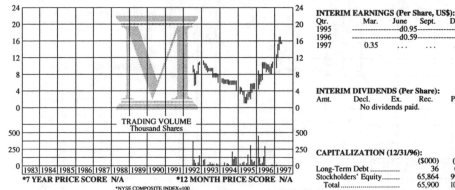

INTERIM EARNINGS (Per Share, US$):

Qtr.	Mar.	June	Sept.	Dec.
1995		-------------d0.95-------------		
1996		-------------d0.59-------------		
1997	0.35	...	...	...

INTERIM DIVIDENDS (Per Share):

Amt.	Decl.	Ex.	Rec.	Pay.
	No dividends paid.			

CAPITALIZATION (12/31/96):

	($000)	(%)
Long-Term Debt	36	0.1
Stockholders' Equity.........	65,864	99.9
Total	65,900	100.0

RECENT DEVELOPMENTS: For the first quarter ended 3/31/97, the Company produced net income of £3.4 million (US$5.5 million) compared with a net loss of £1.8 million in the same prior-year period. Revenues soared to £5.4 million (US$8.8 million) from £17,000 the year before. This increase reflected an up-front license fee of £5.0 million as well as initial contract development payments, both payable to CNTBY under its collaborative agreement with Glaxco Wellcome plc. Operating expenses rose 28.4% to £2.5 million (US$4.2 million) from £2.0 million in 1995 primarily due to higher research and development expenditure. Operating income totaled £2.8 million (US$4.7 million) versus a loss of £2.0 million a year earlier. Net interest and similar income amounted to £545,000 (US$894,000) compared with £152,000 the prior year. During the quarter, Cantab formed Phogen, a 50%-owned joint venture with Marie Curie Cancer Care.

BUSINESS

CANTAB PHARMACEUTICALS PLC, through its subsidiary, Cantab Pharmaceuticals Research Ltd., is engaged in the research and development of proprietary biopharmaceuticals which utilize the highly selective properties of the human immune system for the treatment of diseases. The Company's activities are currently focused on the research and development of products in two principal areas: leucocyte modulators, designed to regulate the function of specific components of the immune system to prevent an undesirable immune response, and therapeutic antigens, designed to activate the immune system to combat specific diseases.

ANNUAL EARNINGS

	12/31/96	12/31/95	12/31/96	12/31/95
	--------------US $--------------		--------------British £--------------	
Earnings Per Share	d0.59	d0.95	d0.35	d0.61

ANNUAL FINANCIAL DATA

RECORD OF EARNINGS (IN THOUSANDS):

Total Revenues	5,278	1,173	3,115	755
Costs & Expenses	15,110	11,894	8,917	7,659
Operating Income	d9,831	d10,722	d5,802	d6,904
Net Income	d7,613	d9,537	d4,493	d6,141
Average Shares Outstg	13,040	10,015	13,040	10,015

BALANCE SHEET (IN THOUSANDS):

Cash & Cash Equivalents	61,465	17,342	36,273	11,167
Receivables, Net	1,456	971	859	625
Gross Property	9,918	8,378	5,853	5,395
Accumulated Depreciation	4,111	2,806	2,426	1,807
Long-Term Debt	36	207	21	133
Stockholders' Equity	65,864	21,021	38,869	13,536
Total Assets	68,727	23,885	40,559	15,380
Total Current Assets	62,920	18,313	37,132	11,792
Total Current Liabilities	2,828	2,559	1,669	1,648
Net Working Capital	60,092	15,754	35,463	10,144
Year End Shs Outstg	15,722	10,760	15,722	10,760

STATISTICAL RECORD:

Book Value Per Share	4.19	1.95		

Converted at 1996, US$1.6945= 1 British pound; 1995, US$1.5530= 1 British pound.

OFFICERS:
J. Collins, Chmn.
J. Sikorski, C.E.O.
N. L. Hart, Fin. Dir. & Sec.

INCORPORATED: NY, Dec., 1991

PRINCIPAL OFFICE: 184 Cambridge Science Park, Milton Road, Cambridge CB4 4GN United Kingdom

TELEPHONE NUMBER: (44) 01223 42413
FAX: (44) 01223 423458
NO. OF EMPLOYEES: 85 (avg.)
ANNUAL MEETING: In May
SHAREHOLDERS: N/A
INSTITUTIONAL HOLDINGS:
No. of Institutions: N/A
Shares Held: N/A

AMERICAN DEPOSITARY RECEIPTS: (Sponsored) Each American Depositary Receipt represents one ordinary share of par £0.05.

DEPOSITARY BANK(S): The Bank of New York, (212) 815-2175

CARLTON COMMUNICATIONS PLC

YIELD   2.8%
P/E RATIO   15.8

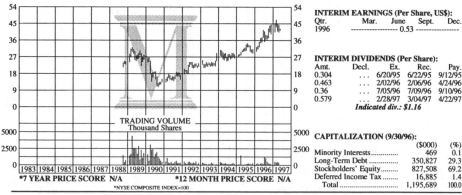

INTERIM EARNINGS (Per Share, US$):

Qtr.	Mar.	June	Sept.	Dec.
1996	------------------ 0.53 ------------------

INTERIM DIVIDENDS (Per Share):

Amt.	Decl.	Ex.	Rec.	Pay.
0.304	...	6/20/95	6/22/95	9/12/95
0.463	...	2/02/96	2/06/96	4/24/96
0.36	...	7/05/96	7/09/96	9/10/96
0.579	...	2/28/97	3/04/97	4/22/97

Indicated div.: $1.16

TRADING VOLUME
Thousand Shares

*7 YEAR PRICE SCORE N/A   *12 MONTH PRICE SCORE N/A

*NYSE COMPOSITE INDEX=100

CAPITALIZATION (9/30/96):

	($000)	(%)
Minority Interests.............	469	0.1
Long-Term Debt	350,827	29.3
Stockholders' Equity........	827,508	69.2
Deferred Income Tax	16,885	1.4
Total	1,195,689	100.0

RECENT DEVELOPMENTS: For the year ended 9/30/96, income including discontinued operations jumped 19.6% to £197.6 million from £165.2 million a year earlier. Sales were £1.68 billion, up 6.2% from £1.58 billion in the previous year. Gross profit as a percentage of sales was 34.8% in 1996 versus 35.3% in 1995. Operating profit was £291.0 million compared with £248.5 million the year before, an increase of 17.1%. Television sales climbed 2.4% to £686.0 million and operating profit rose 5.4% to £129.4 million. Video revenues increased 8.7% to £515.3 million and operating profit jumped 20.6% to £73.2 million. The film division reported 17.6% higher sales to £296.2 million and 26.7% higher operating profit to £52.7 million.

BUSINESS

CARLTON COMMUNICATIONS PLC carries its operations out through four operating divisions: Broadcast Television; Video and Audio Production and Distribution; Film and Television Services; and Video and Sound Products. The Broadcast Television division supplies the London region with original, rebroadcast and news programs through the Central Independent Television, ITN, GMTV and London News Network stations. The Video and Audio Production and Distribution division produces prerecorded videocassettes; markets and distributes a wide range of video titles; and engages in the compilation of albums and re-recordings of popular titles. The Film and Television Services division is engaged in the processing of motion picture films; the provision of physical distribution of prints to theatres; the provision of ancillary services such as print rejuvenation, archival storage and antipiracy control; and post production of commercials and television programs. The Video and Sound Products division is engaged in the design and manufacture of image processing products, including graphic design workstations and editing systems; the design, manufacture and marketing of digital video effect devices, digital disk recorders and vision mixers; and the design and manufacture of analogue and digital professional audio mixing consoles.

ANNUAL EARNINGS

	9/30/96	9/30/95	9/30/96	9/30/95
	------------US $------------		------------British £------------	
Earnings Per Share	0.53	1.14	0.34	0.72

ANNUAL FINANCIAL DATA

RECORD OF EARNINGS (IN MILLIONS):

Total Revenues	2,623	2,501	1,678	1,580
Costs & Expenses	2,168	2,107	1,387	1,331
Operating Income	455	393	291	249
Income Bef Income Tax	461	588	295	247
Income Tax	152	129	97	81
Net Income	309	262	198	165
Average Shares Outstg (000)	579,140	230,365	579,140	230,365

BALANCE SHEET (IN MILLIONS):

Cash & Cash Equivalents	554	604	354	382
Receivables, Net	990	876	633	553
Inventories	87	107	56	68
Gross Property	744	669	476	422
Accumulated Depreciation	350	303	224	192
Long-Term Debt	351	352	224	223
Stockholders' Equity	828	740	529	467
Total Assets	2,119	2,055	1,356	1,298
Total Current Assets	1,631	1,587	1,043	1,003
Total Current Liabilities	873	888	559	561
Net Working Capital	758	700	485	442
Year End Shs Outstg (000)	580,123	231,321	580,123	231,321

STATISTICAL RECORD:

Return on Equity %	37.3	35.4		
Return on Assets %	14.6	12.7		
Operating Profit Margin %	17.3	15.7		
Net Profit Margin %	11.8	10.5		
Book Value Per Share	1.43	3.20		

Converted at 1996, US$1.563= 1 British pound; 1995, US$1.583= 1 British pound

OFFICERS:
M. Green, Chmn.
B. A. Cragg, Fin. Dir.
J. F. de Moller, Managing Dir.
D. Abdoo, Sec.

INCORPORATED: England, 1939

PRINCIPAL OFFICE: 25 Knightsbridge
London United Kingdom

TELEPHONE NUMBER: 0171-663-6363

NO. OF EMPLOYEES: 10,607

ANNUAL MEETING: In Feb.

SHAREHOLDERS: 21,448

INSTITUTIONAL HOLDINGS:
No. of Institutions: 23
Shares Held: 2,011,511

AMERICAN DEPOSITARY RECEIPTS: (Sponsored) Each American Depositary Receipt represents 5 ordinary shares of par £0.05.

DEPOSITARY BANK(S): J.P. Morgan, (212) 648-3206

CBT GROUP, PLC

YIELD ...
P/E RATIO 19.3

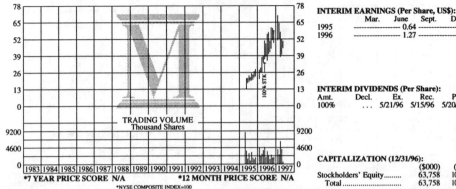

INTERIM EARNINGS (Per Share, US$):

	Mar.	June	Sept.	Dec.
1995	------------------	0.64	------------------	
1996	------------------	1.27	------------------	

TRADING VOLUME
Thousand Shares

INTERIM DIVIDENDS (Per Share):

Amt.	Decl.	Ex.	Rec.	Pay.
100%	...	5/21/96	5/15/96	5/20/96

1983 1984 1985 1986 1987 1988 1989 1990 1991 1992 1993 1994 1995 1996 1997
*7 YEAR PRICE SCORE N/A   *12 MONTH PRICE SCORE N/A
*NYSE COMPOSITE INDEX=100

CAPITALIZATION (12/31/96):

	($000)	(%)
Stockholders' Equity.........	63,758	100.0
Total	63,758	100.0

RECENT DEVELOPMENTS: For the year ended 12/31/96, net income more than doubled to US$12.6 million compared with US$5.6 million in the corresponding period a year earlier. Revenues were US$66.3 million versus US$40.2 million in 1995. Results for all periods have been restated to reflect two acquisitions the Company made during 1996 that were accounted for as poolings of interests. Revenues and earnings benefited from strengthening demand for the Company's products. At year end, the Company's library of interactive education software numbered 328 titles, which represents an increase of 99% over the 165 titles a year earlier. Driving the increase in new titles over the past year were expanded partnership agreements with the Company's existing partners Oracle, Microsoft, IBM, Novell and Sybase/Powersoft.

BUSINESS

CBT GROUP, PLC is a provider of interactive software designed to meet business information technology education and training needs. In addition, the Company develops, publishes and markets a broad library of over 328 software titles focused on client/server technologies and delivered on networked and stand-alone PCs and internet and corporate intranet technologies.

ANNUAL EARNINGS

	12/31/96	12/31/95	12/31/96	12/31/95
	------------US $------------		------------IR£------------	
Earnings Per Share	1.27	0.64	0.77	0.40

ANNUAL FINANCIAL DATA

RECORD OF EARNINGS (IN THOUSANDS):

	12/31/96	12/31/95	12/31/96	12/31/95
Total Revenues	66,324	40,192	40,012	25,117
Costs & Expenses	53,579	34,191	32,323	21,367
Operating Income	12,745	6,001	7,689	3,750
Income Bef Income Tax	14,958	6,851	9,024	4,281
Income Tax	2,385	1,277	1,439	798
Net Income	12,573	5,574	7,585	3,483
Average Shares Outstg	9,865	8,742	9,865	8,742

BALANCE SHEET (IN THOUSANDS):

Cash & Cash Equivalents	46,821	47,233	28,246	29,517
Receivables, Net	19,940	13,362	12,029	8,350
Inventories	264	220	159	137
Gross Property	9,742	3,697	5,877	2,310
Accumulated Depreciation	3,173	1,567	1,914	979
Stockholders' Equity	63,758	48,053	38,464	30,029
Total Assets	84,911	65,622	51,225	41,009
Total Current Assets	70,547	61,659	42,560	38,532
Total Current Liabilities	21,137	17,553	12,752	10,969
Net Working Capital	49,410	44,106	29,808	27,563
Year End Shs Outstg	8,931	8,742	8,931	8,742

STATISTICAL RECORD:

Return on Equity %	19.7	11.6
Return on Assets %	14.8	8.5
Operating Profit Margin %	19.2	14.9
Net Profit Margin %	19.0	13.9
Book Value Per Share	7.14	5.50

Converted at 1996, US$1.6576= 1 Irish pound; 1995, US$1.6002= 1 Irish pound

OFFICERS:
W. G. McCabe, Chmn.
J. J. Buckley, C.E.O. & Pres.
G. M. Priest, V.P. Fin. & C.F.O.
J. P. Hayes, Contr.

INCORPORATED: Ireland Aug. 8, 1989

PRINCIPAL OFFICE: 1005 Hamilton Court
Menlo Park California, 94025

TELEPHONE NUMBER: (415) 614-5900

NO. OF EMPLOYEES: 481

ANNUAL MEETING: N/A

SHAREHOLDERS: 23

INSTITUTIONAL HOLDINGS:
No. of Institutions: 66
Shares Held: 14,183,923

AMERICAN DEPOSITARY RECEIPTS: Each American Depositary Receipt represents two ordinary shares of par IR£0.375.

DEPOSITARY BANK(S): The Bank of New York, (212) 815-2175

CENTRAL PACIFIC MINERALS N.L.

YIELD ...
P/E RATIO ...

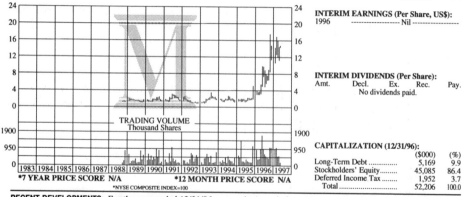

7 YEAR PRICE SCORE N/A   **12 MONTH PRICE SCORE N/A**

*NYSE COMPOSITE INDEX=100

INTERIM EARNINGS (Per Share, US$):
1996 ------------------- Nil -----------------

INTERIM DIVIDENDS (Per Share):
Amt.   Decl.   Ex.   Rec.   Pay.
No dividends paid.

CAPITALIZATION (12/31/96):

	($000)	(%)
Long-Term Debt	5,169	9.9
Stockholders' Equity.........	45,085	86.4
Deferred Income Tax	1,952	3.7
Total	52,206	100.0

RECENT DEVELOPMENTS: For the year ended 12/31/96, net income was A$38,000 with a loss of A$2.6 million in the corresponding period a year earlier. Revenues more than doubled to A$4.5 million versus A$2.0 million in 1995. Operating profit before tax was A$334,000 compared with a loss of $433,000 in 1995. Net investment earnings increased by A$937,000 to A$1.7 million in 1996. The increase in investment earnings is largely attributable to the improving investment climate that prevailed throughout 1996, as well as the additional A$13.1 million in new equity funds available for investment for part of the year. Operating costs increased 14% due to increased activity associated with the Company's Stuart Project, which included the expansion of operations in Brisbane.

BUSINESS

CENTRAL PACIFIC MINERALS N.L. and its affiliate Southern Pacific Petroleum NL are engaged in exploration in Australia. The principal resources and assets of the Company comprise entitlement to eight Queensland oil shale deposits. In total, these deposits contain in-situ resources of 28.6 million barrels of shale oil of which 25.6 million barrels are net to CPM/SPP.

ANNUAL EARNINGS

	12/31/96	12/31/95	12/31/96	12/31/95
	US $		A$	
Earnings Per Share	...	d0.02	...	d0.03

ANNUAL FINANCIAL DATA

RECORD OF EARNINGS (IN THOUSANDS):				
Other Operating Revenues	3,596	1,511	4,488	2,032
Income Bef Income Tax	266	d322	334	d433
Income Tax	235	1,604	296	2,158
Net Income	30	d1,926	38	d2,591
BALANCE SHEET (IN THOUSANDS):				
Cash & Cash Equivalents	21,070	5,570	26,493	7,491
Receivables, Net	337	332	424	447
Gross Property	1,013	961	1,274	1,293
Accumulated Depreciation	378	343	475	462
Long-Term Debt	5,169	9,192	6,500	12,363
Stockholders' Equity	45,085	32,252	56,689	43,378
Total Assets	61,150	51,147	76,889	68,792
Total Current Assets	21,407	7,064	26,917	9,501
Total Current Liabilities	2,220	2,431	2,791	3,270
Net Working Capital	19,187	4,633	24,126	6,231
Year End Shs Outstg	104,404	101,309	104,404	101,309
STATISTICAL RECORD:				
Return on Equity %	0.07	...		
Return on Assets %	0.05	...		
Operating Profit Margin %	0.11	0.11		
Net Profit Margin %	0.46	...		
Book Value Per Share	0.55	0.43		

Converted at 1996, US$0.7953= 1 Australian $; 1995, US$0.7435= 1 Australian $

OFFICERS:
I. McFarlane, Chmn. & Managing Dir.
V. H. Kuss, Fin. Dir. & Sec.
J. V. Browning
B. C. Wright

INCORPORATED: Feb., 1968

PRINCIPAL OFFICE: 10th Floor, National Mutual Centre, 15 London Circuit, Canberra City, ACT 2600, Australia

TELEPHONE NUMBER: (06) 2740 777

NO. OF EMPLOYEES: N/A

ANNUAL MEETING: In Apr.

SHAREHOLDERS: N/A

INSTITUTIONAL HOLDINGS:
No. of Institutions: 12
Shares Held: 1,567,878

AMERICAN DEPOSITARY RECEIPTS:
(Unsponsored) Each ADR represents two ordinary shares of par A$0.50.

DEPOSITARY BANK(S): The Bank of New York, (212) 815-2175; Bankers Trust Co., (212) 250-8500; Citibank N.A., (212) 657-7800; J.P. Morgan, (212) 648-3206

COFLEXIP SA

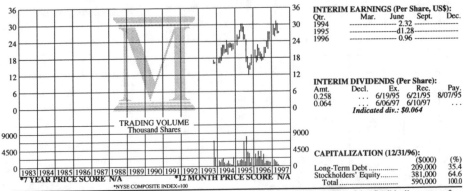

INTERIM EARNINGS (Per Share, US$):

Qtr.	Mar.	June	Sept.	Dec.
1994		2.32		
1995		d1.28		
1996		0.96		

INTERIM DIVIDENDS (Per Share):

Amt.	Decl.	Ex.	Rec.	Pay.
0.258	...	6/19/95	6/21/95	8/07/95
0.064	...	6/06/97	6/10/97	...

Indicated div.: $0.064

CAPITALIZATION (12/31/96):

	($000)	(%)
Long-Term Debt	209,000	35.4
Stockholders' Equity........	381,000	64.6
Total	590,000	100.0

TRADING VOLUME
Thousand Shares

1983 1984 1985 1986 1987 1988 1989 1990 1991 1992 1993 1994 1995 1996 1997

*7 YEAR PRICE SCORE N/A   *12 MONTH PRICE SCORE N/A
*NYSE COMPOSITE INDEX=100

RECENT DEVELOPMENTS: For the year ended 12/31/96, net income was FFr76.0 million (US$15.0 million) compared with a net loss of FFr102.0 million in the prior year. Net operating revenues increased 20.8% to FFr4.91 billion (US$945.0 million) from FFr4.06 billion the year before. The higher revenues were attributed to a high level of activity in Brazil, which represents 25.0% of revenues, as well as increases in the North Sea and worldwide, partially offset by a decrease in Asia-Pacific revenues. The Company reported record sales of its flexible lines, manufactured in Brazil and exported from France, and received a significant contribution from its Sunrise 2000 product charter contract. For the fourth quarter ended 12/31/96, net income was FFr50.0 million (US$10.0 million) compared with a net loss of FFr148.0 million in the corresponding year-earlier quarter. Net operating revenues grew 75.4% to FFr1.47 billion (US$283.0 million) from FFr837.0 million in the comparable period the year before.

BUSINESS

COFLEXIP SA is the parent company of a group of companies operating in the subsea oilfield services industry. Activities include the design, manufacture, and installation of offshore flexible pipe, which is used as an alternative to rigid steel pipe, for the offshore transportation of oil and gas. The group also provides integrated subsea construction, flexible flowline installation and pipelaying services. Other activities include the manufacture of subsea umbilicals, the design and manufacture of remotely-operated vehicles (ROVs), and the installation and maintenance of submarine telecommunications and power cables. In addition, the group manufactures certain composite materials and products for use in the offshore oil industry. In the flexible pipe and umbilicals segment, the Company provides installation, project management, and engineering services for offshore oil and gas projects and conducts business activities such as the manufacture of drilling and refining equipment, and of onshore flexible pipe. In the robotics segment, the Company designs and manufactures remotely operated vehicles (ROVs) for underwater operations through its subsidiary Perry Tritech.

ANNUAL EARNINGS

	12/31/96	12/31/95	12/31/96	12/31/95
	----------US $----------		------------FFr------------	
Earnings Per Share	0.96	d1.28	4.99	d6.30

ANNUAL FINANCIAL DATA

RECORD OF EARNINGS (IN THOUSANDS):

	12/31/96	12/31/95	12/31/96	12/31/95
Total Revenues	945,000	828,267	4,906,000	4,062,123
Costs & Expenses	886,000	815,361	4,601,000	3,998,828
Operating Income	59,000	12,906	305,000	63,295
Income Bef Income Tax	31,000	d13,073	163,000	d64,114
Income Tax	...	7,846	...	38,482
Minority Interests	...	cr210	...	cr1,029
Net Income	15,000	d20,710	76,000	d101,567
Discontinued Operations	d5,000	d16,232	d24,000	d79,610
Average Shares Outstg	...	16,128	...	16,128

BALANCE SHEET (IN THOUSANDS):

Cash & Cash Equivalents	99,000	76,822	514,000	376,764
Receivables, Net	...	131,064	...	642,785
Inventories	...	100,071	...	490,786
Gross Property	① 529,000	785,710	① 2,748,000	3,853,409
Accumulated Depreciation	...	254,408	...	1,247,711
Long-Term Debt	209,000	97,913	1,086,000	480,200
Stockholders' Equity	381,000	349,149	1,976,000	1,712,354
Total Assets	1,128,000	1,050,994	5,858,000	5,154,457
Total Current Assets	499,000	401,117	2,589,000	1,967,222
Total Current Liabilities	475,000	394,216	2,469,000	1,933,379
Net Working Capital	24,000	6,901	120,000	33,843
Year End Shs Outstg	...	15,768	...	15,768

① Net

STATISTICAL RECORD:

Return on Equity %	3.94	...
Return on Assets %	1.33	...
Operating Profit Margin %	6.24	1.56
Net Profit Margin %	1.59	...
Book Value Per Share	...	22.14

Converted at 1996, US$0.1926= 1 French franc; 1995, US$0.2039= 1 French franc. Figures for 12/31/96 are preliminary.

OFFICERS:
P. M. Valentin, Chmn. & C.E.O.

INCORPORATED: 1971

PRINCIPAL OFFICE: 23, avenue de Neuilly, Paris F-75116 France

TELEPHONE NUMBER: 33 1 40 67 60 00

NO. OF EMPLOYEES: 2,543 (avg.)

ANNUAL MEETING: In May

SHAREHOLDERS: N/A

INSTITUTIONAL HOLDINGS:
No. of Institutions: 47
Shares Held: 82,132,179

AMERICAN DEPOSITARY RECEIPTS: (Sponsored) Each American Depositary Receipt represents one half of one ordinary share of par FFr10.

DEPOSITARY BANK(S): The Bank of New York, (212) 815-2175

COLT TELECOM GROUP PLC

YIELD ...
P/E RATIO ...

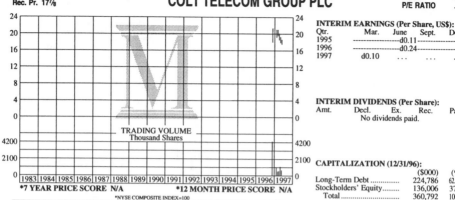

*7 YEAR PRICE SCORE N/A *12 MONTH PRICE SCORE N/A

*NYSE COMPOSITE INDEX=100

INTERIM EARNINGS (Per Share, US$):

Qtr.	Mar.	June	Sept.	Dec.
1995	--------------d0.11----------------			
1996	--------------d0.24----------------			
1997	d0.10	...	...	...

INTERIM DIVIDENDS (Per Share):

Amt.	Decl.	Ex.	Rec.	Pay.
	No dividends paid.			

CAPITALIZATION (12/31/96):

	($000)	(%)
Long-Term Debt	224,786	62.3%
Stockholders' Equity	136,006	37.7
Total	360,792	100.0

RECENT DEVELOPMENTS: For the quarter ended 3/31/97, the Company reported a net loss of £6.7 million (US$10.8 million) versus a net loss of £2.9 million the year before. Total turnover advanced to £15.0 million (US$24.3 million) from £4.9 million a year earlier. Turnover from switched services rose to £12.0 million (US$ 19.5 million) from £3.5 million the previous year due to growth in carrier revenue and an increase in the number of switched customers and increased customer usage. Turnover from non-switched services grew to £2.9 million (US$4.7 million) from £1.3 million in the prior year. COLT reported an operating loss of £4.2 million (US$6.8 million for the period. The Company has signed a major contract with Nortel for two new switches and a next generation Intelligent Network platform, which should enhance its existing network and provide a broader range of services for its customers.

BUSINESS

COLT TELECOM GROUP PLC provides telecommunications services in London and Frankfurt and is constructing networks in several other European markets. The Company's customers are primarily large business and government end users and telecommunications carriers. The Company offers a broad range of telecommunication services including private wire services, switched telephony services for directly connected customers, local area network interconnect services, video transmission services, and in London, switch telephony services for customers indirectly connected to the Company's network by dialing a four digit access code.

ANNUAL EARNINGS

	12/31/96	12/31/95	12/31/96	12/31/95
	----------US $----------		----------British £----------	
Earnings Per Share	d0.24	d0.11	d0.14	d0.07

ANNUAL FINANCIAL DATA

RECORD OF EARNINGS (IN THOUSANDS):

Total Revenues	59,272	14,272	34,979	9,190
Costs & Expenses	64,659	18,588	38,158	11,969
Depreciation & Amort	9,916	3,570	5,852	2,299
Operating Income	d15,303	d7,888	d9,031	d5,079
Net Income	d18,994	d8,163	d11,209	d5,256
Average Shares Outstg	81,609	80,000	81,609	80,000

BALANCE SHEET (IN THOUSANDS):

Cash & Cash Equivalents	267,629	3,623	157,940	2,333
Receivables, Net	22,306	4,513	13,164	2,906
Gross Property	123,385	55,667	72,815	35,845
Accumulated Depreciation	15,217	5,038	8,980	3,244
Long-Term Debt	224,786	39,247	132,656	25,272
Stockholders' Equity	136,006	10,045	80,263	6,468
Total Assets	401,539	60,781	236,966	39,138
Total Current Assets	293,370	10,121	173,131	6,517
Total Current Liabilities	40,748	11,489	24,047	7,398
Net Working Capital	252,623	d1,368	149,084	d881
Year End Shs Outstg	106,700	80,000	106,700	80,000

STATISTICAL RECORD:

Book Value Per Share	1.27	0.13		

Converted at 1996, US$1.6945= 1 British pound; 1995, US$1.5530= 1 British pound.

OFFICERS:
J. P. Hynes, Chmn.
P. W. Chisholm, Pres. & C.E.O.
L. M. Ingeneri, C.F.O.

INCORPORATED: United Kingdom

PRINCIPAL OFFICE: Bishopsgate Court, 4 Norton Folgate London E1 6DQ United Kingdom

TELEPHONE NUMBER: 44-171-190-3900

NO. OF EMPLOYEES: 326

ANNUAL MEETING: In June

SHAREHOLDERS: N/A

INSTITUTIONAL HOLDINGS:
No. of Institutions: 27
Shares Held: 4,187,534

AMERICAN DEPOSITARY RECEIPTS: (Sponsored). Each ADR represents four ordinary shares of Co.

DEPOSITARY BANK(S): The Bank of New York, (212) 815-2175

COMPANIA CERVECERIAS UNIDAS S.A.

YIELD 1.3%
P/E RATIO 24.6

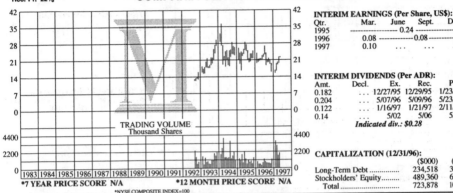

*7 YEAR PRICE SCORE N/A   *12 MONTH PRICE SCORE N/A
*NYSE COMPOSITE INDEX=100

TRADING VOLUME
Thousand Shares

INTERIM EARNINGS (Per Share, US$):

Qtr.	Mar.	June	Sept.	Dec.
1995	---------------- 0.24 ----------------			
1996	0.08	------------- 0.08 -------------		
1997	0.10	...	...	...

INTERIM DIVIDENDS (Per ADR):

Amt.	Decl.	Ex.	Rec.	Pay.
0.182	...	12/27/95	12/29/95	1/23/96
0.204	...	5/07/96	5/09/96	5/23/96
0.122	...	1/16/97	1/21/97	2/11/97
0.14	...	5/02	5/06	5/28

Indicated div.: $0.28

CAPITALIZATION (12/31/96):

	($000)	(%)
Long-Term Debt	234,518	32.4
Stockholders' Equity.........	489,360	67.6
Total	723,878	100.0

RECENT DEVELOPMENTS: During the first quarter of 1997, net income increased 35.7% to Ch$12,414 million (US$29.9 million) compared with Ch$9,152 million (US$20.0 million) during the first quarter of 1996. Sales were up 10.5% to Ch$71,220 million (US$171.3 million) in the first quarter of 1997 versus Ch$64,481 million (US$155.1 million). Volumes increased 9.1%. Higher volumes were driven mainly by volume increases in the beer segment in Argentina (51.3%), and the mineral water (25.1%) and wine segments in Chile (51.5%). Operating income increased 31.0% to Ch$15,618 million (US$37.6 million) in the first quarter of 1997 versus Ch$11,923 million (US$28.7 million) in the first quarter of 1996. Operating margin increased to 21.9% in the first quarter of 1997 versus 18.5% in the first quarter of 1996. This improvement in operating margin is explained by cost of sales and SG&A increasing by only 6.4% and 5.1%, respectively, rates inferior to the 10.5% increase in sales. The Company incurred non-operating losses of Ch$36 million (US$100,000) in the first quarter of 1997 versus a non-operating loss of Ch$1,470 million (US$3.5 million) in the first quarter of 1996.

BUSINESS

COMPANIA CERVECERIAS UNIDAS S.A. ("CCU") is a diversified beverage company operating principally in Chile and Argentina. CCU is the largest Chilean brewer (91% market share), the second-largest brewer in Argentina (11% market share), the second largest Chilean soft drink producer (28% market share), the largest Chilean mineral water producer (66% market share) and the third-largest wine producer in Chile (11% market share). In Chile the Company produces five proprietary beer brands, distributes imported Budweiser, and imports and locally produces Guinness and Paulaner beers. CCU's soft drink business includes proprietary brands and brands produced under license from PepsiCo and Cadbury Schweppes. In Argentina CCU produces Budweiser, under a license agreement with Anheuser-Busch, as well as four proprietary brands. Vina San Pedro, CCU's winery, produces and markets a full range of wine products for both the domestic and export markets. Additionally, CCU owns approximately one third of the largest brewery in Croatia, Karlovacka Pivovara, whose results are not consolidated into the Company's financial statements. CCU also produces plastic bottles and crates for use in its businesses and, in the case of crates, for sale to third parties.

ANNUAL EARNINGS

	12/31/96	12/31/95	12/31/96	12/31/95
	------------- US $ -------------		------- Chilean Pesos -------	
Earnings Per Share	0.16	0.24	69.40	102.28

ANNUAL FINANCIAL DATA

RECORD OF EARNINGS (IN THOUSANDS):

	12/31/96	12/31/95	12/31/96	12/31/95
Total Revenues	533,947	468,951	226,858,178	199,243,423
Costs & Expenses	468,853	406,765	199,201,737	172,822,409
Operating Income	65,094	62,186	27,656,441	26,421,014
Income Bef Income Tax	55,485	73,699	23,573,800	31,312,335
Income Tax	5,456	5,946	2,318,106	2,526,218
Minority Interests	7,254	4,829	3,082,008	2,051,616
Net Income	42,775	62,924	18,173,686	26,734,501

BALANCE SHEET (IN THOUSANDS):

Cash & Cash Equivalents	43,543	81,609	18,500,044	34,673,373
Receivables, Net	131,430	117,341	55,840,864	49,854,807
Inventories	69,064	67,681	29,343,162	28,755,499
Net Property	560,296	522,045	238,052,787	221,801,059
Long-Term Debt	234,518	259,860	99,639,495	110,406,920
Stockholders' Equity	489,360	421,271	207,914,530	178,985,216
Total Assets	978,272	925,473	415,638,251	393,205,606
Total Current Assets	323,712	297,469	137,535,578	126,385,805
Total Current Liabilities	167,998	163,370	71,377,127	69,411,146
Net Working Capital	155,715	134,099	66,158,451	56,974,659
Year End Shs Outstg	304,030	261,394	304,030	261,394

STATISTICAL RECORD:

Return on Equity %	8.7	14.9
Return on Assets %	4.4	6.8
Operating Profit Margin %	12.2	13.3
Net Profit Margin %	8.0	13.4
Book Value Per Share	1.61	1.61

Converted at 1996, US$0.0024= 1 Chilean peso; 1994, US$0.0025= 1 Chilean peso

OFFICERS:
G. Luksic Craig, Chairman
F. Perez Mackenna, Gen. Mgr.
R. Reyes Mercandino, C.F.O.
INCORPORATED: Jan., 1902
PRINCIPAL OFFICE: Bandera 84, 6th floor
Santiago Chile

TELEPHONE NUMBER: 56-2-670-3000
NO. OF EMPLOYEES: 5,419
ANNUAL MEETING: In Apr.
SHAREHOLDERS: 6,775
INSTITUTIONAL HOLDINGS:
No. of Institutions: 27
Shares Held: 8,336,553

**AMERICAN DEPOSITARY
RECEIPTS:** (Sponsored) Each American Depositary Receipt represents five ordinary shares with no par.

DEPOSITARY BANK(S): J.P. Morgan, (212) 648-3206

CONCORDIA PAPER (HOLDINGS) LIMITED

YIELD ...
P/E RATIO ...

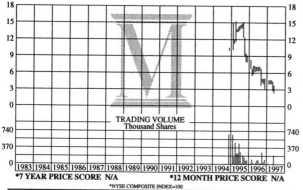

TRADING VOLUME
Thousand Shares

1983|1984|1985|1986|1987|1988|1989|1990|1991|1992|1993|1994|1995|1996|1997

*7 YEAR PRICE SCORE N/A   ***12 MONTH PRICE SCORE N/A**

*NYSE COMPOSITE INDEX=100

INTERIM EARNINGS (Per Share, US$):

Qtr.	Mar.	June	Sept.	Dec.
1994	----------- 0.18 -----------			
1995	----------- d0.05 -----------			
1996	----------- d0.07 -----------			

INTERIM DIVIDENDS (Per Share):

Amt.	Decl.	Ex.	Rec.	Pay.
No dividends paid.				

CAPITALIZATION (12/31/96):

	($000)	(%)
Long-Term Debt	54,585	65.7
Stockholders' Equity........	27,412	33.0
Deferred Income Tax	1,066	1.3
Total	83,063	100.0

RECENT DEVELOPMENTS: For the year ended 12/31/96, the Company reported a net loss of HK$24.9 million. This compares with a net loss of HK$15.7 million in 1995. Net sales for the year grew 45.4% to HK$835.3 million from HK$574.6 million the previous year. During the year, sales growth in the Greater Hong Kong market was 27.0%. In addition, production output increased 61.0% over 1995 levels. Selling, general and administrative expenses decreased 9.8% to HK$67.3 million, which contributed to a significant improvement in operating income. Interest expense, however, more than doubled to HK$33.6 million compared with HK$15.4 million and interest income fell to HK$127,000 from HK$2.7 million, leading to the greater net loss. For the fourth quarter ended 12/31/96, net loss was US$870,000 compared with a net loss of US$4.5 million a year earlier. Net sales grew 27.1% to US$26.7 million from US$21.0 million the year before.

BUSINESS

CONCORDIA PAPER (HOLDINGS) LIMITED is a holding company. Through its subsidiaries, the Company is engaged in the manufacture of high-quality recycled machine-coated grey-back duplex boxboard, which is used primarily for the packaging of light durable consumer goods.

ANNUAL EARNINGS

	12/31/96	12/31/95	12/31/96	12/31/95
	----------US $-----------		----------HK$----------	
Earnings Per Share	d0.07	d0.05	d0.55	d0.35

ANNUAL FINANCIAL DATA

RECORD OF EARNINGS (IN THOUSANDS):

Total Revenues	107,916	74,292	835,263	574,574
Costs & Expenses	107,268	75,030	830,245	580,277
Operating Income	648	d737	5,018	d5,703
Income Bef Income Tax	d3,675	d2,379	d28,445	d18,399
Income Tax	cr433	cr361	cr3,352	cr2,791
Minority Interests	cr30	11	cr229	86
Net Income	d3,212	d2,029	d24,864	d15,694
Average Shares Outstg	45,450	45,450	45,450	45,450

BALANCE SHEET (IN THOUSANDS):

Cash & Cash Equivalents	1,668	396	12,911	3,060
Receivables, Net	9,597	6,391	74,279	49,427
Inventories	14,389	10,789	111,371	83,442
Gross Property	104,857	97,809	811,585	756,452
Accumulated Depreciation	21,254	17,141	164,502	132,565
Long-Term Debt	54,585	40,116	422,483	310,255
Stockholders' Equity	27,412	30,648	212,166	237,030
Total Assets	110,283	100,073	853,580	773,959
Total Current Assets	26,632	19,358	206,133	149,712
Total Current Liabilities	27,478	28,010	212,678	216,628
Net Working Capital	d846	d8,652	d6,545	d66,916
Year End Shs Outstg	45,450	45,450	45,450	45,450

STATISTICAL RECORD:

Operating Profit Margin %	0.60	...		
Book Value Per Share	0.60	0.67		

Converted at 1996, US$0.1292= 1 Hong Kong $; 1995, US$0.1293= 1 Hong Kong $

OFFICERS:
A. Cheng, Chairman
J. Lau, Managing Dir. & C.E.O. & Sec.

INCORPORATED: Bermuda, Sept., 1994

PRINCIPAL OFFICE: Cedar House, 41 Cedar Avenue, Hamilton Bermuda HM 12

TELEPHONE NUMBER: N/A

NO. OF EMPLOYEES: 600

ANNUAL MEETING: In Jun.

SHAREHOLDERS: N/A

INSTITUTIONAL HOLDINGS:
No. of Institutions: 8
Shares Held: 665,178

AMERICAN DEPOSITARY RECEIPTS: (Sponsored) Each American Depositary Share represents five ordinary shares of par US$0.10.

DEPOSITARY BANK(S): Citibank N.A., (212) 657-7800

CORTECS INTERNATIONAL LIMITED

YIELD ...
P/E RATIO ...

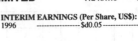

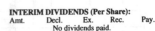

1983 1984 1985 1986 1987 1988 1989 1990 1991 1992 1993 1994 1995 1996 1997

*7 YEAR PRICE SCORE N/A   ***12 MONTH PRICE SCORE N/A**

*NYSE COMPOSITE INDEX=100

INTERIM EARNINGS (Per Share, US$):
1996 -----------------$d0.05-----------------

INTERIM DIVIDENDS (Per Share):

Amt.	Decl.	Ex.	Rec.	Pay.
	No dividends paid.			

CAPITALIZATION (6/30/96):

	($000)	(%)
Minority Interests.............	d39	0.0
Long-Term Debt	2,166	1.5
Stockholders' Equity........	142,190	98.5
Total	144,317	100.0

RECENT DEVELOPMENTS: For the half-year ended 12/31/96, net loss was £4.3 million compared with a loss of £1.6 million in the corresponding half-year period of 1995. Turnover was £4.0 million, down 18.4% from £4.9 million in the year-earlier period. The decrease in turnover was primarily attributed to a decrease in immediately-due payments in the prior-year period. The Company has increased its research and development spending. The Company has capitalized on its increased research and development spending by exploiting the adaptability of its technology platforms and creating product opportunities. The Company plans to seek U.K. PLC status and is now in discussions with the London Stock Exchange regarding U.K. residency for DLVRY.

BUSINESS

CORTECS INTERNATIONAL LIMITED and its subsidiaries develop new pharmaceutical delivery systems for the human and animal healthcare industries and rapid diagnostic technologies. The Company establishes relationships with major international companies to achieve registration, manufacture and distribution of the resulting products in world markets. Group entities are also involved in the development of pharmaceuticals and diagnostic technologies, their manufacture and distribution and the purchase, development and sale of pharmaceutical rights.

ANNUAL EARNINGS

	6/30/96	6/30/95	6/30/96	6/30/95
	-------------US $--------------		-------------A$-------------	
Earnings Per Share	d0.05	d0.05	d0.06	d0.07

ANNUAL FINANCIAL DATA

RECORD OF EARNINGS (IN THOUSANDS):

	6/30/96	6/30/95	6/30/96	6/30/95
Total Revenues	18,088	11,988	22,969	16,891
Income Bef Income Tax	d6,246	d6,372	d7,932	d8,979
Minority Interests	cr39	cr776	cr50	cr1,094
Net Income	d6,207	d5,596	d7,882	d7,885
Average Shares Outstg	97,963	78,432	97,963	78,432

BALANCE SHEET (IN THOUSANDS):

Cash & Cash Equivalents	90,974	10,686	115,523	15,057
Receivables, Net	2,710	2,798	3,441	3,943
Inventories	1,877	1,978	2,384	2,787
Gross Property	4,898	4,084	6,220	5,755
Accumulated Depreciation	2,185	2,344	2,774	3,303
Long-Term Debt	2,166	2,266	2,750	3,193
Stockholders' Equity	142,190	58,606	180,559	82,578
Total Assets	164,387	75,491	208,746	106,370
Total Current Assets	95,562	15,462	121,348	21,787
Total Current Liabilities	4,815	5,546	6,114	7,814
Net Working Capital	90,747	9,917	115,234	13,973
Year End Shs Outstg	115,061	78,622	115,061	78,622

STATISTICAL RECORD:

Return on Equity %	...	...		
Return on Assets %	...	...		
Operating Profit Margin %	...	...		
Net Profit Margin %	...	...		
Book Value Per Share	1.24	0.75		

Converted at 1996, US$0.7875= 1 Australian $; 1995, US$0.7097= 1 Australian $

OFFICERS:
G. N. Travers, Exec. Chmn. & C.E.O.
M. J. Flynn, Pres.
G. Hill, Managing Dir.
J. Pockson, Finance Dir.

INCORPORATED: 1985

PRINCIPAL OFFICE: Level 2, 220 St George's Terrace Perth Australia

TELEPHONE NUMBER: 61 9 481 1314

NO. OF EMPLOYEES: 193

ANNUAL MEETING: In Nov.

SHAREHOLDERS: 5,213 ordinary; 9 preference

INSTITUTIONAL HOLDINGS:
No. of Institutions: 7
Shares Held: 33,081

AMERICAN DEPOSITARY RECEIPTS: (Sponsored) Each American Depositary Receipt represents five shares of par A$0.50.

DEPOSITARY BANK(S): The Bank of New York, (212) 815-2175

CRH PLC

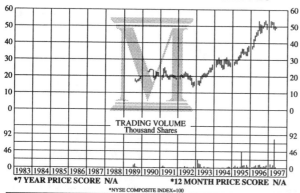

| 1983 | 1984 | 1985 | 1986 | 1987 | 1988 | 1989 | 1990 | 1991 | 1992 | 1993 | 1994 | 1995 | 1996 | 1997 |

*7 YEAR PRICE SCORE N/A   *12 MONTH PRICE SCORE N/A

*NYSE COMPOSITE INDEX=100

TRADING VOLUME Thousand Shares

INTERIM EARNINGS (Per Share,):

| 1995 | ------------------ 0.57 ------------------ |
| 1996 | ------------------ 0.67 ------------------ |

INTERIM DIVIDENDS (Per Share):

Amt.	Decl.	Ex.	Rec.	Pay.
0.220	...	9/19/95	9/21/95	11/20/95
0.508	...	3/15/96	3/19/96	5/28/96
0.255	...	9/20	9/24	11/22
0.590	...	3/12/97	3/14/97	5/28/97

Indicated div.: $0.845

CAPITALIZATION (12/31/96):

	($000)	(%)
Minority Interests	16,394	0.6
Long-Term Debt	1,570,853	52.0
Stockholders' Equity	1,379,931	45.7
Deferred Income Tax	52,093	1.7
Total	3,019,271	100.0

RECENT DEVELOPMENTS: For the year ended 12/31/96, net income increased 17.9% to IR£148.7 million from IR£126.2 million in 1995. Revenues climbed 27.1% to IR£2.43 billion from IR£1.91 billion. Trading profit, including gains from the disposal of fixed assets, grew 21.1% to IR£206.5 million. The improved results primarily reflected acquisitions and expansion in North America. Revenues from North American operations soared 71.5% to IR£1.02 billion and trading profit jumped 56.2% to IR£91.3 million. Revenues from Ireland increased 15.7% to IR£321.9 million, while trading profit grew 18.4% to IR£57.0 million. Revenues in Britain and Northern Ireland rose 20.8% to IR£463.7 million; hovever, trading profit fell 10.9% to IR£15.1 million. Revenues from Mainland Europe slipped 5.0% to IR£619.0 million and trading profit declined 8.4% to IR£43.1 million. The Company expects to continue to expand through acquisitions, but not at the robust pace CRH experienced in 1996.

BUSINESS

CRH plc is a holding company. Through its subsidiaries, the Company is engaged in the manufacture and supply of a wide range of materials for the construction industry. CRH's activities fall into two business segments: building materials, and merchanting and do-it-yourself. The building materials segment is engaged in the production of cement, readymixed concrete, aggregates, concrete products and a variety of construction-related products and services. The merchanting and do-it-yourself segment is engaged in the marketing and sale of builders' supplies to the construction industry and materials for the do-it-yourself market. The Company has operations in a total of 792 locations in 12 countries in North and South America and Europe.

ANNUAL EARNINGS

	12/31/96	12/31/95	12/31/96	12/31/95
	------------US $------------		------------Irish £-------	
Earnings Per Share	0.67	0.57	0.41	0.36

ANNUAL FINANCIAL DATA

RECORD OF EARNINGS (IN MILLIONS):

	12/31/96	12/31/95	12/31/96	12/31/95
Total Revenues	4,024	3,057	2,428	1,911
Costs & Expenses	3,683	2,786	2,222	1,741
Operating Income	341	271	206	169
Income Bef Income Tax	303	243	183	152
Income Tax	72	53	43	33
Eq. Earnings in Affils.	18	14	11	9
Minority Interests	2	2	1	1
Net Income	247	202	149	126
Average Shares Outstg (000)	366,347	354,866	366,347	354,866

BALANCE SHEET (IN MILLIONS):

Cash & Cash Equivalents	1,147	754	692	471
Receivables, Net	760	494	459	309
Inventories	435	330	262	206
Gross Property	2,443	1,851	1,474	1,157
Accumulated Depreciation	830	723	501	452
Long-Term Debt	1,571	724	948	453
Stockholders' Equity	1,380	1,096	832	685
Total Assets	4,121	2,855	2,486	1,784
Total Current Assets	2,342	1,578	1,413	986
Total Current Liabilities	1,048	944	632	590
Net Working Capital	1,294	635	781	397
Year End Shs Outstg (000)	380,288	358,519	380,288	358,519

STATISTICAL RECORD:

Return on Equity %	17.90	18.43		
Return on Assets %	5.99	7.08		
Operating Profit Margin %	8.48	8.87		
Net Profit Margin %	6.14	6.61		
Book Value Per Share	3.62	3.06		

Converted at 1996, US$1.6576= 1 Irish pound; 1995, US$1.6002= 1 Irish pound

OFFICERS:
A. D. Barry, Chmn.
D. Godson, C.E.O.
H. P. Sheridan, Fin. Dir.

INCORPORATED: Ireland, 1970

PRINCIPAL OFFICE: Belgard Castle, Clondalkin, Dublin 22 Ireland

TELEPHONE NUMBER: +(353)-1-404-1000

NO. OF EMPLOYEES: 19,000 (approx.)

ANNUAL MEETING: In May

SHAREHOLDERS: 13,074

INSTITUTIONAL HOLDINGS:
No. of Institutions: 1,886
Shares Held: 33,050,000

AMERICAN DEPOSITARY RECEIPTS: Each American Depositary Receipt represents five ordinary shares of par value IR£0.25.

DEPOSITARY BANK(S): Citibank N.A., (212) 657-2175

NASDAQ SYMBOL CSKKY
Rec. Pr. 23½

CSK CORPORATION

YIELD 0.3%
P/E RATIO ...

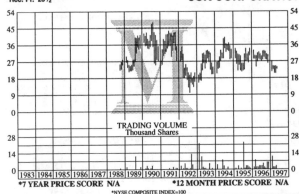

*7 YEAR PRICE SCORE N/A   *12 MONTH PRICE SCORE N/A
*NYSE COMPOSITE INDEX=100

TRADING VOLUME
Thousand Shares

INTERIM EARNINGS (Per Share, US$):
1995	------------------d1.55------------------
1996	------------------d1.15------------------

INTERIM DIVIDENDS (Per Share):

Amt.	Decl.	Ex.	Rec.	Pay.
0.04	...	9/26/95	9/28/95	12/21/95
0.041	...	3/26/96	3/28/96	7/11/96
0.04	...	9/25	9/27	12/23
0.037	...	3/25/97	3/28/97	...

Indicated div.: $0.074

CAPITALIZATION (3/31/96):

	($000)	(%)
Long-Term Debt	402,244	25.7
Stockholders' Equity.........	1,161,989	74.3
Total	1,564,232	100.0

RECENT DEVELOPMENTS: For the six months ended 9/30/96, net income jumped 42.2% to Y1.48 billion from Y1.04 billion in the first half of fiscal 1996. Total revenues climbed 30.4% to Y42.6 billion. Operating income surged to Y1.40 billion from Y586 million. The improved results were driven by increased demand for multimedia services, PC networks, and client/server systems. Sales in the software business/systems development and services unit rose 8.5% to Y18.26 billion. The information management services/computer room management services unit grew sales by 7.1% to Y5.04 billion. Computer and other products sales jumped 77.8% to Y16.15 billion. Other revenues increased 24% to Y3.16 billion. To expand new business opportunities, CSK established a new General Marking Division to focus on systems integration and outsourcing businesses.

BUSINESS

CSK CORPORATION operates as an independent computer multiservice company in Japan. The Company's activities are divided into three areas: Computer services, consisting of programming and software development, facilities management and data entry services; computer and other product sales; and computer leasing. Computer services are user-oriented and include individualized programming for business and technical computing services, such as process control and telecommunications. The Company's stations programmers and system engineers to clients on a long-term basis. CSK is also involved in research and development, and has developed an information storage and retrieval system using laser cards.

ANNUAL EARNINGS

	3/31/96	3/31/95	3/31/96	3/31/95
	-------------US $-------------		-------------Yen-------------	
Earnings Per Share	d1.15	d1.55	d121.81	d126.71

ANNUAL FINANCIAL DATA

RECORD OF EARNINGS (IN MILLIONS):

Total Revenues	963	987	103,563	85,106
Costs & Expenses	953	983	102,507	84,721
Operating Income	10	4	1,056	385
Income Bef Income Tax	d14	d30	d1,466	d3,205
Income Tax	8	8	850	654
Eq. Earnings in Affils.	d51	d49	d5,495	d4,267
Net Income	d73	d76	d7,811	d8,126

BALANCE SHEET (IN MILLIONS):

Cash & Cash Equivalents	706	576	75,867	49,662
Receivables, Net	214	154	23,061	13,236
Inventories	68	55	7,355	4,716
Net Property	254	321	27,264	27,709
Long-Term Debt	402	496	43,252	42,747
Stockholders' Equity	1,162	1,558	124,945	134,310
Total Assets	2,444	2,329	262,805	200,777
Total Current Assets	1,028	942	110,504	81,236
Total Current Liabilities	828	209	89,071	18,015
Net Working Capital	199	733	21,433	63,221
Year End Shs Outstg (000)	64,133	64,133	64,133	64,133

STATISTICAL RECORD:

Return on Equity %	...	...		
Return on Assets %	...	...		
Operating Profit Margin %	1.02	0.45		
Net Profit Margin %	...	...		
Book Value Per Share	18.12	24.29		

Converted at 1996, US$0.0093= 1 Japanese Yen; 1995, US$0.0116= 1 Japanese Yen

OFFICERS:
I. Okawa, Chmn.
Y. Fukushima, Pres.
M. Aozono, Exec. V.P.
K. Kashima, Exec. V.P.

INCORPORATED: Japan, Oct., 1968

PRINCIPAL OFFICE: Shinjuku Sumitomo Bldg. 16th floor 2-6-1 Nishi-Shinjuku Shinjuku-ku Tokyo Japan

TELEPHONE NUMBER: (03) 3344-1811

NO. OF EMPLOYEES: 5,340

ANNUAL MEETING: In Jun.

SHAREHOLDERS: N/A

INSTITUTIONAL HOLDINGS:
No. of Institutions: 4
Shares Held: 156,191

AMERICAN DEPOSITARY RECEIPTS: (Sponsored) Each American Depositary Receipt represents one common share.

DEPOSITARY BANK(S): The Bank of New York, (212) 815-2175

DAIEI, INC.

YIELD 2.6%
P/E RATIO N.M.

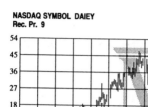

*7 YEAR PRICE SCORE N/A   *12 MONTH PRICE SCORE N/A
*NYSE COMPOSITE INDEX=100

TRADING VOLUME
Thousand Shares

INTERIM EARNINGS (Per Share, US$):

Qtr.	May	Aug.	Nov.	Feb.
1996	------------------ 0.07 -----------------			

INTERIM DIVIDENDS (Per Share):

Amt.	Decl.	Ex.	Rec.	Pay.
0.127	...	8/28/95	8/30/95	12/13/95
0.118	...	2/26/96	2/28/96	6/12/96
0.114	...	8/27	8/29	12/16
0.114	...	2/25/97	2/27/97	...

Indicated Div.:$0.23

CAPITALIZATION (2/29/96):

	($000)	(%)
Minority Interests............	89,196	1.4
Long-Term Debt..............	4,354,515	68.7
Stockholders' Equity........	1,362,319	21.5
Deferred Income Tax	530,385	8.4
Total................	6,336,415	100.0

RECENT DEVELOPMENTS: For the year ended 2/29/96, net income was ¥5.08 billion compared with a net loss of ¥50.66 billion a year earlier. Total revenues were ¥3,156.98 billion, down 2.1% from ¥3,223.87 billion in the prior year. Total costs and expenses fell 3.1% to ¥3,073.85 billion from ¥3,171.53 billion in 1995. Operating income was ¥76.76 billion compared with ¥52.30 billion the year before, an increase of 46.8%. During the year, the Company was actively engaged in building new stores and refurbishing existing stores. Efforts to reduce structural costs included retooling the Company's nationwide distribution network by constructing an information transfer system, as well as establishing and expanding distribution centers. The Company also expanded its supply of processed food products and household sundry items to Maruetsu Co., Ltd., and it continued to pursue the reconstruction of its communication and distribution ties with this company.

BUSINESS

DAIEI, INC. is a retail company engaged in the sale of foodstuffs, clothing and personal care products, including cashmere sweaters, acrylic fiber sweaters, and ram's wool sweaters; household items such as sundry goods, color films, disposable cameras, concentrated detergent, videotapes, hangers, and aluminum pans; hobbies, sporting items, and other merchandise items, including camping products, barbecue sets, trekking shoes, sports bicycles, outdoor equipment, and liquid fertilizer, through its network of superstores, convenience stores, specialty stores and shopping centers.

ANNUAL EARNINGS

	2/29/96	2/28/95	2/29/96	2/28/95
	------------US $-------------		------------Yen------------	
Earnings Per Share	0.07	d0.76	7.20	d73.37

ANNUAL FINANCIAL DATA

RECORD OF EARNINGS (IN MILLIONS):

	2/29/96	2/28/95	2/29/96	2/28/95
Total Revenues	29,991	33,206	3,156,976	3,223,869
Costs & Expenses	29,202	32,667	3,073,854	3,171,531
Operating Income	729	539	76,761	52,296
Income Bef Income Tax	482	323	50,748	d31,353
Income Tax	248	21	26,083	2,039
Eq. Earnings in Affils.	d118	d170	d12,399	d16,519
Minority Interests	d7	d6	d755	d611
Net Income	48	d522	5,083	d50,655
BALANCE SHEET (IN MILLIONS):				
Cash & Cash Equivalents	1,006	1,635	105,869	158,786
Receivables, Net	721	867	75,886	84,184
Inventories	1,438	1,751	151,379	170,034
Gross Property	10,436	10,706	1,098,491	1,039,384
Accumulated Depreciation	3,942	3,919	414,911	380,501
Long-Term Debt	4,355	5,426	458,370	526,754
Stockholders' Equity	1,362	1,514	143,402	146,980
Total Assets	20,314	22,849	2,138,337	2,218,354
Total Current Assets	3,817	5,103	401,837	495,475
Total Current Liabilities	12,436	13,408	1,309,092	1,301,770
Net Working Capital	d8,619	d8,305	d907,255	d806,295
Year End Shs Outstg (000)	713,696	713,696	713,696	713,696
STATISTICAL RECORD:				
Return on Equity %	3.52	...		
Return on Assets %	0.24	...		
Operating Profit Margin %	2.63	1.62		
Net Profit Margin %	0.16	...		
Book Value Per Share	1.91	2.12		

Converted at 1996, US$0.0095= 1 Japanese Yen; 1995, US$0.0103= 1 Japanese Yen

OFFICERS:
I. Nakauchi, Chmn., Pres. & C.E.O.
H. Kawashima, Exec. Vice-Chmn.
J. Nakauchi, Exec. V.P. & C.O.O.
S. Tanishima, V.P.

INCORPORATED: Apr., 1957

PRINCIPAL OFFICE: 4-1-1, Minatojima Nakamachi, Chuo-ku, Kobe 650 Japan

TELEPHONE NUMBER: 078-302-5001

NO. OF EMPLOYEES: 16,612

ANNUAL MEETING: In May

SHAREHOLDERS: N/A

INSTITUTIONAL HOLDINGS:
No. of Institutions: 5
Shares Held: 561,250

AMERICAN DEPOSITARY RECEIPTS: Each American Depositary Receipt represents two common shares.

DEPOSITARY BANK(S): The Bank of New York, (212) 815-2175; Bankers Trust Co., (212) 250-8500; Citibank N.A., (212) 657-7800

DANKA BUSINESS SYSTEMS PLC

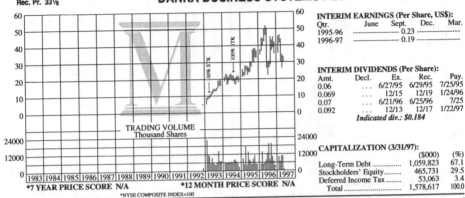

INTERIM EARNINGS (Per Share, US$):

Qtr.	June	Sept.	Dec.	Mar.
1995-96		0.23		
1996-97		0.19		

INTERIM DIVIDENDS (Per Share):

Amt.	Decl.	Ex.	Rec.	Pay.
0.06	...	6/27/95	6/29/95	7/25/95
0.069	...	12/15	12/19	1/24/96
0.07	...	6/21/96	6/25/96	7/25
0.092	...	12/13	12/17	1/22/97

Indicated div.: $0.184

CAPITALIZATION (3/31/97):

	($000)	(%)
Long-Term Debt	1,059,823	67.1
Stockholders' Equity	465,731	29.5
Deferred Income Tax	53,063	3.4
Total	1,578,617	100.0

*7 YEAR PRICE SCORE N/A   *12 MONTH PRICE SCORE N/A

*NYSE COMPOSITE INDEX=100

RECENT DEVELOPMENTS: For the year ended 3/31/97, earnings before extraordinary items slid 8.6% to $42.4 million from $46.3 million in the equivalent 1996 period. Revenues soared 69.4% to $2.10 billion compared with $1.24 billion the year before. The improvement in revenues was primarily attributed to acquisitions, principally from the acquisition of the Kodak businesses. Earnings included restructuring charges of $35.0 million and $8.5 million for 1997 and 1996, respectively, related to the projected integration of the Kodak businesses and the restructuring of the Group's North American operations. Earnings from operations were $101.9 million compared with $96.2 million in 1996. Earnings before extraordinary items excluded charges of $578,000 and $1.1 million for 1997 and 1996, respectively, for the extinguishment of debt.

BUSINESS

DANKA BUSINESS SYSTEMS PLC headquartered in London, England and St. Petersburg, Florida, is one of the world's largest independent suppliers of photocopiers, facsimiles and other automated office equipment. Danka employs over 20,000 people and provides office products and services globally in over 30 countries throughout the world. Danka's ADS's are listed on NASDAQ and its Ordinary Shares are listed on the London Stock Exchange. Effective, 12/31/96, the Company acquired the sales, marketing and equipment service operations of Kodak's Office Imaging business, as well as Kodak's facilities management business, formerly known as Kodak Imaging Services.

ANNUAL EARNINGS

	3/31/97	3/31/96	3/31/97	3/31/96
	US $		British £	
Earnings Per Share	0.19	0.23	0.12	0.15

ANNUAL FINANCIAL DATA

RECORD OF EARNINGS (IN MILLIONS):

	3/31/97	3/31/96	3/31/97	3/31/96
Total Revenues	2,101	1,240	1,288	807
Costs & Expenses	1,980	1,130	1,214	735
Amortization	19	14	12	9
Operating Income	102	96	63	62
Income Bef Income Tax	68	74	42	48
Income Tax	26	28	16	18
Net Income	42	46	26	30
Net Extraordinary Items	d1	d1	d1	d1
Average Shares Outstg (000)	225,071	198,458	225,071	198,458

BALANCE SHEET (IN MILLIONS):

Cash & Cash Equivalents	74	38	45	25
Receivables, Net	847	247	519	161
Inventories	489	215	300	140
Net Property	88	43	54	28
Long-Term Debt	1,060	318	650	207
Stockholders' Equity	466	442	286	288
Total Assets	2,459	1,092	1,508	710
Total Current Assets	1,450	510	889	332
Total Current Liabilities	881	292	540	190
Net Working Capital	569	218	349	142
Year End Shs Outstg (000)	...	219,112	...	219,112

STATISTICAL RECORD:

Return on Equity %	9.09	10.48		
Return on Assets %	1.72	4.25		
Operating Profit Margin %	4.85	7.75		
Net Profit Margin %	2.02	3.74		
Book Value Per Share	...	2.02		

Converted at 1997, US$1.6310= 1 British pound; 1996, US$1.5373= 1 British pound

OFFICERS:
M. A. Vaughan-Lee, Chmn.
D. M. Doyle, Chief Exec.
D. C. Snell, Fin. Dir.

INCORPORATED: United Kingdom, 1986

PRINCIPAL OFFICE: Masters House, 107
Hammersmith Road, London, W1H 0QH
United Kingdom

TELEPHONE NUMBER: 44-171-603-1515

NO. OF EMPLOYEES: 22,000

ANNUAL MEETING: In Jul.

SHAREHOLDERS: 5,221

INSTITUTIONAL HOLDINGS:
No. of Institutions: 100
Shares Held: 40,345,704

AMERICAN DEPOSITARY RECEIPTS: (Sponsored) Each American Depositary Receipt represents four ordinary shares of par £0.0125. ADRs split 2-for-1 on Aug. 16, 1994.

DEPOSITARY BANK(S): The Bank of New York, (212) 815-2175

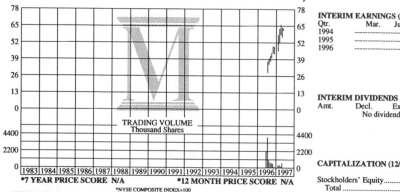

DASSAULT SYSTEMES, S.A.

YIELD ...
P/E RATIO 9.5

INTERIM EARNINGS (Per Share, FFr):

Qtr.	Mar.	June	Sep.	Dec.
1994		3.06		
1995		4.31		
1996		6.66		

TRADING VOLUME
Thousand Shares

INTERIM DIVIDENDS (Per Share):

Amt.	Decl.	Ex.	Rec.	Pay.
	No dividends paid.			

*7 YEAR PRICE SCORE N/A   *12 MONTH PRICE SCORE N/A
*NYSE COMPOSITE INDEX=100

CAPITALIZATION (12/31/95):

	($000)	(%)
Stockholders' Equity	303,922	100.0
Total	303,922	100.0

RECENT DEVELOPMENTS: For the year ended 12/31/96, net income was FF 342.5 million compared with FF 221.3 million in the prior year. Total revenues rose 22.8% to FF 1.39 billlion from FF 1.14 billion a year earlier. The increase in revenues was supported by a 49.2% jump in software revenues and a 24.6% rise in service and other revenues. Operating income was up 34.0% to FF 460.9 million. For the quarter ended 12/31/96, net income advanced 27.9% to FF 132.9 million from FF 103.9 million in the corresponding 1995 period. Revenues were FF 435.6 million, up 17.1% from FF 372.0 million in the equivalent quarter a year earlier. Gross profit, as a percentage of revenues was 86.7% compared to 87.6% a year ago. Operating income was FF 191.5 million, up 21.5%.

BUSINESS

DASSAULT SYSTEMES S.A. develops computer aided design (CAD), computer aided manufacturing (CAM), and computer aided engineering (CAE) software products. The Company's CAD/CAM/CAE product portfolio has over 100 products, and offers a full range of design, analysis, manufacturing and post-production support applications. The products are marketed and sold worldwide through a mutually non-exclusive agreement with IBM since 1981. The Company also markets and distributes a small percentage of its products directly to certain customers and serves as an agent for IBM in France and the United States. Approximately 80% of Dassault's revenues are in the form of royalties received from IBM's licensing of the Company's products. Other revenues come from software and technology-related consulting and support services.

ANNUAL EARNINGS

	12/31/95	12/31/94	12/31/95	12/31/94
	US $		FFr	
Earnings Per Share	0.88	0.57	4.31	3.06

ANNUAL FINANCIAL DATA

RECORD OF EARNINGS (IN THOUSANDS):

Total Revenues	231,584	187,626	1,135,773	1,001,741
Costs & Expenses	161,458	146,437	791,851	781,833
Operating Income	70,126	41,189	343,922	219,908
Income Bef Income Tax	77,089	44,285	378,075	236,439
Income Tax	31,965	14,813	156,770	79,087
Net Income	45,124	29,472	221,305	157,352
Average Shares Outstg (OOO)	51,389	51,389	51,389	51,389

BALANCE SHEET (IN THOUSANDS):

Cash & Cash Equivalents	276,151	200,350	1,354,345	1,069,674
Receivables, Net	88,787	56,416	435,446	301,209
Gross Property	135,247	120,417	663,302	642,908
Accumulated Depreciation	66,109	47,243	324,223	252,233
Stockholders' Equity	303,922	257,071	1,490,544	1,372,510
Total Assets	456,973	361,705	2,241,164	1,931,153
Total Current Assets	370,619	261,166	1,817,652	1,394,374
Total Current Liabilities	102,901	58,053	504,663	309,945
Net Working Capital	267,718	203,114	1,312,989	1,084,429
Year End Shs Outstg	51,389	51,389	51,389	51,389

STATISTICAL RECORD:

Return on Equity %	14.85	11.46		
Return on Assets %	9.87	8.15		
Operating Profit Margin %	30.28	21.95		
Net Profit Margin %	19.48	15.71		
Book Value Per Share	5.91	5.00		

Converted at 1995, US$0.2039= 1 French francs; 1994, US$0.1873= 1 French francs

OFFICERS:
C. Edelstenne, Chmn. & C.E.O.
B. Charles, Pres.
F. Bernard, Special Advisor
T. de Tersant, Exec. V.P.

INCORPORATED: France, 1981

PRINCIPAL OFFICE: 9, quai Marcel Dassault
B.P. 310 92156 Suresnes Cedex France

TELEPHONE NUMBER: 33-1-40-99-40-99

NO. OF EMPLOYEES: 1,066

ANNUAL MEETING: In May

SHAREHOLDERS: N/A

INSTITUTIONAL HOLDINGS:
No. of Institutions: 11
Shares Held: 806,825

AMERICAN DEPOSITARY RECEIPTS: Each American Depositary Receipt represents one common share of Co., par FFr10.

DEPOSITARY BANK(S): J.P. Morgan, (212) 648-3206

DE BEERS CONSOLIDATED MINES LTD.

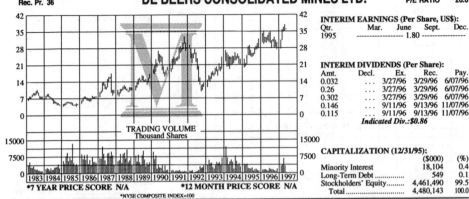

INTERIM EARNINGS (Per Share, US$):

Qtr.	Mar.	June	Sept.	Dec.
1995		1.80		

INTERIM DIVIDENDS (Per Share):

Amt.	Decl.	Ex.	Rec.	Pay.
0.032	...	3/27/96	3/29/96	6/07/96
0.26	...	3/27/96	3/29/96	6/07/96
0.302	...	3/27/96	3/29/96	6/07/96
0.146	...	9/11/96	9/13/96	11/07/96
0.115	...	9/11/96	9/13/96	11/07/96

Indicated Div.:$0.86

CAPITALIZATION (12/31/95):

	($000)	(%)
Minority Interest	18,104	0.4
Long-Term Debt	549	0.1
Stockholders' Equity	4,461,490	99.5
Total	4,480,143	100.0

*7 YEAR PRICE SCORE N/A   *12 MONTH PRICE SCORE N/A

*NYSE COMPOSITE INDEX=100

RECENT DEVELOPMENTS: For the year ended 12/31/95, net income was R2.49 billion compared with income of R1.75 billion, before an extraordinary charge, a year earlier. Total revenues were R2.06 billion, up 48.6% from R1.39 billion in the prior year. Revenues from the diamond account were R1.20 billion compared with R576.0 million in the previous year. Results included equity earnings in affiliated companies of R1.28 billion and R963.0 million for 1996 and 1995, respectively.

BUSINESS

DE BEERS CONSOLIDATED MINES LTD. is a holding company. Through its subsidiaries, the Company is engaged in the mining of gem and industrial diamonds; the manufacturing of synthetic diamond and abrasive products; the marketing through the Central Selling Organization of diamonds produced by the Company and other producers; the manufacture and marketing of synthetic diamond and related hard materials for use in industry; and the management of a portfolio of international investments in mining, industrial and finance companies. The Company owns or leases six diamond mines in South Africa.

ANNUAL EARNINGS

	12/31/95	12/31/94	12/31/95	12/31/94
	------------US $------------		------------Rand------------	
Earnings Per Share	1.80	1.30	6.56	4.61

ANNUAL FINANCIAL DATA

RECORD OF EARNINGS (IN THOUSANDS):

	12/31/95	12/31/94	12/31/95	12/31/94
Total Revenues	564,784	391,129	2,059,000	1,386,000
Costs & Expenses	128,372	131,787	468,000	467,000
Operating Income	616,626	417,092	2,248,000	1,478,000
Income Bef Income Tax	435,863	258,777	1,589,000	917,000
Income Tax	100,394	34,993	366,000	124,000
Eq. Earnings in Affils.	350,007	271,759	1,276,000	963,000
Minority Interests	2,194	1,129	d8,000	d4,000
Net Income	683,281	494,414	2,491,000	1,752,000
Net Extraordinary Items	...	d6,773	...	d24,000

BALANCE SHEET (IN THOUSANDS):

Cash & Cash Equivalents	189,816	137,431	692,000	487,000
Receivables, Net	515,410	460,550	1,879,000	1,632,000
Gross Property	884,892	882,722	3,226,000	3,128,000
Accumulated Depreciation	479,202	475,507	1,747,000	1,685,000
Long-Term Debt	549	847	2,000	3,000
Stockholders' Equity	4,461,490	4,042,797	16,265,000	14,326,000
Total Assets	4,967,573	4,424,896	18,110,000	15,680,000
Total Current Assets	705,225	597,982	2,571,000	2,119,000
Total Current Liabilities	505,535	381,252	1,843,000	1,351,000
Net Working Capital	199,690	216,730	728,000	768,000
Year End Shs Outstg	104,234	107,236	104,234	107,236

STATISTICAL RECORD:

Return on Equity %	15.32	12.23
Return on Assets %	13.75	11.17
Operating Profit Margin %	109.2	106.6
Net Profit Margin %	121.0	126.4
Book Value Per Share	42.80	37.70

Converted at 1995, US$0.2743= 1 South African Rand; 1994, US$0.2822= 1 South African Rand

OFFICERS:
J.O. Thompson, Chairman
G. P. Kell, Grp. Fin. Mgr.
R. W. Ketley, Sec.

INCORPORATED: South Africa, Mar., 1888

PRINCIPAL OFFICE: 36 Stockdale Street
Kimberley South Africa

TELEPHONE NUMBER: (0531) 807-111

NO. OF EMPLOYEES: 9,178

ANNUAL MEETING: In May

SHAREHOLDERS: 24,641

INSTITUTIONAL HOLDINGS:
No. of Institutions: 52
Shares Held: 10,496,017

AMERICAN DEPOSITARY RECEIPTS: (Unsponsored) Each American Depositary Receipt represents one deferred linked unit of par R0.05. American Depositary Receipts split 10-for-1, June 30, 1969.

DEPOSITARY BANK(S): The Bank of New York, (212) 815-2175; Bankers Trust Co., (212) 250-8500; Citibank (212) 250-8500

DIGITALE TELEKABEL AB

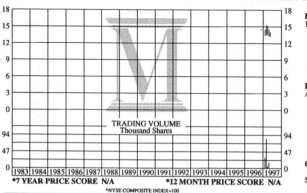

7 YEAR PRICE SCORE N/A   **12 MONTH PRICE SCORE N/A**
*NYSE COMPOSITE INDEX=100

INTERIM EARNINGS (Per Share):
1996 ----------------d0.24----------------

INTERIM DIVIDENDS (Per Share):

Amt.	Decl.	Ex.	Rec.	Pay.
	No dividends paid.			

CAPITALIZATION (8/31/96):

	($000)	(%)
Stockholders' Equity	241	100.0
Total	241	100.0

RECENT DEVELOPMENTS: For the period of 7/8/96 to 8/31/96, the Company incurred a net loss of $96,967. Total revenues for the period were $18. The Company is a new enterprise and has not commenced significant commercial operations. The Company is using proceeds from the December, 1996 initial public offering of 329,700 American Depositary Shares (ADS) to construct and acquire cable television systems in new and refurbished multifam- ily buildings and for general corporate purposes, including working capital and acquisitions. The Company received approximately $3.4 million from the ADS offering. Approximately 90.0% of the proceeds have been allocated towards working capital and general corporate purposes, including the construction of systems to provide service to the approximately 2,100 units that the Company had con- tracted with by 11/30/96.

BUSINESS

DIGITALE TELEKABEL AB com- menced operations on July 8, 1996. Digitale Telekabel AB is the succes- sor company of Deutsche Telekabel AG i.L. The Company is engaged in the provision of third-party cable tele- vision and radio programming ("Cable Services") to multifamily dwelling units through agreements with developers of new residential units and operators of existing apart- ments or condominiums. The Com- pany offers developers and operators a means of providing Cable Services to unit occupants through a "turn key operation," including, where neces- sary, the design, construction and test- ing of a system capable of the receipt of a signal either from a satellite or transmission through the cable of Deutche Telekon AG or one of its competitors. As of 11/30/96, the Company had entered into contracts to provide cable service to approxi- mately 2,100 dwelling units in Germany.

ANNUAL EARNINGS

	8/31/96 ------US $------	8/31/96 -------DM-------
Earnings Per Share	d0.24	d0.36

ANNUAL FINANCIAL DATA

RECORD OF EARNINGS (AS PRESENTED):

Total Revenues	18	27
Costs & Expenses	95,423	141,472
Depreciation & Amort	1,562	2,316
Net Income	d96,967	d143,761
Average Shares Outstg (000)	400	400

BALANCE SHEET (AS PRESENTED):

Cash & Cash Equivalents	53,781	79,735
Receivables, Net	33,305	49,377
Gross Property	66,220	98,176
Accumulated Depreciation	1,559	2,311
Stockholders' Equity	241,051	357,377
Total Assets	303,095	449,362
Total Current Assets	87,824	130,206
Total Current Liabilities	62,044	35,972
Net Working Capital	25,780	94,234
Year End Shs Outstg (000)	400	400

STATISTICAL RECORD:

Return on Equity %	...	
Return on Assets %	...	
Operating Profit Margin %	...	
Net Profit Margin %	...	
Book Value Per Share	0.60	

Converted at 1996, US$0.6745= 1 Deutsche Mark

OFFICERS:
H. Brinkmeier, Chmn.
P. Heidenfelder

INCORPORATED: Germany, July 1996

PRINCIPAL OFFICE: Rennbahnstrasse 72-74 Frankfurt am Main Germany, 60528

TELEPHONE NUMBER: 011-49-69-967-4500

NO. OF EMPLOYEES: 5

ANNUAL MEETING: N/A

SHAREHOLDERS: N/A

INSTITUTIONAL HOLDINGS:
No. of Institutions: N/A
Shares Held: N/A

AMERICAN DEPOSITARY RECEIPTS: Each American Depositary Receipt represents one ordinary share of par DM5.

DEPOSITARY BANK(S): The Bank of New York, (212) 815-2175

DR. SOLOMON'S GROUP, PLC

YIELD ...
P/E RATIO ...

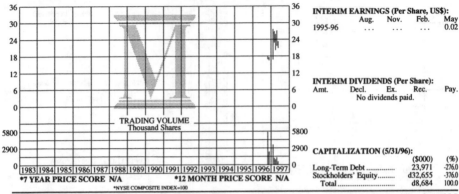

TRADING VOLUME
Thousand Shares

INTERIM EARNINGS (Per Share, US$):

	Aug.	Nov.	Feb.	May
1995-96	...	...	...	0.02

INTERIM DIVIDENDS (Per Share):

Amt.	Decl.	Ex.	Rec.	Pay.
No dividends paid.				

CAPITALIZATION (5/31/96):

	($000)	(%)
Long-Term Debt	23,971	-276.0
Stockholders' Equity	d32,655	-376.0
Total	d8,684	100.0

RECENT DEVELOPMENTS: For the quarter ended 11/30/96, net income more than tripled to £745.0 million from £137.0 million in the same period of 1995. Sales leapt 89.5% to £8.7 million compared with £4.6 million the year before. Results were favorably affected by the contributions from the Company's operations in the United States and Germany, and by the growth of SOLLY's business from distributors and republishers in the rest of the world. Bookings advanced 76.8% year-over-year to £10.1 million from £5.7 million. Operating profit rocketed to £1.9 million versus £406,000 a year earlier. Results should be favorably affected by the introduction of new products, including Dr. Solomon's Software Control System for the management of the Company's anti-virus solutions across enterprise networks utilizing Windows NT servers.

BUSINESS

DR. SOLOMONS'S GROUP, PLC markets and supports anti-virus software programs for personal computers and PC networks. The Company's products are designed to provide effective and easy-to-use software solutions to the risks posed by the proliferation of new and increasingly sophisticated types of computer viruses. SOLLY's principal product line is the "Dr. Solomon's Anti-Virus Toolkit" family of anti-virus software programs. The Toolkit identifies and eradicates more than 10,000 known computer viruses, while minimizing false alarms, maximizing speed of operation and minimizing obtrusiveness in use of system resources.

ANNUAL EARNINGS

	5/31/96 US $	5/31/96 British £
Earnings Per Share	0.02	0.01

ANNUAL FINANCIAL DATA

RECORD OF EARNINGS (IN THOUSANDS):

	US $	British £
Total Revenues	13,268	8,631
Costs & Expenses	10,624	6,911
Operating Income	2,644	1,720
Income Bef Income Tax	1,654	1,076
Income Tax	853	555
Net Income	801	521
Average Shares Outstg	32,400	32,400

BALANCE SHEET (IN THOUSANDS):

Cash & Cash Equivalents	8,040	5,230
Receivables, Net	9,740	6,336
Inventories	407	265
Gross Property	7,273	4,731
Accumulated Depreciation	4,249	2,764
Long-Term Debt	23,971	15,593
Stockholders' Equity	d32,655	d21,242
Total Assets	21,212	13,798
Total Current Assets	18,188	11,831
Total Current Liabilities	26,551	17,271
Net Working Capital	d8,363	d5,440
Year End Shs Outstg	82,400	32,400

STATISTICAL RECORD:

Return on Equity %	...
Return on Assets %	...
Operating Profit Margin %	19.93
Net Profit Margin %	6.04
Book Value Per Share	...

Converted at 1996, US$1.5373= 1 British pound. Results are for the period 2/7/96 to 5/31/96.

OFFICERS:
T. H. Osborne, Chmn.
G. M. Leary, C.E.O.
D. R. Stephens, Fin, Dir.
K. E. Perrett, Oper. Dir.

INCORPORATED: United Kingdom

PRINCIPAL OFFICE: Alton House, Gatehouse Way, Aylesbury United Kingdom, HP19 3XU

TELEPHONE NUMBER: 011-44-1296-318700

NO. OF EMPLOYEES: 300

ANNUAL MEETING: N/A

SHAREHOLDERS: N/A

INSTITUTIONAL HOLDINGS:
No. of Institutions: 27
Shares Held: 6,644,915

AMERICAN DEPOSITARY RECEIPTS: (Sponsored) Each American Depositary Receipt represents 3 ordinary shares of par £0.01.

DEPOSITARY BANK(S): The Bank of New York, (212) 815-2175

DRIEFONTEIN CONSOLIDATED LTD.

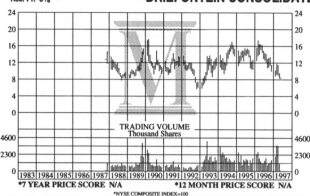

*7 YEAR PRICE SCORE N/A   *12 MONTH PRICE SCORE N/A
*NYSE COMPOSITE INDEX=100

TRADING VOLUME
Thousand Shares

INTERIM EARNINGS (Per Share, US$):
1996   ----------------- 0.90 -----------------

INTERIM DIVIDENDS (Per Share):

Amt.	Decl.	Ex.	Rec.	Pay.
0.284	...	6/28/95	6/30/95	8/17/95
0.127	...	12/27/95	12/29/95	2/23/96
0.209	...	6/26/96	6/28/96	8/22/96
0.166	...	12/24/96	12/27/96	2/21/97

Indicate div.: $0.332

CAPITALIZATION (6/30/96):

	($000)	(%)
Stockholders' Equity	880,103	100.0
Total	880,103	100.0

RECENT DEVELOPMENTS: For the year ended 6/30/96, profit after tax declined 7.5% to R$792.7 million compared with R$857.4 million in the same period of 1995. Working revenue was R$2.36 billion, down 7.1% from R$2.54 billion a year earlier. Working profit was R$878.8 million, down 26.9% from R$1.20 billion in 1995. Profit before tax was R$943.2 million, down 27.6% from R$1.30 billion the year before. A substantial increase in capital expenditure was required to ensure the long-term life of the operations but an even more significant reduction in working profit was suffered by each of the two operating divisions. A reduced mining tax charge cushioned the effect on the consolidated profit after tax. The Company anticipates the milling rate at East Driefontein Division to increase progressively to previously attained levels of 240,000 tons per month as the area affected by fire in is rehabilitated.

BUSINESS

DRIEFONTEIN CONSOLIDATED LTD. conducts gold mining operations through two mines at East Driefontein and West Driefontein that operate independently and are both situated on the Wet Wits Line in the vicinity of Carletonville. Additionally, the Company owns mineral rights in the Oberholzer and Potchefstroom districts. The Company is a member of the Gold Fields Group of companies, which acts as administrative and technical advisers and as secretaries to the Company.

ANNUAL EARNINGS

	6/30/96	6/30/95	6/30/96	6/30/95
	--------------US $-------------		--------------Rand---------	
Earnings Per Share	0.90	1.16	3.89	4.20

ANNUAL FINANCIAL DATA

RECORD OF EARNINGS (IN THOUSANDS):

Total Revenues	545,591	698,991	2,361,865	2,541,785
Costs & Expenses	342,598	368,209	1,483,108	1,338,942
Operating Income	202,993	330,782	878,757	1,202,843
Income Bef Income Tax	217,871	358,042	943,164	1,301,971
Income Tax	34,752	122,259	150,442	444,577
Net Income	183,119	235,783	792,722	857,394

BALANCE SHEET (IN THOUSANDS):

Cash & Cash Equivalents	49,803	157,580	215,599	573,017
Receivables, Net	19,473	21,027	84,297	76,463
Inventories	11,115	12,502	48,119	45,460
Gross Property	861,646	882,341	3,730,069	3,208,511
Stockholders' Equity	880,103	911,088	3,809,969	3,313,047
Total Assets	978,888	1,122,623	4,237,612	4,082,264
Total Current Assets	81,231	192,177	351,651	698,824
Total Current Liabilities	98,786	211,535	427,643	769,217
Net Working Capital	d17,554	d19,358	d75,992	d70,393
Year End Shs Outstg	204,000	204,000	204,000	204,000

STATISTICAL RECORD:

Return on Equity %	20.81	25.88	
Return on Assets %	18.71	21.00	
Operating Profit Margin %	37.21	47.32	
Net Profit Margin %	33.56	33.73	
Book Value Per Share	4.31	4.47	

Converted at 1996, US$0.2310= 1 South African Rand; 1995, US$0.2750= 1 South African Rand

OFFICERS:
A. H. Munro, Chairman
K. C. Spencer, Managing Director

INCORPORATED: Jun., 1981

PRINCIPAL OFFICE: 75 Fox Street
Johannesburg, 2001 South Africa

TELEPHONE NUMBER: 011-639-9111

NO. OF EMPLOYEES: 30,211

ANNUAL MEETING: In Oct.

SHAREHOLDERS: 5,216

INSTITUTIONAL HOLDINGS:
No. of Institutions: 33
Shares Held: 7,594,134

AMERICAN DEPOSITARY RECEIPTS:
(Sponsored) One American Dep Receipt rep.
1 ord shr of par R0.50.

DEPOSITARY BANK(S): The Bank of New York, (212) 815-2175; J.P. Morgan, (212) 648-3206

DURBAN ROODEPOORT DEEP, LIMITED

YIELD ...
P/E RATIO ...

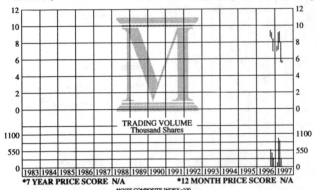

INTERIM EARNINGS (Per Share, US$):

Qtr.	Mar.	June	Sept.	Dec.
1995		d1.26		
Qtr.	Sept.	Dec.	Mar.	June
1995-96	...	...	0.18	

INTERIM DIVIDENDS (Per Share):

Amt.	Decl.	Ex.	Rec.	Pay.
	No dividends paid.			

CAPITALIZATION (6/30/96):

	($000)	(%)
Stockholders' Equity	41,710	100.0
Total	41,710	100.0

RECENT DEVELOPMENTS: For the six months ended 6/30/96, net income totaled US$2.1 million. Total revenues for the period were US$18.9 million. The six-month period ended 6/30/96 represents a transitional period reflecting the Company's fiscal year-end change from December to June. For the year ended 12/31/95, the Company incurred a net loss of US$8.1 million. This compares with a net loss of US$8.9 million in 1994. Total revenues decreased 36.3% to US$31.5 million from US$49.5 million the year before. The 1995 results included a US$10.4 million expense, related to the cancellation of management agreements with Randgold and Rooiwater, as well as US$599,000 in business combination expenses, related to the acquisition of Rand Leases. The Company acquired the entire issued capital share of Rand Leases on 1/1/95 in exchange for approximately 2.9 million ordinary shares.

BUSINESS

DURBAN ROODEPOORT DEEP, LIMITED operates a gold mine at Roodepoort, 22 kilometers west of Johannesburg, South Africa.

ANNUAL EARNINGS

	① 6/30/96	12/31/95	① 6/30/96	12/31/95
	------US $------		------Rand------	
Earnings Per Share	0.18	d1.26	0.78	d4.59

ANNUAL FINANCIAL DATA

RECORD OF EARNINGS (IN THOUSANDS):

	① 6/30/96	12/31/95	① 6/30/96	12/31/95
Total Revenues	18,928	31,526	81,939	114,933
Costs & Expenses	14,763	28,876	63,909	105,272
Depreciation & Amort	1,122	932	4,857	3,398
Operating Income	3,043	1,718	13,173	6,263
Income Bef Income Tax	3,038	d10,876	13,152	d39,650
Income Tax	931	cr2,820	4,030	cr10,281
Net Income	2,107	d8,056	9,121	d29,369
Average Shares Outstg	6,619	6,403	6,619	6,403

① For six months due to fiscal year-end change.

BALANCE SHEET (IN THOUSANDS):

Cash & Cash Equivalents	10,909	12,433	47,225	45,326
Receivables, Net	1,617	1,779	7,000	6,486
Inventories	897	1,372	3,883	5,002
Gross Property	60,843	70,282	263,390	256,223
Accumulated Depreciation	25,547	29,254	110,593	106,650
Stockholders' Equity	41,710	48,087	180,563	175,308
Total Assets	52,062	61,533	225,377	224,327
Total Current Assets	13,423	15,584	58,108	56,814
Total Current Liabilities	4,751	5,997	20,567	21,863
Net Working Capital	8,672	9,587	37,541	34,951
Year End Shs Outstg	6,640	6,600	6,640	6,600

STATISTICAL RECORD:

Return on Equity %	5.05	...		
Return on Assets %	4.05	...		
Operating Profit Margin %	16.08	5.45		
Net Profit Margin %	11.13	...		
Book Value Per Share	6.28	7.29		

Converted at 1996, US$0.2310= 1 South African Rand; 1995, US$0.2743= 1 South African Rand

OFFICERS:
R.A.R. Kebble, Chairman
F.H. Coetzee, Managing Dir.
H. van Rensburg, Financial Mgr.

INCORPORATED: South Africa, 1895

PRINCIPAL OFFICE: Randgold House, 5 Press Avenue, Selby, Johannesburg South Africa 2135

TELEPHONE NUMBER: (011) 837-0706

NO. OF EMPLOYEES: 1,317

ANNUAL MEETING: In Nov.

SHAREHOLDERS: N/A

INSTITUTIONAL HOLDINGS:
No. of Institutions: 13
Shares Held: 1,069,630

AMERICAN DEPOSITARY RECEIPTS: (Sponsored) Each American Depositary Receipt represents one ordinary share.

DEPOSITARY BANK(S): The Bank of New York, (212) 815-2175

ECSOFT GROUP PLC

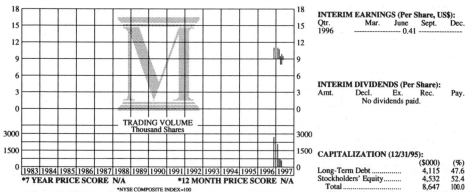

INTERIM EARNINGS (Per Share, US$):

Qtr.	Mar.	June	Sept.	Dec.
1996	------------------ 0.41 ------------------

INTERIM DIVIDENDS (Per Share):

Amt.	Decl.	Ex.	Rec.	Pay.
	No dividends paid.			

TRADING VOLUME
Thousand Shares

*7 YEAR PRICE SCORE N/A   *12 MONTH PRICE SCORE N/A
*NYSE COMPOSITE INDEX=100

CAPITALIZATION (12/31/95):

	($000)	(%)
Long-Term Debt	4,115	47.6
Stockholders' Equity........	4,532	52.4
Total	8,647	100.0

RECENT DEVELOPMENTS: For the year ended 12/31/96, net income soared to $2.1 million. This compares with $52,000 the previous year. The 1995 net income reflects a nonrecurring expense of $1.3 million. Revenues for the year were up 41.9% to $50.6 million from $35.6 million a year earlier. The improved 1996 operating results were attributed to an acceleration in the adoption of client/server and distributed computing for mission-critical applications in major European corporations. The Company also exper-ienced strong growth in its electronic commerce services. The Company's first-quarter acquisition of Digitus Ltd. resulted in a $2.2 million, or 4.4%, contribution to 1996 revenues. For the fourth quarter ended 12/31/96, net income declined 26.3% to $839,000 from $1.1 million in the comparable quarter the year before. Revenues for the quarter were up 39.7% to $14.9 million compared with $10.6 million in the corresponding prior-year period.

BUSINESS

ECSOFT GROUP PLC and its subsidiaries are principally engaged in the provision of information technology consulting services and applications development implementation and integration services. The Company provides services for client/server technologies as well as corporate mainframe and mid-range systems. The Company's areas of expertise include business process re-engineering, object technology, workflow and groupware, enterprise client/server, rightsizing legacy systems, Intranet and data warehousing.

ANNUAL EARNINGS

ANNUAL FINANCIAL DATA

	12/31/95	12/31/94	12/31/95	12/31/94
	-------------US $-------------		-------------ECU-----------	
RECORD OF EARNINGS (IN THOUSANDS):				
Total Revenues	35,402	14,417	27,669	11,760
Costs & Expenses	32,287	17,536	25,234	14,305
Depreciation & Amort	554	435	433	355
Operating Income	2,194	d3,723	1,715	d3,037
Income Bef Income Tax	2,290	d3,661	1,790	d2,986
Income Tax	591	153	462	125
Net Income	1,699	d3,814	1,328	d3,111
BALANCE SHEET (IN THOUSANDS):				
Cash & Cash Equivalents	1,906	1,950	1,490	1,591
Receivables, Net	7,961	8,705	6,222	7,101
Gross Property	2,649	2,381	2,070	1,942
Accumulated Depreciation	773	417	604	340
Long-Term Debt	4,115	4,080	3,216	3,328
Stockholders' Equity	4,532	2,782	3,542	2,269
Total Assets	18,416	19,157	14,393	15,627
Total Current Assets	9,868	10,656	7,712	8,692
Total Current Liabilities	9,095	9,893	7,108	8,070
Net Working Capital	773	763	604	622
Year End Shs Outstg	4,208	...	4,208	...
STATISTICAL RECORD:				
Return on Equity %	37.49	...		
Return on Assets %	9.23	...		
Operating Profit Margin %	6.20	...		
Net Profit Margin %	4.80	...		
Book Value Per Share	1.08	...		

Converted at 1995, US$1.2795= 1 European Currency Unit; 1994, US$1.2259= 1 European Currency Unit

OFFICERS:
T. Laugerud, Pres. & C.E.O.
P. Harris, C.F.O.
G. Tubb, V.P. Mktg. & Managing Dir.

INCORPORATED: United Kingdom

PRINCIPAL OFFICE: 269 High Street, Berkhamsted United Kingdom HP4 1EG

TELEPHONE NUMBER: +44 (0) 1442 872111

NO. OF EMPLOYEES: 248

ANNUAL MEETING: N/A

SHAREHOLDERS: N/A

INSTITUTIONAL HOLDINGS:
No. of Institutions: 20
Shares Held: 2,980,300

AMERICAN DEPOSITARY RECEIPTS: Each American Depositary Receipt represents one ordinary share.

DEPOSITARY BANK(S): The Bank of New York, (212) 815-2175

EIDOS PLC

YIELD ...
P/E RATIO 63.2

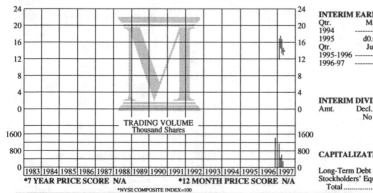

*7 YEAR PRICE SCORE N/A   *12 MONTH PRICE SCORE N/A

*NYSE COMPOSITE INDEX=100

TRADING VOLUME
Thousand Shares

INTERIM EARNINGS (Per Share, US$):

Qtr.	Mar.	June	Sept.	Dec.
1994	-------------------d0.06--------------------			
1995	d0.05		...	...
Qtr.	June	Sept.	Dec.	Mar.
1995-1996	-------------------d0.57------------------			
1996-97	-----------0.36------------			...

INTERIM DIVIDENDS (Per Share):

Amt.	Decl.	Ex.	Rec.	Pay.
	No dividends paid.			

CAPITALIZATION (3/31/96):

	($000)	(%)
Long-Term Debt	886	30.5
Stockholders' Equity........	2,021	69.5
Total	2,907	100.0

RECENT DEVELOPMENTS: For the quarter ended 12/31/96, the Company produced a net profit of £7.5 million compared with a net loss of £1.0 million in the corresponding period of the previous year. Earnings for 1996 included non-recurring reorganization costs of £220,000. Revenues soared to £32.1 million from £1.2 million the year before. Gross profit as a percentage of revenues was 53.6%. Selling and marketing expenses amounted to £4.1 million. General and administrative expenses were £4.7 million, including a foreign exchange loss of £1.6 million. Operating profit totaled £8.0 million. During its third quarter, the Company released eight new games across 14 formats, including Clam Machinehead, Hulk, Jetfighter 3, and Tomb Raider. In addition, Eidos sold 75% of the Silicon Dreams games development division to Geoff Brown. Also, EIDSY entered into publishing and distribution agreements with US design studio ION Storm and US-based Looking Glass Technologies. In addition, EIDSY entered into an agreement with MGM to market the James Bond range among other products.

BUSINESS

EIDOS PLC and its subsidiaries are engaged in the development and publishing of interactive software products and advanced video compression technologies. Through acquisitions, the Company has established a diversified interactive software portfolio that includes many popular multimedia personal computer and dedicated console titles. The Company and its collaborative partners are developing over 35 titles for three platforms: the MPC, Sony PlayStation and Sega Saturn. The Company has built a library of proprietary technologies for use in software development, including 3D models, texture maps, development tools, game engines and compression-decompression algorithms.

ANNUAL EARNINGS

	① 3/31/96	12/31/94	① 3/31/96	12/31/94
	-------------US $-------------		---------------£---------------	
Earnings Per Share	d0.64	d0.06	d0.42	d0.04

ANNUAL FINANCIAL DATA

RECORD OF EARNINGS (IN THOUSANDS):

Total Revenues	5,662	398	3,706	254
Costs & Expenses	7,333	472	4,800	302
Depreciation & Amortization	1,314	102	860	65
Operating Income	d2,985	d177	d1,954	d113
Income Bef Income Tax	d2,977	d167	d1,949	d107
Net Income	d2,977	d167	d1,949	d107
Average Shares Outstg	4,649	2,752	4,649	2,752

① For 15 months due to fiscal year-end change.

BALANCE SHEET (IN THOUSANDS):

Cash & Cash Equivalents	718	604	470	386
Receivables, Net	4,033	77	2,640	49
Inventories	173	11	113	7
Gross Property	3,615	228	2,366	146
Accumulated Depreciation	463	135	303	86
Long-Term Debt	886	33	580	21
Stockholders' Equity	2,021	823	1,323	526
Total Assets	9,846	972	6,445	621
Total Current Assets	4,924	692	3,223	442
Total Current Liabilities	6,939	116	4,542	74
Net Working Capital	d2,015	576	d1,319	368
Year End Shs Outstg	7,366	2,668	7,366	2,668

STATISTICAL RECORD:

Book Value Per Share	0.27	0.31		

Converted at 1996, US$1.5277= 1 British pound; 1994, US$1.5650= 1 British pound.

OFFICERS:
I. Livingstone, Chmn.
C. H. Cornwall, C.E.O.
INCORPORATED: England & Wales, May 1990
PRINCIPAL OFFICE: Ferry House, 51-57 Lacy Road, Putney, SW15 1PR United Kingdom

TELEPHONE NUMBER: 44-181-780-2222
NO. OF EMPLOYEES: 385 (approx.)
ANNUAL MEETING: N/A
SHAREHOLDERS: N/A
INSTITUTIONAL HOLDINGS:
No. of Institutions: 7
Shares Held: 1,444,350

AMERICAN DEPOSITARY RECEIPTS: Each American Depositary Share represents one ordinary share of par £0.10.

DEPOSITARY BANK(S): J.P. Morgan, (212) 648-3206

ERICSSON (L.M.) TELEPHONE COMPANY

YIELD 0.1%
P/E RATIO 31.7

INTERIM EARNINGS (Per Share, US$):

1995	------------------ 0.87 ------------------
1996	------------------ 1.06 ------------------

INTERIM DIVIDENDS (Per Share):

Amt.	Decl.	Ex.	Rec.	Pay.
4-for-1	...	6/16/95	6/20/95	6/21/95
0.217	...	5/09/96	5/13/96	5/30/96
0.277	...	4/28/97	4/30/97	5/16/97

Indicated div.: $0.277

TRADING VOLUME
Thousand Shares

*7 YEAR PRICE SCORE N/A   *12 MONTH PRICE SCORE N/A

*NYSE COMPOSITE INDEX=100

CAPITALIZATION (12/31/96):

	($000)	(%)
Long-Term Debt	1,951,144	23.3
Minority Interest	497,860	6.0
Stockholders' Equity........	5,906,576	70.7
Total	8,355,580	100.0

RECENT DEVELOPMENTS: For the year ended 12/31/96, net income advanced 30.7% to SEK 7,110 million versus SEK 5,439 million the previous year. The 1996 results included a net capital gain of SEK 341 million related to the sale of Ericsson's shareholding in Selga AB, and the divestment of On-site paging operations. Net sales grew 25.8% to SEK 124,266 million from SEK 98,780 million. The growth in revenues was led by the Radio Communications unit as demand for mobile telecommunications continued to be strong. The number of subscribers in this segment grew approximately 50.0% to 137 million during 1996. The Public Telecommunications unit also experienced solid growth as sales increased 7.0% and orders booked jumped 56.0% from 1995. The Business Networks unit's sales climbed 13.0% from 1995. The Microwave Systems division reported strong sales growth, while the Components segment reported modestly higher sales for 1996.

BUSINESS

L.M. ERICSSON TELEPHONE COMPANY is the parent company of a group engaged in the development, production and marketing of systems, products and services handling voice, data, image and text in public and private communication networks. The Company's range of telecommunications products includes systems and services for switching and handling voice and data in public and private telecommunication networks, systems for mobile radio and telephone, telecommunications power equipment, and telecommunications and power cable. The Company also provides defense electronics and communication systems, network engineering and specialized circuitry components. The Company primarily operates through the business areas of Radio Communications, Public Telecommunications, Business Networks, Components and Microwave Systems. The Company's products and services are marketed throughout the world.

ANNUAL EARNINGS

	12/31/96	12/31/95	12/31/96	12/31/95
	----------US $----------		----------SEK----------	
Earnings Per Share	1.06	0.87	7.27	5.83

ANNUAL FINANCIAL DATA

RECORD OF EARNINGS (IN MILLIONS):

Total Revenues	18,354	14,902	125,883	99,681
Costs & Expenses	16,785	13,682	115,125	91,517
Operating Income	1,569	1,221	10,758	8,164
Income Bef Income Tax	1,480	1,138	10,152	7,615
Income Tax	444	325	3,042	2,176
Net Income	1,036	813	7,110	5,439
Average Shares Outstg (000)	986,000	943,000	986,000	943,000

BALANCE SHEET (IN MILLIONS):

Cash & Cash Equivalents	2,779	2,300	19,060	15,385
Receivables, Net	5,159	3,794	35,384	25,379
Inventories	2,860	2,893	19,619	19,351
Gross Property	2,589	2,320	17,754	15,521
Accumulated Depreciation	2,709	2,389	18,581	15,980
Long-Term Debt	1,951	1,864	13,364	12,467
Stockholders' Equity	5,898	5,122	40,456	34,263
Total Assets	16,352	13,579	112,152	90,832
Total Current Assets	12,331	10,141	84,577	67,834
Total Current Liabilities	8,008	6,332	54,922	42,353
Net Working Capital	4,324	3,809	29,655	25,481
Year End Shs Outstg (000)	961,000	958,000	961,000	958,000

STATISTICAL RECORD:

Return on Equity %	20.09	17.65
Return on Assets %	7.25	6.66
Operating Profit Margin %	8.55	8.19
Net Profit Margin %	6.46	6.07
Book Value Per Share	42.10	35.77

Converted at 1996, US$0.146= 1 Swedish Krona; 1995, US$0.149= 1 Swedish Krona

OFFICERS:
L. Ramqvist, Pres. & C.E.O.
C. W. Ros, Sr. Exec. V.P. & C.F.O.
K. Hellstrom, Exec. V.P.
A. Igel, Exec. V.P.

INCORPORATED: Sweden Jul., 1918

PRINCIPAL OFFICE: S-125-25 Stockholm Sweden

TELEPHONE NUMBER: +46-8-719-0000

NO. OF EMPLOYEES: 93,949

ANNUAL MEETING: In Apr.

SHAREHOLDERS: 133,239

INSTITUTIONAL HOLDINGS:
No. of Institutions: 276
Shares Held: 217,631,529

AMERICAN DEPOSITARY RECEIPTS: (Sponsored) Each American Depositary Receipt represents one common B share of par value SEK10. American Depositary Receipts split 5-for-1 on Sept. 20, 1990; 4-for-1 on June 21, 1995.

DEPOSITARY BANK(S): Citibank, (212) 657-7800

ETHICAL HOLDINGS PLC

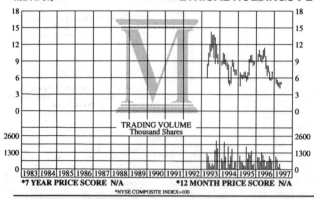

INTERIM EARNINGS (Per Share, US$):

Qtr.	Nov.	Feb.	May	Aug.
1995-96		---------d1.10---------		
1996-97	d0.14	d0.27	...	...

INTERIM DIVIDENDS (Per Share):

Amt.	Decl.	Ex.	Rec.	Pay.
		No dividends paid.		

TRADING VOLUME
Thousand Shares

| 1983 | 1984 | 1985 | 1986 | 1987 | 1988 | 1989 | 1990 | 1991 | 1992 | 1993 | 1994 | 1995 | 1996 | 1997 |

*7 YEAR PRICE SCORE N/A   *12 MONTH PRICE SCORE N/A

*NYSE COMPOSITE INDEX=100

CAPITALIZATION (8/31/96):

	($000)	(%)
Long-Term Debt	12,913	35.3
Capital Lease Obligs.........	370	1.0
Stockholders' Equity.........	23,312	63.7
Total	36,595	100.0

RECENT DEVELOPMENTS: For the quarter ended 2/28/97, ETHCY incurred a net loss of £2.5 million (US$4.0 million) versus a net loss of £1.3 million in the same prior-year period. Net losses for 1997 and 1996 included a foreign exchange gain of £98,000 (US$160,000) and a foreign exchange loss of £105,000, respectively. The increase in net loss was partially due to higher-than-expected losses from associated companies. Total revenues climbed 10.8% to £3.2 million (US$5.2 million) from £2.9 million in 1995. Research and development expenses grew 27.3% to £2.9 million (US$4.8 million) from £2.3 million a year earlier. Interest and investment expense amounted to £529,000 (US$863,000) versus income of £109,000 in 1995. Operating loss totaled £1.6 million (US$2.7 million) versus a loss of £1.3 million the prior year. On 3/10/97, ETHCY announced the introduction in the United Kingdom of its oestrogen-progestogen combination patch for use in hormone replacement therapy.

BUSINESS

ETHICAL HOLDINGS PLC is a global pharmaceutical company that develops pharmaceutical products across a range of therapeutic areas utilizing its proprietary oral and transdermal drug delivery technologies. The Company's drug delivery technologies include transdermal delivery systems, oral controlled-release tablets and topical formulations. The Company also develops phytomedicines (plant-based medicines) derived from plants primarily found in China.

The Company has 11 transdermal patch products, 12 controlled-release tablets and an undisclosed number of schein multi-products. The Company's subsidiary, Bioanalytical Research Ltd., provides analytical and clinical research services to the Company and to clients in the pharmaceutical, food, and agrochemical industries.

ANNUAL EARNINGS

	8/31/96	8/31/95	8/31/96	8/31/95
	-------------US $--------------		-------------British £-------------	
Earnings Per Share	d1.10	0.31	d0.70	0.20

ANNUAL FINANCIAL DATA

RECORD OF EARNINGS (IN THOUSANDS):

	8/31/96	8/31/95	8/31/96	8/31/95
Total Revenues	21,478	29,134	13,759	18,796
Costs & Expenses	39,743	24,402	25,460	15,743
Operating Income	d18,265	4,732	d11,701	3,053
Eq. Earnings in Affils.	d200	84	d128	54
Income Bef Income Tax	d16,760	5,587	d10,737	3,579
Income Tax	cr1,144	1,449	cr733	935
Net Income	d15,616	4,098	d10,004	2,644
Average Shares Outstg	14,242	13,096	14,242	13,096

BALANCE SHEET (IN THOUSANDS):

Cash & Cash Equivalents	4,783	13,332	3,064	8,601
Receivables, Net	14,800	14,199	9,481	9,160
Inventories	1,350	754	865	486
Gross Property	10,314	6,914	6,607	4,461
Accumulated Depreciation	4,001	2,942	2,563	1,898
Long-Term Debt	13,283	260	8,509	168
Stockholders' Equity	23,312	28,856	14,934	18,617
Total Assets	44,882	36,076	28,752	23,275
Total Current Assets	20,933	28,285	13,410	18,248
Total Current Liabilities	8,127	6,727	5,206	4,340
Net Working Capital	12,806	21,558	8,204	13,908
Year End Shs Outstg	14,815	13,826	14,815	13,826

STATISTICAL RECORD:

Return on Equity %	...	14.20		
Return on Assets %	...	11.36		
Operating Profit Margin %		16.24		
Net Profit Margin %	...	14.07		
Book Value Per Share	1.57	2.09		

Converted at 1996, US$1.5610= 1 British pound; 1995, US$1.5500= 1 British pound.

OFFICERS:
G. W. Guy, Chmn. & C.E.O.
D. H. Barry, C.O.O.
M. P. O'Sullivan, C.F.O.
A.A. Booth, Sec.
INCORPORATED: United Kingdom, 1985
PRINCIPAL OFFICE: Stibbington Hall, Stibbington, Cambridgeshire PE8 6LP United Kingdom

TELEPHONE NUMBER: 44-1780-781000
FAX: 44-1780-781029
NO. OF EMPLOYEES: 164 (avg.)
ANNUAL MEETING: N/A
SHAREHOLDERS: N/A
INSTITUTIONAL HOLDINGS:
No. of Institutions: 17
Shares Held: 4,653,724

AMERICAN DEPOSITARY RECEIPTS: Each American Depositary Receipt represents one ordinary share of par £0.10.

DEPOSITARY BANK(S): Citibank, (212) 250-8500

FLAMEL TECHNOLOGIES S.A.

YIELD ...
P/E RATIO ...

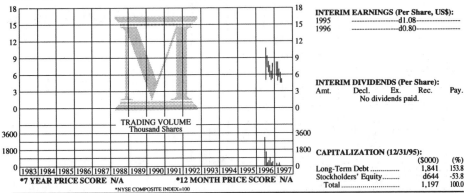

INTERIM EARNINGS (Per Share, US$):
1995 ------------------d1.08------------------
1996 ------------------d0.80------------------

INTERIM DIVIDENDS (Per Share):

Amt.	Decl.	Ex.	Rec.	Pay.
No dividends paid.				

TRADING VOLUME
Thousand Shares

| 1983 | 1984 | 1985 | 1986 | 1987 | 1988 | 1989 | 1990 | 1991 | 1992 | 1993 | 1994 | 1995 | 1996 | 1997 |

*7 YEAR PRICE SCORE N/A   ***12 MONTH PRICE SCORE N/A**

*NYSE COMPOSITE INDEX=100

CAPITALIZATION (12/31/95):

	($000)	(%)
Long-Term Debt	1,841	153.8
Stockholders' Equity........	d644	-53.8
Total	1,197	100.0

RECENT DEVELOPMENTS: For the year ended 12/31/96, FLMLY reported a net loss of US$6.9 million compared with a net loss of US$6.8 million in 1995. Earnings for 1996 and 1995 included a foreign exchange gain of US$64,000 and a foreign exchange loss of US$87,000, respectively. Total revenue grew 73.9% to US$4.9 million from US$2.8 million a year earlier. License and research revenue rose 67.4% to US$3.9 million from US$2.3 million in 1995. Product sales totaled US$733,000 versus none the

prior year. Cost of goods sold amounted to US$1.1 million compared with none the year before. Loss from operations was US$8.9 million versus a loss of US$6.7 million the previous year. For the quarter ended 12/31/96, the Company incurred a net loss of US$1.6 million versus a net loss of US$1.5 m illion in the same prior-year period. Total revenue remained relatively the same at US$1.2 million compared with the year before.

BUSINESS

FLAMEL TECHNOLOGIES S.A. is a drug delivery company engaged in the development and commercialization of controlled-release pharmaceutical products based upon its proprietary polymer-based Micropump microencapsulation technology. This technology is designed to permit both controlled release of drugs and targeting to the small intestine--the preferred site of absorption for many drugs. The Company's expertise in advance polymer technologies and innovative biomaterials has permitted FLMLY to develop additional technology platforms including: nanoencapsulation of proteins and peptides, soft-tissue surgical adhesives and specialty materials for ophthalmic lenses. The Company's products include ASACARD, VIROPUMP and ATENAX.

ANNUAL EARNINGS

	12/31/95	12/31/94	12/31/95	12/31/94
	-------------US $-------------		------------FFr------------	
Earnings Per Share	d1.08	d0.77	d5.30	d4.11

ANNUAL FINANCIAL DATA

RECORD OF EARNINGS (IN THOUSANDS):

Total Revenues	2,829	2,626	13,874	14,020
Costs & Expenses	9,547	7,041	46,822	37,592
Operating Income	d6,718	d4,415	d32,948	d23,572
Income Bef Income Tax	d6,826	d4,534	d33,477	d24,207
Income Tax	cr75	5	cr368	27
Net Income	d6,751	d4,539	d33,109	d24,234
Average Shares Outstg	6,238	5,924	6,238	5,924

BALANCE SHEET (IN THOUSANDS):

Cash & Cash Equivalents	961	826	4,713	4,410
Receivables, Net	470	1,089	2,305	5,814
Inventories	76	26	373	139
Gross Property	6,417	5,424	31,471	28,959
Accumulated Depreciation	5,292	3,974	25,954	21,217
Long-Term Debt	1,841	6,500	9,029	34,704
Stockholders' Equity	d644	d5,261	d3,158	d28,089
Total Assets	3,934	4,442	19,294	23,716
Total Current Assets	1,791	2,034	8,784	10,860
Total Current Liabilities	2,674	3,123	13,114	16,674
Net Working Capital	d883	d1,089	d4,331	d5,814
Year End Shs Outstg	6,726	3,221	6,726	3,221

Converted at 1995, US$0.2039= 1 French franc; 1994, US$0.1873= 1 French franc.

OFFICERS:
G. Soula, Pres. & C.E.O.
P. Perrin, C.F.O.
B. Morra Ph.D., Pres. & C.O.O.

INCORPORATED: France, August 1990

PRINCIPAL OFFICE: Parc Club due Moulin a Vent 33, avenue du Docteur Georges Levy, Venissieux Cedex, 69693 France

TELEPHONE NUMBER: (33) 78.77.68.04

NO. OF EMPLOYEES: 49

ANNUAL MEETING: N/A

SHAREHOLDERS: N/A

INSTITUTIONAL HOLDINGS:
No. of Institutions: 6
Shares Held: 575,090

AMERICAN DEPOSITARY RECEIPTS: (Sponsored) Each American Depositary Receipt represents one Ordinary share of par FFr0.80.

DEPOSITARY BANK(S): The Bank of New York, (212) 815-2175

FREE STATE CONSOLIDATED GOLD MINES LTD.

YIELD 13.1%
P/E RATIO 49.1

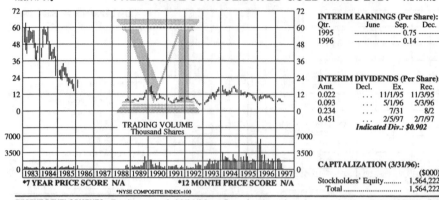

TRADING VOLUME
Thousand Shares

| 1983 | 1984 | 1985 | 1986 | 1987 | 1988 | 1989 | 1990 | 1991 | 1992 | 1993 | 1994 | 1995 | 1996 | 1997 |

*7 YEAR PRICE SCORE N/A   *12 MONTH PRICE SCORE N/A

*NYSE COMPOSITE INDEX=100

INTERIM EARNINGS (Per Share):

Qtr.	June	Sep.	Dec.	Mar.
1995	---------------- 0.75 ----------------			
1996	---------------- 0.14 ----------------			

INTERIM DIVIDENDS (Per Share):

Amt.	Decl.	Ex.	Rec.	Pay.
0.022	...	11/1/95	11/3/95	1/3/96
0.093	...	5/1/96	5/3/96	7/1
0.234	...	7/31	8/2	9/30
0.451	...	2/5/97	2/7/97	3/31/97

Indicated Div.: $0.902

CAPITALIZATION (3/31/96):

	($000)	(%)
Stockholders' Equity.........	1,564,222	100.0
Total.............................	1,564,222	100.0

RECENT DEVELOPMENTS: For the year ended 3/31/96, profit available was R62.8 million compared with R309.7 million in the prior year. Turnover was down slightly to R4,195.5 million from R4,518.1 million a year earlier. The decline in operating results was attributed primarily to a 10.9% drop in gold production to 90 tons for 1996. The drop in gold production was due to the elimination of uneconomic mining operations, long weekends and the addition of statutory public holidays. Working costs increased by 4%, which together with a decrease in volume, resulted in a 17% increase in unit cost per kilogram produced. Operating profit was R214.2 million compared with R642.6 million a year earlier. In line with the decline in operating profit, capital expenditures decreased 24.6% to R185.3 million.

BUSINESS

FREE STATE CONSOLIDATED GOLD MINES LTD. is an investment holding company. Through its subsidiaries, the Company is principally engaged in gold mining operations in the Odendaaisrus, Ventersburg and Welkom districts of the OFS. The Company holds minor investments in Johannesburg stock exchange-quoted mining and mining finance companies. In addition, the Company's subsidiaries are engaged in uranium mining.

ANNUAL EARNINGS

	3/31/96	3/31/95	3/31/96	3/31/95
	--------------US $--------------		--------------Rand------------	
Earnings Per Share	0.14	0.75	0.55	2.70

ANNUAL FINANCIAL DATA

RECORD OF EARNINGS (IN THOUSANDS):

	3/31/96	3/31/95	3/31/96	3/31/95
Total Revenues	1,053,910	1,258,430	4,195,500	4,518,600
Income Bef Income Tax	67,799	186,400	269,900	669,300
Income Tax	10,852	34,395	43,200	123,500
Eq. Earnings in Affils.	d41,172	d66,255	d163,900	d237,900
Net Income	15,775	85,750	62,800	307,900
Average Shs Outstg	114,209	114,209	114,209	114,209

BALANCE SHEET (IN THOUSANDS):

Cash & Cash Equivalents	23,186	23,979	92,300	86,100
Receivables, Net	88,724	154,679	353,200	555,400
Gross Property	1,574,999	1,694,617	6,269,900	6,084,800
Stockholders' Equity	1,564,222	1,688,573	6,227,000	6,063,100
Total Assets	1,742,072	1,923,655	6,935,000	6,907,200
Total Current Assets	126,580	191,719	503,900	688,400
Total Current Liabilities	106,710	169,913	424,800	610,100
Net Working Capital	19,870	21,807	79,100	78,300
Year End Shs Outstg	118,983	118,983	118,983	118,983

STATISTICAL RECORD:

Return on Equity %	1.01	5.08
Return on Assets %	0.91	4.46
Operating Profit Margin %	5.11	14.22
Net Profit Margin %	1.50	6.80
Book Value Per Share	13.14	14.19

Converted at 1996, US$0.2512= 1 South African Rand; 1995, US$0.2785= 1 South African Rand

OFFICERS:
R. M. Godsell, Chairman
N. Mayer, Managing Dir.
K. H. Williams, Mktg. Dir.
A. G. Knowles, Consulting Geologist

INCORPORATED: Jan., 1948

PRINCIPAL OFFICE: 44 Main Street
Johannesburg South Africa

TELEPHONE NUMBER: 638-9111

NO. OF EMPLOYEES: 70,000

ANNUAL MEETING: In June

SHAREHOLDERS: N/A

INSTITUTIONAL HOLDINGS:
No. of Institutions: 37
Shares Held: 11,312,578

AMERICAN DEPOSITARY RECEIPTS: (Unspon)Each Amer. Depos. Receipt represents 1 ord. share of R0.50.

DEPOSITARY BANK(S): The Bank of New York, (212) 815-2175; Bankers Trust Co., (212) 250-8500; Citibank N.A., (212) 657-7800.

FUJI PHOTO FILM CO., LTD.

YIELD 0.3%
P/E RATIO 29.7

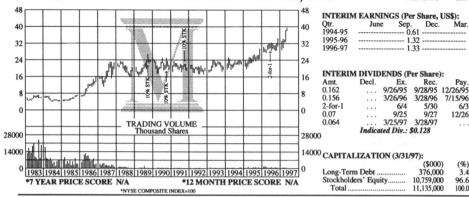

INTERIM EARNINGS (Per Share, US$):

Qtr.	June	Sep.	Dec.	Mar.
1994-95	------------------	0.61	------------------	
1995-96	------------------	1.32	------------------	
1996-97	------------------	1.33	------------------	

INTERIM DIVIDENDS (Per Share):

Amt.	Decl.	Ex.	Rec.	Pay.
0.162	...	9/26/95	9/28/95	12/26/95
0.156	...	3/26/96	3/28/96	7/15/96
2-for-1	...	6/4	5/30	6/3
0.07	...	9/25	9/27	12/26
0.064	...	3/25/97	3/28/97	...

Indicated Div.: $0.128

CAPITALIZATION (3/31/97):

	($000)	(%)
Long-Term Debt	376,000	3.4
Stockholders' Equity	10,759,000	96.6
Total	11,135,000	100.0

RECENT DEVELOPMENTS: For the year ended 3/31/97, net income was ¥85,349 million compared with ¥72,870 million in the prior year, a 17.1% increase. Net sales were ¥1,252,117 million, up 15.4% from ¥1,084,957 million in 1996. Operating income reached ¥164,696 million, up 23.4%. For 1997, revenues and earnings were stronger due partially to a modest improvement in the Japanese econ-omy. Overseas, the Company benefited from increased sales volumes, supported by firm demand for color film and color print paper and the successful introduction of new products. The decline in the yen also contributed to stronger sales overseas. Domestic sales experienced only a slight increase as escalating price wars drove down retail prices.

BUSINESS

FUJI PHOTO FILM CO., LTD., is a multinational manufacturer of photographic products, with growing involvement in imaging and information systems. The Company operates throughout the world, generating approximately 35% of its worldwide sales outside of Japan. The Company's principal businesses are Imaging Systems, Photofinishing Systems and Information Systems. Imaging Systems (accounting for 36% of 1997 sales) consists primarily of photographic films for amateurs and professionals, optical products, motion picture films, electronic imaging systems and magnetic tapes. Photofinishing Systems (17%) consists primarily of photographic paper, photofinishing equipment and chemicals, and photographic developing and printing services. Information Systems (47%) in comprised of materials and equipment for graphic arts and printing, office automation and medical imaging systems, as well as industrial materials and data media.

ANNUAL EARNINGS

	3/31/97	3/31/96	3/31/97	3/31/96
	----US $----		----Yen----	
Earnings Per Share	1.33	1.32	165.85	141.60

ANNUAL FINANCIAL DATA

RECORD OF EARNINGS (IN MILLIONS):

	3/31/97	3/31/96	3/31/97	3/31/96
Total Revenues	10,017	10,090	1,252,117	1,084,957
Costs & Expenses	8,699	8,849	1,087,421	951,527
Operating Income	1,318	1,241	164,696	133,440
Income Bef Income Tax	1,283	1,058	160,320	113,717
Income Tax	684	623	85,488	66,986
Eq. Earnings in Affils.	84	81	10,517	8,713
Net Income	683	678	85,349	72,870
Aver. Shs. Outstg. (000)	514,626	514,626	514,626	514,626

BALANCE SHEET (IN MILLIONS):

Cash & Cash Equivalents	5,658	6,760	707,209	726,868
Receivables, Net	1,927	2,033	240,833	218,574
Inventories	1,751	1,865	218,836	200,539
Gross Property	10,166	11,010	1,270,748	1,183,895
Accumulated Depreciation	6,660	7,212	832,553	775,498
Long-Term Debt	376	594	47,036	63,919
Stockholders' Equity	10,759	11,648	1,344,931	1,252,518
Total Assets	15,884	17,176	1,985,496	1,846,887
Total Current Assets	9,723	11,046	1,215,354	1,187,714
Total Current Liabilities	3,601	3,697	450,137	397,524
Net Working Capital	6,122	7,349	765,217	790,190
Year End Shs Outstg (000)	514,626	514,626	514,626	514,626

STATISTICAL RECORD:

Return on Equity %	6.35	5.82		
Return on Assets %	4.30	3.95		
Operating Profit Margin %	13.16	12.30		
Net Profit Margin %	6.82	6.72		
Book Value Per Share	20.91	22.63		

Converted at 1997, US$0.0080= 1 Japanese Yen; 1996, US$0.0093= 1 Japanese Yen

OFFICERS:
M. Ohnishi, Chmn. & C.E.O
M. Muneyuki, Pres.
H. Ueda, Exec. V.P.
T. Omura, Exec. V.P.

INCORPORATED: Japan, Jan., 1934

PRINCIPAL OFFICE: 26-30 Nishiazabu 2-chome, Minato-ku Tokyo 106 Japan

TELEPHONE NUMBER: (03)3406-2111

NO. OF EMPLOYEES: 32,228

ANNUAL MEETING: In June

SHAREHOLDERS: 37,779

INSTITUTIONAL HOLDINGS:
No. of Institutions: 45
Shares Held: 11,902,411

AMERICAN DEPOSITARY RECEIPTS: Each American Depositary Receipt represents one common sh. of par Y50.

DEPOSITARY BANK(S): The Bank of New York, (212) 815-2175; Bankers Trust Co., (212) 250-8500; Citibank (212) 657-7800; J.P. Morgan, (212) 648-3206

FUTUREMEDIA PLC

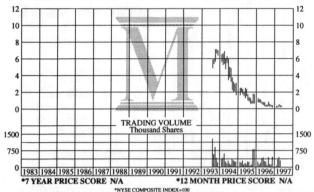

7 YEAR PRICE SCORE N/A   **12 MONTH PRICE SCORE N/A**

NYSE COMPOSITE INDEX=100

INTERIM EARNINGS (Per Share, US$):

Qtr.	July	Oct.	Jan.	Apr.
1996		----------d0.35----------		

INTERIM DIVIDENDS (Per Share):

Amt.	Decl.	Ex.	Rec.	Pay.
	No dividends paid.			

CAPITALIZATION (4/30/96):

	($000)	(%)
Long-Term Debt	620	25.7
Stockholders' Equity........	1,790	74.3
Total	2,410	100.0

RECENT DEVELOPMENTS: For the quarter ended 1/31/97, net loss was £171,000 compared with a loss of £134,000 in the same period the previous year. Sales were £809,000, down 18.4% from £991,000 the year before. Operating loss was £145,000 compared with £147,000 in 1995. The decline in results is being addressed through, according to management, a three-stage recovery plan. Stage one is to eliminate or reduce overhead costs bringing the Company's annual operating expenses down below £2 million. Stage two is to rebuild the Company's sales order book. Stage three is to grow sales revenues while holding the Company's annual operating expenses below £2 million and to increase profitability through achieving higher gross margins. Stage one has been completed. Stage two is well under way and the sales order book has increased significantly over this past year. At the end of October 1996 the sales order backlog surged to £2.2 million compared with £248,000 in the same period of 1995. Additionally, the Company has consistently maintained the order backlog above £2 million since October.

BUSINESS

FUTUREMEDIA PLC is primarily engaged in the production of interactive multimedia courseware and the distribution of its own products and complementary products from other suppliers predominantly to commercial end-users. The main elements of the services provided by the Company are: (i) the production (including, as applicable, script-writing, retention of actors, filming and editing) of training packages tailored to meet customers' specific requirements; (ii) off the shelf sales of mainly in-house developed generic training packages and the systems on which they operate; and (iii) production of interactive communication systems and interactive merchandising to meet particular requirements in the point-of-sale and point-of-information markets.

ANNUAL EARNINGS

	4/30/96	4/30/95	4/30/96	4/30/95
	--------US $--------		--------£--------	
Earnings Per Share	d0.35	d0.37	d0.23	d0.23

ANNUAL FINANCIAL DATA

RECORD OF EARNINGS (IN THOUSANDS):

	4/30/96	4/30/95	4/30/96	4/30/95
Total Revenues	5,750	9,068	3,803	5,625
Costs & Expenses	8,184	11,552	5,413	7,166
Operating Income	d2,434	d2,484	d1,610	d1,541
Income Bef Income Tax	d2,539	d2,529	d1,692	d1,569
Income Tax	cr79	32	cr52	20
Eq. Earnings in Affils.	d20	...	d13	...
Net Income	d2,480	d2,561	d1,640	d1,589
Average Shares Outstg	7,138	6,777	7,138	6,777
BALANCE SHEET (IN THOUSANDS):				
Cash & Cash Equivalents	423	679	280	421
Receivables, Net	1,005	1,683	665	1,044
Inventories	461	713	305	442
Gross Property	4,279	4,854	2,830	3,011
Accumulated Depreciation	2,404	2,257	1,590	1,400
Long-Term Debt	620	814	410	505
Stockholders' Equity	1,790	4,038	1,184	2,505
Total Assets	4,615	7,652	3,052	4,747
Total Current Assets	1,982	3,355	1,311	2,081
Total Current Liabilities	2,183	2,787	1,444	1,729
Net Working Capital	d201	567	d133	352
Year End Shs Outstg	7,780	6,780	7,780	6,780
STATISTICAL RECORD:				
Return on Equity %	...	...		
Return on Assets %	...	...		
Operating Profit Margin %	...	...		
Net Profit Margin %	...	...		
Book Value Per Share	0.23	0.60		

Converted at 1996, US$1.512= 1 British pound; 1995, US$1.612= 1 British pound

OFFICERS:
P. Copeland, Chmn.
N. Burton, C.E.O.
P. Lingard, C.F.O.
INCORPORATED: Feb., 1982
PRINCIPAL OFFICE: Media House, Arundel Road, Walberton, Arundel, West Sussex, BN18 0QP United Kingdom

TELEPHONE NUMBER: 01243 555 000
NO. OF EMPLOYEES: 62
ANNUAL MEETING: In Jan.
SHAREHOLDERS: N/A
INSTITUTIONAL HOLDINGS:
No. of Institutions: N/A
Shares Held: N/A

AMERICAN DEPOSITARY RECEIPTS: (Sponsored) Each American Depositary Receipt represents one ordinary share of par £0.011.

DEPOSITARY BANK(S): The Bank of New York, (212) 815-2175

GENERAL CABLE, PLC

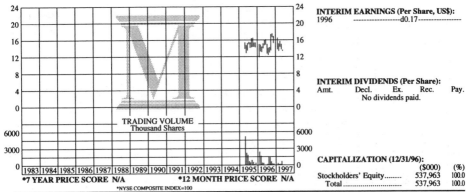

*7 YEAR PRICE SCORE N/A   *12 MONTH PRICE SCORE N/A
*NYSE COMPOSITE INDEX=100

INTERIM EARNINGS (Per Share, US$):
1996 ------------------d0.17----------------

INTERIM DIVIDENDS (Per Share):

Amt.	Decl.	Ex.	Rec.	Pay.
No dividends paid.				

CAPITALIZATION (12/31/96):

	($000)	(%)
Stockholders' Equity........	537,963	100.0
Total	537,963	100.0

RECENT DEVELOPMENTS: For the year ended 12/31/96, net loss was £28.7 million compared with a loss of £18.1 million in 1995. Turnover increased 81.6% to £55.7 million versus £30.7 million a year earlier. Gross profit was £19.1 million compared with £9.4 million in 1995. Operating loss was £26.2 million compared with £20.2 million the year before. Loss on ordinary activities before taxation was £29.8 million from £21.2 million in 1995. The increase in the net loss was primarily attributed to increases in depreciation arising from network build's continuing to exceed operating cash flow growth. Additionally, the loss was increased by including an additional 50% of the loss of the Yorkshire Cable Group from the effective date of acquisition, 8/6/96. The Company anticipates that continued network expansion will lead to further strong growth in operating cash flow, in addition to increased depreciation charges, but interest charges will become a more important component of results as the network build will be funded largely through increased borrowing.

BUSINESS

GENERAL CABLE, PLC is a holding company. Through its subsidiaries, the Company acquires long term investment interests in the United Kingdom cable communications industry through subsidiary and associated undertakings which develop, own and operate integrated broadband telecommunications networks in the United Kingdom delivering voice, data and entertainment services.

ANNUAL EARNINGS

	12/31/96	12/31/95	12/31/96	12/31/95
	--------------US $--------------		--------------£--------------	
Earnings Per Share	d0.17	d0.12	d0.10	d0.08

ANNUAL FINANCIAL DATA

RECORD OF EARNINGS (IN THOUSANDS):

	12/31/96	12/31/95	12/31/96	12/31/95
Total Revenues	94,440	47,669	55,733	30,695
Costs & Expenses	132,086	76,773	77,950	49,435
Depreciation & Amort	6,817	2,241	4,023	1,443
Operating Income	d44,464	d31,344	d26,240	d20,183
Income Bef Income Tax	d50,520	d32,880	d29,814	d21,172
Income Tax	1,793	cr2,864	1,058	cr1,844
Minority Interests	cr3,735	cr1,853	cr2,204	cr1,193
Net Income	d48,578	d28,164	d28,668	d18,135
Average Shares Outstg	505,374	349,077	505,374	349,077
BALANCE SHEET (IN THOUSANDS):				
Cash & Cash Equivalents	280,487	30,057	165,528	19,354
Receivables, Net	31,870	19,894	18,808	12,810
Gross Property	820,568	280,913	484,254	180,884
Accumulated Depreciation	123,561	44,670	72,919	28,764
Stockholders' Equity	537,963	373,059	317,476	240,218
Total Assets	1,082,774	470,469	638,993	302,942
Total Current Assets	312,947	50,699	184,684	32,646
Total Current Liabilities	133,882	53,321	79,010	34,334
Net Working Capital	179,065	d2,621	105,674	d1,688
Year End Shs Outstg	618,648	393,490	618,648	393,490
STATISTICAL RECORD:				
Return on Equity %	...	...		
Return on Assets %	...	...		
Operating Profit Margin %	...	...		
Net Profit Margin %	...	...		
Book Value Per Share	0.87	0.95		

Converted at 1996, US$1.6945= 1 British pound; 1995, US$1.5530= 1 British pound

OFFICERS:
A. Cleaver, Non-Exec. Chmn.
P. X. Galteau, Managing Dir.
D. J. Miller, Finance Dir.
I. Gray, C.O.O.
INCORPORATED: United Kingdom, 1989
PRINCIPAL OFFICE: 37 Old Queen Street, London United Kingdom, SW1H 9JA

TELEPHONE NUMBER: 44-171-393-2828
NO. OF EMPLOYEES: 687
ANNUAL MEETING: N/A
SHAREHOLDERS: N/A
INSTITUTIONAL HOLDINGS:
No. of Institutions: 14
Shares Held: 2,530,548

AMERICAN DEPOSITARY RECEIPTS: Each American Depositary Receipt represents 5 ordinary shares of par value £1.

DEPOSITARY BANK(S): The Bank of New York, (212) 815-2175

GENSET

INTERIM EARNINGS (Per Share, US$):

Qtr.	Mar.	June	Sept.	Dec.
1994		d1.06		
1995		d1.62		
1996		d2.25		
1997	d0.70	...	...	...

INTERIM DIVIDENDS (Per Share):

Amt.	Decl.	Ex.	Rec.	Pay.
No dividends paid.				

TRADING VOLUME
Thousand Shares

1983 1984 1985 1986 1987 1988 1989 1990 1991 1992 1993 1994 1995 1996 1997

*7 YEAR PRICE SCORE N/A   *12 MONTH PRICE SCORE N/A

*NYSE COMPOSITE INDEX=100

CAPITALIZATION (12/31/96):

	($000)	(%)
Long-Term Debt	8,115	7.0
Stockholders' Equity	107,927	93.0
Total	116,042	100.0

RECENT DEVELOPMENTS: For the quarter ended 3/31/97, Genset incurred a net loss of FF26.8 million (US$4.8 million) versus a net loss of FF17.7 million (US$3.1 million) in the same prior-year period. Total revenues rose 84.3% to FF15.1 million (US$2.7 million) from FF8.2 million (US$1.5 million) in 1996. Net sales grew 6.8% to FF8.6 million (US$1.5 million) versus the prior year. Research and development revenues soared to FF6.5 million (US$1.2 million) from FF143,000 a year earlier. This increase was primarily due to GENXY's major genomics programs with Synthelabo and Johnson & Johnson. Research and development expenses more than doubled to FF31.7 million (US$5.6 million) from FF15.2 million (US$2.7 million) in 1996 due to costs related to the rapid expansion of gene discovery programs. General and administrative expenses grew 56.6% to FF10.5 million (US$1.9 million) due to the expansion of patent and licensing activities, as well as investor relations and business development activities.

BUSINESS

GENSET is engaged in the systematic and comprehensive analysis of the human genome to identify and patent genes and regulatory regions related to selected common diseases. The Company's objective is to apply its genomics technology to discover drugs for such diseases and to enter into strategic partnerships with pharmaceutical companies which will develop and market these drugs.

ANNUAL EARNINGS

	12/31/96	12/31/95	12/31/96	12/31/95
	---US $---		---FFr---	
Earnings Per Share	d2.25	d1.62	d11.66	d7.96

ANNUAL FINANCIAL DATA

RECORD OF EARNINGS (IN THOUSANDS):

	12/31/96	12/31/95	12/31/96	12/31/95
Total Revenues	9,352	5,661	48,561	27,762
Costs & Expenses	27,930	14,593	145,035	71,567
Operating Income	d18,579	d8,932	d96,474	d43,805
Income Bef Income Tax	d16,735	d8,756	d86,900	d42,944
Income Tax Benefit	4,201	1,619	21,815	7,942
Net Income	d12,534	d7,137	d65,085	d35,002
Average Shares Outstg	5,580	4,396	5,580	4,396

BALANCE SHEET (IN THOUSANDS):

Cash & Cash Equivalents	100,036	9,213	519,470	45,184
Receivables, Net	2,795	2,658	14,511	13,037
Inventories	544	619	2,827	3,038
Gross Property	20,588	11,890	106,909	58,313
Accumulated Depreciation	7,768	5,280	40,337	25,893
Long-Term Debt	8,115	7,312	42,142	35,860
Stockholders' Equity	107,927	11,743	560,443	57,591
Total Assets	127,606	23,247	662,633	114,010
Total Current Assets	107,767	12,489	559,612	61,253
Total Current Liabilities	11,564	4,192	60,048	20,559
Net Working Capital	96,203	8,298	499,564	40,694
Year-end Shares Outstg.	6,770	6,705	6,770	6,705

STATISTICAL RECORD:

Return on Equity %	...	...		
Return on Assets %	...	...		
Operating Profit Margin %	...	...		
Net Profit Margin %	...	...		
Book Value Per Share	15.94	1.75		

Converted at 1996, US$0.1926 = 1 French franc; 1995, US$0.2039 = 1 French franc

OFFICERS:
P. Brandys, Chmn. & C.E.O.
D.A. Smeltzer, Chief Financial Officer
C. Faure-Cachard, Dir. of Admin. & Fin.

INCORPORATED: France, Sept. 1989

PRINCIPAL OFFICE: 24, rue Royale 75008 Paris France

TELEPHONE NUMBER: +331 55 04 59 00

FAX: +331 55 04 59 29

NO. OF EMPLOYEES: 290

ANNUAL MEETING: In May

SHAREHOLDERS: N/A

INSTITUTIONAL HOLDINGS:
No. of Institutions: N/A
Shares Held: N/A

**AMERICAN DEPOSITARY
RECEIPTS:** (Unsponsored) Three American Depositary Receipts represent one share of par FFr17.

DEPOSITARY BANK(S): The Bank of New York, (212) 815-2175

GETTY COMMUNICATIONS, PLC

YIELD ...
P/E RATIO 58.1

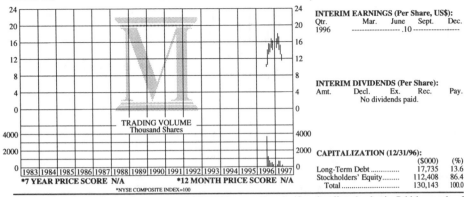

*7 YEAR PRICE SCORE N/A   *12 MONTH PRICE SCORE N/A
*NYSE COMPOSITE INDEX=100

INTERIM EARNINGS (Per Share, US$):

Qtr.	Mar.	June	Sept.	Dec.
1996	----------------- .10 -----------------			

INTERIM DIVIDENDS (Per Share):

Amt.	Decl.	Ex.	Rec.	Pay.
	No dividends paid.			

CAPITALIZATION (12/31/96):

	($000)	(%)
Long-Term Debt	17,735	13.6
Stockholders' Equity	112,408	86.4
Total	130,143	100.0

RECENT DEVELOPMENTS: For the quarter ended 3/31/97, net income advanced 71.5% to £770,000 (US$1.3 million) from £449,000 in the same prior-year period. Sales climbed 15.6% to £14.1 million (US$23.0 million) from £12.2 million in 1996. This increase reflected growth in volume at Tony Stone Images, as well as recent acquisitions by the Company. In addition, Hulton Getty, which was merged with Tony Stone Images in the United Kingdom to form Getty Images, performed well; however, the strength of the sterling significantly affected sales in British pounds of non-United Kingdom operations. On 3/26/97, the Company announced the acquisition of the Liaison Agency, the New York-based photo agency. On 4/7/97, GETTY announced the formation of a development partnership with IBM to create a digital image distribution system that will improve protection for visual copyright holders and speed the development of digital image delivery.

BUSINESS

GETTY COMMUNICATIONS, PLC's principal business is the marketing of reproduction rights of images and visual content collections. The Company, through its subsidiaries, provides visual content to advertising and design agencies, magazine, newspapers, book and new media publishers, broadcasters and other corporations. The Company markets reproduction and broadcasting rights to still and moving images through an international network of wholly-owned offices.

ANNUAL EARNINGS

	12/31/96	① 12/31/95	12/31/96	① 12/31/95
	--------------US $--------------		--------------British £-------------	
Earnings Per Share	0.10	0.06	0.06	0.04
① 9 mos. ended.				

ANNUAL FINANCIAL DATA

RECORD OF EARNINGS (IN THOUSANDS):

Total Revenues	92,308	52,675	54,475	33,918
Costs & Expenses	75,361	43,139	44,474	27,778
Depreciation & Amort	8,296	4,928	4,896	3,173
Operating Income	8,650	4,608	5,105	2,967
Income Bef Income Tax	6,200	3,195	3,659	2,057
Income Tax	3,238	1,843	1,911	1,187
Net Income	2,962	1,351	1,748	870
Average Shares Outstg	27,832	23,057	27,832	23,057

BALANCE SHEET (IN THOUSANDS):

Cash & Cash Equivalents	58,360	1,899	34,441	1,223
Receivables, Net	20,434	17,533	12,059	11,290
Gross Property	49,442	21,330	29,178	13,735
Accumulated Depreciation	16,074	9,234	9,486	5,946
Long-Term Debt	17,735	8,706	10,466	5,606
Stockholders' Equity	112,408	27,019	66,337	17,398
Total Assets	161,899	71,042	95,544	45,745
Total Current Assets	82,495	23,177	48,684	14,924
Total Current Liabilities	31,757	35,317	18,741	22,741
Net Working Capital	50,738	d12,140	29,943	d7,817
Year End Shs Outstg	37,388	23,057	37,388	23,057

STATISTICAL RECORD:

Return on Equity %	2.64	5.00		
Return on Assets %	1.83	1.90		
Operating Profit Margin %	9.37	8.75		
Net Profit Margin %	3.21	2.57		
Book Value Per Share	3.01	1.17		

Converted at 1996, US$1.6945= 1 British pound; 1995, US$1.5530= 1 British pound.

OFFICERS:
M. H. Getty, Chmn.
J. D. Klein, C.E.O.
L. J. Gould, C.F.O.

INCORPORATED: England, Jan., 1995

PRINCIPAL OFFICE: 101 Bayham Street, London NW1 OAG United Kingdom

TELEPHONE NUMBER: (44) 171-544-3456

NO. OF EMPLOYEES: 650

ANNUAL MEETING: N/A

SHAREHOLDERS: N/A

INSTITUTIONAL HOLDINGS:
No. of Institutions: 20
Shares Held: 4,424,300

AMERICAN DEPOSITARY RECEIPTS: Each American Depositary Share represents two Cl. A ordinary shares of par £0.01.

DEPOSITARY BANK(S): The Bank of New York, (212) 815-2175

GOLD FIELDS OF SOUTH AFRICA LTD.

YIELD 1.5%
P/E RATIO 26.9

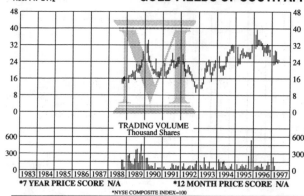

TRADING VOLUME
Thousand Shares

1983 1984 1985 1986 1987 1988 1989 1990 1991 1992 1993 1994 1995 1996 1997

*7 YEAR PRICE SCORE N/A   *12 MONTH PRICE SCORE N/A

*NYSE COMPOSITE INDEX=100

INTERIM EARNINGS (Per Share, US$):

Qtr.	Sept.	Dec.	Mar.	June
1995		1.14		
1996		0.91		

INTERIM DIVIDENDS (Per Share):

Amt.	Decl.	Ex.	Rec.	Pay.
0.303	...	8/30/95	9/1/95	10/5/95
0.201	...	2/7/96	2/9/96	3/21/96
0.31	...	9/4	9/6	10/10
0.179	...	2/5/97	2/7/97	3/20/97

Indicated div.: $0.358

CAPITALIZATION (6/30/96):

	($000)	(%)
Long-Term Debt	43,890	5.8
Stockholders' Equity	714,252	93.9
Deferred Income Tax	2,772	0.3
Total	760,914	100.0

RECENT DEVELOPMENTS: As of 6/30/96, net income dropped 5.2% to R381.0 million from R402.0 million in 1995. Total income fell 1.4% to R702.0 million from R712.0 million the year before. Income from investments decreased 20.2% to R312.0 million from R391.0 million the prior year. Surplus on realization of investments advanced to R84.0 million from R17.0 million in 1995. Administration, technical and general expenses increased 12.3% to R164.0 million from R146.0 million a year earlier. Operating income declined 21.0% to R226.0 million from R286.0 million in 1995. Results for the year ended 6/30/96 reflected continued low levels of labor productivity and underground fires. The underground fires had a significant impact on gold production, particularly at GLDFY's East and West Driefontein divisions of Driefontein Consolidated. In addition, GLDFY suffered a setback due to protest marches, which were accompanied by unlawful stayaways from work for one day at all but two of GLDFY's operations.

BUSINESS

GOLD FIELDS OF SOUTH AFRICA, LTD. is a mining finance company. Through its subsidiaries and associates, the Company is engaged in the investment, mining and the processing of metals and minerals in Southern Africa. The Company is also engaged in the discovery and development of new projects in the energy, precious and base metal fields on a worldwide basis. The Company's principal asset and major source of income is its substantial portfolio of investments, mainly in precious metal mining companies. The Company acts as administrative and technical advisers and secretaries to most of the companies in which it is invested.

ANNUAL EARNINGS

	6/30/96	6/30/95	6/30/96	6/30/95
	-----US $-----		-----Rand-----	
Earnings Per Share	0.91	1.14	3.93	4.14

ANNUAL FINANCIAL DATA

RECORD OF EARNINGS (IN THOUSANDS):

	6/30/96	6/30/95	6/30/96	6/30/95
Total Revenues	162,162	195,800	702,000	712,000
Costs & Expenses	109,956	117,150	476,000	426,000
Operating Income	52,206	78,650	226,000	286,000
Income Bef Income Tax	104,181	133,650	451,000	486,000
Income Tax	8,085	12,100	35,000	44,000
Minority Interests	8,085	11,000	35,000	40,000
Net Income	88,011	110,550	381,000	402,000
Average Shares Outstg	97,000	97,000	97,000	97,000

BALANCE SHEET (IN THOUSANDS):

Cash & Cash Equivalents	129,591	82,225	561,000	299,000
Inventories	13,398	6,875	58,000	25,000
Gross Property	99,561	92,862	431,000	402,000
Accumulated Depreciation	34,188	37,125	148,000	135,000
Long-Term Debt	43,890	17,600	190,000	64,000
Stockholders' Equity	714,252	795,300	3,092,000	2,892,000
Total Assets	880,803	951,500	3,813,000	3,460,000
Total Current Assets	203,049	163,075	879,000	593,000
Total Current Liabilities	63,525	73,700	275,000	268,000
Net Working Capital	139,524	89,375	604,000	325,000
Year End Shs Outstg	97,000	97,000	97,000	97,000

STATISTICAL RECORD:

Return on Equity %	12.32	13.90
Return on Assets %	9.99	11.62
Operating Profit Margin %	32.19	40.17
Net Profit Margin %	54.27	56.46
Book Value Per Share	7.36	8.20

Converted at 1996, US$0.2310= 1 South African Rand; 1995, US$0.2750= 1 South African Rand

OFFICERS:
A.J. Wright, C.E.O.
J.G. Hopwood, Exec. Dir.—Corp. Fin.

INCORPORATED: Republic of South Africa, Nov., 1932

PRINCIPAL OFFICE: 75 Fox Street, Johannesburg, 2001 South Africa

TELEPHONE NUMBER: (011) 639-9111
FAX: (011) 639-2101/2
NO. OF EMPLOYEES: 724
ANNUAL MEETING: In Oct.
SHAREHOLDERS: N/A
INSTITUTIONAL HOLDINGS:
No. of Institutions: 8
Shares Held: 1,502,074

**AMERICAN DEPOSITARY
RECEIPTS:** (Sponsored) One American Depositary Receipt represents one ordinary share of R0.05. American Depositary Receipt split 5-for-1 on Oct. 31, 1983.

DEPOSITARY BANK(S): The Bank of New York, (212) 815-2175; J.P. Morgan, (212) 648-3206

GREAT CENTRAL MINES N.L.

YIELD 1.7%
P/E RATIO 42.0

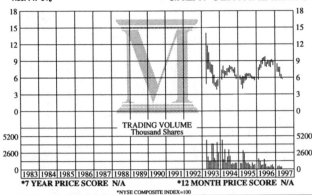

TRADING VOLUME
Thousand Shares

|1983|1984|1985|1986|1987|1988|1989|1990|1991|1992|1993|1994|1995|1996|1997|

*7 YEAR PRICE SCORE N/A   *12 MONTH PRICE SCORE N/A

*NYSE COMPOSITE INDEX=100

INTERIM EARNINGS (Per Share):
1994-95 ------------------ 0.01 ------------------
1995-96 ------------------ 0.14 ------------------

INTERIM DIVIDENDS (Per Share):

Amt.	Decl.	Ex.	Rec.	Pay.
0.051	...	8/30/96	9/04/96	10/21/96
0.05	...	3/19/97	3/21/97	4/21/97

Indicated div.: $0.10

CAPITALIZATION (6/30/96):

	($000)	(%)
Long-Term Debt	45,716	18.2
Stockholders' Equity	206,150	81.8
Total	251,866	100.0

RECENT DEVELOPMENTS: For the three months ended 3/31/97, gold sales totaled A$48.1 million at an average price of A$581 (US$454) per ounce. Gold production was 92,759 ounces, down 24.4% compared with 122,645 ounces in the corresponding quarter the previous year. Production from the Company's Bronzewing mine was 44,723 ounces versus 61,643 ounces a year ago, while production from the Company's Jundee mine slid to 48,036 ounces from 61,002 ounces in the same quarter in 1996. The average cash operating cost jumped 33.0% to A$310 (US$243) compared with $233 the year before. In April, the Company reported that production levels have improved due to increased underground output at the Bronzewing mine. The Company expects production for the year ended 6/30/97 to be between 460,000 ounces and 480,000 ounces compared with 362,362 ounces in the same prior-year period.

BUSINESS

GREAT CENTRAL MINES N.L. is engaged in gold mining and mineral exploration. The Company wholly owns and operates two major gold mines, the Bronzewing gold mine, which commenced production in November 1994 and the Jundee gold mine which commenced production in December 1995.

ANNUAL EARNINGS

	6/30/96	6/30/95	6/30/96	6/30/95
	-------------US $-----------		---------------A $-------------	
Earnings Per Share	0.14	0.01	0.18	0.01

ANNUAL FINANCIAL DATA

RECORD OF EARNINGS (IN THOUSANDS):

Total Revenues	156,264	25,800	198,430	36,354
Income Bef Income Tax	36,323	5,997	46,125	8,450
Net Income	36,323	5,997	46,125	8,450
Average Shares Outstg	252,037	241,839	252,037	241,839

BALANCE SHEET (IN THOUSANDS):

Cash & Cash Equivalents	7,326	5,348	9,303	7,536
Receivables, Net	12,533	1,186	15,915	1,671
Inventories	28,082	2,302	35,660	3,243
Gross Property	82,310	34,243	104,521	48,250
Accumulated Depreciation	10,560	1,573	13,410	2,216
Long-Term Debt	45,716	57,745	58,052	81,365
Stockholders' Equity	206,150	151,275	261,778	213,153
Total Assets	329,774	225,151	418,760	317,248
Total Current Assets	49,453	10,739	62,797	15,132
Total Current Liabilities	77,325	16,131	98,190	22,730
Net Working Capital	d27,872	d5,392	d35,393	d7,598
Year End Shs Outstg	254,033	249,533	254,033	249,533

STATISTICAL RECORD:

Return on Equity %	17.62	3.96		
Return on Assets %	11.01	2.66		
Net Profit Margin %	23.24	23.24		
Book Value Per Share	0.81	0.61		

Converted at 1996, US$0.7875= 1 Australian $; 1995, US$0.7097= 1 Australian $

OFFICERS:
J. Gutnick, Chmn.
D. Burvill
P. Hepburn-Brown
I. Currie
I. Herbison

INCORPORATED: 1985

PRINCIPAL OFFICE: 8th Floor, 580 St. Kilda Road, Melbourne Australia

TELEPHONE NUMBER: 61-3-9276-7888

NO. OF EMPLOYEES: N/A

ANNUAL MEETING: In October

SHAREHOLDERS: 1,293

INSTITUTIONAL HOLDINGS:
No. of Institutions: 9
Shares Held: 493,476

AMERICAN DEPOSITARY RECEIPTS: (Sponsored) Each American Depositary Receipt represents one ordinary share of par A$0.20.

DEPOSITARY BANK(S): The Bank of New York, (212) 815-2175

GREAT WALL ELECTRONIC INTERNATIONAL LTD.

YIELD ...
P/E RATIO 9.7

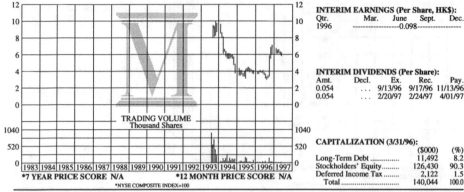

*7 YEAR PRICE SCORE N/A *12 MONTH PRICE SCORE N/A
*NYSE COMPOSITE INDEX=100

INTERIM EARNINGS (Per Share, HK$):

Qtr.	Mar.	June	Sept.	Dec.
1996		-0.098		

INTERIM DIVIDENDS (Per Share):

Amt.	Decl.	Ex.	Rec.	Pay.
0.054	...	9/13/96	9/17/96	11/13/96
0.054	...	2/20/97	2/24/97	4/01/97

CAPITALIZATION (3/31/96):

	($000)	(%)
Long-Term Debt	11,492	8.2
Stockholders' Equity	126,430	90.3
Deferred Income Tax	2,122	1.5
Total	140,044	100.0

RECENT DEVELOPMENTS: For the six months ended 9/30/96, net profit attributable to shareholders advanced 20.4% to HK$38.6 million compared with HK$32.0 million in the same period of 1995. Turnover was HK$1.55 billion, up 1.7% from HK$1.53 billion a year earlier. Operating profit was HK$40.5 million versus HK$17.1 million in 1995. Profit before taxation increased 43.5% to HK$43.4 million compared with HK$30.2 million the year before.

The recent price war among major television producers has effected the results of the Group's associated companies and in turn the Group's results for the current period. As a result, the price war has forced some weaker competitors out of the market recently and the downward pressure on prices has been released. This should enable the surviving players, including the Group's assoc. companies, to achieve more sales in the coming Chinese New Year.

BUSINESS

GREAT WALL ELECTRONIC INTERNATIONAL LTD. is an investment holding company. Through its subsidiaries, the Company is engaged in the manufacture, marketing and sale of consumer electronic products.

ANNUAL EARNINGS

	3/31/96	3/31/95	3/31/96	3/31/95
	--US $--		--HK$--	
Earnings Per Share	0.01	0.02	0.10	0.12

ANNUAL FINANCIAL DATA

RECORD OF EARNINGS (IN THOUSANDS):

	3/31/96	3/31/95	3/31/96	3/31/95
Total Revenues	438,251	403,037	3,389,416	3,117,065
Income Bef Income Tax	9,482	20,782	73,335	160,728
Income Tax	1,829	1,977	14,143	15,293
Eq. Earnings in Affils.	3,510	d562	27,144	d4,343
Minority Interests	cr525	3,558	cr4,060	27,519
Net Income	11,688	14,685	90,396	113,573
Average Shares Outstg	925,859	929,606	925,859	929,606

BALANCE SHEET (IN THOUSANDS):

	3/31/96	3/31/95	3/31/96	3/31/95
Cash & Cash Equivalents	10,918	9,841	84,438	76,108
Receivables, Net	66,596	58,473	515,053	452,231
Inventories	77,883	95,400	602,345	737,820
Gross Property	147,007	146,734	1,136,946	1,134,836
Accumulated Depreciation	41,687	30,432	322,407	235,362
Long-Term Debt	11,492	28,019	88,878	216,701
Stockholders' Equity	126,430	116,814	977,802	903,433
Total Assets	290,865	304,808	2,249,534	2,357,373
Total Current Assets	161,128	173,785	1,246,153	1,344,045
Total Current Liabilities	145,779	149,041	1,127,449	1,152,677
Net Working Capital	15,348	24,744	118,704	191,368
Year End Shs Outstg	925,859	925,859	925,859	925,859

STATISTICAL RECORD:

	3/31/96	3/31/95
Return on Equity %	9.24	12.57
Return on Assets %	4.02	4.82
Operating Profit Margin %	...	...
Net Profit Margin %	2.67	3.64
Book Value Per Share	1.06	0.98

Converted at 1996, US$0.1293= 1 Hong Kong $; 1995, US$0.1293= 1 Hong Kong $

OFFICERS:
Wong Kwok Wing, Chmn.
Cheung Ki Sui
Leung Chor Chiu
Tse On Kin

INCORPORATED: Bermuda, Dec., 1989

PRINCIPAL OFFICE: Cedar House, 41 Cedar Avenue Hamilton Bermuda

TELEPHONE NUMBER: N/A

NO. OF EMPLOYEES: N/A

ANNUAL MEETING: In Sep.

SHAREHOLDERS: N/A

INSTITUTIONAL HOLDINGS:
No. of Institutions: 1
Shares Held: 300

AMERICAN DEPOSITARY RECEIPTS: (Sponsored) Each American Depositary Receipt represents fifty ordinary shares of par HK$0.10.

DEPOSITARY BANK(S): Citibank, (212) 657-7800

HARMONY GOLD MINING CO., LTD.

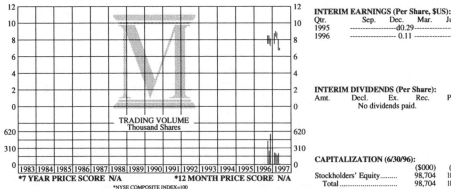

7 YEAR PRICE SCORE N/A   **12 MONTH PRICE SCORE N/A**

*NYSE COMPOSITE INDEX=100

INTERIM EARNINGS (Per Share, $US):

Qtr.	Sep.	Dec.	Mar.	June
1995	------------------d0.29-----------------			
1996	------------------ 0.11 -----------------			

INTERIM DIVIDENDS (Per Share):

Amt.	Decl.	Ex.	Rec.	Pay.
	No dividends paid.			

CAPITALIZATION (6/30/96):

	($000)	(%)
Stockholders' Equity........	98,704	100.0
Total	98,704	100.0

RECENT DEVELOPMENTS: For the year ended 6/30/96, net income was R13.9 million (US$3.2 million) compared with a loss of R3.3 million (dUS$926,000) in the prior year. Results for 1996 included employee termination costs of R33.9 million (US$8.8 million) and equity losses of R2.5 million (US$649,000). These charges were partially offset by a R4.6 million (US$1.2 million) reversal of a provision for the Tailings dam spill. Revenues were down 2.0% to R890.2 million (US$205.6 million) from R908.5 million (US$249.8 million) a year earlier. Revenues from product sales decreased 3.3% due primarily to a 16% reduction in underground volumes. Recovered grade from underground sources improved 7% to 3.51 grams per ton (0.102 oz per ton). Capital expenditures for 1996 reached R40.3 million (US$10.5 million).

BUSINESS

HARMONY GOLD MINING COM-PANY, LTD. is a holding company. Through its subsidiary, the Company is engaged in gold mining and related activities, including exploration, extraction, processing, refining and rehabilitation. Gold bullion, the Company's principal product, is produced and sold in South Africa.

ANNUAL EARNINGS

	6/30/96	6/30/95	6/30/96	6/30/95
	------------US $-------------		------------Rand------------	
Earnings Per Share	0.11	d0.29	0.49	d1.04

ANNUAL FINANCIAL DATA

RECORD OF EARNINGS (IN THOUSANDS):

	6/30/96	6/30/95	6/30/96	6/30/95
Total Revenues	205,636	249,834	890,197	908,489
Costs & Expenses	200,487	251,507	867,907	914,570
Operating Income	5,264	d1,672	22,290	d6,081
Income Bef Income Tax	5,149	d1,672	22,290	d6,081
Income Tax	1,931	cr756	8,360	cr2,749
Net Income	3,218	d926	13,930	d3,332
Average Shares Outstg	28,652	27,629	28,652	27,629

BALANCE SHEET (IN THOUSANDS):

Cash & Cash Equivalents	27,197	38,385	117,735	139,583
Receivables	6,680	11,372	29,698	41,353
Inventories	12,575	14,405	54,438	52,381
Gross Property	226,757	261,634	981,633	951,395
Accumulated Depreciation	107,547	119,525	465,572	434,635
Stockholders' Equity	98,704	110,817	427,288	402,972
Total Assets	186,749	210,932	808,436	767,027
Total Current Assets	46,632	64,162	201,871	233,317
Total Current Liabilities	35,258	36,653	152,630	133,285
Net Working Capital	11,375	27,509	49,241	100,032
Year End Shs Outstg	28,863	28,562	28,863	28,562

STATISTICAL RECORD:

Return on Equity %	3.26	...		
Return on Assets %	1.72	...		
Operating Profit Margin %	2.56	...		
Net Profit Margin %	1.56	...		
Book Value Per Share	3.42	3.83		

Converted at 1996, US$0.2310= 1 South African Rand; 1995, US$0.2750= 1 South African Rand

OFFICERS:
L. Hewitt, Chmn.
Z. B. Swanepoel, Managing Dir.
C. P. Booyens, Fin. Dir.
R. A. L. Atkinson

INCORPORATED: South Africa, Aug. 1950

PRINCIPAL OFFICE: 5 Press Avenue, Selby, Johannesburg Republic of South Africa

TELEPHONE NUMBER: (011) 837-0706

NO. OF EMPLOYEES: 12,500

ANNUAL MEETING: In Nov.

SHAREHOLDERS: N/A

INSTITUTIONAL HOLDINGS:
No. of Institutions: 15
Shares Held: 3,328,350

AMERICAN DEPOSITARY RECEIPTS: Each American Depositary Receipt represents one ordinary share of par R0.50.

DEPOSITARY BANK(S): The Bank of New York, (212) 815-2175

HIBERNIA FOODS PLC

YIELD ...
P/E RATIO ...

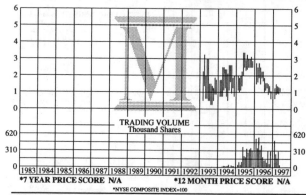

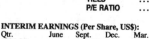

7 YEAR PRICE SCORE N/A   *12 MONTH PRICE SCORE N/A

*NYSE COMPOSITE INDEX=100

INTERIM EARNINGS (Per Share, US$):

Qtr.	June	Sept.	Dec.	Mar.
1994-95		0.19		
1995-96		d0.20		

INTERIM DIVIDENDS (Per Share):

Amt.	Decl.	Ex.	Rec.	Pay.
	No dividends paid.			

CAPITALIZATION (3/31/96):

	($000)	(%)
Long-Term Debt	714	8.0
Stockholders' Equity	8,195	92.0
Total	8,910	100.0

RECENT DEVELOPMENTS: For the six months ended 9/30/96, HIBNY incurred a net loss of US$983,000 versus a net loss of US$349,000 in 1995. Revenues soared to US$25.0 million from US$8.41 million the prior year. This growth was due to a rapid increase in the level of exports to Russia, which developed into Hibernia's main market. In addition, the Bovine Spongiform Encephalopathy ("B.S.E.") crisis caused a deferral of shipments to the 1996 period due to the temporary prohibition of purchases by certain markets. B.S.E., also known as "Mad Cow Disease," is a disease of the nervous system, which affects cattle and might be associated with Creutzfeldt Jakob Disease. During the quarter, HIBNY announced that it will pursue other lines of business outside the beef industry; however, HIBNY will be actively involved in the beef processing and exporting industry mainly through its Tipperary beef processing subsidiary.

BUSINESS

HIBERNIA FOODS PLC is engaged in the purchase of beef in Ireland and other countries for export to wholesale customers in North & South Africa, the Middle East, the Commonwealth of Independent States, and the Far East, as well as to wholesale customers elsewhere in the European community. The Company trades in both fresh and frozen beef, and to date all of the beef traded has been in boneless form. The Company is also engaged in processing beef at its Dublin based processing place. During 1996, the Company announced that it will pursue other lines of business outside the beef industry due to Bovine Spongiform Encephalopathy ("B.S.E."), also known as "Mad Cow Disease." B.S.E. is a disease of the nervous system, which affects cattle and might be associated with Creutzfeldt Jakob Disease. The Company will be actively involved in the beef processing and exporting industry mainly through its Tipperary beef processing subsidiary.

ANNUAL EARNINGS

	3/31/96	⏢ 3/31/95	3/31/96	⏢ 3/31/95
	US $		IR£	
Earnings Per Share	d0.20	0.19	d0.13	0.12

⏢ 15 mnths. ended due to fiscal year-end change.

ANNUAL FINANCIAL DATA

RECORD OF EARNINGS (IN THOUSANDS):

Total Revenues	26,315	50,275	16,710	30,986
Costs & Expenses	27,019	49,612	17,157	30,578
Operating Income	d537	977	d341	602
Income Bef Income Tax	d856	698	d543	430
Income Tax	7	148	4	91
Minority Interests	cr53	2	cr34	1
Net Income	d809	548	d514	338
Average Shares Outstg	4,075	2,862	4,075	2,862

BALANCE SHEET (IN THOUSANDS):

Cash & Cash Equivalents	1,528	1,215	970	749
Receivables, Net	11,923	10,314	7,571	6,357
Inventories	5,917	1,840	3,757	1,134
Gross Property	1,744	1,669	1,107	1,029
Accumulated Depreciation	...	140	...	86
Long-Term Debt	714	275	454	170
Stockholders' Equity	8,195	3,237	5,204	1,995
Total Assets	24,372	17,640	15,476	10,872
Total Current Assets	22,628	16,110	14,369	9,929
Total Current Liabilities	15,392	14,000	9,774	8,629
Net Working Capital	7,236	2,110	4,595	1,301
Year End Shs Outstg	5,622	3,462	5,622	3,462

STATISTICAL RECORD:

Return on Equity %	...	16.93		
Return on Assets %	...	3.11		
Operating Profit Margin %	...	1.32		
Net Profit Margin %	...	1.09		
Book Value Per Share	1.46	0.94		

Converted at 1996, US$1.5748= 1 Irish pound; 1995, US$1.6225= 1 Irish pound.

OFFICERS:
O. Murphy, Chmn. & C.E.O.
C. Delves, C.F.O.
P. Connolly, Corporate Sec.

INCORPORATED: Ireland, Aug., 1991

PRINCIPAL OFFICE: 15 Fitzwilliam Square, Dublin, 2 Ireland

TELEPHONE NUMBER: (1) 661-1030
FAX: (1) 661-1029
NO. OF EMPLOYEES: 17 (avg.)
ANNUAL MEETING: N/A
SHAREHOLDERS: 500
INSTITUTIONAL HOLDINGS:
No. of Institutions: 3
Shares Held: 419,000

AMERICAN DEPOSITARY RECEIPTS: (Sponsored) Each American Depositary Receipt represents one ordinary share of par IR£0.07.

DEPOSITARY BANK(S): The Bank of New York, (212) 815-2175

HIGHVELD STEEL AND VANADIUM CO.

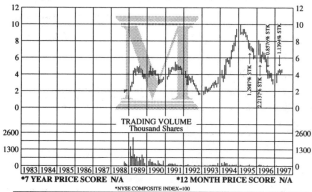

INTERIM EARNINGS (Per Share, $US):

Qtr.	Mar.	June	Sep.	Dec.
1994	------------------	0.37	------------------	
1995	------------------	0.60	------------------	

INTERIM DIVIDENDS (Per Share):

Amt.	Decl.	Ex.	Rec.	Pay.
1.2987%	...	8/16/95	8/18/95	10/05/95
2.2137%	...	2/28/96	3/01/96	4/26/96
0.8576%	...	8/21/96	8/23/96	10/18/96
1.1394%	...	3/12/97	3/14/97	5/09/97

TRADING VOLUME
Thousand Shares

CAPITALIZATION (12/31/95):

	($000)	(%)
Long-Term Debt	204,534	28.5
Stockholders' Equity........	414,369	57.7
Deferred Income Tax	99,425	13.8
Total	718,328	100.0

7 YEAR PRICE SCORE N/A   **12 MONTH PRICE SCORE N/A**

NYSE COMPOSITE INDEX=100

RECENT DEVELOPMENTS: For the year ended 12/31/95, net income was R200.8 million. This compares with R118.0 million in the prior year. Revenues advanced 18.5% to R2.54 billion from R2.14 billion in 1994. The increase in revenues and earnings was attributed to increased volumes produced and higher U.S. dollar export prices for most of the group's products. Total steel sales for the year amounted to R1.15 billion, up 4.0% from R1.10 billion a year ago. Operating income reached R245.0 million compared to R126.2 million a year earlier. Production volumes of total ore mined were up 9.6% to 2.2 million tons. Ferroalloys production increased 10.8% to 275,240 tons while stainless steel production jumped 32.1% to 178,180 tons. Total rolled product amounted to 737,853 tons, up 3.6% from 1994.

BUSINESS

HIGHVELD STEEL AND VANA-DIUM COMPANY is a holding company. The Company produces steel, vanadium products, ferro-alloys, carbonaceous products and metal containers and closures. Ore for the steelworks and the Vantra division is obtained from the Company's own mine. The Company's products include vanadium pentoxide, liquid pig iron, vanadium-bearing slag, manganese alloys, drums, pails and crown closures. Through its subsidiaries, the Company also operates a passenger bus service, mainly for the transportation of Highveld employees.

ANNUAL EARNINGS

	12/31/95	12/31/94	12/31/95	12/31/94
	----------US $----------		----------Rand----------	
Earnings Per Share	0.60	0.37	2.18	1.31

ANNUAL FINANCIAL DATA

RECORD OF EARNINGS (IN THOUSANDS):

	12/31/95	12/31/94	12/31/95	12/31/94
Total Revenues	695,361	603,379	2,535,039	2,138,125
Income Bef Income Tax	71,710	42,629	261,430	151,060
Income Tax	16,618	9,317	60,585	33,016
Net Income	55,092	33,312	200,845	118,044
Average Shares Outstg	91,888	89,945	91,888	89,945
BALANCE SHEET (IN THOUSANDS):				
Cash & Cash Equivalents	30,028	137,642	109,473	487,746
Receivables, Net	114,013	106,324	415,651	376,768
Inventories	185,509	90,613	676,301	321,095
Gross Property	803,611	702,509	2,929,680	2,489,400
Accumulated Depreciation	181,599	169,160	662,046	599,434
Long-Term Debt	204,534	202,428	745,659	717,322
Stockholders' Equity	414,369	373,065	1,510,642	1,321,989
Total Assets	718,328	648,068	2,618,769	2,296,485
Total Current Assets	329,551	334,579	1,201,425	1,185,609
Total Current Liabilities	238,955	227,449	871,146	805,986
Net Working Capital	90,596	107,130	330,279	379,623
Year End Shs Outstg	92,847	90,884	92,847	90,884
STATISTICAL RECORD:				
Return on Equity %	13.30	8.93		
Return on Assets %	7.67	5.14		
Operating Profit Margin %	9.71	9.71		
Net Profit Margin %	7.92	5.52		
Book Value Per Share	4.46	4.10		

Converted at 1995, US$0.2743= 1 South African Rand; 1994, US$0.2822= 1 South African Rand

OFFICERS:
T. E. Jones, Managing Dir.
E. Barnardo
J. A. Chegwidden
L. Matteucci

INCORPORATED: May, 1960

PRINCIPAL OFFICE: Portion 29 of the farm Schoongezicht No. 308 J.S.District Witbank Mpumalanga South Africa

TELEPHONE NUMBER: 27-135-909911

NO. OF EMPLOYEES: 6,956

ANNUAL MEETING: In Apr.

SHAREHOLDERS: 1,771

INSTITUTIONAL HOLDINGS:
No. of Institutions: 5
Shares Held: 77,001

AMERICAN DEPOSITARY RECEIPTS: (Unsponsored) Each American Depositary Receipt represents one ordinary share of par R1.

DEPOSITARY BANK(S): The Bank of New York, (212) 815-2175; Bankers Trust Co., (212) 250-8500; Citibank, (212) 657-7800

INSIGNIA SOLUTIONS, PLC

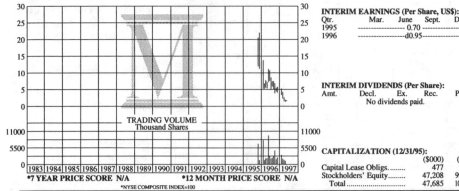

*7 YEAR PRICE SCORE N/A   ***12 MONTH PRICE SCORE N/A**

*NYSE COMPOSITE INDEX=100

INTERIM EARNINGS (Per Share, US$):

Qtr.	Mar.	June	Sept.	Dec.
1995		0.70		
1996		d0.95		

INTERIM DIVIDENDS (Per Share):

Amt.	Decl.	Ex.	Rec.	Pay.
No dividends paid.				

CAPITALIZATION (12/31/95):

	($000)	(%)
Capital Lease Obligs.	477	1.0
Stockholders' Equity	47,208	99.0
Total	47,685	100.0

RECENT DEVELOPMENTS: For the year ended 12/31/96, INSGY incurred a net loss of $10.8 million versus net income of $5.3 million in 1995. Revenues fell 19.7% to $44.2 million from $55.1 million in 1995. Results for the first and second quarters of 1996 were restated to reflect the recent discovery of irregularities in the reporting of sales contracts and reseller inventories by certain individuals in INSGY's U.S. channel sales organization. For the quarter ended 12/31/96, INSGY reported a net loss of $6.1 million versus net income of $630,000 in the same prior-year period. Revenues fell 48.8% to $7.2 million from $14.0 million in 1995. The decrease in 1996 revenues for the year and fourth quarter reflected a decline in the sales of INSGY's SoftWindows(TM) for Macintosh and UNIX product lines. Also, 1996 revenues from INSGY's NTRIGUE(TM) product were relatively small.

BUSINESS

INSIGNIA SOLUTIONS, PLC is engaged in the development, marketing and support of cross-platform compatibility software solutions. The Company provides compatibility solutions for enterprise desktops, including UNIX workstations, Macintosh computers, PCs, X terminals and network computers.

ANNUAL EARNINGS

	12/31/95	12/31/94	12/31/95	12/31/94
	--- US $ ---		--- British £ ---	
Earnings Per Share	0.70	0.66	0.45	0.42

ANNUAL FINANCIAL DATA

RECORD OF EARNINGS (IN THOUSANDS):

	12/31/95	12/31/94	12/31/95	12/31/94
Total Revenues	85,563	61,600	55,095	39,361
Costs & Expenses	75,269	52,119	48,467	33,303
Operating Income	10,293	9,481	6,628	6,058
Income Bef Income Tax	11,663	9,320	7,510	5,955
Income Tax	3,499	1,878	2,253	1,200
Net Income	8,164	7,442	5,257	4,755
Average Shares Outstg	11,643	11,390	11,643	11,390

BALANCE SHEET (IN THOUSANDS):

Cash & Cash Equivalents	57,459	22,251	36,999	14,218
Receivables, Net	9,568	5,406	6,161	3,454
Inventories	519	310	334	198
Property, Net	6,231	4,179	4,012	2,670
Capital Lease Obligs.	477	606	307	387
Stockholders' Equity	47,208	10,185	30,398	6,508
Total Assets	77,301	34,220	49,775	21,866
Total Current Assets	69,455	28,824	44,723	18,418
Total Current Liabilities	29,585	23,319	19,050	14,900
Net Working Capital	39,870	5,506	25,673	3,518
Year End Shs Outstg	41,142	9,468	41,142	9,468

STATISTICAL RECORD:

Return on Equity %	17.29	73.06		
Return on Assets %	10.56	21.75		
Operating Profit Margin %	12.03	15.39		
Net Profit Margin %	9.54	12.08		
Book Value Per Share	1.15	0.79		

Converted at 1995, US$1.5530= 1 British pound; 1994, US$1.5650= 1 British pound

OFFICERS:
N.V. Bearsted, Chmn.
R. P. Lee, Vice-Chmn.
R.M. Noling, Pres. & C.E.O.
R. D. Friedberger, Sr. V.P., C.F.O. & Sec.

INCORPORATED: England, Nov. 1985

PRINCIPAL OFFICE: Kingsmead Business Park, London Road, High Wycombe, Buckinghamshire HP11 1JU, United Kingdom

TELEPHONE NUMBER: 44-131-458-6849

NO. OF EMPLOYEES: 265

ANNUAL MEETING: N/A

SHAREHOLDERS: N/A

INSTITUTIONAL HOLDINGS:
No. of Institutions: 9
Shares Held: 1,083,457

AMERICAN DEPOSITARY RECEIPTS: Each American Depostary receipt repersents one ordinary share of par £0.20.

DEPOSITARY BANK(S): The Bank of New York, (212) 815-2175

INSTRUMENTARIUM OY

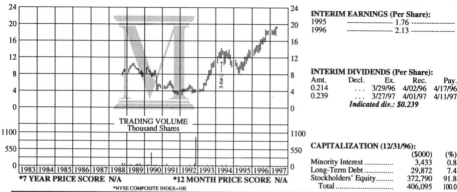

INTERIM EARNINGS (Per Share):
1995	1.76
1996	2.13

INTERIM DIVIDENDS (Per Share):

Amt.	Decl.	Ex.	Rec.	Pay.
0.214	...	3/29/96	4/02/96	4/17/96
0.239	...	3/27/97	4/01/97	4/11/97

Indicated div.: $0.239

CAPITALIZATION (12/31/96):

	($000)	(%)
Minority Interest	3,433	0.8
Long-Term Debt	29,872	7.4
Stockholders' Equity	372,790	91.8
Total	406,095	100.0

TRADING VOLUME
Thousand Shares

1983|1984|1985|1986|1987|1988|1989|1990|1991|1992|1993|1994|1995|1996|1997
*7 YEAR PRICE SCORE N/A   *12 MONTH PRICE SCORE N/A
*NYSE COMPOSITE INDEX=100

RECENT DEVELOPMENTS: For the year ended 12/31/96, profit for the period nearly doubled to FIM275.4 million from FIM139.6 million the previous year. Net sales advanced 8.7% to FIM2.34 billion from FIM2.15 billion the year before. Earnings from 1996 benefited from extraordinary income of FIM76.3 million resulting primarily from the reversal of writedowns of shares in fixed assets. The 1995 results were negatively affected by extraordinary expenses of FIM7.7 million from the closure or divestment of business operations. Net sales from the Company's anaesthesia and critical care equipment segment climbed 19% to FIM845.0 million, driven by strong sales of the AS/3™ Anaesthesia System family of products. Net sales from the optical retail segment grew 16.0% to FIM460.0 million, due primarily to the 1995 acquisition of the Keskus-Optiikka chain. Gross margin rose 8.3% to FIM1.14 billion from FIM1.05 billion a year earlier. Operating profit totaled FIM232.0 million, up 24.6% compared with FIM186.1 million in 1995.

BUSINESS

INSTRUMENTARIUM OY is the parent company of a group engaged in the production and distribution of health care products. The group operates through four divisions; the Medical Equipment and Supplies, the Optical Retail, the Anaesthesia and Critical Care Equipment, and the Distribution of Consumer and Commercial Products. The Medical Equipment and Supplies division is engaged in the manufacture and marketing of diagnostic imaging equipment, specializing in medical and dental X-rays systems; in the manufacture and marketing of hospital and nursing home furniture; and in the marketing and distribution of medical and laboratory equipment and supplies. The Optical Retail Division is engaged in the retail sale of ophthalmic optics products and services primarily in Finland, Sweden and Estonia. The Distribution of Consumer and Commercial Products Division is engaged in the wholesale of information technology products; the import, wholesale and manufacture of cosmetics and personal hygiene products; and the import and wholesale of wireless communications products such as car, hand-portable and radio phones. The Anaesthesia and Critical Care Equipment Division is engaged in the wholesale of patient care and safety products such as anaesthesia and intensive care equipment.

ANNUAL EARNINGS

Earnings Per Share	12/31/96	12/31/95	12/31/96	12/31/95
	------------US $------------		-------Finnish Markka--------	
	2.13	1.76	9.88	8.17

ANNUAL FINANCIAL DATA

RECORD OF EARNINGS (IN THOUSANDS):

Total Revenues	513,961	499,172	2,388,296	2,187,434
Costs & Expenses	458,996	451,773	2,132,880	1,979,726
Depreciation & Amort	5,043	4,923	23,435	21,575
Operating Income	49,922	42,476	231,981	186,133
Income Bef Income Tax	58,817	51,391	273,313	225,201
Income Tax	15,696	17,964	72,937	78,720
Minority Interests	257	cr194	1,196	cr848
Net Income	42,864	33,620	199,180	147,329
Net Extraordinary Items	16,409	d1,759	76,251	d7,706
Average Shares Outstg	20,159	20,150	20,159	20,150

BALANCE SHEET (IN THOUSANDS):

Cash & Cash Equivalents	90,681	97,877	421,381	428,907
Receivables, Net	137,387	147,010	638,417	644,214
Inventories	94,033	97,946	436,956	429,212
Gross Property	67,438	73,435	313,375	321,799
Long-Term Debt	29,872	41,895	138,809	183,589
Stockholders' Equity	372,790	344,042	1,732,294	1,507,633
Total Assets	529,336	538,749	2,459,739	2,360,862
Total Current Assets	322,101	342,832	1,496,754	1,502,333
Total Current Liabilities	95,403	117,671	443,324	515,650
Net Working Capital	226,698	225,161	1,053,430	986,683
Year End Shs Outstg	20,164	20,150	20,164	20,150

STATISTICAL RECORD:

Return on Equity %	11.50	9.77
Return on Assets %	8.10	6.24
Operating Profit Margin %	9.71	8.51
Net Profit Margin %	8.34	6.74
Book Value Per Share	18.49	17.07

Converted at 1996, US$0.2152= 1 Finnish Markka; 1995, US$0.2282= 1 Finnish Markka

OFFICERS:
M. Talonen, Chmn. & Pres.
M. Salmivuori, C.F.O.
G. von Hertzen
O. Riikkala
INCORPORATED: Finland, 1900
PRINCIPAL OFFICE: Kuortaneenkatu 2, P.O. Box 100, Helsinki Finland FIN-00031

TELEPHONE NUMBER: 358-9-394-11
NO. OF EMPLOYEES: 2,628
ANNUAL MEETING: In March
SHAREHOLDERS: 10,178
INSTITUTIONAL HOLDINGS:
No. of Institutions: 5
Shares Held: 126,600

AMERICAN DEPOSITARY RECEIPTS: Two American Depositary Receipts represent one Series B share of par FIM10.

DEPOSITARY BANK(S): J.P. Morgan, (212) 648-3206

INSTRUMENTATION LABORATORY S.P.A.

YIELD ...
P/E RATIO 77.5

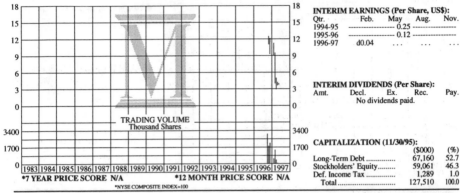

*7 YEAR PRICE SCORE N/A   *12 MONTH PRICE SCORE N/A

*NYSE COMPOSITE INDEX=100

INTERIM EARNINGS (Per Share, US$):

Qtr.	Feb.	May	Aug.	Nov.
1994-95	-------------------- 0.25 --------------------
1995-96	-------------------- 0.12 --------------------
1996-97	d0.04	...	...	...

INTERIM DIVIDENDS (Per Share):

Amt.	Decl.	Ex.	Rec.	Pay.
No dividends paid.				

CAPITALIZATION (11/30/95):

	($000)	(%)
Long-Term Debt	67,160	52.7
Stockholders' Equity	59,061	46.3
Def. Income Tax	1,289	1.0
Total	127,510	100.0

RECENT DEVELOPMENTS: For the quarter ended 2/28/97, ILABY incurred a net loss of Lit1.18 billion (US$698,000) versus net income of Lit848.0 million in the same prior-year period. This loss was primarily due to a weak market in Italy during December 1996, industry pricing pressures, and higher income tax expense. Net sales and revenues advanced 15.0% to Lit112.88 billion (US$66.8 million) from Lit98.15 billion the year before. This increase reflected ILABY's acquisitions of Mallinckrodt Sensor Systems, Inc. and Chromogenix Holding AB in September 1996, and an increase in overall unit placements of core instruments. Operating income fell 24.6% to Lit5.58 billion (US$3.3 million), while interest expense grew 7.8% to Lit5.33 billion (US$3.2 million) versus 1995. For the year ended 11/30/96, net income dropped 54.8% to Lit2.21 billion (US$1.5 million) from Lit4.88 billion the previous year. Net sales and revenues fell 5.5% to Lit388.91 billion (US$256.5 million) from Lit411.44 billion the year before.

BUSINESS

INSTRUMENTATION LABORA-TORY S.P.A. is a developer, manufacturer and distributor of in vitro diagnostics instruments and related reagents, controls and other consumables and services for use primarily in hospitals and independent clinical laboratories. The Company's product lines include critical care systems, hemostatis systems and clinical chemistry systems.

ANNUAL EARNINGS

	11/30/95	11/30/94	11/30/95	11/30/94
	------------US $------------		------------Lit------------	
Earnings Per Share	0.25	0.09	420.17	147.38

ANNUAL FINANCIAL DATA

RECORD OF EARNINGS (IN THOUSANDS):

Total Revenues	246,866	233,218	411,443,000	388,697,000
Costs & Expenses	214,738	205,624	357,896,000	342,706,000
Depreciation & Amort	7,368	9,362	12,280,000	15,604,000
Operating Income	24,760	18,232	41,267,000	30,387,000
Income Bef Income Tax	5,575	2,598	9,292,000	4,330,000
Income Tax	2,648	1,571	4,414,000	2,619,000
Net Income	2,927	1,027	4,878,000	1,711,000

BALANCE SHEET (IN THOUSANDS):

Cash & Cash Equivalents	4,274	4,646	7,124,000	7,744,000
Receivables, Net	120,009	111,140	200,015,000	185,233,000
Inventories	48,182	44,308	80,304,000	73,847,000
Gross Property	56,345	52,079	93,908,000	86,798,000
Accumulated Depreciation	20,443	15,130	34,071,000	25,217,000
Long-Term Debt	67,160	68,714	111,934,000	114,523,000
Stockholders' Equity	59,061	57,098	98,435,000	95,163,000
Total Assets	243,600	233,420	406,000,000	389,034,000
Total Current Assets	175,595	163,242	292,658,000	272,070,000
Total Current Liabilities	109,740	99,697	182,900,000	166,161,000
Net Working Capital	65,855	63,545	109,758,000	105,909,000
Year End Shs Outstg	11,000	11,000	11,000	11,000

STATISTICAL RECORD:

Return on Equity %	4.96	1.80		
Return on Assets %	1.20	0.44		
Operating Profit Margin %	10.03	7.82		
Net Profit Margin %	1.19	0.44		
Book Value Per Share	5.37	5.19		

Converted at 1995, US$0.0006= 1 Italian Lira; 1994, US$0.0006= 1 Italian Lira.

OFFICERS:
J. M. Rubiralta, Chmn., Pres. & C.E.O.
F. Rubiralta, Vice-Chmn.
J. L. Martin, C.F.O. & Sr. V.P.

INCORPORATED: Italy, 1991

PRINCIPAL OFFICE: Viale Monza 338, Milano, 20128 Italy

TELEPHONE NUMBER: 39-2-252-22-56

NO. OF EMPLOYEES: 1,230 (approx.)

ANNUAL MEETING: N/A

SHAREHOLDERS: N/A

INSTITUTIONAL HOLDINGS:
No. of Institutions: 14
Shares Held: 4,001,175

AMERICAN DEPOSITARY RECEIPTS: (Sponsored) Each American Depositary Share represents one common share of par Lit2,500.

DEPOSITARY BANK(S): The Bank of New York, (212) 815-2175

ISRAEL LAND DEVELOPMENT CO. LTD.

YIELD ...
P/E RATIO 36.01

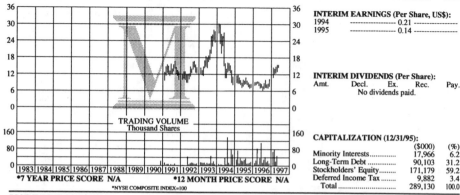

INTERIM EARNINGS (Per Share, US$):
1994 ------------------ 0.21 ------------------
1995 ------------------ 0.14 ------------------

INTERIM DIVIDENDS (Per Share):

Amt.	Decl.	Ex.	Rec.	Pay.
		No dividends paid.		

TRADING VOLUME
Thousand Shares

| 1983 | 1984 | 1985 | 1986 | 1987 | 1988 | 1989 | 1990 | 1991 | 1992 | 1993 | 1994 | 1995 | 1996 | 1997 |

*7 YEAR PRICE SCORE N/A   *12 MONTH PRICE SCORE N/A
*NYSE COMPOSITE INDEX=100

CAPITALIZATION (12/31/95):

	($000)	(%)
Minority Interests.............	17,966	6.2
Long-Term Debt	90,103	31.2
Stockholders' Equity........	171,179	59.2
Deferred Income Tax	9,882	3.4
Total	289,130	100.0

RECENT DEVELOPMENTS: For the year ended 12/31/96, net income climbed 7.4% to NIS14.9 million (US$4.6 million) versus NIS13.9 million (US$4.3 million) in 1995. Earnings for 1996 and 1995 included ILDCY's share in gains of subsidiaries of US$2.8 million and US$2.1 million, respectively. Earnings for 1996 increased primarily due to capital gains of NIS11.5 million (approximately US$3.4 million), which resulted from the Company's dilution of its holdings in MATAV-Cable Systems Media, Ltd. Total revenue improved 10.0% to NIS993.4 million (US$305.6 million) from NIS902.9 million (US$277.7 million) in 1995. General and administrative expenses were NIS30.2 million (approximately US$9.3 million), which included the costs of entrepreneurship and international activity of the ILDCY.

BUSINESS

ISRAEL LAND DEVELOPMENT COMPANY LIMITED, through its subsidiaries, is engaged in five main business activities: Publishing and other commercial media - the ownership and management of a major Israeli daily newspaper, magazines, commercial and cable television, other media businesses and a leisure products subsidiary which includes a record company, book publishing house, multimedia products, and a music, book and video distribution center. Insurance - the ownership and management of a multi-line insurance company. Real Estate - real estate development and property management. Hotels - the ownership and managment of a hotel chain. Emergency Medical Care - the ownership and management of a mobile emergency intensive care service.

ANNUAL EARNINGS

	12/31/95	12/31/94	12/31/95	12/31/94
	-----------US $-----------		-----------NIS-----------	
Earnings Per Share	0.14	0.21	0.45	0.64

ANNUAL FINANCIAL DATA

RECORD OF EARNINGS (IN THOUSANDS):

Total Revenues	258,095	253,999	812,385	766,443
Costs & Expenses	250,600	245,848	788,794	741,847
Operating Income	7,495	8,151	23,591	24,596
Income Bef Income Tax	7,495	10,971	23,591	33,104
Income Tax	5,036	4,338	15,851	13,090
Eq. Earnings in Affils.	1,933	711	6,083	2,146
Minority Interests	393	1,410	1,238	4,254
Net Income	3,998	5,934	12,585	17,906

BALANCE SHEET (IN THOUSANDS):

Cash & Cash Equivalents	20,974	28,753	66,018	86,761
Receivables, Net	59,671	55,346	187,822	167,006
Inventories	19,889	12,633	62,604	38,119
Gross Property	316,491	290,377	996,195	876,214
Accumulated Depreciation	119,267	111,100	375,409	335,245
Long-Term Debt	90,103	87,638	283,611	264,447
Stockholders' Equity	171,179	174,377	538,807	526,184
Total Assets	535,492	503,302	1,685,526	1,518,715
Total Current Assets	133,715	145,350	420,884	438,593
Total Current Liabilities	86,169	71,005	271,228	214,257
Net Working Capital	47,546	74,345	149,656	224,336
Year End Shs Outstg	28,269	28,269	28,269	28,269

STATISTICAL RECORD:

Return on Equity %	2.34	3.40		
Return on Assets %	0.75	1.18		
Operating Profit Margin %	2.90	3.21		
Net Profit Margin %	1.55	2.34		
Book Value Per Share	6.06	6.17		

Converted at 1995, US$0.3177= 1 New Israeli Shekel; 1994, US$0.3314= 1 New Israeli Shekel

OFFICERS:
J. Nimrodi, Chmn. & Pres.
O. Nimrodi, C.E.O.
R. Weissberg, V.P. & C.F.O.
S. Marfogel, V.P. & Comptroller

INCORPORATED: Israel, 1909

PRINCIPAL OFFICE: 194 Hayarkon Street, Tel Aviv 63405 Israel

TELEPHONE NUMBER: (972)-3-520-0222

FAX: (972)-3-520-0241

NO. OF EMPLOYEES: 1,950

ANNUAL MEETING: N/A

SHAREHOLDERS: N/A

INSTITUTIONAL HOLDINGS:
No. of Institutions: 2
Shares Held: 336,490

AMERICAN DEPOSITARY RECEIPTS: (Sponsored) Each American Depositary Receipt represents three ordinary shares of par NIS1.

DEPOSITARY BANK(S): The Bank of New York, (212) 815-2175

ITO-YOKADO CO., LTD.

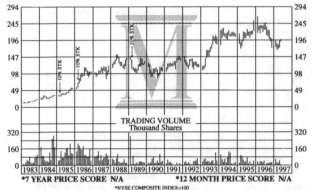

INTERIM EARNINGS (Per Share):

1995	---------------- 1.80 ----------------
1996	---------------- 1.78 ----------------
1997	---------------- 1.73 ----------------

INTERIM DIVIDENDS (Per Share):

Amt.	Decl.	Ex.	Rec.	Pay.
0.534	...	8/28/95	8/30/95	11/28/95
0.562	...	2/26/96	2/28/96	6/4/96
0.487	...	8/27	8/29	11/26
0.496	...	2/25/97	2/27/97	6/3/97

Indicated div.: $0.992

TRADING VOLUME
Thousand Shares

| 1983 | 1984 | 1985 | 1986 | 1987 | 1988 | 1989 | 1990 | 1991 | 1992 | 1993 | 1994 | 1995 | 1996 | 1997 |

*7 YEAR PRICE SCORE N/A   ***12 MONTH PRICE SCORE N/A**

*NYSE COMPOSITE INDEX=100

CAPITALIZATION (2/29/96):

	($000)	(%)
Long-Term Debt	2,168,879	21.2
Stockholders' Equity	7,806,939	76.4
Deferred Income Tax	238,640	2.3
Total	10,214,457	100.0

RECENT DEVELOPMENTS: For the fiscal year ended 2/28/97, net income slipped 3.1% to Y74.33 billion ($614.3 million) from Y76.68 billion the previous year. Revenues advanced 4.4% to Y3,018.86 billion ($24.95 billion) from Y2,892.06 billion the year before. Operating income was up 0.8% to Y220.41 billion ($1.82 billion) from Y218.60 billion the prior year. Revenues from the superstore and other retail operations segment inched down 0.5% to Y1,892.20 billion, while operating income declined 13.4% to Y78.40 billion. Results were hampered by lower profit margins generated from the sale of slow-selling merchandise from inventory. Revenues from convenience store operations rose 15.9% to Y1,015.30 billion, while operating income grew 10.6% to Y132.60 billion. During fiscal 1997, the Company added 502 stores to the Seven-Eleven Japan chain. Revenues from restaurant operations increased 2.0% to Y131.70 billion, while operating income climbed 15.9% to Y9.40 billion.

BUSINESS

ITO-YOKADO CO., LTD. operates approximately 12,000 7-Eleven convenience stores in Japan and North America, as well as clothing stores, discount stores, supermarkets, hypermarkets, and restaurants. The Company owns approximately 64% of 7-Eleven's parent company, Southland Corporation, and is the Japanese franchisee for US-based chains like Robinson's department stores, Oshman's Sporting Goods, and Denny's restaurants.

ANNUAL EARNINGS

	2/29/96	2/28/95	2/29/96	2/28/95
	US $		Yen	
Earnings Per Share	1.78	1.80	187.59	174.40

ANNUAL FINANCIAL DATA

RECORD OF EARNINGS (IN MILLIONS):

	2/29/96	2/28/95	2/29/96	2/28/95
Total Revenues	27,475	29,653	2,892,062	2,878,902
Costs & Expenses	24,649	26,659	2,594,666	2,588,258
Depreciation & Amort	749	816	78,794	79,242
Operating Income	2,077	2,177	218,602	211,402
Income Bef Income Tax	1,990	2,083	209,481	202,224
Income Tax	1,012	1,092	106,495	106,022
Eq. Earnings in Affils.	21	22	2,198	2,108
Minority Interests	272	278	28,585	27,020
Net Income	728	734	76,682	71,290
Average Shares Outstg (000)	408,769	408,770	408,769	408,770

BALANCE SHEET (IN MILLIONS):

Cash & Cash Equivalents	3,739	3,844	393,583	373,201
Receivables, Net	326	342	34,334	33,220
Inventories	807	840	84,985	81,578
Gross Property	12,807	13,145	1,348,128	1,276,192
Accumulated Depreciation	5,303	5,318	558,202	516,328
Long-Term Debt	2,169	2,773	228,303	269,229
Stockholders' Equity	7,807	7,779	821,783	755,286
Total Assets	16,339	17,045	1,719,871	1,654,876
Total Current Assets	5,169	5,318	544,064	516,346
Total Current Liabilities	3,934	4,139	414,083	401,874
Net Working Capital	1,235	1,179	129,981	114,472
Year End Shs Outstg (000)	407,496	407,071	407,496	407,071

STATISTICAL RECORD:

Return on Equity %	9.32	9.44
Return on Assets %	4.46	4.31
Operating Profit Margin %	7.56	7.34
Net Profit Margin %	2.65	2.48
Book Value Per Share	19.16	19.11

Converted at 1996, US$0.0095= 1 Japanese Yen; 1995, US$0.0103= 1 Japanese Yen

OFFICERS:
M. Ito, Honorary Chmn.
T. Suzuki, Pres. & C.E.O.
H. Morita, Exec. V.P.
H. Masukawa, Exec. V.P.

INCORPORATED: N/A

PRINCIPAL OFFICE: 1-4, Shibakoen 4-chome, Minato-ku, Tokyo Japan

TELEPHONE NUMBER: 03-3459-2111

NO. OF EMPLOYEES: 36,932

ANNUAL MEETING: In May

SHAREHOLDERS: 7,946

INSTITUTIONAL HOLDINGS:
No. of Institutions: 22
Shares Held: 466,121

AMERICAN DEPOSITARY RECEIPTS: Each American Depositary Receipt represents four common shs. of Co.

DEPOSITARY BANK(S): J.P. Morgan, (212) 648-3206

JAPAN AIRLINES COMPANY, LTD.

YIELD 0.7%
P/E RATIO ...

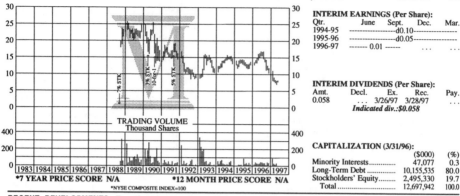

*7 YEAR PRICE SCORE N/A   *12 MONTH PRICE SCORE N/A
*NYSE COMPOSITE INDEX=100

INTERIM EARNINGS (Per Share):

Qtr.	June	Sept.	Dec.	Mar.
1994-95			d0.10	
1995-96			d0.05	
1996-97	0.01		...	...

INTERIM DIVIDENDS (Per Share):

Amt.	Decl.	Ex.	Rec.	Pay.
0.058	...	3/26/97	3/28/97	...

Indicated div.:$0.058

CAPITALIZATION (3/31/96):

	($000)	(%)
Minority Interests..............	47,077	0.3
Long-Term Debt	10,155,535	80.0
Stockholders' Equity........	2,495,330	19.7
Total	12,697,942	100.0

RECENT DEVELOPMENTS: For the six months ended 9/30/96, net income fell 71.3% to ¥2,649 million from ¥9,232 million a year earlier. Operating revenues rose 6.9% to ¥600,081 million. Domestic passenger operating revenues advanced 4.5% to ¥148,369 million. The Company noted that it took advantage of the shift to a new fare-determination system in June 1996 to introduce several new discount fare packages. These efforts, coupled with solid travel demand in Japan, led to a 2.8% rise in domestic passenger volume to 9.3 million. International passenger operating revenues gained 8.1% to ¥319,500 million. Domestic and international cargo operating revenues rose 3.7% and 10.6% to ¥13,727 million and ¥65,207 million, respectively. International transport cargo volume was essentially unchanged at 1,757.2 million ton-kilometers.

BUSINESS

JAPAN AIRLINES COMPANY, LTD. is engaged in regularly scheduled and unscheduled air transport services and aircraft maintenance. The Company's international route network covers 39 cities outside of Japan. The Company also provides new travel products such as personalized and flexible overseas vacation packages and combination air travel and convenient lodging at one of its group hotels. The Company operates an express luggage delivery system and provides inbound cargo services to Europe and the United States. The Company is also engaged in air cargo services for manufactured and agricultural goods, and importing cargo from Europe such as flowers and root vegetables, and textiles.

ANNUAL EARNINGS

	3/31/96	3/31/95	3/31/96	3/31/95
	------------US $------------		-------------Yen-------------	
Earnings Per Share	d0.05	d0.10	d5.11	d8.22

ANNUAL FINANCIAL DATA

RECORD OF EARNINGS (IN MILLIONS):

Total Revenues	13,476	15,642	1,449,041	1,348,417
Costs & Expenses	12,434	14,574	1,336,947	1,256,343
Depreciation & Amort.	881	1,215	94,779	104,705
Operating Income	161	d147	17,315	d12,630
Income Bef Income Tax	d79	d223	d8,540	d19,249
Income Tax	45	cr15	4,842	cr1,319
Eq. Earnings in Affils.	19	2	2,032	202
Minority Interests	cr21	cr36	cr2,252	cr3,107
Net Income	d85	d170	d9,098	d14,620
Average Shares Outstg.	1,779	1,779	1,779	1,779

BALANCE SHEET (IN MILLIONS):

Cash & Cash Equivalents	1,897	3,493	204,029	301,092
Receivables, Net	1,875	1,879	201,607	161,993
Inventories	448	586	48,207	50,506
Property, Net	11,075	13,808	1,190,812	1,190,328
Long-Term Debt	10,156	13,588	1,091,993	1,171,365
Stockholders' Equity	2,495	3,246	268,315	279,846
Total Assets	19,633	25,007	2,111,053	2,155,761
Total Current Assets	5,074	6,965	545,565	600,390
Total Current Liabilities	6,005	6,966	645,693	600,512
Net Working Capital	d931	d1	d100,128	d122
Year End Shs Outstg (000)	1,779	1,779	1,779	1,779

STATISTICAL RECORD:

Operating Profit Margin %	1.19	...		
Net Profit Margin %	...	...		
Book Value Per Share	1.40	1.82		

Converted at 1996, US$0.0093= 1 Japanese Yen; 1995, US$0.0116= 1 Japanese Yen

OFFICERS:
S. Yamaji, Chmn.
A. Kondo, Pres.
T. Kuribayashi, Exec. V.P.
A. Kouno, Exec. V.P.

INCORPORATED: Aug., 1951

PRINCIPAL OFFICE: Tokyo Bldg., 7-3 Marunouchi 2-chome Chiyoda-ku, Tokyo

TELEPHONE NUMBER: 03-5460-3191

NO. OF EMPLOYEES: 20,030

ANNUAL MEETING: In Jun.

SHAREHOLDERS: 206,757

INSTITUTIONAL HOLDINGS:
No. of Institutions: 4
Shares Held: 2,525,926

AMERICAN DEPOSITARY RECEIPTS: Each ADR represents 2 com. shares. ADRs split 5-for-1 on 6/25/82, and 10-for-1 on 9/7/90.

DEPOSITARY BANK(S): Bank of New York, (212) 815-2175; Bankers Trust, (212) 250-8500; Citibank, (212) 657-7800; J.P. Morgan, (212) 648-3206; Security Pacific

KIRIN BREWERY COMPANY, LTD.

YIELD 0.9%
P/E RATIO 32.2

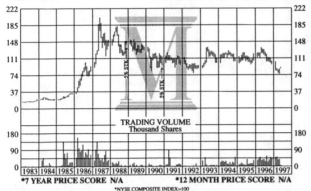

*7 YEAR PRICE SCORE N/A   *12 MONTH PRICE SCORE N/A
*NYSE COMPOSITE INDEX=100

INTERIM EARNINGS (Per Share, US$):
1996 ------------------ 0.28 ------------------

INTERIM DIVIDENDS (Per Share):

Amt.	Decl.	Ex.	Rec.	Pay.
0.476	...	6/27/95	6/29/95	9/29/95
0.458	...	1/03/96	1/05/96	4/15/96
0.441	...	6/25	6/27	9/30
0.527	...	12/26	12/30	4/15/97
0.401	...	3/26/97	3/28/97	...

Indicated div.: $0.802

CAPITALIZATION (12/31/96):

	($000)	(%)
Long-Term Debt	162,029	2.4
Stockholders' Equity	6,473,714	97.6
Total	6,635,743	100.0

RECENT DEVELOPMENTS: For the year ended 12/31/96, net income declined 16.5% to ¥34.39 billion compared with ¥40.07 billion in 1995. Sales fell 2.3% to ¥1,596.36 billion from ¥1,633.30 billion a year earlier. Beer and others segment sales declined 3.7% and 4.6% to ¥1,294.64 billion and ¥132.05 billion, respectively, while the soft drinks' segments sales advanced 5.8% to ¥242.19 billion. Operating income at the beer and others segments declined 27.4% and 24.5% to ¥52.72 billion and ¥7.47 billion, respectively. Operating income at the soft drinks segment rose 2.9% to ¥12.69 billion. Results in 1996 included extraordinary income of ¥5.63 billion, offset by extraordinary expenses totaling ¥9.86 billion. Results in 1995 included extraordinary income of ¥3.01 billion, offset by extraordinary expenses of ¥8.36 billion.

BUSINESS

KIRIN BREWERY COMPANY, LTD. is engaged in the manufacture of beer, non-alcoholic beverages such as canned teas, coffees, carbonated drinks, sports drinks, Tropicana fruit juices, oolong teas, dairy products, pharmaceuticals and agricultural produces; and the distribution of Coca-Cola, Scotch whiskeys, French wines, brandies and champagnes. The Company also engages in providing engineering and information system services; and the operation of pizza restaurants called "Shakey's Pizza" and beer pubs called "Kirin City" and "Giraffe." The Company markets its alcohol products under the name of "Kirin Lager," "Kirin Ichiban Shibori," "Kirin Beer Factory," "Kirin Fuyu Jitate," "Kirin Akiaji," "Kirin Derauma," "Kirin Icebeer," "Kirin Kansai Flavor Fresh Beer," "Kirin Black Beer," "Kirin Beer Light," and "Kirin Stout."

ANNUAL EARNINGS

	12/31/96	12/31/95	12/31/96	12/31/95
	US $		Yen	
Earnings Per Share	0.28	0.37	32.69	38.08

ANNUAL FINANCIAL DATA

RECORD OF EARNINGS (IN MILLIONS):

	12/31/96	12/31/95	12/31/96	12/31/95
Total Revenues	13,888	15,843	1,596,355	1,633,295
Costs & Expenses	13,306	15,046	1,529,430	1,551,106
Operating Income	582	797	66,925	82,189
Income Bef Extraord Items	534	862	67,426	88,894
Income Bef Income Tax	573	855	65,876	88,170
Income Tax	257	425	29,593	43,833
Eq. Earnings in Affils.	24	17	2,721	1,804
Minority Interests	17	14	1,945	1,441
Net Income	299	389	34,386	40,067

BALANCE SHEET (IN MILLIONS):

	12/31/96	12/31/95	12/31/96	12/31/95
Cash & Cash Equivalents	3,287	3,410	377,760	351,573
Receivables, Net	1,825	2,040	209,793	210,330
Inventories	488	521	56,053	53,699
Gross Property	4,738	5,234	544,572	539,550
Long-Term Debt	162	710	18,624	73,167
Stockholders' Equity	6,474	6,998	744,105	721,475
Total Assets	13,269	14,309	1,525,119	1,475,147
Total Current Assets	6,107	6,476	701,998	667,652
Total Current Liabilities	4,444	4,211	510,800	434,136
Net Working Capital	1,663	2,265	191,198	233,516
Year End Shs Outstg	1,052	1,052	1,052	1,052

STATISTICAL RECORD:

	12/31/96	12/31/95
Return on Equity %	4.62	5.56
Return on Assets %	2.25	2.72
Operating Profit Margin %	4.19	5.03
Net Profit Margin %	2.15	2.45
Book Value Per Share	6.15	6.65

Converted at 1996, US$0.0087= 1 Japanese Yen; 1995, US$0.0097= 1 Japanese Yen

OFFICERS:
K. Manabe, Chmn.
Y. Sato, Pres.
S. Furuya, Exec. V.P.

INCORPORATED: Feb., 1907

PRINCIPAL OFFICE: 10-1, Shinkawa 2-chome, Chuo-ku, Tokyo 104 Japan

TELEPHONE NUMBER: 03-5540-3411

NO. OF EMPLOYEES: 8,380

ANNUAL MEETING: In Mar.

SHAREHOLDERS: 143,714

INSTITUTIONAL HOLDINGS:
No. of Institutions: 10
Shares Held: 716,043

AMERICAN DEPOSITARY RECEIPTS: Each American Depositary Receipt represents 10 common shares of par Y50.

DEPOSITARY BANK(S): Bank of New York, (212) 815-2175; Bankers Trust Co., (212) 250-8500; Citibank, (212) 657-7800; J.P. Morgan, (212) 648-3206, Security Pacific.

KLOOF GOLD MINING CO., LTD.

YIELD 3.5%
P/E RATIO 10.4

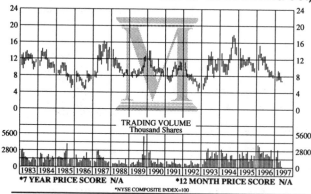

INTERIM EARNINGS (Per Share, US$):
1996 ------------------ 0.65 ------------------

INTERIM DIVIDENDS (Per Share):

Amt.	Decl.	Ex.	Rec.	Pay.
0.235	...	6/28/95	6/30/95	8/17/95
0.113	...	12/27/95	12/29/95	2/23/96
0.115	...	6/26/96	6/28/96	8/22/96
0.122	...	12/24/96	12/27/96	2/21/97

Indicated div.:$0.237

TRADING VOLUME
Thousand Shares

*7 YEAR PRICE SCORE N/A   *12 MONTH PRICE SCORE N/A
*NYSE COMPOSITE INDEX=100

CAPITALIZATION (6/30/96):

	($000)	(%)
Stockholders' Equity........	960,549	100.0
Total..............................	960,549	100.0

RECENT DEVELOPMENTS: For the year ended 6/30/96, net income was R$388.2 million compared with R$575.1 million in the corresponding period a year earlier. Revenues were R$1.97 billion, down 5% versus $2.07 billion in 1995. Lower earnings resulted from an unusually high incidence of seismic activity in the Companys 34, 43 and 50 longwalls. In addition, several higher grade faces were affected and lower than expected values were encountered in the 21 longwall. Production interruptions over the Christmas and New Year holiday period had an adverse effect on production. Stoping resumed in the No. 3 subvertical shaft area below the 35 level during the first quarter of the year, but was delayed due to an ore-pass scaling and blockages. During the year, 1.9 million metric tons were mined compared with 2.1 million metric tons, which yielded 25,461 kilograms of fine gold versus 29,131 kilograms of fine gold.

BUSINESS

KLOOF GOLD MINING CO., LTD. conducts gold mining operations in the vicinity of Westonaria. The Company operates the Kloof, Leeudoorn and Libanon Mines. Ore reserves total 1,125,000 tons.

ANNUAL EARNINGS

	6/30/96	6/30/95	6/30/96	6/30/95
	------------US $------------		------------Rand------------	
Earnings Per Share	0.65	1.14	2.80	4.15

ANNUAL FINANCIAL DATA

RECORD OF EARNINGS (IN THOUSANDS):

Total Revenues	454,294	569,825	1,966,641	2,072,090
Costs & Expenses	366,018	400,380	1,584,494	1,455,927
Operating Income	88,276	169,445	382,147	616,163
Income Bef Income Tax	96,284	182,400	416,814	663,274
Income Tax	6,604	24,245	28,590	88,162
Net Income	89,680	158,156	388,224	575,112

BALANCE SHEET (IN THOUSANDS):

Cash & Cash Equivalents	16,847	65,530	72,931	238,292
Receivables, Net	19,849	19,639	85,926	71,413
Inventories	1,381	1,901	5,978	6,913
Gross Property	986,168	1,096,974	4,269,124	3,988,995
Stockholders' Equity	960,549	1,074,864	4,158,219	3,908,595
Total Assets	1,033,366	1,194,995	4,473,446	4,345,436
Total Current Assets	47,198	98,021	204,322	356,441
Total Current Liabilities	72,817	120,131	315,227	436,841
Net Working Capital	d25,619	d22,110	d110,905	d80,400
Year End Shs Outstg	138,600	138,600	138,600	138,600

STATISTICAL RECORD:

Return on Equity %	9.3	14.7		
Return on Assets %	8.7	13.2		
Operating Profit Margin %	19.4	29.7		
Net Profit Margin %	19.7	27.7		
Book Value Per Share	6.93	7.76		

Converted at 1996, US$0.2310= 1 South African Rand; 1995, US$0.2750= 1 South African Rand

OFFICERS:
A. H. Munro, Chmn. & Manag. Dir.
M. J. Adan
J. W. Dowsley
J. G. Hopwood

INCORPORATED: Jun., 1964

PRINCIPAL OFFICE: 75 Fox Street Johannesburg South Africa

TELEPHONE NUMBER: (011) 639-9111

NO. OF EMPLOYEES: 30,874

ANNUAL MEETING: In Oct.

SHAREHOLDERS: 6,011

INSTITUTIONAL HOLDINGS:
No. of Institutions: 39
Shares Held: 6,769,037

AMERICAN DEPOSITARY RECEIPTS: (Sponsored) Each American Depositary Receipt represents one ordinary share of par £0.25.

DEPOSITARY BANK(S): The Bank of New York, (212) 815-2175; J.P. Morgan, (212) 648-3206

NASDAQ SYMBOL LBMSY
Rec. Pr. 4¾

LEARMONTH & BURCHETT MANAGEMENT SYSTEMS PLC

YIELD ...
P/E RATIO ...

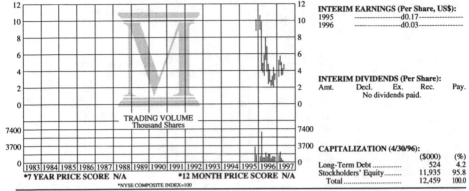

*7 YEAR PRICE SCORE N/A   ***12 MONTH PRICE SCORE N/A**
*NYSE COMPOSITE INDEX=100

INTERIM EARNINGS (Per Share, US$):
| 1995 | --------------d0.17-------------- |
| 1996 | --------------d0.03-------------- |

INTERIM DIVIDENDS (Per Share):

Amt.	Decl.	Ex.	Rec.	Pay.
		No dividends paid.		

CAPITALIZATION (4/30/96):

	($000)	(%)
Long-Term Debt	524	4.2
Stockholders' Equity........	11,935	95.8
Total	12,459	100.0

RECENT DEVELOPMENTS: For the quarter ended 1/31/97, net income was $4.3 million compared with a loss of $955,000 in the same period a year earlier. The current-quarter results included a $3.5 million restructuring benefit related to the sale of the Company's Systems Engineer product line and recovery of lease costs. Total revenues fell 42.1% to $5.6 million from $9.6 million in the year-earlier quarter. The lower revenues reflected the sale of the Systems Engineer product line. Product licenses declined 43.7% to $3.4 million, while service revenues dropped 39.4% to $2.2 million. The improved earnings were attributed to growth of license revenues, increased margins for implementation services business and increased operating margins. During the quarter, the Company expanded its customer base through the addition of new strategic customers such as Highmark (Blue Cross Blue Shield), Kaiser Permanente, Information Resources, Inc. and Case Corporation.

BUSINESS

LEARMONTH & BURCHETT MANAGEMENT SYSTEMS PLC designs, develops, markets and supports client/server software development management tools. The Company also provides services such as maintenance software development management tools. LBMSY's process management tools include; Process Engineer, PE/Process Library, PE/Process Manageer, PE/Project Manager, PE Activity Manager, PE/Web Publisher, PE/RADPath and Client/Server Guidelines. The Company's model management tools include; Systems Engineer, SE/Repository, SE/Server Builder and SE/Object Manager. The Company's object management tools include Insight. The Company sold its Systems Engineer product line to focus its efforts in the Process Management marketplace.

ANNUAL EARNINGS

	4/30/96	4/30/95	4/30/94
		---US $---	
Earnings Per Share	d0.03	d0.17	d0.06

ANNUAL FINANCIAL DATA

RECORD OF EARNINGS (IN THOUSANDS):

	4/30/96	4/30/95	4/30/94
Total Revenues	41,158	40,486	36,650
Costs & Expenses	42,109	44,342	38,056
Operating Income	d951	d3,856	d1,406
Income Bef Income Tax	d784	d3,803	d1,428
Income Tax	...	cr36	cr272
Net Income	d784	d3,767	d1,156
Income from Disc. Ops.	...	d4,908	155
Average Shares Outstg	23,639	21,844	18,760

BALANCE SHEET (IN THOUSANDS):

Cash & Cash Equivalents	10,960	5,026	...
Receivables, Net	9,579	10,634	...
Gross Property	5,447	4,897	...
Accumulated Depreciation	2,465	3,147	...
Long-Term Debt	524	369	...
Stockholders' Equity	11,935	490	...
Total Assets	27,179	20,315	...
Total Current Assets	24,037	18,405	...
Total Current Liabilities	12,571	15,680	...
Net Working Capital	11,466	2,725	...
Year End Shs Outstg	25,531	22,549	...

STATISTICAL RECORD:

Return on Equity %	...	...	...
Return on Assets %	...	...	...
Operating Profit Margin %	...	...	...
Net Profit Margin %	...	...	...
Book Value Per Share	0.47	0.02	...

OFFICERS:
J. P. Bantleman, C.E.O.
S. E. Odom, Sr. V.P., C.F.O. & Sec.
P. Combe, Sr. V.P.-North Amer. Oper.
D. B. Rodway, Sr. V.P.-Devel.
INCORPORATED: England, 1983
PRINCIPAL OFFICE: 1800 West Loop South
6th floor Houston, Texas United States
77027

TELEPHONE NUMBER: 713-625-9300
NO. OF EMPLOYEES: 276
ANNUAL MEETING: In Aug.
SHAREHOLDERS: N/A
INSTITUTIONAL HOLDINGS:
No. of Institutions: 8
Shares Held: 4,024,645

AMERICAN DEPOSITARY RECEIPTS: (Sponsored) Each American Depositary Receipt represents two ordinary shares of Co.

DEPOSITARY BANK(S): J.P. Morgan, (212) 250-8500

192

LIHIR GOLD, LIMITED

YIELD ...
P/E RATIO ...

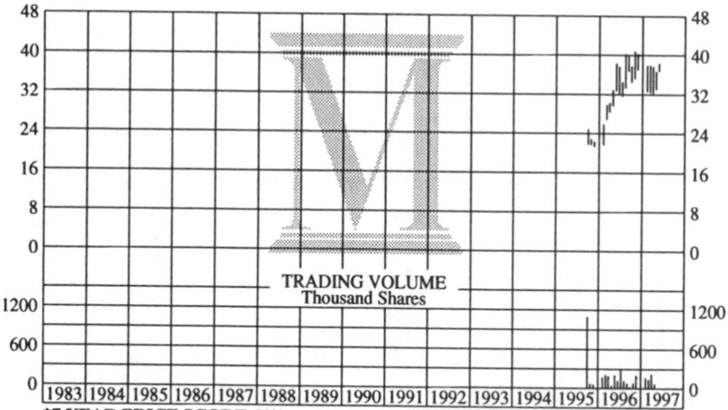

*7 YEAR PRICE SCORE N/A   *12 MONTH PRICE SCORE N/A
*NYSE COMPOSITE INDEX=100

INTERIM EARNINGS (Per Share):
... ...

INTERIM DIVIDENDS (Per Share):
Amt.   Decl.   Ex.   Rec.   Pay.
No dividends paid.

CAPITALIZATION (12/31/96):

	($000)	(%)
Long-Term Debt	60,081	8.8
Stockholders' Equity	622,153	91.2
Total	682,234	100.0

RECENT DEVELOPMENTS: Good progress was made in the construction of the Lihir project during 1996. At year end, construction of the processing facilities and the associated infrastructure was on schedule for initial processing of oxide ore in May 1997. Processing of sulphide ore through all three autoclaves is scheduled for October 1997. Nearly all major items of equipment are on site. At the end of December 1996, engineering was essentially complete, including 3,000 design drawings and almost 2,000 piping isometrics. Concurrently, construction was 67.0% complete and close to the peak of activity. The Thiess-Roche Lihir Joint Venture, the Company's mining contractor, completed the mining infrastructure. This included the first barge wharf, heavy equipment workshop and offices. No revenues or income were reported for fiscal years ending 12/31/96 or 12/31/95.

BUSINESS

LIHIR GOLD LIMITED was established to develop one of the largest undeveloped gold resources located on Lihir Island, Papua New Guinea. The project will have an estimated life of 36 years.

ANNUAL EARNINGS

ANNUAL FINANCIAL DATA

	12/31/96	12/31/95	12/31/96	12/31/95
	-------US $-------		-------Kina-------	
BALANCE SHEET (IN THOUSANDS):				
Cash & Cash Equivalents	44,062	362,615	59,463	484,132
Receivables, Net	42	419	57	560
Long-Term Debt	60,081	...	81,081	...
Stockholders' Equity	622,153	620,486	839,613	828,419
Total Assets	735,946	630,912	993,179	842,339
Total Current Assets	44,104	363,034	59,520	484,692
Total Current Liabilities	53,711	10,426	72,485	13,920
Net Working Capital	d9,607	352,608	d12,965	470,772
Outstanding Shares	900,000	...	900,000	...
STATISTICAL RECORD:				
Return on Equity %	...	...		
Return on Assets %	...	...		
Operating Profit Margin %	...	...		
Net Profit Margin %	...	...		
Book Value Per Share	0.69	...		

Converted at 1996, US$0.7410= 1 Papua New Guinea Kina; 1995, US$0.7490= 1 Papua New Guinea Kina 7

OFFICERS:
R. Garnaut, Chmn.
J. O'Reilly, C.E.O.

INCORPORATED: Papua New Guinea, Mar., 1995

PRINCIPAL OFFICE: Level 7, Pacific Place Corner Champion Parade & Musgrave Streets, P.O. Box 789, Port Moresby Papua New Guinea

TELEPHONE NUMBER: 675-321-7711

NO. OF EMPLOYEES: 700

ANNUAL MEETING: N/A

SHAREHOLDERS: N/A

INSTITUTIONAL HOLDINGS:
No. of Institutions: 3
Shares Held: 335,000

AMERICAN DEPOSITARY RECEIPTS: (Sponsored) Each American Depositary Receipt represents twenty ordinary shares of par Ka0.10.

DEPOSITARY BANK(S): The Bank of New York, (212) 815-2175

LONDON & OVERSEAS FREIGHTERS

YIELD ...
P/E RATIO 67.5

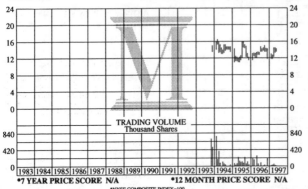

7 YEAR PRICE SCORE N/A **12 MONTH PRICE SCORE N/A**
NYSE COMPOSITE INDEX=100

INTERIM EARNINGS (Per Share, US$):

Qtr.	June	Sept.	Dec.	Mar.
1995	------------------ 0.11 ------------------			
1996	------------------ 0.02 ------------------			

INTERIM DIVIDENDS (Per Share):

Amt.	Decl.	Ex.	Rec.	Pay.
0.02	...	7/21/95	7/25/95	7/27/95
0.02	...	9/22/95	9/26/95	10/18/95
0.02	...	12/26/95	12/28/95	1/19/96

CAPITALIZATION (3/31/96):

	($000)	(%)
Long-Term Debt	106,753	47.6
Stockholders' Equity	117,460	52.4
Total	224,213	100.0

RECENT DEVELOPMENTS: For the three months ended 12/31/96, net income was $596,000 compared with $29,000 in the year-earlier period. Total charter revenues increased 30.4% to $15.2 million. Voyage charter income led the improved results with a 46.3% increase in revenues to $10.7 million. Time charter revenues rose 3.6% to $4.5 million. Operating income surged 79.8% to $2.5 million. Operating income for the Suezmax fleet jumped to $2.1 million from $940,000 as the current quarter represented three vessels compared with approximately two vessels in the year-earlier period. The average daily time charter equivalent for the Suezmax fleet increased to $26,000 versus $23,500 in the year-earlier quarter. The Suezmax fleet benefited from improved profitability of the London Pride under its Chevron time charter. The Panamax fleet's net operating income fell 11.0% to $427,000, reflecting weakness in the voyage market. The average daily time charter equivalent earned fell to $13,000 from $13,500 last year

BUSINESS

LONDON & OVERSEAS FREIGHTERS LIMITED owns and operates a fleet of tankers that transport crude oil and oil products to and from ports, primarily in the United States. The Company's fleet is comprised of three Panamax tankers and three Suezmax tankers, and is engaged in delivering cargos to port-based discharging facilities that larger vessels are not able or not permitted to enter. The Company also operates in the voyage charter market.

ANNUAL EARNINGS

	3/31/96	3/31/95	3/31/94	3/31/93	3/31/92	3/31/91
				---US $---		
Earnings Per Share	0.02	0.11	0.10	0.04	...	...

ANNUAL FINANCIAL DATA

RECORD OF EARNINGS (IN THOUSANDS):

	3/31/96	3/31/95	3/31/94	3/31/93	3/31/92	3/31/91
Total Revenues	33,532	29,192	25,010	14,779	15,637	15,441
Costs & Expenses	26,683	19,937	17,659	12,007	11,460	10,400
Operating Income	6,849	9,255	7,351	2,772	4,177	5,041
Income Bef Income Tax	1,845	8,408	4,169	1,094	3,527	3,875
Income Tax	29	23	cr10	86	72	102
Net Income	1,816	8,385	4,170	1,008	3,455	3,773
Average Shares Outstg	74,497	74,381	40,805	23,386	22,512	21,696

BALANCE SHEET (IN THOUSANDS):

Cash & Cash Equivalents	14,773	32,154	60,730	461	1,233	1,727
Receivables, Net	4,314	442	706	1,045	918	421
Inventories	1,602	496	547	352	215	290
Gross Property	256,211	124,375	124,075	47,660	47,099	46,865
Accumulated Depreciation	36,343	26,164	19,624	14,171	11,270	8,452
Long-Term Debt	106,753	52,056	57,011	50,519	10,000	15,000
Stockholders' Equity	117,460	115,959	108,537	36,774	32,041	30,662
Total Assets	242,021	178,665	179,870	94,803	47,017	48,989
Total Current Assets	21,234	33,540	62,526	1,989	2,697	2,723
Total Current Liabilities	16,042	10,125	13,409	7,218	4,762	2,572
Net Working Capital	5,192	23,415	49,117	d5,229	d2,065	151
Year End Shs Outstg	73,726	73,351	73,126	23,126	...	...

STATISTICAL RECORD:

Return on Equity %	1.5	7.2	3.8	2.7	10.8	12.3
Return on Assets %	0.7	4.7	2.3	1.1	7.3	7.7
Operating Profit Margin %	20.4	31.7	29.4	18.8	26.7	32.6
Net Profit Margin %	5.4	28.7	16.7	6.8	22.1	24.2
Book Value Per Share	1.59	1.58	1.48	1.59	...	...

OFFICERS:
I. A. McGrath, Non-Exec. Chmn.
M. A. Kulukundis, Pres. & C.E.O.
H. D. Spiers, V.P. & C.F.O.

INCORPORATED: Bermuda, June 1992

PRINCIPAL OFFICE: Mercury House 101 Front Street Hamilton HM12 Bermuda

TELEPHONE NUMBER: (441) 295-9500

NO. OF EMPLOYEES: N/A

ANNUAL MEETING: In July

SHAREHOLDERS: N/A

INSTITUTIONAL HOLDINGS:
No. of Institutions: 5
Shares Held: 2,428,100

AMERICAN DEPOSITARY RECEIPTS: (Sponsored) Each American Depositary Receipt represents ten ordinary shares of par US$0.25.

DEPOSITARY BANK(S): The Bank of New York, (212) 815-2175

LONDON INTERNATIONAL GROUP PLC

YIELD 0.8%
P/E RATIO 32.2

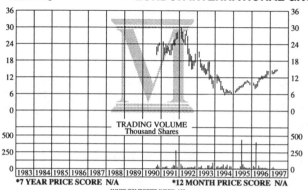

TRADING VOLUME
Thousand Shares

1983|1984|1985|1986|1987|1988|1989|1990|1991|1992|1993|1994|1995|1996|1997
*7 YEAR PRICE SCORE N/A   *12 MONTH PRICE SCORE N/A
*NYSE COMPOSITE INDEX=100

INTERIM EARNINGS (Per Share, US$):

1994-95	------------------ 0.06 ------------------
1995-96	------------------ 0.09 ------------------

INTERIM DIVIDENDS (Per Share):

Amt.	Decl.	Ex.	Rec.	Pay.
0.082	...	8/31/95	6/29/95	9/05/95
0.041	...	1/29/96	1/31/96	3/08/96
0.123	...	6/14/96	6/18/96	9/03/96
0.061	...	12/13/96	12/17/96	3/10/97

Indicated div.: $0.122

CAPITALIZATION (3/31/96):

	($000)	(%)
Long-Term Debt	31,776	13.8
Stockholders' Equity........	197,532	85.8
Deferred Income Tax	917	0.4
Total	230,225	100.0

RECENT DEVELOPMENTS: For the year ended 3/31/96, net profit advanced 66.7% to £19.5 million from £11.7 million the previous year. Total turnover declined 2.7% to £309.6 million from £318.1 million the year before. Turnover on continuing operations improved 8.0% to £309.6 million from £286.7 million in 1995. This increase was primarily due to growth in sales for family planning, surgical gloves, household and industrial gloves, and film barrier technology. Gross profit climbed 9.0% to £171.7 million, or 55.5% of total turnover, from £157.5 million, or 49.5% of total turnover, a year earlier. This improvement reflected price increases, particularly in condoms and surgical gloves, improved sales mix, and major restructuring activities during 1994 and 1995. Operating profit grew 46.9% to £31.3 million compared with £23.9 million the prior year. Profit on ordinary activities before taxation rose 72.4% to £26.2 million from £15.2 million the previous year.

BUSINESS

LONDON INTERNATIONAL GROUP PLC manufactures and sells consumer goods and services, including condoms, sold under such names as Durex, Ramses, Kingtex, Kohinoor, RAPS and Hatu; surgical, consumer and industrial gloves, sold under the Biogel and Marigold names; and health and beauty aids, such as cough and cold medicine, baby care products and toiletries sold under the Woodward's, Sauber, Manan, Mister Baby, Mother's Choice and Buttercup brand names.

ANNUAL EARNINGS

	3/31/96	3/31/95	3/31/96	3/31/95
	-------------US $-------------		-------------British £-------------	
Earnings Per Share	0.09	0.06	0.06	0.04

ANNUAL FINANCIAL DATA

RECORD OF EARNINGS (IN THOUSANDS):

Total Revenues	473,434	516,126	309,900	318,400
Costs & Expenses	425,617	481,599	278,600	297,100
Operating Income	47,817	34,527	31,300	21,300
Income Bef Income Tax	40,026	24,639	26,200	15,200
Income Tax	10,083	5,511	6,600	3,400
Minority Interests	153	162	100	100
Net Income	29,790	18,966	19,500	11,700
Average Shares Outstg	338,756	291,069	338,756	291,069

BALANCE SHEET (IN THOUSANDS):

Cash & Cash Equivalents	49,039	41,011	32,100	25,300
Receivables, Net	172,172	153,995	112,700	95,000
Inventories	78,065	77,484	51,100	47,800
Gross Property	166,978	157,075	109,300	96,900
Accumulated Depreciation	76,079	63,381	49,800	39,100
Long-Term Debt	31,776	41,173	20,800	25,400
Stockholders' Equity	197,532	181,552	129,300	112,000
Total Assets	460,296	447,720	301,300	276,200
Total Current Assets	304,929	277,029	199,600	170,900
Total Current Liabilities	197,379	185,442	129,200	114,400
Net Working Capital	107,550	91,587	70,400	56,500
Year End Shs Outstg	339,060	338,332	339,060	338,332

STATISTICAL RECORD:

Return on Equity %	15.08	10.45
Return on Assets %	6.47	4.24
Operating Profit Margin %	10.10	6.69
Net Profit Margin %	6.30	3.68
Book Value Per Share	0.58	0.54

Converted at 1996, US$1.5277= 1 British pound; 1995, US$1.6210= 1 British pound.

OFFICERS:
M. R. Moore, Chmn.
N. R. Hodges, Group Chief Exec.
J. M. Tyrrell, Fin. Dir.

INCORPORATED: United Kingdom, Nov., 1950

PRINCIPAL OFFICE: 35 New Bridge Street, London EC4V 6BJ United Kingdom

TELEPHONE NUMBER: 44-171-489-1977
FAX: 44-171-489-0962
NO. OF EMPLOYEES: 220
ANNUAL MEETING: In Aug.
SHAREHOLDERS: N/A
INSTITUTIONAL HOLDINGS:
No. of Institutions: 3
Shares Held: 83,544

**AMERICAN DEPOSITARY
RECEIPTS:** (Sponsored) Each American Depositary Receipt represents five ordinary shares of par £0.10.

DEPOSITARY BANK(S): The Bank of New York, (212) 815-2175

LONDON PACIFIC GROUP, LIMITED

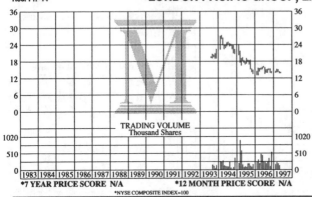

INTERIM EARNINGS (Per Share):

Qtr.	Mar.	June	Sept.	Dec.
1995		0.46		
1996		0.46		

INTERIM DIVIDENDS (Per Share):

Amt.	Decl.	Ex.	Rec.	Pay.
0.332	...	11/10/95	11/14/95	12/01/95
0.556	...	3/01/96	3/05/96	4/08/96
0.332	...	8/16	8/20	9/09
0.556	...	3/07/97	3/11/97	4/14/97

Indicated div.: $1.112

TRADING VOLUME
Thousand Shares

7 YEAR PRICE SCORE N/A   **12 MONTH PRICE SCORE N/A**

*NYSE COMPOSITE INDEX=100

CAPITALIZATION (12/31/96):

	($000)	(%)
Stockholders' Equity	354,512	99.8
Deferred Income Tax	777	0.2
Total	355,289	100.0

RECENT DEVELOPMENTS: For the year ended 12/31/96, profit after taxation was US$25.1 million compared with US$129.1 million in 1995. The 1996 results included exceptional charges totaling US$8.7 million, while the 1995 results included profit on disposal of discontinued operations of US$113.9 million and an exceptional charge of US$9.3 million. Total revenues grew 9.4% to US$130.9 million, driven by higher investment revenues. Total net operating income increased 21.4% to US$45.2 million from US$37.2 million the year before. Investment revenues soared to US$11.1 million from US$1.0 million in 1995. Sales of fixed annuities declined 39.0% to US$108.5 million, primarily due to weak market conditions. The launch of variable annuities in Febuary of 1996 led to US$4.4 million in premium volume for 1996. The Company has signed selling agreements with 42 firms located in most U.S. States. Revenues from other products jumped to US$17.1 million from US$3.1 million in 1995.

BUSINESS

LONDON PACIFIC GROUP LIMITED is in the business of fund management; life insurance and annuities; development capital investment; trust administration; and fee based advisory services. The fund management businesses earn asset-based fees and offer specialist investment management skills to a mix of institutional and retail clients. Life insurance and annuities consist solely of the US based London Pacific Life & Annuity Company and maintains a balanced investmentportfolio, consisting primarily of investment-grade securities. Development capital provides a range of financing and consulting services to private US companies. Trust administration provides recordkeeping, administration and trust services to the sponsors of, and participants in, qualified employee benefit plans. Fee-based advisory services provide a range of investment services to retail and institutional clients.

ANNUAL EARNINGS

	12/31/96	12/31/95	12/31/96	12/31/95
	US $		British £	
Earnings Per Share	0.46	2.38	0.27	1.53

ANNUAL FINANCIAL DATA

RECORD OF EARNINGS (IN THOUSANDS):

Total Revenues	45,181	37,230	26,663	23,973
Costs & Expenses	3,790	3,733	2,237	2,404
Operating Income	41,391	33,497	24,427	21,569
Income Bef Income Tax	33,168	138,195	19,574	88,986
Income Tax	8,081	9,122	4,769	5,874
Net Income	25,087	129,073	14,805	83,112
Average Shares Outstg	54,980	54,166	54,980	54,166

BALANCE SHEET (IN THOUSANDS):

Cash & Cash Equivalents	196,397	250,671	115,903	161,411
Receivables, Net	79,661	40,995	47,959	26,945
Gross Property	6,445	5,305	3,803	3,416
Accumulated Depreciation	3,937	3,291	2,323	2,119
Stockholders' Equity	354,512	344,807	209,213	222,026
Total Assets	1,703,223	1,551,622	1,005,148	999,113
Total Current Assets	277,663	292,517	163,861	188,356
Total Current Liabilities	168,070	56,831	99,186	36,594
Net Working Capital	109,593	235,686	64,676	151,762
Year End Shs Outstg	68,326	68,136	68,326	68,136

STATISTICAL RECORD:

Return on Equity %	7.08	37.43
Return on Assets %	1.47	8.32
Operating Profit Margin %	91.61	89.97
Net Profit Margin %	55.53	346.69
Book Value Per Share	5.19	5.06

Converted at 1996, US$1.6945= 1 British pound; 1995, US$1.5530= 1 British pound

OFFICERS:
A. I. Trueger, Exec. Chmn.
V. A. Hebert, Deputy Chmn.

INCORPORATED: The Channel Islands, 1985

PRINCIPAL OFFICE: Minden House, 6 Minden Place, St. Helier Jersey JE2 4WQ, Channel Islands

TELEPHONE NUMBER: (01534) 607700
NO. OF EMPLOYEES: N/A
ANNUAL MEETING: In Mar.
SHAREHOLDERS: N/A
INSTITUTIONAL HOLDINGS:
No. of Institutions: 10
Shares Held: 1,430,449

AMERICAN DEPOSITARY RECEIPTS: (Sponsored) Each American Depositary Receipt represents 4 ordinary shares of par US$0.05.

DEPOSITARY BANK(S): The Bank of New York, (212) 815-2175

LVMH MOET HENNESSY LOUIS VUITTON

YIELD   0.8%
P/E RATIO   30.2

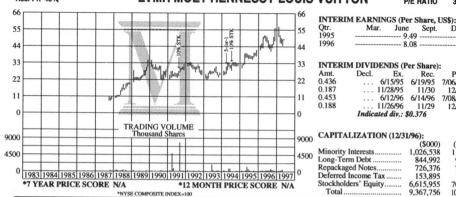

TRADING VOLUME
Thousand Shares

| 1983 | 1984 | 1985 | 1986 | 1987 | 1988 | 1989 | 1990 | 1991 | 1992 | 1993 | 1994 | 1995 | 1996 | 1997 |

*7 YEAR PRICE SCORE N/A   *12 MONTH PRICE SCORE N/A

*NYSE COMPOSITE INDEX=100

INTERIM EARNINGS (Per Share, US$):

Qtr.	Mar.	June	Sept.	Dec.
1995		9.49		
1996		8.08		

INTERIM DIVIDENDS (Per Share):

Amt.	Decl.	Ex.	Rec.	Pay.
0.436	...	6/15/95	6/19/95	7/06/95
0.187	...	11/28/95	11/30	12/11
0.453	...	6/12/96	6/14/96	7/08/96
0.188	...	11/26/96	11/29	12/31

Indicated div.: $0.376

CAPITALIZATION (12/31/96):

	($000)	(%)
Minority Interests	1,026,538	11.0
Long-Term Debt	844,992	9.0
Repackaged Notes	726,376	7.8
Deferred Income Tax	153,895	1.6
Stockholders' Equity	6,615,955	70.6
Total	9,367,756	100.0

RECENT DEVELOPMENTS: For the year ended 12/31/96, net income before unusual items, increased 6.2% to FFr4.30 billion (US$820.0 million). The Company reported negative unusual items of FFr615.0 million (US$117.0 million) that primarily reflect the effect on consolidation of the sale of part of the Company's stake in Guinness PLC. Consolidated net sales in 1996 were up 4.6% to FFr31.14 billion (US$5.94 billion). Economic environments in which the Company operated in 1996 revealed sluggish growth in western Europe, sustained growth in the United States and the United Kingdom, and a moderate gain combined with deflationary trends in Japan. Sales were higher in the second half of the year, particularly in December, when sales growth for the month was 13.0%. Pursuing its development in luxury goods activities, the Company acquired a 61.25% stake in DFS, a leading worldwide distributor of luxury goods, as well as Celine and Loewe S.A.

BUSINESS

LVMH MOET HENNESSY LOUIS VUITTON is the world's leading luxury products group, with preeminent positions in the champagne and wines, cognac and spirits, luggage and leather products, perfumes and beauty products, and high fashion sectors. The Company's brand offerings include Moet & Chandon, Dom Perignon, Veuve Clicquot Ponsardin, and Pommery champagnes and wines, and Hennessy, Hine and Pellisson cognac and spirits. The Company also produces sparkling and still wines as well as wine barrels. The Company holds a 14% interest in the British beverage group, Guinness PLC, producer of Guinness beer, Dewar's, Bell's and Johnnie Walker Scotch whiskies, and Tanqueray gin. The Company is active in luggage and leather goods through Louis Vuitton. In the Perfumes and Beauty Products sector, the Company's operations are carried on through its holdings in Parfums Christian Dior, Guerlain, Parfums Givenchy, and Kenzo. The Company operates in high fashion through Givenchy, Kenzo and Christian Lacroix and in five jewelry and timepieces through Fred. The Company also operates in the financial and economic media sector through its holdings in La Tribune Desfosses, and Investir.

ANNUAL EARNINGS

	12/31/96	12/31/95	12/31/96	12/31/95
	US $		FFr	
Earnings Per Share	8.08	9.49	42.38	46.52

ANNUAL FINANCIAL DATA

RECORD OF EARNINGS (IN MILLIONS):

	12/31/96	12/31/95	12/31/96	12/31/95
Total Revenues	5,939	6,071	31,142	29,775
Costs & Expenses	4,600	4,602	24,120	22,569
Operating Income	1,339	1,469	7,022	7,206
Income Bef Income Tax	1,270	1,353	6,659	6,636
Income Tax	481	548	2,520	2,687
Eq. Earnings in Affils.	174	147	913	719
Minority Interests	113	127	595	621
Net Income	702	825	3,683	4,047
Average Shares Outstg (000)	87,000	87,000	87,000	87,000

BALANCE SHEET (IN MILLIONS):

Cash & Cash Equivalents	1,309	2,127	6,865	10,431
Receivables, Net	1,232	1,210	6,460	5,935
Inventories	2,807	2,906	14,721	14,253
Gross Property	2,702	2,652	14,168	13,008
Accumulated Depreciation	1,106	1,031	5,801	5,055
Long-Term Debt	845	766	4,431	3,759
Stockholders' Equity	6,616	6,320	34,693	30,996
Total Assets	15,255	13,016	79,993	63,833
Total Current Assets	6,254	7,115	32,796	34,896
Total Current Liabilities	5,273	3,103	27,652	15,218
Net Working Capital	981	4,012	5,144	19,678
Year End Shs Outstg (000)	87,390	87,237	87,390	87,237

STATISTICAL RECORD:

Return on Equity %	10.61	13.05		
Return on Assets %	4.60	6.34		
Operating Profit Margin %	22.55	24.20		
Net Profit Margin %	11.82	13.59		
Book Value Per Share	75.71	72.45		

Converted at 1996, US$0.1907= 1 French franc; 1995, US$0.2039= 1 French franc

OFFICERS:
B. Arnault, Chmn. & C.E.O.
A. Bernheim, Vice-Chmn.
F. Chandon de Briailles, Vice-Chmn.

INCORPORATED: N/A

PRINCIPAL OFFICE: 30, avenue Hoche, Paris France, F-75008

TELEPHONE NUMBER: (33) 1 44 13 22 22

NO. OF EMPLOYEES: 20,644 (avg.)

ANNUAL MEETING: N/A

SHAREHOLDERS: N/A

INSTITUTIONAL HOLDINGS:
No. of Institutions: 28
Shares Held: 2,543,215

AMERICAN DEPOSITARY RECEIPTS: (Sponsored) Each American Depositary Receipt represents one-fifth of a common share of par FFr10.

DEPOSITARY BANK(S): The Bank of New York, (212) 815-2175

MACRONIX INTERNATIONAL CO. LTD

YIELD ...
P/E RATIO 12.5

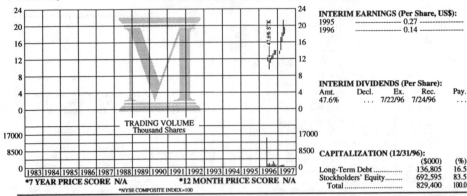

INTERIM EARNINGS (Per Share, US$):
1995 ------------------ 0.27 ------------------
1996 ------------------ 0.14 ------------------

INTERIM DIVIDENDS (Per Share):

Amt.	Decl.	Ex.	Rec.	Pay.
47.6%	...	7/22/96	7/24/96	...

TRADING VOLUME
Thousand Shares

*7 YEAR PRICE SCORE N/A
*12 MONTH PRICE SCORE N/A
*NYSE COMPOSITE INDEX=100

CAPITALIZATION (12/31/96):

	($000)	(%)
Long-Term Debt	136,805	16.5
Stockholders' Equity	692,595	83.5
Total	829,400	100.0

RECENT DEVELOPMENTS: For the year ended 12/31/96, net income advanced 8.9% to NT$3.36 billion compared with NT$3.09 billion in the same period of 1995. Sales were NT$10.19 billion, up 15.0% compared with NT$8.87 billion a year earlier. Operating income jumped 21.0% to NT$3.30 billion. Results for 1995 have been restated. The improvement in sales was achieved despite steadily dropping DRAM prices that sent revenues plummeting by up to 50% throughout the IC industry. MXICY was listed on the NASDAQ stock exchange during May 1996. MXICY plans to aggressively pursue collaboration opportunities with prominent corporations to jointly develop cutting edge, high value-added memory products. MXICY is introducing new facilities that will bring its production capabilities up to the 0.35 micron level. Equipment was installed and tested last year, and mass production in MXICY's new 8-inch fab should begin in April of 1997, providing new business momentum for the second half of the year.

BUSINESS

MACRONIX INTERNATIONAL CO. LTD. is an investment holding company and an independent semiconductor designer, developer, manufacturer and marketer of nonvolatile memory integrated circuits, including mask read-only memory, erasable programmable ROM and flash memory products, and of logic products including audio, network, clock generator and graphic applications devices. Through a subsidiary, Macronix acts as a sales agent of its products.

ANNUAL EARNINGS

	12/31/96	12/31/95	12/31/96	12/31/95
	------------US $------------		------------NT$------------	
Earnings Per Share	0.14	0.27	3.90	7.31

ANNUAL FINANCIAL DATA

RECORD OF EARNINGS (IN THOUSANDS):

Total Revenues	371,084	324,498	10,194,605	8,866,064
Costs & Expenses	250,806	224,552	6,890,263	6,135,297
Operating Income	120,278	99,946	3,304,342	2,730,767
Income Bef Income Tax	118,303	92,053	3,250,091	2,515,104
Income Tax	cr4,023	cr20,938	cr110,520	cr572,076
Net Income	122,326	112,991	3,360,611	3,087,180

BALANCE SHEET (IN THOUSANDS):

Cash & Cash Equivalents	224,165	162,933	6,158,379	4,451,726
Receivables, Net	64,722	58,647	1,778,067	1,602,374
Inventories	87,737	42,106	2,410,353	1,150,443
Gross Property	773,111	359,502	21,239,310	9,822,454
Accumulated Depreciation	139,412	95,464	3,830,000	2,608,310
Long-Term Debt	136,805	68,897	3,758,389	1,882,423
Stockholders' Equity	692,595	407,928	19,027,333	11,145,573
Total Assets	1,083,169	601,611	29,757,391	16,437,458
Total Current Assets	401,631	282,454	11,033,805	7,717,329
Total Current Liabilities	235,144	120,329	6,459,992	3,287,670
Net Working Capital	166,487	162,126	4,573,813	4,429,659
Year End Shs Outstg	941,677	500,000	941,677	500,000

STATISTICAL RECORD:

Return on Equity %	17.66	27.70		
Return on Assets %	11.29	18.78		
Operating Profit Margin %	32.41	30.80		
Net Profit Margin %	32.96	34.82		
Book Value Per Share	0.74	0.82		

Converted at 1996, US$0.0364= 1 New Taiwanese$; 1995, US$0.0366= 1 New Taiwanese$

OFFICERS:
Ding-Hua Hu, Chmn.
Miin Wu, Pres.
Tom Yiu, Sr. V.P.
P. Yeh, Fin. Dir.
INCORPORATED: Republic of Taiwan, 1989
PRINCIPAL OFFICE: No. 3 Creation Road, III Science-Based Industrial Park, Hsinchu China (Rep. Of Taiwan)

TELEPHONE NUMBER: (886-35) 788-888
NO. OF EMPLOYEES: 1,754
ANNUAL MEETING: N/A
SHAREHOLDERS: N/A
INSTITUTIONAL HOLDINGS:
No. of Institutions: 12
Shares Held: 834,663

AMERICAN DEPOSITARY RECEIPTS: Each American Depositary Receipt represents 10 common shares of par value NT$10.

DEPOSITARY BANK(S): The Bank of New York, (212) 815-2175

M.A.I.D., PLC

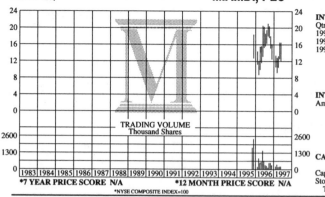

*7 YEAR PRICE SCORE N/A *12 MONTH PRICE SCORE N/A
*NYSE COMPOSITE INDEX=100

TRADING VOLUME
Thousand Shares

INTERIM EARNINGS (Per Share, US$):

Qtr.	Mar.	June	Sept.	Dec.
1994	---------------- 0.02 ----------------			
1995	---------------- d0.06 ----------------			
1996	---------------- d0.14 ----------------			

INTERIM DIVIDENDS (Per Share):

Amt.	Decl.	Ex.	Rec.	Pay.
	No dividends paid.			

CAPITALIZATION (12/31/96):

	($000)	(%)
Capital Lease Obligs.	1,349	3.0
Stockholders' Equity	44,193	97.0
Total	45,542	100.0

RECENT DEVELOPMENTS: For the year ended 12/31/96, the Company incurred a net loss of $18.6 million. This compares with a net loss of $14.7 million in 1995. Revenues for the year grew 57.8% to $34.2 million from $21.7 million in the prior year. Usage and subscription revenues accelerated 64.0% in 1996, compared with a 42.0% growth rate in 1995. The Company made several infrastructure moves during the year, including the opening of seven offices in North America, four offices in Europe, three offices in Asia, and the moving of its U.S. headquarters from New York City to Cary, N.C. to take advantage of lower overhead costs and greater availability of skilled personnel. In early 1997, the Company opened an additional office in Germany. For the fourth quarter ended 12/31/96, the Company reported a net loss of $4.8 million compared with a net loss of $3.7 million in the corresponding period a year earlier. Revenues increased 63.1% to $10.0 million from $6.1 million the previous year.

BUSINESS

M.A.I.D., PLC is an online information company that carries market research reports, business news, company statistics, stockbroker research and up-to-date stock market and commodity prices. The Company has regional headquarters in London; Cary, North Carolina; and Hong Kong.

ANNUAL EARNINGS

	12/31/96	12/31/95	12/31/96	12/31/95
	----------US $----------		----------British £----------	
Earnings Per Share	d0.14	d0.06	d0.08	d0.04

ANNUAL FINANCIAL DATA

RECORD OF EARNINGS (IN THOUSANDS):

	12/31/96	12/31/95	12/31/96	12/31/95
Total Revenues	36,335	21,186	21,443	13,642
Costs & Expenses	45,997	26,457	27,145	17,036
Depreciation & Amort	3,677	1,155	2,170	744
Operating Income	d13,339	d6,426	d7,872	d4,138
Income Bef Income Tax	d11,919	d6,282	d7,034	d4,045
Income Tax	278	cr646	164	cr416
Minority Interests	47	8	28	5
Net Income	d12,244	d5,644	d7,226	d3,634
Average Shares Outstg	92,364	82,183	92,364	82,183

BALANCE SHEET (IN THOUSANDS):

Cash & Cash Equivalents	13,620	34,217	8,038	22,033
Receivables, Net	11,312	5,741	6,676	3,697
Inventories	176	157	104	101
Gross Property	21,654	14,000	12,779	9,015
Accumulated Depreciation	9,808	4,766	5,788	3,069
Long-Term Debt	1,349	2,550	796	1,642
Stockholders' Equity	44,193	49,205	26,080	31,684
Total Assets	57,113	60,621	33,705	39,035
Total Current Assets	27,566	41,810	16,268	26,922
Total Current Liabilities	11,331	8,711	6,687	5,609
Net Working Capital	16,235	33,099	9,581	21,313
Year End Shs Outstg	92,598	91,717	92,598	91,717

STATISTICAL RECORD:

Book Value Per Share	0.48	0.54		

Converted at 1996, US$1.6945= 1 British pound; 1995, US$1.5530= 1 British pound

OFFICERS:
M.S. Mander, Chmn.
D.M. Wagner, C.E.O.
D.G. Mattley, Fin. Dir.
D.B. Smith, Managing Dir.

INCORPORATED: 1985

PRINCIPAL OFFICE: The Communications Building, 48 Leicester Square, London WC2H 7DB England

TELEPHONE NUMBER: 071-930-6900

NO. OF EMPLOYEES: 460

ANNUAL MEETING: In May

SHAREHOLDERS: 41; 20 ADR holders

INSTITUTIONAL HOLDINGS:
No. of Institutions: 2
Shares Held: 275,400

AMERICAN DEPOSITARY RECEIPTS: Each American Depositary Receipt represents four ordinary shares.

DEPOSITARY BANK(S): The Bank of New York, (212) 815-2175

MAKITA CORP.

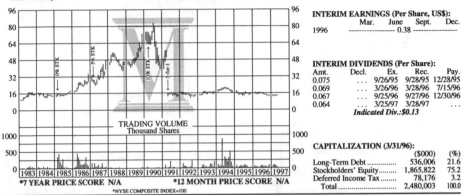

INTERIM EARNINGS (Per Share, US$):

	Mar.	June	Sept.	Dec.
1996	----	0.38	-----	

INTERIM DIVIDENDS (Per Share):

Amt.	Decl.	Ex.	Rec.	Pay.
0.075	...	9/26/95	9/28/95	12/28/95
0.069	...	3/26/96	3/28/96	7/15/96
0.067	...	9/25/96	9/27/96	12/30/96
0.064	...	3/25/97	3/28/97	...

Indicated Div.:$0.13

CAPITALIZATION (3/31/96):

	($000)	(%)
Long-Term Debt	536,006	21.6
Stockholders' Equity.........	1,865,822	75.2
Deferred Income Tax	78,176	3.2
Total.....................	2,480,003	100.0

*7 YEAR PRICE SCORE N/A   ***12 MONTH PRICE SCORE N/A**

*NYSE COMPOSITE INDEX=100

RECENT DEVELOPMENTS: For the first half of the fiscal year ended 9/30/96, net income improved 6.0% to ¥3.36 billion (US$30.3 million) compared with ¥3.17 billion in the same period of 1995. Earnings included foreign currency translation adjustments, which reduced 1996 results by ¥181.0 million (US$1.63 million), but enhanced 1995 results by ¥79.0 million. Net sales increased 19.0% to ¥88.50 billion (US$797.3 million) from ¥74.34 billion the year before.

The stronger results were attributable to stabilization of the U.S. economy, which offset slowdowns in capital investments and exports. Recoveries in the economies of the United Kingdom, Germany and Japan had a favorable effect on results. Gross profit rose 7.8% to ¥27.88 billion (US$251.1 million) versus ¥25.86 billion a year earlier. Operating income slipped 2.7% to ¥7.55 billion (US$68.0 million) from ¥7.76 billion in the prior year.

BUSINESS

MAKITA CORP. is primarily a manufacturer of electric power tools and parts. The Company's operations are carried out through four operating groups: Portable Woodworking Tools, Portable General Purpose Tools, Stationary Woodworking Machines and Other Products. The Portable Woodworking Tools group manufactures circular saws, jig saws, chain saws, electric planers, routers, and air nailers. The Portable General Purpose Tools group manufactures cordless drills, hammer drills, rotary hammers, grinders, drills, sanders, screwdrivers, and cutters. The Stationary Woodworking Machines group manufactures table saws, planer-jointers, and band saws. The Other Products group manufactures vacuum cleaners and generators for industrial use and various products for home and garden use, including cordless vacuum cleaners, automatic drapery openers, lawn mowers and hedge trimmers.

ANNUAL EARNINGS

	3/31/96	3/31/95	3/31/96	3/31/95
	----US $----		----Yen----	
Earnings Per Share	0.38	0.47	40.9	40.3

ANNUAL FINANCIAL DATA

RECORD OF EARNINGS (IN THOUSANDS):

	3/31/96	3/31/95	3/31/96	3/31/95
Total Revenues	1,478,384	1,906,762	158,966,000	164,376,000
Costs & Expenses	1,338,949	1,705,571	143,973,000	147,032,000
Operating Income	139,435	201,190	14,993,000	17,344,000
Income Bef Income Tax	132,990	156,008	14,300,000	13,449,000
Income Tax	69,155	77,801	7,436,000	6,707,000
Net Income	63,835	78,207	6,864,000	6,742,000

BALANCE SHEET (IN THOUSANDS):

	3/31/96	3/31/95	3/31/96	3/31/95
Cash & Cash Equivalents	1,090,378	1,195,310	117,245,000	103,044,000
Receivables, Net	319,660	369,321	34,372,000	31,838,000
Inventories	585,593	547,079	62,967,000	47,162,000
Gross Property	1,454,483	1,685,596	156,396,000	145,310,000
Accumulated Depreciation	664,308	764,289	71,431,000	65,887,000
Long-Term Debt	536,006	528,682	57,635,000	45,576,000
Stockholders' Equity	1,865,822	2,150,048	200,626,000	185,349,000
Total Assets	3,211,876	3,488,178	345,363,000	300,705,000
Total Current Assets	2,024,684	2,172,413	217,708,000	187,277,000
Total Current Liabilities	530,760	498,568	57,071,000	42,980,000
Net Working Capital	1,493,924	1,673,845	160,637,000	144,297,000
Year End Shs Outstg	161,005	161,005	161,005	161,005

STATISTICAL RECORD:

	3/31/96	3/31/95
Return on Equity %	3.42	3.64
Return on Assets %	1.99	2.24
Operating Profit Margin %	9.43	10.55
Net Profit Margin %	4.32	4.10
Book Value Per Share	11.59	13.35

Converted at 1996, US$0.0093= 1 Japanese Yen; 1995, US$0.0116= 1 Japanese Yen

OFFICERS:
M. Goto, Pres.
T. Inagaki, Sr. Managing Dir.

INCORPORATED: Japan, 1938

PRINCIPAL OFFICE: 3-11-8, Sumiyoshi-cho
Anjo, Aichi 446, Japan

TELEPHONE NUMBER: 0566-98-1711
NO. OF EMPLOYEES: 7,444
ANNUAL MEETING: In Jun.
SHAREHOLDERS: N/A
INSTITUTIONAL HOLDINGS:
No. of Institutions: 9
Shares Held: 1,113,738
AMERICAN DEPOSITARY RECEIPTS: Each
American Depositary Receipt represents one
common sh. of par ¥50.

DEPOSITARY BANK(S): The Bank of New
York, (212) 815-2175

MATAV-CABLE SYSTEMS MEDIA LTD.

YIELD ...
P/E RATIO 12.18

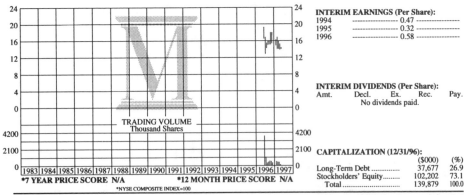

INTERIM EARNINGS (Per Share):

1994	------------------ 0.47 ------------------
1995	------------------ 0.32 ------------------
1996	------------------ 0.58 ------------------

INTERIM DIVIDENDS (Per Share):

Amt.   Decl.   Ex.   Rec.   Pay.
No dividends paid.

CAPITALIZATION (12/31/96):

	($000)	(%)
Long-Term Debt	37,677	26.9
Stockholders' Equity........	102,202	73.1
Total	139,879	100.0

TRADING VOLUME
Thousand Shares

1983 1984 1985 1986 1987 1988 1989 1990 1991 1992 1993 1994 1995 1996 1997
*7 YEAR PRICE SCORE N/A   *12 MONTH PRICE SCORE N/A
*NYSE COMPOSITE INDEX=100

RECENT DEVELOPMENTS: For the year ended 12/31/96, net income grew to NIS46.0 million (US$14.2 million) from NIS21.9 million in 1995. Earnings for 1996 and 1995 included capital losses of NIS20,000 (US$6,000) and NIS119,000, respectively. Also, earnings for 1996 and 1995 included shares in profits of associated companies of NIS1.4 million (US$411,000) and shares in losses of associated companies of NIS1.0 million, respectively. Revenue advanced 12.6% to NIS300.4 million (US$92.4 million) versus NIS266.7 million in 1995. For the quarter ended 12/31/96, net income increased to NIS16.2 million (US$5.0 million) from NIS7.9 million in the same prior-year period. Revenue advanced 13.1% to NIS78.3 million (US$24.1 million) from NIS69.3 million in 1995. On 3/19/97, MATVY signed an agreement with Trefoil Capital Investors and Shamrock Holdings, Inc. to acquire approximately 11.8% of the outstanding shares of R.P. Telekom S.A. for approximately US$17.0 million.

BUSINESS

MATAV-CABLE SYSTEMS MEDIA LTD. is engaged in providing broadband Cable TV services in Israel. As one of five CATV operators in Israel, the Company operates in exclusive franchise areas which cover approximately 25% of Israel's households. The Company provides CATV services to about 25% of all CATV subscribers in Israel.

ANNUAL EARNINGS

	12/31/96	12/31/95	12/31/96	12/31/95
	-------------US $-------------		-------------NIS------------	
Earnings Per Share	0.58	0.32	1.87	1.01

ANNUAL FINANCIAL DATA

RECORD OF EARNINGS (IN THOUSANDS):

	12/31/96	12/31/95	12/31/96	12/31/95
Total Revenues	92,209	84,725	300,354	266,683
Costs & Expenses	64,291	63,755	209,418	200,678
Operating Income	27,917	20,970	90,936	66,005
Income Bef Income Tax	21,494	11,985	70,012	37,725
Income Tax	7,791	4,726	25,378	14,877
Eq. Earnings in Affils.	410	d321	1,337	d1,009
Minority Interests	cr24	cr14	cr77	cr43
Net Income	14,137	6,952	46,048	21,882
Average Shares Outstg	24,610	21,622	24,610	21,622

BALANCE SHEET (IN THOUSANDS):

Cash & Cash Equivalents	26,136	25	85,133	79
Receivables, Net	12,677	13,267	41,294	41,758
Gross Property	233,955	222,974	762,069	701,837
Accumulated Depreciation	78,301	60,736	255,051	191,175
Long-Term Debt	37,677	73,094	122,726	230,073
Stockholders' Equity	102,202	42,750	332,904	134,561
Total Assets	205,014	184,264	667,797	579,995
Total Current Assets	38,813	13,292	126,427	41,837
Total Current Liabilities	56,444	58,289	183,856	183,471
Net Working Capital	d17,631	d44,997	d57,429	d141,634
Year End Shs Outstg	27,022	21,622	27,022	21,622

STATISTICAL RECORD:

Return on Equity %	13.83	16.26
Return on Assets %	6.90	3.77
Operating Profit Margin %	30.28	24.75
Net Profit Margin %	15.33	8.21
Book Value Per Share	3.78	1.98

Converted at 1996, US$0.3070= 1 New Israeli Shekel; 1995, US$0.3177= 1 New Israeli Shekel

OFFICERS:
S. Dankner, Chmn.
R. Avi-Tal, Pres. & C.E.O.
A. Weich, Couns. & Sec.

INCORPORATED: Israel, 1987

PRINCIPAL OFFICE: 42 Pinkas Street North, Industrial Area, Netanya, 42134 Israel

TELEPHONE NUMBER: 972-9-602-160

NO. OF EMPLOYEES: 404

ANNUAL MEETING: N/A

SHAREHOLDERS: 12

INSTITUTIONAL HOLDINGS:
No. of Institutions: 18
Shares Held: 1,848,313

AMERICAN DEPOSITARY RECEIPTS: Each American Depositary Share represents two common shares of par value NIS1.

DEPOSITARY BANK(S): The Bank of New York, (212) 815-2175

MEMTEC LIMITED

YIELD 0.3%
P/E RATIO 23.3

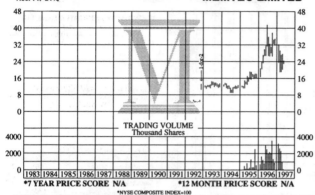

INTERIM EARNINGS (Per Share, US$):

Qtr.	Sept.	Dec.	Mar.	June
1994-95	-------------------	0.39	-------------------	
1995-96	-------------------	1.18	-------------------	
1996-97	0.21	0.24	...	...

INTERIM DIVIDENDS (Per Share):

Amt.	Decl.	Ex.	Rec.	Pay.
0.063	...	10/13/95	10/17/95	11/20/95
0.069	...	11/05/96	11/07/96	12/03/96

Indicated Div.: $0.069

TRADING VOLUME
Thousand Shares

7 YEAR PRICE SCORE N/A   **12 MONTH PRICE SCORE N/A**

NYSE COMPOSITE INDEX=100

CAPITALIZATION (6/30/96):

	($000)	(%)
Long-Term Debt	66,165	27.4
Stockholders' Equity........	171,536	70.9
Deferred Income Tax	4,190	1.7
Total	241,891	100.0

RECENT DEVELOPMENTS: For the three months ended 12/31/96, net income was $2.5 million compared with $5.1 million in the corresponding period a year earlier. Sales were $59.3 million versus $40.0 million in 1995. Seitz accounted for 37% of the sales growth. Earnings for 1995 benefited from an income tax benefit of $3.5 million. Operating profit for the three months leaped 90% to $4.2 million from $2.2 million. Gross profit as a percentage of net sales was unchanged from the prior comparable period at 36%. A strong gross profit margin by Seitz offset a decline in the gross profit margin of Fluid Dynamics. Backlog at December 31, 1996 was $79.0 million, an increase of 16% over the prior year.

BUSINESS

MEMTEC LIMITED manufactures and markets worldwide in excess of 5,000 industrial filtration products across its three principal product lines - Memcor, Fluid Dynamics and Filterite. Memcor large volume purification products include a proprietary line of continuous microfiltration systems used for water purification, waste treatment and beverage filtration. Fluid Dynamics metal fiber media products are high pressure, high temperature, metallic fiber filters and filtration equipment used by plastic film and fiber manufacturers, chemical processors, automotive airbag providers and others. Filterite products encompass a range of filter housings and disposable cartridge filters for varied industrial uses to purify liquid and gas steams.

ANNUAL EARNINGS

	6/30/96	6/30/95	6/30/96	6/30/95
	--------------US $--------------		--------------A$--------------	
Earnings Per Share	1.18	0.39	1.50	0.55

ANNUAL FINANCIAL DATA

RECORD OF EARNINGS (IN THOUSANDS):

	6/30/96	6/30/95	6/30/96	6/30/95
Total Revenues	174,506	145,029	221,595	204,353
Costs & Expenses	161,231	135,446	204,738	190,850
Depreciation & Amort	2,683	2,720	3,407	3,833
Operating Income	10,592	6,863	13,450	9,670
Income Bef Income Tax	7,911	1,259	10,055	1,774
Income Tax	cr3,160	1,259	cr4,013	1,774
Net Income	11,071	3,035	14,058	4,276
Average Shares Outstg	9,384	77,888	9,384	77,888

BALANCE SHEET (IN THOUSANDS):

	6/30/96	6/30/95	6/30/96	6/30/95
Cash & Cash Equivalents	28,067	4,320	35,641	6,087
Receivables, Net	44,499	29,247	56,023	39,373
Inventories	44,987	27,527	57,126	38,787
Gross Property	121,431	72,221	154,198	101,763
Accumulated Depreciation	29,759	22,914	37,789	32,287
Long-Term Debt	66,165	16,340	84,019	23,024
Stockholders' Equity	171,536	126,288	217,823	177,946
Total Assets	299,792	182,239	380,688	256,783
Total Current Assets	130,139	68,941	165,256	97,141
Total Current Liabilities	50,707	35,516	64,390	50,044
Net Working Capital	79,432	33,425	100,866	47,097
Year End Shs Outstg	10,237	79,004	10,237	79,004

STATISTICAL RECORD:

	6/30/96	6/30/95
Return on Equity %	6.45	2.40
Return on Assets %	3.69	1.67
Operating Profit Margin %	6.07	4.73
Net Profit Margin %	6.34	2.09
Book Value Per Share	16.76	1.60

Converted at 1996, US$0.7875= 1 Australian $; 1995, US$0.7097= 1 Australian $

OFFICERS:
D. M. Hanley, Chmn. & C.E.O.
A. L. Denver, Pres. & C.O.O.
D. M. McGarvey, Fin. Contr. & Corp. Sec.
R.C. Postema, Gen. Couns. & Corp. Sec.

INCORPORATED: 1982

PRINCIPAL OFFICE: 1 Memtec Parkway, South Windsor NSW 2756 Australia

TELEPHONE NUMBER: +61 45 77 6800

NO. OF EMPLOYEES: 1,688

ANNUAL MEETING: In Nov.

SHAREHOLDERS: 3,170

INSTITUTIONAL HOLDINGS:
No. of Institutions: 31
Shares Held: 6,264,510

AMERICAN DEPOSITARY RECEIPTS: (Sponsored) Each American Depositary Receipt represents one ordinary share of par A$2.50.

DEPOSITARY BANK(S): The Bank of New York, (212) 815-2175

MICRO FOCUS GROUP PLC

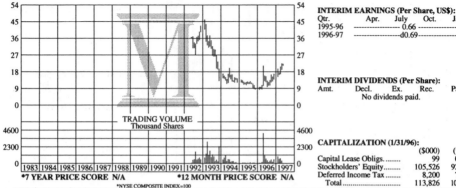

INTERIM EARNINGS (Per Share, US$):

Qtr.	Apr.	July	Oct.	Jan.
1995-96		0.66		
1996-97		d0.69		

INTERIM DIVIDENDS (Per Share):

Amt.	Decl.	Ex.	Rec.	Pay.
		No dividends paid.		

CAPITALIZATION (1/31/96):

	($000)	(%)
Capital Lease Obligs.	99	0.1
Stockholders' Equity	105,526	92.6
Deferred Income Tax	8,200	7.2
Total	113,826	100.0

TRADING VOLUME
Thousand Shares

1983 1984 1985 1986 1987 1988 1989 1990 1991 1992 1993 1994 1995 1996 1997

*7 YEAR PRICE SCORE N/A   *12 MONTH PRICE SCORE N/A

*NYSE COMPOSITE INDEX=100

RECENT DEVELOPMENTS: For the year ended 1/31/97, the Company reported a net loss of £7.3 million ($10.5 million) compared with a net loss of £6.5 million ($10.4 million) the year before. Net revenues declined 5.4% to £73.1 million ($115.4 million) from £77.3 million ($122.0 million). The results included restructuring charges of £5.2 million ($8.0 million) in 1996 and £6.7 million ($10.5 million) in 1995. The lower revenues and widened loss were attributed to poor results in the first half of the year. During the second half of the year, the Company initiated new cost cutting efforts that included reducing the workforce and lowering expense levels. On 3/26/97, the Company announced an agreement to acquire Millennium Limited, a privately held Year 2000 consulting company, for approximately £4.0 million ($6.4 million). Millennium Limited had revenues of approximately £1.0 million ($1.6 million) in 1996. The transaction is expected to be completed in the second quarter of 1997.

BUSINESS

MICRO FOCUS GROUP PLC is engaged in the design, development and marketing of compilers and programmer productivity tools for the development and deployment of business applications across a wide range of computer equipment from personal computer workstations to mainframe computers. These include tools for rightsizing, cross-platform development and deployment, client-server computing and offloading mainframe development, and maintenance of mission-critical applications. The Company sells its products directly to users of IBM PC's, Personal System/2's and clones, and to users of a wide range of UNIX computers including IBM RS6000/AIX. Some of the Company's products, principally those for the UNIX and Japanese markets, are also distributed through computer manufacturers for onward sale on their computer equipment. Product users include corporate data processing departments, independent software vendors, individual software developers and value added resellers.

ANNUAL EARNINGS

	1/31/96	1/31/95	1/31/96	1/31/95
	------US $------		------British £------	
Earnings Per Share	d0.66	0.51	d0.44	0.32

ANNUAL FINANCIAL DATA

RECORD OF EARNINGS (IN THOUSANDS):

	1/31/96	1/31/95	1/31/96	1/31/95
Total Revenues	116,157	142,827	77,258	89,885
Costs & Expenses	129,139	130,859	85,892	82,353
Operating Income	d12,981	11,968	d8,634	7,532
Income Bef Income Tax	d9,836	13,861	d6,542	8,723
Income Tax	cr108	6,567	cr72	4,133
Net Income	d9,728	7,294	d6,470	4,590
Average Shares Outstg	14,843	14,336	14,843	14,336

Note: 1995 results exclude a $10.5 mill. charge.

BALANCE SHEET (IN THOUSANDS):

Cash & Cash Equivalents	58,594	88,703	38,972	55,823
Receivables, Net	20,751	24,849	13,802	15,638
Inventories	2,562	2,835	1,704	1,784
Gross Property	68,537	60,479	45,585	38,061
Accumulated Depreciation	31,085	24,771	20,675	15,589
Capital Lease Obligs.	99	307	66	193
Stockholders' Equity	105,526	115,768	70,187	72,856
Total Assets	154,679	183,447	102,879	115,448
Total Current Assets	81,908	116,386	54,478	73,245
Total Current Liabilities	40,853	58,302	27,172	36,691
Net Working Capital	41,055	58,084	27,306	36,554
Year End Shs Outstg	15,144	14,364	15,144	14,364

STATISTICAL RECORD:

Return on Equity %	...	6.3		
Return on Assets %	...	4.0		
Operating Profit Margin %	...	8.4		
Net Profit Margin %	...	5.1		
Book Value Per Share	6.97	8.06		

Converted at 1996, US$1.5035= 1 British pound; 1995, US$1.5890= 1 British pound

OFFICERS:
B. Reynolds, Chmn.
P. A. O'Grady, C.E.O.
R. A. Connors, Secretary

INCORPORATED: UK, Mar., 1983

PRINCIPAL OFFICE: Speen Court, 7 Oxford Road, Newbury, Berkshire RG14 1PB United Kingdom

TELEPHONE NUMBER: +44 1635-32646

NO. OF EMPLOYEES: 708

ANNUAL MEETING: In Jun.

SHAREHOLDERS: N/A

INSTITUTIONAL HOLDINGS:
No. of Institutions: 9
Shares Held: 1,761,375

AMERICAN DEPOSITARY RECEIPTS: (Sponsored) Each American Depositary Receipt represents one ordinary share of par £0.10.

DEPOSITARY BANK(S): The Bank of New York, (212) 815-2175

MID-STATES PLC

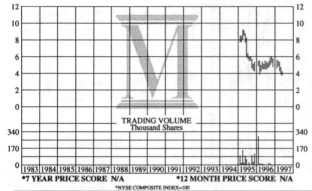

TRADING VOLUME
Thousand Shares

1983|1984|1985|1986|1987|1988|1989|1990|1991|1992|1993|1994|1995|1996|1997

*7 YEAR PRICE SCORE N/A   ***12 MONTH PRICE SCORE N/A**

*NYSE COMPOSITE INDEX=100

INTERIM EARNINGS (Per Share, £):

Qtr.	Mar.	June	Sept.	Dec.
1994	------------------ 0.10 ------------------			
1995	------------------d0.06------------------			

INTERIM DIVIDENDS (Per Share):

Amt.	Decl.	Ex.	Rec.	Pay.
0.027	...	9/06/96	9/10/96	10/21/96
0.028	...	4/25/97	4/29/97	8/04/97

Indicated div.: $0.03

CAPITALIZATION (12/31/95):

	($000)	(%)
Minority Interests.............	638	1.5
Stockholders' Equity........	40,954	98.5
Total	41,592	100.0

RECENT DEVELOPMENTS: For the year ended 12/31/95, the Company reported a net loss of £305,000 compared with a net profit of £5.0 million the year before. Results for the 1995 year-end period included £2.0 million in restructuring charges. Turnover rose 3.7% to £80.5 million from £77.6 million a year earlier. As a percentage of turnover, gross profit margin was 36.7% versus 37.5% the previous year.

Operating profit fell to £1.9 million from £6.8 million the year before. The Company incurred an additional £940,000 in operational expenses related to severance costs, store closing expenditures and disposal of properties. Net profit before taxes was £689,000 compared with £5.9 million a year earlier.

BUSINESS

MID-STATES PLC is engaged in the wholesale and retail distribution of automotive replacement parts in the United States. This activity is carried out through the Company's wholly-owned subsidiary, Mid-State Automotive Distributors, Inc. and its subsidiaries.

ANNUAL EARNINGS

	12/31/95	12/31/94	12/31/95	12/31/94
	--------------US $--------------		--------------British £--------------	
Earnings Per Share	d0.09	0.16	d0.06	0.10

ANNUAL FINANCIAL DATA

RECORD OF EARNINGS (IN THOUSANDS):

Total Revenues	124,957	121,403	80,462	77,574
Costs & Expenses	122,920	112,159	79,150	71,667
Operating Income	2,945	10,665	1,898	6,815
Income Bef Income Tax	1,070	9,273	689	5,925
Income Tax	1,559	1,377	1,004	880
Minority Interests	cr16	28	cr10	18
Net Income	d474	7,867	d305	5,027
Average Shares Outstg	52,596	50,416	52,596	50,416

BALANCE SHEET (IN THOUSANDS):

Cash & Cash Equivalents	152	94	98	60
Receivables, Net	15,951	16,123	10,271	10,302
Inventories	57,779	59,168	37,205	37,807
Gross Property	22,661	21,597	14,592	13,800
Accumulated Depreciation	7,765	6,057	5,000	3,870
Stockholders' Equity	40,954	40,843	26,371	26,098
Total Assets	88,779	90,925	57,166	58,099
Total Current Assets	73,882	75,384	47,574	48,169
Total Current Liabilities	18,468	34,394	11,892	21,977
Net Working Capital	55,414	40,990	35,682	26,192
Year End Shs Outstg	52,716	50,416	52,716	50,416

STATISTICAL RECORD:

Return on Equity %	...	19.26		
Return on Assets %	...	8.65		
Operating Profit Margin %	2.36	8.78		
Net Profit Margin %	...	6.48		
Book Value Per Share	0.78	0.81		

Converted at 1995, US$1.5530= 1 British pound; 1994, US$1.5650= 1 British pound

OFFICERS:
A. I. Wilkes, Non-Exec. Chmn.
W. D. Eberle, Deputy Chmn.
W. E. Cherry, Co-Chief Exec.
B. Keith, Jr., Co-Chief Exec.

INCORPORATED: United Kingdom

PRINCIPAL OFFICE: Masters House 107 Hammersmith Road London United Kingdom W14 0QH

TELEPHONE NUMBER: 0171-603 1515

NO. OF EMPLOYEES: 1,141 (avg.)

ANNUAL MEETING: In April

SHAREHOLDERS: N/A

INSTITUTIONAL HOLDINGS:
No. of Institutions: 1
Shares Held: 10,000

AMERICAN DEPOSITARY RECEIPTS: Each American Depositary Receipt represents 8 ordinary shares of par £0.10.

DEPOSITARY BANK(S): The Bank of New York, (212) 815-2175

NASDAQ SYMBOL MNRCY
Rec. Pr. 22¾

MINORCO

YIELD 3.7%
P/E RATIO 15.2

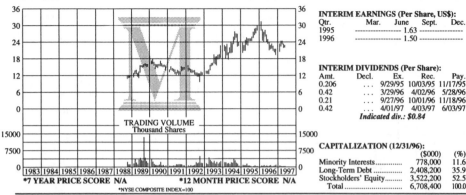

*7 YEAR PRICE SCORE N/A   *12 MONTH PRICE SCORE N/A

*NYSE COMPOSITE INDEX=100

INTERIM EARNINGS (Per Share, US$):

Qtr.	Mar.	June	Sept.	Dec.
1995	------------------	1.63	------------------	
1996	------------------	1.50	------------------	

INTERIM DIVIDENDS (Per Share):

Amt.	Decl.	Ex.	Rec.	Pay.
0.206	...	9/29/95	10/03/95	11/17/95
0.42	...	3/29/96	4/02/96	5/28/96
0.21	...	9/27/96	10/01/96	11/18/96
0.42	...	4/01/97	4/03/97	6/03/97

Indicated div.: $0.84

CAPITALIZATION (12/31/96):

	($000)	(%)
Minority Interests.............	778,000	11.6
Long-Term Debt.............	2,408,200	35.9
Stockholders' Equity.........	3,522,200	52.5
Total...............................	6,708,400	100.0

RECENT DEVELOPMENTS: For the year ended 12/31/96, net earnings were $335.7 million compared with $365.0 million the year before. Results for the recent year-end period included $44.3 million in restructuring and impairment charges relating to the Company's mining operations at Hudson Bay Mining and Smelting Co., Ltd. and Mineracao Morro Velho S.A., and the write-down of certain cost accounted investments. These charges were partially offset by gains from a reduction in the Company's holding in Aylesford Newsprint Holdings Ltd. and the Frantschach A.G. group, and from the sale of certain of Minorco's investments. Sales increased 18.0% to $5.01 billion from $4.25 billion a year earlier. Operating earnings were $604.7 million versus $599.2 million the previous year.

BUSINESS

MINORCO is the parent company of a natural resource group engaged in the mining and processing of gold, base metals, and industrial minerals such as copper, nickel and zinc; the manufacture of paper and packaging; and the distribution of agricultural products. The Company has quarry operations that extract sand, gravel, and limestone for industrial use (i.e. ready-mix concrete, hydrated lime, ground lime, and screened lime). Minorco is also a manufacturer of nitrogen fertilizers, feed additives, ammonia, and methanol. Through its subsidiaries, Minorco is engaged in the manufacture of automotive exhaust emission catalysts, catalytic control systems for industrial companies; chemicals, pharmaceutical compounds, and electronic materials; and the marketing and fabrication of precious materials, pigments, additives, thickeners, and absorbents for the plastics, paper, and paint industries.

ANNUAL EARNINGS

	12/31/96	12/31/95	12/31/94	6/30/93	6/30/92	6/30/91
	----------------------------US $----------------------------					
Earnings Per Share	1.50	1.63	0.86	1.48	1.50	1.32

ANNUAL FINANCIAL DATA

RECORD OF EARNINGS (IN MILLIONS):

	12/31/96	12/31/95	12/31/94	6/30/93	6/30/92	6/30/91
Total Revenues	5,014	4,247	4,636	2,776	1,667	771
Costs & Expenses	4,409	3,648	4,385	2,697	1,634	728
Operating Income	605	599	251	79	32	43
Income Bef Income Tax	600	665	220	248	208	211
Income Tax	127	125	96	64	37	29
Eq. Earnings in Affils.	108	121	135	92	95	64
Minority Interests	137	175	66	24	10	22
Net Income	336	365	193	252	256	224

BALANCE SHEET (IN MILLIONS):

Cash & Cash Equivalents	1,965	1,428	1,633	1,873	1,778	1,890
Receivables, Net	777	692	585	667	416	410
Inventories	878	808	620	501	266	257
Gross Property	6,280	5,671	4,241	3,066	1,277	924
Accumulated Depreciation	2,232	1,964	1,792	1,401	481	410
Long-Term Debt	2,408	2,238	1,661	1,049	407	381
Stockholders' Equity	3,522	3,387	3,113	3,707	2,870	2,809
Total Assets	8,667	7,940	6,287	5,921	4,132	3,870
Total Current Assets	3,620	2,928	2,838	3,042	2,459	2,557
Total Current Liabilities	869	918	783	689	699	545
Net Working Capital	2,751	2,011	2,055	2,352	1,760	2,011
Year End Shs Outstg (000)	225,558	225,547	225,318	170,312	170,312	170,312

STATISTICAL RECORD:

Return on Equity %	8.40	10.71	6.20	6.80	8.91	7.99
Return on Assets %	3.41	4.57	3.07	4.25	6.19	5.80
Operating Profit Margin %	12.07	14.10	5.41	2.85	1.92	5.58
Net Profit Margin %	6.70	8.59	4.16	9.08	15.36	29.05
Book Value Per Share	15.62	15.02	13.82	21.77	16.85	16.49

OFFICERS:
J. O. Thompson, Chmn.
H. R. Slack, Pres. & C.E.O.
P. G. Whitcutt, V.P.-Corp. Fin.
A. R. Attwood, Treas.

INCORPORATED: Sept., 1987

PRINCIPAL OFFICE: 9, rue Sainte Zithe L-2763 Luxembourg City Luxembourg

TELEPHONE NUMBER: (352) 404 110-1

NO. OF EMPLOYEES: 19,891

ANNUAL MEETING: In May

SHAREHOLDERS: N/A

INSTITUTIONAL HOLDINGS:
No. of Institutions: 34
Shares Held: 4,275,156

**AMERICAN DEPOSITARY
RECEIPTS:** (Sponsored) Each American Depositary Receipt represents one ordinary share of par US$1.40.

DEPOSITARY BANK(S): The Bank of New York, (212) 815-2175; J.P. Morgan, (212) 648-3206

MITSUI & COMPANY, LTD.

YIELD 0.71
P/E RATIO 43.09

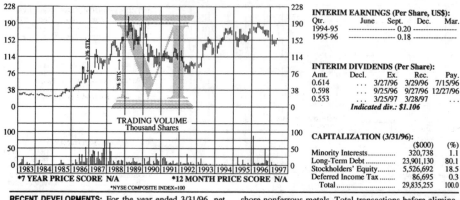

INTERIM EARNINGS (Per Share, US$):

Qtr.	June	Sept.	Dec.	Mar.
1994-95	-----	0.20	-----	-----
1995-96	-----	0.18	-----	-----

INTERIM DIVIDENDS (Per Share):

Amt.	Decl.	Ex.	Rec.	Pay.
0.614	...	3/27/96	3/29/96	7/15/96
0.598	...	9/25/96	9/27/96	12/27/96
0.553	...	3/25/97	3/28/97	...

Indicated div.: $1.106

CAPITALIZATION (3/31/96):

	($000)	(%)
Minority Interests	320,738	1.1
Long-Term Debt	23,901,130	80.1
Stockholders' Equity	5,526,692	18.5
Deferred Income Tax	86,695	0.3
Total	29,835,255	100.0

RECENT DEVELOPMENTS: For the year ended 3/31/96, net income increased 16.0% to ¥30,383 million compared with ¥26,203 million in 1995. Revenue - gross trading profit - advanced 1.5% to ¥537,641 million. The total trading transactions rose 2.8% to ¥17,520 billion due to, according to the Co., increases in offshore energy transactions and chemicals in all types of business that were partially offset by decreases in export machinery transactions and in off- shore nonferrous metals. Total transactions before eliminations decreased 0.9% to ¥14,162 billion. In North America, total trading rose 8.1% to ¥2,017 billion, reflecting stable economic growth in the United States. Transactions in Europe increased 11.6% to ¥3,662 billion, due mainly to higher energy transactions. Transactions in Asia and Oceania advanced 13.2% to ¥955 billion, due primarily to an increase in energy business in Asia.

BUSINESS

MITSUI & COMPANY, LTD. is engaged in the provision of services to facilitate trade and promote the development of commerce and industry around the world. The Company's main services include assistance in basic trading activities, arranging transportation and documentation procedures, distribution in Japan and overseas, provision of finance for trade transactions, and supplying information on market conditions, prices and business opportunities worldwide. The Company trades the following products: (1) Iron ore, nonferrous metals, and other raw metals. (2) Coals, petroleum, natural gases, and their by-products. (3) Various machinery (measuring and medical equipment included), telecommunication equipment, anti-pollution devices, vehicles, vessels, airplanes, and rockets. (4) Various chemicals, salt, fertilizers, high-pressured gases, drugs, and poisons. (5) Foods, sugar, oil, processed foods, and alcohols. (6) Various fibers and furs. (7) Lumbers, cement, and construction materials. (8) Rubber, paper pulp, paper, and tobacco.

ANNUAL EARNINGS

	3/31/96	3/31/95	3/31/96	3/31/95
	US $		Yen	
Earnings Per Share	0.18	0.20	19.56	16.87

ANNUAL FINANCIAL DATA

RECORD OF EARNINGS (IN MILLIONS):

Total Revenues	5,000	6,144	537,641	529,644
Costs & Expenses	4,306	5,466	463,009	471,187
Operating Income	694	678	74,632	58,457
Income Bef Income Tax	582	583	62,581	50,264
Income Tax	337	343	36,228	29,531
Eq. Earnings in Affils.	38	63	4,045	5,470
Net Income	283	304	30,383	26,203

BALANCE SHEET (IN MILLIONS):

Cash & Cash Equivalents	12,110	16,413	1,302,201	1,414,916
Receivables, Net	23,949	27,573	2,575,186	2,297,787
Inventories	4,361	5,637	468,896	485,914
Gross Property	7,404	8,750	796,110	754,353
Accumulated Depreciation	2,458	2,812	264,337	242,388
Long-Term Debt	23,901	29,930	2,570,014	2,580,198
Stockholders' Equity	5,527	6,642	594,268	572,549
Total Assets	68,434	83,077	7,358,484	7,161,805
Total Current Assets	43,926	52,947	4,723,195	4,564,372
Total Current Liabilities	37,728	45,099	4,056,827	3,887,802
Net Working Capital	6,197	7,848	666,368	676,570
Year End Shs Outstg	1,553	1,553	1,553	1,553

STATISTICAL RECORD:

Return on Equity %	5.12	4.58		
Return on Assets %	0.41	0.37		
Operating Profit Margin %	13.88	11.04		
Net Profit Margin %	5.66	4.95		
Book Value Per Share	3.56	4.28		

Converted at 1996, US$0.0093= 1 Japanese Yen; 1995, US$0.0116= 1 Japanese Yen

OFFICERS:
N. Kumagai, Chmn.
S. Ueshima, Pres. & C.E.O.

INCORPORATED: Jul., 1947

PRINCIPAL OFFICE: 2-1, Ohtemachi 1-chome Chiyoda-ku Tokyo Japan

TELEPHONE NUMBER: 81 (3) 3285-1111

NO. OF EMPLOYEES: 11,378

ANNUAL MEETING: In Jun.

SHAREHOLDERS: 137,922

INSTITUTIONAL HOLDINGS:
No. of Institutions: 5
Shares Held: 204,141

AMERICAN DEPOSITARY RECEIPTS: Each American Depositary Receipt represents twenty common shares of par ¥50.

DEPOSITARY BANK(S): Citibank N.A., (212) 657-7800

MULTICANAL PARTICIPACOES, S.A

YIELD ...
P/E RATIO ...

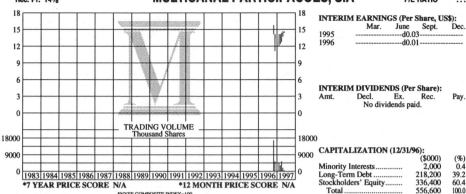

INTERIM EARNINGS (Per Share, US$):

	Mar.	June	Sept.	Dec.
1995		d0.03		
1996		d0.01		

INTERIM DIVIDENDS (Per Share):

Amt.	Decl.	Ex.	Rec.	Pay.
	No dividends paid.			

CAPITALIZATION (12/31/96):

	($000)	(%)
Minority Interests	2,000	0.4
Long-Term Debt	218,200	39.2
Stockholders' Equity	336,400	60.4
Total	556,600	100.0

*7 YEAR PRICE SCORE N/A   ***12 MONTH PRICE SCORE N/A**

*NYSE COMPOSITE INDEX=100

RECENT DEVELOPMENTS: For the year ended 12/31/96, equity adjusted EBITDA reached $67.5 million compared with $24.2 million in the corresponding period a year earlier. Net revenues increased 123% to $204.4 million versus $91.6 million in 1995. Equity adjusted EBITDA benefited from subscriber growth of 127% to 683,400 equity subscribers. The Company built more than 3,827 miles of network and ended the year passing 1.75 million equity homes. In addition, 294,800 new equity subscribers were connected, essentially doubling the size of the Company. At the end of the year, the basic programming package accounted for 21% of its subscriber base, while the advance package represented 79%. Revenue per subscriber remained virtually flat at $43.30 for 1996 versus $44.00 in 1995. The figures used in comparison are based on US GAAP and pro forma to reflect the Multicanal reorganization.

BUSINESS

MULTICANAL PARTICIPACOES, S.A. is a holding company. Through its subsidiaries and associated companies, MPARY is engaged in cable television broadcasting on a subscription or fee basis, with ownership interests in 13 cable television systems serving 17 cities located primarily in the Southeast and Central-West regions of Brazil. Cable television channels provided include: CNN International(TM), Globo News(TM), Discovery Channel - Brasil(TM), MTV(TM), Warner Channel(TM), Sony Entertainment Television(TM), USA Channel(TM), Cartoon Network(TM), Tele Cine(TM), TNT(TM), Shoptime(TM), Multishow(TM), SPORTV ESPN International(TM) and GNT Globosat(TM).

ANNUAL EARNINGS

	12/31/96	12/31/95	12/31/96	12/31/95
	---US $---		---Reais---	
Earnings Per Share	d0.01	d0.03	d0.01	d0.03

ANNUAL FINANCIAL DATA

RECORD OF EARNINGS (IN THOUSANDS):				
Total Revenues	223,900	101,900	232,654	99,047
Costs & Expenses	164,600	91,400	171,036	88,841
Depreciation & Amort	35,400	19,600	36,784	19,051
Operating Income	4,400	d19,400	4,572	18,857
Income Bef Income Tax	d18,400	d25,800	d19,119	d25,078
Income Tax	cr4,300	cr1,800	cr4,468	cr1,750
Minority Interests	cr1,200	4,000	cr1,247	3,888
Net Income	d12,900	d28,000	d13,404	d27,216
Avg End Shs Outstg (000)	934,636	884,367	934,636	884,367
BALANCE SHEET (IN THOUSANDS):				
Cash & Cash Equivalents	135,600	2,300	140,902	2,236
Receivables, Net	54,800	17,100	56,943	16,621
Gross Property	336,100	167,000	349,242	162,324
Accumulated Depreciation	38,200	12,600	39,694	12,247
Long-Term Debt	218,200	37,500	226,732	36,450
Stockholders' Equity	336,400	74,300	349,553	72,220
Total Assets	684,000	265,800	710,744	258,358
Total Current Assets	198,000	22,200	205,742	21,578
Total Current Liabilities	71,900	115,400	74,711	112,169
Net Working Capital	126,100	d93,200	131,031	d90,590
STATISTICAL RECORD:				
Return on Equity %	...	...		
Return on Assets %	...	...		
Operating Profit Margin %	...	...		
Net Profit Margin %	2.0	...		
Book Value Per Share	0.36	0.08		

Converted at 1996, US$0.9624= 1 Brazilian Reais; 1995, US$1.0288= 1 Brazilian Reais

OFFICERS:
A. Dias Leite Neto, Pres.
L. C. de Souza Alves, Exec. V.P.
R. Waddington, C.F.O.
J. F. de Araujo Lima Neto

INCORPORATED: 1994

PRINCIPAL OFFICE: Av. Rio Branco 1-6 andar Rio de Janeiro Brazil

TELEPHONE NUMBER: 21-276-6000

NO. OF EMPLOYEES: 954

ANNUAL MEETING: N/A

SHAREHOLDERS: N/A

INSTITUTIONAL HOLDINGS:
No. of Institutions: 22
Shares Held: 6,432,512

AMERICAN DEPOSITARY RECEIPTS: Each American Depositary Share represents 10 non-voting preferred shares of no par.

DEPOSITARY BANK(S): The Bank of New York, (212) 815-2175

NEC CORPORATION

YIELD 0.6%
P/E RATIO 30.0

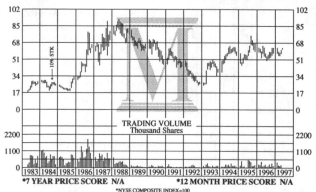

TRADING VOLUME
Thousand Shares

*7 YEAR PRICE SCORE N/A   *12 MONTH PRICE SCORE N/A

INTERIM EARNINGS (Per Share, US$):

1996	0.42
1997	0.42

INTERIM DIVIDENDS (Per Share):

Amt.	Decl.	Ex.	Rec.	Pay.
0.209	...	9/27/95	9/28/95	12/18/95
0.232	...	3/26/96	3/28/96	7/11/96
0.206	...	9/25	9/27	12/23
0.177	...	3/25/97	3/28/97	...

Indicated div.: $0.354

CAPITALIZATION (3/31/97):

	($000)	(%)
Long-Term Debt	11,115,000	56.3
Minority Interest	529	2.7
Stockholders' Equity	8,092,000	41.0
Total	19,736,000	100.0

RECENT DEVELOPMENTS: For the fiscal year ended 3/31/97, net income climbed 18.7% to Y91.6 billion from Y77.2 billion the year before. Total revenues increased 12.5% to Y4,948.4 billion from Y4,397.2 billion. Income before income taxes declined 19.9% to Y121.2 billion as nonoperating expenses jumped 41.1% to Y178.9 billion. The improved sales were attributed to higher domestic sales of communication systems and equipment. Sales of communi- cations systems and equipment jumped 37.5% to Y1,686.6 billion, led by sales of mobile communications and transmission systems in Japan. Sales of computers and industrial electronic systems rose 7.0% to Y2,078.5 billion, reflecting higher sales of PC's. Sales of electron devices slipped 6.8% to Y963.2 billion, resulting from lower prices for memory devices. Net income also benefited from increased earnings from minority interests.

BUSINESS

NEC CORPORATION is an international supplier of electronic products that comprise primarily communications systems and equipment, computers and industrial electronic systems, and electron devices. All of the Company's activities are based on its synergistic business concept of C&C, the integration of computers and communications. NEC operates in Japan through a network of 128 consolidated subsidiaries, 62 manufacturing plants and more than 430 sales offices. Internationally, the Company operates 102 subsidiaries and affiliates in 31 countries and operates 45 plants in 19 countries, along with marketing, services and research and development facilities in 30 countries.

ANNUAL EARNINGS

	3/31/97	3/31/96	3/31/97	3/31/96
	US $		Yen	
Earnings Per Share	0.42	0.42	51.78	45.21

ANNUAL FINANCIAL DATA

RECORD OF EARNINGS (IN MILLIONS):

Total Revenues	39,907	41,174	4,948,437	4,427,272
Costs & Expenses	38,425	40,332	4,760,656	4,275,954
Operating Income	1,482	2,056	187,781	221,111
Income Bef Income Tax	978	1,422	121,222	151,318
Income Tax	201	710	24,900	76,376
Eq. Earnings in Affils.	2	58	277	6,253
Minority Interests	40	37	5,018	4,029
Net Income	739	717	91,581	77,166

BALANCE SHEET (IN MILLIONS):

Cash & Cash Equivalents	3,708	4,465	459,796	480,119
Receivables, Net	9,123	10,620	1,131,258	1,141,936
Inventories	7,588	9,713	940,867	1,044,368
Net Property	10,811	11,335	1,340,596	1,218,817
Long-Term Debt	11,115	9,340	1,378,265	1,004,350
Stockholders' Equity	8,092	8,173	1,003,371	878,852
Total Assets	38,703	43,553	4,799,165	4,683,120
Total Current Assets	21,186	25,629	2,627,033	2,755,812
Total Current Liabilities	18,967	22,431	2,351,967	2,411,980
Net Working Capital	2,219	3,198	275,066	343,832
Year End Shs Outstg (000)	1,565,639	1,546,187	1,565,639	1,546,187

STATISTICAL RECORD:

Return on Equity %	9.13	8.77		
Return on Assets %	1.91	1.65		
Operating Profit Margin %	3.71	4.99		
Net Profit Margin %	1.85	1.74		
Book Value Per Share	5.19	5.29		

Converted at 1997, US$0.0081= 1 Japanese Yen; 1996, US$0.0093= 1 Japanese Yen

OFFICERS:
T. Sekimoto, Chmn.
H. Kaneko, Pres.
S. Yokoyama, Sr. Exec. V.P.
H. Sasaki, Sr. Exec. V.P.

INCORPORATED: Japan, July, 1899

PRINCIPAL OFFICE: 7-1, Shiba 5-chome Minato-ku Tokyo Japan

TELEPHONE NUMBER: (03) 3798-6531

NO. OF EMPLOYEES: 152,719

ANNUAL MEETING: In Jun.

SHAREHOLDERS: N/A

INSTITUTIONAL HOLDINGS:
No. of Institutions: 23
Shares Held: 1,124,104

AMERICAN DEPOSITARY RECEIPTS: Each American Depositary Receipt represents 5 common shares of par Y50. Issuable by The Bank of New York, New York, Depositary and Paying Agent. ADR's split 5-for-1 on Oct. 1, 1982

DEPOSITARY BANK(S): The Bank of New York, (212) 815-2175

NERA AS

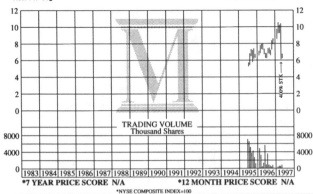

*7 YEAR PRICE SCORE N/A   *12 MONTH PRICE SCORE N/A

*NYSE COMPOSITE INDEX=100

INTERIM EARNINGS (Per Share, US$):

1995	------------------ 0.30 ------------------
1996	------------------ 0.24 ------------------

INTERIM DIVIDENDS (Per Share):

Amt.	Decl.	Ex.	Rec.	Pay.
0.304	...	5/16/96	5/20/96	6/14/96
400% Stk	...	4/25/97	4/23/97	4/24/97
0.292	...	4/21	4/23	5/27

Indicated div.: $0.292

CAPITALIZATION (12/31/96):

	($000)	(%)
Long-Term Debt	76,059	37.8
Stockholders' Equity.........	117,480	58.5
Deferred Income Tax	7,438	3.7
Total	200,977	100.0

RECENT DEVELOPMENTS: For the quarter ended 3/31/97, net income was NOK29.1 million, up slightly from NOK19.9 million in the year-earlier period. Sales declined 13.9% to NOK541.0 million from NOK628.0 million. Higher sales in the mobile satellite communications segment were offset by lower sales for transmission systems. The operating margin before research and development expenses was 14.3% compared with 13.7% in the same period of 1996. Operating income was NOK29.8 million, down 15.6% from NOK35.3 million. However, financial expenses fell to NOK3.4 million from NOK8.8 million, which boosted earnings. During the quarter, the Company received new orders totaling NOK684.0 million, down from 8.3% from NOK746.0 million in the same period of 1996. The decline in orders reflected lower orders for transmission systems and special telecommunications systems, while orders for mobile satellite telecommunications was higher than last year.

BUSINESS

NERA AS is the parent company of a group primarily engaged in the design, development, manufacture and marketing of wireless telecommunications equipment and systems and related services. The Company's products include mobile satellite terminals, land earth stations, global satellite communication networks, microwave radio relay systems, telephone handsets, personal security alarms, and telecommunications management networks. The Company also provides airtime billing services, principally for the International Maritime Satellite Organization (INMARSAT). Under the trade name "Contec," Nera AS provides engineering consultancy services, such as software and hardware electronic design, and the design of test procedures for electronic products. Under the trade name "Informema," the Company provides profiling and image development, including preparation of manuals, graphics and logos.

ANNUAL EARNINGS

	12/31/96	12/31/95	12/31/96	12/31/95
	------------US $------------		------------NOK------------	
Earnings Per Share	0.24	0.30	1.55	1.92

400% stk. div. 4/24/97

ANNUAL FINANCIAL DATA

RECORD OF EARNINGS (IN THOUSANDS):

Total Revenues	408,134	374,234	2,629,727	2,367,072
Costs & Expenses	369,281	336,445	2,379,394	2,128,053
Depreciation & Amort	12,190	8,855	78,542	56,010
Operating Income	26,660	28,934	171,791	183,009
Income Bef Income Tax	21,753	24,292	140,159	153,653
Income Tax	5,941	5,847	38,280	36,922
Net Income	15,812	18,445	101,879	116,731
Average Shares Outstg	65,750	60,850	65,750	60,850

BALANCE SHEET (IN THOUSANDS):

Cash & Cash Equivalents	16,930	20,529	109,083	129,851
Receivables, Net	103,562	78,777	667,282	498,271
Inventories	87,631	85,648	564,633	541,732
Gross Property	73,639	77,649	472,865	491,138
Accumulated Depreciation	28,121	27,686	181,193	175,118
Long-Term Debt	76,059	43,183	490,068	273,138
Stockholders' Equity	117,480	107,930	756,957	682,670
Total Assets	328,237	280,534	2,114,926	1,774,408
Total Current Assets	257,804	216,654	1,661,110	1,370,360
Total Current Liabilities	127,260	122,071	819,977	772,115
Net Working Capital	130,544	94,583	841,133	598,245
Year End Shs Outstg	65,740	65,740	65,740	65,740

STATISTICAL RECORD:

Return on Equity %	68.37	65.04
Return on Assets %	24.47	25.02
Operating Profit Margin %	22.34	21.56
Net Profit Margin %	19.68	18.76
Book Value Per Share	1.79	1.64

Converted at 1996, US$0.1552= 1 Norwegian Krone; 1995, US$0.1581= 1 Norwegian Krone

OFFICERS:
F. Botnevik, Exec. Chmn.
A. Birkland, Pres.
M. L. Braime, Managing Dir.

INCORPORATED: Norway, 1987

PRINCIPAL OFFICE: Kokstadveien 23
Kokstad Norway

TELEPHONE NUMBER: +45-55-22-5100

NO. OF EMPLOYEES: 2,094

ANNUAL MEETING: N/A

SHAREHOLDERS: 1,200 (approx.)

INSTITUTIONAL HOLDINGS:
No. of Institutions: 11
Shares Held: 1,084,130 (adj.)

AMERICAN DEPOSITARY RECEIPTS: Each American Depository Receipt represents one ordinary share of par NOK10.

DEPOSITARY BANK(S): The Bank of New York, (212) 815-2175

NICE-SYSTEMS LIMITED

YIELD ...
P/E RATIO 33.04

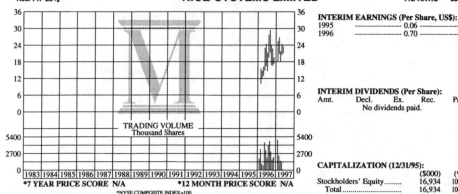

*7 YEAR PRICE SCORE N/A   *12 MONTH PRICE SCORE N/A
*NYSE COMPOSITE INDEX=100

INTERIM EARNINGS (Per Share, US$):
1995 ------------------ 0.06 ------------------
1996 ------------------ 0.70 ------------------

INTERIM DIVIDENDS (Per Share):

Amt.	Decl.	Ex.	Rec.	Pay.
		No dividends paid.		

CAPITALIZATION (12/31/95):

	($000)	(%)
Stockholders' Equity	16,934	100.0
Total	16,934	100.0

RECENT DEVELOPMENTS: For the year ended 12/31/96, net income soared to US$5.2 million from US$318,000 in 1995. Earnings for 1996 and 1995 included equity in losses of an affiliate of US$283,000 and US$47,000, respectively. Revenues advanced 89.7% to US$39.8 million from US$21.0 million a year earlier. Gross profit as a percentage of revenues grew to 55.0% from 47.4% the year before. NICEY reported operating income of US$4.3 million versus a loss of US$131,000 the prior year. For the quarter ended 12/31/96, net income climbed to US$1.9 million from US$481,000 in the same prior-year period. Revenues increased 87.7% to US$11.6 million from US$6.2 million a year earlier. Gross profit as a percentage of revenues rose to 55.6% from 49.6% the year before. Operating income totaled US$1.5 million versus US$197,000 the prior year.

BUSINESS

NICE SYSTEMS LTD. is engaged in the development, design, manufacture, marketing and servicing of digital recording and retrieval systems, which are known as voice logging systems, that simultaneously record and monitor communications from multiple channels and provide data archiving and retrieval features.

ANNUAL EARNINGS

	12/31/95	12/31/94	12/31/95	12/31/94
	--------------US $------------		--------------NIS------------	
Earnings Per Share	0.06	d0.53	0.19	d1.60

ANNUAL FINANCIAL DATA

RECORD OF EARNINGS (IN THOUSANDS):

	12/31/95	12/31/94	12/31/95	12/31/94
Total Revenues	20,993	8,997	66,078	27,148
Costs & Expenses	21,124	11,408	66,490	34,424
Operating Income	d131	d2,411	d412	d7,275
Income Bef Income Tax	539	d2,389	1,697	d7,209
Income Tax	201	218	633	658
Eq. Earnings in Affils.	d47	d189	d148	d570
Minority Interests	cr27	cr49	cr85	cr148
Net Income	318	d2,747	1,001	d8,289
Income from Disc. Ops.	...	19,461	...	58,724
Average Shares Outstg	5,277	5,209	5,277	5,209

BALANCE SHEET (IN THOUSANDS):

Cash & Cash Equivalents	8,147	13,324	25,644	40,205
Receivables, Net	7,886	3,691	24,822	11,138
Inventories	2,285	1,108	7,192	3,343
Gross Property	4,946	3,353	15,568	10,118
Accumulated Depreciation	1,335	948	4,202	2,861
Stockholders' Equity	16,934	20,651	53,302	62,314
Total Assets	23,559	24,415	74,155	73,672
Total Current Assets	18,318	18,123	57,658	54,686
Total Current Liabilities	5,229	2,749	16,459	8,295
Net Working Capital	13,089	15,374	41,199	46,391
Year End Shs Outstg	5,227	5,191	5,227	5,191

STATISTICAL RECORD:

Return on Equity %	1.88	...		
Return on Assets %	1.35	...		
Operating Profit Margin %	...	...		
Net Profit Margin %	1.51	...		
Book Value Per Share	3.24	3.98		

Converted at 1995, US$0.3177= 1 New Israeli Shekel; 1994, US$0.3314= 1 New Israel Shekel

OFFICERS:
D. Arzi, Chmn.
B. Levin, Pres.
H. Miron, C.F.O. & V.P.

INCORPORATED: Israel, 1986

PRINCIPAL OFFICE: Atidim Industrial Park, Neveh Sharett, P.O. Box 58070, Tel-Aviv Israel 61580

TELEPHONE NUMBER: 972-3-645-3700

NO. OF EMPLOYEES: N/A

ANNUAL MEETING: N/A

SHAREHOLDERS: N/A

INSTITUTIONAL HOLDINGS:
No. of Institutions: 24
Shares Held: 1,783,944

AMERICAN DEPOSITARY RECEIPTS: Each American Depositary Receipt represents one ordinary share of par value NIS1.00.

DEPOSITARY BANK(S): The Bank of New York, (212) 815-2175

NISSAN MOTOR CO., LTD.

YIELD ...
P/E RATIO ...

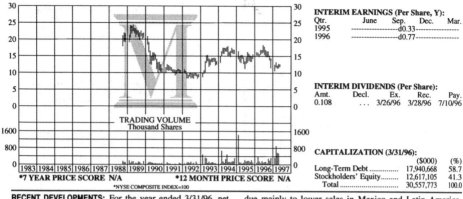

*7 YEAR PRICE SCORE N/A   *12 MONTH PRICE SCORE N/A
*NYSE COMPOSITE INDEX=100

INTERIM EARNINGS (Per Share, Y):

Qtr.	June	Sep.	Dec.	Mar.
1995	------------------d0.33------------------			
1996	------------------d0.77------------------			

INTERIM DIVIDENDS (Per Share):

Amt.	Decl.	Ex.	Rec.	Pay.
0.108	...	3/26/96	3/28/96	7/10/96

CAPITALIZATION (3/31/96):

	($000)	(%)
Long-Term Debt	17,940,668	58.7
Stockholders' Equity........	12,617,105	41.3
Total	30,557,773	100.0

RECENT DEVELOPMENTS: For the year ended 3/31/96, net loss was Y 88,418 million compared with a loss of Y 166,054 million in the previous year. Net sales rose 3.5% to Y 6,039,107 million. Despite the increase in net sales, Nissan's consolidated unit sales of vehicles was down 1.1% to 2.7 million units. Supported by new model introductions, domestic unit volume sales increased 7.8% to 1.15 million. Overseas unit sales decreased 6.8% to 1.53 million units due mainly to lower sales in Mexico and Latin America. U.S. unit sales decreased by 1.9% as overall market demand declined. In Europe, unit sales were up 4 thousand units in spite of severe competition. Operating income reached Y 43,235 million compared with a loss of Y 102,717 million a year ago. In 1996, Nissan reduced its long-term debt levels to Y 1,929,104 million from Y 2,209,829 million in 1995.

BUSINESS

NISSAN MOTOR COMPANY LTD. is the parent company of a group engaged in the vehicle design, research and development, production, parts procurement, marketing, financing and sale of Nissan passenger cars, commercial vehicles, and related components. The Company also manufactures aerospace equipment, textile machinery, engine-driven and battery-driven forklifts, industrial machinery, forklift trucks, boats and marine equipment.

ANNUAL EARNINGS

	3/31/96	3/31/95	3/31/96	3/31/95
	----------US $----------		----------Yen----------	
Earnings Per Share	d0.33	d0.77	d35.19	d66.09

ANNUAL FINANCIAL DATA

RECORD OF EARNINGS (IN MILLIONS):

	3/31/96	3/31/95	3/31/96	3/31/95
Total Revenues	56,164	67,676	6,039,107	5,834,123
Costs & Expenses	55,762	68,867	5,995,872	5,936,840
Operating Income	402	d1,192	43,235	d102,717
Income Bef Income Tax	d861	d2,470	d92,534	d212,929
Income Tax	116	34	12,504	2,901
Eq. Earnings in Affils.	52	192	5,540	16,592
Net Income	d822	d1,926	d88,418	d166,054

BALANCE SHEET (IN MILLIONS):

Cash & Cash Equivalents	5,244	6,904	563,889	595,191
Receivables, Net	12,637	9,113	1,358,786	785,589
Inventories	6,674	8,014	717,691	690,880
Gross Property	56,090	72,456	6,031,159	6,246,182
Accumulated Depreciation	26,983	33,702	2,901,371	2,905,308
Long-Term Debt	17,941	25,634	1,929,104	2,209,829
Stockholders' Equity	12,617	16,577	1,356,678	1,429,065
Total Assets	65,952	83,438	7,091,594	7,192,914
Total Current Assets	28,280	32,861	3,040,857	2,832,819
Total Current Liabilities	32,983	38,159	3,546,606	3,289,546
Net Working Capital	d4,703	d5,298	d505,749	d456,727
Year End Shs Outstg (000)	2,512,828	2,512,712	2,512,828	2,512,712

STATISTICAL RECORD:

Return on Equity %	...	...		
Return on Assets %	...	...		
Operating Profit Margin %	0.72	...		
Net Profit Margin %	...	...		
Book Value Per Share	5.02	6.60		

Converted at 1996, US$0.0093= 1 Japanese Yen; 1995, US$0.0116= 1 Japanese Yen

OFFICERS:
Y. Tsuji, Chmn.
Y. Hanawa, Pres.

INCORPORATED: Dec., 1933

PRINCIPAL OFFICE: 17-1, Ginza 6-chome
Chuo-ku, Tokyo Japan

TELEPHONE NUMBER: (03) 3543-3523
NO. OF EMPLOYEES: 139,856
ANNUAL MEETING: In June
SHAREHOLDERS: 109,083
INSTITUTIONAL HOLDINGS:
No. of Institutions: 13
Shares Held: 3,920,165
AMERICAN DEPOSITARY RECEIPTS: (Sponsored) Each Amer. Depos.
Receipt rep. 2 com shs.

DEPOSITARY BANK(S): The Bank of New York, (212) 815-2175; J.P. Morgan, (212) 648-3206

NORD PACIFIC LIMITED

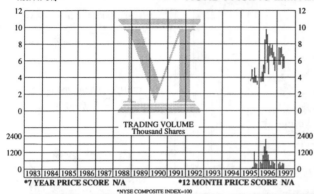

INTERIM EARNINGS (Per Share, US$):

Qtr.	Mar.	June	Sept.	Dec.
1995	------------------	0.12	------------------	
1996	------------------	0.06	------------------	
1997	Nil	...	...	...

INTERIM DIVIDENDS (Per Share):

Amt.	Decl.	Ex.	Rec.	Pay.
		No dividends paid.		

TRADING VOLUME
Thousand Shares

*7 YEAR PRICE SCORE N/A   *12 MONTH PRICE SCORE N/A

*NYSE COMPOSITE INDEX=100

CAPITALIZATION (12/31/96):

	($000)	(%)
Long-Term Debt	3,334	10.7
Stockholders' Equity........	24,209	77.4
Deferred Income Tax	3,740	12.0
Total	31,283	100.0

RECENT DEVELOPMENTS: For the year ended 12/31/96, net income dropped 44.1% to US$617,000 from US$1.1 million in 1995. Earnings for 1996 included a loss of US$304,000 related to copper contracts, as well as a gain of US$383,000 related to forward currency exchange. Earnings for 1995 included a loss of US$657,000 related to forward currency exchange. Revenues rose 14.9% to US$16.2 million from US$14.1 million the year before. Operating earnings grew 12.1% to US$3.4 million from US$3.0 million in 1995, primarily due to an increase in production levels from NORPY's join-venture share of the Girilambone copper mine in Australia. For the quarter ended 12/31/96, NORPY reported net income of US$278,000 versus a net loss of US$298,000 in the same prior-year period, due to increased production of copper. Earnings for 1996 included a gain of US$74,000 related to copper contracts. Revenues advanced 49.8% to US$4.7 million from US$3.2 million in 1995.

BUSINESS

NORD PACIFIC LIMITED is engaged in the production of copper and the exploration for and development of base and precious metals and strategic minerals, including gold, silver, nickel and cobalt in Australia and Papau New Guinea, Mexico, Canada, and the United States.

ANNUAL EARNINGS

	12/31/96	12/31/95	12/31/94	12/31/93	12/31/92	12/31/91	12/31/90
				US $			
Earnings Per Share	0.06	0.12	0.43	d0.06	d0.45	d3.15	d14.45

Note: 1-for-5 reverse stk. split, 3/10/97.

ANNUAL FINANCIAL DATA

RECORD OF EARNINGS (IN THOUSANDS):

	12/31/96	12/31/95	12/31/94	12/31/93	12/31/92	12/31/91	12/31/90
Total Revenues	16,178	14,074	11,293	4,674	64	2,459	8,725
Costs & Expenses	12,775	11,038	10,059	6,787	1,934	3,976	17,173
Operating Income	3,403	3,036	1,234	d2,113	d1,870	d1,517	d8,448
Income Bef Income Tax	3,237	2,223	3,989	d3,037	d2,221	d1,879	d8,639
Income Tax	2,620	1,120	...	...	...	...	...
Net Income	617	1,103	3,989	d3,037	d2,221	d1,879	d8,639
Average Shares Outstg	10,053	9,559	10,800	5,153	4,856	599	598
BALANCE SHEET (IN THOUSANDS):							
Cash & Cash Equivalents	439	3,656	7,149	304	18	645	145
Receivables, Net	1,932	1,261	1,287	1,038	202	138	292
Inventories	326	271	224	390	...	...	423
Gross Property	9,861	9,139	7,669	6,950	3,051	1,125	1,055
Accumulated Depreciation	4,450	3,220	2,057	1,068	656	626	485
Long-Term Debt	3,334	1,500	3,173	12,877	5,578	2,397	1,500
Stockholders' Equity	24,209	23,460	22,813	3,441	3,261	6,073	8,080
Total Assets	39,741	34,666	32,850	22,605	10,827	11,732	13,444
Total Current Assets	4,062	6,730	9,957	1,773	261	783	871
Total Current Liabilities	7,150	6,790	5,940	4,895	1,911	3,154	3,794
Net Working Capital	d3,088	d60	4,017	d3,122	d1,650	d2,371	d2,923
Year End Shs Outstg	9,516	9,492	9,489	5,585	4,873	599	598
STATISTICAL RECORD:							
Return on Equity %	2.55	4.70	17.49	...	...	...	...
Return on Assets %	1.55	3.18	12.14	...	...	...	...
Operating Profit Margin %	21.03	21.16	10.93	...	...	...	...
Net Profit Margin %	3.81	7.84	35.32	...	...	...	...
Book Value Per Share	2.54	2.47	2.40	2.31	0.67	10.14	13.51

OFFICERS:
E. F. Cruft, Chmn. & C.E.O.
W. P. Carson, Pres.
M. R. Welch, V.P.—Devel.
T. H. Lang, V.P. & Treas.

INCORPORATED: Bermuda, Aug., 1988

PRINCIPAL OFFICE: 22 Church Street, Hamilton HM 11 Bermuda

TELEPHONE NUMBER: (411) 292-2363
FAX: (411) 295-4614
NO. OF EMPLOYEES: N/A
ANNUAL MEETING: N/A
SHAREHOLDERS: N/A
INSTITUTIONAL HOLDINGS:
No. of Institutions: 6
Shares Held: 187,885 (adj.)

AMERICAN DEPOSITARY RECEIPTS: Each American Depositary Receipt represents 1 ordinary share of par US$0.05.

DEPOSITARY BANK(S): The Bank of New York, (212) 815-2175

NYNEX CABLECOMMS GROUP, PLC

YIELD ...
P/E RATIO ...

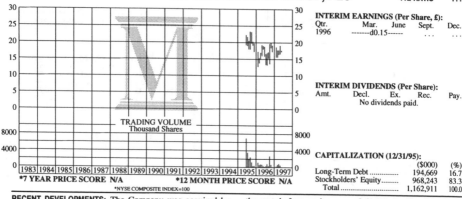

*7 YEAR PRICE SCORE N/A   *12 MONTH PRICE SCORE N/A
*NYSE COMPOSITE INDEX=100

INTERIM EARNINGS (Per Share, £):

Qtr.	Mar.	June	Sept.	Dec.
1996	------d0.15------		...	...

INTERIM DIVIDENDS (Per Share):

Amt.	Decl.	Ex.	Rec.	Pay.
	No dividends paid.			

CAPITALIZATION (12/31/95):

	($000)	(%)
Long-Term Debt	194,669	16.7
Stockholders' Equity........	968,243	83.3
Total	1,162,911	100.0

RECENT DEVELOPMENTS: The Company was acquired by Cable & Wireless Communications plc on 4/28/97. For the year ended 12/31/96, the Company incurred a net loss of £22.8 million compared with a net loss of £0.4 million a year earlier. Total revenue was £151.2 million, up 77.9% from £85.1 million in the prior year. Revenues from cable television were £62.4 million compared with £38.7 million the year before, an increase of 61.2%. Residential telephony revenues advanced 93.9% to £70.6 million from £36.4 million in the previous year. Business telephony revenues more than doubled to £13.1 million from £5.3 million a year ago. Installation revenues were £5.2 million, a gain of 11.5% over £4.6 million in 1995.

BUSINESS

NYNEX CABLECOMMS GROUP, PLC is a provider of cable television and telecommunications services in the United Kingdom. The Company is licensed to provide these services in 16 franchise areas, covering approximately 2.7 million homes and 167,500 businesses. The Company's franchise homes are equivalent to approximately 15.0% of the total homes in the United Kingdom under franchise at 12/31/96. The Company has approximately 2.3 million equity homes, making it the third largest multiple systems operator in the United Kingdom on the basis of the total number of equity homes.

ANNUAL EARNINGS

Earnings Per Share	12/31/95	12/31/94	12/31/95	12/31/94
	--------------US $--------------		--------------British £--------------	
	Nil	...	Nil	...

ANNUAL FINANCIAL DATA

RECORD OF EARNINGS (IN MILLIONS):

	12/31/95	12/31/94	12/31/95	12/31/94
Total Revenues	132	64	85	41
Costs & Expenses	205	140	132	90
Depreciation & Amort	51	30	33	19
Operating Income	d124	d106	d80	d68
Income Bef Income Tax	d30	d110	d19	d70
Income Tax	cr29	cr33	cr19	cr21
Net Income	d1	d78	0	d50
BALANCE SHEET (IN MILLIONS):				
Cash & Cash Equivalents	15	65	10	42
Receivables, Net	68	28	44	18
Gross Property	1,431	806	921	515
Accumulated Depreciation	97	45	62	29
Long-Term Debt	195	81	125	52
Stockholders' Equity	968	456	623	291
Total Assets	1,556	965	1,002	616
Total Current Assets	87	95	56	61
Total Current Liabilities	180	138	116	88
Net Working Capital	d93	d43	d60	d28
Year End Shs Outstg (000)	925,000	...	925,000	...
STATISTICAL RECORD:				
Return on Equity %	...	...		
Return on Assets %	...	...		
Operating Profit Margin %	...	...		
Net Profit Margin %	...	...		
Book Value Per Share	1.05	...		

Converted at 1995, US$1.5530= 1 British pound; 1994, US$1.5650= 1 British pound

OFFICERS:
R. W. Blackburn, Chmn.
C. Bland, Deputy Chmn.
J. F. Killian, Pres. & C.E.O.
N. P. Mearing-Smith, C.F.O.

INCORPORATED: United Kingdom, Feb., 1995

PRINCIPAL OFFICE: The Tolworth Tower, Ewell Road, Surbiton United Kingdom

TELEPHONE NUMBER: 0181-873-2000

NO. OF EMPLOYEES: 2,964

ANNUAL MEETING: N/A

SHAREHOLDERS: N/A

INSTITUTIONAL HOLDINGS:
No. of Institutions: 10
Shares Held: 2,146,250

AMERICAN DEPOSITARY RECEIPTS: Each American Depositary Share represents 10 units, each unit being a "paired" security consisting of one ordinary share, par value 0.10 per share, of NYNC and one share of common stock par value US $0.01 per share.

DEPOSITARY BANK(S): The Bank of New York, (212) 815-2175

OCE N.V.

YIELD 1.3%
P/E RATIO 22.8

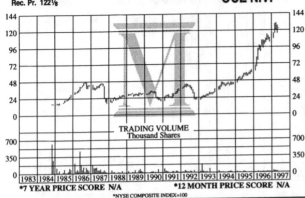

*7 YEAR PRICE SCORE N/A   *12 MONTH PRICE SCORE N/A
*NYSE COMPOSITE INDEX=100

TRADING VOLUME
Thousand Shares

1983 | 1984 | 1985 | 1986 | 1987 | 1988 | 1989 | 1990 | 1991 | 1992 | 1993 | 1994 | 1995 | 1996 | 1997

INTERIM EARNINGS (Per Share, US$):

	Feb.	May	Aug.	Nov.
1996	----------------- 5.36 -----------------

INTERIM DIVIDENDS (Per Share):

Amt.	Decl.	Ex.	Rec.	Pay.
0.485	...	10/17/95	10/19/95	11/16/95
0.789	...	4/12/96	4/16/96	5/20/96
0.533	...	10/18	10/22	12/04
0.811	...	4/11/97	4/15/97	...

Indicated Div.:$1.62

CAPITALIZATION (11/30/96):

	($000)	(%)
Long-Term Debt	711,362	45.5
Minority Interest	51,243	3.3
Stockholders' Equity	789,922	50.6
Capital Lease Oblgs.	9,636	0.6
Total	1,562,163	100.0

RECENT DEVELOPMENTS: For the year ended 11/30/96, net income advanced 56.5% to NLG169.65 million from NLG108.3 million in 1995. Net sales climbed 42.3% to NLG4.17 billion versus NLG2.93 billion the year before. This reflected a 43.5% jump in earnings from sales, rentals and service to NLG4.05 billion and a 11.8% rise in interest income from financial leases. Sales in the engineering systems market increased by 15.0% to NLG1.37 billion. This growth was mainly attributable to the large number of orders of digital copiers/printers for the high volume segment and the similarly digital Oce 9400 family for the low and medium volume segments. Strong demand in the medium, high, and very high volume segments for analogue copiers contributed to the 19% increase in sales of office systems to NLG2.08 billion. Gross margin climbed 35.9% to NLG1.74 billion. Separately, OCENY changed its name to Oce N.V. effective April 15, 1997.

BUSINESS

OCE N.V., formerly OCE-VAN DER GRINTEN N.V., is a holding company, which through its subsidiaries, is engaged in the development, production and marketing of copiers and copying supplies for office systems; copiers and copying supplies for design engineering; laser printing systems; plotter systems and plotter materials for design engineering; and photosensitive materials and graphic films. Co's sales percentages by division include: Engineering Systems (33%), Office Systems (46%) and Printing Systems (21%).

ANNUAL EARNINGS

	11/30/96	11/30/95	11/30/96	11/30/95
	-------------US $-------------		-------------Guilders-------------	
Earnings Per Share	5.36	4.18	9.06	6.64

ANNUAL FINANCIAL DATA

RECORD OF EARNINGS (IN THOUSANDS):				
Total Revenues	2,469,062	1,846,003	4,174,238	2,932,491
Costs & Expenses	2,280,389	1,706,557	3,855,265	2,710,972
Operating Income	188,673	139,446	318,973	221,519
Income Bef Income Tax	126,879	82,874	214,504	131,651
Income Tax	25,762	15,456	43,553	24,553
Eq. Earnings in Affils.	460	732	777	1,163
Minority Interests	cr1,327	5	dr2,244	8
Net Income	102,904	68,145	169,484	108,269
Average Shares Outstg	18,284	16,306	18,284	16,306
BALANCE SHEET (IN THOUSANDS):				
Cash & Cash Equivalents	34,363	15,603	58,094	24,786
Receivables, Net	933,546	678,343	1,578,269	1,077,590
Inventories	468,183	356,181	791,518	565,816
Gross Property	1,189,825	856,194	2,011,538	1,447,496
Accumulated Depreciation	673,748	523,131	1,139,050	884,414
Long-Term Debt	711,362	653,950	1,202,640	1,038,840
Stockholders' Equity	789,922	664,365	1,335,455	1,055,385
Total Assets	2,731,520	1,980,831	4,617,955	3,348,829
Total Current Assets	1,453,680	1,069,403	2,457,617	1,698,814
Total Current Liabilities	937,834	674,784	1,585,518	1,071,936
Net Working Capital	515,847	394,620	872,099	626,878
Year End Shs Outstg	19,742	16,316	19,742	16,316
STATISTICAL RECORD:				
Return on Equity %	13.03	10.26		
Return on Assets %	3.32	2.90		
Operating Profit Margin %	7.64	7.55		
Net Profit Margin %	4.17	3.69		
Book Value Per Share	40.01	40.72		

Converted at 1996, US$0.5915= 1 Netherlands guilder; 1995, US$0.6295= 1 Netherlands guilder

OFFICERS:
J. V. Pennings, Chmn.
E. C. de la Houssaye
R. L. van Iperen
H. J. Meertens

INCORPORATED: Netherlands, 1877

PRINCIPAL OFFICE: St. Urbanusweg 43
Venlo Netherlands 5900

TELEPHONE NUMBER: 31-77-3592222

NO. OF EMPLOYEES: 16,495

ANNUAL MEETING: In Apr.

SHAREHOLDERS: N/A

INSTITUTIONAL HOLDINGS:
No. of Institutions: 7
Shares Held: 79,792

AMERICAN DEPOSITARY
RECEIPTS: (Sponsored) Each American
Depositary Receipt represents one ordinary
share of par NLG4.

DEPOSITARY BANK(S): J. P. Morgan, (212)
648-3206

OLS ASIA HOLDINGS, LIMITED

YIELD 2.9%
P/E RATIO 45.8

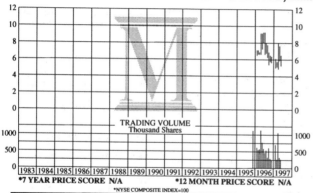

TRADING VOLUME
Thousand Shares

| 1983 | 1984 | 1985 | 1986 | 1987 | 1988 | 1989 | 1990 | 1991 | 1992 | 1993 | 1994 | 1995 | 1996 | 1997 |

*7 YEAR PRICE SCORE N/A   ***12 MONTH PRICE SCORE N/A**

*NYSE COMPOSITE INDEX=100

INTERIM EARNINGS (Per Share, US$):

Qtr.	Mar.	Jun.	Sept.	Dec.
1996	------------------ 0.12 ------------------			

INTERIM DIVIDENDS (Per Share):

Amt.	Decl.	Ex.	Rec.	Pay.
0.106	...	9/30/96	10/02/96	10/28/96
0.157	...	4/09/97	4/11/97	6/02/97

Indicated div.: $0.16

CAPITALIZATION (12/31/95):

	($000)	(%)
Stockholders' Equity........	29,768	100.0
Total	29,768	100.0

RECENT DEVELOPMENTS: For the year ended 12/31/96, net earnings were A$10.5 million (US$8.2 million) compared with A$8.8 million (US$6.5 million) the year before. Sales revenue grew 36.4% to A$93.4 million (US$73.3million) from A$68.4 million (US$50.8 million) a year earlier. Operating profit was A$11.3 million (US$8.9 million), up 15.8% from A$9.8 million (US$7.2 million) the previous year. Results benefited from a rebound in Hong Kong's property and stock markets. During the year, the Company was awarded 17 contracts in Hong Kong and three in the People's Republic of China that are valued at A$44.5 million (US$34.8 million). These contracts included the renovation of the Honest Motor Building, Telford Centre, Cityplaza and interior work for Joyce Boutique, Banque Nationale de Paris and the Shanghai Stock Exchange.

BUSINESS

OLS ASIA HOLDINGS LIMITED is a holding company that, through its subsidiaries, provides an integrated construction service. The Company's operations include new development, interior decoration, and electrical and mechanical installation.

ANNUAL EARNINGS

	12/31/95	12/31/94	12/31/95	12/31/94
	--------------US $-------------		--------------A$-------------	
Earnings Per Share	d0.75	d1.09	d1.01	d1.41

ANNUAL FINANCIAL DATA

RECORD OF EARNINGS (IN THOUSANDS):

Total Revenues	51,374	57,633	69,098	74,308
Cost & Expenses	44,120	51,733	59,341	66,701
Operating Income	7,254	5,900	9,757	7,607
Income Bef Income Tax	d43,638	d51,440	d58,693	d66,323
Income Tax	1,174	1,127	1,579	1,453
Net Income	d44,812	d52,567	d60,272	d67,776
Average Shares Outstg	60,000	48,123	60,000	48,123

BALANCE SHEET (IN THOUSANDS):

Cash & Cash Equivalents	16,312	10,001	21,940	12,895
Receivables, Net	23,799	12,717	32,009	16,396
Inventories	2,175	1,287	2,925	1,659
Gross Property	1,468	1,299	1,974	1,675
Accumulated Depreciation	634	429	853	553
Stockholders' Equity	29,768	16,288	40,037	21,000
Total Assets	48,588	29,548	65,350	38,097
Total Current Assets	42,286	24,005	56,874	30,950
Total Current Liabilities	18,701	13,185	25,153	17,000
Net Working Capital	23,585	10,820	31,721	13,950
Year End Shs Outstg	60,000	60,000	60,000	60,000

STATISTICAL RECORD:

Return on Equity %	...	...		
Return on Assets %	...	...		
Operating Profit Margin %	14.1	10.2		
Net Profit Margin %	...	...		
Book Value Per Share	0.67	0.35		

Converted at 1995, US$0.7435= 1 Australian $; 1994, US$0.7756= 1 Australian $

OFFICERS:
Wing Fung Siu, Chmn. & Managing Dir.
Lau Po, Deputy Chmn.
Wai Kan Leung, Sec. & C.F.O.

INCORPORATED: Bermuda, Aug. 2, 1994

PRINCIPAL OFFICE: AS & K Services Ltd. Cedar House, 41 Cedar Avenue Hamilton Bermuda

TELEPHONE NUMBER: N/A

NO. OF EMPLOYEES: 99

ANNUAL MEETING: N/A

SHAREHOLDERS: N/A

INSTITUTIONAL HOLDINGS:
No. of Institutions: N/A
Shares Held: N/A

AMERICAN DEPOSITARY RECEIPTS: Each American Depositary Receipt represents the right to receive five Class A shares, A$0.20 par value. Each Class A share will convert automatically into one ordinary share, A$0.20 par value on Dec. 15, 1998.

DEPOSITARY BANK(S): The Bank of New York, (212) 815-2175

NASDAQ SYMBOL ORNGY
Rec. Pr. 17¾

ORANGE, PLC

YIELD ...
P/E RATIO ...

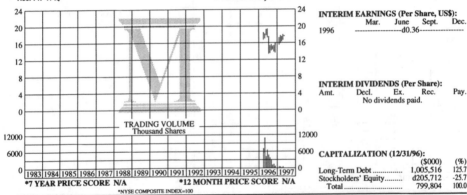

*7 YEAR PRICE SCORE N/A   *12 MONTH PRICE SCORE N/A

*NYSE COMPOSITE INDEX=100

INTERIM EARNINGS (Per Share, US$):

	Mar.	June	Sept.	Dec.
1996		-----d0.36-----		

INTERIM DIVIDENDS (Per Share):

Amt.   Decl.   Ex.   Rec.   Pay.
No dividends paid.

CAPITALIZATION (12/31/96):

	($000)	(%)
Long-Term Debt	1,005,516	125.7
Stockholders' Equity	d205,712	-25.7
Total	799,804	100.0

RECENT DEVELOPMENTS: For the year ended 12/31/96, the Company reported a loss of £229.1 million compared with £140.5 million in the corresponding period a year earlier. Sales were £619.0 million versus £228.7 million in 1995. Earnings for 1995 are proforma results. Higher sales resulted from the doubling of the Company's PCS subscriber base as well as the acquisition of the service provider businesses in France and Germany. Earnings were pressured by increasing distribution and administration costs in absolute terms. Gross profit improved from a loss of £12.3 million in 1995 to a profit of £16.3 million in 1996. Capital expenditures during the year were £219.9 million related to the expansion of the Company's PCS network increasing from £168.0 million in 1995.

BUSINESS

ORANGE, PLC is engaged in the operation of the Orange digital PCN telecommunication network in the United Kingdom and the sale and marketing of Orange services. Under the brand name "Orange," the Company offers a broad range of mobile voice and data communications services. The Company also operates as a service provider for other cellular network operators in the United Kingdom, France and Germany and operates a nationwide paging network in the United Kingdom.

ANNUAL EARNINGS

	12/31/96	12/31/95	12/31/96	12/31/95
	US $		British £	
Earnings Per Share	d0.36	d1.43	d0.21	d0.92

ANNUAL FINANCIAL DATA

RECORD OF EARNINGS (IN THOUSANDS):

Total Revenues	1,048,896	355,171	619,000	228,700
Costs & Expenses	1,349,669	538,115	796,500	346,500
Operating Income	d300,774	d182,943	d177,500	d117,800
Income Bef Income Tax	d388,210	d218,197	d229,100	d140,500
Net Income	d388,210	d218,197	d229,100	d140,500
Average Shares Outstg	1,855,899	...	1,855,899	...

BALANCE SHEET (IN THOUSANDS):

Cash & Cash Equivalents	22,367	129,831	13,200	83,600
Receivables, Net	167,925	44,882	99,100	28,900
Inventories	26,604	50,162	15,700	32,300
Gross Property	1,383,559	920,929	816,500	593,000
Accumulated Depreciation	291,793	164,618	172,200	106,000
Long-Term Debt	1,005,516	1,619,313	593,400	1,042,700
Stockholders' Equity	d205,712	d893,596	d121,400	d575,400
Total Assets	1,526,406	1,141,921	900,800	735,300
Total Current Assets	255,192	242,734	150,600	156,300
Total Current Liabilities	669,328	356,414	395,000	229,500
Net Working Capital	d414,136	d113,680	d244,400	d73,200
Year End Shs Outstg	2,030,072	238,052	2,030,072	238,052

STATISTICAL RECORD:

Return on Equity %	...	...		
Return on Assets %	...	...		
Operating Profit Margin %	...	...		
Net Profit Margin %	...	...		
Book Value Per Share	d0.10	d3.75		

Converted at 1996, US$1.6945= 1 British pound; 1995, US$1.5530= 1 British pound

OFFICERS:
C. Fok, Non-Exec. Chmn.
H. R. Snook, Managing Dir.
G. Howe, Fin. Dir.

INCORPORATED: 1995

PRINCIPAL OFFICE: St James Court, Great Park Road,Almondsbury Park, Bradley Stoke Bristol BS12 4QJ U.K.

TELEPHONE NUMBER: 44-1454-624600

NO. OF EMPLOYEES: 3,592

ANNUAL MEETING: In May

SHAREHOLDERS: 25,522

INSTITUTIONAL HOLDINGS:
No. of Institutions: 13
Shares Held: 1,883,393

AMERICAN DEPOSITARY RECEIPTS: (Sponsored) Each American Depositary Receipt represents five ordinary shares of par £0.20.

DEPOSITARY BANK(S): The Bank Of New York, (212) 815-2175

OZEMAIL, LIMITED

YIELD ...
P/E RATIO N.M.

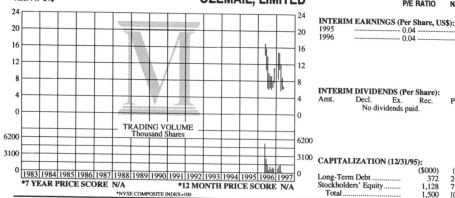

*7 YEAR PRICE SCORE N/A   *12 MONTH PRICE SCORE N/A

*NYSE COMPOSITE INDEX=100

INTERIM EARNINGS (Per Share, US$):

1995	------------------- 0.04 -------------------
1996	------------------- 0.04 -------------------

INTERIM DIVIDENDS (Per Share):

Amt.	Decl.	Ex.	Rec.	Pay.
		No dividends paid.		

CAPITALIZATION (12/31/95):

	($000)	(%)
Long-Term Debt	372	24.8
Stockholders' Equity.........	1,128	75.2
Total	1,500	100.0

RECENT DEVELOPMENTS: For the year ended 12/31/96, net income climbed 8.5% to A$434,000 (US$344,000) from A$400,000 (US$298,000) in 1995. Earnings for 1996 included a foreign exchange gain of A$867,000, an investment gain of A$112,000, and a loss of A$506,000 related to a partnership. Net revenues advanced to A$27.8 million (US$22.0 million) from A$8.9 million (US$22.0 million) in 1995. Operating loss amounted to A$1.5 million (US$1.2 million) versus operating income of $824,000 (US$613,000) in the prior year. For the quarter ended 12/31/96, OZEMY incurred a net loss of A$588,000 (US$467,000) versus a net loss of A$683,000 (US$508,000) in the same prior-year period. Net loss for 1996 included roll-out and start-up costs related to OzEmail Phone, OzEmail Fax, and Web Wide Media. Net revenues rose to A$9.2 million (US$7.3 million) from A$2.6 million (US$2.0 million) in 1995. This increase primarily reflected revenue from the provision of Internet services to Government schools in the State of New South Wales, Australia.

BUSINESS

OZEMAIL, LIMITED, through its subsidiaries, provides Internet services in Australia and New Zealand, providing access to a network that is regionally focused, Internet implementation services and customer support. The Company's Internet services are designed to meet the different needs of its residential and enterprise customers, ranging from low-cost dial-up to high performance continuous access services.

ANNUAL EARNINGS

	12/31/95	12/31/94	12/31/95	12/31/94
	------------US $------------		------------A$------------	
Earnings Per Share	0.04	d0.07	0.05	d0.09

ANNUAL FINANCIAL DATA

RECORD OF EARNINGS (IN THOUSANDS):

Total Revenues	6,593	537	8,868	692
Costs & Expenses	5,981	506	8,044	652
Operating Income	613	31	824	40
Income Bef Income Tax	575	d480	774	d619
Income Tax	323	12	434	15
Minority Interests	cr45	...	cr60	...
Net Income	297	d492	400	d634
Average Shares Outstg	7,440	7,440	7,440	7,440

BALANCE SHEET (IN THOUSANDS):

Cash & Cash Equivalents	7	22	9	28
Receivables, Net	1,619	411	2,178	530
Gross Property	2,665	262	3,585	338
Accumulated Depreciation	336	14	452	18
Long-Term Debt	372	...	500	...
Stockholders' Equity	1,128	14	1,517	18
Total Assets	4,111	717	5,529	925
Total Current Assets	1,670	465	2,246	599
Total Current Liabilities	2,611	703	3,512	907
Net Working Capital	d941	d239	d1,266	d308
Year End Shs Outstg	7,000	7,000	7,000	7,000

STATISTICAL RECORD:

Return on Equity %	26.33	...		
Return on Assets %	7.22	...		
Operating Profit Margin %	9.30	5.77		
Net Profit Margin %	4.50	...		
Book Value Per Share	0.16	0.20		

Converted at 1995, US$0.7435= 1 Australian $; 1994, US$0.7756= 1 Australian $

OFFICERS:
S. Howard, C.E.O.
D. Spence, C.O.O.
J. Worton, C.F.O.
INCORPORATED: Australia, 1994
PRINCIPAL OFFICE: MDIS House, 39 Herbert Street, St. Leonards 2065, Sydney Australia

TELEPHONE NUMBER: 011-612-391-0400
NO. OF EMPLOYEES: 134
ANNUAL MEETING: N/A
SHAREHOLDERS: N/A
INSTITUTIONAL HOLDINGS:
No. of Institutions: 14
Shares Held: 1,936,600

AMERICAN DEPOSITARY RECEIPTS: (Sponsored) Each American Depositary Receipt represents one ord. share of A$0.04.

DEPOSITARY BANK(S): The Bank of New York, (212) 815-2175

PACIFIC DUNLOP LIMITED

YIELD   0.9%
P/E RATIO   ...

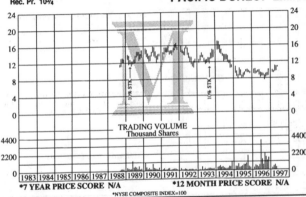

TRADING VOLUME
Thousand Shares

| 1983 | 1984 | 1985 | 1986 | 1987 | 1988 | 1989 | 1990 | 1991 | 1992 | 1993 | 1994 | 1995 | 1996 | 1997 |

*7 YEAR PRICE SCORE N/A   *12 MONTH PRICE SCORE N/A
*NYSE COMPOSITE INDEX=100

INTERIM EARNINGS (Per Share, US$):

Qtr.	Sept.	Dec.	Mar.	June
1994-95	--------------	0.09	--------------	
1995-96	--------------	d0.13	--------------	
1996-97	------- 0.07 ------		...	...

INTERIM DIVIDENDS (Per Share):

Amt.	Decl.	Ex.	Rec.	Pay.
0.293	...	6/02/95	6/08/95	7/13/95
0.327	...	10/10	10/12	11/13
0.325	...	6/04/96	6/06/96	7/11/96
0.089	...	10/08	10/10	11/26
0.05	...	6/05/97	6/09/97	7/11/97

Indicated div.: $0.10

CAPITALIZATION (6/30/96):

	($000)	(%)
Long-Term Debt	828,548	37.0
Stockholders' Equity	1,411,643	63.0
Total	2,240,190	100.0

RECENT DEVELOPMENTS: For the six months ended 12/31/96, net profit attributable to shareholders totaled A$84.0 million, down 28.8% compared with A$118.0 million in the corresponding prior-year period. Operating revenue decreased 13.4% to A$3.17 billion from A$3.66 billion the previous year. The lower revenues were attributed to the effect of a stronger Australian dollar against the U.S. dollar as well as the inclusion in the prior year of A$331.0 million in revenues from businesses that the Company has since sold. The Company has divested more than A$1.70 billion of businesses over an eighteen-month period, dating back to June 1995, reducing the number of business groups from nine to six. All of the Company's reporting businesses reported operating growth, with the exception of GNB Technologies, whose growth was hindered by costs associated with modifications to the Columbus lead smelter in the United States.

BUSINESS

PACIFIC DUNLOP LIMITED is principally engaged in the following: Batteries: manufacturing and marketing of automotive, traction, stationary and submarine batteries and power packs; a recycler of lead in the U.S.A. and New Zealand. Pacific Brands: import, manufacture and marketing of a wide range of popular brands of clothing, footwear and sporting goods. Distribution: marketing and distribution of electrical cable, fittings, accessories, electrical installtion materials, automotive parts, earthmoving and similar equipment; pallet hire. Industrial and Electrical: manufacture and marketing of electrical accessories, power cables, telecommunications and optical fibre cables; polystyrene and polyurethane foam products for the furniture, bedding, automotive and packaging industries. Ansell: manufacture and marketing of latex dipped products including household, industrial surgical and examinations gloves, condoms and balloons. Medical: scientific health care technology; products and equipment; research and development. Pacific Brands Food: manufacturing, processing and distribution of foods and allied products. Tyres: manufacturing and marketing of tyres for vehicles and aircraft, and retailing of tyres, batteries and related automotive products through the Company's 50% interest in South Pacific Tyres, a partnership with the Goodyear Tire & Rubber Co. of the U.S.A.

ANNUAL EARNINGS

	6/30/96	6/30/95	6/30/96	6/30/95
	--------------US $--------------		--------------A$--------------	
Earnings Per Share	d0.13	0.09	d0.16	0.12

ANNUAL FINANCIAL DATA

RECORD OF EARNINGS (IN MILLIONS):

Total Revenues	5,100	5,193	6,476	7,317
Costs & Expenses	4,631	4,816	5,880	6,785
Operating Income	469	377	596	532
Income Bef Income Tax	d16	131	d21	184
Income Tax	83	58	106	81
Minority Interests	5	6	6	9
Net Income	d105	67	d133	94
Average Shares Outstg (000)	812,071	770,162	812,071	770,162

BALANCE SHEET (IN MILLIONS):

Cash & Cash Equivalents	1,176	612	1,493	862
Receivables, Net	812	1,518	1,031	2,139
Inventories	799	823	1,015	1,159
Gross Property	1,663	1,693	2,111	2,386
Accumulated Depreciation	688	669	873	942
Long-Term Debt	829	925	1,052	1,303
Stockholders' Equity	1,412	1,602	1,793	2,257
Total Assets	4,682	4,938	5,945	6,958
Total Current Assets	2,836	3,013	3,602	4,245
Total Current Liabilities	2,225	2,294	2,825	3,233
Net Working Capital	611	719	776	1,013
Year End Shs Outstg (000)	1,013,000	1,060,000	1,013,000	1,060,000

STATISTICAL RECORD:

Return on Equity %	...	4.18		
Return on Assets %	...	1.36		
Operating Profit Margin %	9.20	7.26		
Net Profit Margin %	...	1.29		
Book Value Per Share	1.39	1.51		

Converted at 1996, US$0.7875= 1 Australian $; 1995, US$0.7097= 1 Australian $

OFFICERS:
M. Chadwick, Managing Dir.
P. Dainty, Exec. Gen. Mgr.
P. Gay, Exec. Gen. Mgr.
I. Veal, Exec. Gen. Mgr.

INCORPORATED: Aug., 1920

PRINCIPAL OFFICE: Level 41, 101 Collins Street, Melbourne Australia, 3000

TELEPHONE NUMBER: (61 3) 9270 7270

NO. OF EMPLOYEES: 40,000

ANNUAL MEETING: In Nov.

SHAREHOLDERS: 111,426

INSTITUTIONAL HOLDINGS:
No. of Institutions: 22
Shares Held: 11,991,889

AMERICAN DEPOSITARY RECEIPTS: (Sponsored) Each American Depositary Receipt represents four ordinary shares of par A$0.50.

DEPOSITARY BANK(S): J.P. Morgan, (212) 648-3206

PELSART RESOURCES N.L.

YIELD ...
P/E RATIO ...

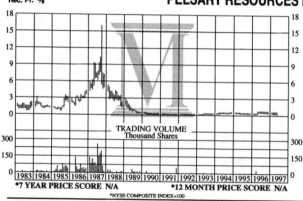

7 YEAR PRICE SCORE N/A   **12 MONTH PRICE SCORE N/A**
*NYSE COMPOSITE INDEX=100

INTERIM EARNINGS (Per Share, US$):

Qtr.	Sep.	Dec.	Mar.	June
1995	------------------ Nil ------------------			
Qtr.	Mar.	June	Sep.	Dec.
1996	------------------ Nil ------------------			

INTERIM DIVIDENDS (Per Share):

Amt.	Decl.	Ex.	Rec.	Pay.
	No dividends paid.			

CAPITALIZATION (12/31/96):

	($000)	(%)
Long-Term Debt	7,813	36.1
Stockholders' Equity	13,835	63.9
Total	21,648	100.0

RECENT DEVELOPMENTS: For the 18 months ended 12/31/96, net loss was A$3.4 million. This compares with income of A$1.8 million for the twelve months ended 6/30/95. Results for 1996 included unusual charges of A$2.4 million for the provisions for non-recoverable loans, and 1995 results included gains of A$1.7 million for reversal of provisions for non-recoverable loans and mine closure costs, partially offset by a charge of A$183,000 for provisions for decreases in the value of exploration expenditures. Revenues were A$379,000 million, up 24.3% from $305,000. Operating loss before unusual items and income taxes was $967,000 compared with a profit of $319,000 in 1995. The Company changed its fiscal year ended from 6/30 to 12/31.

BUSINESS

PELSART RESOURCES N.L. and its subsidiaries are engaged in mineral exploration and development, gold and zircon production in Indonesia and the derivation of petroleum royalties from certain Australian production permits.

ANNUAL EARNINGS

	12/31/96 [1]	6/30/95	12/31/96	6/30/95
	----------US $----------		----------A$----------	
Earnings Per Share	Nil	Nil	Nil	Nil

ANNUAL FINANCIAL DATA

RECORD OF EARNINGS (IN THOUSANDS):

	12/31/96	6/30/95	12/31/96	6/30/95
Total Revenues	301	216	379	305
Income Bef Income Tax	d2,713	1,282	d3,411	1,807
Income Tax	...	cr16	...	cr22
Minority Interests	...	cr9	...	cr12
Net Income	d2,713	1,307	d3,411	1,841

[1] Results for 12/31/96 reflect an 18-month period.

BALANCE SHEET (IN THOUSANDS):

	12/31/96	6/30/95	12/31/96	6/30/95
Cash & Cash Equivalents	1,805	1,131	2,269	1,593
Receivables, Net	219	138	275	194
Gross Property	2,475	1,757	3,112	2,475
Accumulated Depreciation	1,161	617	1,460	869
Long-Term Debt	7,813	212	9,824	299
Stockholders' Equity	13,835	14,767	17,396	20,807
Total Assets	22,449	15,904	28,227	22,410
Total Current Assets	2,213	1,682	2,782	2,370
Total Current Liabilities	801	914	1,007	1,288
Net Working Capital	1,412	768	1,775	1,082
Year End Shs Outstg	649,939	649,938	649,939	649,938

STATISTICAL RECORD:

	12/31/96	6/30/95
Return on Equity %	8.49	...
Return on Assets %	5.23	...
Operating Profit Margin %	...	...
Net Profit Margin %	389.71	...
Book Value Per Share	0.02	0.02

Converted at 1996, US$0.7953= 1 Australian $; 1995, US$0.7097= 1 Australian $.

OFFICERS:
R. Kasenda, Chmn.
S. Nursalim
Y. T. See
F. H. Lee

INCORPORATED: Oct., 1985

PRINCIPAL OFFICE: Suite 81, City West Centre, Corner Sutherland Street & Railway Parade, West Perth Australia, 6005

TELEPHONE NUMBER: (09) 481 0896

NO. OF EMPLOYEES: N/A

ANNUAL MEETING: In May

SHAREHOLDERS: 3,924

INSTITUTIONAL HOLDINGS:
No. of Institutions: 1
Shares Held: 1,199

AMERICAN DEPOSITARY RECEIPTS: (Unsponsored) Each American Depositary Receipt represents one ordinary share of A$0.20.

DEPOSITARY BANK(S): The Bank of New York, (212) 815-2175; J.P. Morgan, (212) 648-3206

PETSEC ENERGY LTD.

YIELD ...
P/E RATIO 17.4

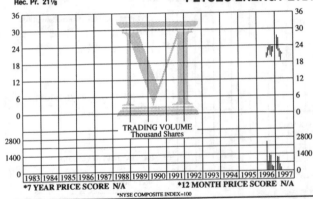

INTERIM EARNINGS (Per Share):

Qtr.	Sept.	Dec.	Mar.	June
1995-96	------------------- 0.13 -------------------
Qtr.	Mar.	June	Sept.	Dec.
1996	...	...	------- 0.14 -------
1997	0.07	...	...	...

INTERIM DIVIDENDS (Per Share):

Amt.	Decl.	Ex.	Rec.	Pay.
	No dividends paid.			

CAPITALIZATION (12/31/96):

	($000)	(%)
Long-Term Debt	36,958	21.2
Stockholders' Equity........	105,551	60.6
Deferred Income Tax	31,568	18.1
Total..............................	174,077	100.0

RECENT DEVELOPMENTS: For the three months ended 3/31/97, net income totaled $6.6 million, or $0.06 per share, compared with $1.1 million, or $0.01 per share, in the corresponding quarter the previous year. Oil and gas sales, net of royalties, more than doubled to $30.9 million versus $13.7 million a year earlier. Net sales of oil jumped 89.4% to $16.0 million from $8.4 million a year ago, while net sales of gas soared to $14.9 million from $5.3 million the year before. Income from operations was $11.0 million, up significantly compared with $2.8 million the prior year. Strong financial performance was attributed to increased production levels and higher oil and gas prices. In the first quarter of 1997, the average sales price of oil climbed 18.2% to $21.40 per Bbl from $18.11 per Bbl in the same quarter in 1996. The average sales price of gas surged 37.3% to $2.54 per Mcf from $1.85 per Mcf the previous year. Total production advanced 83.2% to 10,351 MMcfe from 5,651 MMcfe the year before.

BUSINESS

PETSEC ENERGY LTD. (formerly Petroleum Securities Australia Limited) is an independent oil and gas exploration and production company with its operations located in the Gulf of Mexico.

ANNUAL EARNINGS

	① 12/31/96	6/30/96	① 12/31/96	6/30/96
	------------US $------------		---------Australian $---------	
Earnings Per Share	0.14	0.13	0.18	0.16

ANNUAL FINANCIAL DATA

RECORD OF EARNINGS (IN THOUSANDS):

	① 12/31/96	6/30/96	① 12/31/96	6/30/96
Total Revenues	58,631	100,435	73,722	127,536
Costs & Expenses	13,462	16,078	16,927	20,416
Depreciation & Amort.	15,446	23,094	19,422	29,326
Operating Income	29,729	61,911	37,381	78,617
Income Bef Income Tax	21,547	18,765	27,093	23,829
Income Tax	6,582	6,232	8,276	7,914
Minority Interests	...	1,813	...	2,302
Net Income	14,965	10,720	18,817	13,613
Net Extraordinary Items	...	d5,298	...	d6,728
Average Shares Outstg	104,997	86,297	104,997	86,297

① For six months due to fiscal year-end change.

BALANCE SHEET (IN THOUSANDS):

Cash & Cash Equivalents	12,514	3,557	15,735	4,517
Receivables, Net	12,186	9,293	15,322	11,800
Inventories	45	42	57	53
Gross Property	29,138	21,729	36,638	27,593
Accumulated Depreciation	7,539	5,876	9,480	7,461
Long-Term Debt	36,958	52,239	46,471	66,335
Stockholders' Equity	105,551	59,396	132,718	75,423
Total Assets	200,497	153,918	252,102	195,451
Total Current Assets	24,745	12,891	31,114	16,370
Total Current Liabilities	24,879	20,031	31,283	25,436
Net Working Capital	d134	d7,139	d169	d9,066
Year End Shs Outstg	106,631	97,417	106,631	97,417

STATISTICAL RECORD:

Return on Equity %	14.18	18.05		
Return on Assets %	7.46	6.96		
Operating Profit Margin %	50.71	61.64		
Net Profit Margin %	25.52	10.67		
Book Value Per Share	0.99	0.61		

Converted at 1996, US$0.7953= 1 Australian $; 1996, US$0.7875= 1 Australian $

OFFICERS:
A. J. Fletcher, Chmn.
T. N. Fern, Managing Dir.
G. H. Fulcher, Sec.

INCORPORATED: N/A

PRINCIPAL OFFICE: Level 13, 1 Alfred Street, Sydney NSW 1225 Australia

TELEPHONE NUMBER: 02-9247-4605

NO. OF EMPLOYEES: 47

ANNUAL MEETING: In November

SHAREHOLDERS: 4,043

INSTITUTIONAL HOLDINGS:
No. of Institutions: N/A
Shares Held: N/A

AMERICAN DEPOSITARY RECEIPTS: Each American Depositary Receipt represents 5 ordinary shares of par value A$0.20.

DEPOSITARY BANK(S): The Bank of New York, (212) 815-2175

PLANNING SCIENCES INTERNATIONAL PLC

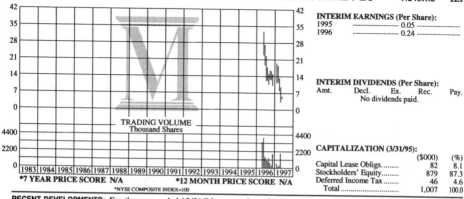

*7 YEAR PRICE SCORE N/A   ***12 MONTH PRICE SCORE N/A**
NYSE COMPOSITE INDEX=100

INTERIM EARNINGS (Per Share):

1995	------------------ 0.05 ------------------
1996	------------------ 0.24 ------------------

INTERIM DIVIDENDS (Per Share):

Amt.	Decl.	Ex.	Rec.	Pay.
	No dividends paid.			

CAPITALIZATION (3/31/95):

	($000)	(%)
Capital Lease Obligs.........	82	8.1
Stockholders' Equity.........	879	87.3
Deferred Income Tax	46	4.6
Total	1,007	100.0

RECENT DEVELOPMENTS: For the year ended 12/31/96, net income more than doubled to $2.5 million compared with $898,000 the previous year. Revenues leaped 58.4% to $26.0 million from $16.4 million the year before. License revenues jumped 64.9% to $16.9 million from $10.2 million the prior year, while service and other revenues surged 47.7% to $9.1 million from $6.2 million in 1995. Gross profit soared 60.0% to $20.2 million, or 77.9% of revenues, from $12.6 million, or 77.1% of revenues, a year earlier. Income from operations totaled $2.7 million, up 85.8% compared with $1.5 million the previous year. For the three months ended 12/31/96, net income was $944,000, up significantly versus $334,000 in the corresponding prior-year quarter. Revenues were up 87.0% to $8.2 million from $4.4 million the previous year.

BUSINESS

PLANNING SCIENCES INTERNA-TIONAL PLC develops, markets and supports high performance client/server decision support software for business, planning and decision making. Its principal product is marketed under the name Gentium. The Company's revenues are derived from license revenues for its Gentium software as well as software support and maintenance, training and consulting revenues from Gentium licenses.

ANNUAL EARNINGS

	3/31/95 ------US $------	3/31/95 --British £--
Earnings Per Share	0.05	0.03

ANNUAL FINANCIAL DATA

RECORD OF EARNINGS (IN THOUSANDS):

Total Revenues	10,762	6,639
Costs & Expenses	10,015	6,178
Operating Income	747	461
Income Bef Income Tax	670	413
Income Tax	254	157
Net Income	416	257
Average Shares Outstg	7,896	7,896

BALANCE SHEET (IN THOUSANDS):

Cash & Cash Equivalents	720	444
Receivables, Net	4,391	2,709
Gross Property	1,833	1,131
Accumulated Depreciation	1,155	713
Capital Lease Obligs.	82	51
Stockholders' Equity	879	542
Total Assets	6,091	3,758
Total Current Assets	5,413	3,339
Total Current Liabilities	5,084	3,136
Net Working Capital	329	203
Year End Shs Outstg	4,867	4,867

STATISTICAL RECORD:

Return on Equity %	47.33
Return on Assets %	6.83
Operating Profit Margin %	6.94
Net Profit Margin %	3.87
Book Value Per Share	0.18

Converted at 1995, US$1.6210= 1 British pound

OFFICERS:
P. R. Rolph, Chmn. & C.E.O.

INCORPORATED: 1983

PRINCIPAL OFFICE: Tuition House, St. George's Road, London United Kingdom

TELEPHONE NUMBER: 011-44-181-971-4000

NO. OF EMPLOYEES: 121

ANNUAL MEETING: N/A

SHAREHOLDERS: N/A

INSTITUTIONAL HOLDINGS:
No. of Institutions: 23
Shares Held: 2,744,200

AMERICAN DEPOSITARY RECEIPTS: Each American Depositary share represents 1 ordinary share of par £0.15.

DEPOSITARY BANK(S): The Bank of New York, (212) 815-2175

PROFESSIONAL STAFF, PLC

YIELD ...
P/E RATIO 13.8

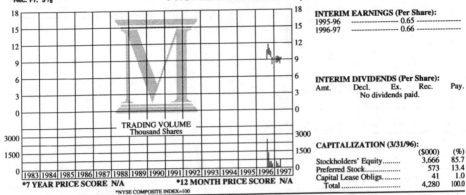

TRADING VOLUME
Thousand Shares

*7 YEAR PRICE SCORE N/A   *12 MONTH PRICE SCORE N/A

*NYSE COMPOSITE INDEX=100

INTERIM EARNINGS (Per Share):

1995-96	------------------ 0.65 ------------------
1996-97	------------------ 0.66 ------------------

INTERIM DIVIDENDS (Per Share):

Amt.	Decl.	Ex.	Rec.	Pay.
	No dividends paid.			

CAPITALIZATION (3/31/96):

	($000)	(%)
Stockholders' Equity........	3,666	85.7
Preferred Stock.................	573	13.4
Capital Lease Obligs........	41	1.0
Total	4,280	100.0

RECENT DEVELOPMENTS: For the twelve months ended 3/31/97, net income rose 22.5% to $3.8 million from $3.1 million the previous year. Revenue climbed 22.9% to $32.3 million from $26.3 million in the corresponding period the year before. Gross profit totaled 9.9 million, or 30.7% of revenue, up 17.5% compared with $8.4 million, or 32.1% of revenue, a year earlier. Operating income advanced 11.8% to $5.0 million from $4.5 million in the same prior-year period. Results benefited from strong fourth quarter demand for temporary scientific professionals and the Company's cost-effective delivery systems. For the three months ended 3/31/97, net income jumped 55.2% to $1.1 million from $685,000 the previous year. Revenue was up 17.6% to $8.3 million from $7.0 million in the fourth quarter in 1996. Operating income grew 24.2% to $1.3 million from $1.0 million the prior year. The 1996 figures used for comparison were restated to reflect discontinued operations.

BUSINESS

PROFESSIONAL STAFF, PLC, through its principal operating subsidiary, Lab Staff, is a provider of laboratory scientists and technicians throughout the United Kingdom. A second operating subsidiary, Executives On Assignment, provides senior executives for temporary assignments.

ANNUAL EARNINGS

	3/31/96	3/31/95	3/31/96	3/31/95
	------US $------		------British £------	
Earnings Per Share	ⓘ 0.65	...	ⓘ 0.43	...
ⓘ Pro forma				

ANNUAL FINANCIAL DATA

RECORD OF EARNINGS (IN THOUSANDS):

Total Revenues	27,442	23,147	17,963	14,279
Costs & Expenses	23,581	20,431	15,436	12,604
Operating Income	3,861	2,716	2,527	1,675
Income Bef Income Tax	3,188	2,846	2,087	1,756
Income Tax	1,436	1,147	940	708
Net Income	1,752	1,699	1,147	1,048
Average Shares Outstg	...	...	...	...

BALANCE SHEET (IN THOUSANDS):

Cash & Cash Equivalents	4,263	2,135	2,791	1,317
Receivables, Net	4,095	4,331	2,680	2,672
Gross Property	2,263	787	1,481	486
Accumulated Depreciation	237	383	155	236
Long-Term Debt	41	87	27	54
Stockholders' Equity	4,239	1,954	2,775	1,205
Total Assets	10,604	6,952	6,941	4,289
Total Current Assets	8,575	6,542	5,613	4,036
Total Current Liabilities	5,566	4,899	3,644	3,022
Net Working Capital	3,009	1,643	1,970	1,014
Year End Shs Outstg	352	352	352	352

STATISTICAL RECORD:

Return on Equity %	41.33	86.94
Return on Assets %	16.52	24.43
Operating Profit Margin %	14.07	11.73
Net Profit Margin %	6.38	7.34
Book Value Per Share	12.04	5.55

Converted at 1996, US$1.5277= 1 British pound; 1995, US$1.6210= 1 British pound

---

OFFICERS:
M. N. Buswell, Chmn.
B. R. Culver, Dep. Chmn.
B. Blackden, Managing Dir.
K. Worrall, Fin. Dir.

INCORPORATED: N/A

PRINCIPAL OFFICE: Buckland House, Waterside Drive, Slough, Berkshire United Kingdom SL36EZ

TELEPHONE NUMBER: 01753-580540

NO. OF EMPLOYEES: 823

ANNUAL MEETING: N/A

SHAREHOLDERS: N/A

INSTITUTIONAL HOLDINGS:
No. of Institutions: 10
Shares Held: 962,700

AMERICAN DEPOSITARY RECEIPTS: One American Depositary Receipt represents one ordinary share of par 0.10.

DEPOSITARY BANK(S): The Bank of New York, (212) 815-2175

P.T. PASIFIK SATELIT NUSANTARA

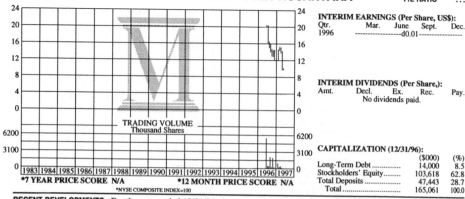

*7 YEAR PRICE SCORE N/A   *12 MONTH PRICE SCORE N/A
*NYSE COMPOSITE INDEX=100

INTERIM EARNINGS (Per Share, US$):

Qtr.	Mar.	June	Sept.	Dec.
1996		--------d0.01--------		

INTERIM DIVIDENDS (Per Share,):

Amt.	Decl.	Ex.	Rec.	Pay.
	No dividends paid.			

CAPITALIZATION (12/31/96):

	($000)	(%)
Long-Term Debt	14,000	8.5
Stockholders' Equity........	103,618	62.8
Total Deposits	47,443	28.7
Total	165,061	100.0

RECENT DEVELOPMENTS: For the year ended 12/31/96, the Company incurred a net loss of $474,692 compared with a net loss of $4.6 million in the prior year. Results included a loss of $948,003 incurred by the Asia Cellular Satellite Project, which is one-third owned by the Company. Revenues were $11.8 million compared with $2.2 million a year earlier. The significant increase in revenues resulted from the leasing of satellite transponders on Palapa C1. Transponder leasing revenue increased six-fold to $11.6 million from $1.8 million in the previous year. Operating profit soared to $6.1 million from $1.2 million the year before.

BUSINESS

P.T. PASIFIK SATELIT NUSANTARA is a private satellite company which provides communications services in the Asia-Pacific region. The Company is engaged in the provision of satellite transponder capacity and related services to telecommunications providers and to broadcasting customers such as STAR TV, a subsidiary of News Corporation; NBC Asia, an affiliate of the National Broadcasting Company; TVB International, an affiliate of a large producer and distributor of Cantonese language programming; and RCTI, an Indonesian broadcaster. In addition, the Company is also developing an innovative, low-cost, small aperture terminal designed to provide business communications and rural telephone services.

ANNUAL EARNINGS

	12/31/96	12/31/95	12/31/96	12/31/95
	--------------US $--------------		-------------Rp-------------	
Earnings Per Share	d0.01	d0.09	d25.0	d225.0

ANNUAL FINANCIAL DATA

RECORD OF EARNINGS (IN THOUSANDS):

	12/31/96	12/31/95	12/31/96	12/31/95
Total Revenues	11,768	2,246	29,419,810	5,615,065
Costs & Expenses	11,005	7,328	27,512,638	18,318,758
Operating Income	763	d5,081	1,907,173	d12,703,693
Income Bef Income Tax	d475	d4,625	d1,186,730	d11,562,218
Eq. Earnings in Affils.	d948	d217	d2,370,008	d542,150
Net Income	d475	d4,625	d1,186,730	d11,562,218

BALANCE SHEET (IN THOUSANDS):

Cash & Cash Equivalents	11,789	2,345	29,472,525	5,862,703
Receivables, Net	377	63	942,578	157,403
Gross Property	101,302	61,237	253,254,875	153,091,970
Accumulated Depreciation	4,495	730	11,236,993	1,825,228
Long-Term Debt	14,000	24,500	35,000,000	61,250,000
Stockholders' Equity	103,618	2,109	259,044,645	5,273,555
Total Assets	190,188	115,796	475,470,508	289,489,768
Total Current Assets	14,874	3,365	37,185,183	8,412,938
Total Current Liabilities	69,940	86,636	174,849,720	216,591,213
Net Working Capital	d55,066	d83,271	d137,664,538	d208,178,275
Year End Shs Outstg	78,786	14,367	78,786	14,367

STATISTICAL RECORD:

Return on Equity %	...	...		
Return on Assets %	...	...		
Operating Profit Margin %	6.48	...		
Net Profit Margin %	...	...		
Book Value Per Share	1.32	0.15		

Converted at 1996, US$0.0004= 1 Indonesian Rupiah; 1995, US$0.0004= 1 Indonesian Rupiah.

OFFICERS:
A. R. Adiwoso, Pres. & C.E.O.
A. K. Perangin Angin, V.P.
K. B. Smyth, V.P.

INCORPORATED: Indonesia, July, 1991

PRINCIPAL OFFICE: Sentra Mulia Suite 1201, Jalan H.R. Rasuna Said Kav. X-6 No. 8, Jakarta Indonesia

TELEPHONE NUMBER: (65-21) 522-9292

NO. OF EMPLOYEES: 36

ANNUAL MEETING: N/A

SHAREHOLDERS: N/A

INSTITUTIONAL HOLDINGS:
No. of Institutions: 12
Shares Held: 2,699,931

AMERICAN DEPOSITARY RECEIPTS: Each American Depositary Receipt represents three shares of par Rp250.

DEPOSITARY BANK(S): The Bank of New York, (212) 815-2175

RANK GROUP PLC (THE)

YIELD 5.9%
P/E RATIO 14.3

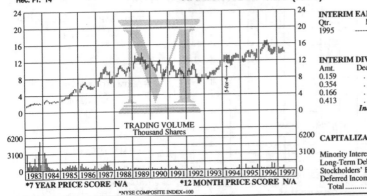

7 YEAR PRICE SCORE N/A **12 MONTH PRICE SCORE N/A**
NYSE COMPOSITE INDEX=100

TRADING VOLUME
Thousand Shares

INTERIM EARNINGS (Per Share, US$):

Qtr.	Mar.	June	Sept.	Dec.
1995	------------------	0.98	------------------	

INTERIM DIVIDENDS (Per Share):

Amt.	Decl.	Ex.	Rec.	Pay.
0.159	...	9/22/95	9/26/95	10/25/95
0.354	...	3/29/96	4/02/96	5/06/96
0.166	...	9/20	9/24	10/23
0.413	...	3/27/97	4/01/97	5/08/97

Indicated Div.: $0.83

CAPITALIZATION (12/31/95):

	($000)	(%)
Minority Interests	38,825	0.9
Long-Term Debt	1,049,828	24.9
Stockholders' Equity	3,109,106	73.8
Deferred Income Tax	17,083	0.4
Total	4,214,842	100.0

RECENT DEVELOPMENTS: For the fourteen months ended 12/31/95, net income was £525.0 million compared with income of £168.0 million, including discontinued operations, a year earlier. Sales from continuing operations were £2.6 million, up 20.5% from £2.2 million in the previous year. Sales from the film and television division jumped 25.1% to £851.0 million and operating profit increased 37.3% to £92.0 million. Recreation sales grew 18.8% to £867.0 million, while operating profit declined 14.5% to £59.0 million. The leisure division reported 36.8% higher sales to £368.0 million and 51.0% higher operating profit to £77.0 million. Results for 1994 are for the twelve months ended 10/31/94.

BUSINESS

THE RANK GROUP PLC is engaged in the supply of products and services to the film and television industries, owns holiday businesses and operates organized recreation and leisure facilities in the United Kingdom and overseas. Subsidiaries operations include: film processing and exhibition; film production studio operation; post-production facility operation; design, manufacture and marketing of high performance, high resolution cathode ray tube products; design, manufacture and marketing of broadcast equipment and software based television graphic products; investment in and international distribution of feature films; design, manufacture and marketing of high precision metrology instruments; video duplication; manufacture of entertainment lighting and lighting control equipment; hotel ownership; amusement machine hire and sales; amusement center operation, casino operation and club management; restaurant and resort management; and investment holding. Associate company operations are comprised of Rank Xerox companies and Universal Studios Florida. The business of Rank Xerox and its associates is the research, development, manufacture, marketing and maintenance of document processing systems and equipment. Universal Studios Florida operates a television and film studio and motion picture theme park.

ANNUAL EARNINGS

	12/31/95	10/31/94	12/31/95	10/31/94
	----- US $ -----		----- British £ -----	
Earnings Per Share	0.93	0.28	0.60	0.18

ANNUAL FINANCIAL DATA

RECORD OF EARNINGS (IN MILLIONS):

	12/31/95	10/31/94	12/31/95	10/31/94
Total Revenues	4,060	3,568	2,614	2,199
Costs & Expenses	3,654	3,208	2,353	1,977
Operating Income	405	360	261	222
Income Bef Income Tax	710	96	457	59
Income Tax	202	180	130	111
Eq. Earnings in Affils.	312	365	201	225
Minority Interests	5	8	3	5
Net Income	815	273	525	168
Average Shares Outstg (000)	830,700	824,400	830,700	824,400

BALANCE SHEET (IN MILLIONS):

Cash & Cash Equivalents	486	214	313	132
Receivables, Net	840	703	541	433
Inventories	235	230	151	142
Gross Property	3,437	3,251	2,213	2,004
Accumulated Depreciation	840	793	541	489
Long-Term Debt	1,050	1,251	676	771
Stockholders' Equity	3,109	2,529	2,002	1,559
Total Assets	5,175	4,919	3,332	3,032
Total Current Assets	1,561	1,147	1,005	707
Total Current Liabilities	918	1,003	591	618
Net Working Capital	643	144	414	89
Year End Shs Outstg (000)	832,600	829,200	832,600	829,200

STATISTICAL RECORD:

Return on Equity %	26.2	10.8		
Return on Assets %	15.8	5.5		
Operating Profit Margin %	10.0	10.1		
Net Profit Margin %	20.1	7.6		
Book Value Per Share	3.73	3.05		

Converted at 1995, US$1.5530= 1 British pound; 1994, US$1.5650= 1 British pound
Results for 12/31/95 are for a fourteen-month period.

OFFICERS:

D. Henderson, Chmn.
A. H. Teare, Chief Exec.
M. B. Gifford, Managing Dir.
A. Crichton-Miller

INCORPORATED: Feb., 1937

PRINCIPAL OFFICE: 6 Connaught Place London United Kingdom W2 2EZ

TELEPHONE NUMBER: 44-171-706-1111

NO. OF EMPLOYEES: 37,451

ANNUAL MEETING: In Apr.

SHAREHOLDERS: 43,883

INSTITUTIONAL HOLDINGS:
No. of Institutions: 18
Shares Held: 2,380,674

AMERICAN DEPOSITARY RECEIPTS: (Sponsored) Each American Depositary Receipt represents 1 ordinary share of par £0.10.

DEPOSITARY BANK(S): J.P. Morgan, (212) 648-3206

REUTERS HOLDINGS PLC

YIELD 2.8%
P/E RATIO 21.6

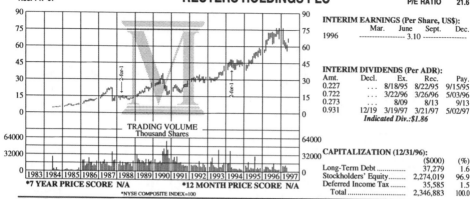

INTERIM EARNINGS (Per Share, US$):

	Mar.	June	Sept.	Dec.
1996	-------------	3.10	-------------	

INTERIM DIVIDENDS (Per ADR):

Amt.	Decl.	Ex.	Rec.	Pay.
0.227	...	8/18/95	8/22/95	9/15/95
0.722	...	3/22/96	3/26/96	5/03/96
0.273	...	8/09	8/13	9/13
0.931	12/19	3/19/97	3/21/97	5/02/97

Indicated Div.:$1.86

TRADING VOLUME
Thousand Shares

1983 1984 1985 1986 1987 1988 1989 1990 1991 1992 1993 1994 1995 1996 1997

*7 YEAR PRICE SCORE N/A   ***12 MONTH PRICE SCORE N/A**

*NYSE COMPOSITE INDEX=100

CAPITALIZATION (12/31/96):

	($000)	(%)
Long-Term Debt	37,279	1.6
Stockholders' Equity	2,274,019	96.9
Deferred Income Tax	35,585	1.5
Total	2,346,883	100.0

RECENT DEVELOPMENTS: For the year ended 12/31/96, net income was £491.0 million compared with £414.0 million in the corresponding period a year earlier. Sales were £2.91 billion versus £2.70 billion in 1995. Sales and earnings benefited from increased sales of subscription-based services and usage revenues. The Company's fastest-growing product line was transaction-based products revenue, which grew 21% to £813.0 million. Instinet posted another excellent year for revenues, growing 42% to £346.0 million. Flat markets led to slower growth in Reuters foreign exchange dealing products particularly in the second half of the year. User accesses grew 11% to 362,000 at the end of 1996. Information products accesses, which include Quotron, datafeed and Pocketwatch access, grew 10%, while datafeed accesses grew 30%.

BUSINESS

REUTERS HOLDINGS PLC supplies the global business community and the news media with real-time financial data, transaction systems, information management systems, access to numerical and textual historical databases, news, graphics, photos and news video. Information is obtained from around 260 exchanges and over-the-counter markets, form 4,800 subscribers who contribute data directly to Reuters and from a network of 1,960 journalists, photographers and cameramen. Some 362,000 clients access Reuters information, some using their own terminals to do so. Additional information about Reuters can be found on the World Wide Web at www.reuters.com

ANNUAL EARNINGS

	12/31/96	12/31/95	12/31/96	12/31/95
	US $		British £	
Earnings Per Share	3.10	2.63	0.304	0.258

ANNUAL FINANCIAL DATA

RECORD OF EARNINGS (IN MILLIONS):

	12/31/96	12/31/95	12/31/96	12/31/95
Total Revenues	4,938	4,198	2,914	2,703
Costs & Expenses	3,372	2,954	1,990	1,902
Depreciation & Amort	480	388	283	250
Operating Income	1,086	856	641	551
Income Bef Income Tax	1,200	949	701	599
Income Tax	356	287	210	185
Eq. Earnings in Affils.	d12	d19	d7	d12
Net Income	832	643	491	414
Average Shares Outstg (000)	1,616,000	1,605,000	1,616,000	1,605,000

BALANCE SHEET (IN MILLIONS):

Cash & Cash Equivalents	1,857	1,441	1,096	928
Receivables, Net	664	654	392	421
Inventories	37	33	22	21
Gross Property	1,187	1,084	775	698
Long-Term Debt	37	53	22	34
Stockholders' Equity	2,274	1,598	1,342	1,029
Total Assets	3,962	3,269	2,338	2,105
Total Current Assets	2,559	2,128	1,510	1,370
Total Current Liabilities	1,669	1,527	985	983
Net Working Capital	890	601	525	387
Year End Shs Outstg (000)	1,688,000	1,677,100	1,688,600	1,677,100

STATISTICAL RECORD:

Return on Equity %	45.6	50.4
Return on Assets %	21.0	19.7
Operating Profit Margin %	22.0	20.4
Net Profit Margin %	16.9	15.3
Book Value Per Share	1.29	0.89

Converted at 1996, US$1.6945= 1 British pound; 1995, US$1.5530= 1 British pound

OFFICERS:
Sir Christopher Hogg, Chmn.
P. Job, C.E.O.
R. Rowley, Fin. Dir.
M. Wood, Editor in Chief

INCORPORATED: 1916

PRINCIPAL OFFICE: 85 Fleet Street, London EC4P 4AJ United Kingdom

TELEPHONE NUMBER: 44-0171-250-1122

NO. OF EMPLOYEES: 14,917

ANNUAL MEETING: In Apr.

SHAREHOLDERS: N/A

INSTITUTIONAL HOLDINGS:
No. of Institutions: 263
Shares Held: 47,878,617

AMERICAN DEPOSITARY RECEIPTS: (Sponsored) Each American Depositary Receipt represents six ordinary shares. In Apr. 1994, ADRs split 2-for-1.

DEPOSITARY BANK(S): J.P. Morgan, (212) 648-3206

REXAM PLC

YIELD 4.4%
P/E RATIO ...

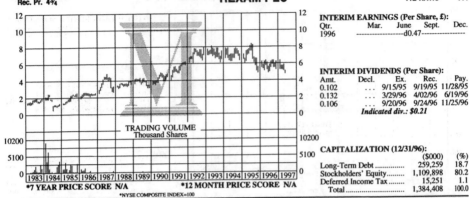

*7 YEAR PRICE SCORE N/A   *12 MONTH PRICE SCORE N/A
*NYSE COMPOSITE INDEX=100

TRADING VOLUME
Thousand Shares

INTERIM EARNINGS (Per Share, £):

Qtr.	Mar.	June	Sept.	Dec.
1996			d0.47	

INTERIM DIVIDENDS (Per Share):

Amt.	Decl.	Ex.	Rec.	Pay.
0.102	...	9/15/95	9/19/95	11/28/95
0.132	...	3/29/96	4/02/96	6/19/96
0.106	...	9/20/96	9/24/96	11/25/96

Indicated div.: $0.21

CAPITALIZATION (12/31/96):

	($000)	(%)
Long-Term Debt	259,259	18.7
Stockholders' Equity	1,109,898	80.2
Deferred Income Tax	15,251	1.1
Total	1,384,408	100.0

RECENT DEVELOPMENTS: For the year ended 12/31/96, the Company reported a loss including exceptional items and discontinued operations of £238.0 million compared with income of £132.0 million including discontinued operations a year earlier. Total turnover was £2.31 billion, down 3.5% from £2.39 billion in the prior year. In January 1997, the Company signed a letter of intent to sell Otis Specialty Papers for a total consideration of £36.0 million, and sold PT Rexam Mulox for £1.3 million. In March 1997, the Company announced the disposal of Rexam Digital Imaging for £1.1 million.

BUSINESS

REXAM PLC, formerly Bowater plc, is a United Kingdom based holding company for an international group of manufacturing, packaging, print and coated products. The businesses within the group, which include engineered building products, are linked across the world by common or related technologies or markets.

ANNUAL EARNINGS

	12/31/96	12/31/95	12/31/96	12/31/95
	----US $----		----British £----	
Earnings Per Share	d0.80	0.40	d0.47	0.26

ANNUAL FINANCIAL DATA

RECORD OF EARNINGS (IN MILLIONS):

	12/31/96	12/31/95	12/31/96	12/31/95
Total Revenues	3,909	3,713	2,307	2,391
Costs & Expenses	3,494	3,241	2,062	2,087
Depreciation & Amort	193	166	114	107
Operating Income	222	306	131	197
Income Bef Income Tax	d322	280	d190	180
Income Tax	81	73	48	47
Minority Interests	...	2	...	1
Net Income	d403	205	d238	132
Average Shares Outstg (000)	503,400	501,900	503,400	501,900

BALANCE SHEET (IN MILLIONS):

Cash & Cash Equivalents	574	820	339	528
Receivables, Net	734	820	433	528
Inventories	329	394	194	254
Gross Property	2,476	2,406	1,461	1,549
Accumulated Depreciation	1,149	1,020	678	657
Long-Term Debt	259	677	153	436
Stockholders' Equity	1,110	1,089	655	701
Total Assets	3,023	3,469	1,784	2,234
Total Current Assets	1,652	2,042	975	1,315
Total Current Liabilities	1,357	1,478	801	952
Net Working Capital	295	564	174	363
Year End Shs Outstg (000)	504,260	503,650	504,260	503,650

STATISTICAL RECORD:

Return on Equity %	...	18.8		
Return on Assets %	...	5.9		
Operating Profit Margin %	5.7	8.2		
Net Profit Margin %	...	5.5		
Book Value Per Share	2.20	2.16		

Converted at 1996, US$1.6945= 1 British pound; 1995, US$1.5530= 1 British pound

OFFICERS:
J. Lancaster, Chmn.
R. Borjesson, C.E.O. & Managing Dir.
M. Hartnall, Fin. Dir.
K. Abbott

INCORPORATED: England, 1923

PRINCIPAL OFFICE: 114 Knightsbridge, London United Kingdom

TELEPHONE NUMBER: 0171-584-7070

NO. OF EMPLOYEES: 24,100

ANNUAL MEETING: In May

SHAREHOLDERS: 27,406

INSTITUTIONAL HOLDINGS:
No. of Institutions: 4
Shares Held: 713,400

AMERICAN DEPOSITARY RECEIPTS: (Sponsored) Each American Depositary Receipt represents one ordinary share of par £0.50.

DEPOSITARY BANK(S): J.P. Morgan, (212) 648-3206

NASDAQ SYMBOL SAESY
Rec. Pr. 9

SAES GETTERS S.P.A.

YIELD 1.9%
P/E RATIO 18.4

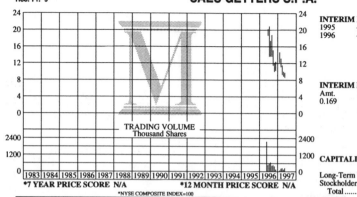

7 YEAR PRICE SCORE N/A **12 MONTH PRICE SCORE N/A**
*NYSE COMPOSITE INDEX=100

INTERIM EARNINGS (Per Share, US$):

1995	------------------ 0.80 ------------------
1996	------------------ 0.58 ------------------

INTERIM DIVIDENDS (Per Share):

Amt.	Decl.	Ex.	Rec.	Pay.
0.169	...	5/14/97	5/16/97	6/13/97

Indicated div.: $0.169

CAPITALIZATION (12/31/96):

	($000)	(%)
Long-Term Debt	2,048	1.3
Stockholders' Equity.........	158,084	98.7
Total	160,132	100.0

RECENT DEVELOPMENTS: For the year ended 12/31/96, net income fell 34.1% to Lit17.71 billion from Lit26.87 billion the previous year. Total net sales increased 5.4% to Lit181.83 billion from Lit172.52 billion a year earlier. Results benefited from a stronger Italian Lire in 1996 compared with 1995 combined with strong sales growth in the Company's gas purification division. Gross profit slipped 4.5% to Lit90.95 billion, or 50.0% of total net sales, from Lit95.20 billion, or 55.2% of total net sales, the year before.

Research and development expenses jumped 64.8% to Lit15.45 billion from Lit9.38 billion in 1995 reflecting advanced product development and higher leasing costs. Operating income dropped 39.5% to Lit25.90 billion from Lit42.84 billion the prior year. For the three months ended 12/31/96, net income was Lit4.09 billion, down 57.5% versus Lit9.63 billion a year earlier. Total net sales rose 7.0% to Lit47.11 billion from Lit44.02 billion the previous year.

BUSINESS

SAES GETTERS S.P.A. and its subsidiaries are engaged in the manufacture of getters, a metal alloy component that is used to maintain very high vacuums. Getters are used in cathode-ray tubes found in TV sets and computers, as well as lamps and fluorescent vacuum displays. Getters are also essential to the production of semiconductors, where it is necessary to maintain high vacuum and purified gas environments.

ANNUAL EARNINGS

	12/31/96	12/31/95	12/31/96	12/31/95
	------------US $------------		---------Italian Lire---------	
Earnings Per Share	0.58	0.80	822	1,334

ANNUAL FINANCIAL DATA

RECORD OF EARNINGS (IN THOUSANDS):

Total Revenues	127,282	103,512	181,832,000	172,520,000
Costs & Expenses	109,155	77,809	155,936,000	129,682,000
Operating Income	18,127	25,703	25,896,000	42,838,000
Income Bef Income Tax	20,200	25,615	28,857,000	42,692,000
Income Tax	7,803	9,495	11,147,000	15,825,000
Net Income	12,397	16,120	17,710,000	26,867,000

BALANCE SHEET (IN THOUSANDS):

Cash & Cash Equivalents	82,572	30,863	117,960,000	51,439,000
Receivables, Net	42,724	30,110	61,034,000	50,183,000
Inventories	34,388	21,255	49,125,000	35,425,000
Gross Property	74,647	59,345	106,639,000	98,909,000
Accumulated Depreciation	38,638	32,319	55,197,000	53,865,000
Long-Term Debt	2,047	2,216	2,925,000	3,694,000
Stockholders' Equity	158,084	74,685	225,834,000	124,475,000
Total Assets	220,921	115,996	315,602,000	193,326,000
Total Current Assets	160,876	82,717	229,823,000	137,862,000
Total Current Liabilities	52,137	32,242	74,481,000	53,736,000
Net Working Capital	108,739	50,476	155,342,000	84,126,000
Year End Shares Outstg	13,656	13,656	13,656	13,656

STATISTICAL RECORD:

Return on Equity %	7.84	21.58
Return on Assets %	5.61	13.90
Operating Profit Margin %	14.24	24.83
Net Profit Margin %	9.74	15.57
Book Value Per Share	11.58	5.47

Converted at 1996, US$0.0007= 1 Italian Lire; 1995, US$0.0006= 1 Italian Lire

OFFICERS:
P. della Porta, Chmn., Pres. & C.E.O.
M. della Porta, Vice-Chmn. & Managing Dir.
G. Canale, Managing Director
G. Rolando, Gen. Mgr. & Group C.F.O.
INCORPORATED: N/A
PRINCIPAL OFFICE: Viale Italia 77, 20020 Lainate Italy

TELEPHONE NUMBER: 39-2-931-781
NO. OF EMPLOYEES: 800 (approx.)
ANNUAL MEETING: In April
SHAREHOLDERS: N/A
INSTITUTIONAL HOLDINGS:
No. of Institutions: 14
Shares Held: 1,478,400

AMERICAN DEPOSITARY RECEIPTS: Each American Depository Share represents one savings share of par Lit1,000 each.

DEPOSITARY BANK(S): Citibank N.A., (212) 657-7800

227

SANTOS, LTD.

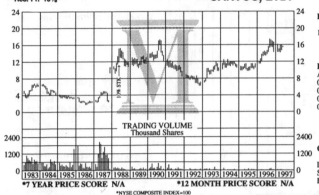

INTERIM EARNINGS (Per Share, US$):

	Mar.	June	Sept.	Dec.
1996	------------------ 0.29 ------------------			

INTERIM DIVIDENDS (Per Share):

Amt.	Decl.	Ex.	Rec.	Pay.
0.324	...	10/31/95	11/02/95	12/12/95
0.38	...	3/26/96	3/28/96	5/13/96
0.347	...	10/22/96	10/24/96	11/26/96
0.405	...	4/08/97	4/10/97	5/13/97

Indicated div.:$0.81

TRADING VOLUME
Thousand Shares

*7 YEAR PRICE SCORE N/A   *12 MONTH PRICE SCORE N/A
*NYSE COMPOSITE INDEX=100

CAPITALIZATION (12/31/96):

	($000)	(%)
Long-Term Debt	867,036	35.0
Stockholders' Equity.........	1,261,584	50.9
Deferred Income Tax	349,932	14.1
Total	2,478,552	100.0

RECENT DEVELOPMENTS: For the year ended 12/31/96, net income leaped 40% to A$195.0 million compared with A$110.6 million in the corresponding period a year earlier. Revenues were A$814.5 million versus A$751.3 million in 1995. Revenues and earnings benefited from strong sales gains, higher prices received for all products and lower exploration write-downs. The Parker and Parsley Australasia acquisition contributed to the result, as did foreign exchange gains on US dollar debt that offset the impact of a stronger Australian dollar on revenue. Reserves increased by 157 million barrels of oil equivalent (boe) to a record 860 boe at the end of 1996. Reserve additions during the year were five times the 1996 level of production. Total reserves now represent almost 22 years of future production, up from 19 years in 1995.

BUSINESS

SANTOS, LTD. and its subsidiaris are engaged in gas and petroleum exploration; the production, treatment and marketing of natural gas, crude oil, condensate, naphtha and liquid petroleum gas; and the transportation by pipeline of crude oil. The Company and its joint venture partners produce one-third of the natural gas consumed in Australia, as well as crude oil, condensate and LPG for Australian and Asian markets. The Company is also involved in exploration and production in the U.S., the U.K., Indonesia and Papua New Guinea.

ANNUAL EARNINGS

	12/31/96	12/31/95	12/31/96	12/31/95
	------------US $------------		------------A$------------	
Earnings Per Share	0.29	0.16	0.36	0.21

ANNUAL FINANCIAL DATA

RECORD OF EARNINGS (IN THOUSANDS):

	12/31/96	12/31/95	12/31/96	12/31/95
Total Revenues	647,772	558,592	814,500	751,300
Income Bef Income Tax	263,960	179,184	331,900	241,000
Income Tax	108,161	96,952	136,000	130,400
Net Income	155,799	82,231	195,900	110,600

BALANCE SHEET (IN THOUSANDS):

Cash & Cash Equivalents	120,886	65,279	152,000	87,800
Receivables, Net	103,707	89,369	130,400	120,200
Inventories	57,739	45,130	72,600	60,700
Gross Property	3,897,050	3,198,463	4,900,100	4,301,900
Accumulated Depreciation	1,832,928	1,576,443	2,304,700	2,120,300
Long-Term Debt	867,036	542,086	1,090,200	729,100
Stockholders' Equity	1,261,584	1,129,600	1,586,300	1,519,300
Total Assets	2,738,536	2,167,674	3,443,400	2,915,500
Total Current Assets	282,332	199,778	355,000	268,700
Total Current Liabilities	201,131	149,964	252,900	201,700
Net Working Capital	81,200	49,815	102,100	67,000
Year End Shs Outstg	429,126	401,101	429,126	401,101

STATISTICAL RECORD:

Return on Equity %	12.35	7.28		
Return on Assets %	5.69	3.79		
Operating Profit Margin %	4.02	4.02		
Net Profit Margin %	24.05	14.72		
Book Value Per Share	2.94	2.82		

Converted at 1996, US$0.7953= 1 Australian $; 1995, US$0.7435= 1 Australian $

OFFICERS:
J. A. Uhrig, Chmn.
N. R. Adler, Managing Dir.
J. W. McArdle, Exec. Dir.

INCORPORATED: Mar., 1954

PRINCIPAL OFFICE: Santos House, 91 King William Street, Adelaide South Australia 5000

TELEPHONE NUMBER: (08) 218 5111

NO. OF EMPLOYEES: 1,461

ANNUAL MEETING: In May

SHAREHOLDERS: 55,684

INSTITUTIONAL HOLDINGS:
No. of Institutions: 8
Shares Held: 286,085

AMERICAN DEPOSITARY RECEIPTS: (Sponsored) Each American Depository Receipt represents four ordinary shares of par A$0.25. American Depository Receipts underwent a 1-for-4 reverse split on Dec. 14, 1987.

DEPOSITARY BANK(S): J.P. Morgan, (212) 648-3206

SANYO ELECTRIC CO., LTD.

YIELD 0.8%
P/E RATIO ...

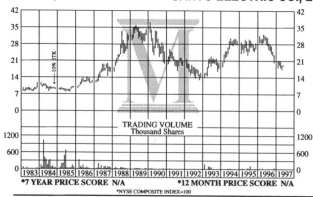

INTERIM EARNINGS (Per Share, US$):

	June	Sept.	Dec.	Mar.
1996		d0.02		

INTERIM DIVIDENDS (Per Share):

Amt.	Decl.	Ex.	Rec.	Pay.
0.11	...	8/04/95	8/08/95	8/17/95
0.09	...	11/27	11/29	3/15/96
0.055	...	5/28/96	5/30/96	7/16
0.083	...	11/08	11/13	12/26
0.077	...	4/01/97	4/03/97	...

Indicated Div.:$0.154

TRADING VOLUME
Thousand Shares

1983 1984 1985 1986 1987 1988 1989 1990 1991 1992 1993 1994 1995 1996 1997

*7 YEAR PRICE SCORE N/A   ***12 MONTH PRICE SCORE N/A**

*NYSE COMPOSITE INDEX=100

CAPITALIZATION (3/31/96):

	($000)	(%)
Long-Term Debt	3,394,203	31.1
Stockholders' Equity	7,529,541	68.9
Total	10,923,744	100.0

RECENT DEVELOPMENTS: For the six months ended 9/30/96, the Company reported net income of ¥8.17 billion (US$73.6 million). Net sales amounted to ¥883.34 billion (US$7.96 billion). Operating income was ¥30.4 million (US$273.6 million). The video equipment business segment, which posted sales of ¥116.02 billion (US$1.05 billion), reflected strong sales of digital still cameras. The trend toward increasing purchases of large refrigerators to replace small models contributed to sales of the home appliances business segment, which reported sales of ¥179.86 billion (US$1.62 billion). Sales of ¥148.51 billion (US$1.34 billion) in the industrial and commercial equipment business segment reflected favorable sales of three-way, multi-type air conditioners for buildings and commercial-use kitchen equipment for hotels.

BUSINESS

SANYO ELECTRIC CO., LTD. is engaged in the manufacturing, marketing, and after-sales servicing of a broad range of electronic products, including video equipment, audio equipment, home appliances, industrial equipment, electronic components, information systems, electronic devices, batteries and other products. The Company's principal business segments are listed as follows: (1) Video Equipment, (2) Audio Equipment, (3) Home Appliances, (4) Industrial Equipment, (5) Information Systems and Electronic Devices, and (6) Batteries and Other Products. The Company encompasses 76 manufacturing companies, 33 sales companies, and 21 other companies based in 28 countries.

ANNUAL EARNINGS

	① 3/31/96	11/30/95	① 3/31/96	11/30/95
	US $		Yen	
Earnings Per Share	d0.02	0.08	d1.92	7.97

① For four months due to fiscal year-end change.

ANNUAL FINANCIAL DATA

RECORD OF EARNINGS (IN THOUSANDS):

	3/31/96	11/30/95	3/31/96	11/30/95
Total Revenues	4,878,808	17,074,403	524,603,000	1,742,286,000
Costs & Expenses	4,753,249	16,492,440	511,102,000	1,682,902,000
Operating Income	125,559	581,963	13,501,000	59,384,000
Income Bef Income Tax	32,411	403,691	3,485,000	41,193,0000
Income Tax	76,771	282,436	8,255,000	28,820,000
Eq. Earnings in Affils.	9,598	31,144	1,032,000	3,178,000
Net Income	d34,763	152,400	d3,738,000	15,551,000
Average Shares Outstg	1,950,926	1,950,286	1,950,926	1,950,286

BALANCE SHEET (IN THOUSANDS):

Cash & Cash Equivalents	6,731,721	6,979,864	723,841,000	712,231,000
Receivables, Net	4,220,814	4,588,076	453,851,000	468,171,000
Inventories	3,085,926	2,954,112	331,820,000	301,440,000
Gross Property	12,077,064	12,554,261	1,298,609,000	1,281,047,000
Accumulated Depreciation	6,945,761	7,195,268	746,856,000	734,211,000
Long-Term Debt	3,394,202	3,403,030	364,968,000	347,248,000
Stockholders' Equity	7,529,540	7,870,321	809,628,000	803,094,000
Total Assets	22,899,781	23,632,612	2,462,342,000	2,411,491,000
Total Current Assets	14,482,007	14,924,371	1,557,205,000	1,522,895,000
Total Current Liabilities	10,981,533	11,304,026	1,180,810,000	1,153,472,000
Net Working Capital	3,500,473	3,620,345	376,395,000	369,423,000
Year End Shs Outstg	1,950,929	1,950,919	1,950,929	1,950,919

STATISTICAL RECORD:

Return on Equity %	...	1.91		
Return on Assets %	...	0.64		
Operating Profit Margin %	2.57	3.41		
Net Profit Margin %	...	0.89		
Book Value Per Share	3.86	4.03		

Converted at 1996, US$0.0093 = 1 Japanese Yen; 1995, US$0.0098 = 1 Japanese Yen

OFFICERS:
S. Iue, Chmn. & Rep. Dir.
M. Yamano, Vice-Chmn. & Rep. Dir.
Y. Takano, Pres. & Rep. Dir.
M. Sugimoto, Exec. V.P. & Rep. Dir.

INCORPORATED: Japan, Apr., 1950

PRINCIPAL OFFICE: 5-5 Keihan-Hondori 2-chome, Moriguchi Japan

TELEPHONE NUMBER: 06-991-1181

NO. OF EMPLOYEES: 56,612

ANNUAL MEETING: In Jun.

SHAREHOLDERS: 220,319

INSTITUTIONAL HOLDINGS:
No. of Institutions: 5
Shares Held: 752,136

AMERICAN DEPOSITARY RECEIPTS:
(Sponsored) Each Amer. Dep. Receipt represents one ordinary share of par ¥50.

DEPOSITARY BANK(S): The Bank of New York, (212) 815-2175; Bankers Trust Co., (212) 250-8500; J.P. Morgan, (212) 648-3206

SASOL LTD.

YIELD 4.2%
P/E RATIO 14.44

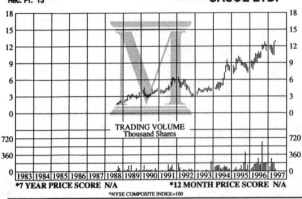

TRADING VOLUME
Thousand Shares

*7 YEAR PRICE SCORE N/A   *12 MONTH PRICE SCORE N/A
*NYSE COMPOSITE INDEX=100

INTERIM EARNINGS (Per Share, US$):

	Sept.	Dec.	Mar.	June
1996	------------------ 0.90 ------------------			

INTERIM DIVIDENDS (Per Share):

Amt.	Decl.	Ex.	Rec.	Pay.
0.319	...	7/27/95	7/31/95	8/14/95
0.117	...	9/27	9/29	11/13
0.113	...	3/13/96	3/15/96	4/29/96
0.138	...	10/02	10/04	10/25
0.134	...	3/12/97	3/14/97	4/28/97
			Indicated div.:$0.54	

CAPITALIZATION (6/25/96):

	($000)	(%)
Minority Interests.............	7,806	0.3
Long-Term Debt	235,851	7.7
Stockholders' Equity........	2,439,271	79.7
Deferred Income Tax	376,314	12.3
Total......................	3,059,242	100.0

RECENT DEVELOPMENTS: For the six months ended 12/25/96, net income leaped to R$1.3 million compared with R$1.0 million in the corresponding period a year earlier. Sales were R$7.9 million versus R$6.8 million in 1995. Results for 1995 were restated to reflect changes in accounting methods. Higher operating profits at Sasol Synthetic Fuels were largely due to continued stable plant operation and a weaker rand versus dollar exchange rate.

Sasol Chemical Industries posted a 30% increase in operating profits due to increased volumes and prices. Improvement at Sasol Oil was due to higher rand refining margins and the favorable effect of the change to the FIFO method of accounting. Sasol Mining is recovering from difficult mining conditions. The group's export and foreign sales increased by 31%, predominantly due to price and volume increases, and a weaker rand.

BUSINESS

SASOL LTD. is a holding company engaged in the production and marketing of liquid fuels, pipeline gas, waxes, plastics, petrochemicals, fertilizers, mining explosives and polymers derived from coal and crude oil. SASOL is also engaged in the mining of coal which it converts into oil and gas. The Company is a member of the Johannesburg Stock Exchange listed under the Coal, Chemical and Crude-oil sector.

ANNUAL EARNINGS

	6/25/96	6/25/95	6/25/96	6/25/95
	-------------US $-------------		-------------Rand-------------	
Earnings Per Share	0.90	0.87	3.90	3.19

ANNUAL FINANCIAL DATA

RECORD OF EARNINGS (IN MILLIONS):

Total Revenues	3,110	3,260	13,545	11,955
Income Bef Income Tax	793	773	3,449	2,830
Income Tax	212	255	924	934
Minority Interests	8	8	34	29
Net Income	537	508	2,333	1,859
Average Shares Outstg (000)	594,000	576,000	594,000	576,000

BALANCE SHEET (IN MILLIONS):

Cash & Cash Equivalents	565	583	2,460	2,137
Receivables, Net	530	581	2,309	2,132
Inventories	316	439	1,378	1,609
Gross Property	4,368	4,822	19,024	17,683
Accumulated Depreciation	1,717	1,902	7,477	6,976
Long-Term Debt	236	317	1,021	1,151
Stockholders' Equity	2,439	2,459	10,624	9,018
Total Assets	4,165	4,641	18,140	17,020
Total Current Assets	1,411	1,603	6,147	5,878
Total Current Liabilities	826	1,102	3,599	4,041
Net Working Capital	585	501	2,548	1,837
Year End Shs Outstg (000)	603,000	586,000	603,000	586,000

STATISTICAL RECORD:

Return on Equity %	21.8	20.4
Return on Assets %	12.8	10.8
Operating Profit Margin %	9.8	9.8
Net Profit Margin %	17.1	15.4
Book Value Per Share	17.6	15.4

Converted at 1996, US$0.2310= 1 South African Rand; 1995, US$0.2750= 1 South African Rand

OFFICERS:
P. du P. Kruger, Chmn.
P. V. Cox, C.O.O.
N. L. Joubert, Sec.

INCORPORATED: Jun., 1979

PRINCIPAL OFFICE: 1 Sturdee Avenue
Rosebank South Africa

TELEPHONE NUMBER: (011) 441-3111

NO. OF EMPLOYEES: 25,000

ANNUAL MEETING: In Oct.

SHAREHOLDERS: 15,455

INSTITUTIONAL HOLDINGS:
No. of Institutions: 9
Shares Held: 885,220

**AMERICAN DEPOSITARY
RECEIPTS:** (Sponsored) Each American Depositary Receipt represents one ordinary share of no par value.

DEPOSITARY BANK(S): The Bank of New York, (212) 815-2175; DST Systems Inc.

SAVILLE SYSTEMS, PLC

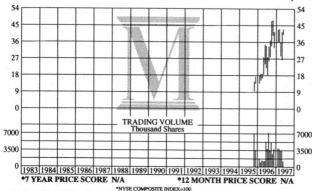

7 YEAR PRICE SCORE N/A   **12 MONTH PRICE SCORE N/A**

*NYSE COMPOSITE INDEX=100

TRADING VOLUME
Thousand Shares

INTERIM EARNINGS (Per Share):

Qtr.	Mar.	June	Sept.	Dec.
1995	0.13	0.12	0.07	0.08
1996	0.11	0.14	0.17	0.19
1997	0.23	...	...	...

INTERIM DIVIDENDS (Per Share):

Amt.	Decl.	Ex.	Rec.	Pay.
No dividends paid.				

CAPITALIZATION (12/31/96):

	($000)	(%)
Minority Interest	320	0.7
Stockholders' Equity	46,611	99.3
Total	46,931	100.0

RECENT DEVELOPMENTS: For the three months ended 3/31/97, net income more than doubled to $4.4 million, or $0.23 per share, compared with $2.0 million, or $0.11 per share, in the corresponding quarter a year earlier. Total revenues soared 90.7% to $20.1 million from $10.6 million the previous year. Services revenue surged 82.8% to $16.5 million from $9.0 million a year ago, while license fees revenue leapt to $3.6 million from $1.5 million the year before. Income from operations totaled $5.4 million, up significantly compared with $2.2 million the prior year. During the first quarter, the Company closed contracts with EnerTel and Citizens Utilities located in Europe and the U.S., respectively. On 4/23/97, the Company announced it had entered into the Asia/Pacific market with a new office located in Singapore.

BUSINESS

SAVILLE SYSTEMS PLC creates customized billing solutions for service providers in the global telecommunications industry. The Company utilizes its library of proprietary software to provide its customers with customized, flexible, cost-effective billing systems. The Company typically continues its relationships with customers by implementing new systems as the customers enter new service categories or geographic markets and by further developing and enhancing installed systems in response to its customers' needs. In addition, SAVLY offers its customers the option of having the Company operate the billing system in one of it's in-house service bureaus. The Company's principal markets are currently located in the United States, Europe and Canada.

ANNUAL EARNINGS

	12/31/96	12/31/95	12/31/96	12/31/95
	-----------US $-----------		---------Irish £---------	
Earnings Per Share	0.61	0.40	0.37	0.25

ANNUAL FINANCIAL DATA

RECORD OF EARNINGS (IN THOUSANDS):

Total Revenues	53,920	30,296	32,529	18,933
Costs & Expenses	40,650	22,180	24,573	13,861
Operating Income	13,270	8,116	8,006	5,072
Income Bef Income Tax	14,761	8,324	8,905	5,202
Income Tax	3,052	1,872	1,841	1,170
Minority Interests	140	70	84	44
Net Income	11,569	6,382	6,979	3,988
Average Shares Outstg	18,948	16,151	18,948	16,151

BALANCE SHEET (IN THOUSANDS):

Cash & Cash Equivalents	35,395	23,722	21,353	14,824
Receivables, Net	15,308	8,177	9,235	5,110
Gross Property	5,684	2,978	3,429	1,861
Accumulated Depreciation	1,409	643	850	402
Long-Term Debt	...	44	...	27
Stockholders' Equity	46,611	30,924	28,120	19,325
Total Assets	56,489	36,031	34,079	22,517
Total Current Assets	52,214	32,955	31,500	20,594
Total Current Liabilities	9,558	4,846	5,766	3,028
Net Working Capital	42,656	28,109	25,734	17,566
Year End Shs Outstg	18,112	17,576	18,112	17,576

STATISTICAL RECORD:

Return on Equity %	24.82	20.64		
Return on Assets %	20.48	17.71		
Operating Profit Margin %	24.61	26.79		
Net Profit Margin %	21.46	21.07		
Book Value Per Share	2.57	1.76		

Converted at 1996, US$1.6576= 1 Irish pound; 1995, US$1.6002= 1 Irish pound

OFFICERS:
B. A. Saville, Chmn.
J. J. Boyle, III, Pres. & C.E.O.
M. J. Venator, C.O.O.
C. A. Hanson, C.F.O.

INCORPORATED: Ireland, June, 1993

PRINCIPAL OFFICE: IDA Business Park, Dangan Galway Ireland

TELEPHONE NUMBER: 011-353-91-526611

NO. OF EMPLOYEES: 641

ANNUAL MEETING: In April

SHAREHOLDERS: N/A

INSTITUTIONAL HOLDINGS:
No. of Institutions: 56
Shares Held: 9,269,832

AMERICAN DEPOSITARY RECEIPTS: Each American Depositary Receipt represents 1 ordinary share of par US$0.0025.

DEPOSITARY BANK(S): The Bank of New York, (212) 815-2175

SAWAKO CORPORATION

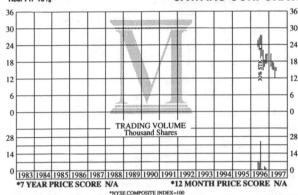

*7 YEAR PRICE SCORE N/A *12 MONTH PRICE SCORE N/A
*NYSE COMPOSITE INDEX=100

TRADING VOLUME
Thousand Shares

INTERIM EARNINGS (Per Share, US$):

Qtr.	Oct.	Jan.	Apr.	Jul.
1996		0.60		

INTERIM DIVIDENDS (Per Share):

Amt.	Decl.	Ex.	Rec.	Pay.
0.137	...	7/26/96	7/30/96	11/15/96
30%	...	7/26/96	7/30/96	10/04/96

Indicated Div.:$0.105

CAPITALIZATION (7/31/96):

	($000)	(%)
Stockholders' Equity	74,724	100.0
Total	74,724	100.0

RECENT DEVELOPMENTS: For the year ended 7/31/96, net income jumped 19.7% to ¥744.4 million from ¥621.8 million a year earlier. Total revenue was ¥15.65 bilion, up 29.7% from ¥12.06 billion in the prior year. A major contribution to the increase in total revenue was made by revenues from sales of units in a condominium project and the expansion of the Company's operations to Kobe, Hyogo Prefecture, and Kariya, Aichi Prefecture, where it opened branch offices during fiscal 1996. Gross profit as a percentage of sales was 18.1% in 1996 versus 17.2% in 1995. Operating income was ¥1.57 billion compared with ¥1.25 billion the year before, an increase of 25.9%. Operating profit margin decreased to 10.0% from 10.3% in the previous year due to the increase in the ratio of selling, general and administrative expenses to total revenue.

BUSINESS

SAWAKO CORPORATION is a regional contractor based in Nagoya. The Company is engaged in the construction of rental multi-unit residental buildings for individual landowners seeking to develop their property to generate rental income and tax savings. The Company specializes in constructing modern multi-unit apartment buildings, built with reinforced concrete or wood, and also builds steel-frame office and other commercial and public-sector buildings. The Company's services are provided in the following three phases: (1) Pre-construction advisory services, which are generally provided by the Company for a proposal designed to meet the customer's specific business needs and assistance to the customer in obtaining financing. (2) Construction work, for which the Company charges a fixed construction price. (3) Post-construction services, which involve assistance by the Company of the customer in tenant recruitment and building maintenance.

ANNUAL EARNINGS

	7/31/96	7/31/95	7/31/96	7/31/95
	US $		Yen	
Earnings Per Share	0.60	0.69	63.99	60.69

ANNUAL FINANCIAL DATA

RECORD OF EARNINGS (IN THOUSANDS):

	7/31/96	7/31/95	7/31/96	7/31/95
Total Revenues	143,959	137,519	15,647,719	12,063,078
Costs & Expenses	129,523	123,316	14,078,607	10,817,198
Operating Income	14,436	14,203	1,569,112	1,245,880
Income Bef Income Tax	14,505	14,982	1,576,578	1,314,204
Income Tax	7,656	7,893	832,176	692,358
Net Income	6,848	7,089	744,402	621,846
Average Shares Outstg	11,633	10,246	11,633	10,246

BALANCE SHEET (IN THOUSANDS):

Cash & Cash Equivalents	45,300	28,095	4,923,947	2,464,492
Receivables, Net	20,060	10,190	2,180,401	893,823
Inventories	10,072	...	1,094,747	...
Gross Property	2,273	2,056	247,073	180,319
Accumulated Depreciation	1,123	1,008	122,114	88,459
Stockholders' Equity	74,724	50,363	8,122,140	4,417,783
Total Assets	115,171	82,298	12,518,541	7,219,085
Total Current Assets	106,697	73,897	11,597,483	6,482,198
Total Current Liabilities	38,248	30,156	4,157,340	2,645,241
Net Working Capital	68,449	43,741	7,440,143	3,836,957
Year End Shs Outstg	9,650	6,500	9,650	6,500

STATISTICAL RECORD:

Return on Equity %	9.17	14.08
Return on Assets %	5.95	8.61
Operating Profit Margin %	10.03	10.33
Net Profit Margin %	4.76	5.15
Book Value Per Share	7.74	7.75

Converted at 1996, US$0.0092= 1 Japanese Yen; 1995, US$0.0114= 1 Japanese Yen

OFFICERS:
J. Ohira, Pres. & Rep. Dir.
S. Kondo, Managing Dir.
K. Nishimoto, Managing Dir.
M. Sumiya, Managing Dir.

INCORPORATED: Japan, May, 1990

PRINCIPAL OFFICE: 15-8 Nakata 2-chome Chikusa-ku Nagoya Japan

TELEPHONE NUMBER: (052) 732-5701

NO. OF EMPLOYEES: 190

ANNUAL MEETING: In Oct.

SHAREHOLDERS: N/A

INSTITUTIONAL HOLDINGS:
No. of Institutions: 2
Shares Held: 8,400

**AMERICAN DEPOSITARY
RECEIPTS:** (Sponsored) Each American Depositary Receipt represents one common share of par Y50.

DEPOSITARY BANK(S): The Bank of New York, (212) 815-2175

SELECT APPOINTMENTS (HOLDINGS) PLC

YIELD 1.0
P/E RATIO 27.0

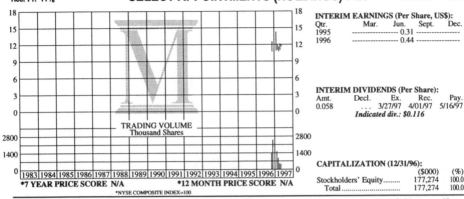

INTERIM EARNINGS (Per Share, US$):

Qtr.	Mar.	Jun.	Sept.	Dec.
1995		0.31		
1996		0.44		

INTERIM DIVIDENDS (Per Share):

Amt.	Decl.	Ex.	Rec.	Pay.
0.058	...	3/27/97	4/01/97	5/16/97

Indicated div.: $0.116

TRADING VOLUME
Thousand Shares

CAPITALIZATION (12/31/96):

	($000)	(%)
Stockholders' Equity	177,274	100.0
Total	177,274	100.0

1983|1984|1985|1986|1987|1988|1989|1990|1991|1992|1993|1994|1995|1996|1997
*7 YEAR PRICE SCORE N/A   *12 MONTH PRICE SCORE N/A
*NYSE COMPOSITE INDEX=100

RECENT DEVELOPMENTS: For the year ended 12/31/96, net earnings were $17.3 million compared with $10.3 million the year before. Sales results benefited from internal growth and acquisitions. Sales jumped 62.9% to $584.1 million. Sales for North America increased 54.7% to $282.3 million. Europe's sales soared 76.6% to $257.6 million. Sales for Australasia and Asia rose 46.3% to $44.2 million. Operating profit advanced 67.3% to $28.6 million.

During the year, the Company opened 82 new offices, including 41 offices acquired through acquisitions. The Company completed eight acquisitions in six countries during the year, including Toner Corporation, a California-based information technology company. Select also acquired Japan-based Niscom Services Inc., which also operates in the information technology market.

BUSINESS

SELECT APPOINTMENTS (HOLD-INGS) PLC is a provider of international staffing services. The principal activities of the Company and its subsidiaries is the provision of professional temporary, contract and permanent staffing services to both service and manufacturing industries including medical, computer, accounting, legal, technical and industrial industries. The Company operates over 350 offices in 21 countries.

ANNUAL EARNINGS

	12/31/96	12/31/95	12/31/96	12/31/95
	---US $---		---British £---	
Earnings Per Ordinary Share	0.22	0.15	0.01	0.01

ANNUAL FINANCIAL DATA

RECORD OF EARNINGS (IN THOUSANDS):

	12/31/96	12/31/95	12/31/96	12/31/95
Total Revenues	584,090	358,561	369,920	226,737
Costs & Expenses	555,506	341,473	348,821	214,027
Operating Income	28,584	17,088	21,099	12,710
Income Bef Income Tax	25,928	15,152	19,424	11,486
Income Tax	8,742	4,857	5,795	3,690
Eq. Earnings in Affils.	d406	d642	485	1,024
Minority Interests	121	28	181	388
Net Income	17,307	10,323	13,933	8,432
Average Shares Outstg	78,868	66,691	78,868	66,691

BALANCE SHEET (IN THOUSANDS):

Cash & Cash Equivalents	22,756	12,790	14,656	8,238
Receivables, Net	108,024	63,105	75,480	48,606
Accumulated Depreciation	15,735	10,255	9,195	6,604
Stockholders' Equity	177,274	100,820	28,984	17,367
Total Assets	305,788	173,129	105,874	65,522
Total Current Assets	156,099	86,213	91,665	56,844
Total Current Liabilities	102,845	63,009	63,053	43,650
Net Working Capital	53,254	23,204	28,612	13,194
Year End Shs Outstg	87,565,250	70,953,227	87,565,250	70,953,227

STATISTICAL RECORD:

Return on Equity %	9.76	10.24		
Return on Assets %	5.66	5.96		
Operating Profit Margin %	4.89	4.76		
Net Profit Margin %	2.96	2.88		
Book Value Per Share	0.02	0.01		

Converted at 1996, US$1.6945 = 1 British pound; 1995, US$1.5530 = 1 British pound

OFFICERS:
A. V. Martin, Chmn.
C. K. Z. Miles, Finance Dir. & Sec.
M. J. Franks, Non-Exec. Dir.
R. C. G. MacLeod, Non-Exec. Dir.
P. Kaminsky, Non-Exec. Dir.

INCORPORATED: United Kingdom

PRINCIPAL OFFICE: Ziggurat Grosvenor Road St. Albans, Hertfordshire United Kingdom AL1 3HW

TELEPHONE NUMBER: 44-1727-842999

NO. OF EMPLOYEES: 1,487

ANNUAL MEETING: In May

SHAREHOLDERS: N/A

INSTITUTIONAL HOLDINGS:
No. of Institutions: 9
Shares Held: 2,515,409

AMERICAN DEPOSITARY RECEIPTS: Each American Depositary Share represents two ordinary shares.

DEPOSITARY BANK(S): The Bank of New York, (212) 815-2175; Independent Registrars Group, Ltd., Kent, United Kingdom

SELECT SOFTWARE TOOLS PLC

YIELD ...
P/E RATIO ...

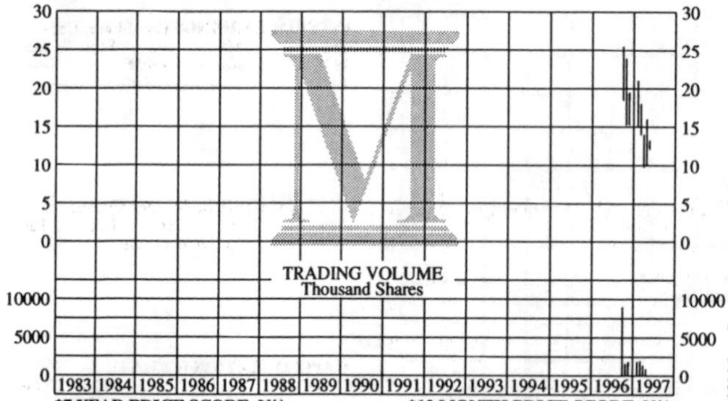

*7 YEAR PRICE SCORE N/A   *12 MONTH PRICE SCORE N/A

*NYSE COMPOSITE INDEX=100

INTERIM EARNINGS (Per Share):

Qtr.	Mar.	June	Sept.	Dec.
1994		d0.09		
1995		d0.35		
1996		d0.20		

INTERIM DIVIDENDS (Per Share):

Amt.	Decl.	Ex.	Rec.	Pay.
	No dividends paid.			

CAPITALIZATION (12/31/95):

	($000)	(%)
Long-Term Debt	363	-14.7
Stockholders' Equity	d3,016	121.9
Preferred Stock	178	-7.2
Total	d2,475	100.0

RECENT DEVELOPMENTS: For the year ended 12/31/96, the Company reported a net loss of $1.7 million, or $0.20 per share, compared with a net loss of $3.0 million, or $0.35 per share, the previous year. Total revenues more than doubled to $14.3 million versus $5.7 million in the corresponding prior-year period. Earnings for 1996 were negatively affected by a one-time charge of $2.1 million, taken in the fourth quarter, related to the acquisition of System Engineer in December 1996. Revenues from license fees totaled $10.6 million versus $4.4 million in 1995, while services and maintenance revenues jumped to $3.7 million from $1.3 million the year before. Gross profit was $11.6 million, or 81.0% of total revenues, compared with $4.5 million, or 78.4% of total revenues, a year earlier. For the three months ended 12/31/96, net loss totaled $1.7 million versus a loss of $767,000 the previous year. Total revenues were $4.8 million, up significantly from $1.8 million the prior year.

BUSINESS

SELECT SOFTWARE TOOLS PLC develops, markets and supports object-oriented modeling tools which enable the user to develop high-end client/server software applications. The Company offers two main product lines: its principal object-oriented product, SELECT enterprise, and a range of more general analysis and design tools consisting of SELECT OMT Professional, SELECT SSADM Professional and SELECT Yourdon.

ANNUAL EARNINGS

	12/31/95	12/31/94	12/31/95	12/31/94
	US $		British £	
Earnings Per Share	d0.35	d0.09	d0.23	d0.06

ANNUAL FINANCIAL DATA

RECORD OF EARNINGS (IN THOUSANDS):

	12/31/95	12/31/94	12/31/95	12/31/94
Total Revenues	5,732	3,153	3,691	2,015
Costs & Expenses	8,396	3,806	5,406	2,432
Operating Income	d2,664	d653	d1,715	d417
Net Income	d2,989	d766	d1,925	d489
Average Shares Outstg	8,528	8,528	8,528	8,528

BALANCE SHEET (IN THOUSANDS):

Cash & Cash Equivalents	25	92	16	59
Receivables, Net	1,225	933	789	596
Gross Property	1,347	753	867	481
Accumulated Depreciation	487	227	314	145
Long-Term Debt	363	444	234	284
Stockholders' Equity	d3,016	d1,038	d1,942	d663
Total Assets	2,735	1,964	1,761	1,255
Total Current Assets	1,351	1,173	870	750
Total Current Liabilities	5,210	2,558	3,355	1,635
Net Working Capital	d3,859	d1,385	d2,485	d885
Year End Shs Outstg	7,154	6,493	7,154	6,493

Converted at 1995, US$1.5530= 1 British pound; 1994, US$1.5650= 1 British pound

OFFICERS:
M.E. Jackson, Chmn.
S. Frost, C.E.O.
J.R. Davison, C.F.O.
A.B. Grisewood, Sec.

INCORPORATED: 1988

PRINCIPAL OFFICE: Westmoreland House, 80-86 Bath Road, Cheltenham, Gloucestershire GL53 7JT United Kingdom

TELEPHONE NUMBER: 44-1242-229700

NO. OF EMPLOYEES: 102

ANNUAL MEETING: N/A

SHAREHOLDERS: N/A

INSTITUTIONAL HOLDINGS:
No. of Institutions: 31
Shares Held: 3,496,640

AMERICAN DEPOSITARY RECEIPTS: Each American Depositary Receipt represents one ordinary share, par value £0.001.

DEPOSITARY BANK(S): The Bank of New York, (212) 815-2175

SENETEK PLC

YIELD ...
P/E RATIO ...

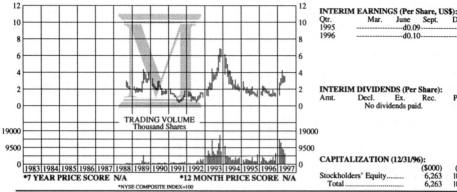

*7 YEAR PRICE SCORE N/A   *12 MONTH PRICE SCORE N/A
*NYSE COMPOSITE INDEX=100

TRADING VOLUME
Thousand Shares

INTERIM EARNINGS (Per Share, US$):

Qtr.	Mar.	June	Sept.	Dec.
1995		------------------d0.09------------------		
1996		------------------d0.10------------------		

INTERIM DIVIDENDS (Per Share):

Amt.	Decl.	Ex.	Rec.	Pay.
	No dividends paid.			

CAPITALIZATION (12/31/96):

	($000)	(%)
Stockholders' Equity........	6,263	100.0
Total	6,263	100.0

RECENT DEVELOPMENTS: For the year ended 12/31/96, the Company incurred a net loss of $4.0 million, or $0.10 per share. This compares with a net loss of $3.7 million, or $0.09 per share, the previous year. Revenues advanced to $6.5 million from $1.9 million the year before. For the quarter ended 12/31/96, the Company reported a net loss of $1.3 million, or $0.03 per share, versus a net loss of $809,000, or $0.02 per share, in the corresponding period of the prior year. Revenues dropped 11.6% to $1.6 million. This compares with $1.9 million a year earlier. Senetek expects to commercialize new products in 1997 that will include various regulatory approvals in Europe and the United States.

BUSINESS

SENETEK PLC is engaged in research in the life sciences, health care, and biotechnology fields, with particular emphasis on research relating to the diagnosis and treatment of diseases related to senescence or ageing. The Company's research and development activities are conducted through research groups at the University of Aarhus, with clinical associates of the University of Copenhagen in various hospitals in Denmark, and at other clinical or contract research centers in the United Kingdom, Europe and in the United States. The main areas in which the Company is involved are the treatment of male sexual dysfunction, the development, manufacture and sale of a self-administered automatic injector syringe, and the proposed establishment of distribution arrangements for the sale of the Company's product known as Factor X, designed to be applicable to age-related skin disorders including premature aging.

ANNUAL EARNINGS

	12/31/96	12/31/95	12/31/96	12/31/95
	-------------US $-------------		----------British £----------	
Earnings Per Share	d0.10	d0.09	d0.06	d0.09

ANNUAL FINANCIAL DATA

RECORD OF EARNINGS (IN THOUSANDS):

	12/31/96	12/31/95	12/31/96	12/31/95
Total Revenues	6,486	1,931	3,828	1,243
Costs & Expenses	10,552	5,835	6,227	3,757
Operating Income	d4,066	d3,904	d2,400	d2,514
Net Income	d4,020	d3,721	d2,372	d2,396
Average Shares Outstg	41,235	40,490	41,235	40,490

BALANCE SHEET (IN THOUSANDS):

Cash & Cash Equivalents	2,975	2,237	1,756	1,440
Receivables, Net	859	841	507	542
Inventories	1,657	1,231	978	793
Gross Property	1,679	1,396	991	899
Accumulated Depreciation	497	310	293	200
Stockholders' Equity	6,263	6,745	3,696	4,343
Total Assets	9,841	7,905	5,808	5,090
Total Current Assets	5,629	4,427	3,322	2,851
Total Current Liabilities	3,578	1,160	2,112	747
Net Working Capital	2,051	3,267	1,210	2,104
Year End Shares Outstg	43,899	40,606	43,899	40,606

STATISTICAL RECORD:

Book Value Per Share	0.14	0.17		

Converted at 1996, US$1.6945= 1 British pound; 1995, US$1.5530= 1 British pound

---

OFFICERS:
A. J. Cataldo, Chmn. & C.E.O.
P. A. Logan, C.F.O. & Sec.

INCORPORATED: England, 1985

PRINCIPAL OFFICE: 23 Palace Street, London, SW1E 5HW United Kingdom

TELEPHONE NUMBER: (0171) 828-4800

NO. OF EMPLOYEES: 23

ANNUAL MEETING: In May

SHAREHOLDERS: 1,618 (approx.)

INSTITUTIONAL HOLDINGS:
No. of Institutions: 6
Shares Held: 123,450

AMERICAN DEPOSITARY RECEIPTS: Each ADS represents one ordinary share, one A and one B warrants (or evidence of rights to receive one ordinary share) deposited with the Custodian.

DEPOSITARY BANK(S): The Bank of New York, (212) 815-2175

SIGNET GROUP PLC

YIELD ...
P/E RATIO 6.5

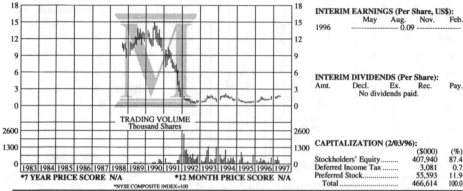

TRADING VOLUME
Thousand Shares

| 1983 | 1984 | 1985 | 1986 | 1987 | 1988 | 1989 | 1990 | 1991 | 1992 | 1993 | 1994 | 1995 | 1996 | 1997 |

*7 YEAR PRICE SCORE N/A   *12 MONTH PRICE SCORE N/A
*NYSE COMPOSITE INDEX=100

INTERIM EARNINGS (Per Share, US$):

	May	Aug.	Nov.	Feb.
1996	------------------ 0.09 ------------------			

INTERIM DIVIDENDS (Per Share):

Amt.	Decl.	Ex.	Rec.	Pay.
	No dividends paid.			

CAPITALIZATION (2/03/96):

	($000)	(%)
Stockholders' Equity	407,940	87.4
Deferred Income Tax	3,081	0.7
Preferred Stock	55,593	11.9
Total	466,614	100.0

RECENT DEVELOPMENTS: For the six months ended 8/3/96, the Company reported a net loss of £21.5 million compared with a net loss of £33.1 million in the corresponding period of 1995. Sales improved 7.2% to £369.6 million versus £344.9 million in the prior year. Operating profit climbed to £10.0 million from an operating loss of £2.9 million in 1995. Sales in the United Kingdom and Eire rose to £134.2 million from £126.2 million a year earlier. This was attributable to a 3.0% increase in sales of H Samuel and an 18.0% increase in sales of Ernest Jones. Sales in the United States improved to £235.4 million compared with £218.7 million the year before. U.S. sales benefited from the refocusing of marketing and promotional activity, as well as from improved product ranges, which are being introduced. Separately, in February 1997, the Company entered into a new three-year voluntary £360.0 million multi-currency credit facility with a new syndicate of banks.

BUSINESS

SIGNET GROUP PLC is a holding company, which through its subsidiaries, is engaged in the retailing of jewelry, watches and gifts throughout the United Kingdom and the United States.

ANNUAL EARNINGS

	2/03/96	1/28/95	2/03/96	1/28/95
	-------------US $-------------		-------------British £-------------	
Earnings Per Share	0.09	0.02	0.08	0.09

ANNUAL FINANCIAL DATA

RECORD OF EARNINGS (IN THOUSANDS):

Total Revenues	1,345,154	1,446,184	894,682	924,079
Costs & Expenses	1,249,022	1,376,599	830,743	879,616
Operating Income	96,132	69,585	63,939	44,463
Income Bef Income Tax	37,612	12,744	25,016	8,143
Income Tax	11,275	9,064	7,499	5,792
Net Income	26,337	3,679	17,517	2,351
Average Shares Outstg	293,059	293,058	293,059	293,058

BALANCE SHEET (IN THOUSANDS):

Cash & Cash Equivalents	231,153	221,385	153,743	141,460
Receivables, Net	343,547	362,631	228,498	231,713
Inventories	511,182	528,679	339,995	337,814
Gross Property	560,287	570,419	372,655	364,485
Accumulated Depreciation	335,273	321,925	222,995	205,703
Stockholders' Equity	407,940	389,516	271,327	248,892
Total Assets	1,314,612	1,365,057	874,368	872,241
Total Current Assets	1,085,882	1,112,695	722,236	710,987
Total Current Liabilities	272,290	927,762	181,104	592,819
Net Working Capital	813,592	184,933	541,132	118,168
Year End Shs Outstg	293,063	293,059	293,063	293.059

STATISTICAL RECORD:

Return on Equity %	6.46	0.94
Return on Assets %	2.00	0.27
Operating Profit Margin %	7.15	4.81
Net Profit Margin %	1.96	0.25
Book Value Per Share	1.39	1.33

Converted at 1996, US$1.5035= 1 British pound; 1995, US$1.5650= 1 British pound. Results for 1995 are restated.

OFFICERS:
J. McAdam, Chmn. & C.E.O.
J. Gillum, Non-exec. Dep. Chmn.
L. Cooklin, Exec. Dir.
W. Boyd, Finance Dir.

INCORPORATED: United Kingdom, 1950

PRINCIPAL OFFICE: Zenith House, The Hyde, London United Kingdom

TELEPHONE NUMBER: 0181-905-9000

NO. OF EMPLOYEES: 11,995

ANNUAL MEETING: In Jun.

SHAREHOLDERS: 166

INSTITUTIONAL HOLDINGS:
No. of Institutions: 4
Shares Held: 1,447,748

AMERICAN DEPOSITARY RECEIPTS: (Sponsored) Each American Depositary Receipt represents three ordinary shares of par £0.10 each.

DEPOSITARY BANK(S): The Bank of New York, (212) 815-2175

SMALLWORLDWIDE PLC

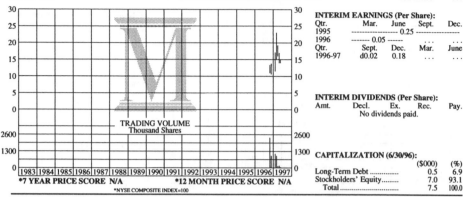

INTERIM EARNINGS (Per Share):

Qtr.	Mar.	June	Sept.	Dec.
1995			0.25	
1996		0.05		

Qtr.	Sept.	Dec.	Mar.	June
1996-97	d0.02	0.18	...	...

INTERIM DIVIDENDS (Per Share):

Amt.	Decl.	Ex.	Rec.	Pay.
		No dividends paid.		

TRADING VOLUME
Thousand Shares

| 1983 | 1984 | 1985 | 1986 | 1987 | 1988 | 1989 | 1990 | 1991 | 1992 | 1993 | 1994 | 1995 | 1996 | 1997 |

*7 YEAR PRICE SCORE N/A   *12 MONTH PRICE SCORE N/A
*NYSE COMPOSITE INDEX=100

CAPITALIZATION (6/30/96):

	($000)	(%)
Long-Term Debt	0.5	6.9
Stockholders' Equity	7.0	93.1
Total	7.5	100.0

RECENT DEVELOPMENTS: For the three months ended 12/31/96, net income fell 35.1% to $1.3 million from $1.9 million in the corresponding prior-year quarter. Total revenues climbed 44.3% to $13.3 million from $9.2 million the previous year. The 1995 results are presented on a pro forma basis to reflect the 1995 and early 1996 acquisitions of the German, Spanish, Australian and Swedish distributors as if they occured on 1/1/95. Licenses revenue surged 47.4% to $8.6 million, services and maintenance revenue rose 38.7% to $4.5 million, and other revenues were up 42.4% to $235,000. Higher revenues were attributed to increased sales to existing customers combined with sales from many new customers. Gross profit totaled $9.1 million, or 68.0% of total revenues, versus $7.0 million, or 75.7% of total revenues, a year earlier. Income from operations slipped 6.3% to $2.0 million from $2.2 million the prior year. For the six months ended 12/31/96, net income dropped 45.6% to $1.1 million from $1.9 million the previous year. Total revenues jumped 62.9% to $22.5 million from $13.8 million in 1995.

BUSINESS

SMALLWORLDWIDE PLC develops, markets and supports client/server software for the spatial design, engineering and management of complex physical networks. The Company's product Smallworld GIS, is used primarily by telecommunications companies and utilities to plan, design, build and manage their complex infrastructures, with the objective of increasing their overall efficiency, profitability and competitiveness. Smallworld GIS employs unique object-oriented development and spatial database technologies that enable users to rapidly develop applications to meet their scalability, performance and integration requirements. Smallworld GIS integrates with its users' other management information systems, such as resource planning, customer information and network monitoring systems, to create comprehensive network management systems.

ANNUAL EARNINGS

	① 6/30/96	① 12/31/95	① 6/30/96	① 12/31/95
		US $		British £
Earnings Per Share	0.05	0.25	0.03	0.16

① For 12 months ended

ANNUAL FINANCIAL DATA

RECORD OF EARNINGS (AS PRESENTED):

Total Revenues	18,758	17,980	12,116	11,578
Costs & Expenses	18,058	17,681	11,664	11,385
Operating Income	700	299	452	193
Income Bef Income Tax	585	242	378	156
Income Tax	391	cr1,000	253	cr644
Net Income	281	1,326	125	800
Net Extraordinary Items	87	84	56	54
Average Shares Outstg (000)	6,098	5,247	6,098	5,247

BALANCE SHEET (AS PRESENTED):

Cash & Cash Equivalents	733	1,547	473	996
Receivables, Net	1,128	1,152	729	742
Inventories	1,160	953	749	614
Gross Property	6,205	4,881	4,008	3,143
Accumulated Depreciation	3,365	2,900	2,173	1,867
Long-Term Debt	516	122	333	79
Stockholders' Equity	7,598	6,985	4,908	4,498
Total Assets	19,631	14,896	12,680	9,592
Total Current Assets	13,881	10,341	8,966	6,659
Total Current Liabilities	10,674	6,887	6,894	4,435
Net Working Capital	3,207	3,454	2,071	2,224
Year End Shs Outstg (000)	7,063	...	7,063	...

STATISTICAL RECORD:

Return on Equity %	3.69	18.98		
Return on Assets %	1.43	8.90		
Operating Profit Margin %	3.73	1.66		
Net Profit Margin %	1.50	7.37		
Book Value Per Share	1.08	...		

Converted at 1996, US$1.5482= 1 British pound; 1995, US$1.5530= 1 British pound

OFFICERS:
R. G. Newell, Chmn.
A. P. Stafford
T. Cadman
R. T. Green
INCORPORATED: Oct., 1996
PRINCIPAL OFFICE: Elizabeth House, 1 High Street, Chesterton United Kingdom

TELEPHONE NUMBER: 44-1223-301-144
NO. OF EMPLOYEES: 223
ANNUAL MEETING: N/A
SHAREHOLDERS: N/A
INSTITUTIONAL HOLDINGS:
No. of Institutions: 16
Shares Held: 2,161,525

AMERICAN DEPOSITARY RECEIPTS: One American Depositary Receipt represents one ordinary share of par £0.01.

DEPOSITARY BANK(S): The Bank of New York, (212) 815-2175

SOUTHERN PACIFIC PETROLEUM N.L.

YIELD ...
P/E RATIO ...

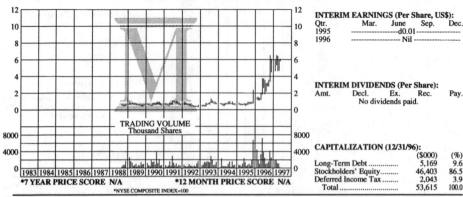

*7 YEAR PRICE SCORE N/A   *12 MONTH PRICE SCORE N/A
*NYSE COMPOSITE INDEX=100

TRADING VOLUME
Thousand Shares

INTERIM EARNINGS (Per Share, US$):

Qtr.	Mar.	June	Sep.	Dec.
1995		d0.01		
1996		Nil		

INTERIM DIVIDENDS (Per Share):

Amt.	Decl.	Ex.	Rec.	Pay.
	No dividends paid.			

CAPITALIZATION (12/31/96):

	($000)	(%)
Long-Term Debt	5,169	9.6
Stockholders' Equity	46,403	86.5
Deferred Income Tax	2,043	3.9
Total	53,615	100.0

RECENT DEVELOPMENTS: For the year ended 12/31/96, operating profit after income tax was A$130,000. This compares with a loss of A$2.6 million in the prior year. Operating profit before tax improved substantially to A$550,000 from a loss of A$457,000 in 1995. Income amounted to A$2.6 million, more than double A$1.3 million a year earlier. The increase in income was attributed primarily to stronger investment earnings, which more than doubled to A$1.7 million from A$762,000 due largely to an improved investment climate during 1996 and the addition of A$14.0 million in new equity funds available. Operating costs advanced by 13% due primarily to increased activity associated with the Staurt Project, a oil shale deposit under development near Gladstone, Queensland.

BUSINESS

SOUTHERN PACIFIC PETRO-LEUM N.L. and its 39.3%-owned affiliate, Central Pacific Minerals N.L., are engaged in the exploration and evaluation of oil shale and other mineral deposits predominantly in Australia. Through the joint interests of the Company and Central Pacific, the two companies now comprise eight Australian oil share deposits with net interest in these resources approximating 25.63 billion barrels.

ANNUAL EARNINGS

	12/31/96	12/31/95	12/31/96	12/31/95
	US $		A$	
Earnings Per Share	Nil	d0.01	Nil	d0.01

ANNUAL FINANCIAL DATA

RECORD OF EARNINGS (IN THOUSANDS):

	12/31/96	12/31/95	12/31/96	12/31/95
Income Bef Income Tax	437	d340	550	d457
Income Tax	334	1,598	420	2,149
Net Income	103	d1,938	130	d2,606

BALANCE SHEET (IN THOUSANDS):

Cash & Cash Equivalents	21,070	5,570	26,493	7,491
Receivables, Net	1,266	764	1,592	1,027
Gross Property	1,688	1,535	2,123	2,064
Accumulated Depreciation	894	793	1,124	1,067
Long-Term Debt	5,169	9,192	6,500	12,363
Stockholders' Equity	46,403	32,618	58,346	43,871
Total Assets	61,541	51,062	77,381	68,678
Total Current Assets	22,336	7,495	28,085	10,081
Total Current Liabilities	1,202	1,987	1,511	2,672
Net Working Capital	21,134	5,509	26,574	7,409
Year End Shs Outstg	230,183	208,248	230,183	208,248

STATISTICAL RECORD:

Return on Equity %	0.22	...		
Return on Assets %	0.17	...		
Net Profit Margin %	0.88	0.88		
Book Value Per Share	0.20	0.16		

Converted at 1996, US$0.7953= 1 Australian $; 1995, US$0.7435= 1 Australian $

OFFICERS:
I. McFarlane, Chmn. & Managing Dir.
N. J. Paterson
V. H. Kuss
B. C. Wright

INCORPORATED: In Australia, 1968

PRINCIPAL OFFICE: C/- Phipson Nominees Pty. Ltd., 10th Floor National Mutual Centre, 15 London Circuit Canberra City, ACT 2600 Australia

TELEPHONE NUMBER: (06) 2740 777

NO. OF EMPLOYEES: N/A

ANNUAL MEETING: In April

SHAREHOLDERS: 6,757

INSTITUTIONAL HOLDINGS:
No. of Institutions: 17
Shares Held: 9,769,752

AMERICAN DEPOSITARY RECEIPTS: Each American Depositary Share represents two shares of par value A$0.50.

DEPOSITARY BANK(S): The Bank of New York, (212) 815-2175; Bankers Trust Co., (212) 250-8500; Citibank N.A., (212) 657-7800; J.P. Morgan, (212) 648-3206

ST. HELENA GOLD MINES LTD.

YIELD 1.9%
P/E RATIO ...

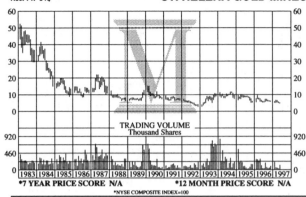

INTERIM EARNINGS (Per Share, US$):

Qtr.	Sept.	Dec.	Mar.	June
1995	------------------ 0.99 ------------------			
1996	------------------ d0.25 ------------------			

INTERIM DIVIDENDS (Per Share):

Amt.	Decl.	Ex.	Rec.	Pay.
0.257	...	8/02/95	8/04/95	10/02/95
0.102	...	2/05/97	2/07/97	3/31/97

Indicated div.: $0.102

CAPITALIZATION (6/30/96):

	($000)	(%)
Stockholders' Equity........	87,309	100.0
Total	87,309	100.0

RECENT DEVELOPMENTS: For the fiscal year ended 6/30/96, the Company incurred a net loss of R10.4 million compared with net income of R34.6 million the year before. Turnover declined 13.2% to R213.8 million from R246.3 million. The net working loss was R14.8 million compared with net working income of R50.4 million. The poor results were attributed to disruptions caused by two fires early in the fiscal year, which led to lower gold output levels and higher costs. Gold output for the year was down 19.6% to 4,477 kilograms, reflecting a 10.4% decline in tons milled to 735,000 and a 10.3% decline in the gold yield to 6.1 grams per ton from 6.8 grams per ton the year earlier. The Company's primary focus for 1997 is to improve productivity through education and training.

BUSINESS

ST. HELENA GOLD MINES LTD. is engaged in the mining of gold and the recover of silver as a by-product. The Company operates a gold mine in the Welkon area, Free State. The Company also operates the Oryx Mine, situated in the Theunissen area, Free State, which has not yet attained a meaningful level of production. Since its inception, the Company has produced more than 882 tons of gold.

ANNUAL EARNINGS

	6/30/96	6/30/95	6/30/96	6/30/95
	------------US $------------		------------Rand------------	
Earnings Per Share	d0.25	0.99	d1.08	3.60

ANNUAL FINANCIAL DATA

RECORD OF EARNINGS (IN THOUSANDS):

Total Revenues	49,397	67,729	213,840	246,287
Costs & Expenses	52,808	53,792	228,606	195,730
Operating Income	d3,411	13,938	d14,766	50,557
Income Bef Tax & Cap. Exp.	d389	20,026	d1,683	72,821
Capital Expenditures	2,018	10,551	8,734	38,367
Income Tax	...	cr3	...	cr10
Net Income	d2,406	9,478	d10,417	34,464

BALANCE SHEET (IN THOUSANDS):

Cash & Cash Equivalents	6,291	16,009	27,234	58,215
Receivables, Net	3,361	2,857	14,548	10,390
Inventories	656	1,122	2,838	4,080
Gross Property	84,639	98,840	366,403	359,419
Stockholders' Equity	87,309	104,926	377,962	381,548
Total Assets	95,001	119,180	411,260	433,381
Total Current Assets	10,362	20,340	44,857	73,962
Total Current Liabilities	7,692	14,254	33,298	51,833
Net Working Capital	2,670	6,085	11,559	22,129
Year End Shs Outstg	9,625	9,625	9,625	9,625

STATISTICAL RECORD:

Return on Equity %	...	9.03		
Return on Assets %	...	7.95		
Operating Profit Margin %	...	20.60		
Net Profit Margin %	...	14.00		
Book Value Per Share	9.07	10.90		

Converted at 1996, US$0.2310= 1 South African Rand; 1995, US$0.2750= 1 South African Rand

OFFICERS:
T. G. Dale, Managing Dir.
B. D. Abbott, Fin. Director
T. F. Kok, Human Resources Dir.
P. D. Robinson, Dir. Safety & Ops.

INCORPORATED: South Africa, Feb., 1946

PRINCIPAL OFFICE: Gencor Ltd., 6 Hollard Street Johannesburg 2001 South Africa

TELEPHONE NUMBER: (011) 376-9111

NO. OF EMPLOYEES: 3,611

ANNUAL MEETING: In Oct.

SHAREHOLDERS: 1,018

INSTITUTIONAL HOLDINGS:
No. of Institutions: 12
Shares Held: 1,269,936

AMERICAN DEPOSITARY RECEIPTS: (Unsponsored) Each ADR represents one ordinary share of par R1.

DEPOSITARY BANK(S): The Bank of New York, (212) 815-2175; Bankers Trust Co., (212) 250-8500; Citibank N.A., (212) 657-7800

STOLT-NIELSEN S.A.

YIELD ...
P/E RATIO 10.61

INTERIM EARNINGS (Per Share):

Qtr.	Feb.	May.	Aug.	Nov.
1994	------------------ 0.77 ------------------			
1995	------------------ 2.34 ------------------			
1996	------------------ 1.72 ------------------			

INTERIM DIVIDENDS (Per Share):

Amt.	Decl.	Ex.	Rec.	Pay.
0.25	...	5/15/96	5/17/96	6/05/96
0.25	...	12/03/96	12/05/96	12/19/96
0.25	...	5/08/97	5/12/97	5/28/97

TRADING VOLUME
Thousand Shares

*7 YEAR PRICE SCORE N/A   *12 MONTH PRICE SCORE N/A
*NYSE COMPOSITE INDEX=100

CAPITALIZATION (11/30/96):

	($000)	(%)
Long-Term Debt	675,939	42.1
Stockholders' Equity	884,820	57.1
Total Deposits	12,905	0.8
Total	1,549,978	100.0

RECENT DEVELOPMENTS: For the year ended 11/30/96, net income was $91.9 million, down 12.5% from $105.0 million a year earlier. Results for 1996 included a provision of $3.9 million related to the restructuring of the Company's seafood operations and a loss of $2.2 million from the disposal of Sogetram, Stolt Comex Seaway's French civil engineering business. Operating revenues were up 3.2% to $1.35 billion from $1.31 billion in the prior year. Revenues from transportation services were up 3.1% to $890.2 million due primarily to a 15.3% increase in revenues from the Company's tank container operations. Revenues from subsea services were down 4.2% to $313.5 million, while seafood revenues increased 24.2% to $146.9 million. The decline in earnings for 1996 were attributed to disappointing results from Stolt Comex Seaway and Stolt Sea Farm.

BUSINESS

STOLT-NIELSEN S.A. is a holding company. Through its subsidiaries, the Company provides transportation services for bulk liquid chemicals, edible oils, acids and other specialty liquids. The Company, through its parcel, tanker, tank container, terminal, rail and barge services, provides integrated transportation for its customers. The Company also owns 60% of Stolt Comex Seaway S.A., a subsea services contractor that specializes in providing engineering, flowline lay, construction, inspection and maintenance services to the offshore oil and gas industry. Stolt Sea Farm, wholly-owned by the Company, produces and markets high-quality Atlantic Salmon, salmon trout, turbot and halibut.

ANNUAL EARNINGS

	11/30/96	11/30/95	11/30/94	11/30/93	11/30/92	11/30/91	11/30/90
	------------------------------US $------------------------------						
Earnings Per Share	1.72	2.34	0.59	0.09	d0.11	1.74	3.18

ANNUAL FINANCIAL DATA

RECORD OF EARNINGS (IN MILLIONS):

	11/30/96	11/30/95	11/30/94	11/30/93	11/30/92	11/30/91	11/30/90
Total Revenues	1,351	1,309	1,078	1,107	1,105	730	616
Costs & Expenses	1,214	1,132	1,003	1,049	1,033	654	539
Operating Income	136	177	75	58	72	76	77
Income Bef Income Tax	95	114	30	10	7	47	88
Income Tax	3	9	4	6	10	1	2
Net Income	92	105	34	4	d6	48	87
Net Extraordinary Items	...	...	5	3	43	...	...
Average Shares Outstg (000)	53,404	44,840	44,751	44,450	28,829	26,874	26,976

BALANCE SHEET (IN MILLIONS):

Cash & Cash Equivalents	7	14	16	9	22	27	50
Receivables, Net	225	179	143	185	205	73	58
Inventories	101	93	72	63	68	37	...
Gross Property	2,177	1,833	1,664	1,484	1,496	1,189	984
Accumulated Depreciation	724	639	546	465	406	354	306
Long-Term Debt	676	610	584	575	658	413	265
Stockholders' Equity	885	640	535	482	487	435	401
Total Assets	1,978	1,687	1,529	1,443	1,610	1,120	885
Total Current Assets	397	351	281	302	345	173	136
Total Current Liabilities	355	394	364	358	435	220	168
Net Working Capital	42	d44	d83	d56	d90	d47	d33
Year End Shs Outstg (000)	54,400	30,342	30,110	30,069	30,031	27,870	27,084

STATISTICAL RECORD:

Return on Equity %	10.39	16.41	6.35	0.84	...	11.03	21.70
Return on Assets %	4.65	6.23	2.22	0.28	...	4.29	9.83
Operating Profit Margin %	10.08	13.52	7.00	5.25	6.49	10.39	12.52
Net Profit Margin %	6.81	8.03	3.15	0.37	...	6.58	14.12
Book Value Per Share	16.27	21.10	17.77	16.04	16.21	15.60	14.80

OFFICERS:
J. Stolt-Nielsen Jr., Chmn. & C.E.O.
C. J. Wright, Pres. & C.O.O.
J. C. Engelhardtsen, C.F.O.

INCORPORATED: Luxembourg, 1974

PRINCIPAL OFFICE: C/O Stolt-Nielsen Ltd.
Aldwych House71-91 Aldwych London
United Kingdom

TELEPHONE NUMBER: 44-171-611-8962

NO. OF EMPLOYEES: N/A

ANNUAL MEETING: In June

SHAREHOLDERS: N/A

INSTITUTIONAL HOLDINGS:
No. of Institutions: 26
Shares Held: 8,404,454

AMERICAN DEPOSITARY RECEIPTS: Each American depository share represents one common class B-share.

DEPOSITARY BANK(S): Citibank N.A., (212) 657-7800

SWEDISH MATCH, AB

YIELD 3.4%
P/E RATIO 9.4

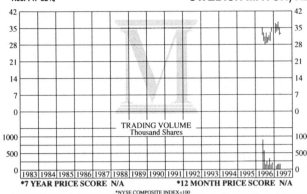

INTERIM EARNINGS (Per Share, US$):
1995 ------------------ 0.35 ------------------
1996 ------------------ 0.35 ------------------

INTERIM DIVIDENDS (Per Share):

Amt.	Decl.	Ex.	Rec.	Pay.
1.236	. . .	5/8/97	5/12/97	5/30/97

Indicated div.: $1.236

TRADING VOLUME
Thousand Shares

1000
500

1983|1984|1985|1986|1987|1988|1989|1990|1991|1992|1993|1994|1995|1996|1997
*7 YEAR PRICE SCORE N/A   *12 MONTH PRICE SCORE N/A
*NYSE COMPOSITE INDEX=100

CAPITALIZATION (12/31/96):

	($000)	(%)
Minority Interests..............	7,873	2.0
Long-Term Debt	583	0.2
Stockholders' Equity........	337,381	86.4
Deferred Income Tax	44,615	11.4
Total	390,452	100.0

RECENT DEVELOPMENTS: For the year ended 12/31/96, net income rose slightly to SEK 1.11 billion compared with SEK 1.10 billion 1995. Total revenues declined slightly to 7.42 billion from SEK 7.44 billion. Operating income slipped 4.9% to SEK 1.60 billion from SEK 1.68 billion. The 1996 results included a nonrecurring charge of SEK 123.0 million for the shutdown of certain tobacco plants, while the 1995 results included a SEK 189.0 million gain related to the sale of an investment in UST, Inc. and certain licensing rights. The 1996 earnings benefited from SEK 18 million in earnings from minority interest compared with a loss of SEK 6.0 million in 1995. Revenue growth was achieved in Sweden, led by increased sales of moist snuff products. However, sales in Western Europe, excluding Sweden, Eastern Europe, North Amercia and Latin America were lower than 1995, primarily due to lower cigarette sales. On 1/1/97, The Company established a new organizational structure to enhance growth prospects.

BUSINESS

SWEDISH MATCH is an international group that produces and markets a broad range of tobacco products as well as matches and disposable lighters. The Company operates through seven global product divisions: Division Chewing Tobacco, which manufactures and sells chewing tobacco; Division Cigarettes, which manufactures and sells cigarettes, roll-your-own tobacco and tobacco accessories; Division Cigars, which manufactures and sells cigars and cigarillos; Division Lighters, which manufactures and sells disposable lighters; Division Matches, which manufactures and sells matches; Division Pipe Tobacco, which manufactures and sells pipe tobacco; Division Snuff, which manufactures and sells moist snuff products. The divisions market their products through seven sales regions for marketing to consumers and one global unit for advertising products for company sales.

ANNUAL EARNINGS

	12/31/96	12/31/95	12/31/96	12/31/95
	-------------US $-------------		-------------SEK-------------	
Earnings Per Share	0.35	0.35	2.39	2.37

ANNUAL FINANCIAL DATA

RECORD OF EARNINGS (IN MILLIONS):

Total Revenues	1,081	1,112	7,416	7,435
Costs & Expenses	793	847	5,439	5,668
Depreciation & Amort	39	44	270	294
Operating Income	233	252	1,600	1,683
Income Bef Income Tax	223	236	1,530	1,576
Income Tax	64	71	439	473
Minority Interests	cr3	1	cr18	6
Net Income	162	164	1,109	1,097

BALANCE SHEET (IN MILLIONS):

Cash & Cash Equivalents	137	120	942	804
Receivables, Net	229	217	1,570	1,454
Inventories	202	229	1,388	1,532
Gross Property	595	592	4,079	3,957
Accumulated Depreciation	312	292	2,139	1,955
Long-Term Debt	1	1	4	9
Stockholders' Equity	337	233	2,314	1,557
Total Assets	1,003	994	6,877	6,646
Total Current Assets	590	583	4,050	3,903
Total Current Liabilities	585	701	4,014	4,686
Net Working Capital	5	d117	36	d783
Year End Shs Outstg (000)	463,558	463,558	463,558	463,558

STATISTICAL RECORD:

Return on Equity %	47.93	70.46		
Return on Assets %	16.13	16.51		
Operating Profit Margin %	21.58	22.64		
Net Profit Margin %	14.95	14.76		
Book Value Per Share	0.73	0.50		

Converted at 1996, US$0.1458= 1 Swedish Krona; 1995, US$0.1495= 1 Swedish Krona

OFFICERS:
G. Linden, Pres. & C.E.O.
M. Rossi, Exec. V.P. & Deputy to the Pres.
H. van den Berg, Exec. V.P. & Chief Commercial Officer
W. G. McClure III, Exec. V.P. & C.O.O.
INCORPORATED: Sweden, 1915
PRINCIPAL OFFICE: SE-118 85 Stockholm Sweden

TELEPHONE NUMBER: +46-8-658-0200
NO. OF EMPLOYEES: 6,580
ANNUAL MEETING: In May
SHAREHOLDERS: N/A
INSTITUTIONAL HOLDINGS:
No. of Institutions: 19
Shares Held: 494,335

AMERICAN DEPOSITARY RECEIPTS: Each American Depositary Receipt represents 10 shares of par SEK2.

DEPOSITARY BANK(S): Citibank N.A., (212) 657-7800

TELEFONOS DE MEXICO, S.A. DE C.V.

YIELD ...
P/E RATIO 13.3

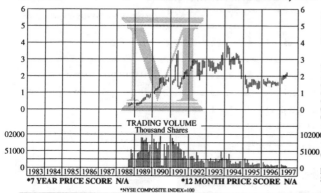

02000
51000

TRADING VOLUME
Thousand Shares

| 1983 | 1984 | 1985 | 1986 | 1987 | 1988 | 1989 | 1990 | 1991 | 1992 | 1993 | 1994 | 1995 | 1996 | 1997 |

*7 YEAR PRICE SCORE N/A   *12 MONTH PRICE SCORE N/A
*NYSE COMPOSITE INDEX=100

INTERIM EARNINGS (Per Share, US$):

Qtr.	Mar.	June	Sept.	Dec.
1995	------------------ 0.15 ------------------			
1996	------------------ 0.16 ------------------			

INTERIM DIVIDENDS (Per Share):

Amt.	Decl.	Ex.	Rec.	Pay.
0.018	...	6/17/96	6/19/96	6/27/96
0.018	...	11/15	11/19	11/29
0.018	...	6/16/97	6/18/97	6/26/97
0.018	...	9/15	9/17	9/25
0.018	...	12/15	12/17	12/26

Indicated div.: $0.054

CAPITALIZATION (12/31/96):

	($000)	(%)
Long-Term Debt	1,250,056	9.9
Stockholders' Equity	11,374,917	90.1
Total	12,624,973	100.0

RECENT DEVELOPMENTS: For the year ended 12/31/96, net income declined 2.4% to Ps.11.6 billion compared with Ps.11.9 billion in the same period of 1995. Operating revenues slid 1.0% to Ps.52.7 billion, while operating income decreased 14.1% to Ps.20.3 billion. Results for 1996 included Ps.3.8 billion in non-recurring charges. Domestic long distance minutes increased 7.9% to 7.87 billion minutes and international long distance minutes were up 16.2% to 3.51 billion minutes. During 1996, the decrease of the customer growth rate persisted. Demand for new lines incrementally exceeded the number of disconnections because of non payment. TFONY's network was prepared within the times set for interconnection to the different networks of new operators, beginning in the cities of Queretaro and Monterrey. On 12/19/96, the Telecommunications Attention Center for Operators was inaugurated in Mexico City in order to provide quality service to TFONY's customers through new long distance services.

BUSINESS

TELEFONOS DE MEXICO, S.A. DE C.V. is engaged in the telecommunications services industry. The Company operates under a licensing agreement granted by the Ministry of Communications and Transportation. The Company owns all public exchanges, the nationwide network of local telephone lines, and the principal public long distance telephone transmission facilities in Mexico. The Company also provides telephone related services such as directory services, and delivers cellular mobile telephone services to 657,000 subscribers in Mexico.

ANNUAL EARNINGS

	12/31/96	12/31/95	12/31/96	12/31/95
	---------------US $---------------		------------Pesos------------	
Earnings Per Share	0.16	0.15	1.267	1.171

ANNUAL FINANCIAL DATA

	12/31/96	12/31/95	12/31/96	12/31/95
RECORD OF EARNINGS (IN MILLIONS):				
Total Revenues	6,721	6,919	52,714	53,224
Costs & Expenses	3,178	3,226	24,927	24,812
Depreciation & Amort	1,396	1,197	10,948	9,208
Operating Income	2,147	2,496	16,839	19,204
Income Bef Income Tax	2,230	1,729	18,939	14,472
Income Tax	705	140	5,532	1,078
Eq. Earnings in Affils.	d45	d44	d356	d340
Net Income	1,479	1,545	11,600	11,884
Average Shares Outstg.	9,154	10,150	9,154	10,150
BALANCE SHEET (IN MILLIONS):				
Cash & Cash Equivalents	649	1,162	5,087	8,938
Receivables, Net	1,603	1,350	12,569	10,385
Gross Property	17,039	18,806	133,638	144,665
Accumulated Depreciation	5,459	5,185	42,818	39,882
Long-Term Debt	1,250	1,943	9,804	14,946
Stockholders' Equity	11,375	13,119	89,215	100,916
Total Assets	14,240	16,872	111,682	129,787
Total Current Assets	2,443	2,676	19,158	20,587
Total Current Liabilities	1,529	1,603	11,989	12,329
Net Working Capital	914	1,074	7,168	8,258
Year End Shs Outstg (000)	8,875	9,654	8,875	9,654
STATISTICAL RECORD:				
Return on Equity %	13.00	11.78		
Return on Assets %	10.39	9.16		
Operating Profit Margin %	31.94	36.08		
Net Profit Margin %	22.01	22.33		
Book Value Per Share	10.05	10.45		

Converted at 1996, US$0.1275= 1 Mexican Peso; 1995, US$0.1300= 1 Mexican Peso

OFFICERS:
J. Chico Pardo, Gen. Dir.
A. Cerezo
I. Ambe Attar
J. Elguea Solis
INCORPORATED: Dec., 1947
PRINCIPAL OFFICE: Parque Via 190, Oficina 1001, Colonia Cuauhtemoc, Mexico City 06599 Mexico

TELEPHONE NUMBER: 5-703-3990; 222-5462
NO. OF EMPLOYEES: N/A
ANNUAL MEETING: In Apr.
SHAREHOLDERS: N/A
INSTITUTIONAL HOLDINGS:
No. of Institutions: 23
Shares Held: 1,859,501

AMERICAN DEPOSITARY RECEIPTS: (Unsponsored) Each American Depositary Receipt represents one Series A share without par value.

DEPOSITARY BANK(S): The Bank of New York, (212) 815-2175; Bankers Trust Co., (212) 250-8500; Citibank N.A., (212) 657-7800; J.P. Morgan, (212) 648-3206

TELEWEST COMMUNICATIONS PLC

YIELD ...
P/E RATIO ...

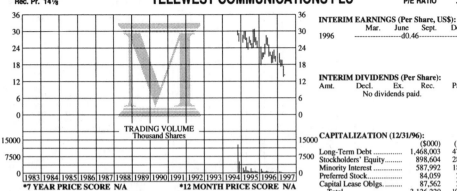

*7 YEAR PRICE SCORE N/A   *12 MONTH PRICE SCORE N/A

*NYSE COMPOSITE INDEX=100

INTERIM EARNINGS (Per Share, US$):

	Mar.	June	Sept.	Dec.
1996	------------------d0.46----------------			

INTERIM DIVIDENDS (Per Share):

Amt.	Decl.	Ex.	Rec.	Pay.
	No dividends paid.			

CAPITALIZATION (12/31/96):

	($000)	(%)
Long-Term Debt	1,468,003	47.0
Stockholders' Equity.........	898,604	28.7
Minority Interest	587,992	18.8
Preferred Stock.................	84,059	2.7
Capital Lease Oblgs.	87,562	2.8
Total	3,126,220	100.0

RECENT DEVELOPMENTS: For the year ended 12/31/96, the Company reported an increase in net loss to £250.9 million compared with a net loss of £115.4 million in the same period of 1995. Earnings were unfavorably affected by programming fees, which as a percentage of revenues, increased to 58.0% from 50.0% the year before. This was partly attributable the Company's decision to provide more channels in the basic cable television package with no price increase. Total revenues more than doubled to £290.3 million from £144.8 million the year before. Cable television revenues leapt 87.3% to £121.2 million. Residential telephone revenues more than doubled to £125.0 million versus £57.6 million in 1995. Business telephone revenues surged 98.9% to £34.6 million. Other revenues advanced 86.3% to £9.5

BUSINESS

TELEWEST COMMUNICATIONS PLC. is a provider of cable television and residential and business cable telephone services in the UK. The Company owns and operates 16 cable franchises (which operate under the name "United Artists Communications") and has minority interests in three UK cable operators, which own and operate 7 additional cable franchises. The owned and operated franchises and the affiliated franchises together include approximately 479,465 residential telephone lines and 21,721 business telephone lines.

ANNUAL EARNINGS

	12/31/96	12/31/95	12/31/96	12/31/95
	------------US $------------		------------British £------------	
Earnings Per Share	d0.46	d0.20	d0.27	d0.13

ANNUAL FINANCIAL DATA

RECORD OF EARNINGS (IN THOUSANDS):

Total Revenues	491,856	224,850	290,266	144,784
Costs & Expenses	710,872	354,947	419,517	228,556
Operating Income	d219,016	d130,098	d129,251	d83,772
Income Bef Income Tax	d423,461	d178,075	d249,903	d114,665
Income Tax	1,389	1,072	820	690
Minority Interests	305	25	180	16
Net Income	d425,155	d179,171	d250,903	d115,371
Average Shares Outstg	925,425	865,424	925,425	865,424

BALANCE SHEET (IN THOUSANDS):

Cash & Cash Equivalents	134,062	721,862	79,116	464,818
Receivables, Net	113,411	85,384	66,929	54,980
Inventories	90	62	53	40
Gross Property	2,974,583	1,934,960	1,755,434	1,245,950
Accumulated Depreciation	522,313	282,867	308,240	182,142
Long-Term Debt	1,555,565	1,234,737	918,008	795,066
Stockholders' Equity	982,663	1,307,155	579,913	841,697
Total Assets	2,898,785	2,756,069	1,710,702	1,774,674
Total Current Assets	247,563	807,308	146,098	519,838
Total Current Liabilities	359,969	213,916	212,434	137,744
Net Working Capital	d112,406	593,392	d66,336	382,094
Year End Shs Outstg	927,567	919,963	927,567	919,963

STATISTICAL RECORD:

Return on Equity %	...	...		
Return on Assets %	...	...		
Operating Profit Margin %	...	...		
Net Profit Margin %	...	...		
Book Value Per Share	0.06	1.42		

Converted at 1996, US$1.6945= 1 British pound; 1995, US$1.5530= 1 British pound

OFFICERS:
S. Davidson, C.E.O.
C. Burdick, fin. Dir.
V. Hull, Couns. & Sec.
S. Galpert, Sr. V.P.-Fin.

INCORPORATED: United Kingdom, Jan., 1994

PRINCIPAL OFFICE: Genesis Business Park Albert Drive Woking United Kingdom

TELEPHONE NUMBER: 0148-3075-0900

NO. OF EMPLOYEES: 4,962

ANNUAL MEETING: In May

SHAREHOLDERS: 94

INSTITUTIONAL HOLDINGS:
No. of Institutions: 15
Shares Held: 1,689,792

AMERICAN DEPOSITARY RECEIPTS: Each American Depositary Receipt represents ten ordinary shs. of par £0.10.

DEPOSITARY BANK(S): The Bank of New York, (212) 815-2175

TEVA PHARMACEUTICAL INDUSTRIES LTD.

YIELD	0.5%
P/E RATIO	43.2

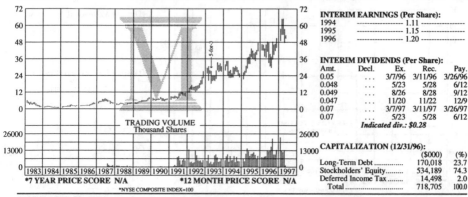

INTERIM EARNINGS (Per Share):

1994	1.11
1995	1.15
1996	1.20

INTERIM DIVIDENDS (Per Share):

Amt.	Decl.	Ex.	Rec.	Pay.
0.05	...	3/7/96	3/11/96	3/26/96
0.048	...	5/23	5/28	6/12
0.049	...	8/26	8/28	9/12
0.047	...	11/20	11/22	12/9
0.07	...	3/7/97	3/11/97	3/26/97
0.07	...	5/23	5/28	6/12

Indicated div.: $0.28

TRADING VOLUME
Thousand Shares

CAPITALIZATION (12/31/96):

	($000)	(%)
Long-Term Debt	170,018	23.7
Stockholders' Equity	534,189	74.3
Deferred Income Tax	14,498	2.0
Total	718,705	100.0

*7 YEAR PRICE SCORE N/A *12 MONTH PRICE SCORE N/A

*NYSE COMPOSITE INDEX=100

RECENT DEVELOPMENTS: For the year ended 12/31/96, net income rose 4.4% to $73.4 million from $70.3 million the previous year. Sales totaled $953.8 million, up 17.6% compared with $811.3 million the year before. Earnings for 1996 were negatively affected by pretax non-recurring merger charges of $19.8 million. Results for 1995 were restated to reflect the acquisition of Biocraft Laboratories Inc. and were negatively affected by a pretax charge of $4.7 million stemming from the write-off of debt in the fourth quarter. Gross profit climbed 21.2% to $359.7 million from

$296.8 million a year earlier. As a percentage of sales, gross profit was 37.7% versus 36.6% in 1995 due to an improved product mix coupled with the introduction of new products, primarily in the U.S. Operating income grew 10.1% to $109.5 million from $99.4 million the prior year. For the quarter ended 12/31/96, net income more than doubled to $30.3 million compared with $14.8 million the previous year. Sales advanced 20.6% to $277.7 million from $230.2 million the year before.

BUSINESS

TEVA PHARMACEUTICAL INDUSTRIES LTD. and its subsidiaries develop, manufacture and market branded, generic (off-patent) and branded generic pharmaceutical products, and bulk pharmaceutical chemicals. The Company utilizes its integrated production, manufacturing and research facilities to enter into niche markets with generic drugs or proprietary products on a worldwide basis. The Company also manufactures and sells hospital supplies, veterinary products and yeast and alcohol. The Company manufactures COPAXONE,® recently approved by authorities in the U.S., Israel and Argentina for treatment of multiple sclerosis.

ANNUAL EARNINGS

	12/31/96	12/31/95
	US $	
Earnings Per Share	1.20	1.15

ANNUAL FINANCIAL DATA

RECORD OF EARNINGS (IN THOUSANDS):

	12/31/96	12/31/95
Total Revenues	953,783	811,280
Costs & Expenses	844,279	711,832
Operating Income	109,504	99,448
Income Bef Income Tax	93,324	91,482
Income Tax	20,898	22,174
Eq. Earnings in Affils.	529	27
Minority Interests	467	967
Net Income	[1] 73,422	[2] 70,302

[1] Incl. merger-related expenses of $19,790,000 [2] Incl. General Health Fund write-off expenses of $4,745,000

BALANCE SHEET (IN THOUSANDS):

Cash & Cash Equivalents	61,178	64,865
Receivables, Net	328,069	239,750
Inventories	328,625	232,095
Gross Property	647,952	556,644
Accumulated Depreciation	234,246	178,626
Long-Term Debt	184,516	113,595
Stockholders' Equity	534,189	482,467
Total Assets	1,241,415	1,039,437
Total Current Assets	725,874	546,983
Total Current Liabilities	521,708	438,696
Net Working Capital	204,166	108,287
Year End Shs Outstg	62,774	62,695

STATISTICAL RECORD:

Return on Equity %	13.74	14.57
Return on Assets %	5.91	6.76
Operating Profit Margin %	11.48	12.26
Net Profit Margin %	7.70	8.67
Book Value Per Share	8.51	7.70

OFFICERS:
E. Hurvitz, Pres. & C.E.O.
D. S. Suesskind, C.F.O.
U. Karniel, Sec. & Couns.

INCORPORATED: 1935

PRINCIPAL OFFICE: 5 Basel Street, P.O. Box 3190, Petach Tikva, 49131 Israel

TELEPHONE NUMBER: 972-3-926-7267
NO. OF EMPLOYEES: 5,900
ANNUAL MEETING: In October
SHAREHOLDERS: 16,446
INSTITUTIONAL HOLDINGS:
No. of Institutions: 263
Shares Held: 25,700,000

AMERICAN DEPOSITARY RECEIPTS: (Sponsored) Each American Depositary Receipt represents one ordinary share of NIS0.10.

DEPOSITARY BANK(S): The Bank of New York, (212) 815-5133

THORN PLC

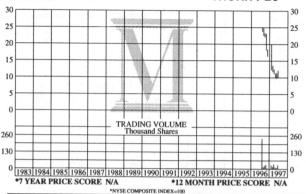

*7 YEAR PRICE SCORE N/A   *12 MONTH PRICE SCORE N/A

*NYSE COMPOSITE INDEX=100

INTERIM EARNINGS (Per Share, US$):
1996 ------------------ 0.27 ------------------

INTERIM DIVIDENDS (Per Share):

Amt.	Decl.	Ex.	Rec.	Pay.
0.255	...	1/10/97	1/14/97	3/17/97
0.6609	...	7/16	7/18	10/10

Indicated div.: $1.32

CAPITALIZATION (3/31/96):

	($000)	(%)
Long-Term Debt	2,140,000	99.7
Deferred Income Tax	7,333	0.3
Total	2,147,333	100.0

RECENT DEVELOPMENTS: For the year ended 3/31/97, group turnover increased 1.5% to £1.56 billion from the year before. Operating profit, before exceptional items, slipped 1.7% to £184.1 million. Operating profit excluded a £32.9 million charge for possible future lease obligations, a £17.1 million provision for a class action lawsuit in which Thorn is a defendant, and a £10.9 million provision for the reduction in the market value of Thorn plc shares held by the Employee Benefit Trust. Operating profit was pressured by weak volumes during the second half of the year, the negative effect of currency translations and investments in store expansions. The finance charge for the year, excluding non-recurring pre-demerger charges, was £13.1 million, down from £16.5 million the previous year. During the year, the Company opened 32 new Crazy George's stores in the United Kingdom and 73 additional rural rental-purchase stores in the United States.

BUSINESS

THORN PLC and its subsidiaries are engaged in consumer rental and rental-purchase of high quality durable goods. The Company offers a variety of consumer goods and services to customers who cannot or do not choose to buy them outright. Thorn markets its products and services to hotels and other institutional customers in Europe and Australasia through its business-to-business division. In addition, Thorn has an electrical and music retail operation in Denmark. The Company's principal rental and rental purchase brands include Radio Rentals, Crazy George's and Easiview in the UK, DER in Denmark, Thorn in Sweden, Norway and Finland, Skala in Benelux, Visea in France, Rent-A-Center, Remco and U-Can Rent in the US, Radio Rentals and Redihire in Australia, and DTR in New Zealand. Products currently available for rent include the following: televisions, VCRs, audio equipment, domestic appliances, home entertainment centres, furniture, personal computers and related office equipment, jewelry, air-conditioners, and mobile telephones.

ANNUAL EARNINGS

	3/31/96	3/31/95	3/31/96	3/31/95
	----------US $----------		--------British £--------	
Earnings Per Share	0.27	...	0.18	...

ANNUAL FINANCIAL DATA

RECORD OF EARNINGS (IN MILLIONS):

	3/31/96	3/31/95	3/31/96	3/31/95
Total Revenues	2,349	2,620	1,537	1,616
Costs & Expenses	2,109	2,558	1,380	1,578
Operating Income	240	62	157	38
Income Bef Income Tax	143	d9	94	d5
Income Tax	27	15	18	10
Net Income	116	d24	76	d15

BALANCE SHEET (IN MILLIONS):

Cash & Cash Equivalents	318	300	208	185
Receivables, Net	222	182	146	112
Inventories	72	88	47	54
Gross Property	3,164	3,110	2,071	1,919
Accumulated Depreciation	1,731	1,741	1,133	1,074
Long-Term Debt	2,140	692	1,401	427
Total Assets	5,139	2,975	3,364	1,835
Total Current Assets	3,706	1,606	2,426	991
Total Current Liabilities	2,090	1,994	1,368	1,230
Net Working Capital	1,615	d388	1,057	d239
Year End Shs Outstg (000)	434,500	...	434,500	...

STATISTICAL RECORD:

Return on Assets %	2.26	...		
Operating Profit Margin %	10.22	2.35		
Net Profit Margin %	4.95	...		

Converted at 1996, US$1.5277= 1 British pound; 1995, US$1.6210= 1 British pound

OFFICERS:
C. Southgate, Chmn.
M. Metcalf, C.E.O.
S. Marshall, Finance Dir.
H. Jenkins, Deputy Chmn.
INCORPORATED: United Kingdom, March 29, 1996
PRINCIPAL OFFICE: Thorn House, 124 Bridge Road, Chertsey, Surrey KT16 8LZ

TELEPHONE NUMBER: 01932 573700
NO. OF EMPLOYEES: 17,772
ANNUAL MEETING: In July
SHAREHOLDERS: 45,187
INSTITUTIONAL HOLDINGS:
No. of Institutions: 10
Shares Held: 686,815

AMERICAN DEPOSITARY RECEIPTS: Each American Depositary Share represents 4 ordinary shares of par value £0.25.

DEPOSITARY BANK(S): J.P. Morgan (212) 648-3206

NASDAQ SYMBOL TKIOY
Rec. Pr. 50¾

TOKIO MARINE & FIRE INSURANCE CO., LTD.

YIELD	0.6%
P/E RATIO	101.5

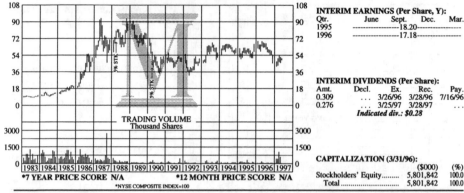

*7 YEAR PRICE SCORE N/A   *12 MONTH PRICE SCORE N/A

*NYSE COMPOSITE INDEX=100

INTERIM EARNINGS (Per Share, Y):

Qtr.	June	Sept.	Dec.	Mar.
1995	------------------18.20------------------			
1996	------------------17.18------------------			

INTERIM DIVIDENDS (Per Share):

Amt.	Decl.	Ex.	Rec.	Pay.
0.309	...	3/26/96	3/28/96	7/16/96
0.276	...	3/25/97	3/28/97	...

Indicated div.: $0.28

CAPITALIZATION (3/31/96):

	($000)	(%)
Stockholders' Equity	5,801,842	100.0
Total	5,801,842	100.0

RECENT DEVELOPMENTS: For the year ended 3/31/96, net income was ¥26.63 billion (US $248.0 million) compared with ¥28.16 billion (US $327.0 million) the year before. Results for the recent and prior-year periods included net extraordinary gains of ¥10.69 billion and ¥1.27 billion, respectively. The extraordinary items consisted of gains realized from the sale of marketable securities and real estate, partially offset by losses on the disposal of fixed assets, devaluation of marketable securities and real estate, and sale of marketable securities. Total revenue increased 4.1% to ¥1,814.94 billion (US $16.88 billion). Net premiums written rose 3.3% to ¥1,278.57 billion (US $11.89 billion) from ¥1,237.50 billion a year earlier.

BUSINESS

TOKIO MARINE AND FIRE INSURANCE CO., LTD. is a non-life insurance company engaged in writing marine, fire and casualty, personal accidents, burglary, glasses, flight, flood, animal, workers' compensation, liability, machinery, construction, nuclear power, auto and allied lines of insurance principally covering risks located in Japan and hull and cargo risks for Japanese businesses. Also, the Company provides insurance services in the United States, United Kingdom, Canada, Brazil and various countries in Southeast Asia.

ANNUAL EARNINGS

	3/31/96	3/31/95	3/31/96	3/31/95
	----------US $----------		----------Yen----------	
Earnings Per Share	0.16	0.21	17.18	18.20

ANNUAL FINANCIAL DATA

RECORD OF EARNINGS (IN MILLIONS):

	3/31/96	3/31/95	3/31/96	3/31/95
Total Revenues	16,879	20,220	1,814,942	1,743,069
Costs & Expenses	16,091	19,329	1,730,194	1,666,305
Operating Income	788	890	84,748	76,763
Non-Operating Income	67	4	7,161	379
Income Tax	680	743	73,156	64,057
Net Income	248	327	26,627	28,161

BALANCE SHEET (IN MILLIONS):

Cash & Cash Equivalents	6,102	6,516	656,106	561,703
Receivables, Net	1,399	1,579	150,440	136,162
Gross Property	3,237	4,077	348,117	351,501
Stockholders' Equity	5,802	7,041	623,853	607,006
Total Assets	46,689	55,896	5,020,338	4,818,630
Total Current Assets	7,501	8,095	806,546	697,866
Total Current Liabilities	37,290	44,609	4,009,722	3,845,616
Year End Shs Outstg (000)	1,549,692	1,547,070	1,549,692	1,547,070

STATISTICAL RECORD:

Return on Equity %	4.3	4.6		
Return on Assets %	0.5	0.6		
Operating Profit Margin %	4.7	4.4		
Net Profit Margin %	1.5	1.6		
Book Value Per Share	3.74	4.55		

Converted at 1996, US$0.0093= 1 Japanese Yen; 1995, US$0.0116= 1 Japanese Yen

OFFICERS:
S. Kono, Chairman
K. Higuchi, President

INCORPORATED: Japan, 1879

PRINCIPAL OFFICE: 2-1 Marunouchi 1-chome Chiyoda-ku Tokyo 100 Japan

TELEPHONE NUMBER: (03) 3212-6211

NO. OF EMPLOYEES: 14,029

ANNUAL MEETING: In June

SHAREHOLDERS: 113,077
INSTITUTIONAL HOLDINGS:
No. of Institutions: 4,029
Shares Held: 1,209,767,174

AMERICAN DEPOSITARY RECEIPTS: Each American Depositary Receipt represents 5 common shs. of Co.

DEPOSITARY BANK(S): Citibank N.A., (212) 657-7800

246

TOYOTA MOTOR CORPORATION

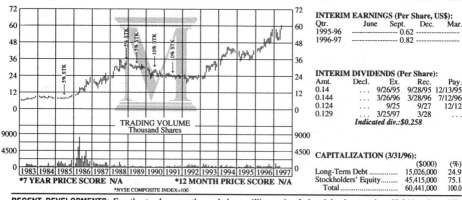

INTEREST EARNINGS (Per Share, US$):

Qtr.	June	Sept.	Dec.	Mar.
1995-96	------------------ 0.62 ------------------			
1996-97	------------------ 0.82 ------------------			

INTERIM DIVIDENDS (Per Share):

Amt.	Decl.	Ex.	Rec.	Pay.
0.14	...	9/26/95	9/28/95	12/13/95
0.144	...	3/26/96	3/28/96	7/12/96
0.124	...	9/25	9/27	12/12
0.129	...	3/25/97	3/28	...

Indicated div.:$0.258

TRADING VOLUME
Thousand Shares

*7 YEAR PRICE SCORE N/A   ***12 MONTH PRICE SCORE N/A**

*NYSE COMPOSITE INDEX=100

CAPITALIZATION (3/31/96):

	($000)	(%)
Long-Term Debt	15,026,000	24.9
Stockholders' Equity.........	45,415,000	75.1
Total	60,441,000	100.0

RECENT DEVELOPMENTS: For the twelve months ended 3/31/97, net income leaped 50.2% to Y385.92 billion compared with Y256.98 billion in 1996. Revenues were Y12,243.83 billion, up 14.2% versus Y10,718.74 billion in the prior year. Worldwide, Toyota vehicle sales were up 9.9% to 4.6 million units in fiscal 1997. During the period, sales in Japan, the Company's largest market, rose 7.7% to 2.2 million units. Overseas sales increased 12.2% to 2.3 million units. Industrial sales stood at 69,044 units, while sales of the Company's prefabricated houses amounted to 3,713 units. Cost of sales increased 10.1% on an annualized basis, while the Company's operating income nearly doubled to Y665.11 billion versus Y348.07 billion in the previous term. Selling, general and administrative expenses amounted to 13.7% of net sales, compared with 12.6% in the year-earlier period.

BUSINESS

TOYOTA MOTOR CORPORATION is a worldwide manufacturer, distributer and marketer of passenger cars, trucks, buses, mini-vans, commercial vehicles and automotive replacement parts and accessories. The Company's brand names include Century, Celsior, Crown, Soarer, Supra, Starlet, Chaser, Cresta, Camry, Vista, and Corolla; and automotive replacement parts and accessories. In addition, TOYOY manufactures industrial equipment, including shovel loaders, forklifts, towing tractors, and automatic-guided vehicles and other kinds of equipment for automating factory operations. The Company also provides financing to its dealers and their customers and operates vehicle leasing and rental outlets, both domestically and overseas. Other activities include the manufacture and marketing of prefabricated homes; cellular car telephone services; and telephone and proprietary telecommunications services.

ANNUAL EARNINGS

	3/31/97	3/31/96	3/31/97	3/31/96
	---------------US $---------------		-------------Yen-------------	
Earnings Per Share	0.82	0.62	102.25	66.55

ANNUAL FINANCIAL DATA

RECORD OF EARNINGS (IN MILLIONS):

Total Revenues	97,951	99,684	12,243,834	10,718,739
Costs & Expenses	92,630	96,447	11,578,719	10,370,670
Operating Income	5,321	3,237	665,114	348,069
Income Bef Income Tax	5,666	3,913	708,299	420,801
Income Tax	2,833	1,707	354,113	183,531
Eq. Earnings in Affils.	303	231	37,854	24,886
Minority Interests	47	49	5,893	5,239
Net Income	3,087	2,390	385,915	256,977

BALANCE SHEET (IN MILLIONS):

Cash & Cash Equivalents	14,836	12,858	1,854,529	1,382,550
Receivables, Net	11.262	11,543	1,407,782	1,241,162
Inventories	4,493	4,886	561,621	525,353
Net Property	327,952	32,339	4,094,024	3,477,288
Long-Term Debt	15,026	18,105	1,878,310	1,946,732
Stockholders' Equity	45,415	49,448	5,676,824	5,316,997
Total Assets	101,639	105,485	12,704,833	11,342,448
Total Current Assets	46,719	46,489	5,839,920	4,998,830
Total Current Liabilities	37,439	34,034	4,679,937	3,659,565
Net Working Capital	9,280	12,455	1,159,983	1,339,265
Year End Shs Outstg	3,774	3,751	3,774	3,751

STATISTICAL RECORD:

Return on Equity %	6.80	4.83		
Return on Assets %	3.04	2.27		
Operating Profit Margin %	5.43	3.25		
Net Profit Margin %	3.15	2.40		
Book Value Per Share	12.03	13.18		

Converted at 1997, US$0.0080= 1 Japanese Yen; 1996, US$0.0093= 1 Japanese Yen

OFFICERS:
S. Toyoda, Chmn. & Representative Dir.
I. Isomura, Vice-Chmn. & Representative Dir.
H. Okuda, Pres. & Representative Dir.

INCORPORATED: Aug., 1937

PRINCIPAL OFFICE: 1, Toyota-cho Toyota Japan

TELEPHONE NUMBER: (0565) 28-2121

NO. OF EMPLOYEES: 70,000

ANNUAL MEETING: In Jun.

SHAREHOLDERS: 107,140

INSTITUTIONAL HOLDINGS:
No. of Institutions: 51
Shares Held: 5,930,183

AMERICAN DEPOSITARY RECEIPTS: Each American Depositary Receipt represents 2 common shs. of Co.

DEPOSITARY BANK(S): The Bank of New York, (212) 815-2175; Bankers Trust Co., (212) 250-8500; Citibank N.A., (212) 657-7800; J.P. Morgan, (212) 648-3206

NASDAQ SYMBOL TGBRY
Rec. Pr. 1⅛

TRANS-GLOBAL RESOURCES N.L.

YIELD ...
P/E RATIO ...

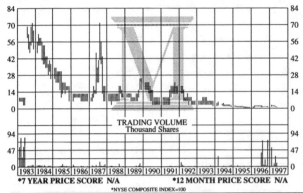

1983 1984 1985 1986 1987 1988 1989 1990 1991 1992 1993 1994 1995 1996 1997
*7 YEAR PRICE SCORE N/A   *12 MONTH PRICE SCORE N/A
*NYSE COMPOSITE INDEX=100

TRADING VOLUME
Thousand Shares

INTERIM EARNINGS (Per Share):
1994-95 ----------------- Nil -----------------
1995-96 -----------------d0.01-----------------

INTERIM DIVIDENDS (Per Share):
Amt.   Decl.   Ex.   Rec.   Pay.
No dividends paid.

CAPITALIZATION (6/30/96):

	($000)	(%)
Stockholders' Equity........	3,618	100.0
Total.............................	3,618	100.0

RECENT DEVELOPMENTS: For the year ended 6/30/96, the Company incurred a net loss of A$978,578 (US$770,630) compared with a net loss of A$1.7 million (US$1.2 million) the previous year. Earnings for 1995 included abnormal items of A$1.1 million (US$749,958). Operating revenue soared to A$401,822 (US$316,435) from A$22,040 (US$15,642) the year before. During September 1996, Atomer Holdings Pty Ltd, a 20%-owned subsidiary of Trans-Global, was sold to a Canadian company for consideration of A$400,000. On 2/26/97, the Company announced that it entered into an agreement to sell all of its Ghanaian assets to Earth King Resources, Inc. for 8.5 million shares in Earth King. Under this transaction, the Company will own approximately 78% of Earth King.

BUSINESS

TRANS-GLOBAL RESOURCES N.L. is a mining company engaged in the exploration for and development of gold, silver, copper, titanium, iron and other mineral prospects in Australia, Northern Chile, the United States, Ghana, West Africa, and Zimbabwe.

ANNUAL EARNINGS

	6/30/96	6/30/95	6/30/96	6/30/95
	---------US $---------		---------A $---------	
Earnings Per Share	d0.01	Nil	d0.02	d0.01

ANNUAL FINANCIAL DATA

RECORD OF EARNINGS (IN THOUSANDS):

Total Revenues	316	16	402	22
Costs & Expenses	881	458	1,119	645
Depreciation & Amort	5	4	7	5
Operating Income	d771	d1,183	d979	d1,667
Net Income	d771	d1,183	d979	d1,667
Average Shares Outstg	53,003	272,158	53,003	272,158

BALANCE SHEET (IN THOUSANDS):

Cash & Cash Equivalents	597	21	758	30
Receivables, Net	394	104	500	146
Gross Property	12	31	16	44
Accumulated Depreciation	8	11	10	16
Stockholders' Equity	3,618	1,849	4,595	2,605
Total Assets	3,720	2,271	4,724	3,200
Total Current Assets	1,085	144	1,378	203
Total Current Liabilities	101	422	129	595
Net Working Capital	983	d278	1,249	d392
Year End Shs Outstg	73,157	296,700	73,157	296,700

STATISTICAL RECORD:

Book Value Per Share	0.05	0.01		

Converted at 1996, US$0.7875= 1 Australian $; 1995, US$0.7097= 1 Australian $

OFFICERS:
B. J. Frost, Chmn.
D. A. Lenigas, Exec. Dir.
R. C. Davey, Exec. Dir.
D. P. Rodli, Non-Exec. Dir.

INCORPORATED: Australia, Sept., 1970

PRINCIPAL OFFICE: Suite 2, 1233 High Street, Armadale Australia

TELEPHONE NUMBER: 61-3-9824866

NO. OF EMPLOYEES: N/A

ANNUAL MEETING: In November

SHAREHOLDERS: 3,509

INSTITUTIONAL HOLDINGS:
No. of Institutions: 4
Shares Held: 90

AMERICAN DEPOSITARY RECEIPTS: (Sponsored) Each American Depositary Receipt represents ten ordinary shares of par A$2.50.

DEPOSITARY BANK(S): The Bank of New York, (212) 815-2175

248

TRANSCOM INTERNATIONAL, LIMITED

YIELD   ...
P/E RATIO   ...

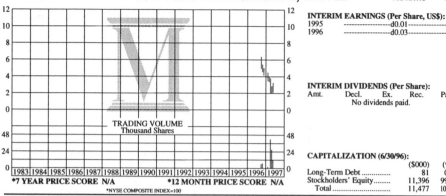

INTERIM EARNINGS (Per Share, US$):
1995 ------------------d0.01------------------
1996 ------------------d0.03------------------

INTERIM DIVIDENDS (Per Share):

Amt.	Decl.	Ex.	Rec.	Pay.
		No dividends paid.		

*7 YEAR PRICE SCORE N/A   *12 MONTH PRICE SCORE N/A
*NYSE COMPOSITE INDEX=100

CAPITALIZATION (6/30/96):

	($000)	(%)
Long-Term Debt	81	0.7
Stockholders' Equity.........	11,396	99.3
Total	11,477	100.0

RECENT DEVELOPMENTS: For the year ended 6/30/96, the Company reported a loss of A$7.9 million compared with a loss of A$2.3 million in the corresponding period a year earlier. Revenues were A$2.6 million, up 67% versus A$1.6 million in 1995. Revenues for the Company's natural gas vehicle segment rose 31% to A$634,084 compared with A$485,565 in the comparable period a year earlier. The vehicle systems data communications segment posted revenues of A$1.2 million versus A$560,660 in 1995. Other revenues advanced 51% to A$774,469. The Company announced that it signed a letter of intent to acquire Collins Motor Corporation Ltd. Under the acquisition plan TRIXY will give each Collins shareholder one share of its stock for each Collins share held. The acquisition plan is subject to approval by shareholders and the federal court in Australia.

BUSINESS

TRANSCOM INTERNATIONAL, LIMITED is a producer of products and services for the Company's Electronic Control Systems Technology (ECST) products. ECST is a generic technology which is applied by the Company to natural gas vehicle engines and mobile data transfer computing products. The Company's patented natural gas vehicle system enables heavy duty engines to run on clean natural gas. The Company's patented radio area network data technology enables the transfer of computer data from mobile locations via wireless networks.

ANNUAL EARNINGS

	6/30/96	6/30/95	6/30/96	6/30/95
	-----------US $-----------		-----------A$-----------	
Earnings Per Share	① d0.03	d0.01	① d0.04	d0.01

① Incl. abnormal charges of US$3.7 mill.(A$4.8 mill.).

ANNUAL FINANCIAL DATA

RECORD OF EARNINGS (IN THOUSANDS):

Total Revenues	2,055	1,106	2,609	1,558
Income Bef Income Tax	d6,404	d2,117	d8,132	d2,982
Minority Interests	cr208	cr505	cr264	cr711
Net Income	d6,196	d1,612	d7,868	d2,271
Average Shares Outstg	195,901	163,173	195,901	163,173

BALANCE SHEET (IN THOUSANDS):

Cash & Cash Equivalents	8,757	3,293	11,120	4,640
Receivables, Net	435	165	552	233
Inventories	39	63	50	89
Gross Property	1,830	889	2,323	1,252
Accumulated Depreciation	382	155	485	219
Long-Term Debt	81	113	102	159
Stockholders' Equity	11,396	8,410	14,471	11,849
Total Assets	16,966	13,999	21,544	19,725
Total Current Assets	9,489	5,154	12,049	7,262
Total Current Liabilities	913	1,409	1,160	1,986
Net Working Capital	8,576	3,744	10,890	5,276
Year End Shs Outstg	232,673	166,856	232,673	166,856

STATISTICAL RECORD:

Return on Equity %	...	...		
Return on Assets %	...	...		
Operating Profit Margin %	...	...		
Net Profit Margin %	...	...		
Book Value Per Share	0.05	0.05		

Converted at 1996, US$0.7875= 1 Australian $; 1995, US$0.7097= 1 Australian $

OFFICERS:
H. W. Sorensen, Chmn.
P. F. Malone, Managing Dir.
D. V. Martino, Director
S. Cassim, Director

INCORPORATED: N/A

PRINCIPAL OFFICE: 22 Hasler Road, Herdsman WA 6016 Australia

TELEPHONE NUMBER: (619) 244-1166

NO. OF EMPLOYEES: 40

ANNUAL MEETING: N/A

SHAREHOLDERS: 3,514

INSTITUTIONAL HOLDINGS:
No. of Institutions: N/A
Shares Held: N/A

AMERICAN DEPOSITARY RECEIPTS: Each ADR equals 50 ord. shares.

DEPOSITARY BANK(S): Bankers Trust Co., (212) 250-8500

TRANZ RAIL HOLDINGS, LIMITED

YIELD 5.8%
P/E RATIO 16.7

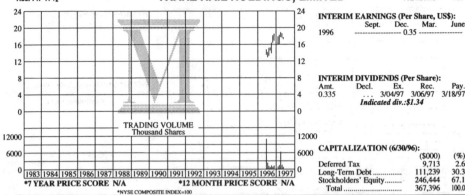

INTERIM EARNINGS (Per Share, US$):

	Sept.	Dec.	Mar.	June
1996	------------------ 0.35 ------------------			

INTERIM DIVIDENDS (Per Share):

Amt.	Decl.	Ex.	Rec.	Pay.
0.335	...	3/04/97	3/06/97	3/18/97

Indicated div.:$1.34

TRADING VOLUME
Thousand Shares

*7 YEAR PRICE SCORE N/A   *12 MONTH PRICE SCORE N/A

*NYSE COMPOSITE INDEX=100

CAPITALIZATION (6/30/96):

	($000)	(%)
Deferred Tax	9,713	2.6
Long-Term Debt	111,239	30.3
Stockholders' Equity	246,444	67.1
Total	367,396	100.0

RECENT DEVELOPMENTS: For the quarter ended 12/31/96, net income advanced to NZ$14.7 million compared with NZ$13.1 million in the corresponding period a year earlier. Revenues were NZ$150.9 million flat for the period. Earnings benefited from a reduction of interest expense. Revenue gains in coal, up 19%, and manufactured products, up 5%, represented the strongest sectors in the Company's customer base, while Interisland and Rail passenger volumes increased 6% and 4%, respectively, over the prior year period. Net interest expense and deferred financing costs decreased NZ$2.4 million to NZ$6.4 million, which included a NZ$1.4 million one-time pre-tax charge related to the retirement of the Company's bank debt.

BUSINESS

TRANZ RAIL HOLDINGS, LIMITED is a transport company providing a range of services to grow the freight and passenger markets. TNZRY'S business is conducted through Tranz Link, which markets and manages all aspects of freight transport; Tranz Scenic, which operates the company's eight long distance rail services; Tranz Metro, which offers urban commuter rail services in Auckland and Wellington; and Interisland Travel, which markets interisland passenger services, commercial vehicle services and ferry services.

ANNUAL EARNINGS

	6/30/96	6/30/95	6/30/96	6/30/95
	US $		NZ$	
Earnings Per Share	0.35	0.44	0.51	0.66

ANNUAL FINANCIAL DATA

RECORD OF EARNINGS (IN THOUSANDS):

	6/30/96	6/30/95	6/30/96	6/30/95
Total Revenues	391,743	372,681	571,637	556,989
Costs & Expenses	297,324	284,721	433,860	425,528
Depreciation & Amort	18,461	17,510	26,939	26,169
Operating Income	75,957	70,451	110,838	105,292
Income Bef Income Tax	50,113	65,760	73,126	98,281
Income Tax	16,410	16,483	23,946	24,635
Net Income	33,703	49,277	49,180	73,646

BALANCE SHEET (IN THOUSANDS):

Cash & Cash Equivalents	59	3,431	86	5,128
Receivables, Net	41,024	34,062	59,863	50,907
Inventories	35,013	27,678	51,092	41,366
Gross Property	455,106	383,806	664,097	573,616
Accumulated Depreciation	87,384	70,134	127,512	104,819
Long-Term Debt	111,239	220,931	162,321	330,191
Stockholders' Equity	246,444	88,962	359,615	132,957
Total Assets	446,436	387,552	651,447	579,214
Total Current Assets	76,096	65,171	111,041	97,401
Total Current Liabilities	58,489	52,682	85,348	78,735
Net Working Capital	17,607	12,489	25,693	18,666
Year End Shs Outstg	126,173	91,512	126,173	91,512

STATISTICAL RECORD:

Return on Equity %	13.68	55.39
Return on Assets %	9.10	15.29
Operating Profit Margin %	19.39	18.90
Net Profit Margin %	8.60	13.22
Book Value Per Share	1.95	0.97

Converted at 1996, US$0.6853= 1 New Zealand $; 1995, US$0.6691= 1 New Zealand $

OFFICERS:
E. A. Burkhardt, Chmn.
A. F. Small, Managing Dir.
R. G. Russ, Exec. Manager & C.F.O.

INCORPORATED: 1993

PRINCIPAL OFFICE: Wellington Railway Station, Bunny Street, Wellington New Zealand

TELEPHONE NUMBER: 644-498-3000

NO. OF EMPLOYEES: 4,780

ANNUAL MEETING: In Dec.

SHAREHOLDERS: N/A

INSTITUTIONAL HOLDINGS:
No. of Institutions: 36
Shares Held: 5,441,954

AMERICAN DEPOSITARY RECEIPTS: Each American Depositary Receipt represents 3 ordinary shares of no par value.

DEPOSITARY BANK(S): The Bank of New York, (212) 815-2175

TRINITY BIOTECH PLC

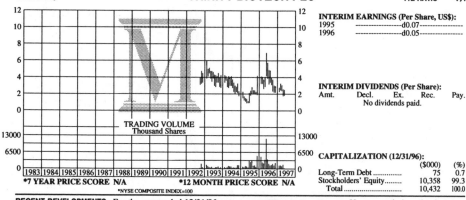

INTERIM EARNINGS (Per Share, US$):
1995	------------------d0.07------------------
1996	------------------d0.05------------------

INTERIM DIVIDENDS (Per Share):

Amt.	Decl.	Ex.	Rec.	Pay.
	No dividends paid.			

TRADING VOLUME
Thousand Shares

CAPITALIZATION (12/31/96):

	($000)	(%)
Long-Term Debt	75	0.7
Stockholders' Equity........	10,358	99.3
Total	10,432	100.0

RECENT DEVELOPMENTS: For the year ended 12/31/96, net loss totaled $776,000, or $0.05 per share, compared with a loss of $831,000, or $0.07 per share, the previous year. Earnings in 1996 were negatively affected by a $350,000 provision for legal fees that was recorded in the fourth quarter coupled with an unfavorable foreign currency exchange rate. Revenues fell 27.8% to $7.2 million from $9.9 million the year before. Lower revenues stemmed from the timing of shipments to the Company's U.S. OTC pregnancy test customer. However, during the last two quarters, shipments to this customer increased and are expected to continue to increase for the remainder of 1997. Gross profit was $1.9 million, down 1.9% versus $2.0 million a year earlier. For the three months ended 12/31/96, net loss totaled $779,000 compared with a net loss of $359,000 the prior year. Revenues slipped 22.4% to $2.1 million from $2.7 million in the same quarter in 1995.

BUSINESS

TRINITY BIOTECH PLC and its subsidiaries are engaged in the developing, manufacturing and marketing of rapid on-site whole blood and saliva-based tests for the diagnosis of Human Immune Deficiency Virus (HIV), hepatitis and other infectious diseases, and the marketing of pregnancy tests.

ANNUAL EARNINGS

	12/31/96	12/31/95	12/31/96	12/31/95
	--------------US $--------------		----------Irish £----------	
Earnings Per Share	d0.05	d0.07	d0.03	d0.05

ANNUAL FINANCIAL DATA

RECORD OF EARNINGS (IN THOUSANDS):
Total Revenues	7,007	9,908	4,227	6,192
Costs & Expenses	7,294	10,193	4,401	6,370
Operating Income	d1,134	d938	d684	d586
Income Bef Income Tax	d776	d831	d468	d519
Net Income	d776	d831	d468	d519
Average Shares Outstg	16,120	11,136	16,120	11,136
BALANCE SHEET (IN THOUSANDS):				
Cash & Cash Equivalents	5,482	7,518	3,307	4,698
Receivables, Net	2,873	379	1,734	237
Inventories	514	269	310	168
Gross Property	2,228	1,734	1,344	1,084
Accumulated Depreciation	983	810	593	506
Long-Term Debt	75	. . .	45	. . .
Stockholders' Equity	10,358	7,500	6,249	4,687
Total Assets	13,348	9,173	8,052	5,732
Total Current Assets	9,468	8,208	5,712	5,129
Total Current Liabilities	2,915	1,673	1,759	1,045
Net Working Capital	6,552	6,535	3,953	4,084
Year End Shs Outstg	16,299	15,316	16,299	15,316
STATISTICAL RECORD:				
Book Value Per Share	0.64	0.49		

Converted at 1996, US$1.6576= 1 Irish pound; 1995, US$1.6002= 1 Irish pound

OFFICERS:
R. O'Caoimh, Chmn. & C.E.O.
B. K. Farrell, Pres.
J. Walsh, C.O.O.
J. O'Connell, C.F.O. & Sec.
INCORPORATED: Ireland, Jan. 22, 1992
PRINCIPAL OFFICE: Three Rock Road, Sandyford Industrial Estate, Dublin 18 Ireland

TELEPHONE NUMBER: 353-1-295-5111

NO. OF EMPLOYEES: 52

ANNUAL MEETING: In April

SHAREHOLDERS: N/A

INSTITUTIONAL HOLDINGS:
No. of Institutions: 2
Shares Held: 18,452

AMERICAN DEPOSITARY RECEIPTS: (Sponsored) Each American Depositary Receipt represents one class 'A' ordinary share of par IR£0.01.

DEPOSITARY BANK(S): The Bank of New York, (212) 815-2175

UNITED NEWS & MEDIA, P.L.C.

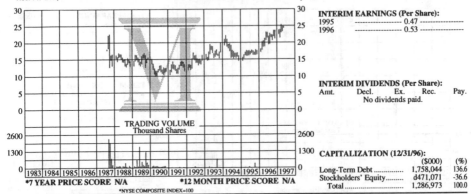

INTERIM EARNINGS (Per Share):

1995	------------------ 0.47 ------------------
1996	------------------ 0.53 ------------------

INTERIM DIVIDENDS (Per Share):

Amt.	Decl.	Ex.	Rec.	Pay.
		No dividends paid.		

CAPITALIZATION (12/31/96):

	($000)	(%)
Long-Term Debt	1,758,044	136.6
Stockholders' Equity	d471,071	-36.6
Total	1,286,973	100.0

TRADING VOLUME
Thousand Shares

*7 YEAR PRICE SCORE N/A   *12 MONTH PRICE SCORE N/A

*NYSE COMPOSITE INDEX=100

RECENT DEVELOPMENTS: For the year ended 12/31/96, net income advanced 5.2% to £152.4 million ($258.2 million) from £144.9 million ($225.0 million) the previous year. Total revenues rose 5.3% to £1.99 billion ($3.37 billion) from £1.89 billion ($2.94 billion) a year earlier. Earnings in 1996 included extraordinary charges totaling £43.7 million ($74.0 million). The 1995 results have been restated to reflect the 4/2/96 merger with MAI plc. The Company experienced strong sales and earnings growth in its busi-

ness services and broadcasting divisions. Profits from the consumer publishing division were boosted by a new pricing strategy and new product offerings in the U.K.; however, these gains were more than offset by higher paper costs. Sluggish activity in world financial markets negatively affected earnings in the financial services division. However, results benefited from cost controls, elimination of unprofitable businesses and the development of new products.

BUSINESS

UNITED NEWS & MEDIA, P.L.C. is an international media and information group with interests in: consumer publishing, including Express Newspapers, regional newspapers in the U.K., and advertising publications in the U.S. and Europe; broadcasting and entertainment, including the Meridian and Anglia ITV companies and a 29% share in Channel 5 in the U.K.; financial services, including the world's largest integrated money and securities broker; business services, including the Miller Freeman trade magazines and exhibitions business, NOP Information Group, PR Newswire and the Visual Communications Group stock photography business.

ANNUAL EARNINGS

	12/31/96	12/31/95	12/31/96	12/31/95
	----------US $----------		----------British £--------	
Earnings Per Share	0.53	0.47	0.31	0.30

ANNUAL FINANCIAL DATA

RECORD OF EARNINGS (IN THOUSANDS):				
Total Revenues	3,373,241	2,937,344	1,990,700	1,891,400
Costs & Expenses	3,088,226	2,600,343	1,822,500	1,674,400
Operating Income	285,015	337,001	168,200	217,000
Eq. Earnings in Affils.	d69,983	21,431	d41,300	13,800
Income Bef Income Tax	396,174	334,361	233,800	215,300
Income Tax	128,613	109,176	75,900	70,300
Minority Interests	9,320	155	5,500	100
Net Income	258,242	225,030	152,400	144,900
BALANCE SHEET (IN THOUSANDS):				
Cash & Cash Equivalents	752,019	610,640	443,800	393,200
Receivables, Net	666,786	1,120,024	393,500	721,200
Inventories	174,195	163,376	102,800	105,200
Gross Property	1,178,355	1,122,664	695,400	722,900
Accumulated Depreciation	562,066	471,801	331,700	303,800
Long-Term Debt	1,758,044	1,333,095	1,037,500	858,400
Stockholders' Equity	d471,071	527,709	d278,000	339,800
Total Assets	2,706,455	2,814,813	1,597,200	1,812,500
Total Current Assets	1,592,999	1,894,039	940,100	1,219,600
Total Current Liabilities	1,159,038	861,294	684,000	554,600
Net Working Capital	433,961	1,032,745	256,100	665,000
Year End Shs Outstg	491,153	245,720	491,153	245,720
STATISTICAL RECORD:				
Return on Equity %	...	42.64		
Return on Assets %	9.54	7.99		
Operating Profit Margin %	8.45	11.47		
Net Profit Margin %	7.66	7.66		
Book Value Per Share	...	2.14		

Converted at 1996, US$1.6945= 1 British pound; 1995, US$1.5530= 1 British pound

OFFICERS:
The Lord Stevens of Ludgate, Chmn.
C. Hollick, Group Chief Executive
D. Arculus, Chief Operating Officer
C. Stern, Finance Director
INCORPORATED: N/A
PRINCIPAL OFFICE: Ludgate House, 245 Blackfriars Road, London SE1 9UY United Kingdom

TELEPHONE NUMBER: 44-171-921-5000
NO. OF EMPLOYEES: 18,318
ANNUAL MEETING: In May
SHAREHOLDERS: N/A
INSTITUTIONAL HOLDINGS:
No. of Institutions: 4
Shares Held: 216,980

AMERICAN DEPOSITARY RECEIPTS: (Sponsored) Each American Depositary Receipt represents two ordinary shares of par £0.25.

DEPOSITARY BANK(S): The Bank of New York, (212) 815-2175

VAAL REEFS EXPLORATION AND MINING CO. LTD.

YIELD 7.3%
P/E RATIO ...

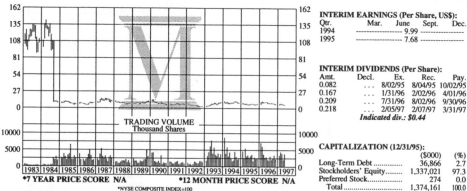

INTERIM EARNINGS (Per Share, US$):

Qtr.	Mar.	June	Sept.	Dec.
1994	------------------	9.99	------------------	
1995	------------------	7.68	------------------	

INTERIM DIVIDENDS (Per Share):

Amt.	Decl.	Ex.	Rec.	Pay.
0.082	...	8/02/95	8/04/95	10/02/95
0.167	...	1/31/96	2/02/96	4/01/96
0.209	...	7/31/96	8/02/96	9/30/96
0.218	...	2/05/97	2/07/97	3/31/97

Indicated div.: $0.44

CAPITALIZATION (12/31/95):

	($000)	(%)
Long-Term Debt	36,866	2.7
Stockholders' Equity.........	1,337,021	97.3
Preferred Stock.................	274	0.0
Total	1,374,161	100.0

*7 YEAR PRICE SCORE N/A   *12 MONTH PRICE SCORE N/A

*NYSE COMPOSITE INDEX=100

RECENT DEVELOPMENTS: For the year ended 12/31/96, net profit was R406.4 million (US$149.1 million) compared with R211.3 million (US$64.8 million) the year before. Results for the 1996 year-end period included an appropriation of R327.4 million for capital expenditures, while the 1995 year-end period included an appropriation of R324.1 million. Revenue increased 19.8% to R3.68 billion (US$860.3 million) from R3.07 billion (US$846.3 million) a year earlier. Cost of sales increased 11.0% to R2.60 billion (US$663.2 million) from R2.35 billion (US$702.2 million) the previous year. Operating profit was R1.08 billion (US$197.1 million) versus R724.3 million (US$144.1 million) in the prior-year period. Profit before taxation was R805.6 million (US$133.5 million) compared with R574.6 million (US$102.8 million) the year before.

BUSINESS

VAAL REEFS EXPLORATION AND MINING CO. LTD. conducts gold-mining operations. The Company also produces uranium oxide and sulphuric acid.

ANNUAL EARNINGS

	12/31/95	12/31/94	12/31/95	12/31/94
	----------US $----------		----------Rand----------	
Earnings Per Share	7.68	9.99	28.00	35.40

ANNUAL FINANCIAL DATA

RECORD OF EARNINGS (IN MILLIONS):

Total Revenues	842	877	3,071	3,109
Costs & Expenses	644	618	2,347	2,192
Operating Income	199	259	724	917
Income Bef Income Tax	158	210	575	744
Income Tax	11	19	39	67
Net Income	58	67	211	238
Average Shares Outstg (000)	19,115	19,115	19,115	19,115

BALANCE SHEET (IN MILLIONS):

Cash & Cash Equivalents	9	14	31	50
Receivables, Net	37	83	135	292
Inventories	60	52	219	183
Gross Property	1,326	1,257	4,833	4,453
Long-Term Debt	37	33	134	115
Stockholders' Equity	1,337	1,278	4,874	4,529
Total Assets	1,509	1,448	5,501	5,132
Total Current Assets	114	154	416	547
Total Current Liabilities	135	138	493	489
Net Working Capital	d21	16	d77	58
Year End Shs Outstg (000)	19,115	19,115	19,115	19,115

STATISTICAL RECORD:

Return on Equity %	10.98	14.94		
Return on Assets %	9.73	13.19		
Operating Profit Margin %	23.58	29.50		
Net Profit Margin %	17.43	21.77		
Book Value Per Share	69.95	66.86		

Converted at 1995, US$0.2743= 1 South African Rand; 1994, US$0.2822= 1 South African Rand

OFFICERS:
R. M. Godsell, Chmn.
R. J. Fisher, C.O.O.

INCORPORATED: South Africa, May 29, 1944

PRINCIPAL OFFICE: 44 Main Street Johannesburg, 2001 South Africa

TELEPHONE NUMBER: (011) 638-9111

NO. OF EMPLOYEES: 48,000

ANNUAL MEETING: In April

SHAREHOLDERS: 4,654

INSTITUTIONAL HOLDINGS:
No. of Institutions: 36
Shares Held: 12,432,495

AMERICAN DEPOSITARY RECEIPTS: (Sponsored) Ten ADR's represent one ordinary share of par R0.50.

DEPOSITARY BANK(S): The Bank of New York, (212) 815-2175; Bankers Trust Co., (212) 250-8500; Citibank N.A., (212) 657-7800

VOLVO (A B)

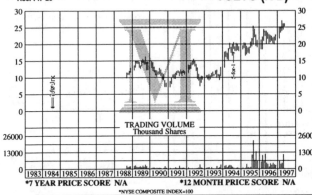

INTERIM EARNINGS (Per Share, SEK):

Qtr.	Mar.	June	Sept.	Dec.
1994		-31.80-		
1995		-20.20-		
1996		-26.90-		

INTERIM DIVIDENDS (Per Share):

Amt.	Decl.	Ex.	Rec.	Pay.
0.497	...	4/25/96	4/29/96	5/16/96
0.476	...	4/24/97	4/28/97	5/15/97

Indicated div.:$0.48

TRADING VOLUME
Thousand Shares

1983|1984|1985|1986|1987|1988|1989|1990|1991|1992|1993|1994|1995|1996|1997

*7 YEAR PRICE SCORE N/A   ***12 MONTH PRICE SCORE N/A**

*NYSE COMPOSITE INDEX=100

CAPITALIZATION (12/31/96):

	($000)	(%)
Minority Interests	73,584	0.6
Long-Term Debt	2,651,956	22.8
Stockholders' Equity	8,449,000	72.8
Deferred Income Tax	437,124	3.8
Total	11,611,664	100.0

RECENT DEVELOPMENTS: For the year ended 12/31/96, net income was SEK 12.48 billion compared with SEK 9.26 billion the year before. Results for the prior-year period included a net non-recurring gain of SEK 1.22 billion related to the sales of Procordia Food, Abba Seafood, Alfred Berg Holding, and Falcon Holding, partially offset by a write-down of acquired shares in Volvo Construction Equipment. Total sales declined 9.0% to SEK 156.06 billion from SEK 171.51 billion the previous year, reflecting a decline in sales for the automotive operations. Operating income was SEK 3.71 billion versus SEK 10.24 billion a year earlier. The decline in operating income was attributed to a decrease in income for Volvo Truck's North American operations, which incurred substantial losses due to lower volume of sales and higher costs of production and product development.

BUSINESS

AB VOLVO is the parent company of groups engaged in the manufacture, sale and export of motor vehicles including cars, trucks and buses. The Company operates through the following business areas: Volvo Car Group, which is engaged in the development and production of cars and the production of niche models such as convertibles and coupes; Volvo Truck Group, which is engaged in the development, production and marketing of trucks; Volvo Bus Group, which is engaged in the development, production and marketing of buses; Volvo Construction Equipment Group, which is engaged in the development, production and marketing of construction equipment; Volvo Penta Group, which is engaged in the development, production and marketing of gas turbines for industrial, mobile and marine operations, diesel engine components, and hydrostatic drive systems, the development, production and marketing of electrically controlled marine diesel engines, and maintenance and repair services; and Volvo Aero Group, which is engaged in the development, manufacture and sale of marine, military and industrial engines, aircraft engines, and aerospace equipment.

ANNUAL EARNINGS

	12/31/96	12/31/95	12/31/96	12/31/95
	---US $---		---SEK---	
Earnings Per Share	3.86	2.98	26.90	20.20

ANNUAL FINANCIAL DATA

RECORD OF EARNINGS (IN MILLIONS):

	12/31/96	12/31/95	12/31/96	12/31/95
Total Revenues	22,754	25,641	156,060	171,511
Costs & Expenses	21,432	23,446	146,999	156,831
Depreciation & Amort	780	846	5,351	5,656
Operating Income	541	1,349	3,710	10,239
Income Bef Income Tax	2,029	1,741	14,203	13,048
Income Tax	266	559	1,825	3,741
Eq. Earnings in Affils.	42	210	290	1,402
Minority Interests	14	7	99	d45
Net Income	1,790	1,385	12,477	9,262
Average Shares Outstg (000)	463,558	457,984	463,558	457,984

BALANCE SHEET (IN MILLIONS):

Cash & Cash Equivalents	3,887	3,484	26,661	23,306
Receivables, Net	4,663	4,321	31,979	28,906
Inventories	3,375	3,577	23,148	23,929
Gross Property	9,570	9,108	65,641	60,926
Accumulated Depreciation	4,989	4,931	34,215	32,985
Long-Term Debt	2,652	2,524	18,189	16,885
Stockholders' Equity	8,438	7,654	57,876	51,200
Total Assets	20,581	20,736	141,159	138,699
Total Current Assets	11,925	11,383	81,788	76,141
Total Current Liabilities	8,521	8,935	58,446	59,769
Net Working Capital	3,403	2,448	23,342	16,372
Year End Shs Outstg (000)	463,558	463,558	463,558	463,558

STATISTICAL RECORD:

Return on Equity %	21.22	18.09		
Return on Assets %	8.70	6.68		
Operating Profit Margin %	2.38	5.26		
Net Profit Margin %	7.87	5.40		
Book Value Per Share	18.20	16.51		

Converted at 1996, US$0.1458= 1 Swedish Krona; 1995, US$0.1495= 1 Swedish Krona

OFFICERS:
L. Johansson, Pres. & C.E.O.
L. Jeansson, Dep. C.E.O. & Exec. V.P.
P.E. Mohlin, Exec. V.P.
S. Langenius, Exec. V.P.

INCORPORATED: Sweden, 1915

PRINCIPAL OFFICE: S-405 08 Gothenburg
Sweden

TELEPHONE NUMBER: 46-31-59-00-00

NO. OF EMPLOYEES: 70,330

ANNUAL MEETING: In April

SHAREHOLDERS: 176,850

INSTITUTIONAL HOLDINGS:
No. of Institutions: 47
Shares Held: 18,951,715

AMERICAN DEPOSITARY RECEIPTS: Each American Depositary Receipt represents one Class B share of par SEK5.

DEPOSITARY BANK(S): Citibank N.A., (212) 657-7800

WACOAL CORP.

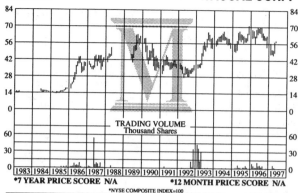

*7 YEAR PRICE SCORE N/A   *12 MONTH PRICE SCORE N/A

*NYSE COMPOSITE INDEX=100

INTERIM EARNINGS (Per Share, Y):

Qtr.	June	Sept.	Dec.	Mar.
1994	-----------------	167	-----------------	
1995	-----------------	211	-----------------	
1996	-----------------	228	-----------------	

INTERIM DIVIDENDS (Per Share):

Amt.	Decl.	Ex.	Rec.	Pay.
		No dividends paid.		

CAPITALIZATION (3/31/96):

	($000)	(%)
Long-Term Debt	12,257	0.9
Stockholders' Equity........	1,311,002	98.7
Deferred Income Tax	5,608	0.4
Total	1,328,868	100.0

RECENT DEVELOPMENTS: For the year ended 3/31/96, net income was ¥7.23 billion (US $67.5 million) compared with ¥6.69 billion the year before. Total revenues rose 4.1% to ¥162.17 billion (US $1.52 billion) from ¥155.74 billion a year earlier. Net sales increased 3.9% to ¥159.16 billion (US $1.49 billion) from ¥153.17 billion the previous year. Sales of foundation garments and lingerie increased 4.5% to ¥112.23 billion, while sales of hosiery products increased 48.6% to ¥1.96 billion. As a percentage of total revenues, gross profit margin improved to 47.3% from 46.6% the year before. Total costs and expenses rose 3.4% to ¥147.76 billion (US $1.38 billion) from ¥142.94 billion a year earlier. Income before taxes was ¥14.41 billion (US $134.7 million) versus ¥12.81 billion the previous year.

BUSINESS

WACOAL CORP. is an independent designer and manufacturer of intimate apparel, including foundation garments, lingerie and nightwear. The Company also designs and manufactures sportswear, such as leotards and body-shaping swimsuits, womens' outerwear, shoes, bridal wear, and support stockings. Wacoal also manufactures children's underwear and develops a line of skin and hair-care products. Through its subsidiaries, the Company supplies displays and mannequins, as well as interior fabrics and interior design services to building contractors.

ANNUAL EARNINGS

	3/31/96	3/31/95	3/31/96	3/31/95
	-----------US $-----------		-----------Yen-----------	
Earnings Per Share	0.44	0.50	46.93	43.43

ANNUAL FINANCIAL DATA

RECORD OF EARNINGS (IN MILLIONS):

Total Revenues	1,508	1,807	162,166	155,742
Costs & Expenses	1,374	1,658	147,758	142,935
Operating Income	134	149	14,408	12,807
Income Bef Income Tax	134	149	14,408	12,807
Income Tax	67	71	7,181	6,119
Net Income	67	78	7,227	6,688
Average Shares Outstg (000)	154,117	154,117	154,117	154,117

BALANCE SHEET (IN MILLIONS):

Cash & Cash Equivalents	557	630	59,861	54,328
Receivables, Net	197	215	21,230	18,561
Inventories	226	259	24,290	22,322
Gross Property	759	943	81,598	81,276
Accumulated Depreciation	285	343	30,684	29,578
Long-Term Debt	12	20	1,318	1,702
Stockholders' Equity	1,311	1,573	140,968	135,574
Total Assets	1,837	2,138	197,577	184,309
Total Current Assets	1,085	1,220	116,705	105,153
Total Current Liabilities	389	414	41,861	35,720
Net Working Capital	696	805	74,844	69,433
Year End Shs Outstg (000)	154,117	154,117	154,117	154,117

STATISTICAL RECORD:

Return on Equity %	5.13	4.93		
Return on Assets %	3.66	3.63		
Operating Profit Margin %	8.88	8.22		
Net Profit Margin %	4.46	4.29		
Book Value Per Share	8.51	10.21		

Converted at 1996, US$0.0093= 1 Japanese Yen; 1995, US$0.0116= 1 Japanese Yen

OFFICERS:
K. Tsukamoto, Chmn.
Y. Tsukamoto, Pres.
T. Terade, Exec. V.P.
T. Ohashi, Sr. Managing Dir.

INCORPORATED: Nov., 1949

PRINCIPAL OFFICE: 29 Nakajima-Cho, Kisshoin, Minami-ku Kyoto 601 Japan

TELEPHONE NUMBER: (075) 682-5111

NO. OF EMPLOYEES: 5,057

ANNUAL MEETING: In June

SHAREHOLDERS: 9,467

INSTITUTIONAL HOLDINGS:
No. of Institutions: 4
Shares Held: 64,600

AMERICAN DEPOSITARY RECEIPTS: (Sponsored) Each American Depositary Receipt represents five common shares of par Y50.

DEPOSITARY BANK(S): Chase Mellon Shareholder Services, New York

WATERFORD WEDGWOOD PLC

YIELD 0.8%
P/E RATIO 22.3

INTERIM EARNINGS (Per Share, US$):

1995	------------------ 0.05 ------------------
1996	------------------ 0.06 ------------------

INTERIM DIVIDENDS (Per Share):

Amt.	Decl.	Ex.	Rec.	Pay.
0.043	...	10/05/95	10/10/95	12/15/95
0.161	...	4/15/96	4/17/96	6/17/96
0.051	...	10/18	10/22	12/16

Indicated div.: $0.102

*7 YEAR PRICE SCORE N/A   *12 MONTH PRICE SCORE N/A

*NYSE COMPOSITE INDEX=100

CAPITALIZATION (12/31/95):

	($000)	(%)
Long-Term Debt	100,493	29.6
Stockholders' Equity.........	236,670	69.7
Capital Lease Oblgs.	2,240	0.7
Total	339,402	100.0

RECENT DEVELOPMENTS: For the year ended 12/31/96, the Company reported pre-tax profit of IR£34.9 million, up 24.2% from IR£28.1 million in 1995. Total revenues grew 9.1% to IR£376.3 million compared with IR£345.0 million. Operating profit climbed 17.7% to IR£39.2 million from IR£33.3 million the year before. Earnings per share increased to 4.0 pence from 3.4 pence in 1995. During 1996, the Company began full production of a new 18 tonne tank furnance at its main Kilberry plant. This furnace provides combined potential yield of 36 tonnes per day. The new furnance also improves crystal yield quality, reduces waste and produces crystal more cost effectively. Revenues and earnings also benefited from continued emphasis on new product development, increased marketing initiatives and enhanced customer service. Manufacturing efficiences at the Company's Irish manufacturing facilities also contributed to improved profit margins.

BUSINESS

WATERFORD WEDGEWOOD is a holding company that operates two independent and autonomous businesses: the Waterford Crystal Group and the Wedgwood Group. The Waterford Crystal Group business consists of the manufacture, marketing, distribution and retailing of high quality crystal products, including stemware, giftware, bone china tableware and lightingware. The Company's product line is sold under the Waterford(R), Marquis(R) and Stuart(R) brand names. The Wedgwood Group business consists the manufacture, distribution and retailing of high-quality ceramic tableware and giftware by Wedgwood and Johnson Brothers and the distribution of the Group's crystal products in Japan, Canada and Australia. Products are sold under the Wedgwood(R), Johnson Brothers(R), Franciscan(R), Coalport(R) and Mason's Ironstone(TM) brand names.

ANNUAL EARNINGS

	12/31/95	12/31/94	12/31/95	12/31/94
	------------US $------------		------------IR£------------	
Earnings Per Share	0.05	0.05	0.03	0.03

ANNUAL FINANCIAL DATA

RECORD OF EARNINGS (IN THOUSANDS):

Total Revenues	551,269	502,158	344,500	325,000
Costs & Expenses	497,982	458,431	311,200	296,700
Operating Income	53,287	43,726	33,300	28,300
Income Bef Income Tax	44,966	34,919	28,100	22,600
Income Tax	6,401	3,090	4,000	2,000
Net Income	38,565	31,829	24,100	20,600
Average Shares Outstg	710,900	710,900	710,900	710,900

BALANCE SHEET (IN THOUSANDS):

Cash & Cash Equivalents	43,365	66,594	27,100	43,100
Receivables, Net	84,971	80,345	53,100	52,000
Inventories	153,939	141,995	96,200	91,900
Gross Property	312,199	281,054	195,100	181,900
Accumulated Depreciation	132,177	130,406	82,600	84,400
Long-Term Debt	100,493	124,072	61,400	78,400
Stockholders' Equity	236,670	204,880	147,900	132,600
Total Assets	466,618	443,753	291,600	287,200
Total Current Assets	282,275	288,934	176,400	187,000
Total Current Liabilities	117,935	102,904	73,700	66,600
Net Working Capital	164,341	186,030	102,700	120,400
Year End Shs Outstg	710,900	710,900	710,900	710,900

STATISTICAL RECORD:

Return on Equity %	16.29	15.54
Return on Assets %	8.26	7.17
Operating Profit Margin %	9.67	8.71
Net Profit Margin %	7.00	6.34
Book Value Per Share	0.20	0.19

Converted at 1995, US$1.6002= 1 Irish pounds; 1994, US$1.5451= 1 Irish pounds

OFFICERS:
A. J. O'Reilly, Non-Exec. Chmn.
R. A. Barnes, Finance Dir.
C. J. Johnson
P. R. O'Donoghue

INCORPORATED: Ireland, 1983

PRINCIPAL OFFICE: Kilbarry Waterford Ireland

TELEPHONE NUMBER: +35-3147-81855

NO. OF EMPLOYEES: 7,777

ANNUAL MEETING: In Apr.

SHAREHOLDERS: N/A

INSTITUTIONAL HOLDINGS:
No. of Institutions: 7
Shares Held: 174,123

AMERICAN DEPOSITARY RECEIPTS: (Sponsored) Each American Depositary Receipt represents ten ordinary shares of par IR£0.05.

DEPOSITARY BANK(S): J.P. Morgan, (212) 815-2175

WESTERN DEEP LEVELS LTD.

YIELD   5.5%
P/E RATIO   ...

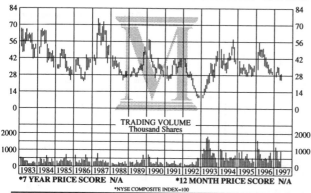

INTERIM EARNINGS (Per Share, US$):

1995 ---------------- 0.95 ----------------

INTERIM DIVIDENDS (Per Share):

Amt.	Decl.	Ex.	Rec.	Pay.
0.257	...	8/02/95	8/04/95	10/02/95
0.587	...	1/31/96	2/02/96	4/01/96
0.689	...	7/31	8/02	9/30
0.789	...	2/05/97	2/07/97	3/31/97

Indicated div.:$1.58

CAPITALIZATION (12/31/95):

	($000)	(%)
Stockholders' Equity	1,062,583	100.0
Total	1,062,583	100.0

TRADING VOLUME
Thousand Shares

*7 YEAR PRICE SCORE N/A   *12 MONTH PRICE SCORE N/A

*NYSE COMPOSITE INDEX=100

RECENT DEVELOPMENTS: For the year ended 12/31/96, net income was R188.1 million compared with R95.8 million in the corresponding period a year earlier. Earnings per share advanced to R6.79 from R3.46. Turnover was R1.82 billion, up 14% versus R1.59 billion in 1995. Operating profit increased to R400.8 million compared with R251.4 million, reflecting in part an 18% increase in the price of gold. Gold produced was almost two tons lower at 34 tons. The mining rate at the Company's high-grade East Mine was significantly reduced during the second and third quarters due to a major seismic event on May 5, 1996. Gold production from the East Mine returned to normal levels in the fourth quarter.

BUSINESS

WESTERN DEEP LEVELS LTD. conducts gold mining operations in the Oberholzer and Potchefstroom districts, Gauteng and North West Province, respectively.

ANNUAL EARNINGS

	12/31/95	12/31/94	12/31/95	12/31/94
	------------US $------------		------------Rand------------	
Earnings Per Share	0.95	1.42	3.46	5.02

ANNUAL FINANCIAL DATA

RECORD OF EARNINGS (IN THOUSANDS):

	12/31/95	12/31/94	12/31/95	12/31/94
Total Revenues	436,987	475,309	1,593,100	1,684,300
Costs & Expenses	368,028	339,995	1,341,700	1,204,800
Operating Income	68,959	135,315	251,400	479,500
Income Bef Income Tax	79,218	148,663	288,800	526,800
Income Tax	6,583	25,200	24,000	89,300
Net Income	26,278	39,226	95,800	139,000

BALANCE SHEET (IN THOUSANDS):

Cash & Cash Equivalents	8,476	7,732	30,900	27,400
Receivables, Net	51,568	76,843	188,000	272,300
Inventories	3,538	...	12,900	...
Gross Property	1,057,042	1,039,766	3,853,600	3,684,500
Stockholders' Equity	1,062,583	1,046,595	3,873,800	3,708,700
Total Assets	1,125,590	1,129,167	4,103,500	4,001,300
Total Current Assets	63,994	84,575	233,300	299,700
Total Current Liabilities	63,007	82,572	229,700	292,600
Net Working Capital	987	2,004	3,600	7,100
Year End Shs Outstg	27,713	27,713	27,713	27,713

STATISTICAL RECORD:

Return on Equity %	6.84	11.80		
Return on Assets %	6.45	10.93		
Operating Profit Margin %	15.78	28.47		
Net Profit Margin %	16.62	25.98		
Book Value Per Share	38.34	37.77		

Converted at 1995, US$0.2743= 1 South African Rand; 1994, US$0.2822= 1 South African Rand

OFFICERS:
R. M. Godsell, Chmn. & C.E.O.
K. Dicks, C.O.O.

INCORPORATED: South Africa, 1957

PRINCIPAL OFFICE: 44 Main Street
Johannesburg South Africa

TELEPHONE NUMBER: (011) 638-911

NO. OF EMPLOYEES: 25,439

ANNUAL MEETING: In Apr.

SHAREHOLDERS: 2,434

INSTITUTIONAL HOLDINGS:
No. of Institutions: 29
Shares Held: 2,750,284

AMERICAN DEPOSITARY RECEIPTS: Each American Depositary Receipt represents one ordinary share of par value R2.

DEPOSITARY BANK(S): The Bank of New York, (212) 815-2175; Bankers Trust Co., (212) 250-8500; Citibank (212) 657-7800; and DST Systems Inc.

WPP GROUP PLC

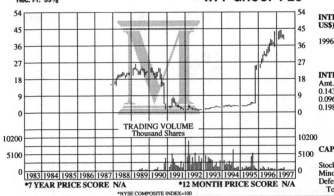

INTERIM EARNINGS (Earnings Per ADR, US$):

	Mar.	June	Sept.	Dec.
1996	----	2.25	----	

INTERIM DIVIDENDS (Per ADR):

Amt.	Decl.	Ex.	Rec.	Pay.
0.143	...	6/14/96	6/18/96	7/22/96
0.096	...	10/25/96	10/29/96	12/06/96
0.198	...	6/11/97	6/13/97	7/21/97

Indicated Div.:0.40

TRADING VOLUME
Thousand Shares

CAPITALIZATION (12/31/96):

	($000)	(%)
Stockholders' Equity	37,787	60.6
Minority Interest	7,795	12.5
Deferred Income Tax	16,776	26.9
Total	62,358	100.0

*7 YEAR PRICE SCORE N/A   *12 MONTH PRICE SCORE N/A

*NYSE COMPOSITE INDEX=100

RECENT DEVELOPMENTS: For the year ended 12/31/96, net income advanced 45.6% to £100.0 million from £68.7 million in 1995. Gross billings improved 8.1% to £7.08 billion versus £6.55 billion in the prior year and revenue increased 8.8% to £1.69 billion from £1.55 billion. This included a 12.2% rise in revenue from the United States to £667.0 million and a 7.1% increase in United Kingdom revenues to £317.0 million. Revenue from advertising climbed 7.6% to £930.0 million, and from information and consultancy by 9.9% to £273.0 million. The public relations and public affairs business increased revenues by 8.9% to £106.0 million, whilst specialist communications showed an advance of 11.0% to £382.0 million. Operating income jumped 22.0% to £182.4 million from £149.5 million and group operating margins increased to 10.8% from 9.6% in the prior year. Average net debt fell from £214.0 million to £145.0 million.

BUSINESS

WPP GROUP PLC is a holding company, which through its subsidiaries, is engaged in the provision of marketing services. These services include media advertising, which includes planning, production and placing of advertising for a wide range of advertisers; public lobbying and government relations; market research, such as consumer, media, corporate communication and policy research; non-media advertising, including graphic design, packaging and corporate identity design, and sales promotion consultancy; and specialist communications, such as direct mail and direct marketing, healthcare advertising, investor communications and real estate advertising. The Company has 800 offices in 90 countries.

ANNUAL EARNINGS

	12/31/96	12/31/95	12/31/96	12/31/95
	US $		British £	
Earnings Per Share	0.22	0.14	0.13	0.09

ANNUAL FINANCIAL DATA

RECORD OF EARNINGS (IN THOUSANDS):

	12/31/96	12/31/95	12/31/96	12/31/95
Gross billings	12,003,838	10,176,964	7,084,000	6,553,100
Net revenues	2,865,908	2,414,760	1,691,300	1,554,900
Operating Income	309,077	232,174	182,400	149,500
Income Bef Income Tax	259,767	176,576	153,300	113,700
Income Tax	85,742	67,090	50,600	43,200
Minority Interests	4,575	2,795	2,700	1,800
Net Income	169,450	106,691	100,000	68,700
Average Shares Outstg	767,570	756,641	767,570	756,641

BALANCE SHEET (IN THOUSANDS):

Cash & Cash Equivalents	698,473	583,928	412,200	376,000
Receivables, Net	1,368,648	1,307,626	807,700	842,000
Inventories	159,452	143,653	94,100	92,500
Gross Property	485,644	441,363	286,600	284,200
Accumulated Depreciation	250,786	225,185	148,000	145,000
Stockholders' Equity	37,787	d96,907	22,300	d62,400
Total Assets	3,210,739	2,921,504	1,894,800	1,881,200
Total Current Assets	2,305,198	2,106,955	1,360,400	1,356,700
Total Current Liabilities	2,555,306	2,363,200	1,508,000	1,521,700
Net Working Capital	d250,108	d256,245	d147,600	d165,000
Year End Shs Outstg	741,415	736,987	741,415	736,987

STATISTICAL RECORD:

Return on Equity %	448.43	...		
Return on Assets %	5.28	3.65		
Operating Profit Margin %	10.78	9.61		
Net Profit Margin %	5.91	4.42		
Book Value Per Share	0.05	...		

Converted at 1996, US$1.6945= 1 British pound; 1995, US$1.5530= 1 British pound

OFFICERS:
H. Maxwell, Chmn.
M. Sorrell, C.E.O.
P. Richardson, Group Fin. Director
B. Brooks, Group Dir.-Human Resources

INCORPORATED: United Kingdom, 1971

PRINCIPAL OFFICE: 27 Farm Street London, W1X 6RD United Kingdom

TELEPHONE NUMBER: 071-408-2204

NO. OF EMPLOYEES: 22,102

ANNUAL MEETING: In Jun.

SHAREHOLDERS: 278 (ADRs)

INSTITUTIONAL HOLDINGS:
No. of Institutions: 24
Shares Held: 1,835,277

AMERICAN DEPOSITARY RECEIPTS: (Sponsored) Each American Depositary Receipt represents ten ordinary shares of par £0.10.

DEPOSITARY BANK(S): Citibank N.A., (212) 657-7800

XEIKON N.V.

YIELD ...
P/E RATIO N.M.

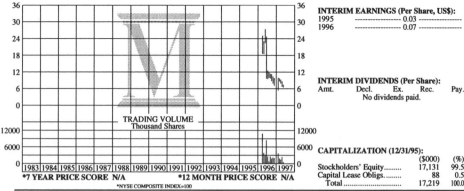

*7 YEAR PRICE SCORE N/A   *12 MONTH PRICE SCORE N/A
*NYSE COMPOSITE INDEX=100

INTERIM EARNINGS (Per Share, US$):

| 1995 | ------------------ 0.03 ------------------ |
| 1996 | ------------------ 0.07 ------------------ |

INTERIM DIVIDENDS (Per Share):

Amt.	Decl.	Ex.	Rec.	Pay.
		No dividends paid.		

CAPITALIZATION (12/31/95):

	($000)	(%)
Stockholders' Equity........	17,131	99.5
Capital Lease Obligs.........	88	0.5
Total	17,219	100.0

RECENT DEVELOPMENTS: For the twelve months ended 12/31/96, net earnings more than doubled to $1.9 million compared with $706,000 the previous year. Revenues totaled $72.6 million, down 10.5% versus $81.1 million the year before. Results were negatively affected by the appreciation in the value of the U.S. dollar compared with the Belgian franc. Gross profit surged 45.1% to $17.7 million, or 24.4% of revenues, from $12.2 million, or 15.1% of revenues, a year earlier. Operating income slid 39.3% to $868,000 from $1.4 million the prior year. The Company shipped a record 72 digital printing systems during the fourth quarter and 256 in 1996. For the three months ended 12/31/96, net income surged 48.2% to $723,000 from $488,000 the previous year. Revenues fell 16.3% to $18.8 million from $22.5 million in the corresponding quarter the year before.

BUSINESS

XEIKON N.V. develops, produces, and markets an innovative digital color printing system and sells related consumables specifically designed to meet the quality, speed, reliability, cost, variable content, and on-demand requirements of the short-run color printing (SRCP) market. The Company's line of consumables includes toners, developers and usage parts. The SRCP market consists of color print jobs with run lengths ranging from a few to 5,000 copies and includes printed materials such as product catalogs, marketing brochures, direct mailings, newsletters, and event-related items. The primary users of the Company's digital color press, the DCP-1, are commercial printers, in-plant print shops, prepress service bureaus, and color trade shops. The Company's proprietary One-Pass Duplex Color® technology allows reliable printing of full-color two-sided pages at a high output speed. The Company sells its DCP-1 to value added distributors under the Xeikon® brand name and to Agfa-Gevaert N.V. and International Business Machines (IBM) under original equipment manufacturer (OEM) agreements for resale under the OEM name. In 1995, Agfa-Gevaert and IBM were the Company's largest customers, accounting for approx. 43% and 16% of revenues, respectively.

ANNUAL EARNINGS

	12/31/95	12/31/94	12/31/95	12/31/94
	-------------US $-------------		-------------BFr-----------	
Earnings Per Share	0.03	...	0.88	...

ANNUAL FINANCIAL DATA

RECORD OF EARNINGS (IN THOUSANDS):

	12/31/95	12/31/94	12/31/95	12/31/94
Total Revenues	81,121	20,769	2,385,912	661,433
Costs & Expenses	79,690	27,651	2,343,824	880,605
Operating Income	1,431	d6,882	42,088	d219,172
Net Income	706	d6,510	20,765	d207,325
Average Shares Outstg	23,823	...	23,823	...

BALANCE SHEET (IN THOUSANDS):

Cash & Cash Equivalents	17	7,450	500	237,261
Receivables, Net	19,672	11,998	578,588	382,102
Inventories	22,714	16,938	668,059	539,427
Gross Property	5,070	2,549	149,118	81,178
Accumulated Depreciation	3,270	1,687	96,176	53,726
Capital Lease Obligs.	88	...	2,588	...
Long-Term Debt	...	1,037	...	33,025
Stockholders' Equity	17,131	15,162	503,853	482,866
Total Assets	46,681	37,324	1,372,971	1,188,662
Total Current Assets	43,882	36,462	1,290,647	1,161,210
Total Current Liabilities	29,462	21,125	866,529	672,771
Net Working Capital	14,420	15,337	424,118	488,439
Year End Shs Outstg	28,473	...	28,473	...

STATISTICAL RECORD:

Return on Equity %	4.12	...
Return on Assets %	1.51	...
Operating Profit Margin %	1.76	...
Net Profit Margin %	0.87	...
Book Value Per Share	0.60	...

Converted at 1995, US$0.0340= 1 Belgian franc; 1994, US$0.0314= 1 Belgian franc

OFFICERS:
L. De Schamphelaere, Chmn., Pres. & C.E.O.
A. Buts, C.O.O. & Sec.
M. Blanpain, C.F.O.
E. De Cock, Sr. V.P.

INCORPORATED: 1988

PRINCIPAL OFFICE: 72 Vredebaan, Mortsel
Belgium B-2640

TELEPHONE NUMBER: 3443-1311

NO. OF EMPLOYEES: 163

ANNUAL MEETING: In March

SHAREHOLDERS: N/A

INSTITUTIONAL HOLDINGS:
No. of Institutions: 20
Shares Held: 3,079,983

AMERICAN DEPOSITARY RECEIPTS: Each American Depositary Receipt represents one share of common stock with no par value.

DEPOSITARY BANK(S): The Bank of New York, (212) 815-2175

XENOVA GROUP PLC

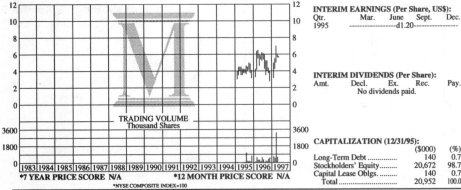

INTERIM EARNINGS (Per Share, US$):

Qtr.	Mar.	June	Sept.	Dec.
1995	------------------d1.20------------------			

INTERIM DIVIDENDS (Per Share):

Amt.	Decl.	Ex.	Rec.	Pay.
	No dividends paid.			

TRADING VOLUME
Thousand Shares

*7 YEAR PRICE SCORE N/A   *12 MONTH PRICE SCORE N/A
*NYSE COMPOSITE INDEX=100

CAPITALIZATION (12/31/95):

	($000)	(%)
Long-Term Debt	140	0.7
Stockholders' Equity.........	20,672	98.7
Capital Lease Oblgs.	140	0.7
Total	20,952	100.0

RECENT DEVELOPMENTS: For the quarter ended 3/31/97, net loss amounted to £2.6 million compared with a loss of £1.4 million in the same period of 1996. Revenues were £205,000, down 46.6% from £384,000 a year earlier. The decline in revenues was primarily attributed to an anticipated decline in research payments from earlier collaborations and the phasing of payments from more recent agreements. Total operating expenses surged 61.8% to £3.3 million. The operating expenses increased due to an increase in clinical trial and drug development activity, including the establishment of the U.S. subsidiary, MetaXen, and investment in the development of the Group's natural compound libraries. The Company plans to continue to progress its portfolio of three drugs in clinical and preclinical development and its drug discovery programs. Recently, new drug discovery agreements were completed with Bristol-Myers Squibb and Zeneca. The Group received an equity investment of £1.0 million from Warner-Lambert, in support of the development of XNVAY's QTC drug discovery system.

BUSINESS

XENOVA GROUP PLC is an emerging pharmaceutical company specializing in the discovery and development of new small molecule drugs derived from naturally occurring micro-organisms, such as fungi and bacteria, and from plants and plant extracts. The Company has developed an integrated group of proprietary platform technologies to identify rapidly and efficiently candidate compounds, or leads, for new drugs from such natural sources. The Company's high-throughput screening technology, called ASSET(TM), and extensive natural products chemistry capabilities, in conjunction with its proprietary bio-informatics system, enable the Company to screen its natural product resources and identify novel chemical compounds that may lead to the development of new drugs for major diseases for which traditional drug discovery has been largely unsuccessful.

ANNUAL EARNINGS

	12/31/95	12/31/94	12/31/95	12/31/94
	-------------US $------------		--------British £----------	
Earnings Per Share	d1.20	d1.37	d0.77	d0.88

ANNUAL FINANCIAL DATA

RECORD OF EARNINGS (IN THOUSANDS):

	12/31/95	12/31/94	12/31/95	12/31/94
Total Revenues	2,778	3,067	1,789	1,960
Costs & Expenses	16,344	17,270	10,524	11,035
Operating Income	d13,565	d14,202	d8,735	d9,075
Income Bef Income Tax	d12,412	d12,855	d7,992	d8,214
Net Income	d12,412	d12,855	d7,992	d8,214
Average Shares Outstg	10,365	9,300	10,365	9,300

BALANCE SHEET (IN THOUSANDS):

Cash & Cash Equivalents	20,500	24,556	13,200	15,691
Receivables, Net	1,294	1,388	833	887
Gross Property	8,498	8,304	5,472	5,306
Accumulated Depreciation	6,355	5,370	4,092	3,431
Long-Term Debt	140	424	90	271
Stockholders' Equity	20,672	25,184	13,311	16,092
Total Assets	23,936	28,879	15,413	18,453
Total Current Assets	21,793	25,945	14,033	16,578
Total Current Liabilities	3,125	3,271	2,012	2,090
Net Working Capital	18,669	22,674	12,021	14,488
Year End Shs Outstg	12,564	9,993	12,564	9,993

STATISTICAL RECORD:

Return on Equity %	...	...		
Return on Assets %	...	...		
Operating Profit Margin %	...	...		
Net Profit Margin %	...	...		
Book Value Per Share	1.64	2.52		

Converted at 1995, US$1.5530= 1 British pound; 1994, US$1.5650= 1 British pound

OFFICERS:
J. B. Jackson, Chmn.
L. J. Nisbet, C.E.O. & Managing Dir.
P. Bevan, Research Dir.
G. McMillan, Commercial Dir.
INCORPORATED: England, Mar., 1992
PRINCIPAL OFFICE: 240 Bath Road, Slough United Kingdom SL1 4EF

TELEPHONE NUMBER: 01753 692229
NO. OF EMPLOYEES: 123
ANNUAL MEETING: N/A
SHAREHOLDERS: N/A
INSTITUTIONAL HOLDINGS:
No. of Institutions: 5
Shares Held: 1,809,766

AMERICAN DEPOSITARY RECEIPTS: Each American Depositary Receipt Unit represents 1 ordinary share and 1 conversion right of par £0.10.

DEPOSITARY BANK(S): The Bank of New York, (212) 815-2175

Foreign Securities

Company Name	Country	
Abacan Resource Corporation	Hong Kong	ABAC
Accugraph Corporation	Canada	ACCU
AES China Generating Co. LTD.	Israel	
Air Canada Corporation	Canada	ACNA
Abacus Knowledge Systems Limited	Canada	ALDN
Algoma Steel, Inc.	Canada	ALGS
Alliance Communications Corp.	Canada	ALLI
American Eco Corporation	Canada	ECGO
American Sensors, Inc.	Netherlands	SNIF
Amtryc Computing Limited	Canada	ADYN
Amvescap Signal N.V.	Israel	ASIG
Arakis Energy Corporation	Israel	AKSE
Arel Communications & Software Ltd.	Taiwan	ARLC
Aptas Advertising Limited	Netherlands	RELE
ASE Test Limited	Netherlands	ASTS
ASM International N.V.	Netherlands	ASMI
ASM Lithography Holding N.V.	Canada	ASML
Baan Company N.V.	Bahamas	BAAN
Ballard Power Systems, Inc.	Canada	BLDP
Basic Petroleum International Limited	Netherlands	BPIL
Battery Technologies, Inc.	Belize	BTID
BE Semiconductor Industries NV	Canada	BESI
BGI Corporation	Canada	BHIK
Big Rock Brewery Ltd.	Canada	BEER
Biochem Pharma Inc.	Hong Kong	BCHX
Biomira Inc.	Canada	BIOM
Benson Electronics International, Inc.	Canada	BNSO
Boliden Mining Corporation	United Kingdom	CALV
Cam-Net Enterprises Inc.	Bermuda	CNED
Cayman Water Company, Ltd.	Canada	CWCO
Central European Media Enterprises Ltd.		
Chai-Na-Ta Corp.		
CHC Insurance Company, Ltd.		
CHC Helicopter Corporation		
Check Point Software		

Foreign Securities

In addition to the ADR listings, 279[2] foreign companies list their shares directly on The Nasdaq Stock Market, and 181 of them are profiled here. Some of the largest issuers are Canada's BioChem Pharma, Methanex and MacMillan Bloedel; Israel's Scitex Limited and ECI Telecom; Singapore's Creative Technology; and Taiwan's ASE Test Limited. These foreign issuers are based in 18 countries throughout the world, with the highest number coming from Canada, 87, and then Israel, 42.[2] Nasdaq has more foreign listings than the New York and American Stock Exchanges combined.

The following pages profile only the Nasdaq National Market foreign companies. The typical Nasdaq National Market foreign issuer trades more than 78,000 shares per day, has 11 market makers and a share price of over $10.

The profile pages are arranged alphabetically by company.

[2] As of December 31, 1996.

Foreign Securities by Company

(as of December 31, 1996)

NAME	COUNTRY	SYMBOL
Abacan Resource Corporation	Canada	ABACF
Accugraph Corporation	Canada	ACCUF
AES China Generating Co. LTD.	Hong Kong	CHGNF
Air Canada Corporation	Canada	ACNAF
Aladdin Knowledge Systems Limited	Israel	ALDNF
Algoma Steel, Inc.	Canada	ALGSF
Alliance Communications Corp.	Canada	ALLIF
American Eco Corporation	Canada	ECGOF
American Sensors, Inc.	Canada	SNIFF
Andyne Computing Limited	Canada	ADYNF
Ansaldo Signal, N.V.	Netherlands	ASIGF
Arakis Energy Corporation	Canada	AKSEF
Arel Communications & Software Ltd.	Israel	ARLCF
Ariely Advertising, Limited	Israel	RELEF
ASE Test, Limited	Taiwan	ASTSF
ASM International N.V.	Netherlands	ASMIF
ASM Lithography Holding N.V.	Netherlands	ASMLF
Baan Company N.V.	Netherlands	BAANF
Ballard Power Systems, Inc.	Canada	BLDPF
Basic Petroleum International Limited	Bahamas	BPILF
Battery Technologies, Inc.	Canada	BTIOF
BE Semiconductor Industries NV	Netherlands	BESIF
BHI Corporation	Belize	BHIKF
Big Rock Brewery Ltd.	Canada	BEERF
Biochem Pharma Inc.	Canada	BCHXF
Biomira Inc.	Canada	BIOMF
Bonso Electronics International, Inc.	Hong Kong	BNSOF
Caledonia Mining Corporation	Canada	CALVF
Call-Net Enterprises Inc.	Canada	CNEBF
Cayman Water Company, Ltd.	United Kingdom	CWCOF
Central European Media Enterprises Ltd.	Bermuda	CETV
Chai-Na-Ta Corp.	Canada	CCCFF
Chandler Insurance Company, Ltd.	Cayman Islands	CHANF
CHC Helicopter Corporation	Canada	FLYAF
Check Point Software Technologies, Ltd.	Israel	CHKPF
Cimatron, Limited	Israel	CIMTF
Cinar Films, Inc.	Canada	CINRF
Cinram International Inc.	Canada	CNRMF
Clearly Canadian Beverage Corp.	Canada	CLCDF
Clearnet Communications Inc.	Canada	CLNTF
Cognos Incorporated	Canada	COGNF
Comcast UK Cable Partners Limited	United Kingdom	CMCAF
Commodore Holdings Limited	United Kingdom	CCLNF
Computalog Ltd.	Canada	CLTDF
Core Laboratories, N.V.	Netherlands	CRLBF
Corel Corporation	Canada	COSFF
Cott Corporation	Canada	COTTF
Counsel Corporation	Canada	CXSNF
Creative Technology Ltd.	Singapore	CREAF
Cronos Group (The)	Luxembourg	CRNSF

Foreign Securities by Company (Continued)

NAME	COUNTRY	SYMBOL
Deswell Industries, Inc.	United Kingdom	DSWLF
Discreet Logic, Inc.	Canada	DSLGF
Diversinet Corp.	Canada	DVNTF
Draxis Health Inc.	Canada	DRAXF
Dreco Energy Services Ltd.	Canada	DREAF
DSG International Limited	United Kingdom	DSGIF
ECI Telecom Ltd.	Israel	ECILF
EduSoft Ltd.	Israel	EDUSF
Elamex S.A. de C.V.	Mexico	ELAMF
Elbit Ltd.	Israel	ELBTF
Elbit Medical Imaging Ltd.	Israel	EMITF
Elbit Systems Ltd.	Israel	ESLTF
Elbit Vision Systems, Limited	Israel	EVSNF
Elron Electronic Industries Ltd.	Israel	ELRNF
EMCO Limited	Canada	EMLTF
ESC Medical Systems, Limited	Israel	ESCMF
Ezcony Interamerica Inc.	United Kingdom	EZCOF
Fantom Technologies Inc.	Canada	FTMTF
First Dynasty Mines Ltd.	Canada	FDYMF
Fletcher's Fine Foods Ltd.	Canada	FLCHF
Flextronics International Ltd.	Singapore	FLEXF
Frisco Bay Industries Ltd.	Canada	FBAYF
Fulcrum Technologies Inc.	Canada	FULCF
Gaming Lottery Corporation	British Virgin Islands	GLCCF
Gandalf Technologies Inc.	Canada	GANDF
GCR Holdings, Limited	Bermuda	GCREF
Gemstar International Group, Limited	United Kingdom	GMSTF
Gilat Satellite Networks Ltd.	Israel	GILTF
Globalstar Telecommunications, Limited	United Kingdom	GSTRF
Goran Capital, Inc.	Canada	GNCNF
GrandeTel Technologies, Inc.	Canada	GTTIF
Heidemij N.V.	Netherlands	HEIDF
Highway Holdings Limited	Hong Kong	HIHOF
Hollinger Inc.	Canada	HLGRF
Home Centers, (DIY), Limited	Israel	HOMEF
Hummingbird Communications, Limited	Canada	HUMCF
Hyal Pharmaceutical Corporation	Canada	HYALF
ICTS International N.V.	Netherlands	ICTSF
I.I.S. Intelligent Information Systems Limited	Israel	IISLF
Imax Corporation	Canada	IMAXF
Imperial Ginseng Products, Limited	Canada	IGPFF
Indigo N.V.	Netherlands	INDGF
Intelect Communications Systems, Limited	Bermuda	ICOMF
International Murex Technologies Corporation	Canada	MURXF
International Petroleum Corporation	United Arab Emirates	IRPPF
International Verifact, Inc.	Canada	IVIAF
IPC Holdings, Limited	Bermuda	IPCRF
IPL Energy Inc.	Canada	IPPIF
ISG International Software Group Ltd.	Israel	SISGF
I.S.G. Technologies Inc.	Canada	ISGTF

Foreign Securities by Company (Continued)

NAME	COUNTRY	SYMBOL
IWI Holding, Limited	United Kingdom	JEWLF
Jannock Limited	Canada	JANNF
JetForm Corporation	Canada	FORMF
LanOptics Ltd.	Israel	LNOPF
Laser Industries Limited	Israel	LASRF
Lernout & Hauspie Speech Products, N.V.	Belgium	LHSPF
Liquidation World, Inc.	Canada	LIQWF
Livent, Inc.	Canada	LVNTF
Logal Educational Software & Systems, Limited	Israel	LOGLF
Mackenzie Financial Corporation	Canada	MKFCF
MacMillan Bloedel Limited	Canada	MMBLF
Madge Networks, N.V.	Netherlands	MADGF
Magal Security Systems Ltd.	Israel	MAGSF
Magic Software Enterprises Ltd.	Israel	MGICF
MDSI Mobile Data Solutions, Inc.	Canada	MDSIF
Memco Software Limited	Israel	MEMCF
Methanex Corporation	Canada	MEOHF
Metrowerks Corporation	Canada	MTWKF
Millicom International Cellular S.A.	Luxembourg	MICCF
Miramar Mining Corporation	Canada	MAENF
M-Systems Flash Disk Pioneers Ltd.	Israel	FLSHF
Nam Tai Electronics, Inc.	United Kingdom	NTAIF
New Dimension Software Ltd.	Israel	DDDDF
Nobel Insurance Limited	United Kingdom	NOBLF
Nur Advanced Technologies, Ltd	Israel	NURTF
Olicom A/S	Denmark	OLCMF
Open Text Corporation	Canada	OTEXF
Optima Petroleum Corporation	Canada	OPPCF
Optimal Robotics Corp.	Canada	OPMRF
Orbotech Ltd.	Israel	ORBKF
Orckit Communications, Limited	Israel	ORCTF
Orthofix International N.V.	Netherlands	OFIXF
Oshap Technologies Ltd.	Israel	OSHSF
PC DOCS Group International	Canada	DOCSF
Petromet Resources Limited	Canada	PNTGF
Plaintree Systems, Inc.	Canada	LANPF
QIAGEN N.V.	Netherlands	QGENF
QLT Phototherapeutics, Inc.	Canada	QLTIF
Quality Dino Entertainment Ltd	Canada	RCORF
Q-Zar, Inc.	Canada	QZARF
Rada Electronic Industries Limited	Israel	RADIF
Radica Games Limited	Hong Kong	RADAF
REPAP Enterprises, Inc.	Canada	RPAPF
Revenue Properties Company Limited	Canada	RPCLF
Russel Metals, Inc.	Canada	RUSAF
Sand Technology Systems International Inc.	Canada	SNDCF
Sapiens International Corporation N.V.	Netherlands	SPNSF
Scandinavian Broadcasting System SA	Sweden	SBTVF
ScanVec Company, Ltd.	Israel	SVECF
Scitex Corporation Ltd.	Israel	SCIXF

Foreign Securities by Company (Continued)

NAME	COUNTRY	SYMBOL
Semi-Tech Corporation	Canada	SEMCF
Simware, Inc.	Canada	SIMWF
SoftQuad International, Inc.	Canada	SWEBF
Spectral Diagnostics Inc.	Canada	DIAGF
Spectrum Signal Processing Inc.	Canada	SSPIF
Steiner Leisure Limited	Bahamas	STNRF
Stolt Comex Seaway S.A.	Luxembourg	SCSWF
Sutton Resources, Ltd.	Canada	STTZF
Tadiran Telecommunications, Limited	Israel	TTELF
Taro Pharmaceutical Industries Ltd.	Israel	TAROF
Taseko Mines Limited	Canada	TKOCF
TAT Technologies Ltd.	Israel	TATTF
Tecnomatix Technologies Ltd.	Israel	TCNOF
Tee-Comm Electronics Inc.	Canada	TENXF
Teledata Communications Ltd.	Israel	TLDCF
Tesco Corporation	Canada	TESOF
Tesma International, Inc.	Canada	TSMAF
3Dlabs Inc., Ltd.	Bermuda	TDDDF
Toolex Alpha, N.V.	Netherlands	TLXAF
Tower Semiconductor Ltd.	Israel	TSEMF
Tramford International, Ltd.	Hong Kong	TRFDF
Triple P, N.V.	Netherlands	TPPPF
TTI Team Telecom International Ltd.	Israel	TTILF
Vengold, Inc.	Canada	VENGF
Venture Seismic, Limited	Canada	VSEIF
Visible Genetics, Inc.	Canada	VGINF
Vitran Corporation, Inc.	Canada	VTNAF
VocalTec, Limited	Israel	VOCLF
Wescast Industries Inc.	Canada	WCSTF
Wiztec Solutions, Limited	Israel	WIZTF
ZAG Industries Ltd.	Israel	ZAGIF

Foreign Securities by Country

(as of December 31, 1996)

COUNTRY	COMPANY NAME	SYMBOL
Bahamas	Basic Petroleum International Limited	BPILF
Bahamas	Steiner Leisure Limited	STNRF
Belgium	Lernout & Hauspie Speech Products, N.V.	LHSPF
Belize	BHI Corporation	BHIKF
Bermuda	Central European Media Enterprises Ltd.	CETV
Bermuda	GCR Holdings, Limited	GCREF
Bermuda	Intelect Communications Systems, Limited	ICOMF
Bermuda	IPC Holdings, Limited	IPCRF
Bermuda	3Dlabs Inc., Ltd.	TDDDF
British Virgin Islands	Gaming Lottery Corporation	GLCCF
Canada	Abacan Resource Corporation	ABACF
Canada	Accugraph Corporation	ACCUF
Canada	Air Canada Corporation	ACNAF
Canada	Algoma Steel, Inc.	ALGSF
Canada	Alliance Communications Corp.	ALLIF
Canada	American Eco Corporation	ECGOF
Canada	American Sensors, Inc.	SNIFF
Canada	Andyne Computing Limited	ADYNF
Canada	Arakis Energy Corporation	AKSEF
Canada	Ballard Power Systems, Inc.	BLDPF
Canada	Battery Technologies, Inc.	BTIOF
Canada	Big Rock Brewery Ltd.	BEERF
Canada	Biochem Pharma Inc.	BCHXF
Canada	Biomira Inc.	BIOMF
Canada	Caledonia Mining Corporation	CALVF
Canada	Call-Net Enterprises Inc.	CNEBF
Canada	Chai-Na-Ta Corp.	CCCFF
Canada	CHC Helicopter Corporation	FLYAF
Canada	Cinar Films, Inc.	CINRF
Canada	Cinram International Inc.	CNRMF
Canada	Clearly Canadian Beverage Corp.	CLCDF
Canada	Clearnet Communications Inc.	CLNTF
Canada	Cognos Incorporated	COGNF
Canada	Computalog Ltd.	CLTDF
Canada	Corel Corporation	COSFF
Canada	Cott Corporation	COTTF
Canada	Counsel Corporation	CXSNF
Canada	Discreet Logic, Inc.	DSLGF
Canada	Diversinet Corp.	DVNTF
Canada	Draxis Health Inc.	DRAXF
Canada	Dreco Energy Services Ltd.	DREAF
Canada	EMCO Limited	EMLTF
Canada	Fantom Technologies Inc.	FTMTF
Canada	First Dynasty Mines Ltd.	FDYMF
Canada	Fletcher's Fine Foods Ltd.	FLCHF
Canada	Frisco Bay Industries Ltd.	FBAYF
Canada	Fulcrum Technologies Inc.	FULCF
Canada	Gandalf Technologies Inc.	GANDF
Canada	Goran Capital, Inc.	GNCNF
Canada	GrandeTel Technologies, Inc.	GTTIF

Foreign Securities by Country (Continued)

COUNTRY	COMPANY NAME	SYMBOL
Canada	Hollinger Inc.	HLGRF
Canada	Hummingbird Communications, Limited	HUMCF
Canada	Hyal Pharmaceutical Corporation	HYALF
Canada	Imax Corporation	IMAXF
Canada	Imperial Ginseng Products, Limited	IGPFF
Canada	International Murex Technologies Corporation	MURXF
Canada	International Verifact, Inc.	IVIAF
Canada	IPL Energy Inc.	IPPIF
Canada	I.S.G. Technologies Inc.	ISGTF
Canada	Jannock Limited	JANNF
Canada	JetForm Corporation	FORMF
Canada	Liquidation World, Inc.	LIQWF
Canada	Livent, Inc.	LVNTF
Canada	Mackenzie Financial Corporation	MKFCF
Canada	MacMillan Bloedel Limited	MMBLF
Canada	MDSI Mobile Data Solutions, Inc.	MDSIF
Canada	Methanex Corporation	MEOHF
Canada	Metrowerks Corporation	MTWKF
Canada	Miramar Mining Corporation	MAENF
Canada	Open Text Corporation	OTEXF
Canada	Optima Petroleum Corporation	OPPCF
Canada	Optimal Robotics Corp.	OPMRF
Canada	PC DOCS Group International	DOCSF
Canada	Petromet Resources Limited	PNTGF
Canada	Plaintree Systems, Inc.	LANPF
Canada	QLT Phototherapeutics, Inc.	QLTIF
Canada	Quality Dino Entertainment Ltd	RCORF
Canada	Q-Zar, Inc.	QZARF
Canada	REPAP Enterprises, Inc.	RPAPF
Canada	Revenue Properties Company Limited	RPCLF
Canada	Russel Metals, Inc.	RUSAF
Canada	Sand Technology Systems International Inc.	SNDCF
Canada	Semi-Tech Corporation	SEMCF
Canada	Simware, Inc.	SIMWF
Canada	SoftQuad International, Inc.	SWEBF
Canada	Spectral Diagnostics Inc.	DIAGF
Canada	Spectrum Signal Processing Inc.	SSPIF
Canada	Sutton Resources, Ltd.	STTZF
Canada	Taseko Mines Limited	TKOCF
Canada	Tee-Comm Electronics Inc.	TENXF
Canada	Tesco Corporation	TESOF
Canada	Tesma International, Inc.	TSMAF
Canada	Vengold, Inc.	VENGF
Canada	Venture Seismic, Limited	VSEIF
Canada	Visible Genetics, Inc.	VGINF
Canada	Wescast Industries Inc.	WCSTF
Canada	Vitran Corporation, Inc.	VTNAF
Cayman Islands	Chandler Insurance Company, Ltd.	CHANF
Denmark	Olicom A/S	OLCMF
Hong Kong	AES China Generating Co. LTD.	CHGNF

COUNTRY	COMPANY NAME	SYMBOL
Hong Kong	Bonso Electronics International, Inc.	BNSOF
Hong Kong	Highway Holdings Limited	HIHOF
Hong Kong	Radica Games Limited	RADAF
Hong Kong	Tramford International, Ltd.	TRFDF
Israel	Aladdin Knowledge Systems Limited	ALDNF
Israel	Arel Communications & Software Ltd.	ARLCF
Israel	Ariely Advertising, Limited	RELEF
Israel	Check Point Software Technologies, Ltd.	CHKPF
Israel	Cimatron, Limited	CIMTF
Israel	ECI Telecom Ltd.	ECILF
Israel	EduSoft Ltd.	EDUSF
Israel	Elbit Ltd.	ELBTF
Israel	Elbit Medical Imaging Ltd.	EMITF
Israel	Elbit Systems Ltd.	ESLTF
Israel	Elbit Vision Systems, Limited	EVSNF
Israel	Elron Electronic Industries Ltd.	ELRNF
Israel	ESC Medical Systems, Limited	ESCMF
Israel	Gilat Satellite Networks Ltd.	GILTF
Israel	Home Centers, (DIY), Limited	HOMEF
Israel	I.I.S. Intelligent Information Systems Limited	IISLF
Israel	ISG International Software Group Ltd.	SISGF
Israel	LanOptics Ltd.	LNOPF
Israel	Laser Industries Limited	LASRF
Israel	Logal Educational Software & Systems, Limited	LOGLF
Israel	Magal Security Systems Ltd.	MAGSF
Israel	Magic Software Enterprises Ltd	MGICF
Israel	Memco Software Limited	MEMCF
Israel	M-Systems Flash Disk Pioneers Ltd.	FLSHF
Israel	New Dimension Software Ltd.	DDDDF
Israel	Nur Advanced Technologies, Ltd	NURTF
Israel	Orbotech Ltd.	ORBKF
Israel	Orckit Communications, Limited	ORCTF
Israel	Oshap Technologies Ltd.	OSHSF
Israel	Rada Electronic Industries Limited	RADIF
Israel	ScanVec Company, Ltd.	SVECF
Israel	Scitex Corporation Ltd.	SCIXF
Israel	Tadiran Telecommunications, Limited	TTELF
Israel	Taro Pharmaceutical Industries Ltd.	TAROF
Israel	TAT Technologies Ltd.	TATTF
Israel	Tecnomatix Technologies Ltd.	TCNOF
Israel	Teledata Communications Ltd.	TLDCF
Israel	Tower Semiconductor Ltd.	TSEMF
Israel	TTI Team Telecom International Ltd.	TTILF
Israel	VocalTec, Limited	VOCLF
Israel	Wiztec Solutions, Limited	WIZTF
Israel	ZAG Industries Ltd.	ZAGIF
Luxembourg	Cronos Group (The)	CRNSF
Luxembourg	Millicom International Cellular S.A.	MICCF
Luxembourg	Stolt Comex Seaway S.A.	SCSWF
Mexico	Elamex S.A. de C.V.	ELAMF

Foreign Securities by Country (Continued)

COUNTRY	COMPANY NAME	SYMBOL
Netherlands	Ansaldo Signal, N.V.	ASIGF
Netherlands	ASM International N.V.	ASMIF
Netherlands	ASM Lithography Holding N.V.	ASMLF
Netherlands	Baan Company N.V.	BAANF
Netherlands	BE Semiconductor Industries NV	BESIF
Netherlands	Core Laboratories, N.V.	CRLBF
Netherlands	Heidemij N.V.	HEIDF
Netherlands	ICTS International N.V.	ICTSF
Netherlands	Indigo N.V.	INDGF
Netherlands	Madge Networks, N.V.	MADGF
Netherlands	Orthofix International N.V.	OFIXF
Netherlands	QIAGEN N.V.	QGENF
Netherlands	Sapiens International Corporation N.V.	SPNSF
Netherlands	Toolex Alpha, N.V.	TLXAF
Netherlands	Triple P, N.V.	TPPPF
Singapore	Creative Technology Ltd.	CREAF
Singapore	Flextronics International Ltd.	FLEXF
Sweden	Scandinavian Broadcasting System SA	SBTVF
Taiwan	ASE Test, Limited	ASTSF
United Arab Emirates	International Petroleum Corporation	IRPPF
United Kingdom	Cayman Water Company, Ltd.	CWCOF
United Kingdom	Comcast UK Cable Partners Limited	CMCAF
United Kingdom	Commodore Holdings Limited	CCLNF
United Kingdom	Deswell Industries, Inc.	DSWLF
United Kingdom	DSG International Limited	DSGIF
United Kingdom	Ezcony Interamerica Inc.	EZCOF
United Kingdom	Gemstar International Group, Limited	GMSTF
United Kingdom	Globalstar Telecommunications, Limited	GSTRF
United Kingdom	IWI Holding, Limited	JEWLF
United Kingdom	Nam Tai Electronics, Inc.	NTAIF
United Kingdom	Nobel Insurance Limited	NOBLF

ABACAN RESOURCE CORPORATION

YIELD ...
P/E RATIO ...

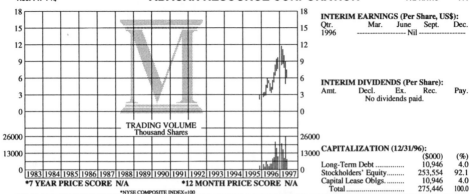

*7 YEAR PRICE SCORE N/A   *12 MONTH PRICE SCORE N/A
*NYSE COMPOSITE INDEX=100

TRADING VOLUME
Thousand Shares

INTERIM EARNINGS (Per Share, US$):

Qtr.	Mar.	June	Sept.	Dec.
1996	------------------- Nil -------------------			

INTERIM DIVIDENDS (Per Share):

Amt.	Decl.	Ex.	Rec.	Pay.
	No dividends paid.			

CAPITALIZATION (12/31/96):

	($000)	(%)
Long-Term Debt	10,946	4.0
Stockholders' Equity........	253,554	92.1
Capital Lease Oblgs.	10,946	4.0
Total	275,446	100.0

RECENT DEVELOPMENTS: As of 12/31/96, the Company was in the pre-production stage of its development. Since all of Abacan's activities are related to oil and gas exploration and development and are still at a pre-production stage, all costs are being capitalized. These costs will be amortized over the life of the reserves on a unit of production basis. Accordingly, there is no statement of loss or deficit. During September 1996, the Company, through its wholly-owned subsidiary, Liberty Technical Services Ltd., and its Nigerian partner, Amni International Petroleum Develop-

ment Company Limited, concluded a $30.0 million secured debt financing from MeesPierson N.V. and ING Bank N.V., of the Netherlands. Proceeds from the loan are being used to meet financial commitments associated with the development of the NGO field; repayment will be made from net proceeds of production. Also during September 1996, the Company executed a one-year agreement with Total International Limited of France for the purchase of all of the crude oil and condensate produced from the NGO field by Liberty and Amni.

BUSINESS

ABACAN RESOURCE CORPORA-TION is engaged in the acquisition, exploration and development of oil and gas prospects in West Africa.

ANNUAL EARNINGS

ANNUAL FINANCIAL DATA

	12/31/96	12/31/95	12/31/96	12/31/95
	------------US $------------		------------C $------------	
BALANCE SHEET (IN THOUSANDS):				
Cash & Cash Equivalents	64,045	33,753	87,601	46,054
Receivables, Net	4,131	77	5,650	105
Gross Property	162	147	222	201
Accumulated Depreciation	49	36	67	49
Long-Term Debt	10,946	5,094	14,972	6,950
Stockholders' Equity	253,554	130,212	346,812	177,667
Total Assets	335,840	139,640	459,363	190,531
Total Current Assets	68,176	33,830	93,251	46,159
Total Current Liabilities	71,340	4,334	97,579	5,913
Net Working Capital	d3,164	29,496	d4,328	40,246
Year End Shs Outstg	109,414	...	109,414	...
STATISTICAL RECORD:				
Return on Equity %	...	...		
Return on Assets %	...	...		
Operating Profit Margin %	...	...		
Net Profit Margin %	...	...		
Book Value Per Share	2.32	2.32		

Converted at 1996, US$0.7311= 1 Canadian $; 1995, US$0.7329= 1 Canadian $

OFFICERS:
W. G. Cherwayko, Pres. & C.E.O.
F. Elliott, Exploration Mgr.
A. Le Bis, Geophysical Mgr.
G.B. Singer, V.P.-Fin. & C.F.O.
INCORPORATED: Feb. 10, 1995
PRINCIPAL OFFICE: 1750, 800-5th Avenue S.W., Calgary, Alberta, T2P 3T6 Canada

TELEPHONE NUMBER: 403-262-1220
NO. OF EMPLOYEES: 12
ANNUAL MEETING: In Jun.
SHAREHOLDERS: 1,980
INSTITUTIONAL HOLDINGS:
No. of Institutions: 65
Shares Held: 45,024,238

REGISTRAR(S): N/A

TRANSFER AGENT(S): Montreal Trust Company, Calgary.

ACCUGRAPH CORPORATION

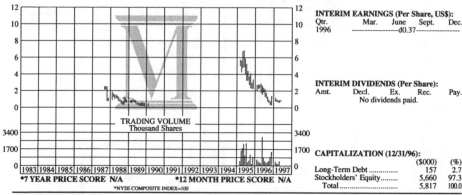

*7 YEAR PRICE SCORE N/A   *12 MONTH PRICE SCORE N/A
*NYSE COMPOSITE INDEX=100

TRADING VOLUME
Thousand Shares

INTERIM EARNINGS (Per Share, US$):

Qtr.	Mar.	June	Sept.	Dec.
1996	---------------d0.37----------------			

INTERIM DIVIDENDS (Per Share):

Amt.	Decl.	Ex.	Rec.	Pay.
		No dividends paid.		

CAPITALIZATION (12/31/96):

	($000)	(%)
Long-Term Debt	157	2.7
Stockholders' Equity........	5,660	97.3
Total	5,817	100.0

RECENT DEVELOPMENTS: For the year ended 12/31/96, the Company reported a loss of $7.3 million compared with income of $2.0 million in the corresponding period a year earlier. Sales were $16.2 million versus $22.7 million in 1995. Earnings were pressured by a $3.9 million charge for unusual items. Operating loss before unusual items was $3.2 million compared with operating income of $2.0 million. Currently, the Company is taking steps to refocus its operations and improve profitability. During the year, the Company's work force was reduced by 42%, days sales outstanding decreased 55% and quarterly expenses were reduced by 39%. For the fourth quarter ended 12/31/96, the Company reported a net loss of $2.6 million compared with income of $1.1 million in 1995. Sales slipped 62% to $4.5 million versus $7.3 million a year earlier. Earnings were pressured by a $3.4 million charge for unusual items.

BUSINESS

ACCUGRAPH CORPORATION and its wholly-owned subsidiary Accugraph Corp. (United States) develop and support computer based software products to design and manage graphic information, focusing primarily on applications in the areas of telecommunications, facilities management, and computer network management.

ANNUAL EARNINGS

	12/31/96	12/31/95	12/31/96	12/31/95
	------------US $------------		------------C $------------	
Earnings Per Share	d0.37	0.10	d0.51	0.14

ANNUAL FINANCIAL DATA

RECORD OF EARNINGS (IN THOUSANDS):

	12/31/96	12/31/95	12/31/96	12/31/95
Total Revenues	16,151	22,746	22,091	31,036
Costs & Expenses	19,438	20,761	26,587	28,327
Operating Income	d3,287	1,985	d4,496	2,708
Income Bef Income Tax	d7,142	1,985	d9,769	2,708
Income Tax	151	32	207	44
Net Income	d7,293	1,953	d9,975	2,665
Average Shares Outstg	19,877	19,753	19,877	19,753

BALANCE SHEET (IN THOUSANDS):

Cash & Cash Equivalents	960	1,748	1,313	2,385
Receivables, Net	3,576	8,806	4,891	12,015
Gross Property	4,220	6,373	5,772	8,696
Accumulated Depreciation	1,753	3,426	2,398	4,675
Long-Term Debt	157	220	215	300
Stockholders' Equity	5,660	12,943	7,742	17,660
Total Assets	9,210	15,877	12,597	21,663
Total Current Assets	5,139	11,051	7,029	15,078
Total Current Liabilities	3,226	2,714	4,413	3,703
Net Working Capital	1,913	8,337	2,617	11,375
Year End Shs Outstg	19,891	19,872	19,891	19,872

STATISTICAL RECORD:

Return on Equity %	...	15.09		
Return on Assets %	...	12.30		
Operating Profit Margin %	...	8.73		
Net Profit Margin %	...	8.59		
Book Value Per Share	0.28	0.65		

Converted at 1996, US$0.7311= 1 Canadian $; 1995, US$0.7329= 1 Canadian $

OFFICERS:
P. D. Damp, Chmn. & C.E.O.
Z. Rana, Sr. V.P.
G. Shroyer, V.P. & C.F.O.
P. Thrasher, V.P.

INCORPORATED: Canada, Sept. 1976

PRINCIPAL OFFICE: 5822 Cromo Drive, El Paso TX 79912

TELEPHONE NUMBER: 915-581-1171

NO. OF EMPLOYEES: 129

ANNUAL MEETING: In Jun.

SHAREHOLDERS: 270

INSTITUTIONAL HOLDINGS:
No. of Institutions: 7
Shares Held: 4,251,900

REGISTRAR(S): Montreal Trust Company of Canada, Toronto.

TRANSFER AGENT(S): Montreal Trust Company of Canada, Toronto.

AES CHINA GENERATING CO. LTD.

YIELD   ...
P/E RATIO   72.6

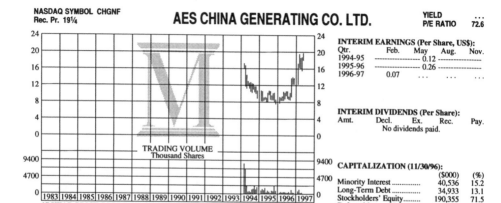

INTERIM EARNINGS (Per Share, US$):

Qtr.	Feb.	May	Aug.	Nov.
1994-95	----------------	0.12	----------------	
1995-96	----------------	0.26	----------------	
1996-97	0.07	...	...	...

INTERIM DIVIDENDS (Per Share):

Amt.	Decl.	Ex.	Rec.	Pay.
	No dividends paid.			

CAPITALIZATION (11/30/96):

	($000)	(%)
Minority Interest	40,536	15.2
Long-Term Debt	34,933	13.1
Stockholders' Equity........	190,355	71.5
Deferred Income Tax	387	0.1
Total	266,211	100.0

RECENT DEVELOPMENTS: For the three months ended 2/28/97, net income totaled $1.1 million, or $0.07 per share, versus $316,000, or $0.02 per share, in the corresponding quarter the previous year. Total revenues were $2.5 million, up significantly compared with $424,000 in the first quarter in 1996. Costs of sales jumped to $1.7 million versus $231,000 the year before. The increases in revenues and costs of sales were attributed to the commencement of operations of the Wuxi Tin Hill project. Development, selling, general and administrative expenses fell 17.8% to $1.6 million from $2.0 million a year ago, due to the capitalization of development costs related to the Yangcheng Sun City project, which has achieved certain project-related milestones. Operating loss totaled $856,000 compared with a loss of $1.8 million a year earlier.

BUSINESS

AES CHINA GENERATING CO. LTD. develops, acquires, finances, constructs, owns and manages electric power generation facilities in the People's Republic of China.

ANNUAL EARNINGS

	11/30/96	11/30/95
	------------------------------US $------------------------------	
Earnings Per Share	0.26	0.12

ANNUAL FINANCIAL DATA

RECORD OF EARNINGS (IN THOUSANDS):

Total Revenues	9,212	1,382
Operating Income	345	d8,512
Income Bef Income Tax	4,804	2,223
Income Tax	387	...
Minority Interests	277	85
Net Income	4,140	2,138
Average Shares Outstg	15,670	17,391

BALANCE SHEET (IN THOUSANDS):

Cash & Cash Equivalents	65,195	170,288
Receivables, Net	7,095	756
Inventories	765	31
Gross Property	165,743	47,256
Accumulated Depreciation	3,143	665
Long-Term Debt	34,933	6,666
Stockholders' Equity	190,355	187,585
Total Assets	280,698	229,871
Total Current Assets	73,929	171,497
Total Current Liabilities	14,487	16,538
Net Working Capital	59,442	154,959
Year End Shs Outstg	15,634	17,716

STATISTICAL RECORD:

Return on Equity %	2.17	1.14
Return on Assets %	1.47	0.93
Operating Profit Margin %	3.75	...
Net Profit Margin %	44.94	N.M.
Book Value Per Share	12.18	10.59

OFFICERS:
R. W. Sant, Chmn.
D. W. Bakke, Vice-Chmn.
R. F. Hemphill, Vice-Chmn.
P. T. Hanrahan, Pres. & C.E.O.
J. A. Safford, V.P., C.F.O. & Sec.

INCORPORATED: Bermuda, Dec., 1993

PRINCIPAL OFFICE: 3/F., Jinqiao Building, #1 Jianguomenwai Avenue, Beijing 100020 Peoples Rep. of China

TELEPHONE NUMBER: 8610-508-9619

NO. OF EMPLOYEES: 69

ANNUAL MEETING: In March

SHAREHOLDERS: 171 (approx.)

INSTITUTIONAL HOLDINGS:
No. of Institutions: N/A
Shares Held: N/A

REGISTRAR(S): First Union National Bank of North Carolina, Charlotte, NC.

TRANSFER AGENT(S): First Union National Bank of North Carolina, Charlotte, NC.

AIR CANADA CORPORATION

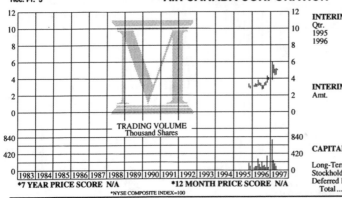

*7 YEAR PRICE SCORE N/A   *12 MONTH PRICE SCORE N/A
*NYSE COMPOSITE INDEX=100

INTERIM EARNINGS (Per Share, US$):

Qtr.	Mar.	June	Sep.	Dec.
1995		0.26		
1996		0.63		

INTERIM DIVIDENDS (Per Share):

Amt.	Decl.	Ex.	Rec.	Pay.
		No dividends paid.		

CAPITALIZATION (12/31/96):

	($000)	(%)
Long-Term Debt	2,171,000	78.1
Stockholders' Equity	584,000	21.0
Deferred Income Tax	25,000	0.9
Total	2,780,000	100.0

RECENT DEVELOPMENTS: For the year ended 12/31/96, net income more than doubled to C$149.0 million compared C$62.0 million a year earlier. The 1996 results included non-recurring gains of C$129.0 million from the sale of Continental Airlines holdings. Revenues advanced 8.3% to C$4.88 billion. The increase in revenues was attributed primarily to an 11% increase in revenues from passenger routes, which benefited from strong growth in international markets, particularly transborder. Cargo revenues climbed 7.4% to C$347.0 million, supported by an 11% rise in cargo traffic, partially offset by a 4% decline in cargo yields, excluding subsidiaries. Operating income was down 21.8% to C$215.0 million, due primarily to reduced contributions from domestic operations and a rapid runup in fuel prices, which alone accounted for C$40.0 million in additional expenses when compared with 1995. Lower contributions from subsidiaries, notably AirBC in Western Canada, were also a factor in lower operating income.

BUSINESS

AIR CANADA CORPORATION is a Canadian-based international air carrier providing scheduled and charter air transportation for passengers and for cargo. The airline's passenger route network, including regional airline subsidiaries, provides air transportation services to 120 cities worldwide. The Company serves directly 17 cities in Canada with an additional 40 Canadian communities served by its regional airlines. The Company also provides air transportation services to 35 cities in the United States and to 22 cities in Europe, Asia, the Middle East and the Caribbean. Charter passenger services are also offered to six international destinations. The airline's cargo division serves directly over 67 destinations in Canada and internationally. The Company operates a large aircraft and engine maintenance business providing maintenance services to airlines and other customers. The Company is traded on the NASDAQ Stock Market under Class A non-voting common shares.

ANNUAL EARNINGS

	12/31/96	12/31/95	12/31/96	12/31/95
	---US $---		---C $---	
Earnings Per Share	0.63	0.26	0.86	0.36

ANNUAL FINANCIAL DATA

RECORD OF EARNINGS (IN MILLIONS):

	12/31/96	12/31/95	12/31/96	12/31/95
Total Revenues	3,568	3,302	4,880	4,507
Costs & Expenses	2,989	2,729	4,088	3,724
Deprec, Amort & Aircraft Rent	422	372	577	508
Operating Income	157	202	215	275
Income Bef Income Tax	112	60	153	82
Income Tax	3	15	4	20
Net Income	109	45	149	62
Average Shares Outstg (000)	155,400	144,000	155,400	144,000

BALANCE SHEET (IN MILLIONS):

Cash & Cash Equivalents	333	568	455	775
Receivables, Net	285	298	390	408
Inventories	144	129	197	176
Gross Property	2,061	2,016	2,819	2,751
Accumulated Depreciation	1,285	1,168	1,758	1,594
Long-Term Debt	2,171	2,020	2,969	2,756
Stockholders' Equity	584	485	799	662
Total Assets	3,938	3,955	5,386	5,397
Total Current Assets	776	1,013	1,062	1,382
Total Current Liabilities	812	1,111	1,111	1,516
Net Working Capital	d36	d98	d49	d134
Year End Shs Outstg (000)	156,000	155,000	156,000	155,000

STATISTICAL RECORD:

Return on Equity %	18.7	9.3		
Return on Assets %	2.8	1.1		
Operating Profit Margin %	4.4	6.1		
Net Profit Margin %	3.1	1.4		
Book Value Per Share	3.74	3.13		

Converted at 1996, US$0.7311= 1 Canadian $; 1995, US$0.7329= 1 Canadian $

OFFICERS:
J. F. Fraser, Chmn.
R. L. Durrett, Pres. & C.E.O.
M. R. Peterson, Sr. V.P.-Fin. & C.F.O.
R. A. Milton, Exec. V.P. & C.O.O.

INCORPORATED: On Apr. 10, 1937

PRINCIPAL OFFICE: P.O. Box 14000, Saint-Laurent, H4Y 1H4 Canada

TELEPHONE NUMBER: 514-422-5000
NO. OF EMPLOYEES: 19,900
ANNUAL MEETING: In May
SHAREHOLDERS: N/A
INSTITUTIONAL HOLDINGS:
No. of Institutions: 6
Shares Held: 8,450,307 (Cl. A non-voting common)

REGISTRAR(S): The R-M Trust Company, Halifax, Montreal, Toronto, Winnipeg, Regina, Calgary, Vancouver.

TRANSFER AGENT(S): The R-M Trust Company, Halifax, Montreal, Toronto, Winnipeg, Regina, Calgary, Vancouver.

ALADDIN KNOWLEDGE SYSTEMS LIMITED

YIELD ...
P/E RATIO ...

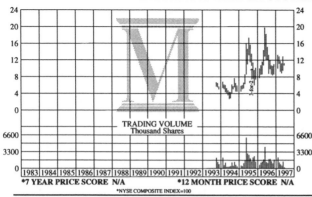

TRADING VOLUME
Thousand Shares

| 1983 | 1984 | 1985 | 1986 | 1987 | 1988 | 1989 | 1990 | 1991 | 1992 | 1993 | 1994 | 1995 | 1996 | 1997 |

*7 YEAR PRICE SCORE N/A   *12 MONTH PRICE SCORE N/A

*NYSE COMPOSITE INDEX=100

INTERIM EARNINGS (Per Share, US$):

	Mar.	June	Sept.	Dec
1996		-----------------d0.31-----------------		

INTERIM DIVIDENDS (Per Share):

Amt.	Decl.	Ex.	Rec.	Pay.
3-for-2	8/15/95	9/18/95	8/25/95	9/15/95

CAPITALIZATION (12/31/95):

	($000)	(%)
Stockholders' Equity.........	15,826	100.0
Total	15,826	100.0

RECENT DEVELOPMENTS: For the year ended 12/31/96, the Company reported a loss of $3.1 million, or a loss of $0.31 per share, compared with income of $6.0 million, or $0.61 per share, in the corresponding period a year earlier. Sales were $28.7 million versus $24.8 million in 1995. Earnings were affected by reorganization expenses associated with the Aladdin-Fastmerger. Without taking the reorganization expenses associated with FAST, net income for the year would have been $6.9 million. For the quarter ended 12/31/96, net income advanced 16% to $2.1 million, or $0.21 per share, compared with $1.8 million, or $0.18 per share, in 1995. Sales rose 20% to $8.4 million versus $7.0 million a yearearlier. Higher sales and earnings reflect growing demand for HASP in North America.

BUSINESS

ALADDIN KNOWLEDGE SYSTEMS LIMITED designs, develops, manufactures and markets a family of proprietary software security products that combine hardware and software to prevent unauthorized use of computer programs. ALDNF's primary product system is sold under the name HASP (Hardware Against Software Piracy). The Company markets its HASP family of products to software development houses that develop and market software products for use with IBM, IBM-compatible, NEC and Macintosh personal computers and to distributors of software products that run on such hardware platforms.

ANNUAL EARNINGS

	12/31/95	12/31/94	12/31/95	12/31/94
	--------------US $------------		-------------NIS------------	
Earnings Per Share	0.51	0.38	1.61	1.15

ANNUAL FINANCIAL DATA

RECORD OF EARNINGS (IN THOUSANDS):

	12/31/95	12/31/94	12/31/95	12/31/94
Total Revenues	11,345	7,385	35,710	22,284
Costs & Expenses	8,226	5,089	25,892	15,356
Operating Income	3,119	2,296	9,817	6,928
Income Bef Income Tax	3,591	2,561	11,303	7,728
Income Tax	207	127	652	383
Net Income	3,384	2,434	10,652	7,345
Average Shares Outstg	6,676	6,457	6,676	6,457

BALANCE SHEET (IN THOUSANDS):

Cash & Cash Equivalents	10,223	8,783	32,178	26,504
Receivables, Net	3,275	1,803	10,308	5,441
Inventories	953	750	3,000	2,262
Gross Property	2,098	1,100	6,604	3,320
Accumulated Depreciation	500	244	1,574	735
Stockholders' Equity	15,826	11,143	49,814	33,622
Total Assets	17,826	12,342	56,110	37,242
Total Current Assets	14,451	11,337	45,486	34,206
Total Current Liabilities	1,795	1,044	5,650	3,151
Net Working Capital	12,656	10,293	39,836	31,055
Year End Shs Outstg	6,583	6,441	6,583	6,441

STATISTICAL RECORD:

Return on Equity %	21.38	21.84		
Return on Assets %	18.98	19.72		
Operating Profit Margin %	27.49	31.09		
Net Profit Margin %	29.83	32.96		
Book Value Per Share	2.40	1.73		

Converted at 1995, US$0.3177= 1 New Israeli Shekel; 1994, US$0.3314= 1 New Israeli Shekel

OFFICERS:
Y. Margalit, Chmn. & Pres.
D. Margalit, Exec. V.P.

INCORPORATED: 1985

PRINCIPAL OFFICE: 15 Beit Oved Street
P.O. Box 11141, Tel Aviv Israel

TELEPHONE NUMBER: 972-3-537-5795

NO. OF EMPLOYEES: N/A

ANNUAL MEETING: N/A

SHAREHOLDERS: N/A

INSTITUTIONAL HOLDINGS:
No. of Institutions: N/A
Shares Held: N/A

REGISTRAR(S): American Stock Transfer and Trust Co., New York.

TRANSFER AGENT(S): American Stock Transfer and Trust Co., New York.

ALGOMA STEEL INC.

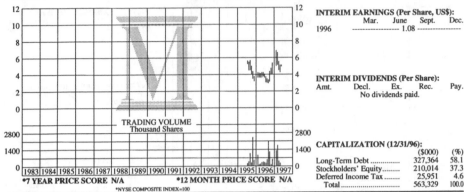

7 YEAR PRICE SCORE N/A   **12 MONTH PRICE SCORE N/A**
*NYSE COMPOSITE INDEX=100

INTERIM EARNINGS (Per Share, US$):

	Mar.	June	Sept.	Dec.
1996	---------------- 1.08 ----------------

INTERIM DIVIDENDS (Per Share):

Amt.	Decl.	Ex.	Rec.	Pay.
	No dividends paid.

CAPITALIZATION (12/31/96):

	($000)	(%)
Long-Term Debt	327,364	58.1
Stockholders' Equity	210,014	37.3
Deferred Income Tax	25,951	4.6
Total	563,329	100.0

RECENT DEVELOPMENTS: For the year ended 12/31/96, net income decreased 38.1% to C$67.8 million from C$109.6 million in 1995. Results for 1996 included an after-tax gain of $4.8 million on the sale of fixed assets. The 1995 results included a loss of C$3.5 million on the retirement of preferred shares. Revenues inched up 1.7% to C$1.23 billion from C$1.21 billion the year before. Income from operations declined 36.4% to C$121.2 million versus C$190.7 million a year earlier. Raw steel production improved 6.1% to 2.4 million net tons from 2.2 million net tons in 1995. Steel shipments increased 4.6% to 2.1 million net tons from 2.0 net tons in 1995. For the fourth quarter ended 12/31/96, net income leapt to C$27.5 million from C$1.8 million in the equivalent period of 1995. Revenues increased 4.5% to C$305.1 million versus C$292.0 million in 1995. On 2/18/97, ALGSF completed an equity offering of 6.0 million shares at $8.75 per share. Proceeds amounted to approximately $50.0 million.

BUSINESS

ALGOMA STEEL INC. is a vertically integrated steel producer, which accounts for approximately 16.0% of Canadian raw steel production. From its location in Sault Ste. Marie, the Company is positioned to access the extensive steel markets within a 400 mile radius of its plant. In 1996, the Company produced approximately 2.4 million tons of raw steel and shipped over 2.1 million tons of finished products. ALGSF's principal product is sheet, which represents 61.0% of its annual production, with plate, structural and seamless tubular products accounting for the balance. The principal markets for the Company's products are steel centers, the automotive industry, steel fabricators and manufacturers, pipe and tube manufacturers and the oil and gas exploration industry. As of 12/31/96, virtually all of the Company's production is sold in Canada and the U.S., with approximately 12.0% of its steel sales to customers in the U.S.

ANNUAL EARNINGS

	12/31/96	12/31/95	12/31/96	12/31/95
	----------US $----------		----------C $----------	
Earnings Per Share	1.08	1.88	1.48	3.14

ANNUAL FINANCIAL DATA

RECORD OF EARNINGS (IN THOUSANDS):

	12/31/96	12/31/95	12/31/96	12/31/95
Total Revenues	897,696	885,096	1,227,871	1,207,663
Costs & Expenses	769,459	710,608	1,052,468	969,584
Depreciation & Amort	39,658	34,763	54,244	47,432
Operating Income	88,579	139,725	121,159	190,647
Income Bef Income Tax	67,832	121,614	92,781	165,936
Income Tax	18,278	35,199	25,000	48,027
Net Income	49,555	86,416	67,781	117,909
Average Shares Outstg	45,800	35,000	45,000	35,000

BALANCE SHEET (IN THOUSANDS):

Cash & Cash Equivalents	2,266	14,104	3,100	19,244
Receivables, Net	120,065	104,198	164,225	142,172
Inventories	277,455	272,162	379,504	371,350
Gross Property	774,447	591,102	1,059,290	806,525
Accumulated Depreciation	252,039	235,458	344,740	321,269
Long-Term Debt	327,364	284,875	447,769	388,695
Stockholders' Equity	210,014	160,855	287,258	219,477
Total Assets	984,818	898,727	1,347,036	1,226,261
Total Current Assets	401,514	395,061	549,192	539,038
Total Current Liabilities	168,872	188,204	230,983	256,793
Net Working Capital	232,643	206,857	318,209	282,245
Year End Shs Outstg	45,840	45,840	45,840	45,840

STATISTICAL RECORD:

Return on Equity %	23.60	53.72		
Return on Assets %	5.03	9.62		
Operating Profit Margin %	9.87	15.79		
Net Profit Margin %	5.52	9.76		
Book Value Per Share	4.58	3.50		

Converted at 1996, US$0.7311= 1 Canadian $; 1995, US$0.7329= 1 Canadian $

OFFICERS:
H. E. Joudrie, Chmn.
A. Adam, Pres. & C.E.O.
P. C. Finley, Gen. Couns. & Sec.
G. P. Manchester, Dir. of Fin. & Contr.

INCORPORATED: Canada, Dec., 1934

PRINCIPAL OFFICE: 105 West Street P.O. Box 1400 Sault Ste. Marie Canada P6A 5P2

TELEPHONE NUMBER: 705-945-2351

NO. OF EMPLOYEES: 5,300

ANNUAL MEETING: In Apr.

SHAREHOLDERS: N/A

INSTITUTIONAL HOLDINGS:
No. of Institutions: 10
Shares Held: 11,876,278

REGISTRAR(S):

TRANSFER AGENT(S): Montreal Trust Company, Toronto.

NASDAQ SYMBOL ALLIF
Rec. Pr. 8⅝

ALLIANCE COMMUNICATIONS CORP.

YIELD ...
P/E RATIO 11.2

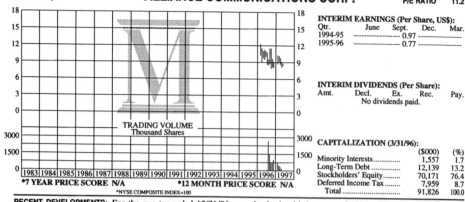

*7 YEAR PRICE SCORE N/A ***12 MONTH PRICE SCORE N/A**

*NYSE COMPOSITE INDEX=100

TRADING VOLUME
Thousand Shares

INTERIM EARNINGS (Per Share, US$):

Qtr.	June	Sept.	Dec.	Mar.
1994-95		0.97		
1995-96		0.77		

INTERIM DIVIDENDS (Per Share):

Amt.	Decl.	Ex.	Rec.	Pay.
	No dividends paid.			

CAPITALIZATION (3/31/96):

	($000)	(%)
Minority Interests..............	1,557	1.7
Long-Term Debt	12,139	13.2
Stockholders' Equity..........	70,171	76.4
Deferred Income Tax	7,959	8.7
Total	91,826	100.0

RECENT DEVELOPMENTS: For the quarter ended 12/31/96, net earnings fell 7.6% to C$4.1 million from C$4.4 million in the corresponding period of 1995. Total revenues dropped 30.6% to C$65.0 million from C$93.6 million the year before. Alliance television revenues decreased 38.0% to C$22.7 million from C$36.7 million in 1995 primarily due to the timing of deliveries. Alliance motion pictures revenues declined 32.3% to C$26.3 million from C$38.9 million a year earlier. This decrease reflected no new deliv- eries in the third quarter of 1996 versus one delivery of an in-house produced motion picture in the same prior-year period. For the nine months ended 12/31/96, net earnings grew to C$11.3 million from C$5.5 million in 1995. Total revenues fell 9.0% to C$183.1 million from C$201.2 mil- lion the prior year. On 2/27/97, ALLIF formed a joint venture with Electric Pictures, the United Kingdom distrib- utor of independent films. This is ALLIF's first direct investment in the British film industry.

BUSINESS

ALLIANCE COMMUNICATIONS CORP. is a fully integrated supplier of entertainment products. The Com- pany has five divisions which are: Alliance Television Group, Alliance Motion Picture Group, Alliance Mul- timedia, Alliance Equicap and Alli- ance Broadcasting. The Company's origins are in the television and motion picture industry, domestic dis- tribution, international distributions, and structured production financing. In fiscal 1995, the Company expanded into broadcasting with the acquisition of a 55% equity ownership in SHOW- CASE Television Inc. and a 23% equity ownership in Budapest TV3, as well as music publishing with the acquisition of a 75% equity ownership in Partisan Music Productions Inc.

ANNUAL EARNINGS

	3/31/96	3/31/95	3/31/96	3/31/95
	----- US $ -----		----- C $ -----	
Earnings Per Share	0.77	0.97	1.05	1.36

ANNUAL FINANCIAL DATA

RECORD OF EARNINGS (IN THOUSANDS):

	3/31/96	3/31/95	3/31/96	3/31/95
Total Revenues	197,863	167,105	268,945	233,811
Costs & Expenses	184,694	151,952	251,045	212,610
Depreciation & Amort	3,706	3,691	5,038	5,164
Operating Income	9,463	11,462	12,862	16,037
Income Bef Income Tax	9,463	11,462	12,862	16,037
Income Tax	1,424	2,614	1,935	3,658
Minority Interests	413	cr426	562	cr596
Net Income	7,626	9,273	10,365	12,975
Average Shares Outstg	9,840	9,543	9,840	9,543

BALANCE SHEET (IN THOUSANDS):

Cash & Cash Equivalents	3,745	13,479	5,090	18,860
Receivables, Net	162,306	140,072	220,614	195,987
Gross Property	7,927	5,626	10,775	7,872
Accumulated Depreciation	2,889	1,539	3,927	2,154
Long-Term Debt	12,139	11,793	16,500	16,500
Stockholders' Equity	70,171	59,929	95,380	83,852
Total Assets	175,757	161,607	238,898	226,118
Total Current Assets	167,244	154,210	227,326	215,769
Total Current Liabilities	59,870	58,483	81,378	81,829
Net Working Capital	107,374	95,727	145,948	133,940
Year End Shs Outstg	9,894	9,776	9,894	9,776

STATISTICAL RECORD:

Return on Equity %	10.87	15.47		
Return on Assets %	4.34	5.74		
Operating Profit Margin %	4.78	6.86		
Net Profit Margin %	3.85	5.55		
Book Value Per Share	7.09	6.13		

Converted at 1996, US$0.7357= 1 Canadian C $; 1995, US$0.7147= 1 Canadian C $

OFFICERS:
R. Lantos, Chmn. & C.E.O.
V. Loewy, Vice-Chmn.
G. Burger, Exec. V.P.
R. Doronuik, C.F.O.

INCORPORATED: Canada

PRINCIPAL OFFICE: 121 Bloor Street East, Toronto, M4W 3M5 Canada

TELEPHONE NUMBER: 416-967-1174
FAX: 416-960-0971
NO. OF EMPLOYEES: N/A
ANNUAL MEETING: In Sep.
SHAREHOLDERS: N/A
INSTITUTIONAL HOLDINGS:
No. of Institutions: 12
Shares Held: 1,259,475

REGISTRAR(S): The Montreal Trust Company of Canada, Toronto.

TRANSFER AGENT(S): The Montreal Trust Company of Canada, Toronto.

AMERICAN ECO CORPORATION

YIELD ...
P/E RATIO 9.4

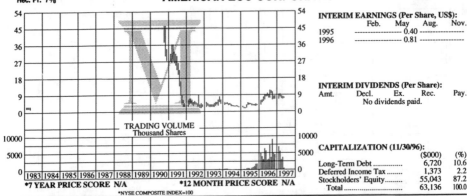

INTERIM EARNINGS (Per Share, US$):

	Feb.	May	Aug.	Nov.
1995			0.40	
1996			0.81	

INTERIM DIVIDENDS (Per Share):

Amt.	Decl.	Ex.	Rec.	Pay.
	No dividends paid.			

CAPITALIZATION (11/30/96):

	($000)	(%)
Long-Term Debt	6,720	10.6
Deferred Income Tax	1,373	2.2
Stockholders' Equity	55,043	87.2
Total	63,136	100.0

*7 YEAR PRICE SCORE N/A   *12 MONTH PRICE SCORE N/A

*NYSE COMPOSITE INDEX=100

RECENT DEVELOPMENTS: For the quarter ended 2/28/97, net income leaped 97% to US$3.6 million compared with US$1.8 million in the corresponding period a year earlier. Earnings per share were US$0.25, rising 20% from US$0.20 per share in the year-earlier period. Revenues were US$45.2 million, up 13% versus US$40.0 million in 1996. Earnings and revenues benefited from improving demand for the Company's services. The Company announced its intentions to acquire Chempower Inc. for US$6.20 per share in cash. The two companies have agreed to general terms of a financing arrangement that includes the deferring of the payment of a portion of the total consideration for up to one year. Chempower is a manufacturing, construction and environmental services company for the power generation industry. For the year ended 11/30/96, net income was US$8.8 million compared with US$2.9 million in 1995. Revenues rose 256% to US$119.5 million.

BUSINESS

AMERICAN ECO CORPORATION

is a provider of single source construction, project management, industrial maintenance, demolition, and environmental remediation services. The Company's customers are in the refining, chemical processing, forest products, utility and manufacturing industries as well as commercial and governmental markets.

ANNUAL EARNINGS

	11/30/96	11/30/95	11/30/96	11/30/95
	US $		C $	
Earnings Per Share	0.81	0.40	0.60	0.54

ANNUAL FINANCIAL DATA

RECORD OF EARNINGS (IN THOUSANDS):

	11/30/96	11/30/95	11/30/96	11/30/95
Total Revenues	119,529	46,684	89,169	63,198
Costs & Expenses	109,343	42,517	81,570	57,557
Depreciation & Amort	2,232	1,107	1,665	1,499
Operating Income	7,954	3,060	5,934	4,142
Income Bef Income Tax	7,954	3,060	5,934	4,142
Income Tax	809	208	604	282
Net Income	8,763	2,852	6,537	3,861
Average Shares Outstg	10,847	7,217	10,847	7,217

BALANCE SHEET (IN THOUSANDS):

	11/30/96	11/30/95	11/30/96	11/30/95
Cash & Cash Equivalents	497	1,070	371	1,448
Receivables, Net	20,918	5,535	15,605	7,493
Inventories	6,807	1,923	5,078	2,603
Net Property	33,238	5,844	24,796	4,317
Long-Term Debt	6,720	2,100	5,013	2,843
Stockholders' Equity	55,043	18,736	41,062	25,363
Total Assets	104,484	31,061	77,945	42,048
Total Current Assets	44,255	16,693	33,014	22,598
Total Current Liabilities	40,975	10,054	30,567	13,610
Net Working Capital	3,280	8,859	2,447	8,859

STATISTICAL RECORD:

	11/30/96	11/30/95
Return on Equity %	15.9	15.22
Return on Assets %	8.39	9.18
Operating Profit Margin %	6.65	6.55
Net Profit Margin %	7.33	6.11
Book Value Per Share	5.07	2.11

Converted at 1996, US$0.7460= 1 Canadian $; 1995, US$0.7387= 1 Canadian $

OFFICERS:
M. E. McGinnis, Chmn., Pres. & C.E.O.
D. L. Norris, Sr. V.P. & C.F.O.
B. Rich, Secretary

INCORPORATED: Canada, 1987

PRINCIPAL OFFICE: 154 University Ave,
Suite 200, Toronto, Ontario Canada M5

TELEPHONE NUMBER: 416-340-2727

NO. OF EMPLOYEES: 1,800

ANNUAL MEETING: In May

SHAREHOLDERS: N/A

INSTITUTIONAL HOLDINGS:
Shares Held: 560,866

REGISTRAR(S): N/A

TRANSFER AGENT(S): The R-M Trust
Company, Toronto.

AMERICAN SENSORS INC.

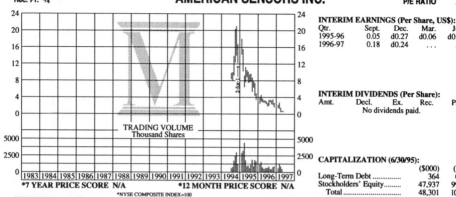

INTERIM EARNINGS (Per Share, US$):

Qtr.	Sept.	Dec.	Mar.	Jun.
1995-96	0.05	d0.27	d0.06	d0.81
1996-97	0.18	d0.24	...	...

INTERIM DIVIDENDS (Per Share):

Amt.	Decl.	Ex.	Rec.	Pay.
		No dividends paid.		

CAPITALIZATION (6/30/95):

	($000)	(%)
Long-Term Debt	364	0.8
Stockholders' Equity	47,937	99.2
Total	48,301	100.0

TRADING VOLUME
Thousand Shares

1983 1984 1985 1986 1987 1988 1989 1990 1991 1992 1993 1994 1995 1996 1997

*7 YEAR PRICE SCORE N/A   *12 MONTH PRICE SCORE N/A

*NYSE COMPOSITE INDEX=100

RECENT DEVELOPMENTS: For the quarter ended 12/31/96, SNIF reported a net loss of US$2.4 million compared with a net loss of US$2.9 million the year before. Sales declined 24.6% to US$19.5 million. The decrease in sales was attributed to delays in SNIF's new product development program, which included delays in the launch of its battery-powered semiconductor carbon monoxide detector. Gross profit was US$6.5 million, down 3.9% from US$6.8 million a year earlier due to unusually high production costs. SNIF plans to take a restructuring charge against operations in its next quarter relating to production alternatives, inventory reduction, manufacturing and operational logistics and expense infrastructure. For the six months ended 12/31/96, SNIF reported a net loss of US$634,000 versus a net loss of US$2.4 million the previous year. Sales declined 10.7% to US$47.4 million. For the year ended 6/30/96, SNIF reported a net loss of US$11.1 million compared with net income of US$2.2 million a year earlier. Sales advanced 71.4% to US$78.3 million.

BUSINESS

AMERICAN SENSORS INC. is engaged in the business of developing, manufacturing and marketing products to monitor indoor air quality. The Company currently produces a line of detectors which signal the presence of hazardous gases in residential, marine and industrial environments.

ANNUAL EARNINGS

	6/30/95	6/30/94	6/30/95	6/30/94
	---US $---		---C $---	
Earnings Per Share	0.25	0.23	0.34	0.32

ANNUAL FINANCIAL DATA

RECORD OF EARNINGS (IN THOUSANDS):

	6/30/95	6/30/94	6/30/95	6/30/94
Total Revenues	45,691	11,946	62,702	16,514
Costs & Expenses	43,289	10,810	59,406	14,943
Operating Income	2,402	1,136	3,296	1,570
Income Bef Income Tax	2,402	1,136	3,296	1,570
Income Tax	200	...	274	...
Net Income	2,202	1,136	3,022	1,570
Average Shares Outstg	8,914	4,880	8,914	4,880

BALANCE SHEET (IN THOUSANDS):

Cash & Cash Equivalents	7,865	8,410	10,793	11,626
Receivables, Net	5,613	6,151	7,703	8,503
Inventories	32,410	1,579	44,476	2,183
Gross Property	8,016	829	11,000	1,146
Accumulated Depreciation	1,092	153	1,499	212
Long-Term Debt	364	...	500	...
Stockholders' Equity	47,937	16,242	65,784	22,452
Total Assets	62,332	18,578	85,539	25,682
Total Current Assets	47,065	16,196	64,588	22,389
Total Current Liabilities	14,031	2,336	19,255	3,229
Net Working Capital	33,034	13,860	45,333	19,160
Year End Shs Outstg	10,143	8,031	10,143	8,031

STATISTICAL RECORD:

Return on Equity %	4.59	6.99
Return on Assets %	3.53	6.11
Operating Profit Margin %	5.26	9.51
Net Profit Margin %	4.82	9.51
Book Value Per Share	4.73	2.02

Converted at 1995, US$0.7287= 1 Canadian $; 1994, US$0.7234= 1 Canadian $

OFFICERS:
W. L. Koyle, Chmn.
M. Lupynec, Pres. & C.E.O.
R. S. Gill, V.P. & C.F.O.
J. F. Walsh, V.P.
INCORPORATED: Ontario, May, 1993
PRINCIPAL OFFICE: 100 Tempo Avenue
Toronto, Ontario Canada M2H 2N8

TELEPHONE NUMBER: 416-496-5900
NO. OF EMPLOYEES: 494
ANNUAL MEETING: In Sept. (tentative)
SHAREHOLDERS: N/A
INSTITUTIONAL HOLDINGS:
No. of Institutions: 6
Shares Held: 280,360

REGISTRAR(S): Equity Transfer, Toronto, Ontario, Canada

TRANSFER AGENT(S): Equity Transfer, Toronto, Ontario, Canada

ANDYNE COMPUTING LIMITED

YIELD ...
P/E RATIO ...

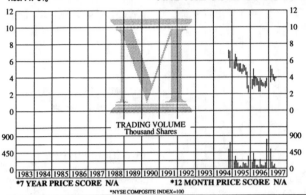

*7 YEAR PRICE SCORE N/A   *12 MONTH PRICE SCORE N/A
*NYSE COMPOSITE INDEX=100

TRADING VOLUME
Thousand Shares

INTERIM EARNINGS (Per Share, US $):

Qtr.	Dec.	Mar.	June	Sept.
1994-95	------------------d0.04------------------			
1995-96	------------------d0.26------------------			
1996-97	0.04	...	...	...

INTERIM DIVIDENDS (Per Share):

Amt.	Decl.	Ex.	Rec.	Pay.
	No dividends paid.			

CAPITALIZATION (9/30/96):

	($000)	(%)
Stockholders' Equity	7,986	100.0
Total	7,986	100.0

RECENT DEVELOPMENTS: For the three months ended 12/31/96, net earnings totaled C$355,000 versus a net loss of C$250,000 the previous year. Total sales jumped 56.6% to C$5.1 million from C$3.3 million a year earlier. Products sales climbed 35.7% to C$4.0 million from C$2.9 million the year before. Higher products sales were generated by the Company's international distributors and French subsidiary, Andyne France. International product sales, as a percentage of total product sales, grew to approximately 39% versus approximately 31% in the same year-earlier quarter. Services sales more than tripled to C$1.2 million compared with C$343,000 the prior year due to increased maintenance revenues stemming from a larger customer base. Gross margin surged 67.3% to C$4.5 million from C$2.7 million in 1995. Income from operations was C$414,000 compared with a loss of C$288,000 the previous year.

BUSINESS

ANDYNE COMPUTING LIMITED is engaged in the development, marketing and support of software applications that provide a visual interface for information access and reporting. ADYNF's products, Andyne GQL and Andyne PaBLO, exploit client/server computing technology to provide powerful access by end-users to database information stored on server computers. The Company's products are designed for medium to large business, government and institutional organizations that require on-line access to data stored in relational databases.

ANNUAL EARNINGS

	9/30/96	9/30/95	9/30/96	9/30/95
	----------US $----------		----------C $----------	
Earnings Per Share	d0.26	d0.04	d0.36	d0.06

ANNUAL FINANCIAL DATA

RECORD OF EARNINGS (IN THOUSANDS):

	9/30/96	9/30/95	9/30/96	9/30/95
Total Revenues	12,119	8,160	16,517	10,950
Costs & Expenses	10,983	8,510	14,969	11,420
Depreciation & Amort	696	387	948	519
Operating Income	440	d737	600	d989
Income Bef Income Tax	d2,230	d519	d3,040	d697
Income Tax	cr291	cr181	cr396	cr243
Net Income	d1,940	d338	d2,644	d454
Net Extraordinary Items	d2,812	...	d3,832	...
Average Shares Outstg	7,404	7,153	7,404	7,153

BALANCE SHEET (IN THOUSANDS):

Cash & Cash Equivalents	2,896	2,844	3,947	3,817
Receivables, Net	4,335	4,249	5,909	5,702
Inventories	225	101	307	135
Gross Property	3,335	2,445	4,546	3,281
Accumulated Depreciation	1,407	844	1,917	1,132
Stockholders' Equity	7,986	10,081	10,884	13,528
Total Assets	10,613	12,051	14,465	16,172
Total Current Assets	8,005	7,666	10,911	10,287
Total Current Liabilities	2,627	1,727	3,581	2,318
Net Working Capital	5,378	5,938	7,330	7,969
Year End Shs Outstg	7,404	7,404	7,404	7,404

STATISTICAL RECORD:

Operating Profit Margin %	3.63	...		
Book Value Per Share	1.08	1.36		

Converted at 1996, US$0.7337= 1 Canadian $; 1995, US$0.7452= 1 Canadian $

OFFICERS:
A. C. Thompson, Chmn., Pres. & C.E.O.
C. J. McCann, V.P., C.F.O. & Treas.
D. L. Weinstein, Sec.

INCORPORATED: Nov. 26, 1976

PRINCIPAL OFFICE: 552 Princess Street, Kingston, Ontario Canada K7L 1C7

TELEPHONE NUMBER: 613-548-4355

NO. OF EMPLOYEES: N/A

ANNUAL MEETING: N/A

SHAREHOLDERS: N/A

INSTITUTIONAL HOLDINGS:
No. of Institutions: 3
Shares Held: 137,343

REGISTRAR(S): The R-M Trust Company, Toronto; Chemical Mellon Shareholder Services, New York

TRANSFER AGENT(S): The R-M Trust Company, Toronto; Chemical Mellon Shareholder Services, New York.

ANSALDO SIGNAL N.V.

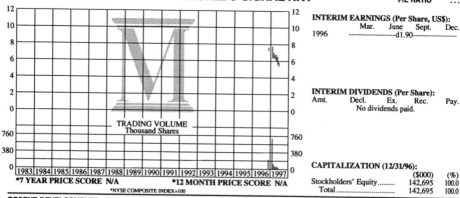

7 YEAR PRICE SCORE N/A   **12 MONTH PRICE SCORE N/A**
*NYSE COMPOSITE INDEX=100

TRADING VOLUME
Thousand Shares

INTERIM EARNINGS (Per Share, US$):

	Mar.	June	Sept.	Dec.
1996	----------------d1.90----------------			

INTERIM DIVIDENDS (Per Share):

Amt.	Decl.	Ex.	Rec.	Pay.
	No dividends paid.			

CAPITALIZATION (12/31/96):

	($000)	(%)
Stockholders' Equity	142,695	100.0
Total	142,695	100.0

RECENT DEVELOPMENTS: For the year ended 12/31/96, the Company reported a net loss of $38.9 million compared with net income of $6.4 million in the same period of 1995. Earnings included a $17.3 million reorganization charge and a $15.1 million write-off of intangible assets related to in-process technology. Revenues rose 18.1% to $353.5 million from $299.3 million the year before. Gross profit declined 9.0% to $56.9 million from $62.5 million a year earlier. In March 1997, ASIGF announced the elimination of several divisions within the Company, a reduction in operating costs, the elimination of several corporate management positions and their related staff, and a shift in strategy from focusing on growth to focusing on customer performance and investor profitability. The Company expects to regain some positive earnings momentum in the third and fourth quarters of 1997 via a mandate to reduce costs, increase efficiency, and maximize internal synergies brought on by the merger with Union Switch and Signal.

BUSINESS

ANSALDO SIGNAL N.V., an Ansaldo/Finmeccanica-affiliated company, was formed by the amalgamation of five sister companies: Union Switch & Signal in the U.S.; Ansaldo Segnalamento Ferroviario S.p.A. of Italy; CSEE Transport S.A. of France; AT Signal Systems A.B. of Sweden; and Ansaldo Trasporti Signaling Ltd., an Irish limited liability company. The chief business of the amalgamated companies is the design, engineering, production, and distribution of railway signaling devices.

ANNUAL EARNINGS

	12/31/96	12/31/95	12/31/96	12/31/95
	--------------US $--------------		------------NLG------------	
Earnings Per Share	d1.90	...	d3.32	...

ANNUAL FINANCIAL DATA

RECORD OF EARNINGS (IN THOUSANDS):

	12/31/96	12/31/95	12/31/96	12/31/95
Total Revenues	353,500	299,347	616,821	481,343
Costs & Expenses	371,539	287,446	648,297	462,206
Operating Income	d18,039	11,901	d31,476	19,137
Income Bef Income Tax	d41,002	6,999	d71,544	11,254
Income Tax	cr2,714	3,508	cr4,736	5,641
Eq. Earnings in Affils.	d608	2,917	d1,061	4,690
Net Income	d38,896	6,408	d67,869	10,304
Avg.Shs. Oustg.	20,488	...	20,488	...

BALANCE SHEET (IN THOUSANDS):

Cash & Cash Equivalents	89	...	155	...
Stockholders' Equity	142,695	...	248,988	...
Total Assets	149,977	...	261,694	...
Total Current Assets	89	...	155	...
Total Current Liabilities	7,282	...	12,706	...
Net Working Capital	d7,193	...	d12,551	...
Year End Shs Outstg	20,449	...	20,449	...

STATISTICAL RECORD:

Return on Equity %	...	...		
Return on Assets %	...	...		
Operating Profit Margin %	...	3.98		
Net Profit Margin %	...	2.14		
Book Value Per Share	6.98	...		

Converted at 1996, US$0.5731= 1 Netherlands guilder; 1995, US$0.6219= 1 Netherlands guilder

OFFICERS:
J. N. Sanders, Chairman
J. A. Kirby, V.P. & C.F.O.
M. P. Rivera, V.P. & Gen. Coun.

INCORPORATED: Netherlands, Nov. 13, 1996

PRINCIPAL OFFICE: Ansaldo Signal, N.V. c/o Union Switch & Signal, Inc., 1901 Main Street, Suite 1150 Columbia SC 29201

TELEPHONE NUMBER: 803-929-1200

NO. OF EMPLOYEES: N/A

ANNUAL MEETING: N/A

SHAREHOLDERS: N/A

INSTITUTIONAL HOLDINGS:
No. of Institutions: N/A
Shares Held: N/A

REGISTRAR(S): Sun Trust Bank, Atlanta, GA

TRANSFER AGENT(S): Sun Trust Bank, Atlanta, GA

ARAKIS ENERGY CORPORATION

YIELD ...
P/E RATIO ...

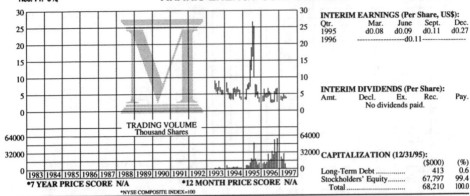

INTERIM EARNINGS (Per Share, US$):

Qtr.	Mar.	June	Sept.	Dec.
1995	d0.08	d0.09	d0.11	d0.27
1996	------------------d0.11------------------			

INTERIM DIVIDENDS (Per Share):

Amt.   Decl.   Ex.   Rec.   Pay.
No dividends paid.

CAPITALIZATION (12/31/95):

	($000)	(%)
Long-Term Debt	413	0.6
Stockholders' Equity.........	67,797	99.4
Total	68,210	100.0

RECENT DEVELOPMENTS: For the quarter ended 9/30/96, net loss was $3.0 million, unchanged from the same period of 1995. Revenues leapt to $1.2 million, from $245,040 the year before. Loss from operations before taxes was $2.7 million compared with $3.0 million in 1995. The decline in earnings was primarily attributable to the continued costs associated with the ongoing exploration and development of the Company's Sudan oil concession. During the quarter, the Company began sustained delivery of crude oil through the Early Production System (EPS) in the Heglig Develop- ment Block, to the Government of the Republic of Sudan. As a result, 78,000 barrels of oil were delivered to the Heglig field gate. The Company's EPS has the ability to deliver 25,000 barrels of oil per day. During December 1996, AKSEF formed a consortium, subject to execution of formal agreements, to proceed with an accelerated program of exploration, delineation of recent discoveries and devel- opment on the Company's Sudan concession, in addition to the immediate construction of an export pipeline.

BUSINESS

ARAKIS ENERGY CORPORA- TION, along with its wholly-owned subsidiaries, is engaged in the explo- ration and development of oil and gas reserves internationally, and in the development, production and sale of natural gas and to a lesser extent, the operation and maintenance of gas wells for a fee in the United States.

ANNUAL EARNINGS

	12/31/95	12/31/94	12/31/95	12/31/94
	------------US $------------		------------C $------------	
Earnings Per Share	d0.55	d0.18	d0.75	d0.25

ANNUAL FINANCIAL DATA

RECORD OF EARNINGS (IN THOUSANDS):

Total Revenues	2,059	2,227	2,809	3,124
Costs & Expenses	7,828	5,136	10,680	7,204
Depreciation & Amort	1,090	693	1,487	972
Operating Income	d6,859	d3,601	d9,358	d5,052
Income Bef Income Tax	d14,104	d3,601	d19,245	d5,052
Net Income	d14,104	d3,601	d19,245	d5,052
Average Shares Outstg	25,884	20,607	25,884	20,607

BALANCE SHEET (IN THOUSANDS):

Cash & Cash Equivalents	5,293	3,403	7,222	4,773
Receivables, Net	3,154	890	4,304	1,248
Gross Property	69,667	47,994	95,056	67,322
Accumulated Depreciation	1,850	1,936	2,524	2,716
Long-Term Debt	413	3,236	563	4,539
Stockholders' Equity	67,797	43,697	92,505	61,295
Total Assets	77,267	50,691	105,427	71,106
Total Current Assets	8,607	4,634	11,744	6,500
Total Current Liabilities	6,719	3,758	9,168	5,272
Net Working Capital	1,888	875	2,576	1,228
Year End Shs Outstg	30,875	21,947	30,875	21,947

STATISTICAL RECORD:

Return on Equity %	...	...		
Return on Assets %	...	...		
Operating Profit Margin %	...	...		
Net Profit Margin %	...	...		
Book Value Per Share	2.20	1.99		

Converted at 1995, US$0.7329= 1 Canadian $; 1994, US$0.7129= 1 Canadian $

OFFICERS:
L. R. Khan, Chmn.
J. G. McLeod, Exec. V.P.
P. L. Holstein, Exec. V.P.
D. Robinson, V.P.
INCORPORATED: Canada, 1991
PRINCIPAL OFFICE: 540- 5th Avenue, S.W.
Suite 320 Calgary Canada

TELEPHONE NUMBER: 403-263-2471
NO. OF EMPLOYEES: 175
ANNUAL MEETING: In Jun.
SHAREHOLDERS: 730
INSTITUTIONAL HOLDINGS:
No. of Institutions: 37
Shares Held: 13,075,635

REGISTRAR(S): Pacific Corporate Trust Company, Vancouver.

TRANSFER AGENT(S): Pacific Corporate Trust Company, Vancouver.

AREL COMMUNICATIONS & SOFTWARE

YIELD ...
P/E RATIO ...

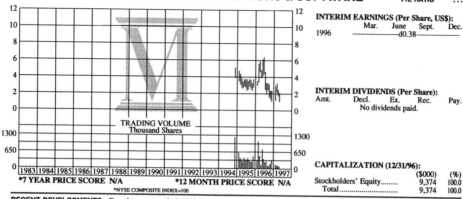

7 YEAR PRICE SCORE N/A　　**12 MONTH PRICE SCORE N/A**

*NYSE COMPOSITE INDEX=100

INTERIM EARNINGS (Per Share, US$):

	Mar.	June	Sept.	Dec.
1996		----d0.38----		

INTERIM DIVIDENDS (Per Share):

Amt.	Decl.	Ex.	Rec.	Pay.
		No dividends paid.		

CAPITALIZATION (12/31/96):

	($000)	(%)
Stockholders' Equity	9,374	100.0
Total	9,374	100.0

RECENT DEVELOPMENTS: For the year ended 12/31/96, the Company reported a net loss of $2.1 million compared with net income of $1.4 million in the corresponding period of 1995. Results included a charge of $280,000 related to the formation of Arel Net Ltd., the acquisition of i-Fax core technology, and the receipt of technical expertise from Elron Electronic Industries Ltd. The increase in cost of sales and services, which was associated with the development of new products and the expansion of ARLCF's marketing activities, had a negative effect on earnings. Revenues and sales from services declined 25.5% to $5.0 million from $6.3 million a year earlier. This was related to price erosion, an increase in competition and the cancellation of a major product.

BUSINESS

AREL COMMUNICATIONS AND SOFTWARE LTD is engaged in designing, developing, marketing, producing, integrating and supporting, on a worldwide basis, software for a family of message-switching wide-area network systems called ARCOM, as well as software for a family of products in the interactive distance earning market.

ANNUAL EARNINGS

	12/31/96	12/31/95	12/31/96	12/31/95
	----US $----		----NIS----	
Earnings Per Share	d0.38	0.25	d1.24	0.79

ANNUAL FINANCIAL DATA

RECORD OF EARNINGS (IN THOUSANDS):

Total Revenues	5,001	6,276	16,290	19,756
Costs & Expenses	7,249	5,019	23,612	15,797
Operating Income	d2,248	1,258	d7,322	3,959
Income Bef Income Tax	d2,036	1,583	d6,632	4,983
Income Tax	...	179	...	563
Minority Interests	18	...	59	...
Net Income	d2,054	1,404	d6,691	4,420
Average Shares Outstg	5,400	5,583	5,400	5,583

BALANCE SHEET (IN THOUSANDS):

Cash & Cash Equivalents	6,660	7,055	21,695	22,206
Receivables, Net	2,998	3,829	9,764	12,052
Inventories	130	137	422	430
Gross Property	1,759	1,451	5,730	4,566
Accumulated Depreciation	591	326	1,924	1,026
Stockholders' Equity	9,374	11,068	30,535	34,838
Total Assets	11,203	12,342	36,492	38,849
Total Current Assets	9,788	11,021	31,881	34,689
Total Current Liabilities	1,264	1,166	4,117	3,669
Net Working Capital	8,524	9,855	27,764	31,020
Year End Shs Outstg	5,400	5,400	5,400	5,400

STATISTICAL RECORD:

Return on Equity %	...	12.69		
Return on Assets %	...	11.38		
Operating Profit Margin %	...	20.04		
Net Profit Margin %	...	22.37		
Book Value Per Share	1.74	2.05		

Converted at 1996, US$0.3070= 1 New Israeli Shekel; 1995, US$0.3177= 1 New Israeli Shekel

OFFICERS:
S. Klier, Chmn.
I. Gross, Pres.
R. Ben-Nun, C.E.O.
S. Tauber, Fin. Contr.

INCORPORATED: Israel, 1982

PRINCIPAL OFFICE: 3 Hayarden Street, P.O. Box 76, Yavne 70600 Israel

TELEPHONE NUMBER: 972-8-420880

NO. OF EMPLOYEES: 45

ANNUAL MEETING: N/A

SHAREHOLDERS: 44

INSTITUTIONAL HOLDINGS:
No. of Institutions: N/A
Shares Held: N/A

REGISTRAR(S): N/A

TRANSFER AGENT(S): N/A

ARIELY ADVERTISING LTD.

YIELD 12.2%
P/E RATIO 6.1

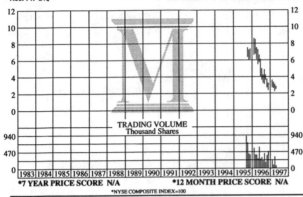

TRADING VOLUME
Thousand Shares

1983 1984 1985 1986 1987 1988 1989 1990 1991 1992 1993 1994 1995 1996 1997
*7 YEAR PRICE SCORE N/A   *12 MONTH PRICE SCORE N/A
*NYSE COMPOSITE INDEX=100

INTERIM EARNINGS (Per Share, US$):
1995 ------------------ 1.02 ------------------
1996 ------------------ 0.45 ------------------

INTERIM DIVIDENDS (Per Share):

Amt.	Decl.	Ex.	Rec.	Pay.
0.32	3/28/96	4/09/96	4/11/96	5/01/96
0.335	3/17/97	3/25/97	3/27/97	4/17/97

Indicated div.:$0.34

CAPITALIZATION (12/31/95):

	($000)	(%)
Minority Interests.............	36	0.6
Stockholders' Equity.........	5,816	99.4
Total..............................	5,852	100.0

RECENT DEVELOPMENTS: For the year ended 12/31/96, net income was NIS 4.5 million (US$1.4 million) compared with NIS 7.7 million (US$2.4 million) the year before. Commission and fees declined 11.8% to NIS 123.0 million (US$37.8 million) from NIS 139.4 million (US$42.9 million) a year earlier. Gross profit was NIS 21.7 million (US$6.7 million), down 8.4% from NIS 23.7 million (US$7.3 million) the previous year. Operating income was NIS 8.7 million (US$2.7 million) versus NIS 12.4 million (US$3.8 million) the year before. For the quarter ended 12/31/96, net income was NIS 789,000 (US$243,000) compared with NIS 2.0 million (US$600,000) the previous year. Commissions and fees were NIS 28.4 million (US$8.7 million), down 3.3% from NIS 29.4 million (US$9.0 million) a year earlier. Operating income was NIS 1.7 million (US$525,000) versus NIS 2.6 million (US$811,000) in the comparable prior-year period.

BUSINESS

ARIELY ADVERTISING LTD. provides a broad range of advertising services in Israel, including market analysis, the development of marketing strategies and creative concepts, media planning and the placement of advertisements in various media such as television, magazines, newspapers, radio and billboards.

ANNUAL EARNINGS

	12/31/95	12/31/94	12/31/95	12/31/94
	----------US $----------		-----------NIS-----------	
Earnings Per Share	1.02	0.06	3.21	0.18

ANNUAL FINANCIAL DATA

RECORD OF EARNINGS (IN THOUSANDS):

Total Revenues	40,057	30,644	126,084	92,468
Costs & Expenses	36,490	29,817	114,857	89,973
Operating Income	3,567	827	11,227	2,495
Income Bef Income Tax	3,464	445	10,903	1,343
Income Tax	1,150	301	3,620	908
Eq. Earnings in Affils.	8	d125	25	d377
Minority Interests	110	cr84	345	cr254
Net Income	2,212	103	6,963	312
Average Shares Outstg	2,169	1,680	2,169	1,680

BALANCE SHEET (IN THOUSANDS):

Cash & Cash Equivalents	6,135	174	19,312	524
Receivables, Net	6,173	5,904	19,429	17,814
Gross Property	2,455	2,362	7,728	7,128
Accumulated Depreciation	1,243	1,117	3,914	3,370
Long-Term Debt	...	371	...	1,121
Stockholders' Equity	5,816	d900	18,307	d2,716
Total Assets	14,298	7,942	45,005	23,965
Total Current Assets	12,635	6,383	39,769	19,260
Total Current Liabilities	7,861	6,760	24,745	20,398
Net Working Capital	4,773	d377	15,024	d1,138
Year End Shs Outstg	2,950	1,383	2,950	1,383

STATISTICAL RECORD:

Return on Equity %	38.03	...		
Return on Assets %	15.47	1.30		
Operating Profit Margin %	8.90	2.70		
Net Profit Margin %	5.52	0.34		
Book Value Per Share	1.97	...		

Converted at 1995, US$0.3177= 1 New Israeli Shekel; 1994, US$0.3314= 1 New Israeli Shekel

OFFICERS:
U. Ariely, Chmn.
A. Tal-Shir, Managing Dir.
V. Viduchinsky, C.F.O.

INCORPORATED: Dec., 1965

PRINCIPAL OFFICE: 140 Rothchild Blvd. Tel Aviv 65272 Israel

TELEPHONE NUMBER: 972-3-563-9001

NO. OF EMPLOYEES: 101

ANNUAL MEETING: N/A

SHAREHOLDERS: N/A

INSTITUTIONAL HOLDINGS:
No. of Institutions: N/A
Shares Held: N/A

REGISTRAR(S):

TRANSFER AGENT(S): American Stock Transfer & Trust Company, New York, NY

ASE TEST, LIMITED

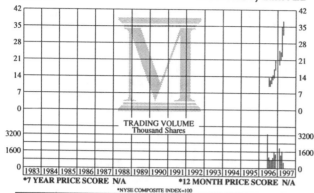

*7 YEAR PRICE SCORE N/A   *12 MONTH PRICE SCORE N/A

*NYSE COMPOSITE INDEX=100

TRADING VOLUME
Thousand Shares

1983 1984 1985 1986 1987 1988 1989 1990 1991 1992 1993 1994 1995 1996 1997

INTERIM EARNINGS (Per Share, US$):

	Mar.	June	Sept.	Dec.
1995		---------------- 0.92 ----------------		

INTERIM DIVIDENDS (Per Share):

Amt.	Decl.	Ex.	Rec.	Pay.
	No dividends paid.			

CAPITALIZATION (12/31/95):

	($000)	(%)
Long-Term Debt	18,769	29.7
Stockholders' Equity........	44,441	70.3
Total	63,210	100.0

RECENT DEVELOPMENTS: For the year ended 12/31/96, the Company reported a 30.4% increase in net income to $14.9 million. Moreover, sales jumped 35.7% to $48.2 million. For the fourth quarter ended 12/31/96, net income improved to T$130.2 million. Sales climbed 20.5% to T$380.6 million ($13.8 million). Income before taxes improved 35.6% to T$128.2 million ($4.7 million). As a result of the industry's being more cautious in capacity expansion and inventory control, the Company does not expect to see sequential growth in the short term. Separately, the Company acquired 100% of ASE Malaysia from ASTSF's parent company ASE Inc. 2311.TW. The transaction was valued at $98.4 million. The acquisition of ASE Malaysia fits into the Company's growth strategy as it adds to its testing capacity and expands its customer base.

BUSINESS

ASE TEST LTD. is an integrated-circuit testing firm which is 79.6% owned by Taiwan's integrated-circuit packaging firm Advanced Semiconductor Engineering Inc 2311.TW.

ANNUAL EARNINGS

	12/31/95	12/31/94	12/31/95	12/31/94
	---------US $---------		-----------NT$-----------	
Earnings Per Share	0.92	0.42	25.13	10.98

ANNUAL FINANCIAL DATA

RECORD OF EARNINGS (IN THOUSANDS):

	12/31/95	12/31/94	12/31/95	12/31/94
Total Revenues	35,705	19,043	975,558	501,131
Costs & Expenses	25,336	14,498	692,233	381,535
Operating Income	10,370	4,545	283,325	119,596
Income Bef Income Tax	9,947	3,822	271,789	100,591
Income Tax	cr1,533	cr227	cr41,878	cr5,978
Net Income	11,480	4,050	313,667	106,569
Average Shares Outstg	12,480	9,711	12,480	9,711

BALANCE SHEET (IN THOUSANDS):

Cash & Cash Equivalents	1,830	8,983	49,992	236,403
Receivables, Net	8,439	4,624	230,582	121,682
Inventories	320	324	8,754	8,532
Gross Property	72,551	39,840	1,982,271	1,048,428
Accumulated Depreciation	13,692	8,470	374,110	222,887
Long-Term Debt	18,769	8,795	512,826	231,443
Stockholders' Equity	44,441	32,702	1,214,226	860,579
Total Assets	73,568	48,243	2,010,063	1,269,553
Total Current Assets	12,634	14,869	345,186	391,283
Total Current Liabilities	10,220	6,713	279,231	176,645
Net Working Capital	2,414	8,156	65,955	214,638
Year End Shs. Outstg	62,400	48,000	62,400	48,000

STATISTICAL RECORD:

Return on Equity %	25.83	12.38		
Return on Assets %	15.60	8.39		
Operating Profit Margin %	29.04	23.87		
Net Profit Margin %	32.15	21.27		
Book Value Per Share	0.71	0.68		

Converted at 1995, US$0.0366=1 New Taiwanese $; 1994, US$0.0380=1 New Taiwanese $

OFFICERS:
J. C. S. Chang, Chmn.
D. Pan, Pres.
J. Tung, Acting C.F.O.
T. H. Tsai, Fin. Dir.

INCORPORATED: Singapore, 1996

PRINCIPAL OFFICE: 2/F 25 Kai-Far Road Nantze Export Processing Zone, Kaohsiung China (Rep. Of Taiwan)

TELEPHONE NUMBER: 8867-363-6641

NO. OF EMPLOYEES: 656

ANNUAL MEETING: N/A

SHAREHOLDERS: N/A

INSTITUTIONAL HOLDINGS:
No. of Institutions: N/A
Shares Held: N/A

REGISTRAR(S): Bank of New York, New York.

TRANSFER AGENT(S): Bank of New York, New York.

ASM INTERNATIONAL N.V.

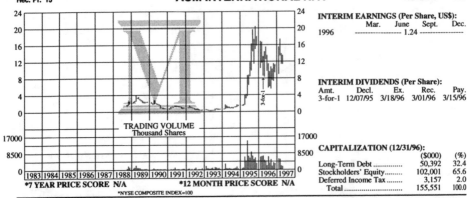

*7 YEAR PRICE SCORE N/A   *12 MONTH PRICE SCORE N/A
*NYSE COMPOSITE INDEX=100

INTERIM EARNINGS (Per Share, US$):

	Mar.	June	Sept.	Dec.
1996		---- 1.24 ----		

INTERIM DIVIDENDS (Per Share):

Amt.	Decl.	Ex.	Rec.	Pay.
3-for-1	12/07/95	3/18/96	3/01/96	3/15/96

CAPITALIZATION (12/31/96):

	($000)	(%)
Long-Term Debt	50,392	32.4
Stockholders' Equity........	102,001	65.6
Deferred Income Tax	3,157	2.0
Total	155,551	100.0

RECENT DEVELOPMENTS: For the year ended 12/31/96, net income declined 7.0% to NLG68.4 million compared with NLG73.6 million in the same period of 1995. Net sales slipped 1.9% to NLG658.2 million from NLG670.9 million the year before. The 7.0% increase in front-end sales to NLG361.2 million was related to stronger sales for the Eagle 10, a PECVD product manufactured in Japan; epitaxial reactors; and A600 UHV products. A large cancellation of shipments mid-year for the A400 vertical furnace kept the shipments of this product below the 1995 level. At the same time, the customer base for this product was significantly enlarged. However, back-end operations fell 10.0% to NLG297.0 million. This reflected a decrease in sales and the expenses associated with the development and introduction of new products. Front-end and back-end equipment operations accounted for 55.0% and 45.0% of total revenues, respectively, compared with 51.0% and 49.0% in 1995.

BUSINESS

ASM INTERNATIONAL N.V., headquartered in Bilthoven, the Netherlands, designs, manufactures and markets equipment and materials used to produce semiconductor devices. The Company provides production solutions for semiconductor wafer processing, assembly and packaging through its facilities in the United States, Europe, Japan and South East Asia.

ANNUAL EARNINGS

	12/31/96	12/31/95	12/31/96	12/31/95
	------------US $------------		------------Guilders------------	
Earnings Per Share	1.24	4.37	2.17	7.02

ANNUAL FINANCIAL DATA

RECORD OF EARNINGS (IN THOUSANDS):

	12/31/96	12/31/95	12/31/96	12/31/95
Total Revenues	377,039	417,203	658,238	670,852
Costs & Expenses	320,260	340,024	559,113	546,750
Operating Income	56,778	77,179	99,125	124,102
Income Bef Income Tax	52,694	68,625	91,994	110,348
Income Tax	2,565	4,106	4,476	6,603
Minority Interests	dr10,948	dr18,760	dr19,114	dr30,166
Net Income	39,181	45,759	68,402	73,579
Average Shares Outstg	31,565	10,476	31,565	10,476

BALANCE SHEET (IN THOUSANDS):

Cash & Cash Equivalents	32,855	36,568	57,358	58,801
Receivables, Net	95,352	93,218	166,466	149,893
Inventories	80,404	69,017	140,370	110,977
Gross Property	219,487	183,085	383,183	294,397
Accumulated Depreciation	95,332	85,114	166,431	136,862
Long-Term Debt	50,392	53,368	87,975	85,815
Stockholders' Equity	102,001	45,755	178,075	73,573
Total Assets	350,542	320,571	611,980	515,471
Total Current Assets	226,387	222,600	395,228	357,936
Total Current Liabilities	138,972	170,216	242,618	273,703
Net Working Capital	87,415	52,385	152,610	84,233
Year End Shs Outstg	33,058	10,461	33,058	10,461

STATISTICAL RECORD:

Return on Equity %	38.41	100.01		
Return on Assets %	11.18	14.27		
Operating Profit Margin %	15.06	18.50		
Net Profit Margin %	10.39	10.97		
Book Value Per Share	3.09	4.37		

Converted at 1996, US$0.5728= 1 Netherlands guilder; 1995, US$0.6219= 1 Netherlands guilder

OFFICERS:
A. H. del Prado, Pres. & C.E.O.
R. de Jong, V.P. & C.F.O.
D. Queyssac, C.O.O.-Front End Opers.
P. L. See Pong, V.P.
F. Tomino, V.P.

INCORPORATED: Netherlands, 1968

PRINCIPAL OFFICE: Jan van Eycklaan 10
3723 BC Bilthoven Netherlands NL-3723

TELEPHONE NUMBER: 31 030-2298411

NO. OF EMPLOYEES: 4,037

ANNUAL MEETING: I May

SHAREHOLDERS: N/A

INSTITUTIONAL HOLDINGS:
No. of Institutions: N/A
Shares Held: N/A

REGISTRAR(S): Citibank, New York, NY, USA, ABN AMRO Bank, Breda, Netherlands

TRANSFER AGENT(S): Citibank, New York, NY, USA, ABN AMRO Bank, Breda, Netherlands

ASM LITHOGRAPHY HOLDING N.V.

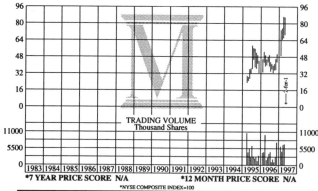

INTERIM EARNINGS (Per Share):

Qtr.	Mar.	June	Sep.	Dec.
1995		1.26		
1996		1.82		

INTERIM DIVIDENDS (Per Share):

Amt.	Decl.	Ex.	Rec.	Pay.
2-for-1	...	5/12/97	5/09/97	5/14/97

TRADING VOLUME
Thousand Shares

1983 1984 1985 1986 1987 1988 1989 1990 1991 1992 1993 1994 1995 1996 1997

*7 YEAR PRICE SCORE N/A   *12 MONTH PRICE SCORE N/A
*NYSE COMPOSITE INDEX=100

CAPITALIZATION (12/31/96):

	($000)	(%)
Stockholders' Equity	369,213	100.0
Total	369,213	100.0

RECENT DEVELOPMENTS: For the year ended 12/31/96, net income was NLG 217.7 million, up 65.7% from NLG 131.4 million in the prior year. Results for 1996 and 1995 included charges of NLG 40.1 million and NLG 36.3 million, respectively, for technical development credits. Net sales climbed 45.1% to NLG 1.33 billion. The increase in sales was attributed primarily to stronger units sales, up 15.8% to 205 units in 1996, as well as an increase in the average unit sales prices for wafer steppers. The increase in average unit sales prices resulted from higher base prices and a change in the sales mix, reflecting increased unit sales of more advanced wafer steppers and higher sales of units incorporating factory-installed options. Gross profit rose 59.2% to NLG 534.6 million from NLG 335.8 million due primarily to increased sales, higher average prices and decreased cost per comparable unit.

BUSINESS

ASM LITHOGRAPHY HOLDING, N.V. is a holding company. Through its subsidiaries, the Company develops, markets and services advanced photolithography projection systems, known as wafer steppers, that are essential to the fabrication of modern integrated circuits (ICs). The Company supplies wafer steppers to IC manufacturers throughout the U.S., Asia and Western Europe and also provides its customers with a full range of support services.

ANNUAL EARNINGS

	12/31/96	12/31/95	12/31/96	12/31/95
	--US $--		--Guilders--	
Earnings Per Share	1.82	1.26	3.18	2.03

ANNUAL FINANCIAL DATA

RECORD OF EARNINGS (IN THOUSANDS):

Total Revenues	763,041	570,727	1,331,427	917,715
Costs & Expenses	570,600	440,783	995,637	708,768
Operating Income	192,441	129,944	335,790	208,947
Income Bef Income Tax	192,219	129,358	335,402	208,004
Income Tax	67,447	47,633	117,688	76,593
Net Income	124,772	81,725	217,714	131,411
Average Shares Outstg	68,510	64,750	68,510	64,750

BALANCE SHEET (IN THOUSANDS):

Cash & Cash Equivalents	94,911	49,789	165,610	80,060
Receivables, Net	237,888	168,415	415,089	270,807
Inventories	192,480	143,163	335,857	230,203
Gross Property	123,939	84,353	216,260	135,638
Accumulated Depreciation	46,911	38,557	81,854	61,998
Stockholders' Equity	369,213	188,815	644,238	303,610
Total Assets	615,111	409,874	1,073,304	659,067
Total Current Assets	528,435	363,687	922,065	584,800
Total Current Liabilities	241,092	208,306	420,680	334,951
Net Working Capital	287,344	155,381	501,385	249,849
Year End Shs Outstg	69,000	69,000	69,000	69,000

STATISTICAL RECORD:

Return on Equity %	33.79	43.28		
Return on Assets %	20.28	19.94		
Operating Profit Margin %	25.22	22.77		
Net Profit Margin %	16.35	14.32		
Book Value Per Share	5.35	2.74		

Converted at 1996, US$0.5731= 1 Netherlands guilder; 1995, US$0.6219= 1 Netherlands guilder

OFFICERS:
H. Bodt, Chairman
W. D. Maris, Pres. & C.E.O.
G. S. A. J. Verdonschot, C.F.O.
S. Wittekoek, Chief Exec. Scientist

INCORPORATED: Netherlands, 1984

PRINCIPAL OFFICE: De Run 1110, 5503 LA Veldhoven, NL-55031 Netherlands

TELEPHONE NUMBER: 31-40-230-3000

NO. OF EMPLOYEES: 1,423

ANNUAL MEETING: In Apr.

SHAREHOLDERS: N/A

INSTITUTIONAL HOLDINGS:
No. of Institutions: N/A
Shares Held: N/A

REGISTRAR(S): N/A

TRANSFER AGENT(S): Nederlands Centraal Instituut voor Giraal Effectenverkeer; Citibank, N.A., New York (for shares traded in the United States).

BAAN COMPANY N.V.

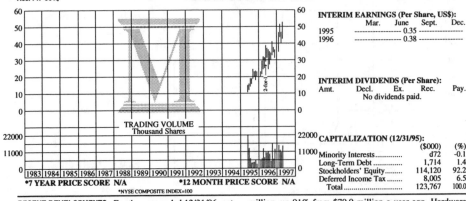

7 YEAR PRICE SCORE N/A   **12 MONTH PRICE SCORE N/A**
*NYSE COMPOSITE INDEX=100

INTERIM EARNINGS (Per Share, US$):

	Mar.	June	Sept.	Dec.
1995		------ 0.35 ------		
1996		------ 0.38 ------		

INTERIM DIVIDENDS (Per Share):

Amt.	Decl.	Ex.	Rec.	Pay.
No dividends paid.				

CAPITALIZATION (12/31/95):

	($000)	(%)
Minority Interests............	d72	-0.1
Long-Term Debt..............	1,714	1.4
Stockholders' Equity........	114,120	92.2
Deferred Income Tax.......	8,005	6.5
Total	123,767	100.0

RECENT DEVELOPMENTS: For the year ended 12/31/96, net income more than doubled to $36.3 million compared with $15.3 million in the corresponding period a year earlier. Revenues increased 79.4% to $388.0 million versus $216.2 million in 1995. License revenue increased 98% to $224.2 million for 1996 compared with $113.0 million in 1995. Service and maintenance revenues for the year were $152.4 million, up 91% from $79.9 million a year ago. Hardware and other revenues slipped to $11.3 million versus $23.4 million. For the quarter ended 12/31/96, net income more than doubled to $15.8 million compared with $6.8 million a year earlier. Revenues rose 64% to $123.9 million versus $75.6 million in 1995.

BUSINESS

BAAN COMPANY N.V. is a holding company. Through its subsidiaries, the Company is engaged in the provision of open systems, client/server-based Enterprise Resource Planning (ERP) software which permits the enterprise-wide management of resources and the integration of sales forecasting, component procurement, inventory management, manufacturing control, project management, distribution, transportation, finance, and other functions. BAANF'S principal source of revenues consists of license fees and related services, including consulting, implementation, training, and maintenance, as well as the resale of third party hardware on an original equipment manufacturer (OEM) basis.

ANNUAL EARNINGS

	12/31/95	12/31/94	12/31/95	12/31/94
	------US $------		------NLG------	
Earnings Per Share	0.35	0.08	0.56	0.14

ANNUAL FINANCIAL DATA

RECORD OF EARNINGS (IN THOUSANDS):

Total Revenues	216,210	122,924	347,660	213,373
Costs & Expenses	188,028	115,416	302,344	200,340
Depreciation & Amort	4,701	2,172	7,559	3,770
Operating Income	23,481	5,336	37,757	9,262
Income Bef Income Tax	25,168	4,345	40,470	7,542
Income Tax	9,817	2,171	15,785	3,768
Minority Interests	72	976	116	1,694
Net Income	15,279	1,198	24,569	2,080
Average Shares Outstg	44,522	39,694	44,522	39,694

BALANCE SHEET (IN THOUSANDS):

Cash & Cash Equivalents	35,727	6,885	57,448	11,951
Receivables, Net	87,226	34,431	140,257	59,766
Gross Property	42,371	29,452	68,132	51,123
Accumulated Depreciation	13,990	13,717	22,496	23,810
Long-Term Debt	1,714	2,005	2,756	3,480
Stockholders' Equity	114,120	27,811	183,502	48,275
Total Assets	186,621	77,587	300,082	134,676
Total Current Assets	131,067	46,695	210,753	81,054
Total Current Liabilities	59,327	41,409	95,396	71,878
Net Working Capital	71,740	5,286	115,356	9,175

STATISTICAL RECORD:

Return on Equity %	13.39	4.31		
Return on Assets %	8.19	1.54		
Operating Profit Margin %	10.86	4.34		
Net Profit Margin %	7.07	1.06		
Book Value Per Share	2.56	0.70		

Converted at 1995, US$0.6219= 1 Netherlands guilder; 1994, US$0.5761= 1 Netherlands guilder

OFFICERS:
J. Baan, Managing Dir. & Chmn.
J. G. Baan, Managing Dir. & Vice-Chmn.
T. C. Tinsley, Managing Dir. & Pres.

INCORPORATED: 1978

PRINCIPAL OFFICE: Zonneoordlaan 17 BG
Ede NL-6710 Netherlands

TELEPHONE NUMBER: 083-805-8888

NO. OF EMPLOYEES: 1,525

ANNUAL MEETING: N/A

SHAREHOLDERS: N/A

INSTITUTIONAL HOLDINGS:
No. of Institutions: N/A
Shares Held: N/A

REGISTRAR(S): Citibank N.A., New York, New York, and Barneveld Register, Barneveld.

TRANSFER AGENT(S): Citibank N.A., New York, New York, and Barneveld Register, Barneveld.

BALLARD POWER SYSTEMS, INC.

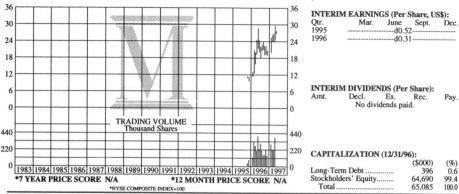

INTERIM EARNINGS (Per Share, US$):

Qtr.	Mar.	June	Sept.	Dec.
1995	---------------------d0.52----------------			
1996	---------------------d0.31----------------			

TRADING VOLUME
Thousand Shares

INTERIM DIVIDENDS (Per Share):

Amt.	Decl.	Ex.	Rec.	Pay.
	No dividends paid.			

1983 1984 1985 1986 1987 1988 1989 1990 1991 1992 1993 1994 1995 1996 1997

*7 YEAR PRICE SCORE N/A   *12 MONTH PRICE SCORE N/A

*NYSE COMPOSITE INDEX=100

CAPITALIZATION (12/31/96):

	($000)	(%)
Long-Term Debt	396	0.6
Stockholders' Equity.........	64,690	99.4
Total	65,085	100.0

RECENT DEVELOPMENTS: For the year ended 12/31/96, net loss was C$6.1 million compared with C$7.4 million in the same period of 1995. Total revenues were C$38.4 million, up 56.5% to C$24.5 million a year earlier. Revenues increased 22.7% to C$25.8 million compared with C$21.1 million in 1995. Investment income was C$2.7 million, up 81.9% from C$1.5 million the year before. Research and product development expenses increased 20.2% to C$15.4 million from C$12.8 million in 1995. Costs of revenues and expenses were C$44.5 million, up 39.6% from C$31.9 mil-

lion a year earlier. The improvement in revenues was primarily attributed to the number and value of long term fuel cell development and demonstration programs. BLDPF benefited from utilizing lower cost materials, improving product designs and automating the manufacturing process. In December 1996, the Company formed a subsidiary, Ballard Generation Systems. The subsidiary will be used to interact with strategic partners to manufacture, market and distribute fuel cell power systems to users.

BUSINESS

BALLARD POWER SYSTEMS, INC. develops and manufactures fuel cell power systems. These zero emission engines, which convert fuel into electricity without combustion, are used in: stationary power plants to provide electricity for buildings and equipment and in transportation vehicles including buses and automobiles. The Company commenced developing proton exchange membrane (PEM) fuel cells in 1983. Since 1989 the Company has been focused on commercializing this technology.

ANNUAL EARNINGS

	12/31/96	12/31/95	12/31/96	12/31/95
	--------------US $-------------		-----------C $-----------	
Earnings Per Share	d0.31	d0.52	d0.43	d0.71

ANNUAL FINANCIAL DATA

RECORD OF EARNINGS (IN THOUSANDS):

Total Revenues	28,052	17,966	38,370	24,514
Costs & Expenses	32,543	23,376	44,512	31,895
Operating Income	d4,490	d5,410	d6,142	d7,381
Income Bef Income Tax	d4,490	d5,410	d6,142	d7,381
Net Income	d4,490	d5,410	d6,142	d7,381
Average Shares Outstg	10,456	7,649	10,456	7,649

BALANCE SHEET (IN THOUSANDS):

Cash & Cash Equivalents	55,939	21,414	76,513	29,218
Receivables, Net	7,811	4,772	10,684	6,511
Inventories	1,769	2,001	2,419	2,730
Gross Property	16,135	9,909	22,070	13,520
Accumulated Depreciation	3,451	3,055	4,720	4,168
Long-Term Debt	396	803	541	1,096
Stockholders' Equity	64,690	24,924	88,483	34,007
Total Assets	78,323	35,399	107,130	48,300
Total Current Assets	65,638	28,545	89,780	38,948
Total Current Liabilities	12,791	9,627	17,495	13,136
Net Working Capital	52,848	18,918	72,285	25,812
Year End Shs Outstg	11,225	9,007	11,225	9,007

STATISTICAL RECORD:

Return on Equity %	...	...		
Return on Assets %	...	...		
Operating Profit Margin %	...	...		
Net Profit Margin %	...	...		
Book Value Per Share	5.76	2.77		

Converted at 1996, US$0.7311= 1 Canadian $; 1995, US$0.7329= 1 Canadian $

OFFICERS:
G. E. Ballard, Chmn.
F. A. Rasul, Pres. & C.E.O.
P. F. Howard, V.P.
K. B. Prater, V.P.
INCORPORATED: 1983
PRINCIPAL OFFICE: 9000 Glenlyon Parkway
Burnaby, British Columbia Canada

TELEPHONE NUMBER: 604-454-0900
NO. OF EMPLOYEES: N/A
ANNUAL MEETING: In May
SHAREHOLDERS: N/A
INSTITUTIONAL HOLDINGS:
No. of Institutions: 10
Shares Held: 989,004

REGISTRAR(S): Montreal Trust Company,
Vancouver, British, Columbia.

TRANSFER AGENT(S): Montreal Trust
Company, Vancouver, British, Columbia.

BASIC PETROLEUM INTERNATIONAL LTD.

YIELD ...
P/E RATIO 12.1

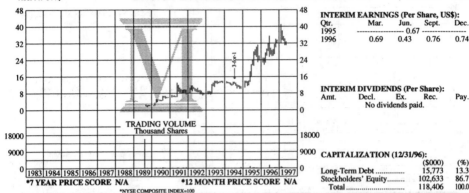

7 YEAR PRICE SCORE N/A   **12 MONTH PRICE SCORE N/A**
NYSE COMPOSITE INDEX=100

TRADING VOLUME
Thousand Shares

1983 1984 1985 1986 1987 1988 1989 1990 1991 1992 1993 1994 1995 1996 1997

INTERIM EARNINGS (Per Share, US$):

Qtr.	Mar.	Jun.	Sept.	Dec.
1995	------------------- 0.67 -------------------			
1996	0.69	0.43	0.76	0.74

INTERIM DIVIDENDS (Per Share):

Amt.	Decl.	Ex.	Rec.	Pay.
	No dividends paid.			

CAPITALIZATION (12/31/96):

	($000)	(%)
Long-Term Debt	15,773	13.3
Stockholders' Equity	102,633	86.7
Total	118,406	100.0

RECENT DEVELOPMENTS: For the year ended 12/31/96, net profit was $18.1 million compared with $8.4 million the year before. Total revenue from petroleum operations soared 77.2% to $80.8 million from $45.6 million a year earlier. Exploration and production revenue advanced 82.0% to $64.5 million, while refinery revenue jumped 60.6% to $16.4 million. Operating profit was $26.7 million, an increase of 85.1% over operating profit of $14.4 million

the previous year. The Government of Guatemala has approved the Company's agreement with Mexpetrol Guatemala for the purchase of Contract 5-93, which covers an exploration area of 629,467 acres located in the Central Peten area. The Company continues to wait for a completed contract from the Goverment of Guatemala relating to Area A-1-95, which covers 206,000 acres also located in the Central Peten area.

BUSINESS

BASIC PETROLEUM INTERNA-TIONAL LIMITED is an independent petroleum company engaged in the exploration, development and production of oil properties in the Central American country of Guatemala. The Company has interests in three contract areas located in two dinstinct geologic regions of Guatemala: Contracts 2-85, which includes the Xan field, and 1-92 in northwest Guatemala; and Contract 1-85 in central Guatemala, which encompasses the Rubelsanto, West Chinaja, Caribe and Tierra Blanca production fields.

ANNUAL EARNINGS

	12/31/96	12/31/95	12/31/94	12/31/93	12/31/92	12/31/91	12/31/90
				---US $---			
Earnings Per Share	1.26	0.67	0.05	0.65	0.95	1.13	1.98

ANNUAL FINANCIAL DATA

RECORD OF EARNINGS (IN THOUSANDS):

	12/31/96	12/31/95	12/31/94	12/31/93	12/31/92	12/31/91	12/31/90
Total Revenues	80,847	45,625	28,005	27,661	24,667	19,616	22,217
Costs & Expenses	49,596	31,481	24,471	23,796	20,175	14,964	14,139
Depreciation & Amort	10,399	4,370	2,748	2,097	2,208	1,330	1,272
Operating Income	20,853	9,773	785	1,768	2,284	3,322	6,806
Income Bef Income Tax	18,122	8,412	632	2,460	3,601	4,127	7,227
Net Income	18,122	8,412	632	2,460	3,601	4,127	7,227
Average Shares Outstg (000)	6,905	6,282	6,035	...	...	...	...

BALANCE SHEET (IN THOUSANDS):

Cash & Cash Equivalents	7,619	103	3,356	695	2,472	6,740	8,000
Receivables, Net	12,596	8,206	3,551	3,003	2,502	2,508	1,314
Inventories	10,292	8,136	6,779	5,804	7,452	5,077	6,300
Gross Property	296,719	251,983	...	...	...	...	...
Accumulated Depreciation	186,732	176,428	...	...	...	...	...
Long-Term Debt	15,773	21,880	...	...	...	...	...
Stockholders' Equity	102,633	55,537	47,135	39,988	37,476	32,171	28,044
Total Assets	140,495	92,000	53,388	46,681	40,656	36,308	31,585
Total Current Assets	30,508	16,445	13,686	9,526	12,629	14,508	15,685
Total Current Liabilities	22,089	14,582	6,253	6,693	3,179	4,137	3,540
Net Working Capital	8,419	1,863	7,432	2,833	9,450	10,371	12,145
Year End Shs Outstg	7,429	6,324	6,258	1,908	1,901	1,830	1,830

STATISTICAL RECORD:

Return on Equity %	17.66	15.15	1.34	6.15	9.61	12.83	25.77
Return on Assets %	12.90	9.14	1.18	5.27	8.86	11.37	22.88
Operating Profit Margin %	25.79	21.42	2.80	6.39	9.26	16.93	30.63
Net Profit Margin %	22.42	18.44	2.26	8.89	14.60	21.04	32.53
Book Value Per Share	13.82	8.78	7.53	20.96	19.71	17.58	15.33

OFFICERS:
G. E. Beaux, C.E.O.
R. Sosa, Pres.
S. A. De Toledo, Sr. V.P. & C.F.O.
M. R. Bonner, V.P.-Inv. Rel. & Sec.

INCORPORATED: Bahamas, Oct., 1967

PRINCIPAL OFFICE: P.O. Box N3242 East Bay Street Nassau Bahamas

TELEPHONE NUMBER: (809) 393-8622

NO. OF EMPLOYEES: 482

ANNUAL MEETING: In April

SHAREHOLDERS: 3,014

INSTITUTIONAL HOLDINGS:
No. of Institutions: 25
Shares Held: 1,557,974

REGISTRAR(S): The R-M Trust Company, Ontario, Canada

TRANSFER AGENT(S): The R-M Trust Company, Ontario, Canada

BATTERY TECHNOLOGIES, INC.

YIELD ...
P/E RATIO ...

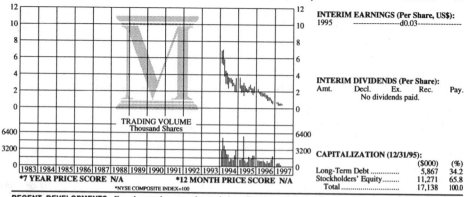

INTERIM EARNINGS (Per Share, US$):
1995 ----------------d0.03----------------

INTERIM DIVIDENDS (Per Share):

Amt.	Decl.	Ex.	Rec.	Pay.
	No dividends paid.			

CAPITALIZATION (12/31/95):

	($000)	(%)
Long-Term Debt	5,867	34.2
Stockholders' Equity	11,271	65.8
Total	17,138	100.0

*7 YEAR PRICE SCORE N/A   *12 MONTH PRICE SCORE N/A

*NYSE COMPOSITE INDEX=100

RECENT DEVELOPMENTS: For the twelve months ended 12/31/95, the Company reported a loss of C$1.4 compared with income of C$441,000 in the corresponding period a year earlier. Revenues were C$19.8 million, up over 70.5% versus C$11.6 million in 1994. Higher revenues resulted from equipment sales activity and the substantial completion during the year of the initial turnkey production equipment for Korean licensee and Malaysian sub-license. The Company recorded licenses fee revenues of C$2.2 million from the sale of a new license in South East Asia, the continued recognition of sales of licenses in Hong Kong, and the initial deposit on the sale of a non-exclusive license for Russia. The Company posted royalty income of C$962,000 from its Canadian and U.S. licenses currently in production, representing an annual increase of 17%.

BUSINESS

BATTERY TECHNOLOGIES, INC. is engaged in the research, development and commercialization of electrochemical energy technology. The Company's primary product is a rechargeable alkaline manganese (RAM) battery system.

ANNUAL EARNINGS

	12/31/95	12/31/94	12/31/95	12/31/94
	----US $----		----C $----	
Earnings Per Share	d0.03	0.01	d0.04	0.02

ANNUAL FINANCIAL DATA

RECORD OF EARNINGS (IN THOUSANDS):

	12/31/95	12/31/94	12/31/95	12/31/94
Total Revenues	14,497	8,272	19,780	11,604
Costs & Expenses	4,179	3,669	5,702	5,147
Depreciation & Amort	1,221	1,158	1,666	1,624
Operating Income	d608	399	d830	560
Income Bef Income Tax	d1,044	334	d1,425	468
Income Tax	cr45	19	cr61	27
Net Income	d1,000	314	d1,364	441
Average Shares Outstg	30,038	28,764	30,038	28,764

BALANCE SHEET (IN THOUSANDS):

Cash & Cash Equivalents	3,264	1,978	4,453	2,774
Receivables, Net	11,032	5,837	15,052	8,188
Gross Property	1,270	933	1,733	1,309
Accumulated Depreciation	419	222	572	311
Long-Term Debt	5,867	3,864	8,005	5,420
Stockholders' Equity	11,271	10,867	15,379	15,244
Total Assets	25,397	18,759	34,653	26,314
Total Current Assets	14,795	7,907	20,187	11,091
Total Current Liabilities	8,259	4,028	11,269	5,650
Net Working Capital	6,536	3,879	8,918	5,441
Year End Shs Outstg	30,562	29,732	30,562	29,732

STATISTICAL RECORD:

Return on Equity %	...	2.89		
Return on Assets %	...	1.68		
Operating Profit Margin %	...	4.82		
Net Profit Margin %	...	3.80		
Book Value Per Share	0.37	0.37		

Converted at 1995, US$0.7329= 1 Canadian $; 1994, US$0.7129= 1 Canadian $

OFFICERS:
B. J. Reiter, Chmn.
D. W. Hartford, Pres. & C.E.O.
S. W. Massel, C.F.O.
L. Eaton-Serbert, V.P.
L. Zelenka, Contr.

INCORPORATED: Canada 1986

PRINCIPAL OFFICE: 1595 16th Avenue, Suite 601 Richmond Hill Ontario Canada L4B3N9

TELEPHONE NUMBER: 905-881-5100

NO. OF EMPLOYEES: N/A

ANNUAL MEETING: In May

SHAREHOLDERS: N/A

INSTITUTIONAL HOLDINGS:
No. of Institutions: 6
Shares Held: 820,100

REGISTRAR(S): N/A

TRANSFER AGENT(S): The R-M Trust Company, Toronto.

BE SEMICONDUCTOR INDUSTRIES NV

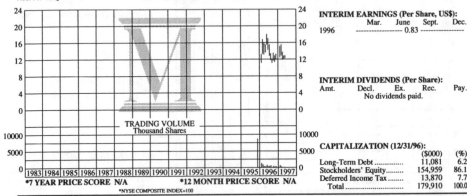

*7 YEAR PRICE SCORE N/A   *12 MONTH PRICE SCORE N/A

*NYSE COMPOSITE INDEX=100

INTERIM EARNINGS (Per Share, US$):

	Mar.	June	Sept.	Dec.
1996	----------------	0.83	----------------	

INTERIM DIVIDENDS (Per Share):

Amt.	Decl.	Ex.	Rec.	Pay.
	No dividends paid.			

CAPITALIZATION (12/31/96):

	($000)	(%)
Long-Term Debt	11,081	6.2
Stockholders' Equity.........	154,959	86.1
Deferred Income Tax	13,870	7.7
Total	179,910	100.0

RECENT DEVELOPMENTS: For the year ended 12/31/96, net income jumped 30.4% to NLG37.8 million from pro forma net income NLG29.0 million in the corresponding period of 1995. The 1995 historical results included nonrecurring charges of NLG55.7 million. Net sales climbed 24.8% to NLG480.0 million versus NLG384.5 million a year earlier. This was due to increased shipments of automated plating and packaging equipment, partly offset by a decrease in sales of leadframes and plating services. Higher sales and manufacturing efficiencies contributed to the 30.9% increase in gross profit to NLG173.0 million compared with NLG132.2 million in 1995. As a percentage of sales, gross margin for the year improved to 36.0% from 34.4% the year before. The 1995 results, which are pro forma, reflects the acquisition of Meco International as if the transaction had occurred on Jan. 1, 1995.

BUSINESS

BE SEMICONDUCTOR INDUSTRIES NV is a holding company which, through its subsidiaries, is engaged in the design, development, manufacture, marketing and servicing of automated molding, trim and form, and plating systems which are integral in the "back-end" assembly operations of semiconductor chip production. The Company also provides leadframes and connector plating services to major semiconductor and connector manufacturers.

ANNUAL EARNINGS

	12/31/96	12/31/95	12/31/96	12/31/95
	----------US $----------		----------Guilders----------	
Earnings Per Share	0.83	0.72	1.44	1.15

ANNUAL FINANCIAL DATA

RECORD OF EARNINGS (IN THOUSANDS):

	12/31/96	12/31/95	12/31/96	12/31/95
Total Revenues	277,909	239,783	479,976	384,492
Costs & Expenses	238,312	208,626	411,588	334,533
Operating Income	35,251	26,476	60,882	42,454
Income Bef Income Tax	33,678	24,221	58,166	38,838
Income Tax	11,820	6,164	20,415	9,883
Net Income	21,858	18,057	37,751	28,955

BALANCE SHEET (IN THOUSANDS):

Cash & Cash Equivalents	26,483	20,526	45,704	32,913
Receivables, Net	61,718	58,846	106,593	96,964
Inventories	44,273	47,239	76,464	75,747
Gross Property	93,812	77,767	162,023	124,700
Accumulated Depreciation	42,632	36,261	73,630	58,145
Long-Term Debt	11,081	14,606	19,139	23,421
Stockholders' Equity	154,959	126,496	267,630	202,837
Total Assets	242,729	235,898	419,218	378,263
Total Current Assets	139,486	128,567	240,906	206,157
Total Current Liabilities	63,419	80,539	109,531	129,143
Net Working Capital	76,067	48,028	131,375	77,014
Year End Shs Outstg	26,394	24,600	26,394	24,600

STATISTICAL RECORD:

Return on Equity %	14.11	14.27		
Return on Assets %	9.01	7.65		
Operating Profit Margin %	12.68	11.04		
Net Profit Margin %	7.87	7.53		
Book Value Per Share	5.87	5.14		

Converted at 1996, US$0.5790= 1 Netherlands guilder; 1995, US$0.6236= 1 Netherlands guilder.

OFFICERS:
R. W. Blickman, Pres. & C.E.O.
H. G. van der Sande, Contr.

INCORPORATED: Netherlands, May, 1995

PRINCIPAL OFFICE: Edisonstraat 90
Zevenaar PZ Netherlands

TELEPHONE NUMBER: 31-316-59-7511

NO. OF EMPLOYEES: 1,303

ANNUAL MEETING: In May

SHAREHOLDERS: N/A

INSTITUTIONAL HOLDINGS:
No. of Institutions: 6
Shares Held: 979,940

REGISTRAR(S): The Bank of New York, N.Y.

TRANSFER AGENT(S): The Bank of New York, N.Y.

BHI CORPORATION

YIELD 1.4%
P/E RATIO 7.9

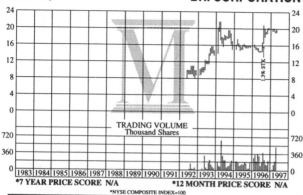

*7 YEAR PRICE SCORE N/A   ***12 MONTH PRICE SCORE N/A**
*NYSE COMPOSITE INDEX=100

TRADING VOLUME
Thousand Shares

INTERIM EARNINGS (Per Share, US$):

Qtr.	July	Oct.	Jan.	Apr.
1994-95		1.68		
1995-96		1.09		
1996-97		2.48		

INTERIM DIVIDENDS (Per Share):

Amt.	Decl.	Ex.	Rec.	Pay.
1.3%	6/15/96	8/07/96	8/09/96	9/03/96
0.27	12/14/96	2/05/97	2/07/97	3/03/97

Indicated div.: $0.27

CAPITALIZATION (4/30/97):

	($000)	(%)
Long-Term Debt	604	0.3
Stockholders' Equity	90,459	39.2
Total Deposits	139,550	60.5
Total	230,613	100.0

RECENT DEVELOPMENTS: For the twelve months ended 4/30/97, the Company reported net income of $17.7 million, or $2.48 per share, compared with $7.8 million, or $1.09 per share, in the corresponding prior-year period. The 1996 results were negatively affected by restructuring and special charges totaling $6.8 million. Higher earnings were fueled by strong growth in banking and financial services coupled with increased earnings from the Company's strategic regional investments, especially NUMAR. Results from banking and financial services benefited from continued growth in both lending and non-interest income from fees and services. Net interest income climbed 18%, while non-interest income rose 24% from the year before. Earnings from the Company's investments in telecommunications rose slightly due to strong growth in cellular and other new service revenues. Strong results from NUMAR stemmed from demand for refined and packaged products in both the domestic Costa Rican and export markets.

BUSINESS

BHI CORPORATION is a corporation operating financial and other service businesses in Central America and the Caribbean. The financial services businesses include The Belize Bank, a 10-branch commercial bank; international business company formation and trust formation; company and ship registration services; and computer services. The Company's equity investments in telecommunications, energy and agro-processing include 26% of Belize Telecommunications Ltd. and 20% of Belize Energy Ltd. in Belize; 23% of Energia Global Inc., which develops and invests in private power projects in the region and operates two hydro electric facilities in Costa Rica; and 23% of NUMAR, a major provider of vegetable oil products and animal feed in Costa Rica. The Company's other services include construction and engineering services and ownership of the premier hotel in Belize City.

ANNUAL EARNINGS

	4/30/97	4/30/96
	US $	
Earnings Per Share	2.48	1.09

ANNUAL FINANCIAL DATA

RECORD OF EARNINGS (IN THOUSANDS):

	4/30/97	4/30/96
Total Revenues	24,314	22,438
Costs & Expenses	16,123	14,378
Net Income	17,684	7,772
Average Shares Outstg	7,125	7,130

BALANCE SHEET (IN THOUSANDS):

Cash & Cash Equivalents	14,305	24,914
Gross Property	① 22,483	27,014
Accumulated Depreciation	...	6,523
Long-Term Debt	604	708
Stockholders' Equity	90,459	71,069
Total Assets	247,212	229,560
Total Current Assets	42,948	51,590
Total Current Liabilities	146,715	139,299
Net Working Capital	d103,767	d87,709
Year End Shs Outstg	7,462	7,285
① Net		

STATISTICAL RECORD:

Return on Equity %	19.55	10.94
Return on Assets %	7.15	3.39
Net Profit Margin %	72.73	34.64
Book Value Per Share	12.12	9.76

OFFICERS:
M. A. Ashcroft, Chmn.
A. G. Forrest, C.E.O.
I. G. Robinson, C.F.O.
P. T. Osborne, Sec.

INCORPORATED: Jan., 1987

PRINCIPAL OFFICE: 60 Market Square, Belize City Belize

TELEPHONE NUMBER: 501-2-72660

NO. OF EMPLOYEES: 397

ANNUAL MEETING: N/A

SHAREHOLDERS: 851 (approx.)

INSTITUTIONAL HOLDINGS:
No. of Institutions: N/A
Shares Held: N/A

REGISTRAR(S): The Belize Bank Limited, Belize City.

TRANSFER AGENT(S): The Belize Bank Limited, Belize City.

BIG ROCK BREWERY LTD.

YIELD ...
P/E RATIO 68.1

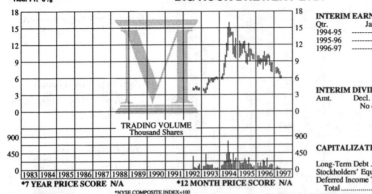

INTERIM EARNINGS (Per Share, US$):

Qtr.	Jan.	Sept.	Dec.	Mar.
1994-95	----------	0.29	----------	
1995-96	----------	0.22	----------	
1996-97	----------	0.09	----------	

INTERIM DIVIDENDS (Per Share):

Amt.	Decl.	Ex.	Rec.	Pay.
		No dividends paid.		

TRADING VOLUME
Thousand Shares

1983|1984|1985|1986|1987|1988|1989|1990|1991|1992|1993|1994|1995|1996|1997

*7 YEAR PRICE SCORE N/A   *12 MONTH PRICE SCORE N/A
*NYSE COMPOSITE INDEX=100

CAPITALIZATION (3/31/97):

	($000)	(%)
Long-Term Debt	8,276	36.7
Stockholders' Equity.........	12,628	56.1
Deferred Income Tax	1,625	7.2
Total	22,529	100.0

RECENT DEVELOPMENTS: For the year ended 3/31/97, net income dropped 60.5% to C$515,149 compared with C$1.3 million the previous year. Earnings for 1997 included a writedown of $500,000 associated with surplus facilities and equipment. Total revenue advanced 10.6% to C$15.1 million versus C$13.7 million a year earlier. Sales increased 10.0% to C$24.2 million compared with C$22.0 million in 1996. Gross profit climbed 13.1% to C$7.8 mil- lion, or 51.3% of total revenue, from C$6.9 million, or 50.2% of total revenue, the year before. Selling, general and administrative expenses grew 27.5% to C$4.7 million from C$3.7 million a year earlier. Interest on long-term debt climbed to C$545,093 compared with C$108,737 the prior year. Income before income taxes declined 60.7% to C$840,149 from C$2.1 million the previous year.

BUSINESS

BIG ROCK BREWERY LTD. is engaged in the brewing of beer using malted barley, hops, water and yeast. The Company is a regional producer and marketer of specialty draught and bottled beer. Products are currently available in five provinces, two territories and 23 U.S. states.

ANNUAL EARNINGS

	3/31/97	3/31/96	3/31/97	3/31/96
	------------US $------------		------------C $------------	
Earnings Per Share	0.09	0.22	0.12	0.30

ANNUAL FINANCIAL DATA

RECORD OF EARNINGS (IN THOUSANDS):

Total Revenues	17,495	16,154	24,164	21,957
Costs & Expenses	16,290	14,079	22,500	19,137
Depreciation & Amort	596	501	823	681
Operating Income	608	1,574	840	2,140
Income Bef Income Tax	608	1,574	840	2,140
Income Tax	235	615	325	836
Net Income	373	959	515	1,304
Average Shares Outstg	...	4,419	...	4,419

BALANCE SHEET (IN THOUSANDS):

Cash & Cash Equivalents	164	161	226	218
Receivables, Net	1,360	1,168	1,879	1,587
Inventories	1,376	1,263	1,900	1,717
Gross Property	① 20,595	17,105	① 28,446	23,251
Accumulated Depreciation	...	1,493	...	2,029
Long-Term Debt	8,276	6,947	11,431	9,443
Stockholders' Equity	12,628	8,493	17,442	11,544
Total Assets	23,796	18,424	32,867	25,043
Total Current Assets	3,096	2,765	4,276	3,758
Total Current Liabilities	1,267	1,560	1,750	2,121
Net Working Capital	1,830	1,205	2,527	1,638
Year End Shs Outstg	...	4,426	...	4,426
① Net				

STATISTICAL RECORD:

Return on Equity %	2.95	11.29		
Return on Assets %	1.57	5.21		
Operating Profit Margin %	3.48	9.74		
Net Profit Margin %	2.13	5.94		
Book Value Per Share		1.92		

Converted at 1997, US$0.7240= 1 Canadian $; 1996, US$0.7357= 1 Canadian $

OFFICERS:
E. E. McNally, Chmn., Pres. & C.E.O.
B. Pieper, Brewmaster
B. A. Boulet, C.F.O.

INCORPORATED: Canada, 1985

PRINCIPAL OFFICE: 5555 76th Avenue S.E., Calgary, Alberta T2C 4L8 Canada

TELEPHONE NUMBER: 403-720-3239

FAX: 403-236-7523

NO. OF EMPLOYEES: N/A

ANNUAL MEETING: In August

SHAREHOLDERS: N/A

INSTITUTIONAL HOLDINGS:
No. of Institutions: N/A
Shares Held: N/A

REGISTRAR(S): N/A

TRANSFER AGENT(S): R-M Trust Company, Calgary, Alberta T2P 2Z3.

BIOCHEM PHARMA INC.

YIELD ...
P/E RATIO 96.2

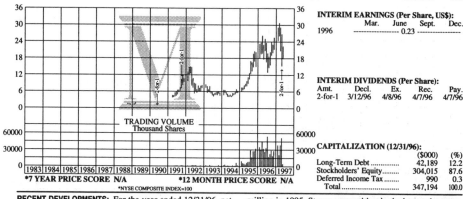

INTERIM EARNINGS (Per Share, US$):

	Mar.	June	Sept.	Dec.
1996	----------------	0.23	----------------	

TRADING VOLUME
Thousand Shares

*7 YEAR PRICE SCORE N/A   *12 MONTH PRICE SCORE N/A

*NYSE COMPOSITE INDEX=100

INTERIM DIVIDENDS (Per Share):

Amt.	Decl.	Ex.	Rec.	Pay.
2-for-1	3/12/96	4/8/96	4/7/96	4/7/96

CAPITALIZATION (12/31/96):

	($000)	(%)
Long-Term Debt	42,189	12.2
Stockholders' Equity........	304,015	87.6
Deferred Income Tax	990	0.3
Total	347,194	100.0

RECENT DEVELOPMENTS: For the year ended 12/31/96, net income advanced to C$33.4 million compared with a net loss of C$5.0 million in the equivalent period of 1995. Results included the Company's share of the loss reported by its affiliate North American Vaccine, Inc., which amounts to C$4.1 million in 1996, net of gain on dilution, and C$8.1 million in 1995. Total operating revenue jumped 24.7% to C$233.6 million from C$187.4 million the year before. Sales slipped to C$156.9 million from C$162.5 million in 1995. Strong competition in the hematology sector of the business caused diagnostic product sales to decrease to C$141.3 million from C$156.9 million. Royalties more than quadrupled to C$57.1 million compared with C$12.6 million a year earlier. This was primarily due to strong worldwide sales of 3TC/Epivir, which had worldwide sales of C$429.3 million in its first full year of sales, is used in a combination treatment for people living with HIV.

BUSINESS

BIOCHEM PHARMA INC. is an international biopharmaceutical company, which through its subsidiaries, BioChem Therapeutic Inc., BioChem ImmunoSystems Inc., IAF BioVac Inc. and its foreign subsidiaries, is engaged in the research, development, manufacturing, and marketing of products for the prevention, detection, and treatment of a broad range of human diseases. BCHXF's subsidiaries are divided into three groups: therapeutic, diagnostic and vaccine. The Company's therapeutic research and development focuses on four areas: antivirals, anti-cancer, pain control and anti-thrombosis. The Company's diagnostic subsidiary, is focused on the research, development, production and commercialization of new diagnostic products for various diseases and allergies and on a new generation of cost effective, versatile laboratory analyzers. BCHXF's vaccine subsidiary, is engaged in research and development, production and marketing of vaccines against human disease. BioChem Pharma also owns 36.0% of publicly-traded North American Vaccine, Inc.

ANNUAL EARNINGS

	12/31/96	12/31/95	12/31/96	12/31/95
	------------US $-----------		------------C $-----------	
Earnings Per Share	0.23	d0.04	0.31	d0.05

ANNUAL FINANCIAL DATA

RECORD OF EARNINGS (IN THOUSANDS):

	12/31/96	12/31/95	12/31/96	12/31/95
Total Revenues	170,798	137,339	233,618	187,391
Costs & Expenses	133,785	121,140	182,992	165,288
Operating Income	37,013	16,199	50,626	22,103
Income Bef Income Tax	28,636	6,641	39,169	9,061
Income Tax	1,061	3,989	1,451	5,443
Eq. Earnings in Affils.	d3,007	d5,937	d4,113	d8,101
Minority Interests	d154	d355	d211	d484
Net Income	24,414	d3,640	33,394	d4,967
Average Shares Outstg	106,486	97,044	106,486	97,044

BALANCE SHEET (IN THOUSANDS):

Cash & Cash Equivalents	230,114	46,467	314,751	63,401
Receivables, Net	66,654	56,178	91,170	76,651
Inventories	23,397	21,748	32,003	29,674
Gross Property	75,355	62,664	103,071	85,501
Accumulated Depreciation	20,418	15,685	27,928	21,401
Long-Term Debt	42,189	51,055	57,706	69,662
Stockholders' Equity	304,015	98,644	415,832	134,594
Total Assets	418,383	209,038	572,265	285,220
Total Current Assets	322,154	126,021	440,643	171,949
Total Current Liabilities	56,953	50,924	77,901	69,483
Net Working Capital	265,201	75,097	362,742	102,466
Year End Shs Outstg	108,030	98,566	108,030	98,566

STATISTICAL RECORD:

Return on Equity %	8.03	...		
Return on Assets %	5.84	...		
Operating Profit Margin %	21.67	11.80		
Net Profit Margin %	14.29	...		
Book Value Per Share	2.81	1.00		

Converted at 1996, US$0.7311= 1 Canadian $; 1995, US$0.7329= 1 Canadian $

OFFICERS:
F. Bellini, Pres. & C.E.O.
G. Dionne, Exec. V.P.
F. Legault, Sr. V.P.-Admin. & Treas.
C. A. Tessier, V.P. & Corp. Sec.

INCORPORATED: Canada, 1986

PRINCIPAL OFFICE: 275 Armand-Frappier Blvd., Laval, Quebec Canada H7V 4A7

TELEPHONE NUMBER: 514-978-7771

NO. OF EMPLOYEES: 1,000

ANNUAL MEETING: In May

SHAREHOLDERS: N/A

INSTITUTIONAL HOLDINGS:
No. of Institutions: 116
Shares Held: 48,597,364 (adj.)

REGISTRAR(S): General Trust of Canada, Montreal.

TRANSFER AGENT(S): General Trust of Canada, Montreal.

BIOMIRA INC.

YIELD ...
P/E RATIO ...

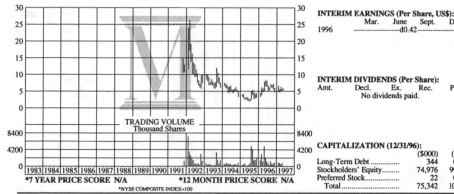

INTERIM EARNINGS (Per Share, US$):

	Mar.	June	Sept.	Dec.
1996	-----------------d0.42-----------------			

INTERIM DIVIDENDS (Per Share):

Amt.	Decl.	Ex.	Rec.	Pay.
		No dividends paid.		

TRADING VOLUME
Thousand Shares

1983 1984 1985 1986 1987 1988 1989 1990 1991 1992 1993 1994 1995 1996 1997
*7 YEAR PRICE SCORE N/A   *12 MONTH PRICE SCORE N/A
*NYSE COMPOSITE INDEX=100

CAPITALIZATION (12/31/96):

	($000)	(%)
Long-Term Debt	344	0.5
Stockholders' Equity........	74,976	99.5
Preferred Stock................	22	0.0
Total	75,342	100.0

RECENT DEVELOPMENTS: For the year ended 12/31/96, the Company reported a loss of C$21.8 million compared with C$21.4 million in the corresponding period a year earlier. Revenues were C$9.4 million versus C$7.7 million in 1995. Revenues benefited from an increase in TRUQUANT BR product sales following the April 1996 U.S. Food and Drug Administration marketing approval. TRUQUANT BR is blood test used for the detection of recurrent breast cancer. For the three months ended 12/31/96, the Company reported a loss of C$5.6 million compared with a loss of C$5.8 million in 1995. Revenues rose 55% to C$3.2 million versus C$2.0 million a year earlier.

BUSINESS

BIOMIRA INC. is a biotechnology, healthcare company utilizing proprietary and patentable methods in the development, manufacture and sale of products for the diagnosis and therapy of cancer. The Company is also involved in the manufacture and sale of diagnostic test kits for sexually transmitted and infectious diseases, including hepatitis.

ANNUAL EARNINGS

	12/31/96	12/31/95	12/31/96	12/31/95
	-------------US $-------------		-------------C $-------------	
Earnings Per Share	d0.42	d0.57	d0.57	d0.78

ANNUAL FINANCIAL DATA

RECORD OF EARNINGS (IN THOUSANDS):

	12/31/96	12/31/95	12/31/96	12/31/95
Total Revenues	6,888	5,640	9,421	7,695
Costs & Expenses	19,490	19,280	26,659	26,307
Depreciation & Amort	3,320	2,010	4,541	2,743
Operating Income	d15,923	d15,651	d21,779	d21,355
Income Bef Income Tax	d15,954	d15,692	d21,822	d21,411
Net Income	d15,954	d15,692	d21,822	d21,411
Average Shares	37,954,978	27,449,561	37,954,978	27,449,561

BALANCE SHEET (IN THOUSANDS):

Cash & Cash Equivalents	69,017	26,964	94,402	36,791
Receivables, Net	1,646	1,320	2,252	1,801
Inventories	1,712	1,157	2,341	1,579
Gross Property	12,783	12,396	17,484	16,914
Accumulated Depreciation	10,266	8,924	14,042	12,176
Long-Term Debt	344	314	471	428
Stockholders' Equity	74,998	36,382	102,583	49,611
Total Assets	77,935	38,914	106,599	53,096
Total Current Assets	72,806	29,809	99,584	40,673
Total Current Liabilities	2,592	2,218	3,545	3,027
Net Working Capital	70,214	27,591	96,039	37,646
Year End Shs Outstg	44,316,412	33,365,061	44,316,412	33,365,061

STATISTICAL RECORD:

Return on Equity %	...	...		
Return on Assets %	...	...		
Operating Profit Margin %	...	...		
Net Profit Margin %	...	...		
Book Value Per Share	d0.74	d0.74		

Converted at 1996, US$0.7311= 1 Canadian $; 1995, US$0.7329= 1 Canadian $

OFFICERS:
E. E. Baker, Chmn.
A. McPherson, Pres. & C.E.O.
B. M. Longenecker, Sr. V.P.
R. D. Aubrey, V.P.

INCORPORATED: Aug., 1985

PRINCIPAL OFFICE: Edmonton Research Park 2011 - 94th Street Edmonton Canada

TELEPHONE NUMBER: 403-450-3761

NO. OF EMPLOYEES: N/A

ANNUAL MEETING: In May

SHAREHOLDERS: N/A

INSTITUTIONAL HOLDINGS:
No. of Institutions: 20
Shares Held: 3,489,171

REGISTRAR(S): The Montreal Trust Company of Canada, Calgary; United Missouri Trust Co., New York.

TRANSFER AGENT(S): The Montreal Trust Company of Canada, Calgary; United Missouri Trust Co., New York.

BONSO ELECTRONICS INTERNATIONAL, INC.

YIELD ...
P/E RATIO 8.93

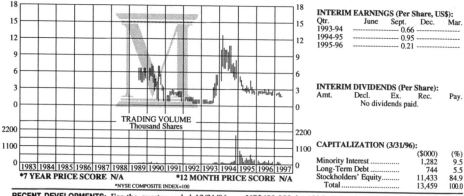

INTERIM EARNINGS (Per Share, US$):

Qtr.	June	Sept.	Dec.	Mar.
1993-94			0.66	
1994-95			0.95	
1995-96			0.21	

INTERIM DIVIDENDS (Per Share):

Amt.	Decl.	Ex.	Rec.	Pay.
		No dividends paid.		

CAPITALIZATION (3/31/96):

	($000)	(%)
Minority Interest	1,282	9.5
Long-Term Debt	744	5.5
Stockholders' Equity	11,433	84.9
Total	13,459	100.0

*7 YEAR PRICE SCORE N/A   *12 MONTH PRICE SCORE N/A
*NYSE COMPOSITE INDEX=100

RECENT DEVELOPMENTS: For the quarter ended 12/31/96, net income dropped 50.2% to US$133,000 from US$267,000 in the same prior-year period. Earnings for 1996 and 1995 included foreign exhange losses of US$36,000 and US$31,000, respectively. Sales climbed 12.5% to US$4.8 million from US$4.3 million the year before. Gross profit as a percentage of sales fell to 27.4% from 32.9% the prior year. For the nine months ended 12/31/96, net income decreased 54.1% to US$229,000 from US$499,000 in 1995. Sales improved 14.6% to US$12.7 million from US$11.1 million a year earlier. This increase reflected sales growth from both existing and new customers. Gross profit as a percentage of sales fell to 28.7% from 34.6% primarily due to the write-off of inventory in the second quarter of 1996, and the preparation for BNSOF's move to its new factory on 1/8/97. The new factory will permit Bonso to approximately triple its productive capacity.

BUSINESS

BONSO ELECTRONICS INTERNATIONAL INC. is engaged in the design, development, manufacture, assembly, and marketing of electronic scales and balances for kitchen, bathroom, office, jewelry, laboratory, pocket, postal and industrial use. In addition, the Company also produces bicycle computers, pedometers, joysticks, digital thermometers, blood pressure meters and other health care products.

ANNUAL EARNINGS

	3/31/96	3/31/95	3/31/94	3/31/93	3/31/92	3/31/91
			US$			
Earnings Per Share	0.21	0.95	0.66	0.04	0.01	0.02

ANNUAL FINANCIAL DATA

RECORD OF EARNINGS (IN THOUSANDS):

	3/31/96	3/31/95	3/31/94	3/31/93	3/31/92	3/31/91
Total Revenues	14,248	13,266	12,549	8,600	7,841	7,535
Costs & Expenses	13,364	11,886	11,072	8,187	7,715	7,432
Operating Income	885	1,380	1,477	413	126	102
Income Bef Income Tax	521	1,863	1,067	425	101	164
Income Tax	cr96	67	72	109	2	cr5
Minority Interests	10	cr46	cr29	...	...	...
Net Income	608	1,843	1,024	316	99	169
Average Shares Outstg	2,826	1,950	1,543	9,000	9,000	9,000

BALANCE SHEET (IN THOUSANDS):

Cash & Cash Equivalents	1,717	2,822	612	601	298	...
Receivables, Net	2,762	3,768	1,826	1,560	976	...
Inventories	6,515	4,265	3,533	3,005	2,390	...
Gross Property	10,559	7,936	8,369	3,022	2,689	...
Accumulated Depreciation	3,251	2,507	2,219	1,815	1,493	...
Long-Term Debt	744	68	1,789	376	...	...
Stockholders' Equity	11,433	10,764	3,459	2,531	2,225	...
Total Assets	20,700	18,278	12,906	6,967	4,860	...
Total Current Assets	10,994	10,855	5,971	5,166	3,664	...
Total Current Liabilities	7,193	6,136	6,285	3,963	2,636	...
Net Working Capital	3,801	4,719	d314	1,203	1,029	...
Year End Shs Outstg	2,826	2,826	1,500	9,000	9,000	9,000

STATISTICAL RECORD:

Return on Equity %	5.31	17.12	29.60	12.49	4.46	4.46
Return on Assets %	2.93	10.08	7.93	4.54	2.04	2.04
Operating Profit Margin %	6.21	10.40	11.77	4.80	1.61	1.36
Net Profit Margin %	4.26	13.89	8.16	3.68	1.27	2.24
Book Value Per Share	4.05	3.81	2.31	0.28	0.25	0.25

OFFICERS:
A. So, Chmn., C.E.O., C.F.O., Pres., Treas. & Sec.

INCORPORATED: British Virgin Islands, Aug., 1988

PRINCIPAL OFFICE: Flat A-D, 8th Floor, Universal Industrial Centre, 23-25 Shan Mei Street, Fo TanSha Tin Town, New Territories Hong Kong

TELEPHONE NUMBER: (852) 605-5822

NO. OF EMPLOYEES: N/A

FAX: (852) 691-1724

ANNUAL MEETING: N/A

SHAREHOLDERS: N/A

INSTITUTIONAL HOLDINGS:
No. of Institutions: 1
Shares Held: 107,000

REGISTRAR(S): N/A

TRANSFER AGENT(S): American Securities Transfer, Inc., Denver, Colorado.

CALEDONIA MINING CORPORATION

YIELD ...
P/E RATIO 7.14

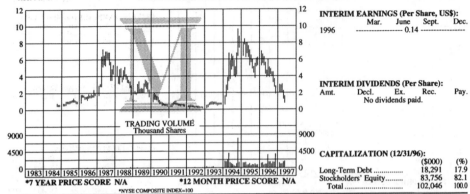

7 YEAR PRICE SCORE N/A   **12 MONTH PRICE SCORE N/A**
NYSE COMPOSITE INDEX=100

INTERIM EARNINGS (Per Share, US$):

	Mar.	June	Sept.	Dec.
1996	------------------ 0.14 ------------------			

INTERIM DIVIDENDS (Per Share):

Amt.	Decl.	Ex.	Rec.	Pay.
	No dividends paid.			

CAPITALIZATION (12/31/96):

	($000)	(%)
Long-Term Debt	18,291	17.9
Stockholders' Equity........	83,756	82.1
Total	102,046	100.0

RECENT DEVELOPMENTS: For the year ended 12/31/96, CALVF reported income from continuing operations of C$4.2 million compared with a loss from continuing operations of C$7.3 million in 1995. Results excluded a loss of C$8.0 million in 1996 and C$1.1 million in 1995 from the write-off of the discontinued operations of CALVF's interest in Renaissance Stone Masonry Rt., Hungary. This was part of the Company's decision to focus its management and financial resources on those assets that show excellent promise. CALVF reported a significant cobalt discovery at the Bopalo prospect in Zambia. A strong cobalt geochemical anomaly was tested with three shallow reverse circulation drill holes. All three holes intersected significant cobalt mineralization over widths of between 13 and 24 meters. On 3/25/97, CALVF entered into an agreement with IBK Capital Corp. of Toronto whereby IBK Capital will raise up to C$20.0 million by way of a private placement of 7.0% unsecured five-year convertible debentures.

BUSINESS

CALEDONIA MINING CORPORATION OF TORONTO, along with its subsidiaries and investee companies, is currently engaged in the mining, exploration and development of related projects in Canada, Great Britain, Spain, South Africa, Zambia, and other areas of Africa.

ANNUAL EARNINGS

	12/31/96	12/31/95	12/31/96	12/31/95
	--------------US $--------------		--------------C $--------------	
Earnings Per Share	0.10	d0.20	0.14	d0.27

ANNUAL FINANCIAL DATA

RECORD OF EARNINGS (IN THOUSANDS):

	12/31/96	12/31/95	12/31/96	12/31/95
Total Revenues	17,856	15,532	24,423	21,192
Costs & Expenses	13,622	19,977	18,632	27,258
Depreciation & Amort	728	827	996	1,128
Operating Income	3,506	d5,272	4,795	d7,194
Income Bef Income Tax	3,506	d5,272	4,795	d7,194
Income Tax	403	63	551	86
Minority Interests	1	cr21	1	cr29
Net Income	3,102	d5,314	4,243	d7,251
Income from Disc. Ops.	d5,850	d772	d8,001	d1,054
Average Shares Outstg	30,672	27,195	30,672	27,195

BALANCE SHEET (IN THOUSANDS):

Cash & Cash Equivalents	10,576	1,617	14,466	2,206
Receivables, Net	1,112	1,315	1,521	1,794
Inventories	1,355	1,182	1,853	1,613
Net Property	42,236	34,231	55,869	46,706
Accumulated Depreciation	1,391	...	1,902	...
Long-Term Debt	18,291	14,922	25,018	20,360
Stockholders' Equity	83,756	65,672	114,561	89,606
Total Assets	113,587	85,482	155,365	116,635
Total Current Assets	13,565	4,221	18,554	5,759
Total Current Liabilities	10,016	3,415	13,700	4,659
Net Working Capital	3,549	806	4,854	1,100
Year End Shs Outstg	32,603	27,670	32,603	27,670

STATISTICAL RECORD:

Return on Equity %	3.70	...		
Return on Assets %	2.73	...		
Operating Profit Margin %	19.63	...		
Net Profit Margin %	17.37	...		
Book Value Per Share	2.57	2.37		

Converted at 1996, US$0.7311= 1 Canadian $; 1995, US$0.7329= 1 Canadian $

OFFICERS:
S. Hayden, Non-Exec. Chmn.
E. F. Merringer, Vice-Chmn. & Sec.
R. J. Fiorini, Pres. & C.E.O.
F. C. Harvey, Tech. Dir.
J. Johnstone, V.P. & C.O.O.
INCORPORATED: 1992
PRINCIPAL OFFICE: Suite 16 2150 Winston Park Drive Oakville Canada

TELEPHONE NUMBER: 905-829-4848
NO. OF EMPLOYEES: N/A
ANNUAL MEETING: N/A
SHAREHOLDERS: N/A
INSTITUTIONAL HOLDINGS:
No. of Institutions: N/A
Shares Held: N/A

REGISTRAR(S): Equity Transfer Services Inc., Toronto, Ontario.

TRANSFER AGENT(S): Equity Transfer Services Inc., Toronto, Ontario.

CALL-NET ENTERPRISES INC.

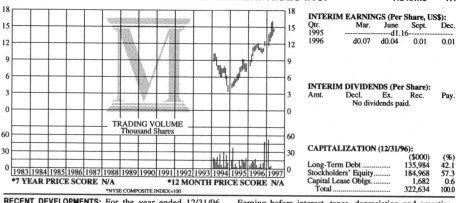

INTERIM EARNINGS (Per Share, US$):

Qtr.	Mar.	June	Sept.	Dec.
1995	------------d1.16------------			
1996	d0.07	d0.04	0.01	0.01

INTERIM DIVIDENDS (Per Share):

Amt.	Decl.	Ex.	Rec.	Pay.
	No dividends paid.			

TRADING VOLUME
Thousand Shares

| 1983 | 1984 | 1985 | 1986 | 1987 | 1988 | 1989 | 1990 | 1991 | 1992 | 1993 | 1994 | 1995 | 1996 | 1997 |

*7 YEAR PRICE SCORE N/A   *12 MONTH PRICE SCORE N/A

*NYSE COMPOSITE INDEX=100

CAPITALIZATION (12/31/96):

	($000)	(%)
Long-Term Debt	135,984	42.1
Stockholders' Equity	184,968	57.3
Capital Lease Oblgs.	1,682	0.6
Total	322,634	100.0

RECENT DEVELOPMENTS: For the year ended 12/31/96, Call-Net reported a net loss of C$7.1 million compared with a net loss of C$64.7 million in 1995. Revenues jumped 55.8% to C$712.6 million from C$457.5 million the year before. The growth in revenues reflected a 70.3% increase in total minutes billed to 2.81 billion from 1.65 billion and increased customer acceptance of the Company's business and residential long-distance products.

Earning before interest, taxes, depreciation and amortization (EBITDA) improved to C$43.1 million, a significant improvement from the negative C$15.7 million EBITDA reported in 1995. Gross margins improved to 37.6% versus 34.0% in 1995. Contingent upon regulatory approvals, the Company intends to launch competitive on-line, mobile and local services in the Canadian telecommunications market during 1997.

BUSINESS

CALL-NET ENTERPRISES INC. is a telecommunications holding company. Through its operating subsidiaries, the Company is engaged in long distance and wireless telecommunications. It's holdings are divided into three investments: Sprint Canada Inc., MicroCell Telecommunications Inc. and 100% ownership of a local telecommunications service company. Sprint Canada Inc. is a long distance company that provides voice, data and network management services to consumers, business and government. The Company owns 100% of Sprint Canada Inc. MicroCell Telecommunications Inc. provides digital wireless telecommunictions services, known as personal communications service (PCS). The Company has a 19% non-controlling interest in MicroCell Telecommunications Inc. The local telecommunications company was formed in Jan. 1996, and plans to offer service in 1997, depending on regulatory decisions.

ANNUAL EARNINGS

	12/31/96	12/31/95	12/31/96	12/31/95
	------------US $------------		------------C $------------	
Earnings Per Share	d0.10	d1.16	d0.14	d1.58

ANNUAL FINANCIAL DATA

RECORD OF EARNINGS (IN THOUSANDS):

	12/31/96	12/31/95	12/31/96	12/31/95
Total Revenues	520,982	335,273	712,600	457,461
Costs & Expenses	489,471	346,848	669,500	473,254
Depreciation & Amort	24,273	21,029	33,200	28,693
Operating Income	7,238	d32,604	9,900	d44,486
Net Income	d5,191	d47,456	d7,100	d64,751
Average Shares Outstg	50,063	41,025	50,623	41,025

BALANCE SHEET (IN THOUSANDS):

Cash & Cash Equivalents	124,360	131,648	170,100	179,626
Receivables, Net	86,124	66,621	117,800	90,900
Gross Property	162,231	118,880	221,900	162,205
Accumulated Depreciation	38,163	22,131	52,200	30,197
Long-Term Debt	135,984	120,649	186,000	164,619
Stockholders' Equity	184,968	182,828	253,000	249,458
Total Assets	420,748	384,595	575,500	524,758
Total Current Assets	211,873	199,546	289,800	272,269
Total Current Liabilities	98,114	78,531	134,200	107,151
Net Working Capital	113,759	121,015	155,600	165,118
Year End Shs Outstg	17,376	16,903	17,376	16,903

STATISTICAL RECORD:

Operating Profit Margin %	1.4	...		
Book Value Per Share	10.65	10.82		

Converted at 1996, US$0.7311= 1 Canadian $; 1995, US$0.7329= 1 Canadian $

OFFICERS:
J. Koor, Chmn. & Pres.
D. Parkes, Sr. V.P.
P. Bates, Sr. V.P.
R. Boron, Sr. V.P. & Chief Counsel

INCORPORATED: Canada, Jan. 1986

PRINCIPAL OFFICE: 2550 Victoria Park Avenue, Suite 400, North York, Ontario M2J 5A9 Canada

TELEPHONE NUMBER: 416-496-4925

NO. OF EMPLOYEES: N/A

ANNUAL MEETING: In May

SHAREHOLDERS: N/A

INSTITUTIONAL HOLDINGS:
No. of Institutions: N/A
Shares Held: N/A

REGISTRAR(S): The R-M Trust Company, Toronto, Montreal and Vancouver.

TRANSFER AGENT(S): The R-M Trust Company, Toronto, Montreal and Vancouver.

CAYMAN WATER COMPANY, LIMITED

YIELD ...
P/E RATIO 18.1

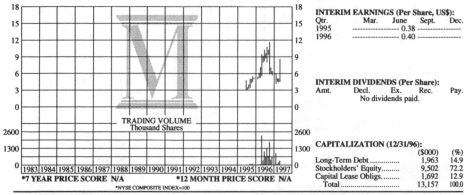

INTERIM EARNINGS (Per Share, US$):

Qtr.	Mar.	June	Sept.	Dec.
1995		------ 0.38 ------		
1996		------ 0.40 ------		

INTERIM DIVIDENDS (Per Share):

Amt.   Decl.   Ex.   Rec.   Pay.
No dividends paid.

CAPITALIZATION (12/31/96):

	($000)	(%)
Long-Term Debt	1,963	14.9
Stockholders' Equity........	9,502	72.2
Capital Lease Obligs........	1,692	12.9
Total	13,157	100.0

*7 YEAR PRICE SCORE N/A   *12 MONTH PRICE SCORE N/A

*NYSE COMPOSITE INDEX=100

RECENT DEVELOPMENTS: For the year ended 12/31/96, net income was $1.1 million, down 10.2% compared with $1.3 million in 1995. The 1995 results excluded a $400,000 exceptional charge for the write-down of assets. Revenues grew 7.3% to $6.4 million from $5.9 million. Water sales rose 6.4% to $6.2 million, reflecting increased tourist properties that use the Company's water. Interest income jumped to $42,760 from $1,368. Connection charges declined slightly to $23,076 compared with $23,748 in 1995. Other income increased 16.0% to $148,671 from $128,203. Direct expense rose 6.8% to $4.2 million, resulting from the purchase of additional water products for resale. Indirect expenses jumped 41.1% to $995,180, reflecting expenses associated with the successful application for a NASDAQ National Market quotation and the underwriting of 575,000 shares of common stock.

BUSINESS

CAYMAN WATER COMPANY LIMITED operates a public water utility in certain areas on Grand Cayman Island under a license from the Government of the Cayman Islands. The Company, which was established in 1973, provides water services to both the major residential area of West Bay and the Seven Miles Beach region, which includes most of the Island's hotels, condominiums and restaurants, as well as the Cayman Island's 18 hole championship golf course. The Cayman Islands are comprised of three islands; Grand Cayman, Cayman Brac and Little Cayman and has a populataion of approximately 32,000.

ANNUAL EARNINGS

	12/31/96	12/31/95	12/31/94	12/31/93	12/31/92
			----US $----		
Earnings Per Share	0.40	0.38	0.25	0.30	0.16

ANNUAL FINANCIAL DATA

RECORD OF EARNINGS (IN THOUSANDS):

	12/31/96	12/31/95	12/31/94	12/31/93	12/31/92
Total Revenues	6,365	5,934	5,387	5,101	3,053
Costs & Expenses ①	5,227	4,666	4,906	4,555	2,765
Operating Income ①	1,138	1,268	481	547	289
Net Income	1,138	868	481	547	334
① Incl. Interest Exp.					

BALANCE SHEET (IN THOUSANDS):

Cash & Cash Equivalents	1,122	89	101	75	249
Receivables, Net	637	691	480	655	299
Inventories	46	63	340	290	275
Gross Property	16,845	15,716	15,245	14,112	10,340
Accumulated Depreciation	4,267	3,528	5,134	5,327	3,791
Long-Term Debt	1,963	2,137	2,309	2,467	1,819
Stockholders' Equity	9,502	6,466	5,355	4,172	3,157
Total Assets	14,676	13,570	11,347	10,109	7,757
Total Current Assets	1,967	1,240	1,153	1,234	1,017
Total Current Liabilities	1,371	2,662	1,769	1,843	1,193
Net Working Capital	596	d1,421	d616	d610	d176
Year End Shs Outstg	2,938	2,325	2,160	1,758	1,758

STATISTICAL RECORD:

Return on Equity %	12.0	13.4	9.0	13.1	10.6
Return on Assets %	7.8	6.4	4.2	5.4	4.3
Operating Profit Margin %	17.9	21.4	8.9	10.7	9.4
Net Profit Margin %	17.9	14.6	8.9	10.7	10.9
Book Value Per Share	3.23	2.78	2.48	2.37	1.80

OFFICERS:
J. M. Parker, Chmn. & C.E.O.
P. D. Ribbins, Pres. & C.O.O.
A. S. Bodden, V.P.-Fin. & Sec.
G. S. Mctaggart, V.P.-Oper.

INCORPORATED: Cayman Islands, Aug. 1973

PRINCIPAL OFFICE: Trafalgar Place, West Bay Road, PO Box 1114 GT, Grand Cayman Cayman Islands

TELEPHONE NUMBER: (345) 945-4277

NO. OF EMPLOYEES: N/A

ANNUAL MEETING: In Apr.

SHAREHOLDERS: N/A

INSTITUTIONAL HOLDINGS:
No. of Institutions: N/A
Shares Held: N/A

REGISTRAR(S): Amercian Stock Transfer & Trust Co., New York, NY

TRANSFER AGENT(S): American Stock Transfer & Trust Co., New York, NY

CENTRAL EUROPEAN MEDIA ENTERPRISES LTD.

YIELD ...
P/E RATIO ...

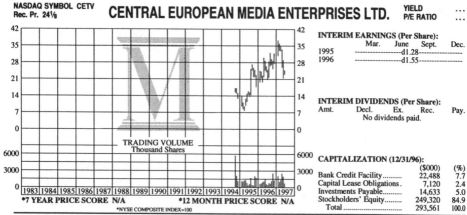

*7 YEAR PRICE SCORE N/A *12 MONTH PRICE SCORE N/A

*NYSE COMPOSITE INDEX=100

TRADING VOLUME
Thousand Shares

INTERIM EARNINGS (Per Share):

	Mar.	June	Sept.	Dec.
1995	----------------d1.28----------------
1996	----------------d1.55----------------

INTERIM DIVIDENDS (Per Share):

Amt.	Decl.	Ex.	Rec.	Pay.
No dividends paid.

CAPITALIZATION (12/31/96):

	($000)	(%)
Bank Credit Facility...........	22,488	7.7
Capital Lease Obligations .	7,120	2.4
Investments Payable........	14,633	5.0
Stockholders' Equity.........	249,320	84.9
Total	293,561	100.0

RECENT DEVELOPMENTS: For the year ended 12/31/96, the Company reported a loss of $30.0 million compared with a loss of $18.7 million in the corresponding period a year earlier. Revenues were $136.0 million, up 37% versus $98.9 million in 1995. The increased loss reflected growing losses at PRO TV and POP TV, which were operational for all of 1996 compared with one month in 1995 and, to a lesser extent, increased corporate and development expenses. The increase in revenues was primarily attributa-

ble to the increase in revenues from PRO TV and POP TV, which were operational for all of 1996 compared with one month in 1995, and the increase in Nova TV's net revenues. SG&A expenses increased 176% to $21.4 million primarily attributable to the addition of stations. Interest expense decreased 5.8% to $4.7 million due to lower debt levels at Nova TV. Interest income grew to $2.9 million from $1.2 million in the prior year.

BUSINESS

CENTRAL EUROPEAN MEDIA ENTERPRISES LTD. is engaged in the owning, operating and development of national and regional private commercial television stations in the newly emerging markets of Central Europe (including the Czech Republic, Slovakia, Hungary, Romania, Slovenia and Poland) and regional private commercial television stations in Germany.

ANNUAL EARNINGS

	12/31/96	12/31/95	12/31/94
	-------------------------------US $-------------------------------
Earnings Per Share	d1.55	d1.28	d3.45

ANNUAL FINANCIAL DATA

RECORD OF EARNINGS (IN THOUSANDS):

	12/31/96	12/31/95	12/31/94
Total Revenues	135,985	98,919	53,566
Cost & Expenses	19,531	16,344	10,517
Operating Income	9,996	22,308	957
Equity Loss in Affiliates	17,867	14,816	13,677
Net Interest Expense	1,794	3,721	1,813
Income Bef Income Tax	d12,526	4,095	d14,778
Income Tax	16,405	16,340	3,331
Minority Interests	1,072	6,491	2,396
Net Income	d30,003	d18,736	d20,505
Average Shares Outstg	19,373	14,678	...

BALANCE SHEET (IN THOUSANDS):

	12/31/96	12/31/95	12/31/94
Cash & Cash Equivalents	84,152	68,078	51,327
Receivables, Net	37,342	32,475	13,775
Gross Property	81,299	61,980	34,696
Accumulated Depreciation	22,317	10,281	3,477
Long-Term Debt	29,608	15,513	16,448
Stockholders' Equity	249,320	138,936	62,631
Total Assets	365,130	222,027	115,332
Total Current Assets	146,159	116,728	71,447
Total Current Liabilities	60,506	46,453	18,161
Net Working Capital	85,653	70,275	53,286
Year End Shs Outstg	24,742	18,373	5,942

STATISTICAL RECORD:

	12/31/96	12/31/95	12/31/94
Return on Equity %	...	...	...
Return on Assets %	...	...	...
Operating Profit Margin %	7.4	22.6	1.8
Net Profit Margin %	...	...	...
Book Value Per Share	10.08	7.56	10.54

OFFICERS:
R. S. Lauder, Chmn.
L. M. Fertig, Pres. & C.E.O.
J. A. Schwallie, V.P.--Fin. & C.F.O.

INCORPORATED: Bermuda, 1994

PRINCIPAL OFFICE: 18 D'Arblay Street
London   England, W1V 3FP

TELEPHONE NUMBER: 44-171-292-7900
FAX: 44-171-292-7903
NO. OF EMPLOYEES: 2,498
ANNUAL MEETING: In May
SHAREHOLDERS: 55
INSTITUTIONAL HOLDINGS:
No. of Institutions: N/A
Shares Held: N/A

REGISTRAR(S): American Stock Transfer
and Trust Co.

TRANSFER AGENT(S): American Stock
Transfer and Trust Co.

NASDAQ SYMBOL CCCFF
Rec. Pr. 6¼

CHAI-NA-TA CORP.

YIELD ...
P/E RATIO 5.34

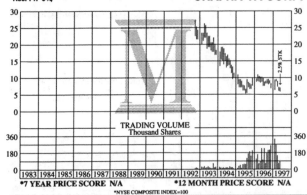

*7 YEAR PRICE SCORE N/A   ***12 MONTH PRICE SCORE N/A**

NYSE COMPOSITE INDEX=100

INTERIM EARNINGS (Per Share, US$):

Qtr.	2/28	5/31	8/31	11/30
1995	---------------- 1.02 ------------------				
1996	0.03	0.00	d0.03	1.17

INTERIM DIVIDENDS (Per Share):

Amt.	Decl.	Ex.	Rec.	Pay.
2.5%	4/28/97	5/06/97	5/08/97	5/22/97

CAPITALIZATION (11/30/96):

	($000)	(%)
Long-Term Debt	21,611	36.9
Stockholders' Equity........	28,577	48.8
Deferred Income Tax	8,430	14.4
Total	58,617	100.0

RECENT DEVELOPMENTS: For the year ended 11/30/96, net income increased 21.6% to C$6.2 million compared with C$5.1 million in 1995. Revenues climbed 33.0% to C$34.4 million from C$25.9 million. Gross profit improved 19.6% to C$16.0 million from C$13.4 million. The improved results were attributed to a record harvest, growth of value-added programs in North America and China and a new product launch in Mexico. Ginseng crops increased to 25,455 compared with 24,229 in 1995. Acres under cultiva-

tion rose to 1,470 from 1,410 the year before. The Company completed a 1-for-4 stock consolidation in October, 1996. The Company continues to focus on its vertical integration strategy to increase revenues. For the fourth quarter ended 11/30/96, net income jumped 57.7% to C$6.3 million compared with C$4.0 million in the year-earlier quarter. Revenues advanced 42.2% to C$23.1 million from C$16.3 million.

BUSINESS

CHAI-NA-TA CORP. is engaged in the production, processing and distribution of North American Ginseng, a root crop that is predominantly used by Asians for its medicinal and therapeutic properties. The Company operates several farms in the southern British Columbia area and one in southern Ontario. Crops are harvested and exported to the Orient for further processing and sale, and a portion of the product is sold at the wholesale level. The remaining is further processed, and distributed through Company's processing operations in mainland China and its marketing company in Hong Kong.

ANNUAL EARNINGS

	11/30/96	11/30/95	11/30/96	11/30/95
	--------------US $-------------		--------------C $-------------	
Earnings Per Share	1.19	1.02	1.60	1.38

ANNUAL FINANCIAL DATA

RECORD OF EARNINGS (IN THOUSANDS):

Total Revenues	25,685	19,116	34,430	25,878
Costs & Expenses	18,691	12,849	25,055	17,394
Operating Income	6,993	6,267	9,374	8,484
Income Bef Income Tax	6,924	6,088	9,282	8,241
Income Tax	2,283	2,290	3,060	3,100
Net Income	4,642	3,798	6,222	5,141
Average Shares Outstg	3,886	3,726	3,886	3,726

BALANCE SHEET (IN THOUSANDS):

Cash & Cash Equivalents	6,336	1,406	8,493	1,904
Receivables, Net	18,227	8,757	24,434	11,855
Inventories	2,295	2,933	3,077	3,971
Gross Property	16,863	19,292	22,605	26,116
Accumulated Depreciation	6,022	4,854	8,073	6,571
Long-Term Debt	21,611	9,186	28,969	12,435
Stockholders' Equity	28,577	21,696	38,307	29,370
Total Assets	63,450	51,684	85,054	69,966
Total Current Assets	32,921	19,264	44,130	26,078
Total Current Liabilities	2,947	12,879	3,950	17,435
Net Working Capital	29,974	6,385	40,180	8,643
Year End Shs Outstg	3,924	3,647	3,924	3,647

STATISTICAL RECORD:

Return on Equity %	16.24	17.50
Return on Assets %	7.32	7.35
Operating Profit Margin %	27.23	32.78
Net Profit Margin %	18.07	19.87
Book Value Per Share	7.28	5.95

Converted at 1996, US$0.7460= 1 Canadian $; 1995, US$0.7387= 1 Canadian $

OFFICERS:
J. B. Abernethy, Chmn.
G. A. Gill, Pres. & C.E.O.
J. S. Crowder, V.P.
B. D. Jones, V.P.
INCORPORATED: Canada, Aug., 1981
PRINCIPAL OFFICE: 5965-205A Street, Langley, British Columbia Canada V3A 8C4

TELEPHONE NUMBER: 604-533-8883
NO. OF EMPLOYEES: 100
ANNUAL MEETING: In May
SHAREHOLDERS: 447 (approx.)
INSTITUTIONAL HOLDINGS:
No. of Institutions: 4
Shares Held: 502,617 (adj.)

REGISTRAR(S): N/A

TRANSFER AGENT(S): The Montreal Trust Company, Vancouver.

CHANDLER INSURANCE COMPANY, LTD.

NASDAQ SYMBOL CHANF
Rec. Pr. 4½

YIELD ...
P/E RATIO 32.1

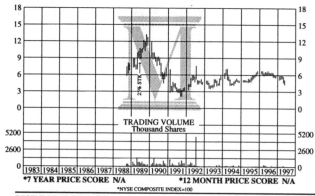

7 YEAR PRICE SCORE N/A   **12 MONTH PRICE SCORE N/A**
*NYSE COMPOSITE INDEX=100

INTERIM EARNINGS (Per Share, US$):
1996 ------------------ 0.14 ------------------

INTERIM DIVIDENDS (Per Share):
Amt.   Decl.   Ex.   Rec.   Pay.
No dividends paid.

CAPITALIZATION (12/31/96):

	($000)	(%)
Long-Term Debt	2,907	3.9
Stockholders' Equity	72,547	96.1
Total	75,454	100.0

RECENT DEVELOPMENTS: For the year ended 12/31/96, net income was $972,000 compared with $3.8 million a year earlier. Earnings for 1996 were affected by charges totaling $1.5 million for the settlement attributed to legal proceedings and related matters arising from the termination of an underwriting and production contract with the Company's former underwriting manager for a portion of the Company's surety bond business. In addition, legal expenses related to these matters were $441,000 for 1996. The Company's results for 1996 also reflected a charge totaling $1.1 million from an arbitration award that was lower than expected. Legal expenses related to the arbitration award were $527,000 in 1996. Total revenues were $100.2 million, up 8.7% from $92.2 million in the prior year.

BUSINESS

CHANDLER INSURANCE COMPANY, LTD. is a holding company. Through its subsidiaries, the Company is engaged in various property and casualty insurance and reinsurance operations. The Company's insurance products are underwritten by National American Insurance Company, a wholly owned subsidiary. National American primarily provides property and casualty coverage for long-haul trucking companies, nursing homes, school districts and municipalities, and surety bonds for small contractors. Through its wholly owned subsidiary, LaGere & Walkingstick Insurance Agency, Inc., the Company represents various insurance companies that provide a variety of property-casualty, life and accident and health coverages. LaGere also acts as a surplus lines broker specializing in risk management and brokering insurance for high risk ventures.

ANNUAL EARNINGS

	12/31/96	12/31/95	12/31/94	12/31/93	12/31/92	12/31/91
			--US $--			
Earnings Per Share	0.14	0.54	0.36	0.53	0.24	0.09

ANNUAL FINANCIAL DATA

RECORD OF EARNINGS (IN THOUSANDS):

	12/31/96	12/31/95	12/31/94	12/31/93	12/31/92	12/31/91
Total Revenues	100,245	92,235	93,133	94,621	103,325	162,669
Costs & Expenses	99,590	87,645	90,816	91,953	102,878	161,559
Operating Income	655	4,590	2,317	2,668	447	1,110
Income Bef Income Tax	655	4,590	2,317	2,668	447	1,110
Income Tax	cr317	812	cr157	cr1,030	cr1,222	443
Net Income	972	3,778	2,474	3,698	1,669	667
Average Shares Outstg	6,942	6,942	6,942	6,942	6,942	7,151

BALANCE SHEET (IN THOUSANDS):

Investments	111,247	114,037	116,081	135,624	151,237	167,772
Cash & Cash Equivalents	7,889	8,524	8,420	10,398	7,799	22,286
Receivables, Net	30,413	35,058	33,606	31,107	32,921	35,915
Gross Property	12,926	12,285	12,515	12,250	13,605	13,147
Accumulated Depreciation	6,992	6,097	6,094	5,087	4,808	3,383
Long-Term Debt	2,907	225	...	...	...	880
Stockholders' Equity	72,547	73,450	63,459	68,182	61,585	59,916
Total Assets	206,827	246,949	261,364	286,447	234,485	268,824
Year End Shs Outstg	6,942	6,942	6,942	6,942	6,942	6,942

STATISTICAL RECORD:

Return on Equity %	1.34	5.14	3.90	5.42	2.71	1.11
Return on Assets %	0.47	1.53	0.95	1.29	0.71	0.25
Operating Profit Margin %	0.65	4.98	2.49	2.82	0.43	0.68
Net Profit Margin %	0.97	4.10	2.66	3.91	1.62	0.41
Book Value Per Share	10.45	10.58	9.14	9.82	8.87	8.63

OFFICERS:
W. B. LaGere, Chmn. & Chief Exec.
B. T. Walkingstick, President
B. B. Watson, Exec. V.P.
M. T. Paden, V.P.-Fin., C.F.O. & Treas.
INCORPORATED: Cayman Islands, Sept., 1983
PRINCIPAL OFFICE: Anderson Square, Fifth Floor, P.O. Box 1854, Grand Cayman Cayman Islands

TELEPHONE NUMBER: 345-949-8177
NO. OF EMPLOYEES: 361
ANNUAL MEETING: In May
SHAREHOLDERS: 170
INSTITUTIONAL HOLDINGS:
No. of Institutions: 6
Shares Held: 998,976

REGISTRAR(S): NationsBank of Texas, Dallas.

TRANSFER AGENT(S): NationsBank of Texas, Dallas.

303

CHC HELICOPTER CORPORATION

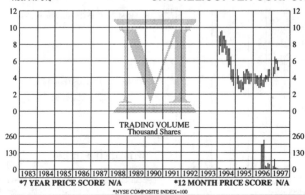

TRADING VOLUME
Thousand Shares

*7 YEAR PRICE SCORE N/A   *12 MONTH PRICE SCORE N/A
*NYSE COMPOSITE INDEX=100

INTERIM EARNINGS (Per Share, US$):

Qtr.	July	Oct.	Jan.	Apr.
1994-95		d0.10		
1995-96		0.48		
1996-97	0.56	0.47	d0.20	0.03

INTERIM DIVIDENDS (Per Share):

Amt.	Decl.	Ex.	Rec.	Pay.
0.10	7/26/93	9/3/93	9/10/93	9/28/93
0.10	9/22/94	10/3/94	10/7/94	11/7/94
0.10	9/18/95	9/27/95	9/29/95	10/30/95
0.10	6/27/96	7/5/96	7/9/96	8/6/96

Indicated div.:$0.10

CAPITALIZATION (4/30/97):

	($000)	(%)
Long-Term Debt	219,665	67.7
Stockholders' Equity	104,664	32.3
Total	324,329	100.0

RECENT DEVELOPMENTS: For the year ended 4/30/97, net income was C$10.1 million compared with income of C$7.6 million in the prior year. Revenues rose 5.3% to C$351.7 million from C$334.2 million a year earlier. The improvement in earnings was attributed to the Company's overhaul and repair segment, where business rose 30% over prior-year levels. Also contributing to the Company's strong earnings performance was its helicopter operations as business activity remained solid through much of 1997. Cash flow from operations before interest and taxes was C$53.8 million compared with C$47.3 million in the previous year, a 13.7% increase. For the quarter ended 4/30/97, net income was $400,000, down 33.3% from $600,000 in 1996. Revenues rose 7.2% to $79.0 million.

BUSINESS

CHC HELICOPTER CORPORA-TION is a holding company, and through its subsidiaries, is engaged in providing helicopter transportation and aviation repair and overhaul services worldwide. The Company's helicopter operations (65% of 1997 revenues), with 222 light, medium and heavy helicopters worldwide as of 4/30/97, make it one of the largest commerical helicopter operators. In Canada, the Company serves both public and private interests active in oil and gas, mining, forestry (including reforestation, logging and fire fighting), construction, rail, power line and emergency response. The Company also trains helicopter pilots at flight training schools in Penticton, British Columbia and Toronto, Ontario. Internationally, the Company operates light, medium and heavy helicopters that are primarily used to support offshore oil and gas activities by transporting people and cargo. The Company's aviation repair and overhaul operations (35% of 1997 revenues) service both helicopter and fixed wing aircraft worldwide.

ANNUAL EARNINGS

	4/30/97	4/30/96	4/30/97	4/30/96
	US $		C $	
Earnings Per Share	0.62	0.48	0.86	0.65

ANNUAL FINANCIAL DATA

RECORD OF EARNINGS (IN THOUSANDS):

	4/30/97	4/30/96	4/30/97	4/30/96
Total Revenues	251,712	245,491	351,749	334,183
Costs & Expenses	212,890	210,041	297,498	285,925
Depreciation & Amort	6,596	5,991	9,217	8,156
Operating Income	32,482	30,789	45,391	41,913
Income Bef Income Tax	13,795	10,647	19,277	14,493
Income Tax	6,585	5,053	9,202	6,879
Net Income	7,210	5,593	10,075	7,614
Average Shares Outstg	11,700	11,660	11,700	11,660

BALANCE SHEET (IN THOUSANDS):

Cash & Cash Equivalents	632	661	883	900
Receivables, Net	35,697	33,352	49,884	45,402
Inventories	81,040	71,487	113,248	97,314
Property and Equipment, Net	213,788	207,554	298,754	282,540
Long-Term Debt	157,192	164,037	219,665	223,301
Stockholders' Equity	74,898	70,298	104,664	95,696
Total Assets	358,335	339,805	500,748	462,571
Total Current Assets	121,013	108,334	169,107	147,473
Total Current Liabilities	79,224	61,840	110,710	84,182
Net Working Capital	41,789	46,494	58,397	65,291
Year End Shs Outstg	11,700	11,708	11,700	11,708

STATISTICAL RECORD:

Return on Equity %	9.6	8.0		
Return on Assets %	2.0	1.6		
Operating Profit Margin %	12.9	4.3		
Net Profit Margin %	2.9	2.3		
Book Value Per Share	6.40	6.00		

Converted at 1997, US$0.7156= 1 Canadian $; 1996, US$0.7346= 1 Canadian $

OFFICERS:
C. L. Dobbin, Chmn.
R. Palladina, Pres. & C.E.O.
M. D. Dobbin, Sr. V.P.
M. Parsons, C.F.O. & Sec.

INCORPORATED: N/A

PRINCIPAL OFFICE: Hangar No. 1 St. John's Airport, P.O. Box 5188 St. John's Canada

TELEPHONE NUMBER: 709-570-0700

NO. OF EMPLOYEES: 1,529

ANNUAL MEETING: In Sept.

SHAREHOLDERS: N/A

INSTITUTIONAL HOLDINGS:
No. of Institutions: 5
Shares Held: 2,948,200

REGISTRAR(S): The R-M Trust Company, Toronto.

TRANSFER AGENT(S): The R-M Trust Company, Toronto.

CHECK POINT SOFTWARE

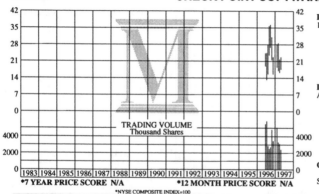

INTERIM EARNINGS (Per Share, US$):
1996 ------------------ 0.43 ------------------

INTERIM DIVIDENDS (Per Share):

Amt.	Decl.	Ex.	Rec.	Pay.
		No dividends paid.		

CAPITALIZATION (12/31/95):

	($000)	(%)
Stockholders' Equity.........	5,040	100.0
Total	5,040	100.0

TRADING VOLUME
Thousand Shares

1983 1984 1985 1986 1987 1988 1989 1990 1991 1992 1993 1994 1995 1996 1997

*7 YEAR PRICE SCORE N/A   *12 MONTH PRICE SCORE N/A

*NYSE COMPOSITE INDEX=100

RECENT DEVELOPMENTS: For the year ended 12/31/96, net income more than tripled to $15.2 million from $4.8 million in the same period of 1995. Revenues leapt to $31.9 million from $9.5 million in the prior year. Gross profit rocketed to $29.9 million from $9.0 million a year earlier. Operating income soared to $4.9 million from $1.5 million the year before. The total number of units shipped grew 200% year-over-year. The four-fold growth in total installed base units was mainly due to the significant increase in resellers, distributors and systems integrators carrying the Company's products, which broadened its reach worldwide. Additionally, CHKPF established national two-tier distribution through new partnerships with Westcon and Ingram Micro during the fourth quarter of 1996. Revenues from Sunsoft, Inc. accounted for 42.0% of the Company's total revenues in fiscal 1996, down from 58.0% in fiscal 1995.

BUSINESS

CHECK POINT SOFTWARE TECHNOLOGIES LTD. develops, markets and supports network security software products that enable connectivity with security and manageability. The Company's revenues are derived from sales of the Firewall-1 family of software products and related maintenance agreements.

ANNUAL EARNINGS

	12/31/95	12/31/94	12/31/93
		----US $----	
Earnings Per Share	0.14	0.00	0.00

ANNUAL FINANCIAL DATA

RECORD OF EARNINGS (IN THOUSANDS):

Total Revenues	9,546	794	...
Costs & Expenses	4,686	717	119
Operating Income	4,860	77	d119
Income Bef Income Tax	4,837	24	d117
Income Tax	cr10	...	...
Net Income	4,847	24	d117
Average Shares Outstg	33,812	33,730	33,482

BALANCE SHEET (IN THOUSANDS):

Cash & Cash Equivalents	3,634	121	...
Receivables, Net	3,058	458	...
Gross Property	474	94	...
Accumulated Depreciation	86	12	...
Stockholders' Equity	5,040	d62	...
Total Assets	7,102	661	...
Total Current Assets	6,692	580	...
Total Current Liabilities	1,953	712	...
Net Working Capital	4,739	d133	...
Year End Shs Outstg	29,700	27,090	...

STATISTICAL RECORD:

Return on Equity %	96.15	...	...
Return on Assets %	66.49	3.68	...
Operating Profit Margin %	50.91	9.75	...
Net Profit Margin %	50.77	3.07	...
Book Value Per Share	0.17	...	...

OFFICERS:
G. Shwed, Pres. & C.E.O.
H. Schwartz, C.F.O. & V.P.-Fin.
S. Kramer, V.P.
M. Nacht, V.P.
D. Triant, Pres. & C.E.O. of CP Inc.

INCORPORATED: Isreal, July, 1993

PRINCIPAL OFFICE: 3 (A) Jabotinsky Street
Diamond Tower Ramat-Gan 52520 Israel

TELEPHONE NUMBER: 9723-613-1833

NO. OF EMPLOYEES: 49

ANNUAL MEETING: N/A

SHAREHOLDERS: N/A

INSTITUTIONAL HOLDINGS:
No. of Institutions: N/A
Shares Held: N/A

REGISTRAR(S): N/A

TRANSFER AGENT(S): American Stock
Transfer & Trust Company.

CIMATRON, LIMITED

YIELD ...
P/E RATIO 10.58

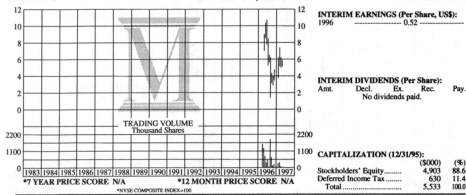

7 YEAR PRICE SCORE N/A **12 MONTH PRICE SCORE N/A**

*NYSE COMPOSITE INDEX=100

TRADING VOLUME
Thousand Shares

INTERIM EARNINGS (Per Share, US$):
1996 ------------------ 0.52 ------------------

INTERIM DIVIDENDS (Per Share):
Amt.   Decl.   Ex.   Rec.   Pay.
No dividends paid.

CAPITALIZATION (12/31/95):

	($000)	(%)
Stockholders' Equity	4,903	88.6
Deferred Income Tax	630	11.4
Total	5,533	100.0

RECENT DEVELOPMENTS: For the year ended 12/31/96, net income surged 62.1% to $3.9 million from $2.4 million in the comparable period of 1995. Total revenues advanced 32.8% to $18.1 million from $13.6 million the year before. Total international revenues jumped 37.9% to $14.3 million versus $10.4 million a year earlier. This reflected a 31.9% improvement in product revenues to $11.9 million and a 78.6% leap in service revenues to $2.4 million. Total Israel revenues climbed 16.5% to $3.7 million from $3.2 million in 1995. This was related to a 1.4% rise in product revenues to $2.2 million and a 49.1% climb in service revenues to $1.5 million. Gross profit increased 36.0% to $14.6 million compared with $10.8 million in the prior year. For the fourth quarter ended 12/31/96, net income more than doubled to $1.9 million from $808,000 in 1995. Revenues grew 49.6% to $5.0 million.

BUSINESS

CIMATRON Ltd. designs, develops, manufactures, markets and supports a family of modular, high performance, fully integrated computer-aided design/computer-aided manufacturing software products.

ANNUAL EARNINGS

	12/31/95	12/31/94	12/31/95	12/31/94
	------------US $------------		------------NIS------------	
Earnings Per Share	0.40	0.15	1.26	0.45

ANNUAL FINANCIAL DATA

RECORD OF EARNINGS (IN THOUSANDS):				
Total Revenues	13,611	9,087	42,842	27,420
Costs & Expenses	10,165	7,752	31,996	23,392
Operating Income	3,446	1,335	10,847	4,028
Income Bef Income Tax	3,465	1,360	10,907	4,104
Income Tax	1,050	480	3,305	1,448
Net Income	2,415	880	7,602	2,655
Average Shares Outstg	6,000	6,000	6,000	6,000
BALANCE SHEET (IN THOUSANDS):				
Cash & Cash Equivalents	235	318	740	960
Receivables, Net	6,292	3,424	19,805	10,332
Inventories	230	60	724	181
Gross Property	4,235	3,386	13,330	10,217
Accumulated Depreciation	2,214	1,748	6,969	5,275
Stockholders' Equity	4,903	3,036	15,433	9,161
Total Assets	10,003	6,265	31,486	18,905
Total Current Assets	6,757	3,802	21,268	11,473
Total Current Liabilities	3,270	2,286	10,293	6,898
Net Working Capital	3,487	1,516	10,976	4,575
Year End Shs Outstg	6,000	...	6,000	...
STATISTICAL RECORD:				
Return on Equity %	49.26	28.99		
Return on Assets %	24.14	14.05		
Operating Profit Margin %	25.32	14.69		
Net Profit Margin %	17.74	9.68		
Book Value Per Share	0.82	...		

Converted at 1995, US$0.3177= 1 New Israeli Shekel; 1994, US$0.3314= 1 New Israeli Shekel

OFFICERS:
Y. Frenkel, Chmn.
M. Yoeli, Pres. & C.E.O.
A. Feldman, Exec. V.P.
E. Lebel, V.P. & C.F.O.

INCORPORATED: Israel, 1992

PRINCIPAL OFFICE: Clal Computer House
11 Gush Etzion Street Givat Shmuel Israel

TELEPHONE NUMBER: 972-3-531-2121

NO. OF EMPLOYEES: 117

ANNUAL MEETING: N/A

SHAREHOLDERS: N/A

INSTITUTIONAL HOLDINGS:
No. of Institutions: N/A
Shares Held: N/A

REGISTRAR(S): N/A

TRANSFER AGENT(S): N/A

CINAR FILMS, INC.

YIELD ...
P/E RATIO 12.28

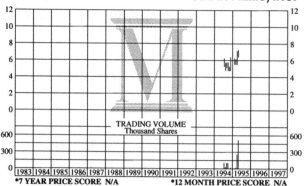

1983 1984 1985 1986 1987 1988 1989 1990 1991 1992 1993 1994 1995 1996 1997

*7 YEAR PRICE SCORE N/A   *12 MONTH PRICE SCORE N/A

*NYSE COMPOSITE INDEX=100

TRADING VOLUME
Thousand Shares

INTERIM EARNINGS (Per Share, US$):

	Feb.	May	Aug.	Nov.
1996	------------------ 0.58 ------------------			

INTERIM DIVIDENDS (Per Share):

Amt.	Decl.	Ex.	Rec.	Pay.
	No dividends paid.			

CAPITALIZATION (11/30/96):

	($000)	(%)
Stockholders' Equity........	92,486	98.2
Deferred Income Tax	1,671	1.8
Total	94,157	100.0

RECENT DEVELOPMENTS: For the year ended 11/30/96, net income leapt 60.9% to C$8.5 million compared with C$5.3 million in the same period of 1995. Revenues advanced 37.6% to C$57.9 million versus C$42.1 million the year before. Gross profit increased 47.6% to C$15.5 million from C$10.5 million a year earlier. The Company donated a part of its collection of animal scripts, storyboards, draw-ings, backgrounds and cells to the CinJmathPque QuJecoise. The donation was valued by independent evaluators at $8.1 million, creating a tax deduction for the Company. As a result, earnings per share includes $0.06 generated by the utilization of 23.0% of the tax deduction. The balance of this tax deduction will be carried forward to future years.

BUSINESS

CINAR FILMS INC. is an integrated family entertainment company, involved in the development, production, post-production, and worldwide distribution of non-violent, animated and live-action programming, as well as entertainment and educational products for children and families. CINRF's divisions and subsidiaries include CINAR Animation, a full-ser-vice animation studio; CINAR Stu-dios, a modern sound recording, mix-ing, audio and video post-production facility; as well as CINAR Music, a music creation, recording and publish-ing division. Through co-production relationships with major production companies, broadcasters and publish-ing companies located throughout the world, CINRF's productions are seen daily in Canada, the U.S. and in over 100 countries around the world.

ANNUAL EARNINGS

	11/30/96	11/30/95	11/30/96	11/30/95
	----------US $----------		----------C $----------	
Earnings Per Share	0.58	0.44	0.78	0.59

ANNUAL FINANCIAL DATA

RECORD OF EARNINGS (IN THOUSANDS):

Total Revenues	43,220	31,104	57,935	42,107
Costs & Expenses	33,853	25,182	45,380	34,089
Depreciation & Amort	636	336	852	455
Operating Income	8,730	5,587	11,703	7,563
Income Bef Income Tax	8,730	5,587	11,703	7,563
Income Tax	2,419	1,703	3,242	2,306
Net Income	6,312	3,883	8,461	5,257
Average Shares Outstg	10,912	8,843	10,912	8,943

BALANCE SHEET (IN THOUSANDS):

Cash & Cash Equivalents	37,264	17,561	49,952	23,773
Receivables, Net	20,340	8,502	27,265	11,509
Gross Property	6,949	4,242	9,315	5,742
Accumulated Depreciation	3,640	2,953	4,879	3,998
Stockholders' Equity	92,486	35,684	123,976	48,306
Total Assets	110,835	49,490	148,572	66,996
Total Current Assets	89,427	47,853	119,876	64,780
Total Current Liabilities	16,627	12,641	22,288	17,113
Net Working Capital	72,801	35,212	97,588	47,667
Year End Shs Outstg	12,640	9,861	12,640	9,861

STATISTICAL RECORD:

Return on Equity %	6.82	10.88		
Return on Assets %	5.69	7.85		
Operating Profit Margin %	20.20	17.96		
Net Profit Margin %	14.60	12.48		
Book Value Per Share	7.32	3.62		

Converted at 1996, US$0.7460= 1 Canadian $; 1995, US$0.7387= 1 Canadian $

OFFICERS:
M. Charest, Chmn. & C.E.O.
R. A. Weinberg, Pres.
H. H. Panju, V.P. & C.F.O.
M. Corbeil, V.P. & General Counsel

INCORPORATED: Canada, Dec., 1976

PRINCIPAL OFFICE: 1055 boul. Rene-Levesque Est Montreal Canada H2L 455

TELEPHONE NUMBER: 514-843-7070

NO. OF EMPLOYEES: 200

ANNUAL MEETING: In Mar.

SHAREHOLDERS: N/A

INSTITUTIONAL HOLDINGS:
No. of Institutions: N/A
Shares Held: N/A

REGISTRAR(S): Montreal Trust, Montreal.

TRANSFER AGENT(S): Montreal Trust, Montreal.

CINRAM INTERNATIONAL INC.

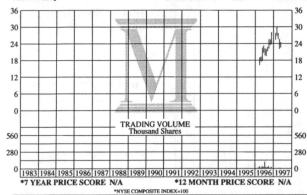

INTERIM EARNINGS (Per Share, US$):

Qtr.	Mar.	June	Sept.	Dec.
1995	0.11	0.12	0.18	0.34
1996	0.14	0.14	0.23	0.45

INTERIM DIVIDENDS (Per Share):

Amt.	Decl.	Ex.	Rec.	Pay.
0.04	3/07/96	3/12/97	3/15/97	3/31/97
0.04	3/06/97	6/11	6/15	6/30
0.04	3/06	9/11	9/15	9/30
0.04	3/06	12/11	12/15	12/31
0.04	3/06	3/11/98	3/15/98	3/31/98

Indicated div.:$0.16

TRADING VOLUME
Thousand Shares

| 1983 | 1984 | 1985 | 1986 | 1987 | 1988 | 1989 | 1990 | 1991 | 1992 | 1993 | 1994 | 1995 | 1996 | 1997 |

*7 YEAR PRICE SCORE N/A *12 MONTH PRICE SCORE N/A

*NYSE COMPOSITE INDEX=100

CAPITALIZATION (12/31/96):

	($000)	(%)
Long-Term Debt	10,149	3.8
Stockholders' Equity	252,066	94.2
Deferred Income Tax	5,250	2.0
Total	267,465	100.0

RECENT DEVELOPMENTS: For the year ended 12/31/96, net income increased 35.7% to C$31.2 million from C$23.0 million the year before. Net sales climbed 26.2% to C$340.7 million. The improved results were attributed to acquisitions and increased demand for CD's and VHS video cassettes, despite lower selling prices. Audio CD sales rose 18.0%, while CD-ROM sales grew 23.0%, including a 90.0% increase in sales of CDs in Latin America. Cinram recently completed the acquisition of cer-

tain assets relating to the CD and CD-ROM manufacturing business of Disc Manufacturing Inc. The Company also purchased the videocassette duplication and distribution business of Videoprint Ltd. On 1/7/97, Cinram announced an agreement with Pacific Ocean Post to form a joint venture, called Cinram POP-DVD centre, to provide services for DVD authoring and multiplexing for motion picture clients and other services.

BUSINESS

CINRAM INTERNATIONAL INC. is engaged in the manufacture of pre-recorded compact discs and cassettes. The Company's product line also includes pre-recorded audio and VHS video cassettes and CD-ROMs. Through one of its U.S. facilities, Cinram designs and builds manufacturing systems for the international optical disc industry. The Company also has facilities in Canada, Europe and Latin America.

ANNUAL EARNINGS

	12/31/96	12/31/95	12/31/96	12/31/95
	----US $----		----C $----	
Earnings Per Share	0.96	0.75	1.31	1.02

ANNUAL FINANCIAL DATA

RECORD OF EARNINGS (IN THOUSANDS):

Total Revenues	249,099	197,942	340,718	270,081
Costs & Expenses	214,296	173,377	293,115	236,563
Operating Income	34,803	24,565	47,603	33,518
Income Bef Income Tax	35,414	25,754	48,439	35,140
Income Tax	12,610	8,904	17,248	12,149
Net Income	22,804	16,850	31,191	22,991
Average Shares Outstg	23,875	22,588	23,875	22,588

BALANCE SHEET (IN THOUSANDS):

Cash & Cash Equivalents	173,932	38,811	237,905	52,955
Receivables, Net	55,757	51,207	76,264	69,869
Inventories	16,983	16,160	23,229	22,049
Gross Property	147,543	122,144	201,810	166,658
Accumulated Depreciation	56,741	48,466	77,611	66,129
Long-Term Debt	10,149	9,830	13,882	13,413
Stockholders' Equity	252,066	102,782	344,776	140,240
Total Assets	346,341	189,638	473,726	258,750
Total Current Assets	247,844	106,836	339,002	145,772
Total Current Liabilities	78,876	71,667	107,887	97,785
Net Working Capital	168,968	35,170	231,115	47,987
Year End Shs Outstg	23,901	23,848	23,901	23,848

STATISTICAL RECORD:

Return on Equity %	9.05	16.39
Return on Assets %	6.58	8.89
Operating Profit Margin %	13.97	12.41
Net Profit Margin %	9.15	8.51
Book Value Per Share	10.55	4.31

Converted at 1996, US$0.7311= 1 Canadian $; 1995, US$0.7329= 1 Canadian $

OFFICERS:
I. Philosophe, Chmn., Pres. & C.E.O.
J. Philosophe, Exec. V.P.
L. Ritchie, Exec. V.P., C.F.O. & Sec.

INCORPORATED: Canada, 1969

PRINCIPAL OFFICE: 2255 Markham Road
Scarborough, Ontario Canada M1B 2W3

TELEPHONE NUMBER: (416) 298-8190

NO. OF EMPLOYEES: N/A

ANNUAL MEETING: In Jun.

SHAREHOLDERS: 4,500

INSTITUTIONAL HOLDINGS:
No. of Institutions: NA
Shares Held: NA

REGISTRAR(S): Montreal Trust Company of Canada, Toronto.

TRANSFER AGENT(S): Montreal Trust
Company of Canada, Toronto.

CLEARLY CANADIAN BEVERAGE CORP.

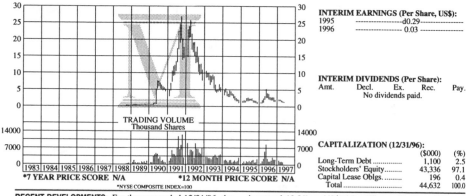

INTERIM EARNINGS (Per Share, US$):

1995	---------------d0.29----------------
1996	----------------- 0.03 -----------------

INTERIM DIVIDENDS (Per Share):

Amt.	Decl.	Ex.	Rec.	Pay.
	No dividends paid.			

TRADING VOLUME
Thousand Shares

CAPITALIZATION (12/31/96):

	($000)	(%)
Long-Term Debt	1,100	2.5
Stockholders' Equity.........	43,336	97.1
Capital Lease Oblgs.	196	0.4
Total	44,632	100.0

1983 1984 1985 1986 1987 1988 1989 1990 1991 1992 1993 1994 1995 1996 1997
*7 YEAR PRICE SCORE N/A   ***12 MONTH PRICE SCORE N/A**
*NYSE COMPOSITE INDEX=100

RECENT DEVELOPMENTS: For the year ended 12/31/96, the Company posted net income of US$450,000 versus a loss of US$4.0 million the year before. Results included inventory write-offs of US$127,000 in 1996 and US$589,000 in 1995. The 1995 results also included restructuring charges of US$580,000. Sales rose 3.9% to US$50.1 million. Gross profit as a percentage of sales increased to 33.6%, or US$16.8 million, versus 22.0%, or US$12.1 million the previous year. Selling, administrative and general expenses increased 13.8% to US$16.8 million, reflecting additional costs associated with the operation of recently acquired distribution territories in the U.S. and Canada as well as increased marketing and promotion expenses. The Company recently completed several acquisitions of distribution rights from former master distributors in the U.S. and Canadian markets and now has approximately 80.0% of the North American market.

BUSINESS

CLEARLY CANADIAN BEVER-AGE CORP. bottles, packages, markets and distributes an alternative beverage called Clearly Canadian. Clearly Canadian is the result of the Company's combining natural spring water from company-owned locations in British Columbia and natural fruit oils to produce a beverage that is free of artificial colors and caffeine. Clearly Canadian distributes its line of premium beverages, including Clearly Canadian sparkling flavored water, Orbitz and Clearly Canadian Natural Artesian Water in the United States, Canada, Japan, Great Britain and other countries worldwide. The Company also designs, develops and distributes hobby or home brew equipment, small breweries, supplies and concentrate.

ANNUAL EARNINGS

	12/31/96	12/31/95	12/31/96	12/31/95
	-------------US $-------------		-------------C $-------------	
Earnings Per Share	0.03	d0.29	0.03	d0.38

ANNUAL FINANCIAL DATA

RECORD OF EARNINGS (IN THOUSANDS):

	12/31/96	12/31/95	12/31/96	12/31/95
Total Revenues	50,082	48,185	68,592	65,746
Costs & Expenses	49,480	50,815	67,727	69,335
Operating Income	602	d2,630	865	d3,589
Income Bef Income Tax	504	d3,799	690	d5,184
Income Tax	54	170	73	232
Net Income	450	d3,969	617	d5,416
Average Shares Outstg	23,010	13,459	23,010	13,459

BALANCE SHEET (IN THOUSANDS):

Cash & Cash Equivalents	11,254	4,705	15,414	6,420
Receivables, Net	9,392	6,211	12,264	8,474
Inventories	4,847	4,600	6,638	6,277
Gross Property	12,582	7,795	17,233	10,636
Accumulated Depreciation	2,634	2,003	3,608	2,733
Long-Term Debt	1,100	1,895	1,500	2,585
Stockholders' Equity	43,366	28,451	59,396	38,820
Total Assets	52,101	36,484	71,360	49,781
Total Current Assets	27,495	22,702	37,658	26,656
Total Current Liabilities	7,439	5,891	10,196	8,038
Net Working Capital	20,056	16,811	27,462	18,618
Year End Shs Outstg	23,010	13,429	23,010	13,429

STATISTICAL RECORD:

Return on Equity %	1.04	...		
Return on Assets %	0.86	...		
Operating Profit Margin %	1.20	...		
Net Profit Margin %	0.89	...		
Book Value Per Share	1.88	2.12		

Converted at 1996, US$0.7301= 1 Canadian $; 1994, US$0.7329= 1 Canadian $

OFFICERS:
D. L. Mason, Pres. & C.E.O.
D. B. Horton, C.F.O. & Sec.
G. D. Forman, C.O.O.
S. R. Ross, Exec. V.P.

INCORPORATED: Mar., 1981

PRINCIPAL OFFICE: 1900-999 W. Hastings Street Vancouver Canada V6C 2W2

TELEPHONE NUMBER: 604-683-0312

NO. OF EMPLOYEES: N/A

ANNUAL MEETING: In Sep.

SHAREHOLDERS: N/A

INSTITUTIONAL HOLDINGS:
No. of Institutions: 9
Shares Held: 60,351

REGISTRAR(S): The Montreal Trust Company, Vancouver.

TRANSFER AGENT(S): The Montreal Trust Company, Vancouver.

CLEARNET COMMUNICATIONS INC.

YIELD ...
P/E RATIO ...

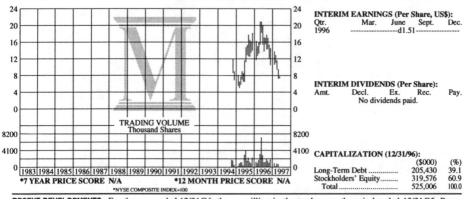

*7 YEAR PRICE SCORE N/A   *12 MONTH PRICE SCORE N/A
*NYSE COMPOSITE INDEX=100

INTERIM EARNINGS (Per Share, US$):

Qtr.	Mar.	June	Sept.	Dec.
1996		d1.51		

INTERIM DIVIDENDS (Per Share):

Amt.	Decl.	Ex.	Rec.	Pay.
	No dividends paid.			

CAPITALIZATION (12/31/96):

	($000)	(%)
Long-Term Debt	205,430	39.1
Stockholders' Equity	319,576	60.9
Total	525,006	100.0

RECENT DEVELOPMENTS: For the year ended 12/31/96, the Company posted a net loss of C$74.8 million versus a loss of C$13.1 million in 1995. Revenues were C$38.8 million compared with C$22.0 million a year earlier. Results for the period ended 12/31/95 were for an eight month period. The Company changed its fiscal year end to December 31 from April 30 effective 12/31/95. For comparative purposes, for the year ended 12/31/96, the Company posted a net loss of C$74.8 million compared with a loss C$17.1 million in the twelve month period ended 12/31/95. Revenues advanced 20.6% to C$38.8 million. Network revenue rose 5.3% to C$15.6 million, while equipment sales, rental and service revenue advanced 33.7% to C$23.1 million. The Company attributed the increase in network revenue primarily to the increase in analogue average revenue per subscriber unit and the Mike digital network launch in October 1996 that brought in 5,065 subscribers by 12/31/96.

BUSINESS

CLEARNET COMMUNICATIONS INC. is a wireless communications company that commercially launched its digital business communications service in October 1996, under the trade name "Mike™", in a continuous corridor from Windsor to Quebec City. The Company continues to operate its analogue Specialized Mobile Radio ("SMR") network services across Canada and its multi-location mobile communications sales and service dealership division, Clearnet Business Communications Centre, formerly MOCO Canada.

ANNUAL EARNINGS

	12/31/96	☐ 12/31/95	12/31/96	☐ 12/31/95
	US $		C $	
Earnings Per Share	d1.51	d0.32	d2.07	d0.43

ANNUAL FINANCIAL DATA

RECORD OF EARNINGS (IN THOUSANDS):

Total Revenues	28,339	16,130	38,762	22,008
Costs & Expenses	57,005	21,116	77,972	28,812
Depreciation & Amort	19,918	3,900	27,244	5,322
Operating Income	d48,585	d8,887	d66,454	d12,126
Income Bef Income Tax	d53,809	d9,432	d73,600	d12,869
Income Tax	886	184	1,212	251
Net Income	d54,695	d9,616	d74,812	d13,120
Average Shares Outstg	36,225	30,734	36,225	30,734

☐ For eight months due to fiscal year-end change.

BALANCE SHEET (IN THOUSANDS):

Cash & Cash Equivalents	254,062	199,605	347,506	272,349
Receivables, Net	10,624	4,808	14,531	6,560
Inventories	12,019	3,166	16,440	4,320
Gross Property	204,293	105,822	279,432	144,388
Accumulated Depreciation	19,827	7,393	27,119	10,088
Long-Term Debt	205,430	175,403	280,987	239,327
Stockholders' Equity	319,576	208,862	437,117	284,980
Total Assets	587,465	439,247	803,536	599,327
Total Current Assets	279,599	210,867	382,436	287,716
Total Current Liabilities	61,426	52,599	84,019	71,768
Net Working Capital	218,173	158,268	298,417	215,948
Year End Shs Outstg	40,007	30,769	40,007	30,769

STATISTICAL RECORD:

Book Value Per Share	7.99	6.79		

Converted at 1996, US$0.7311= 1 Canadian $; 1995, US$0.7329= 1 Canadian $

OFFICERS:
R. C. Simmonds, Chmn. & V.P.
G. A. Cope, Pres. & C.E.O.
R. G. McFarlane, V.P., C.F.O. & Sec.-Treas.

INCORPORATED: N/A

PRINCIPAL OFFICE: 1305 Pickering Parkway, Suite 300, Pickering Ontario, Canada L1V 3P2

TELEPHONE NUMBER: 905-837-3007

NO. OF EMPLOYEES: 680

ANNUAL MEETING: In May

SHAREHOLDERS: N/A

INSTITUTIONAL HOLDINGS:
No. of Institutions: 31
Shares Held: 6,142,274

REGISTRAR(S): Montreal Trust Company of Canada, Toronto; Bank of Nova Scotia Trust Co., New York.

TRANSFER AGENT(S): Montreal Trust Company of Canada, Toronto; Bank of Nova Scotia Trust Co., New York.

COGNOS INCORPORATED

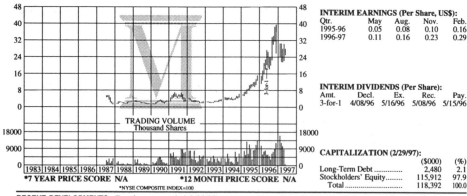

INTERIM EARNINGS (Per Share, US$):

Qtr.	May	Aug.	Nov.	Feb.
1995-96	0.05	0.08	0.10	0.16
1996-97	0.11	0.16	0.23	0.29

INTERIM DIVIDENDS (Per Share):

Amt.	Decl.	Ex.	Rec.	Pay.
3-for-1	4/08/96	5/16/96	5/08/96	5/15/96

TRADING VOLUME
Thousand Shares

1983 1984 1985 1986 1987 1988 1989 1990 1991 1992 1993 1994 1995 1996 1997

*7 YEAR PRICE SCORE N/A   *12 MONTH PRICE SCORE N/A

*NYSE COMPOSITE INDEX=100

CAPITALIZATION (2/29/97):

	($000)	(%)
Long-Term Debt	2,480	2.1
Stockholders' Equity.........	115,912	97.9
Total	118,392	100.0

RECENT DEVELOPMENTS: For the year ended 2/28/97, net income more than doubled to US$36.8 million from US$17.5 million the previous year. Revenue advanced 30.2% to US$198.2 million from US$152.2 million the year before. Operating income increased to US$41.7 million from US$20.0 million a year earlier. Income before taxes grew 94.7% to US$45.8 million from US$23.5 million the prior year. The improvement in results for fiscal 1997 was primarily due to the development of new and enhanced products, growth in Cognos' customer base and expansion of Cognos' distribution channels. For the quarter ended 2/28/97, net income climbed 78.9% to US$13.3 million from US$7.4 million in the corresponding period of the previous year. Revenue improved 31.0% to US$58.3 million from US$44.5 million the year before. On 4/9/97, the Company acquired Right Information Systems, Ltd. for approximately $8.0 million.

BUSINESS

COGNOS INCORPORATED develops, markets and supports complementary lines of software tools that are designed to meet complex business-critical needs, while protecting the training and technology investments customers have made in their existing technologies. The Corporation's business intelligence tools, which include PowerPlay(R), Impromptu(R), Scenario(R), 4Thought(R), and PowerPlay Server Web Edition(R), give individual users the ability to independently access, explore, analyze, and report corporate data. The Corporation's client/server application development tools, which include Axiant(R) and PowerHouse Series 8(R), are designed to increase the productivity of system analysts and developers. Cognos products are distributed both directly and through resellers worldwide.

ANNUAL EARNINGS

	2/29/97	2/28/96	2/29/97	2/28/96
	--------------US $--------------		------------C $------------	
Earnings Per Share	0.80	0.40	1.09	0.55

Note: 3-for-1 stk. split, 5/15/96.

ANNUAL FINANCIAL DATA

RECORD OF EARNINGS (IN THOUSANDS):

	2/29/97	2/28/96	2/29/97	2/28/96
Total Revenues	198,185	152,186	271,152	209,478
Costs & Expenses	156,468	132,211	214,075	181,983
Operating Income	41,717	19,975	57,076	27,495
Income Bef Income Tax	45,814	23,526	62,682	32,383
Income Tax	9,025	5,996	12,348	8,253
Net Income	36,789	17,530	50,344	24,129
Average Shares Outstg.	46,052	44,301	46,052	44,301
BALANCE SHEET (IN THOUSANDS):				
Cash & Cash Equivalents	119,228	79,381	163,125	109,265
Receivables, Net	47,029	36,837	64,344	50,400
Inventories	697	908	954	1,250
Gross Property	51,853	44,986	70,944	61,922
Accumulated Depreciation	33,017	29,437	45,173	40,519
Long-Term Debt	2,655	2,744	3,633	3,777
Stockholders' Equity	115,192	78,297	158,588	107,773
Total Assets	189,152	140,010	258,793	192,719
Total Current Assets	169,817	120,319	232,340	165,615
Total Current Liabilities	66,090	54,170	90,423	74,563
Net Working Capital	103,727	66,149	141,917	91,052
Year End Shs Outstg	43,589	42,261	43,589	42,261
STATISTICAL RECORD:				
Return on Equity %	31.74	22.39		
Return on Assets %	19.45	12.52		
Operating Profit Margin %	21.05	13.13		
Net Profit Margin %	18.56	11.52		
Book Value Per Share	2.66	1.85		

Converted at 1997, US$0.7309= 1 Canadian $; 1996, US$0.7265= 1 Canadian $

OFFICERS:
R. Zambonini, Pres. & C.E.O.
D.M. Moore, Sr. V.P.—Fin. & Admin. & C.F.O.

INCORPORATED: Canada, Dec. 1969

PRINCIPAL OFFICE: 3755 Riverside Drive, P.O. Box 9707, Station T, Ottawa, Ontario Canada K1G 4K9

TELEPHONE NUMBER: 613-738-1440
FAX: 613-738-0002
NO. OF EMPLOYEES: 1,227
ANNUAL MEETING: In June
SHAREHOLDERS: 690
INSTITUTIONAL HOLDINGS:
No. of Institutions: 80
Shares Held: 26,660,145

REGISTRAR(S): N/A

TRANSFER AGENT(S): The Montreal Trust Company, Toronto; ChaseMellon Shareholder Services, New York.

COMCAST UK CABLE PARTNERS LTD.

YIELD ...
P/E RATIO ...

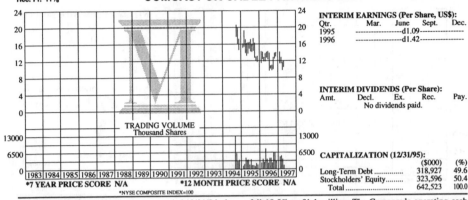

*7 YEAR PRICE SCORE N/A *12 MONTH PRICE SCORE N/A
*NYSE COMPOSITE INDEX=100

INTERIM EARNINGS (Per Share, US$):

Qtr.	Mar.	June	Sept.	Dec.
1995		d1.09		
1996		d1.42		

INTERIM DIVIDENDS (Per Share):

Amt.	Decl.	Ex.	Rec.	Pay.
		No dividends paid.		

CAPITALIZATION (12/31/95):

	($000)	(%)
Long-Term Debt	318,927	49.6
Stockholders' Equity	323,596	50.4
Total	642,523	100.0

RECENT DEVELOPMENTS: For the year ended 12/31/96, the Company reported a net loss of £40.6 million compared with a loss of £29.0 million the year before. Revenues skyrocketed to £32.4 million from £2.8 million. Service revenues jumped to £31.4 million from £1.5 million, reflecting the consolidation of the Cambridge franchise operating results effective 4/1/96 and the continued growth of cable and telephone subscribers. Consulting fee revenues fell 18.5% to £1.1 million. The Company's operating cash flow deficit was £7.9 million versus £8.8 million in 1995. The operating cash flow deficit continues to reflect costs associated with the ongoing construction of cable and telephone networks at Teesside. During 1996, Comcast UK's franchises grew rapidly as Cable TV subscribers increased 32.0%, residential telephone subscribers grew by 46.0% and business telephone subscribers climbed 42.0%.

BUSINESS

COMCAST UK CABLE PARTNERS LTD. is a holding company and was formed to develop, construct, manage and operate Comcast Corporation's interest in the United Kingdom cable television and telecommunications industry. Through its subsidiaries, the Company is engaged in integrated cable television, business telecommunications and residential telephone systems in three major metropolitan areas: Birmingham, northern London and Cambridge.

ANNUAL EARNINGS

	12/31/95	12/31/94	12/31/95	12/31/94
	US $		British £	
Earnings Per Share	d1.09	d0.85	d0.70	d0.54

ANNUAL FINANCIAL DATA

RECORD OF EARNINGS (IN THOUSANDS):

	12/31/95	12/31/94	12/31/95	12/31/94
Total Revenues	4,415	2,122	2,843	1,356
Costs & Expenses	22,755	6,542	14,652	4,180
Operating Income	d18,339	d4,420	d11,809	d2,824
Eq. Earnings in Affils.	d36,770	d25,492	d23,677	d16,289
Net Income	d44,978	d25,456	d28,962	d16,266
Average Shares Outstg	41,245	30,117	41,245	30,117

BALANCE SHEET (IN THOUSANDS):

Cash & Cash Equivalents	340,838	178,748	219,471	114,216
Receivables, Net	1,180	2,718	760	1,737
Gross Property	74,156	3,014	47,750	1,926
Accumulated Depreciation	1,918	88	1,235	56
Long-Term Debt	318,927	13,547	205,362	8,656
Stockholders' Equity	323,596	371,504	208,368	237,383
Total Assets	670,411	398,667	431,688	254,739
Total Current Assets	347,919	182,891	224,030	116,863
Total Current Liabilities	24,497	12,911	15,774	8,250
Net Working Capital	323,422	169,979	208,256	108,613
Year End Shs Outstg	28,372	28,372	28,372	28,372

STATISTICAL RECORD:

Book Value Per Share	11.41	13.09		

Converted at 1995, US$1.5530= 1 British pound; 1994, US$1.5650= 1 British pound

OFFICERS:
B. L. Roberts, Pres.
J. R. Alchin, Sr. V.P. & Treas.
L. S. Smith, Sr. V.P.
S. L. Wang, Sr. V.P. & Sec.

INCORPORATED: Bermuda, Sept. 1992

PRINCIPAL OFFICE: Clarendon House, 2 Church Street West, Hamilton HM11 Bermuda

TELEPHONE NUMBER: 441-295-5950

NO. OF EMPLOYEES: 1,730

ANNUAL MEETING: N/A

SHAREHOLDERS: N/A

INSTITUTIONAL HOLDINGS:
No. of Institutions: N/A
Shares Held: N/A

REGISTRAR(S): N/A

TRANSFER AGENT(S): The First National Bank of Boston, United States.

COMMODORE HOLDINGS LIMITED

YIELD ...
P/E RATIO 8.5

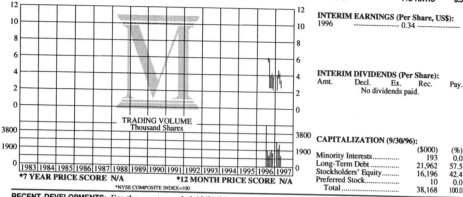

*7 YEAR PRICE SCORE N/A   *12 MONTH PRICE SCORE N/A
*NYSE COMPOSITE INDEX=100

INTERIM EARNINGS (Per Share, US$):
1996 ------------------ 0.34 ------------------

INTERIM DIVIDENDS (Per Share):

Amt.	Decl.	Ex.	Rec.	Pay.
		No dividends paid.		

CAPITALIZATION (9/30/96):

	($000)	(%)
Minority Interests.............	193	0.0
Long-Term Debt	21,962	57.5
Stockholders' Equity.........	16,196	42.4
Preferred Stock...............	10	0.0
Total	38,168	100.0

RECENT DEVELOPMENTS: For the quarter ended 12/31/96, net income more than doubled to $174,847 compared with $51,771 in the corresponding period a year earlier. Earnings per share were $0.04, versus $0.00 per share in the year-earlier period. Revenues were $12.1 million, up 58% versus $7.7 million in 1995. Earnings and revenues benefited from the Company's having two vessels in service for the quarter compared with only one vessel in service for the year-earlier period. Operating expenses rose 57.7% to $11.7 million primarily due to the Company's having two vessels in service. Marketing, selling and administrative expenses rose 15.7% to $1.7 million compared with $1.5 million in the corresponding period a year earlier.

BUSINESS

COMMODORE HOLDINGS LIMITED is a holding company. Through its subsidiary, the Company is engaged in the operation of cruise ships. The Enchanted Isle offers cruises to the Caribbean from New Orleans. The Universe Explorer is chartered to Sea-Comm Ltd., which is a joint-venture company between the Company and Seawise Foundation Inc. Seawise operates the educational Semester-at-Sea program during a portion of the year and Sea-Comm operates cruises to Alaska during the balance of the year.

ANNUAL EARNINGS

	9/30/96	9/30/95
	US $	
Earnings Per Share	0.34	0.06

ANNUAL FINANCIAL DATA

RECORD OF EARNINGS (IN THOUSANDS):

	9/30/96	9/30/95
Total Revenues	47,817	7,256
Costs & Expenses	42,728	6,605
Depreciation & Amort	1,614	198
Operating Income	3,475	453
Income Bef Income Tax	2,009	320
Income Tax	...	8
Net Income	2,009	312
Average Shares Outstg	5,440	4,378

BALANCE SHEET (IN THOUSANDS):

Cash & Cash Equivalents	4,889	3,638
Receivables, Net	2,799	79
Inventories	1,830	691
Gross Property	37,927	33,283
Accumulated Depreciation	1,779	198
Long-Term Debt	21,962	24,500
Stockholders' Equity	16,196	12,519
Total Assets	53,285	44,097
Total Current Assets	12,102	6,158
Total Current Liabilities	14,933	7,078
Net Working Capital	d2,832	d920
Year End Shs Outstg	5,582	4,932

STATISTICAL RECORD:

Return on Equity %	12.4	2.49
Return on Assets %	3.8	0.7
Operating Profit Margin %	7.27	6.24
Net Profit Margin %	4.20	4.30
Book Value Per Share	2.90	2.54

OFFICERS:
J. I. Binder, Chmn.
F. A. Mayer, Vice-Chmn. & C.E.O.
J. R. Sullivan, Pres.
A. Pritzker, V.P. Fin. & C.F.O.

INCORPORATED: Bermuda Apr. 13, 1995.

PRINCIPAL OFFICE: 4000 Hollywood Boulevard, Suite 385-S South Tower Hollywood FL 33021

TELEPHONE NUMBER: 954-967-2100

NO. OF EMPLOYEES: 551

ANNUAL MEETING: In Feb.

SHAREHOLDERS: N/A

INSTITUTIONAL HOLDINGS:
No. of Institutions: N/A
Shares Held: N/A

REGISTRAR(S): Stock Trans, Inc., Ardmore, PA.

TRANSFER AGENT(S): Stock Trans, Inc., Ardmore, PA.

COMPUTALOG LTD.

YIELD ...
P/E RATIO 15.1

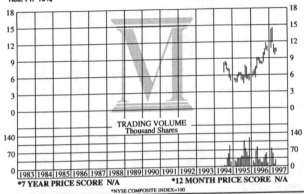

INTERIM EARNINGS (Per Share, US$):
1995	0.73
1996	0.89

INTERIM DIVIDENDS (Per Share):

Amt.	Decl.	Ex.	Rec.	Pay.
	No dividends paid.			

TRADING VOLUME
Thousand Shares

| 1983 | 1984 | 1985 | 1986 | 1987 | 1988 | 1989 | 1990 | 1991 | 1992 | 1993 | 1994 | 1995 | 1996 | 1997 |

*7 YEAR PRICE SCORE N/A   ***12 MONTH PRICE SCORE N/A**

*NYSE COMPOSITE INDEX=100

CAPITALIZATION (12/31/96):
	($000)	(%)
Stockholders' Equity	71,720	99.0
Deferred Income Tax	754	1.0
Total	72,474	100.0

RECENT DEVELOPMENTS: For the year ended 12/31/96, net income climbed 41.0% to c$10.7 million compared with c$7.6 million the previous year. Revenues increased 36.2% to c$147.9 million from c$108.6 million. Net income before taxes and minority interest jumped 68.1% to c$15.7 million. The improved results were attributed to the acquisitions of Norjet Geotechnologies Inc. on 3/7/96 and The Bob Fournet Company on 5/1/96, along with equipment sales to international joint ventures and increased levels of drilling activity in western Canada. The average western Canada drilling rig count grew 14.0% to 320, while the total number of oil and natural gas wells completed in Canada during 1996 increased 24.0% to 9,973. On 3/19/97, the Company finalized definitive agreements with Geoservices Group of Paris related to the establishment of United GeoCom Drilling Services. United GeoCom was formed to combine each company's Canadian directional drilling services operations.

BUSINESS

COMPUTALOG LTD. is engaged in electric wireline logging and directional drilling services and the development, manufacture and international sale of wireline logging products to the petroleum resource industry. The Company offers wireline services in Canada, the United States and Venezuela and, through a 49.0% joint venture in Argentina. Drilling services are offered in North America through the United GeoCom Drilling Services joint ventures. Wireline products are manufactured in the USA and through a 50.1% joint venture in China and directional drilling products are designed and assembled in Canada.

ANNUAL EARNINGS

	12/31/96	12/31/95	12/31/96	12/31/95
	---US $---		---C $---	
Earnings Per Share	0.89	0.73	1.22	1.00

ANNUAL FINANCIAL DATA

RECORD OF EARNINGS (IN THOUSANDS):
	12/31/96	12/31/95	12/31/96	12/31/95
Total Revenues	108,163	79,621	147,945	108,638
Costs & Expenses	88,783	66,913	121,438	91,299
Depreciation & Amort	7,894	5,860	10,797	7,995
Income Bef Income Tax	11,486	6,848	15,710	9,344
Income Tax	3,748	1,310	5,126	1,787
Minority Interests	cr54	...	cr74	...
Net Income	7,792	5,539	10,658	7,557

BALANCE SHEET (IN THOUSANDS):
Cash & Cash Equivalents	1,853	6,785	2,534	9,258
Receivables, Net	27,772	14,756	37,986	20,134
Inventories	10,605	9,576	14,506	13,066
Gross Property	81,765	70,400	111,838	96,057
Accumulated Depreciation	36,005	35,799	49,248	48,846
Stockholders' Equity	71,720	52,583	98,099	71,747
Total Assets	96,632	66,522	132,174	90,765
Total Current Assets	40,912	31,803	55,959	43,394
Total Current Liabilities	23,429	13,621	32,046	18,585
Net Working Capital	17,483	18,183	23,913	24,809
Year End Shs Outstg	11,047	7,561	11,047	7,561

STATISTICAL RECORD:
Return on Equity %	10.9	10.5		
Return on Assets %	8.1	8.3		
Operating Profit Margin %	10.6	8.6		
Net Profit Margin %	7.2	7.0		
Book Value Per Share	6.49	6.95		

Converted at 1996, US$0.7311= 1 Canadian C $; 1995, US$0.7329= 1 Canadian C $

CORE LABORATORIES N.V.

YIELD ...
P/E RATIO 25.2

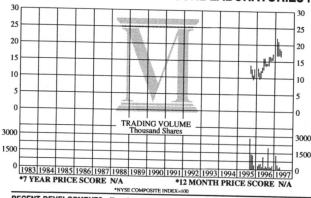

INTERIM EARNINGS (Per Share, US$):

Qtr.	Mar.	June	Sept.	Dec.
1995	----------------- 0.52 -----------------			
1996	----------------- 0.72 -----------------			

INTERIM DIVIDENDS (Per Share):

Amt.	Decl.	Ex.	Rec.	Pay.
	No dividends paid.			

TRADING VOLUME
Thousand Shares

1983 1984 1985 1986 1987 1988 1989 1990 1991 1992 1993 1994 1995 1996 1997
*7 YEAR PRICE SCORE N/A   *12 MONTH PRICE SCORE N/A
*NYSE COMPOSITE INDEX=100

CAPITALIZATION (12/31/96):

	($000)	(%)
Long-Term Debt	11,594	19.0
Minority Interest	212	0.3
Stockholders' Equity........	47,411	77.5
Deferred Income Tax	1,970	3.2
Total	61,187	100.0

RECENT DEVELOPMENTS: For the year ended 12/31/96, net income jumped 55.7% to $8.0 million compared with $5.1 million, before an extraordinary item, in 1995. Revenues increased 17.0% to $93.7 million from $80.1 million. The improved results reflected continued internal growth of developed technologies, as well as acquired technologies. On 12/31/96, the Company completed the acquisition of Pro Technics, a worldwide provider of services that measure the effectiveness of well stimulations and completions through their proprietary technology. The combined company's 1996 revenues increased 20.3% to $105.4 million. During the first quarter of 1997, Core acquired all of the outstanding shares of Scott Pickford plc, a London-based provider of geological, geophysical and engineering services and products. Core Laboratories also acquired Saybolt International B.V. in the second quarter of 1997. Saybolt provides analytical and field services used to characterize crude oil and its derivatives.

BUSINESS

CORE LABORATORIES N.V. is a major provider of petroleum reservoir description data and production management services for maximizing hydrocarbon recovery from new and existing fields. The Company is the world's largest provider of petroleum reservoir rock and fluids analyses and multidisciplinary reservoir discription studies. Core is also a major provider of field services evaluating the efficiencies of well completions and stimulations and the effectiveness of enhanced oil recovery projects. In addition, the Company manufactures and sells petroleum reservoir rock and fluids analysis and other integrated systems.

ANNUAL EARNINGS

	12/31/96	12/31/95	12/31/96	12/31/95
	------------US $------------		------------NLG------------	
Earnings Per Share	0.72	0.52	1.26	0.90

ANNUAL FINANCIAL DATA

RECORD OF EARNINGS (IN THOUSANDS):

Total Revenues	105,368	87,593	183,856	140,847
Costs & Expenses	93,184	77,637	162,596	124,838
Operating Income	12,184	9,956	21,260	16,009
Income Bef Income Tax	11,396	6,956	19,885	10,290
Income Tax	3,719	2,174	6,489	3,496
Net Income	7,677	4,782	13,396	7,689
Average Shares Outstg	10,691	8,594	10,691	8,594

BALANCE SHEET (IN THOUSANDS):

Cash & Cash Equivalents	2,935	4,940	5,121	7,943
Receivables, Net	27,993	24,331	45,012	42,455
Inventories	9,472	8,559	16,528	13,763
Gross Property	35,814	25,822	62,492	41,521
Accumulated Depreciation	8,109	3,972	14,149	6,387
Long-Term Debt	11,594	13,541	20,230	21,774
Stockholders' Equity	47,411	39,665	82,727	63,780
Total Assets	79,691	71,379	139,053	114,776
Total Current Assets	42,550	39,932	74,245	64,210
Total Current Liabilities	17,345	15,473	30,265	24,880
Net Working Capital	25,205	24,459	43,980	39,329
Year End Shs Outstg	10,593	10,579	10,593	10,579

STATISTICAL RECORD:

Return on Equity %	16.2	12.1
Return on Assets %	9.6	6.7
Operating Profit Margin %	11.5	11.3
Net Profit Margin %	7.3	5.5
Book Value Per Share	4.48	3.75

Converted at 1996, US$0.5731= 1 Netherlands guilder; 1995, US$0.6219= 1 Netherlands guilder

OFFICERS:
S. D. Weinroth, Chmn.
D. M. Demshur, Pres. & C.E.O.
J. R. Perna, Sr. V.P.
R. L. Bergmark, C.F.O. & Treas.

INCORPORATED: Netherlands, 1994

PRINCIPAL OFFICE: Herengracht 424
Amsterdam Netherlands 1017 BZ

TELEPHONE NUMBER: 20-420-3191

NO. OF EMPLOYEES: 1,200 (approx.)

ANNUAL MEETING: N/A

SHAREHOLDERS: 72 (approx.)

INSTITUTIONAL HOLDINGS:
No. of Institutions: 15
Shares Held: 1,958,092

REGISTRAR(S): The American Stock
Transfer Company, New York.

TRANSFER AGENT(S): The American Stock
Transfer Company, New York.

COREL CORPORATION

YIELD ...
P/E RATIO ...

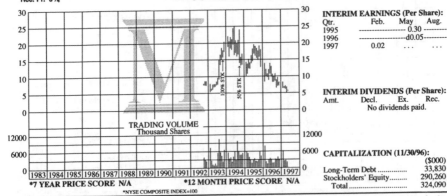

INTERIM EARNINGS (Per Share):

Qtr.	Feb.	May	Aug.	Nov.
1995		0.30		
1996		d0.05		
1997	0.02	...	...	...

INTERIM DIVIDENDS (Per Share):

Amt.	Decl.	Ex.	Rec.	Pay.
		No dividends paid.		

CAPITALIZATION (11/30/96):

	($000)	(%)
Long-Term Debt	33,830	10.4
Stockholders' Equity	290,260	89.6
Total	324,090	100.0

RECENT DEVELOPMENTS: On 4/7/97, the Company agreed to sell its Corel CD Home Collection software line to Hoffmann & Associates Inc. of Toronto for $1.0 million in cash and up to a 25% stake in Hoffmann. For the three months ended 2/28/97, net income totaled $1.0 million, or $0.02 per share, compared with a net loss of $6.6 million, or $0.13 per share, the previous year. Sales were $93.7 million, up significantly versus $36.4 million a year earlier. Gross profit totaled $69.0 million, or 73.6% of sales, compared with $27.0 million, or 74.1% of sales, the year before. Income from operations was $3.5 million versus a loss from operations of $11.2 million the prior year. In March 1997, the Company announced that it plans to spin off its Video and Networking groups into a new company to be called Corel Computer Corporation.

BUSINESS

COREL CORPORATION develops and markets productivity applications, graphics and Internet software. The Company's product line includes CorelDRAW™, the Corel® WordPerfect® Suite, Corel® Office Professional, CorelVIDEO™, Corel-CAD™ and over 50 multimedia software titles. The Company ships its products in over 17 languages through a network of more than 160 distributors in 70 countries worldwide.

ANNUAL EARNINGS

	11/30/96	11/30/95	11/30/96	11/30/95
	----US $----		----C $----	
Earnings Per Share	d0.05	0.30	d0.06	0.41

ANNUAL FINANCIAL DATA

RECORD OF EARNINGS (IN THOUSANDS):

Total Revenues	334,245	196,379	448,050	265,844
Costs & Expenses	320,155	170,111	429,162	230,284
Depreciation & Amort	19,081	9,468	25,578	12,817
Operating Income	d4,991	16,800	d6,690	22,743
Income Bef Income Tax	d3,600	21,823	d4,826	29,542
Income Tax	cr850	7,339	cr1,139	9,935
Net Income	d2,750	14,484	d3,686	19,607
Average Shares Outstg	57,289	48,412	57,289	48,412

BALANCE SHEET (IN THOUSANDS):

Cash & Cash Equivalents	6,924	81,816	9,282	110,757
Receivables, Net	136,691	65,425	183,232	88,568
Inventories	30,390	16,224	40,737	21,963
Gross Property	297,969	88,854	399,422	120,284
Accumulated Depreciation	95,694	39,854	128,276	53,952
Long-Term Debt	33,830	...	45,349	...
Stockholders' Equity	290,260	195,858	389,088	265,139
Total Assets	398,478	221,346	534,153	299,643
Total Current Assets	195,333	172,346	261,840	233,310
Total Current Liabilities	74,388	22,993	99,716	31,126
Net Working Capital	120,945	149,353	162,125	202,184
Year End Shs Outstg	60,041	49,300	60,041	49,300

STATISTICAL RECORD:

Return on Equity %	...	7.40		
Return on Assets %	...	6.54		
Operating Profit Margin %	...	8.55		
Net Profit Margin %	...	7.38		
Book Value Per Share	4.83	3.97		

Converted at 1996, US$0.7460= 1 Canadian $; 1995, US$0.7387= 1 Canadian $

OFFICERS:
M. C. Cowpland, Chmn., Pres. & C.E.O.
C. A. Norris, V.P.-Fin. & C.F.O.
P. R. Beirne, Chf. Engineer
P. C. LaBarge, Sec. & Treas.

INCORPORATED: May, 1985

PRINCIPAL OFFICE: 1600 Carling Avenue, Ottawa, Ontario Canada K1Z 8R7

TELEPHONE NUMBER: 613-728-3733

NO. OF EMPLOYEES: 1,700

ANNUAL MEETING: In April

SHAREHOLDERS: N/A

INSTITUTIONAL HOLDINGS:
No. of Institutions: 21
Shares Held: 2,225,657

REGISTRAR(S): Montreal Trust Company, Toronto; The Bank of New York, New York.

TRANSFER AGENT(S): Montreal Trust Company, Toronto; The Bank of New York, New York.

COTT CORPORATION

YIELD ...
P/E RATIO 26.8

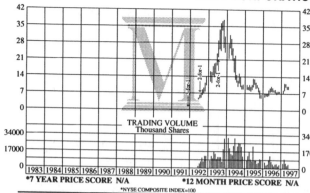

*7 YEAR PRICE SCORE N/A   *12 MONTH PRICE SCORE N/A

*NYSE COMPOSITE INDEX=100

TRADING VOLUME
Thousand Shares

INTERIM EARNINGS (Per Share, C $):

Qtr.	Apr.	Jul.	Oct.	Jan.
1994-95		0.56		
1995-96		d0.41		
1996-97		0.47		

INTERIM DIVIDENDS (Per Share):

Amt.	Decl.	Ex.	Rec.	Pay.
0.025	2/07/96	2/16/96	2/20/96	2/29/96

Last Dividend Paid.

CAPITALIZATION (1/25/97):

	($000)	(%)
Long-Term Debt	205,511	46.2
Stockholders' Equity	239,187	53.8
Total	444,697	100.0

RECENT DEVELOPMENTS: For the year ended 1/25/97, income from continuing operations was C$29.5 million compared with a loss of C$25.0 million a year ago. The results for the year ended 1/25/97 included pre-tax charges of C$12.1 million due to the restructuring of certain operations. Sales advanced 5.8% to C$1.35 billion from C$1.28 billion in the prior year. The increase in sales was fueled by a 9% increase in case sales, partially offset by a slight decline in average selling prices. Case sales in the U.S. were 6% over 1995 volumes and respresented 53% of the Company's total soft drink volumes. In Canada, which accounted for 24% of total soft drink volumes, case sales increased 5%. European case sales rose 39% and represented 16% of total soft drink volumes. Gross profit margin, as a percentage of sales, was 15.9% compared to 11.6% a year earlier.

BUSINESS

COTT CORPORATION is the parent company of a group engaged in the bottling and canning of a range of soft drinks, mineral water and spring water under its own brand names and under the private labels of major grocery store chains. The Company also offers its customers the full-time services of a team of product developers who can customize soft-drink concentrates, flavors and formulas to meetclient's needs. The Company also offers its customers the services of designer packaging and operates research, manufacturing, marketing and customer service facilities in Canada, the United States, the United Kingdom, South Africa and Australia. The Company's product line includes soft drinks, "new age" clear beverages, juice, juice-based beverages, iced teas, and water. While the majority of these products are produced under private label for retailers, The Company also sells proprietary beverages, which include its own and licensed brands products including "VESS" and "STARS & STRIPES" soft drinks in the United States and "RC" and "DIET RITE" soft drinks in certain regions of Canada.

ANNUAL EARNINGS

	1/25/97	1/27/96	1/25/97	1/27/96
	---------US $---------		---------C $---------	
Earnings Per Share	0.34	d0.30	0.47	d0.41

ANNUAL FINANCIAL DATA

RECORD OF EARNINGS (IN THOUSANDS):

	1/25/97	1/27/96	1/25/97	1/27/96
Total Revenues	988,131	924,449	1,351,567	1,277,393
Costs & Expenses	913,908	905,500	1,250,045	1,268,911
Depreciation & Amort	26,965	18,684	36,883	25,818
Operating Income	47,258	d12,546	64,639	d17,336
Income Bef Income Tax	29,697	d26,625	40,619	d36,790
Income Tax	8,715	cr7,256	11,921	cr10,026
Eq. Earnings in Affils.	1,015	913	1,388	1,261
Minority Interests	448	cr373	613	cr516
Net Income	21,548	d18,083	29,473	d24,987
Income from Disc. Ops.	3,338	d3,176	4,566	d4,388

BALANCE SHEET (IN THOUSANDS):

Cash & Cash Equivalents	63,226	71,356	86,481	98,599
Receivables, Net	104,976	102,723	143,586	141,942
Inventories	112,023	113,867	153,225	157,340
Gross Property	233,118	186,827	318,859	258,156
Accumulated Depreciation	45,412	31,026	62,115	42,871
Long-Term Debt	205,511	196,749	281,098	271,866
Stockholders' Equity	239,187	203,984	327,160	281,862
Total Assets	594,967	549,870	813,797	759,804
Total Current Assets	284,756	292,422	389,490	404,065
Total Current Liabilities	146,030	144,121	199,740	199,145
Net Working Capital	138,726	148,301	189,750	204,920
Year End Shs Outstg	62,142	60,702	62,142	60,702

STATISTICAL RECORD:

Return on Equity %	9.01	...		
Return on Assets %	3.62	...		
Operating Profit Margin %	4.78	...		
Net Profit Margin %	2.18	...		
Book Value Per Share	3.85	3.36		

Converted at 1997, US$0.7311= 1 Canadian $; 1996, US$0.7237= 1 Canadian $

OFFICERS:
G. N. Pencer, Chmn. & C.E.O.
S. S. Pencer, Sr. Vice-Chmn.
F. D. Latta, Vice-Chmn.
P. K. Henderson, Exec. V.P.-Fin. & Adm. & C.F.O.

INCORPORATED: Jul., 1955

PRINCIPAL OFFICE: 207 Queen's Quay West, Suite 800, Toronto, Ontario Canada M5J 147

TELEPHONE NUMBER: 514-428-1000

NO. OF EMPLOYEES: 2,000

ANNUAL MEETING: In June

SHAREHOLDERS: N/A

INSTITUTIONAL HOLDINGS:
No. of Institutions: 49
Shares Held: 14,137,409

REGISTRAR(S): Montreal Trust.

TRANSFER AGENT(S): Montreal Trust.

COUNSEL CORPORATION

YIELD ...
P/E RATIO 11.7

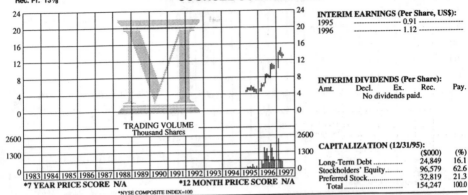

INTERIM EARNINGS (Per Share, US$):
1995 ------------------ 0.91 ------------------
1996 ------------------ 1.12 ------------------

INTERIM DIVIDENDS (Per Share):
Amt.   Decl.   Ex.   Rec.   Pay.
No dividends paid.

CAPITALIZATION (12/31/95):

	($000)	(%)
Long-Term Debt	24,849	16.1
Stockholders' Equity	96,579	62.6
Preferred Stock	32,819	21.3
Total	154,247	100.0

RECENT DEVELOPMENTS: For the year ended 12/31/96, net income jumped 46.8% to $28.5 million from $19.4 million in 1995. Total revenues more than doubled to $352.2 million from $173.1 million. The improved results were driven by acquisitions. Revenues from consolidated specialty retail pharmacy operations were $155.1 million and earnings were $10.8 million compared with no operations in this segment in 1995. Total home health care revenues slipped 3.3% to $84.4 million and earnings fell 35.5% to $7.7 million. The decrease in this segment was caused by a change to the equity method of accounting. Institutional pharmacy earnings soared to $2.2 million from $95,000 in 1995. Clinical laboratory operations, for which the Company reported no operating results in 1995, reported revenues of $7.8 million and earnings of $877,000. Long-term care earnings jumped to $889,000 from $143,000.

BUSINESS

COUNSEL CORPORATION is an entrepreneurial management and business development company that operates in two health care niches in the United States - home health care and institutional pharmacy. American HomePatient, Inc., 66% owned by Co., provides home health care services and products through 144 locations in 20 states. Its main services are respiratory and infusion therapy and the sale or rental of home medical equipment. Premier Pharmacy/Choice Drug Systems, Inc., 25% owned by the Company., provides pharmaceutical and health care products and services to nursing homes, assisted living centers and managed care markets. Counsel Management Services Inc. (CMSI), wholly-owned by the Company., provides real estate asset and property management services across Canada for Counsel Real Estate Investment Trust, various real estate partnerships, and institutional and individual owners.

ANNUAL EARNINGS

	12/31/95	12/31/94	12/31/95	12/31/94
	---------US $---------		---------C $---------	
Earnings Per Share	0.91	0.35	1.24	0.49

ANNUAL FINANCIAL DATA

RECORD OF EARNINGS (IN THOUSANDS):

	12/31/95	12/31/94	12/31/95	12/31/94
Total Revenues	216,719	217,030	295,700	304,432
Costs & Expenses	5,923	7,491	8,082	10,508
Depreciation & Amort	4,615	8,388	6,297	11,766
Operating Income	206,180	201,150	281,321	282,158
Income Bef Income Tax	32,385	17,287	44,187	24,249
Income Tax	12,242	6,383	16,703	8,953
Minority Interests	729	4,239	995	5,946
Net Income	19,414	6,666	26,489	9,350
Average Shares Outstg	21,385	19,282	21,385	19,282

BALANCE SHEET (IN THOUSANDS):

Cash & Cash Equivalents	19,679	12,562	26,851	17,621
Receivables, Net	9,816	49,457	13,393	69,374
Inventories	4,862	11,222	6,634	15,742
Gross Property	38,378	47,429	52,364	66,530
Accumulated Depreciation	7,009	7,016	9,563	9,841
Long-Term Debt	24,849	49,815	33,905	69,877
Stockholders' Equity	96,579	81,108	131,776	113,772
Total Assets	142,474	219,154	194,397	307,412
Total Current Assets	35,252	88,738	48,099	124,475
Total Current Liabilities	13,642	59,650	18,614	83,673
Net Working Capital	21,610	29,088	29,485	40,802
Year End Shs Outstg	21,289	21,437	21,289	21,437

STATISTICAL RECORD:

Return on Equity %	20.1	8.2		
Return on Assets %	13.6	3.0		
Operating Profit Margin %	95.1	92.7		
Net Profit Margin %	9.0	3.1		
Book Value Per Share	6.20	5.30		

Converted at 1995, US$0.7329= 1 Canadian C $; 1994, US$0.7129= 1 Canadian C $

OFFICERS:
A. Silber, Chmn. & C.E.O.
E. Sonshine, Vice-Chmn.
M. Perlis, Pres.
S. Wintraub, Sr. V.P. & Sec.

INCORPORATED: Canada June, 1990

PRINCIPAL OFFICE: The Exchange Tower, Suite 1300, P.O. Box 435, 2 First Canadian Place Toronto Canada

TELEPHONE NUMBER: 416-866-3000

NO. OF EMPLOYEES: N/A

ANNUAL MEETING: In Jun.

SHAREHOLDERS: N/A

INSTITUTIONAL HOLDINGS:
No. of Institutions: 9
Shares Held: 3,758,567

REGISTRAR(S): Montreal Trust Company, Toronto and The Bank of Nova Scotia Trust Company of New York, New York.

TRANSFER AGENT(S): Montreal Trust Company, Toronto and The Bank of Nova Scotia Trust Company of New York, New York.

CREATIVE TECHNOLOGY LTD.

YIELD ...
P/E RATIO ...

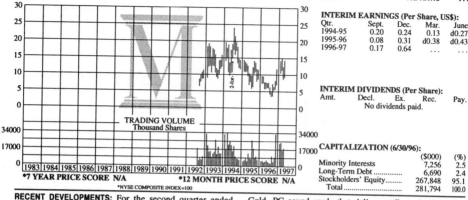

*7 YEAR PRICE SCORE N/A *12 MONTH PRICE SCORE N/A

*NYSE COMPOSITE INDEX=100

INTERIM EARNINGS (Per Share, US$):

Qtr.	Sept.	Dec.	Mar.	June
1994-95	0.20	0.24	0.13	d0.27
1995-96	0.08	0.31	d0.38	d0.43
1996-97	0.17	0.64	...	...

INTERIM DIVIDENDS (Per Share):

Amt.	Decl.	Ex.	Rec.	Pay.
		No dividends paid.		

CAPITALIZATION (6/30/96):

	($000)	(%)
Minority Interests	7,256	2.5
Long-Term Debt	6,690	2.4
Stockholders' Equity.........	267,848	95.1
Total	281,794	100.0

RECENT DEVELOPMENTS: For the second quarter ended 12/31/96, net income more than doubled to US$56.9 million from US$27.0 million in the comparable year-earlier quarter. Sales decreased 11.3% to US$386.0 million compared with US$435.0 million the previous year. The improvement in net income reflects a significant leap in gross profit as a percentage of sales to 28.3% from 20.8% in the corresponding quarter the year before. The Company has introduced the Sound Blaster(R) AWE64 and AWE64 Gold, PC sound cards that deliver audio technology that provides a more flexible, professional-quality audio solution while maintaining compatibility with previous Sound Blaster products. The Company is heavily involved in a direction strategy to offer solutions that bring audio, video, 3D graphics and commerce together over the Internet. Among the Company's new technologies is "Passport," which offers audio, graphics and communications solutions for the PC.

BUSINESS

CREATIVE TECHNOLOGY LTD. develops, manufactures, and markets a family of audio boards, video cards, desktop video communications tools, multimedia kits and productivity software. The Company designs this array of multimedia products for use on IBM compatible PCs. The Company's Sound Blaster platform is comprised of a sound card, software drivers and bundled software applications that enable IBM compatible PCs to produce high quality sound for various applications. The Company has expanded on its 8-bit sound boards with a series of 16-bit offerings that produce CD quality sound. The Company also offers video products which enable PC users to digitize, capture and display live video or television broadcasts in a resizable window while simultaneously performing other tasks on the PC.

ANNUAL EARNINGS

	6/30/96	6/30/95	6/30/96	6/30/95
	----------US $----------		----------S$----------	
Earnings Per Share	d0.43	0.30	d0.61	0.42

ANNUAL FINANCIAL DATA

RECORD OF EARNINGS (IN MILLIONS):

Total Revenues	1,308	1,202	1,846	1,680
Costs & Expenses	1,305	1,147	1,842	1,602
Depreciation & Amort	18	17	25	24
Operating Income	d15	38	d21	53
Income Bef Income Tax	d30	33	d42	46
Income Tax	9	6	12	8
Minority Interests	cr1	1	cr1	1
Net Income	d38	27	d53	37
Average Shares Outstg (000)	87,984	89,422	87,984	89,422

BALANCE SHEET (IN MILLIONS):

Cash & Cash Equivalents	196	127	277	178
Receivables, Net	105	147	149	205
Inventories	166	262	234	366
Gross Property	102	82	144	114
Accumulated Depreciation	33	20	47	28
Long-Term Debt	7	102	9	142
Stockholders' Equity	268	302	378	423
Total Assets	593	661	837	924
Total Current Assets	494	568	698	794
Total Current Liabilities	312	253	440	353
Net Working Capital	183	315	258	440
Year End Shs Outstg (000)	88,212	87,637	88,212	87,637

STATISTICAL RECORD:

Return on Equity %	...	8.76		
Return on Assets %	...	4.01		
Operating Profit Margin %	...	3.16		
Net Profit Margin %	...	2.25		
Book Value Per Share	3.04	3.45		

Converted at 1996, US$0.7085= 1 Singapore $; 1995, US$0.7158= 1 Singapore $

OFFICERS:
S. W. Hoo, Chmn. & C.E.O.
T. Lip-Bu, Dir.
T. C. Choy, Dir.
L. K. Nam, Dir.

INCORPORATED: Jul., 1983

PRINCIPAL OFFICE: 67 Ayer Rajah Crescent #03-18 Singapore 139950

TELEPHONE NUMBER: 65-773 0233

NO. OF EMPLOYEES: N/A

ANNUAL MEETING: In Dec.

SHAREHOLDERS: 344 (approx.)

INSTITUTIONAL HOLDINGS:
No. of Institutions: N/A
Shares Held: N/A

REGISTRAR(S): First Interstate Bank Registrars, Los Angeles, CA

TRANSFER AGENT(S): First Interstate Bank Registrars, Los Angeles, CA

NASDAQ SYMBOL CRNSF
Rec. Pr. 5

CRONOS GROUP (THE)

YIELD ...
P/E RATIO 4.1

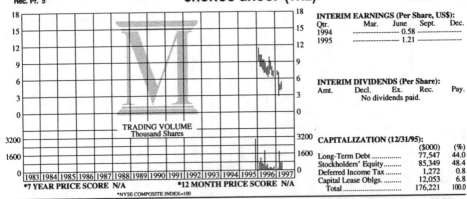

7 YEAR PRICE SCORE N/A   **12 MONTH PRICE SCORE N/A**

*NYSE COMPOSITE INDEX=100

INTERIM EARNINGS (Per Share, US$):

Qtr.	Mar.	June	Sept.	Dec.
1994		0.58		
1995		1.21		

INTERIM DIVIDENDS (Per Share):

Amt.	Decl.	Ex.	Rec.	Pay.
	No dividends paid.			

CAPITALIZATION (12/31/95):

	($000)	(%)
Long-Term Debt	77,547	44.0
Stockholders' Equity	85,349	48.4
Deferred Income Tax	1,272	0.8
Capital Lease Oblgs.	12,053	6.8
Total	176,221	100.0

RECENT DEVELOPMENTS: For the year ended 12/31/95, net income soared 87.1% to $7.4 million from $3.9 million a year earlier. Total revenues were $160.6 million, up 21.6% from $132.0 million in the prior year. Gross lease revenue jumped 20.7% to $150.4 million from $124.7 million in 1994. Operating income was $21.8 million compared with $17.1 million the year before, an increase of 43.3%. Reve-

nues from total managed containers increased 20.7% to $126.2 million and operating profit improved 28.8% to $8.8 million. Revenue from owned containers grew 25.0% to $32.5 million and operating profit advanced 22.8% to $23.4 million. Results included equity in earnings of affiliates of $1.9 million and $1.4 million for 1995 and 1994, respectively.

BUSINESS

THE CRONOS GROUP is a holding company. Through its subsidiaries, the Company acts as a lessor of intermodal marine containers to ocean carriers throughout the world, owning and managing a fleet of dry cargo, refrigerated and tank containers. Through an extensive global network of offices and agents, the Company leases both its own and other owners' containers to over 300 ocean carriers and transport operators, including all of the 20 largest ocean carriers. The Company specifically targets three market segments: the dry cargo container market, the refrigerated container market, and the tank container market for liquids. The Company employs master leases for its dry cargo containers, while its refrigerated and tank containers are leased through term leases. All containers, whether owned or managed, are operated as part of a single fleet. The Company purchases new containers for its own account and for resale to its managed container programs.

ANNUAL EARNINGS

	12/31/95	12/31/94	12/31/95	12/31/94
	----US $----		----LFr----	
Earnings Per Share	1.21	0.58	35.59	18.53

ANNUAL FINANCIAL DATA

RECORD OF EARNINGS (IN THOUSANDS):

Total Revenues	160,595	132,025	4,723,382	4,218,051
Costs & Expenses	128,144	106,219	3,768,941	3,393,578
Depreciation & Amort	10,676	8,711	314,000	278,307
Operating Income	21,775	17,075	640,491	546,166
Income Bef Income Tax	10,537	6,966	309,912	224,710
Income Tax	3,175	3,031	93,382	96,837
Net Income	7,362	3,935	216,529	126,935
Average Shs. Outstg.(000)	5,383	5,215	5,383	5,215

BALANCE SHEET (IN THOUSANDS):

Cash & Cash Equivalents	24,243	7,493	713,029	239,393
Receivables, Net	45,393	44,448	1,335,088	1,420,064
Inventories	7,910	3,590	232,647	114,696
Gross Property	163,246	145,809	4,801,353	4,658,435
Accumulated Depreciation	29,374	19,381	863,941	619,201
Long-Term Debt	77,547	75,496	2,280,794	2,412,013
Capital Lease Oblgs.	12,053	18,082	354,500	577,700
Stockholders' Equity	85,349	53,186	2,510,265	1,699,233
Total Assets	266,485	222,337	7,837,794	7,103,419
Total Current Assets	77,546	55,531	2,280,765	1,774,153
Total Current Liabilities	72,400	55,816	2,129,412	1,783,259
Net Working Capital	5,146	d285	151,353	d9,105
Year End Shs Outstg	8,615	5,215	8,615	5,215

STATISTICAL RECORD:

Return on Equity %	8.63	7.40		
Return on Assets %	2.76	1.77		
Operating Profit Margin %	13.56	12.95		
Net Profit Margin %	4.58	2.98		
Book Value Per Share	9.91	10.20		

Converted at 1995, US$0.0340= 1 Luxembourgian franc; 1994, US$0.0313= 1 Luxembourgian franc

OFFICERS:
S. M. Palatin, Chmn. & C.E.O.
L. P. Sargent, Deputy Chmn. & Sec.
E. A. Eriksen, C.O.O.
A. D. Ponniah, C.F.O.

INCORPORATED: Luxembourg, 1990

PRINCIPAL OFFICE: 35, rue Glesener
Luxembourg, L-1631

TELEPHONE NUMBER: 352-451451

NO. OF EMPLOYEES: 137

ANNUAL MEETING: In Jun.

SHAREHOLDERS: N/A

INSTITUTIONAL HOLDINGS:
No. of Institutions: N/A
Shares Held: N/A

REGISTRAR(S): The First National Bank of Boston.

TRANSFER AGENT(S): The First National Bank of Boston.

320

DESWELL INDUSTRIES, INC.

YIELD 2.7%
P/E RATIO 13.3

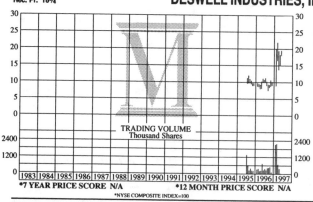

*7 YEAR PRICE SCORE N/A   *12 MONTH PRICE SCORE N/A

*NYSE COMPOSITE INDEX=100

INTERIM EARNINGS (Per Share, US$):

1994-95	------------------ 1.18 -----------------
1995-96	------------------ 1.41 -----------------

INTERIM DIVIDENDS (Per Share):

Amt.	Decl.	Ex.	Rec.	Pay.
0.35	7/19/96	7/25/96	7/29/96	8/13/96
0.25	11/20	12/2	12/4	12/18

Indicated div.: $0.50

CAPITALIZATION (3/31/96):

	($000)	(%)
Minority Interests..............	1,884	8.2
Stockholders' Equity........	21,075	91.8
Deferred Income Tax	11	0.0
Total..............................	22,970	100.0

RECENT DEVELOPMENTS: For the third quarter ended 12/31/96, net income was up 51.3% to $2.7 million. This compares with $1.8 million in the corresponding quarter a year earlier. Net sales grew 71.3% to $13.3 million from $7.8 million in the comparable period the year before. The improved operating results were attributed to increased volume from existing customers and additional production capacity, as well as benefits from the Company's acquisi-tion of Kwanta Precision Metal Products Co. Ltd. In its first three months as a subsidiary, Kwanta contributed $790,000 to third-quarter revenues. During the quarter, the Company leased 40,000 square feet of factory space in Shenzhen, China to meet the demand for its injection-molded plastic products, bringing total production space to 225,000 square feet. The Company has also completed construction of a Kwanta factory in Douggan, China.

BUSINESS

DESWELL INDUSTRIES, INC. is a holding company. Through its subsidiaries, the Company is engaged in the manufacturing of plastic parts and components that are used in the manufacture of consumer and industrial products, including cases and key tops for calculators and personal organizers; cases for flashlights, telephones, paging machines, projectors and alarm clocks; grips and rods for fishing tackle; and toner cartridges and cases for photocopy machines. In addition, the Company manufactures printed circuit board assemblies and finished products such as telephones, telephone answering machines, audio equipment and computer peripherals, such as CD-ROM drives and LAN and sound cards.

ANNUAL EARNINGS

	3/31/96	3/31/95	3/31/94
	------------------US $------------------		
Earnings Per Share	1.41	1.18	0.89

ANNUAL FINANCIAL DATA

RECORD OF EARNINGS (IN THOUSANDS):

	3/31/96	3/31/95	3/31/94
Total Revenues	30,580	21,006	16,165
Costs & Expenses	21,993	15,294	12,057
Depreciation & Amort	1,400	1,103	756
Operating Income	7,187	4,609	3,352
Income Bef Income Tax	7,417	4,483	3,211
Income Tax	220	92	37
Minority Interests	1,286	381	142
Net Income	5,911	4,010	3,032
Average Shares Outstg	4,198	3,400	3,400
BALANCE SHEET (IN THOUSANDS):			
Cash & Cash Equivalents	11,168	2,049	673
Receivables, Net	4,408	3,283	2,823
Inventories	2,932	2,058	1,123
Gross Property	11,601	6,964	5,280
Accumulated Depreciation	4,232	3,097	2,146
Long-Term Debt	. . .	179	716
Stockholders' Equity	21,075	7,271	4,489
Total Assets	26,620	12,203	8,832
Total Current Assets	19,003	8,073	5,465
Total Current Liabilities	3,650	4,109	3,402
Net Working Capital	15,353	3,964	2,063
Year End Shs Outstg	4,550	3,400	3,400
STATISTICAL RECORD:			
Return on Equity %	28.05	55.15	67.54
Return on Assets %	22.21	32.86	34.33
Operating Profit Margin %	23.50	21.94	20.74
Net Profit Margin %	19.33	19.09	18.76
Book Value Per Share	4.63	2.14	1.32

OFFICERS:
R. Lau, Chmn. & C.E.O.
L. Chin-Pang, Gen. Mgr., C.F.O. & Sec.

INCORPORATED: Br. Virgin Is., Dec., 1993

PRINCIPAL OFFICE: Unit 514-517, Hong Leong Ind. Complex, No. 4 Wang Kwong Rd., Kowloon Bay Hong Kong

TELEPHONE NUMBER: (852) 2796-6993

NO. OF EMPLOYEES: 1,500 (approx.)

ANNUAL MEETING: In Sept.

SHAREHOLDERS: N/A

INSTITUTIONAL HOLDINGS:
No. of Institutions: 2
Shares Held: 45,800

REGISTRAR(S): U.S. Stock Transfer Corp., Glendale, Ca

TRANSFER AGENT(S): U.S. Stock Transfer Corp., Glendale, CA

DISCREET LOGIC, INC.

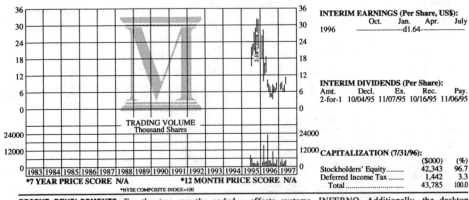

INTERIM EARNINGS (Per Share, US$):

	Oct.	Jan.	Apr.	July
1996	---------------d1.64---------------			

INTERIM DIVIDENDS (Per Share):

Amt.	Decl.	Ex.	Rec.	Pay.
2-for-1	10/04/95	11/07/95	10/16/95	11/06/95

TRADING VOLUME
Thousand Shares

CAPITALIZATION (7/31/96):

	($000)	(%)
Stockholders' Equity........	42,343	96.7
Deferred Income Tax	1,442	3.3
Total	43,785	100.0

*7 YEAR PRICE SCORE N/A   *12 MONTH PRICE SCORE N/A

*NYSE COMPOSITE INDEX=100

RECENT DEVELOPMENTS: For the two months ended 12/31/96, net income advanced to $2.0 million from $775,000 in the comparable three month period of 1995. Total revenues declined 33.3% to $16.8 million from $25.2 million the year before. Earnings were enhanced by increasing market acceptance for the high-end editing product, FIRE, with revenues of $4.1 million, and stronger demand for the Company's premier solution-independent effects systems, INFERNO. Additionally, the desktop effects product line continued to grow in revenues. This reflected first commercial shipments of FLINT RT, the desktop visual effects system featuring PEBBLES real-time acquisition and playback, and expansion of the indirect distribution channel. In January 1997, the Company changed its fiscal year end from July 31 to June 30.

BUSINESS

DISCREET LOGIC INC. develops, assembles, markets and supports non-linear, digital image processing systems for creating, editing and compositing special visual effects for film and video. The Company's systems are utilized by creative professionals in production and post-production to create special visual effects for various applications, including feature films, television programs, commercials and music videos. DSLGF sells its systems and other products through its direct sales organization, as well as through distributors and resellers. DSLGF markets and sells its systems directly in North America and in certain European and Pacific Rim countries.

ANNUAL EARNINGS

	7/31/96	7/31/95	7/31/96	7/31/95
	--------------US $--------------		--------------C $--------------	
Earnings Per Share	d1.64	0.31	d0.87	0.42

ANNUAL FINANCIAL DATA

RECORD OF EARNINGS (IN THOUSANDS):

	7/31/96	7/31/95	7/31/96	7/31/95
Total Revenues	83,997	64,549	61,066	88,229
Costs & Expenses	50,788	51,088	74,812	69,831
Operating Income	d49,914	13,460	d32,652	18,399
Income Bef Income Tax	d42,100	13,290	d31,047	18,166
Income Tax	1,435	5,490	1,043	7,504
Minority Interests	...	15	...	20
Net Income	d44,141	7,785	d32,091	10,641
Average Shares Outstg	26,837	24,886	26,837	24,886

BALANCE SHEET (IN THOUSANDS):

Cash & Cash Equivalents	21,658	40,987	29,779	56,024
Receivables, Net	16,074	15,019	22,032	20,650
Inventories	15,829	9,562	21,765	13,070
Gross Property	18,259	8,336	25,105	11,394
Accumulated Depreciation	8,221	1,577	11,304	2,155
Stockholders' Equity	42,343	50,124	58,219	68,513
Total Assets	80,148	76,858	110,199	105,055
Total Current Assets	60,393	67,320	83,037	92,017
Total Current Liabilities	36,363	25,473	49,997	34,818
Net Working Capital	24,030	41,847	33,039	57,199
Year End Shs Outstg	27,699	25,167	27,699	25,167

STATISTICAL RECORD:

Return on Equity %	...	15.53		
Return on Assets %	...	10.13		
Operating Profit Margin %	...	20.85		
Net Profit Margin %	...	12.06		
Book Value Per Share	1.53	1.99		

Converted at 1996, US$0.7273= 1 Canadian $; 1995, US$0.7316= 1 Canadian $

OFFICERS:
R. J. Szalwinski, Chmn. & C.E.O.
F. Plamondon, V.P. & C.F.O.

INCORPORATED: Canada, Sept., 1991

PRINCIPAL OFFICE: 5505 Boulevard St. Laurent, Suite 5200 Montreal Canada H2T 1S6

TELEPHONE NUMBER: 514-272-0525

NO. OF EMPLOYEES: 259

ANNUAL MEETING: In Jan.

SHAREHOLDERS: 223

INSTITUTIONAL HOLDINGS:
No. of Institutions: 19
Shares Held: 3,230,498

REGISTRAR(S): The First National Bank of Boston, Boston.

TRANSFER AGENT(S): The First National Bank of Boston, Boston.

DIVERSINET CORP.

YIELD ...
P/E RATIO ...

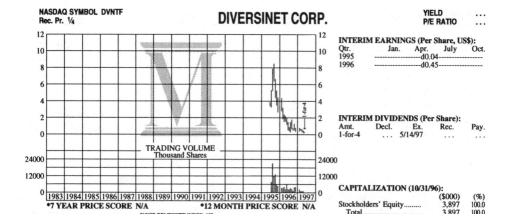

*7 YEAR PRICE SCORE N/A   *12 MONTH PRICE SCORE N/A

INTERIM EARNINGS (Per Share, US$):

Qtr.	Jan.	Apr.	July	Oct.
1995		----------------d0.04-----------------		
1996		----------------d0.45-----------------		

INTERIM DIVIDENDS (Per Share):

Amt.	Decl.	Ex.	Rec.	Pay.
1-for-4	...	5/14/97	...	...

CAPITALIZATION (10/31/96):

	($000)	(%)
Stockholders' Equity........	3,897	100.0
Total.............................	3,897	100.0

RECENT DEVELOPMENTS: For the three months ended 1/31/97, net loss improved to $321,127 from a loss of $5.6 million in the prior-year quarter. Revenues were down 56.1% to $657,530. Revenues were primarily generated from sales of the IPS 950 system in the home based business market. Gross profit was down 64.8% to $244,564 from $694,546 in the equivalent period a year earlier. Bottom-line performance improved as a result of the Company's restructuring, which reduced operating costs to $565,691 from $5.6 million in 1996. On 5/12/97, shareholders of the Company approved the consolidation of the Company's shares on a 1-for-4 basis. The consolidation was recommended by the Company due to NASDAQ's new rules to de-list from the National Market System companies whose shares trade at less than $1.00.

BUSINESS

DIVERSINET CORP. (formerly Instant Publisher Inc.) creates, produces and markets a small format turnkey printing system that provides typesetting, database merge, artwork and color printing functionality. A niche machine, this printing system allows businesses to produce business cards, labels, invitations, bar codes, bumper stickers, tickets and tags, with sequential numbering and variable data options, on demand.

ANNUAL EARNINGS

	10/31/96	10/31/95	10/31/96	10/31/95
	------------US $------------		------------C $------------	
Earnings Per Share	d0.45	d0.04	d0.61	d0.05

ANNUAL FINANCIAL DATA

RECORD OF EARNINGS (IN THOUSANDS):

	10/31/96	10/31/95	10/31/96	10/31/95
Total Revenues	1,460	6,755	1,963	9,197
Costs & Expenses	5,999	8,110	8,070	11,041
Operating Income	d4,540	d1,355	d6,106	d1,844
Income Bef Income Tax	d21,322	d1,742	d28,682	d2,372
Net Income	d21,322	d1,742	d28,682	d2,372
Average Shares Outstg	47,287	43,810	47,287	43,810
BALANCE SHEET (IN THOUSANDS):				
Cash & Cash Equivalents	3,997	17,389	5,377	23,675
Receivables, Net	359	2,274	483	3,096
Inventories	504	197	678	268
Gross Property	139	27	187	37
Accumulated Depreciation	83	...	111	...
Stockholders' Equity	3,897	19,337	5,242	26,327
Total Assets	5,028	21,009	6,764	28,602
Total Current Assets	4,898	19,880	6,588	27,066
Total Current Liabilities	1,131	1,671	1,521	2,276
Net Working Capital	3,767	18,208	5,067	24,790
Year End Shs Outstg	57,501	47,266	57,501	47,266
STATISTICAL RECORD:				
Return on Equity %	...	...		
Return on Assets %	...	...		
Operating Profit Margin %	...	...		
Net Profit Margin %	...	...		
Book Value Per Share	0.07	0.41		

Converted at 1996, US$0.7434= 1 Canadian $; 1995, US$0.7345= 1 Canadian $

OFFICERS:
J. Wiseman, Pres. & C.E.O.
E. Swartz, Sec.

INCORPORATED: Canada

PRINCIPAL OFFICE: 160 Nashdene Road
Toronto, Ontario Canada M1V 4C4

TELEPHONE NUMBER: 416-754-9293

NO. OF EMPLOYEES: N/A

ANNUAL MEETING: N/A

SHAREHOLDERS: N/A

INSTITUTIONAL HOLDINGS:
No. of Institutions: N/A
Shares Held: N/A

REGISTRAR(S): Equity Transfer Services Inc., Toronto.

TRANSFER AGENT(S): Equity Transfer Services Inc., Toronto.

DRAXIS HEALTH INC.

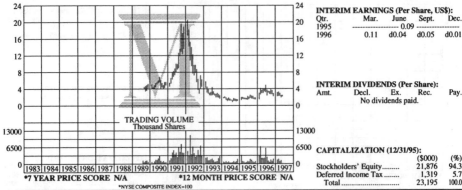

*7 YEAR PRICE SCORE N/A   *12 MONTH PRICE SCORE N/A

*NYSE COMPOSITE INDEX=100

INTERIM EARNINGS (Per Share, US$):

Qtr.	Mar.	June	Sept.	Dec.
1995		d0.09		
1996	0.11	d0.04	d0.05	d0.01

INTERIM DIVIDENDS (Per Share):

Amt.	Decl.	Ex.	Rec.	Pay.
	No dividends paid.			

CAPITALIZATION (12/31/95):

	($000)	(%)
Stockholders' Equity	21,876	94.3
Deferred Income Tax	1,319	5.7
Total	23,195	100.0

RECENT DEVELOPMENTS: For the year ended 12/31/96, the Company reported a net loss of C$166,418 versus net income of C$2.4 million in 1995. The 1996 results included a reversal of C$696,556 of deferred taxes on prior dilution gains and a C$6.1 million gain from the sale of shares of DUSA Pharmaceuticals, Inc. The 1995 results included C$5.4 million in gains related to investments in DUSA. Revenues declined 6.2% to C$15.6 million from C$16.6 million. The Company reported a loss from operations of C$5.4 million compared with income from operations of C$549,992 in 1995. The results were negatively affected by the consolidation of its Deprenyl Animal Health, Inc. (DAHI) subsidiary. In January, the Company's Canadian pharmacy operations acquired the exclusive Canadian marketing rights to the Mylan formulation of the cancer drug, paclitaxel, from Mylan Laboratories. In February, Draxis acquired Spectropharm, a Montreal-based dermatology company. Spectropharm's 1996 sales totaled C$3.0 million.

BUSINESS

DRAXIS HEALTH INC. is a Canadian-based health care company engaged in the research and development, marketing and sales of prescription neurological products, and prescription, consumer and over-the-counter dermatological products. The Company also markets specialized products for the treatment of other chronic and degenerative diseases. The Company's dermatological products are used in the treatment of psoriasis and dry skin disorders. The pipeline of drugs for the Canadian market includes drugs for narcolepsy, osteoporosis, renal osteodystrophy, keloids and ALA Photo Dynamic Therapy, and its various potential applications. In the United States, the Company's focus is on foot care products and consumer nutriceuticals.

ANNUAL EARNINGS

	12/31/95	12/31/94	12/31/95	12/31/94
	---US $---		---C $---	
Earnings Per Share	0.09	0.04	0.12	0.06

ANNUAL FINANCIAL DATA

RECORD OF EARNINGS (IN THOUSANDS):				
Total Revenues	12,189	12,181	16,631	17,086
Costs & Expenses	10,833	8,038	14,780	11,275
Depreciation & Amort	942	618	1,285	867
Operating Income	414	3,525	565	4,945
Income Bef Income Tax	4,408	3,518	6,015	4,935
Income Tax	1,513	1,240	2,064	1,740
Eq. Earnings in Affils.	d1,124	d1,494	d1,533	d2,095
Net Income	1,772	784	2,417	1,099
Average Shares Outstg	20,058	19,927	20,058	19,927
BALANCE SHEET (IN THOUSANDS):				
Cash & Cash Equivalents	12,171	8,881	16,606	12,458
Receivables, Net	1,214	1,730	1,656	2,427
Inventories	516	723	705	1,014
Gross Property	743	635	1,013	891
Accumulated Depreciation	344	312	469	438
Stockholders' Equity	21,876	19,361	29,849	27,159
Total Assets	25,690	23,570	35,052	33,062
Total Current Assets	14,484	12,009	19,763	16,845
Total Current Liabilities	2,495	3,089	3,404	4,333
Net Working Capital	11,990	8,920	16,359	12,512
Year End Shs Outstg	20,127	20,019	20,127	20,019
STATISTICAL RECORD:				
Return on Equity %	8.1	4.0		
Return on Assets %	6.9	3.3		
Operating Profit Margin %	3.4	28.9		
Net Profit Margin %	14.5	6.4		
Book Value Per Share	1.09	0.97		

Converted at 1995, US$0.7329= 1 Canadian $; 1994, US$0.7129= 1 Canadian $

OFFICERS:
B. M. King, Chmn.
J. P. Doherty, Vice-Chmn.
M. Barkin, Pres., C.E.O. & C.O.O.
J. H. Le Saux, V.P., Gen. Couns. & Sec.

INCORPORATED: Canada, Oct. 1987

PRINCIPAL OFFICE: 6870 Goreway Drive
Mississauga, Ontario Canada L4V 1P1

TELEPHONE NUMBER: 905-677-5500

NO. OF EMPLOYEES: N/A

ANNUAL MEETING: In Jun.

SHAREHOLDERS: N/A

INSTITUTIONAL HOLDINGS:
No. of Institutions: 11
Shares Held: 749,222

REGISTRAR(S): The Montreal Trust Company, Toronto, Ontario

TRANSFER AGENT(S): The Montreal Trust Company, Toronto, Ontario

DRECO ENERGY SERVICES LTD.

NASDAQ SYMBOL DREAF
Rec. Pr. 32⅛

YIELD ...
P/E RATIO 16.1

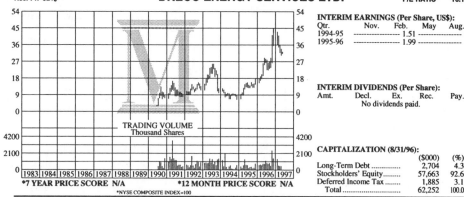

*7 YEAR PRICE SCORE N/A   *12 MONTH PRICE SCORE N/A
*NYSE COMPOSITE INDEX=100

INTERIM EARNINGS (Per Share, US$):

Qtr.	Nov.	Feb.	May	Aug.
1994-95	-------------------	1.51	-----------------	
1995-96	-------------------	1.99	-----------------	

INTERIM DIVIDENDS (Per Share):

Amt.	Decl.	Ex.	Rec.	Pay.
	No dividends paid.			

CAPITALIZATION (8/31/96):

	($000)	(%)
Long-Term Debt	2,704	4.3
Stockholders' Equity	57,663	92.6
Deferred Income Tax	1,885	3.1
Total	62,252	100.0

RECENT DEVELOPMENTS: For the first quarter ended 11/30/96, net income was $1.6 million. This compares with $3.4 million in the corresponding quarter a year earlier. Revenue for the period fell 39.4% to $20.2 million from $33.4 million in the comparable period the previous year. Drilling and Well Servicing Equipment revenue dropped 53.8% to $12.6 million, primarily due to the absence of a large individual contract. Meanwhile, Downhole Products revenue rose 24.6% to $7.6 million. On 12/2/96, the Company completed the acquisition of Vector Oil Tool Ltd. for a consideration of 425,000 shares of stock and $1.5 million in cash. The transaction was accounted for using the purchase method, with results of operations from Vector to be included in the Company's financial statements from 12/1/96.

BUSINESS

DRECO ENERGY SERVICES LTD., together with its subsidiaries, is engaged in the design and manufacture of oilfield equipment for the worldwide petroleum exploration and production industry. The Company operates in two principal business segments: Drilling and Well Servicing Equipment; and Downhole Products. Through its Drilling and Well Servicing Equipment segment, the Company designs, manufactures and markets products used in the original construction, modernization, repair and support of land and offshore drilling and well servicing rigs under its DRECO(R) and KREMCO(R) trade names. Through its Downhole Products segment, the Company designs, assembles and markets drilling and well servicing rigs utilizing several of the Company's propriety products as well as components manufactured by others. In addition, the Company has continued its focus on providing conventional designs of its products to customers in countries where the oil and gas drilling industry is being developed, expanded or modernized.

ANNUAL EARNINGS

	8/31/96	8/31/95	8/31/96	8/31/95
	------------US $------------		------------C $------------	
Earnings Per Share	1.99	1.51	2.72	2.03

ANNUAL FINANCIAL DATA

RECORD OF EARNINGS (IN THOUSANDS):

	8/31/96	8/31/95	8/31/96	8/31/95
Total Revenues	126,335	86,875	172,920	116,877
Costs & Expenses	106,810	73,643	146,115	99,116
Depreciation & Amort	4,859	4,558	6,651	6,132
Operating Income	16,689	10,059	22,843	13,533
Income Bef Income Tax	18,535	12,196	25,370	16,408
Income Tax	6,304	2,938	8,629	3,953
Net Income	12,231	9,258	16,741	12,455
Average Shares Outstg	6,159	6,145	6,159	6,145

BALANCE SHEET (IN THOUSANDS):

Cash & Cash Equivalents	2,605	21,391	3,566	28,778
Receivables, Net	38,966	17,946	53,334	24,144
Inventories	11,581	10,175	15,851	13,689
Gross Property	47,914	40,573	65,582	54,585
Accumulated Depreciation	22,865	20,700	31,296	27,849
Long-Term Debt	2,704	1,987	3,701	2,673
Stockholders' Equity	57,663	45,707	78,926	61,492
Total Assets	79,677	74,305	109,057	99,966
Total Current Assets	54,628	54,432	74,771	73,230
Total Current Liabilities	17,425	24,690	23,850	33,217
Net Working Capital	37,203	29,742	50,921	40,013
Year End Shs Outstg	6,204	6,154	6,204	6,154

STATISTICAL RECORD:

Return on Equity %	21.21	20.26		
Return on Assets %	15.35	12.46		
Operating Profit Margin %	13.21	11.58		
Net Profit Margin %	9.68	10.66		
Book Value Per Share	9.29	7.43		

Converted at 1996, US$0.7306= 1 Canadian dollar; 1995, US$0.7433= 1 Canadian dollar

OFFICERS:
F. W. Pheasey, Chmn.
R. L. Phillips, Pres. & C.E.O.
G. J. Knoll, C.O.O.
J. E. Devaney, V.P., C.F.O. & Treas.

INCORPORATED: N/A

PRINCIPAL OFFICE: Suite 1340 Weber Centre, 5555 Calgary Trail, Edmonton, Alberta Canada T6H 5P9

TELEPHONE NUMBER: (403) 944-3900

NO. OF EMPLOYEES: 713

ANNUAL MEETING: In Jan.

SHAREHOLDERS: 1,237

INSTITUTIONAL HOLDINGS:
No. of Institutions: 35
Shares Held: 3,938,527

REGISTRAR(S):

TRANSFER AGENT(S): The Bank of New York, New York, NY; Montreal Trust, Edmonton, Alberta

325

DSG INTERNATIONAL LIMITED

YIELD   ...
P/E RATIO   12.3

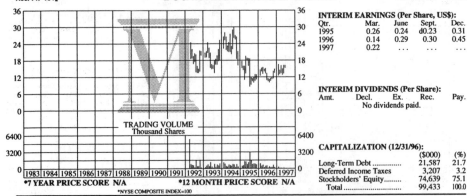

*7 YEAR PRICE SCORE N/A   *12 MONTH PRICE SCORE N/A
*NYSE COMPOSITE INDEX=100

INTERIM EARNINGS (Per Share, US$):

Qtr.	Mar.	June	Sept.	Dec.
1995	0.26	0.24	d0.23	0.31
1996	0.14	0.29	0.30	0.45
1997	0.22	...	...	...

INTERIM DIVIDENDS (Per Share):

Amt.	Decl.	Ex.	Rec.	Pay.
	No dividends paid.			

CAPITALIZATION (12/31/96):

	($000)	(%)
Long-Term Debt	21,587	21.7
Deferred Income Taxes	3,207	3.2
Stockholders' Equity.........	74,639	75.1
Total	99,433	100.0

RECENT DEVELOPMENTS: For the quarter ended 3/31/97, net income advanced 30.0% to $1.5 million versus $1.1 million in the same quarter of 1996. Revenues declined 8.6% to $56.8 million from $62.1 million. Operating income surged 73.4% to $3.3 million. The lower revenues reflected intense price and promotional competition in the North American and European markets. However, lower fluff wood pulp prices more than offset the higher advertising and promotional expenses and aggressive price cuts.

Gross profit margin as a percentage of net sales improved to 36.1% from 30.0% in the year-ago quarter. Selling, general and administration expenses as a percentage of net sales rose to 30.3% from 27.0% in the year-ago period. To counter the aggressive competition in North America and expand sales in Asia, the Company recently entered into a joint-venture agreement with its vendor in Indonesia to start up a manufacturing facility, which is scheduled to operate early in 1998.

BUSINESS

DSG INTERNATIONAL LIMITED is an international manufacturer and distributor of disposable diapers, adult incontinence, feminine hygiene and training pants products. The Company has eleven manufacturing plants in Hong Kong, the United States, Australia, England, Singapore, Switzerland, Canada, China and Thailand. Its products are marketed under brand names which include FITTI(R), PET PET(R), COSIES(R), COSIFITS(R), BABY LOVE(R), TOGS(R), CARES(R), VLESI(R), DISPO 123(R) and CERTAINTY(R). The Company distributes its products throughout Asia, Australia, North America and Europe. The Company's largest market is North America, which accounted for approximately 39.0% of 1996 total sales.

ANNUAL EARNINGS

	12/31/96	12/31/95	12/31/96	12/31/95
	--------------US $-------------		-------------HK$------------	
Earnings Per Share	1.18	0.58	9.13	4.49

ANNUAL FINANCIAL DATA

RECORD OF EARNINGS (IN THOUSANDS):

	12/31/96	12/31/95	12/31/96	12/31/95
Total Revenues	236,050	245,881	1,827,003	1,901,632
Costs & Expenses	220,067	236,823	1,703,297	1,831,578
Operating Income	15,983	9,058	123,706	70,054
Income Bef Income Tax	15,351	7,732	118,815	59,799
Income Tax	6,185	3,267	47,871	25,267
Minority Interests	...	cd222	...	cr1,717
Net Income	9,166	4,687	70,944	36,249
Average Shares Outstg	7,747	8,109	7,747	8,109

BALANCE SHEET (IN THOUSANDS):

Cash & Cash Equivalents	8,605	15,573	66,610	120,441
Receivables, Net	38,857	29,717	300,749	229,830
Inventories	23,990	21,399	185,680	165,499
Gross Property	100,380	97,821	776,931	756,543
Accumulated Depreciation	38,297	28,630	296,415	221,423
Long-Term Debt	21,587	16,470	167,081	127,378
Stockholders' Equity	74,639	83,706	577,698	647,378
Total Assets	141,910	154,393	1,098,369	1,194,068
Total Current Assets	73,838	68,727	571,499	531,531
Total Current Liabilities	42,124	49,150	326,036	380,124
Net Working Capital	31,714	19,577	245,463	151,408
Year End Shs Outstg	6,678	7,922	6,678	7,922

STATISTICAL RECORD:

Return on Equity %	12.28	5.60		
Return on Assets %	6.46	3.04		
Operating Profit Margin %	6.77	3.68		
Net Profit Margin %	3.88	1.91		
Book Value Per Share	11.18	10.57		

Converted at 1996, US$0.1292= 1 Hong Kong $; 1995, US$0.1293= 1 Hong Kong $

OFFICERS:
B. S. Wang, Chmn. & C.E.O. & Pres.
P. K. Leung, Secretary
T. Y. Leung, C.F.O.

INCORPORATED: Virgin Islands, 1991

PRINCIPAL OFFICE: 17th Floor Watson Centre16-22 Kung Yip Street Kwai Chung Hong Kong

TELEPHONE NUMBER: (852) 2427-6951

NO. OF EMPLOYEES: 1,317

ANNUAL MEETING: In Jun.

SHAREHOLDERS: 41

INSTITUTIONAL HOLDINGS:
No. of Institutions: N/A
Shares Held: N/A

REGISTRAR(S): N/A

TRANSFER AGENT(S): ChaseMellon
Shareholder Services, Encino, CA.

ECI TELECOM LTD.

YIELD 0.6%
P/E RATIO 17.3

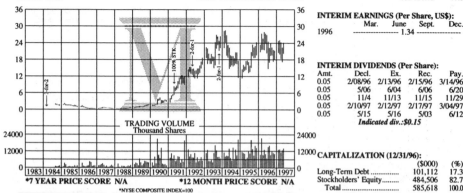

| | 1983 | 1984 | 1985 | 1986 | 1987 | 1988 | 1989 | 1990 | 1991 | 1992 | 1993 | 1994 | 1995 | 1996 | 1997 |

TRADING VOLUME
Thousand Shares

*7 YEAR PRICE SCORE N/A   *12 MONTH PRICE SCORE N/A
*NYSE COMPOSITE INDEX=100

INTERIM EARNINGS (Per Share, US$):

	Mar.	June	Sept.	Dec.
1996	------------------	1.34	------------------	

INTERIM DIVIDENDS (Per Share):

Amt.	Decl.	Ex.	Rec.	Pay.
0.05	2/08/96	2/13/96	2/15/96	3/14/96
0.05	5/06	6/04	6/06	6/20
0.05	11/4	11/13	11/15	11/29
0.05	2/10/97	2/12/97	2/17/97	3/04/97
0.05	5/15	5/16	5/03	6/12
	Indicated div.:$0.15			

CAPITALIZATION (12/31/96):

	($000)	(%)
Long-Term Debt	101,112	17.3
Stockholders' Equity	484,506	82.7
Total	585,618	100.0

RECENT DEVELOPMENTS: For the year ended 12/31/96, net income advanced 15.6% to $101.5 million from $87.9 million in the comparable period of 1995. Total revenues increased 30.4% to $588.7 million versus $451.4 million the year before. The improved results were primarily attributable to growth in sales of the Company's digital circuit multiplication equipment (DCME), which climbed 21.0% to $177.5 million. This growth was related to an increase in internet traffic, the adoption of the DTX-240 and 360 solution by global carriers, and the positive reception of ECILF's DCME solutions by emerging telecommunication carriers. Sales in Europe jumped 29.6% to $284.9 million, while North American sales rose 12.0% to $127.2 million. Sales in the Asia/Pacific region leapt 72.8% to $117.6 million. Operating income rose 8.9% to $98.6 million compared with $90.5 million a year earlier.

BUSINESS

ECI TELECOM LTD. is engaged in designing, developing, manufacturing and marketing of digital communication systems and data transmission systems for improving and expanding transmisssion infrastructure of both access and core networks on domestic and international routes. These systems provide capacity expansion, flexibility and management functions to better utilize existing and new telecommunications networks. The Company's subsidiary, Telematics International, designs, manufactures, sells and supports a complete line of wide area networking products designed for voice and data communications applications and networks worldwide.

ANNUAL EARNINGS

	12/31/96	12/31/95	12/31/96	12/31/95
	--------------US $--------------		-------------NIS------------	
Earnings Per Share	1.34	1.16	4.22	3.65

ANNUAL FINANCIAL DATA

RECORD OF EARNINGS (IN THOUSANDS):

	12/31/96	12/31/95	12/31/96	12/31/95
Total Revenues	588,733	451,421	1,917,697	1,420,903
Costs & Expenses	490,143	360,887	1,596,557	1,135,936
Operating Income	98,590	90,534	321,140	284,967
Income Bef Income Tax	102,039	94,425	332,375	297,214
Income Tax	512	6,574	1,668	20,692
Net Income	101,527	87,851	330,707	276,522
Average Shares Outstg	75,863	75,837	75,863	75,837

BALANCE SHEET (IN THOUSANDS):

Cash & Cash Equivalents	128,369	123,122
Receivables, Net	184,110	149,312
Inventories	176,826	101,070
Gross Property	N/A	133,504
Accumulated Depreciation	N/A	48,836
Long-Term Debt	101,112	1,360
Stockholders' Equity	484,506	391,519
Total Assets	709,730	501,145
Total Current Assets	515,185	379,485
Total Current Liabilities	122,112	106,810
Net Working Capital	393,073	272,675
Year End Shs Outstg	N/A	75,563

STATISTICAL RECORD:

Return on Equity %	20.95	22.44
Return on Assets %	14.31	17.53
Operating Profit Margin %	16.75	20.06
Net Profit Margin %	17.24	19.46
Book Value Per Share	N/A	5.18

Converted at 1996, US$0.3070= 1 New Israeli Shekel; 1994, US$0.3177= 1 New Israeli Shekel.

OFFICERS:
D. Rubner, Pres. & C.E.O.
D. Inbar, Sr. V.P. & C.F.O.

INCORPORATED: April, 1961

PRINCIPAL OFFICE: 30 Hasivim Street, Petah Tikva, 49133 Israel

TELEPHONE NUMBER: 972-3-926-6585

NO. OF EMPLOYEES: 3,300

ANNUAL MEETING: In July

SHAREHOLDERS: N/A

INSTITUTIONAL HOLDINGS:
No. of Institutions: 92
Shares Held: 35,154,754

REGISTRAR(S): N/A

TRANSFER AGENT(S): American Stock Transfer & Trust Co., New York.

EDUSOFT LTD.

YIELD ...
P/E RATIO 9.9

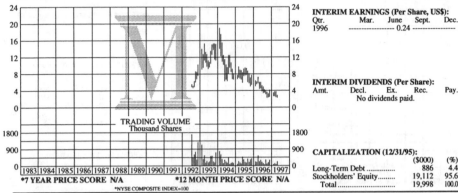

*7 YEAR PRICE SCORE N/A   *12 MONTH PRICE SCORE N/A

*NYSE COMPOSITE INDEX=100

INTERIM EARNINGS (Per Share, US$):

Qtr.	Mar.	June	Sept.	Dec.
1996		0.24		

INTERIM DIVIDENDS (Per Share):

Amt.	Decl.	Ex.	Rec.	Pay.
	No dividends paid.			

CAPITALIZATION (12/31/95):

	($000)	(%)
Long-Term Debt	886	4.4
Stockholders' Equity	19,112	95.6
Total	19,998	100.0

RECENT DEVELOPMENTS: For the year ended 12/31/96, net income decreased 36.5% to $1.1 million compared with $1.8 million in the same period of 1995. Revenues were $10.4 million, down 5.8% from $11.0 million the year before. Operating income plummeted 50.2% to $838,000 from $1.7 million the year before. Income before taxes was $1.3 million, down 31.8% from $2.0 million in 1995. The decline in revenues was primarily attributed to projects in Latin America, that due to local economic conditions, did not materialize. However, the Company is experiencing a revitalization in this market that management believes will possibly be reflected in increased sales in 1997. Of total revenues in 1996, Europe accounted for 33%, North America 23%, South America 20% and Asia 17%. The Companys research and development expenditures surged 49.2% to $1.3 million compared with $870,000. This increase reflects the development of the newly released Hotelier multimedia product, which offers an English learning environment for the hospitality industry.

BUSINESS

EDUSOFT LTD. develops, publishes, markets and supports personal computer based educational software products for science, technology, language learning and early childhood. The software is used to provide students with interactive, self-paced and individual computer-based instruction to supplement and enhance classroom teaching. A wide varitey of the products are marketed to schools, colleges, industrial training centers and government agencies. The Company distributes its software products, which are available in many languages, throughout the United States, Europe and Latin America. The Company currently sells over 90 interactive, full-color, software products in the fields of science, technology, English as a Second Language('ESL') learning and early childhood. These products are available in one or more of 15 languages and have been sold in over 35 countries to schools, home users, training centers and governments. The Company's products operate mostly on IBM-compatible personal computers and networks.

ANNUAL EARNINGS

	12/31/95	12/31/94	12/31/95	12/31/94
	----US $----		----NIS----	
Earnings Per Share	0.38	0.37	1.20	1.12

ANNUAL FINANCIAL DATA

RECORD OF EARNINGS (IN THOUSANDS):

	12/31/95	12/31/94	12/31/95	12/31/94
Total Revenues	10,986	10,028	34,580	30,260
Costs & Expenses	9,304	8,577	29,285	25,881
Operating Income	1,682	1,451	5,294	4,378
Income Bef Income Tax	1,975	1,785	6,217	5,386
Income Tax	169	cr20	532	cr60
Eq. Earnings in Affils.	...	d103	...	d311
Net Income	1,806	1,702	5,685	5,136
Average Shares Outstg	4,810	4,641	4,810	4,641

BALANCE SHEET (IN THOUSANDS):

	12/31/95	12/31/94	12/31/95	12/31/94
Cash & Cash Equivalents	10,312	9,751	32,458	29,424
Receivables, Net	5,238	4,567	16,487	13,781
Inventories	231	280	727	845
Gross Property	1,534	1,017	4,828	3,069
Accumulated Depreciation	557	354	1,753	1,068
Long-Term Debt	886	1,329	2,789	4,010
Stockholders' Equity	19,112	16,901	60,157	50,999
Total Assets	22,782	21,105	71,709	63,684
Total Current Assets	16,310	15,492	51,338	46,747
Total Current Liabilities	2,461	2,600	7,746	7,846
Net Working Capital	13,849	12,892	43,591	38,902
Year End Shs Outstg	4,720	4,676	4,720	4,676

STATISTICAL RECORD:

	12/31/95	12/31/94
Return on Equity %	9.45	10.07
Return on Assets %	7.93	8.06
Operating Profit Margin %	15.31	14.47
Net Profit Margin %	16.44	16.97
Book Value Per Share	4.05	3.61

Converted at 1995, US$0.3177= 1 New Israeli New Shekel; 1994, US$0.3314= 1 New Israeli New Shekel

OFFICERS:
M. Hasfari, Pres. & C.E.O.
A. Genish, C.F.O.
G. Nimoy, V.P.

INCORPORATED: 1991

PRINCIPAL OFFICE: 19 Weissburg Street, Tel Aviv Israel 61130

TELEPHONE NUMBER: 972-3-648-2131

NO. OF EMPLOYEES: 62

ANNUAL MEETING: In Aug.

SHAREHOLDERS: 66

INSTITUTIONAL HOLDINGS:
No. of Institutions: N/A
Shares Held: N/A

REGISTRAR(S): American Stock Transfer & Trust Co., New York.

TRANSFER AGENT(S): American Stock Transfer & Trust Co., New York.

ELAMEX, S.A. DE C.V.

YIELD ...
P/E RATIO 7.0

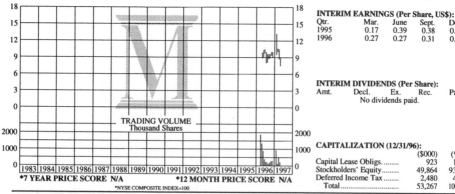

*NYSE COMPOSITE INDEX=100

INTERIM EARNINGS (Per Share, US$):

Qtr.	Mar.	June	Sept.	Dec.
1995	0.17	0.39	0.38	0.25
1996	0.27	0.27	0.31	0.29

INTERIM DIVIDENDS (Per Share):

Amt.	Decl.	Ex.	Rec.	Pay.
	No dividends paid.			

CAPITALIZATION (12/31/96):

	($000)	(%)
Capital Lease Obligs.........	923	1.7
Stockholders' Equity........	49,864	93.6
Deferred Income Tax	2,480	4.7
Total	53,267	100.0

*7 YEAR PRICE SCORE N/A   *12 MONTH PRICE SCORE N/A

RECENT DEVELOPMENTS: For the year ended 12/31/96, net income rose 27.7% to US$7.9 million from US$6.2 million in 1995. Sales rose 21.9% to US$118.9 million. Gross profit gained 24.8% to US$18.7 million, while operating income rose 18.0% to US$10.4 million. Weighted average shares outstanding totaled 6.9 million versus 5.0 million in 1995. The Company attributed the strong revenue and income growth to increased sales to existing customers and the addition of new customers, along with improved effi-ciencies and economies of scale. For the three months ended 12/31/96, net income rose 69.1% to US$2.1 million from US$1.3 million a year earlier. Sales advanced 31.4% to US$32.2 million. Gross profit declined 3.1% to US$4.2 million, while operating income fell 35.7% to US$1.7 million. The Company attributed the declines to a governmentally mandated wage increase, originally not expected until 1997. In addition, the Company noted that there was a shift towards more turnkey sales with less assembly content.

BUSINESS

ELAMEX, S.A. DE C.V. is a provider of contract assembly services and turnkey manufacturing services to Original Equipment Manufacturers primarily located in the United States. The Company assembles printed cir-cuit boards with computer-automated equipment using surface mount and pin-through-hole interconnection technologies, and produces wire cable assemblies, plastic over-molded SMT printed circuit boards and fiber optic cable and connector assemblies. The Company is also engaged in the man-ufacture of switchboard components, outlet strips, smoke detectors, auto-matic timer switches and the refur-bishment of telephones. The Com-pany is also engaged in the assembly of tube assemblies and surgery sets and the manufacture of microbiologi-cal test equipment.

ANNUAL EARNINGS

	12/31/96	12/31/95	12/31/96	12/31/95
	------------US $------------		------------Pesos------------	
Earnings Per Share	1.15	1.20	9.02	9.23

ANNUAL FINANCIAL DATA

RECORD OF EARNINGS (IN THOUSANDS):

	12/31/96	12/31/95	12/31/96	12/31/95
Total Revenues	118,919	97,544	932,697	750,335
Costs & Expenses	108,553	88,755	851,394	682,732
Operating Income	10,366	8,788	81,303	67,603
Income Bef Income Tax	10,503	7,936	82,373	61,047
Income Tax	2,575	1,727	20,197	13,285
Net Income	7,927	6,209	62,176	47,763
Average Shares Outstg	6,881	5,000	6,881	5,000
BALANCE SHEET (IN THOUSANDS):				
Cash & Cash Equivalents	6,270	2,849	49,175	21,913
Receivables, Net	15,992	15,692	125,427	120,711
Inventories	16,200	11,358	127,060	87,371
Gross Property	40,036	32,814	314,004	252,415
Accumulated Depreciation	11,425	8,791	89,607	67,625
Long-Term Debt	...	15,677	...	122,957
Capital Lease Obligs	923	181	7,239	1,392
Stockholders' Equity	49,864	23,196	391,089	178,433
Total Assets	67,976	55,110	533,146	423,927
Total Current Assets	38,955	30,586	305,528	235,277
Total Current Liabilities	14,496	15,156	113,695	116,581
Net Working Capital	24,459	15,430	191,833	118,696
Year End Shs Outstg	7,400	5,000	7,400	5,000
STATISTICAL RECORD:				
Return on Equity %	15.90	26.77		
Return on Assets %	11.66	11.27		
Operating Profit Margin %	8.72	9.01		
Net Profit Margin %	6.67	6.37		
Book Value Per Share	6.74	4.64		

Converted at 1996, US$0.1275= 1 Mexican Peso; 1995, US$0.1300= 1 Mexican Peso

OFFICERS:
E. S. Vallina, Chmn.
F. Barrio, Vice-Chmn.
J. Alvarez-Morodo, Vice-Chmn. & Sec.
H. M. Raynal, Pres. & C.E.O.
INCORPORATED: Oct., 1995
PRINCIPAL OFFICE: Avenida Insurgentes No. 4145-B Ote. Ciudad Juarez, Chihuahua Mexico C.P. 32340

TELEPHONE NUMBER: (16) 16-43-33
NO. OF EMPLOYEES: 5,040
ANNUAL MEETING: In Apr.
SHAREHOLDERS: 1,098 (approx.)
INSTITUTIONAL HOLDINGS:
No. of Institutions: N/A
Shares Held: N/A

REGISTRAR(S):

TRANSFER AGENT(S):

ELBIT LTD.

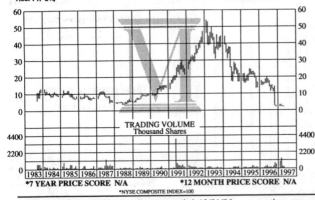

*7 YEAR PRICE SCORE N/A   *12 MONTH PRICE SCORE N/A
*NYSE COMPOSITE INDEX=100

TRADING VOLUME
Thousand Shares

1983 1984 1985 1986 1987 1988 1989 1990 1991 1992 1993 1994 1995 1996 1997

INTERIM EARNINGS (Per Share, US$):

Qtr.	Mar.	June	Sept.	Dec.
1995		0.86		
1996		d0.53		

INTERIM DIVIDENDS (Per Share):

Amt.	Decl.	Ex.	Rec.	Pay.
	No dividends paid.			

CAPITALIZATION (12/31/95):

	($000)	(%)
Long-Term Debt	41,825	8.3
Minority Interest	101,092	20.2
Stockholders' Equity	350,203	69.9
Deferred Income Taxes	7,941	1.6
Total	501,061	100.0

RECENT DEVELOPMENTS: For the year ended 12/31/96, Elbit Ltd. reported a net loss of $11.3 million, unchanged from a net loss of $11.3 million in 1995. The results reflect the demerger of Elbit into three independent companies. Net revenues fell 41.5% to $33.6 million from $57.4 million, resulting primarily from lower levels of television sales by the video division and the focusing of its sales in only the Israeli market. Operating loss from continuing operations narrowed to $6.7 million from $13.4 million. Other income was $3.5 million versus $1.6 million in 1995. During 1996, the Company executed its strategy of disposing its non-strategic assets, which included the sale of its holdings in Inframetrics, Fiboronics, and the public offering of EVS. Ebbit realized cash reserves of approximately $29.0 million, which is expected to be used toward investment in the Communications sector.

BUSINESS

ELBIT LTD. focuses on providing connectivity and communications systesm for public and private networks through its new subsidiary ELBIT.COM Ltd. ELBIT.COM Ltd. intends to implement communication access solutions using ATM technology and over Cable TV infrastructure. To focus on expanding its communications activities, the Company has been actively divesting non-strategic assets. During 1996, Elbit Ltd, completed the spinoff of its medical imaging and defense systems. Elbit Ltd. is 40% owned by Elron Electronic Industries.

ANNUAL EARNINGS

	12/31/95	12/31/94	12/31/95	12/31/94
	US $		NIS	
Earnings Per Share	0.86	1.57	2.71	4.74

ANNUAL FINANCIAL DATA

RECORD OF EARNINGS (IN THOUSANDS):

Total Revenues	968,089	758,486	3,047,180	2,288,733
Costs & Expenses	944,313	711,576	2,972,342	2,147,182
Operating Income	23,776	46,910	74,838	141,551
Income Bef Income Tax	28,425	43,932	89,471	132,565
Income Tax	2,493	7,147	7,847	21,566
Minority Interests	7,579	6,774	23,856	20,441
Net Income	18,353	30,011	57,768	90,558
Average Shares Outstg	21,294	19,107	21,294	19,107

BALANCE SHEET (IN THOUSANDS):

Cash & Cash Equivalents	111,115	148,330	349,748	447,586
Receivables, Net	286,140	250,551	900,661	756,038
Inventories	205,301	174,566	646,210	526,753
Gross Property	246,682	238,808	776,462	720,604
Accumulated Depreciation	147,638	142,764	464,709	430,791
Long-Term Debt	41,825	41,195	131,649	124,306
Stockholders' Equity	350,203	327,146	1,102,307	987,164
Total Assets	886,649	851,853	2,790,837	2,570,468
Total Current Assets	656,178	606,564	2,065,401	1,830,308
Total Current Liabilities	372,006	365,997	1,170,935	1,104,396
Net Working Capital	284,172	240,567	894,466	725,911
Year End Shs Outstg	21,386	20,532	21,386	20,532

STATISTICAL RECORD:

Return on Equity %	5.24	9.17	
Return on Assets %	2.07	3.52	
Operating Profit Margin %	2.46	6.18	
Net Profit Margin %	1.90	3.96	
Book Value Per Share	16.38	15.93	

Converted at 1995, US$0.3177= 1 New Israeli New Shekel; 1994, US$0.3314= 1 New Israeli New Shekel

OFFICERS:
U. Gill, Pres. & C.E.O.
Y. Baruchi, Gen. Manager & C.O.O.
S. Haruvi, Exec. V.P.
J. Ackerman, Sr. V.P.

INCORPORATED: Israel, 1966

PRINCIPAL OFFICE: Advanced Technology Center, Haifa, Israel

TELEPHONE NUMBER: 972-4-315315

NO. OF EMPLOYEES: 3,061

ANNUAL MEETING: In Jun.

SHAREHOLDERS: N/A

INSTITUTIONAL HOLDINGS:
No. of Institutions: N/A
Shares Held: N/A

REGISTRAR(S): The American Stock Transfer & Trust Co., New York.

TRANSFER AGENT(S): The American Stock Transfer & Trust Co., New York.

ELBIT MEDICAL IMAGING, LTD.

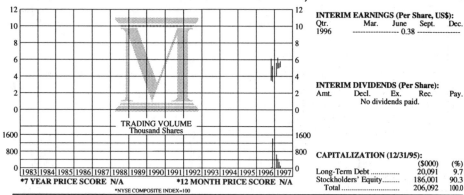

*7 YEAR PRICE SCORE N/A   *12 MONTH PRICE SCORE N/A
*NYSE COMPOSITE INDEX=100

INTERIM EARNINGS (Per Share, US$):

Qtr.	Mar.	June	Sept.	Dec.
1996	-------------------	0.38	-------------------	

INTERIM DIVIDENDS (Per Share):

Amt.	Decl.	Ex.	Rec.	Pay.
	No dividends paid.			

CAPITALIZATION (12/31/95):

	($000)	(%)
Long-Term Debt	20,091	9.7
Stockholders' Equity.........	186,001	90.3
Total	206,092	100.0

RECENT DEVELOPMENTS: For the year ended 12/31/96, net income was $8.1 million, up 50.0% from $5.4 million in the same period of 1995. Total revenues declined 2.5% to $525.2 million compared with $538.6 million the prior year. Research and development increased 12.9% to $38.6 million compared with $34.2 million a year earlier. Operating income was $13.1 million, up 6.5% from $12.3 million in 1995. The 1995 sales included revenues of $47.2 million generated by Omker, a trading company based in Hungary, in which EMITF previously held a majority interest. Effec-

tive 1/1/96, EMITF reduced its ownership of Omker to 44%, no longer a controlling interest. Consequently, sales of Omker are no longer consolidated. During November 1996, Elbit Ltd., a holding company, demerged into three separate entities. EMITF emerged as one of the three independent companies. The improvement in results was primarily attributed to operating and strategic initiatives implemented in all three of the Company's subsidiaries, Elbit Ultrasound Ltd., Elscint Ltd. and Elbit Medical Services Ltd.

BUSINESS

ELBIT MEDICAL IMAGING, LTD. is a developer, manufacturer and marketer of medical imaging products. The Company conducts its diagnostic systems and equipment activities through its subsidiaries and affiliates.

ANNUAL EARNINGS

	12/31/95	12/31/94	12/31/95	12/31/94
	------------US $------------		------------NIS------------	
Earnings Per Share	0.26	0.51	0.82	1.54

ANNUAL FINANCIAL DATA

RECORD OF EARNINGS (IN THOUSANDS):

	12/31/95	12/31/94	12/31/95	12/31/94
Total Revenues	538,684	342,677	1,695,574	1,034,028
Costs & Expenses	526,430	326,062	1,657,003	983,893
Operating Income	12,254	16,615	38,571	50,136
Income Bef Income Tax	14,397	18,649	45,316	56,273
Income Tax	2,105	1,431	6,626	4,318
Minority Interests	6,859	7,464	21,590	22,523
Net Income	5,433	9,754	17,101	29,433
Average Shares Outstg	21,294	19,107	21,294	19,107

BALANCE SHEET (IN THOUSANDS):

Cash & Cash Equivalents	45,830	63,258	144,256	190,881
Receivables, Net	220,951	191,260	695,471	577,127
Inventories	129,495	105,062	407,602	317,025
Gross Property	132,009	128,294	415,515	387,127
Accumulated Depreciation	82,580	81,004	259,931	244,430
Long-Term Debt	20,091	16,907	63,239	51,017
Stockholders' Equity	186,001	173,034	585,461	522,130
Total Assets	498,073	447,885	1,567,746	1,351,494
Total Current Assets	396,719	361,251	1,248,722	1,090,075
Total Current Liabilities	187,366	159,506	589,758	481,310
Net Working Capital	209,353	201,745	658,964	608,766
Year End Shs Outstg	21,386	21,386	21,386	21,386

STATISTICAL RECORD:

Return on Equity %	2.92	5.64		
Return on Assets %	1.09	2.18		
Operating Profit Margin %	2.27	4.85		
Net Profit Margin %	1.01	2.85		
Book Value Per Share	8.70	8.09		

Converted at 1995, US$0.3177= 1 New Israeli Shekel; 1994, US$0.3314= 1 New Israeli Shekel

OFFICERS:
E. Gill, Pres. & C.E.O.
O. Tamir, V.P. & C.F.O.
P. Kirshen, V.P. & General Counsel
D. E. McNulty
INCORPORATED: Israel, 1996
PRINCIPAL OFFICE: Advanced Technology Center, Haifa Israel 31053

TELEPHONE NUMBER: (972-4) 8315315
NO. OF EMPLOYEES: 3,061
ANNUAL MEETING: June
SHAREHOLDERS: N/A
INSTITUTIONAL HOLDINGS:
No. of Institutions: N/A
Shares Held: N/A

REGISTRAR(S): American Stock Transfer & Trust Co.

TRANSFER AGENT(S): American Stock Transfer & Trust Co.

ELBIT SYSTEMS, LTD.

YIELD 1.8%
P/E RATIO 13.4

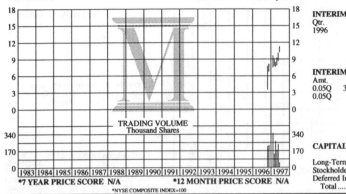

340

170

0

| 1983 | 1984 | 1985 | 1986 | 1987 | 1988 | 1989 | 1990 | 1991 | 1992 | 1993 | 1994 | 1995 | 1996 | 1997 |

*7 YEAR PRICE SCORE N/A   *12 MONTH PRICE SCORE N/A

*NYSE COMPOSITE INDEX=100

INTERIM EARNINGS (Per Share, US$):

Qtr.	Mar.	June	Sept.	Dec.
1996	------------------ 0.84 ------------------			

INTERIM DIVIDENDS (Per Share):

Amt.	Decl.	Ex.	Rec.	Pay.
0.05Q	3/04/97	5/07/97	4/30/97	5/14/97
0.05Q	5/7	6/26	6/30	7/14

Indicated div.:$0.200

CAPITALIZATION (12/31/96):

	($000)	(%)
Long-Term Debt	4,628	5.3
Stockholders' Equity........	77,626	89.4
Deferred Income Tax	4,579	5.3
Total	86,833	100.0

RECENT DEVELOPMENTS: For the year ended 12/31/96, net income decreased 25.5% to $18.0 million compared with $24.2 million in the same period of 1995. Revenues were $307.5 million, up 2.6% from $299.9 million the year before. Gross profit was down 5.4% to $76.1 million from $80.4 million in 1995. The decline in gross profit was primarily attributed to the continuous freeze of the U.S. Dollar/Israeli Shekel exchange rate and the mix of types of projects. Research and development increased 19.3% to $21.8 million compared with $18.2 million the year before. Operating income was $23.1 million, down 21.1% from $29.2 million in 1995. The Company experienced a decline in earnings that was primarily the result of increased research and development expenditures invested to maintain the Company's technological advantages in future markets, and the result of investments in new electronic systems developed in response to customers anticipated needs.

BUSINESS

ELBIT SYSTEMS LTD. is engaged in integrated upgrade programs for combat aircraft, helicopters, tanks and other platforms. On January 1, 1996, the Company commenced operations following the completion of the demerger of Elbit Ltd. As a result of the demerger, the Company received the defense-related businesses of Elbit Ltd. The Company is an Israeli corporation, 40.0% owned by Elron Electronic Industries Ltd.

ANNUAL EARNINGS

	12/31/96	12/31/95	12/31/96	12/31/95
	------------US $------------		------------NIS------------	
Earnings Per Share	0.84	1.14	2.74	3.59

ANNUAL FINANCIAL DATA

RECORD OF EARNINGS (IN THOUSANDS):

Total Revenues	307,508	299,858	1,001,655	943,840
Costs & Expenses	284,449	270,619	926,544	851,807
Operating Income	23,059	29,239	75,111	92,033
Income Bef Income Tax	23,821	30,752	77,593	96,796
Income Tax	5,812	6,579	18,932	20,708
Net Income	18,009	24,173	58,661	76,088
Average Shares Outstg	21,386	21,294	21,386	21,294

BALANCE SHEET (IN THOUSANDS):

Cash & Cash Equivalents	23,374	21,153	76,137	66,582
Receivables, Net	66,721	48,512	217,332	152,698
Inventories	73,280	51,721	238,697	162,798
Gross Property	67,179	62,672	218,824	197,268
Accumulated Depreciation	41,671	38,618	135,736	121,555
Long-Term Debt	4,628	4,628	15,075	14,567
Stockholders' Equity	77,626	61,366	252,853	193,157
Total Assets	241,354	201,837	786,169	635,307
Total Current Assets	163,375	121,386	532,166	382,077
Total Current Liabilities	145,968	120,765	475,466	380,123
Net Working Capital	17,407	621	56,700	1,955
Year End Shs Outstg	21,386	21,386	21,386	21,386

STATISTICAL RECORD:

Return on Equity %	23.20	39.39		
Return on Assets %	7.46	11.98		
Operating Profit Margin %	7.50	9.75		
Net Profit Margin %	5.86	8.06		
Book Value Per Share	3.63	2.87		

Converted at 1996, US$0.3070= 1 New Israeli Shekel; 1995, US$0.3177= 1 New Israeli Shekel

OFFICERS:
E. Gill, Chmn.
J. Ackerman, Pres. & C.E.O.
I. Farchi, C.F.O.
D. B. Temin, Gen. Couns.

INCORPORATED: N/A

PRINCIPAL OFFICE: Advanced Technology Center P.O.B. 539, Haifa Israel

TELEPHONE NUMBER: 972-4-8315315

NO. OF EMPLOYEES: N/A

ANNUAL MEETING: N/A

SHAREHOLDERS: N/A

INSTITUTIONAL HOLDINGS:
No. of Institutions: N/A
Shares Held: N/A

REGISTRAR(S): American Stock Transfer and Trust Co., New York.

TRANSFER AGENT(S): American Stock Transfer and Trust Co., New York.

ELBIT VISION SYSTEMS LTD.

YIELD ...
P/E RATIO 71.1

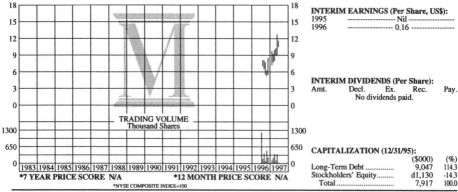

*7 YEAR PRICE SCORE N/A   ***12 MONTH PRICE SCORE N/A**
*NYSE COMPOSITE INDEX=100

INTERIM EARNINGS (Per Share, US$):
1995 ------------------ Nil ------------------
1996 ------------------ 0.16 ------------------

INTERIM DIVIDENDS (Per Share):

Amt.	Decl.	Ex.	Rec.	Pay.

No dividends paid.

CAPITALIZATION (12/31/95):

	($000)	(%)
Long-Term Debt	9,047	114.3
Stockholders' Equity........	d1,130	-14.3
Total...........................	7,917	100.0

RECENT DEVELOPMENTS: For the year ended 12/31/96, net income was $1.2 million compared with a loss of $25,000 in the same period of 1995. Net sales were $16.5 million, up 63.6% from $10.1 million the year before. Gross profit was $7.6 million, up 65.5% from $4.6 million in 1995. Research and development expenses were $2.6 million, up 73.7% from $1.5 million a year earlier. Results for 1996 excluded a one-time royalty payment of $823,000 for licensed technology. The improvement in earnings and sales was primarily attributed to the steady worldwide acceptance of EVSNF's I-TEX Inspected label by strong customers in the textile industry. The Company recently received a significant follow-on order from Mount Vernon Mills, Inc., a leading U.S. textile manufacturer. A series of orders received recently from major textile manufacturers worldwide includes orders for the Company's recently introduced PRINTEX and SVA systems.

BUSINESS

ELBIT VISION SYSTEMS LTD. is engaged in the design, development, manufacture, marketing and support of automatic vision inspection and quality monitoring systems. The Company's systems are designd to increase the accuracy, consistency and speed of the detection and identification of defects in the manufacturing process in order to reduce labor costs, improve product quality and increase manufacturing efficiency.

ANNUAL EARNINGS

	12/31/95	12/31/94	12/31/95	12/31/94
	-------------US $------------		-------------NIS------------	
Earnings Per Share	Nil	d0.03	Nil	d0.09

ANNUAL FINANCIAL DATA

RECORD OF EARNINGS (IN THOUSANDS):

	12/31/95	12/31/94	12/31/95	12/31/94
Total Revenues	10,116	6,973	31,841	21,041
Costs & Expenses	9,696	6,996	30,519	21,110
Operating Income	420	d23	1,322	d69
Income Bef Income Tax	d25	d135	d79	d407
Income Tax	...	80	...	241
Net Income	d25	d215	d79	d649
Average Shares Outstg	6,676	6,676	6,676	6,676
BALANCE SHEET (IN THOUSANDS):				
Cash & Cash Equivalents	1	223	3	673
Receivables, Net	2,786	1,686	8,769	5,088
Inventories	7,868	4,916	24,766	14,834
Gross Property	790	457	2,487	1,379
Accumulated Depreciation	123	9	387	27
Long-Term Debt	9,047	7,209	28,477	21,753
Stockholders' Equity	d1,130	d1,657	d3,557	d5,000
Total Assets	12,090	7,861	38,055	23,721
Total Current Assets	10,655	6,825	33,538	20,594
Total Current Liabilities	3,521	1,761	11,083	5,314
Net Working Capital	7,134	5,064	22,455	15,281
Year End Shs Outstg	6,572	1,095	6,572	1,095
STATISTICAL RECORD:				
Return on Equity %	...	...		
Return on Assets %	...	...		
Operating Profit Margin %	4.15	...		
Net Profit Margin %	...	...		
Book Value Per Share	d0.17	d1.51		

Converted at 1995, US$0.3177= 1 New Israeli Shekel; 1994, US$0.3314= 1 New Israeli Shekel

---

OFFICERS:
E. Gill, Chmn.
J. Barath, Pres. & C.E.O.
A. Harel, C.F.O.
H. Avni, V.P.-Engineering

INCORPORATED: 1994

PRINCIPAL OFFICE: New Industrial Park, P.O. Box 140, Yoqneam Israel

TELEPHONE NUMBER: 972-4-993-6400

NO. OF EMPLOYEES: 51

ANNUAL MEETING: N/A

SHAREHOLDERS: N/A

INSTITUTIONAL HOLDINGS:
No. of Institutions: N/A
Shares Held: N/A

REGISTRAR(S): N/A

TRANSFER AGENT(S): N/A

ELRON ELECTRONIC INDUSTRIES

YIELD 1.8%
P/E RATIO 24.3

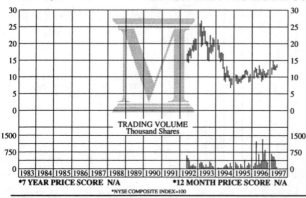

TRADING VOLUME
Thousand Shares

| 1983 | 1984 | 1985 | 1986 | 1987 | 1988 | 1989 | 1990 | 1991 | 1992 | 1993 | 1994 | 1995 | 1996 | 1997 |

*7 YEAR PRICE SCORE N/A   *12 MONTH PRICE SCORE N/A
*NYSE COMPOSITE INDEX=100

INTERIM EARNINGS (Per Share, US$):
1995 ------------------ 0.51 ------------------
1996 ------------------ 0.56 ------------------

INTERIM DIVIDENDS (Per Share):

Amt.	Decl.	Ex.	Rec.	Pay.
0.06	11/08/95	11/30/95	12/04/95	12/18/95
0.06	3/12/96	3/28/96	4/01/96	4/15/96
0.06	5/14/96	5/30/96	6/03/96	6/17/96
0.06	8/08/96	9/12/96	9/16/96	9/30/96
0.06	11/13	...	12/9	12/23
0.06	3/11/97	3/20/97	3/24/97	4/07/97

Indicated div.:$0.24

CAPITALIZATION (12/31/96):

	($000)	(%)
Stockholders' Equity	201,347	100.0
Total	201,347	100.0

RECENT DEVELOPMENTS: For the year ended 12/31/96, net income rose 9.5% to $11.3 million compared with $10.3 million in 1995. The Company derives its earnings from three main sources: its share of net income of affiliated companies, a gain on equity from change in holdings in affiliated companies, and other income resulting primarily from the sales of investments or holdings. Elron's net income from affiliated companies amounted to $2.8 mil-

lion, down 40.4% from $4.7 million in 1995. The decrease reflects losses from new emerging companies. The Company's gain from changes in holdings in affiliated companies was $690,000 compared with $3.8 million, resulting from changes in Elron's holding in Zoran, which completed an initial public offering in 1995. Other income jumped 57.4% to $11.4 million, reflecting the sale and increase in value of 650,000 Orbotech shares.

BUSINESS

ELRON ELECTRONIC INDUS-TRIES is an industrial holding company. Through its subsidiaries, the Company designs, develops, manufactures, markets and services electronic systems and products for diagnostic medical imaging, advanced defense electronics, data communications and manufacturing automation. In addition, the Company also produces semiconductor products, software products and sophisticated productivity tools, such as CAIS (Computer-Aided Intelligent Service) which assists managers in developing rapid solutions to relevant business problems through quick access to pertinent technical and logistical information, and CBT (Computer Based Training) which provides multimedia training and reduces development and revision time of user documentation and training manuals.

ANNUAL EARNINGS

	12/31/96	12/31/95	12/31/96	12/31/95
	---US $---		---NIS---	
Earnings Per Share	0.56	0.51	1.82	1.61

ANNUAL FINANCIAL DATA

RECORD OF EARNINGS (IN THOUSANDS):				
Total Revenues	14,859	15,719	48,401	49,477
Costs & Expenses	3,580	5,415	11,661	17,044
Operating Income	11,279	10,304	36,739	32,433
Net Income	11,279	10,304	36,739	32,433
Average Shares Outstg	20,287	20,287	20,287	20,287
BALANCE SHEET (IN THOUSANDS):				
Cash & Cash Equivalents	11,604	8,450	37,798	26,597
Receivables, Net	435	457	1,417	1,438
Gross Property	950	1,122	3,094	3,532
Accumulated Depreciation	381	390	1,241	1,228
Stockholders' Equity	201,347	196,903	655,853	619,777
Total Assets	203,278	199,377	662,143	627,564
Total Current Assets	12,039	8,907	39,215	28,036
Total Current Liabilities	1,931	2,474	6,290	7,787
Net Working Capital	10,108	6,433	32,925	20,249
Year End Shs Outstg	20,287	20,287	20,287	20,287
STATISTICAL RECORD:				
Return on Equity %	5.6	5.2		
Return on Assets %	5.5	5.2		
Operating Profit Margin %	75.9	65.6		
Net Profit Margin %	75.9	65.6		
Book Value Per Share	9.92	9.71		

Converted at 1996, US$0.3070= 1 New Israeli Shekel; 1995, US$0.3177= 1 New Israeli Shekel

OFFICERS:
U. Galil, Chmn., Pres. & C.E.O.
J. Ben-Zvi, Sr. V.P.
A. Peri, V.P.-Tech.
D. Birger, V.P.-Fin. & Sec.

INCORPORATED: Israel, 1962

PRINCIPAL OFFICE: Advanced Technology Center P.O. Box 1573 Haifa Israel 31015

TELEPHONE NUMBER: 972-4-854-5000

NO. OF EMPLOYEES: 50 (approx.)

ANNUAL MEETING: In Jun.

SHAREHOLDERS: N/A

INSTITUTIONAL HOLDINGS:
No. of Institutions: N/A
Shares Held: N/A

REGISTRAR(S): N/A

TRANSFER AGENT(S): The American Stock and Transfer & Trust Co., New York.

EMCO LIMITED

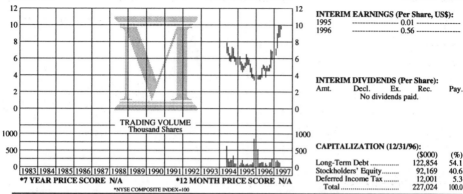

*7 YEAR PRICE SCORE N/A   *12 MONTH PRICE SCORE N/A
*NYSE COMPOSITE INDEX=100

INTERIM EARNINGS (Per Share, US$):

1995	------------------- 0.01 -------------------
1996	------------------- 0.56 -------------------

INTERIM DIVIDENDS (Per Share):

Amt.	Decl.	Ex.	Rec.	Pay.
	No dividends paid.			

CAPITALIZATION (12/31/96):

	($000)	(%)
Long-Term Debt	122,854	54.1
Stockholders' Equity........	92,169	40.6
Deferred Income Tax	12,001	5.3
Total	227,024	100.0

RECENT DEVELOPMENTS: For the year ended 12/31/96, net income from continuing operations soared to C$17.8 million from C$199,000 in 1995. The 1996 results included a pre-tax gain of C$6.9 million from the sale of businesses. The 1995 results excluded a C$19.2 million loss from discontinued operations. Revenues increased 4.6% to C$1.14 billion from C$1.09 billion. The higher revenues were attributed to strong growth at Emco Building products. Operating earnings jumped 78.7% to C$46.2 million. Reve-

nues at Emco Building Products grew 23.5% to C$289.5 million and operating income soared to C$24.0 million from C$5.9 million in 1995. Emco Distribution reported a 1.1% increase in revenues to C$752.8 million and a 9.1% improvement in operating profit to C$28.0 million. Revenues at Emco Custom Products declined 12.1% to C$102.4 million; however, operating income jumped 61.4% to C$6.5 million. Earnings also benefited from a 21.9% decline in interest expense to C$19.3 million.

BUSINESS

EMCO LIMITED manufactures and distributes building materials and engineered products and is organized into three operating groups: Emco Distribution Group, Emco Building Products Group and Emco Custom Products Group. The Distribution Group distributes plumbing, heating, air conditioning and pipe valves and fittings through 106 branches and three regional distribution centers throughout Canada. Its products are sold primarily to residential, industrial and commercial construction sectors and to governments, institutions and retail outlets. The Building Products Group manufactures and distributes roofing and wood fibre products, and residential and commercial sinkware, windows and patio doors. It also markets and distributes air barrier wrap, hardwood flooring, and a retail line of plumbing and heating products. The Custom Products Group provides contract manufacturing and engineering services for original equipment manufacturers who are increasingly using outside services for specialized components. Major customers are hardware, electronic, electrical and automotive manufacturers.

ANNUAL EARNINGS

	12/31/96	12/31/95	12/31/96	12/31/95
	------------US $------------		------------C $------------	
Earnings Per Share	0.56	0.01	0.76	0.01

ANNUAL FINANCIAL DATA

RECORD OF EARNINGS (IN THOUSANDS):

	12/31/96	12/31/95	12/31/96	12/31/95
Total Revenues	830,957	796,494	1,136,584	1,086,771
Costs & Expenses	786,344	767,437	1,075,563	1,047,124
Depreciation & Amort	10,852	10,122	14,843	13,811
Operating Income	33,761	18,935	46,178	25,836
Income Bef Income Tax	24,134	664	33,011	906
Income Tax	11,113	518	15,200	707
Net Income	13,022	146	17,811	199
Income from Disc. Ops.	...	d14,182	...	d19,350

BALANCE SHEET (IN THOUSANDS):

Receivables, Net	108,611	105,951	148,559	144,564
Inventories	109,004	118,986	149,096	162,350
Gross Property	157,148	163,649	214,947	223,289
Accumulated Depreciation	60,980	65,158	83,408	88,904
Long-Term Debt	122,854	173,186	168,040	236,303
Stockholders' Equity	92,169	79,010	126,069	107,804
Total Assets	334,202	348,190	457,122	475,085
Total Current Assets	220,402	231,641	301,466	316,061
Total Current Liabilities	107,178	94,318	146,598	128,692
Net Working Capital	113,224	137,323	154,868	187,369
Year End Shs Outstg	23,319	23,239	23,319	23,239

STATISTICAL RECORD:

Return on Equity %	14.1	0.2		
Return on Assets %	3.9	...		
Operating Profit Margin %	4.1	2.4		
Net Profit Margin %	1.6	...		
Book Value Per Share	3.95	3.40		

Converted at 1996, US$0.7311= 1 Canadian $; 1995, US$0.7329= 1 Canadian $

OFFICERS:
F. M. Hennessey, Chmn. & C.E.O.
D. E. Speers, Pres. & C.O.O.
R. B. Grogan, V.P. & C.F.O.

INCORPORATED: Canada, 1906

PRINCIPAL OFFICE: 620 Richmond Street
P.O. Box 5252, London Ontario, Canada

TELEPHONE NUMBER: (519) 645-3900

NO. OF EMPLOYEES: 3,500

ANNUAL MEETING: In May

SHAREHOLDERS: N/A

INSTITUTIONAL HOLDINGS:
No. of Institutions: 5
Shares Held: 1,770,400

REGISTRAR(S): Montreal Trust Company of Canada, Toronto, Montreal.

TRANSFER AGENT(S): Montreal Trust Company of Canada, Toronto, Montreal.

ESC MEDICAL SYSTEMS LIMITED

YIELD ...
P/E RATIO 49.1

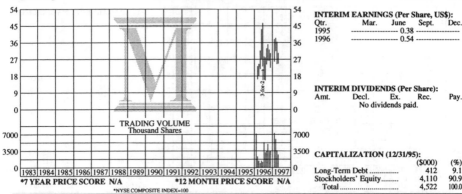

7 YEAR PRICE SCORE N/A　　**12 MONTH PRICE SCORE N/A**
*NYSE COMPOSITE INDEX=100

TRADING VOLUME
Thousand Shares

1983 1984 1985 1986 1987 1988 1989 1990 1991 1992 1993 1994 1995 1996 1997

INTERIM EARNINGS (Per Share, US$):

Qtr.	Mar.	June	Sept.	Dec.
1995		0.38		
1996		0.54		

INTERIM DIVIDENDS (Per Share):

Amt.	Decl.	Ex.	Rec.	Pay.
	No dividends paid.			

CAPITALIZATION (12/31/95):

	($000)	(%)
Long-Term Debt	412	9.1
Stockholders' Equity	4,110	90.9
Total	4,522	100.0

RECENT DEVELOPMENTS: For the year ended 12/31/96, net income advanced to $9.2 million compared with $2.8 million in the same period of 1995. Sales increased to $32.9 million from $8.4 million a year before. Gross profit rose to $25.4 million compared with $6.3 million in 1995. Results for 1996 included a non-recurring expense of $3.5 million associated with the purchase of L.B.T. Ltd. The substantial improvement in sales was primarily attributable to the strong worldwide acceptance of the Company's PhotoDerm VL and PhotoDerm PL systems. In addition, sales of the EpiLight(TM) hair removal system, the Derma(TM) 20 Er: Yag Laser System and the Topaz(TM) 30 continue to generate incremental revenues internationally and, upon FDA approval, should provide tremendous opportunities for the Company in the U.S. There is strong demand for the EpiLight internationally and it offers a unique alternative to hair removal. Clinical trials conducted in the U.S. for EpiLight have been very positive and served as the basis of the EpiLight 510 (k) FDA filing in August of 1996.

BUSINESS

ESC MEDICAL SYSTEMS LIMITED is engaged in the development, manufacture and marketing of medical devices utilizing proprietary intense pulsed light source technology for non-invasive treatment of varicose veins and other benign vascular lesions, as well as other clinical applications.

ANNUAL EARNINGS

	12/31/95	12/31/94	12/31/95	12/31/94
	US $		NIS	
Earnings Per Share	0.38	d0.19	3.21	d0.57

ANNUAL FINANCIAL DATA

RECORD OF EARNINGS (IN THOUSANDS):

Total Revenues	8,398	1,134	26,435	3,423
Costs & Expenses	5,734	1,630	18,048	4,918
Operating Income	2,665	d495	8,387	d1,495
Income Bef Income Tax	2,775	d500	8,736	d1,509
Income Tax	24	...	74	...
Minority Interests	cr14	...	cr44	...
Net Income	2,766	d500	8,706	d1,509

BALANCE SHEET (IN THOUSANDS):

Cash & Cash Equivalents	3,353	1,248	10,553	3,765
Receivables, Net	1,635	209	5,147	631
Inventories	380	95	1,196	286
Gross Property	578	226	1,818	681
Accumulated Depreciation	84	44	265	132
Long-Term Debt	412	459	1,297	1,386
Stockholders' Equity	4,110	631	12,935	1,903
Total Assets	6,717	1,734	21,144	5,231
Total Current Assets	5,368	1,552	16,897	4,682
Total Current Liabilities	2,168	643	6,824	1,942
Net Working Capital	3,200	908	10,073	2,740
Year End Shs Outstg	7,650	1,061	7,650	1,061

STATISTICAL RECORD:

Return on Equity %	67.30	...		
Return on Assets %	41.18	...		
Operating Profit Margin %	31.73	...		
Net Profit Margin %	32.94	...		
Book Value Per Share	0.54	0.59		

Converted at 1995, US$0.3177= 1 New Israeli Shekel; 1994, US$0.3314= 1 New Israeli Shekel

OFFICERS:
G. Tolkowsky, Chmn.
Dr. S. Eckhouse, Pres. & C.E.O.
H. Bachrach, Exec. V.P.
N. Bauch, V.P. & C.F.O.
INCORPORATED: Israel, Apr., 1992
PRINCIPAL OFFICE: 9 Haezel Street, Tirat Carmel Israel 30200

TELEPHONE NUMBER: 972-4-574-123
NO. OF EMPLOYEES: 55
ANNUAL MEETING: N/A
SHAREHOLDERS: 17
INSTITUTIONAL HOLDINGS:
No. of Institutions: N/A
Shares Held: N/A

REGISTRAR(S): N/A

TRANSFER AGENT(S): N/A

EZCONY INTERAMERICA INC.

NASDAQ SYMBOL EZCOF
Rec. Pr. 2 7/8

YIELD ...
P/E RATIO 12.0

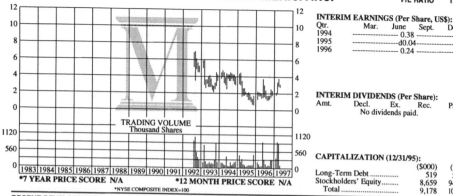

*7 YEAR PRICE SCORE N/A   *12 MONTH PRICE SCORE N/A
*NYSE COMPOSITE INDEX=100

TRADING VOLUME
Thousand Shares

INTERIM EARNINGS (Per Share, US$):

Qtr.	Mar.	June	Sept.	Dec.
1994		0.38		
1995		d0.04		
1996		0.24		

INTERIM DIVIDENDS (Per Share):

Amt.	Decl.	Ex.	Rec.	Pay.
	No dividends paid.			

CAPITALIZATION (12/31/95):

	($000)	(%)
Long-Term Debt	519	5.7
Stockholders' Equity	8,659	94.3
Total	9,178	100.0

RECENT DEVELOPMENTS: For the year ended 12/31/96, net income was $1.1 million compared with a loss of $163,026, from continuing operations, in the same period of 1995. The 1995 results exclude a one-time charge of $118.1 million from discontinued operations. The 1995 results include income of $726,454 due to the reversal of litigation costs and excess accruals relating to the prior class action suit. Net sales were $111.9 million, up 41.3% from $79.2 million in 1995. The Company benefited from strong sales and

earnings. This reflected the Company's strategic planning process. The Company plans to continue evolving and seeking out various business opportunities for its distribution of branded consumer electronics available in Latin America. For the quarter ended 12/31/96, net income climbed to $459,598 from a loss of $92,552 in 1995. Net sales were $34.6 million, up 32.9% from $26.0 million in 1995. On a quarterly basis, this is EZCOF's first full year of consistent net profit.

BUSINESS

EZCONY INTERAMERICA INC. is engaged in the wholesale distribution to Latin American markets of a range of major brand name (Sony, AIWA, Pioneer, Mitsubishi, Brother, Philips and Sanyo) consumer electronic products, including televisions, video cassette recorders, home and automobile audio equipment, personal portable stereos, cassette recorders, compact disc players and camcorders. The Company also has established a cellular communications division which distributes cellular products in Latin America. In addition, the Company is engaged in the localizing and distribution of CD-ROM software and related hardware products. The Company purchases most of its major brand name consumer electronics directly from manufacturers. The Company's products are distributed to a variety of customers, including wholesalers and distributors who resell the Company's products to retail markets.

ANNUAL EARNINGS

	12/31/95	12/31/94	12/31/93	12/31/92	12/31/91
			US $		
Earnings Per Share	d0.04	0.38	d1.74	0.28	0.86

ANNUAL FINANCIAL DATA

RECORD OF EARNINGS (IN THOUSANDS):

	12/31/95	12/31/94	12/31/93	12/31/92	12/31/91
Total Revenues	79,198	104,509	101,385	110,993	125,012
Costs & Expenses	79,828	103,041	106,490	108,970	120,857
Operating Income	d630	1,467	d5,105	2,023	4,155
Income Bef Income Tax	d49	1,799	d7,997	860	2,809
Income Tax	115	109	cr162	cr148	230
Net Income	d163	1,690	d7,835	1,008	2,579
Income from Disc. Ops.	d118	d465	119	...	...
Average Shares Outstg	4,500	4,500	4,500	3,574	3,000

BALANCE SHEET (IN THOUSANDS):

Cash & Cash Equivalents	7,267	7,823	9,546	8,426	5,545
Receivables, Net	13,917	7,898	9,787	20,592	13,096
Inventories	6,079	15,360	15,256	14,974	9,704
Gross Property	2,291	2,410	2,286	2,223	1,101
Accumulated Depreciation	948	850	698	476	366
Long-Term Debt	519	574	622	665	...
Stockholders' Equity	8,659	8,940	7,715	15,431	5,657
Total Assets	30,349	34,083	37,463	46,976	29,659
Total Current Assets	28,585	32,172	35,469	44,898	28,861
Total Current Liabilities	21,171	24,569	29,126	30,880	24,002
Net Working Capital	7,414	7,602	6,342	14,018	4,860
Year End Shs Outstg	4,500	4,500	4,500	3,574	3,000

STATISTICAL RECORD:

Return on Equity %	...	18.90	...	6.53	45.59
Return on Assets %	...	4.96	...	2.15	8.70
Operating Profit Margin %	...	1.40	...	1.82	3.32
Net Profit Margin %	...	1.62	...	0.91	2.06
Book Value Per Share	1.92	1.99	1.71	4.32	1.89

OFFICERS:
M. E. Cohen, Chmn.
E. Cohen, Pres. & C.E.O.
E. H. Gateno, Exec. V.P. & C.O.O.
J.A. Galea, C.F.O.
INCORPORATED: Nov., 1990
PRINCIPAL OFFICE: Craigmuir Chambers, P.O. Box 71, Road Town, Tortola British Virgin Islands

TELEPHONE NUMBER: (507) 41-6566
NO. OF EMPLOYEES: 106
ANNUAL MEETING: In May
SHAREHOLDERS: 89
INSTITUTIONAL HOLDINGS:
No. of Institutions: N/A
Shares Held: N/A

REGISTRAR(S): Mellon Securities Trust Co.

TRANSFER AGENT(S): Mellon Securities Trust Co.

FANTOM TECHNOLOGIES INC.

YIELD ...
P/E RATIO 12.2

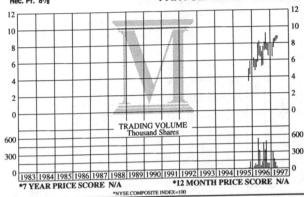

*7 YEAR PRICE SCORE N/A   *12 MONTH PRICE SCORE N/A
*NYSE COMPOSITE INDEX=100

INTERIM EARNINGS (Per Share, C $):

Qtr.	Sept.	Dec.	Mar.	June
1995-96	0.11	0.19	0.20	0.22
1996-97	0.12	0.19	0.24	...

INTERIM DIVIDENDS (Per Share):

Amt.	Decl.	Ex.	Rec.	Pay.
	No dividends paid.			

CAPITALIZATION (6/30/96 US $):

	($000)	(%)
Long-Term Debt	278	1.9
Stockholders' Equity.........	14,636	97.5
Deferred Income Tax	90	0.6
Total	15,004	100.0

RECENT DEVELOPMENTS: On 5/1/97, the Company changed its name to Fantom Technologies Inc. For the quarter ended 3/31/97, net income was C$2.0 million compared with C$1.4 million the year before. Sales advanced 57.4% to C$39.3 million from C$25.0 million a year earlier. The increase in sales was attributed to the continued success of the FANTOM line of vacuums in the U.S. market, which was driven by the Company's advertising and promotional activity in the U.S. Income before taxes was C$3.1 million versus C$1.4 million the previous year. For the nine months ended 3/31/97, net income was C$4.6 million compared with C$3.4 million the year before. Sales jumped 63.0% to C$102.7 million from C$63.0 million a year earlier.

BUSINESS

FANTOM TECHNOLOGIES INC. (formerly Iona Appliances Inc.) designs, manufactures and markets vacuum cleaners and carpet dry-cleaning machines based on proprietary, dual-cyclonic vacuuming technology. The Company's main product line consists of the FANTOM, FANTOM THUNDER, and FANTOM FURY vacuums. These vacuums are sold in the U.S. and Canada via direct-response television and through mass merchandisers, catalog and catalog/showroom retailers, major warehouse clubs and independent vacuum dealers.

ANNUAL EARNINGS

	6/30/96	6/30/95	6/30/96	6/30/95
	--------US $--------		--------C $--------	
Earnings Per Share	0.53	0.35	0.72	0.48

ANNUAL FINANCIAL DATA

RECORD OF EARNINGS (IN THOUSANDS):

	6/30/96	6/30/95	6/30/96	6/30/95
Total Revenues	72,178	43,301	98,429	59,422
Costs & Expenses	67,987	41,097	92,714	56,398
Operating Income	4,191	2,203	5,715	3,024
Income Bef Income Tax	4,191	2,203	5,715	3,024
Income Tax	370	0	504	0
Net Income	3,821	2,203	5,211	3,024
Average Shares Outstg	7,233	6,303	7,233	6,303

BALANCE SHEET (IN THOUSANDS):

Cash & Cash Equivalents	249	370	340	508
Receivables, Net	13,870	8,433	18,914	11,572
Inventories	10,174	6,188	13,875	8,492
Gross Property	7,693	3,803	10,491	5,219
Accumulated Depreciation	1,968	1,685	2,683	2,312
Long-Term Debt	278	20	379	27
Stockholders' Equity	14,636	5,850	19,959	8,028
Total Assets	31,288	17,824	42,667	24,460
Total Current Assets	25,562	15,351	34,859	21,066
Total Current Liabilities	16,283	11,954	22,205	16,404
Net Working Capital	9,279	3,397	12,653	4,662
Year End Shs Outstg	6,663	5,050	6,663	5,050

STATISTICAL RECORD:

Return on Equity %	26.11	22.72
Return on Assets %	12.21	7.46
Operating Profit Margin %	5.81	5.09
Net Profit Margin %	5.29	3.07
Book Value Per Share	3.00	1.59

Converted at 1996, US$0.7333= 1 Canadian $; 1995, US$0.7287= 1 Canadian $

OFFICERS:
K. Kelman, Chmn.
A. D. Millman, Pres. & C.E.O.
W. J. Palmer, Sec.

INCORPORATED: Ontario, 1982

PRINCIPAL OFFICE: 1110 Hansler Road P.O. Box 1004 Welland, Ontario Canada L3B 5S1

TELEPHONE NUMBER: 905-734-7476

NO. OF EMPLOYEES: 400 (approx.)

ANNUAL MEETING: In Oct.

SHAREHOLDERS: 70

INSTITUTIONAL HOLDINGS:
No. of Institutions: 4
Shares Held: 2,599,540

REGISTRAR(S): The R-M Trust Company, Toronto, Ontario, Canada

TRANSFER AGENT(S): The R-M Trust Company, Toronto, Ontario, Canada

FIRST DYNASTY MINES LTD.

YIELD ...
P/E RATIO ...

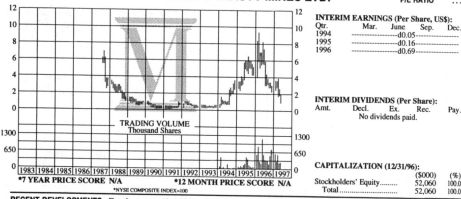

TRADING VOLUME
Thousand Shares

INTERIM EARNINGS (Per Share, US$):

Qtr.	Mar.	June	Sep.	Dec.
1994		d0.05		
1995		d0.16		
1996		d0.69		

INTERIM DIVIDENDS (Per Share):

Amt.	Decl.	Ex.	Rec.	Pay.
		No dividends paid.		

CAPITALIZATION (12/31/96):

	($000)	(%)
Stockholders' Equity	52,060	100.0
Total	52,060	100.0

RECENT DEVELOPMENTS: For the year ended 12/31/96, the Company posted a net loss of US$33.1 million compared with a loss of US$6.2 million in 1995. Total revenues were up significantly to US$11.3 million from US$2.9 million in the prior year. Results for 1996 included an impairment of US$25.7 million for the investment value of the Sembakung oilfield in Indonesia and an impairment of US$400,000 for deferred mineral acquisition and explora-

tion expenditures due to the relinquishment of exploration blocks 10 and 11 in Myanmar. Revenues from oil and gas sales were US$9.6 million compared with US$2.5 million in the previous year. Interest revenues more than tripled to US$1.7 million from US$424,000. As of 12/31/96, cash and cash equivalents amounted to US$4.8 million, down 29.0% from the prior year.

BUSINESS

FIRST DYNASTY MINES LTD. is engaged in the business of acquiring, exploring and developing mineral resource properties and operating an oil and gas field. The Company owns and operates gold exploration prospects located in the Yukon Territory of Canada, Myanmar and Indonesia.

ANNUAL EARNINGS

	12/31/96	12/31/95	12/31/96	12/31/95
	US $		C $	
Earnings Per Share	d0.69	d0.16	d0.94	d0.22

ANNUAL FINANCIAL DATA

RECORD OF EARNINGS (IN THOUSANDS):				
Total Revenues	11,256	2,911	15,396	3,972
Costs & Expenses	39,484	7,469	54,006	10,191
Depreciation & Amort	4,800	1,433	6,565	1,955
Income Bef Income Tax	d33,076	d6,188	d45,241	d8,443
Net Income	d33,076	d6,188	d45,241	d8,443
BALANCE SHEET (IN THOUSANDS):				
Cash & Cash Equivalents	4,839	6,812	6,619	9,295
Receivables, Net	320	4,295	438	5,860
Inventories	...	811	...	1,107
Gross Property	5,624	402	7,693	549
Accumulated Depreciation	75	39	103	53
Long-Term Debt	...	1,650	...	2,251
Stockholders' Equity	52,060	61,029	71,208	83,271
Total Assets	53,018	67,467	72,518	92,055
Total Current Assets	5,625	12,439	7,694	16,972
Total Current Liabilities	958	4,788	1,310	6,533
Net Working Capital	4,667	7,651	6,384	10,439
Year End Shs Outstg	48,812	46,835	48,812	46,835
STATISTICAL RECORD:				
Return on Equity %	...	...		
Return on Assets %	...	...		
Operating Profit Margin %	...	...		
Net Profit Margin %	...	...		
Book Value Per Share	1.07	1.30		

Converted at 1996, US$0.7311= 1 Canadian $; 1995, US$0.7329= 1 Canadian $

OFFICERS:
M. P. Randolph, Pres.
B. R. Aitken, Sr. V.P.-Fin. & Mktg.
J. D. Lewins, Sr. V.P.-Engr. & Constr.
G. F. Lister, Sr. V.P.-Corp. Dev.

INCORPORATED: Apr. 1949, Canada

PRINCIPAL OFFICE: No. 1 Temasek Avenue #37-02 Millenia Tower Singapore 39192

TELEPHONE NUMBER: (65) 337-9028

NO. OF EMPLOYEES: N/A

ANNUAL MEETING: In June

SHAREHOLDERS: 380

INSTITUTIONAL HOLDINGS:
No. of Institutions: 9
Shares Held: 6,641,525

REGISTRAR(S): The R-M Trust Company, Vancouver.

TRANSFER AGENT(S): The R-M Trust Company, Vancouver.

FLETCHER'S FINE FOODS LTD.

YIELD ...
P/E RATIO 76.0

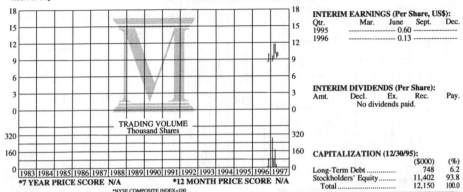

*7 YEAR PRICE SCORE N/A   *12 MONTH PRICE SCORE N/A

*NYSE COMPOSITE INDEX=100

TRADING VOLUME
Thousand Shares

INTERIM EARNINGS (Per Share, US$):

Qtr.	Mar.	June	Sept.	Dec.
1995		0.60		
1996		0.13		

INTERIM DIVIDENDS (Per Share):

Amt.	Decl.	Ex.	Rec.	Pay.
	No dividends paid.			

CAPITALIZATION (12/30/95):

	($000)	(%)
Long-Term Debt	748	6.2
Stockholders' Equity.........	11,402	93.8
Total	12,150	100.0

RECENT DEVELOPMENTS: For the year ended 12/31/96, net income declined 50.7% to C$628,000 compared with earnings before a gain on debt forgiveness of C$1.3 million in 1995. Total sales were C$300.6 million, up 11.5% from C$269.7 million a year earlier. Total gross profit declined 8.7% to C$22.4 million compared with C$24.5 million in 1995. The gain on debt forgiveness was C$2.3 million in 1995. During 1996, the Company recorded a gain of C$608,000 and a loss of C$11,000 for the cessation of Golden Gate operations. The decline in earnings was primarily attributable to the Fresh Pork Division experiencing high price hog prices throughout most of the year. The Prepared Food Division benefited from improving margins and consolidation trends that are eradicating industry overcapacity. On 2/24/97, FLCHF completed its acquisition of the Grimm's Food Group, one of Western Canada's premier delicatessen suppliers.

BUSINESS

FLETCHER'S FINE FOODS LTD. is primarily engaged in the manufacture and sale of fresh and prepared pork products in addition to specialty meats and delicatessen items. The fresh pork operations consist of processing hogs into a variety of fresh pork products including bacon, hams, fresh and smoked sausages, weiners, delicatessen and luncheon meats and specialty products, including appetizers, meat pastries, chili and lasagna. FLCHF markets its fresh pork and prepared food products to wholesale, retail and food service customers in western Canada, the Pacific Northwest and Japan and certain other Pacific Rim countries. FLCHF's branded products are sold under the Fletcher's, Smoke House, Lean'N'Tasty, Goodlife, and High Health brand names.

ANNUAL EARNINGS

	12/30/95	12/31/94	12/30/95	12/31/94
	----US $----		----C $----	
Earnings Per Share	0.60	...	0.82	...

ANNUAL FINANCIAL DATA

RECORD OF EARNINGS (IN THOUSANDS):

	12/30/95	12/31/94	12/30/95	12/31/94
Total Revenues	197,630	177,047	269,655	248,348
Costs & Expenses	193,911	167,822	264,580	235,408
Depreciation & Amort	1,398	1,111	1,907	1,559
Operating Income	2,322	8,114	3,168	11,381
Income Bef Income Tax	474	3,014	647	4,228
Income Tax	cr460	1,638	cr627	2,297
Net Income	2,656	1,377	3,624	1,931
Average Shares Outstg	1,555	...	1,555	...

BALANCE SHEET (IN THOUSANDS):

Cash & Cash Equivalents	461	1,125	629	1,578
Receivables, Net	12,060	10,740	16,455	15,065
Inventories	8,278	6,509	11,295	9,130
Gross Property	33,425	29,933	45,606	41,987
Accumulated Depreciation	22,646	20,821	30,899	29,206
Long-Term Debt	748	8,789	1,020	12,328
Stockholders' Equity	11,402	d5,923	15,557	d8,308
Total Assets	33,173	28,205	45,262	39,564
Total Current Assets	20,940	18,503	28,571	25,955
Total Current Liabilities	15,964	13,672	21,782	19,178
Net Working Capital	4,976	4,831	6,789	6,777
Year End Shs Outstg	3,044	166	3,044	166

STATISTICAL RECORD:

Return on Equity %	23.29	...		
Return on Assets %	8.00	4.88		
Operating Profit Margin %	1.17	4.58		
Net Profit Margin %	1.34	0.78		
Book Value Per Share	3.75	...		

Converted at 1995, US$0.7329= 1 Canadian $; 1994, US$0.7129= 1 Canadian $

OFFICERS:
D. Lowen, Chmn.
F. Knoedler, Pres. & C.E.O.
G. Paleologou, C.F.O. & V.P.

INCORPORATED: Canada, 1917

PRINCIPAL OFFICE: 2600 Manulife Place, 10180-101 Street, Edmonton, Alberta Canada T5J 3Y2

TELEPHONE NUMBER: 403-477-5901

NO. OF EMPLOYEES: 1,500

ANNUAL MEETING: N/A

SHAREHOLDERS: N/A

INSTITUTIONAL HOLDINGS:
No. of Institutions: 10
Shares Held: 1,800,000

REGISTRAR(S): Montreal Trust Co. of Canada.

TRANSFER AGENT(S): Montreal Trust Co. of Canada.

FLEXTRONICS INTERNATIONAL LTD.

YIELD   ...
P/E RATIO   ...

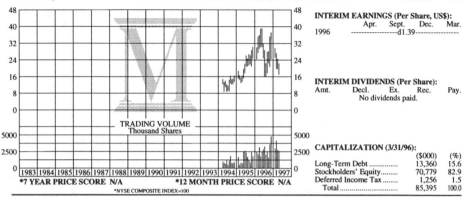

INTERIM EARNINGS (Per Share, US$):

	Apr.	Sept.	Dec.	Mar.
1996		----------d1.39----------

INTERIM DIVIDENDS (Per Share):

Amt.	Decl.	Ex.	Rec.	Pay.
	No dividends paid.

CAPITALIZATION (3/31/96):

	($000)	(%)
Long-Term Debt	13,360	15.6
Stockholders' Equity	70,779	82.9
Deferred Income Tax	1,256	1.5
Total	85,395	100.0

RECENT DEVELOPMENTS: For the quarter ended 12/31/96, net income dropped to US$68,000 compared with US$5.0 million in the equivalent period of 1995. Earnings for 1996 included a US$2.3 million provision for plant closings. Net sales declined 7.8% to US$121.5 million from $131.8 million a year earlier. This was primarily due to reduced sales to certain customers, including Visioneer and Apple Computer. The 0.7% reduction in gross profit margin to 8.3% was mainly due to a US$900,000 inventory write down relating to the closure of the Texas and nChip facilities. For the nine months ended 12/31/96, net income fell 9.4% to US$10.5 million versus US$11.6 million in the same period of 1995. However, net sales jumped 12.3% to US$362.3 million from US$322.6 million in the prior year.

BUSINESS

FLEXTRONICS INTERNATIONAL LTD. offers advanced contract manufacturing services of electronics for OEM's in the medical, consumer, computer and communications industries. The Company offers a range of services including printed circuit board (PCB) and multichip module (MCM) design, materials procurement and management, advanced packaging fabrication, PCB assembly, final system build, distribution, and warranty repair. The Company has facilities in North America, Europe and Asia. Company acquired nChip in 1995.

ANNUAL EARNINGS

	3/31/96	3/31/95	3/31/96	3/31/95
	------------US $------------	----------Singapore $--------
Earnings Per Share	d1.39	0.51	d1.96	0.72

ANNUAL FINANCIAL DATA

RECORD OF EARNINGS (IN THOUSANDS):

	3/31/96	3/31/95	3/31/96	3/31/95
Total Revenues	448,346	237,386	631,029	334,111
Operating Income	d11,775	10,207	d16,573	14,366
Income Bef Income Tax	d13,621	7,619	d19,171	10,754
Income Tax	3,791	1,463	5,336	2,065
Net Income	d17,412	6,156	d24,507	8,689
Average Shares Outstg	12,536	12,103	12,536	12,103

BALANCE SHEET (IN THOUSANDS):

	3/31/96	3/31/95	3/31/96	3/31/95
Cash & Cash Equivalents	6,546	4,751	9,213	6,706
Receivables, Net	78,114	44,250	109,942	62,456
Inventories	52,637	30,193	74,084	42,615
Gross Property	98,998	47,532	139,336	67,088
Accumulated Depreciation	37,896	21,774	53,337	30,733
Long-Term Debt	13,360	...	18,804	...
Stockholders' Equity	70,779	57,717	99,619	81,464
Total Assets	214,588	116,117	302,024	163,891
Total Current Assets	141,384	83,941	198,992	118,477
Total Current Liabilities	113,708	50,516	160,039	71,300
Net Working Capital	27,676	33,425	38,953	47,177
Year End Shs Outstg	13,213	11,603	13,213	11,603

STATISTICAL RECORD:

	3/31/96	3/31/95
Return on Equity %	...	10.67
Return on Assets %	...	5.30
Operating Profit Margin %	...	4.30
Net Profit Margin %	...	2.59
Book Value Per Share	5.36	4.97

Converted at 1996, US$0.7105= 1 Singapore $; 1995, US$0.7085= 1 Singapore $

OFFICERS:
M. E. Marks, Chmn. & C.E.O.
T. S. Lam, Pres. & C.O.O.
D. P. Stradford, Sr. V.P.
G. C. Peng, C.F.O.

INCORPORATED: Singapore, May, 1990

PRINCIPAL OFFICE: 514 Chai Chee Lane, #04-13, Bedok Industrial Estate Singapore 1646

TELEPHONE NUMBER: +65-449-5255

NO. OF EMPLOYEES: 3,994

ANNUAL MEETING: In Aug.

SHAREHOLDERS: 609

INSTITUTIONAL HOLDINGS:
No. of Institutions: N/A
Shares Held: N/A

REGISTRAR(S): The First National Bank of Boston, Massachussetts.

TRANSFER AGENT(S): The First National Bank of Boston, Massachussetts.

FRISCO BAY INDUSTRIES LTD.

YIELD ...
P/E RATIO ...

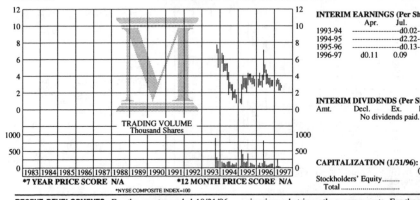

*7 YEAR PRICE SCORE N/A   *12 MONTH PRICE SCORE N/A
*NYSE COMPOSITE INDEX=100

TRADING VOLUME
Thousand Shares

INTERIM EARNINGS (Per Share, C$):

	Apr.	Jul.	Oct.	Jan.
1993-94			d0.02	
1994-95			d2.22	
1995-96			d0.13	
1996-97	d0.11	0.09	0.05	...

INTERIM DIVIDENDS (Per Share):

Amt.	Decl.	Ex.	Rec.	Pay.
	No dividends paid.

CAPITALIZATION (1/31/96):

	($000)	(%)
Stockholders' Equity	6,947	100.0
Total	6,947	100.0

RECENT DEVELOPMENTS: For the quarter ended 10/31/96, net earnings were C$119.5 million compared with a loss of C$269.8 million in the prior-year period. Sales advanced 21.1% to C$6.9 million from C$5.7 million in the corresponding 1995 quarter. The improved performance in operating results was attributed to the Company's continued commitment to increase revenues, improve operating efficiencies and stringently manage costs. For the nine months ended 10/31/96, net income was C$65.0 million compared with a loss of C$749.7 million in the comparable period a year earlier. Sales reached C$19.2 million, an increase of 17.7% over 1995 results. Gross profit as a percentage of sales was 39.1% compared with 41.7% a year earlier.

BUSINESS

FRISCO BAY INDUSTRIES LTD. is engaged in the design, development and marketing of efficiency-enhancing integrated systems and services, predominantly for banks and other financial institutions. The Company's systems include self-service and financial transaction processing systems, computerized time management systems, integrated security systems and offsite data storage and disaster planning and recovery systems. The Company's products, systems and services are designed to help financial and other institutions improve their competitiveness and the cost-effectiveness of their operations. The principal markets for the Company's products are the United States and Canada.

ANNUAL EARNINGS

	1/31/96	1/31/95	1/31/96	1/31/95
	US $		C $	
Earnings Per Share	d0.09	d1.57	d0.13	d2.22

ANNUAL FINANCIAL DATA

RECORD OF EARNINGS (IN THOUSANDS):

	1/31/96	1/31/95	1/31/96	1/31/95
Total Revenues	16,988	15,212	23,473	21,519
Costs & Expenses	17,211	18,707	23,781	26,464
Operating Income	d223	d3,495	d308	d4,945
Income Bef Income Tax	d223	d3,495	d308	d4,945
Income Tax	cr13	cr9	cr18	cr13
Net Income	d210	d3,486	d291	d4,932
Average Shares Outstg	2,221	2,221	2,221	2,221

BALANCE SHEET (IN THOUSANDS):

	1/31/96	1/31/95	1/31/96	1/31/95
Cash & Cash Equivalents	531	1,504	733	2,128
Receivables, Net	4,486	4,292	6,199	6,071
Inventories	3,196	3,855	4,416	5,454
Gross Property	2,462	2,327	3,402	3,292
Accumulated Depreciation	1,847	1,642	2,553	2,323
Long-Term Debt	...	283	...	400
Stockholders' Equity	6,947	6,991	9,599	9,890
Total Assets	11,384	13,101	15,730	18,533
Total Current Assets	8,285	10,130	11,448	14,330
Total Current Liabilities	4,437	5,827	6,131	8,243
Net Working Capital	3,848	4,303	5,317	6,086
Year End Shs Outstg	2,221	2,221	2,221	2,221

STATISTICAL RECORD:

	1/31/96	1/31/95	1/31/96	1/31/95
Return on Equity %	...	...		
Return on Assets %	...	...		
Operating Profit Margin %	...	...		
Net Profit Margin %	...	...		
Book Value Per Share	3.13	3.15		

Converted at 1996, US$0.7237= 1 Canadian $; 1995, US$0.7069= 1 Canadian $

OFFICERS:
B. E. Katsof, Chmn. & C.E.O.
R. G. Waxman, Vice-Chmn.
P. Matteau, Pres.
M. Matthew, V.P. & Asst. Sec.

INCORPORATED: 1970

PRINCIPAL OFFICE: 160 Graveline Street, St. Laurent, Quebec, Canada H4T 1R7

TELEPHONE NUMBER: 514-738-7300

NO. OF EMPLOYEES: 175

ANNUAL MEETING: In July

SHAREHOLDERS: 32

INSTITUTIONAL HOLDINGS:
No. of Institutions: 1
Shares Held: 29,700

REGISTRAR(S): American Stock Transfer & Trust Company, New York.

TRANSFER AGENT(S): American Stock Transfer & Trust Company, New York.

FULCRUM TECHNOLOGIES INC.

YIELD ...
P/E RATIO ...

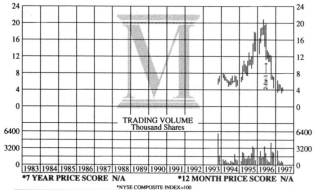

7 YEAR PRICE SCORE N/A   **12 MONTH PRICE SCORE N/A**
*NYSE COMPOSITE INDEX=100

TRADING VOLUME
Thousand Shares

INTERIM EARNINGS (Per Share, US$):

Qtr.	Mar.	June	Sept.	Dec.
1996		------------------d0.53-----------------		

INTERIM DIVIDENDS (Per Share):

Amt.	Decl.	Ex.	Rec.	Pay.
	No dividends paid.			

CAPITALIZATION (12/31/96):

	($000)	(%)
Stockholders' Equity........	29,070	100.0
Total	29,070	100.0

RECENT DEVELOPMENTS: For the year ended 12/31/96, loss from operations was C$14.9 million, including the non-recurring charge in the fourth quarter of C$13.9 million related to the write-off or significant write-down of previously capitalized research and development costs and acquired technologies, compared with an operating income of C$8.0 million in 1995. After-tax loss was C$11.0 million compared with net income of C$5.3 million in 1995. Revenues increased 40% to C$60.2 million in 1996 compared with the previous year. In the future, the Company intends to expense research and development costs as incurred. FULCF's earnings were lower than anticipated and as a result of delays in the deployment of Microsoft Exchange, sales of its Fulcrum FIND! product have been substantially lower than expected. The Company benefited from strong revenue growth and an increase in overall market share. During the fourth quarter, the Company signed more than 100 new accounts.

BUSINESS

FULCRUM TECHNOLOGIES INC. is engaged in the development, marketing, licensing and support of software that indexes and retrieves information contained in electronically-stored documents. This software is used with a variety of document formats and operates in heterogeneous computing environments that include multiple operating systems, networks and graphical user interfaces. FULCF's products include a full-text indexing and retrieval engine and related application development tools. These products are used by large and medium-sized organizations to provide desktop access. FULCF's software is scalable and designed for client/server architectures. Its new products are based on emerging industry standards, such as Structured Query Language (SQL) Access Group's Call Level Interface and Microsoft Corp.'s Open Date Base Connectivity specifications.

ANNUAL EARNINGS

	12/31/96	12/31/95	12/31/96	12/31/95
	------------US $------------		------------C $------------	
Earnings Per Share	d0.53	0.28	d0.73	0.38

ANNUAL FINANCIAL DATA

RECORD OF EARNINGS (IN THOUSANDS):

	12/31/96	12/31/95	12/31/96	12/31/95
Total Revenues	43,998	31,467	60,181	42,935
Costs & Expenses	54,867	25,618	75,047	34,954
Operating Income	d10,869	5,849	d14,866	7,981
Income Bef Income Tax	d11,921	6,190	d16,306	8,446
Income Tax	cr3,917	2,280	cr5,357	3,111
Minority Interests	20	...	27	...
Net Income	d8,025	3,910	d10,976	5,335
Average Shares Outstg	15,029	13,884	15,029	13,884

BALANCE SHEET (IN THOUSANDS):

Cash & Cash Equivalents	2,511	16,577	3,435	22,619
Receivables, Net	18,621	14,374	25,470	19,612
Gross Property	12,234	7,823	16,734	10,674
Accumulated Depreciation	5,690	3,439	7,783	4,692
Stockholders' Equity	29,070	35,675	39,762	48,677
Total Assets	41,220	50,513	56,381	68,922
Total Current Assets	22,635	32,615	30,960	44,501
Total Current Liabilities	11,857	13,506	16,218	18,428
Net Working Capital	10,778	19,109	14,742	26,073
Year End Shs Outstg	15,166	14,728	15,166	14,728

STATISTICAL RECORD:

Return on Equity %	...	10.96		
Return on Assets %	...	7.74		
Operating Profit Margin %	...	18.59		
Net Profit Margin %	...	12.43		
Book Value Per Share	1.92	2.42		

Converted at 1996, US$0.7311= 1 Canadian $; 1995, US$0.7329= 1 Canadian $

OFFICERS:
E. R. Goodwin, Chmn. & C.E.O.
M. Laginski, Pres. & C.O.O.
A. Wolff, V.P.-Fin. & C.F.O.
D. Keys, V.P.-Corp. Dev. & Gen. Couns.

INCORPORATED: Sep., 1983

PRINCIPAL OFFICE: 785 Carling Avenue, Ottawa Canada K1S 5H4

TELEPHONE NUMBER: 613-238-1761

NO. OF EMPLOYEES: 300

ANNUAL MEETING: In Jun.

SHAREHOLDERS: N/A

INSTITUTIONAL HOLDINGS:
No. of Institutions: 7
Shares Held: 829,975

REGISTRAR(S): The R-M Trust Co., Toronto.

TRANSFER AGENT(S): The R-M Trust Co., Toronto.

GAMING LOTTERY CORPORATION

YIELD ...
P/E RATIO ...

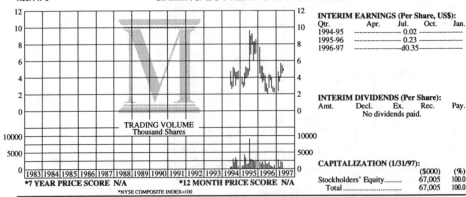

*7 YEAR PRICE SCORE N/A   *12 MONTH PRICE SCORE N/A
*NYSE COMPOSITE INDEX=100

TRADING VOLUME
Thousand Shares

INTERIM EARNINGS (Per Share, US$):

Qtr.	Apr.	Jul.	Oct.	Jan.
1994-95	---------------- 0.02 ----------------			
1995-96	---------------- 0.23 ----------------			
1996-97	----------------d0.35----------------			

INTERIM DIVIDENDS (Per Share):

Amt.	Decl.	Ex.	Rec.	Pay.
	No dividends paid.			

CAPITALIZATION (1/31/97):

	($000)	(%)
Stockholders' Equity.........	67,005	100.0
Total	67,005	100.0

RECENT DEVELOPMENTS: For the year ended 1/31/97, loss from continuing operations was US$8.9 million compared with income of US$4.9 million in 1996. Revenues dropped 60.4% to US$2.3 million from US$5.7 million a year earlier. Results excluded a gain of US$23.4 million from the sale of discontinued operations, partially offset by a loss from discontinued operations of $2.2 million. These gains and losses reflect the Company's commenced plan to dispose of its subsidiaries engaged in the manufacture and supply of paper related gaming products. As a part of this strategy, the Company had identified the following subsidiaries for divestiture: Specialty Manufacturing, Inc., ANCI, Inc., Printing Associates, Inc., and Laserdata Technology Inc. As of 2/7/97, the Company had completed the sale of these subsidiaries, which resulted in total realized proceeds of over C$60.0 million.

BUSINESS

GAMING LOTTERY CORPORA-TION is engaged in the development and marketing of a virtual reality three-dimensional digital casino and entertainment website known as Galaxiworld.

ANNUAL EARNINGS

	1/31/97	1/31/96	1/31/95
	----------------------US $----------------------		
Earnings Per Share	d0.35	0.23	0.02

ANNUAL FINANCIAL DATA

RECORD OF EARNINGS (IN THOUSANDS):

	1/31/97	1/31/96	1/31/95
Total Revenues	2,266	5,727	916
Costs & Expenses	5,696	849	632
Operating Income	d3,430	4,878	284
Income Bef Income Tax	d8,930	4,878	284
Income Tax	...	134	...
Net Income	d8,930	4,743	284
Net Discontinued Operations	21,182	...	...
Average Shares Outstg	25,431	21,002	16,957

BALANCE SHEET (IN THOUSANDS):

Cash & Cash Equivalents	30,526	36,215	...
Receivables, Net	...	4,882	...
Inventories	...	5,202	...
Property and Equipment, Net	...	14,752	...
Long-Term Debt	...	888	...
Stockholders' Equity	67,005	58,139	...
Total Assets	75,465	64,615	...
Total Current Assets	31,965	47,344	...
Total Current Liabilities	8,461	4,715	...
Net Working Capital	23,504	42,629	...
Year End Shs Outstg	24,927	25,984	...

STATISTICAL RECORD:

Return on Equity %	...	8.2	...
Return on Assets %	...	7.3	...
Operating Profit Margin %	...	85.2	31.0
Net Profit Margin %	...	82.8	31.0
Book Value Per Share	2.69	2.24	...

OFFICERS:
J. Banks, Pres. & C.E.O.
L. Weltman, Exec. V.P. & C.F.O.
D. Webster, Sec.

INCORPORATED: N/A

PRINCIPAL OFFICE: 30 DeCastro St., P.O. Box 961, Road Town, Tortola British Virgin Islands

TELEPHONE NUMBER: 809-494-7400

NO. OF EMPLOYEES: N/A

ANNUAL MEETING: In July

SHAREHOLDERS: 777

INSTITUTIONAL HOLDINGS:
No. of Institutions: 5
Shares Held: 52,345

REGISTRAR(S): Equity Transfer Service Inc., Toronto.

TRANSFER AGENT(S): Equity Transfer Service Inc., Toronto.

GANDALF TECHNOLOGIES INC.

YIELD ...
P/E RATIO 100

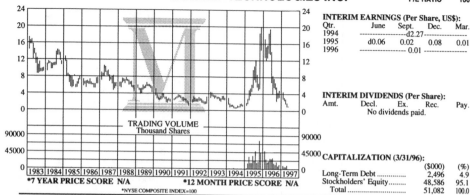

*7 YEAR PRICE SCORE N/A   *12 MONTH PRICE SCORE N/A

*NYSE COMPOSITE INDEX=100

TRADING VOLUME
Thousand Shares

INTERIM EARNINGS (Per Share, US$):

Qtr.	June	Sept.	Dec.	Mar.
1994		--------d2.27--------		
1995	d0.06	0.02	0.08	0.01
1996		----------- 0.01 -----------		

INTERIM DIVIDENDS (Per Share):

Amt.	Decl.	Ex.	Rec.	Pay.
	No dividends paid.			

CAPITALIZATION (3/31/96):

	($000)	(%)
Long-Term Debt	2,496	4.9
Stockholders' Equity	48,586	95.1
Total	51,082	100.0

RECENT DEVELOPMENTS: For the year ended 3/31/96, net income was $260,000 compared with $1.4 million the year before. Results for the current and prior-year period included restructuring charges of $1.5 million and $685,000, respectively. Net income for the prior-year period also included a gain of $2.0 million from the sale of a portfolio investment. Total revenues declined 3.3% to $116.5 million from $120.5 million a year earlier. Product revenues decreased 3.3% to $81.1 million, while service revenues declined 3.4% to $35.5 million. As a percentage of total revenues, gross profit margin improved to 45.9% from 44.4% the year before. Income from operations fell to $488,000 from $2.0 million the previous year.

BUSINESS

GANDALF TECHNOLOGIES INC. designs, supplies, markets and services equipment that is designed to transport information in a manner that is efficient, cost effective, secure and reliable. The Company creates value for its customers through its ability to integrate a variety of technologies and a range of telephone company services with its customers' information applications. The Company accomplishes this through four lines of business: Access, Concentration, Backbone and Service.

ANNUAL EARNINGS

	3/31/96	3/31/95	3/31/96	3/31/95
	-------US $-------		-------C $-------	
Earnings Per Share	0.01	0.05	0.01	0.07

ANNUAL FINANCIAL DATA

RECORD OF EARNINGS (IN THOUSANDS):

Total Revenues	116,533	120,511	158,397	168,618
Costs & Expenses	116,045	118,489	157,734	165,788
Operating Income	488	2,022	663	2,829
Net Income	260	1,406	353	1,967
Average Shares Outstg	40,359	28,589	40,359	28,589

BALANCE SHEET (IN THOUSANDS):

Cash & Cash Equivalents	13,602	11,817	18,489	16,534
Receivables, Net	28,694	26,880	39,002	37,610
Inventories	13,491	15,230	18,338	21,310
Gross Property	65,147	62,766	88,551	87,821
Accumulated Depreciation	48,894	44,147	66,459	61,770
Long-Term Debt	2,496	11,928	3,393	16,690
Stockholders' Equity	48,586	34,442	66,041	48,191
Total Assets	79,375	81,508	107,890	114,045
Total Current Assets	57,654	56,195	78,366	78,627
Total Current Liabilities	28,293	35,138	38,457	49,165
Net Working Capital	29,361	21,057	39,909	29,463
Year End Shs Outstg	42,940	35,238	42,940	35,238

STATISTICAL RECORD:

Return on Equity %	0.54	4.08
Return on Assets %	0.33	1.72
Operating Profit Margin %	0.42	1.68
Net Profit Margin %	0.22	1.17
Book Value Per Share	1.13	0.98

Converted at 1996, US$0.7357= 1 Canadian $; 1995, US$0.7147= 1 Canadian $

OFFICERS:
T. A. Vassiliades, Chmn., Pres. & C.E.O.
W. MacDonald, V.P.-Fin. & C.F.O.
M. Chawner, V.P. & Chief Tech. Off.

INCORPORATED: Canada, April, 1971

PRINCIPAL OFFICE: 130 Colonnade Road
South Nepean, Ontario Canada K2E 7M4

TELEPHONE NUMBER: 613-274-6500

NO. OF EMPLOYEES: 700 (approx.)

ANNUAL MEETING: In Aug.

SHAREHOLDERS: 1,867

INSTITUTIONAL HOLDINGS:
No. of Institutions: 24
Shares Held: 9,248,105

REGISTRAR(S): N/A

TRANSFER AGENT(S): The R-M Trust Company, Toronto; Chemical Mellon Shareholder Services, NJ.

GCR HOLDINGS LIMITED

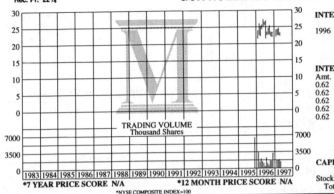

INTERIM EARNINGS (Per Share):

	Sept.	Dec.	Mar.	June
1996	------------------	3.63	------------------	

INTERIM DIVIDENDS (Per Share):

Amt.	Decl.	Ex.	Rec.	Pay.
0.62	1/25/96	2/12/96	2/14/96	2/27/96
0.62	4/18	4/29	5/01	5/15
0.62	7/25	8/01	8/05	8/20
0.62	10/31	11/12	11/14	11/27
0.62	1/23/97	2/10/97	2/12/97	2/25/97

Indicated div.:$2.480

TRADING VOLUME
Thousand Shares

1983|1984|1985|1986|1987|1988|1989|1990|1991|1992|1993|1994|1995|1996|1997

*7 YEAR PRICE SCORE N/A   *12 MONTH PRICE SCORE N/A

*NYSE COMPOSITE INDEX=100

CAPITALIZATION (9/30/96):

	($000)	(%)
Stockholders' Equity	417,037	100.0
Total	417,037	100.0

RECENT DEVELOPMENTS: For the quarter ended 3/31/97, net income was $17.2 million compared with $26.4 million in the corresponding period a year earlier. Total revenues were $29.9 million versus $38.6 million in 1996. Lower earnings resulted from higher incurred losses, which amounted to $5.8 million compared with $3.2 million a year ago. Earned premiums of $24.0 million were down 28% compared to $30.6 million in 1996. Earned premiums were negatively affected by a one time adjustment from certain proportional contracts. Investment income of $6.5 million was down 15.5% compared with the prior year as a result of utilization of invested assets to repay debt in February 1996. The Company did not experience any new catastrophic losses during the first half of fiscal 1997.

BUSINESS

GCR HOLDINGS LIMITED, through Global Capital Re subsidiary, provides property catastrophe and, to a limited extent, other short-tail property reinsurance on a worldwide basis. In fiscal year 1996, approximately 68% of this reinsurance covered property catastrophe risks, of which 92% was written on an excess-of-loss basis. Substantially all reinsurance written by Global Capital Re was written for primary insurers rather than reinsurers. Global Capital Re had 234 clients on September 30, 1996, around the world. At that date, approximately 48.7% of Global Capital Re's clients were based in the United States and approximately 56% of its premiums written on policies in force related to U.S. risks. The balance of Global Capital Re's clients and covered risks were located in the largest international insurance markets, principally in Europe, Japan, Australia and New Zealand.

ANNUAL EARNINGS

	9/30/96	9/30/95	9/30/94
	------------------US $------------------		
Earnings Per Share	3.63	3.94	1.32

ANNUAL FINANCIAL DATA

RECORD OF EARNINGS (IN THOUSANDS):

	9/30/96	9/30/95	9/30/94
Total Revenues	153,261	153,578	67,113
Costs & Expenses	62,499	62,922	37,298
Operating Income	90,762	90,656	29,815
Net Income	90,762	90,656	29,815
Average Shares Outstg	24,990	23,010	22,685

BALANCE SHEET (IN THOUSANDS):

Cash & Cash Equivalents	14,070	41,490	121,496
Receivables, Net	45,542	49,716	37,859
Stockholders' Equity	417,037	356,397	468,067
Total Assets	516,840	597,641	534,014
Total Current Assets	59,612	91,206	159,355
Total Current Liabilities	2,840	146,166	882
Net Working Capital	56,772	d54,960	158,473
Year End Shs Outstg	24,674	22,362	22,562

STATISTICAL RECORD:

Return on Equity %	21.76	25.44	6.37
Return on Assets %	17.56	15.17	5.58
Operating Profit Margin %	61.65	60.31	44.43
Net Profit Margin %	59.22	59.03	44.43
Book Value Per Share	16.90	15.94	20.75

OFFICERS:
L. S. Doyle, Pres. & C.E.O.
R. L. Nason, Sr. V.P.
S. S. Outerbridge, Sr. V.P.
F. W. Deichmann, C.F.O.
W. G. Fanning, Chief Actuary

INCORPORATED: 1993

PRINCIPAL OFFICE: Sofia House, 3rd Floor
48 Church Street Hamilton Bermuda

TELEPHONE NUMBER: 441-299-9415

NO. OF EMPLOYEES: 16

ANNUAL MEETING: N/A

SHAREHOLDERS: 482

INSTITUTIONAL HOLDINGS:
No. of Institutions: N/A
Shares Held: N/A

REGISTRAR(S): First Chicago Trust Co. of New York, New York.

TRANSFER AGENT(S): First Chicago Trust Co. of New York, New York.

GEMSTAR INTERNATIONAL GROUP LIMITED

YIELD ...
P/E RATIO 22.18

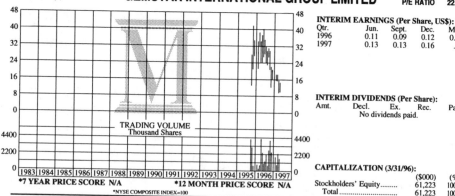

*7 YEAR PRICE SCORE N/A   *12 MONTH PRICE SCORE N/A
*NYSE COMPOSITE INDEX=100

INTERIM EARNINGS (Per Share, US$):

Qtr.	Jun.	Sept.	Dec.	Mar.
1996	0.11	0.09	0.12	0.20
1997	0.13	0.13	0.16	...

INTERIM DIVIDENDS (Per Share):

Amt.	Decl.	Ex.	Rec.	Pay.
	No dividends paid.			

CAPITALIZATION (3/31/96):

	($000)	(%)
Stockholders' Equity	61,223	100.0
Total	61,223	100.0

RECENT DEVELOPMENTS: For the quarter ended 12/31/96, net earnings were $5.3 million compared with a net loss of $28.0 million the year before. Revenues advanced 35.9% to $19.1 million from $14.1 million a year earlier. The increase in revenues was attributed to continued increases in the incorporation of the Company's VCR Plus+ system by manufacturers of VCRs and televisions worldwide. Earnings from operations were $6.1 million versus a loss from operations of $27.4 million the previous year. Results for the prior-year period have been restated to reflect the Company's acquisition of VideoGuide, Inc., which was completed in December 1996. During the quarter, JVC and Magnavox introduced the Company's TV Guide Plus+ system in the U.S. and Canada by incorporating the feature in selected television models. The Company merged with StarSight Telecast, Inc.

BUSINESS

GEMSTAR INTERNATIONAL GROUP LIMITED develops, markets and licenses proprietary technologies and systems that simplify and enhance the viewing and recording of video and television programming. The Company's products include: VCR Plus+ Instant Programming System, which allows a user to record a television program by entering a PlusCode Number found in television program listings; Index Plus+, a video tape indexing system built into new VCRs that features an on-screen directory of video tape content by titles automatically captured from the broadcast; and TV Guide Plus+, a subscription-free on-screen interactive television guide built into new televisions and VCRs.

ANNUAL EARNINGS

	3/31/96	3/31/95	3/31/94
	----------------US $----------------		
Earnings Per Share	0.52	0.32	0.18

ANNUAL FINANCIAL DATA

RECORD OF EARNINGS (IN THOUSANDS):

	3/31/96	3/31/95	3/31/94
Total Revenues	53,436	41,744	27,025
Costs & Expenses	33,881	29,999	20,611
Operating Income	19,555	11,745	6,414
Income Bef Income Tax	21,580	12,500	7,200
Income Tax	5,497	3,681	2,238
Net Income	16,083	8,819	4,962
Income from Disc. Ops.	...	5,197	6,726
Average Shares Outstg	30,983	27,684	27,684

BALANCE SHEET (IN THOUSANDS):

Cash & Cash Equivalents	63,079	12,735	21,976
Receivables, Net	...	2,414	...
Stockholders' Equity	61,223	8,904	22,895
Total Assets	78,440	23,189	41,355
Total Current Assets	66,813	16,185	34,020
Total Current Liabilities	12,279	11,000	13,647
Net Working Capital	54,534	5,185	20,373
Year End Shs Outstg	30,462	23,500	23,500

STATISTICAL RECORD:

Return on Equity %	26.27	99.05	21.67
Return on Assets %	20.50	38.03	12.00
Operating Profit Margin %	36.60	28.14	23.73
Net Profit Margin %	30.10	21.13	18.36
Book Value Per Share	2.01	0.38	0.97

OFFICERS:
T. L. Lau, Chmn.
H. C. Yuen, C.E.O.
E. M. Leung, C.F.O.
L. Goldberg, Sec.

INCORPORATED: British Virgin Islands, April, 1992

PRINCIPAL OFFICE: 135 North Los Robles Avenue Suite 800 Pasadena CA 91101

TELEPHONE NUMBER: (818) 792-5700

NO. OF EMPLOYEES: N/A

ANNUAL MEETING: In June

SHAREHOLDERS: N/A

INSTITUTIONAL HOLDINGS:
No. of Institutions: N/A
Shares Held: N/A

REGISTRAR(S): ChaseMellon Shareholder Services

TRANSFER AGENT(S): ChaseMellon Shareholder Services

GILAT SATELLITE NETWORKS LTD.

YIELD ...
P/E RATIO 60.0

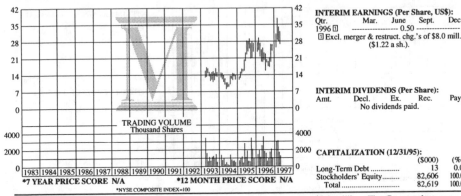

*7 YEAR PRICE SCORE N/A   *12 MONTH PRICE SCORE N/A
*NYSE COMPOSITE INDEX=100

INTERIM EARNINGS (Per Share, US$):

Qtr.	Mar.	June	Sept.	Dec.
1996 ①		---- 0.50 ----		

① Excl. merger & restruct. chg.'s of $8.0 mill. ($1.22 a sh.).

INTERIM DIVIDENDS (Per Share):

Amt.	Decl.	Ex.	Rec.	Pay.
	No dividends paid.			

CAPITALIZATION (12/31/95):

	($000)	(%)
Long-Term Debt	13	0.0
Stockholders' Equity.........	82,606	100.0
Total	82,619	100.0

RECENT DEVELOPMENTS: For the year ended Dec. 31, 1996, net income decreased 36.6% to $5.5 million compared with $8.6 million in 1995. Sales advanced 35.9% to $74.1 million compared with $54.5 million a year earlier. Gross profit was $31.2 million, up 35.3% from $23.0 million in 1995. The results for 1995 have been restated to reflect the acquisition of Skydata, Inc. The decline in earnings was primarily attributed to merger and restructuring expenses that amounted to $8.0 million. The Company's revenues benefited from the growth in Gilat's sales and from sales attributed to Skydata. As of 12/31/96, GILTF had backlogs of US$18.6 million. The Company has received orders for Skystar Advantage(TM), a trademark of GE Capital Spacenet Services, Inc. and is joint development of GE Capital Spacenet Services, Inc. and GILTF, for more than 5,000 Skystar Advantage (TM) VSAT sites.

BUSINESS

GILAT SATELLITE NETWORKS LTD. designs, develops, manufactures, markets and supports very small aperture terminal ('VSAT') satellite earth stations, hub equipment and related software products. The Company's products are incorporated primarily into private telecommunications networks which provide satellite-based communication between a central location ('hub') and a large number of geographically-dispersed locations. GILTF's main product is a two-way VSAT used primarily for point-of-sale and other transaction-oriented applications, such as credit card authorization, inventory control, prescription verification and state and national computerized on-line lottery systems. GILTF also produces the one-way VSAT for data broadcasting applications, and the rural telephony two-way VSAT product designed to provide dial tone service to remote locations.

ANNUAL EARNINGS

	12/31/95	12/31/94	12/31/95	12/31/94
	US $		NLG	
Earnings Per Share	0.95	0.73	1.53	1.27

ANNUAL FINANCIAL DATA

RECORD OF EARNINGS (IN THOUSANDS):

	12/31/95	12/31/94	12/31/95	12/31/94
Total Revenues	41,732	27,009	67,104	46,882
Costs & Expenses	34,077	20,994	54,795	36,442
Operating Income	7,655	6,015	12,309	10,441
Income Bef Income Tax	8,496	6,102	13,661	10,592
Net Income	8,496	6,102	13,661	10,592
Average Shares Outstg	8,942	8,398	8,942	8,398

BALANCE SHEET (IN THOUSANDS):

Cash & Cash Equivalents	34,541	8,490	55,541	14,731
Receivables, Net	21,245	8,599	34,161	14,926
Inventories	10,449	8,841	16,802	15,346
Gross Property	20,723	10,794	33,322	18,736
Accumulated Depreciation	2,360	1,187	3,795	2,060
Long-Term Debt	13	50	21	87
Stockholders' Equity	82,606	36,632	132,828	63,586
Total Assets	92,335	41,278	148,472	71,651
Total Current Assets	71,862	25,930	115,552	45,010
Total Current Liabilities	9,334	4,230	15,009	7,342
Net Working Capital	62,528	21,700	100,543	37,667
Year End Shs Outstg	10,034	8,349	10,034	8,349

STATISTICAL RECORD:

Return on Equity %	10.28	16.66		
Return on Assets %	9.20	14.78		
Operating Profit Margin %	18.34	22.27		
Net Profit Margin %	20.36	22.59		
Book Value Per Share	8.23	4.39		

Converted at 1995, US$0.6219= 1 Netherlands guilder; 1994, US$0.5761= 1 Netherlands guilder

OFFICERS:
Y. Gat, Chmn. & C.E.O.
A. Levinberg, Pres. & C.O.O.
Y. Leibovitch, C.F.O. & V.P.-Finan. & Admin.
E. Kahani, Contr.
INCORPORATED: 1987
PRINCIPAL OFFICE: Gilat House Yegia Kapayim St.Daniv Park, Kiryat Arye Petah Tikva Israel 49130

TELEPHONE NUMBER: (972)3-925-2000
NO. OF EMPLOYEES: N/A
ANNUAL MEETING: N/A
SHAREHOLDERS: N/A
INSTITUTIONAL HOLDINGS:
No. of Institutions: N/A
Shares Held: N/A

REGISTRAR(S): N/A

TRANSFER AGENT(S): American Stock Transfer & Trust Co., New York.

GLOBALSTAR TELECOMMUNICATIONS, LIMITED

YIELD ...
P/E RATIO ...

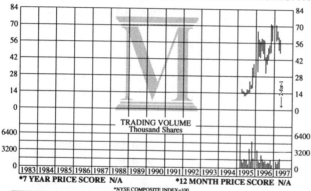

*7 YEAR PRICE SCORE N/A   *12 MONTH PRICE SCORE N/A

*NYSE COMPOSITE INDEX=100

TRADING VOLUME
Thousand Shares

INTERIM EARNINGS (Per Share, US$):
1996 -----------------d0.76-----------------

INTERIM DIVIDENDS (Per Share):

Amt.	Decl.	Ex.	Rec.	Pay.
2-for-1	4/08/97	5/29/97	5/12/97	5/28/97

CAPITALIZATION (12/31/96):

	($000)	(%)
Long-Term Debt	300,358	62.4
Stockholders' Equity.........	180,639	37.6
Total	480,997	100.0

RECENT DEVELOPMENTS: For the year ended 12/31/96, the Company reported a net loss of $15.1 million compared with a loss of $12.6 million in 1995. As of 12/31/96, the Company maintained a 21.3% ownership interest in the ordinary partnership interests of Globalstar, L.P. For the year ended 12/31/96, Globalstar L.P. posted a net loss of $54.6 million compared with $68.2 million in the year-earlier period. Globalstar L.P. attributed the results to a decrease in development costs partially offset by a decrease in interest income. The net loss applicable to ordinary part-

nership interest was $72.0 million during the current period reflecting $17.3 million of preferred distributions on the redeemable preferred partnership interests. Globalstar L.P. noted that it is expending significant funds for the design, construction, testing and deployment of the Globalstar System and expects such losses to continue until commencement of commercial operations. Globalstar L.P. does not expect to launch satellites until the second half of 1997, to commence operations before the second half of 1998 or to have positive cash flow before 1999.

BUSINESS

GLOBALSTAR TELECOMMUNI-CATIONS, LIMITED plans to operate in one industry segment, telecommunications. On 2/14/95, the Company completed an initial public offering of 10,000,000 shares of common stock. Effective 2/22/95, the Company purchased 10,000,000 ordinary partnership interests from Globalstar, L.P., a development stage limited partnership. At 12/31/96, Company had a 21.3% ownership interest in the ordinary partnership interests of Globalstar, and its sole business is acting as a general partner in Globalstar. The Globalstar System is designed to enable local service providers to offer low-cost, high quality wireless voice telephony and data services in virtually every populated area of the world.

ANNUAL EARNINGS

	12/31/96	12/31/95	12/31/94
		------US $------	
Earnings Per Share	d0.76	d0.63	...

ANNUAL FINANCIAL DATA

RECORD OF EARNINGS (IN THOUSANDS):

	12/31/96	12/31/95	12/31/94
Income Bef Income Tax	0	0	...
Eq. Earnings in Affils.	d15,080	d12,632	...
Net Income	d15,080	d12,632	...

BALANCE SHEET (IN THOUSANDS):

Long-Term Debt	300,358	...	...
Stockholders' Equity	180,639	173,118	124
Total Assets	482,676	173,118	190
Total Current Assets	...	...	190
Total Current Liabilities	1,679	...	66
Net Working Capital	...	...	124
Year End Shs Outstg	20,000	20,000	24

STATISTICAL RECORD:

Return on Equity %	...	...	...
Return on Assets %	...	...	...
Operating Profit Margin %	...	...	...
Net Profit Margin %	...	...	...
Book Value Per Share	9.03	8.66	5.17

OFFICERS:
B. L. Schwartz, Chmn. & C.E.O.
M. B. Targoff, Pres. & C.O.O.
M. P. DeBlasio, Sr. V.P. & C.F.O.
D. G. Dwyre, Sr. V.P.
INCORPORATED: Bermuda, Nov. 1994
PRINCIPAL OFFICE: 600 Third Avenue New York NY 10016

TELEPHONE NUMBER: 212-697-1105
NO. OF EMPLOYEES: 140
ANNUAL MEETING: N/A
SHAREHOLDERS: 390 (approx.)
INSTITUTIONAL HOLDINGS:
No. of Institutions: N/A
Shares Held: N/A

REGISTRAR(S): The Bank of New York

TRANSFER AGENT(S): The Bank of New York

GORAN CAPITAL, INC.

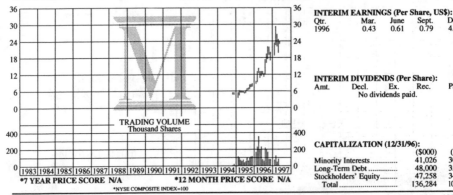

*7 YEAR PRICE SCORE N/A   *12 MONTH PRICE SCORE N/A

*NYSE COMPOSITE INDEX=100

INTERIM EARNINGS (Per Share, US$):

Qtr.	Mar.	June	Sept.	Dec.
1996	0.43	0.61	0.79	4.10

INTERIM DIVIDENDS (Per Share):

Amt.	Decl.	Ex.	Rec.	Pay.
	No dividends paid.			

CAPITALIZATION (12/31/96):

	($000)	(%)
Minority Interests.............	41,026	30.1
Long-Term Debt	48,000	35.2
Stockholders' Equity........	47,258	34.7
Total	136,284	100.0

RECENT DEVELOPMENTS: For the year ended 12/31/96, income before an unusual item advanced 83.1% to $13.1 million compared with $7.2 million in 1995. Consolidated gross premium revenue improved to $307.6 million compared with $151.7 million a year earlier. Premiums earned and net investment and other income was $230.8 million compared with $82.0 million in 1995. Profit from operations was $29.0 million compared with $11.4 million a year earlier. The Company's results excluded an unusual gain of $18.2 million in 1996 related to the initial public offering of Symons International Group Inc. in November 1996. The improvement in results was attributed to increases in sales and earnings of GNCNF's crop insurance subsidiary, IGF Insurance Company, of Des Moines, Iowa. Additionally, GGS Holdings Inc., GNCNF's nonstandard automobile insurance division, more than doubled its premium income to $187.2 million in 1996. The Company continued to benefit from the growth and earnings of Granite Reinsurance Company Ltd., Goran's reinsurance division.

BUSINESS

GORAN CAPITAL INC. is a holding company that owns subsidiaries engaged in a number of business activities. The most important of these is the property and casualty insurance business conducted in 31 US states, Canada and Barbados, on both a direct and reinsurance basis through a number of subsidiaries. The Company's principal US subsidiaries offer consumers a full range of niche insurance products and crop insurance, through independent agents and brokers. The Company's Canadian subsidiary underwrites finite (limited risk) reinsurance in Bermuda, the United States and Canada.

ANNUAL EARNINGS

	12/31/96	12/31/95	12/31/96	12/31/95
	----US $----		----C $----	
Earnings Per Share	5.92	1.43	8.07	1.96

ANNUAL FINANCIAL DATA

RECORD OF EARNINGS (IN THOUSANDS):

	12/31/96	12/31/95	12/31/96	12/31/95
Total Revenues	230,752	81,974	315,623	111,849
Costs & Expenses	206,697	72,306	282,721	98,657
Operating Income	24,055	9,668	32,902	13,191
Income Bef Income Tax	24,055	9,668	32,902	13,191
Income Tax	8,127	2,497	11,116	3,407
Minority Interests	2,801	...	3,831	...
Net Income	13,127	7,171	17,955	9,784
Net Extraordinary Items	18,169	...	24,852	...
Average Shares Outstg	5,286	5,012	5,286	5,012

BALANCE SHEET (IN THOUSANDS):

Cash & Cash Equivalents	206,671	54,366	282,685	74,179
Receivables, Net	101,249	47,301	138,489	64,540
Gross Property	8,779	3,819	12,023	5,214
Accumulated Depreciation	3,978	1,731	5,448	2,363
Long-Term Debt	48,000	16,896	65,654	23,054
Stockholders' Equity	47,258	12,622	64,640	17,222
Total Assets	381,342	160,816	521,600	219,424
Total Current Assets	307,920	101,667	421,174	138,719
Total Current Liabilities	26,806	10,484	36,665	14,305
Net Working Capital	281,114	91,183	384,508	124,414
Year End Shs Outstg	5,406	5,060	5,406	5,060

STATISTICAL RECORD:

Return on Equity %	43.84	80.86
Return on Assets %	4.84	6.92
Operating Profit Margin %	10.42	11.79
Net Profit Margin %	5.69	8.75
Book Value Per Share	8.74	2.49

Converted at 1996, US$0.7311= 1 Canadian C $; 1995, US$0.7329= 1 Canadian C $

OFFICERS:
G. G. Symons, Chmn.
A. G. Symons, Pres. & C.E.O.
D. H. Symons, V.P. & C.O.O.
G. P. Hutchcraft, V.P. & C.F.O.
INCORPORATED: Canada
PRINCIPAL OFFICE: 181 University Avenue, Suite 1101, Toronto Canada M5H 3M7

TELEPHONE NUMBER: 416-594-1155
NO. OF EMPLOYEES: N/A
ANNUAL MEETING: In May
SHAREHOLDERS: 105
INSTITUTIONAL HOLDINGS:
No. of Institutions: 1
Shares Held: 500

REGISTRAR(S): Montreal Trust Company of Canada, Toronto.

TRANSFER AGENT(S): Chemical Bank, London.

GRANDETEL TECHNOLOGIES, INC.

YIELD ...
P/E RATIO ...

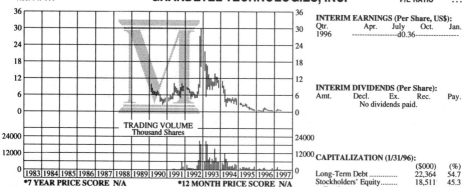

*7 YEAR PRICE SCORE N/A   *12 MONTH PRICE SCORE N/A

*NYSE COMPOSITE INDEX=100

TRADING VOLUME
Thousand Shares

INTERIM EARNINGS (Per Share, US$):

Qtr.	Apr.	July	Oct.	Jan.
1996	------------------d0.36----------------			

INTERIM DIVIDENDS (Per Share):

Amt.	Decl.	Ex.	Rec.	Pay.
No dividends paid.				

CAPITALIZATION (1/31/96):

	($000)	(%)
Long-Term Debt	22,364	54.7
Stockholders' Equity........	18,511	45.3
Total	40,875	100.0

RECENT DEVELOPMENTS: For the year ended 1/31/96, net loss was C$10.1 million compared to a loss of C$75.1 million in the same period of 1995. Sales were C$15.4 million, down 45.5% from C$28.2 million a year earlier. Operating loss was C$11.7 million versus a loss of C$50.2 million in 1995. Sales in the United States decreased to C$4.8 million from C$8.9 million in 1995. Results for 1995 have been restated. The decline in results was primarily attributed to the winding down of the consumer electronic products distribution business, which mostly consisted of televisions and low-end audio and video products in North America. The Company switched to the manufacture and sale of higher margin consumer electronic products, mainly telephones, and sales are made directly to customers in North America and Europe from Hong Kong or China. Sales to China increased slightly to C$4.7 million from C$4.2 million. The Company continues to focus on business operations in China.

BUSINESS

GRANDETEL TECHNOLOGIES, INC. is a communications and distribution company focused on the consumer electronics, fax, paging and cellular telephone markets. The Company distributes a broad line of consumer electronic products in Canada, Mexico and the United States. GTTIF sells fax machines and cellular telephone systems in China.

ANNUAL EARNINGS

	1/31/96	1/31/95	1/31/96	1/31/95
	-------------US $-------------		-------------C $-------------	
Earnings Per Share	d0.36	d3.10	d0.50	d4.38

ANNUAL FINANCIAL DATA

RECORD OF EARNINGS (IN THOUSANDS):

	1/31/96	1/31/95	1/31/96	1/31/95
Total Revenues	11,114	19,915	15,357	28,173
Costs & Expenses	19,605	56,729	27,090	78,387
Operating Income	d8,491	d36,340	d11,733	d50,214
Interest Expenses	1,806	1,824	2,496	2,520
Other Income	3,022	16,217	4,176	22,409
Net Income	d7,275	d53,119	d10,053	d75,143
Average Shares Outstg	20,014	17,139	20,014	17,139

BALANCE SHEET (IN THOUSANDS):

Cash & Cash Equivalents	14,450	31,451	19,967	44,492
Receivables, Net	3,444	3,296	4,759	4,663
Inventories	11,067	7,161	15,292	10,130
Gross Property	5,069	3,813	7,004	5,394
Accumulated Depreciation	999	878	1,380	1,242
Long-Term Debt	22,364	22,382	30,902	31,662
Stockholders' Equity	18,511	25,188	25,578	35,631
Total Assets	51,504	63,084	71,168	89,241
Total Current Assets	29,611	42,523	40,916	60,154
Total Current Liabilities	10,630	15,515	14,688	21,948
Net Working Capital	18,981	27,008	26,228	38,206

STATISTICAL RECORD:

Return on Equity %	...	...		
Return on Assets %	...	...		
Operating Profit Margin %	...	...		
Net Profit Margin %	...	...		
Book Value Per Share	0.01	0.01		

Converted at 1996, US$0.7237= 1 Canadian $; 1995, US$0.7069= 1 Canadian $

OFFICERS:
C. Ho, Chmn. & C.E.O.
J. T. Evans, Vice Chmn. & Sec.
P. K. Law, Pres. & Managing Dir.
K. Yuen, C.F.O.

INCORPORATED: 1972

PRINCIPAL OFFICE: 135-13500 Maycrest Way, Richmond, British Columbia Canada V6V 2N8

TELEPHONE NUMBER: (604) 278-8788

NO. OF EMPLOYEES: N/A

ANNUAL MEETING: In Jul.

SHAREHOLDERS: N/A

INSTITUTIONAL HOLDINGS:
No. of Institutions: 4
Shares Held: 117,150

REGISTRAR(S): N/A

TRANSFER AGENT(S): Corporate Stock Transfer, Denver.

HEIDEMIJ N.V.

YIELD ...
P/E RATIO 9.2

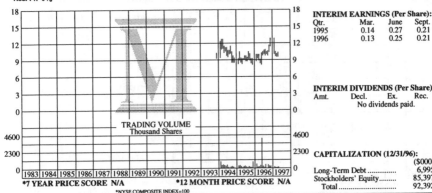

18 ... 18
15 ... 15
12 ... 12
9 ... 9
6 ... 6
3 ... 3
0 ... 0

TRADING VOLUME
Thousand Shares
4600 ... 4600
2300 ... 2300
0 ... 0

1983 1984 1985 1986 1987 1988 1989 1990 1991 1992 1993 1994 1995 1996 1997
*7 YEAR PRICE SCORE N/A   *12 MONTH PRICE SCORE N/A
*NYSE COMPOSITE INDEX=100

INTERIM EARNINGS (Per Share):

Qtr.	Mar.	June	Sept.	Dec.
1995	0.14	0.27	0.21	0.29
1996	0.13	0.25	0.21	0.28

INTERIM DIVIDENDS (Per Share):

Amt.	Decl.	Ex.	Rec.	Pay.
No dividends paid.				

CAPITALIZATION (12/31/96):

	($000)	(%)
Long-Term Debt	6,995	7.6
Stockholders' Equity	85,397	92.4
Total	92,392	100.0

RECENT DEVELOPMENTS: For the year ended 12/31/96, net income, before an extraordinary charge, totaled $16.6 million, or $1.07 per share, compared with $17.0 million, or $0.96 per share, in the corresponding prior-year period. Gross revenue climbed 14.1% to $645.4 million from $565.7 million the previous year, while net revenue grew 12.5% to $439.6 million from $390.6 million in 1995. Revenue growth in 1996 was fueled by acquisitions completed during the year, partially offset by adverse foreign currency exchange rates. Gross margin advanced 12.9% to $145.3 million, or 22.5% of gross revenue, from $128.7 million, or 22.8% of gross revenue, a year earlier. Operating income rose 7.9% to $28.6 million from $26.5 million the year before. For the three months ended 12/31/96, net income, before an extraordinary charge, was $5.3 million, down slightly versus $5.4 million the prior year. Gross revenue increased 8.7% to $165.5 million from $152.3 million the previous year.

BUSINESS

HEIDEMIJ N.V. is the holding company of the Heidemij group. Through its subsidiaries, the Company is engaged in international consultation, engineering, contracting and project management services for the maintenance and improvement of the environment. The Company's core activities are divided under its divisional subsidiary groups. Heidemij Advies B.V. and its subsidiaries are engaged in contracting and consultation services in land use planning, the environment, infrastructure, construction, and real estate projects. Heidemij Realisatie B.V. and its subsidiaries are engaged in contracting and project management services in environment, infrastructure, green amenities, sports and environmental projects. Holding Grabowsky & Poort B.V. and its subsidiaries are engaged in engineering, construction, infrastructure, hydraulic engineering, and environmental projects. Geraghty & Miller Inc. and its subsidiaries are engaged in environmental engineering in the United States. This division is also involved in soil and groundwater remediation, groundwater extraction, and air quality preservation. Euroconsult B.V. and its subsidiaries are engaged in engineering, contracting, and consultation services in regard to rural and urban development in Africa, Asia, Latin America and Eastern Europe.

ANNUAL EARNINGS

	12/31/96	12/31/95	12/31/96	12/31/95
	---US $---		---Guilders---	
Earnings Per Share	0.86	0.90	1.50	1.45

ANNUAL FINANCIAL DATA

RECORD OF EARNINGS (IN THOUSANDS):

	12/31/96	12/31/95	12/31/96	12/31/95
Total Revenues	624,219	559,949	1,089,198	900,384
Costs & Expenses	582,095	520,468	1,015,696	836,900
Depreciation & Amort	14,409	13,331	25,142	21,436
Operating Income	27,715	26,150	48,360	42,048
Income Bef Income Tax	25,277	24,556	44,105	39,486
Income Tax	8,148	7,021	14,218	11,290
Eq. Earnings in Affils.	258	1,190	451	1,914
Minority Interests	cr1,290	cr1,922	cr2,251	cr3,091
Net Income	18,677	20,648	32,589	33,201
Net Extraordinary Items	d1,117	...	d1,949	...

BALANCE SHEET (IN THOUSANDS):

Cash & Cash Equivalents	18,606	21,133	32,466	33,981
Receivables, Net	155,796	167,322	271,848	269,050
Inventories	19,091	1,055	33,311	1,696
Gross Property	138,294	132,869	241,309	213,650
Accumulated Depreciation	82,750	72,916	144,390	117,247
Long-Term Debt	6,995	11,631	12,205	18,702
Stockholders' Equity	85,397	104,354	149,000	167,798
Total Assets	273,004	264,312	476,363	425,008
Total Current Assets	193,493	189,510	337,625	304,727
Total Current Liabilities	158,326	126,483	276,263	203,381
Net Working Capital	35,167	63,027	61,362	101,346
Year End Shs Outstg	18,846	18,633	18,846	18,633

STATISTICAL RECORD:

Return on Equity %	21.87	19.79		
Return on Assets %	6.84	7.81		
Operating Profit Margin %	4.44	4.67		
Net Profit Margin %	2.99	3.69		
Book Value Per Share	4.53	5.60		

Converted at 1996, US$0.5731= 1 Netherlands guilder; 1995, US$0.6219= 1 Netherlands guilder

OFFICERS:
F. P. Luttmer, Chmn.
J. Faber
H. L. Noy

INCORPORATED: 1888

PRINCIPAL OFFICE: Utrechtseweg 68, P.O. Box 33, 6800 LE Arnhem The Netherlands

TELEPHONE NUMBER: 31-26-3-778-911

NO. OF EMPLOYEES: 5,996

ANNUAL MEETING: In May

SHAREHOLDERS: N/A

INSTITUTIONAL HOLDINGS:
No. of Institutions: N/A
Shares Held: N/A

REGISTRAR(S): ABN AMRO Bank, Amsterdam; Bank of New York, New York.

TRANSFER AGENT(S): ABN AMRO Bank, Amsterdam; Bank of New York, New York.

HIGHWAY HOLDINGS

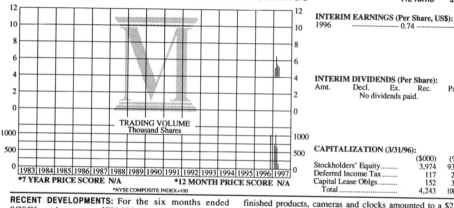

7 YEAR PRICE SCORE N/A   **12 MONTH PRICE SCORE N/A**
*NYSE COMPOSITE INDEX=100

INTERIM EARNINGS (Per Share, US$):
1996 ------------------ 0.74 ------------------

INTERIM DIVIDENDS (Per Share):

Amt.	Decl.	Ex.	Rec.	Pay.
	No dividends paid.			

CAPITALIZATION (3/31/96):

	($000)	(%)
Stockholders' Equity........	3,974	93.7
Deferred Income Tax	117	2.7
Capital Lease Oblgs.	152	3.6
Total	4,243	100.0

RECENT DEVELOPMENTS: For the six months ended 9/30/96, net income was $789,000 compared with $693,000 in the corresponding period a year earlier. Revenues were $9.7 million, up 31% versus $7.4 million in 1995. Higher earnings and sales resulted from improved demand from the Companys hi-tech customers. Sales of metal stamped parts amounted to $7.7 million, an increase of $2.5 million, or 47%, compared with the year-earlier period. Sales of finished products, cameras and clocks amounted to a $2.0 million decrease of $155,000, or 7%, versus the six months ended 9/30/95, and represented 21% of the Company's total sales. The Company posted a gross profit margin of 26.8% versus a gross profit margin of 22.7% in 1995. The increase in gross profit resulted from a reduction in raw material prices that was not passed along to customers.

BUSINESS

HIGHWAY HOLDINGS is an integrated manufacturer of high quality metal parts, cameras and clocks for major Japanese, German and United States original equipment manufacturers and contract manufacturers. In addition, the Company manufactures and supplies a wide variety of high quality metal parts and components which are used by the Company's customers in the manufacturing of such products as photocopiers, laser printers, compact disc players, laser disc players, cassette players, computer equipment, electronic components, electrical connectors, cameras, clocks, automobiles and car audio and other audio equipment.

ANNUAL EARNINGS

	3/31/96	3/31/95
	-------------US $-------------	
Earnings Per Share	0.74	0.31

ANNUAL FINANCIAL DATA

RECORD OF EARNINGS (IN THOUSANDS):

Total Revenues	13,773	9,752
Costs & Expenses	12,444	8,777
Operating Income	1,329	975
Income Bef Income Tax	1,414	1,025
Income Tax	43	138
Eq. Earnings in Affils.	16	d3
Minority Interests	471	519
Net Income	916	365
Average Shares Outstg	1,244	1,162

BALANCE SHEET (IN THOUSANDS):

Cash & Cash Equivalents	1,279	1,194
Receivables, Net	2,189	1,606
Inventories	2,196	1,782
Gross Property	3,923	2,480
Accumulated Depreciation	1,201	912
Capital Lease Oblig.	152	212
Stockholders' Equity	3,974	2,715
Total Assets	8,582	6,204
Total Current Assets	5,764	4,625
Total Current Liabilities	2,924	1,949
Net Working Capital	2,840	2,676
Year End Shs Outstg	1,398	1,111

STATISTICAL RECORD:

Return on Equity %	23.05	13.44
Return on Assets %	10.67	5.88
Operating Profit Margin %	9.65	10.00
Net Profit Margin %	6.65	3.74
Book Value Per Share	2.84	2.44

OFFICERS:
R. W. Kohl, Chmn. & C.E.O.
S. Saito, Managing Dir.
M. P. Majzner, C.F.O. & Sec.
M. Tsang Shu Mui, Factory Mgr.

INCORPORATED: 1990

PRINCIPAL OFFICE: Flat E and G, 7/F, Phase 2 Kingsway Industrial Building 173-175 Wo Y: Hop Road Kwa: Chung, N.T. HongKong

TELEPHONE NUMBER: (852) 2494-0923

NO. OF EMPLOYEES: 41

ANNUAL MEETING: N/A

SHAREHOLDERS: N/A

INSTITUTIONAL HOLDINGS:
No. of Institutions: N/A
Shares Held: N/A

REGISTRAR(S): U.S. Stock Transfer Corporation, Glendale, CA.

TRANSFER AGENT(S): U.S. Stock Transfer Corporation, Glendale, CA.

HOLLINGER INC.

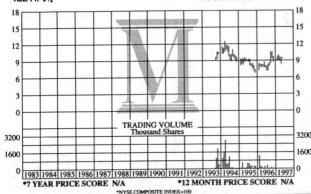

INTERIM EARNINGS (Per Share, C$):

Qtr.	Mar.	June	Sept.	Dec.
1996	------------------ 0.58 ------------------			

INTERIM DIVIDENDS (Per Share):

Amt.	Decl.	Ex.	Rec.	Pay.
0.15	5/29/96	8/22/96	8/26/96	9/10/96
0.15	9/10	11/21	11/25	12/10
0.15	1/07/97	2/24/97	2/26/97	3/10/97
0.15	2/19	5/21	5/26	6/10
2.50E	4/22	5/05	5/07	5/12

Indicated div.:$0.60

TRADING VOLUME
Thousand Shares

| 1983 | 1984 | 1985 | 1986 | 1987 | 1988 | 1989 | 1990 | 1991 | 1992 | 1993 | 1994 | 1995 | 1996 | 1997 |

*7 YEAR PRICE SCORE N/A   ***12 MONTH PRICE SCORE N/A**

*NYSE COMPOSITE INDEX=100

CAPITALIZATION (12/31/96):

	($000)	(%)
Minority Interests	641,079	32.0
Long-Term Debt	769,360	38.4
Stockholders' Equity	454,848	22.7
Deferred Income Tax	137,690	6.9
Total	2,002,977	100.0

RECENT DEVELOPMENTS: For the year ended 12/31/96, net income was C$46.3 million compared with income of C$18.9 million, before discontinued operations, a year earlier. Included in results were unusual gains of C$36.5 million and C$9.8 million for 1996 and 1995, respectively. Results also included net foreign currency losses of C$948,000 versus net foreign currency gains of C$1.3 million in 1995. Total revenues were C$1.89 billion, up 23.9% from C$1.53 billion in the prior year. Total expenses rose 22.5% to C$1.68 billion from C$1.37 billion a year ago. Publishing operating profit was C$235.6 million compared with C$161.7 million the year before, an increase of 45.7%. Comparisons were made with restated prior-year figures to reflect new accounting standards for financial instruments.

BUSINESS

HOLLINGER INC. is a Canadian based multinational newspaper company which, directly and through subsidiaries and associated companies, is engaged primarily in the publishing, printing and distribution of newspapers and magazines in Canada, the United States, the United Kingdom, Australia and Israel. The Company also acquires underperforming newspaper properties with a view to improving the operation and enhancing profitability and value. Geographic contributions to revenue for 1996 were as follows: Canada, 21%; United States, 43%; United Kingdom, 35%; and other Countries, 1%.

ANNUAL EARNINGS

	12/31/96	12/31/95	12/31/96	12/31/95
	-----------US $-----------		-----------C $-----------	
Earnings Per Share	0.37	0.05	0.58	0.07

ANNUAL FINANCIAL DATA

RECORD OF EARNINGS (IN MILLIONS):

Total Revenues	1,382	1,119	1,891	1,526
Costs & Expenses	1,230	1,007	1,683	1,374
Depreciation & Amort	84	66	116	91
Operating Income	68	45	93	62
Income Bef Income Tax	85	62	116	85
Income Tax	40	25	55	34
Minority Interests	d38	d30	d52	d41
Net Income	34	14	46	19
Income from Disc. Ops.	...	d2	...	d2
Net Extraordinary Items	cr27	cr7	cr36	cr10
Average Shares Outstg (000)	41,191	40,866	56,341	55,759

BALANCE SHEET (IN MILLIONS):

Cash & Cash Equivalents	150	0	205	0
Receivables, Net	352	177	482	241
Inventories	32	32	44	44
Gross Property	3,009	1,419	4,116	1,936
Accumulated Depreciation	640	278	875	379
Long-Term Debt	966	355	1,321	707
Stockholders' Equity	455	355	622	485
Total Assets	3,456	2,117	4,727	2,888
Total Current Assets	534	209	731	285
Total Current Liabilities	1,115	738	1,526	541
Net Working Capital	d581	d529	d795	d256
Year End Shs Outstg (000)	41,301	40,935	56,492	55,853

STATISTICAL RECORD:

Return on Equity %	1.6	1.5		
Return on Assets %	0.2	0.3		
Operating Profit Margin %	4.9	4.0		
Net Profit Margin %	0.5	0.6		
Book Value Per Share	11.02	8.67		

Converted at 1996, US$0.7311= 1 Canadian C $; 1995, US$0.7329= 1 Canadian C $

OFFICERS:
C. M. Black, Chmn. & C.E.O.
D. S. Chant, Deputy Chmn.
F. D. Radler, Pres. & C.O.O.
J. A. Boultbee, V.P., Fin.

INCORPORATED: Canada, Sept., 1985

PRINCIPAL OFFICE: 10 Toronto Street Toronto Canada MSC2B7

TELEPHONE NUMBER: 416-363-8721

NO. OF EMPLOYEES: N/A

ANNUAL MEETING: In May

SHAREHOLDERS: 2,345

INSTITUTIONAL HOLDINGS:
No. of Institutions: 11
Shares Held: 512,801

REGISTRAR(S): Montreal Trust Company of Canada, Toronto, Montreal, Vancouver; The Bank of Nova Scotia Trust Company of New York, New York.

TRANSFER AGENT(S): Montreal Trust Company of Canada, Toronto, Montreal, Vancouver; The Bank of Nova Scotia Trust Company of New York, New York.

HOME CENTERS (DIY) LIMITED

YIELD ...
P/E RATIO 10.5

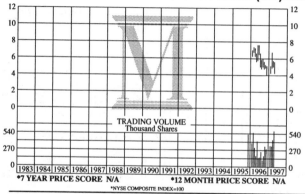

*7 YEAR PRICE SCORE N/A   *12 MONTH PRICE SCORE N/A
*NYSE COMPOSITE INDEX=100

INTERIM EARNINGS (Per Share, US$):
1996 ------------------ 0.43 ------------------

INTERIM DIVIDENDS (Per Share):

Amt.	Decl.	Ex.	Rec.	Pay.
No dividends paid.				

CAPITALIZATION (12/31/96):

	($000)	(%)
Long-Term Debt	1,887	10.6
Stockholders' Equity........	15,849	89.3
Deferred Income Tax	10	0.1
Total	17,746	100.0

RECENT DEVELOPMENTS: For the year ended 12/31/96, net income fell 8.4% to NIS6.9 million from NIS7.5 million a year earlier. Results for 1995 were restated and included a tax gain of NIS2.8 million arising from the extinguishment of the Company's deferred tax valuation allowance. Total sales were NIS272.8 million, up 20.3% from NIS226.7 million in the previous year. Operating income was NIS10.7 million compared with NIS8.7 million the year before, an increase of 22.6%. For the quarter ended 12/31/96, net income jumped 31.5% to NIS1.6 million from NIS1.2 million in the corresponding 1995 quarter. Total revenues were NIS72.8 million, a gain of 24.5% over NIS58.4 million in the fourth quarter of 1995. Comparisons were made with restated prior-year figures.

BUSINESS

HOME CENTERS (DIY) LIMITED is engaged in warehouse-type home improvement centers located in Israel, offering a selection of home improvement products such as tools, paints, plumbing, faucets, electrical and building materials. In addition, the Company offers housewares, ready-to-assemble furniture and kitchen cabinetry, automotive accessories and sporting goods. Also, integrated into the Company's stores are leased departments that offer home electronic, appliances, lighting, carpets, bathroom fixtures, bedding and linens.

ANNUAL EARNINGS

	12/31/96	12/31/95	12/31/96	12/31/95
	------------US $------------		------------NIS------------	
Earnings Per Share	0.43	1.99	1.39	6.26

ANNUAL FINANCIAL DATA

RECORD OF EARNINGS (IN THOUSANDS):

Total Revenues	83,902	178,911	273,296	563,144
Costs & Expenses	80,621	171,041	262,609	538,373
Operating Income	3,281	7,870	10,687	24,772
Income Bef Income Tax	3,321	6,545	10,818	20,601
Income Tax	1,212	cr221	3,948	cr696
Net Income	2,109	6,766	6,856	21,297
Average Shares Outstg	4,945	3,398	4,945	3,398

BALANCE SHEET (IN THOUSANDS):

Cash & Cash Equivalents	389	16,400	1,267	51,621
Receivables, Net	13,725	26,112	44,707	82,191
Inventories	13,366	28,795	43,537	90,636
Gross Property	21,616	33,889	70,410	106,670
Accumulated Depreciation	3,705	5,888	12,068	18,533
Long-Term Debt	1,887	4,269	6,147	13,437
Stockholders' Equity	15,849	40,394	51,625	127,145
Total Assets	46,851	101,630	152,609	319,893
Total Current Assets	27,480	71,307	89,511	224,448
Total Current Liabilities	28,724	56,279	93,564	177,145
Net Working Capital	d1,244	15,028	d4,052	47,302
Year End Shs Outstg	4,720	4,720	4,720	4,720

STATISTICAL RECORD:

Return on Equity %	13.31	16.75		
Return on Assets %	4.50	6.66		
Operating Profit Margin %	3.91	4.40		
Net Profit Margin %	2.51	3.78		
Book Value Per Share	3.36	8.56		

Converted at 1996, US$0.3070= 1 New Israeli Shekel; 1995, US$0.3177= 1 New Israeli Shekel

OFFICERS:
L. Kushner, Chmn.
A. Meidan, Pres. & C.E.O.
R. Mamon, C.F.O.

INCORPORATED: Isreal, Nov., 1992

PRINCIPAL OFFICE: 68 Mivtza Kadesh Street, Bnei-Brak Israel 51205

TELEPHONE NUMBER: 972-3-579-9678

NO. OF EMPLOYEES: 490

ANNUAL MEETING: N/A

SHAREHOLDERS: 62

INSTITUTIONAL HOLDINGS:
No. of Institutions: N/A
Shares Held: N/A

REGISTRAR(S): American Stock Transfer & Trust Company, New York.

TRANSFER AGENT(S): American Stock Transfer & Trust Company, New York.

HUMMINGBIRD COMMUNICATIONS LTD.

YIELD ...
P/E RATIO 12.1

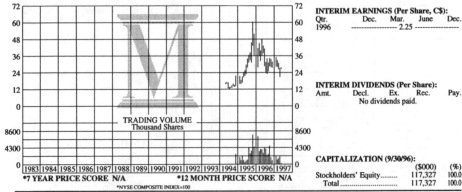

INTERIM EARNINGS (Per Share, C$):

Qtr.	Dec.	Mar.	June	Dec.
1996	------------------- 2.25 -------------------			

INTERIM DIVIDENDS (Per Share):

Amt.	Decl.	Ex.	Rec.	Pay.
	No dividends paid.			

CAPITALIZATION (9/30/96):

	($000)	(%)
Stockholders' Equity........	117,327	100.0
Total	117,327	100.0

RECENT DEVELOPMENTS: For the quarter ended 12/31/96, net income was $6.8 million compared with a loss of $200,000 in the corresponding 1995 quarter. Results for 1995 included a $5.3 million write-off of acquired research and development related to the acquisition of Common Ground Software, Inc. Sales were $22.3 million, up 36.8% from $16.3 million in the year-earlier quarter. Gross profit was $21.6 million compared with $15.5 million the year before, an increase of 39.4%. Expenses fell 23.4% to $9.8 million from $12.8 million in the prior-year quarter. The Company recently signed an agreement to purchase from McGill University and PolarSoft Inc. the TN3270 and TN5250 terminal emulation software, a product that is used by a large number of organizations for enterprise-host connectivity.

BUSINESS

HUMMINGBIRD COMMUNICA-TIONS LTD. is a computer software development company that designs, manufactures and markets a complete line of PC X servers as well as X development tool kits for various computer platforms. The Company sells its products through accredited distributors and resellers, original equipment manufacturers, value-added resellers and systems integrators and through its own direct sales force to major accounts. The Company's customers include Boeing, Chevron, EDS, the Federal Reserve Board, Ford Motor Company, Hewlett-Packard, the Mayo Clinic, Merrill Lynch, NASA, Procter & Gamble, Reuters, the Tennessee Valley Authority, Texas Instruments, the US Armed Forces and Wal-Mart.

ANNUAL EARNINGS

	9/30/96	9/30/95	9/30/96	9/30/95
	-------------US $-------------		-------------C $-------------	
Earnings Per Share	1.65	1.22	2.25	1.64

ANNUAL FINANCIAL DATA

RECORD OF EARNINGS (IN THOUSANDS):

	9/30/96	9/30/95	9/30/96	9/30/95
Total Revenues	74,881	47,486	102,060	63,722
Costs & Expenses	32,215	20,299	43,907	27,239
Depreciation & Amort	4,184	1,379	5,703	1,850
Operating Income	38,483	25,809	52,450	34,633
Income Bef Income Tax	43,606	27,729	59,433	37,210
Income Tax	21,009	12,624	28,635	16,940
Net Income	22,596	15,105	30,798	20,270
Average Shares Outstg	13,673	12,330	13,673	12,330

BALANCE SHEET (IN THOUSANDS):

Cash & Cash Equivalents	96,850	80,058	132,002	107,432
Receivables, Net	13,983	8,585	19,058	11,521
Inventories	495	346	674	464
Gross Property	4,998	2,639	6,812	3,541
Accumulated Depreciation	1,554	621	2,118	833
Stockholders' Equity	117,327	93,946	159,911	126,068
Total Assets	131,897	104,478	179,770	140,201
Total Current Assets	113,686	90,856	154,949	121,922
Total Current Liabilities	14,571	10,532	19,859	14,133
Net Working Capital	99,116	80,324	135,090	107,789
Year End Shs Outstg	13,777	13,579	13,777	13,579

STATISTICAL RECORD:

Return on Equity %	19.26	16.08
Return on Assets %	17.13	14.46
Operating Profit Margin %	51.39	54.35
Net Profit Margin %	30.18	31.81
Book Value Per Share	8.52	6.92

Converted at 1996, US$0.7337= 1 Canadian $; 1995, US$0.7452= 1 Canadian $

OFFICERS:
F. Sorkin, Chmn., Pres. & C.E.O.
A. B. Litwin, Exec. V.P. & Sec.
J. Adamek, Sr. V.P.
I.P.S. Duggal, C.F.O. & Contr.

INCORPORATED: Canada, 1984

PRINCIPAL OFFICE: 1 Sparks Avenue, North York, Ontario, Canada M2H 2W1

TELEPHONE NUMBER: 416-496-2200

NO. OF EMPLOYEES: 330 (approx.)

ANNUAL MEETING: In Mar.

SHAREHOLDERS: N/A

INSTITUTIONAL HOLDINGS:
No. of Institutions: 27
Shares Held: 3,259,025

REGISTRAR(S): The R-M Trust Co., Ontario.

TRANSFER AGENT(S): The R-M Trust Co., Ontario.

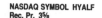

NASDAQ SYMBOL HYALF
Rec. Pr. 3⅝

HYAL PHARMACEUTICAL CORP.

YIELD ...
P/E RATIO ...

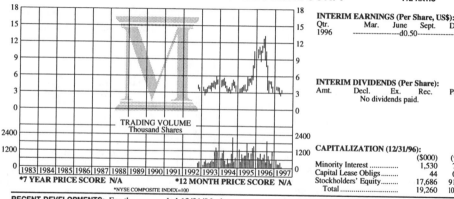

*7 YEAR PRICE SCORE N/A *12 MONTH PRICE SCORE N/A

*NYSE COMPOSITE INDEX=100

INTERIM EARNINGS (Per Share, US$):

Qtr.	Mar.	June	Sept.	Dec.
1996	----------------d0.50----------------			

INTERIM DIVIDENDS (Per Share):

Amt.	Decl.	Ex.	Rec.	Pay.
No dividends paid.				

CAPITALIZATION (12/31/96):

	($000)	(%)
Minority Interest	1,530	7.9
Capital Lease Obligs........	44	0.2
Stockholders' Equity........	17,686	91.9
Total	19,260	100.0

RECENT DEVELOPMENTS: For the year ended 12/31/96, the Company reported a net loss of C$15.8 million compared with C$11.6 million in the corresponding period a year earlier. Revenues dropped 3% to C$2.1 million. Interest income generated from the investment of cash reserves from equity offerings continues to be the main source for the Company and was consistent with 1995. Product sales were positively affected by the sale of product for clinical use. These increases were partially offset by lower licensing revenues. Research and development expenses in 1996 increased by 39% to C$13.4 million compared with C$9.6 million in 1995. This increase reflects costs related to the clinical trial activities for Solarase, Hyanalgese-D, and to a lesser extent, Cardi-Clear.

BUSINESS

HYAL PHARMACEUTICAL CORP. is a drug delivery Company engaged in the research, development and worldwide commercialization of pharmaceutical formulations utilizing its proprietary Hyaluronan Induced Targeting (HIT) and Hyaluronan Improved Liposome Technology (HILT). Hyal licenses its product innovations to major pharmaceutical companies that in turn manufacture, market and sell the resulting drugs to hospitals, physicians and consumers. Hyal seeks global licensing partners for its products and technologies in return for up from licensing fees and royalties on sales. The Company's operating plans, sales prospects and profitability are predicated on successful licensing and marketing of its human products and development of pharmaceutical technologies for human applications. HYAL F is in the process of developing and obtaining regulatory approvals and the initiation of distribution arrangements for its products. The Company's products, among other things, are used for the topical treatment of basal cell carcinoma (skin cancer), actinic keratosis (precancerous lesions), and painful conditions of arthritis and neuropathies, and also for the injectable treatment of moderate to severe chronic pain.

ANNUAL EARNINGS

	12/31/96	12/31/95	12/31/96	12/31/95
	-----------US $-----------		-----------C $-----------	
Earnings Per Share	d0.50	d0.44	d0.69	d0.60

ANNUAL FINANCIAL DATA

RECORD OF EARNINGS (IN THOUSANDS):

	12/31/96	12/31/95	12/31/96	12/31/95
Total Revenues	1,506	1,564	2,060	2,134
Costs & Expenses	13,327	10,109	18,229	13,793
Depreciation & Amort	330	308	451	420
Operating Income	d12,151	d8,853	d16,620	d12,079
Minority Interest	583	457	797	623
Net Income	d11,569	d8,484	d15,824	d11,575
Average Shares Outstg	22,906	19,343	22,906	19,343
BALANCE SHEET (IN THOUSANDS):				
Cash & Cash Equivalents	18,200	19,871	24,894	27,113
Receivables, Net	240	243	329	331
Inventories	265	362	362	494
Gross Property	969	616	1,326	840
Accumulated Depreciation	425	335	582	457
Capital Lease Obligs	44	54	60	74
Stockholders' Equity	17,686	19,307	24,191	26,344
Total Assets	21,364	23,109	29,221	31,531
Total Current Assets	18,830	20,594	25,755	28,100
Total Current Liabilities	2,104	1,810	2,877	2,470
Net Working Capital	16,726	18,784	22,878	25,630
Year End Shs Outstg	25,835	22,587	25,835	22,587
STATISTICAL RECORD:				
Return on Equity %	...	...		
Return on Assets %	...	...		
Operating Profit Margin %	...	...		
Net Profit Margin %	...	...		
Book Value Per Share	0.94	1.17		

Converted at 1996, US$0.7311= 1 Canadian $; 1995, US$0.7329= 1 Canadian $

OFFICERS:
D. C. Webster, Chmn.
S. S. Asculai, Pres. & C.E.O.
G. H. Kidd, Exec. V.P.
M. A. Byrne, V.P. & Corp. Sec.
M. D. Cohen, M.D., Sr.V.P. & Chief Medical Officer

INCORPORATED: 1968

PRINCIPAL OFFICE: 2425 Skymark Avenue
Mississauga, Ontario Canada L4W 4Y6

TELEPHONE NUMBER: 905-625-8181

NO. OF EMPLOYEES: 29

ANNUAL MEETING: In Jun.

SHAREHOLDERS: N/A

INSTITUTIONAL HOLDINGS:
No. of Institutions: 7
Shares Held: 87,667

REGISTRAR(S): The R-M Trust Company, Toronto.

TRANSFER AGENT(S): The R-M Trust Company, Toronto.

357

ICTS INTERNATIONAL N.V.

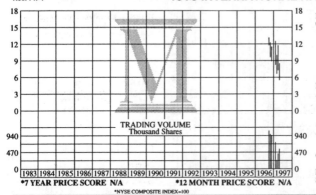

18 15 12 9 6 3 0

TRADING VOLUME
Thousand Shares

940
470
0

1983|1984|1985|1986|1987|1988|1989|1990|1991|1992|1993|1994|1995|1996|1997

*7 YEAR PRICE SCORE N/A   *12 MONTH PRICE SCORE N/A

*NYSE COMPOSITE INDEX=100

INTERIM EARNINGS (Per Share, US$):

Qtr.	Mar.	June	Sept.	Dec.
1996	------------------	1.33	------------------	

INTERIM DIVIDENDS (Per Share):

Amt.	Decl.	Ex.	Rec.	Pay.
	No dividends paid.			

CAPITALIZATION (12/31/95):

	($000)	(%)
Long Term Debt	237	6.8
Stockholders' Equity	3,237	93.2
Total	3,474	100.0

RECENT DEVELOPMENTS: For the year ended 12/31/96, net income advanced to $6.8 million from $1.1 million in the prior year. Revenues were $38.9 million, up 30.6% from $29.8 million a year earlier. Gross profit grew 32.9% to $6.3 million from $4.8 million in the previous year. For the quarter ended 12/31/96, net income was $5.0 million compared with $430,000 in the corresponding 1995 quarter. Revenues jumped 37.0% to $10.4 million from $7.6 million in the fourth quarter of 1995. In March 1997, the Company signed a five-year contract with a major U.S. carrier for the installation and operation of its Automated Profiling System in all the carrier's European operations.

BUSINESS

ICTS INTERNATIONAL N.V. is engaged in providing aviation security services, primarily serving the European operations of the major U.S. carriers. The Company's principal service is the implementation of passenger risk evaluation and classification procedures, generally described as "profiling." The Company is also engaged in security consulting, training and auditing for airlines, airports and in the provision of other security services.

ANNUAL EARNINGS

	12/31/95	12/31/94	12/31/95	12/31/94
	-------------US $-------------		-----------Guilders-----------	
Earnings Per Share	0.28	d0.09	0.45	d0.16

ANNUAL FINANCIAL DATA

RECORD OF EARNINGS (IN THOUSANDS):

	12/31/95	12/31/94	12/31/95	12/31/94
Total Revenues	29,826	23,738	47,959	41,205
Costs & Expenses	28,192	23,701	45,332	41,140
Operating Income	1,634	37	2,627	64
Income Bef Income Tax	1,329	d242	2,137	d420
Income Tax	339	37	545	64
Eq. Earnings in Affils.	123	d91	198	d158
Net Income	1,113	d370	1,790	d642
Average Shares Outstg	4,025	4,025	4,025	4,025

BALANCE SHEET (IN THOUSANDS):

Cash & Cash Equivalents	1,899	1,344	3,054	2,333
Receivables, Net	4,713	3,376	7,578	5,860
Gross Property	1,263	1,032	2,031	1,791
Accumulated Depreciation	738	576	1,187	1,000
Long Term Debt	237	402	381	698
Stockholders' Equity	3,237	2,124	5,205	3,687
Total Assets	13,908	11,608	22,364	20,149
Total Current Assets	7,856	5,750	12,632	9,981
Total Current Liabilities	8,799	8,090	14,149	14,043
Net Working Capital	d943	d2,340	d1,516	d4,062
Year End Shs Outstg	4,000	4,000	4,000	4,000

STATISTICAL RECORD:

Return on Equity %	34.38	...		
Return on Assets %	8.00	...		
Operating Profit Margin %	5.48	0.16		
Net Profit Margin %	3.73	...		
Book Value Per Share	0.81	0.53		

Converted at 1995, US$0.6219= 1 Netherlands guilder; 1994, US$0.5761= 1 Netherlands guilder

OFFICERS:
L. Zouker, C.E.O.
Y. Navon, C.O.O.
J. Yahav, V.P.-Intl.
J. Neuhaus, C.F.O. & Treas.

INCORPORATED: Netherlands

PRINCIPAL OFFICE: Binderij 7G ZH
Amstelveen Netherlands NL-1185

TELEPHONE NUMBER: 20-643-8449

NO. OF EMPLOYEES: 1,200 (approx.)

ANNUAL MEETING: N/A

SHAREHOLDERS: 5,400,000

INSTITUTIONAL HOLDINGS:
No. of Institutions: N/A
Shares Held: N/A

REGISTRAR(S): American Stock Transfer & Trust Company of New York, New York.

TRANSFER AGENT(S): American Stock Transfer & Trust Company of New York, New York.

I.I.S. INTELLIGENT INFORMATION

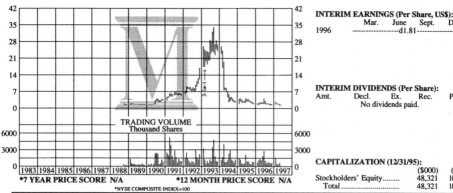

INTERIM EARNINGS (Per Share, US$):

	Mar.	June	Sept.	Dec.
1996		----------------d1.81----------------		

INTERIM DIVIDENDS (Per Share):

Amt.	Decl.	Ex.	Rec.	Pay.
	No dividends paid.			

TRADING VOLUME
Thousand Shares

1983 1984 1985 1986 1987 1988 1989 1990 1991 1992 1993 1994 1995 1996 1997

*7 YEAR PRICE SCORE N/A   *12 MONTH PRICE SCORE N/A

*NYSE COMPOSITE INDEX=100

CAPITALIZATION (12/31/95):

	($000)	(%)
Stockholders' Equity........	48,321	100.0
Total	48,321	100.0

RECENT DEVELOPMENTS: For the year ended 12/31/96, the Company reported a loss of $25.2 million compared with $18.8 million in the corresponding period a year earlier. Revenues were $63.0 million versus $76.5 million in 1995. Earnings were pressured by management changes and restructuring in the first three quarters of 1996. Restructuring and reorganization expenses totaled $9.6 million for the period. Gross profit for the year declined 34% to $12.5 million from $16.8 million in 1995. For the quarter ended 12/31/96, the Company reported a loss of $3.5 million compared with $3.9 million in the year-earlier period. Revenues were $14.8 million, down 29% to $20.8 million in 1995. Maintenance and services revenues totaled $1.9 million, down from $3.2 million in the year-earlier period. Gross profit for the quarter fell to $2.6 million versus $4.0 million.

BUSINESS

I.I.S. INTELLIGENT INFORMA-TION and its subsidiaries design, develop, manufacture, market and service data communication, networking and intelligent peripheral products serving a variety of hosts, local area networks ("LANs") and wide area networks ("WANs") within the midrange and mainframe International Business Machines Corp., IBM-compatible, UNIX-compatible and Digital Equipment Corp. environments.

ANNUAL EARNINGS

	12/31/95	12/31/94	12/31/95	12/31/94
	-------------US $-------------		-----------NIS-----------	
Earnings Per Share	d1.35	d0.66	d4.25	d1.99

ANNUAL FINANCIAL DATA

RECORD OF EARNINGS (IN THOUSANDS):

	12/31/95	12/31/94	12/31/95	12/31/94
Total Revenues	76,481	91,781	240,733	276,949
Costs & Expenses	98,150	101,819	308,939	307,239
Operating Income	d21,669	d10,038	d68,206	d30,290
Income Bef Income Tax	d18,372	d9,007	d57,828	d27,179
Income Tax	400	226	1,259	682
Net Income	d18,772	d9,233	d59,087	d27,861
Average Shares Outstg	13,948	13,939	13,948	13,939

BALANCE SHEET (IN THOUSANDS):

Cash & Cash Equivalents	13,321	3,907	41,929	11,789
Receivables, Net	22,137	30,372	69,679	91,648
Inventories	20,046	26,282	63,097	79,306
Gross Property	12,840	11,915	40,415	35,954
Accumulated Depreciation	6,590	5,341	20,743	16,116
Stockholders' Equity	48,321	66,976	152,096	202,100
Total Assets	67,633	83,606	212,883	252,281
Total Current Assets	55,504	60,561	174,706	182,743
Total Current Liabilities	19,093	16,556	60,098	49,958
Net Working Capital	36,411	44,005	114,608	132,785
Year End Shs Outstg	13,948	13,944	13,948	13,944

STATISTICAL RECORD:

Return on Equity %	...	...		
Return on Assets %	...	...		
Operating Profit Margin %	...	...		
Net Profit Margin %	...	...		
Book Value Per Share	3.46	4.80		

Converted at 1995, US$0.3177= 1 Israeli Shekel; 1994, US$0.3314= 1 Israeli Shekel

OFFICERS:
J. Herbst, Chmn. & C.E.O.
J. Shemesh, Pres. & V.P.
Y. Feigenbaum, C.O.O. & Man. Dir., V.P.
I. Eder, V.P. & C.F.O.
E. Shopira, E.V.P.

INCORPORATED: 1980

PRINCIPAL OFFICE: Yokneam Industrial Park, P.O. Box 110, Yokneam Israel

TELEPHONE NUMBER: 972-4-989 2077

NO. OF EMPLOYEES: 450

ANNUAL MEETING: In Jul.

SHAREHOLDERS: 500 (approx.)

INSTITUTIONAL HOLDINGS:
No. of Institutions: 5
Shares Held: 76,010

REGISTRAR(S): N/A

TRANSFER AGENT(S): American Stock Transfer & Trust Co., New York.

IMAX CORPORATION

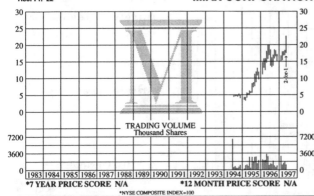

INTERIM EARNINGS (Per Share, US$):

Qtr.	Mar.	June	Sept.	Dec.
1996	0.10	0.11	0.14	0.16

INTERIM DIVIDENDS (Per Share):

Amt.	Decl.	Ex.	Rec.	Pay.
2-for-1	5/06/97	5/27/97	5/22/97	5/23/97

TRADING VOLUME
Thousand Shares

1983|1984|1985|1986|1987|1988|1989|1990|1991|1992|1993|1994|1995|1996|1997
*7 YEAR PRICE SCORE N/A   *12 MONTH PRICE SCORE N/A
*NYSE COMPOSITE INDEX=100

CAPITALIZATION (12/31/96):

	($000)	(%)
Minority Interest	1,593	0.7
Long-Term Debt	165,867	72.3
Stockholders' Equity	54,841	23.9
Deferred Income Tax	6,081	2.6
Preferred Stock..................	1,184	0.5
Total	229,566	100.0

RECENT DEVELOPMENTS: For the year ended 12/31/96, net income advanced to $15.4 million from $3.7 million a year earlier. Total revenues were $129.8 million, up 46.7% from $88.5 million in the previous year. Systems revenues soared 65.4% to $86.0 million from $52.0 million as the Company recognized revenues on 26 theatre systems as compared with 11 theatre systems in 1995. Revenues from films declined 1.6% to $28.4 million from $28.8 million in the previous year. Earnings from operations were $36.9 million compared with $12.9 million the year before. During 1996, the Company signed contracts for 29 IMAX theatre systems valued at a record $89.6 milllion, a 38.8% over the $64.6 million in 1995. As of 12/31/96, there was a backlog of 45 theater systems (including three upgrades) representing projected revenues of $131.8 million. Not included in backlog are signings for 29 IMAX Ridefilm systems, including six upgrades.

BUSINESS

IMAX CORPORATION is engaged in the design, manufacture and marketing of proprietary projection and sound systems for IMAX theaters; the development, production and distribution of films shown in the IMAX theater network; the design and supply of motion simulation theaters and production of films for movie rides; and the provision of other services to the IMAX theater network including designing and manufacturing IMAX camera equipment for rental to film makers, providing film post-production image quality assurance and providing ongoing maintenance services for the IMAX projection and sound systems. As of 3/31/97, there were 153 IMAX theatres in operation in 22 countries.

ANNUAL EARNINGS

	12/31/96	12/31/95	12/31/96	12/31/95
	US $		C $	
Earnings Per Share	0.51	0.12	0.69	0.16

ANNUAL FINANCIAL DATA

RECORD OF EARNINGS (IN THOUSANDS):

	12/31/96	12/31/95	12/31/96	12/31/95
Total Revenues	129,838	88,497	177,593	120,749
Costs & Expenses	90,245	73,081	123,437	99,715
Amort of Intangibles	2,708	2,541	3,704	3,467
Operating Income	36,885	12,875	50,451	17,567
Income Bef Income Tax	30,580	9,108	41,827	12,427
Income Tax	13,579	5,458	18,573	7,447
Minority Interests	1,593	...	2,179	...
Net Income	15,408	3,650	21,075	4,980
Average Shares Outstg	29,924	29,394	29,924	29,394
BALANCE SHEET (IN THOUSANDS):				
Cash & Cash Equivalents	102,589	50,747	140,321	69,241
Receivables, Net	17,995	10,526	24,614	14,362
Inventories	21,292	18,730	29,123	25,556
Net investment in leases	34,494	21,765	47,181	29,697
Gross Property	49,716	34,578	68,002	47,180
Accumulated Depreciation	11,925	6,855	16,311	9,353
Film Assets	19,050	6,733	26,057	9,187
Long-Term Debt	165,867	69,597	226,873	94,961
Stockholders' Equity	54,841	57,486	75,012	78,436
Total Assets	308,744	194,515	422,301	265,405
Total Current Assets	148,203	84,286	202,712	115,003
Total Current Liabilities	65,061	55,581	88,991	75,837
Net Working Capital	83,142	28,705	113,722	39,166
Year End Shs Outstg	27,886	28,154	27,886	28,154
STATISTICAL RECORD:				
Return on Equity %	28.10	6.35		
Return on Assets %	4.99	1.88		
Operating Profit Margin %	28.41	14.55		
Net Profit Margin %	11.87	4.12		
Book Value Per Share	1.97	2.04		

Converted at 1996, US$0.7311= 1 Canadian $; 1995, US$0.7329= 1 Canadian $

OFFICERS:
B. J. Wechsler, Chmn. & Co. C.E.O.
R. L. Gelfond, Vice-Chmn. & Co. C.E.O.
J. M. Davison, Exec. V.P. Operations & C.F.O.

INCORPORATED: N/A

PRINCIPAL OFFICE: 2525 Speakman Drive
Sheridan Science and Technology Park
Mississauga, Ontario, Canada L5K 1B1

TELEPHONE NUMBER: 905-403-6500

NO. OF EMPLOYEES: 361

ANNUAL MEETING: In May

SHAREHOLDERS: N/A

INSTITUTIONAL HOLDINGS:
No. of Institutions: 54
Shares Held: 7,200,000

REGISTRAR(S): Chemical Mellon
Shareholder Services, New York and
Montreal Trust, Ontario.

TRANSFER AGENT(S): Chemical Mellon
Shareholder Services, New York and
Montreal Trust, Ontario.

IMPERIAL GINSENG PRODUCTS LTD.

YIELD ...
P/E RATIO 0.9

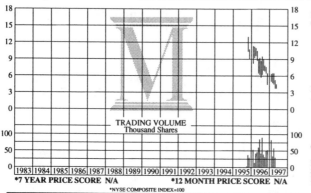

INTERIM EARNINGS (Per Share, C$):

Qtr.	Sept.	Dec.	Mar.	Jun.
1994-95	d0.62	0.73	0.55	d0.03
1995-96	d0.26	d1.54	2.27	0.90
1996-97	0.38	2.70	...	...

INTERIM DIVIDENDS (Per Share):

Amt.	Decl.	Ex.	Rec.	Pay.
	No dividends paid.			

TRADING VOLUME
Thousand Shares

1983|1984|1985|1986|1987|1988|1989|1990|1991|1992|1993|1994|1995|1996|1997
*7 YEAR PRICE SCORE N/A   *12 MONTH PRICE SCORE N/A
*NYSE COMPOSITE INDEX=100

CAPITALIZATION (6/30/96):

	($000)	(%)
Long-Term Debt	13,562	47.5
Stockholders' Equity........	14,503	50.8
Deferred Income Tax	494	1.7
Total	28,559	100.0

RECENT DEVELOPMENTS: For the quarter ended 12/31/96, the Company reported a net loss of C$4.0 million (US$2.8 million) compared with a net loss of C$1.4 million (US$1.4 million) the year before. Total revenue declined 45.5% to C$1.9 million (US$1.4 million) from C$3.5 million (US$2.6 million) a year earlier. Results for the recent quarter were negatively affected by bad debt expense associated with the cancellation of a ginseng sales agreement that was entered into in the Spring of 1996. Lower ginseng prices also contributed to the quarter's performance. During the quarter, the Company launched a new product, the Imperial Life brand of fresh, or non-dried, North American ginseng roots. The Company expects to expand distribution of fresh roots in Canada, the U.S. and overseas.

BUSINESS

IMPERIAL GINSENG PRODUCTS LTD. cultivates, processes and markets ginseng products throughout North America and Asia. The Company produces two forms of ginseng: American Ginseng and Asian Ginseng. American Ginseng is used to reduce stress, strengthen internal organs and as a cooling tonic. Asian Ginseng is used as a tonic for blood. Imperial produces the ginseng in teas, candies, capsules and fresh roots.

ANNUAL EARNINGS

	6/30/96	6/30/95	6/30/96	6/30/95
	--- US $ ---		--- C $ ---	
Earnings Per Share	1.00	0.46	1.37	0.63

ANNUAL FINANCIAL DATA

RECORD OF EARNINGS (IN THOUSANDS):

	6/30/96	6/30/95	6/30/96	6/30/95
Total Revenues	13,808	9,113	18,830	12,506
Costs & Expenses	11,845	8,056	16,154	11,056
Depreciation & Amort	149	245	203	337
Operating Income	1,814	811	2,473	1,113
Income Bef Income Tax	1,814	811	2,473	1,113
Income Tax	329	232	449	319
Minority Interests	...	cr104	...	cr143
Net Income	1,484	683	2,024	937
Average Shares Outstg	1,478	1,478	1,478	1,478

BALANCE SHEET (IN THOUSANDS):

Cash & Cash Equivalents	2,564	1,321	3,496	1,814
Receivables, Net	6,308	5,131	8,603	7,041
Inventories	56	90	76	124
Gross Property	5,761	5,392	7,856	7,399
Accumulated Depreciation	1,421	920	1,938	1,262
Long-Term Debt	13,562	9,425	18,494	12,934
Stockholders' Equity	14,503	12,937	19,778	17,754
Total Assets	29,641	23,948	40,421	32,864
Total Current Assets	11,859	11,460	16,173	15,727
Total Current Liabilities	1,026	1,373	1,400	1,885
Net Working Capital	10,833	10,087	14,773	13,842
Year End Shs Outstg	1,478	1,478	1,478	1,478

STATISTICAL RECORD:

Return on Equity %	10.23	5.28		
Return on Assets %	5.01	2.85		
Operating Profit Margin %	13.13	8.90		
Net Profit Margin %	10.75	7.49		
Book Value Per Share	9.81	8.75		

Converted at 1996, US$0.7333= 1 Canadian $; 1995, US$0.7287= 1 Canadian $

OFFICERS:
S. P. McCoach, C.E.O. & Sec.
H. R. Cartwright, Pres.
L. Hill, C.F.O.
J. Chang, V.P.

INCORPORATED: Canada, April, 1989

PRINCIPAL OFFICE: Suite 1601 650 West Georgia Street Vancouver Canada V6B 4N7

TELEPHONE NUMBER: 604-689-8863

NO. OF EMPLOYEES: N/A

ANNUAL MEETING: In Dec.

SHAREHOLDERS: N/A

INSTITUTIONAL HOLDINGS:
No. of Institutions: N/A
Shares Held: N/A

REGISTRAR(S): Pacific Corporate Trust, Vancouver, British Columbia

TRANSFER AGENT(S): Pacific Corporate Trust, Vancouver, British Columbia

INDIGO N.V.

YIELD ...
P/E RATIO ...

7 YEAR PRICE SCORE N/A
12 MONTH PRICE SCORE N/A
NYSE COMPOSITE INDEX=100

TRADING VOLUME
Thousand Shares

INTERIM EARNINGS (Per Share, US$):

1996	------------------d1.33------------------

INTERIM DIVIDENDS (Per Share):

Amt.	Decl.	Ex.	Rec.	Pay.
	No dividends paid.			

CAPITALIZATION (12/31/96):

	($000)	(%)
Conv. Pfd. Stk.................	175	0.3
Stockholders' Equity........	56,818	99.7
Total	56,993	100.0

RECENT DEVELOPMENTS: For the year ended 12/31/96, the Company incurred a net loss of $73.8 million compared with a net loss of $40.5 million the year before. Results for 1996 included litigation settlement expenses totaling $6.8 million. Total revenues were $103.9 million, down 37.3% from $165.8 million a year earlier. The decline in revenues resulted from the continuation of the slower-than-expected development of the short-run color printing market during most of 1996, the weakness of the Company's sales activity in North America, as well as the impact of a reduced level of activity with the Company's Japanese distributor. Product sales fell 31.1% to $100.4 million from $145.7 million in the prior year. Revenues from license fees, royalties and other was $3.4 million versus $20.0 million in 1995.

BUSINESS

INDIGO N.V., a Netherlands corporation with wholly-owned subsidiaries in Israel and the United States, is engaged in the research, development, production, marketing, distribution and service of electronic color printing products. These products include the E-PRINT 1000+ Digital Offset color press for short-run commercial printing; the Omnius One-Shot Color press for label, packaging and decorative printing; peripherals such as the E-RIP group of off-line image processors and Imaging Products including Indigo's proprietary ElectroInk products. Indigo's Digital Offset color technology combines the quality of liquid ink based offset printing with the performance advantages of electronic imaging. Indigo, E-PRINT, E PRINT 1000+, ElectroInk, Digital Offset Color, Omnius, One-Shot Color, and E-RIP are trademarks or registered trademarks of the Company.

ANNUAL EARNINGS

	12/31/96	12/31/95	12/31/94
		----US $----	
Earnings Per Share	d1.33	d0.95	d0.46

ANNUAL FINANCIAL DATA

RECORD OF EARNINGS (IN THOUSANDS):

Total Revenues	103,873	165,766	80,758
Costs & Expenses	173,829	200,123	99,953
Operating Income	d69,956	d34,357	d19,195
Income Bef Income Tax	d70,207	d36,637	d18,569
Income Tax	3,602	3,870	2,358
Net Income	d79,281	d40,507	d20,927
Net Extraordinary Items	...	...	d6,975
Average Shares Outstg	59,823	42,622	45,380

BALANCE SHEET (IN THOUSANDS):

Cash & Cash Equivalents	70,600	36,122	34,047
Receivables, Net	21,811	27,892	37,103
Inventories	27,380	41,734	17,425
Gross Property	a24,574	45,667	28,193
Accumulated Depreciation	...	18,140	11,583
Long-Term Debt	...	30,000	...
Stockholders' Equity	56,993	14,437	26,803
Total Assets	163,666	137,479	110,959
Total Current Assets	136,043	106,836	89,638
Total Current Liabilities	102,830	90,859	65,607
Net Working Capital	33,213	15,977	24,031
Year End Shs Outstg	55,603	53,846	50,232

STATISTICAL RECORD:

Return on Equity %	...	...	...
Return on Assets %	...	...	...
Operating Profit Margin %	...	...	...
Net Profit Margin %	...	...	...
Book Value Per Share	1.02	0.27	0.53
a-Gross property and equipment.			

OFFICERS:
B. Landa, Chmn.
S. Nimrodi, C.F.O.

INCORPORATED: Netherlands, 1977

PRINCIPAL OFFICE: Limburglaan 5, Maastricht Netherlands 6229 GA

TELEPHONE NUMBER: N/A

NO. OF EMPLOYEES: 800

ANNUAL MEETING: In June

SHAREHOLDERS: N/A

INSTITUTIONAL HOLDINGS:
No. of Institutions: N/A
Shares Held: N/A

REGISTRAR(S): N/A

TRANSFER AGENT(S): The Bank of New York, New York.

INTELECT COMMUNICATIONS SYSTEMS LTD.

YIELD ...
P/E RATIO ...

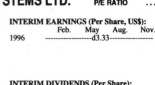

INTERIM EARNINGS (Per Share, US$):

	Feb.	May	Aug.	Nov.
1996		----d3.33----		

INTERIM DIVIDENDS (Per Share):

Amt.	Decl.	Ex.	Rec.	Pay.
No dividends paid.				

TRADING VOLUME
Thousand Shares

1983 1984 1985 1986 1987 1988 1989 1990 1991 1992 1993 1994 1995 1996 1997

*7 YEAR PRICE SCORE N/A   *12 MONTH PRICE SCORE N/A

*NYSE COMPOSITE INDEX=100

CAPITALIZATION (12/31/96):

	($000)	(%)
Long-Term Debt	18,210	69.3
Stockholders' Equity	7,731	29.4
Deferred Income Tax	267	1.0
Capital Lease Oblgs.	59	0.2
Total	26,267	100.0

RECENT DEVELOPMENTS: For the year ended 12/31/96, the Company reported a net loss of $35.0 million. The net loss included asset writedowns of $4.2 million associated with the videoconferencing business where market information was delayed by the condition of purchased technology, a $1.8 million charge for liquidating European operations and an expense of $56,000 from discontinued operations. Reve-nues for the year were $10.0 million. Gross loss amounted to $949,000. Comparisons to 1995 results are not possible nor meaningful, as the Company changed its line of business and acquired new business operations. Near-term results should be favorably affected by the customers' response to the functionality and cost-effectiveness of ICOMF's new products.

BUSINESS

INTELECT COMMUNICATIONS SYSTEMS LIMITED is an international provider of multi/media voice, data and video products for communications-critical applications. ICOMF's products include digital switching and fiber optic multiplexing equipment.

ANNUAL EARNINGS

	12/31/96	① 12/31/95	10/31/95	10/31/94
		----US $----		
Earnings Per Share	d3.33	d0.26	d1.12	d0.26

ANNUAL FINANCIAL DATA

RECORD OF EARNINGS (IN THOUSANDS):

Net Revenues	10,005	924	2,198	20
Costs & Expenses	52,901	3,700	7,392	588
Income From Contin. Ops.	d42,896	d2,776	d5,194	d38
Income Tax	87	...	...	...
Net Income	d43,039	d3,012	12,822	2,872
Average Shares Outstg	12,943	11,385	11,451	11,061

BALANCE SHEET (IN THOUSANDS):

Cash & Cash Equivalents	5,717	15,039	20,936	2,571
Receivables, Net	2,427	1,975	713	28
Inventories	2,978	2,537	2,814	...
Gross Property	5,379	2,028	1,442	...
Accumulated Depreciation	1,094	189	162	...
Long-Term Debt	18,210	368	365	...
Stockholders' Equity	7,731	25,540	28,266	11,903
Total Assets	36,018	31,239	35,722	12,172
Total Current Assets	11,594	19,957	24,587	2,599
Total Current Liabilities	9,810	5,331	7,091	269
Net Working Capital	1,784	14,626	17,496	2,330
Year End Shs Outstg	15,028	11,385	11,385	10,583

STATISTICAL RECORD:

Return on Equity %	...	...	45.4	24.1
Return on Assets %	...	...	35.9	23.6
Operating Profit Margin %	...	...	...	...
Net Profit Margin %	...	...	N.A.	N.A.
Book Value Per Share	0.51	2.24	2.48	1.12

① For two months.

OFFICERS:
H. M. Frietsch, Chmn. & C.E.O.
A. v. Liechenstein
P. P. Sudan Jr.

INCORPORATED: Bermuda, Apr., 1980

PRINCIPAL OFFICE: 1100 Executive Drive
Richardson TX 75081

TELEPHONE NUMBER: 972-367-2100

NO. OF EMPLOYEES: 300

ANNUAL MEETING: August 13, 1997

SHAREHOLDERS: 8,600

INSTITUTIONAL HOLDINGS:
No. of Institutions: N/A
Shares Held: N/A

REGISTRAR(S): American Stock Transfer &
Trust Co., New York

TRANSFER AGENT(S): American Stock
Transfer & Trust Co., New York

NASDAQ SYMBOL MURXF
Rec. Pr. 7

INTERNATIONAL MUREX TECHNOLOGIES CORP.

YIELD ...
P/E RATIO 63.6

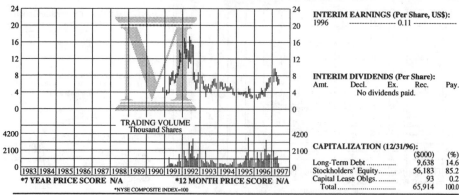

7 YEAR PRICE SCORE N/A   **12 MONTH PRICE SCORE N/A**

*NYSE COMPOSITE INDEX=100

INTERIM EARNINGS (Per Share, US$):
1996 ------------------ 0.11 ------------------

INTERIM DIVIDENDS (Per Share):
Amt.   Decl.   Ex.   Rec.   Pay.
No dividends paid.

CAPITALIZATION (12/31/96):

	($000)	(%)
Long-Term Debt	9,638	14.6
Stockholders' Equity	56,183	85.2
Capital Lease Oblgs.	93	0.2
Total	65,914	100.0

RECENT DEVELOPMENTS: For the year ended 12/31/96, net income was $1.8 million compared with a loss of $6.6 million in 1995. Revenues increased 9.2% to $100.9 million. Results in 1996 included restructuring expenses of $2.1 million, while results in 1995 included a charge of $3.1 million related to the settlement of litigation. The Company noted that its screening business remained strong during 1996 and was further enhanced by new products introduced during the year. In February 1996, the Company announced its expansion into the emerging diagnostics monitoring market. In 1996, the Companys monitoring products business increased to in excess of $9.0 million and management anticipates continued rapid growth in this area in 1997. In addition, the Company noted that it will continue to actively seek out acquisitions, strategic business alliances and other opportunities that will support the Companys future.

BUSINESS

INTERNATIONAL MUREX TECH- NOLOGIES CORP., through its subsidiaries, develops, manufactures and markets medical diagnostic products and provides medical services for the screening, diagnosis and monitoring of infectious diseases and other medical conditions. The Company performs research, develops and manufactures in vitro diagnostic products in the United Kingdom and markets them throughout the world, using 15 distribution centers supporting a direct sales force in 35 countries and a distributor network in more than 100 countries. The Company also distributes products manufactured by third parties.

ANNUAL EARNINGS

	12/31/96	12/31/95	12/31/96	12/31/95
	--US $--		--C $--	
Earnings Per Share	0.11	d0.40	0.15	d0.55

ANNUAL FINANCIAL DATA

RECORD OF EARNINGS (IN THOUSANDS):

	12/31/96	12/31/95	12/31/96	12/31/95
Total Revenues	100,851	92,394	137,944	126,066
Costs & Expenses	97,425	96,272	133,258	131,358
Operating Income	3,426	d3,878	4,686	d5,291
Income Bef Income Tax	2,865	d6,128	3,919	d8,361
Income Tax	1,016	482	1,390	658
Net Income	1,849	d6,610	2,529	d9,019
Average Shares Outstg	16,511	16,381	16,511	16,381

BALANCE SHEET (IN THOUSANDS):

Cash & Cash Equivalents	9,723	15,771	13,299	21,519
Receivables, Net	33,718	34,836	46,120	47,532
Inventories	21,534	16,941	29,454	23,115
Gross Property	27,425	22,682	37,512	30,948
Accumulated Depreciation	17,334	13,451	23,709	18,353
Long-Term Debt	9,731	246	13,310	336
Stockholders' Equity	56,183	49,531	76,847	67,582
Total Assets	95,113	85,748	130,096	116,998
Total Current Assets	70,597	70,399	96,563	96,055
Total Current Liabilities	29,122	35,891	39,833	48,971
Net Working Capital	41,475	34,508	56,730	47,084
Year End Shs Outstg	16,293	16,689	16,293	16,689

STATISTICAL RECORD:

Return on Equity %	3.29	...		
Return on Assets %	1.94	...		
Operating Profit Margin %	3.40	...		
Net Profit Margin %	1.83	...		
Book Value Per Share	3.45	2.97		

Converted at 1996, US$0.7311= 1 Canadian $; 1995, US$0.7329= 1 Canadian $

OFFICERS:
F. M. Warren, Chmn.
C. R. Cusick, Vice-Chmn., Pres. & C.E.O.
S. C. Ramsey, V.P. & C.F.O.
J. Gilmer, Corp. Sec.

INCORPORATED: In Canada

PRINCIPAL OFFICE: 2255 B. Queen Street East Suite 828 Toronto, Ontario Canada M4E 1G3

TELEPHONE NUMBER: 519-836-8016

NO. OF EMPLOYEES: 641

ANNUAL MEETING: In May

SHAREHOLDERS: 702 (approx.)

INSTITUTIONAL HOLDINGS:
No. of Institutions: 12
Shares Held: 4,455,013

REGISTRAR(S): N/A

TRANSFER AGENT(S): The Bank of New York, New York.

NASDAQ SYMBOL IRPPF
Rec. Pr. 4⅜

INTERNATIONAL PETROLEUM CORP.

YIELD ...
P/E RATIO ...

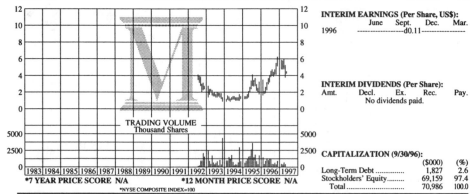

*7 YEAR PRICE SCORE N/A   *12 MONTH PRICE SCORE N/A

*NYSE COMPOSITE INDEX=100

TRADING VOLUME
Thousand Shares

INTERIM EARNINGS (Per Share, US$):

	June	Sept.	Dec.	Mar.
1996		d0.11		

INTERIM DIVIDENDS (Per Share):

Amt.	Decl.	Ex.	Rec.	Pay.
	No dividends paid.			

CAPITALIZATION (9/30/96):

	($000)	(%)
Long-Term Debt	1,827	2.6
Stockholders' Equity........	69,159	97.4
Total	70,986	100.0

RECENT DEVELOPMENTS: For the year ended 9/30/96, the Company reported a net loss of $4.4 million compared with net income of $490,801 in the corresponding period of 1995. The 1995 results included a $7.9 million gain from the sale of the Welton subsidiary and a $1.7 million loss on the sale of the Sands subsidiary. Total revenues declined 27.0% to $12.9 million from $17.7 million a year earlier. This was partly attributable to the reduction in condensate

sales revenues from the Bukha Field to $9.4 million from $10.6 million in 1995. A total of 507,792 net barrels of condensate were sold at an average price of $18.48 per barrel compared with 629,213 net barrels at an average price of $16.85 per barrel in the previous year. Moreover, liquid propane gas sales declined to 63,759 barrels at an average price of $10.54 per barrel versus 66,990 barrels at an average price of $10.01 per barrel in 1995.

BUSINESS

INTERNATIONAL PETROLEUM CORP. is engaged in the acquisition, exploration and development of interests in oil and gas projects with land holdings in seven countries. The Company also has investments in projects with similar objectives. Currently, IRPPF is enaged in a major development project in Malaysia.

ANNUAL EARNINGS

	9/30/96	9/30/95	9/30/96	9/30/95
	--------------US $--------------		------------C $------------	
Earnings Per Share	d0.11	0.01	d0.15	0.01

ANNUAL FINANCIAL DATA

RECORD OF EARNINGS (IN THOUSANDS):

Total Revenues	12,927	17,707	17,619	23,761
Costs & Expenses	13,468	18,915	18,357	25,383
Depreciation & Amort	3,822	5,650	5,210	7,582
Operating Income	d4,363	d6,859	d5,947	d9,204
Income Bef Income Tax	d4,553	301	d6,206	404
Minority Interests	cr138	cr189	cr188	cr254
Net Income	d4,416	491	d6,018	659
Average Shares Outstg	41,706	40,477	41,706	40,477

BALANCE SHEET (IN THOUSANDS):

Cash & Cash Equivalents	26,267	14,393	35,801	19,314
Receivables, Net	6,420	17,426	8,750	23,800
Inventories	289	267	394	359
Gross Property	1,605	1,426	2,188	1,913
Accumulated Depreciation	1,278	1,044	1,742	1,400
Long-Term Debt	1,827	6,622	2,490	8,886
Stockholders' Equity	69,159	68,100	94,261	91,385
Total Assets	92,246	91,686	125,727	123,035
Total Current Assets	33,202	46,265	45,253	62,084
Total Current Liabilities	9,857	8,251	13,435	11,073
Net Working Capital	23,345	38,014	31,819	51,012
Year End Shs Outstg	43,992	41,402	43,992	41,402

STATISTICAL RECORD:

Return on Equity %	...	0.72		
Return on Assets %	...	0.54		
Operating Profit Margin %	...	...		
Net Profit Margin %	...	2.77		
Book Value Per Share	1.57	1.64		

Converted at 1996, US$0.7337= 1 Canadian $; 1995, US$0.7452= 1 Canadian $

OFFICERS:
A. H. Lundin, Chmn.
I. H. Lundin, Pres. & C.E.O.
N. R. McCue, Ex. V.P. & C.F.O.
S. M. Kansky, Corp. Sec.

INCORPORATED: Jun., 1985

PRINCIPAL OFFICE: Suite 1320, 885 West Georgia Street, Vancouver British Columbia, Canada V6C 3E8

TELEPHONE NUMBER: 604-689-7842

NO. OF EMPLOYEES: N/A

ANNUAL MEETING: In Feb.

SHAREHOLDERS: N/A

INSTITUTIONAL HOLDINGS:
No. of Institutions: 2
Shares Held: 428,000

REGISTRAR(S): Montreal Trust Co. of Canada, Toronto; Independent Registrars Group Limited, Kent, England.

TRANSFER AGENT(S): Montreal Trust Co. of Canada, Toronto; Independent Registrars Group Limited, Kent, England.

INTERNATIONAL VERIFACT, INC.

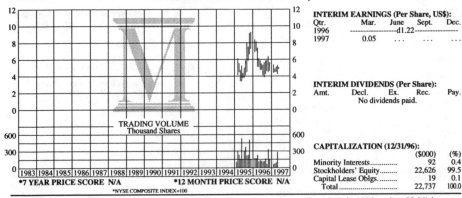

INTERIM EARNINGS (Per Share, US$):

Qtr.	Mar.	June	Sept.	Dec.
1996		-----d1.22-----		
1997	0.05	...	...	...

INTERIM DIVIDENDS (Per Share):

Amt.	Decl.	Ex.	Rec.	Pay.
		No dividends paid.		

CAPITALIZATION (12/31/96):

	($000)	(%)
Minority Interests.............	92	0.4
Stockholders' Equity........	22,626	99.5
Capital Lease Oblgs.	19	0.1
Total.............................	22,737	100.0

*7 YEAR PRICE SCORE N/A   *12 MONTH PRICE SCORE N/A
*NYSE COMPOSITE INDEX=100

RECENT DEVELOPMENTS: For the quarter ended 3/31/97, net income was $401,000 compared with a net loss of $10.5 million in the corresponding 1996 quarter. Results for the 1996 quarter included a $9.3 million write-off of goodwill. Total revenues were $15.3 million, up 69.1% from $9.0 million in the year-earlier quarter. The significant increase in revenues was attributable to a recovery of Canadian revenues from order delays in 1996, and an 80.0% increase in U.S. revenues, including sales from National Transaction Network, which was acquired in September 1996. Gross profit as a percentage of sales was 34.5% versus 30.9% in the 1996 quarter. Results increased significantly due to the Company's new contracts with the Bank of Montreal and its U.S. partners.

BUSINESS

INTERNATIONAL VERIFACT, INC. is primarily engaged in the design, development, sale and export of electronic payment solutions for use in electronic funds transfer and point of sale applications. Hardware and software products include point-of-sale debit/credit/EFT/EBT termi-nals, check readers, smart card readers and secure PIN entry devices. The Company's customers include super-markets, the hospitality industry, the retail petroleum industry, department stores, super drugstores and ware-house chains. Products are sold through processors, independent sales organizations and value added resellers.

ANNUAL EARNINGS

	12/31/96	12/31/95	12/31/96	12/31/95
	----US $----		----C $----	
Earnings Per Share	d1.22	0.38	d1.67	0.52

ANNUAL FINANCIAL DATA

RECORD OF EARNINGS (IN THOUSANDS):

	12/31/96	12/31/95	12/31/96	12/31/95
Total Revenues	34,947	44,349	47,801	60,511
Costs & Expenses	34,479	39,951	47,160	54,511
Depreciation & Amort	1,189	2,000	1,626	2,729
Operating Income	d720	2,397	d985	3,271
Earnings Bef. Minority Int.	d8,574	2,510	d11,727	3,425
Eq. Earnings in Affils.	d147	...	d201	...
Minority Interests	cr20	...	cr27	...
Net Income	d8,701	2,510	d11,901	3,425
Average Shares Outstg	7,120	6,591	7,120	6,591

BALANCE SHEET (IN THOUSANDS):

Cash & Cash Equivalents	10,559	4,557	14,443	6,218
Receivables, Net	6,918	10,320	9,463	14,081
Inventories	6,967	4,029	9,529	5,498
Gross Property	6,339	4,511	8,670	6,155
Accumulated Depreciation	3,989	2,754	5,456	3,758
Capital Lease Obligations	19	21	26	29
Stockholders' Equity	22,626	21,912	30,948	29,897
Total Assets	32,380	30,088	44,290	41,054
Total Current Assets	24,745	19,069	33,846	26,018
Total Current Liabilities	9,643	8,156	13,190	11,128
Net Working Capital	15,102	10,913	20,656	14,890
Year End Shs Outstg	8,636	6,776	8,636	6,776

STATISTICAL RECORD:

Return on Equity %	...	11.5		
Return on Assets %	...	8.3		
Operating Profit Margin %	...	5.4		
Net Profit Margin %	...	5.7		
Book Value Per Share	2.6	3.2		

Converted at 1996, US$0.7311= 1 Canadian $; 1995, US$0.7329= 1 Canadian $

OFFICERS:
G. Whitton, Chmn.
L. B. Thomson, Pres. & C.E.O.
R. G. Bowen, V.P. Sales
N. J. Dawson, V.P. Operations
D. H. Groves, V.P. Engineering
P. H. Henry, V.P.-Fin. & Admin.

INCORPORATED: Canada, Apr., 1983

PRINCIPAL OFFICE: 79 Torbarrie Road, Toronto Canada

TELEPHONE NUMBER: 416-245-6700

NO. OF EMPLOYEES: 175

ANNUAL MEETING: In May

SHAREHOLDERS: N/A

INSTITUTIONAL HOLDINGS:
No. of Institutions: 3
Shares Held: 274,680

REGISTRAR(S): N/A

TRANSFER AGENT(S): Montreal Trust Company, Toronto.

IPC HOLDINGS, LIMITED

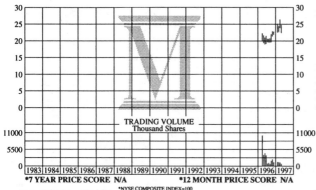

TRADING VOLUME
Thousand Shares

1983 1984 1985 1986 1987 1988 1989 1990 1991 1992 1993 1994 1995 1996 1997
*7 YEAR PRICE SCORE N/A   *12 MONTH PRICE SCORE N/A
*NYSE COMPOSITE INDEX=100

INTERIM EARNINGS (Per Share, US$):

1995	0.47	0.98	0.38	1.05
1996	1.03	0.89	0.74	0.88

INTERIM DIVIDENDS (Per Share):

Amt.	Decl.	Ex.	Rec.	Pay.
0.287	7/25/96	9/06/96	9/10/96	9/26/96
0.318	10/29	11/29	12/03	12/19
0.318	2/28/97	3/07/97	3/11/97	3/27/97
0.318	4/25	6/06	6/10	6/26
1.00E	4/25	6/06	6/10	6/26

Indicated div.:$1.27

CAPITALIZATION (12/31/96):

	($000)	(%)
Stockholders' Equity.........	496,135	100.0
Total.............................	496,135	100.0

RECENT DEVELOPMENTS: For the year ended 12/31/96, net income jumped 24.6% to $92.6 million from $74.3 million in the prior year. Results included net realized capital gains of $3.9 million versus $3.0 million in 1995. Total revenues were $146.4 million, up 14.9% from $127.4 million a year earlier. Premiums written increased 7.2% to $111.6 million from $104.1 million in the previous year. The increase in premiums written resulted from new business and larger signings on existing business, which more than offset the effect of rate reductions. Net investment income was $28.9 million compared with $22.9 million the year before, an increase of 26.4%.

BUSINESS

IPC HOLDINGS, LIMITED is a holding company. Through its wholly-owned subsidiary, International Property Catastrophe Reinsurance Company, Ltd. (IPC RE), the Company provides property catastrophe reinsurance and, to a limited extent, marine, aviation, property-per-risk excess and other short-tail property reinsurance on a worldwide basis. Approximately 46.0% of premiums written in 1996 related to U.S. risks. The balance of IPC RE's covered risks are located principally in Europe, Japan and Australia/New Zealand.

ANNUAL EARNINGS

	12/31/96	12/31/95	12/31/94
		----US $----	
Earnings Per Share	3.55	2.90	1.85

ANNUAL FINANCIAL DATA

RECORD OF EARNINGS (IN THOUSANDS):

	12/31/96	12/31/95	12/31/94
Total Revenues	146,396	127,369	90,376
Income Bef Income Tax	92,565	74,285	46,433
Net Income	92,565	74,285	46,433
Average Shares Outstg	26,081	25,619	25,130

BALANCE SHEET (IN THOUSANDS):

Cash & Cash Equivalents	38,812	30,461	28,737
Receivables, Net	25,687	25,451	19,285
Stockholders' Equity	496,135	434,292	347,183
Total Assets	548,081	485,248	387,327
Total Current Assets	544,548	481,885	384,947
Total Current Liabilities	51,946	50,956	40,144
Net Working Capital	492,602	430,929	344,803
Year End Shs Outstg	25,000	25,000	25,000

STATISTICAL RECORD:

Return on Equity %	18.65	17.10	13.37
Return on Assets %	16.88	15.30	11.98
Operating Profit Margin %	63.22	58.32	51.37
Net Profit Margin %	63.22	58.32	51.37
Book Value Per Share	19.85	17.37	13.89

OFFICERS:
J. P. Dowling, Pres. & C.E.O.
J. P. Bryce, Sr. V.P.
J. R. Weale, V.P. & C.F.O.
D. J. Higginbottom, V.P. & Sec.
P. J. Cozens, V.P.

INCORPORATED: Bermuda, May 20, 1993

PRINCIPAL OFFICE: American International Building, 29 Richmond Road, Pembroke HM 08 Bermuda,

TELEPHONE NUMBER: 441-295-2121

NO. OF EMPLOYEES: 15

ANNUAL MEETING: In June

SHAREHOLDERS: 208

INSTITUTIONAL HOLDINGS:
No. of Institutions: N/A
Shares Held: N/A

REGISTRAR(S): N/A

TRANSFER AGENT(S): Harris Trust Co. of New York, N.Y.

IPL ENERGY INC.

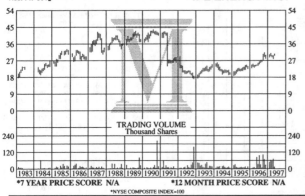

INTERIM EARNINGS (Per Share):

1995		1.68
1996		2.12

INTERIM DIVIDENDS (Per Share):

Amt.	Decl.	Ex.	Rec.	Pay.
0.5	5/2/96	5/13/96	5/15/96	6/1/96
0.515	8/8	8/16	8/20	9/1
0.515	11/5	11/13	11/15	12/1
0.515	1/13/97	2/12/97	2/14/97	3/1/97
0.515	5/1	5/14	5/16	6/1

Indicated div.:$2.06

TRADING VOLUME
Thousand Shares

`1983 1984 1985 1986 1987 1988 1989 1990 1991 1992 1993 1994 1995 1996 1997`

*7 YEAR PRICE SCORE N/A   ***12 MONTH PRICE SCORE N/A**

NYSE COMPOSITE INDEX=100

CAPITALIZATION (12/31/96):

	($000)	(%)
Long-Term Debt	2,148,703	62.4
Stockholders' Equity	1,020,616	29.6
Deferred Income Tax	273,139	7.9
Total	3,442,458	100.0

RECENT DEVELOPMENTS: For the year ended 12/31/96, net earnings increased 38.3% to C$180.3 million ($131.8 million) from C$130.4 million ($95.6 million) the previous year. Earnings from the pipeline segment were C$92.6 million, up 15.5% versus C$80.2 million the year before. Results from the Company's liquids pipeline business benefited from record deliveries of 1.9 million barrels per day in 1996 compared with 1.7 million barrels per day in 1995. Earnings from the gas distribution segment totaled C$111.8 million versus C$75.5 million the prior year, an increase of 48.1%. Operating revenue rose 5.8% to C$2.46 billion ($1.80 billion) from C$2.32 billion ($1.70 billion) a year earlier. Cash from operating activities climbed 14.5% to C$538.0 million from C$470.0 million in 1995. For the three months ended 12/31/96, net loss was C$3.5 million compared with a loss of C$1.3 million in the corresponding quarter a year earlier. Operating revenue grew 2.6% to C$327.4 million from C$319.0 million the previous year

BUSINESS

IPL ENERGY INC. is a major North American provider of energy services and delivery and is engaged in the transportation of liquid hydrocarbons and the distribution of natural gas to residential, commercial and industrial users. The Company is exploring several opportunities to expand its business in North America and selected opportunities internationally.

ANNUAL EARNINGS

	12/31/96	12/31/95	12/31/96	12/31/95
	US $		C $	
Earnings Per Share	2.12	1.68	2.90	2.30

ANNUAL FINANCIAL DATA

RECORD OF EARNINGS (IN THOUSANDS):

Total Revenues	1,796,971	1,702,380	2,457,900	2,322,800
Costs & Expenses	1,199,443	1,201,077	1,640,600	1,638,800
Depreciation & Amort	173,271	162,337	237,000	221,500
Operating Income	424,257	338,966	580,300	462,500
Income Bef Income Tax	249,086	165,562	340,700	225,900
Income Tax	101,111	54,528	138,300	74,400
Minority Interests	16,157	15,464	22,100	21,100
Net Income	131,817	95,570	180,300	130,400
Average Shares Outstg	62,165	56,791	62,165	56,791

BALANCE SHEET (IN THOUSANDS):

Cash & Cash Equivalents	10,089	23,306	13,800	31,800
Receivables, Net	264,000	204,406	361,100	278,900
Gross Property	4,438,069	4,012,188	6,070,400	5,474,400
Accumulated Depreciation	923,672	803,771	1,263,400	1,096,700
Long-Term Debt	2,148,703	1,871,753	2,939,000	2,553,900
Stockholders' Equity	1,020,616	802,965	1,396,000	1,095,600
Total Assets	4,211,940	3,794,223	5,761,100	5,177,000
Total Current Assets	478,139	442,452	654,000	603,700
Total Current Liabilities	734,756	651,402	1,005,000	888,800
Net Working Capital	d256,616	d208,950	d351,000	d285,100
Year End Shs Outstg	67,490	60,873	67,490	60,873

STATISTICAL RECORD:

Return on Equity %	12.92	11.90		
Return on Assets %	3.13	2.52		
Operating Profit Margin %	23.61	19.91		
Net Profit Margin %	7.34	5.61		
Book Value Per Share	15.12	13.19		

Converted at 1996, US$0.7311= 1 Canadian $; 1995, US$0.7329= 1 Canadian $

OFFICERS:
B. F. MacNeill, Pres. & C.E.O.
D. P. Truswell, Sr. V.P. & C.F.O.
M. F. Belich, Sr. V.P. & General Counsel

INCORPORATED: Apr., 1949

PRINCIPAL OFFICE: 2900,421-7 Avenue
S.W., Calgary, Alberta Canada

TELEPHONE NUMBER: 403-231-3900

NO. OF EMPLOYEES: 5,000 (approx.)

ANNUAL MEETING: In May

SHAREHOLDERS: 10,060

INSTITUTIONAL HOLDINGS:
No. of Institutions: 23
Shares Held: 4,938,730

REGISTRAR(S): The R-M Trust Company,
Toronto; ChaseMellon Shareholder Services
L.L.C., New York.

TRANSFER AGENT(S): The R-M Trust
Company, Toronto; ChaseMellon
Shareholder Services L.L.C., New York.

ISG INTERNATIONAL SOFTWARE GROUP LTD.

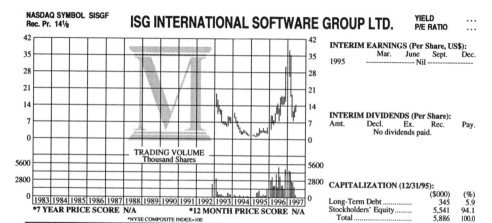

INTERIM EARNINGS (Per Share, US$):

	Mar.	June	Sept.	Dec.
1995	------------------ Nil ------------------			

INTERIM DIVIDENDS (Per Share):

Amt.	Decl.	Ex.	Rec.	Pay.
		No dividends paid.		

*7 YEAR PRICE SCORE N/A *12 MONTH PRICE SCORE N/A
*NYSE COMPOSITE INDEX=100

CAPITALIZATION (12/31/95):

	($000)	(%)
Long-Term Debt	345	5.9
Stockholders' Equity........	5,541	94.1
Total	5,886	100.0

RECENT DEVELOPMENTS: For the year ended 12/31/96, the Company reported a net loss of $1.7 million compared with net income of $13,000 in 1995. The increasing costs related to the introduction of the Company's new ISG Navigator, the first object-linking and embedding database (OLE DB), and the decline in the CorVision business had an unfavorable effect on earnings. Revenues decreased 17.5% to $10.5 million versus $12.7 million in the prior year. This decrease was primarily attributable to a reduction in the CorVision-based consulting business. The Company plans to rebuild the consulting business around the ISG Navigator product in 1997. Results should receive a boost from strategic alliances with Microsoft Corp. and Digital Equipment Corporation. Gross profit fell to $6.6 million from $8.4 million in 1995.

BUSINESS

ISG INTERNATIONAL SOFTWARE GROUP LTD. is the leading provider of Universal Data Access middleware based on Microsoft's new OLE DB standard and standards-based (OLE DB, ODBC and ActiveX) development and integration tools. SISGF products are available on multiple platforms and provide simultaneous database-independent access to many databases and file systems. The Company's principal products are: ISG Navigator; CorVision10; and APTuser. SISGF has sales and support offices in the United States, Israel, United Kingdom, Hong Kong, and Australia.

ANNUAL EARNINGS

	12/31/95	12/31/94	12/31/95	12/31/94
	------------US $------------		------------NIS------------	
Earnings Per Share	0.00	① d1.32	0.00	① d3.9
① Bef. extraord. gain.				

ANNUAL FINANCIAL DATA

RECORD OF EARNINGS (IN THOUSANDS):

	12/31/95	12/31/94	12/31/95	12/31/94
Total Revenues	12,743	14,103	40,110	42,556
Costs & Expenses	12,710	20,307	40,006	61,276
Operating Income	33	d6,204	104	d18,721
Income Bef Income Tax	13	d6,681	41	d20,160
Income Tax	...	cr18	...	cr54
Minority Interests	...	cr11	...	cr33
Net Income	13	d6,652	41	d20,072
Net Extraordinary Items	...	561	...	1,693

BALANCE SHEET (IN THOUSANDS):

Cash & Cash Equivalents	2,483	2,827	7,816	8,530
Receivables, Net	4,537	4,593	14,281	13,859
Inventories	...	258	...	779
Gross Property	3,733	3,859	11,750	11,645
Accumulated Depreciation	1,936	1,937	6,094	5,845
Long-Term Debt	345	442	1,086	1,334
Stockholders' Equity	5,541	3,786	17,441	11,424
Total Assets	12,879	11,861	40,538	35,791
Total Current Assets	7,020	7,678	22,096	23,168
Total Current Liabilities	6,932	7,518	21,819	22,686
Net Working Capital	88	160	277	483
Year End Shs Outstg	5,882	5,079	5,882	5,079

STATISTICAL RECORD:

Return on Equity %	0.23	...		
Return on Assets %	0.10	...		
Operating Profit Margin %	0.26	...		
Net Profit Margin %	0.10	...		
Book Value Per Share	0.94	0.75		

Converted at 1995, US$0.3177= 1 New Israeli Shekel; 1994, US$0.3314= 1 New Israeli Shekel

OFFICERS:
A. Gonen, Pres. & C.E.O.
S. Baumgarten, V.P. & C.F.O.
I. Sagie, V.P.

INCORPORATED: Israel, Oct., 1988

PRINCIPAL OFFICE: Carmel Business Park
Einstein Building Tirat Hacarmel 39101
Israel

TELEPHONE NUMBER: 972-4-857-6744

NO. OF EMPLOYEES: 144

ANNUAL MEETING: N/A

SHAREHOLDERS: 66

INSTITUTIONAL HOLDINGS:
No. of Institutions: N/A
Shares Held: N/A

REGISTRAR(S): American Stock Transfer & Trust Co., New York.

TRANSFER AGENT(S): American Stock Transfer & Trust Co., New York.

NASDAQ SYMBOL ISGTF
Rec. Pr. 2⅝

I.S.G. TECHNOLOGIES INC.

YIELD ...
P/E RATIO ...

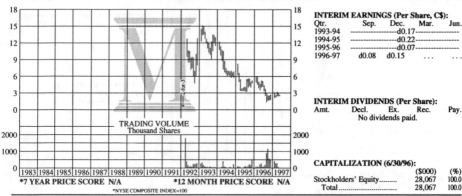

TRADING VOLUME
Thousand Shares

| 1983 | 1984 | 1985 | 1986 | 1987 | 1988 | 1989 | 1990 | 1991 | 1992 | 1993 | 1994 | 1995 | 1996 | 1997 |

*7 YEAR PRICE SCORE N/A   *12 MONTH PRICE SCORE N/A
*NYSE COMPOSITE INDEX=100

INTERIM EARNINGS (Per Share, C$):

Qtr.	Sep.	Dec.	Mar.	Jun.
1993-94	----------------d0.17----------------			
1994-95	----------------d0.22----------------			
1995-96	----------------d0.07----------------			
1996-97	d0.08	d0.15	...	...

INTERIM DIVIDENDS (Per Share):

Amt.	Decl.	Ex.	Rec.	Pay.
	No dividends paid.			

CAPITALIZATION (6/30/96):

	($000)	(%)
Stockholders' Equity........	28,067	100.0
Total..............................	28,067	100.0

RECENT DEVELOPMENTS: For the quarter ended 12/31/96, net loss was C$1.8 million compared with income of C$88,000, including restructuring charges of C$550,000, in the corresponding quarter a year earlier. Results for 1996 included charges of C$875,000 associated with the writeoff of excess inventory of the Pulsus product line and proxy costs of C$646,000. Total revenues slipped 11.9% to C$6.3 million. The decline in revenues was attributed to the Company's battle with a dissident shareholder, which seriously impaired ISGTF's ability to generate revenues according to management. However growth trends have resumed and halfway through the third quarter of fiscal 1997 the Company's management had seen clear indications that a recovery is underway.

BUSINESS

ISG TECHNOLOGIES, INC. is engaged in the development, production and sale of visualization software for the medical imaging market. Visualization includes the rapid digital display manipulation and analysis of medical images made possible through efficient image transmission and management. The Company's visualization products and services include: Software platforms comprised of standard software tools that accelerate the development of medical imaging software applications; Image-Guided Surgery Systems that enable precise and less invasive neurosurgery and spine surgery; and Radiology Applications Software used to collect, report and analyse diagnostic information. The Company also develops software products outsourced by large medical imaging companies, through its Contract Research & Development operations. The Company's Services operations include technical, application, clinical development, and marketing services.

ANNUAL EARNINGS

Earnings Per Share	6/30/96	6/30/95	6/30/96	6/30/95
	------------US $------------		------------C $------------	
	d0.05	d0.16	d0.07	d0.22

ANNUAL FINANCIAL DATA

RECORD OF EARNINGS (IN THOUSANDS):

Total Revenues	21,092	15,011	28,763	20,600
Costs & Expenses	20,836	17,004	28,414	23,335
Depreciation & Amort	1,259	974	1,717	1,337
Operating Income	d1,003	d2,967	d1,368	d4,072
Income Bef Income Tax	d661	d1,994	d901	d2,736
Net Income	d661	d1,994	d901	d2,736
Average Shares Outstg	12,603	12,580	12,603	12,580

BALANCE SHEET (IN THOUSANDS):

Cash & Cash Equivalents	9,689	13,513	13,213	18,544
Receivables, Net	9,003	7,997	12,278	10,975
Inventories	3,703	2,561	5,050	3,515
Gross Property	4,326	4,368	5,899	5,994
Accumulated Depreciation	1,541	1,941	2,101	2,663
Stockholders' Equity	28,067	28,645	38,275	39,310
Total Assets	30,906	30,983	42,147	42,518
Total Current Assets	24,200	25,515	33,002	35,015
Total Current Liabilities	2,839	2,338	3,872	3,208
Net Working Capital	21,361	23,178	29,130	31,807
Year End Shs Outstg	12,605	12,580	12,605	12,580

STATISTICAL RECORD:

Return on Equity %	...	...		
Return on Assets %	...	...		
Operating Profit Margin %	...	...		
Net Profit Margin %	...	...		
Book Value Per Share	2.23	2.28		

Converted at 1996, US$0.7333= 1 Canadian $; 1995, US$0.7287= 1 Canadian $

OFFICERS:
M. M. Greenberg, Chmn. & C.E.O.
D. Dekel, V.P.
G. McDonald, V.P.
C. Hall, V.P.

INCORPORATED: Canada, 1982

PRINCIPAL OFFICE: 6509 Airport Road,
Mississauga, Ontario Canada, L4V 1S7

TELEPHONE NUMBER: 905-672-2100

NO. OF EMPLOYEES: N/A

ANNUAL MEETING: In Dec.

SHAREHOLDERS: N/A

INSTITUTIONAL HOLDINGS:
No. of Institutions: 2
Shares Held: 229,700

REGISTRAR(S): The Montreal Trust,
Toronto; Bank of Boston, Boston.

TRANSFER AGENT(S): The Montreal Trust,
Toronto; Bank of Boston, Boston.

IWI HOLDING, LIMITED

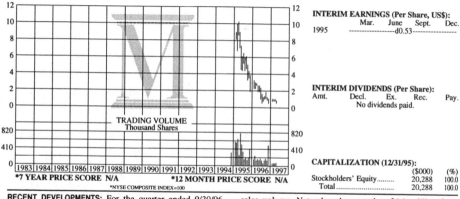

*7 YEAR PRICE SCORE N/A   *12 MONTH PRICE SCORE N/A

*NYSE COMPOSITE INDEX=100

TRADING VOLUME
Thousand Shares

INTERIM EARNINGS (Per Share, US$):

	Mar.	June	Sept.	Dec.
1995		----d0.53----		

INTERIM DIVIDENDS (Per Share):

Amt.	Decl.	Ex.	Rec.	Pay.
	No dividends paid.			

CAPITALIZATION (12/31/95):

	($000)	(%)
Stockholders' Equity........	20,288	100.0
Total..............................	20,288	100.0

RECENT DEVELOPMENTS: For the quarter ended 9/30/96, the Company reported a net loss of $3.4 million compared with a net income of $509,000 in the same period of 1995. The loss was primarily attributable to an aggressive inventory reduction program coupled with low sales volume. The return of approximately $1.0 million in inventory by a Canadian customer facing bankruptcy negatively affected sales volume. Net sales plummeted to $4.1 million from $12.7 million in the prior year. Loss from operations increased to $2.8 million versus income from operations of $975,000 the year before. For the nine months ended 9/30/96, the Company reported a net loss of $4.7 million compared with net income of $507,000 in the equivalent period of 1995.

BUSINESS

IWI HOLDING, LIMITED is a holding company, which through its subsidiaries, is engaged in the design, assembly, merchandising and wholesale distribution of jewelry. In addition, the Company imports pearls for assembly and resale. JEWLF's principal products are rings, pendants, earrings, bracelets, necklaces, pins, and brooches made of diamonds, other precious or semi-precious stones, pearls, silver and gold. A substantial part of the Company's sales are made in the United States and Canada under the tradename of "World Pacific Jewelry."

ANNUAL EARNINGS

	12/31/95	12/31/94	12/31/93	12/31/92
		----US $----		
Earnings Per Share	d0.53	2.34	1.93	1.40

ANNUAL FINANCIAL DATA

RECORD OF EARNINGS (IN THOUSANDS):

	12/31/95	12/31/94	12/31/93	12/31/92
Total Revenues	41,710	41,902	35,616	33,402
Costs & Expenses	42,822	38,556	32,763	31,428
Operating Income	d1,112	3,346	2,852	1,974
Income Bef Income Tax	d2,013	3,079	2,274	1,227
Income Tax	cr629	788	514	18
Net Income	d1,384	2,291	1,760	1,209
Average Shares Outstg	2,626	980	911	864
BALANCE SHEET (IN THOUSANDS):				
Cash & Cash Equivalents	196	435	228	2,850
Receivables, Net	20,445	16,048	9,342	9,968
Inventories	18,060	10,498	8,969	9,003
Gross Property	3,858	2,096	1,060	723
Accumulated Depreciation	926	569	552	499
Long-Term Debt	...	...	3,645	...
Stockholders' Equity	20,288	20,035	4,205	1,631
Total Assets	44,137	31,695	19,652	22,144
Total Current Assets	39,975	27,724	19,143	21,919
Total Current Liabilities	23,293	11,660	11,802	16,168
Net Working Capital	16,682	16,064	7,341	5,751
Year End Shs Outstg	2,644	2,419	919	876
STATISTICAL RECORD:				
Return on Equity %	...	11.43	41.86	74.13
Return on Assets %	...	7.23	8.96	5.46
Operating Profit Margin %	...	7.99	8.01	5.91
Net Profit Margin %	...	5.47	4.94	3.62
Book Value Per Share	7.67	8.28	4.58	1.86

OFFICERS: D. F. Chu, Chairman
B. W. Anderson, Pres. & C.E.O.
J. K. Lau, Sr. V.P., C.O.O. & Sec.
R. W. Sigman, V.P.-Fin. & C.F.O.
R. J. Mick, V.P. & Gen. Mgr.

INCORPORATED: British Virgin Islands, Feb. 22, 1993

PRINCIPAL OFFICE: P.O. Box 3340, Dawson Building, Road Town, Tortola British Virgin Islands

TELEPHONE NUMBER: 809-494-4974

NO. OF EMPLOYEES: 180

ANNUAL MEETING: In Oct.

SHAREHOLDERS: 1,500

INSTITUTIONAL HOLDINGS:
No. of Institutions: N/A
Shares Held: N/A

REGISTRAR(S): N/A

TRANSFER AGENT(S): N/A

JANNOCK LIMITED

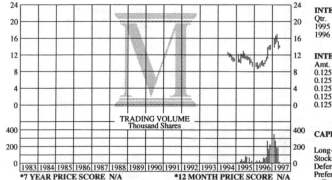

400
200
0
1983|1984|1985|1986|1987|1988|1989|1990|1991|1992|1993|1994|1995|1996|1997
*7 YEAR PRICE SCORE N/A   *12 MONTH PRICE SCORE N/A
*NYSE COMPOSITE INDEX=100

TRADING VOLUME
Thousand Shares

INTERIM EARNINGS (Per Share, C$):

Qtr.	Mar.	June	Sept.	Dec.
1995	d0.13	0.35	0.34	0.05
1996	d0.25	0.66	0.83	0.41

INTERIM DIVIDENDS (Per Share):

Amt.	Decl.	Ex.	Rec.	Pay.
0.125	5/06/96	5/30/96	6/03/96	7/01/96
0.125	7/23	8/29	9/03	10/01
0.125	10/22	11/27	12/02	1/02/97
0.125	2/25/97	2/27/97	3/03/97	4/01
0.125	4/29	5/30	6/03	7/01

Indicated div.:$0.50

CAPITALIZATION (12/31/96):

	($000)	(%)
Long-Term Debt	132,841	34.3
Stockholders' Equity	237,462	61.4
Deferred Income Tax	2,924	0.8
Preferred Stock	13,525	3.5
Total	386,752	100.0

RECENT DEVELOPMENTS: For the year ended 12/31/96, net income advanced to $50.7 million from $19.7 million in the previous year. Results for 1996 included an unusual gain of $2.6 million generated from the sale of the Company's insulation business net of charges for restructuring undertaken by the Vinyl Group. Results for 1995 included an unusual loss of $6.0 million related to restructuring of the Company's Canadian brick operations. Income from builders' sales of completed units in a property development site amounted to $1.5 million in 1996 versus $5.3 million in 1995. Sales were $1.24 billion, up 8.4% from $1.15 billion a year earlier. During 1996, the U.S. accounted for approximately 50.0% of sales and 54.0% of earnings.

BUSINESS

JANNOCK LIMITED manufactures and distributes building products for North American construction markets. The Company presently serves five construction market sectors: new residential, renovation and repair; commercial/industrial; agricultural and infrastructure. The Company's operations are organized into three buisness groups: vinyl, metal and brick. These groups operate more than 60 manufacturing plants across North America.

ANNUAL EARNINGS

	12/31/96	12/31/95	12/31/96	12/31/95
	---US $---		---C $---	
Earnings Per Share	1.21	0.45	1.65	0.61

ANNUAL FINANCIAL DATA

RECORD OF EARNINGS (IN THOUSANDS):

	12/31/96	12/31/95	12/31/96	12/31/95
Total Revenues	906,052	841,516	1,239,300	1,148,200
Costs & Expenses	852,170	813,226	1,165,600	1,109,600
Operating Income	69,080	40,608	94,500	55,400
Income Bef Income Tax	55,775	23,896	76,300	32,600
Income Tax	18,716	9,454	25,600	12,900
Net Income	37,062	14,440	50,700	19,700
Net Extraordinary Items	1,901	d4,397	2,600	d6,000
Average Shs Outstg.(000)	30,727	32,295	30,727	32,295

BALANCE SHEET (IN THOUSANDS):

Cash & Cash Equivalents	7,823	5,717	10,700	7,800
Receivables, Net	145,562	120,489	199,100	164,400
Inventories	106,594	106,051	145,800	144,700
Gross Property	420,383	402,948	575,000	549,800
Accumulated Depreciation	244,407	222,582	334,300	303,700
Long-Term Debt	132,841	146,067	181,700	199,300
Stockholders' Equity	237,462	210,635	324,800	287,399
Total Assets	535,823	512,517	732,900	699,300
Total Current Assets	266,778	239,658	364,900	327,000
Total Current Liabilities	147,390	135,953	201,600	185,500
Net Working Capital	119,389	103,705	163,300	141,500
Year End Shs. Outstg.(000)	30,289	30,278	30,289	30,278

STATISTICAL RECORD:

Return on Equity %	14.76	6.43		
Return on Assets %	6.91	2.81		
Operating Profit Margin %	7.62	4.82		
Net Profit Margin %	4.10	1.71		
Book Value Per Share	7.84	6.96		

Converted at 1996, US$0.7311= 1 Canadian $; 1995, US$0.7329= 1 Canadian $

OFFICERS:
R. F. Bennett, Chmn.
R. J. Atkinson, Pres. & C.E.O.
V. C. Hepburn, Exec. V.P.
B. W. Jamieson, V.P.-Fin. & C.F.O.

INCORPORATED: Canada

PRINCIPAL OFFICE: Suite 5205, Scotia Plaza, 40 King Street West, Toronto Ontario, Canada M5H 3Y2

TELEPHONE NUMBER: 416-364-8586

NO. OF EMPLOYEES: 5,000

ANNUAL MEETING: In Apr.

SHAREHOLDERS: 2,025

INSTITUTIONAL HOLDINGS:
No. of Institutions: 8
Shares Held: 289,465

REGISTRAR(S): Montreal Trust Company; Montreal, Toronto, and Vancouver.

TRANSFER AGENT(S): Montreal Trust Company; Montreal, Toronto, and Vancouver.

JETFORM CORPORATION

YIELD ...
P/E RATIO 37.4

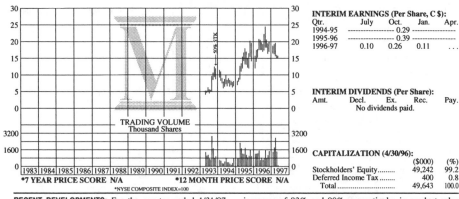

INTERIM EARNINGS (Per Share, C $):

Qtr.	July	Oct.	Jan.	Apr.
1994-95		0.29		
1995-96		0.39		
1996-97	0.10	0.26	0.11	...

INTERIM DIVIDENDS (Per Share):

Amt.	Decl.	Ex.	Rec.	Pay.
No dividends paid.				

CAPITALIZATION (4/30/96):

	($000)	(%)
Stockholders' Equity	49,242	99.2
Deferred Income Tax	400	0.8
Total	49,643	100.0

*7 YEAR PRICE SCORE N/A   *12 MONTH PRICE SCORE N/A

*NYSE COMPOSITE INDEX=100

RECENT DEVELOPMENTS: For the quarter ended 1/31/97, net income was C$1.6 million, up 45.5% from C$1.1 million in the prior-year period. Revenues nearly doubled to C$22.3 million from C$11.6 million in the corresponding 1996 quarter. The improvement in operating results was attributed to steady growth in all areas of the business as product revenues jumped 85.2% to $16.3 million. Growth was particularly strong in North America and Europe with increases of 83% and 90%, respectively, in product sales over the comparable quarter in 1996. Operating income reached C$3.5 million compared with C$1.4 million a year earlier. For the nine months ended 1/31/97, net loss was $147.3 million compared with an income of $2.7 million in 1996. Revenues advanced 85.6% to $55.8 million. Results for 1997 included charges totaling $154.0 million.

BUSINESS

JETFORM CORPORATION is a provider of software products used to design, fill, route, print and manage electronic forms. JetForm(R) technology allows organizations to replace existing pre-printed paper form processes or to implement new forms-based processes using client/server electronic forms solutions. The Company's products are available for many different commonly used computer platforms and operating systems; including DOS, Microsoft Windows, Windows 95, Windows NT, IBM OS/2, Apple Macintosh, IBM AS/400, DEC VAX and ALPHA VMS, HP3000, SUN, IBM RS/6000, HPUX and several other Unix systems. The Company also provides support, training, consulting, software development and other services related to its electronic forms products. The Company's products include JetForm Design™, JetForm Filler™, JetForm Workflow™, JetForm Central™ and JetForm BizForms™.

ANNUAL EARNINGS

	4/30/96	4/30/95	4/30/96	4/30/95
	---US $---		---C $---	
Earnings Per Share	0.29	0.21	0.39	0.29

ANNUAL FINANCIAL DATA

RECORD OF EARNINGS (IN THOUSANDS):

	4/30/96	4/30/95	4/30/96	4/30/95
Total Revenues	31,922	19,182	43,455	26,009
Costs & Expenses	25,513	16,914	34,731	22,934
Depreciation & Amort	2,639	882	3,593	1,196
Operating Income	3,769	1,386	5,131	1,879
Income Bef Income Tax	4,846	2,547	6,597	3,453
Income Tax	1,799	515	2,449	698
Net Income	3,047	2,032	4,148	2,755
Average Shares Outstg	10,651	9,559	10,651	9,559

BALANCE SHEET (IN THOUSANDS):

Cash & Cash Equivalents	14,837	21,200	20,198	28,746
Receivables, Net	16,169	9,034	22,011	12,249
Inventories	1,313	766	1,787	1,039
Gross Property	9,563	3,919	13,018	5,314
Accumulated Depreciation	2,623	1,370	3,570	1,857
Stockholders' Equity	49,242	34,433	67,033	46,689
Total Assets	61,560	38,093	83,801	51,651
Total Current Assets	33,754	31,558	45,944	42,790
Total Current Liabilities	11,917	3,548	16,223	4,811
Net Working Capital	21,837	28,010	29,726	37,979
Year End Shs Outstg	9,237	8,140	9,237	8,140

STATISTICAL RECORD:

Return on Equity %	6.2	5.9		
Return on Assets %	4.9	5.3		
Operating Profit Margin %	11.8	7.2		
Net Profit Margin %	9.5	10.6		
Book Value Per Share	5.33	4.23		

Converted at 1996, US$0.7346= 1 Canadian $; 1995, US$0.7375= 1 Canadian $

OFFICERS:
A. E. Ostrovsky, Chmn.
J. Kelly, Pres. & C.E.O.
J. Gleed, Exec. V.P. & Chief Tech. Officer
L. K. Boyd, Sr. V.P.

INCORPORATED: Jun., 1982

PRINCIPAL OFFICE: 560 Rochester St. Suite 400 Ottawa Canada, K1S 5K2

TELEPHONE NUMBER: 613-230-3676

NO. OF EMPLOYEES: 368

ANNUAL MEETING: In Sept.

SHAREHOLDERS: 155

INSTITUTIONAL HOLDINGS:
No. of Institutions: 17
Shares Held: 3,069,592

REGISTRAR(S): N/A

TRANSFER AGENT(S): American Stock Transfer & Trust Co., New York.

LANOPTICS LTD.

YIELD ...
P/E RATIO ...

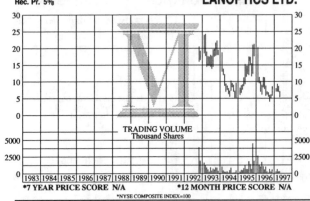

*7 YEAR PRICE SCORE N/A   *12 MONTH PRICE SCORE N/A
*NYSE COMPOSITE INDEX=100

TRADING VOLUME
Thousand Shares

INTERIM EARNINGS (Per Share, US$):
1995 ------------------ 0.70 ------------------
1996 ------------------d0.62------------------

INTERIM DIVIDENDS (Per Share):

Amt.	Decl.	Ex.	Rec.	Pay.
No dividends paid.				

CAPITALIZATION (12/31/96):

	($000)	(%)
Stockholders' Equity........	35,998	100.0
Total	35,998	100.0

RECENT DEVELOPMENTS: For the year ended 12/31/96, the Company posted a net loss of US$3.8 million compared with income of US$4.3 million in 1995. Sales declined 11.8% to US$20.6 million from US$23.3 million a year earlier. Results in 1996 included an inventory write down of US$1.8 million. In addition, the Company noted that results included US$400,000 for a reversal of amounts accrued due to delays in marketing grant approval by the Israeli government. Research and development costs as a percentage of sales, less royalty-bearing grants, totaled 18.9% (US$3.9 million) compared with 12.4% (US$2.9 million) in 1995. Selling, general and administrative expenses as a percentage of revenues increased to 50.4% compared with 34.5% a year earlier. For the three months ended 12/31/96, the Company reported a net loss of US$1.4 million compared with income of US$996,000 in the corresponding period of 1995. Sales declined 2.6% to US$5.4 million from US$5.6 million in the year-ago period.

BUSINESS

LANOPTICS LTD. and its subsidiaries, develop, manufacture and market intelligent networking solutions for IBM mainframe-based corporations, providing enterprise-wide connectivity and facilitating migration to client/server environments utilizing the Token Ring environment. These concentrators are devices that connect users in a local area network (LAN) and allow such users to communicate with each other, share resources and data bases, and run applications across the network. The Company places primary emphasis on products for the IBM environment and the Token Ring protocol promoted by IBM, while also offering a line of concentrator modules compatible with the Ethernet protocol. The Company's principal products for LANs are StackNetro, a family of stackable networking platforms, and StarView, the Company's proprietary network management system for its networking platform.

ANNUAL EARNINGS

	12/31/96	12/31/95	12/31/96	12/31/95
	-------------US $-------------		-------------NIS-------------	
Earnings Per Share	d0.62	0.70	d2.01	2.19

ANNUAL FINANCIAL DATA

RECORD OF EARNINGS (IN THOUSANDS):

	12/31/96	12/31/95	12/31/96	12/31/95
Total Revenues	20,583	23,328	67,046	73,428
Costs & Expenses	25,615	20,192	83,436	63,557
Operating Income	d5,032	3,136	d16,391	9,871
Income Bef Income Tax	d3,803	4,337	d12,388	13,651
Net Income	d3,803	4,337	d12,388	13,651
Average Shares Outstg	6,153	6,224	6,153	6,224

BALANCE SHEET (IN THOUSANDS):

Cash & Cash Equivalents	15,205	21,579	49,528	67,923
Receivables, Net	8,997	7,245	29,306	22,805
Inventories	6,447	8,194	21,000	25,792
Gross Property	5,520	4,178	17,980	13,151
Accumulated Depreciation	2,103	1,421	6,850	4,473
Stockholders' Equity	35,998	39,796	117,257	125,263
Total Assets	40,007	44,775	130,316	140,935
Total Current Assets	30,649	37,018	99,834	116,519
Total Current Liabilities	2,987	4,353	9,730	13,702
Net Working Capital	27,662	32,665	90,104	102,817
Year End Shs Outstg	6,113	6,112	6,113	6,112

STATISTICAL RECORD:

Return on Equity %	...	10.9		
Return on Assets %	...	9.7		
Operating Profit Margin %	...	13.4		
Net Profit Margin %	...	18.6		
Book Value Per Share	5.89	6.51		

Converted at 1996, US$0.307= 1 New Israeli Shekel; 1995, US$0.318= 1 New Israeli Shekel

OFFICERS:
E. Fruchter, Chmn.
E. Harry, Pres. & C.E.O.
K. Sarid, C.F.O. & Sec.
E. Rom, Exec. V.P.
INCORPORATED: 1989
PRINCIPAL OFFICE: LanOptics Building, Ramat Gabriel Industrial Park, P.O. Box 184, Migdal Ha-Emek 10551 Israel

TELEPHONE NUMBER: 972-6-6449-944
NO. OF EMPLOYEES: 156
ANNUAL MEETING: N/A
SHAREHOLDERS: 39
INSTITUTIONAL HOLDINGS:
No. of Institutions: N/A
Shares Held: N/A

REGISTRAR(S): N/A

TRANSFER AGENT(S): American Stock Transfer & Trust Co., New York.

LASER INDUSTRIES LIMITED

YIELD ...
P/E RATIO 10.7

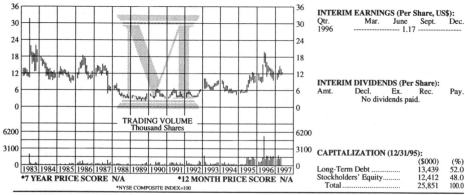

*7 YEAR PRICE SCORE N/A *12 MONTH PRICE SCORE N/A
*NYSE COMPOSITE INDEX=100

INTERIM EARNINGS (Per Share, US$):

Qtr.	Mar.	June	Sept.	Dec.
1996	-----------------	1.17	-----------------	

INTERIM DIVIDENDS (Per Share):

Amt.	Decl.	Ex.	Rec.	Pay.
		No dividends paid.		

CAPITALIZATION (12/31/95):

	($000)	(%)
Long-Term Debt	13,439	52.0
Stockholders' Equity........	12,412	48.0
Total	25,851	100.0

RECENT DEVELOPMENTS: For the year ended 12/31/96, net income was $8.8 million compared with a net loss of $2.3 million a year earlier. Sales were $58.7 million, up 17.2% from $50.1 million in the prior year. Operating income was $9.4 million compared with $7.3 million the year before, an increase of 28.1%. Gross profit increased 20.1% to $37.9 million from $31.6 million in 1995. For the quarter ended 12/31/96, net income was $2.5 million compared with a net loss of $6.4 million in the corresponding 1995 quarter. Net sales jumped 14.4% to $15.5 million from $13.5 million in the fourth quarter of 1995. Results for fiscal and fourth quarter 1995 included litigation settlement expenses totaling $8.1 million.

BUSINESS

LASER INDUSTRIES LTD. designs, develops manufactures and markets a broad range of complete surgical laser systems in a wide variety of technologies, complemented by customer service and support programs. It also offers a range of application driven accessories designed for integration with its surgical laser systems. The laser systems and accessories are sold under the trade name "SHARPLAN."

ANNUAL EARNINGS

	12/31/95	12/31/94	12/31/95	12/31/94
	-------------US $------------		-------------NIS------------	
Earnings Per Share	d0.37	0.67	d1.16	2.02

ANNUAL FINANCIAL DATA

RECORD OF EARNINGS (IN MILLIONS):

	12/31/95	12/31/94	12/31/95	12/31/94
Total Revenues	50	41	158	122
Costs & Expenses	43	35	135	106
Operating Income	7	5	23	16
Income Bef Income Tax	d2	4	d7	12
Net Income	d2	4	d7	12
Average Shares Outstg (000)	6,249	5,987	6,249	5,987

BALANCE SHEET (IN MILLIONS):

Cash & Cash Equivalents	5	6	14	18
Receivables, Net	11	10	36	29
Inventories	12	9	38	29
Gross Property	20	18	62	56
Accumulated Depreciation	16	15	52	46
Long-Term Debt	13	11	42	32
Stockholders' Equity	12	11	39	34
Total Assets	40	36	126	108
Total Current Assets	30	26	94	80
Total Current Liabilities	14	13	43	40
Net Working Capital	16	13	51	39
Year End Shs Outstg (000)	6,307	5,890	6,307	5,890

STATISTICAL RECORD:

Return on Equity %	...	36.1		
Return on Assets %	...	11.3		
Operating Profit Margin %	14.6	13.4		
Net Profit Margin %	...	10.0		
Book Value Per Share	2.0	1.9		

Converted at 1995, US$0.3177= 1 New Israeli Shekel; 1994, US$0.3314= 1 New Israeli Shekel

OFFICERS:
B. Givli, Chmn. & C.E.O.
Y. Sutton, Pres. & C.O.O.
H. Solomon, Sec. & Couns.

INCORPORATED: Israel, 1973

PRINCIPAL OFFICE: Atidim Science Based Industrial Park Neve Sharett, P.O. Box 13135 Tel Aviv Israel

TELEPHONE NUMBER: 972-3-645-4545

NO. OF EMPLOYEES: N/A

ANNUAL MEETING: N/A

SHAREHOLDERS: N/A

INSTITUTIONAL HOLDINGS:
No. of Institutions: 14
Shares Held: 1,615,622

REGISTRAR(S): N/A

TRANSFER AGENT(S): American Stock Transfer and Trust Co., New York.

NASDAQ SYMBOL LHSPF
Rec. Pr. 20½

LERNOUT & HAUSPIE SPEECH

YIELD ...
P/E RATIO ...

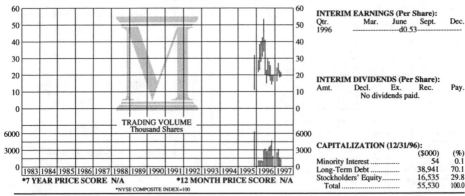

*7 YEAR PRICE SCORE N/A *12 MONTH PRICE SCORE N/A

*NYSE COMPOSITE INDEX=100

INTERIM EARNINGS (Per Share):

Qtr.	Mar.	June	Sept.	Dec.
1996		d0.53		

INTERIM DIVIDENDS (Per Share):

Amt.	Decl.	Ex.	Rec.	Pay.
	No dividends paid.			

CAPITALIZATION (12/31/96):

	($000)	(%)
Minority Interest	54	0.1
Long-Term Debt	38,941	70.1
Stockholders' Equity	16,535	29.8
Total	55,530	100.0

RECENT DEVELOPMENTS: For the year ended 12/31/96, income was $3.6 million before an extraordinary charge compared with a net loss of $14.0 million a year earlier. Income for 1996 excluded a one-time write-off of $11.5 million of acquired in-process research and development for Berkeley Speech Technologies, but included a $500,000 tax charge related to the Company's recent acquisitions. Total net revenues advanced to $31.0 million from $7.7 million in the prior year. License revenues more than tripled to $20.3 million from $5.9 million in 1995. Engineering revenues increased to $3.8 million from $1.9 million in the prior year. Service revenues totaled $6.9 million. The Company's operating loss amounted to $7.0 million from $10.9 million a year ago.

BUSINESS

LERNOUT & HAUSPIE SPEECH and its subsidiaries are engaged in the international development and licensing of advanced speech technologies, including automatic speech recognition, text-to-speech and digitized speech compression. The Company licenses its multilingual, multi-platform technologies to original equipment manufacturers, component manufacturers, and software vendors for use in a broad range of applications in four markets: computers and multimedia, telecommunications, automotive electronics, and consumer electronics.

ANNUAL EARNINGS

	12/31/96	12/31/95	12/31/96	12/31/95
	US $		BFr	
Earnings Per Share	d0.53	d1.67	d16.99	d49.12

ANNUAL FINANCIAL DATA

RECORD OF EARNINGS (IN THOUSANDS):

	12/31/96	12/31/95	12/31/96	12/31/95
Total Revenues	31,014	7,722	994,038	227,118
Costs & Expenses	38,515	18,585	1,234,455	546,618
Operating Income	d7,501	d10,863	d240,417	d319,500
Income Bef Income Tax	d7,376	d13,975	d236,410	d411,029
Income Tax	579	...	18,558	...
Eq. Earnings in Affils.	16	...	513	...
Net Income	d7,939	d13,975	d254,455	d411,029
Average Shares Outstg	14,900	8,355	14,900	8,355

BALANCE SHEET (IN THOUSANDS):

Cash & Cash Equivalents	28,650	22,543	918,269	663,029
Gross Property	9,125	5,560	292,468	163,529
Accumulated Depreciation	3,826	2,996	122,628	88,118
Stockholders' Equity	16,535	18,889	529,968	555,559
Total Assets	79,874	32,792	2,560,064	964,471
Total Current Assets	43,229	29,301	1,385,545	861,794
Total Current Liabilities	24,344	10,679	780,256	314,088
Net Working Capital	18,885	18,622	605,288	547,706
Year End Shs Outstg	15,452	14,338	15,452	14,338

STATISTICAL RECORD:

Return on Equity %	...	...		
Return on Assets %	...	...		
Operating Profit Margin %	...	...		
Net Profit Margin %	...	...		
Book Value Per Share	1.07	1.32		

Converted at 1996, US$0.0312= 1 Belgian franc; 1995, US$0.0340= 1 Belgian franc

---

OFFICERS:
P. Hauspie, Chmn.
J. Lernout, Co.-Chmn.
N. Willaert, Vice-Chmn. & Managing Dir.
G. Bastiaens, Pres.

INCORPORATED: Belgium, Dec., 1987

PRINCIPAL OFFICE: Sint-Krispijnstraat 7
Ieper Belgium

TELEPHONE NUMBER: 32-57-228-888

NO. OF EMPLOYEES: 155

ANNUAL MEETING: In May

SHAREHOLDERS: 16

INSTITUTIONAL HOLDINGS:
No. of Institutions: N/A
Shares Held: N/A

REGISTRAR(S): N/A

TRANSFER AGENT(S): Chemical Mellon
Shareholder Services, East Hartford, CT

LIQUIDATION WORLD, INC.

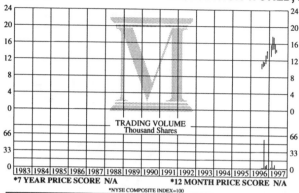

INTERIM EARNINGS (Per Share):
1995 ---------------- 0.58 ----------------
1996 ---------------- 0.75 ----------------

TRADING VOLUME
Thousand Shares

| 1983 | 1984 | 1985 | 1986 | 1987 | 1988 | 1989 | 1990 | 1991 | 1992 | 1993 | 1994 | 1995 | 1996 | 1997 |

*7 YEAR PRICE SCORE N/A   *12 MONTH PRICE SCORE N/A
*NYSE COMPOSITE INDEX=100

INTERIM DIVIDENDS (Per Share):
Amt.   Decl.   Ex.   Rec.   Pay.
No dividends paid.

CAPITALIZATION (10/06/96):

	($000)	(%)
Stockholders' Equity	15,919	100.0
Total	15,919	100.0

RECENT DEVELOPMENTS: For the thirteen weeks ended 1/5/97, net earnings advanced 30.4% to C$1.1 million, or C$0.30 per share, from C$879,473, or C$0.29 per share, in the corresponding prior-year period. Sales totaled C$23.0 million, up 23.5% compared with C$18.6 million the previous year. The Company reported higher sales and earnings despite severe winter weather conditions which closed most of the Company's outlets in British Columbia for at least a day. Gross profit jumped 36.7% to C$9.2 million, or 40.0% of sales, from C$6.7 million, or 36.2% of sales, the year before. Earnings before income taxes climbed 28.0% to C$2.0 million from C$1.5 million a year earlier. During the first quarter, the Company opened four new outlets in Wainwright and Edmonton, Alberta and Lloydminster and Saskatoon, Saskatchewan. In the second quarter, a temporary outlet was opened in Kent, Washington that may become permanent depending on market acceptance and the Company's ability to obtain a longer-term lease at a favorable rate.

BUSINESS

LIQUIDATION WORLD INC. is engaged in the marketing of consumer and business related merchandise acquired from bankruptcies, receiverships, close-outs, inventory overruns, insurance claims and other distress situations. The Company also operates in the rent-to-own furniture and appliance business through its associated company. The Company operates 43 retail outlets located in Alberta, British Columbia, Ontario, Saskatchewan, Washington state and Idaho.

ANNUAL EARNINGS

	10/06/96	10/01/95	10/06/96	10/01/95
	--------US $--------		--------C $--------	
Earnings Per Share	0.75	0.58	1.02	0.78

ANNUAL FINANCIAL DATA

RECORD OF EARNINGS (IN THOUSANDS):

	10/06/96	10/01/95	10/06/96	10/01/95
Total Revenues	52,610	41,931	71,705	56,268
Costs & Expenses	47,888	38,597	65,269	51,795
Depreciation & Amort	263	169	359	227
Operating Income	4,459	3,164	6,077	4,246
Income Bef Income Tax	4,478	3,158	6,104	4,238
Income Tax	1,896	1,391	2,584	1,867
Net Income	2,583	1,767	3,520	2,371

BALANCE SHEET (IN THOUSANDS):

Cash & Cash Equivalents	3,233	...	4,407	...
Receivables, Net	143	143	194	191
Inventories	13,520	11,571	18,427	15,527
Gross Property	2,340	1,377	3,190	1,848
Accumulated Depreciation	698	517	952	694
Stockholders' Equity	15,919	7,835	21,697	10,514
Total Assets	19,000	12,962	25,897	17,394
Total Current Assets	17,309	12,072	23,592	16,199
Total Current Liabilities	3,081	5,127	4,199	6,880
Net Working Capital	14,228	6,945	19,392	9,319
Year End Shs Outstg	3,774	3,062	3,774	3,062

STATISTICAL RECORD:

Return on Equity %	16.22	22.55
Return on Assets %	13.59	13.63
Operating Profit Margin %	8.48	7.55
Net Profit Margin %	4.91	4.21
Book Value Per Share	4.22	2.56

Converted at 1996, US$0.7337= 1 Canadian $; 1995, US$0.7452= 1 Canadian $

OFFICERS:
D. Gillespie, Pres. & C.E.O.
W. Mantika, V.P.
A. Searby, C.F.O.

INCORPORATED: Canada, Dec. 1986

PRINCIPAL OFFICE: 3900 - 29 Street N.E., Calgary, Alberta Canada T1Y 6B6

TELEPHONE NUMBER: 403-250-1222

NO. OF EMPLOYEES: 744

ANNUAL MEETING: N/A

SHAREHOLDERS: 126

INSTITUTIONAL HOLDINGS:
No. of Institutions: 1
Shares Held: 213,800

REGISTRAR(S): N/A

TRANSFER AGENT(S): Montreal Trust, Toronto.

LIVENT INC.

YIELD ...
P/E RATIO 16.8

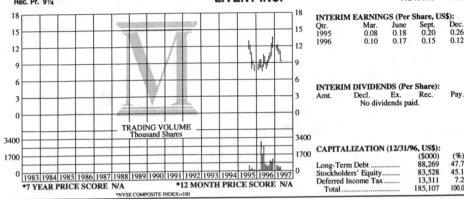

TRADING VOLUME
Thousand Shares

| 1983 | 1984 | 1985 | 1986 | 1987 | 1988 | 1989 | 1990 | 1991 | 1992 | 1993 | 1994 | 1995 | 1996 | 1997 |

*7 YEAR PRICE SCORE N/A   *12 MONTH PRICE SCORE N/A
*NYSE COMPOSITE INDEX=100

INTERIM EARNINGS (Per Share, US$):

Qtr.	Mar.	June	Sept.	Dec.
1995	0.08	0.18	0.20	0.26
1996	0.10	0.17	0.15	0.12

INTERIM DIVIDENDS (Per Share):

Amt.	Decl.	Ex.	Rec.	Pay.
		No dividends paid.		

CAPITALIZATION (12/31/96, US$):

	($000)	(%)
Long-Term Debt	88,269	47.7
Stockholders' Equity........	83,528	45.1
Deferred Income Tax	13,311	7.2
Total	185,107	100.0

RECENT DEVELOPMENTS: For the year ended 12/31/96, net income declined 6.1% to C$11.1 million from C$11.8 million in 1995. Revenues rose 14.0% to C$331.7 million. Amortization of preproduction costs increased 41.2% to C$45.8 million from C$32.4 million in the year-ago period. The weighted average number of shares outstanding increased to 14.8 million from 12.0 million in 1995 as a result of the U.S. equity financing that closed at the beginning of the second quarter of 1996. The Company noted that it plans an extensive expansion of its North American production activities in 1997. All three companies of Show Boat will be touring, and are scheduled to play in 17 different cities in North America compared with five cities in 1996. The Company opened its first company of Ragtime in Metropolitan Toronto at the Ford Centre for the Performing Arts in November 1996 and a second company of Ragtime opened in Los Angeles in late May 1997.

BUSINESS

LIVENT INC. is a vertically integrated producer of live theatrical entertainment as well as an operator of theaters in North American markets. Livent acquires domestic and international rights to musical works and produces, licenses and markets such properties for live theater and other forms of entertainment. In Canada, the Company owns the 2,200-seat Pantages Theatre in Toronto and the 1,849-seat Ford Centre For The Performing Arts in Vancouver, and it manages the three-theater, 3,000-seat Ford Centre For The Performing Arts in Metropolitan Toronto. In the U.S. it has two theaters in development the Ford Center for the Performing Arts in both New York and Chicago. In addition, the Company generates revenue from corporate sponsorships and from a broad range of merchandise associated with each musical production and from concessions at the Company managed theaters.

ANNUAL EARNINGS

	12/31/96	12/31/95	12/31/96	12/31/95
	----------US $--------		----------C $----------	
Earnings Per Share	0.55	0.72	0.75	0.98

ANNUAL FINANCIAL DATA

RECORD OF EARNINGS (IN THOUSANDS):

	12/31/96	12/31/95	12/31/96	12/31/95
Total Revenues	242,530	213,241	331,733	290,955
Costs & Expenses	192,226	171,873	262,928	234,511
Depreciation & Amort	36,417	26,206	49,811	35,756
Operating Income	13,886	15,163	18,994	20,689
Income Bef Income Tax	10,393	13,372	14,216	18,245
Income Tax	2,312	4,748	3,162	6,478
Net Income	8,081	8,624	11,054	11,767
Average Shares Outstg	14,780	11,961	14,780	11,961
BALANCE SHEET (IN THOUSANDS):				
Cash & Cash Equivalents	16,855	...	23,054	...
Receivables, Net	23,574	19,364	32,244	26,421
Inventories	1,131	1,538	1,547	2,098
Gross Property	105,334	65,295	144,075	89,092
Accumulated Depreciation	7,950	6,061	10,875	8,270
Long-Term Debt	88,269	32,668	120,735	44,573
Stockholders' Equity	83,528	45,378	114,249	61,916
Total Assets	223,752	138,516	306,048	188,997
Total Current Assets	47,232	25,227	64,604	34,420
Total Current Liabilities	38,645	48,468	52,858	66,132
Net Working Capital	8,587	d23,242	11,746	d31,712
Year End Shs Outstg	15,726	11,962	15,726	11,962
STATISTICAL RECORD:				
Return on Equity %	9.7	19.0		
Return on Assets %	3.6	6.2		
Operating Profit Margin %	5.7	7.1		
Net Profit Margin %	3.3	4.0		
Book Value Per Share	5.31	3.79		

Converted at 1996, US$0.7311= 1 Canadian $; 1995, US$0.7329= 1 Canadian $

OFFICERS:
G. H. Drabinsky, Chmn. & C.E.O.
M. I. Gottlieb, Pres.
R. Topol, Sr. Exec. V.P. & C.O.O.
J. M. Banks, Sec. & Couns.

INCORPORATED: Dec., 1989

PRINCIPAL OFFICE: 165 Avenue Road, Suite 600, Toronto, Ontario M5R 3S4 Canada

TELEPHONE NUMBER: 416-324-5800

NO. OF EMPLOYEES: N/A

ANNUAL MEETING: In May

SHAREHOLDERS: N/A

INSTITUTIONAL HOLDINGS:
No. of Institutions: 15
Shares Held: 2,001,866

REGISTRAR(S): Montreal Trust Co., Toronto.

TRANSFER AGENT(S): Montreal Trust Co., Toronto.

LOGAL EDUCATIONAL SOFTWARE & SYSTEMS LTD.

YIELD ...
P/E RATIO ...

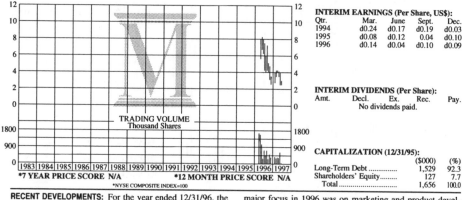

*7 YEAR PRICE SCORE N/A   *12 MONTH PRICE SCORE N/A

*NYSE COMPOSITE INDEX=100

INTERIM EARNINGS (Per Share, US$):

Qtr.	Mar.	June	Sept.	Dec.
1994	d0.24	d0.17	d0.19	d0.03
1995	d0.08	d0.12	0.04	d0.10
1996	d0.14	d0.04	d0.10	d0.09

INTERIM DIVIDENDS (Per Share):

Amt.	Decl.	Ex.	Rec.	Pay.
	No dividends paid.			

CAPITALIZATION (12/31/95):

	($000)	(%)
Long-Term Debt	1,529	92.3
Shareholders' Equity........	127	7.7
Total	1,656	100.0

RECENT DEVELOPMENTS: For the year ended 12/31/96, the Company posted a net loss of US$2.1 million compared with a loss of US$1.1 million in 1995. Revenues increased 31.6% to US$6.7 million from US$5.1 million a year earlier. Results in 1996 included a restructuring charge of US$197,000. Product sales rose 30.2% to US$5.2 million, while services revenues advanced 36.6% to US$1.5 million. Gross profit as a percentage of revenues declined to 65.7% from 66.1% in 1995. The Company noted that its major focus in 1996 was on marketing and product development. The Company brought in a new head of marketing and shifted from a product to a sales orientation and focused on telesales and indirect sales. The Company recently launched the first phase of LOGAL.net. The Company has taken 600 interactive, simulation-based high-school/college math and science lessons, and made them available on the Internet to schools and individuals.

BUSINESS

LOGAL EDUCATIONAL SOFTWARE & SYSTEMS LTD. designs, creates, publishes, and markets interactive simulation-based, educational software for curriculum in high schools and colleges. In addition, the Company offers probeware products that complement the science product line and are used for computer-based experiments. The Company sells its products through its own sales force and distributors and has strategic alliances with Prentice-Hall, Computer Curriculum Corporation, and Houghton Mifflin Company.

ANNUAL EARNINGS

	12/31/95	12/31/94	12/31/95	12/31/94
	------------- US $ -------------		--------------- NIS --------------	
Earnings Per Share	d0.25	d0.50	d0.78	d1.51

ANNUAL FINANCIAL DATA

RECORD OF EARNINGS (IN THOUSANDS):

	12/31/95	12/31/94	12/31/95	12/31/94
Total Revenues	5,102	2,147	16,059	6,479
Costs & Expenses	6,048	3,816	19,037	11,515
Operating Income	d946	d1,669	d2,978	d5,036
Net Income	d1,084	d1,728	d3,412	d5,214
Average Shares Outstg	4,306	3,449	4,306	3,449

BALANCE SHEET (IN THOUSANDS):

Cash & Cash Equivalents	596	887	1,876	2,676
Receivables, Net	1,908	1,419	6,006	4,282
Inventories	469	329	1,476	993
Gross Property	1,412	808	4,444	2,438
Accumulated Depreciation	401	203	1,262	613
Long-Term Debt	1,529	1,403	4,813	4,234
Stockholders' Equity	127	187	400	564
Total Assets	4,291	3,324	13,506	10,030
Total Current Assets	2,973	2,635	9,358	7,951
Total Current Liabilities	2,118	1,563	6,667	4,716
Net Working Capital	855	1,072	2,691	3,235
Year End Shs Outstg	3,800	3,255	3,800	3,255

STATISTICAL RECORD:

Book Value Per Share	0.03	0.06		

Converted at 1995, US$0.3177= 1 New Israeli Shekel; 1994, US$0.3314= 1 New Israeli Shekel

OFFICERS:
A.I. Mlavsky, Chmn.
Y. Givol, Pres. & C.E.O.
A. Ben-Nun, V.P. & C.F.O.

INCORPORATED: Israel, 1991

PRINCIPAL OFFICE: P.O. Box 295 Hatzor
Israel 10352

TELEPHONE NUMBER: 011 972 6 693 8880

NO. OF EMPLOYEES: 100

ANNUAL MEETING: N/A

SHAREHOLDERS: N/A

INSTITUTIONAL HOLDINGS:
No. of Institutions: N/A
Shares Held: N/A

REGISTRAR(S):

TRANSFER AGENT(S): American Stock &
Transfer Company

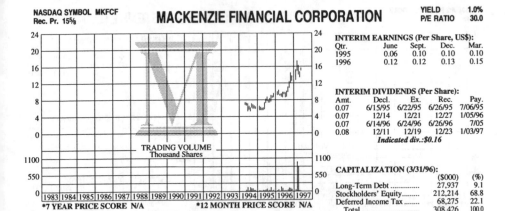

MACKENZIE FINANCIAL CORPORATION

YIELD 1.0%
P/E RATIO 30.0

INTERIM EARNINGS (Per Share, US$):

Qtr.	June	Sept.	Dec.	Mar.
1995	0.06	0.10	0.10	0.10
1996	0.12	0.12	0.13	0.15

INTERIM DIVIDENDS (Per Share):

Amt.	Decl.	Ex.	Rec.	Pay.
0.07	6/15/95	6/22/95	6/26/95	7/06/95
0.07	12/14	12/21	12/27	1/05/96
0.07	6/14/96	6/24/96	6/26/96	7/05
0.08	12/11	12/19	12/23	1/03/97

Indicated div.:$0.16

TRADING VOLUME
Thousand Shares

1983 1984 1985 1986 1987 1988 1989 1990 1991 1992 1993 1994 1995 1996 1997
*7 YEAR PRICE SCORE N/A   ***12 MONTH PRICE SCORE N/A**
*NYSE COMPOSITE INDEX=100

CAPITALIZATION (3/31/96):

	($000)	(%)
Long-Term Debt	27,937	9.1
Stockholders' Equity	212,214	68.8
Deferred Income Tax	68,275	22.1
Total	308,426	100.0

RECENT DEVELOPMENTS: For the year ended 3/31/96, net income jumped 38.2% to C$40.7 million from C$29.5 million a year earlier. Net income benefited from improved profitability of the Company's Canadian and U.S. mutual fund businesses and the trust business. Results included a loss on the sale of investments of C$64,000 and C$19,000 in 1996 and 1995, respectively. Total revenues were C$269.4 million, up 21.6% from C$221.6 million in the prior year. The Company reported equity in earnings of affiliated companies of C$5.2 million in 1996 versus C$785,000 in 1995. Total expenses increased 20.9% to C$202.9 million from C$167.8 million in the previous year.

BUSINESS

MACKENZIE FINANCIAL CORPORATION is the parent company of a group engaged in the management and distribution of public mutual funds in both Canada and the United States. Through its subsidiaries, the Company also provides investment management services to other public mutual funds and private accounts. In Canada, the Company provides investment management, administration and marketing services to 35 mutual funds comprising four distinct fund groups. In the United States, the Company provides similar services to 16 mutual funds comprising three distinct fund groups.

ANNUAL EARNINGS

	3/31/96	3/31/95	3/31/96	3/31/95
	--------US $--------		--------C $--------	
Earnings Per Share	0.50	0.36	0.68	0.50

ANNUAL FINANCIAL DATA

RECORD OF EARNINGS (IN THOUSANDS):

	3/31/96	3/31/95	3/31/96	3/31/95
Total Revenues	198,204	157,874	269,409	220,896
Costs & Expenses	115,359	95,001	156,802	132,924
Depreciation & Amort	33,920	24,472	46,106	34,241
Operating Income	48,925	38,402	66,501	53,731
Income Bef Income Tax	48,925	38,402	66,501	53,731
Income Tax	22,809	17,915	31,003	25,066
Eq. Earnings in Affils.	3,848	561	5,230	785
Net Income	29,964	21,048	40,728	29,450

BALANCE SHEET (IN THOUSANDS):

Cash & Cash Equivalents	75,915	103,242	103,188	144,455
Receivables, Net	73,449	36,819	61,781	51,517
Gross Property	44,939	34,536	61,084	48,323
Accumulated Depreciation	25,869	18,309	35,162	25,618
Long-Term Debt	27,937	31,578	37,973	44,184
Stockholders' Equity	212,214	181,687	288,452	254,215
Total Assets	564,628	442,087	767,471	618,563
Total Current Assets	149,365	140,061	203,024	195,972
Total Current Liabilities	47,648	41,353	64,765	57,861
Net Working Capital	101,717	98,708	138,259	138,111
Year End Shs Outstg	43,869	42,356	43,869	42,356

STATISTICAL RECORD:

Return on Equity %	14.12	11.58
Return on Assets %	5.31	4.76
Operating Profit Margin %	24.68	24.32
Net Profit Margin %	15.12	13.33
Book Value Per Share	3.56	3.07

Converted at 1996, US$0.7357= 1 Canadian $; 1995, US$0.7147= 1 Canadian $

OFFICERS:
W. G. Crerar, Chmn.
N. Lovatt, Vice-Chmn.
A. Christ, Pres. & C.E.O.
P. F. Cunningham, Exec. V.P.

INCORPORATED: Canada, 1968

PRINCIPAL OFFICE: 150 Bloor Street West, Suite 400, Toronto Canada M5S 3B5

TELEPHONE NUMBER: 416-922-5322

NO. OF EMPLOYEES: N/A

ANNUAL MEETING: In Sep.

SHAREHOLDERS: N/A

INSTITUTIONAL HOLDINGS:
No. of Institutions: 5
Shares Held: 5,258,625

REGISTRAR(S): N/A

TRANSFER AGENT(S): The R-M Trust Company, Toronto.

MACMILLAN BLOEDEL LIMITED

YIELD 1.4%
P/E RATIO 54.3

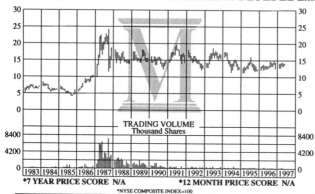

TRADING VOLUME
Thousand Shares

| 1983 | 1984 | 1985 | 1986 | 1987 | 1988 | 1989 | 1990 | 1991 | 1992 | 1993 | 1994 | 1995 | 1996 | 1997 |

*7 YEAR PRICE SCORE N/A   *12 MONTH PRICE SCORE N/A
*NYSE COMPOSITE INDEX=100

INTERIM EARNINGS (Per Share, US$):

Qtr.	Mar.	June	Sept.	Dec.
1995		1.61		
1996		0.26		

INTERIM DIVIDENDS (Per Share):

Amt.	Decl.	Ex.	Rec.	Pay.
0.15	4/18/96	5/6/96	5/8/96	6/12/96
0.15	6/18	8/12	8/14	9/11
0.15	9/18	11/7	11/12	12/11
0.15	2/11/97	2/21/97	2/25/97	3/18/97
0.05	4/30	5/20	5/22	6/17

Indicated div.:$0.200

CAPITALIZATION (12/31/96):

	($000)	(%)
Long-Term Debt	1,069,453	38.5
Stockholders' Equity	1,460,007	52.5
Deferred Income Tax	250,036	9.0
Total	2,779,496	100.0

RECENT DEVELOPMENTS: For the year ended 12/31/96, net earnings totaled C$51.0 million. This compares with C$280.0 million in 1995. Total sales for the year were C$5.04 billion, down 4.0% from C$5.25 billion the year before. The Company's largest business segment, Building Materials, posted a 2.6% sales gain to C$3.49 billion, while its other business segments posted sales declines for the year. The primary contributor to the gain in Building

Materials sales was C$1.15 billion in sales of lumber, up 31.7% over the prior year. Sales in the Paper segment were down 21.5% to C$715.0 million, primarily due to a 43.0% decline in standard newsprint paper sales to C$257.0 million. Packaging sales decreased 12.6% to C$911.0 million due primarily to a 23.3% decline in containerboard sales and an 8.3% drop in corrugated container sales.

BUSINESS

MACMILLAN BLOEDEL LIMITED, together with its subsidiaries, is one of the largest forest products companies in Canada and has integrated operations in Canada and the United States, as well as major investments in Canada, the United States and Mexico. The Company also has major joint venture investments in North America. The Company manages two million hectares of productive timberlands which supply most of its fiber requirements. Of these timberlands, 1.1 million hectares are in British Columbia where approximately 40% of the Company's property, plant and equipment and the Company's head office are located. The products of the Company and its affiliated companies are marketed throughout the world and include lumber, panelboards, engineered lumber, newsprint, groundwood printing papers, containerboard, corrugated containers and SpaceKraft.

ANNUAL EARNINGS

	12/31/96	12/31/95	12/31/96	12/31/95
	US $		C $	
Earnings Per Share	0.26	1.61	0.36	2.20

ANNUAL FINANCIAL DATA

RECORD OF EARNINGS (IN MILLIONS):

	12/31/96	12/31/95	12/31/96	12/31/95
Total Revenues	3,687	3,851	5,043	5,254
Costs & Expenses	3,448	3,349	4,716	4,570
Depreciation & Amort	184	165	251	225
Operating Income	56	336	76	459
Income Bef Income Tax	31	263	43	359
Income Tax	cr1	103	cr2	141
Eq. Earnings in Affils.	4	45	6	62
Net Income	37	205	51	280

BALANCE SHEET (IN MILLIONS):

Cash & Cash Equivalents	38	23	52	32
Receivables, Net	388	514	531	701
Inventories	650	619	889	844
Gross Property	3,895	3,514	5,327	4,795
Accumulated Depreciation	1,579	1,426	2,160	1,946
Long-Term Debt	1,069	1,115	1,463	1,522
Stockholders' Equity	1,460	1,540	1,997	2,101
Total Assets	3,531	3,863	4,830	5,271
Total Current Assets	1,094	1,183	1,497	1,614
Total Current Liabilities	679	893	929	1,219
Net Working Capital	415	289	568	395
Year End Shs Outstg (000)	124,377	124,336	124,377	124,336

STATISTICAL RECORD:

Return on Equity %	2.55	13.33		
Return on Assets %	1.06	5.31		
Operating Profit Margin %	1.51	8.74		
Net Profit Margin %	1.01	5.33		
Book Value Per Share	11.74	12.39		

Converted at 1996, US$0.7311= 1 Canadian $; 1995, US$0.7329= 1 Canadian $

OFFICERS:
R. F. Haskayne, Chmn.
R. B. Findlay, Pres. & C.E.O.
R. D. Tuckey, Exec. V.P.
G.M. Ferguson, Sr. V.P.-Fin. & C.F.O.

INCORPORATED: Jul., 1911

PRINCIPAL OFFICE: 925 West Georgia St., Vancouver, British Columbia Canada V6C 3L2

TELEPHONE NUMBER: (604) 661-8000

NO. OF EMPLOYEES: 13,497

ANNUAL MEETING: In Apr.

SHAREHOLDERS: N/A

INSTITUTIONAL HOLDINGS:
No. of Institutions: 38
Shares Held: 33,695,330

REGISTRAR(S): Montreal Trust Company of Canada (Vancouver, Calgary, Regina, Winnipeg, Toronto and Montreal); Bank of Nova Scotia Trust Company of New York (USA).

TRANSFER AGENT(S): Montreal Trust Company of Canada (Vancouver, Calgary, Regina, Winnipeg, Toronto and Montreal); Bank of Nova Scotia Trust Company of New York (USA).

MADGE NETWORKS N. V.

YIELD ...
P/E RATIO ...

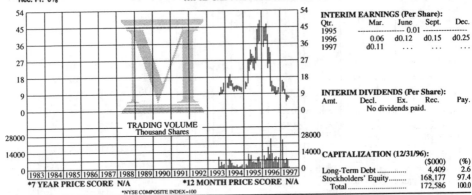

*7 YEAR PRICE SCORE N/A   *12 MONTH PRICE SCORE N/A

*NYSE COMPOSITE INDEX=100

INTERIM EARNINGS (Per Share):

Qtr.	Mar.	June	Sept.	Dec.
1995	-------- 0.01 --------			
1996	0.06	d0.12	d0.15	d0.25
1997	d0.11	...	...	...

INTERIM DIVIDENDS (Per Share):

Amt.	Decl.	Ex.	Rec.	Pay.
	No dividends paid.			

CAPITALIZATION (12/31/96):

	($000)	(%)
Long-Term Debt	4,409	2.6
Stockholders' Equity	168,177	97.4
Total	172,586	100.0

RECENT DEVELOPMENTS: For the quarter ended 3/31/97, net loss was $4.8 million, or d$.011 per share, compared with income of $2.7 million, or $0.06 per share, for the same period last year. Madge reported revenues of $107.4 million for the first fiscal quarter ended 3/31/97, down from $132.8 million for the same period in 1996. Historical financial results have been restated to reflect the acquisition of Teleos Communications, Inc., which was completed in February 1996 and accounted for as a pooling-of-interests. The Company experienced strong volume growth and sta-

ble revenue in its adapter business, but that growth was offset by weakness in its systems business. Madge's systems business was affected by macro-economic conditions in geographic regions such as Germany, Japan and Korea; the strength of the dollar overseas; and internal organizational restructuring in the Americas. During the quarter, Madge introduced the 3LS™ switch, the industry's first, all-silicon IP/IPX third layer switch for its LANswitch™ chassis, and grew its PCI adapter business.

BUSINESS

MADGE NETWORKS N.V. is a major global supplier of end-to-end switched networking solutions for large enterprises, with a special focus on multiservice networking, i.e., networks which will be able to support integrated data, video and voice. The Company, an orginator of ATM, Ethernet, ISDN and Token Ring technology, offers a range of products from desktop connections through LAN and WAN switches and enterprise network management software. It serves its multinational customer base in more than 20 countries worldwide from five major business centers located in Hong Kong, London, San Jose, Tel Aviv and Tokyo.

ANNUAL EARNINGS

	12/31/96	12/31/95	12/31/96	12/31/95
	------------US $------------		------------NLG------------	
Earnings Per Share	d0.47	d0.05	d0.82	d0.08

ANNUAL FINANCIAL DATA

RECORD OF EARNINGS (IN THOUSANDS):

	12/31/96	12/31/95	12/31/96	12/31/95
Total Revenues	482,101	427,350	841,216	687,168
Costs & Expenses	508,918	407,239	888,009	654,830
Operating Income	d26,817	20,111	d46,793	32,338
Income Bef Income Tax	d24,551	25,216	d42,839	40,547
Income Tax	cr4,054	27,201	cr7,074	43,739
Net Income	d20,497	d1,985	d35,765	d3,192
Average Shares Outstg	43,976	42,777	43,976	42,777

BALANCE SHEET (IN THOUSANDS):

Cash & Cash Equivalents	38,020	114,006	66,341	183,319
Receivables, Net	107,197	96,025	187,408	154,405
Inventories	53,374	51,501	93,132	82,812
Gross Property	131,621	79,717	229,665	128,183
Accumulated Depreciation	62,768	35,212	109,524	56,620
Long-Term Debt	4,409	4,507	7,693	7,247
Stockholders' Equity	168,177	175,863	293,451	282,783
Total Assets	294,455	324,278	513,793	521,431
Total Current Assets	218,463	277,118	381,195	445,599
Total Current Liabilities	121,869	143,908	212,649	231,401
Net Working Capital	96,594	133,210	168,547	214,198
Year End Shs Outstg	44,460	43,393	44,460	43,393

STATISTICAL RECORD:

Return on Equity %	...	...		
Return on Assets %	...	...		
Operating Profit Margin %	...	4.71		
Net Profit Margin %	...	...		
Book Value Per Share	3.78	4.05		

Converted at 1996, US$0.5731= 1 Netherlands guilders; 1995, US$0.6219= 1 Netherlands guilders

OFFICERS:
R. H. Madge, Chmn. & C.E.O.
M. E. Jones, C.O.O. & Group Pres.
K. R. Evans, V.P.-Fin. & Admin. & C.F.O.
INCORPORATED: Apr., 1993
PRINCIPAL OFFICE: Transpolis Schiphol Airport, Polaris Avenue 23, 2132 JH Hoofddorp The Netherlands

TELEPHONE NUMBER: +31 23 568 55 24
NO. OF EMPLOYEES: 440
ANNUAL MEETING: June 26, 1997
SHAREHOLDERS: 511
INSTITUTIONAL HOLDINGS:
No. of Institutions: 31
Shares Held: 4,847,040

REGISTRAR(S): Chase Mellon Shareholder Services

TRANSFER AGENT(S): Chase Mellon Shareholder Services

MAGAL SECURITY SYSTEMS LTD.

YIELD ...
P/E RATIO 20.8

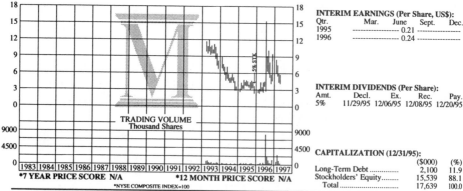

INTERIM EARNINGS (Per Share, US$):

Qtr.	Mar.	June	Sept.	Dec.
1995		0.21		
1996		0.24		

INTERIM DIVIDENDS (Per Share):

Amt.	Decl.	Ex.	Rec.	Pay.
5%	11/29/95	12/06/95	12/08/95	12/20/95

CAPITALIZATION (12/31/95):

	($000)	(%)
Long-Term Debt	2,100	11.9
Stockholders' Equity	15,539	88.1
Total	17,639	100.0

RECENT DEVELOPMENTS: For the year ended 12/31/96, net income increased 12.8% to US$1.2 million compared with US$1.1 million in 1995. Revenues advanced 6.4% to US$18.2 million from US$17.1 million a year earlier. Research and development expenses totaled US$2.0 million, essentially unchanged from the prior year. As a percentage of revenues, research and development expenses totaled 11.2% compared with 11.8% in 1995. Selling, general and administrative expenses as a percentage of revenues were 23.1% versus 25.2% in 1995. For the three

months ended 12/31/96, net income increased 32.8% to US$478,000 compared with US$360,000 in the corresponding period of 1995. Revenues advanced 14.6% to US$5.2 million from US$4.5 million in the year-ago period. On 2/7/97, the Company issued 2,000,000 shares at the price of US$5.50 through an underwriting managed by Josephthal Lyon & Ross. The net proceeds to the Company were approximately US$10.0 million. Also, on 2/18/97, the Company finalized its acquisition of Senstar Corporation. The effective date of the acquisition is 1/1/97.

BUSINESS

MAGAL SECURITY SYSTEMS LTD. and its subsidiaries are engaged in the developing, manufacturing and marketing of computerized security systems used to automatically detect and deter human intrusions, and to locate and identify explosive devices in luggage, packages and other parcels.

ANNUAL EARNINGS

	12/31/95	12/31/94	12/31/95	12/31/94
	---US $---		---NIS---	
Earnings Per Share	0.21	0.36	0.66	1.09

ANNUAL FINANCIAL DATA

RECORD OF EARNINGS (IN THOUSANDS):

	12/31/95	12/31/94	12/31/95	12/31/94
Total Revenues	17,083	16,836	53,771	50,803
Costs & Expenses	15,741	14,831	49,547	44,753
Operating Income	1,342	2,005	4,224	6,050
Income Bef Income Tax	1,222	1,708	3,846	5,154
Income Tax	161	3	507	9
Net Income	1,061	1,705	3,340	5,145
Average Shares Outstg	4,977	4,977	4,977	4,977

BALANCE SHEET (IN THOUSANDS):

Cash & Cash Equivalents	4,310	4,361	13,566	13,159
Receivables, Net	8,928	8,629	28,102	26,038
Inventories	5,464	4,267	17,199	12,876
Gross Property	5,608	5,518	17,652	16,651
Accumulated Depreciation	2,027	1,716	6,380	5,178
Long-Term Debt	2,100	2,100	6,610	6,337
Stockholders' Equity	15,539	14,428	48,911	43,537
Total Assets	23,666	22,513	74,492	67,933
Total Current Assets	18,768	17,370	59,075	52,414
Total Current Liabilities	5,964	5,916	18,772	17,852
Net Working Capital	12,804	11,454	40,302	34,562
Year End Shs Outstg	5,229	4,980	5,229	4,980

STATISTICAL RECORD:

Return on Equity %	6.8	11.8		
Return on Assets %	4.5	7.6		
Operating Profit Margin %	7.9	11.9		
Net Profit Margin %	6.2	10.1		
Book Value Per Share	2.97	2.90		

Converted at 1995, US$0.3177= 1 New Israeli Shekel; 1994, US$0.3314= 1 New Israeli Shekel

OFFICERS:
J. Even-Ezra, C.E.O. & Chmn.
I. Dekel, Pres.

INCORPORATED: 1984, Israel

PRINCIPAL OFFICE: P.O. Box 70, Industrial Zone, Yahud Israel 56000

TELEPHONE NUMBER: 027-3-5394144
NO. OF EMPLOYEES: N/A
ANNUAL MEETING: N/A
SHAREHOLDERS: N/A
INSTITUTIONAL HOLDINGS:
No. of Institutions: N/A
Shares Held: N/A

REGISTRAR(S): American Stock Transfer and Trust Co., New York.

TRANSFER AGENT(S): American Stock Transfer and Trust Co., New York.

MAGIC SOFTWARE ENTERPRISES LTD

YIELD ...
P/E RATIO 20.8

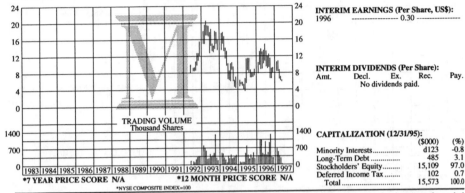

INTERIM EARNINGS (Per Share, US$):
1996 ------------------ 0.30 -----------------

INTERIM DIVIDENDS (Per Share):
Amt.   Decl.   Ex.   Rec.   Pay.
No dividends paid.

CAPITALIZATION (12/31/95):

	($000)	(%)
Minority Interests..............	d123	-0.8
Long-Term Debt	485	3.1
Stockholders' Equity........	15,109	97.0
Deferred Income Tax	102	0.7
Total	15,573	100.0

TRADING VOLUME
Thousand Shares

1983 1984 1985 1986 1987 1988 1989 1990 1991 1992 1993 1994 1995 1996 1997

*7 YEAR PRICE SCORE N/A   *12 MONTH PRICE SCORE N/A
*NYSE COMPOSITE INDEX=100

RECENT DEVELOPMENTS: For the year ended 12/31/96, the Company posted net income of $1.4 million versus a loss of $438,000 in 1995. Revenues rose 43.5% to $36.4 million. Software sales advanced 44.2% to $28.6 million, while services revenues rose 40.7% to $7.8 million. Gross profit as a percentage of total revenues totaled 69.3% or $25.2 million versus 77.7% or $19.7 million in the year-ago period. Research and development expenses fell 9.3% to $2.6 million. Sales and marketing and general and administrative expenses advanced 19.8% and 9.7%, respectively, to

$16.0 million and $4.1 million. For the three months ended 12/31/96, net income declined 4.6% to $970,000 from $1.0 million a year earlier. Revenues rose 21.8% to $10.8 million. Sales and marketing expenses advanced 36.4% to $5.3 million, while general and administrative expenses rose 6.1% to $1.0 million. The Company noted that it will continue to invest heavily in US sales and marketing in order to achieve high revenue growth, market share, and a critical mass installed base, even at the expense of short-term profitability.

BUSINESS

MAGIC SOFTWARE ENTER-PRISES LTD. designs, develops, markets and supports a family of software products used for the rapid application development and deployment ("RADD") of departmental and enterprise client/server applications. The Company's family of MAGIC products automate the programming cycle, increasing the productivity of analysts and programmers involved in software development, and provide the end-users with the ability to independently access, analyze, and present corporate data. The Company's subsidiaries are engaged in the marketing of the software in the United States, Britain, the Netherlands and Israel.

ANNUAL EARNINGS

	12/31/95	12/31/94	12/31/95	12/31/94
	----------US $----------		----------NIS----------	
Earnings Per Share	d0.10	d0.34	d0.31	d1.03

ANNUAL FINANCIAL DATA

RECORD OF EARNINGS (IN THOUSANDS):				
Total Revenues	25,384	21,372	79,899	64,490
Costs & Expenses	25,613	21,421	80,620	64,638
Operating Income	d229	d49	d721	d148
Income Bef Income Tax	d295	d1,298	d929	d3,917
Income Tax	333	190	1,048	573
Eq. Earnings in Affils.	67	...	211	...
Minority Interests	cr123	cr88	cr387	cr266
Net Income	d438	d1,400	d1,379	d4,225
Average Shares Outstg	4,303	4,158	4,303	4,158
BALANCE SHEET (IN THOUSANDS):				
Cash & Cash Equivalents	824	2,672	2,594	8,063
Receivables, Net	11,244	8,177	35,392	24,674
Inventories	266	198	837	597
Gross Property	7,712	6,385	24,274	19,267
Accumulated Depreciation	1,930	1,174	6,075	3,543
Long-Term Debt	485	...	1,527	...
Stockholders' Equity	15,109	14,889	47,557	44,928
Total Assets	24,559	20,436	77,302	61,666
Total Current Assets	14,041	12,088	44,196	36,476
Total Current Liabilities	7,828	4,712	24,640	14,218
Net Working Capital	6,213	7,376	19,556	22,257
Year End Shs Outstg	4,215	3,952	4,215	3,952
STATISTICAL RECORD:				
Return on Equity %	...	...		
Return on Assets %	...	...		
Operating Profit Margin %	...	...		
Net Profit Margin %	...	...		
Book Value Per Share	3.6	3.8		

Converted at 1995, US$0.318= 1 New Israeli Shekel; 1994, US$0.331= 1 New Israeli Shekel

OFFICERS:
D. Assia, Chmn. & C.E.O.
E. Gonen, Pres. & C.O.O.
I. Teiblum, C.F.O.

INCORPORATED: 1983

PRINCIPAL OFFICE: 5 HaPlada Street, Or Yehuda Israel

TELEPHONE NUMBER: 972-3-751-1914
NO. OF EMPLOYEES: 265
ANNUAL MEETING: N/A
SHAREHOLDERS: 64
INSTITUTIONAL HOLDINGS:
No. of Institutions: 6
Shares Held: 98,000

REGISTRAR(S): American Stock Transfer and Trust Co., N.Y.

TRANSFER AGENT(S): American Stock Transfer and Trust Co., N.Y.

MDSI MOBILE DATA SOLUTIONS,

YIELD ...
P/E RATIO 49.6

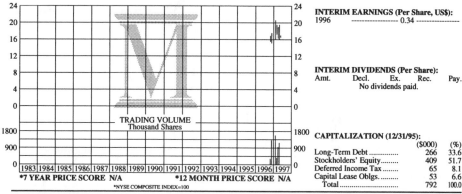

*7 YEAR PRICE SCORE N/A   *12 MONTH PRICE SCORE N/A

TRADING VOLUME
Thousand Shares

| 1983 | 1984 | 1985 | 1986 | 1987 | 1988 | 1989 | 1990 | 1991 | 1992 | 1993 | 1994 | 1995 | 1996 | 1997 |

INTERIM EARNINGS (Per Share, US$):
1996 ------------------ 0.34 -----------------

INTERIM DIVIDENDS (Per Share):
Amt.   Decl.   Ex.   Rec.   Pay.
No dividends paid.

CAPITALIZATION (12/31/95):

	($000)	(%)
Long-Term Debt	266	33.6
Stockholders' Equity........	409	51.7
Deferred Income Tax	65	8.1
Capital Lease Oblgs.	53	6.6
Total	792	100.0

RECENT DEVELOPMENTS: For the year ended 12/31/96, the Company reported a net loss of C$6.0 million versus a loss of C$1.5 million in 1995. Revenues rose to C$45.1 million from C$9.3 million a year earlier. Results in 1996 included acquired R&D costs of C$8.5 million associated with the purchase of Spectronics MicroSystems Limited. Software and services. Revenue more than doubled to C$18.4 million from C$8.6 million in 1995, while maintenance and support revenues rose to C$2.8 million versus C$729,103 in the prior year. Additionally, the Company reported terminals and infrastructure revenues of C$8.7 million in 1996 and third party products and services revenues of C$15.2 million. In November 1996, a U.S. public offering of 1,495,000 shares raised approximately C$30.0 million. A portion of the proceeds were used to repay C$8.6 million in notes arising from the acquisition of Spectronics.

BUSINESS

MDSI MOBILE DATA SOLUTIONS, INC. is engaged in the development, marketing and supporting of wireless, mobile data communication software products and provides related professional services to customers who require solutions for increased management control and productivity of mobile field resources. The Company's suite of software products consists principally of Utility Computer-Aided Dispatch (U-CAD), Order Scheduling Systems (OSS), S-2000 Field Service Management, and TechNet Wireless Connectivity products. The Company's revenue is derived from licensing software and providing related services, including training, project management, installation, integration, and customization. In addition, customers can elect to contract with the Company for product support, which includes product and documentation enhancements, as well as telephone support for problem resolution.

ANNUAL EARNINGS

	12/31/95 [1]	6/30/95	12/31/95 [1]	6/30/95
	------------US $-----------		------------C $-----------	
Earnings Per Share	d0.31	0.72	d0.42	0.99

[1] Results represent a six-month time period ended 12/31/95.

ANNUAL FINANCIAL DATA

RECORD OF EARNINGS (IN THOUSANDS):

Total Revenues	3,153	5,829	4,302	8,000
Costs & Expenses	2,969	4,673	4,051	6,412
Operating Income	184	1,157	252	1,588
Income Bef Income Tax	d1,210	1,195	d1,651	1,640
Income Tax	...	471	...	646
Net Income	d1,210	724	d1,651	993

BALANCE SHEET (IN THOUSANDS):

Cash & Cash Equivalents	1,408	984	1,922	1,350
Receivables, Net	2,882	2,195	3,933	3,012
Gross Property	2,139	373	2,919	512
Accumulated Depreciation	1,290	...	1,760	...
Long-Term Debt	266	1,454	363	1,995
Stockholders' Equity	409	525	559	721
Total Assets	6,335	3,598	8,644	4,938
Total Current Assets	4,406	3,225	6,011	4,426
Total Current Liabilities	5,595	1,554	7,635	2,133
Net Working Capital	d1,190	1,671	d1,623	2,293
Year End Shs Outstg	3,690	1,500	3,690	1,500

STATISTICAL RECORD:

Return on Equity %	...	137.8		
Return on Assets %	...	20.1		
Operating Profit Margin %	5.9	19.8		
Net Profit Margin %	...	12.4		
Book Value Per Share	0.11	0.35		

Converted at 1995, US$0.7329= 1 Canadian $; 1995, US$0.7287= 1 Canadian C $

OFFICERS:
E. Dysthe, Chmn. & C.E.O.
K. R. Miller, Pres. & C.F.O.
P. H. Rankin, Sr. V.P.

INCORPORATED: In Canada

PRINCIPAL OFFICE: 135 - 10551 Shellbridge Way, Richmond B.C., Canada V6X 2W9

TELEPHONE NUMBER: 604-270-9939

NO. OF EMPLOYEES: 211

ANNUAL MEETING: In Jun.

SHAREHOLDERS: N/A

INSTITUTIONAL HOLDINGS:
No. of Institutions: 13
Shares Held: 1,068,200

REGISTRAR(S): Montreal Trust Company of Canada, Vancouver.

TRANSFER AGENT(S): Montreal Trust Company of Canada, Vancouver.

MEMCO SOFTWARE, LTD.

YIELD ...
P/E RATIO 43.0

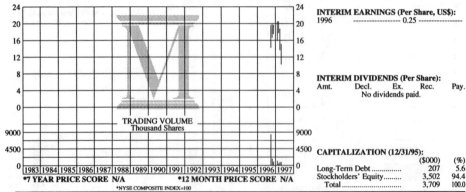

*7 YEAR PRICE SCORE N/A   *12 MONTH PRICE SCORE N/A

*NYSE COMPOSITE INDEX=100

INTERIM EARNINGS (Per Share, US$):
1996 ------------------ 0.25 ------------------

INTERIM DIVIDENDS (Per Share):
Amt.   Decl.   Ex.   Rec.   Pay.
No dividends paid.

CAPITALIZATION (12/31/95):

	($000)	(%)
Long-Term Debt	207	5.6
Stockholders' Equity........	3,502	94.4
Total	3,709	100.0

RECENT DEVELOPMENTS: For the year ended 12/31/96, the Company posted net income of $3.4 million compared with a loss of $2.5 million in 1995. Revenues increased to $15.3 million from $1.5 million a year earlier. Marketing and selling expenses as a percentage of revenues were 48.4%, or $7.4 million, versus $2.4 million in the year-ago period. General and administrative expenses as a percentage of revenues totaled 9.8%, or $1.5 million, versus 34.5%, or $535,000, in 1995. For the three months ended 12/31/96, the Company posted net income of $1.7 million compared with a loss of $384,000 in the comparable period a year earlier. Revenues advanced to $6.2 million from $1.1 million a year earlier. The Company noted that during the quarter ended 12/31/96, it completed an initial public offering of 3,450,000 of its Ordinary Shares on the NASDAQ National Market, raising approximately $46.0 million in net proceeds. In addition, the Company noted that it continued to build its distribution network and recently signed agreements with European distributors in key territories, including Italy, France, the United Kingdom, and other countries.

BUSINESS

MEMCO SOFTWARE LIMITED is a provider of advanced information security solutions. The Company offers a comprehensive product set designed to address enterprise security concerns. The Company's solutions enforce, administer and control security and productivity in distributed environments.

ANNUAL EARNINGS

	12/31/95	12/31/94	12/31/95	12/31/94
	------------US $------------		------------NIS------------	
Earnings Per Share	d0.21	d0.09	d0.66	d0.27

ANNUAL FINANCIAL DATA

RECORD OF EARNINGS (IN THOUSANDS):

	12/31/95	12/31/94	12/31/95	12/31/94
Total Revenues	1,549	440	4,876	1,328
Costs & Expenses	4,010	948	12,622	2,861
Operating Income	d2,461	d508	d7,746	d1,533
Income Bef Income Tax	d2,163	d483	d6,808	d1,457
Income Tax	300	...	944	...
Net Income	d2,463	d483	d7,753	d1,457
Average Shares Outstg	11,953	5,117	11,953	5,117

BALANCE SHEET (IN THOUSANDS):

Cash & Cash Equivalents	9,453	1,137	29,754	3,431
Receivables, Net	1,065	128	3,352	386
Gross Property	700	212	2,203	640
Accumulated Depreciation	115	37	362	112
Long-Term Debt	207	113	652	341
Stockholders' Equity	3,502	1,119	11,023	3,377
Total Assets	11,342	1,614	35,700	4,870
Total Current Assets	10,518	1,265	33,107	3,817
Total Current Liabilities	2,221	264	6,991	797
Net Working Capital	8,297	1,001	26,116	3,021
Year End Shs Outstg	11,672	9,338	11,672	9,338

STATISTICAL RECORD:

Return on Equity %	...	...		
Return on Assets %	...	...		
Operating Profit Margin %	...	...		
Net Profit Margin %	...	...		
Book Value Per Share	0.30	0.12		

Converted at 1995, US$0.3177= 1 New Israeli Shekel; 1994, US$0.3314= 1 New Israeli Shekel

OFFICERS:
I. Mazin, Chmn. & C.E.O.
O. Mazin, C.O.O.
D. Gal, C.F.O.
E. Mashiah, Chief Tech. Officer
INCORPORATED: Sept. 1990
PRINCIPAL OFFICE: Atidim Industrial Park Building 7Neve Sharet Tel Aviv Israel

TELEPHONE NUMBER: 011-972-3-648-7415
NO. OF EMPLOYEES: 70
ANNUAL MEETING: N/A
SHAREHOLDERS: N/A
INSTITUTIONAL HOLDINGS:
No. of Institutions: N/A
Shares Held: N/A

REGISTRAR(S): N/A

TRANSFER AGENT(S): American Stock Transfer & Trust Co., New York, NY.

METHANEX CORPORATION

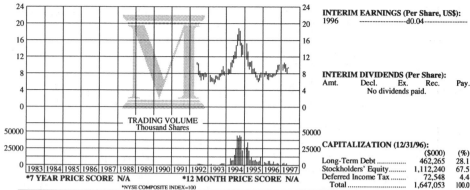

INTERIM EARNINGS (Per Share, US$):
1996 ------------------d0.04----------------

INTERIM DIVIDENDS (Per Share):

Amt.	Decl.	Ex.	Rec.	Pay.
	No dividends paid.			

*7 YEAR PRICE SCORE N/A   *12 MONTH PRICE SCORE N/A

*NYSE COMPOSITE INDEX=100

CAPITALIZATION (12/31/96):

	($000)	(%)
Long-Term Debt	462,265	28.1
Stockholders' Equity........	1,112,240	67.5
Deferred Income Tax	72,548	4.4
Total	1,647,053	100.0

RECENT DEVELOPMENTS: For the year ended 12/31/96, the Company posted a net loss of $7.9 million versus income of $191.7 million in 1995. Revenues fell 24.3% to $945.7 million. Results in 1996 included a write-down of $105.0 million related to facilities that will be idled and replaced by low-cost assets. Results in 1995 included debt retirement costs of $36.5 million. Comparisons were made with restated 1995 results. For the three months ended 12/31/96, the Company posted a net loss of $56.5 million versus income of $4.8 million a year earlier. Revenues rose 22.9% to $264.3 million. Results included the previously mentioned write-down of $105.0 million. Net earnings before the write down totaled $36.9 million versus $4.8 million in the prior period. The Company attributed the gain in operating earnings to record sales volume and strengthening pricing. In the recent quarter (ended 12/31/96), the Company sold a record 1.6 million tons. For 1996, total sales volume was in excess of 6.1 million tons, 15% above 1995.

BUSINESS

METHANEX CORPORATION is a major producer and marketer of methanol. Methanol, typically produced from natural gas, is a basic chemical building block used in the production of formaldehyde, methyl-tertiary-butyl-ether (MTBE), acetic acid and a variety of other chemical intermediaries. These derivatives are ultimately adhesives, paints, inks, urethane and MDI foams, gasoline additives, silicones, PET plastic, polyester, solvents, Spandex, and windshield washer fluid. Methanol is also used directly as a fuel. Based in Vancouver, Canada, Methanex has plants strategically located in New Zealand, the United States, Canada and Chile. Additional methanol is available through marketing agreements with plants located in the United States, Germany and Trinidad. This extensive global marketing and distribution system makes Methanex the largest supplier of Methanol to each of the major international markets. In 1996, Methanex accounted for roughly 38% of the world merchant market for methanol.

ANNUAL EARNINGS

	12/31/96	12/31/95	12/31/96	12/31/95
	------------US $------------		------------C $------------	
Earnings Per Share	d0.04	1.01	d0.05	1.38

ANNUAL FINANCIAL DATA

RECORD OF EARNINGS (IN THOUSANDS):

	12/31/96	12/31/95	12/31/96	12/31/95
Total Revenues	945,707	1,249,179	1,293,540	1,704,433
Costs & Expenses	734,122	848,256	1,004,133	1,157,397
Depreciation & Amort	114,055	97,575	156,005	133,135
Operating Income	97,530	303,348	133,402	413,901
Income Bef Income Tax	d4,838	254,457	d6,617	347,192
Income Tax	3,014	62,719	4,123	85,576
Net Income	d7,852	191,738	d10,740	261,616
Average Shares Outstg	188,981	190,273	188,981	190,273

BALANCE SHEET (IN THOUSANDS):

Cash & Cash Equivalents	383,892	399,645	525,088	545,293
Receivables, Net	207,847	173,045	284,294	236,110
Inventories	68,129	64,223	93,187	87,629
Property	1,020,546	1,014,128	1,395,905	1,383,720
Long-Term Debt	398,241	401,331	544,715	547,593
Stockholders' Equity	1,112,240	1,113,285	1,521,324	1,519,014
Total Assets	1,771,164	1,748,601	2,422,602	2,385,866
Total Current Assets	669,105	650,264	915,203	887,248
Total Current Liabilities	124,111	136,043	169,759	185,623
Net Working Capital	544,994	514,221	745,444	701,625
Year End Shs Outstg	189,119	188,965	189,119	188,965

STATISTICAL RECORD:

Return on Equity %	...	17.2		
Return on Assets %	...	11.0		
Operating Profit Margin %	10.3	24.3		
Net Profit Margin %	...	15.3		
Book Value Per Share	5.9	5.9		

Converted at 1996, US$0.7311= 1 Canadian C $; 1995, US$0.7329= 1 Canadian C $

OFFICERS:
T. Newal, Chmn.
P. Choquette, Pres. & C.E.O.
M. M. Wilson, Exec. V.P.
T. W. Duncan, V.P. & C.F.O.
INCORPORATED: Sep., 1991
PRINCIPAL OFFICE: 1880 Waterfront Centre, 200 Burrard Street Vancouver, British Columbia Canada V6C 3M1

TELEPHONE NUMBER: 604-661-2600
NO. OF EMPLOYEES: 881
ANNUAL MEETING: In May
SHAREHOLDERS: 650 (approx.)
INSTITUTIONAL HOLDINGS:
No. of Institutions: 37
Shares Held: 30,855,654

REGISTRAR(S): R-M Trust Company; Toronto.

TRANSFER AGENT(S): R-M Trust Company; Toronto.

METROWERKS INC.

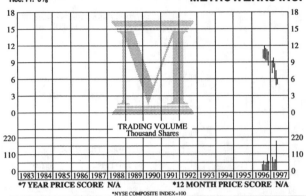

INTERIM EARNINGS (Per Share, US$):

Qtr	Oct.	Jan.	Apr.	July
1994-95	---------- 0.03 ----------			
1995-96	0.02	0.02	d0.01	0.02
1996-97	d0.01	d0.01	...	...

INTERIM DIVIDENDS (Per Share):

Amt.	Decl.	Ex.	Rec.	Pay.
	No dividends paid.			

CAPITALIZATION (7/31/96):

	($000)	(%)
Stockholders' Equity........	16,437	100.0
Total	16,437	100.0

RECENT DEVELOPMENTS: For the quarter ended 1/31/97, the Company posted a net loss of $75,000 versus income of $221,000 a year earlier. Revenues rose 93.7% to $4.7 million. The Company noted that Macintosh-related revenues accounted for 53% of total sales, while embedded and other revenues accounted for 47% of sales. The Company has continued to make progress in diversifying its revenue base and building the infra-structure needed to continue its penetration into the embedded market. In the recent quarter, R&D expenses more than doubled to $1.5 million from $700,000 in the year-ago period reflecting the development of new products, including five new products for the embedded systems market that the Company has indicated will be shipped in the current fiscal year. On 1/27/97, the Company signed a letter of intention to acquire the principle assets of The Latitude Group, Inc. Latitude's principle assets include a porting library that will be used to port Code Warrior to UNIX-based workstations and in transitioning current Mac OS applications to Apple's new Rhapsody OS due out next year.

BUSINESS

METROWERKS INC. develops, markets and supports a complete line of programming tools for building applications for a number of operating systems intended for use on desktop computers or embedded systems, including Windows 95, Windows NT, Mac OS, BeOS, PlayStation OS, Palm OS, and OS-9, running on a number of processors including X86, Power PC, MIPS, 68K and ARM microprocessors.

ANNUAL EARNINGS

	7/31/96	7/31/95	7/31/96	7/31/95
	----------US $----------		----------C $----------	
Earnings Per Share	0.01	0.03	0.01	0.04

ANNUAL FINANCIAL DATA

RECORD OF EARNINGS (IN THOUSANDS):

	7/31/96	7/31/95	7/31/96	7/31/95
Total Revenues	10,619	5,143	14,601	7,030
Costs & Expenses	10,536	4,832	14,486	6,605
Depreciation & Amort	355	155	488	212
Operating Income	d272	156	d374	213
Net Income	105	254	144	347
Average Shares Outstg	10,620	7,956	10,620	7,956

BALANCE SHEET (IN THOUSANDS):

Cash & Cash Equivalents	11,498	4,746	15,809	6,487
Receivables, Net	3,062	797	4,210	1,089
Inventories	254	64	349	87
Gross Property	2,274	570	3,127	779
Accumulated Depreciation	558	213	767	291
Stockholders' Equity	16,437	5,571	22,600	7,615
Total Assets	18,305	6,634	25,168	9,068
Total Current Assets	15,387	5,805	21,156	7,935
Total Current Liabilities	1,868	1,063	2,568	1,453
Net Working Capital	13,519	4,742	18,588	6,482
Year End Shs Outstg	11,497	8,177	11,497	8,177

STATISTICAL RECORD:

Return on Equity %	0.6	4.6		
Return on Assets %	0.6	3.8		
Operating Profit Margin %	...	3.0		
Net Profit Margin %	1.0	4.9		
Book Value Per Share	1.43	0.68		

Converted at 1996, US$0.7273= 1 Canadian $; 1995, US$0.7316= 1 Canadian $

OFFICERS:
J. J. Belanger, Chmn. & C.E.O.
G. P. Galanos, Pres. & Chief Tech. Off.
D. Perkins, Sr. V.P.
J. Welch, V.P.-Fin. & C.F.O.
INCORPORATED: 1995
PRINCIPAL OFFICE: 2201 Danley, Suite 310
Austin TX 78758

TELEPHONE NUMBER: 512-873-4777
NO. OF EMPLOYEES: 175
ANNUAL MEETING: In Oct.
SHAREHOLDERS: N/A
INSTITUTIONAL HOLDINGS:
No. of Institutions: 15
Shares Held: 4,000,000

REGISTRAR(S): Montreal Trust Company of Canada; The Bank of Nova Scotia Trust, New York.

TRANSFER AGENT(S): Montreal Trust Company of Canada; The Bank of Nova Scotia Trust, New York.

MILLICOM INTERNATIONAL CELLULAR S.A.

YIELD ...
P/E RATIO ...

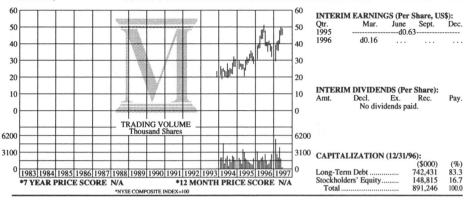

INTERIM EARNINGS (Per Share, US$):

Qtr.	Mar.	June	Sept.	Dec.
1995	----------------d0.63----------------			
1996	d0.16	...	...	...

INTERIM DIVIDENDS (Per Share):

Amt.	Decl.	Ex.	Rec.	Pay.
	No dividends paid.			

TRADING VOLUME
Thousand Shares

| 1983 | 1984 | 1985 | 1986 | 1987 | 1988 | 1989 | 1990 | 1991 | 1992 | 1993 | 1994 | 1995 | 1996 | 1997 |

*7 YEAR PRICE SCORE N/A   ***12 MONTH PRICE SCORE N/A**

*NYSE COMPOSITE INDEX=100

CAPITALIZATION (12/31/96):

	($000)	(%)
Long-Term Debt	742,431	83.3
Stockholders' Equity	148,815	16.7
Total	891,246	100.0

RECENT DEVELOPMENTS: For the quarter ended 3/31/97, loss after taxes was $21.1 million compared with a loss of $7.8 million in the same period of 1996. Revenues increased 61.5% to $70.2 million. The decline in earnings was attributed to the substantial investment undertaken in building MICCF's subscriber base during the second half of 1996 and the first quarter of 1997. In addition, the loss was due to the related network development worldwide and the corresponding increase in interest expense on the funds borrowed to finance this development. The number of MICCF subscribers worldwide rose 93.2% to 582,625 as of 3/31/97. MICCF has initiated a strategic restructuring of its operations. During the quarter, MICCF acquired a Broadband fixed wireless license in the United Kingdom, commenced operations in the Kingdom of Cambodia, and was granted a ten year license extension for operation in Colombia. Also, MICCF's operation in Pakistan recommenced service in Karachi and Hyderabad.

BUSINESS

MILLICOM INTERNATIONAL CELLULAR S.A. is a holding company. Through its subsidiaries, MICCF is engaged in the development and management of cellular phone networks worldwide. MICCF has interests in 30 cellular systems in 20 countries, primarily in emerging markets. Its cellular operations are mostly located in developing countries with new markets for communication services. Upon entering a new market, MICCF will typically establish a joint venture with a local business partner and apply for a cellular telephone license. If the license is granted, MICCF will actively participates with the joint venture partner in the selection of management, the development of business plans, and the initial set-up of the cellular network.

ANNUAL EARNINGS

	12/31/96	12/31/95	12/31/94
	---------------US $---------------		
Earnings Per Share	d0.26	d0.43	0.15

ANNUAL FINANCIAL DATA

RECORD OF EARNINGS (IN THOUSANDS):

	12/31/96	12/31/95	12/31/94
Total Revenues	215,628	131,376	81,377
Costs & Expenses	154,355	92,107	57,313
Depreciation & Amort	27,893	18,601	9,269
Operating Income	33,380	20,668	14,795
Income Bef Income Tax	d5,388	d22,330	20,803
Income Tax	12,717	7,556	10,395
Net Income	d18,105	d29,886	10,408

BALANCE SHEET (IN THOUSANDS):

Cash & Cash Equivalents	158,372	39,321	31,626
Receivables, Net	267,868	41,858	26,380
Inventories	11,458	8,986	6,219
Gross Property	342,269	215,261	102,838
Accumulated Depreciation	60,634	38,150	16,866
Long-Term Debt	742,431	161,045	124,159
Stockholders' Equity	148,815	167,546	126,047
Total Assets	1,063,231	475,438	340,423
Total Current Assets	468,898	107,506	75,364
Total Current Liabilities	171,985	146,847	90,217
Net Working Capital	296,913	d39,341	d14,853
Year End Shs Outstg	48,144	47,995	44,995

STATISTICAL RECORD:

Return on Equity %	...	...	8.26
Return on Assets %	...	...	3.06
Operating Profit Margin %	15.48	15.73	18.18
Net Profit Margin %	...	...	12.79
Book Value Per Share	2.13	3.49	2.80

OFFICERS:
R. Blott, C.E.O.
H. Berk, Sr. V.P.
M. Beula, Sr. V.P.-Fin.
J. Harlton, V.P.-Engineering

INCORPORATED: Jun., 1992

PRINCIPAL OFFICE: 75 Route de Longwy,
P.O. Box 23, L-8080 Bertrange Luxembourg

TELEPHONE NUMBER: 352 4571451

NO. OF EMPLOYEES: N/A

ANNUAL MEETING: May

SHAREHOLDERS: 579

INSTITUTIONAL HOLDINGS:
No. of Institutions: N/A
Shares Held: N/A

REGISTRAR(S): The American Stock Transfer & Trust Co., New York.

TRANSFER AGENT(S): The American Stock Transfer & Trust Co., New York.

MIRAMAR MINING CORPORATION

YIELD ...
P/E RATIO ...

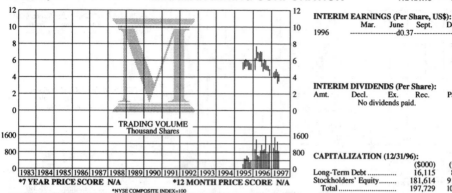

INTERIM EARNINGS (Per Share, US$):

	Mar.	June	Sept.	Dec.
1996	----------------d0.37----------------

INTERIM DIVIDENDS (Per Share):

Amt.	Decl.	Ex.	Rec.	Pay.
No dividends paid.

CAPITALIZATION (12/31/96):

	($000)	(%)
Long-Term Debt	16,115	8.1
Stockholders' Equity	181,614	91.9
Total	197,729	100.0

RECENT DEVELOPMENTS: For the year ended 12/31/96, the Company reported a net loss of C$29.1 million (US$21.3 million) compared with $18.4 million (US$13.4 million) in the equivalent period of 1995. The 1996 results included a C$37.5 million charge for the write-down of mineral properties. Revenues decreased 12.2% to C$76.8 million (US$56.2 million) from C$87.6 million (US$64.2 million) in the prior year. Revenues included gains on dilution in the amounts of C$1.9 million in 1996 and C$9.1 million in 1995. The Cone Mine milled 414,000 tons with an average grade of 0.298 ounces per ton of gold and recovered 111,021 ounces of gold for an annual recovery of 89.3%. Cash operating costs for the year were US$336.00 per ounce, reflecting lower gold production than the year before. Overall gold production in 1997 is expected to be similar to that achieved in 1996, but at a lower cash cost.

BUSINESS

MIRAMAR MINING CORPORA-TION is principally engaged in the business of mining and exploration of gold, silver and copper throughout Canada, the United States, Cuba and Argentina.

ANNUAL EARNINGS

	12/31/96	12/31/95	12/31/96	12/31/95
	US $		C $	
Earnings Per Share	d0.37	0.26	d0.51	0.36

ANNUAL FINANCIAL DATA

RECORD OF EARNINGS (IN THOUSANDS):

	12/31/96	12/31/95	12/31/96	12/31/95
Total Revenues	56,173	64,171	76,833	87,557
Costs & Expenses	72,377	47,281	98,997	64,512
Depreciation & Amort	5,593	3,594	7,650	4,904
Operating Income	d21,797	13,296	d29,814	18,141
Income Bef Income Tax	d21,797	13,296	d29,814	18,141
Minority Interests	cr513	cr185	cr701	cr252
Net Income	d21,285	13,480	d29,113	18,393
Average Shares Outstg	56,635	51,009	56,635	51,009

BALANCE SHEET (IN THOUSANDS):

	12/31/96	12/31/95	12/31/96	12/31/95
Cash & Cash Equivalents	101,302	122,405	138,561	167,014
Receivables, Net	9,169	1,537	12,541	2,097
Inventories	8,517	8,311	11,649	11,340
Gross Property	138,326	135,502	189,202	184,885
Accumulated Depreciation	12,735	7,160	17,419	9,769
Long-Term Debt	16,115	17,189	22,042	23,454
Stockholders' Equity	181,614	203,199	248,412	277,253
Total Assets	249,275	264,680	340,959	361,140
Total Current Assets	119,612	133,063	163,606	181,557
Total Current Liabilities	9,917	9,511	13,565	12,977
Net Working Capital	109,695	123,552	150,041	168,580
Year End Shs Outstg	56,694	56,320	56,694	56,320

STATISTICAL RECORD:

	12/31/96	12/31/95
Return on Equity %	...	6.63
Return on Assets %	...	5.09
Operating Profit Margin %	...	20.72
Net Profit Margin %	...	21.01
Book Value Per Share	3.20	3.61

Converted at 1996, US$0.7311= 1 Canadian $; 1995, US$0.7329= 1 Canadian $

OFFICERS:
W. H. Berkoff, Chmn. & Pres.
S. P. Quin, Exec. V.P.
B. M. Labadie, Sr. V.P.
D. W. Cohen, Sr. V.P.

INCORPORATED: Canada, 1986

PRINCIPAL OFFICE: 311 West First Street
North Vancouver British Columbia, Canada
V7M 1B5

TELEPHONE NUMBER: 604-985-2572

NO. OF EMPLOYEES: N/A

ANNUAL MEETING: In Jun.

SHAREHOLDERS: N/A

INSTITUTIONAL HOLDINGS:
No. of Institutions: 26
Shares Held: 7,364,715

REGISTRAR(S): Pacific Corporate Services Ltd., Vancouver and Toronto.

TRANSFER AGENT(S): Pacific Corporate Services Ltd., Vancouver and Toronto.

M-SYSTEMS FLASH DISK PIONEERS

YIELD ...
P/E RATIO ...

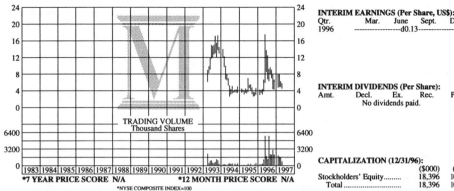

*7 YEAR PRICE SCORE N/A   *12 MONTH PRICE SCORE N/A
*NYSE COMPOSITE INDEX=100

TRADING VOLUME
Thousand Shares

INTERIM EARNINGS (Per Share, US$):

Qtr.	Mar.	June	Sept.	Dec.
1996	------------------d0.13-----------------			

INTERIM DIVIDENDS (Per Share):

Amt.	Decl.	Ex.	Rec.	Pay.
No dividends paid.				

CAPITALIZATION (12/31/96):

	($000)	(%)
Stockholders' Equity.........	18,396	100.0
Total	18,396	100.0

RECENT DEVELOPMENTS: For the year ended 12/31/96, net loss was $987,000 compared with $2.8 million in the same period of 1995. Revenues were $11.8 million, up 79.9% from $6.5 million a year earlier. Gross profit more than doubled to $4.1 million compared with $2.0 million in 1995. The loss in earnings was primarily attributable to continued losses from the Company's subsidiary EUROM FlashWare Solutions Ltd. The Company has decided to close down the active operations of EUROM effective 2/1/97, in order to focus on its core business and minimize expenses. However, the Company is maintaining its ownership of the proprietary voice-chip technology developed by EUROM and will continue to look for opportunities to realize the value of such technology. On 2/3/97, FLSHF signed a letter of intent to acquire C-One Technology, a privately-held Taiwan-based company, and Pretec Electronics Corp., its majority-owned U.S. subsidiary, in exchange for 1.163 million shares of M-Systems.

BUSINESS

M-SYSTEMS FLASH DISK PIONEERS is engaged in the design, development, manufacture and marketing of innovative software and hardware data storage solutions based on Flash memory, utilizing its patented TrueFFS(R) technology. The Company, through its subsidiary, Eurom FlashWare Solutions, is also engaged in the development of a single highly-integrated voice chip for voice recording and playback to be incorporated into a broad range of portable voice applications and products.

ANNUAL EARNINGS

	12/31/96	12/31/95	12/31/96	12/31/95
	------------US $------------		------------NIS------------	
Earnings Per Share	d0.13	d0.44	d0.42	d1.38

ANNUAL FINANCIAL DATA

RECORD OF EARNINGS (IN THOUSANDS):

	12/31/96	12/31/95	12/31/96	12/31/95
Total Revenues	11,750	6,533	38,274	20,563
Costs & Expenses	12,915	9,507	42,068	29,924
Operating Income	d1,165	d2,974	d3,795	d9,361
Income Bef Income Tax	d987	d2,753	d3,215	d8,665
Net Income	d987	d2,753	d3,215	d8,665
Average Shares Outstg	7,393	6,332	7,393	6,332

BALANCE SHEET (IN THOUSANDS):

Cash & Cash Equivalents	14,556	1,694	47,414	5,332
Receivables, Net	2,422	2,748	7,889	8,650
Inventories	2,539	2,210	8,270	6,956
Gross Property	2,076	1,797	6,762	5,656
Accumulated Depreciation	986	613	3,212	1,929
Stockholders' Equity	18,396	6,277	59,922	19,758
Total Assets	20,814	8,032	67,798	25,282
Total Current Assets	19,517	6,652	63,573	20,938
Total Current Liabilities	2,340	1,686	7,622	5,307
Net Working Capital	17,177	4,966	55,951	15,631
Year End Shs Outstg	8,956	6,346	8,956	6,346

STATISTICAL RECORD:

Return on Equity %	...	...		
Return on Assets %	...	...		
Operating Profit Margin %	...	...		
Net Profit Margin %	...	...		
Book Value Per Share	2.05	0.99		

Converted at 1996, US$0.3070= 1 New Israeli Shekel; 1995, US$0.3177= 1 New Israeli Shekel

OFFICERS:
D. Moran, Chmn. & Pres.
A. Mergi, Exec. V.P.
A. Ban, Software Manager
D. Gross, C.F.O. & Pres.

INCORPORATED: Israel, 1989

PRINCIPAL OFFICE: Building No. 7, Atidim Industrial Park, Neve Sharet Tel Aviv Israel 61580

TELEPHONE NUMBER: 972-3-647-7776

NO. OF EMPLOYEES: N/A

ANNUAL MEETING: N/A

SHAREHOLDERS: 23

INSTITUTIONAL HOLDINGS:
No. of Institutions: N/A
Shares Held: N/A

REGISTRAR(S): N/A

TRANSFER AGENT(S): N/A

NAM TAI ELECTRONICS, INC.

YIELD 0.8%
P/E RATIO 9.7

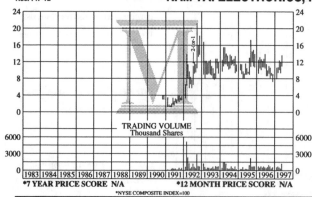

*7 YEAR PRICE SCORE N/A   *12 MONTH PRICE SCORE N/A
*NYSE COMPOSITE INDEX=100

INTERIM EARNINGS (Per Share, US$):
1996 ------------------ 1.24 ------------------

INTERIM DIVIDENDS (Per Share):

Amt.	Decl.	Ex.	Rec.	Pay.
0.03	6/21/96	7/11/96	7/15/96	8/08/96
0.10	5/12/97	5/28/97	5/30/97	6/20/97

Indicated div.:$0.10

CAPITALIZATION (12/31/96):

	($000)	(%)
Stockholders' Equity	66,990	100.0
Total	66,990	100.0

RECENT DEVELOPMENTS: For the year ended 12/31/96, net income declined 17.6% to $9.4 million from $11.4 million in 1995. Sales fell 10.7% to $108.2 million from $121.2 million in the year-earlier period. Gross profit as a percentage of sales improved to 21.0% compared with 19.1% in the prior year; however, selling, general and administrative expenses as a percentage of sales increased to 11.7% from 9.4% a year earlier. Research and development as a percentage of sales totaled less than 1% at $963,000 compared with $945,000 in 1995. For the three months ended 12/31/96, net income increased 51.8% to $3.1 million compared with $2.0 million in the corresponding period of 1995. Sales declined 9.7% to $30.0 million versus $33.2 million a year ago. The Company's financial position remains solid with $25.6 million of working capital and no long-term debt. Order backlog at 12/31/96 totaled $28.5 million compared with $24.8 million at 12/31/95.

BUSINESS

NAM TAI ELECTRONICS, INC. is engaged in the designing, developing, manufacturing, assembling andmarketing of consumer electronic products. These products includecalculators, personal organizers, business card organizers, dictionaries,spell checkers, language translators, scales, LCD modules for telephones, ICcard readers, and health care products such as electronic blood pressuremeters. The Company sells these products under the FORTEC, SANTRON and NAMTAI brandsand also sells to customers who market the products under their own brandnames. In addition, the Company provides silk screening and circuit board assemblyservices to original equipment manufacturers for incorporation into theirfinished products.

ANNUAL EARNINGS

	12/31/96	12/31/95	12/31/94	12/31/93	12/31/92	12/31/91	12/31/90
				US $			
Earnings Per Share	1.16	1.40	1.09	0.87	0.47	1.56	1.13

ANNUAL FINANCIAL DATA

RECORD OF EARNINGS (IN THOUSANDS):

	12/31/96	12/31/95	12/31/94	12/31/93	12/31/92	12/31/91	12/31/90
Total Revenues	108,234	121,240	96,564	70,844	57,955	38,418	37,870
Costs & Expenses	99,701	110,474	88,950	65,028	55,208	36,914	36,615
Operating Income	8,533	10,766	7,614	5,816	2,747	1,504	1,255
Income Bef Income Tax	9,574	10,830	8,198	5,266	2,822	3,547	2,628
Income Tax	158	cr589	173	73	219	128	77
Minority Interests	...	...	cr74	cr4	100	451	400
Net Income	9,416	11,419	8,099	5,197	2,503	2,968	2,151
Income from Disc. Ops.	...	...	...	...	...	...	d84
Net Extraordinary Items	...	...	...	...	...	...	d58
Average Shares Outstg	8,142	8,172	7,460	5,976	5,302	1,899	1,899

BALANCE SHEET (IN THOUSANDS):

	12/31/96	12/31/95	12/31/94	12/31/93	12/31/92	12/31/91	12/31/90
Cash & Cash Equivalents	17,741	17,362	23,681	14,016	9,532	7,076	4,937
Receivables, Net	16,589	17,699	11,744	9,887	7,286	7,463	4,517
Inventories	10,511	10,425	9,087	6,673	5,107	4,480	3,239
Gross Property	46,751	35,365	20,121	11,063	9,404	6,087	7,433
Accumulated Depreciation	10,264	7,730	5,497	3,667	3,067	3,235	2,930
Long-Term Debt	...	...	...	...	...	...	295
Stockholders' Equity	66,990	60,173	48,449	28,162	16,368	11,323	8,544
Total Assets	88,391	79,281	66,287	39,530	29,474	22,980	17,603
Total Current Assets	46,609	47,011	45,520	31,247	23,071	19,543	13,021
Total Current Liabilities	21,401	19,108	17,838	10,644	12,475	10,128	7,261
Net Working Capital	25,208	27,903	27,682	20,603	10,596	9,415	5,760
Year End Shs Outstg	7,837	8,063	7,993	6,499	5,272	1,899	1,899

STATISTICAL RECORD:

	12/31/96	12/31/95	12/31/94	12/31/93	12/31/92	12/31/91	12/31/90
Return on Equity %	14.05	18.98	16.72	18.45	15.29	26.21	25.18
Return on Assets %	10.65	14.40	12.22	13.15	8.49	12.92	12.22
Operating Profit Margin %	7.88	8.88	7.88	8.21	4.74	3.91	3.31
Net Profit Margin %	8.69	9.42	8.39	7.34	4.32	7.73	5.68
Book Value Per Share	8.55	7.52	6.06	4.33	3.10	5.96	4.50

OFFICERS:
M. Shigemori, Gen. Mgr.
J. Chang, Factory Contr.
X. M. Fang, Vice Gen. Mgr.
T. Adachi, Customer Service Mgr.

INCORPORATED: Aug., 1987

PRINCIPAL OFFICE: Unit 513-520 No. 1
Hung To Road Kwun Tong, Kowloon Hong Kong

TELEPHONE NUMBER: N/A

NO. OF EMPLOYEES: 2,250

ANNUAL MEETING: In Jun.

SHAREHOLDERS: N/A

INSTITUTIONAL HOLDINGS:
No. of Institutions: 8
Shares Held: 745,693

REGISTRAR(S): U.S. Stock Transfer Corp., California.

TRANSFER AGENT(S): U.S. Stock Transfer Corp., California.

NEW DIMENSION SOFTWARE LTD.

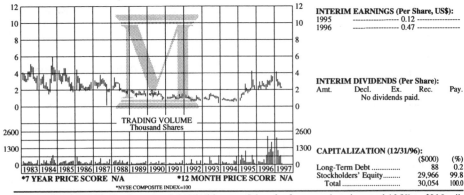

*7 YEAR PRICE SCORE N/A   *12 MONTH PRICE SCORE N/A
*NYSE COMPOSITE INDEX=100

INTERIM EARNINGS (Per Share, US$):

1995	----------- 0.12 -----------
1996	----------- 0.47 -----------

INTERIM DIVIDENDS (Per Share):

Amt.	Decl.	Ex.	Rec.	Pay.
	No dividends paid.			

CAPITALIZATION (12/31/96):

	($000)	(%)
Long-Term Debt	88	0.2
Stockholders' Equity........	29,966	99.8
Total	30,054	100.0

RECENT DEVELOPMENTS: For the year ended 12/31/96, net income soared to $5.5 million from $1.6 million in 1995. Total revenues climbed 21.9% to $43.6 million compared with $35.7 million. Operating profit jumped to $4.1 million from $438,000 the year before. The improved results were attributed to the growing market acceptance for the Company's product line, benefits of a realigned sales operation, increased sales to existing customers and new products.

Sales of software products increased 16.5% to $26.9 million, benefiting from the entrance into new markets, including the Windows NT, SAP R/3 and Internet/Intranet markets. Maintenance fees grew 31.6% to $16.6 million. The Company recently acquired the Central User Registration System (C.U.R.S.) product line, a mainframe-based se curity management product, and customer base from Electronic Data Systems (EDS) Germany.

BUSINESS

NEW DIMENSION SOFTWARE, LTD. and its subsidiaries develop, market and support comprehensive systems software solutions for managing key disciplines within the data center and the accross the computing enterprise. The Company's product line consists of the CONTROL (TM) family of products based on it IOA (R) (Integrated Operations Architecture (R)) for mainframes and non-mainframes. The Company's mainframe products operate on IBM or compatible mainframes running the MVS operating system and Fujitsu mainframs running the MSP operating system. Non-mainframe products operate on various platforms, including HP-UX, Solaris 2.3, RS/6000, Sun OS, VAX/VMS, DOS-, Windows- and OS/2 based personal computers. The Company's products are licensed to more than 1,700 customers in more than 40 countries.

ANNUAL EARNINGS

	12/31/95	12/31/94	12/31/95	12/31/94
	US $		NIS	
Earnings Per Share	0.12	d2.02	0.38	d6.10

ANNUAL FINANCIAL DATA

RECORD OF EARNINGS (IN THOUSANDS):

Total Revenues	35,737	28,240	112,485	85,214
Costs & Expenses	35,299	51,443	111,107	155,231
Operating Income	438	d23,204	1,378	d70,017
Income Bef Income Tax	1,597	d22,503	5,027	d67,904
Income Tax	270	248	850	750
Net Income	1,327	d22,752	4,177	d68,654
Average Shares Outstg	11,218	11,241	11,218	11,241

BALANCE SHEET (IN THOUSANDS):

Cash & Cash Equivalents	14,309	18,330	45,040	55,310
Receivables, Net	11,226	12,603	35,337	38,029
Gross Property	10,657	9,221	33,545	27,824
Accumulated Depreciation	4,604	2,932	14,493	8,847
Long-Term Debt	56	2,283	175	6,890
Stockholders' Equity	23,917	22,301	75,282	67,293
Total Assets	45,263	49,991	142,472	150,849
Total Current Assets	25,536	30,933	80,377	93,339
Total Current Liabilities	18,678	22,444	58,792	67,725
Net Working Capital	6,858	8,489	21,586	25,614
Year End Shs Outstg	11,051	10,974	11,051	10,974

STATISTICAL RECORD:

Return on Equity %	5.55	...		
Return on Assets %	2.93	...		
Operating Profit Margin %	1.23	...		
Net Profit Margin %	3.71	...		
Book Value Per Share	2.16	2.03		

Converted at 1995, US$0.3177= 1 New Israeli New Shekel; 1994, US$0.3314= 1 New Israeli New Shekel

OFFICERS:
D. Barnea, C.E.O.
D. Prashker-Katzman, Pres.
I. Zion, C.F.O.
A. S. Gordon, Chief Tech. Officer

INCORPORATED: Israel, 1983

PRINCIPAL OFFICE: Devora Hanevia Street Building 7, Atidim Neve Sharet Tel Aviv Israel

TELEPHONE NUMBER: (972)-3-645-1111

NO. OF EMPLOYEES: 285

ANNUAL MEETING: In Nov.

SHAREHOLDERS: 75

INSTITUTIONAL HOLDINGS:
No. of Institutions: 12
Shares Held: 275,004

REGISTRAR(S): N/A

TRANSFER AGENT(S): America Stock Transfer & Trust Company, New York.

NOBEL INSURANCE LIMITED

YIELD 1.6%
P/E RATIO 13.5

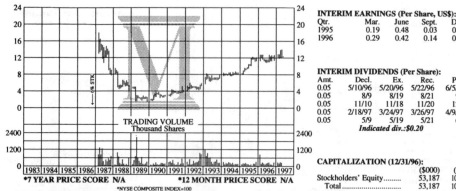

INTERIM EARNINGS (Per Share, US$):

Qtr.	Mar.	June	Sept.	Dec.
1995	0.19	0.48	0.03	0.35
1996	0.29	0.42	0.14	0.06

INTERIM DIVIDENDS (Per Share):

Amt.	Decl.	Ex.	Rec.	Pay.
0.05	5/10/96	5/20/96	5/22/96	6/5/96
0.05	8/9	8/19	8/21	9/4
0.05	11/10	11/18	11/20	12/4
0.05	2/18/97	3/24/97	3/26/97	4/9/97
0.05	5/9	5/19	5/21	6/4

Indicated div.:$0.20

CAPITALIZATION (12/31/96):

	($000)	(%)
Stockholders' Equity	53,187	100.0
Total	53,187	100.0

RECENT DEVELOPMENTS: For the year ended 12/31/96, net income declined 31.2% to $4.3 million. This compares with $6.2 million in 1995. Total revenues were up 18.9% to $72.9 million from $61.3 million a year earlier. Net premiums written totaled $43.2 million, down 9.2% compared with $47.6 million the year before. Premium gains from new business were reported in all of the Company's insurance programs. Changes in major reinsurance programs, however, contributed to the lower net premiums written. The Company wrote a larger portion of surety and personal lines business and a lower proportion of commercial casualty business in 1996 due primarily to increased commissions, fronting and taxes expense. In 1996, the Company had a claims ratio of 76.0% versus 73.0% the previous year.

BUSINESS

NOBEL INSURANCE LIMITED's principal business is the service and underwriting of commercial property, casualty and surety risks for specialized industries, and personal lines property coverages for low-value dwellings. The Company's principal commercial markets consist of distributors, manufacturers and users of explosives; transporters of hazardous materials and general commodities; marketers of propane; and small- to medium-size businesses requiring all forms of surety bonding.

ANNUAL EARNINGS

	12/31/96	12/31/95	12/31/94	12/31/93	12/31/92	12/31/91	12/31/90
				US $			
Earnings Per Share	0.92	1.06	2.37	1.43	2.89	1.30	0.75

ANNUAL FINANCIAL DATA

RECORD OF EARNINGS (IN THOUSANDS):

	12/31/96	12/31/95	12/31/94	12/31/93	12/31/92	12/31/91	12/31/90
Total Revenues	72,858	61,269	50,253	38,193	26,590	22,775	31,209
Costs & Expenses	70,640	57,537	34,878	28,265	7,518	13,676	25,754
Operating Income	2,218	3,732	15,375	9,928	19,072	9,099	5,455
Income Bef Income Tax	2,218	3,732	15,375	9,928	19,072	9,099	5,455
Income Tax	cr2,069	cr2,500	...	...	...	...	...
Minority Interests	...	...	...	...	...	239	763
Net Income	4,287	6,232	15,375	9,928	19,072	8,860	4,692
Average Shares Outstg	4,659	5,901	6,478	6,947	6,599	6,802	6,225
BALANCE SHEET (IN THOUSANDS):							
Cash & Cash Equivalents	3,607	4,848	5,416	4,741	6,739	6,737	5,880
Receivables, Net	57,054	46,485	38,639	24,189	18,185	8,558	6,493
Gross Property	6,164	5,482	3,525	3,371	3,061	3,016	2,879
Accumulated Depreciation	2,119	1,840	1,654	1,689	1,528	1,479	1,135
Long-Term Debt	...	...	...	838	907	727	757
Stockholders' Equity	53,187	64,908	56,548	54,479	46,114	25,711	18,378
Total Assets	222,778	203,388	168,173	153,310	143,873	113,805	115,886
Total Current Assets	94,235	67,689	55,543	40,230	35,044	16,136	13,737
Total Current Liabilities	101,577	91,582	74,026	72,129	73,418	76,591	85,839
Net Working Capital	d7,342	d23,893	d18,483	d31,899	d38,374	d60,455	d72,102
Year End Shs Outstg	4,471	5,542	5,917	7,322	7,307	6,564	6,988
STATISTICAL RECORD:							
Return on Equity %	8.06	9.60	27.19	18.22	41.36	34.46	25.53
Return on Assets %	1.92	3.06	9.14	6.48	13.26	7.79	4.05
Operating Profit Margin %	3.04	6.09	30.60	25.99	71.73	39.95	17.48
Net Profit Margin %	5.88	6.09	30.60	25.99	71.73	38.90	15.03
Book Value Per Share	11.90	11.71	9.56	7.44	6.31	3.92	2.63

OFFICERS:
R. C. Duvall, Chmn.
J. K. Amsbaugh, Pres. & C.E.O.
B. L. Martin, Sr. V.P.
T. D. Nimmo, Sr. V.P. & Treas.

INCORPORATED: Dec., 1978

PRINCIPAL OFFICE: Falconer House, Ground Level, 108 Pitts Bay Road, Hamilton Bermuda HM AX

TELEPHONE NUMBER: (441) 292-7104

NO. OF EMPLOYEES: N/A

ANNUAL MEETING: In May

SHAREHOLDERS: 260 (approx.)

INSTITUTIONAL HOLDINGS:
No. of Institutions: 8
Shares Held: 1,161,830

REGISTRAR(S):

TRANSFER AGENT(S): Harris Trust and Savings Bank, Chicago, IL.

NUR ADVANCED TECHNOLOGIES, LTD

YIELD ...
P/E RATIO ...

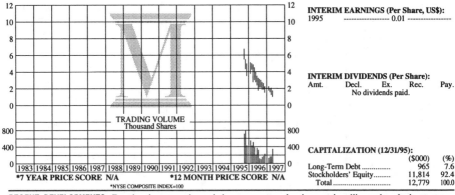

*7 YEAR PRICE SCORE N/A   *12 MONTH PRICE SCORE N/A

*NYSE COMPOSITE INDEX=100

INTERIM EARNINGS (Per Share, US$):
1995 ------------------ 0.01 ----------------

INTERIM DIVIDENDS (Per Share):

Amt.	Decl.	Ex.	Rec.	Pay.
No dividends paid.				

CAPITALIZATION (12/31/95):

	($000)	(%)
Long-Term Debt	965	7.6
Stockholders' Equity........	11,814	92.4
Total	12,779	100.0

RECENT DEVELOPMENTS: For the three months ended 9/30/96, the Company reported a loss of $1.3 million compared with income of $420,000 in the corresponding period a year earlier. Revenues were $4.6 million, up 23% versus $3.7 million in 1995. Gross profits for the quarter rose 12% to $1.4 million. Earnings were pressured by a one-time expense of $287,000, representing a write-off of deferred tax assets and an increase in selling and marketing expense. The increase in selling and marketing expense resulted from the Company's starting maintenance support and logistical services for its products. In addition, research and development expenses increased 183% due to additional resources being allocated to develop new products, one of which the Company plans to introduce in 1997.

BUSINESS

NUR ADVANCED TECHNOLO-GIES, LTD. develops, manufactures, sells and services digital, color, continuous ink-jet printing systems for large format printing. NURTF also sells a specialized ink and manufactures and sells electronic billboards.

ANNUAL EARNINGS

	12/31/95	12/31/94	12/31/95	12/31/94
	------------US $-------------		------------NIS-----------	
Earnings Per Share	0.01	d0.05	0.03	d0.15

ANNUAL FINANCIAL DATA

RECORD OF EARNINGS (IN THOUSANDS):

Total Revenues	13,824	10,010	43,513	30,205
Costs & Expenses	12,334	9,089	38,823	27,426
Operating Income	1,490	921	4,690	2,779
Income Bef Income Tax	1,407	816	4,429	2,462
Income Tax	221	25	696	75
Eq. Earnings in Affils.	d1,125	d987	d3,541	d2,978
Net Income	61	d196	192	d591
Average Shares Outstg	4,904	4,123	4,904	4,123

BALANCE SHEET (IN THOUSANDS):

Cash & Cash Equivalents	4,855	1,084	15,282	3,271
Receivables, Net	8,998	3,736	28,322	11,273
Inventories	723	1,036	2,276	3,126
Gross Property	611	448	1,923	1,352
Accumulated Depreciation	179	76	563	229
Long-Term Debt	965	3,784	3,037	11,418
Stockholders' Equity	11,814	688	37,186	2,076
Total Assets	16,759	7,039	52,751	21,240
Total Current Assets	14,576	5,856	45,880	17,670
Total Current Liabilities	3,979	2,430	12,524	7,333
Net Working Capital	10,597	3,426	33,355	10,338
Year End Shs Outstg	6,880	4,111	6,880	4,111

STATISTICAL RECORD:

Return on Equity %	0.52	...		
Return on Assets %	0.36	...		
Operating Profit Margin %	10.78	9.20		
Net Profit Margin %	0.44	...		
Book Value Per Share	1.72	0.17		

Converted at 1995, US$0.3177= 1 Israeli New Shekel; 1994, US$0.3314= 1 Israeli New Shekel

OFFICERS:
M. Nur, Chmn.
E. Sarig, C.E.O.
V. Herskowits, Sr. V.P.

INCORPORATED: 1987

PRINCIPAL OFFICE: 5 David Navon Street
Moshav Magshmim Petah Tikvah Israel
49001

TELEPHONE NUMBER: 972-3-924-8512

NO. OF EMPLOYEES: 42

ANNUAL MEETING: N/A

SHAREHOLDERS: 44

INSTITUTIONAL HOLDINGS:
No. of Institutions: N/A
Shares Held: N/A

REGISTRAR(S): N/A

TRANSFER AGENT(S):

NASDAQ SYMBOL OLCMF
Rec. Pr. 15½

OLICOM A/S

YIELD ...
P/E RATIO 31.0

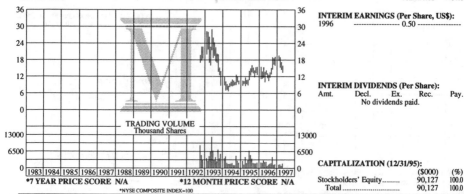

INTERIM EARNINGS (Per Share, US$):
1996 ------------------- 0.50 -----------------

INTERIM DIVIDENDS (Per Share):
Amt. Decl. Ex. Rec. Pay.
No dividends paid.

TRADING VOLUME
Thousand Shares

| 1983 | 1984 | 1985 | 1986 | 1987 | 1988 | 1989 | 1990 | 1991 | 1992 | 1993 | 1994 | 1995 | 1996 | 1997 |

*7 YEAR PRICE SCORE N/A   *12 MONTH PRICE SCORE N/A
*NYSE COMPOSITE INDEX=100

CAPITALIZATION (12/31/95):

	($000)	(%)
Stockholders' Equity	90,127	100.0
Total	90,127	100.0

RECENT DEVELOPMENTS: For the year ended 12/31/96, net income fell 42.0% to $7.4 million from $12.8 million in 1995. Sales rose 32.0% to $168.2 million. Results in 1996 included acquisition related expenses of $3.8 million, special charges of $1.4 million related to a management change, and a gain of $2.9 million on the sale of a minority interest in Contex A/S. Excluding these charges and the gain, earnings per share for 1996 were $0.61 versus $0.87 in 1995. Gross profit as a percentage of net sales fell to 43.4% from 48.9% a year earlier. For the three months ended 12/31/96, net income increased 12.9% to $4.5 million from $4.0 million in the year-earlier period. Sales rose 39.7% to $50.3 million. The Company noted that in the quarter ended 12/31/96, it experienced significant sales increases in all categories of adapter products a well as Lasat-branded products. In the U.S., sales increased by 57% versus the comparable year-earlier period, while European sales of Olicom-branded products were slightly lower.

BUSINESS

OLICOM A/S is engaged in the design, development, marketing, sale and export of Token-Ring local area network hardware and software products, such as adapters, bridges, intelligent wiring hubs, and wiring components, which enable computer users to communicate, exchange data and share computing resources in work groups and enterprise-wide LANs (local area networks), and in wide area networks. The Company is also engaged in the development, production and sale of Ethernet and ATM (asynchronous transfer mode) network adapters, network cards, cable transceivers and other Ethernet and ATM products. The Company has products under the following registered trademarks: PowerMach™, GoCard™, RapidFire™ and Cross-Fire™. The Company's customers fall into three main groups: Fortune 500 companies, the financial sector and airlines. Primary export markets include North America, Europe and Australia.

ANNUAL EARNINGS

	12/31/95	12/31/94	12/31/95	12/31/94
	----------US $----------		----------DKK----------	
Earnings Per Share	0.87	0.66	4.82	3.95

ANNUAL FINANCIAL DATA

RECORD OF EARNINGS (IN THOUSANDS):

Total Revenues	127,469	113,604	706,591	691,022
Costs & Expenses	111,706	96,952	619,213	589,732
Operating Income	15,763	16,652	87,378	101,290
Income Bef Income Tax	19,029	14,933	105,482	90,833
Income Tax	6,223	5,026	34,496	30,572
Income Bef. Acct. Changes	12,806	9,907	70,987	60,262
Effect of Acct. Changes	...	161	...	979
Net Income	12,806	10,068	70,987	59,283
Average Shares Outstg	14,748	15,298	14,748	15,298

BALANCE SHEET (IN THOUSANDS):

Cash & Cash Equivalents	33,065	34,545	183,287	210,128
Receivables, Net	39,292	34,654	217,805	210,791
Inventories	32,259	16,143	178,819	98,193
Gross Property	10,603	10,528	58,775	64,039
Accumulated Depreciation	5,564	4,544	30,843	27,640
Stockholders' Equity	90,127	78,191	499,595	475,614
Total Assets	127,327	108,917	705,804	662,512
Total Current Assets	115,800	97,153	641,907	590,955
Total Current Liabilities	37,200	30,726	206,208	186,898
Net Working Capital	78,600	66,427	435,698	404,057
Year End Shs Outstg	15,837	15,837	15,837	15,837

STATISTICAL RECORD:

Return on Equity %	14.21	12.67		
Return on Assets %	10.06	9.10		
Operating Profit Margin %	12.37	14.66		
Net Profit Margin %	10.05	8.72		
Book Value Per Share	5.69	4.94		

Converted at 1995, US$0.1804= 1 Danish Krone; 1994, US$0.1644= 1 Danish Krone

OFFICERS:
L. S. Nielsen, Pres. & C.E.O.
B. Rinhart, C.F.O.
N. C. Furu, Exec. V.P. & C.O.O.
N. Jorgensen, V.P.-Engineering

INCORPORATED: Denmark, 1985

PRINCIPAL OFFICE: Nybrovej 114, Lyngby
Denmark DK-2800

TELEPHONE NUMBER: 45-27-00-00

NO. OF EMPLOYEES: 303 (avg.)

ANNUAL MEETING: In May

SHAREHOLDERS: 126

INSTITUTIONAL HOLDINGS:
No. of Institutions: N/A
Shares Held: N/A

REGISTRAR(S): American Stock Transfer &
Trust Co., New York.

TRANSFER AGENT(S): American Stock
Transfer & Trust Co., New York.

OPEN TEXT CORPORATION

YIELD ...
P/E RATIO ...

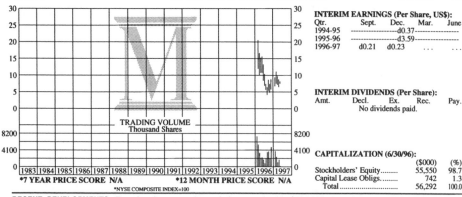

*7 YEAR PRICE SCORE N/A   *12 MONTH PRICE SCORE N/A
*NYSE COMPOSITE INDEX=100

TRADING VOLUME
Thousand Shares

INTERIM EARNINGS (Per Share, US$):

Qtr.	Sept.	Dec.	Mar.	June
1994-95	----------------d0.37----------------			
1995-96	----------------d3.59----------------			
1996-97	d0.21	d0.23	...	...

INTERIM DIVIDENDS (Per Share):

Amt.	Decl.	Ex.	Rec.	Pay.
		No dividends paid.		

CAPITALIZATION (6/30/96):

	($000)	(%)
Stockholders' Equity.........	55,550	98.7
Capital Lease Obligs.........	742	1.3
Total	56,292	100.0

RECENT DEVELOPMENTS: For the three months ended 12/31/96, net loss totaled $3.8 million compared with a loss of $23.3 million the previous year. Total revenues more than doubled to $5.2 million from $2.3 million a year earlier. The 1995 results were negatively affected by a one-time charge of $21.2 million related to the write-off of purchased research and development. License revenue soared 97.9% to $3.1 million from $1.5 million the year before. Service revenue was $2.2 million, up sharply compared with $731,000 the prior year. Revenues benefited from the initial market penetration of the Company's Livelink Intranet suite of products, coupled with the addition of approximately 70 new accounts deploying these products. For the six months ended 12/31/96, net loss was $7.4 million versus a loss of $26.0 million in the comparable prior-year period. Total revenues more than tripled to $9.3 million from $2.9 million a year earlier.

BUSINESS

OPEN TEXT CORPORATION develops, markets, licenses and supports software for use on Intranets, local and wide area private networks, and the Internet that enables users to find electronically stored information, work together in creative and collaborative processes and distribute or make available to users across networks or the Internet the resulting work product and other information. The Company's principal produce line, Livelink Suite, integrates several modular engines including, but not limited to, search, collaboration, workflow and document management engines.

ANNUAL EARNINGS

	6/30/96	6/30/95
	---------------US $---------------	
Earnings Per Share	d3.59	d0.37

ANNUAL FINANCIAL DATA

RECORD OF EARNINGS (IN THOUSANDS):

Total Revenues	9,995	2,479
Costs & Expenses	23,895	3,438
Depreciation & Amort	30,793	144
Operating Income	d44,693	d1,103
Net Income	d43,199	d1,211
Average Shares Outstg	12,042	3,242

BALANCE SHEET (IN THOUSANDS):

Cash & Cash Equivalents	51,139	...
Receivables, Net	6,773	1,777
Gross Property	5,017	818
Accumulated Depreciation	1,481	271
Capital Lease Obligs.	742	157
Stockholders' Equity	55,550	404
Total Assets	66,158	2,597
Total Current Assets	58,758	1,912
Total Current Liabilities	9,866	2,036
Net Working Capital	48,892	d124
Year End Shs Outstg	16,236	6,124

STATISTICAL RECORD:

Book Value Per Share	3.42	0.07

OFFICERS:
D. C. Webster, Chmn.
P. T. Jenkins, Pres. & C.E.O.
K. Soley, C.O.O.
W. Stirlen, C.F.O.

INCORPORATED: June, 1991

PRINCIPAL OFFICE: 185 Columbia Street West, Waterloo, Ontario Canada N2L 5Z5

TELEPHONE NUMBER: 519-888-7111

NO. OF EMPLOYEES: 292

ANNUAL MEETING: In February

SHAREHOLDERS: 2,625

INSTITUTIONAL HOLDINGS:
No. of Institutions: 11
Shares Held: 1,976,118

REGISTRAR(S):

TRANSFER AGENT(S): Montreal Trust, Toronto, Ontario.

OPTIMA PETROLEUM CORPORATION

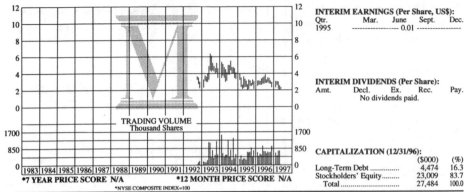

*7 YEAR PRICE SCORE N/A   *12 MONTH PRICE SCORE N/A
*NYSE COMPOSITE INDEX=100

INTERIM EARNINGS (Per Share, US$):

Qtr.	Mar.	June	Sept.	Dec.
1995	-----------------	0.01	-----------------	

INTERIM DIVIDENDS (Per Share):

Amt.	Decl.	Ex.	Rec.	Pay.
		No dividends paid.		

CAPITALIZATION (12/31/96):

	($000)	(%)
Long-Term Debt	4,474	16.3
Stockholders' Equity.........	23,009	83.7
Total	27,484	100.0

RECENT DEVELOPMENTS: For the year ended 12/31/96, net income was C$228,573 compared with a loss of C$1.2 million in the same period of 1995. Operating income increased 90.2% to C$12.9 million compared with C$6.8 million a year earlier. General and administrative expenses were C$1.7 million, up 13.2% from C$1.5 million in 1995. Results for 1995 have been reclassified to conform to the presentation adopted for the current year. The improvement in earnings was primarily attributed to increased oil and gas production and improved commodity prices. Gross natural volumes increased 40% to 3.3 million MCF compared with 2.4 million MCF whereas oil production increased to 153,699 barrels from 71,122 barrels a year earlier. The Company benefited from a combination of higher U.S. oil and gas prices and the increase in production. During 1996, in accordance with its business strategy, the Company completed its program of divestiture of minor U.S. properties with the sale of its interests at Elm Grove, Louisiana.

BUSINESS

OPTIMA PETROLEUM CORPORA-TION, along with its wholly owned U.S. subsidiary, Optima Energy Corporation, is engaged in the business of oil and gas exploration and development in Canada and the United States.

ANNUAL EARNINGS

	12/31/96	12/31/95	12/31/96	12/31/95
	---------------US $---------------		---------------C $---------------	
Earnings Per Share	0.01	d0.10	0.02	d0.13

ANNUAL FINANCIAL DATA

RECORD OF EARNINGS (IN THOUSANDS):

	12/31/96	12/31/95	12/31/96	12/31/95
Total Revenues	9,404	4,956	12,863	6,762
Costs & Expenses	5,034	3,476	6,886	4,743
Depreciation & Amort	4,189	2,367	5,730	3,230
Operating Income	181	d887	247	d1,210
Income Bef Income Tax	202	d828	277	d1,129
Income Tax	35	19	48	26
Net Income	167	d847	229	d1,155
Average Shares Outstg	10,945	9,032	10,945	9,032
BALANCE SHEET (IN THOUSANDS):				
Cash & Cash Equivalents	1,502	750	2,055	1,023
Receivables, Net	1,840	2,174	2,517	2,966
Gross Property	25,416	24,552	34,764	33,500
Long-Term Debt	4,474	5,416	6,120	7,390
Stockholders' Equity	23,009	20,871	31,472	28,478
Total Assets	30,132	28,714	41,215	39,178
Total Current Assets	3,433	2,924	4,696	3,989
Total Current Liabilities	2,491	2,376	3,408	3,242
Net Working Capital	942	547	1,289	747
Year End Shs Outstg	11,319	10,559	11,319	10,559
STATISTICAL RECORD:				
Return on Equity %	0.73	...		
Return on Assets %	0.55	...		
Operating Profit Margin %	1.92	...		
Net Profit Margin %	1.78	...		
Book Value Per Share	2.03	1.98		

Converted at 1996, US$0.7311= 1 Canadian $; 1995, US$0.7329= 1 Canadian $

OFFICERS:
W. C. Leuschner, Chmn.
R. L. Hodgkinson, Pres. & C.E.O.
R. P. Bourgeois, C.F.O. & Sec.

INCORPORATED: Canada, 1983

PRINCIPAL OFFICE: 600-595 Howe Street, Vancouver, British Columbia Canada

TELEPHONE NUMBER: 604-684-6886

NO. OF EMPLOYEES: N/A

ANNUAL MEETING: N/A

SHAREHOLDERS: N/A

INSTITUTIONAL HOLDINGS:
No. of Institutions: 7
Shares Held: 2,190,952

REGISTRAR(S): Montreal Trust Company of Canada, Vancouver.

TRANSFER AGENT(S): Montreal Trust Company of Canada, Vancouver.

OPTIMAL ROBOTICS CORP.

YIELD ...
P/E RATIO ...

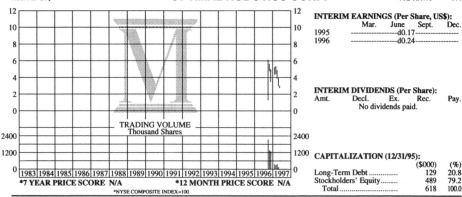

*7 YEAR PRICE SCORE N/A   *12 MONTH PRICE SCORE N/A
*NYSE COMPOSITE INDEX=100

INTERIM EARNINGS (Per Share, US$):

	Mar.	June	Sept.	Dec.
1995	------------------d0.17------------------			
1996	------------------d0.24------------------			

INTERIM DIVIDENDS (Per Share):

Amt.	Decl.	Ex.	Rec.	Pay.
	No dividends paid.			

CAPITALIZATION (12/31/95):

	($000)	(%)
Long-Term Debt	129	20.8
Stockholders' Equity	489	79.2
Total	618	100.0

RECENT DEVELOPMENTS: For the year ended 12/31/96, the Company reported a net loss of C$1.6 million (US$1.2 million) compared with a net loss of C$947,964 in 1995. Results included a foreign exchange gain of C$63,278 (US$142,012) in 1996 and a foreign exchange loss of C$4,710 in 1995. Revenues leapt 79.4% to C$1.4 million (US$1.0 million) from C$764,210 million the year before. Revenues were favorably affected by OPMRF's U-Scan

Express™ System, which continues to increase its penetration of the retail market. The U-Scan Express™ System was designed to reduce the cost of checkout transactions to retailers and increase shoppers' convenience. The Company, which possessed cash of C$14.0 million as of 12/31/96, expects to increase its market penetration not only among food retailers but also in the general retail sector, particularly mass merchandisers.

BUSINESS

OPTIMAL ROBOTICS CORP and its subsidiary are engaged in the development, marketing, assembly, installation and servicing of automated self-service transaction systems designed for use in retail point-of-sale applications. OPMRF's principal product is the U-Scan Express system, an automated self-service checkout system. OPMRF's primary focus is the commercialization of the U-Scan Express™ system for use in express lanes in supermarkets. The U-Scan Express is designed to reduce the cost of checkout transactions to retailers and increase shoppers' convenience by enabling shoppers to scan, bag and pay for their purchases with limited or no assistance from store personnel.

ANNUAL EARNINGS

	12/31/95	12/31/94	12/31/95	12/31/94
	-------------US $-------------		-----------C $-----------	
Earnings Per Share	d0.17	d0.08	d0.23	d0.11

ANNUAL FINANCIAL DATA

RECORD OF EARNINGS (IN THOUSANDS):

Total Revenues	580	58	792	81
Costs & Expenses	1,275	344	1,740	482
Operating Income	d695	d286	d948	d401
Income Bef Income Tax	d695	d286	d948	d401
Income Tax	...	cr19	...	cr26
Income from Contin. Ops.	d695	d268	d948	d375
Income from Disc. Ops.	...	167	...	234
Net Income	d695	d103	d948	d141
BALANCE SHEET (IN THOUSANDS):				
Cash & Cash Equivalents	687	32	938	45
Receivables, Net	653	169	891	237
Gross Property	57	35	78	49
Accumulated Depreciation	27	19	36	27
Long-Term Debt	129	268	176	376
Stockholders' Equity	489	d26	667	d36
Total Assets	1,416	260	1,932	364
Total Current Assets	1,360	216	1,856	304
Total Current Liabilities	297	18	405	25
Net Working Capital	1,064	198	1,451	278
Year End Shs Outstg	4,065	3,431	4,065	3,431
STATISTICAL RECORD:				
Return on Equity %	...	...		
Return on Assets %	...	...		
Operating Profit Margin %	...	...		
Net Profit Margin %	...	...		
Book Value Per Share	0.12	d0.01		

Converted at 1995, US$0.7329= 1 Canadian $; 1994, US$0.7129= 1 Canadian $

OFFICERS:
N. S. Wechsler, Chmn. & C.E.O.
H. L. Ostrin, Vice-Chmn.
H. M. Karp, Exec. V.P. & C.O.O.
G. S. Wechsler, C.F.O., Sec. & Treas.

INCORPORATED: Canada, May 29, 1994

PRINCIPAL OFFICE: 4700 de la Savane
Montreal Quebec, Canada H4P 1T7

TELEPHONE NUMBER: 514-738-8885

NO. OF EMPLOYEES: N/A

ANNUAL MEETING: In Jun.

SHAREHOLDERS: N/A

INSTITUTIONAL HOLDINGS:
No. of Institutions: 5
Shares Held: 1,087,000

REGISTRAR(S): Montreal Trust, Toronto, Canada

TRANSFER AGENT(S): Montreal Trust, Toronto, Canada

ORBOTECH LTD.

YIELD ...
P/E RATIO 9.14

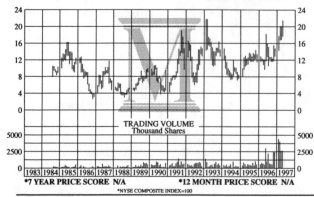

TRADING VOLUME
Thousand Shares

*7 YEAR PRICE SCORE N/A   *12 MONTH PRICE SCORE N/A

INTERIM EARNINGS (Per Share, $US):

Qtr.	Mar.	Jun.	Sep.	Dec.
1995	------------------ 1.17 ------------------			
1996	------------------ 2.16 ------------------			

INTERIM DIVIDENDS (Per Share):

Amt.	Decl.	Ex.	Rec.	Pay.
	No dividends paid.			

CAPITALIZATION (12/31/95):

	($000)	(%)
Stockholders' Equity	66,053	100.0
Total	66,053	100.0

RECENT DEVELOPMENTS: For the year ended 12/31/96, net income was $28.1 million, up 86.9% from $15.0 million a year earlier. The results for 1996 included a net gain of $8.0 million recognized from the sale of Opal holdings. Revenues increased 14.5% to $148.2 million from $129.5 million in the previous year. Operating income rose 62.3% to $20.9 million. For the quarter ended 12/31/96, net income was $13.7 million compared with $3.7 million in the corresponding quarter a year earlier. Revenues rose 97.0% to $38.8 million. The improvement in sales and earnings for the quarter were attributed to stronger sales from ORBKF's subsidiaries in Japan and the Pacific Rim, which experienced a 117% and a 30% increase in revenues, respectively. Plotter sales were especially strong, rising 82% over 1995 sales.

BUSINESS

ORBOTECH LTD. is engaged in the development, manufacture, marketing and servicing of computerized electro-optical systems used for automated inspection and identification of defects in printed circuit boards and liquid crystal flat panel displays. The Company also produces computer-aided manufacturing (CAM) systems for electronic verification, engineering and tooling preparation and laser plotters for the creation of artwork masters.

ANNUAL EARNINGS

	12/31/95	12/31/94	12/31/95	12/31/94
	-------------US $-------------		-------------NIS-------------	
Earnings Per Share	1.17	0.74	3.68	2.23

ANNUAL FINANCIAL DATA

RECORD OF EARNINGS (IN THOUSANDS):

	12/31/95	12/31/94	12/31/95	12/31/94
Total Revenues	129,454	117,950	407,472	355,914
Costs & Expenses	116,593	106,760	366,991	322,148
Operating Income	12,861	11,190	40,482	33,766
Income Bef Income Tax	15,074	10,110	47,447	30,508
Income Tax	1,073	888	3,377	2,680
Net Income	15,019	9,210	47,274	27,791
Average Shares Outstg	12,858	12,491	12,858	12,491
BALANCE SHEET (IN THOUSANDS):				
Cash & Cash Equivalents	12,404	13,395	39,043	40,419
Receivables, Net	31,230	29,489	98,300	88,983
Inventories	31,391	30,371	98,807	91,645
Gross Property	31,722	28,875	99,849	87,130
Accumulated Depreciation	21,282	19,423	66,988	58,609
Long-Term Debt	...	278	...	839
Stockholders' Equity	66,053	50,276	207,910	151,708
Total Assets	105,713	100,455	332,745	303,123
Total Current Assets	75,672	73,704	238,187	222,402
Total Current Liabilities	36,320	46,662	114,322	140,803
Net Working Capital	39,352	27,042	123,865	81,599
Year End Shs Outstg	12,529	12,372	12,529	12,372
STATISTICAL RECORD:				
Return on Equity %	22.74	18.32		
Return on Assets %	14.21	9.17		
Operating Profit Margin %	9.93	9.49		
Net Profit Margin %	11.60	7.81		
Book Value Per Share	5.27	4.06		

Converted at 1995, US$0.3177= 1 New Israeli Shekel; 1994, US$0.3314= 1 New Israeli Shekel

OFFICERS:
Y. Richter, Pres. & C.E.O.
A. Weisberg, C.F.O. & V.P.
D. Falk, Exec. V.P.
H. Kaplan, Sec.

INCORPORATED: Feb., 1981

PRINCIPAL OFFICE: New Industrial Zone, P.O. Box 215 Yavne Israel 70651

TELEPHONE NUMBER: 972-(8)-9428-533

NO. OF EMPLOYEES: N/A

ANNUAL MEETING: In June

SHAREHOLDERS: N/A

INSTITUTIONAL HOLDINGS:
No. of Institutions: N/A
Shares Held: N/A

REGISTRAR(S): American Stock Transfer & Trust Co., New York.

TRANSFER AGENT(S): American Stock Transfer & Trust Co., New York.

NASDAQ SYMBOL ORCTF
Rec. Pr. 13⅜

ORCKIT COMMUNICATIONS, LIMITED

YIELD ...
P/E RATIO ...

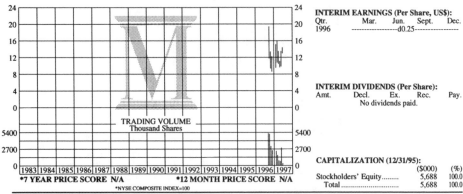

*7 YEAR PRICE SCORE N/A   *12 MONTH PRICE SCORE N/A
*NYSE COMPOSITE INDEX=100

TRADING VOLUME
Thousand Shares

INTERIM EARNINGS (Per Share, US$):

Qtr.	Mar.	Jun.	Sept.	Dec.
1996		------------------d0.25-----------------		

INTERIM DIVIDENDS (Per Share):

Amt.	Decl.	Ex.	Rec.	Pay.
		No dividends paid.		

CAPITALIZATION (12/31/95):

	($000)	(%)
Stockholders' Equity	5,688	100.0
Total	5,688	100.0

RECENT DEVELOPMENTS: For the year ended 12/31/96, the Company reported a net loss of $3.1 million compared with a net loss of $2.2 million the year before. Results for the recent year-end period include $330,000 in charges relating to an agreement to discharge the Company's future royalty obligations to the BIRD Foundation. Total revenues more than doubled to $13.7 million from $6.4 million a year earlier. Sales revenues more than tripled to $11.1 million, while contract engineering revenues declined 12.7% to $2.6 million. During the fourth quarter, the Company began shipping its CopperTrunk ORvision II Asymmetric Digital Subscriber Line (ADSL) and ORmega Symmetric Digital Subscriber Line (SDSL) products. The Company also began shipment of its FastInternet xDSL Broadband Ac cess Multiplexer during the fourth quarter.

BUSINESS

ORCKIT COMMUNICATIONS LTS. designs, develops, manufactures and markets digital subscriber line (DSL) systems that enable telephone companies to cost-effectively provide efficient, high-speed digital transmission of data, voice and video over the last mile of the existing telephone network.

ANNUAL EARNINGS

	12/31/95	12/31/94	12/31/95	12/31/94
	------------US $-------------		------------NIS------------	
Earnings Per Share	d0.19	d0.06	d0.60	d0.18

ANNUAL FINANCIAL DATA

RECORD OF EARNINGS (IN THOUSANDS):

	12/31/95	12/31/94	12/31/95	12/31/94
Total Revenues	6,439	2,870	20,268	8,660
Costs & Expenses	8,681	3,577	27,325	10,794
Operating Income	d2,242	d707	d7,057	d2,133
Income Bef Income Tax	d2,205	d679	d6,941	d2,049
Net Income	d2,205	d679	d6,941	d2,049
Average Shares Outstg	11,653	11,627	11,653	11,627

BALANCE SHEET (IN THOUSANDS):

Cash & Cash Equivalents	2,102	1,637	6,616	4,940
Receivables, Net	4,038	626	12,710	1,889
Inventories	2,992	359	9,418	1,083
Gross Property	1,083	708	3,409	2,136
Accumulated Depreciation	294	136	925	410
Stockholders' Equity	5,688	2,142	17,904	6,463
Total Assets	9,921	3,194	31,228	9,638
Total Current Assets	9,132	2,622	28,744	7,912
Total Current Liabilities	3,284	930	10,337	2,806
Net Working Capital	5,848	1,692	18,407	5,106
Year End Shs Outstg	10,959	8,888	10,959	8,888

STATISTICAL RECORD:

Return on Equity %	...	...		
Return on Assets %	...	...		
Operating Profit Margin %	...	...		
Net Profit Margin %	...	...		
Book Value Per Share	0.52	0.24		

Converted at 1995, US$0.3177= 1 New Israeli Shekel; 1994, US$0.3314= 1 New Israeli Shekel

OFFICERS:
E. Paneth, Chmn. & C.E.O.
I. Tamir, Pres.
U. Feinstein, C.F.O.
B. Rippin, V.P.-Engineering

INCORPORATED: Israel, 1990

PRINCIPAL OFFICE: 38 Nahalat Yitzhak Street Tel Aviv Israel 67448

TELEPHONE NUMBER: 972-3-696-2121

NO. OF EMPLOYEES: 91

ANNUAL MEETING: N/A

SHAREHOLDERS: N/A

INSTITUTIONAL HOLDINGS:
No. of Institutions: N/A
Shares Held: N/A

REGISTRAR(S): N/A

TRANSFER AGENT(S): American Stock Transfer & Trust Co., New York, NY

ORTHOFIX INTERNATIONAL N.V.

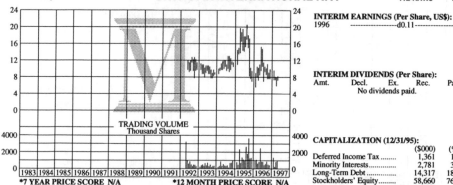

7 YEAR PRICE SCORE N/A   **12 MONTH PRICE SCORE N/A**

NYSE COMPOSITE INDEX=100

INTERIM EARNINGS (Per Share, US$):
1996 ------------------d0.11----------------

INTERIM DIVIDENDS (Per Share):
Amt.	Decl.	Ex.	Rec.	Pay.
		No dividends paid.		

CAPITALIZATION (12/31/95):

	($000)	(%)
Deferred Income Tax	1,361	1.8
Minority Interests............	2,781	3.6
Long-Term Debt	14,317	18.5
Stockholders' Equity........	58,660	76.1
Total	77,119	100.0

RECENT DEVELOPMENTS: For the year ended 12/31/96, the Company reported a net loss of $1.3 million compared with a loss of $19.8 million in 1995. Sales increased 47.7% to $77.2 million from $52.3 million a year earlier. The Company attributed the increase in sales largely to the inclusion of the results of Orthofix Inc. (previously American Medical Electronics Inc.), which was acquired on 8/21/95. Results in 1996 included a restructuring charge of $3.1 million, while results in 1995 included an acquisition-related non-recurring charge of $24.3 million. The Company noted that it expects to incur a further restructuring charge of $900,000 related to severance payments in the first quarter of 1997. U.S. sales were approximately $44.0 million, or 57% of total revenues, compared with $23.0 million, or 44%, in 1995. Non-US sales increased 14% to approximately $33.0 million, versus $29.0 million in 1995.

BUSINESS

ORTHOFIX INTERNATIONAL N.V. is a producer of external fixation devices used in fracture treatment, limb lengthening and bone reconstruction. The Company's external fixation devices are specifically designed to permit controlled micromovement of the bone, which enhances the natural physiological healing process by promoting the formation of callus, the organic material that fuses bone fractures. The Company sells its products in over 80 countries.

ANNUAL EARNINGS

Earnings Per Share	12/31/95	12/31/94	12/31/95	12/31/94
	------------US $------------		------------NAG------------	
	d1.78	0.84	d2.86	1.46

ANNUAL FINANCIAL DATA

RECORD OF EARNINGS (IN THOUSANDS):

	12/31/95	12/31/94	12/31/95	12/31/94
Total Revenues	52,272	39,634	84,052	68,797
Costs & Expenses	43,438	27,290	69,847	47,370
Depreciation & Amort	1,406	660	2,261	1,146
Nonrecurring charges	24,300	...	39,074	...
Operating Income	d16,872	11,684	d27,130	20,281
Income Bef Income Tax	d16,654	12,251	d26,779	21,265
Income Tax	2,564	2,793	4,123	4,848
Minority Interests	cr584	cr396	cr939	cr687
Net Income	d19,802	9,062	d31,841	15,730
Average Shares Outstg	11,114	10,820	11,114	10,820

BALANCE SHEET (IN THOUSANDS):

Cash & Cash Equivalents	7,046	20,491	12,611	36,676
Receivables, Net	19,738	12,805	35,328	22,919
Inventories	9,327	3,553	16,694	6,359
Gross Property	12,840	6,178	20,646	10,724
Accumulated Depreciation	3,446	2,695	5,541	4,678
Long-Term Debt	14,317	953	23,021	1,654
Stockholders' Equity	58,660	43,570	94,324	75,630
Total Assets	103,958	56,740	167,162	98,490
Total Current Assets	42,423	38,929	68,215	67,573
Total Current Liabilities	26,304	8,367	42,296	14,524
Net Working Capital	16,119	30,562	25,919	53,050
Year End Shs Outstg	12,477	10,275	12,477	10,275

STATISTICAL RECORD:

Return on Equity %	...	20.80		
Return on Assets %	...	15.97		
Operating Profit Margin %	...	29.48		
Net Profit Margin %	...	22.86		
Book Value Per Share	4.70	4.24		

Converted at 1995, US$0.6219= 1 Netherlands Antilles guilders; 1994, US$0.5761= 1 Netherlands Antilles guilders

OFFICERS:
R. G. Cooper, Chmn.
E. Wallner, Pres. & C.E.O.
B. Steer, C.O.O.
P. Clarke, Exec. V.P. & C.F.O.

INCORPORATED: Netherlands, 1987

PRINCIPAL OFFICE: 7 Abraham de Veerstraat Curacao Netherlands Antilles

TELEPHONE NUMBER: 559-9-602-738

NO. OF EMPLOYEES: 370

ANNUAL MEETING: N/A

SHAREHOLDERS: N/A

INSTITUTIONAL HOLDINGS:
No. of Institutions: N/A
Shares Held: N/A

REGISTRAR(S): The Bank of New York, New York

TRANSFER AGENT(S): The Bank of New York, New York

OSHAP TECHNOLOGIES LTD.

YIELD ...
P/E RATIO 3.1

TRADING VOLUME
Thousand Shares

| 1983 | 1984 | 1985 | 1986 | 1987 | 1988 | 1989 | 1990 | 1991 | 1992 | 1993 | 1994 | 1995 | 1996 | 1997 |

*7 YEAR PRICE SCORE N/A   *12 MONTH PRICE SCORE N/A
*NYSE COMPOSITE INDEX=100

INTERIM EARNINGS (Per Share, US$):

Qtr.	Mar.	Jun.	Sept.	Dec.
1995	----------------d0.18----------------			
1996	0.02	1.70	0.01	0.04

INTERIM DIVIDENDS (Per Share):

Amt.	Decl.	Ex.	Rec.	Pay.
	No dividends paid.			

CAPITALIZATION (12/31/95):

	($000)	(%)
Minority Interests.............	18,905	47.4
Long-Term Debt	6,748	16.9
Stockholders' Equity........	14,207	35.7
Total	39,860	100.0

RECENT DEVELOPMENTS: For the year ended 12/31/96, net income was $21.9 million compared with a net loss of $1.7 million the year before. Results for the recent year-end period include a gain of approximately $21.4 million from the sale of Tecnomatix shares in May 1996. Revenues declined 45.5% to $20.8 million from $38.2 million a year earlier. The Company reported an operating loss of $1.0 million versus operating income of $1.6 million the previous year. During the fourth quarter, Tecnomatix received a $10.0 million contract with Mazda Motor Corp. and a $3.3 million order from General Motors North America Operations. Decalog received an order from Austria-based Raiffeisen Kapitalanlage, valued at more than $600,000. Decalog also signed a non-exclusive development and marketing agreement with ACT Financial Systems Ltd., valued at over $5.4 million.

BUSINESS

OSHAP TECHNOLOGIES LTD. is a holding company focused primarily on the software business, including computer-aided production engineering software, and products designed for the financial market which include sophisticated content sensitive information switching software and relational database replication software systems. The Company also provides, through its subsidiaries, sophisticated content sensitive information switching software products primarily for financial institutions, relational data base replication systems, software products and consulting services for automating portfolio management and dealing rooms operations within financial institutions, flexible machining centers and automated factory services.

ANNUAL EARNINGS

	12/31/95	12/31/94	12/31/95	12/31/94
	----------US $----------		----------NIS----------	
Earnings Per Share	d0.18	0.15	d0.57	0.45

ANNUAL FINANCIAL DATA

RECORD OF EARNINGS (IN THOUSANDS):

	12/31/95	12/31/94	12/31/95	12/31/94
Total Revenues	38,233	27,620	120,343	83,343
Costs & Expenses	36,629	30,178	115,294	91,062
Operating Income	1,604	d2,558	5,049	d7,719
Income Bef Income Tax	1,672	1,317	5,263	3,974
Income Tax	24	620	76	1,871
Eq. Earnings in Affils.	d1,064	d237	d3,349	d715
Minority Interests	2,240	cr566	7,051	cr1,708
Net Income	d1,656	1,026	d5,212	3,096
Income from Disc. Ops.	...	d1,554	...	d4,689
Average Shares Outstg	9,225	6,854	9,225	6,854

BALANCE SHEET (IN THOUSANDS):

Cash & Cash Equivalents	21,126	16,640	66,497	50,211
Receivables, Net	12,516	13,284	39,396	40,084
Inventories	112	11	353	33
Gross Property	10,893	8,709	34,287	26,279
Accumulated Depreciation	6,102	4,741	19,207	14,306
Long-Term Debt	6,748	7,640	21,240	23,054
Stockholders' Equity	14,207	9,705	44,718	29,285
Total Assets	54,209	48,163	170,630	145,332
Total Current Assets	37,191	32,627	117,063	98,452
Total Current Liabilities	12,609	13,277	39,688	40,063
Net Working Capital	24,582	19,350	77,375	58,389
Year End Shs Outstg	12,424	6,854	12,424	6,854

STATISTICAL RECORD:

Return on Equity %	...	10.57		
Return on Assets %	...	2.13		
Operating Profit Margin %	4.20	...		
Net Profit Margin %	...	3.71		
Book Value Per Share	1.14	1.42		

Converted at 1995, US$0.3177= 1 New Israeli Shekel; 1994, US$0.3314= 1 New Israeli Shekel

OFFICERS:
A. Dovrat, Chmn.
S. Dovrat, Pres. & C.E.O.
A. Zeevi, C.F.O.

INCORPORATED: Israel, Dec., 1981

PRINCIPAL OFFICE: Delta Building 16
Hagalim Avenue Herzeliya Israel 46733

TELEPHONE NUMBER: 972-9-594-894

NO. OF EMPLOYEES: N/A

ANNUAL MEETING: N/A

SHAREHOLDERS: N/A

INSTITUTIONAL HOLDINGS:
No. of Institutions: 9
Shares Held: 1,304,068

REGISTRAR(S): N/A

TRANSFER AGENT(S): American Stock
Transfer & Trust Co., New York, NY

PC DOCS GROUP INTERNATIONAL INC.

YIELD   ...
P/E RATIO   15.7

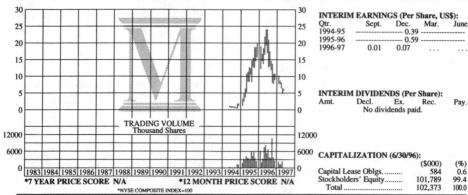

INTERIM EARNINGS (Per Share, US$):

Qtr.	Sept.	Dec.	Mar.	June
1994-95	----------------	0.39	----------------	
1995-96	----------------	0.59	----------------	
1996-97	0.01	0.07	...	...

INTERIM DIVIDENDS (Per Share):

Amt.	Decl.	Ex.	Rec.	Pay.
		No dividends paid.		

TRADING VOLUME
Thousand Shares

1983 1984 1985 1986 1987 1988 1989 1990 1991 1992 1993 1994 1995 1996 1997

*7 YEAR PRICE SCORE N/A   *12 MONTH PRICE SCORE N/A

*NYSE COMPOSITE INDEX=100

CAPITALIZATION (6/30/96):

	($000)	(%)
Capital Lease Oblgs.	584	0.6
Stockholders' Equity	101,789	99.4
Total	102,373	100.0

RECENT DEVELOPMENTS: For the second quarter ended 12/31/96, net earnings declined 16.9% to C$2.1 million compared with C$2.5 million in the corresponding quarter the year before. Total revenues increased 36.3% to C$25.0 million from C$18.3 million in the prior year. Revenues from the Company's two major businesses were up significantly over the previous year. Enterprise document management revenues grew 45.0%, while information management for professionals revenues rose 28.0%. Software sales, which comprise more than half of total revenues, were up 27.6% to C$13.3 million compared with C$10.4 million a year earlier. During the quarter, the Company released DOCS Open 3.5, the DOCS Enterprise Suite, which combines the power of enterprise document management, desktop imaging and document routing. The Company also introduced CyberDOCS, which expands DOCS Open to include support for the Internet and corporate intranets.

BUSINESS

PC DOCS GROUP INTERNATIONAL INC. and its subsidiaries develop, market and support object-oriented enterprise document management systems, information management system for professionals, advanced database and Internet software, as well as retail information management systems.

ANNUAL EARNINGS

	6/30/96	6/30/95	6/30/96	6/30/95
	--------------US $--------------		--------------C $--------------	
Earnings Per Share	0.59	0.39	0.81	0.54

ANNUAL FINANCIAL DATA

RECORD OF EARNINGS (IN THOUSANDS):

	6/30/96	6/30/95	6/30/96	6/30/95
Total Revenues	57,354	34,718	78,213	47,644
Costs & Expenses	39,409	27,005	53,742	37,059
Depreciation & Amort	3,856	2,071	5,258	2,842
Operating Income	14,089	5,642	19,213	7,743
Income Bef Income Tax	13,925	5,510	18,990	7,562
Income Tax	4,456	659	6,077	905
Net Income	9,469	4,851	12,913	6,657
Average Shares Outstg	15,840	12,377	15,840	12,377

BALANCE SHEET (IN THOUSANDS):

Cash & Cash Equivalents	70,302	9,495	95,871	13,030
Receivables, Net	24,660	12,714	33,629	17,448
Gross Property	8,946	5,238	12,199	7,188
Accumulated Depreciation	5,100	3,578	6,955	4,910
Long-Term Debt	584	450	797	618
Stockholders' Equity	101,789	17,419	138,810	23,904
Total Assets	119,078	30,675	162,386	42,095
Total Current Assets	95,929	22,998	130,818	31,560
Total Current Liabilities	16,704	12,805	22,779	17,573
Net Working Capital	79,225	10,192	108,039	13,987
Year End Shs Outstg	19,413	14,733	19,413	14,733

STATISTICAL RECORD:

Return on Equity %	9.30	27.85
Return on Assets %	7.95	15.81
Operating Profit Margin %	24.56	16.25
Net Profit Margin %	16.51	13.97
Book Value Per Share	5.24	1.18

Converted at 1996, US$0.7333= 1 Canadian $; 1995, US$0.7287= 1 Canadian $

OFFICERS:
R. I. Osten, Chmn., Pres. & C.E.O.
P. I. Reece, V.P.-Fin. & C.F.O.
M. Day, Sec. & Gen. Couns.

INCORPORATED: N/A

PRINCIPAL OFFICE: 2005 Sheppard Ave. East, Suite 800, Toronto Canada M2J 5B4

TELEPHONE NUMBER: (416) 497-7700

NO. OF EMPLOYEES: N/A

ANNUAL MEETING: N/A

SHAREHOLDERS: N/A

INSTITUTIONAL HOLDINGS:
No. of Institutions: 17
Shares Held: 1,931,065

REGISTRAR(S): N/A

TRANSFER AGENT(S): Montreal Trust, Toronto; Continental Stock Transfer & Trust Company, New York.

PETROMET RESOURCES LIMITED

YIELD ...
P/E RATIO 19.8

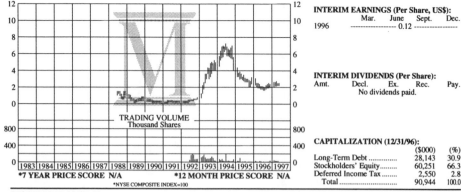

INTERIM EARNINGS (Per Share, US$):

	Mar.	June	Sept.	Dec.
1996	----------------- 0.12 -----------------			

INTERIM DIVIDENDS (Per Share):

Amt.	Decl.	Ex.	Rec.	Pay.
	No dividends paid.			

CAPITALIZATION (12/31/96):

	($000)	(%)
Long-Term Debt	28,143	30.9
Stockholders' Equity........	60,251	66.3
Deferred Income Tax	2,550	2.8
Total	90,944	100.0

*7 YEAR PRICE SCORE N/A ***12 MONTH PRICE SCORE N/A**

*NYSE COMPOSITE INDEX=100

RECENT DEVELOPMENTS: For the year ended 12/31/96, net income more than trippled to C$5.9 million compared with C$1.7 million in the corresponding period a year earlier. Oil and gas sales and royalties jumped to C$23.7 million versus C$16.7 million in 1995. Improved sales and earnings resulted from higher production levels and the Company's emphasis on cost control and efficiency measures. Average daily production increased to 33.1 million cubic feet of natural gas and 859 barrels of oil and natural gas liquids from 27 million cubic feet and 801 barrels, respectively, in 1995. Petromet's current daily production is approximately 40 million cubic feet and 1,000 barrels. During 1996, the Company drilled 29 gross, 21 net, wells, resulting in 17 natural gas wells, 3 oil wells and 9 dry and abandoned wells. The Company announced a large pipeline project and plant expansion at the Bigstone project.

BUSINESS

PETROMET RESOURCES LIM-ITED is engaged in the exploration, development and production of oil and natural gas, principally in Alberta. The Company has grown its average production from 5 million cubic feet of natural gas equivalent per day in 1992 to 42 million cubic feet equivalent per day in 1996 primarily through exploration.

ANNUAL EARNINGS

	12/31/96	12/31/95	12/31/96	12/31/95
	--------------US $-------------		-------------C $-------------	
Earnings Per Share	0.12	0.04	0.17	0.05

ANNUAL FINANCIAL DATA

RECORD OF EARNINGS (IN THOUSANDS):

	12/31/96	12/31/95	12/31/96	12/31/95
Total Revenues	17,293	12,255	23,653	16,721
Costs & Expenses	3,337	3,319	4,564	4,528
Depreciation & Amort	7,075	5,620	9,677	7,668
Operating Income	6,881	3,316	9,412	4,525
Income Bef Income Tax	7,291	1,733	9,972	2,365
Income Tax	2,950	470	4,035	641
Net Income	4,341	1,264	5,937	1,724
Average Shares Outstg	34,347	31,612	34,347	31,612
BALANCE SHEET (IN THOUSANDS):				
Cash & Cash Equivalents	97	2,270	132	3,097
Receivables, Net	4,082	4,293	5,584	5,858
Inventories	972	1,602	1,330	2,186
Gross Property	110,446	93,739	151,068	127,901
Accumulated Depreciation	19,297	12,597	26,395	17,188
Long-Term Debt	28,143	33,398	38,494	45,570
Stockholders' Equity	60,251	48,816	82,412	66,606
Total Assets	96,300	89,307	131,719	121,854
Total Current Assets	5,151	8,165	7,046	11,141
Total Current Liabilities	4,463	4,781	6,105	6,523
Net Working Capital	688	3,385	941	4,618
Year End Shs Outstg	37,032	33,932	37,032	33,932
STATISTICAL RECORD:				
Return on Equity %	7.20	2.59		
Return on Assets %	4.51	1.41		
Operating Profit Margin %	39.79	27.06		
Net Profit Margin %	25.10	10.31		
Book Value Per Share	1.63	1.44		

Converted at 1996, US$0.7311= 1 Canadian $; 1995, US$0.7329= 1 Canadian $

OFFICERS:
P. G. Schoch, Chmn.
L. J. Smith, Pres. & C.E.O.
D. H. Erickson, Sr. V.P.
S. A. Supple, C.F.O.

INCORPORATED: Canada 1981

PRINCIPAL OFFICE: 839-5th Avenue S.W., Suite 350 Calgary Alberta, Canada T2P 3C8

TELEPHONE NUMBER: 403-269-2627

NO. OF EMPLOYEES: 29

ANNUAL MEETING: In May

SHAREHOLDERS: N/A

INSTITUTIONAL HOLDINGS:
No. of Institutions: 6
Shares Held: 7,250,275

REGISTRAR(S): The R-M Trust Company; Toronto and Calgary.

TRANSFER AGENT(S): The R-M Trust Company; Toronto and Calgary.

PLAINTREE SYSTEMS, INC.

YIELD ...
P/E RATIO ...

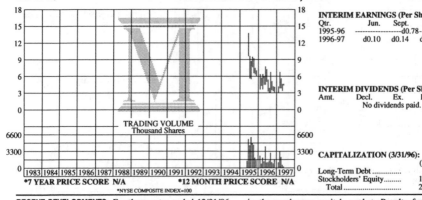

INTERIM EARNINGS (Per Share, C$):

Qtr.	Jun.	Sept.	Dec.	Mar.
1995-96	------------------d0.78-----------------			
1996-97	d0.10	d0.14	d0.32	...

INTERIM DIVIDENDS (Per Share):

Amt.	Decl.	Ex.	Rec.	Pay.
	No dividends paid.			

TRADING VOLUME
Thousand Shares

1983 1984 1985 1986 1987 1988 1989 1990 1991 1992 1993 1994 1995 1996 1997

*7 YEAR PRICE SCORE N/A   *12 MONTH PRICE SCORE N/A

*NYSE COMPOSITE INDEX=100

CAPITALIZATION (3/31/96):

	($000)	(%)
Long-Term Debt	422	2.1
Stockholders' Equity.........	19,608	97.9
Total	20,030	100.0

RECENT DEVELOPMENTS: For the quarter ended 12/31/96, the Company reported a net loss of C$4.9 million compared with a net loss of C$4.8 million the year before. Sales declined 25.6% to C$6.3 million from C$8.5 million a year earlier. The decrease in sales was attributed to a list price reduction in excess of 30.0% for WaveSwitch 1000/4000 series products in response to continued price competition in the workgroup switch market. Results for the recent quarter were negatively affected by lower-than-anticipated sales through the Company's original equipment manufacturers and distributor channels. For the nine months ended 12/31/96, the Company reported a net loss of C$8.3 million versus a net loss of C$6.6 million the year before. Sales climbed slightly to C$22.8 million.

BUSINESS

PLAINTREE SYSTEMS INC. designs, develops, manufactures, markets and supports computer networking products designed to allow its customers to improve the performance and increase the manageability of their existing local area networks, while providing a migration path to emerging networking technologies.

ANNUAL EARNINGS

	3/31/96	3/31/95	3/31/96	3/31/95
	------------US $------------		------------C $------------	
Earnings Per Share	d0.57	d0.04	d0.78	d0.06

ANNUAL FINANCIAL DATA

RECORD OF EARNINGS (IN THOUSANDS):

	3/31/96	3/31/95	3/31/96	3/31/95
Total Revenues	23,114	19,434	31,417	27,192
Costs & Expenses	30,951	19,984	42,070	27,961
Operating Income	d7,837	d549	d10,653	d768
Income Bef Income Tax	d7,766	d444	d10,556	d621
Income Tax	...	3	...	4
Net Income	d7,766	d447	d10,556	d625
Average Shares Outstg	9,938	7,442	9,938	7,442
BALANCE SHEET (IN THOUSANDS):				
Cash & Cash Equivalents	4,676	2,338	6,356	3,271
Receivables, Net	5,632	10,294	7,655	14,403
Inventories	9,096	5,491	12,363	7,683
Gross Property	4,931	2,634	6,702	3,685
Accumulated Depreciation	2,170	1,006	2,949	1,408
Long-Term Debt	422	155	573	217
Stockholders' Equity	19,608	13,661	26,652	19,115
Total Assets	25,162	20,104	34,201	28,129
Total Current Assets	21,404	18,476	29,093	25,852
Total Current Liabilities	5,132	6,287	6,976	8,797
Net Working Capital	16,271	12,189	22,117	17,055
Year End Shs Outstg	10,163	8,790	10,163	8,790
STATISTICAL RECORD:				
Return on Equity %	...	...		
Return on Assets %	...	...		
Operating Profit Margin %	...	...		
Net Profit Margin %	...	...		
Book Value Per Share	1.93	1.55		

Converted at 1996, US$0.7357= 1 Canadian $; 1995, US$0.7147= 1 Canadian $

OFFICERS:
D. M. Delaney, Chmn.
B. V. Walter, Pres. & C.E.O.
A. D. Greenfield, Sr. V.P.
T. J. Branca, V.P. & C.F.O.

INCORPORATED: April, 1988

PRINCIPAL OFFICE: 59 Iber Road Stittsville, Ontario Canada K2S 1E7

TELEPHONE NUMBER: 613-831-8300

NO. OF EMPLOYEES: 160

ANNUAL MEETING: N/A

SHAREHOLDERS: N/A

INSTITUTIONAL HOLDINGS:
No. of Institutions: 6
Shares Held: 3,289,800

REGISTRAR(S): N/A

TRANSFER AGENT(S): Montreal Trust, Toronto, Ontario, Canada

QIAGEN N.V.

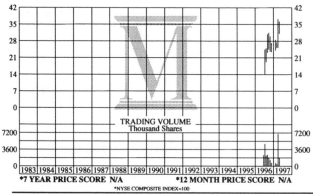

TRADING VOLUME
Thousand Shares

| | 1983 | 1984 | 1985 | 1986 | 1987 | 1988 | 1989 | 1990 | 1991 | 1992 | 1993 | 1994 | 1995 | 1996 | 1997 |

*7 YEAR PRICE SCORE N/A   *12 MONTH PRICE SCORE N/A

*NYSE COMPOSITE INDEX=100

INTERIM EARNINGS (Per Share, US$):

Qtr.	Mar.	Jun.	Sept.	Dec.
1995		0.18		
1996	0.06	0.08	0.09	0.11

INTERIM DIVIDENDS (Per Share):

Amt.	Decl.	Ex.	Rec.	Pay.
	No dividends paid.			

CAPITALIZATION (12/31/95):

	($000)	(%)
Long-Term Debt	1,276	6.8
Stockholders' Equity........	12,208	65.2
Capital Lease Oblgs.	5,248	28.0
Total	23,980	100.0

RECENT DEVELOPMENTS: For the year ended 12/31/96, net income was $5.3 million compared with $2.4 million the year before. Net sales advanced 46.4% to $54.2 million from $37.0 million a year earlier. The increase in sales was attributed to successful new product introductions, including an expanded line of the Company's products for nucleic acid separation. Income from operations was $6.0 million compared with $4.7 million the previous year. During the fourth quarter, the Company introduced new products targeting the market for PCR reagents. The Company also acquired the rights under patents for the purification and stabilization of nucleic acids utilizing a cationic detergent technology. In December 1996, the Company relocated its U.S. sales and distribution headquarters to Valencia, California.

BUSINESS

QIAGEN NV and its subsidiaries are engaged in the production and distribution of biotechnology products, primarily for the separation and purification of nucleic acids (DNA and RNA). The Company produces its products for use in molecular biology reasearch, genetic vaccination research, gene therapy research, DNA sequencing and clinical diagnostic research. In addition, Qiagen also assembles and distributes certain robotic equipment to be used in connection with its products.

ANNUAL EARNINGS

	12/31/95	12/31/94	12/31/95	12/31/94
	US $		Guilders	
Earnings Per Share	0.18	0.10	0.29	0.17

ANNUAL FINANCIAL DATA

RECORD OF EARNINGS (IN THOUSANDS):

	12/31/95	12/31/94	12/31/95	12/31/94
Total Revenues	36,992	24,115	59,482	41,859
Costs & Expenses	22,764	13,362	36,604	23,194
Operating Income	4,678	3,465	22,878	18,665
Income Bef Income Tax	4,525	2,940	7,276	5,103
Income Tax	2,130	1,656	3,425	2,875
Net Income	2,395	1,284	3,851	2,229
Average Shares Outstg	13,623	13,132	13,623	13,132
BALANCE SHEET (IN THOUSANDS):				
Cash & Cash Equivalents	5,305	3,612	8,530	6,270
Receivables, Net	4,680	3,004	9,399	7,323
Inventories	6,152	4,219	9,892	7,323
Gross Property	14,886	11,455	23,936	19,884
Accumulated Depreciation	6,130	4,097	9,857	7,112
Long-Term Debt	6,524	6,515	10,490	11,309
Stockholders' Equity	12,208	9,120	19,630	15,831
Total Assets	26,203	19,450	42,134	33,761
Total Current Assets	17,302	12,050	27,821	20,917
Total Current Liabilities	7,382	3,747	11,870	6,504
Net Working Capital	9,920	8,303	15,951	14,412
Year End Shs Outstg	13,710	12,877	13,710	12,877
STATISTICAL RECORD:				
Return on Equity %	19.62	14.08		
Return on Assets %	9.14	6.60		
Operating Profit Margin %	12.65	14.37		
Net Profit Margin %	6.47	5.32		
Book Value Per Share	0.89	0.71		

Converted at 1995, US$0.6219= 1 Netherlands guilder; 1994, US$0.5761= 1 Netherlands guilder

OFFICERS:
M. Colpan, Managing Dir. & C.E.O.
P. M. Schatz, C.F.O.

INCORPORATED: Amsterdam, April 29, 1996

PRINCIPAL OFFICE: Johaannes Vermeerplein 9-1 Amsterdam Netherlands 1071 DV

TELEPHONE NUMBER: 31 (0) 20 664 5500

NO. OF EMPLOYEES: 334

ANNUAL MEETING: N/A

SHAREHOLDERS: N/A

INSTITUTIONAL HOLDINGS:
No. of Institutions: N/A
Shares Held: N/A

REGISTRAR(S): American Stock Transfer & Trust Co., New York, NY

TRANSFER AGENT(S): American Stock Transfer & Trust Co., New York, NY

QLT PHOTOTHERAPEUTICS, INC.

YIELD ...
P/E RATIO ...

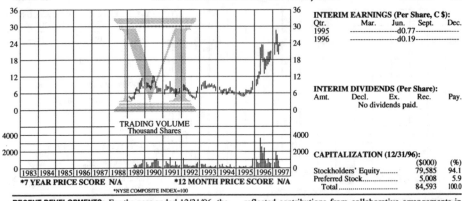

*7 YEAR PRICE SCORE N/A *12 MONTH PRICE SCORE N/A
*NYSE COMPOSITE INDEX=100

TRADING VOLUME
Thousand Shares

INTERIM EARNINGS (Per Share, C $):
Qtr.	Mar.	Jun.	Sept.	Dec.
1995		d0.77		
1996		d0.19		

INTERIM DIVIDENDS (Per Share):
Amt.	Decl.	Ex.	Rec.	Pay.
	No dividends paid.			

CAPITALIZATION (12/31/96):
	($000)	(%)
Stockholders' Equity	79,585	94.1
Preferred Stock	5,008	5.9
Total	84,593	100.0

RECENT DEVELOPMENTS: For the year ended 12/31/96, the Company reported a net loss of C$4.7 million versus a net loss of C$14.7 million the year before. Total revenues were C$13.5 million compared with C$2.5 million a year earlier. For the quarter ended 12/31/96, net income was C$4.0 million compared with a net loss of C$4.2 million in the prior-year period. Total revenues were C$10.9 million versus C$779,000 the previous year. The increase in revenues reflected contributions from collaborative arrangements in the U.S. and Europe and the early sales efforts of the Company's distribution partner, Sanofi Pharmaceuticals, Inc., in the launch of PHOTOFRIN in the U.S. Revenues are expected to continue growing as additional laser placements are made in the U.S. and Japan, and as Beaufour Ipsen, the Company's European partner, launches PHOTOFRIN in Europe in 1997.

BUSINESS

QLT PHOTOTHERAPEUTICS INC. is engaged in the development and commercialization of proprietary pharmaceutical products for photodynamic therapy, a field of medicine that uses light-activated drugs for the treatment of cancer, diseases of the eye and other medical conditions. QLT's lead product, PHOTOFRIN,® has been approved and is being marketed for the treatment of specific cancers in the United States, Canada, Japan, France, and the Netherlands. The Company has a diversified portfolio of photodynamic therapy products, including Benzoporphyrin derivative (verteporfin), a second-generation product which is in Phase III clinical trials for the treatment of age-related macular degeneration (AMD).

ANNUAL EARNINGS

	12/31/96	12/31/95	12/31/96	12/31/95
	US $		C $	
Earnings Per Share	d0.14	d0.54	d0.19	d0.77

ANNUAL FINANCIAL DATA

RECORD OF EARNINGS (IN THOUSANDS):
Total Revenues	9,867	1,855	13,497	2,531
Costs & Expenses	11,937	11,405	16,327	15,561
Depreciation & Amort	1,365	1,217	1,867	1,660
Operating Income	d3,434	d10,766	d4,698	d14,690
Income Bef Income Tax	d3,434	d10,766	d4,698	d14,690
Net Income	d3,434	d10,766	d4,698	d14,690
Average Shares Outstg	24,473	19,788	24,473	19,788

BALANCE SHEET (IN THOUSANDS):
Cash & Cash Equivalents	71,027	8,620	97,151	11,762
Gross Property	5,023	4,230	6,870	5,771
Accumulated Depreciation	3,043	2,547	4,162	3,475
Stockholders' Equity	79,585	15,533	108,857	21,194
Total Assets	82,025	16,621	112,195	22,678
Total Current Assets	78,830	10,086	107,824	13,761
Total Current Liabilities	2,440	1,088	3,338	1,484
Net Working Capital	76,390	8,998	104,486	12,277
Year End Shs Outstg	25,917	19,996	25,917	19,996

STATISTICAL RECORD:
Return on Equity %	...	...		
Return on Assets %	...	...		
Operating Profit Margin %	...	...		
Net Profit Margin %	...	...		
Book Value Per Share	4.20	1.06		

Converted at 1996, US$0.7311= 1 Canadian $; 1995, US$0.7329= 1 Canadian $

OFFICERS:
E. D. Scott, Chmn.
J. G. Levy, Pres. & C.E.O.
K. H. Galbraith, Sr. V.P. & C.F.O.

INCORPORATED: Feb., 1981

PRINCIPAL OFFICE: QLT Place 520 West
6th Avenue Vancouver Canada

TELEPHONE NUMBER: (604) 872-7881

NO. OF EMPLOYEES: 115

ANNUAL MEETING: In May

SHAREHOLDERS: 662

INSTITUTIONAL HOLDINGS:
No. of Institutions: 13
Shares Held: 1,695,100

REGISTRAR(S): Montreal Trust Company,
Vancouver, Canada

TRANSFER AGENT(S): Montreal Trust
Company, Vancouver, Canada

NASDAQ SYMBOL RCORF
Rec. Pr. 5⅜

QUALITY DINO ENTERTAINMENT LTD

YIELD ...
P/E RATIO 14.1

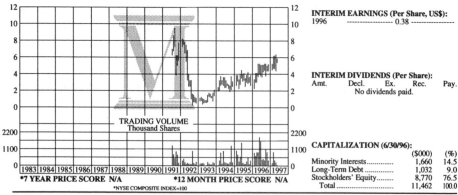

7 YEAR PRICE SCORE N/A **12 MONTH PRICE SCORE N/A**

*NYSE COMPOSITE INDEX=100

INTERIM EARNINGS (Per Share, US$):
1996 ------------------ 0.38 ------------------

INTERIM DIVIDENDS (Per Share):
Amt.	Decl.	Ex.	Rec.	Pay.
No dividends paid.				

CAPITALIZATION (6/30/96):
	($000)	(%)
Minority Interests.............	1,660	14.5
Long-Term Debt	1,032	9.0
Stockholders' Equity........	8,770	76.5
Total............................	11,462	100.0

RECENT DEVELOPMENTS: For the six months ended 12/31/96, net income declined 8.6% to $2.4 million compared with $2.6 million in the corresponding period of 1995. Sales fell 2.2% to $57.6 million from $58.9 million a year earlier. The Company noted that its North American operations reported record sales and net income, with the continued strong sales of the Company's Dance Mix music series, sports videos and consumer products, including the Body Break Ab Master. These gains, however, were more than offset by the decline in sales and earnings in the Company's UK TV-advertised retail music operations. For the quarter ended 12/31/96, net income declined 14.0% to $1.6 million from $1.8 million a year earlier. Sales fell 8.2% to $33.4 million.

BUSINESS

QUALITY DINO ENTERTAIN-MENT LTD and its subsidiaries are primarily engaged in the acquisition, production and distribution of recorded music and consumers products in Europe, North America and Australia. The Company primarily sells its products to wholesalers, record stores, department stores and other retailers or through third parties, and accordingly, is subject to the inherent business risks associated with distributing its products through these channels.

ANNUAL EARNINGS

	6/30/96	6/30/95	6/30/96	6/30/95
	------------US $------------		------------C $------------	
Earnings Per Share	0.38	0.49	0.52	0.67

ANNUAL FINANCIAL DATA

RECORD OF EARNINGS (IN THOUSANDS):
	6/30/96	6/30/95	6/30/96	6/30/95
Total Revenues	95,952	87,579	130,850	120,185
Costs & Expenses	94,053	86,427	128,260	118,604
Operating Income	1,899	1,152	2,590	1,581
Income Bef Income Tax	3,330	3,393	4,541	4,656
Income Tax	135	337	184	462
Minority Interests	1,172	488	1,598	670
Net Income	2,023	2,568	2,759	3,524
Average Shares Outstg	5,311	5,282	5,311	5,282

BALANCE SHEET (IN THOUSANDS):
Cash & Cash Equivalents	1,789	7,528	2,440	10,331
Receivables, Net	24,903	17,965	33,960	24,653
Inventories	9,054	6,944	12,347	9,529
Gross Property	3,839	3,299	5,235	4,527
Accumulated Depreciation	1,999	1,659	2,726	2,277
Long-Term Debt	1,032	1,018	1,407	1,397
Stockholders' Equity	8,770	6,742	11,960	9,252
Total Assets	41,462	37,941	56,542	52,067
Total Current Assets	37,900	34,493	51,684	47,335
Total Current Liabilities	30,000	29,693	40,911	40,748
Net Working Capital	7,900	4,800	10,773	6,587
Year End Shs Outstg	5,321	5,306	5,321	5,306

STATISTICAL RECORD:
Return on Equity %	23.1	38.1		
Return on Assets %	4.9	6.8		
Operating Profit Margin %	2.0	1.3		
Net Profit Margin %	2.1	2.9		
Book Value Per Share	1.65	1.27		

Converted at 1996, US$0.7333= 1 Canadian $; 1995, US$0.7287= 1 Canadian $

OFFICERS:
R. Kives, Chmn., Pres. & C.E.O.
G. J. O'Keefe, Exec. V.P. & C.F.O.
P. Popeski, V.P.
A. Anhang, Sec.

INCORPORATED: Dec., 1984

PRINCIPAL OFFICE: 101-426 Portage Avenue, Winnipeg Canada

TELEPHONE NUMBER: 204-957-1744

NO. OF EMPLOYEES: N/A

ANNUAL MEETING: In Dec.

SHAREHOLDERS: N/A

INSTITUTIONAL HOLDINGS:
No. of Institutions: 1
Shares Held: 258,000

REGISTRAR(S): The Norwest Bank Minnesota, N.A., Minnesota.

TRANSFER AGENT(S): The Norwest Bank Minnesota, N.A., Minnesota.

Q-ZAR, INC.

INTERIM EARNINGS (Per Share, US$):

Qtr.	Mar.	Jun.	Sept.	Dec.
1994		d0.29		
1995		0.45		
1996	0.06	0.12	0.15	0.18

INTERIM DIVIDENDS (Per Share):

Amt.	Decl.	Ex.	Rec.	Pay.
	No dividends paid.			

*7 YEAR PRICE SCORE N/A   *12 MONTH PRICE SCORE N/A

*NYSE COMPOSITE INDEX=100

CAPITALIZATION (12/31/95):

	($000)	(%)
Minority Interests	439	1.3
Stockholders' Equity	32,440	97.0
Total Deposits	550	1.7
Total	33,429	100.0

RECENT DEVELOPMENTS: For the year ended 12/31/96, net earnings were $12.7 million compared with $8.6 million the year before. Revenue soared 94.9% to $47.6 million from $24.4 million a year earlier. As a percentage of revenue, gross profit margin was 81.1% versus 71.2% in the prior-year period. General and administrative expenses grew to 29.1% of revenue from 18.7% the previous year.

For the quarter ended 12/31/96, net earnings were $4.4 million compared with $3.3 million the previous year. Revenue advanced 73.5% to $15.8 million from $9.1 million the year before. As a percentage of revenue, gross profit margin improved to 88.7% from 63.6% in the comparable prior-year period. General and administrative expenses increased to 33.7% of revenue from 11.2% a year earlier.

BUSINESS

Q-ZAR INC. and its subsidiaries are primarily engaged in the business of developing, licensing and franchising Q-Zar Centers, which are interactive entertainment centers. These centers feature an interactive, family-style, live-action laser tag game known as 'Q-Zar' and other related activities, and are located in North America, South America and the Pacific Rim.

ANNUAL EARNINGS

	12/31/95	12/31/94
	US $	
Earnings Per Share	0.45	d0.29

ANNUAL FINANCIAL DATA

RECORD OF EARNINGS (IN THOUSANDS):

	12/31/95	12/31/94
Total Revenues	24,439	9,218
Costs & Expenses	12,789	11,002
Depreciation & Amort	2,342	1,635
Operating Income	9,308	d3,419
Income Bef Income Tax	9,308	d3,419
Income Tax	588	...
Eq. Earnings in Affils.	d130	d343
Minority Interests	cr27	...
Net Income	8,617	d3,762
Average Shares Outstg	19,101	13,128

BALANCE SHEET (IN THOUSANDS):

Cash & Cash Equivalents	357	100
Receivables, Net	12,323	929
Inventories	955	596
Gross Property	6,556	343
Accumulated Depreciation	489	43
Stockholders' Equity	32,440	7,180
Total Assets	43,542	17,201
Total Current Assets	14,967	1,631
Total Current Liabilities	10,663	10,021
Net Working Capital	4,304	d8,390
Year End Shs Outstg	21,479	2,043

STATISTICAL RECORD:

Return on Equity %	26.56	...
Return on Assets %	19.79	...
Operating Profit Margin %	38.09	...
Net Profit Margin %	35.26	...
Book Value Per Share	1.51	3.52

OFFICERS:
T. Butler, Pres. & C.E.O.
J. Cooke, Exec. V.P.
M. Boyle, C.F.O.
R. P. Borden, Sec.

INCORPORATED: May, 1995

PRINCIPAL OFFICE: Suite 200 1701 N. Market Street, Lock Box 53 Dallas TX 75202

TELEPHONE NUMBER: (214) 741-1376

NO. OF EMPLOYEES: N/A

ANNUAL MEETING: In Aug.

SHAREHOLDERS: N/A

INSTITUTIONAL HOLDINGS:
No. of Institutions: 7
Shares Held: 2,968,000

REGISTRAR(S): Equity Transfer Services, Toronto, Ontario, Canada

TRANSFER AGENT(S): Equity Transfer Services, Toronto, Ontario, Canada

RADA ELECTRONIC INDUSTRIES

YIELD ...
P/E RATIO 14.3

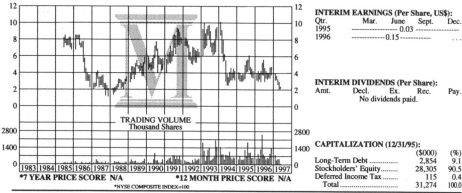

*7 YEAR PRICE SCORE N/A   *12 MONTH PRICE SCORE N/A
*NYSE COMPOSITE INDEX=100

INTERIM EARNINGS (Per Share, US$):

Qtr.	Mar.	June	Sept.	Dec.
1995	------------------- 0.03 -------------------			
1996	------------ 0.15 ------------			...

INTERIM DIVIDENDS (Per Share):

Amt.	Decl.	Ex.	Rec.	Pay.
	No dividends paid.			

CAPITALIZATION (12/31/95):

	($000)	(%)
Long-Term Debt	2,854	9.1
Stockholders' Equity.........	28,305	90.5
Deferred Income Tax	115	0.4
Total	31,274	100.0

RECENT DEVELOPMENTS: For the quarter ended 9/30/96, net income climbed 2.2% to $412,000 from $403,000 in the corresponding 1995 quarter. Sales and contract revenues earned were $8.1 million, up 2.3% from $7.9 million in the year-earlier quarter. Operating income was $785,000 compared with $727,000 the year before, an increase of 8.0%. Financial expenses were down 3.4% to $313,000 from $324,000 in the prior-year quarter. Rada's backlog at the end of the third quarter was $18.0 million. For the nine months ended 9/30/96, net income was $1.0 million compared with income from continuing operations of $52,000 for the same period in 1995. Sales and contract revenues earned jumped 22.9% to $22.2 million from $18.0 million in the comparable 1995 period.

BUSINESS

RADA ELECTRONIC INDUSTRIES and its subsidiaries are engaged in two business segments, an Industry sector and a Commercial sector: the Industry sector is engaged in the development, manufacture, marketing and sale of aerospace, naval and ground electronic equipment, both for commercial and military use; and the Commercial sector is engaged in the distribution and sale of electronic components, personal computers and aircraft parts. The Company's Industrial sector focuses on the development, manufacture and sale of Automated Test Equipment, avionic and airborne equipment, and multi-purpose ruggedized computers and control systems for air, naval and ground applications. The Company's Commercial sector specializes in the marketing, distribution and sale of electronic components and aerospace related products to manufacturers in Israel, Europe and the United States. The Company's products are used in the production of defense related equipment, telecommunications equipment, medical instruments, electronic systems and subsystems, and computer equipment.

ANNUAL EARNINGS

	12/31/95	12/31/94	12/31/95	12/31/94
	--------------US $-------------		--------------NIS-------------	
Earnings Per Share	0.03	d0.17	0.09	d0.51

ANNUAL FINANCIAL DATA

RECORD OF EARNINGS (IN THOUSANDS):

Total Revenues	25,084	23,104	78,955	69,716
Costs & Expenses	23,562	22,756	74,164	68,666
Operating Income	1,522	348	4,791	1,050
Income Bef Income Tax	261	d918	822	d2,770
Income Tax	52	69	164	208
Net Income	209	d987	658	d2,978
Income from Disc. Ops.	2,918	1,156	9,185	3,488
Average Shares Outstg	6,213	5,988	6,213	5,988

BALANCE SHEET (IN THOUSANDS):

Cash & Cash Equivalents	1,748	990	5,502	2,987
Receivables, Net	5,479	9,805	17,246	29,587
Inventories	8,177	9,904	25,738	29,885
Gross Property	19,562	16,017	61,574	48,331
Accumulated Depreciation	8,687	7,429	27,343	22,417
Long-Term Debt	2,854	3,976	8,983	11,998
Stockholders' Equity	28,305	24,164	89,093	72,915
Total Assets	50,675	47,304	159,506	142,740
Total Current Assets	25,337	27,046	79,751	81,611
Total Current Liabilities	19,014	18,743	59,849	56,557
Net Working Capital	6,323	8,303	19,902	25,054
Year End Shs Outstg	6,287	5,935	6,287	5,935

STATISTICAL RECORD:

Return on Equity %	0.7	...		
Return on Assets %	0.4	...		
Operating Profit Margin %	6.1	1.5		
Net Profit Margin %	0.8	...		
Book Value Per Share	4.5	4.1		

Converted at 1995, US$0.3177= 1 New Israeli New Shekel; 1994, US$0.3314= 1 New Israeli New Shekel

OFFICERS:
H. Nissenson, Chmn. & C.E.O.
Y. Grinberg, Vice-Chmn.
A. Werber, C.F.O.
M. Perera, Sec.

INCORPORATED: Israel, 1970

PRINCIPAL OFFICE: 12 Medinat Hayehudim St., Herzliya 46120 Israel

TELEPHONE NUMBER: 972-9-542-182

NO. OF EMPLOYEES: 165

ANNUAL MEETING: N/A

SHAREHOLDERS: 360

INSTITUTIONAL HOLDINGS:
No. of Institutions: 4
Shares Held: 153,554

REGISTRAR(S): N/A

TRANSFER AGENT(S): American Stock Transfer & Trust Co., New York.

NASDAQ SYMBOL RADAF
Rec. Pr. 3⅛

RADICA GAMES LIMITED

YIELD ...
P/E RATIO 13.4

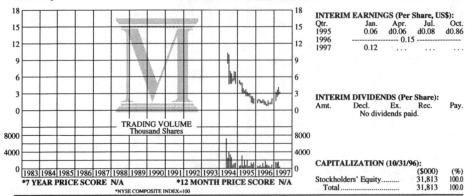

INTERIM EARNINGS (Per Share, US$):

Qtr.	Jan.	Apr.	Jul.	Oct.
1995	0.06	d0.06	d0.08	d0.86
1996		0.15		
1997	0.12	...	...	...

INTERIM DIVIDENDS (Per Share):

Amt.	Decl.	Ex.	Rec.	Pay.
	No dividends paid.			

*7 YEAR PRICE SCORE N/A   *12 MONTH PRICE SCORE N/A
*NYSE COMPOSITE INDEX=100

CAPITALIZATION (10/31/96):

	($000)	(%)
Stockholders' Equity	31,813	100.0
Total	31,813	100.0

RECENT DEVELOPMENTS: For the quarter ended 1/31/97, net income was $2.5 million compared with a loss from continuing operations of $618,000 in the corresponding 1996 quarter. Net sales were $12.7 million, up 39.9% from $9.1 million in the year-earlier quarter. The sales gain resulted from an increase in Original Equipment Manufac-turing production and international business, in addition to sales of new non-discounted products. Gross profit as a percentage of net sales was 43.2% in 1997 versus 32.9% in 1996. The increase in gross margin was due to the sale of the new Sports theme and Heritage theme products at nor-mal margins.

BUSINESS

RADICA GAMES LTD. is engaged in the design, development, manufacture and distribution of a variety of non-gambling casino theme games. The Company's principal products currently include handheld and table-top electronic poker, blackjack, slot and keno games and tabletop mechanical slot machines found in casinos. The Company manufactures its products in its factory in southern China and markets throughout the world. The Company's United States distribution subsidiary markets over 73.0% of the Company's sales in the United States. In 1996, net sales were derived from the following geographic areas: United States, 71.7%; People's Republic of China and Hong Kong, 28.3%.

ANNUAL EARNINGS

	10/31/96	10/31/95	10/31/94	10/31/93	10/31/92	10/31/91
			US $			
Earnings Per Share	0.15	d0.94	0.81	0.51	0.09	0.04

ANNUAL FINANCIAL DATA

RECORD OF EARNINGS (IN THOUSANDS):

	10/31/96	10/31/95	10/31/94	10/31/93	10/31/92	10/31/91
Total Revenues	47,535	52,650	72,092	32,505	9,853	5,154
Income Bef Income Tax	3,086	d22,387	19,110	10,937	1,898	920
Income Tax	cr120	cr897	1,950	860	186	152
Net Income	3,206	d21,490	17,160	10,077	1,712	768
Net Extraordinary Items	d1,712	d233	...	...	...	...
Average Shares Outstg	21,439	22,780	21,308	19,696	18,728	18,000

BALANCE SHEET (IN THOUSANDS):

Cash & Cash Equivalents	8,604	10,985	14,268	4,698	1,084	...
Receivables, Net	9,624	10,242	25,977	7,761	758	...
Inventories	10,984	16,472	33,222	6,459	1,845	...
Gross Property	16,905	17,041	13,399	3,462	1,801	...
Accumulated Depreciation	3,968	2,573	1,668	880	...	...
Long-Term Debt	...	99	73	30	600	...
Stockholders' Equity	31,813	30,297	51,821	10,365	3,187	...
Total Assets	42,725	54,054	87,326	21,826	5,755	...
Total Current Assets	29,759	39,536	75,165	19,076	3,778	...
Total Current Liabilities	10,912	23,658	35,432	11,431	1,891	...
Net Working Capital	18,847	15,878	39,733	7,645	1,887	...
Year End Shs Outstg	20,680	22,780	22,780	20,252	16,696	...

STATISTICAL RECORD:

Return on Equity %	10.08	...	33.11	97.22	53.72	53.72
Return on Assets %	7.50	...	19.65	46.17	29.75	29.75
Operating Profit Margin %	5.3	...	26.4	33.8	19.7	18.5
Net Profit Margin %	6.7	...	23.8	31.0	17.4	14.9
Book Value Per Share	1.54	1.33	2.27	0.51	0.19	0.19

OFFICERS:
J. N. Bengston, Chmn.
D. C. Howell, Exec. V.P. & C.F.O.
R. E. Davids, Pres. & C.E.O.
Lam Siu Wing, V.P.

INCORPORATED: Bermuda, Dec., 1993

PRINCIPAL OFFICE: Suite R, 6/Fl. 2-12 Au Pui Wan St., Fo Tan Hong Kong

TELEPHONE NUMBER: 800-880-6402

NO. OF EMPLOYEES: N/A

ANNUAL MEETING: In Apr.

SHAREHOLDERS: 118

INSTITUTIONAL HOLDINGS:
No. of Institutions: N/A
Shares Held: N/A

REGISTRAR(S): U.S. Stock Transfer Corp., Glendale, CA

TRANSFER AGENT(S): U.S. Stock Transfer Corp., Glendale, CA

REPAP ENTERPRISES, INC.

YIELD ...
P/E RATIO ...

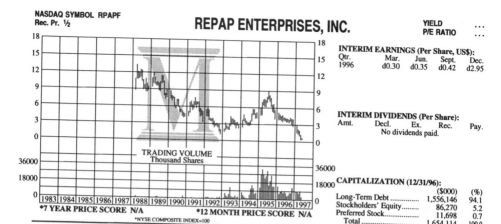

INTERIM EARNINGS (Per Share, US$):

Qtr.	Mar.	Jun.	Sept.	Dec.
1996	d0.30	d0.35	d0.42	d2.95

INTERIM DIVIDENDS (Per Share):

Amt.	Decl.	Ex.	Rec.	Pay.
No dividends paid.				

CAPITALIZATION (12/31/96):

	($000)	(%)
Long-Term Debt	1,556,146	94.1
Stockholders' Equity	86,270	5.2
Preferred Stock	11,698	0.7
Total	1,654,114	100.0

*7 YEAR PRICE SCORE N/A   *12 MONTH PRICE SCORE N/A

*NYSE COMPOSITE INDEX=100

RECENT DEVELOPMENTS: For the year ended 12/31/96, the Company reported a net loss of C$477.0 million compared with net income of C$157.7 million the year before. Results for 1996 include an unusual charge of C$305.5 millionrelated to the impairment of Alcell assets. Revenues declined 17.4% to C$1.72 billion from C$2.08 billion a year earlier, due to lower pulp and coated paper prices. Net sales decreased 19.4% to C$1.53 billion from C$1.90 bil-

lion the previous year. For the quarter ended 12/31/96, theCompany reported a net loss of C$359.3 million versus net income of C$61.1 million the year before. Results for 1996 include an unusual charge of C$305.5 million. Revenues were C$425.0 million, down 5.9% from C$451.8 million a year earlier. Net sales declined 7.9% toC$381.4 million from C$414.3 million the previous year.

BUSINESS

REPAP ENTERPRISES INC. is a forest products holding company. The Company produces high value-added coated paper used for the publication and printing of magazines, catalogs, coupons, inserts and annual reports; premium northern softwood kraft pulp used primarily in printing and writing papers; superior strength kraft paper used for the packaging of compounds such as dry cement and fertilizer; and high value-added lumber.

ANNUAL EARNINGS

Earnings Per Share	12/31/96 ----US $----	12/31/95	12/31/96 ----C $----	12/31/95
	d0.32	0.80	d0.44	1.09

ANNUAL FINANCIAL DATA

RECORD OF EARNINGS (IN THOUSANDS):

	12/31/96	12/31/95	12/31/96	12/31/95
Total Revenues	850,269	1,098,544	1,163,000	1,498,900
Costs & Expenses	709,971	776,801	971,100	1,059,900
Depreciation & Amort	59,804	65,668	81,800	89,600
Operating Income	80,494	256,075	110,100	349,400
Income Bef Income Tax	d44,232	105,611	d60,500	144,100
Income Tax	cr4,752	7,402	cr6,500	10,100
Net Income	d39,479	98,209	d54,000	134,000
Income from Disc. Ops.	d309,255	17,370	d423,000	23,700
Average Shares Outstg	123,432	122,739	123,432	122,739

BALANCE SHEET (IN THOUSANDS):

Cash & Cash Equivalents	17,181	27,484	23,500	37,500
Receivables, Net	155,066	159,845	212,100	218,100
Inventories	236,876	244,276	324,000	333,300
Gross Property	2,390,770	2,457,780	3,270,100	3,353,500
Accumulated Depreciation	664,570	601,418	909,000	820,600
Long-Term Debt	1,556,146	1,451,875	2,128,500	1,981,000
Stockholders' Equity	86,270	436,002	118,000	594,900
Total Assets	2,471,557	2,697,512	3,380,600	3,680,600
Total Current Assets	409,124	431,605	559,600	588,900
Total Current Liabilities	262,684	262,451	359,300	358,100
Net Working Capital	146,439	169,153	200,300	230,800
Year End Shs Outstg	123,437	123,424	123,437	123,424

STATISTICAL RECORD:

Return on Equity %	...	22.52		
Return on Assets %	...	3.64		
Operating Profit Margin %	9.47	23.31		
Net Profit Margin %	...	8.94		
Book Value Per Share	0.70	3.53		

Converted at 1996, US$0.7311= 1 Canadian $; 1995, US$0.7329= 1 Canadian $

OFFICERS:
G. S. Petty, Chmn. & C.E.O.
S. C. Larson, Pres. & C.O.O.
H. R. Papushka, Exec. V.P.
R. H. Sumner, Exec. V.P.

INCORPORATED: 1978

PRINCIPAL OFFICE: 1250 Rene-Levesque Blvd. West Suite 3800 Montreal Canada

TELEPHONE NUMBER: 514-846-1316

NO. OF EMPLOYEES: 3,449

ANNUAL MEETING: In May

SHAREHOLDERS: N/A

INSTITUTIONAL HOLDINGS:
No. of Institutions: 39
Shares Held: 12,406,656

REGISTRAR(S): The Montreal Trust Company, Montreal.

TRANSFER AGENT(S): The Montreal Trust Company, Montreal.

REVENUE PROPERTIES COMPANY

YIELD 4.3%
P/E RATIO N.M.

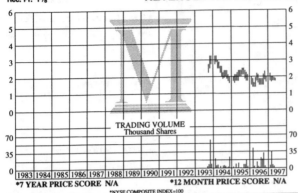

*7 YEAR PRICE SCORE N/A   *12 MONTH PRICE SCORE N/A
*NYSE COMPOSITE INDEX=100

TRADING VOLUME
Thousand Shares

INTERIM EARNINGS (Per Share, US$):

	Mar.	June	Sept.	Dec.
1996	------------------ 0.01 ------------------			

INTERIM DIVIDENDS (Per Share):

Amt.	Decl.	Ex.	Rec.	Pay.
0.07	3/11/96	3/26/96	3/28/96	4/15/96
0.08	3/17/97	3/25/97	3/27/97	4/01/97
	Indicated div.:$0.08			

CAPITALIZATION (12/31/96):

	($000)	(%)
Minority Interests.............	1,512	0.3
Long-Term Debt	364,389	74.7
Stockholders' Equity.........	121,814	25.0
Total	487,715	100.0

RECENT DEVELOPMENTS: For the year ended 12/31/96, net income from continuing operations was C$1.0 million compared with C$4.9 million in the corresponding period a year earlier. Revenues increased 21.5% to C$109.8 million versus C$90.3 million in 1995. Earnings were pressured by non-recurring expenses of C$1.4 million related to retirement compensation, a loss of C$508,000 in the Company's land development project in Guelph and an increase of depreciation expense of C$1.2 million. In addition, the 1995 comparative financial statements include a C$1.0 million lease cancellation payment. Certain comparative figures for 1995 have been restated to give effect, on a retroactive basis, to the Company's adoption of new accounting recommendations for accounting for financial instruments.

BUSINESS

REVENUE PROPERTIES COMPANY is a public real estate company, engaged in the acquisition, development and ownership of income producing properties, in both Canada and the United States. In addition, the Company develops income producing commercial, industrial and residential properties to sell to other builders or for its own use; and also provides a complete range of property management services.

ANNUAL EARNINGS

	12/31/96	12/31/95	12/31/96	12/31/95
	-------------US $-------------		-------------C $-------------	
Earnings Per Share	0.01	0.05	0.01	0.07

ANNUAL FINANCIAL DATA

RECORD OF EARNINGS (IN THOUSANDS):

	12/31/96	12/31/95	12/31/96	12/31/95
Total Revenues	80,243	66,198	109,756	90,323
Costs & Expenses	73,864	59,240	99,163	76,961
Depreciation & Amort	6,600	5,774	9,028	7,878
Operating Income	1,144	4,019	1,565	5,484
Income Bef Income Tax	1,144	4,019	1,565	5,484
Income Tax	401	429	549	585
Minority Interests	12	cr4	16	cr5
Net Income	731	3,594	1,000	4,904
Income from Disc. Ops.	2,031	d440	2,778	d600
Average Shares Outstg	66,121	67,025	66,121	67,025

BALANCE SHEET (IN THOUSANDS):

Cash & Cash Equivalents	59,153	8,061	80,910	10,999
Receivables, Net	2,244	2,651	3,070	3,617
Gross Property	446,144	431,773	610,236	589,129
Accumulated Depreciation	29,137	23,367	39,853	31,883
Long-Term Debt	364,389	348,744	498,412	475,841
Stockholders' Equity	121,814	81,255	166,618	110,868
Total Assets	503,768	445,357	689,055	607,664
Total Current Assets	72,388	18,718	99,013	25,540
Total Current Liabilities	16,052	13,859	21,956	18,910
Net Working Capital	56,336	4,859	77,057	6,630
Year End Shs Outstg	65,757	66,384	65,757	66,384

STATISTICAL RECORD:

Return on Equity %	0.60	4.42		
Return on Assets %	0.15	0.81		
Operating Profit Margin %	. . .	1.79		
Net Profit Margin %	0.91	5.43		
Book Value Per Share	1.85	1.37		

Converted at 1996, US$0.7311= 1 Canadian C $; 1995, US$0.7329= 1 Canadian C $

OFFICERS:
T. I. Sherman, Chmn.
R. E. Tanz, Pres. & Co-C.E.O.
S. A. Tanz, Co-C.E.O.
L. M. Forbes, V.P. & C.F.O.

INCORPORATED: Aug., 1961

PRINCIPAL OFFICE: The Colonnade, 131 Bloor Street West, Suite 300, Toronto Canada

TELEPHONE NUMBER: 416-963-8100

NO. OF EMPLOYEES: N/A

ANNUAL MEETING: In May

SHAREHOLDERS: 3,869

INSTITUTIONAL HOLDINGS:
No. of Institutions: 5
Shares Held: 9,358,252

REGISTRAR(S): Before June 30, 1997, The R-M Trust Company. After June 30, 1997, Montreal Trust Company of Canada, Toronto.

TRANSFER AGENT(S): Before June 30, 1997, The R-M Trust Company. After June 30, 1997, Montreal Trust Company of Canada, Toronto.

NASDAQ SYMBOL RUSAF
Rec. Pr. 3⅛

RUSSEL METALS, INC.

YIELD ...
P/E RATIO ...

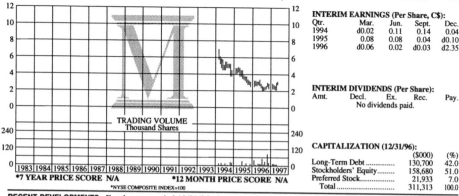

7 YEAR PRICE SCORE N/A   **12 MONTH PRICE SCORE N/A**
*NYSE COMPOSITE INDEX=100

INTERIM EARNINGS (Per Share, C$):

Qtr.	Mar.	Jun.	Sept.	Dec.
1994	d0.02	0.11	0.14	0.04
1995	0.08	0.08	0.04	d0.10
1996	d0.06	0.02	d0.03	d2.35

INTERIM DIVIDENDS (Per Share):

Amt.	Decl.	Ex.	Rec.	Pay.
	No dividends paid.			

CAPITALIZATION (12/31/96):

	($000)	(%)
Long-Term Debt	130,700	42.0
Stockholders' Equity	158,680	51.0
Preferred Stock	21,933	7.0
Total	311,313	100.0

RECENT DEVELOPMENTS: For the year ended 12/31/96, the Company reported a net loss of C$118.5 million compared with net earnings of C$7.0 million the year before. Results for 1996 included C$59.7 million in special charges. Sales and services declined 2.9% to C$1.45 billion from C$1.49 billion a year earlier and included C$78.2 million and C$137.4 million, respectively, from divested operations. Operating income in the Service Center segment declined as a result of lower selling prices and margins. The Spe-cialty Metals and Trading segment's operating income remained relatively flat versus the prior-year period. The Company has entered into a supply agreement with Samuel, Son & Co., Limited for light gauge sheet requirements, and sold its flat rolled processing operations to Samuel. The Company rationalized, closed or sold eight underperforming operations, generating approximately $30.0 million.

BUSINESS

RUSSEL METALS INC. is a processor and distributor of metals and metal products with a network of 45 Canadian and 13 U.S. locations. The Company also operates an international trading business which exports North American steel products to international customers and imports foreign steel products into Canada and the United States. The Company also has investments in the transport sector, represented principally by its investments in The White Pass and Yukon Route, Thunder Bay Terminals Ltd. and Tri-Line Expressway Ltd.

ANNUAL EARNINGS

	12/31/96	12/31/95	12/31/96	12/31/95
	----------US $----------		----------C $----------	
Earnings Per Share	d1.77	0.07	d2.42	0.10

ANNUAL FINANCIAL DATA

RECORD OF EARNINGS (IN MILLIONS):

Total Revenues	1,058	1,093	1,448	1,492
Costs & Expenses	1,051	1,082	1,438	1,476
Operating Income	8	12	10	16
Income Tax	51	4	69	6
Net Income	d87	5	d118	7
Average Shares Outstg (000)	51,008	51,008	51,008	51,008

BALANCE SHEET (IN MILLIONS):

Receivables, Net	169	160	231	218
Inventories	161	178	220	243
Gross Property	195	217	266	296
Accumulated Depreciation	90	98	123	134
Long-Term Debt	131	135	179	184
Stockholders' Equity	181	268	247	366
Total Assets	519	590	710	806
Total Current Assets	332	340	454	464
Total Current Liabilities	208	187	284	255
Net Working Capital	124	153	170	209
Year End Shs Outstg (000)	51,008	51,008	51,008	51,008

STATISTICAL RECORD:

Return on Equity %	...	1.9		
Return on Assets %	...	0.8		
Operating Profit Margin %	0.7	1.1		
Net Profit Margin %	...	0.7		
Book Value Per Share	3.55	5.25		

Converted at 1996, US$0.7311= 1 Canadian C $; 1995, US$0.7329= 1 Canadian C $

OFFICERS:
A. F. Griffiths, Chmn.
E. M. Siegel, Jr., Acting Pres. & C.E.O.,
Exec. V.P. & C.O.O.-Metals Opers.
B. R. Hedges, Sr. V.P. & C.F.O.

INCORPORATED: July, 1929

PRINCIPAL OFFICE: 1900 Minnesota Court
Suite 210 Mississauga Ontario L5N 3C9

TELEPHONE NUMBER: 905-819-7777

NO. OF EMPLOYEES: 2,241

ANNUAL MEETING: In May

SHAREHOLDERS: N/A

INSTITUTIONAL HOLDINGS:
No. of Institutions: 8
Shares Held: 38,198,172

REGISTRAR(S): The R-M Trust Company, Winnipeg, Montreal, Toronto, Regina, Calgary, Vancouver; Mellon Securities Trust Company, New York.

TRANSFER AGENT(S): The R-M Trust Company, Winnipeg, Montreal, Toronto, Regina, Calgary, Vancouver; Mellon Securities Trust Company, New York.

SAND TECHNOLOGY SYSTEMS INTERNATIONAL INC.

YIELD ...
P/E RATIO N.M.

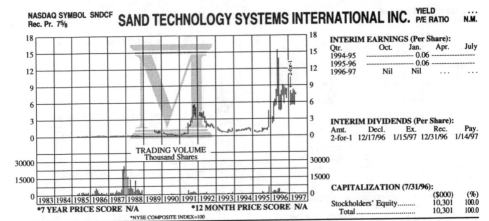

INTERIM EARNINGS (Per Share):

Qtr.	Oct.	Jan.	Apr.	July
1994-95	----------	0.06	----------	
1995-96	----------	0.06	----------	
1996-97	Nil	Nil	...	...

INTERIM DIVIDENDS (Per Share):

Amt.	Decl.	Ex.	Rec.	Pay.
2-for-1	12/17/96	1/15/97	12/31/96	1/14/97

CAPITALIZATION (7/31/96):

	($000)	(%)
Stockholders' Equity	10,301	100.0
Total	10,301	100.0

RECENT DEVELOPMENTS: For the three months ended 1/31/97, net earnings totaled C$9,768 compared with C$133,505 in the corresponding quarter the previous year. Net sales dropped 73.7% to C$1.5 million from C$5.5 million the year before. Loss from operations was C$198,841 compared with earnings from operations of C$25,229 a year earlier. Income from an affiliate climbed 59.7% to C$184,959 from C$115,828 the prior year. Finan-

cial performance was negatively affected by delays in new installations of the Nucleus Server. For the six months ended 1/31/97, net earnings totaled C$24,766 versus C$236,182 the year before. Net sales fell 63.9% to C$2.2 million from C$6.1 million in the same six-month period the prior year. Loss from operations was C$289,328 compared with earnings from operations of C$44,745 a year earlier.

BUSINESS

SAND TECHNOLOGY SYSTEMS INTERNATIONAL INC. is primarily engaged in the sale and service of mainframe peripheral products manufactured by Hitachi, Ltd. and Hitachi Koki Co., Ltd. of Japan through the Company's affiliate in Canada, Hitachi Data Systems Inc. (HDS Canada). HDS Canada was formed to distribute Hitachi-manufactured, IBM-compatible data processing products and related data processing services in Canada. The Company's secondary business is the sale and service of high performance, mainframe channel attached line printers, and a series of remote communications controlled mainframe line printers and non-impact printers in the U.S.A. This business is conducted through The Company's subsidiary, Sand Technology Systems Inc. Also, the Company has a contractual relationship with Nissei Sangyo Co., Ltd. through which it has negotiated a series of non-exclusive product sales agreements that currently cover approximately 13 major products. The Company obtains over 90% of its hardware products from Nissei. The Company continues to import Hitachi and Hitachi Koki products from Nissei, based on firm orders from HDS Canada. This equipment is then sold to HDS Canada by the Company, for resale by HDS Canada into the Canadian marketplace.

ANNUAL EARNINGS

	7/31/96	7/31/95	7/31/96	7/31/95
	---US $---		---C $---	
Earnings Per Share	0.06	0.06	0.08	0.08

Note: 2-for-1 stk. split, 1/97

ANNUAL FINANCIAL DATA

RECORD OF EARNINGS (IN THOUSANDS):

Total Revenues	5,235	11,521	7,198	15,748
Costs & Expenses	5,794	11,932	7,966	16,309
Operating Income	d558	d410	d768	d561
Income Bef Income Tax	d34	117	d47	160
Eq. Earnings in Affils.	523	394	718	539
Net Income	489	511	672	699
Average Shares Outstg	8,864	8,864	8,864	8,864

BALANCE SHEET (IN THOUSANDS):

Cash & Cash Equivalents	6,531	7,546	8,979	10,314
Receivables, Net	826	1,179	1,136	1,612
Inventories	34	149	47	203
Gross Property	292	241	401	330
Accumulated Depreciation	280	214	386	293
Stockholders' Equity	10,301	9,871	14,164	13,492
Total Assets	12,116	11,720	16,659	16,019
Total Current Assets	7,420	8,904	10,202	12,171
Total Current Liabilities	1,390	1,849	1,911	2,527
Net Working Capital	6,030	7,055	8,292	9,643
Year End Shs Outstg	8,864	8,864	8,864	8,864

STATISTICAL RECORD:

Return on Equity %	4.74	5.18		
Return on Assets %	4.03	4.36		
Operating Profit Margin %	...	...		
Net Profit Margin %	9.33	4.44		
Book Value Per Share	1.16	1.11		

Converted at 1996, US$0.7273= 1 Canadian $; 1995, US$0.7316= 1 Canadian $

OFFICERS:
A. G. Ritchie, Chmn., Pres. & C.E.O.
S. Waxman, V.P.-Fin. & Admin.
G. Dube, Sec.

INCORPORATED: Dec., 1982

PRINCIPAL OFFICE: 4141 Sherbrooke Street West, Suite 410, Westmount, Quebec Canada

TELEPHONE NUMBER: 514-939-3477

NO. OF EMPLOYEES: N/A

ANNUAL MEETING: In December

SHAREHOLDERS: N/A

INSTITUTIONAL HOLDINGS:
No. of Institutions: 2
Shares Held: 1,053

REGISTRAR(S): N/A

TRANSFER AGENT(S): Continental Stock Transfer & Trust Company, New York, NY.

SAPIENS INTERNATIONAL

YIELD ...
P/E RATIO ...

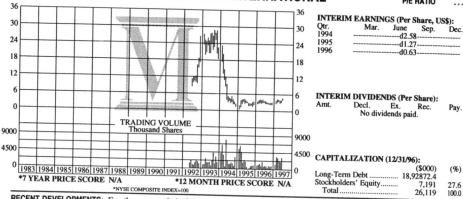

7 YEAR PRICE SCORE N/A   **12 MONTH PRICE SCORE N/A**
*NYSE COMPOSITE INDEX=100

TRADING VOLUME
Thousand Shares

INTERIM EARNINGS (Per Share, US$):

Qtr.	Mar.	June	Sep.	Dec.
1994			d2.58	
1995			d1.27	
1996			d0.63	

INTERIM DIVIDENDS (Per Share):

Amt.	Decl.	Ex.	Rec.	Pay.
	No dividends paid.			

CAPITALIZATION (12/31/96):

	($000)	(%)
Long-Term Debt	18,928	72.4
Stockholders' Equity	7,191	27.6
Total	26,119	100.0

RECENT DEVELOPMENTS: For the year ended 12/31/96, net loss was $6.7 million compared with income of $345,000, including unusual gains of $15.9 million, in the prior year. The 1996 results included a charge of $8.7 million from the settlement of a class action suit. Total revenues reached $39.0 million, up 6.4% from $36.6 million a year earlier. The increase in total revenues was attributed primarily to a 34.3% increase to $13.7 million in revenues from software

licenses. Consulting, maintenance and other revenues were down 4.3% to $25.3 million from $26.4 million in 1995. Operating income was $1.8 million compared with a loss of $12.6 million in the previous year. For the quarter ended 12/31/96, net income was $1.0 million compared with $13.6 million, including unusual gains of $15.9 million, in the corresponding prior-year period. Total revenues rose 10.4% to $10.7 million.

BUSINESS

SAPIENS INTERNATIONAL CORPORATION N.V. is primarily engaged in application development productivity. The Company develops and markets Rapid Application Development tools and provides consulting and support services, enabling its customers worldwide to build, manage and maintain high-quality business solutions in short time frames. The Company also provides comprehensive solutions for the year 2000 date-change problem. The Company's products include the following: SAPIENS® ObjectPool™, an application development environment for both client/server and network-centric applications; ObjectPool™ X-Platform, which allows objects and applications to be distributed across heterogeneous servers in an open system environment; SAPIENS® Object Modeler™, a graphical development workbench; and SAPIENS® Work-Station™, which generates GUI clients for ObjectPool applications. In addition, Sapiens offers SAPIENS Y2K, a year 2000 solution that includes a new toolset based on ObjectPool technology, and FAL-CON, a tool that converts mainframe Assembler programs to ANSI "C" source code and identifies data fields in Assembler code for purposes of year 2000 conversions. The Company sells its products through its subsidiaries as well as distributors, custom software developers, and strategic business partners such as IBM, Hitachi Data Systems and Hewlett Packard. The Company also provides consultation services to its customers.

ANNUAL EARNINGS

	12/31/96	12/31/95	12/31/94
Earnings Per Share		US $	
	d0.63	d1.27	d2.58

ANNUAL FINANCIAL DATA

RECORD OF EARNINGS (IN THOUSANDS):

	12/31/96	12/31/95	12/31/94
Total Revenues	38,987	36,640	33,296
Costs & Expenses	37,194	49,255	64,077
Operating Income	1,793	d12,615	d30,781
Income Bef Income Tax	d6,851	d15,397	d31,047
Income Tax	35	41	33
Eq. Earnings in Affils.	d150	d211	...
Minority Interests	317	83	...
Net Income	d6,719	d15,566	31,235
Net Extraordinary Item	96	15,911	1,686
Average Shares Outstg	12,601	12,268	12,589

BALANCE SHEET (IN THOUSANDS):

Cash & Cash Equivalents	20,547	24,689	37,010
Receivables, Net	13,163	14,154	13,352
Gross Property	4,766	6,202	8,060
Long-Term Debt	18,928	21,953	50,721
Stockholders' Equity	7,191	9,541	d3,371
Total Assets	50,218	55,951	71,595
Total Current Assets	33,710	38,843	50,362
Total Current Liabilities	24,099	24,457	24,245
Net Working Capital	9,611	14,386	26,117
Year End Shs Outstg	12,893	12,228	12,062

STATISTICAL RECORD:

Return on Equity %	...	...	...
Return on Assets %	...	...	...
Operating Profit Margin %	4.6	...	...
Net Profit Margin %	...	...	...
Book Value Per Share	0.56	0.04	...

OFFICERS:
R. Zuckerman, C.E.O.
M. Weiss, C.O.O.
L. Hanover, C.F.O.
S. Kronengold, Gen. Couns. & Sec.

INCORPORATED: Apr., 1990

PRINCIPAL OFFICE: De Ruyterkade 58A
Curacao Netherlands Antilles

TELEPHONE NUMBER: N/A

NO. OF EMPLOYEES: 365

ANNUAL MEETING: June 27, 1997

SHAREHOLDERS: N/A

INSTITUTIONAL HOLDINGS:
No. of Institutions: N/A
Shares Held: N/A

REGISTRAR(S): N/A

TRANSFER AGENT(S): American Stock
Transfer & Trust Co., New York.

SCANDINAVIAN BROADCASTING SYSTEM S.A.

YIELD   ...
P/E RATIO ...

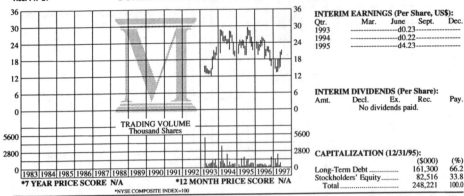

INTERIM EARNINGS (Per Share, US$):

Qtr.	Mar.	June	Sept.	Dec.
1993	----------------d0.23----------------			
1994	----------------d0.22----------------			
1995	----------------d4.23----------------			

INTERIM DIVIDENDS (Per Share):

Amt.	Decl.	Ex.	Rec.	Pay.
	No dividends paid.			

TRADING VOLUME
Thousand Shares

1983│1984│1985│1986│1987│1988│1989│1990│1991│1992│1993│1994│1995│1996│1997

*7 YEAR PRICE SCORE N/A   *12 MONTH PRICE SCORE N/A

*NYSE COMPOSITE INDEX=100

CAPITALIZATION (12/31/95):

	($000)	(%)
Long-Term Debt	161,300	66.2
Stockholders' Equity.........	82,516	33.8
Total..............................	248,221	100.0

RECENT DEVELOPMENTS: For the year ended 12/31/96, the Company reported a net loss of $57.3 million compared with a net loss of $2.8 million the year before. Net revenue advanced 54.2% to $108.8 million from $70.6 million a yearearlier. As a percentage of net revenue, selling, general and administrative expenses rose to 38.3% from 32.3% the previous year. Total operating expenses more than doubled to $166.7 million from $75.2 million the year before. The Company reported an operatingloss of $57.9 million versus an operating loss of $4.6 million a year earlier, due to costs associated with new investments and start-up operations, in addition to increased programming expenses at established operations.

BUSINESS

SCANDINAVIAN BROADCAST-ING SYSTEM S.A. is the parent company of a group engaged in the acquisition, ownership and operation of commercial television and radio broadcasting stations. Through its subsidiaries, the Company owns and operates television stations that broadcast into Sweden, Denmark, Norway, Flemish Belgium and the Netherlands, as well as radio stations that broadcast in Sweden, Denmark and Finland.

ANNUAL EARNINGS

	12/31/95	12/31/94	12/31/93	12/31/92	12/31/91	12/31/90
				---US $---		
Earnings Per Share	d4.23	d0.22	d0.20	d1.23	d2.27	...

ANNUAL FINANCIAL DATA

RECORD OF EARNINGS (IN THOUSANDS):

	12/31/95	12/31/94	12/31/93	12/31/92	12/31/91	12/31/90
Total Revenues	108,788	70,561	50,465	18,623	8,768	4,469
Costs & Expenses	157,797	70,402	46,979	22,423	14,662	11,527
Depreciation & Amort	8,857	4,802	3,034	816	936	982
Operating Income	d57,866	d4,643	452	d4,616	d6,830	d8,040
Income Bef Income Tax	d57,342	2,997	d1,848	d5,672	d8,607	d8,410
Income Taxes	289	d66	...	...	...	...
Minority Interests	282	100	172	...	...	...
Net Income	d57,349	d2,831	d2,020	d5,672	d8,607	d8,410
Net Extraordinary Items	289	d66	d20	...	...	...
Average Shares Outstg	13,551	13,127				

BALANCE SHEET (IN THOUSANDS):

Cash & Cash Equivalents	138,182	72,843	19,830	1,080	2,106	...
Receivables, Net	22,459	7,481	6,133	1,798	1,316	...
Inventories	35,612	10,319	6,332	867	536	...
Gross Property	...	...	...	2,746	2,387	...
Long-Term Debt	161,300	4,265	7,890	9,869	5,444	...
Stockholders' Equity	82,516	127,619	54,291	d10,080	d6,979	...
Total Assets	316,701	166,385	80,661	13,675	9,360	...
Total Current Assets	209,397	98,477	34,018	5,654	4,619	...
Total Current Liabilities	68,480	32,722	18,379	13,244	9,684	...
Net Working Capital	140,917	65,755	15,639	d7,590	d5,065	...
Year End Shs Outstg	13,576	13,478	10,130	4,608	3,795	...

STATISTICAL RECORD:

Return on Equity %	...	...	...	56.27	123.33	123.33
Return on Assets %	...	...	...	...	...	...
Operating Profit Margin %	...	...	0.90	...	...	...
Net Profit Margin %	...	...	...	...	...	...
Book Value Per Share	6.08	9.47	5.36	d2.19	d1.84	d1.84

OFFICERS:
H. Evans Sloan, Chmn. & C.E.O.
M. Lindskog, Pres. & C.O.O.
F. Kastrup, C.F.O.

INCORPORATED: Luxembourg, Oct., 1989

PRINCIPAL OFFICE: 8-10 rue Mathias Hardt
Luxembourg L-1717

TELEPHONE NUMBER: 40 78 78

NO. OF EMPLOYEES: 687 (approx.)

ANNUAL MEETING: N/A

SHAREHOLDERS: 52

INSTITUTIONAL HOLDINGS:
No. of Institutions: N/A
Shares Held: N/A

REGISTRAR(S): State Street Bank Luxembourg, S.A., Luxembourg; State Street Bank and Trust Co., N. Quincy, the United States.

TRANSFER AGENT(S): State Street Bank Luxembourg, S.A., Luxembourg; State Street Bank and Trust Co., N. Quincy, the United States.

SCANVEC COMPANY, LTD.

YIELD ...
P/E RATIO ...

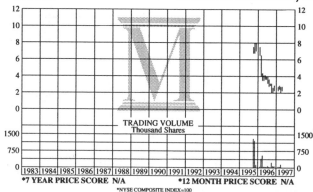

TRADING VOLUME
Thousand Shares

	1983	1984	1985	1986	1987	1988	1989	1990	1991	1992	1993	1994	1995	1996	1997

*7 YEAR PRICE SCORE N/A   *12 MONTH PRICE SCORE N/A

*NYSE COMPOSITE INDEX=100

INTERIM EARNINGS (Per Share, $US):

Qtr.	Mar.	Jun.	Sep.	Dec.
1995	----------	0.53	----------	
1996	----------	d0.17	----------	

INTERIM DIVIDENDS (Per Share):

Amt.	Decl.	Ex.	Rec.	Pay.
	No dividends paid.			

CAPITALIZATION (12/31/95):

	($000)	(%)
Stockholders' Equity	14,214	100.0
Total	14,214	100.0

RECENT DEVELOPMENTS: For the year ended 12/31/96, net loss was $780,966 compared with $2.1 million in the prior year. Sales rose 9.9% to $11.6 million due primarily to a 26% rise in sales to the Asian market and 12% increase in sales to the European market. Sales in the U.S. declined 2%. Earnings were negatively affected by lower than planned sales due to a slow-down in the signmaking market at a time of increased competition. Increased research and development and operating expenses and delays in the release of new products into new markets also contributed to lower earnings. Results for 1996 were also affected by the result of a tax audit by the Israeli tax authority for the years 1990-1995. Following the audit, the Company agreed that $210,000 would be paid in tax in respect of the years up to and including 1996 and a further $45,000 in each of the years 1997 through 1998.

BUSINESS

SCANVEC COMPANY is engaged in the design, manufacture, marketing and support of a family of high performance software products for the sign making & graphic arts industries, for the textile industry and for machining applications in wood and metal carving. The Company's products are PC-based open-architecture solutions sold in 65 countries and 21 languages, by more than 140 distributors, dealers and OEMs around the world.

ANNUAL EARNINGS

	12/31/95	12/31/94	12/31/95	12/31/94
	----US $----		----NIS----	
Earnings Per Share	0.53	0.41	1.67	1.24

ANNUAL FINANCIAL DATA

RECORD OF EARNINGS (IN THOUSANDS):

Total Revenues	10,592	7,795	33,340	23,522
Costs & Expenses	8,580	6,014	27,006	18,148
Operating Income	2,012	1,781	6,334	5,374
Income Bef Income Tax	2,109	1,438	6,638	4,341
Income Tax	360	197	1,132	594
Net Income	1,749	1,242	5,506	3,746
Average Shares Outstg	3,320	3,000	3,320	3,000

BALANCE SHEET (IN THOUSANDS):

Cash & Cash Equivalents	9,489	1,913	29,868	5,771
Receivables, Net	4,218	1,560	13,278	4,707
Inventories	487	178	1,534	537
Gross Property	1,640	781	5,162	2,356
Accumulated Depreciation	334	209	1,051	630
Stockholders' Equity	14,214	3,703	44,741	11,174
Total Assets	16,278	4,809	51,238	14,512
Total Current Assets	14,195	3,650	44,680	11,015
Total Current Liabilities	1,839	876	5,789	2,644
Net Working Capital	12,356	2,774	38,891	8,371
Year End Shs Outstg	4,428	3,000	4,428	3,000

STATISTICAL RECORD:

Return on Equity %	12.31	33.53
Return on Assets %	10.75	25.82
Operating Profit Margin %	19.00	22.84
Net Profit Margin %	16.51	15.93
Book Value Per Share	3.21	1.23

Converted at 1995, US$0.3177= 1 New Israeli Shekel; 1994, US$0.3314= 1 New Israeli Shekel

OFFICERS:
R. Harel, Chmn., C.E.O. & C.F.O.
R. Bachman
A. Sebran

INCORPORATED: Israel, 1990

PRINCIPAL OFFICE: Atidim Industrial Park Building No. 7 Tel Aviv Israel 61581

TELEPHONE NUMBER: 972-3-6474477

NO. OF EMPLOYEES: 116

ANNUAL MEETING: N/A

SHAREHOLDERS: 63

INSTITUTIONAL HOLDINGS:
No. of Institutions: N/A
Shares Held: N/A

REGISTRAR(S): N/A

TRANSFER AGENT(S): N/A

SCITEX CORPORATION LTD.

YIELD 7.6%
P/E RATIO ...

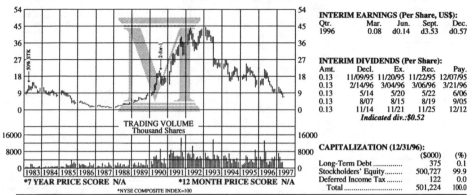

*7 YEAR PRICE SCORE N/A   *12 MONTH PRICE SCORE N/A
*NYSE COMPOSITE INDEX=100

INTERIM EARNINGS (Per Share, US$):

Qtr.	Mar.	Jun.	Sept.	Dec.
1996	0.08	d0.14	d3.53	d0.57

INTERIM DIVIDENDS (Per Share):

Amt.	Decl.	Ex.	Rec.	Pay.
0.13	11/09/95	11/20/95	11/22/95	12/07/95
0.13	2/14/96	3/04/96	3/06/96	3/21/96
0.13	5/14	5/20	5/22	6/06
0.13	8/07	8/15	8/19	9/05
0.13	11/14	11/21	11/25	12/12
	Indicated div.:$0.52			

CAPITALIZATION (12/31/96):

	($000)	(%)
Long-Term Debt	375	0.1
Stockholders' Equity	500,727	99.9
Deferred Income Tax	122	0.0
Total	501,224	100.0

RECENT DEVELOPMENTS: For the year ended 12/31/96, the Company reported a net loss of $178.3 million compared with a net loss of $34.5 million the year before. Total revenues were $695.0 million, down 4.8% from $730.3 million a year earlier. The Company reported an operating loss of $184.6 million versus an operating loss of $54.3 million the previous year. Results for the recent period reflect the severe difficulties the Company experienced in its Graphic Arts business and the transition year for Scitex Digital Video, partially offset by a strong performance at Scitex Digital Printing. During the year, Scitex Digital Video completed the merger of ImMIX and Abekas and launched the new ImMIX Sphere line of video editing workstations.

BUSINESS

SCITEX CORPORATION LTD. develops and markets visual information communication products for the graphic arts, digital printing and digital video markets. The Company's Graphic Arts Group specializes in scanners, color workstations for page assembly and retouching, client-server systems, inkjet color printers, imagesetters and platesetters and on-demand short-run color printing systems. Scitex Digital Printing is dedicated to very high-speed, inkjet printers for long-run variable data applications. Scitex Digital Video focuses on video post-production and on-line systems for non-linear editing and creation of special effects.

ANNUAL EARNINGS

	12/31/96	12/31/95	12/31/96	12/31/95
	US $		NIS	
Earnings Per Share	d4.16	d0.81	d13.55	d2.54

ANNUAL FINANCIAL DATA

RECORD OF EARNINGS (IN THOUSANDS):

	12/31/96	12/31/95	12/31/96	12/31/95
Total Revenues	695,048	728,900	2,264,000	2,294,303
Costs & Expenses	863,404	770,859	2,812,391	2,426,374
Depreciation & Amort	16,221	12,347	52,837	38,864
Operating Income	d184,577	d54,306	d601,228	d170,935
Income Bef Income Tax	d180,132	d46,852	d586,749	d147,472
Income Tax	1,700	13,464	5,537	42,380
Eq. Earnings in Affils.	155	d1,123	505	d3,535
Net Income	d178,277	d34,511	d580,707	d108,628
Average Shares Outstg	42,809	42,800	42,809	42,800

BALANCE SHEET (IN THOUSANDS):

Cash & Cash Equivalents	135,153	154,806	440,238	487,271
Receivables, Net	190,276	332,377	619,792	1,046,198
Inventories	118,826	121,716	387,055	383,116
Gross Property	256,040	250,412	834,007	788,203
Accumulated Depreciation	170,118	152,042	554,130	478,571
Long-Term Debt	375	214	1,221	674
Stockholders' Equity	500,727	700,981	1,631,033	2,206,424
Total Assets	704,734	920,831	2,295,550	2,898,429
Total Current Assets	523,587	703,030	1,705,495	2,212,874
Total Current Liabilities	203,511	219,426	662,902	690,670
Net Working Capital	320,076	483,604	1,042,593	1,522,203
Year End Shs Outstg	42,809	42,809	42,809	42,809

STATISTICAL RECORD:

Return on Equity %	...	...		
Return on Assets %	...	...		
Operating Profit Margin %	...	...		
Net Profit Margin %	...	...		
Book Value Per Share	11.70	16.37		

Converted at 1996, US$0.3070 = 1 New Israeli Shekel; 1995, US$0.3177 = 1 New Israeli Shekel

OFFICERS:
Y. Z. Chelouche, Pres. & C.E.O.
E. Desheh, V.P. & C.F.O.
R. R. Nagle, Dir. Inv. Rel. (U.S.)
(617) 280-7242

INCORPORATED: Israel, 1971

PRINCIPAL OFFICE: P.O. Box 330, Herzlia Industrial Park 46103 Herzlia 'B' Israel 46103

TELEPHONE NUMBER: 972-9-959-7222

NO. OF EMPLOYEES: 3,500

ANNUAL MEETING: In June

SHAREHOLDERS: N/A

INSTITUTIONAL HOLDINGS:
No. of Institutions: 45
Shares Held: 15,666,335

REGISTRAR(S): The American Stock Transfer & Trust Co., New York, NY

TRANSFER AGENT(S): The American Stock Transfer & Trust Co., New York, NY

SEMI-TECH CORPORATION

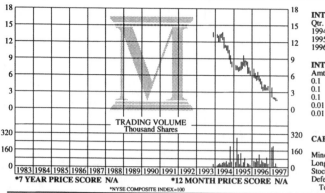

TRADING VOLUME
Thousand Shares

1983|1984|1985|1986|1987|1988|1989|1990|1991|1992|1993|1994|1995|1996|1997

*7 YEAR PRICE SCORE N/A   ***12 MONTH PRICE SCORE N/A**

*NYSE COMPOSITE INDEX=100

INTERIM EARNINGS (Per Share, US$):

Qtr.	June	Sept.	Dec.	Mar.
1994-95	----------------	0.06	----------------	
1995-96	----------------	d0.26	----------------	
1996-97	d0.10	d0.16	...	...

INTERIM DIVIDENDS (Per Share):

Amt.	Decl.	Ex.	Rec.	Pay.
0.1	8/25/95	8/31/95	9/05/95	9/15/95
0.1	11/22/95	11/29/95	12/01/95	12/15/95
0.1	2/16/96	2/28/96	3/01/96	3/15/96
0.01	5/24/96	5/29/96	5/31/96	6/14/96
0.01	8/20/96	8/28/96	8/30/96	9/15/96

Indicated div.:$0.04

CAPITALIZATION (1/31/96):

	($000)	(%)
Minority Interests	d5,172	-0.4
Long-Term Debt	193,950	15.7
Stockholders' Equity	1,044,485	84.7
Deferred Income Tax	259	0.0
Total	1,233,522	100.0

RECENT DEVELOPMENTS: For the quarter ended 9/30/96, the Company reported a loss of $11.1 million compared with a loss of $6.5 million in the corresponding period a year earlier. Revenues were $443.5 million, down 2% versus $451.3 million in 1995. Earnings were pressured by poor operating results for the Companys consumer electronics operations. However, the Company is experiencing a surge in television sales in China. Earnings from Singer remain strong, but were offset somewhat by difficult economic conditions in Europe. The introduction of the digital versatile disk player and its internet connection network computer should drive earnings growth. For the six months ended 9/30/96, the Company reported a loss of $17.6 million compared with income of $13.2 million a year earlier. Revenues were $894.8 million, up 17% versus $767.2 million in 1995. Singer Group reported earning of $28.9 million on sales of $648.0 million.

BUSINESS

SEMI-TECH CORPORATION is an investment holding company. Through its subsidiaries, the Company is engaged in the manufacture, distribution and retailing of sewing machines; consumer durables; consumer electronics including stereos, blenders, toasters, juicers, irons, washers, freezers and air-conditioners; and other hard goods.

ANNUAL EARNINGS

	1/31/96	1/31/95	1/31/96	1/31/95
	US$		HK$	
Earnings Per Share	0.10	0.47	0.74	3.62

ANNUAL FINANCIAL DATA

RECORD OF EARNINGS (IN THOUSANDS):

	1/31/96	1/31/95	1/31/96	1/31/95
Total Revenues	1,112,627	541,379	8,605,000	4,187,000
Income Bef Income Tax	28,317	155,677	219,000	1,204,000
Income Tax	3,103	cr776	24,000	cr6,000
Eq. Earnings in Affils.	2,974	...	23,000	...
Minority Interests	cr5,172	2,069	cr40,000	16,000
Net Income	33,359	154,384	258,000	1,194,000
Average Shares Outstg	45,255	42,669	45,255	42,669

BALANCE SHEET (IN THOUSANDS):

Cash & Cash Equivalents	695,246	793,902	5,377,000	6,140,000
Inventories	468,842	218,258	3,626,000	1,688,000
Gross Property	1,042,934	500,779	8,066,000	3,873,000
Accumulated Depreciation	347,688	233,386	2,689,000	1,805,000
Long-Term Debt	193,950	99,690	1,500,000	771,000
Stockholders' Equity	1,044,485	1,031,038	8,078,000	7,974,000
Total Assets	3,087,167	1,763,393	23,876,000	13,638,000
Total Current Assets	1,574,615	1,267,657	12,178,000	9,804,000
Total Current Liabilities	1,418,162	500,908	10,968,000	3,874,000
Net Working Capital	156,453	766,749	1,210,000	5,930,000
Year End Shs Outstg	46,419	44,738	46,419	44,738

STATISTICAL RECORD:

Return on Equity %	3.19	14.97
Return on Assets %	1.08	8.75
Operating Profit Margin %	3.68	3.68
Net Profit Margin %	3.00	28.52
Book Value Per Share	22.50	23.05

Converted at 1996, US$0.129= 1 Hong Kong $; 1995, US$0.129= 1 Hong Kong $

OFFICERS:
James Henry Ting, Chmn. & Chief Exec.
Frank Edward Holmes, Exec. V.P. &
C.O.O.
Cheuk Hung Tam, Exec. V.P. & C.F.O.
Yim Yong Loh, Sr. V.P.

INCORPORATED: N/A

PRINCIPAL OFFICE: Clarendon House
Church Street Hamilton Bermuda

TELEPHONE NUMBER: N/A

NO. OF EMPLOYEES: N/A

ANNUAL MEETING: In Jul.

SHAREHOLDERS: N/A

INSTITUTIONAL HOLDINGS:
No. of Institutions: 13
Shares Held: 11,781,337

REGISTRAR(S): Central Registration Hong
Kong Ltd., Hong Kong.

TRANSFER AGENT(S): Central Registration
Hong Kong Ltd., Hong Kong.

SIMWARE, INC.

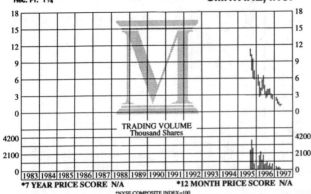

INTERIM EARNINGS (Per Share, US$):
1995-96 ------------------d0.34------------------

INTERIM DIVIDENDS (Per Share):

Amt.	Decl.	Ex.	Rec.	Pay.
	No dividends paid.			

TRADING VOLUME
Thousand Shares

*7 YEAR PRICE SCORE N/A   *12 MONTH PRICE SCORE N/A

*NYSE COMPOSITE INDEX=100

CAPITALIZATION (4/30/96):

	($000)	(%)
Stockholders' Equity........	12,543	100.0
Total..............................	12,543	100.0

RECENT DEVELOPMENTS: For the six months ended 10/31/96, the Company reported a net loss of C$2.2 million compared with income of C$112,000 in the corresponding period of 1995. Total revenues declined 11.2% to C$8.1 million. Product license revenue fell 6.0% to C$4.5 million, maintenance revenue declined 12.2% to C$3.2 million, and professional services revenues dropped 64.5% to C$465,000. Selling and marketing, R&D, and general and administrative expenses totaled 116.9% of total revenues versus 86.1% a year earlier. The Company noted that license revenue from the REXXWARE product family amounted to C$1.2 million, more than double the C$514,000 in the prior year's comparative quarter. Salvo, released in the prior quarter, generated license revenue of approximately C$200,000 and also added 14 new accounts in comparison with the five new accounts closed in the first quarter. A2B license revenue declined 59.8% to C$402,000, reflecting the continuing softness in the general connectivity market. Sim family license revenue fell 48.0% to C$476,000.

BUSINESS

SIMWARE, INC. develops, markets and supports software products for remote connectivity and for automation of local area network administration tasks. Simware, A2B, SimPC, SplitSecond, SimMAC, SimXFER, Sim3278, SimHLLAPI and REXXWARE are registered trademarks of Simware. The Company's A2B remote connectivity products provide remote or mobile end-users with easy to use, single "point and click" access to enterprise applicatons residing on a variety of platforms, including LANs, mainframes, minicomputers, Transmission Control Protocol/ Internet Protocol networks and the Internet. A2B supports a broad range of remote communications technologies, including dial-up, X.25, cellular and wireless networks. The Company's REXXWARE LAN automation product allows network administrators to automate and schedule time consuming tasks, permits existing LAN administration tools to work together and execute tasks in remote servers. In addition, in January 1996, the Company rolled out its Salvo product line that allows Web browser-based access to enterprise information.

ANNUAL EARNINGS

	4/30/96	4/30/95	4/30/96	4/30/95
	------------US $------------		------------C $------------	
Earnings Per Share	d0.34	0.08	d0.46	0.11

ANNUAL FINANCIAL DATA

RECORD OF EARNINGS (IN THOUSANDS):

	4/30/96	4/30/95	4/30/96	4/30/95
Total Revenues	12,972	14,069	17,658	19,076
Costs & Expenses	15,422	13,596	20,994	18,435
Operating Income	d2,451	473	d3,336	641
Income Bef Income Tax	d2,067	468	d2,814	634
Income Tax	24	48	32	65
Net Income	d2,091	420	d2,846	569
Average Shares Outstg	6,165	5,070	6,165	5,070

BALANCE SHEET (IN THOUSANDS):

Cash & Cash Equivalents	10,172	1,378	13,847	1,869
Receivables, Net	4,377	3,474	5,959	4,710
Gross Property	1,575	1,095	2,144	1,485
Stockholders' Equity	12,543	2,269	17,075	3,076
Total Assets	17,846	7,342	24,294	9,955
Total Current Assets	16,058	6,082	21,860	8,247
Total Current Liabilities	5,303	5,073	7,219	6,879
Net Working Capital	10,755	1,009	14,641	1,368
Year End Shs Outstg	6,714	5,143	6,714	5,143

STATISTICAL RECORD:

Return on Equity %	...	18.5		
Return on Assets %	...	5.7		
Operating Profit Margin %	...	3.4		
Net Profit Margin %	...	3.0		
Book Value Per Share	1.87	0.44		

Converted at 1996, US$0.7346= 1 Canadian $; 1995, US$0.7375= 1 Canadian $

OFFICERS:
W. G. Breen, Chmn. & C.E.O.
G. M. Brownlee, Pres. & C.O.O.
C. J. Fedorko, V.P.
J. A. Guillen, V.P.
INCORPORATED: April, 1982
PRINCIPAL OFFICE: 2 Gurdwara Road
Ottawa Ontario, Canada

TELEPHONE NUMBER: 613-727-1779
NO. OF EMPLOYEES: 130
ANNUAL MEETING: In September
SHAREHOLDERS: 137 (approx.)
INSTITUTIONAL HOLDINGS:
No. of Institutions: 6
Shares Held: 371,843

REGISTRAR(S): Chase Mellon Shareholder Services, New York.

TRANSFER AGENT(S): Chase Mellon Shareholder Services, New York.

SOFTQUAD INTERNATIONAL, INC.

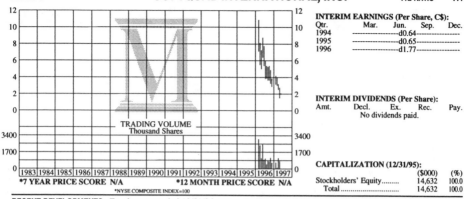

INTERIM EARNINGS (Per Share, C$):

Qtr.	Mar.	Jun.	Sep.	Dec.
1994		d0.64		
1995		d0.65		
1996		d1.77		

TRADING VOLUME
Thousand Shares

INTERIM DIVIDENDS (Per Share):

Amt.	Decl.	Ex.	Rec.	Pay.
	No dividends paid.			

*7 YEAR PRICE SCORE N/A   *12 MONTH PRICE SCORE N/A
*NYSE COMPOSITE INDEX=100

CAPITALIZATION (12/31/95):

	($000)	(%)
Stockholders' Equity	14,632	100.0
Total	14,632	100.0

RECENT DEVELOPMENTS: For the year ended 12/31/96, net loss was C$18.5 million compared with a loss of C$4.2 million in the previous year. The 1996 results included a charge of C$11.8 million related to the amortization of acquired software products. Sales more than doubled to C$16.0 million from C$7.7 million. Despite the substantial increase in sales, the Company announced that it is currently reassessing its cost structure and product strategy and is implementing a restructuring plan in order to reduce expenses and achieve greater profitability. The restructuring is expected to result in workforce reductions, the consolidation of facilities and other cost reduction measures involving cuts in all areas of the Company. The Company is examining the profitability of its product lines on a contribution basis, and expects to be in a position to begin implementing changes in the near-term.

BUSINESS

SOFTQUAD INTERNATIONAL INC. develops, markets and supports digital content authoring and publishing software tools that enable non-technical and technical users to create and distribute standards-based, formatted digital content via the Internet, intranets, CD-ROM and paper. The Company's products are designed for ease of use, high performance and integration with other authoring and programming tools. The Company's suite of products allows users to create and publish vast amounts and various types of digital content, including text, hypertext, graphics, audio, video and 3-D images, which adhere to the open, international publishing standard known as SGML, and its subset HTML. Using these publishing standards, organizations and individuals are able to create and organize digital content that can be broadly accessed, independent of the output medium. HoTMetaL, the Company's HTML product, enables users familiar wih popular word processing software to create and publish content-rich applications on the Web. In addition, the Company also develops and markets SGML authoring, publishing and viewing tools and network monitoring software.

ANNUAL EARNINGS

	12/31/95	12/31/94	12/31/95	12/31/94
	US $		C $	
Earnings Per Share	d0.48	d0.46	d0.65	d0.64

ANNUAL FINANCIAL DATA

RECORD OF EARNINGS (IN THOUSANDS):

Total Revenues	5,761	2,960	7,861	4,152
Costs & Expenses	6,483	3,507	8,846	4,920
Depreciation & Amort	2,354	1,806	3,212	2,534
Operating Income	d3,076	d2,354	d4,197	d3,302
Income Bef Income Tax	d3,076	d2,354	d4,197	d3,302
Net Income	d3,076	d2,354	d4,197	d3,302
Average Shares Outstg	6,413	5,200	6,413	5,200

BALANCE SHEET (IN THOUSANDS):

Cash & Cash Equivalents	1,909	1,193	2,605	1,673
Receivables, Net	2,786	1,143	3,802	1,603
Inventories	101	41	138	58
Gross Property	1,399	685	1,909	961
Accumulated Depreciation	564	361	769	507
Long-Term Debt	. . .	371	. . .	520
Stockholders' Equity	14,632	5,064	19,964	7,104
Total Assets	16,247	6,683	22,168	9,375
Total Current Assets	5,102	2,399	6,961	3,365
Total Current Liabilities	1,615	1,248	2,204	1,751
Net Working Capital	3,486	1,151	4,757	1,614
Year End Shs Outstg	7,386	5,754	7,386	5,754

STATISTICAL RECORD:

Return on Equity %	. . .	. . .		
Return on Assets %	. . .	. . .		
Operating Profit Margin %	. . .	. . .		
Net Profit Margin %	. . .	. . .		
Book Value Per Share	1.98	0.88		

Converted at 1995, US$0.7329= 1 Canadian $; 1994, US$0.7129= 1 Canadian $

OFFICERS:
D. J. Gurney, Chmn. & Pres.
M. Cooperman, C.O.O.
F. Ruffolo, Sec.
S. Wener, C.F.O.

INCORPORATED: April 1982, British Columbia

PRINCIPAL OFFICE: 56 Aberfoyle Crescent 5th Floor Toronto Canada M8X 2W4

TELEPHONE NUMBER: 416-239-4801

NO. OF EMPLOYEES: 105

ANNUAL MEETING: In May

SHAREHOLDERS: N/A

INSTITUTIONAL HOLDINGS:
No. of Institutions: 7
Shares Held: 1,397,385

REGISTRAR(S): N/A

TRANSFER AGENT(S): N/A

NASDAQ SYMBOL DIAGF
Rec. Pr. 5⅜

SPECTRAL DIAGNOSTICS INC.

YIELD ...
P/E RATIO ...

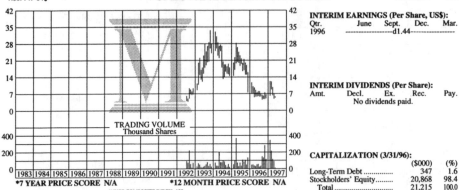

*7 YEAR PRICE SCORE N/A   *12 MONTH PRICE SCORE N/A
*NYSE COMPOSITE INDEX=100

INTERIM EARNINGS (Per Share, US$):

Qtr.	June	Sept.	Dec.	Mar.
1996		d1.44		

INTERIM DIVIDENDS (Per Share):

Amt.	Decl.	Ex.	Rec.	Pay.
	No dividends paid.			

CAPITALIZATION (3/31/96):

	($000)	(%)
Long-Term Debt	347	1.6
Stockholders' Equity........	20,868	98.4
Total	21,215	100.0

RECENT DEVELOPMENTS: For the third quarter ended 12/31/96, net loss was C$3.1 million compared with a loss of C$3.6 million in the same period of 1995. Revenues surged up to C$515,000 from C$70,000 in the prior-year period. The improvement in revenues was primarily attributed to increased sales to hospitals. Recently, the Company successfully closed an account with a hospital estimated to have annual purchases of $200,000. The Company anticipates that the U.S. and Canadian market will increasingly contribute to revenue generation in the near term. DIAGF's targets come from a hospital by hospital sales and marketing campaign. Currently, sales and marketing efforts are underway in the United States by Princeton BioMeditech Corp., DIAGF's manufacturing partner, and Spectral USA, a wholly-owned subsidiary of Spectral Diagnostics Inc. During February 1997, the Company announced that the United States Patent and Trademark Office has issued to DIAGF, U.S. Patent 5,604,105, effecitve 2/18/97.

BUSINESS

SPECTRAL DIAGNOSTICS INC. is engaged in the research, development and commercialization of rapid cardiac diagnostic panel tests which are designed to assist physicians in the rapid diagnosis of chest pain. Products include the Cardiac STATus™ CK-MB/Myoglobin Test for early 'rule-out' of a heart attack, the Cardiac STATys™ Troponin I Test for confirmation of a heart attack and cardiac specificity, the Cardiac Panel™ for differential diagnosis of chest pain and the Anti-Streptokinase Test for thrombolytic selection. Spectral is also a source of cardiac proteins, antibodies and reagents as well as blood to plasma separation membranes through its subsidiary Primecare b.v.

ANNUAL EARNINGS

	3/31/96	3/31/95	3/31/96	3/31/95
	------US $------		------C $------	
Earnings Per Share	d1.44	d0.99	d1.96	d1.34

ANNUAL FINANCIAL DATA

RECORD OF EARNINGS (IN THOUSANDS):

	3/31/96	3/31/95	3/31/96	3/31/95
Total Revenues	453	327	616	458
Costs & Expenses	10,732	7,450	14,588	10,424
Amortization	1,185	728	1,611	1,018
Recoveries & Other Income	1,197	1,438	1,627	1,954
Net Income	d10,267	d6,643	d13,956	d9,030
Average Shares Outstg	7,116	6,721	7,116	6,721

BALANCE SHEET (IN THOUSANDS):

Cash & Cash Equivalents	13,541	22,996	18,406	32,176
Receivables, Net	462	233	628	326
Inventories	338	89	459	125
Gross Property	5,942	2,962	8,077	4,144
Accumulated Depreciation	1,432	784	1,946	1,097
Long-Term Debt	347	89	472	125
Stockholders' Equity	20,868	28,058	28,365	39,258
Total Assets	22,498	29,261	30,580	40,942
Total Current Assets	14,602	23,964	19,848	33,530
Total Current Liabilities	1,282	1,114	1,743	1,559
Net Working Capital	13,320	22,850	18,105	31,971
Year End Shs Outstg	7,181	7,034	7,181	7,034

STATISTICAL RECORD:

Return on Equity %	...	...		
Return on Assets %	...	...		
Operating Profit Margin %	...	...		
Net Profit Margin %	...	...		
Book Value Per Share	2.91	3.99		

Converted at 1996, US$0.7357= 1 Canadian $; 1995, US$0.7147= 1 Canadian $

OFFICERS:
D. C. Ball, Chmn. & C.E.O.
Dr. J. H. Keffer, Chief Medical Officer & V.P.
C. R. Plaxton, Exec. V.P. & C.F.O.
R. Perley, Dir. of Finance

INCORPORATED: Canada, July 29, 1991
PRINCIPAL OFFICE: 135 - 2 The West Mall, Toronto, Ontario Canada M9C 1C2

TELEPHONE NUMBER: 416-626-3233
NO. OF EMPLOYEES: 85
ANNUAL MEETING: In Sep.
SHAREHOLDERS: 94
INSTITUTIONAL HOLDINGS:
No. of Institutions: 3
Shares Held: 79,450

REGISTRAR(S): The Montreal Trust Company of Canada, Toronto.

TRANSFER AGENT(S): The Montreal Trust Company of Canada, Toronto.

SPECTRUM SIGNAL PROCESSING

YIELD ...
P/E RATIO 25.5

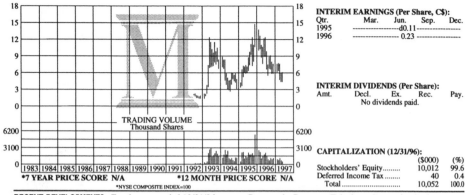

TRADING VOLUME
Thousand Shares

INTERIM EARNINGS (Per Share, C$):

Qtr.	Mar.	Jun.	Sep.	Dec.
1995		d0.11		
1996		0.23		

INTERIM DIVIDENDS (Per Share):

Amt.	Decl.	Ex.	Rec.	Pay.
	No dividends paid.			

CAPITALIZATION (12/31/96):

	($000)	(%)
Stockholders' Equity	10,012	99.6
Deferred Income Tax	40	0.4
Total	10,052	100.0

RECENT DEVELOPMENTS: For the year ended 12/31/96, net income improved substantially to C$2.2 million from a loss of C$1.0 million in the prior year. Sales rose 43.4% to C$36.9 million. The increase in operating results was attributed to record growth in revenues, gross margins and profit after tax. Research and development expenditures were up 10.6% to C$3.8 million as the Company continues to investment heavily in new product devlopment. The Company's Computer Telephony Integration business continues to develop and with Nortel and IBM as key customers, 1996 showed significant progress in terms of product sales. For the quarter ended 12/31/96, net earnings was $1.2 million compared with $85,000 in the corresponding 1995 quarter. Sales rose 71.8% to $13.0 million from $7.6 million in a year earlier.

BUSINESS

SPECTRUM SIGNAL PROCESS-ING INC. is a technology company with three focus areas as business segments: Multimedia & Telephony, Military & Aerospace, and Commercial Digital Signal Processing (DPS). The Company is engaged in designing, manufacturing and marketing digital systems and software process systems for the DSP technology market. Applications for DSP include multimedia, digital cellular telephony, digital audio, medical diagnostics and monitoring, test instruments, defense communications and surveillance, and many industrial uses ranging from the design of more efficient automobile engines to advanced well monitoring techniques for the oil and gas industry.

ANNUAL EARNINGS

	12/31/96	12/31/95	12/31/96	12/31/95
	US $		C $	
Earnings Per Share	0.17	d0.08	0.23	d0.11

ANNUAL FINANCIAL DATA

RECORD OF EARNINGS (IN THOUSANDS):

	12/31/96	12/31/95	12/31/96	12/31/95
Total Revenues	26,988	18,869	36,914	25,746
Costs & Expenses	24,141	19,656	33,020	26,819
Depreciation & Amort	496	424	678	579
Operating Income	2,351	d1,211	3,216	d1,652
Income Bef Income Tax	2,357	d755	3,224	d1,030
Income Tax	785	...	1,074	...
Net Income	1,572	d755	2,150	d1,030
Average Shares Outstg	9,195	9,000	9,195	9,000

BALANCE SHEET (IN THOUSANDS):

Cash & Cash Equivalents	1,490	1,409	2,038	1,922
Receivables, Net	8,403	4,806	11,493	6,557
Inventories	1,752	2,309	2,396	3,150
Gross Property	3,734	2,701	5,107	3,686
Accumulated Depreciation	1,599	1,106	2,187	1,509
Long-Term Debt	...	10	...	13
Stockholders' Equity	10,012	8,097	13,694	11,048
Total Assets	15,118	11,378	20,678	15,525
Total Current Assets	12,161	8,892	16,634	12,132
Total Current Liabilities	5,066	3,272	6,929	4,464
Net Working Capital	7,095	5,620	9,705	7,668
Year End Shs Outstg	9,227	9,164	9,227	9,164

STATISTICAL RECORD:

Return on Equity %	15.70	...
Return on Assets %	10.40	...
Operating Profit Margin %	8.71	...
Net Profit Margin %	5.82	...
Book Value Per Share	1.09	0.88

Converted at 1996, US$0.7311= 1 Canadian $; 1995, US$0.7329= 1 Canadian $

OFFICERS:
M. Mertens, Chmn.
B. Jinks, Pres. & C.E.O.
D. Hobbs, V.P.-Engr.
D. Johnson, V.P.-Logistics

INCORPORATED: Jul., 1987

PRINCIPAL OFFICE: 8525 Baxter Place, 100 Production Court, Burnaby B.C., Canada V5A 4V7

TELEPHONE NUMBER: 604-421-5422

NO. OF EMPLOYEES: N/A

ANNUAL MEETING: In June

SHAREHOLDERS: N/A

INSTITUTIONAL HOLDINGS:
No. of Institutions: 3
Shares Held: 84,728

REGISTRAR(S): Montreal Trust Company of Canada, Vancouver.

TRANSFER AGENT(S): Montreal Trust Company of Canada, Vancouver.

STEINER LEISURE LIMITED

YIELD ...
P/E RATIO 67.1

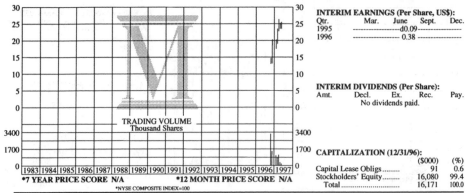

INTERIM EARNINGS (Per Share, US$):

Qtr.	Mar.	June	Sept.	Dec.
1995	------------------d0.09----------------			
1996	------------------ 0.38 ------------------			

INTERIM DIVIDENDS (Per Share):

Amt.	Decl.	Ex.	Rec.	Pay.
	No dividends paid.			

CAPITALIZATION (12/31/96):

	($000)	(%)
Capital Lease Obligs	91	0.6
Stockholders' Equity	16,080	99.4
Total	16,171	100.0

RECENT DEVELOPMENTS: For the three months ended 3/31/97, net income advanced 94.1% to US$2.3 million compared with US$1.2 million in the corresponding period of 1996. Revenues rose 19.2% to US$19.7 million from US$16.5 million a year earlier. Service revenues increased 14.5% to US$11.8 million, while products revenues rose 27.2% to US$7.8 million. The Company attributed the increase in revenues and net income to the introduction of new ships with enlarged and enhanced shipboard spa facilities serviced by the Company and a general increase in the productivity of the Company's shipboard employees. As of 5/1/97, the Company was serving 86 vessels representing 26 cruise lines.

BUSINESS

STEINER LEISURE LIMITED is a provider of spa services and skin and hair care products on board cruise ships worldwide. The Company strives to create an engaging and therapeutic environment where customers can receive body and facial treatments and hair styling comparable in quality to the finest land-based spas and salons. In addition, the Company develops and markets premium priced, high quality personal care products which are sold primarily in connection with the services the Company provides and, to a lesser extent, through third party land-based salon and retail channels. Additionally, the Company offers over 150 different products, including beauty products such as aromatherapy oils, cleansers, creams and other skin care products and accessories and hair care products such as shampoos, moisturizers and lotions.

ANNUAL EARNINGS

	12/31/96	12/31/95	12/31/94
		----------US $----------	
Earnings Per Share	0.38	d0.09	0.05

ANNUAL FINANCIAL DATA

RECORD OF EARNINGS (IN THOUSANDS):

	12/31/96	12/31/95	12/31/94
Total Revenues	69,580	54,412	39,650
Costs & Expenses	59,514	50,957	36,850
Depreciation & Amort	2,477	2,292	1,264
Operating Income	7,589	1,163	1,536
Income Bef Income Tax	7,421	793	1,231
Income Tax	4,950	1,356	910
Net Income	2,471	d563	321
Average Shares Outstg	6,470	6,372	6,372

BALANCE SHEET (IN THOUSANDS):

Cash & Cash Equivalents	13,625	1,397	1,420
Receivables, Net	3,413	2,362	3,373
Inventories	5,232	2,603	2,853
Gross Property	4,307	3,647	3,554
Accumulated Depreciation	2,096	1,389	1,192
Long-Term Debt	...	3,020	4,876
Capital Lease Obligs	91	42	...
Stockholders' Equity	16,080	3,574	5,050
Total Assets	26,656	13,320	16,230
Total Current Assets	23,080	6,706	8,213
Total Current Liabilities	10,485	6,684	6,204
Net Working Capital	12,595	22	2,009
Year End Shs Outstg	7,200	6,372	6,372

STATISTICAL RECORD:

Return on Equity %	15.37	...	6.36
Return on Assets %	9.27	...	1.98
Operating Profit Margin %	10.91	2.14	3.87
Net Profit Margin %	3.55	...	0.81
Book Value Per Share	2.23	0.56	0.79

OFFICERS:
C. E. Warshaw, Chmn. & C.E.O.
L. I. Fluxman, C.O.O. & C.F.O.
M. Steiner Warshaw, Exec. V.P.
A. Jane Francis, Sr. V.P.

INCORPORATED: Nov. 1995, The Bahamas

PRINCIPAL OFFICE: Suite 104A, Saffrey Square, Nassau The Bahamas

TELEPHONE NUMBER: 242-356-0006

NO. OF EMPLOYEES: 832

ANNUAL MEETING: In June

SHAREHOLDERS: 93

INSTITUTIONAL HOLDINGS:
No. of Institutions: N/A
Shares Held: N/A

REGISTRAR(S): American Stock Transfer and Trust Company.

TRANSFER AGENT(S): American Stock Transfer and Trust Company.

STOLT COMEX SEAWAY S.A.

YIELD ...
P/E RATIO ...

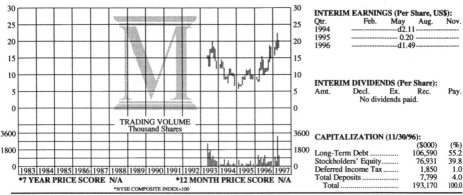

INTERIM EARNINGS (Per Share, US$):

Qtr.	Feb.	May	Aug.	Nov.
1994	---------------- d2.11 ----------------			
1995	---------------- 0.20 ----------------			
1996	---------------- d1.49 ----------------			

INTERIM DIVIDENDS (Per Share):

Amt.	Decl.	Ex.	Rec.	Pay.
	No dividends paid.			

CAPITALIZATION (11/30/96):

	($000)	(%)
Long-Term Debt	106,590	55.2
Stockholders' Equity........	76,931	39.8
Deferred Income Tax	1,850	1.0
Total Deposits	7,799	4.0
Total	193,170	100.0

RECENT DEVELOPMENTS: For the year ended 11/30/96, the Company reported a net loss of $14.9 million compared with net income of $2.0 million the year before. Net operating revenue declined 4.2% to $313.4 million from $327.0 million a year earlier. The decrease in revenue resulted from decreases in net operating revenue from the North Sea and SEAME regions, partially offset by net operating revenue from the inception of operations in the Gulf of Mexico and an increase in net operating revenue from the Asia Pacific region. As a percentage of net operating revenue, gross profit margin fell to 6.8% from 14.0% the previous year. Administrative and general expenses were 9.6% of net operating revenue versus 10.1% a year earlier. The Company reported an operating loss of $3.4 million versus operating income of $19.2 million the year before.

BUSINESS

STOLT COMEX SEAWAY S.A. is a holding company that, through its subsidiaries, acts as a diversified contractor to the offshore oil and gas industry. The Company specializes in engineering, survey and construction services with a focus on subsea activities. Stolt provides subsea services and supplies offshore survey services in 24 countries in Europe, the Middle East, West Africa, Southeast Asia and South America. The Company's operations are divided into three primary categories: subsea services and engineering; marine construction and topside maintenance; and survey and positioning.

ANNUAL EARNINGS

	11/30/96	11/30/95	11/30/96	11/30/95
	-------------- US $ -----------		-------------- British £ ------------	
Earnings Per Share	d1.49	0.20	d0.89	0.13

ANNUAL FINANCIAL DATA

RECORD OF EARNINGS (IN THOUSANDS):

	11/30/96	11/30/95	11/30/96	11/30/95
Total Revenues	313,358	327,042	186,545	209,642
Costs & Expenses	316,795	307,850	188,591	197,340
Operating Income	d3,437	19,192	d2,046	12,303
Income Bef Income Tax	d16,660	6,222	d9,918	3,988
Income Tax	1,758	4,208	1,047	2,697
Net Income	d18,418	2,014	d10,964	1,291
Average Shares Outstg	10,000	10,000	10,000	10,000

BALANCE SHEET (IN THOUSANDS):

Cash & Cash Equivalents	9,547	3,783	5,683	2,425
Receivables, Net	116,057	93,290	69,090	59,801
Inventories	9,477	8,127	5,642	5,210
Gross Property	278,578	232,450	165,840	149,006
Accumulated Depreciation	106,135	80,990	63,183	51,917
Long-Term Debt	106,590	111,412	63,733	71,742
Stockholders' Equity	76,931	90,947	45,798	58,299
Total Assets	357,285	311,348	212,695	199,582
Total Current Assets	147,758	114,705	87,962	73,529
Total Current Liabilities	167,725	102,456	99,848	65,677
Net Working Capital	d19,967	12,249	d11,887	7,852
Year End Shs Outstg	17,003	17,000	17,003	17,000

STATISTICAL RECORD:

Return on Equity %	...	2.21		
Return on Assets %	...	0.65		
Operating Profit Margin %	...	5.87		
Net Profit Margin %	...	0.62		
Book Value Per Share	4.52	5.35		

Converted at 1996, US$1.6798= 1 British pound; 1995, US$1.5600= 1 British pound

OFFICERS:
B. Vossier, C.E.O.
P. Frikstad, C.F.O.
J. Rasmussen, Legal Counsel

INCORPORATED: May, 1993

PRINCIPAL OFFICE: Bucksburn House
Howes Road, Bucksburn Aberdeen Scotland
AB21 9RQ

TELEPHONE NUMBER: 44-0-1224-718 200

NO. OF EMPLOYEES: N/A

ANNUAL MEETING: In May

SHAREHOLDERS: N/A

INSTITUTIONAL HOLDINGS:
No. of Institutions: N/A
Shares Held: N/A

REGISTRAR(S): First Chicago Trust Co., Jersey City, New Jersey

TRANSFER AGENT(S): First Chicago Trust Co., Jersey City, New Jersey

SUTTON RESOURCES, LTD.

YIELD ...
P/E RATIO ...

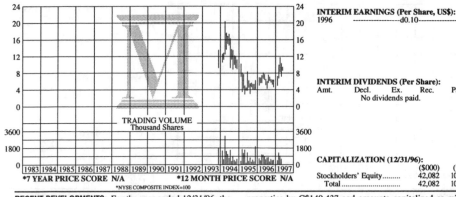

INTERIM EARNINGS (Per Share, US$):
1996 ------------------d0.10------------------

INTERIM DIVIDENDS (Per Share):

Amt.	Decl.	Ex.	Rec.	Pay.
No dividends paid.				

TRADING VOLUME
Thousand Shares

*7 YEAR PRICE SCORE N/A   *12 MONTH PRICE SCORE N/A
*NYSE COMPOSITE INDEX=100

CAPITALIZATION (12/31/96):

	($000)	(%)
Stockholders' Equity	42,082	100.0
Total	42,082	100.0

RECENT DEVELOPMENTS: For the year ended 12/31/96, the Company posted a net loss of C$1.6 million compared with a loss of C$1.7 million a year earlier. The Company posted interest income of C$1.3 million versus interest income of C$326,251 in 1995. During the year ended 12/31/96, the Company re-evaluated the properties located in the Western United States developed through its joint-venture agreement with Crown Resources Corporation and decided to write down deferred exploration expenditures on certain properties by C$149,437 and amounts capitalized as mineral properties by C$39,999 to nominal value. The Company is advancing its Bulyanhulu gold property to the bankable feasability stage during 1997 through an underground development program. The Company has plans to have a fully operating mine producing at Bulyanhulu in 1999. At Kabanga, the Company is planning an aggressive exploration program to add to the nickel reserves, and to develop a production plan.

BUSINESS

SUTTON RESOURCES, LTD., through its subsidiaries, controls gold and nickel properties in Tanzania, South Africa. The Company's operations include the Bulyanhulu Gold Property in the Lake Victoria Goldfields, with a resource of 5.62 million ounces of gold; the Kabanga nickel concession, containing resources of over one billion pounds of nickel, 150 million pounds of copper and 89 million pounds of cobalt; and the Marudi Mountain gold deposit in Guyana, South America, which contains 518,000 ounces of gold. The Company also holds a nickel exploration concession north of its Kabanga nickel property, extending to the Uganda border. In the United States, the Company has conducted joint venture exploration programs on precious metals properties in Washington, Nevada and Colorado. Other operations are located in British Columbia, Canada.

ANNUAL EARNINGS

	12/31/96	12/31/95	12/31/96	12/31/95
	--------------US $--------------		--------------C $--------------	
Earnings Per Share	d0.10	d0.12	d0.14	d0.17

ANNUAL FINANCIAL DATA

RECORD OF EARNINGS (IN THOUSANDS):

Total Revenues	730	d5	999	d7
Costs & Expenses	1,958	1,268	2,678	1,731
Depreciation & Amort	18	15	25	21
Income Bef Income Tax	d1,246	d1,289	d1,704	d1,758
Income Tax	cr48	cr16	cr66	cr22
Net Income	d1,198	d1,272	d1,639	d1,736

BALANCE SHEET (IN THOUSANDS):

Cash & Cash Equivalents	19,453	1,525	26,608	2,080
Receivables, Net	400	168	546	230
Gross Property	113	58	154	80
Accumulated Depreciation	51	32	69	44
Stockholders' Equity	42,082	18,290	57,560	24,955
Total Assets	43,606	18,612	59,644	25,395
Total Current Assets	19,907	1,744	27,229	2,380
Total Current Liabilities	1,524	322	2,084	440
Net Working Capital	18,384	1,422	25,145	1,940
Year End Shs Outstg	12,715	10,409	12,715	10,409

STATISTICAL RECORD:

Return on Equity %	...	...		
Return on Assets %	...	...		
Operating Profit Margin %	...	...		
Net Profit Margin %	...	...		
Book Value Per Share	3.31	1.76		

Converted at 1996, US$0.7311= 1 Canadian $; 1995, US$0.7329= 1 Canadian $

OFFICERS:
R. E. Shklanka, Chmn.
J. M. Kenyon, Pres. & C.E.O.
A. Luteijn, V.P.
J. A. Rubenstein, V.P. & C.F.O.
INCORPORATED: 1979
PRINCIPAL OFFICE: Suite 900, Box 40, 999 West Hastings Street, Vancouver Canada V6C 2W2

TELEPHONE NUMBER: 604-669-9446
NO. OF EMPLOYEES: N/A
ANNUAL MEETING: Apr. 17, 1997
SHAREHOLDERS: N/A
INSTITUTIONAL HOLDINGS:
No. of Institutions: N/A
Shares Held: N/A

REGISTRAR(S): Montreal Trust, Vancouver and Toronto.

TRANSFER AGENT(S): Montreal Trust, Vancouver and Toronto.

TADIRAN TELECOMMUNICATIONS LTD.

YIELD ...
P/E RATIO 11.1

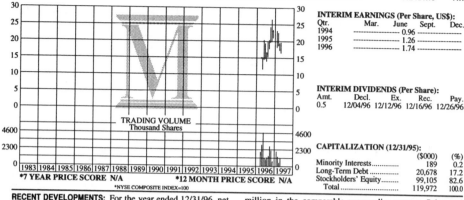

*7 YEAR PRICE SCORE N/A   *12 MONTH PRICE SCORE N/A
*NYSE COMPOSITE INDEX=100

INTERIM EARNINGS (Per Share, US$):

Qtr.	Mar.	June	Sept.	Dec.
1994		0.96		
1995		1.26		
1996		1.74		

INTERIM DIVIDENDS (Per Share):

Amt.	Decl.	Ex.	Rec.	Pay.
0.5	12/04/96	12/12/96	12/16/96	12/26/96

CAPITALIZATION (12/31/95):

	($000)	(%)
Minority Interests	189	0.2
Long-Term Debt	20,678	17.2
Stockholders' Equity	99,105	82.6
Total	119,972	100.0

RECENT DEVELOPMENTS: For the year ended 12/31/96, net income increased 64.1% to $41.4 million compared with $25.2 million a year earlier. Sales and revenues totaled $468.6 million, up 20.9% from $387.5 million the previous year. Sales to Bezeq, Israel's telephone operating company, were up 11.9% to $216.0 million compared with $193.0 million the year before. Export sales grew 46.2% in 1996, reaching $174.0 million. For the fourth quarter ended 12/31/96, net income rose 4.0% to $3.7 million from $3.6 million in the comparable year-earlier quarter. Sales and revenues increased 4.9% to $102.1 million compared with $97.4 million in the corresponding period the previous year. Sales to Bezeq were down for the quarter to $29.0 million versus $43.0 million the year before. The Company has extended its contract through the year 2000 to be a key supplier to Bezeq. During the quarter, the Company received new orders from Jamaica, Belgium, Scotland, Poland and other countries.

BUSINESS

TADIRAN TELECOMMUNICA-TIONS LTD. is a holding company. Through its subsidiaries, the Company is engaged in designing, developing, manufacturing, producing and marketing a wide range of sophisticated telecommunications equipment, defense electronic systems, electrical appliances and consumer electronic products, batteries, and computer software products for both civilian and military markets in Israel and throughout the world.

ANNUAL EARNINGS

	12/31/95	12/31/94	12/31/95	12/31/94
	US $		NIS	
Earnings Per Share	1.26	0.96	3.97	2.90

ANNUAL FINANCIAL DATA

RECORD OF EARNINGS (IN THOUSANDS):				
Total Revenues	387,530	308,419	1,219,799	930,655
Costs & Expenses	352,583	279,964	1,109,799	844,792
Operating Income	34,947	28,455	110,000	85,863
Income Bef Income Tax	30,654	26,022	96,487	78,521
Income Tax	5,588	5,903	17,589	17,812
Eq. Earnings in Affils.	161	d859	507	d2,592
Minority Interests	22	cr15	69	cr45
Net Income	25,205	19,275	79,336	58,162
Average Shares Outstg	20,000	20,000	20,000	20,000
BALANCE SHEET (IN THOUSANDS):				
Cash & Cash Equivalents	6,706	665	21,108	2,007
Receivables, Net	74,584	78,783	234,762	237,728
Inventories	82,738	90,301	260,428	272,483
Gross Property	74,964	65,331	235,958	197,136
Accumulated Depreciation	28,742	23,179	90,469	69,943
Long-Term Debt	20,678	1,305	65,087	3,938
Stockholders' Equity	99,105	81,000	311,945	244,418
Total Assets	240,729	229,085	757,724	691,264
Total Current Assets	180,820	180,775	569,153	545,489
Total Current Liabilities	113,034	140,545	355,788	424,095
Net Working Capital	67,786	40,230	213,365	121,394
Year End Shs Outstg	20,000	20,000	20,000	20,000
STATISTICAL RECORD:				
Return on Equity %	25.43	23.80		
Return on Assets %	10.47	8.41		
Operating Profit Margin %	9.02	9.23		
Net Profit Margin %	6.50	6.25		
Book Value Per Share	4.96	4.05		

Converted at 1995, US$0.3177= 1 New Israeli Shekel; 1994, US$0.3314= 1 New Israeli Shekel

OFFICERS:
I. Zamir, Chmn.
H. Rosen, Pres. & C.E.O.
B. Chelouche, Sec.
M. Sperling, Couns.

INCORPORATED: Dec., 1994

PRINCIPAL OFFICE: 18 Hasivim Street, Petach-Tikva Israel 49104

TELEPHONE NUMBER: 972-3-926-2262

NO. OF EMPLOYEES: 2,300 (approx.)

ANNUAL MEETING: N/A

SHAREHOLDERS: N/A

INSTITUTIONAL HOLDINGS:
No. of Institutions: N/A
Shares Held: N/A

REGISTRAR(S): The Bank of New York.

TRANSFER AGENT(S): The Bank of New York.

TARO PHARMACEUTICAL INDUSTRIES

NASDAQ SYMBOL TAROF
Rec. Pr. 5⅞

YIELD ...
P/E RATIO 28.05

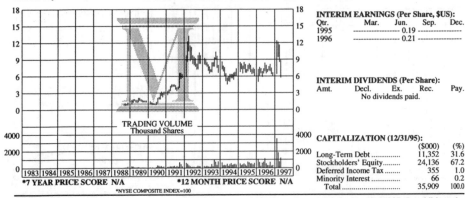

INTERIM EARNINGS (Per Share, $US):

Qtr.	Mar.	Jun.	Sep.	Dec.
1995		0.19		
1996		0.21		

INTERIM DIVIDENDS (Per Share):

Amt.	Decl.	Ex.	Rec.	Pay.
	No dividends paid.			

TRADING VOLUME
Thousand Shares

*7 YEAR PRICE SCORE N/A   *12 MONTH PRICE SCORE N/A

*NYSE COMPOSITE INDEX=100

CAPITALIZATION (12/31/95):

	($000)	(%)
Long-Term Debt	11,352	31.6
Stockholders' Equity	24,136	67.2
Deferred Income Tax	355	1.0
Minority Interest	66	0.2
Total	35,909	100.0

RECENT DEVELOPMENTS: For the year ended 12/31/96, net income was $2.2 million, up 7.8% from $2.0 million in the prior year. Sales advanced 14.0% to $56.5 million from $49.6 million a year earlier. Despite a 37% rise in research and development expenditures for the year, operating results were up due primarily to strong product sales and new product introductions. During 1996, the Company received seven Abbreviated New Drug Approvals (ANDA), and an eighth in January 1997. In addition, the Company entered the U.S. prescription solid dosage form market with its ANDA for Carbamazepine tablets and Clomipramine Hydrochloride capsules. For the quarter ended 12/31/96, net income was $714,000 compared with $124,000 in the corresponding 1995 quarter. Sales rose 20.8% to $15.1 million.

BUSINESS

TARO PHARMACEUTICAL INDUSTRIES LTD. is a vertically integrated international manufacturer and marketer of prescription and over-the-counter pharmaceutical products, with a focus on generic products. In addition to the production of finished dosage form drugs, the Company synthesizes the pharmaceutical chemicals used in their production. The Company's products are sold through wholesalers, generic drug distributors, drug store chains, mass merchandisers, pharmacies and hospitals. The Company also has research and development capabilities in pharmaceutical finished dosage forms and pharmaceutical active ingredients.

ANNUAL EARNINGS

	12/31/95	12/31/94	12/31/95	12/31/94
	US $		NIS	
Earnings Per Share	0.19	0.34	0.60	1.03

ANNUAL FINANCIAL DATA

RECORD OF EARNINGS (IN THOUSANDS):

	12/31/95	12/31/94	12/31/95	12/31/94
Total Revenues	49,581	42,128	156,062	127,121
Costs & Expenses	44,248	35,309	139,276	106,545
Operating Income	5,333	6,819	16,786	20,576
Income Bef Income Tax	3,538	5,568	11,136	16,801
Income Tax	1,501	2,160	4,725	6,518
Minority Interests	12	33	38	100
Net Income	2,025	3,375	6,374	10,184
Average Shares Outstg	10,427	9,874	10,427	9,874

BALANCE SHEET (IN THOUSANDS):

Cash & Cash Equivalents	2,551	2,951	8,030	8,905
Receivables, Net	14,178	13,277	44,627	40,063
Inventories	11,194	8,744	35,234	26,385
Gross Property	22,985	18,252	72,348	55,075
Accumulated Depreciation	6,744	5,291	21,228	15,966
Long-Term Debt	11,352	1,809	35,732	5,459
Stockholders' Equity	24,136	21,831	75,971	65,875
Total Assets	49,532	42,838	155,908	129,264
Total Current Assets	27,923	24,972	87,891	75,353
Total Current Liabilities	13,545	18,920	42,635	57,091
Net Working Capital	14,378	6,052	45,257	18,262
Year End Shs Outstg	9,907	9,886	9,907	9,886

STATISTICAL RECORD:

Return on Equity %	8.39	15.46
Return on Assets %	4.09	7.88
Operating Profit Margin %	10.76	16.19
Net Profit Margin %	4.08	8.01
Book Value Per Share	2.44	2.21

Converted at 1995, US$0.3177= 1 New Israeli Shekel; 1994, US$0.3314= 1 New Israeli Shekel

OFFICERS:
B. Levitt M.D., Chmn.
A. Levitt, Pres.
P. Giallorenzo, Sr. V.P. & C.O.O.
S. Rubinstein, Sr. V.P. & C.O.O.

INCORPORATED: Israel, 1952

PRINCIPAL OFFICE: 14 Hakitor Street Haifa Bay Israel 26110

TELEPHONE NUMBER: 972-4-872-3257

NO. OF EMPLOYEES: N/A

ANNUAL MEETING: N/A

SHAREHOLDERS: 707

INSTITUTIONAL HOLDINGS:
No. of Institutions: N/A
Shares Held: N/A

REGISTRAR(S): N/A

TRANSFER AGENT(S): The American Stock Transfer Co., New York.

TASEKO MINES LIMITED

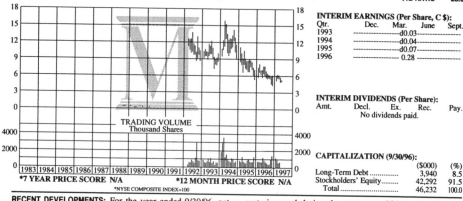

INTERIM EARNINGS (Per Share, C $):

Qtr.	Dec.	Mar.	June	Sept.
1993	---------d0.03---------			
1994	---------d0.04---------			
1995	---------d0.07---------			
1996	--------- 0.28 ---------			

INTERIM DIVIDENDS (Per Share):

Amt.	Decl.	Ex.	Rec.	Pay.
	No dividends paid.			

*7 YEAR PRICE SCORE N/A   ***12 MONTH PRICE SCORE N/A**

*NYSE COMPOSITE INDEX=100

CAPITALIZATION (9/30/96):

	($000)	(%)
Long-Term Debt	3,940	8.5
Stockholders' Equity.........	42,292	91.5
Total	46,232	100.0

RECENT DEVELOPMENTS: For the year ended 9/30/96, net earnings were C$3.5 million compared with a net loss of C$921,619 the year before. Results for the recent period included a gain of C$4.6 million related to financing. Interest revenue soared to C$217,857 from C$38,482 a year earlier. Total expenses rose 31.9% to C$1.3 million from C$960,101 the previous year. Exploration and development costs incurred during the year were C$5.5 million versus C$1.1 million in the prior-year period. During the year, the Company completed C$15.1 million in financing to fund ongoing detailed engineering and environmental studies for the permitting, financing and construction of a major open pit gold and copper mine.

BUSINESS

TASEKO MINES LIMITED is engaged in the exploration and development of its wholly-owned Prosperity Gold-Copper Project (formerly Fish Lake Gold-Copper Project), which is located in south central British Columbia, Canada. The Prosperity Deposit is one of the largest untapped metal resources in the world and contains in excess of 9.4 million ounces of gold and 3.5 billion pounds of copper.

ANNUAL EARNINGS

	9/30/96	9/30/95	9/30/96	9/30/95
	----------US $----------		----------C $----------	
Earnings Per Share	0.21	d0.06	0.28	d0.08

ANNUAL FINANCIAL DATA

RECORD OF EARNINGS (IN THOUSANDS):

	9/30/96	9/30/95	9/30/96	9/30/95
Total Revenues	160	29	218	38
Costs & Expenses	923	711	1,257	953
Depreciation & Amort	6	5	9	7
Operating Income	d769	d687	d1,048	d922
Income Bef Income Tax	2,589	d687	3,529	d922
Net Income	2,589	d687	3,529	d922
Average Shares Outstg	12,446	12,310	12,446	12,310

BALANCE SHEET (IN THOUSANDS):

Cash & Cash Equivalents	7,643	136	10,416	183
Receivables, Net	255	35	347	48
Gross Property	41	23	55	31
Accumulated Depreciation	17	11	24	15
Long-Term Debt	3,940	...	5,370	...
Stockholders' Equity	42,292	32,325	57,642	43,377
Total Assets	44,020	32,622	59,998	43,776
Total Current Assets	7,897	171	10,764	230
Total Current Liabilities	1,648	298	2,246	399
Net Working Capital	6,250	d126	8,518	d169
Year End Shs Outstg	12,565	12,349	12,565	12,349

STATISTICAL RECORD:

Return on Equity %	6.12	...
Return on Assets %	5.88	...
Operating Profit Margin %	...	...
Net Profit Margin %	N.M.	...
Book Value Per Share	4.59	3.51

Converted at 1996, US$0.7337= 1 Canadian $; 1995, US$0.7452= 1 Canadian $

OFFICERS:
R. G. Hunter, Chmn. & C.E.O.
R. A. Dickinson, Pres. & C.F.O.
J. A. Mason, Sec. & Treas.

INCORPORATED: British Columbia

PRINCIPAL OFFICE: 1020 - 800 West Pender Street Vancouver, British Columbia Canada

TELEPHONE NUMBER: 604-684-6365

NO. OF EMPLOYEES: N/A

ANNUAL MEETING: In March

SHAREHOLDERS: N/A

INSTITUTIONAL HOLDINGS:
No. of Institutions: 10
Shares Held: 681,740

REGISTRAR(S): N/A

TRANSFER AGENT(S): The Montreal Trust Company, Vancouver, British Columbia, Canada

TAT TECHNOLOGIES LTD.

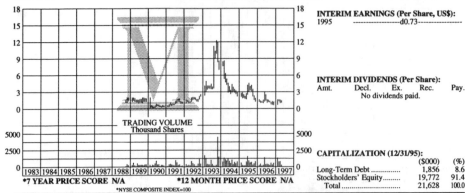

INTERIM EARNINGS (Per Share, US$):
1995 ------------------d0.73------------------

INTERIM DIVIDENDS (Per Share):
Amt.   Decl.   Ex.   Rec.   Pay.
No dividends paid.

*7 YEAR PRICE SCORE N/A   *12 MONTH PRICE SCORE N/A
*NYSE COMPOSITE INDEX=100

CAPITALIZATION (12/31/95):

	($000)	(%)
Long-Term Debt	1,856	8.6
Stockholders' Equity.........	19,772	91.4
Total	21,628	100.0

RECENT DEVELOPMENTS: For the three months ended 9/30/96, the Company reported a loss of $377,000 compared with a loss of $892,000 in the corresponding period a year earlier. Revenues were $4.0 million, up 8% versus $3.7 million in 1995. Earnings were pressured by a substantial expenditure in research and development. Research and development costs more than doubled to $1.6 million compared with $577,000 a year earlier. For the nine months ended 9/30/96, the Company reported a loss of $1.6 million compared with $476,000 in the corresponding period a year earlier. Revenues were $12.5 million, up 3% versus $12.2 million in 1995. Research and development costs more than doubled to $2.8 million compared with $1.2 million a year earlier. Research and development costs are not expected to be reduced before the end of the Company's fiscal year.

BUSINESS

TAT TECHNOLOGIES LTD. is principally engaged in the design, manufacture and sale of heat transfer equipment used in mechanical and electronic systems on board commercial and military aircraft and in a variety of other electronic equipment. The Company is also engaged in the remanufacture, overhaul and repair of heat transfer equipment and other aircraft components manufactured by itself as well as other companies. TATTF also manufactures, sells and services certain related products for use in aircraft and electronic systems. Other activities include the design, development and marketing of hardware and software products for computerized transportation systems that facilitate management of a fleet of vehicles and of specialized, high-performance, computer graphic subsystems used in applications such as medical imaging.

ANNUAL EARNINGS

	12/31/95	12/31/94	12/31/95	12/31/94
	US $		NIS	
Earnings Per Share	d0.73	d0.16	d2.32	d0.48

ANNUAL FINANCIAL DATA

RECORD OF EARNINGS (IN THOUSANDS):

	12/31/95	12/31/94	12/31/95	12/31/94
Total Revenues	16,705	17,559	52,581	52,984
Costs & Expenses	17,528	18,599	55,172	56,123
Operating Income	d823	d1,040	d2,590	d3,138
Income Bef Income Tax	d186	d1,179	d585	d3,558
Income Tax	126	161	397	486
Eq. Earnings in Affils.	d3,460	d428	d10,891	d1,291
Minority Interests	cr229	cr323	cr721	cr975
Net Income	d3,543	d1,445	d11,152	d4,360
Income from Disc. Ops.	d3,034	...	d9,550	...
Average Shares Outstg	8,974	8,969	8,974	8,969

BALANCE SHEET (IN THOUSANDS):

Cash & Cash Equivalents	3,834	10,988	12,068	33,156
Receivables, Net	6,766	5,097	21,297	15,380
Inventories	4,373	2,881	13,765	8,693
Gross Property	9,254	8,054	29,128	24,303
Accumulated Depreciation	3,712	2,994	11,684	9,034
Long-Term Debt	1,856	2,174	5,842	6,560
Stockholders' Equity	19,772	26,293	62,235	79,339
Total Assets	31,325	37,211	98,599	112,284
Total Current Assets	19,026	22,404	59,887	67,604
Total Current Liabilities	4,889	4,088	15,389	12,336
Net Working Capital	14,137	18,316	44,498	55,269
Year End Shs Outstg	8,950	8,903	8,950	8,903

STATISTICAL RECORD:

Return on Equity %	...	...		
Return on Assets %	...	...		
Operating Profit Margin %	...	...		
Net Profit Margin %	...	...		
Book Value Per Share	2.21	2.95		

Converted at 1995, US$0.3177= 1 Israeli Shekel; 1994, US$0.3314= 1 Israeli Shekel

OFFICERS:
S. Ostersetzer, Chmn. & C.E.O.
D. Zeelim, Vice-Chmn.
I. Ofen, Pres. & Managing Dir.
I. Ofer, Treas., Comptroller & C.F.O.

INCORPORATED: 1985

PRINCIPAL OFFICE: P.O. Box 80 Gedera
Israel 70750

TELEPHONE NUMBER: N/A

NO. OF EMPLOYEES: 220

ANNUAL MEETING: N/A

SHAREHOLDERS: 164

INSTITUTIONAL HOLDINGS:
No. of Institutions: N/A
Shares Held: N/A

REGISTRAR(S): N/A

TRANSFER AGENT(S): American Stock
Transfer and Trust Co., New York.

TECNOMATIX TECHNOLOGIES, LTD.

YIELD ...
P/E RATIO 30.6

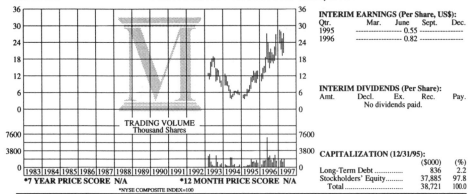

INTERIM EARNINGS (Per Share, US$):

Qtr.	Mar.	June	Sept.	Dec.
1995	------------------	0.55	------------------	
1996	------------------	0.82	------------------	

INTERIM DIVIDENDS (Per Share):

Amt.	Decl.	Ex.	Rec.	Pay.
		No dividends paid.		

TRADING VOLUME
Thousand Shares

*7 YEAR PRICE SCORE N/A   *12 MONTH PRICE SCORE N/A

*NYSE COMPOSITE INDEX=100

CAPITALIZATION (12/31/95):

	($000)	(%)
Long-Term Debt	836	2.2
Stockholders' Equity	37,885	97.8
Total	38,721	100.0

RECENT DEVELOPMENTS: For the year ended 12/31/96, net income was $8.0 million, up 78.1% from $4.5 million in the prior year. Total revenues rose 33.4% to $44.5 million from $33.4 million in 1995. The improvement in revenues was attributed primarily to a high-level of repeat sales to existing customers along with new sales from new customer growth. Software and systems sales advanced 31.0% to $32.5 million, while revenues from maintenance and other services climbed 40.5% to $12.0 million. Gross profit was $38.2 million compared with $27.7 million a year ago, a 37.9% increase. For the quarter ended 12/31/96, net income advanced 67.6% to $2.9 million from $1.7 million in the corresponding 1995 quarter. Total revenues were up 28.7% to $12.8 million.

BUSINESS

TECNOMATRIX TECHNOLOGIES is engaged in the development, marketing and support of Computer-Aided Production Engineering (CAPE) software and tools used in the design, simulation, optimization and off-line programming of automated manufacturing systems. The Company's three main product lines are: ROBCAD for manufacturing processes, VALISYS for quality engineering and EXALINE for printed circuit board assembly. The Company's customers include major worldwide manufacturers in the automotive, aerospace, heavy machinery, electronics and other industries.

ANNUAL EARNINGS

	12/31/95	12/31/94	12/31/95	12/31/94
	----------US $----------		----------NIS----------	
Earnings Per Share	0.55	d0.14	1.73	d0.42

ANNUAL FINANCIAL DATA

RECORD OF EARNINGS (IN THOUSANDS):

	12/31/95	12/31/94	12/31/95	12/31/94
Total Revenues	33,376	23,445	105,055	70,745
Costs & Expenses	29,457	25,449	92,720	76,792
Operating Income	3,919	d2,004	12,336	d6,047
Income Bef Income Tax	4,703	d1,610	14,803	d4,858
Income Tax	24	cr620	76	cr1,871
Net Income	4,487	d1,133	14,123	d3,419
Average Shares Outstg	8,173	7,950	8,173	7,950

BALANCE SHEET (IN THOUSANDS):

Cash & Cash Equivalents	9,880	6,444	31,099	19,445
Receivables, Net	14,581	13,793	45,895	41,620
Inventories	112	11	353	33
Gross Property	9,098	7,076	28,637	21,352
Accumulated Depreciation	5,170	3,986	16,273	12,028
Long-Term Debt	836	717	2,631	2,164
Stockholders' Equity	37,885	32,580	119,248	98,310
Total Assets	46,806	39,802	147,328	120,103
Total Current Assets	35,507	30,182	111,763	91,074
Total Current Liabilities	7,779	6,458	24,485	19,487
Net Working Capital	27,728	23,724	87,277	71,587
Year End Shs Outstg	7,978	7,973	7,978	7,973

STATISTICAL RECORD:

Return on Equity %	11.84	...		
Return on Assets %	9.59	...		
Operating Profit Margin %	11.74	...		
Net Profit Margin %	13.44	...		
Book Value Per Share	4.75	4.09		

Converted at 1995, US$0.3177= 1 New Israeli Shekel; 1994, US$0.3314= 1 New Israeli Shekel

OFFICERS:
S. Dovrat, Chmn.
H. Beit-On, Pres. & C.E.O.
N. Idan, C.F.O. & Sec.
Y. Livne, Exec. V.P. & Chief Technical Officer

INCORPORATED: Isreal, 1992

PRINCIPAL OFFICE: Delta House 16 Hagalim Avenue Herzliya Israel 46733

TELEPHONE NUMBER: 972-9-594777

NO. OF EMPLOYEES: N/A

ANNUAL MEETING: N/A

SHAREHOLDERS: N/A

INSTITUTIONAL HOLDINGS:
No. of Institutions: N/A
Shares Held: N/A

REGISTRAR(S): American Stock Transfer & Trust Co., New York.

TRANSFER AGENT(S): American Stock Transfer & Trust Co., New York.

NASDAQ SYMBOL TENXF
Rec. Pr. 2

TEE-COMM ELECTRONICS INC.

YIELD ...
P/E RATIO ...

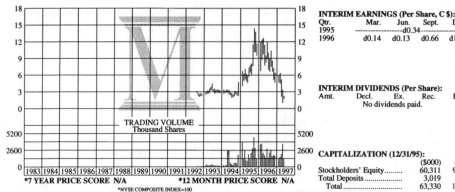

*7 YEAR PRICE SCORE N/A   *12 MONTH PRICE SCORE N/A

*NYSE COMPOSITE INDEX=100

INTERIM EARNINGS (Per Share, C $):

Qtr.	Mar.	Jun.	Sept.	Dec.
1995			d0.34	
1996	d0.14	d0.13	d0.66	d1.18

INTERIM DIVIDENDS (Per Share):

Amt.	Decl.	Ex.	Rec.	Pay.
	No dividends paid.			

CAPITALIZATION (12/31/95):

	($000)	(%)
Stockholders' Equity.........	60,311	95.2
Total Deposits..................	3,019	4.8
Total..............................	63,330	100.0

RECENT DEVELOPMENTS: For the year ended 12/31/96, the Company reported a net loss of $52.4 million compared with a net loss of $7.9 million the year before. Revenue increased 9.8% to $42.9 million from $39.1 million a year earlier. Revenues benefited from the Company's introduction of its own line of digital systems during the summer of 1996. In late summer 1996, the Company's U.S. subsidiary, AlphaStar Television Network Inc., launched its direct-to-home programming service, which stimulated demand for its new systems. For the quarter ended 12/31/96, the Company reported a net loss of $28.6 million versus a net loss of $5.8 million the previous year. Revenue more than doubled to $17.9 million from $8.2 million the year before.

BUSINESS

TEE-COMM ELECTRONICS INC. is a digital satellite communications company. The Company's manufacturing operations are diverse and range from high-tech electronics to fabrication of satellite antennas. The Star Trak line of television receive-only satellite equipment is manufactured on a contract basis in plants in Korea, Taiwan and the United States. Under a non-exclusive license from General Instrument Corp., Tee-Comm manufactures a line of integrated receivers/descramblers which provides the ability to incorporate the VideoCipher module into the receiver unit and permit the user to tune in and descramble all authorized subscription channels. The VideoCipher descrambler is currently the principal means to descramble satellite video signals received in Canada and the United States. The Company also produces a wide range of products including stand alone receivers, low noise amplifiers, satellite dishes and mounts. In addition to its own manufactured products, Tee-Comm distributes a broad range of products in Canada from manufacturers such as Uniden, Drake, Chaparral and Toshiba.

ANNUAL EARNINGS

	12/31/95	12/31/94	12/31/95	12/31/94
	---------US $---------		---------C $---------	
Earnings Per Share	d0.23	0.05	d0.34	0.07

ANNUAL FINANCIAL DATA

RECORD OF EARNINGS (IN THOUSANDS):

Total Revenues	29,055	53,746	39,078	69,296
Costs & Expenses	31,740	49,809	48,837	63,983
Depreciation & Amort	2,605	2,066	3,503	2,664
Operating Income	d5,291	1,871	d13,262	2,649
Income Bef Income Tax	d10,173	1,706	d13,682	2,200
Income Tax	cr4,273	490	cr5,747	632
Net Income	d5,900	1,216	d7,936	1,568
Average Shares Outstg	25,915	22,695	25,915	22,695

BALANCE SHEET (IN THOUSANDS):

Cash & Cash Equivalents	14,005	...	18,836	...
Receivables, Net	4,460	7,623	5,999	9,829
Inventories	35,476	11,248	47,714	14,502
Gross Property	29,472	17,519	39,639	22,588
Accumulated Depreciation	10,421	4,242	14,016	5,470
Stockholders' Equity	60,311	35,817	81,118	46,180
Total Assets	95,031	40,360	127,816	52,037
Total Current Assets	54,378	19,348	73,138	24,946
Total Current Liabilities	34,720	4,542	46,699	5,856
Net Working Capital	19,658	14,806	26,439	19,090

STATISTICAL RECORD:

Return on Equity %	...	3.40		
Return on Assets %	...	3.01		
Operating Profit Margin %	...	3.48		
Net Profit Margin %	...	2.26		
Book Value Per Share	0.05	0.05		

Converted at 1995, US$0.7435= 1 Australian $; 1994, US$0.7756= 1 Australian $

OFFICERS:
A. Bahnman, Chmn. & Pres.
J. Wilkinson, Exec. V.P. & C.O.O.
P. Murphy, V.P. & Gen. Mgr.

INCORPORATED: Oct., 1983

PRINCIPAL OFFICE: 775 Main Street East
Milton, Ontario Canada L9T 3Z3

TELEPHONE NUMBER: 905-878-8181

NO. OF EMPLOYEES: 180 (approx.)

ANNUAL MEETING: In May

SHAREHOLDERS: N/A

INSTITUTIONAL HOLDINGS:
No. of Institutions: 14
Shares Held: 1,234,596

REGISTRAR(S): The Montreal Trust Co. of Canada, Toronto, Ontario, Canada

TRANSFER AGENT(S): The Montreal Trust Co. of Canada, Toronto, Ontario, Canada

NASDAQ SYMBOL TLDCF
Rec. Pr. 21½

TELEDATA COMMUNICATIONS LTD.

YIELD ...
P/E RATIO 32.58

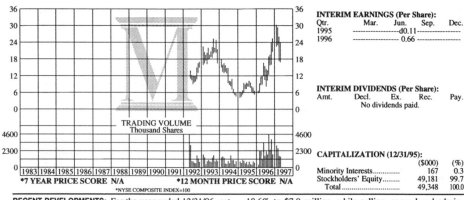

*7 YEAR PRICE SCORE N/A   *12 MONTH PRICE SCORE N/A
*NYSE COMPOSITE INDEX=100

INTERIM EARNINGS (Per Share):

Qtr.	Mar.	Jun.	Sep.	Dec.
1995	------------------d0.11-----------------			
1996	------------------ 0.66 -----------------			

INTERIM DIVIDENDS (Per Share):

Amt.	Decl.	Ex.	Rec.	Pay.
	No dividends paid.			

CAPITALIZATION (12/31/95):

	($000)	(%)
Minority Interests.............	167	0.3
Stockholders' Equity........	49,181	99.7
Total	49,348	100.0

RECENT DEVELOPMENTS: For the year ended 12/31/96, net income was $7.0 million compared with a loss of $1.2 million in the prior year. Sales climbed 77.7% to $57.1 million from $32.1 million in 1995. The Company pointed out that sales and profitability continue to improve, supported by the strong flow of orders for all of the Company's products. Gross profit margin as a percentage of sales was 45.1% compared with 40.0% in 1995. On the expense side, research and development costs were up 18.6% to $7.0 million, while selling, general and administrative costs rose 34.7% to $13.2 million. Operating income reached $5.2 million, up substantially from an operating loss of $2.8 million a year earlier. For the quarter ended 12/31/96, net income was $2.4 million, more than triple $715,000 in the corresponding 1995 quarter. Sales rose 94.7% to $19.6 million from $10.1 million in the prior-year period.

BUSINESS

TELEDATA COMMUNICATIONS LTD. designs, develops, manufactures, markets and supports concentrators and multipexers for incorporation into telephone networks. The Company's products allow telephone operating companies to expand and improve service in the "local loop" (the network of transmission links that connect subscribers to local exchanges) by substantially increasing the number of subscribers that may be served by new and existing network infrastructures. The Company's products are marketed in Israel, Europe, Asia, South America, Central America, and Australia and the surrounding islands. The Company maintains marketing in over 70 countries and has installed equipment in 50 countries.

ANNUAL EARNINGS

	12/31/95	12/31/94	12/31/95	12/31/94
	-------------US $-------------		------------NIS------------	
Earnings Per Share	d0.11	0.06	d0.35	0.18

ANNUAL FINANCIAL DATA

RECORD OF EARNINGS (IN THOUSANDS):

Total Revenues	32,127	28,252	101,125	85,250
Costs & Expenses	34,900	28,727	109,853	86,683
Operating Income	d2,773	d475	d8,729	d1,433
Income Bef Income Tax	d1,183	691	d3,723	2,086
Income Tax	11	43	33	130
Minority Interests	cr6	30	cr18	90
Net Income	d1,188	619	d3,739	1,867
Average Shares Outstg	10,400	10,384	10,400	10,384

BALANCE SHEET (IN THOUSANDS):

Cash & Cash Equivalents	25,903	16,228	81,533	51,080
Receivables, Net	14,310	15,076	45,042	45,492
Inventories	8,668	11,283	27,282	34,046
Gross Property	9,808	9,253	30,871	27,920
Accumulated Depreciation	4,721	3,388	14,861	10,224
Stockholders' Equity	49,181	50,246	154,805	151,618
Total Assets	59,592	59,724	187,574	180,217
Total Current Assets	48,881	42,587	153,858	128,507
Total Current Liabilities	8,977	7,573	28,256	22,853
Net Working Capital	39,904	35,014	125,602	105,655
Year End Shs Outstg	10,411	10,393	10,411	10,393

STATISTICAL RECORD:

Return on Equity %	...	1.23		
Return on Assets %	...	1.04		
Operating Profit Margin %	...	...		
Net Profit Margin %	...	2.19		
Book Value Per Share	4.72	4.83		

Converted at 1995, US$0.3177= 1 New Israeli Shekel; 1994, US$0.3314= 1 New Israeli Shekel

OFFICERS:
U. Levit, Chmn.
L. R. Hartman, Pres.
J. Atsmon, C.E.O.
A. Bergman, Exec. Vice-Pres.

INCORPORATED: Israel, 1981

PRINCIPAL OFFICE: Herzlia Industrial Park
Maskit Street Herzlia-B Israel 46120

TELEPHONE NUMBER: 972-9-591818

NO. OF EMPLOYEES: 232

ANNUAL MEETING: N/A

SHAREHOLDERS: 45

INSTITUTIONAL HOLDINGS:
No. of Institutions: N/A
Shares Held: N/A

REGISTRAR(S): The Bank of New York,
New York.

TRANSFER AGENT(S): The Bank of New
York, New York.

TESCO CORPORATION

YIELD   ...
P/E RATIO   ...

INTERIM EARNINGS (Per Share, C$):
| 1995-96 | ------------------ 0.37 ------------------ |
| 1996-97 | ------------------ 0.60 ------------------ |

TRADING VOLUME
Thousand Shares

INTERIM DIVIDENDS (Per Share):
Amt.   Decl.   Ex.   Rec.   Pay.
No dividends paid.

| 1983 | 1984 | 1985 | 1986 | 1987 | 1988 | 1989 | 1990 | 1991 | 1992 | 1993 | 1994 | 1995 | 1996 | 1997 |

*7 YEAR PRICE SCORE N/A   *12 MONTH PRICE SCORE N/A
*NYSE COMPOSITE INDEX=100

CAPITALIZATION (2/28/97):
	($000)	(%)
Stockholders' Equity.........	63,781	95.4
Deferred Income Tax	3,079	4.6
Total	66,860	100.0

RECENT DEVELOPMENTS: For the year ended 2/28/97, net income more than doubled to C$16.9 million versus C$8.7 million in the same period of 1996. Revenues leapt to C$96.6 million compared with C$41.9 million in the prior year. results were favorably affected by the introduction of two top drive products, the 500EC and the 150HMI. Top drive rental days for the year advanced to 12,300 days from 7,055 days a year earlier. The top drive rental fleet nearly doubled to 79 systems. Sales of 14 top drive systems represented approximately 25.0% of top drive production. Continuing emphasis on research and development in the areas of integrated underbalancing drilling, casing drilling and drilling rig drive systems hold the potential for the creation of additional market for the Company.

BUSINESS

TESCO CORPORATION is an international oilfield service company operating in over twenty countries. Tesco design, manufactures and services highly efficient oilfield equipment that reduces the cost of drilling and producing oil and gas.

ANNUAL EARNINGS

	2/28/97	2/28/96	2/28/97	2/28/96
	--------------US $--------------		--------------C $--------------	
Earnings Per Share	0.48	0.31	0.66	0.43

ANNUAL FINANCIAL DATA

RECORD OF EARNINGS (IN THOUSANDS):
Total Revenues	70,680	30,456	96,610	41,922
Costs & Expenses	46,525	18,851	63,594	25,948
Depreciation & Amort	3,976	1,528	5,434	2,103
Operating Income	20,179	10,077	27,582	13,871
Income Bef Income Tax	20,179	10,077	27,582	13,871
Income Tax	7,828	3,760	10,700	5,175
Net Income	12,351	6,318	16,882	8,696

BALANCE SHEET (IN THOUSANDS):
Cash & Cash Equivalents	3,363	2,973	4,597	4,092
Receivables, Net	21,857	9,423	29,876	12,970
Inventories	8,754	4,455	11,966	6,132
Gross Property	48,947	27,579	66,904	37,962
Accumulated Depreciation	6,104	2,707	8,343	3,726
Stockholders' Equity	63,782	31,670	87,182	43,593
Total Assets	80,048	42,181	109,416	58,061
Total Current Assets	33,975	16,850	46,439	23,194
Total Current Liabilities	13,188	8,772	18,026	12,075
Net Working Capital	20,787	8,078	28,413	11,119
Year End Shs Outstg	27,331	22,626	27,331	22,626

STATISTICAL RECORD:
Return on Equity %	19.36	19.95		
Return on Assets %	15.43	14.98		
Operating Profit Margin %	28.55	33.09		
Net Profit Margin %	17.47	20.74		
Book Value Per Share	2.33	1.40		

Converted at 1997, US$0.7316= 1 Canadian $; 1996, US$0.7265= 1 Canadian $

OFFICERS:
R. M. Tessari, Chmn. & Pres.
P. G. Angman, C.O.O.
M. Hall, Sr. V.P. & Sec.
E. Beierbach, Sr. V.P.
M. Brouse, Sr. V.P
D. Campbell, Sr. V.P.

INCORPORATED: Alberta, Canada

PRINCIPAL OFFICE: 6204 - 6 A Street S.E. Calgary Canada

TELEPHONE NUMBER: 403-233-0757

NO. OF EMPLOYEES: 471

ANNUAL MEETING: June 26, 1997

SHAREHOLDERS: 5,000

INSTITUTIONAL HOLDINGS:
No. of Institutions: 12
Shares Held: 5,304,923

REGISTRAR(S): N/A

TRANSFER AGENT(S): The Montreal Trust Co., Calgary, Bank of Nova Scotia Trust Company, New York.

TESMA INTERNATIONAL, INC.

YIELD 1.4%
P/E RATIO 18.2

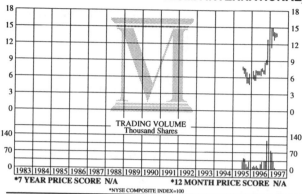

INTERIM EARNINGS (Per Share, C$):

Qtr.	---------------- Oct. ----------------			
1995-96	0.25	0.22	0.33	0.25
1996-97	0.35	0.30	...	...

INTERIM DIVIDENDS (Per Share):

Amt.	Decl.	Ex.	Rec.	Pay.
0.05	3/07/96	3/27/96	3/29/96	4/15/96
0.05	6/06	6/26	6/28	7/15
0.05	10/03	10/10	10/15	10/31
0.05	12/04	12/24	12/27	1/15/97
0.05	3/06/97	3/25/97	3/28/97	4/15

Indicated div.:$0.200

CAPITALIZATION (7/31/96):

	($000)	(%)
Long-Term Debt	11,589	8.6
Stockholders' Equity	107,266	79.5
Deferred Income Tax	16,014	11.9
Total	134,869	100.0

TRADING VOLUME Thousand Shares

*7 YEAR PRICE SCORE N/A   *12 MONTH PRICE SCORE N/A

*NYSE COMPOSITE INDEX=100

RECENT DEVELOPMENTS: For the quarter ended 1/31/97, net income jumped 36.4% to C$6.0 million from C$4.4 million in the corresponding 1996 quarter. Sales were C$118.0 million, up 7.8% from C$109.5 million in the year-earlier period. For the six months ended 1/31/97, net income advanced 53.0% to C$12.7 million from C$8.3 million for the comparable 1996 period. Sales were C$254.3 million, a gain of 16.2% over C$218.8 million in the prior-year period despite flat North American vehicle production volumes. The fiscal 1996 figures were restated to reflect the retroactive adoption of the Canadian Institute of Chartered Accountants' financial instruments guidelines. Higher sales and improved operating performance at several divisions have resulted in better capacity utilization and higher gross margins.

BUSINESS

TESMA INTERNATIONAL INC. is a supplier of engine, powertrain, fueling and cooling components, assemblies, modules and systems for cars and light trucks. The Company designs, engineers and manufactures these products principally for North American, Japanese and European OEMs, including Ford, GM, Chrysler and Volkswagen. The Company's operations are divided into five operating groups: Powertrain Modules Group, Liquid Transfer Technology, Power Transfer Technology, Rotational Products Technology and Rotational Drive Technology.

ANNUAL EARNINGS

	7/31/96	7/31/95	7/31/96	7/31/95
	------------US $------------		------------C $------------	
Earnings Per Share	0.77	0.77	1.05	1.05

ANNUAL FINANCIAL DATA

RECORD OF EARNINGS (IN THOUSANDS):

	7/31/96	7/31/95	7/31/96	7/31/95
Total Revenues	331,343	252,335	455,580	344,908
Costs & Expenses	292,721	223,011	402,476	304,826
Depreciation & Amort	10,785	6,630	14,829	9,062
Operating Income	28,087	21,107	38,618	28,850
Income Bef Income Tax	27,837	19,412	38,275	26,534
Income Tax	11,486	8,800	15,792	12,029
Minority Interests	...	cr297	...	cr406
Net Income	16,352	10,909	22,483	14,911
Average Shares Outstg	17,953	14,224	17,953	14,224

BALANCE SHEET (IN THOUSANDS):

Cash & Cash Equivalents	25,648	34,965	35,264	47,793
Receivables, Net	42,809	34,096	58,860	46,605
Inventories	32,071	28,658	44,096	39,171
Gross Property	131,583	118,093	180,920	161,417
Accumulated Depreciation	53,705	47,757	73,842	65,277
Long-Term Debt	11,589	14,800	15,934	20,230
Stockholders' Equity	107,266	97,140	147,485	132,778
Total Assets	187,950	179,826	258,421	245,798
Total Current Assets	103,912	101,976	142,874	139,388
Total Current Liabilities	53,081	58,835	72,983	80,419
Net Working Capital	50,832	43,142	69,891	58,969
Year End Shs Outstg	17,953	17,953	17,953	17,953

STATISTICAL RECORD:

Return on Equity %	15.24	11.23
Return on Assets %	8.70	6.07
Operating Profit Margin %	8.47	8.36
Net Profit Margin %	4.94	4.32
Book Value Per Share	3.14	2.56

Converted at 1996, US$0.7273= 1 Canadian $; 1995, US$0.7316= 1 Canadian $

OFFICERS:
D. J. Walker, Chmn.
M. Gingl, Pres. & C.E.O.
A. Dobranowski, Exec. V.P. & C.F.O.

INCORPORATED: Canada, June, 1989

PRINCIPAL OFFICE: 300 Edgeley Boulevard Concord Ontario, Canada

TELEPHONE NUMBER: 905-669-5444

NO. OF EMPLOYEES: 2,500

ANNUAL MEETING: In Dec.

SHAREHOLDERS: 93

INSTITUTIONAL HOLDINGS:
No. of Institutions: 1
Shares Held: 2,000

REGISTRAR(S): The Montreal Trust Company of Canada, Toronto and The Bank of Nova Scotia Trust Company of New York, New York.

TRANSFER AGENT(S): The Montreal Trust Company of Canada, Toronto and The Bank of Nova Scotia Trust Company of New York, New York.

3DLABS INC., LTD.

YIELD ...
P/E RATIO 106.58

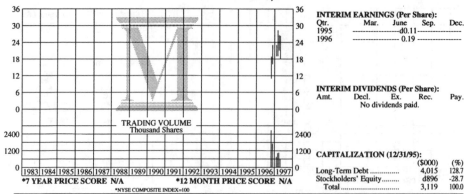

INTERIM EARNINGS (Per Share):

Qtr.	Mar.	June	Sep.	Dec.
1995		-------------------d0.11------------------		
1996		------------------ 0.19 ------------------		

INTERIM DIVIDENDS (Per Share):

Amt.	Decl.	Ex.	Rec.	Pay.
	No dividends paid.			

CAPITALIZATION (12/31/95):

	($000)	(%)
Long-Term Debt	4,015	128.7
Stockholders' Equity........	d896	-28.7
Total.............................	3,119	100.0

RECENT DEVELOPMENTS: For the year ended 12/31/96, net income was $2.6 million compared with a loss of $1.4 million in the prior year. Total revenues more than doubled to $19.7 million from $6.6 million in 1995. The substantial improvement in revenues and earnings was attributed to the tremendous growth in product sales, which resulted in revenues of $16.0 million compared with $3.0 million a year earlier. License, royalty and other revenues were up 11.1% to $3.7 million. Income from operations reached $2.8 million compared to a loss of $1.4 million in the previous year. For the quarter ended 12/31/96, net income was $2.2 million, up from $91,000 in the corresponding 1995 quarter. Revenues more than tripled to $8.6 million from $2.7 million a year earlier.

BUSINESS

3DLABS INC., LTD. designs, develops, sells and licenses semiconductors, software and related technology that enable high performance 3D graphics functions in personal computers. The Company markets a range of 3D graphics processors for use in higher personal computer graphics applications, such as CAD/CAM, 3D animation and scientific visualization, as well as for the mainstream business and consumer personal computer applications such as business presentations, multimedia and personal computer games.

ANNUAL EARNINGS

	12/31/95	12/31/94
	----------------------------US $-----------------------------	
Earnings Per Share	d0.11	...

ANNUAL FINANCIAL DATA

RECORD OF EARNINGS (IN THOUSANDS):

	12/31/95	12/31/94
Total Revenues	6,594	2,080
Costs & Expenses	7,992	5,381
Operating Income	d1,398	d3,301
Income Bef Income Tax	d1,358	d3,197
Net Income	d1,358	d3,197
Average Shares Outstg	12,477	...

BALANCE SHEET (IN THOUSANDS):

	12/31/95	12/31/94
Cash & Cash Equivalents	1,671	2,582
Receivables, Net	973	560
Inventories	37	26
Long-Term Debt	4,015	3,417
Stockholders' Equity	d896	431
Total Assets	5,182	5,731
Total Current Assets	2,942	3,362
Total Current Liabilities	2,063	1,883
Net Working Capital	879	1,480
Year End Shs Outstg	5,658	5,658

STATISTICAL RECORD:

	12/31/95	12/31/94
Return on Equity %	151.62	...
Return on Assets %	...	...
Operating Profit Margin %	...	...
Net Profit Margin %	...	...
Book Value Per Share	...	0.08

OFFICERS:
O. Kent, Chmn., Pres. & C.E.O.
T. S. Donohue, V.P.-Fin. & C.O.O.
N. F. Trevett, V.P.-Mktg.
R. K. Singh, V.P.-Sales

INCORPORATED: Bermunda, Mar. 1994

PRINCIPAL OFFICE: Clarendon House
Church Street Hamilton Bermuda HM11

TELEPHONE NUMBER: N/A

NO. OF EMPLOYEES: 54

ANNUAL MEETING: N/A

SHAREHOLDERS: 10

INSTITUTIONAL HOLDINGS:
No. of Institutions: N/A
Shares Held: N/A

REGISTRAR(S): N/A

TRANSFER AGENT(S): First National Bank
of Boston, Boston Mass.

TOOLEX ALPHA, N.V.

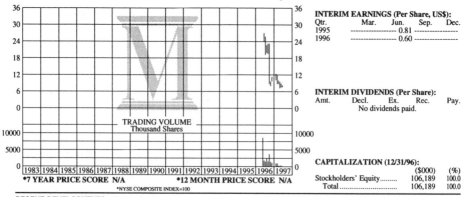

INTERIM EARNINGS (Per Share, US$):

Qtr.	Mar.	Jun.	Sep.	Dec.
1995		0.81		
1996		0.60		

INTERIM DIVIDENDS (Per Share):

Amt.	Decl.	Ex.	Rec.	Pay.
No dividends paid.				

TRADING VOLUME
Thousand Shares

*7 YEAR PRICE SCORE N/A   ***12 MONTH PRICE SCORE N/A**
*NYSE COMPOSITE INDEX=100

CAPITALIZATION (12/31/96):

	($000)	(%)
Stockholders' Equity	106,189	100.0
Total	106,189	100.0

RECENT DEVELOPMENTS: For the year ended 12/31/96, net income was SEK 76.2 million compared with SEK 90.4 million in the prior year. Results for 1996 included nonrecurring charges totaling SEK 10.6 million. Revenues were SEK 577.7 million, down 4.3% from a year earlier. The decline in operating results was attributed partially to a slowdown in growth in the music industry during the second half of the year, resulting in a decrease in compact discs shipped. Gross margin as a percentage of revenues was 38.6%, up slightly from 38.0% in 1995 due primarily to lower component prices and reduced warranty costs, partially offset by direct labor costs and changes in product mix. As a result of the Company's developing and launching more new products in 1996 than in any other year previous to its inception, research and development costs were up 62.8% to SEK 19.7 million.

BUSINESS

TOOLEX ALPHA N.V. is a holding company. Through its subsidiary, Toolex Alpha A.B., the Company designs, produces and installs turnkey production lines used in the replication of music and compact data discs. The Company also produces injection moulding equipment and electroplating equipment that are included in its turnkey systems or sold separately, either to other product line integrators or directly to end-users. Toolex currently exports approximately 95% of its production to over 100 customers in approximately 25 countries. As of 12/31/96, the Company's revenue breakdown was as follows: electroplating, 5%; injection molders, 9%; replication lines, 70%; and other products, 16%.

ANNUAL EARNINGS

	12/31/96	12/31/95	12/31/96	12/31/95
	---US $---		---SEK---	
Earnings Per Share	0.60	0.81	4.11	5.42

ANNUAL FINANCIAL DATA

RECORD OF EARNINGS (IN THOUSANDS):

	12/31/96	12/31/95	12/31/96	12/31/95
Total Revenues	84,230	90,254	577,707	603,708
Costs & Expenses	62,500	64,459	428,670	431,164
Operating Income	21,730	25,795	149,037	172,544
Income Bef Income Tax	17,001	20,224	116,602	135,277
Income Tax	5,886	6,708	40,369	44,867
Net Income	11,115	13,516	76,233	90,410
Average Shares Outstg	19,940	18,815	19,940	18,815

BALANCE SHEET (IN THOUSANDS):

Cash & Cash Equivalents	21,284	10,578	145,979	70,753
Receivables, Net	18,988	19,709	130,234	131,831
Inventories	17,269	8,800	118,440	58,862
Gross Property	2,016	1,544	13,830	10,329
Accumulated Depreciation	1,351	1,180	9,265	7,891
Stockholders' Equity	106,189	37,337	728,322	249,743
Total Assets	124,564	110,137	854,347	736,703
Total Current Assets	60,056	41,516	411,904	277,702
Total Current Liabilities	14,011	23,445	96,098	156,821
Net Working Capital	46,045	18,072	315,806	120,881
Year End Shs Outstg	15,000	15,000	15,000	15,000

STATISTICAL RECORD:

Return on Equity %	10.47	36.20		
Return on Assets %	8.92	12.27		
Operating Profit Margin %	25.80	28.58		
Net Profit Margin %	13.20	14.98		
Book Value Per Share	7.08	2.49		

Converted at 1996, US$0.1458= 1 Swedish Krona; 1995, US$0.1495= 1 Swedish Krona

OFFICERS:
G. Axe, Chmn.
C. Lindell, Exec. V.P.
G. Barsby, Managing Dir.
G. Holmgren, Dir.-Fin.

INCORPORATED: The Netherlands

PRINCIPAL OFFICE: Strawinskylaar 2001, Amsterdam The Netherlands 1077 ZZ

TELEPHONE NUMBER: 31-20-546-0606

NO. OF EMPLOYEES: 111

ANNUAL MEETING: N/A

SHAREHOLDERS: N/A

INSTITUTIONAL HOLDINGS:
No. of Institutions: N/A
Shares Held: N/A

REGISTRAR(S): Citibank N.A.

TRANSFER AGENT(S): Citibank N.A.

TOWER SEMICONDUCTOR LTD.

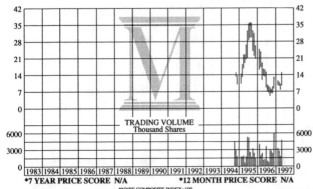

*7 YEAR PRICE SCORE N/A   *12 MONTH PRICE SCORE N/A
*NYSE COMPOSITE INDEX=100

INTERIM EARNINGS (Per Share):

Qtr.	Mar.	Jun.	Sep.	Dec.
1995		1.76		
1996		0.76		

INTERIM DIVIDENDS (Per Share):

Amt.	Decl.	Ex.	Rec.	Pay.
1.50	10/22/96	10/30/96	11/1/96	11/22/96

CAPITALIZATION (12/31/95):

	($000)	(%)
Long-Term Debt	22,207	11.5
Stockholders' Equity	170,351	88.5
Total	192,558	100.0

RECENT DEVELOPMENTS: For the year ended 12/31/96, net income was $10.0 million compared with $20.4 million in the prior-year period. Sales declined 1.7% to $97.9 million from $99.6 million a year earlier. Gross profit as a percentage of sales was 22.6% compared with 31.5% in 1995. The substantial decline in operating results was attributed to difficult market conditions within the semiconductor industry during 1996. Despite these difficult conditions, the Company reacted quickly in streamlining operations, reducing costs, and increasing marketing and sales efforts, which enabled it to maintain profitability for the year. For the quarter ended 12/31/96, net income was $1.2 million, down substantially from $6.4 million achieved in 1995. Sales were down 24.5% to $21.8 million.

BUSINESS

TOWER SEMICONDUCTOR is an independent contract manufacturer of semiconductor integrated circuits (ICs) on silicon wafers. As a foundry, the Company manufactures primarily differentiated ICs which are incorporated into a wide range of products in diverse and rapidly expanding markets, including computer and office equipment, communication products and consumer electronics.

ANNUAL EARNINGS

	12/31/95	12/31/94	12/31/95	12/31/94
	US $		NIS	
Earnings Per Share	1.76	1.03	5.54	3.11

ANNUAL FINANCIAL DATA

RECORD OF EARNINGS (IN THOUSANDS):

Total Revenues	99,621	57,709	313,569	174,137
Costs & Expenses	76,153	46,946	239,701	141,660
Operating Income	23,468	10,763	73,868	32,477
Income Bef Income Tax	25,606	9,989	80,598	30,142
Income Tax	5,167	2,227	16,264	6,720
Net Income	20,439	7,762	64,334	23,422
Average Shares Outstg	11,593	7,551	11,593	7,551

BALANCE SHEET (IN THOUSANDS):

Cash & Cash Equivalents	121,865	38,681	383,585	116,720
Receivables, Net	31,988	13,000	100,686	39,228
Inventories	13,207	9,486	41,571	28,624
Gross Property	84,441	38,288	265,788	115,534
Accumulated Depreciation	13,270	5,193	41,769	15,670
Long-Term Debt	22,207	12,064	69,899	36,403
Stockholders' Equity	170,351	61,688	536,201	186,144
Total Assets	239,991	94,924	755,401	286,433
Total Current Assets	168,459	61,829	530,246	186,569
Total Current Liabilities	44,642	20,626	140,516	62,239
Net Working Capital	123,817	41,203	389,729	124,330
Year End Shs Outstg	13,205	10,000	13,205	10,000

STATISTICAL RECORD:

Return on Equity %	12.00	12.58		
Return on Assets %	8.52	8.18		
Operating Profit Margin %	23.56	18.65		
Net Profit Margin %	20.52	13.45		
Book Value Per Share	12.90	6.17		

Converted at 1995, US$0.3177= 1 New Israeli Shekel; 1994, US$0.3314= 1 New Israeli Shekel

OFFICERS:
G. Morgenstern, Chmn.
R. M. Levin, Co-C.E.O.
Y. Nissan-Cohen, Co-C.E.O.
H. Teman, Finance Manager

INCORPORATED: Israel, 1993

PRINCIPAL OFFICE: Migdal Haemek
Industrial Park, Post Office Box 619, Migdal
Haemek Israel 23105

TELEPHONE NUMBER: 972-6-506-611

NO. OF EMPLOYEES: 715

ANNUAL MEETING: N/A

SHAREHOLDERS: 50

INSTITUTIONAL HOLDINGS:
No. of Institutions: N/A
Shares Held: N/A

REGISTRAR(S): N/A

TRANSFER AGENT(S): American Stock
Transfer & Trust Company.

TRAMFORD INTERNATIONAL LIMITED

YIELD ...
P/E RATIO 31.3

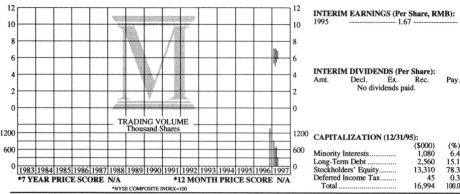

INTERIM EARNINGS (Per Share, RMB):
1995 ------------------ 1.67 ------------------

INTERIM DIVIDENDS (Per Share):

Amt.	Decl.	Ex.	Rec.	Pay.
	No dividends paid.			

CAPITALIZATION (12/31/95):

	($000)	(%)
Minority Interests	1,080	6.4
Long-Term Debt	2,560	15.1
Stockholders' Equity	13,310	78.3
Deferred Income Tax	45	0.3
Total	16,994	100.0

RECENT DEVELOPMENTS: For the five months ended 5/31/96, net income was Rmb9.3 million, down from Rmb13.6 million, for Tramford's predecessor company, in the corresponding 1995 period. Net sales were Rmb900,000 compared with Rmb155,000 in the year-earlier period. Baoquan Bathtub accounted for 86.2% and 98.2% of the Company's net sales in the 1996 and 1995 interim period, respectively. Operating income jumped 30.8% to Rmb17.0 million from Rmb13.0 million for the same period in 1995. Selling, general and administrative expenses decreased by 8.3% to Rmb7.8 million in the 1995 period, due primarily to increased cost controls. Total assets were Rmb267.6 million, up 19.4% from Rmb223.9 million in the prior-year period.

BUSINESS

TRAMFORD INTERNATIONAL LIMITED owns, through its wholly-owned subsidiaries, Jing Tai Industrial Investment Company Limited and Jolly Mind Company Limited, both Hong Kong companies, 95% equity interests in each of Linyl Baoquan Bathtub Company Limited and Linyi Xinhua Building Ceramics Company Limited. Baoquan Bathtub and Xinhua Ceramics are both Sino-foreign equity joint ventures formed under the laws of the People's Republic of China.

ANNUAL EARNINGS

	12/31/95 ------US $------	12/31/95 ------RMB------
Earnings Per Share	0.20	1.67

ANNUAL FINANCIAL DATA

RECORD OF EARNINGS (IN THOUSANDS):

Total Revenues	14,567	121,187
Costs & Expenses	11,928	99,233
Operating Income	2,639	21,954
Income Bef Income Tax	2,690	22,379
Minority Interests	1,080	8,982
Net Income	1,610	13,397
Average Shares Outstg	964	964

BALANCE SHEET (IN THOUSANDS):

Cash & Cash Equivalents	2,241	18,642
Receivables, Net	9,338	77,691
Inventories	3,709	30,860
Gross Property	12,945	107,697
Accumulated Depreciation	425	3,539
Long-Term Debt	2,560	21,296
Stockholders' Equity	13,310	110,729
Total Assets	32,127	267,276
Total Current Assets	18,954	157,686
Total Current Liabilities	9,693	80,639
Net Working Capital	9,261	77,047
Year End Shs Outstg	682	682

STATISTICAL RECORD:

Return on Equity %	12.10
Return on Assets %	5.01
Operating Profit Margin %	18.12
Net Profit Margin %	11.05
Book Value Per Share	19.50

Converted at 1995, US$0.120= 1 Chinese Renminbi

OFFICERS:
W. Xiaolong, Chmn. & Pres.
W. Tian, C.F.O. & Sec.
J. Xiahao, V.P.

INCORPORATED: British Virgin Islands, Sept., 1995

PRINCIPAL OFFICE: c/o Jing Tai Industrial Investment Company Limited, Room 1010-1012, West Tower, Shun Tak Centre, 200 Connaught Road, Central Hong Kong

TELEPHONE NUMBER: 852-2547-9800

NO. OF EMPLOYEES: 2,204

ANNUAL MEETING: N/A

SHAREHOLDERS: N/A

INSTITUTIONAL HOLDINGS:
No. of Institutions: N/A
Shares Held: N/A

REGISTRAR(S): American Stock Transfer & Trust Co.

TRANSFER AGENT(S): American Stock Transfer & Trust Co.

TRIPLE P N.V.

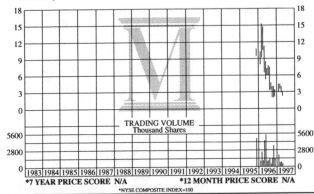

*7 YEAR PRICE SCORE N/A   *12 MONTH PRICE SCORE N/A

*NYSE COMPOSITE INDEX=100

INTERIM EARNINGS (Per Share, US$):

Qtr.	Mar.	June	Sept.	Dec.
1994		d2.11		
1995		0.31		

INTERIM DIVIDENDS (Per Share):

Amt.	Decl.	Ex.	Rec.	Pay.
	No dividends paid.			

CAPITALIZATION (12/31/95):

	($000)	(%)
Stockholders' Equity	10,136	100.0
Total	10,136	100.0

RECENT DEVELOPMENTS: For the year ended 12/31/95, net income was NAG 10.5 million versus a loss of NAG 66.6 million a year earlier. Revenues rose to NAG 347.1 million from NAG 169.5 million in 1994. Results in 1994 included a restructuring charge of NAG 1.7 million and acquired in-process research and development costs of NAG 50.4 million. Application solutions revenues rose 82.0% to NAG 252.0 million, while maintenance and other services' revenues more than tripled to NAG 95.1 million from NAG 31.0 million in the prior year. The Company attributed the revenue gains, in part, to the introduction of new modules for the KOMPAS hospital information system in early 1995, market acceptance of the Company's TIS homecare systems and sales of ROADRUNNER+ to the historic customer base of MAI Systems Corp., which were acquired in October 1994. Research and development expense increased 90.2% to NAG 33.1 million, primarily reflecting higher personnel and personnel-related expenses.

BUSINESS

TRIPLE P N.V. and its subsidiaries are engaged in providing application solutions for client-server and other distributed information and communication networks in the Netherlands, Germany, France, Belgium and the United States. The Company focuses on delivering fully integrated solutions primarily to four vertical markets: healthcare, financial services, transportation and distribution logistics, and printing and publishing.

ANNUAL EARNINGS

	12/31/95	12/31/94	12/31/95	12/31/94
	US $		NAG	
Earnings Per Share	0.31	d2.11	0.56	d3.78

ANNUAL FINANCIAL DATA

RECORD OF EARNINGS (IN THOUSANDS):

	12/31/95	12/31/94	12/31/95	12/31/94
Total Revenues	193,913	94,702	347,079	169,505
Costs & Expenses	185,247	130,259	331,568	233,146
Operating Income	8,666	d35,556	15,511	d63,641
Income Bef Income Tax	6,150	d36,978	11,008	d66,186
Income Tax	302	211	540	377
Net Income	5,848	d37,189	10,468	d66,563
Average Shares Outstg	18,528	17,590	18,528	17,590

BALANCE SHEET (IN THOUSANDS):

Cash & Cash Equivalents	11,403	6,695	20,409	11,984
Receivables, Net	33,478	31,023	59,922	55,528
Inventories	14,222	14,964	25,455	26,784
Gross Property	17,765	15,396	31,797	27,557
Accumulated Depreciation	9,203	5,775	16,472	10,336
Long-Term Debt	...	349	...	625
Stockholders' Equity	10,136	d38,431	18,142	d68,787
Total Assets	75,417	70,010	134,986	125,308
Total Current Assets	64,746	58,585	115,886	104,860
Total Current Liabilities	47,254	83,641	84,579	149,706
Net Working Capital	17,491	d25,055	31,307	d44,846
Year End Shs Outstg	23,115	17,590	23,115	17,590

STATISTICAL RECORD:

Return on Equity %	57.70	96.77
Return on Assets %	7.75	...
Operating Profit Margin %	4.47	...
Net Profit Margin %	3.02	...
Book Value Per Share	0.44	...

Converted at 1995, US$0.5587= 1 Netherlands Antilles guilder; 1994, US$0.5587= 1 Netherlands Antilles guilder

OFFICERS:
F. Khaleghi Yazdi, Managing Dir., Pres. & C.E.O.
J. W. Baud, Chief Oper. Off.
E. H. van Moorsel, Treas.
F. A. van Brussel, Chief Legal Off.

INCORPORATED: 1989

PRINCIPAL OFFICE: Ir. D.S. Tuynmanweg 10, 4131 PN Vianen The Netherlands

TELEPHONE NUMBER: N/A

NO. OF EMPLOYEES: 1,340

ANNUAL MEETING: N/A

SHAREHOLDERS: N/A

INSTITUTIONAL HOLDINGS:
No. of Institutions: N/A
Shares Held: N/A

REGISTRAR(S): The Bank of New York, New York

TRANSFER AGENT(S): The Bank of New York, New York

NASDAQ SYMBOL TTILF
Rec. Pr. 5¼

TTI TEAM TELECOM INTERNATIONAL LTD.

YIELD ...
P/E RATIO 65.63

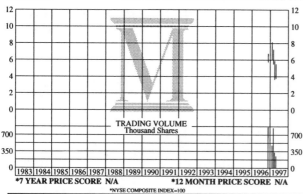

7 YEAR PRICE SCORE N/A   **12 MONTH PRICE SCORE N/A**
*NYSE COMPOSITE INDEX=100

INTERIM EARNINGS (Per Share, US$):

Qtr.	Mar.	June	Sept.	Dec.
1994	---------------- 0.12 ----------------			
1995	0.01	Nil	Nil	0.04
1996	0.02	0.02	...	...

INTERIM DIVIDENDS (Per Share):

Amt.	Decl.	Ex.	Rec.	Pay.
	No dividends paid.			

CAPITALIZATION (12/31/95):

	($000)	(%)
Stockholders' Equity........	1,737	100.0
Total.............................	1,737	100.0

RECENT DEVELOPMENTS: For the year ended 12/31/96, net income more than doubled to $700,254 from $330,996 in 1995. Total revenues jumped 95.7% to $7.8 million compared with $4.0 million a year earlier. Product revenues totaled $3.9 million versus $1.8 million the year before, while service revenues rose 78.0% to $3.9 million from $2.2 million the previous year. The Company invested significantly in research and development in 1996 adding functionality to its product line, especially Device Expert, as well as adding new features to its cellular management product, TCAM. For the fourth quarter ended 12/31/96, net income decreased 6.7% to $251,902 compared with $269,855 in the corresponding prior-year quarter. Total revenues were up 78.0% to $2.3 million from $1.3 million a year earlier. During the quarter, the Company boosted its investment in selling and marketing, opened an office in the United States, and increased its sales force.

BUSINESS

TTI TEAM TELECOM INTERNA-TIONAL LTD. is principally engaged in the development and marketing of advanced, modular, integrated software products and services for operations support systems and network management systems in the telecommunications industry. The Company's solutions, based on its Netrac family of products, enable telecommunications service providers to improve the quality of existing services, streamline their operations, maximize their return on investment in network infrastructure and offer new services over complex networks. The Company's products manage mission-critical functions, such as fault, performance, configuration and security management. The Company also develops advanced software to manage individual components of the network, as well as ancillary equipment such as line testers.

ANNUAL EARNINGS

	12/31/95	12/31/94	12/31/95	12/31/94
	------------US $-----------		------------NIS------------	
Earnings Per Share	0.06	0.12	0.19	0.36

ANNUAL FINANCIAL DATA

RECORD OF EARNINGS (IN THOUSANDS):

Total Revenues	3,989	3,368	12,555	10,162
Costs & Expenses	3,514	2,733	11,061	8,247
Depreciation & Amort	103	91	325	274
Operating Income	371	544	1,169	1,642
Income Bef Income Tax	323	511	1,016	1,543
Income Tax	cr8	14	cr26	41
Net Income	331	498	1,042	1,502
Average Shares Outstg	5,649	4,312	5,649	4,312

BALANCE SHEET (IN THOUSANDS):

Cash & Cash Equivalents	7	45	22	137
Receivables, Net	2,088	1,333	6,572	4,022
Gross Property	756	607	2,378	1,832
Accumulated Depreciation	211	108	666	326
Stockholders' Equity	1,737	1,323	5,467	3,992
Total Assets	3,050	2,127	9,600	6,417
Total Current Assets	2,225	1,408	7,003	4,249
Total Current Liabilities	901	527	2,837	1,591
Net Working Capital	1,324	881	4,166	2,658
Year End Shs Outstg	6,000	4,313	6,000	4,313

STATISTICAL RECORD:

Return on Equity %	19.06	37.63		
Return on Assets %	10.85	23.41		
Operating Profit Margin %	9.30	16.15		
Net Profit Margin %	8.30	14.79		
Book Value Per Share	0.29	0.31		

Converted at 1995, US$0.3177= 1 New Israeli Shekel; 1994, US$0.3314= 1 New Israeli Shekel

OFFICERS:
S. Eisenberg, Chmn.
M. Lipshes, C.E.O.
R. Al-Dor, Pres.
I. Ofer, C.F.O.

INCORPORATED: Israel, Feb., 1990

PRINCIPAL OFFICE: 7 Hamifalim Street
Kiryat Aryeh Petach Tikva, Israel 49513

TELEPHONE NUMBER: 972-3-926-9700

NO. OF EMPLOYEES: 86

ANNUAL MEETING: N/A

SHAREHOLDERS: N/A

INSTITUTIONAL HOLDINGS:
No. of Institutions: N/A
Shares Held: N/A

REGISTRAR(S):

TRANSFER AGENT(S): American Stock
Transfer & Trust Co., New York.

443

VENGOLD INC.

YIELD ...
P/E RATIO ...

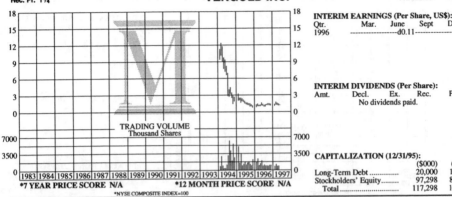

INTERIM EARNINGS (Per Share, US$):

Qtr.	Mar.	June	Sept	Dec.
1996		d0.11		

INTERIM DIVIDENDS (Per Share):

Amt.	Decl.	Ex.	Rec.	Pay.
	No dividends paid.			

CAPITALIZATION (12/31/95):

	($000)	(%)
Long-Term Debt	20,000	17.1
Stockholders' Equity.........	97,298	82.9
Total	117,298	100.0

*7 YEAR PRICE SCORE N/A   *12 MONTH PRICE SCORE N/A

RECENT DEVELOPMENTS: For the year ended 12/31/96, the Company incurred a net loss of $48.1 million compared with a net loss of $4.3 million a year earlier. The loss in 1996 included a $42.2 million provision against the carrying value of the Corporation's mineral properties in the Kilometre 88 region of Venezuela, thus reducing the carrying value to $5.0 million. The Company plans to maintain these mining concessions and continue exploration activity in 1997. The Company also recorded a provision against certain investments of $2.0 million. Exploration and administrative expenses declined 42.2% to $2.6 million from $4.5 million in the prior year.

BUSINESS

VENGOLD INC. is engaged in the acquisition, exploration and development of precious metal properties. The Company is continuing an extensive exploration program on its Venezuelan mining properties in South America with a view to establishing a gold reserve and if successful, to establish the feasibility of production from such reserves.

ANNUAL EARNINGS

	12/31/95	12/31/94	12/31/95	12/31/94
	--------------US $------------		--------------C $------------	
Earnings Per Share	d0.11	0.15	d0.15	0.21

ANNUAL FINANCIAL DATA

RECORD OF EARNINGS (IN THOUSANDS):

	12/31/95	12/31/94	12/31/95	12/31/94
Costs & Expenses	4,518	7,443	6,165	10,441
Income Bef Income Tax	d4,316	3,359	d5,889	4,712
Net Income	d4,316	3,359	d5,889	4,712
Average Shares Outstg	37,900	21,796	37,900	21,796

BALANCE SHEET (IN THOUSANDS):

Cash & Cash Equivalents	33,746	11,321	46,045	15,880
Long-Term Debt	20,000	733	27,289	1,029
Stockholders' Equity	97,298	56,294	132,758	78,964
Total Assets	118,253	58,179	161,349	81,609
Total Current Assets	34,222	11,402	46,694	15,993
Total Current Liabilities	954	1,152	1,302	1,616
Net Working Capital	33,267	10,250	45,391	14,377
Year End Shs Outstg	50,930	21,867	50,930	21,867

STATISTICAL RECORD:

Return on Equity %	...	5.97		
Return on Assets %	...	5.77		
Operating Profit Margin %	...	...		
Net Profit Margin %	...	...		
Book Value Per Share	1.91	2.57		

Converted at 1995, US$0.7329= 1 Canadian $; 1994, US$0.7129= 1 Canadian $

OFFICERS:
J. S. Walton, Chmn.
I. W. Telfer, Pres. & C.E.O.
R. J. Gallagher, V.P.-Opers.
G. A. Ives, V.P.-Fin. & C.F.O.
G. T. Bonifacio, Treas. & Sec.

INCORPORATED: Canada, Oct., 1983

PRINCIPAL OFFICE: 200 Burrard Street, Suite 1788 Vancouver Canada V6C 3L6

TELEPHONE NUMBER: 604-664-7050

NO. OF EMPLOYEES: N/A

ANNUAL MEETING: In May

SHAREHOLDERS: N/A

INSTITUTIONAL HOLDINGS:
No. of Institutions: 12
Shares Held: 15,153,150

REGISTRAR(S): Montreal Trust, Vancouver.

TRANSFER AGENT(S): Montreal Trust, Vancouver.

VENTURE SEISMIC LTD.

YIELD ...
P/E RATIO ...

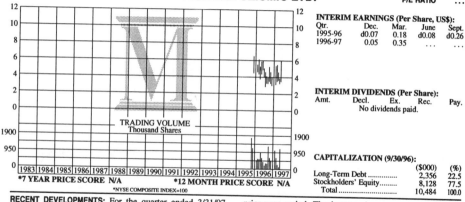

*7 YEAR PRICE SCORE N/A   *12 MONTH PRICE SCORE N/A
*NYSE COMPOSITE INDEX=100

TRADING VOLUME
Thousand Shares

INTERIM EARNINGS (Per Share, US$):

Qtr.	Dec.	Mar.	June	Sept.
1995-96	d0.07	0.18	d0.08	d0.26
1996-97	0.05	0.35	...	...

INTERIM DIVIDENDS (Per Share):

Amt.	Decl.	Ex.	Rec.	Pay.
	No dividends paid.			

CAPITALIZATION (9/30/96):

	($000)	(%)
Long-Term Debt	2,356	22.5
Stockholders' Equity	8,128	77.5
Total	10,484	100.0

RECENT DEVELOPMENTS: For the quarter ended 3/31/97, net income was US$1.1 million compared with US$527,136 in the corresponding 1996 quarter. Total revenues were US$10.1 million, up 72.0% from US$5.9 million in the year-earlier quarter. For the six months ended 3/31/97, net income advanced to US$1.2 million from US$371,811 for the same period in 1996. Total revenues were US$15.7 million compared with US$7.5 million in the prior-year period. The increase in revenue was primarily attributable to increased activity in Canadian-based operations and revenue contributions from the acquisition of Boone Geophysical, Inc. in June 1996. The improved results also reflected the expansion of operations into the U.S., increased equipment capacity and a greater number of three-dimensional projects in the Canadian market.

BUSINESS

VENTURE SEISMIC LTD. is primarily engaged in the acquisition of land and water-based seismic data for use in the exploration for and development and field management of hydrocarbon reservoirs by oil and natural gas producers. The Company offers both traditional two-dimensional and advanced three-dimensional seismic services for land and transition zone surveys. The Company is based in Calgary, Alberta, and remains the solo supplier of radio telemetry data acquisition to Western Canada. In June 1996, the Company increased its United States operating presence with the acquisition of Boone Geophysical, Inc.

ANNUAL EARNINGS

	9/30/96	9/30/95	9/30/96	9/30/95
	US $		C $	
Earnings Per Share	d0.23	0.31	d0.31	0.42

ANNUAL FINANCIAL DATA

RECORD OF EARNINGS (IN THOUSANDS):

	9/30/96	9/30/95	9/30/96	9/30/95
Total Revenues	14,147	9,458	19,282	12,693
Costs & Expenses	13,661	7,828	18,620	10,505
Depreciation & Amort	1,513	902	2,062	1,210
Operating Income	d1,028	728	d1,400	977
Income Bef Income Tax	d1,022	756	d1,393	1,015
Income Tax	cr357	320	cr487	429
Net Income	d665	436	d906	585
Average Shares Outstg	3,098	1,358	3,098	1,358

BALANCE SHEET (IN THOUSANDS):

Receivables, Net	3,211	1,464	4,376	1,964
Inventories	381	59	520	79
Gross Property	12,744	6,839	17,370	9,177
Accumulated Depreciation	3,130	1,767	4,266	2,372
Long-Term Debt	2,356	2,441	3,211	3,275
Stockholders' Equity	8,128	1,291	11,078	1,733
Total Assets	14,933	7,002	20,353	9,396
Total Current Assets	3,749	1,908	5,109	2,560
Total Current Liabilities	4,449	2,816	6,064	3,778
Net Working Capital	d701	d908	d955	d1,218
Year End Shs Outstg	3,098	1,400	3,098	1,400

STATISTICAL RECORD:

Return on Equity %	...	33.79		
Return on Assets %	...	6.23		
Operating Profit Margin %	...	7.70		
Net Profit Margin %	...	4.61		
Book Value Per Share	2.62	0.92		

Converted at 1996, US$0.7337= 1 Canadian $; 1995, US$0.7452= 1 Canadian $

OFFICERS:
B. W. Kozun, Chmn. & Pres.
P. D. McArthur, C.O.O.
G. B. Wiebe, V.P.-Fin. & C.F.O.
J. W. Stenhouse, V.P.-Oper.

INCORPORATED: N/A

PRINCIPAL OFFICE: 3110-80th Avenue S.E., Calgary Alberta, Canada T2C 1J3

TELEPHONE NUMBER: 403-777-9070

NO. OF EMPLOYEES: 200 (approx.)

ANNUAL MEETING: N/A

SHAREHOLDERS: N/A

INSTITUTIONAL HOLDINGS:
No. of Institutions: 1
Shares Held: 1,000

REGISTRAR(S): N/A

TRANSFER AGENT(S): American Stock Transfer & Trust Company, New York.

VISIBLE GENETICS INC.

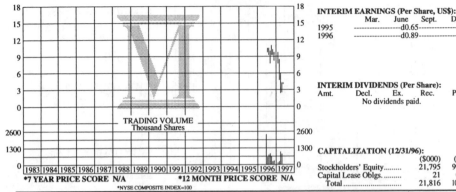

*7 YEAR PRICE SCORE N/A   *12 MONTH PRICE SCORE N/A

*NYSE COMPOSITE INDEX=100

TRADING VOLUME
Thousand Shares

INTERIM EARNINGS (Per Share, US$):

	Mar.	June	Sept.	Dec.
1995	-------------------d0.65-------------------			
1996	-------------------d0.89-------------------			

INTERIM DIVIDENDS (Per Share):

Amt.	Decl.	Ex.	Rec.	Pay.
No dividends paid.				

CAPITALIZATION (12/31/96):

	($000)	(%)
Stockholders' Equity........	21,795	99.9
Capital Lease Oblgs.	21	0.1
Total	21,816	100.0

RECENT DEVELOPMENTS: For the year ended 12/31/96, the Company reported a net loss of $5.2 million compared with a net loss of $2.7 million in 1995. The 1996 results included pre-production plant costs in the amount of $434,659. The increase in net loss was primarily due to start-up costs for VGINF's commercial operations, including the initial manufacturing and sales of its OpenGene DNA sequencing systems. The Company reported revenues of $978,139. The Company did not generate any sales in 1995. For the fourth quarter ended 12/31/96, net loss was $1.5 million compared with $800,000 in 1995. Revenues were $824,000. Separately, VGINF signed a research agreement with Consolidated Laboratory Services. The two companies will develop and carry-out early stage clinical trials on two diagnostic tests for HIV, a quantitative viral load test and a full sequence based test.

BUSINESS

VISIBLE GENETICS INC. is engaged in the development of a proprietary integrated genetic diagnostic system and proprietary application-based products that can identify gene sequences and disease-associated genetic mutations. The Company's application-based products include gene-specific test kits that rely on VGINF's proprietary stratified matrix testing method to identify disease-associated mutations. The Company's product is known as OpenGene(TM), an automated sequencing system and Mircrogel(TM) disposable cassette. OpenGene consists of the following: MicroGene Blaster(TM) automated fluorescence-base DNA sequencer; MicroCel(TM) disposable cassette; Gel Toaster(TM) polymerizing unit; GeneObjects(TM) DNA analysis software framework; Gene-specific diagnostic GeneKits(TM).

ANNUAL EARNINGS

	12/31/96	12/31/95	12/31/96	12/31/95
	-------------US $-------------		-------------C $-------------	
Earnings Per Share	d0.89	d0.65	d1.22	d0.89

ANNUAL FINANCIAL DATA

RECORD OF EARNINGS (IN THOUSANDS):

	12/31/96	12/31/95	12/31/96	12/31/95
Total Revenues	978	...	1,338	...
Costs & Expenses	6,683	2,683	9,141	3,707
Operating Income	d5,705	d2,717	d7,803	d3,707
Net Income	d5,165	d2,724	d7,064	d3,717
Average Shares Outstg	5,791	4,182	5,791	4,182

BALANCE SHEET (IN THOUSANDS):

Cash & Cash Equivalents	18,928	403	25,889	550
Receivables, Net	955	50	1,307	68
Inventories	345	16	472	22
Gross Property	1,178	372	1,611	507
Accumulated Depreciation	310	91	425	124
Capital Lease Oblgs.	21	40	28	55
Stockholders' Equity	21,795	841	29,812	1,148
Total Assets	22,606	1,791	30,920	2,444
Total Current Assets	20,851	1,328	28,520	1,811
Total Current Liabilities	790	909	1,080	1,241
Net Working Capital	20,061	418	27,440	571
Year End Shs Outstg	6,962	4,437	6,962	4,437

STATISTICAL RECORD:

Book Value Per Share	3.13	0.19		

Converted at 1996, US$0.7311= 1 Canadian $; 1995, US$0.7329= 1 Canadian $

OFFICERS:
J. K. Stevens, Chmn., Pres. & C.E.O.
A. W. Cole, Exec. V.P. & Chief Bus. Officer
J. D. Sherman, V.P.-Fin. & C.F.O.
S. Schwartz, Sec.
INCORPORATED: 1993
PRINCIPAL OFFICE: 700 Bay Street, Suite 1000, Box 333 Toronto, Ontario Canada M5G 1Z6

TELEPHONE NUMBER: 416-813-3240
NO. OF EMPLOYEES: 85 (full-time); 30 (part-time)
ANNUAL MEETING: In May
SHAREHOLDERS: N/A
INSTITUTIONAL HOLDINGS:
No. of Institutions: 11
Shares Held: 892,900

REGISTRAR(S): ChaseMellon Shareholder Services, New York, N.Y.

TRANSFER AGENT(S): ChaseMellon Shareholder Services, New York, N.Y.

VITRAN CORPORATION, INC.

YIELD 1.6%
P/E RATIO N.M.

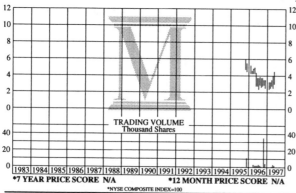

INTERIM EARNINGS (Per Share, US$):

Qtr.	Mar.	June	Sept.	Dec.
1995	----	----	0.23	----
1996	----	----	0.04	----
1997	0.04	...	...	...

INTERIM DIVIDENDS (Per Share):

Amt.	Decl.	Ex.	Rec.	Pay.
0.035	11/07/95	12/13/95	12/15/95	12/31/95
0.035	5/16/96	6/12/96	6/15/96	6/30/96
0.035	12/10	12/17	12/19	12/31
0.035	5/05/97	6/10/97	6/12/97	6/30/97

Indicated div.:$0.07

CAPITALIZATION (12/31/96):

	($000)	(%)
Minority Interest	592	0.8
Long-Term Debt	42,757	55.7
Stockholders' Equity........	33,416	43.5
Total	76,765	100.0

RECENT DEVELOPMENTS: For the quarter ended 3/31/97, net income was C$425,000 compared with a net loss of C$874,000 in the same period of 1996. Revenues increased 15.0% to C$79.8 million. Operating profit improved to C$2.0 million versus a loss of C$765,000. The improved results were attributed to improving economic conditions in Canada and the United States, increased volumes and higher rate levels at the less-than-truckload business units, expansion at The Freight Connection and a return to profit-ability at the U.S. truckload business. Gross profit margins improved to 15.4% from 13.9%, reflecting higher volumes, improved pricing and cost-cutting efforts. Selling, general and administrative expenses as a percentage of revenues declined to 10.6% versus 12.4%, benefiting from ongoing streamlining activities. The Environmental Services Group reported reduced operating losses compared with the year-ago quarter. Meanwhile, the Company continues to seek expansion opportunities.

BUSINESS

VITRAN CORPORATION INC. operates a North American freight distribution system that provides logistical solutions through a network of companies with 70 locations in Canada and the United States. The Company provides a complete range of services for the movement of freight throughout the continent utilizing both highway and rail modes. Services include less than truckload, full-load, intermodal, dedicated contract cartage, warehousing and inventory management. The Environmental Group is a processor and marketer of recyclable material recovered from the consumer, industrial, commercial and institutional waste streams.

ANNUAL EARNINGS

	12/31/96	12/31/95	12/31/96	12/31/95
	------US $------		------C $------	
Earnings Per Share	0.04	0.25	0.05	0.34

ANNUAL FINANCIAL DATA

RECORD OF EARNINGS (IN THOUSANDS):

Total Revenues	221,945	197,250	303,577	269,137
Costs & Expenses	213,215	186,161	291,636	254,006
Depreciation & Amort	5,412	4,668	7,402	6,370
Operating Income	3,319	6,421	4,540	8,761
Income Bef Income Tax	d355	3,727	d485	5,085
Income Tax	cr802	1,372	cr1,097	1,872
Minority Interests	d90	149	d123	203
Net Income	358	2,206	489	3,010

BALANCE SHEET (IN THOUSANDS):

Cash & Cash Equivalents	8,944	13,202	12,234	18,014
Receivables, Net	28,972	24,002	39,628	32,750
Gross Property	47,268	45,532	64,653	62,126
Accumulated Depreciation	12,642	9,154	17,292	12,490
Long-Term Debt	42,757	45,340	58,483	61,864
Stockholders' Equity	33,416	33,546	45,706	45,771
Total Assets	101,410	103,049	138,709	140,605
Total Current Assets	39,824	39,615	54,472	54,053
Total Current Liabilities	24,645	23,660	33,710	32,283
Net Working Capital	15,179	15,955	20,762	21,770
Year End Shs Outstg	9,395	9,354	9,395	9,354

STATISTICAL RECORD:

Return on Equity %	1.07	6.58		
Return on Assets %	0.35	2.14		
Operating Profit Margin %	1.50	3.26		
Net Profit Margin %	0.16	1.12		
Book Value Per Share	3.56	3.59		

Converted at 1996, US$0.7311= 1 Canadian $; 1995, US$0.7329= 1 Canadian $

OFFICERS:
A. F. Griffiths, Chmn.
A. Gnat, Vice-Chmn.
R. D. McGraw, Pres. & C.E.O.
D. Walker, V.P. & C.F.O.

INCORPORATED: Canada, April, 1981

PRINCIPAL OFFICE: 70 University Avenue, Toronto, Ontario Canada M4A 1H9

TELEPHONE NUMBER: 416-752-1411

NO. OF EMPLOYEES: 1,500

ANNUAL MEETING: In May

SHAREHOLDERS: N/A

INSTITUTIONAL HOLDINGS:
No. of Institutions: N/A
Shares Held: N/A

REGISTRAR(S): N/A

TRANSFER AGENT(S): Montreal Trust Company of Canada; Toronto.

VOCALTEC LTD.

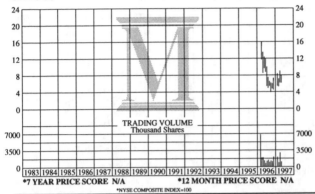

*7 YEAR PRICE SCORE N/A   *12 MONTH PRICE SCORE N/A
*NYSE COMPOSITE INDEX=100

TRADING VOLUME
Thousand Shares

INTERIM EARNINGS (Per Share, US$):

Qtr.	Mar.	June	Sept.	Dec.
1994		d0.23		
1995		d0.23		
1996		d0.86		

INTERIM DIVIDENDS (Per Share):

Amt.	Decl.	Ex.	Rec.	Pay.
	No dividends paid.			

CAPITALIZATION (12/31/96):

	($000)	(%)
Stockholders' Equity	27,218	100.0
Total	27,218	100.0

RECENT DEVELOPMENTS: For the year ended 12/31/96, the Company reported a net loss of $7.2 million. This compares with a net loss of $1.4 million a year earlier. The 1996 loss included a one-time charge of $1.3 million related to the acquisition of Insitu Inc. Also contributing to the 1996 loss were total operating expenses of $14.4 million, compared with $3.5 million in 1995. Net sales soared to $8.5 million from $2.5 million the year before. For the quarter ended 12/31/96, the Company incurred a net loss of $2.4 million compared with a net loss of $525,000 in the corresponding prior-year quarter. Net sales for the quarter soared to $3.0 million from $973,000 the year before. During the quarter, the Company's sales mix shifted as it integrated the first full quarter's contribution from the Internet Telephony Gateway server product. The Company has started a VAR partner program for its Telephony Gateway products in an effort to attract business from corporate telephony integrators and resellers.

BUSINESS

VOCALTEC LTD. develops and markets software that enables voice and audio communications over the Internet. The Company's core products include Internet Phone software and the Internet Phone Telephony Gateway Server. The Company is also pioneering open systems to bridge the Internet to the public switched telephone network.

ANNUAL EARNINGS

	12/31/96	12/31/95	12/31/96	12/31/95
	US $		NIS	
Earnings Per Share	d0.86	d0.23	d2.80	d0.72

ANNUAL FINANCIAL DATA

RECORD OF EARNINGS (IN THOUSANDS):

	12/31/96	12/31/95	12/31/96	12/31/95
Total Revenues	8,495	2,468	27,671	7,769
Costs & Expenses	15,679	3,804	51,072	11,975
Operating Income	d8,496	d1,336	d27,674	d4,206
Net Income	d7,160	d1,368	d23,322	d4,306
Average Shares Outstg	8,290	5,930	8,290	5,930

BALANCE SHEET (IN THOUSANDS):

Cash & Cash Equivalents	22,617	2,063	73,671	6,495
Receivables, Net	5,203	556	16,948	1,751
Inventories	481	...	1,567	...
Gross Property	2,614	487	8,515	1,533
Accumulated Depreciation	381	62	1,241	195
Long-Term Debt	...	384	...	1,209
Stockholders' Equity	27,218	1,311	88,658	4,128
Total Assets	30,773	3,201	100,238	10,076
Total Current Assets	28,301	2,619	92,205	8,244
Total Current Liabilities	3,178	1,370	10,352	4,312
Net Working Capital	25,123	1,249	81,853	3,932
Year End Shs Outstg	8,613	5,767	8,613	5,767

STATISTICAL RECORD:

Book Value Per Share	3.16	0.23

Converted at 1996, US$0.3070= 1 New Israeli Shekel; 1995, US$0.3177= 1 New Israeli Shekel

OFFICERS:
E. A. Ganor, Chmn. & C.E.O.
A. Tal, C.O.O.
A. Cohen, Chief Tech. Off.
Y. Zilka, C.F.O.

INCORPORATED: 1989

PRINCIPAL OFFICE: 4 Ha Mada Street, Herzliya Israel 46733

TELEPHONE NUMBER: 011-972-9-9525-818

NO. OF EMPLOYEES: 79

ANNUAL MEETING: N/A

SHAREHOLDERS: 69

INSTITUTIONAL HOLDINGS:
No. of Institutions: N/A
Shares Held: N/A

REGISTRAR(S): American Stock Transfer & Trust Co., New York, New York.

TRANSFER AGENT(S): American Stock Transfer & Trust Co., New York, New York.

WESCAST INDUSTRIES INC.

YIELD 0.46%
P/E RATIO 13.53

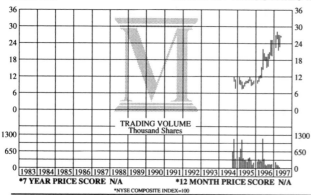

TRADING VOLUME
Thousand Shares

1983 | 1984 | 1985 | 1986 | 1987 | 1988 | 1989 | 1990 | 1991 | 1992 | 1993 | 1994 | 1995 | 1996 | 1997
*7 YEAR PRICE SCORE N/A   *12 MONTH PRICE SCORE N/A
*NYSE COMPOSITE INDEX=100

INTERIM EARNINGS (Per Share, US$):

Qtr.	Mar.	June	Sept.	Dec.
1995	0.23	0.25	0.28	0.45
1996	0.43	0.48	0.42	0.61

INTERIM DIVIDENDS (Per Share):

Amt.	Decl.	Ex.	Rec.	Pay.
0.03	4/19/96	5/2/96	5/6/96	5/21/96
0.03	7/22	8/2	8/6	8/20
0.03	10/18	10/31	11/4	11/19
0.03	1/27/97	2/6/97	2/10/97	2/25/97
0.03	4/18	4/24	4/28	5/13

Indicated div.:$0.12

CAPITALIZATION (12/29/96):

	($000)	(%)
Long-Term Debt	2,209	1.9
Stockholders' Equity........	111,630	96.0
Deferred Income Tax	2,478	2.1
Total	116,317	100.0

RECENT DEVELOPMENTS: For the year ended 12/29/96, net income was up 60.0% to C$28.4 million compared with C$17.7 million the year before. Sales for the year grew 18.2% to C$197.7 million from C$167.3 million a year earlier. Gross profit as a percentage of sales improved to 30.3% compared with 22.7% in 1995. For the fourth quarter ended 12/29/96, net income rose 37.9% to C$9.0 million from C$6.6 million in the comparable prior-year quarter. Sales increased 38.0% to C$55.7 million compared with

C$40.4 million in the corresponding period a year earlier. The higher fourth-quarter sales reflect a 27.3% increase in casting and machining sales to C$46.2 million. Prototype casting sales were C$1.4 million versus C$600,000 in 1995. In addition, sales were fueled by tooling sales for two new machine lines totaling C$4.2 million compared with C$122,000 the previous year. During 1997, the Company plans to build a new plant for its pump business in Stratford, Ontario.

BUSINESS

WESCAST INDUSTRIES INC. is engaged in the supply and manufacture of exhaust manifolds for passenger cars and light trucks in North America. The Company's products are currently sold primarily to Ford Motor Company, General Motors Corporation and Chrysler Corporation.

ANNUAL EARNINGS

	12/29/96	12/31/95	12/29/96	12/31/95
	-----------US $-----------		-----------C $-----------	
Earnings Per Share	1.92	1.21	2.63	1.65

ANNUAL FINANCIAL DATA

RECORD OF EARNINGS (IN THOUSANDS):

	12/29/96	12/31/95	12/29/96	12/31/95
Total Revenues	144,551	122,613	197,717	167,299
Costs & Expenses	102,971	96,463	140,844	131,618
Depreciation & Amort	8,672	5,505	11,861	7,511
Operating Income	32,908	20,646	45,012	28,170
Income Bef Income Tax	32,318	20,268	44,204	27,655
Income Tax	11,583	7,279	15,843	9,932
Net Income	20,735	12,989	28,361	17,723
Average Shares Outstg	10,794	10,741	10,794	10,741

BALANCE SHEET (IN THOUSANDS):

	12/29/96	12/31/95	12/29/96	12/31/95
Cash & Cash Equivalents	26,219	945	35,863	1,290
Receivables, Net	27,342	14,256	37,399	19,452
Inventories	7,323	10,788	10,017	14,719
Gross Property	109,762	90,656	150,132	123,695
Accumulated Depreciation	35,224	27,332	48,180	37,293
Long-Term Debt	2,209	23,574	3,021	32,165
Stockholders' Equity	111,630	52,032	152,688	70,995
Total Assets	138,104	92,204	188,899	125,807
Total Current Assets	61,089	26,197	83,557	35,744
Total Current Liabilities	20,507	14,237	28,050	19,426
Net Working Capital	40,581	11,959	55,507	16,318
Year End Shs Outstg	12,870	10,741	12,870	10,741

STATISTICAL RECORD:

	12/29/96	12/31/95
Return on Equity %	18.57	24.96
Return on Assets %	15.01	14.09
Operating Profit Margin %	22.77	16.84
Net Profit Margin %	14.34	10.59
Book Value Per Share	8.67	4.84

Converted at 1996, US$0.7311= 1 Canadian $; 1995, US$0.7329= 1 Canadian $

OFFICERS:
R. W. LeVan, Chmn. & C.E.O.
N. M. Exel, V.P.-Fin.

INCORPORATED: Canada, 1901

PRINCIPAL OFFICE: P.O. Box 1930, 799 Powerline Road West, Brantford, Ontario Canada N3T 5W5

TELEPHONE NUMBER: 519-759-0452

NO. OF EMPLOYEES: 1,159

ANNUAL MEETING: In Apr.

SHAREHOLDERS: N/A

INSTITUTIONAL HOLDINGS:
No. of Institutions: 10
Shares Held: 1,395,200

REGISTRAR(S): Montreal Trust Company of Canada, Toronto; Bank of Nova Scotia Trust Company of New York, New York

TRANSFER AGENT(S): Montreal Trust Company of Canada, Toronto; Bank of Nova Scotia Trust Company of New York, New York

WIZTEC SOLUTIONS LTD.

YIELD ...
P/E RATIO 19.40

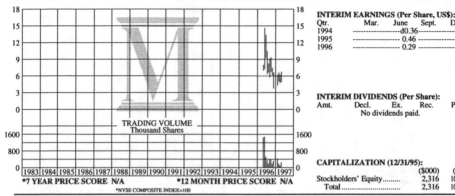

INTERIM EARNINGS (Per Share, US$):

Qtr.	Mar.	June	Sept.	Dec.
1994		----------d0.36----------		
1995		---------- 0.46 ----------		
1996		---------- 0.29 ----------		

INTERIM DIVIDENDS (Per Share):

Amt.	Decl.	Ex.	Rec.	Pay.
		No dividends paid.		

TRADING VOLUME
Thousand Shares

*7 YEAR PRICE SCORE N/A   *12 MONTH PRICE SCORE N/A
*NYSE COMPOSITE INDEX=100

CAPITALIZATION (12/31/95):

	($000)	(%)
Stockholders' Equity........	2,316	100.0
Total	2,316	100.0

RECENT DEVELOPMENTS: For the year ended 12/31/96, net income declined 19.8% to $1.6 million from $2.0 million in 1995. Revenues increased 46.2% to $8.3 million compared with $5.7 million a year earlier. Revenues from the Company's existing customer base, which includes on-going customization, on-site support and maintenance, grew to 72.0% of total revenues, more than five times the previous year's level. During the year, the Company won four new major WIZARD projects; however, overall revenue from new customers decreased primarily due to a backlog of work for projects won in 1995, long-term schedules of new projects and the Company's revenue recognition policy. The 1996 results included six months of operations of Business Systems, Inc. For the fourth quarter ended 12/31/96, net income fell to $146,500. This compares with $774,490 in the corresponding prior-year quarter. Revenues rose 20.8% to $2.3 million from $1.9 million in the comparable period the year before.

BUSINESS

WIZTEC SOLUTIONS LIMITED is engaged in developing, marketing and supporting computer software that provides multi-channel subscription television systems operators with a comprehensive subscriber management system. The Company's software is marketed under the WIZARD® tradename and incorporates subscriber management functions, such as billing, collection, customer service, work order processing, equipment inventory control and customer analysis for target marketing.

ANNUAL EARNINGS

	12/31/95	12/31/94	12/31/95	12/31/94
	-------------US $-------------		-------------NIS------------	
Earnings Per Share	0.46	d0.36	1.45	d1.09

ANNUAL FINANCIAL DATA

RECORD OF EARNINGS (IN THOUSANDS):

Total Revenues	5,698	1,335	17,936	4,030
Costs & Expenses	3,657	2,852	11,511	8,606
Operating Income	2,041	d1,517	6,425	d4,577
Net Income	2,012	d1,500	6,333	d4,526
Average Shares Outstg	4,382	4,202	4,382	4,202

BALANCE SHEET (IN THOUSANDS):

Cash & Cash Equivalents	665	...	2,093	...
Receivables, Net	1,105	159	3,478	479
Gross Property	750	...	2,361	...
Accumulated Depreciation	44	...	139	...
Stockholders' Equity	2,316	151	7,291	455
Total Assets	3,448	802	10,855	2,420
Total Current Assets	1,770	159	5,571	479
Total Current Liabilities	1,132	651	3,563	1,964
Net Working Capital	638	d492	2,008	d1,486
Year End Shs Outstg	4,400	3,636	4,400	3,636

STATISTICAL RECORD:

Return on Equity %	86.86	...
Return on Assets %	58.35	...
Operating Profit Margin %	35.82	...
Net Profit Margin %	35.31	...
Book Value Per Share	0.53	0.04

Converted at 1995, US$0.3177= 1 New Israeli Shekel; 1994, US$0.3314= 1 New Israeli Shekel

OFFICERS:
S. Belis, Chmn.
Y. Polak, Pres. & C.E.O.
D. Zahavi, Contr.

INCORPORATED: Israel, Jan. 27, 1993

PRINCIPAL OFFICE: 39 Hagalim Street, Herzlia Israel 46725

TELEPHONE NUMBER: 972-9-598-740

NO. OF EMPLOYEES: 40

ANNUAL MEETING: N/A

SHAREHOLDERS: N/A

INSTITUTIONAL HOLDINGS:
No. of Institutions: N/A
Shares Held: N/A

REGISTRAR(S):

TRANSFER AGENT(S): American Stock Transfer and Trust Company, New York, NY.

ZAG INDUSTRIES LTD.

YIELD ...
P/E RATIO 14.4

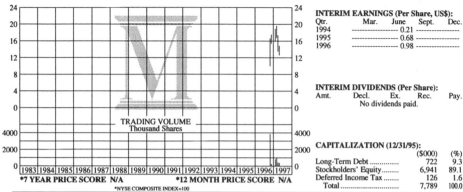

INTERIM EARNINGS (Per Share, US$):

Qtr.	Mar.	June	Sept.	Dec.
1994	----	----	0.21	----
1995	----	----	0.68	----
1996	----	----	0.98	----

INTERIM DIVIDENDS (Per Share):

Amt.	Decl.	Ex.	Rec.	Pay.
		No dividends paid.		

CAPITALIZATION (12/31/95):

	($000)	(%)
Long-Term Debt	722	9.3
Stockholders' Equity	6,941	89.1
Deferred Income Tax	126	1.6
Total	7,789	100.0

7 YEAR PRICE SCORE N/A   *12 MONTH PRICE SCORE N/A*
*NYSE COMPOSITE INDEX=100

RECENT DEVELOPMENTS: For the year ended 12/31/96, net income rose 56.1% to $6.7 million from $4.3 million in the prior year. Sales were up 61.5% to $50.5 million compared with $31.3 million the previous year. The improved sales were attributed to the launch of new products, penetration to new retailers, new strategic alliances and expanded relationships with existing customers. New customers gained included Sam's Club, Home Base and Costco in the United States, and Bauhaus, Halfords and Do-It-All in Europe. For the fourth quarter ended 12/31/96, net income increased 58.1% to $2.9 million compared with $1.9 million in the corresponding year-earlier quarter. Sales grew 45.2% to $15.4 million from 10.6 million the year before. Gross margins for the quarter declined to 37.1% from 41.6% due to start-up expenses associated with the Company's new, wholly-owned manufacturing facility as well as an increase in the prices paid for the Company's main resins, which rose $113 per ton to an average of $851.

BUSINESS

ZAG INDUSTRIES LTD. designs, develops, manufactures and markets plastic consumer products, including a wide range of hardware, storage and gardening accessories. In addition, the Company is developing and has introduced selected products for the fishing and camping markets, and has launched a line of bathroom accessories, through a joint venture with Masco. The Company's products are sold for household and professional use in 39 countries.

ANNUAL EARNINGS

	12/31/95	12/31/94	12/31/95	12/31/94
	----US $----		----NIS----	
Earnings Per Share	0.68	0.21	2.14	0.63

ANNUAL FINANCIAL DATA

RECORD OF EARNINGS (IN THOUSANDS):

	12/31/95	12/31/94	12/31/95	12/31/94
Total Revenues	31,266	9,519	98,414	28,724
Costs & Expenses	24,984	7,791	78,640	23,509
Depreciation & Amort	521	171	1,640	516
Operating Income	5,761	1,557	18,133	4,698
Income Bef Income Tax	5,689	1,368	17,907	4,128
Income Tax	1,411	369	4,441	1,113
Net Income	4,278	999	13,466	3,014
Average Shares Outstg	6,303	4,726	6,303	4,726

BALANCE SHEET (IN THOUSANDS):

Cash & Cash Equivalents	3,397	1,618	10,692	4,882
Receivables, Net	7,698	2,440	24,230	7,363
Inventories	2,408	1,079	7,579	3,256
Gross Property	5,778	1,785	18,187	5,386
Accumulated Depreciation	787	266	2,477	803
Long-Term Debt	722	123	2,273	371
Stockholders' Equity	6,941	2,663	21,848	8,036
Total Assets	18,494	6,656	58,212	20,084
Total Current Assets	13,503	5,137	42,502	15,501
Total Current Liabilities	10,596	3,764	33,352	11,358
Net Working Capital	2,907	1,373	9,150	4,143
Year End Shs Outstg	6,303	6,303	6,303	6,303

STATISTICAL RECORD:

Return on Equity %	61.63	37.51
Return on Assets %	23.13	15.01
Operating Profit Margin %	18.43	16.36
Net Profit Margin %	13.68	10.49
Book Value Per Share	1.10	0.42

Converted at 1995, US$0.3177= 1 New Israeli Shekel; 1994, US$0.3314= 1 New Israeli Shekel

OFFICERS:
Z. Yemini, Chmn. & C.E.O.
S. Schreter, V.P.-Sales
J. Kupperwas, C.F.O. & Sec.
I. Marcus, V.P.-Oper.

INCORPORATED: Israel, 1987

PRINCIPAL OFFICE: New Industrial Zone, 19 Hamelacha Street, Rosh Ha'Ayin Israel 48091

TELEPHONE NUMBER: 972-3-902-0200

NO. OF EMPLOYEES: 87

ANNUAL MEETING: N/A

SHAREHOLDERS: N/A

INSTITUTIONAL HOLDINGS:
No. of Institutions: N/A
Shares Held: N/A

REGISTRAR(S): American Stock Transfer & Trust Company, New York, NY.

TRANSFER AGENT(S): American Stock Transfer & Trust Company, New York, NY.

Notes: